TWENTY
BEST PLAYS

f The Modern American Theatre

Edited with an introduction by
John Gassner

CROWN PUBLISHERS, INC.
New York

Twenty-fourth Printing, August, 1967

CONTENTS

Introduction

AN AMERICAN DECADE

By JOHN GASSNER

It is no secret that America has the youngest national drama of any importance in the world. Although it has been officially in existence since 1787 when an American play on an American subject, Royall Tyler's *The Contrast,* appeared on the local stage, a century had to elapse before the country could boast a playwright of some importance in James A. Herne. Another quarter of a century had to be consumed in tentative efforts to hammer out some heavy artillery that might vie with European achievements, and even then it was impossible to mention such worthies as Fitch, Moody, Thomas and Walter in the same breath with their contemporaries across the Atlantic. Something momentous, it is true, occurred in 1915 when the Washington Square Players (later The Theatre Guild), the Provincetown Players, and the Neighborhood Playhouse arose almost simultaneously. But even then one would have had to be unusually optimistic to conclude that America was on the threshold of an important dramatic period. Moreover, our entry into the World War soon reduced the activities of the nascent organizations, and it was only four or five years later that their playwrights developed their molars.

In 1920, however, American drama attained maturity. On February second appeared Eugene O'Neill's *Beyond the Horizon,* and this event was followed a month later by this dramatist's first version of *Anna Christie* and, eight months later, by *Emperor Jones.* Within three years, moreover, O'Neill was no longer a lone figure: Maxwell Anderson, George Kelly, Elmer Rice, George S. Kaufman, Marc Connelly, Sidney Howard, John Howard Lawson, and Philip Barry were joining him in the theatre, bringing intelligence and observation to bear upon the American scene. A little later arrived those talented recruits Robert Sherwood, Paul Green, and S. N. Behrman, as well as a host of better than average privates.

The years 1920-1929 comprised a period of unparalleled expansion in the economic and social life of the nation. Our pioneering days were now definitely a thing of the past, and the surplus of our energies flowed into the arts. We adopted the best that we could find in European culture without allowing it to stifle native growths. We emancipated ourselves from provincialism and from the gaunt hand of fanatical puritanism, although we allowed it to keep a tight finger on our liquor supply. We began to explore human nature with the lantern of philosophy and the scalpel of modern surgery. The lantern revealed the richness of our resources, dreams, and strivings; the scalpel probed our intestinal tumors of complacency, intolerance, and acquisitiveness. In short, we achieved a criticism of life without which the drama is nothing but evanescent showmanship.

Then on October 29, 1929, amidst a flurry of ticker-tape and a rain of suicides from office windows, the bubble of our financial structure burst with a deafening explosion. Its fragments littered the landscape of the richest country in the world with apple-stands and bread lines. Unwilling to admit defeat, the country fed on windy promises, elected a new administration, and tried to coast along with the aid of relief and federal employment projects. At this writing, a decade is coming to an end without our having repaired the damage to our economic life.

That the theatre should have been severely affected was inevitable. Inflated real estate values on Broadway were deflated; business men who financed commercial productions or supported experimental enterprises retrenched; productions diminished in number, actors became a drug on the market, and the theatre's clientele became smaller as incomes diminished. Playwrights, directors and the better known actors found themselves frequently constrained to transfer their allegiance to the films. All told, the theatre of the thirties was a diminished quantity.

A literal application of economics to the stage could only lead to the conclusion that the American drama was coming to an untimely end. But man is not the passive creature of dollars or even of history; it is, after all, he who *makes* history, and the same exercise of will enables him to rise above defeat. How long he can remain in the slough of a depressed economy without losing his spirit or his sanity or both, it is of course impossible to tell with any precision. It is easier to record the past than to chart the future. But it is with the past that we are concerned here, a past which moreover provides a link with the immediate future—and that is about as far as most of us dare to look. The fact is that the thirties in America witnessed a period of drama equal in quality to the work of the preceding decade. The period has been rightly described by the sagacious critic John Mason Brown as "these full lean years."

2

In the physical theatre—if such a human phenomenon as the theatre may be called physical!—there were notable developments. It is true that the Provincetown Players and the Neighborhood Playhouse had disappeared some years before the stock-market crash; that the Civic Repertory Company came to an end; that the "Little Theatres" which had once dotted the country died or hibernated by the dozens, until in 1932 they omitted their national tournament for the first time since its inception in 1923; that the "road" back of cosmopolitan New York was almost closed for a time to the wagon-cars of Thespis. But there was at least one survivor from the wreckage, and the fertilizing time-spirit soon gave birth to a succession of younger enterprises that kept the drama not only distinctly alive, but also literally kicking.

The survivor, The Theatre Guild, which had shared honors with the Provincetown in the first decade, held its own—albeit sometimes precariously—by virtue of accumulated resources and the ability of its older playwrights. Amid many unwise choices—as is the way of the theatre—it managed to reveal such honorable native plays, in addition to imports, as *Hotel Universe, Elizabeth, the Queen, Green Grow the Lilacs, Mourning Becomes Electra, Reunion in Vienna, American Dream, Biography, Both Your Houses, Ah, Wilderness, Mary of Scotland, They Shall Not Die, Valley Forge, Rain from Heaven, Porgy and Bess, End of Summer,* and *The Philadelphia Story.* The Guild was, moreover, instrumental in founding the American Theatre Society which possesses a substantial subscription audience in a number of cities. Its efforts, combined with the successful tours of its Lunts, Katherine Cornell, Helen Hayes and others, helped considerably to reopen traffic on the road.

New sources of energy, moreover, were quickly forthcoming in response to new promptings. First to emerge was a group of actors and young directors who had been associated with The Theatre Guild for some time. They had tried their wings as early as the winter of 1928 when they worked on Waldo Frank's *New*

Year's Eve and Padraic Colum's *Balloon* for experimental purposes. They became inspired with the ideal of a collective theatre that would perfect ensemble playing and would give itself wholly to the badly shattered world beyond the footlights. They began to hold meetings between November, 1930, and May, 1931, and started rehearsals at Brookfield Center, Connecticut, in June. The play was Paul Green's memorable *House of Connelly*, which they presented a few months later under the auspices of the parent organization. Acting independently thereafter, this company, now known as The Group Theatre, produced the first full-length treatment of the depression, the Siftons' *1931*. This availed them little, nor did its successor Maxwell Anderson's *Night Over Taos*. But in the fall of 1932 John Howard Lawson's *Success Story* was almost faithful to its title. Then Sidney Kingsley's Pulitzer Prize hospital play, *Men in White*, produced in association with a commercial management, added strength to the Group's moorings at the same time that it revealed the potency of planned production by a permanent company.

A crisis impended when the next two productions met with disaster, for it is not usually given to young theatres to weather the Broadway climate. But at this point life came out of the Group's own body, and the company gave birth to a bouncing baby playwright who grew up almost instantaneously and made himself the foremost new dramatist of the thirties. Clifford Odets had worked with the Group as an actor and had shared its aims as a member of the collective from the beginning. He was ideally suited to the theatre he had helped to create along with its more expert actors and its directors, Cheryl Crawford, Harold Clurman, and Lee Strasberg. He found, in turn, that this theatre was suited to his particular style of dramaturgy. The association has continued without interruption, and to it we owe the plays—*Waiting for Lefty, Till the Day I Die, Awake and Sing, Paradise Lost, Golden Boy,* and *Rocket to the Moon*— which, regardless of their limitations, have given the drama of the thirties much of its claim to vitality. The Group, moreover, owes to Clifford Odets much of its present stability. It nearly foundered in 1937 in consequence of four financial failures when *Golden Boy* gave this intrepid company its deserved security under the present management of its able director, Mr. Harold Clurman. Then, profiting by this change in its fortunes, the Group gave another new writer, Irwin Shaw, his first Broadway success with *The Gentle People*, and brought William Saroyan into the theatre with the boldly experimental *My Heart's in the High-lands*.

In the theatre, however, no one works alone. The parturition that brought forth Clifford Odets and Irwin Shaw was a joint delivery. The partner was the New Theatre League, with its increasingly successful organ the New Theatre magazine, itself a joint product of the depression and of earlier attempts to create a working-class theatre. In the benign twenties only a small minority had felt the need for such a forum. After October, 1929, the necessary stimulus was only too abundantly present in unemployed millions, depressed wages, embattled labor unions, darkened theatres, and hungering actors. At first, small radical groups created "agit-prop" ("agitation" and "propaganda") plays. By 1933, however, this movement, known as the League of Workers Theatres, had been penetrated by more expert and less militant members, and the millenium of a social upheaval became a receding expectation.

Recognizing the fact that it was now an association of theatre people united only by an aversion to fascism, by sympathy with the underdog, or simply by a desire to create a vital stage, the movement renamed itself the New Theatre

League. Its productions, mostly one-acters, grew in number until these filled at least a portion of the gap left by the moribund state of the country's Little Theatres. In accordance with the new policy, New Theatre magazine announced an annual award for the best short play of "social significance", promising to produce it at benefit nights with the assistance of sympathetic acting groups.

Clifford Odets, who had been unable to dispose of his full-length script *Awake and Sing*, saw the announcement, locked himself in a hotel room for three days, and turned the scales with his one-acter *Waiting for Lefty*, a kaleidoscopic picture of American life caught within the frame of a taxicab strike. After its premiere by Group Theatre actors, it was produced throughout the country, as well as abroad, winning acclaim from many who were far more impressed with the young author's pungent talent than with his social philosophy. The Group discovered it had an exceptional playwright in its midst, and Odets became its mainstay. This event, little short of momentous, occurred in January, 1935.

Other contests and New Theatre nights followed, one of them in January, 1936 bringing to light Paul Green's notable and provocative chain-gang one-acter *Hymn to the Rising Sun*, which linked a leading figure of the twenties with a movement that was peculiarly a product of the new decade. Then came Irwin Shaw's expressionistic long one-acter *Bury the Dead*, in which the victims of a new war, refusing to be buried, return to wrest a richer life from the world. Thus another powerful playwright was added to the lists. He has not operated long enough to realize himself completely. But, after one slip, *Siege*, he carved out the richly humorous parable of the revolt of the meek against the bullies of the world, *The Gentle People*. It was warmly received in New York despite a mixed press, and it is currently captivating the British people, who have grown restive under too much international hijacking.

In 1937, the New Theatre League began to suffer a recession, but retained sufficient vitality to discover at least one other playwright, Marc Blitzstein.

During this period, the social movement also managed to create a forum for full-length plays, The Theatre Union. For several seasons it became a haven for socially conscious playwrights and provided a popular-priced theatre. Except for a brief foray into the Middle West, it confined its activities to New York; it suffered from sectarian management; and it closed its doors, after some uneven productions, when John Howard Lawson's stirring but special strike drama *Marching Song* ended its run in the spring of 1937.

But this theatre was not padlocked before it had produced an exciting drama of racial conflict in the South, *Stevedore;* a touching picture of the mining regions in Albert Maltz's *Black Pit;* and Albert Bein's vivid epic of harassed Southern mountaineers in the grip of the industrial system, *Let Freedom Ring*. The Theatre Union's example, moreover, inspired the creation of Labor Stage, owned and operated by the progressive International Ladies Garment Workers Union in New York. This organization is still presenting, contrary to expectations, the freshest and most entertaining musical revue of the thirties, *Pins and Needles*.

Still more characteristic of the era was the Federal Theatre, a unit of the Works Progress Administration with which the government strove to stem the tide of unemployment. Started in 1935 under the direction of Miss Hallie Flanagan of Vassar College, and ended with one blow of the congressional axe in the summer of 1939, the project had a chequered career partly perhaps owing to the uneven quality of its personnel, but largely to red tape and continual reorganization. Nevertheless, its services as the first national low-priced theatre in America cannot be discounted; it went far toward filling gaps in the "road" and toward acclimatizing hitherto lethargic citizens to the stage.

It attempted to create a poetic theatre, and succeeded in giving an inkling of its potentialities in this sadly prosaic age with T. S. Eliot's *Murder in the Cathedral*. The Negro Theatre branch introduced a vigorous note with its Haitian version of *Macbeth* and with William Du Bois' *Haiti*. The Children's Theatre showed what could be done in the direction of fostering a feeling for the stage among America's younger millions with *Pinocchio*, as well as with sundry less publicized ventures. Other affiliates sponsored democratic drama with the country-wide production of *It Can't Happen Here*, a much needed warning against fascism in a troubled age. Finally, the subsidized theatre created America's most original contribution to the world's drama, the Living Newspapers—dramatizations of vital facts concerning the problems of agriculture, labor, utilities, venereal disease, and housing. "As American as Walt Disney, the *March of Time* and the *Congressional Record*," the new form created purposeful native *commedia dell' arte* in *Power* and in the more sombre *One-third of a Nation*. Drama of the people and for the people, the Living Newspaper does not appear to advantage on the printed page except for the most imaginative reader. But without regard for literary permanence it tended to enrich the theatre honorably, stirringly, and entertainingly. The absence of the Federal Theatre will, we fear, be deeply felt in the imminent forties.

Not the least of its gifts to the stage, however, was the directorial genius of Orson Welles, which was instrumental in forming another remarkable, if temporarily stalemated, theatrical enterprise. After providing highly original revivals for the Federal Theatre culminating in Marlowe's *Dr. Faustus*, Orson Welles and his partner, John Houseman, created the Mercury Theatre that gave memorable modern productions of *Julius Caesar* and Dekker's *Shoemakers' Holiday*. These respectively illuminated the tragedy of liberalism in an era of dictatorship and demagoguery and glorified the homely democratic spirit. Although primarily a revival theatre, the Mercury moreover brought forth that scintillating sublimation of "agit-pop" in operatic or oratorio form, *The Cradle Will Rock*, memorable equally for its dramatic style and its engaging sceneryless production.

A rich and fruitful life was assured by these various enterprises, though not exactly in proportion to their interest in the reformation of American society or the defence of what was best in it. Nor were the theatre's resources monopolized by the institutional stage. Commercial enterprise had been elevated appreciably in the twenties, and the next decade did not fall below that level. As usual, the ordinary producer promoted the amenities for the greater glory of the box-office, and this, too, was to the good since the playgoer is entitled to relaxation. To provide it is also an art, as well as a function, of the eternal theatre. Moreover, a number of producers did not fail to honor their profession with work of rare distinction. It was Guthrie McClintic who produced the poetic dramas *Winterset* and *High Tor*, Jed Harris *Our Town*, Sam Harris *Of Mice and Men*. Finally, in the fall of 1938 came an association of five older dramatists, The Playwrights' Theatre, devoted to no program other than personal interest and yet achieving thus far one season of uncommon lustre. This group was completely free from concessions to commerce whether its plays were successful as was eminently the case with *Abe Lincoln in Illinois* and *No Time for Comedy* or unsuccessful in the instance of Elmer Rice's *American Landscape*. The chronicle of "these full lean years" is that of a theatre venturesome, spirited, and resourceful despite economic chaos within and beyond its boundaries.

To insist upon this fact is important because it is a tribute to our general resilience, as well as to the particular resilience of the theatre. It is only too easy to lose one's patience with that madcap institution, and he is a poor friend indeed who does not at some time or other pelt it with epithets born of mingled vexation and devotion. But one does not expect perfection from anything so human and therefore so fallible as the stage. All one requires of it is protoplasmic activity, and in this respect the theatre reacted better than prophets of disaster could have predicted. It even displayed that index of vitality "trial and error" or "experiment" in stagecraft. Fantasy found abundant scope in the production of *High Tor*. The only approximation of the famous but ambiguous "Stanislavsky system" in this country came from the Group Theatre. A new technique was evolved by the "Living Newspaper." The "learning play" combination of dramatic and lecture methods was imported on two occasions by the Theatre Union and the Group Theatre, and was modified in the Group's production of *Johnny Johnson*. Largely sceneryless, stylized treatment was accorded to *Our Town* and *The Cradle Will Rock*. Even *surréalisme* was pressed into service, in the Group's staging of *My Heart's in the Highlands*. And these methods, it is important to note, were employed not by long-haired esthetes but by tough-minded organizations addressing the plebes in the name of collective welfare, as well as by a hardboiled producer whose business it is to make the theatre *pay*.

Athens crowned the theatre with glory while fighting for its existence against a host of enemies. Germany advanced stagecraft by leaps and bounds at a time when it suffered the miseries of inflation and national humiliation. America, struggling through a decade of economic distress, likewise affirmed the strength of the human spirit that often proves so painfully blind and bestial under the whiplash of accumulated errors. The approaching decade may confront us with an ominous question mark, and our hearts may falter at the prospect. But it is something to be able to say that we held our own as long as we could, and that as yet we are undefeated and have no intention of surrendering. And, be it known, as this anthology seeks to show, we laughed, too. Moreover, ours was free and hearty laughter.

3

By their fruit ye shall know them. But in the theatre the only fruit that can be packed away and retained is its literary crop—its drama. The most conclusive proof the period's vitality is the quality of its plays, and this anthology collects some of them.

Naturally they fall into two broad groups—serious and light. But this classification tells us nothing about their nature. They were the product of different minds and temperaments, different outlooks and allegiances, different conditioning. For convenience a more definite line may be drawn between those writers who passed their novitiate in the twenties and those who grew to maturity in the next decade. It is not a hard and fast line; for some of the latter wrote farces with as much insouciance as older practitioners, while some of the older dramatists stood on common ground with the younger revolutionists or sociologists. Moreover, neither the young nor the old remained fixed in their respective grooves. Still there were differences.

Generally, the serious dramatists of the previous decade were variously liberal in politics but remained chiefly interested in individual psychology and in personal matters. Thus Eugene O'Neill, their master, continued to work in the spirit of the twenties. His masterpiece, *Mourning Becomes Electra*, was a psychological tragedy of passion, fixations, and complexes; its point of reference with respect to American society was the narrow puritanism and acquisitiveness which his contemporaries had deplored in many a debunking biography or history. *Days Without End* continued this author's concern with problems of faith and dual personality. His sole departure from his norm was an unexpected tribute to normality in *Ah, Wilderness*, a comedy of rare humor and geniality. True, however, to his introspective, Freudian approach, he suggested that radicalism in the young was only a passing phase of the libido. The point was made without malice and with a good deal of tolerance which enhanced the understanding and amiability of the play. But to apply it to the rampant sons of the thirties would have been incongruous in view of the fact that their particular distemper was caused by unemployment and want.

Maxwell Anderson oscillated between the past and the present. He seemed, in fact, to be definitely committed to romanticism with his successes *Elizabeth, the Queen* and *Mary of Scotland*. Although there were contemporary implications in *Night Over Taos, The Wingless Victory, High Tor, The Masque of Kings*, and *Knickerbocker Holiday*, the romantic afflatus was more or less present in all these plays. In addition, he was concerned with a stylistic problem of great importance—how to create poetic drama in a prosaic age. Since it is comparatively easy to write poetic plays when the subject is set in the past, he proceeded cautiously at first with Elizabethan tragedies, *Elizabeth, the Queen* and *Mary of Scotland*. Tactfully he moved closer to our own time and place with *Valley Forge*. Then with one bold leap he applied poetry to a contemporary background of gangsters, East Siders and the Sacco and Vanzetti case in *Winterset*. Fantasy in *High Tor* enabled him to make the same application to a tale about land speculators and a plucky lad who refused to be devoured by the leviathan of our industrial civilization. Musical comedy in *Knickerbocker Holiday* gave him an opportunity to indulge his lyric gift with a travesty on old Peter Stuyvesant, for whom the name of Franklin D. Roosevelt could be substituted by those who were so minded.

The desire to create drama of absolute beauty nevertheless shared interest in Mr. Anderson's mind with a keen awareness of contemporary realities. As a former journalist, he was not inclined to forget them. In 1933 he castigated Congress with the prose satire of *Both Your Houses*. *Night Over Taos* more than hinted that the old order must make room for the new. *Valley Forge* was a reminder that the tree of Liberty is a precious plant nourished by the blood and dreams of the American people. *Winterset*, pointing to an old sore in the American body, was a scathing attack on the perversion of justice by class prejudice; *High Tor* excoriated business ethics; *The Masque of Kings* stressed the futility of revolutions which right one wrong with another and substitute new tyrants for old. *Knickerbocker Holiday* satirized dictatorial ambitions, honored the chronic rebelliousness of the American people, and paid the institution of democracy the left-handed compliment that the tyranny of the majority was less efficient and therefore more tolerable than the rule of a single individual.

No one represented the old-fashioned, but by no means extinct liberal position more consistently than Maxwell Anderson. On the one hand, he spoke up eloquently against social corruption, but on the other hand, he maintained a consistent distrust of government interference and an antipathy to revolutionary action. This he did in defiance of all who favored either the destruction of the *status quo* or the partial socialization of America by reform. If he became a source of irritation to some, he nevertheless represented one segment of opinion. Moreover, his great talent as a showman and dramatist must remain unquestioned. Whatever flaws one will find in his dramatic logic or in his poetic style, he is the master of the period. He is variously derivative, wordy, sentimental, circuitious and tangential. But at his best he is imaginative, fiery, humane, and noble. Or so he was, in the main, in the thirties.

His peers in the serious vein were generally less successful, but almost equally enterprising. Sidney Howard turned out a charming adaptation from the French in *The Late Christopher Bean,* and a creative dramatization of a Sinclair Lewis novel, *Dodsworth.* He remained a man of the twenties: *Dodsworth* was at most a common sense reaction to the adulation of European manners and the passion for self-expression that prevailed in that decade; *Alien Corn* was one of those studies of personal frustration which were dear to it. He came closer to the thirties with his *Yellow Jack,* a drama which moved away from personal complications, honoring the services of science to society in the battle against yellow fever in Cuba. It was a noble and spirited work, and it belonged to the bolder experiments by virtue of its shifting scenes unified by the omission of intermissions. In *The Ghost of Yankee Doodle* this playwright turned to a theme still closer to the problems of the thirties. The war-making of magnates of the press and the dilemma of liberals who are torn between pacifism and profits concerned him here. But the play lacked elevation and excitement, as is often the way of considered and reasoned documents in the theatre. In the main, Sidney Howard failed to catch fire from the period. Nevertheless, he helped to keep the drama intelligent and expert.

Paul Green, Pulitzer Prize winner of 1927, tried to fuse music, symbolism, and drama in several unsuccessful experiments which did not reach Broadway. But he mastered the full-length realistic drama in *The House of Connelly.* This sensitive character play acquired additional interest from its social picture of the decay of the Southern aristocracy and the advent of a more vigorous order. The chain-gang system of the South fired him to write one of the finest American one-acters in *Hymn to the Rising Sun,* a tragedy that wrests poetry from what is sordid and properly colloquial in his material; it is a vivid telescoping of brutal social fact and human psychology. Finally, he topped his efforts to create imaginative drama with *Johnny Johnson,* supported by the notable music of the German refugee Kurt Weill. Moreover, this was no mere exercise in expressionism but a bitter and poignant tragi-comedy of a good man in a vile world, of a homespun lover of peace in the midst of sadists, madmen, and fools.

More definitely irate and embattled were Elmer Rice and John Howard Lawson, who joined hands with the younger rebels. The former poured vitriol, in *The Left Bank,* on the affectations of bohemian artists who coddle their souls in Paris. He followed this with an excellent character play, *Counsellor-at-Law.* By 1933, however, he had worked up a blinding indignation at the state of the nation, and his *We, the People* became a kaleidoscopic and overcrowded indictment. An exposé of fascist justice (*Judgment Day*), a comparison between American and Soviet viewpoints favorable to the latter (*Between Two Worlds*), and a call for a socially responsible liberalism, with American ancestors rising from the grave to instruct the age (*American Landscape*), completed his contribution to the thirties. He was poorly rewarded for his social dramas and their artistry left much to be desired; they were more honorable than satisfying. Intellectually even more inclined to the "left", John Howard Lawson deplored the corruption of character by the profit motive in his generally effective *Success Story.* He decried the waste of American life in his gangster and show-girl melodrama *The Pure in Heart,* and juxtaposed a rich woman and revolutionary lover in *Gentlefolk.* Then realizing that the last two unsuccessful efforts were muddled, and fired by the cause of the working-class, he wrote the panoramic strike play *Marching Song,* too hortatory but poetic and exciting.

4

The twenties had revealed several extremely competent writers of comedy. They continued to function variously, some of them turning to serious drama, others intensifying their interest in ideas or problems, still others remaining content to be merely clever and entertaining. Among the latter, that expert team Mr. and Mrs. Spewack continued to be sharp and ingenious in *Clear All Wires,* as well as in the delightful musical comedy *Leave It to Me.* They achieved a native farce of rare vigor and bite in *Boy Meets Girl* by falling back upon one of the staples of American humor—Hollywood.

Philip Barry, an old friend of the amenities in the twenties, wavered. His temperament deepened, and he produced the psychoanalytical fantasy *Hotel Universe,* an original study of bedevilled members of the upper-class and of the intelligentsia. This was at the beginning of the decade. At its end he added another testament to the serious side of his nature in *Here Come the Clowns.* This was an allegory of the search for the justice of God and of the unequal conflict between love and hatred in the contemporary world. Both works were distinctly flawed; both added considerable nobility and aspiration to the theatre. He also tapped a serious vein in *Tomorrow and Tomorrow,* but with no marked reference to the world beyond the household of a childless couple. His other more moralistic efforts, however, failed, and their author returned to the comic spirit. Without being noticeably ebullient in *The Animal Kingdom,* produced in 1932, he had nevertheless extracted humor out of a predatory wife and an intelligent mistress. In *The Philadelphia Story,* seven years later, Mr. Barry moved into the mansions of our plutocracy to combine an entertaining analysis of a proud girl with a playful plea for tolerance for "the rich and mighty." His contribution to the problems that troubled his contemporaries was the "liberal" point that the upper brackets, as well as the radical movement, did not necessarily teem with ogres.

S. N. Behrman never wavered; his province had been high comedy, and high comedy it continued to be. Less of a master of plot than Philip Barry, he is inimitable in his mastery of dialogue and in his illumination of different viewpoints. And since ideas and viewpoints clashed audibly in the period, he made the time-spirit his own. From the mild flare-up of a wealthy man who marries out of his class in *Brief Moment,* Mr. Behrman moved on to a succession of controversial comedies. In the love story of *Biography* he maintained an understanding balance between the volatile tempérament that is merely amused at self-seeking or toryism and the acerb spirit of a young man who, having suffered from the world's injustice, cannot give quarter. Moving closer to tragedy in *Rain from Heaven,* Mr. Behrman showed the world of the artist and thinker crashing about his ears in the hailstorm of fascism and antisemitism. Recovering his spirits, this inquiring playwright then investigated the failure of wealth and the rebellion of the younger generation in the generally blithe *End of Summer.* Then, after his polished adaption of a French comedy *Amphitryon 38,* he wrote an unintegrated defense of liberalism in *Wine of Choice.* He closed with an amusing triangle woven around a writer of comedies who makes a *gauche* attempt to grapple with social realities foreign to his nature. This last-mentioned work, *No Time for Comedy,* is still running. Sometimes inconsistent, nearly always between two stools as is the case when men consider ideas dispassionately, and generally also more conversational than dramatic, this brilliant author nevertheless was responsible for much of the intelligence and scintillation of the decade's theatre.

The rest of the comic tribe followed individual inclinations. The veteran Rachel Crothers continued to display character and domestic situations with shrewd humor. Without any marked concern for problems now that feminism was an issue of the past, Miss Crothers in *As Husbands Go, When Ladies Meet,* and *Susan and God* kept her weather-eye on the miniature tempests of middle-class women. Marc Connelly, whose comic bent had been charitable and flavorsome, found glorious material in Roark Bradford's *Ol' Man Adam an' his Chillun,* a collection of negro biblical tales. The result was the most lovable play of the thirties *Green Pastures.* Historically never remote, the play was close to the human heart, and the trials it recounted are eternally relevant.

His erstwhile collaborator, the fertile George S. Kaufman continued, with the aid of various collaborators, to reveal the multiple facets of his temperament. Above all, he remained a showman. But the stresses of the period met with a continual response from his nimble spirit, playful on the boards and unencumbered by profundity. While the Hoover administration was waning during 1930-1932 amid clouds of disapproval, Mr. Kaufman (with Morrie Ryskind) delivered himself of that brilliant musical travesty *Of Thee I Sing,* and its less successful sequel *Let 'Em Eat Cake* had reference to the economic upheaval. Both did much to lift musical comedy from the saccharine in which it was usually imbedded. Without benefit of an orchestra, *First Lady* satirized Washington society; and another musical comedy, *I'd Rather Be Right,* dealt ambidextrously with the aims and measures of the New Deal. Turning to the arts, Mr. Kaufman, with Moss Hart, waxed lugubrious (and somewhat autobiographical) in *Merrily We Roll Along* over a writer's loss of his ideals. Then, with Miss Edna Ferber, he described the struggles of the valiant young people who try to remain loyal to the theatre despite its neglect of them in *Stage Door.* This play was not devoid of sentimentality despite its humor, but it touched a raw wound in view of the theatre's doldrums.

Soon Mr. Kaufman hastened to pour balm on all wounds with the madcap, philosophical plea to let life slide in *You Can't Take It With You.* Although strictly considered, most Americans could not afford that luxury, this was an amiable prescription. Coupled with a disarming tolerance, it promoted good feeling and hilarity in the theatre. But this playwright's final contribution noticed that a state of bliss was growing precarious in an era of unsolved problems. His most recent play, *The American Way,* challenged the visible threat of fascism with a glowing chronicle of "the American Way." With a showman's partiality for theatrical effects, he oversimplified matters, sentimentalized, and came perilously close to chauvinism. But there was never any doubt about his intentions, and the total effect was inspiriting.

Most remarkable, however, was the evolution of the youngest of the "old men". After two sentimental melodramas of no great moment—*Waterloo Bridge* and *This is New York*—it seemed as if Robert Sherwood's forte was comedy. He had first attracted attention with his historical comedy *The Road to Rome* in 1927, and his first success in the thirties was the Austrian triangle *Reunion in Vienna.* But it was apparent that his historical bent was considerable and that it was neither antiquarian nor dilettante. He was much concerned with the passing of systems, the death of societies; like John Webster during the twilight of the English renaissance, Sherwood saw the skull beneath the skin. *Reunion in Vienna,* in addition to being excellent comedy when a psychoanalyst was caught in his own cerebral coils, was a vivid picture of the decayed and exiled Hapsburg aristocracy. This was followed by a static eulogy on the dying civilization of Athens, *Acropolis,* which was professionally produced only in London. For all its shortcomings, it was a searching work, and it was not difficult to discover in it an eloquent lament for the passing of European civilization. Then came *The Petrified Forest,* an attempt, as he declared, "to show the passing of an epoch in the terms of melodrama and assembled characters" in an American locale. Its suicidal intellectual clearly symbolized the defeat of spirit by matter, of culture by brute force. The playwright was not, however, happy in his choice of a hero, and his elegiac mood was somewhat maudlin, so that only the melodrama *per se* was completely realized.

Finally, he struck home with *Idiot's Delight,* a satiric and mournful evocation of the madness of war and chauvinism which engulfs even the most intelligent members of society. Once again he showed civilization going to pot in a welter of wasted or corrupted lives. And again the author's past welled up to dilute the force of his meaning and enhance his showmanship; this time it was his tried talent for comedy that brought debit and credit to his pacifist play in the form of savory chorus girl episodes. "The trouble with me," he has said, perhaps with his tongue in his cheek, "is that I start off with a big message and end with nothing but good entertainment." For his final contribution to the thirties, however, Mr. Sherwood needed no such apology. His current *Abe Lincoln in Illinois* has succeeded without concessions to the public. Moreover, he has at least temporarily shed his negativism. His biographical drama is a noble, if at first leisurely and unexciting, affirmation of American ideals through the one national hero who best embodied them both as a political figure and a man.

5

After this chronicle, it might seem that the new blood of the thirties could not have boiled more perceptibly than that which had started flowing in the twenties. And a glance at comedy might confirm the assumption. The most incisive high comedy by the new generation, Clare Boothe's *The Women,* differed at most from the satires of the elders only in its more abundant use of acid. No American writer has ever arranged such an exhibit of parasitism as Miss Boothe's gallery of idle, backbiting and unscrupulous women. If one did not know something about this author's background, one might accuse her of being a "bolshie" and of boring from within. Yet there is no fear of this. She is or seems oblivious of the fact that her only good woman is also useless (and for the most part without the excuse of being interesting). Moreover, the amenities are restored by a happy conclusion. Mark Reed's *Yes, My Darling Daughter* pokes gentle fun at the ex-radicals of Greenwich Village days and generously allows their children a taste of their parents' liberty. But respectability is hardly stormed by this genial comedy, the author's first major contribution to the theatre although he has been writing since 1919—which perhaps entitles him to be listed with the youngsters.

Finally, not even a microscope could reveal any cleavage between that excellent farce of the thirties *Three Men on a Horse* and older products. It consists of those ever-fresh but hardly novel ingredients of American low comedy: salty colloquialism, an amusingly realized background which alternates between the suburbs and a racetrack den, a lovable nitwit, and a series of fortuitous circumstances. The formula also applies, with various modifications, to such other expertly contrived farces of the decade as *Room Service, Brother Rat,* and *Personal Appearance.*

Nor is there anything topical in the content of that two-thirds excellent drama *Our Town* by Thornton Wilder, who as a dramatist (but not as a novelist) belongs to the thirties. This cross-section of small-town life in America is an affirmation of the simple humanity that seeks to round its cycle of life, love, and death quietly. *Our Town* belongs to the classic tradition by its "above-the-battle" viewpoint. If its flavor is wholly and great-heartedly American, if its nostalgic re-collection of vanished tranquility (only a partial reality, as Mr. Wilder knows) has contemporary implications, its prime interest is the most universal of uni-versals "Life". Something to the same effect also appears in the most charming fantasy of recent years *On Borrowed Time,* in which Death reaps his harvest with a gentleness that is rapidly becoming anomalous. These plays did not grapple with the age. Their authors were eager only to make breathing in it more tolerable.

Still, as the first portion of this essay suggested, many of the new playwrights were burning with indignation at the state of the world or were at least sensible of much social injustice and ferment. Even so genial a comedy as Arthur Kober's *Having Wonderful Time* injected into its summer camp antics the ache of the younger generation, deprived of its claim to happiness but struggling for it with pathetic intensity. Less successful plays traced the ravages of the depression with varying seriousness, ranging from tearfully comic imbroglios of *The Three-Cornered Moon* to the tragedy of wasted youth in *Class of 29* and the angry melodrama of the Siftons' *1931.* These works, deficient in the polish that their authors could not, and would not, supply, told a darker and more immediate tale than the survivors of the twenties cared to put on the stage. Depression plays were indeed legion, when one-acters and unproduced scripts are added to the list. Nor were they confined to the doldrums of youth; a jeremiad like *But for the Grace of God* distributed suffering impartially between parent and children.

Tobacco Road is the classic of this school. No other play of the period con-veyed such misery, such degradation, and such hopelessness as Jack Kirkland's dramatization of Erskine Caldwell's inferno of "white trash" life in the South. Fortunately its earthiness produced a naturalistic comedy which could make its gravest implications acceptable as theatre. Historians might be tempted to consider it the corner-stone of the decade's drama on the strength of its long run. It has held the stage since December, 1933, and has been held up as a case-history by nearly every reformer. To suggest that the Rip Van Winkle story of a shiftless farmer and the salacious details stressed by the production have attracted more customers than the social message detracts only slightly from the significance of *Tobacco Road.* Only a sensational play could have made Erskine Caldwell's original material so palatable to the nation.

It is one of several realistic expositions which commanded attention and comment. Such an exposé, in a sense, is that excellent dramatization John Stein-beck's *Of Mice and Men,* which brought the itinerant worker into the limelight. Few plays have conveyed so much pathos as this tragedy of homeless men holding fast to each other and dreaming of a place of their own. Unlike *Tobacco Road,* moreover, Steinbeck's humane treatment of the theme lifts one from the depths; the characters have an inarticulate nobility and the light of common things shines in them. Moreover, as is generally the case with work of singular merit, its poetry of the soul relates it to the efforts of other times and places. There are touches of Gorky in Steinbeck's play, and the material recalls O'Neill's sea-pieces in which wandering men also seek a haven. Despite some contrived melodrama in the murder of a somewhat Hollywoodish "vamp" by a half-wit, and despite the lack of tragic stature in the latter, *Of Mice and Men* was one of the most moving plays of the period.

Exposition was indeed the forte of the younger men, another striking example being Sidney Kingsley's *Dead End,* a pungent drama of slum life. This author's critical viewpoint had been subordinated in *Men in White* to a love story between an interne and a girl. Although a love story between an unemployed architect and a kept woman also played a part—and a distracting one—in *Dead End,* the emphasis rested on a group of children who, but for the grace of God, would grow up into gangsters like the killer who is tracked down on its waterfront. Rounding out the picture, Mr. Kingsley indicated a sharp cleavage between poor and rich in this land of plenty by setting the fire-trap tenements flush against a swanky East River residence. There is war between its residents and the denizens of the slums, and the "dead end" of the street might easily suggest both the trapped lives of its children and the unneccessary impasse of American society. Although somewhat contrived and sentimentally resolved, *Dead End* lived richly in its young ragamuffins while casting the shadow of larger matters upon their pier.

Here, moreover, we find the three main pillars of the younger militant drama—exposition of social evil, economic determinism, and stress upon the struggle of the classes. It is significant that Mr. Kingsley topped *Dead End* with a vitriolic assault, in *Ten Million Ghosts,* on the munitions makers who promote wars for profit but escape its ravages. This unwieldly protest is closely related to the propagandist plays of the radical movement. It is noteworthy that the Theatre Union had raised its curtain two years earlier on a similar play, *Peace on Earth* by Albert Maltz and George Sklar.

Symptomatic was the work of Lillian Hellman. *The Children's Hour* might be classed with the psychological dramas of the twenties. It explored abnormality in a maladjusted child and a homosexually inclined teacher. Yet the play did not confine itself to purely clinical details; Miss Hellman suggested a powerful antagonist in the well-to-do community that accepted a child's testimony and persecuted her victims. This intensely tragic drama, replete with well-drawn characters, was however only the beginning of Miss Hellman's invasion of the social scene. It was followed by the short-lived strike play *Days to Come,* poorly focussed and overcrowded but permeated with her talent for incisive characterization. Finally came *The Little Foxes,* a trenchant account of the making of some American fortunes, the rise of industrialism in the South, and the triumph of the predatory dog-eat-dog dispensation. Miss Hellman's ability to combine intense indignation with a sharp analysis of social fact and of individual character was one of the major accomplishments of the period. Only a slight halting in her third acts, a penchant for inconsequential conversions incompletely rooted in the logic of the play, weakened this author's work.

The writers we have considered above were either more or less associated with the so-called left-wing movement in the theatre or they shared its outlook. But one must know its most active proponents to understand its intellectual basis. The playwrights of the Theatre Union, George Sklar, Albert Maltz, Paul Peters, Victor Wolfson, Michael Blankfort, and Albert Bein, along with the new Theatre League discoveries, Clifford Odets and Irwin Shaw, started with a fixed philosophy. Whether or not they adhered to the party programs of Communism or Socialism, they recognized the Marxist principle that modern society is divided between two camps—capital and labor. In the world-wide depression, the re-arming of the nations, and fascism they discerned the writhings of the dying monster, Capitalism. In the strikes that flared up throughout the nation they saw dress rehearsals for revolution. In racial conflicts they found machiavellian machinations by a frightened master-class. In the plight of the middle-class they located a major symptom of the era of the social wars—namely, the proletarianization of the small business man. Had not Marx predicted that the time would come when there would be only workers and monopolistic capitalists in the world, and that the preponderance of the former would create a socialist society!

Indisputably these younger men were firebrands, and their work suffered from violence and one-sidedness. But out of their fire (and smoke) sometimes came theatrical excitement, a commodity that the stage can rarely afford to neglect. *Stevedore* was a gripping purposeful melodrama; John Wexley's *They Shall not Die* made stirring drama out of the Scottsboro Case; Odets' *Waiting for Lefty* assembled a multitude of complaints into a sweeping call for revolutionary action so striking that the play became a *tour de force*. Moreover, these apostolic youngsters knew how to enrich the stage with vivid pictures of proletarian and lower middle-class life in generally overlooked locales from the South to the Bronx. This trenchant kind of realism had not been seen to much advantage in the theatre since *Street Scene* and O'Neill's early works. A good example was Albert Maltz's harrowing description of life among the miners in *Black Pit*. Still another concomitant of such writing was flavorsome dialogue, for which the stage is ever grateful without respect to creed or party-line; it appeared in *Stevedore, Black Pit* and *Let Freedom Ring*, and it became memorable in the work of Clifford Odets.

Imagination also flourished, along with striking dramatic methods. *Waiting for Lefty* employed the expressionistic device of flash-backs, each realistic in content and background but imaginatively projected. Finally, fantasy prevailed in Irwin Shaw's *Bury the Dead;* the dead returned to life on a future battlefield to signify the common man's refusal to be twice-buried by poverty and war. Although Irwin Shaw's long one-acter was somewhat wordy and disjointed, it proved that a socially minded playwright did not have to keep his nose to the grindstone of literal realism in order to convey his meaning or purpose. And soon there arose two other playwrights, Marc Blitzstein and Archibald MacLeish, one an embattled musician and the other a sympathetic poet, to confirm the point.

Marc Blitzstein turned out a rebellious opus compounded of satire, indignation, and challenge, *The Cradle Will Rock*. All the depreciated stock-in-trade of "agit-prop" was here converted into a pungent and original short opera. Its telescoped scenes must have struck many of us as a welcome relief from at least some of the aerated caterwaulings of the Metropolitan Opera House's repertoire. But even more important was the work of Archibald MacLeish, a notable poet and a man of noble convictions. His *Fall of the City* was significant not only because it was a brilliantly imaginative treatment of fascism or because its poetry was superior to any that had been written for the American stage. (If it was equalled and here and there even surpassed by T. S. Eliot's *Murder in the Cathedral,* one must still give the palm to Mr. MacLeish. Mr. Eliot's contribution mixed prose and verse, reached its highest dramatic moment in the concluding prose section, and treated the medieval matter of St. Becket's martyrdom which belongs to an older poetic tradition.) For the future, the greatest significance of *The Fall of the City* lies in the fact that with it a real poet and an intelligent dramatist invaded the broadcasting studios.

Radio drama had been beneath contempt when suddenly the air vibrated with the fresh and incisive lines of this parable of the masses, here seen submitting to a Leader who is nothing but a piece of empty armor. This was the poet's second play, the first—*Panic*, a tragedy of the stock-market crash—having been written for the stage, where it was somewhat ill at ease. Having found his metier in radio drama, this poet also wrote *Air Raid*. This piece sounded a gripping protest against the massacre of unarmed civilians by those who "make war on life itself". Thanks largely to Archibald MacLeish the air-waves are no longer completely monopolized by Pollyanna and her laxative-sponsored cousins.

Finally, "honey" began to come from the "strong" when the lions of the left stopped pawing the ground and roaring. Irwin Shaw's whimsical *The Gentle People* was quiescent by comparison with his *Bury the Dead*. Although his viewpoint was unaltered, and he still defended the common man and proclaimed his revolt, the treatment was leisurely, unhortatory, and oblique. It is unfair to call Odets' later plays a departure from his earliest work *Awake and Sing*, a poignant and dissolving picture of the poor to which the revolutionary ending was a mere appendage and a not very convincing one. But his later work differed materially from the "direct action" of *Waiting for Lefty*. After a semi-symbolic picture of the destruction of middle-class security in *Paradise Lost*, he wrote his best constructed and least rampant play, *Golden Boy*.

Superficially, this saga of a violinist turned prize-fighter might have come from the Beverly Hills studios. Its background was reminiscent of many a flicker, as was perhaps the rather arbitrary transformation of a violinist into a bruiser. But Odets aimed at something higher. Taking a theme from popular life as ready material for critical interpretation, he dramatized the waste inherent in contemporary life. His Joe Bonaparte may never have become a Heifetz, but he was at least a sensitive and moderately gifted lad. Fear of poverty and obscurity, coupled with the extravagant desires fostered by our high-pressure civilization, made him seek a field for easy success. Then the machinations of a prize-fight promoter, himself a victim of economic pressure, snared him to his doom. The "honey" came from Odets' touching picture of the lad's father, from his understanding of the boy, and from his humane evaluation of the prize-fight addicts. Odets' comet dipped somewhat in his next play *Rocket to the Moon*, the story of a love-harassed and work-driven dentist and his variously capsized neighbors. But here again there was more sweetness than thunder, and once more characterization supplanted direct preachment.

The short cycle of the years closed with the young militants located somewhere in the vicinity of their elders. Simultaneously, the latter moved forward a little in the direction of the "social" school with such work as *Abe Lincoln in Illinois* and *The American Way*. They were intrenching democracy against the assault of social misery and fascism. Thus the progress of America's dramatists brought the two generations together more than might have been expected. And between them they brought the contracted theatre of the decade to fruition. The waste, the stumbling, and the lagging of the theatre notwithstanding, the record of the drama was distinctly honorable.

This collection of twenty plays is an obviously incomplete harvest. To have included more than a portion of the crop would have required a book twice as large and expensive. Moreover, the copyright situation is always an impediment to anthologists, and anyone familiar with our recent drama will know that this problem has been only partially surmounted here. Upon being approached by the publisher to edit and introduce this volume, the present writer had more qualms than he should perhaps confess in public.

Fortunately, however, it has been possible to represent the four main currents of our recent drama. Here are the exaltations and the relaxations of both the survivors from the twenties and the newcomers of the thirties. Five serious plays (*Winterset, High Tor, Idiot's Delight, Johnny Johnson,* and *Green Pastures*) and five comedies (*You Can't Take It With You, End of Summer, The Animal Kingdom, Boy Meets Girl,* with *Stage Door* as a final olio to remind us of some of the ardors and endurances of the theatre) represent the veterans. Three comedies (*The Women, Yes, My Darling Daughter,* and *Three Men on a Horse*) and seven weighty contributions (*The Children's Hour, Tobacco Road, Of Mice and Men, Dead End, Golden Boy, Bury the Dead,* and *The Fall of the City*) testify to the proficiency of the recruits. Regret is in order for our inability to include *Mourning Becomes Electra* because of its length, *Our Town* and two or three of last season's items because they were unavailable, and a few other items for related reasons. But there is, I trust, ample compensation in our ability to present *Winterset, High Tor, Idiot's Delight, The Green Pastures, Of Mice and Men, The Children's Hour, The Fall of the City,* and other notable contributions to the contemporary stage. For this much the editor is grateful. Perhaps the reader will be too.

Winterset

BY MAXWELL ANDERSON

CHARACTERS

TROCK
SHADOW
GARTH
MIRIAMNE
ESDRAS
THE HOBO
FIRST GIRL
SECOND GIRL
JUDGE GAUNT
MIO

CARR
HERMAN
LUCIA
PINY
A SAILOR
STREET URCHIN,
POLICEMAN
RADICAL
SERGEANT

Non-speaking

URCHINS

TWO MEN IN BLUE SERGE

NOTE

WINTERSET

ACT ONE

SCENE I

SCENE: *The scene is the bank of a river under a bridgehead. A gigantic span starts from the rear of the stage and appears to lift over the heads of the audience and out to the left. At the right rear is a wall of solid supporting masonry. To the left an apartment building abuts against the bridge and forms the left wall of the stage with a dark basement window and a door in the brick wall. To the right, and in the foreground, an outcropping of original rock makes a barricade behind which one may enter through a cleft. To the rear, against the masonry, two sheds have been built by waifs and strays for shelter. The river bank, in the foreground, is black rock worn smooth by years of trampling. There is room for exit and entrance to the left around the apartment house, also around the rock to the right. A single street lamp is seen at the left—and a glimmer of apartment lights in the background beyond. It is an early, dark December morning.*

TWO YOUNG MEN IN SERGE *lean against the masonry, matching bills.* TROCK ESTRELLA *and* SHADOW *come in from the left.*

TROCK. Go back and watch the car. (*The* TWO YOUNG MEN *go out.* TROCK *walks to the corner and looks toward the city.*)
You roost of punks and gulls! Sleep it off,
whatever you had last night, get down in warm,
one big ham-fat against another—sleep,
cling, sleep and rot! Rot out your pasty guts
with diddling, you had no brain to begin.
If you had
there'd be no need for us to sleep on iron
who had too much brains for you.

SHADOW. Now look, Trock, look,
what would the warden say to talk like that?

TROCK. May they die as I die!
By God, what life they've left me
they shall keep me well! I'll have that out of them—
these pismires that walk like men!

SHADOW. Because, look, chief,
it's all against science and penology
for you to get out and begin to cuss that way
before your prison vittles are out of you. Hell,
you're supposed to leave the pen full of high thought,
kind of noble-like, loving toward all mankind,
ready to kiss their feet—or whatever parts
they stick out toward you. Look at me!

TROCK. I see you.
And even you may not live as long as you think.

You think too many things are funny. Well, laugh.
But it's not so funny.

SHADOW. Come on, Trock, you know me.
Anything you say goes, but give me leave
to kid a little.

TROCK. Then laugh at somebody else!
It's a lot safer! They've soaked me once too often
in that vat of poisoned hell they keep up-state
to soak men in, and I'm rotten inside, I'm all
one liquid puke inside where I had lungs
once, like yourself! And now they want to get me
and stir me in again—and that'd kill me—
and that's fine for them. But before that happens to me
a lot of these healthy boys'll know what it's like
when you try to breathe and have no place to put air—
they'll learn it from me!

SHADOW. They've got nothing on you, chief.

TROCK. I don't know yet. That's what I'm here to find out.
If they've got what they might have
it's not a year this time—
no, nor ten. It's screwed down under a lid.—
I can die quick enough, without help.

SHADOW. You're the skinny kind
that lives forever.

2

TROCK. He gave me a half a year,
the doc at the gate.

SHADOW. Jesus.

TROCK. Six months I get,
and the rest's dirt, six feet. (LUCIA, *the
street-piano man, comes in right from behind the rock and goes to the shed where
he keeps his piano.* PINY, *the apple woman,
follows and stands in the entrance.* LUCIA
*speaks to Estrella, who still stands facing
Shadow.*)

LUCIA. Morning. (TROCK *and* SHADOW *go out
round the apartment house without speaking.*)

PINY. Now what would you call them?

LUCIA. Maybe someting da river washed up.

PINY. Nothing ever washed him—that black
one.

LUCIA. Maybe not, maybe so. More like his
pa and ma raise-a heem in da cellar .(*He
wheels out the piano.*)

PINY. He certainly gave me a turn. (*She
lays a hand on the rock.*)

LUCIA. You don' live-a right, ol' gal. Take
heem easy. Look on da bright-a side. Never
say-a die. Me, every day in every way I getta
be da regular heller. (*He starts out.*)

CURTAIN

SCENE II

SCENE: *A cellar apartment under the apartment building, floored with cement and
roofed with huge boa constrictor pipes that run slantwise from left to right, dwarfing
the room. An outside door opens to the left and a door at the right rear leads to the
interior of the place. A low squat window to the left. A table at the rear and a few
chairs and books make up the furniture.* GARTH, *son of* ESDRAS, *sits alone, holding a
violin upside down to inspect a crack at its base. He lays the bow on the floor and runs
his fingers over the joint.* MIRIAMNE *enters from the rear, a girl of fifteen.* GARTH *looks
up, then down again.*

MIRIAMNE. Garth—

GARTH. The glue lets go. It's the steam, I
guess.
It splits the hair on your head.

MIRIAMNE. It can't be mended?

GARTH. I can't mend it.
No doubt there are fellows somewhere
who'd mend it for a dollar—and glad to
do it.
That is if I had a dollar.—Got a dollar?
No, I thought not.

MIRIAMNE. Garth, you've sat at home here
three days now. You haven't gone out at all.
Something frightens you.

GARTH. Yes?

MIRIAMNE. And father's frightened.
He reads without knowing where. When a
shadow falls
across the page he waits for a blow to follow
after the shadow. Then in a little while
he puts his book down softly and goes out
to see who passed.

GARTH. A bill collector, maybe.
We haven't paid the rent.

MIRIAMNE. No.

GARTH. You're a bright girl, sis.—
You see too much. You run along and cook.
Why don't you go to school?

MIRIAMNE. I don't like school.
They whisper behind my back.

GARTH. Yes? About what?

MIRIAMNE. What did the lawyer mean
that wrote to you?

GARTH (*rising*). What lawyer?

MIRIAMNE. I found a letter
on the floor of your room. He said, "Don't
get me wrong,
but stay in out of the rain the next few days,
just for instance."

GARTH. I thought I burned that letter.

MIRIAMNE. Afterward you did. And then
what was printed
about the Estrella gang—you hid it from me,

you and father. What is it—about this murder—?

GARTH. Will you shut up, you fool!

MIRIAMNE. But if you know
why don't you tell them, Garth?
If it's true—what they say—
you knew all the time Romagna wasn't
guilty,
and could have said so—

GARTH. Everybody knew
Romagna wasn't guilty! But they weren't
listening
to evidence in his favor. They didn't want it.
They don't want it now.

MIRIAMNE. But was that why
they never called on you?—

GARTH. So far as I know
they never'd heard of me—and I can assure
you
I knew nothing about it—

MIRIAMNE. But something's wrong—
and it worries father—

GARTH. What could be wrong?

MIRIAMNE. I don't know. (*A pause.*)

GARTH. And I don't know. You're a good
kid, Miriamne,
but you see too many movies. I wasn't
mixed up
in any murder, and I don't mean to be.
If I had a dollar to get my fiddle fixed
and another to hire a hall, by God I'd fiddle
some of the prodigies back into Sunday
School
where they belong, but I won't get either,
and so
I sit here and bite my nails—but if you
hoped
I had some criminal romantic past
you'll have to look again!

MIRIAMNE. Oh, Garth, forgive me—
But I want you to be so far above such
things
nothing could frighten you. When you seem
to shrink
and be afraid, and you're the brother I
love,
I want to run there and cry, if there's any
question
they care to ask, you'll be quick and glad
to answer,
for there's nothing to conceal!

GARTH. And that's all true—

MIRIAMNE. But then I remember—
how you dim the lights—
and we go early to bed—and speak in
whispers—
and I could think there's a death somewhere
behind us—
an evil death—

GARTH (*hearing a step*). Now for God's
sake, be quiet! (ESDRAS, *an old rabbi with
a kindly face, enters from the outside. He
is hurried and troubled.*)

ESDRAS. I wish to speak alone with someone
here
if I may have this room. Miriamne—

MIRIAMNE (*turning to go*). Yes, father.
(*The outer door is suddenly thrown open.*
TROCK *appears.*)

TROCK (*after a pause*). You'll excuse me
for not knocking. (SHADOW *follows* TROCK
in.)
Sometimes it's best to come in quiet. Sometimes
it's a good way to go out. Garth's home,
I see.
He might not have been here if I made a
point
of knocking at doors.

GARTH. How are you, Trock?

TROCK. I guess
you can see how I am.
(*To* MIRIAMNE). Stay here. Stay where you
are.
We'd like to make your acquaintance.
—If you want the facts
I'm no better than usual, thanks. Not
enough sun,
my physician tells me. Too much close confinement.
A lack of exercise and an overplus
of beans in the diet. You've done well, no
doubt?

GARTH. I don't know what makes you think
so.

TROCK. Who's the family?

GARTH. My father and my sister.

TROCK. Happy to meet you.
Step inside a minute. The boy and I
have something to talk about.

ESDRAS. No, no—he's said nothing—
nothing, sir, nothing!

TROCK. When I say go out, you go—

ESDRAS (pointing to the door). Miriamne—

GARTH. Go on out, both of you!

ESDRAS. Oh, sir—I'm old—
old and unhappy—

GARTH. Go on! (MIRIAMNE and ESDRAS go
inside.)

TROCK. And if you listen
I'll riddle that door! (SHADOW shuts the door
behind them and stands against it.)
I just got out, you see,
and I pay my first call on you.

GARTH. Maybe you think
I'm not in the same jam you are.

TROCK. That's what I do think.
Who started looking this up?

GARTH. I wish I knew,
and I wish he was in hell! Some damned
professor
with nothing else to do. If you saw his
stuff
you know as much as I do.

TROCK. It wasn't you
turning state's evidence?

GARTH. Hell, Trock, use your brain!
The case was closed. They burned Romagna
for it
and that finished it. Why should I look for
trouble
and maybe get burned myself?

TROCK. Boy, I don't know,
but I just thought I'd find out.

GARTH. I'm going straight, Trock.
I can play this thing, and I'm trying to make
a living.
I haven't talked and nobody's talked to me.
Christ—it's the last thing I'd want!

TROCK. Your old man knows.

GARTH. That's where I got the money that
last time
when you needed it. He had a little saved
up,
but I had to tell him to get it. He's as
safe
as Shadow there.

TROCK (looking at Shadow). There could
be people safer
than that son-of-a-bitch.

SHADOW. Who?

TROCK. You'd be safer dead
along with some other gorillas.

SHADOW. It's beginning to look
as if you'd feel safer with everybody dead,
the whole god-damn world.

TROCK. I would. These Jesus-bitten
professors! Looking up their half-ass cases!
We've got enough without that.

GARTH. There's no evidence
to reopen the thing.

TROCK. And suppose they called on you
and asked you to testify?

GARTH. Why then I'd tell 'em
that all I know is what I read in the papers.
And I'd stick to that.

TROCK. How much does your sister know?

GARTH. I'm honest with you, Trock. She read
my name
in the professor's pamphlet, and she was
scared
the way anybody would be. She got nothing
from me, and anyway she's go to the chair
herself before she'd send me there.

TROCK. Like hell.

GARTH. Besides, who wants to go to trial
again
except the radicals?—You and I won't spill
and unless we did there's nothing to take to
court
as far as I know. Let the radicals go on howling
about getting a dirty deal. They always
howl
and nobody gives a damn. This professor's
red—
everybody knows it.

TROCK. You're forgetting the judge.
Where's the damn judge?

GARTH. What judge?

TROCK. Read the morning papers.
It says Judge Gaunt's gone off his nuts. He's
got

that damn trial on his mind, and been going
round
proving to everybody he was right all the
time
and the radicals were guilty—stopping
people
in the street to prove it—and now he's nuts
entirely
and nobody knows where he is.

GARTH. Why don't they know?

TROCK. Because he's on the loose somewhere!
They've got the police of three cities looking
for him.

GARTH. Judge Gaunt?

TROCK. Yes. Judge Gaunt.

SHADOW. Why should that worry you?
He's crazy, ain't he? And even if he wasn't
he's arguing on your side. You're jittery,
chief.
God, all the judges are looney. You've got
the jitters,
and you'll damn well give yourself away
some time
peeing yourself in public. (TROCK *half turns
toward* SHADOW *in anger.*)
Don't jump the gun now,
I've got pockets in my clothes, too. (*His
hand is in his coat pocket.*)

TROCK. All right. Take it easy. (*He takes
his hand from his pocket, and* SHADOW *does
the same.*) (*To* GARTH)
Maybe you're lying to me and maybe you're
not.
Stay at home a few days.

GARTH. Sure thing. Why not?

TROCK. And when I say stay at home I
mean stay home.
If I have to go looking for you you'll stay
a long time
wherever I find you. (*To* SHADOW)
Come on. We'll get out of here. (*To* GARTH)
Be seeing you. (SHADOW *and* TROCK *go out.
After a pause* GARTH *walks over to his chair
and picks up the violin. Then he puts it
down and goes to the inside door, which he
opens.*)

GARTH. He's gone. (MIRIAMNE *enters,* ESDRAS
behind her.)

MIRIAMNE (*going up to* GARTH.) Let's not
stay here. (*She puts her hands on his
arms.*)

I thought he'd come for something—horrible.
Is he coming back?

GARTH. I don't know.

MIRIAMNE. Who is he, Garth?

GARTH. He'd kill me if I told you who he is,
that is, if he knew.

MIRIAMNE. Then don't say it—

GARTH. Yes, and I'll say it! I was with a
gang one time
that robbed a pay roll. I saw murder done,
and Trock Estrella did it. If that got out
I'd go to the chair and so would he—that's
why
he was here today—

MIRIAMNE. But that's not true—

ESDRAS. He says it
to frighten you, child.

GARTH. Oh, no I don't! I say it
because I've held it in too long! I'm damned
if I sit here forever, and look at the door,
waiting for Trock with his sub-machine gun,
waiting
for police with a warrant!—I say I'm damned, and I am,
no matter what I do! These piddling scales
on a violin—first position, third, fifth,
arpeggios in E—and what I'm thinking
is Romagna dead for the murder—dead
while I sat here
dying inside—dead for the thing Trock did
while I looked on—and I could have saved
him, yes—
but I sat here and let him die instead of me
because I wanted to live! Well, it's no life,
and it doesn't matter who I tell, because
I mean to get it over!

MIRIAMNE. Garth, it's not true!

GARTH. I'd take some scum down with me
if I died—
that'd be one good deed—

ESDRAS. Son, son, you're mad—
someone will hear—

GARTH. Then let them hear! I've lived
with ghosts too long, and lied too long.
God damn you
if you keep me from the truth!—(*He turns
away.*)

Oh, God damn the world!
I don't want to die! (*He throws himself down.*)

ESDRAS. I should have known.
I thought you hard and sullen,
Garth, my son. And you were a child, and
    hurt
with a wound that might be healed.
—All men have crimes,
and most of them are hidden, and many
    are heavy
as yours must be to you. (GARTH *sobs.*)
They walk the streets
to buy and sell, but a spreading crimson
    stain
tinges the inner vestments, touches flesh,
and burns the quick. You're not alone.

GARTH. I'm alone
in this.

ESDRAS. Yes, if you hold with the world that
    only
those who die suddenly should be revenged.
But those whose hearts are cancered, drop
    by drop
in small ways, little by little, till they've
    borne
all they can bear, and die—these deaths will
    go
unpunished now as always. When we're
    young
we have faith in what is seen, but when
    we're old
we know that what is seen is traced in air
and built on water. There's no guilt under
    heaven,
just as there's no heaven, till men believe it—
no earth, till men have seen it, and have a
    word
to say this is the earth.

GARTH. Well, I say there's an earth,
and I say I'm guilty on it, guilty as hell.

ESDRAS. Yet till it's known you bear no guilt
    at all—
unless you wish. The days go by like film,
like a long written scroll, a figured veil
unrolling out of darkness into fire
and utterly consumed. And on this veil,
running in sounds and symbols of men's
    minds
reflected back, life flickers and is shadow
going toward flame. Only what men can see
exists in that shadow. Why must you rise
    and cry out:
That was I, there in the ravelled tapestry,
there, in that pistol flash, when the man was
    killed.
I was there, and was one, and am blood-
    stained!
Let the wind
and fire take that hour to ashes out of time
and out of mind! This thing that men call
    justice,
this blind snake that strikes men down in
    the dark,
mindless with fury, keep your hand back
    from it,
pass by in silence—let it be forgotten, for-
    gotten!—
Oh, my son, my son—have pity!

MIRIAMNE. But if it was true
and someone died—then it was more than
    shadow—
and it doesn't blow away—

GARTH. Well, it was true.

ESDRAS. Say it if you must. If you have heart
    to die,
say it, and let them take what's left—there
    was little
to keep, even before—

GARTH. Oh, I'm a coward—
I always was. I'll be quiet and live. I'll live
even if I have to crawl. I know. (*He gets
up and goes into the inner room.*)

MIRIAMNE. Is it better
to tell a lie and live?

ESDRAS. Yes, child. It's better.

MIRIAMNE. But if I had to do it—
I think I'd die.

ESDRAS. Yes, child. Because you're young.

MIRIAMNE. Is that the only reason?

ESDRAS. The only reason.

CURTAIN

SCENE III

SCENE: *Under the bridge, evening of the same day. When the curtain rises* MIRIAMNE *is sitting alone on the ledge at the rear of the apartment house. A spray of light fall on her from a street lamp above. She shivers a little in her thin coat, but sits still as if heedless of the weather. Through the rocks on the other side a* TRAMP *comes down to the river bank, hunting a place to sleep. He goes softly to the apple-woman's hut and looks in, then turns away, evidently not daring to preempt it. He looks at* MIRIAMNE *doubtfully. The door of the street-piano man is shut. The vagabond passes it and picks carefully among some rags and shavings to the right.* MIRIAMNE *looks up and sees him but makes no sign. She looks down again, and the man curls himself up in a makeshift bed in the corner, pulling a piece of sacking over his shoulders. Two* GIRLS *come in from round the apartment house.*

FIRST GIRL. Honest, I never heard of anything so romantic. Because you never liked him.

SECOND GIRL. I certainly never did.

FIRST GIRL. You've got to tell me how it happened. You've got to.

SECOND GIRL. I couldn't. As long as I live I couldn't. Honest, it was terrible. It was terrible.

FIRST GIRL. What was so terrible?

SECOND GIRL. The way it happened.

FIRST GIRL. Oh, please—not to a soul, never.

SECOND GIRL. Well, you know how I hated him because he had such a big mouth. So he reached over and grabbed me, and I began all falling to pieces inside, the way you do—and I said, "Oh no you don't, mister," and started screaming and kicked a hole through the windshield and lost a shoe, and he let go and was cursing and growling because he borrowed the car and didn't have money to pay for the windshield, and he started to cry, and I got so sorry for him I let him, and now he wants to marry me.

FIRST GIRL. Honest, I never heard of anything so romantic! (*She sees the sleeping Tramp.*) My God, what you won't see! (*They give the Tramp a wide berth, and go out right. The* TRAMP *sits up looking about him.* JUDGE GAUNT, *an elderly, quiet man, well dressed but in clothes that have seen some weather, comes in uncertainly from the left. He holds a small clipping in his hand and goes up to the* HOBO.)

GAUNT (*tentatively*). Your pardon, sir. Your pardon, but perhaps you can tell me the name of this street.

HOBO. Huh?

GAUNT. The name of this street?

HOBO. This ain't no street.

GAUNT. There, where the street lamps are.

HOBO. That's the alley.

GAUNT. Thank you. It has a name, no doubt?

HOBO. That's the alley.

GAUNT. I see. I won't trouble you. You wonder why I ask, I daresay.—I'm a stranger.—Why do you look at me? (*He steps back.*) I—I'm not the man you think. You've mistaken me, sir.

HOBO. Huh?

JUDGE. Perhaps misled by a resemblance. But you're mistaken—I had an errand in this city. It's only by accident that I'm here—

HOBO (*muttering*). You go to hell.

JUDGE (*going nearer to him, bending over him*). Yet why should I deceive you? Before God, I held the proofs in my hands. I hold them still. I tell you the defense was cunning beyond belief, and unscrupulous in its use of propaganda—they gagged at nothing—not even—(*He rises.*) No, no— I'm sorry—this will hardly interest you. I'm sorry. I have an errand. (*He looks toward the street.* ESDRAS *enters from the basement and goes to* MIRIAMNE. *The* JUDGE *steps back into the shadows.*)

ESDRAS. Come in, my daughter. You'll be cold here.

MIRIAMNE. After a while.

ESDRAS. You'll be cold. There's a storm coming.

MIRIAMNE. I didn't want him to see me crying. That was all.

ESDRAS. I know.

MIRIAMNE. I'll come soon. (ESDRAS *turns reluctantly and goes out the way he came.* MIRIAMNE *rises to go, pausing to dry her eyes.* MIO *and* CARR, *road boys of seventeen or so, come round the apartment house. The* JUDGE *has disappeared.*)

CARR. Thought you said you were never coming east again.

MIO. Yeah, but—I heard something changed my mind.

CARR. Same old business?

MIO. Yes. Just as soon not talk about it.

CARR. Where did you go from Portland?

MIO. Fishing—I went fishing. God's truth.

CARR. Right after I left?

MIO. Fell in with a fisherman's family on the coast and went after the beautiful mackerel fish that swim in the beautiful sea. Family of Greeks—Aristides Marinos was his lovely name. He sang while he fished. Made the pea-green Pacific ring with his bastard Greek chanties. Then I went to Hollywood High School for a while.

CARR. I'll bet that's a seat of learning.

MIO. It's the hind end of all wisdom. They kicked me out after a time.

CARR. For cause?

MIO. Because I had no permanent address, you see. That means nobody's paying school taxes for you, so out you go. (*To* MIRIAMNE.) What's the matter, kid?

MIRIAMNE. Nothing. (*She looks up at him, and they pause for a moment.*) Nothing.

MIO. I'm sorry.

MIRIAMNE. It's all right. (*She withdraws her eyes from his and goes out past him. He turns and looks after her.*)

CARR. Control your chivalry.

MIO. A pretty kid.

CARR. A baby.

MIO. Wait for me.

CARR. Be a long wait? (MIO *steps swiftly out after* MIRIAMNE, *then returns.*) Yeah?

MIO. She's gone.

CARR. Think of that.

MIO. No, but I mean—vanished. Presto—into nothing—prodigioso.

CARR. Damn good thing, if you ask me. The homely ones are bad enough, but the lookers are fatal.

MIO. You exaggerate, Carr.

CARR. I doubt it.

MIO. Well, let her go. This river bank's loaded with typhus rats, too. Might as well die one death as another.

CARR. They say chronic alcoholism is nice but expensive. You can always starve to death.

MIO. Not always. I tried it. After the second day I walked thirty miles to Niagara Falls and made a tour of the plant to get the sample of shredded wheat biscuit on the way out.

CARR. Last time I saw you you couldn't think of anything you wanted to do except curse God and pass out. Still feeling low?

MIO. Not much different. (*He turns away, then comes back.*) Talk about the lost generation, I'm the only one fits that title. When the State executes your father and your mother dies of grief, and you know damn well he was innocent, and the authorities of your home town politely inform you they'd consider it a favor if you lived somewhere else—that cuts you off from the world—with a meat-axe.

CARR. They asked you to move?

MIO. It came to that.

CARR. God, that was white of them.

MIO. It probably gave them a headache just to see me after all that agitation. They knew as well as I did my father never staged a hold-up. Anyway, I've got a new interest in life now.

CARR. Yes—I saw her.

MIO. I don't mean the skirt.—No, I got wind of something, out west, some college professor investigating the trial and turning up new evidence. Couldn't find anything he'd written out there, so I beat it east and arrived on this blessed island just in time to find the bums holing up in the public library for the winter. I know now what the unemployed have been doing since the depression started. They've been catching up on their reading in the main reference room. Man, what a stench! Maybe I stank, too, but a hobo has the stench of ten because his shoes are poor.

CARR. Tennyson.

MIO. Right. Jeez, I'm glad we met up again! Never knew anybody else that could track me through the driven snow of Victorian literature.

CARR. Now you're cribbing from some half-forgotten criticism of Ben Jonson's Roman plagiarisms.

MIO. Where did you get your education, sap?

CARR. Not in the public library, sap. My father kept a news-stand.

MIO. Well, you're right again. (*There is a faint rumble of thunder.*) What's that? Winter thunder?

CARR. Or Mister God, beating on His little tocsin. Maybe announcing the advent of a new social order.

MIO. Or maybe it's going to rain coffee and doughnuts.

CARR. Or maybe it's going to rain.

MIO. Seems more likely. (*Lowering his voice.*) Anyhow, I found Professor Hobhouse's discussion of the Romagna case. I think he has something. It occurred to me I might follow it up by doing a little sleuthing on my own account.

CARR. Yes?

MIO. I have done a little. And it leads me to somewhere in that tenement house that backs up against the bridge. That's how I happen to be here.

CARR. They'll never let you get anywhere with it, Mio. I told you that before.

MIO. I know you did.

CARR. The State can't afford to admit it was wrong, you see. Not when there's been that much of a row kicked up over it. So for all practical purposes the State was right and your father robbed the pay roll.

MIO. There's still such a thing as evidence.

CARR. It's something you can buy. In fact, at the moment I don't think of anything you can't buy, including life, honor, virtue, glory, public office, conjugal affection and all kinds of justice, from the traffic court to the immortal nine. Go out and make yourself a pot of money and you can buy all the justice you want. Convictions obtained, convictions averted. Lowest rates in years.

MIO. I know all that.

CARR. Sure.

MIO. This thing didn't happen to you.
They've left you your name
and whatever place you can take. For my heritage
they've left me one thing only, and that's to be
my father's voice crying up out of the earth
and quicklime where they stuck him. Electrocution
doesn't kill, you know. They eviscerate them
with a turn of the knife in the dissecting room.
The blood spurts out. The man was alive. Then into
the lime pit, leave no trace. Make it short shrift
and chemical dissolution. That's what they thought
of the man that was my father. Then my mother—
I tell you these county burials are swift
and cheap and run for profit! Out of the house
and into the ground, you wife of a dead dog. Wait,
here's some Romagna spawn left.
Something crawls here—
something they called a son. Why couldn't he die
along with his mother? Well, ease him out of town,
ease him out, boys, and see you're not too gentle.
He might come back. And, by their own living Jesus,

I will go back, and hang the carrion
around their necks that made it!
Maybe I can sleep then.
Or even live.

CARR. You have to try it?

MIO. Yes.
Yes. It won't let me alone. I've tried to live
and forget it—but I was birthmarked with
   hot iron
into the entrails. I've got to find out who
   did it
and make them see it till it scalds their eyes
and make them admit it till their tongues
   are blistered
with saying how black they lied! (HERMAN,
a gawky shoe salesman, enters from the left.)

HERMAN. Hello. Did you see a couple of girls
go this way?

CARR. Couple of girls? Did we see a couple
of girls?

MIO. No.

CARR. No. No girls. (HERMAN *hesitates, then
goes out right.* LUCIA *comes in from the
left, trundling his piano.* PINY *follows him,
weeping.*)

PINY. They've got no right to do it—

LUCIA. All right, hell what, no matter, I
got to put him away, I got to put him away,
that's what the hell! (TWO STREET URCHINS
follow him in.)

PINY. They want everybody on the relief
rolls and nobody making a living?

LUCIA. The cops, they do what the big boss
says. The big boss, that's the mayor, he says
he heard it once too often, the sextette—

PINY. They want graft, that's all. It's a new
way to get graft—

LUCIA. Oh, no, no, no! He's a good man,
the mayor. He's just don't care for music,
that's all.

PINY. Why shouldn't you make a living on
the street? The National Biscuit Company
ropes off Eighth Avenue—and does the
mayor do anything? No, the police hit you
over the head if you try to go through!

LUCIA. You got the big dough, you get the
pull, fine. No big dough, no pull, what the
hell, get off the city property! Tomorrow I

start cooking chestnuts . . . (*He strokes
the piano fondly. The* TWO GIRLS *and* HER-
MAN *comes back from the right.*) She's a
good little machine, this baby. Cost plenty—
and two new records I only played twice.
See, this one. (*He starts turning the crank,
talking while he plays.*) Two weeks since
they play this one in a picture house. (A
SAILOR *wanders in from the left. One of
the* STREET URCHINS *begins suddenly to
dance a wild rumba, the others watch.*)
Good boy—see, it's a lulu—it itches in the
feet! (HERMAN, *standing with his girl, tosses
the boy a penny. He bows and goes on dancing; the other* URCHIN *joins him. The* SAILOR
tosses a coin.)

SAILOR. Go it, Cuba! Go it! (LUCIA *turns the
crank, beaming.*)

SECOND GIRL. Oh, Herman! (*She throws her
arms round* HERMAN *and they dance.*)

FIRST URCHIN. Hey, pipe the professionals!

FIRST GIRL. Do your glide, Shirley! Do your
glide!

LUCIA. Maybe we can't play in front, maybe
we can play behind! (*The* HOBO *gets up from
his nest and comes over to watch. A* YOUNG
RADICAL *wanders in.*) Maybe you don't
know, folks! Tonight we play good-bye to
the piano! Good-bye forever! No more
piano on the streets! No more music! No
more money for the music-man! Last time,
folks! Good-bye to the piano—good-bye
forever! (MIRIAMNE *comes out the rear
door of the apartment and stands watching. The* SAILOR *goes over to the* FIRST GIRL
and they dance together.) Maybe you don't
know, folks! Tomorrow will be sad as
hell, tonight we dance! Tomorrow no more
Verdi, no more rumba, no more good time!
Tonight we play good-bye to the piano,
good-bye forever! (*The* RADICAL *edges up
to* MIRIAMNE, *and asks her to dance. She
shakes her head and he goes to* PINY, *who
dances with him. The* HOBO *begins to do
a few lonely curvets on the side above.*)
Hoy! Hoy! Pick 'em up and take 'em
around! Use the head, use the feet! Last
time forever! (*He begins to sing to the air.*)

MIO. Wait for me, will you?

CARR. Now's your chance. (MIO *goes over to
MIRIAMNE and holds out a hand, smiling.
She stands for a moment uncertain, then*

dances with him. ESDRAS *comes out to watch.* JUDGE GAUNT *comes in from the left. There is a rumble of thunder.*)

LUCIA. Hoy! Hoy! Maybe it rains tonight, maybe it snows tomorrow! Tonight we dance good-bye. (*He sings the air lustily. A* POLICEMAN *comes in from the left and looks on. Two or three* PEDESTRIANS *follow him.*)

POLICEMAN. Hey you! (LUCIA *goes on singing.*)Hey, you!

LUCIA (*still playing*). What you want?

POLICEMAN. Sign off!

LUCIA. What you mean? I get off the street!

POLICEMAN. Sign off!

LUCIA (*still playing*). What you mean? (*The* POLICEMAN *walks over to him.* LUCIA *stops playing and the* DANCERS *pause.*)

POLICEMAN. Cut it.

LUCIA. Is this a street?

POLICEMAN. I say cut it out. (*The* HOBO *goes back to his nest and sits in it, watching.*)

LUCIA. It's the last time. We dance good-bye to the piano.

POLICEMAN. You'll dance good-bye to something else if I catch you cranking that thing again.

LUCIA. All right.

PINY. I'll bet you don't say that to the National Biscuit Company!

POLICEMAN. Lady, you've been selling apples on my beat for some time now, and I said nothing about it—

PINY. Selling apples is allowed—

POLICEMAN. You watch yourself—(*He takes a short walk around the place and comes upon the* HOBO.) What are you doing here? (*The* HOBO *opens his mouth, points to it, and shakes his head.*) Oh, you are, are you? (*He comes back to* LUCIA.) So you trundle your so-called musical instrument to wherever you keep it, and don't let me hear it again. (*The* RADICAL *leaps on the base of the rock at right. The* FIRST GIRL *turns away from the* SAILOR *toward the* SECOND GIRL *and* HERMAN.)

SAILOR. Hey, captain, what's the matter with the music?

POLICEMAN. Not a thing, admiral.

SAILOR. Well, we had a little party going here—

POLICEMAN. I'll say you did.

SECOND GIRL. Please, officer, we want to dance.

POLICEMAN. Go ahead. Dance.

SECOND GIRL. But we want music!

POLICEMAN (*turning to go*). Sorry. Can't help you.

RADICAL. And there you see it, the perfect example of capitalistic oppression! In a land where music should be free as air and the arts should be encouraged, a uniformed minion of the rich, a guardian myrmidon of the Park Avenue pleasure hunters, steps in and puts a limit on the innocent enjoyments of the poor! We don't go to theatres! Why not? We can't afford it! We don't go to night clubs, where women dance naked and the music drips from saxophones and leaks out of Rudy Vallee—we can't afford that either!—But we might at least dance on the river bank to the strains of a barrel organ—! (GARTH *comes out of the apartment and listens.*)

POLICEMAN. It's against the law!

RADICAL. What law? I challenge you to tell me what law of God or man—what ordinance—is violated by this spontaneous diversion? None! I say none! An official whim of the masters who should be our servants!—

POLICEMAN. Get down! Get down and shut up!

RADICAL. By what law, by what ordinance do you order me to be quiet?

POLICEMAN. Speaking without a flag. You know it.

RADICAL (*pulling out a small American flag*). There's my flag! There's the flag of this United States which used to guarantee the rights of man—the rights of man now violated by every third statute of the commonweal—

POLICEMAN. Don't try to pull tricks on me! I've seen you before! You're not making any speech, and you're climbing down—

JUDGE GAUNT (*who has come quietly forward*). One moment, officer. There is some difference of opinion even on the bench as to the elasticity of police power when applied in minor emergencies to preserve civil order. But the weight of authority would certainly favor the defendant in any equable court, and he would be upheld in his demand to be heard.

POLICEMAN. Who are you?

JUDGE GAUNT. Sir, I am not accustomed to answer that question.

POLICEMAN. I don't know you.

GAUNT. I am a judge of some standing, not in your city, but in another with similar statutes. You are aware, of course, that the bill of rights is not to be set aside lightly by the officers of any municipality—

POLICEMAN (*looking over* GAUNT's *somewhat bedraggled costume*). Maybe they understand you better in the town you come from, but I don't get your drift.— (*To the* RADICAL.) I don't want any trouble, but if you ask for it you'll get plenty. Get down!

RADICAL. I'm not asking for trouble, but I'm staying right here. (*The* POLICEMAN *moves toward him.*)

GAUNT (*taking the policeman's arm, but shaken off roughly*). I ask this for yourself, truly, not for the dignity of the law nor the maintenance of precedent. Be gentle with them when their threats are childish—be tolerant while you can—for your harsh word will return on you in the night—return in a storm of cries!—(*He takes the* POLICEMAN's *arm again.*) Whatever they may have said or done, let them disperse in peace! It is better that they go softly, lest when they are dead you see their eyes pleading, and their outstretched hands touch you, fingering cold on your heart!—I have been harsher than you. I have sent men down that long corridor into blinding light and blind darkness! (*He suddenly draws himself erect and speaks defiantly.*) And it was well that I did so! I have been an upright judge! They are all liars! Liars!

POLICEMAN (*shaking* GAUNT *off so that he falls*). Why, you fool, you're crazy!

GAUNT. Yes, and there are liars on the force! They came to me with their shifty lies! (*He catches at the* POLICEMAN, *who pushes him away with his foot.*)

POLICEMAN. You think I've got nothing better to do than listen to a crazy fool?

FIRST GIRL. Shame, shame!

POLICEMAN. What have I got to be ashamed of? And what's going on here, anyway? Where in hell did you all come from?

RADICAL. Tread on him! That's right! Tread down the poor and the innocent! (*There is a protesting murmur in the crowd.*)

SAILOR (*moving in a little*). Say, big boy, you don't have to step on the guy.

POLICEMAN (*facing them, stepping back*). What's the matter with you? I haven't stepped on anybody!

MIO (*at the right, across from the* POLICEMAN). Listen now, fellows, give the badge a chance.
He's doing his job, what he gets paid to do, the same as any of you. They're all picked men,
these metropolitan police, hand picked for loyalty and a fine up-standing pair of shoulders on their legs—it's not so easy to represent the law. Think what he does for all of us, stamping out crime! Do you want to be robbed and murdered in your beds?

SAILOR. What's eating you?

RADICAL. He must be a capitalist.

MIO. They pluck them fresh from Ireland, and a paucity of headpiece is a prime prerequisite. You from Ireland, buddy?

POLICEMAN (*surly*). Where are you from?

MIO. Buddy, I tell you flat I wish I was from Ireland, and could boast some Tammany connections. There's only one drawback
about working on the force. It infects the brain,
it eats the cerebrum. There've been cases known,

fine specimens of manhood, too, where
autopsies,
conducted in approved scientific fashion,
revealed conditions quite incredible
in policemen's upper layers. In some, a trace,
in others, when they've swung a stick too
long,
there was nothing there!—but nothing! Oh,
my friends,
this fine athletic figure of a man
that stands so grim before us, what will
they find
when they saw his skull for the last inspection?
I fear me a little puffball dust will blow
away
rejoining earth, our mother—and this same
dust,
this smoke, this ash on the wind, will represent
all he had left to think with!

THE HOBO. Hooray! (*The* POLICEMAN *turns
on his heels and looks hard at the* HOBO, *who
slinks away.*)

POLICEMAN. Oh, yeah?

MIO. My theme
gives ears to the deaf and voice to the dumb!
But now
forgive me if I say you were most unkind
in troubling the officer. He's a simple man
of simple tastes, and easily confused
when faced with complex issues. He may
reflect
on returning home, that is, so far as he
is capable of reflection, and conclude
that he was kidded out of his uniform pants,
and in his fury when this dawns on him
may smack his wife down!

POLICEMAN. That'll be about enough from
you, too, professor!

MIO. May I say that I think you have
managed this whole situation rather badly,
from the beginning?—

POLICEMAN. You may not! (TROCK *slips in
from the background. The* TWO YOUNG MEN
IN SERGE *come with him.*)

MIO. Oh, but your pardon, sir! It's apparent
to the least competent among us that you
should have gone about your task more
subtly—the glove of velvet, the hand of iron,
and all that sort of thing—

POLICEMAN. Shut that hole in your face!

MIO. Sir, for that remark I shall be satisfied
with nothing less than an unconditional
apology! I have an old score to settle with
policemen, brother, because they're fools
and fat-heads, and you're one of the most
fatuous fat-heads that ever walked his feet
flat collecting graft! Tell that to your
sergeant back in the booby-hatch.

POLICEMAN. Oh, you want an apology, do
you? You'll get an apology out of the other
side of your mouth! (*He steps toward* MIO.
CARR *suddenly stands in his path.*) Get out
of my way! (*He pauses and looks round
him; the crowd looks less and less friendly.
He lays a hand on his gun and backs to a
position where there is nobody behind him*
Get out of here, all of you! Get out! What
are you trying to do—start a riot?

MIO. There now, that's better! That's in the
best police tradition. Incite a riot yourself
and then accuse the crowd.

POLICEMAN. It won't be pleasant if I decide
to let somebody have it! Get out! (*The onlookers begin to melt away. The* SAILOR *goes
out left with the* GIRLS *and* HERMAN. CARR
and MIO *go out right,* CARR *whistling "The
Star Spangled Banner." The* HOBO *follows
them. The* RADICAL *walks past with his head
in the air.* PINY *and* LUCIA *leave the piano
where it stands and slip away to the left. At
the end the* POLICEMAN *is left standing in the
center, the* JUDGE *near him.* ESDRAS *stands in
the doorway.* MIRIAMNE *is left sitting half
in shadow unseen by* ESDRAS.)

JUDGE GAUNT (*to the* POLICEMAN). Yes, but
should a man die, should it be necessary that
one man die for the good of many, make not
yourself the instrument of death, lest you
sleep to wake sobbing! Nay, it avails nothing
that you are the law—this delicate ganglion
that is the brain, it will not bear these
things—! (*The* POLICEMAN *gives the* JUDGE
*the once-over, shrugs, decides to leave him
there and starts out left.* GARTH *goes to his
father—a fine sleet begins to fall through the
street lights.* TROCK *is still visible.*)

GARTH. Get him in here, quick.

ESDRAS. Who, son?

GARTH. The Judge, damn him!

ESDRAS. Is it Judge Gaunt?

GARTH. Who did you think it was? He's crazy as a bedbug and telling the world. Get him inside! (*He looks round.*)

ESDRAS (*going up to* GAUNT). Will you come in, sir?

GAUNT. You will understand, sir. We old men know how softly we must proceed with these things.

ESDRAS. Yes, surely, sir.

GAUNT. It was always my practice—always. They will tell you that of me where I am known. Yet even I am not free of regret— even I. Would you believe it?

ESDRAS. I believe we are none of us free of regret.

GAUNT. None of us? I would it were true. I would I thought it were true.

ESDRAS. Shall we go in, sir? This is sleet that's falling.

GAUNT. Yes. Let us go in. (ESDRAS *and* GARTH *enter the basement and shut the door.* TROCK *goes out with his men. After a pause* MIO *comes back from the right, alone. He stands at a little distance from* MIRIAMNE.)

MIO. Looks like rain. (*She is silent.*)
You live around here? (*She nods gravely.*)
I guess
you thought I meant it—about waiting here
   to meet me. (*She nods again.*)
I'd forgotten about it till I got that winter
across the face. You'd better go inside.
I'm not your kind. I'm nobody's kind but
   my own.
I'm waiting for this to blow over. (*She rises.*)
I lied. I meant it—
I meant it when I said it—but there's too
   much black
whirling inside me—for any girl to know.
So go on in. You're somebody's angel child
and they're waiting for you.

MIRIAMNE. Yes. I'll go. (*She turns.*)

MIO. And tell them
when you get inside where it's warm,
and you love each other,
and mother comes to kiss her darling, tell
   them
to hang on to it while they can, believe while
   they can
it's a warm safe world, and Jesus finds his
   lambs

and carries them in his bosom.—I've seen
   some lambs
that Jesus missed. If they ever want the truth
tell them that nothing's guaranteed in this
   climate
except it gets cold in winter, nor on this
   earth
except you die sometime. (*He turns away.*)

MIRIAMNE. I have no mother.
And my people are Jews.

MIO. Then you know something about it.

MIRIAMNE. Yes.

MIO. Do you have enough to eat?

MIRIAMNE. Not always.

MIO. What do you believe in?

MIRIAMNE. Nothing.

MIO. Why?

MIRIAMNE. How can one?

MIO. It's easy if you're a fool. You see the
   words
in books. Honor, it says there, chivalry, freedom,
heroism, enduring love—and these
are words on paper. It's something to have
   them there.
You'll get them nowhere else.

MIRIAMNE. What hurts you?

MIO. Just that.
You'll get them nowhere else.

MIRIAMNE. Why should you want them?

MIO. I'm alone, that's why. You see those
   lights,
along the river, cutting across the rain—?
those are the hearths of Brooklyn, and up
   this way
the love-nests of Manhattan—they turn their
   points
like knives against me—outcast of the world,
snake in the streets.—I don't want a handout.
I sleep and eat.

MIRIAMNE. Do you want me to go with
you?

MIO. Where?

MIRIAMNE. Where you go. (*A pause. He goes nearer to her.*)

MIO. Why, you god-damned little fool—
what made you say that?

MIRIAMNE. I don't know.

MIO. If you have a home
stay in it. I ask for nothing. I've schooled
myself
to ask for nothing, and take what I can get,
and get along. If I fell for you, that's my
look-out,
and I'll starve it down.

MIRIAMNE. Wherever you go, I'd go.

MIO. What do you know about loving?
How could you know?
Have you ever had a man?

MIRIAMNE (*after a slight pause*). No. But I
know.
Tell me your name.

MIO. Mio. What's yours?

MIRIAMNE. Miriamne.

MIO. There's no such name.

MIRIAMNE. But there's no such name as Mio!
M.I.O. It's no name.

MIO. It's for Bartolomeo.

MIRIAMNE. My mother's name was Miriam,
so they called me Miriamne.

MIO. Meaning little Miriam?

MIRIAMNE. Yes.

MIO. So now little Miriamne will go in
and take up quietly where she dropped them
all
her small housewifely cares.—When I first
saw you,
not a half-hour ago, I heard myself saying,
this is the face that launches ships for me—
and if I owned a dream—yes, half a dream—
we'd share it. But I have no dream. This
earth
came tumbling down from chaos, fire and
rock,
and bred up worms, blind worms that sting
each other
here in the dark. These blind worms of the
earth
took out my father—and killed him, and set
a sign
on me—the heir of the serpent—and he was
a man
such as men might be if the gods were
men—

but they killed him—
as they'll kill all others like him
till the sun cools down to the stabler mole-
cules,
yes, till men spin their tent-worm webs to
the stars
and what they think is done, even in the
thinking,
and they are the gods, and immortal, and
constellations
turn from them all like mill wheels—still
as they are
they will be, worms and blind. Enduring
love,
oh gods and worms, what mockery!—And
yet
I have blood enough in my veins. It goes
like music,
singing, because you're here. My body turns
as if you were the sun, and warm. This men
called love
in happier times, before the Freudians
taught us
to blame it on the glands. Only go in
before you breathe too much of my atmosphere
and catch death from me.

MIRIAMNE. I will take my hands
and weave them to a little house, and there
you shall keep a dream—

MIO. God knows I could use a dream
and even a house.

MIRIAMNE. You're laughing at me, Mio!

MIO. The worms are laughing.
I tell you there's death about me
and you're a child! And I'm alone and
half mad
with hate and longing. I shall let you love
me
and love you in return, and then, why then
God knows what happens!

MIRIAMNE. Something most unpleasant?

MIO. Love in a box car—love among the
children.
I've seen to much of it. Are we to live
in this same house you make with your two
hands
mystically, out of air?

MLRIAMNE. No roof, no mortgage!
Well, I shall marry a banker out in Flatbush,
it gives hot bread in the morning! Oh, Mio,
Mio,
in all the unwanted places and waste lands

that roll up into the darkness out of sun
and into sun out of darkness, there should
  be one empty
for you and me.

MIO. No.

MIRIAMNE. Then go now and leave me.
I'm only a girl you saw in the tenements,
and there's been nothing said.

MIO. Miriamne. (*She takes a step toward
him.*)

MIRIAMNE. Yes. (*He kisses her lips lightly.*)

MIO. Why, girl, the transfiguration on the
  mount
was nothing to your face. It lights from
  within—
a white chalice holding fire, a flower in
 ·flame,
this is your face.

MIRIAMNE. And you shall drink the flame
and never lessen it. And round your head
the aureole shall burn that burns there now,
forever. This I can give you. And so forever
the Freudians are wrong.

MIO. They're well-forgotten
at any rate.

MIRIAMNE. Why did you speak to me
when you first saw me?

MIO. I knew then.

MIRIAMNE. And I came back
because I must see you again. And we
  danced together
and my heart hurt me. Never, never, never,
though they should bind me down and tear
  out my eyes,
would I ever hurt you now. Take me with
  you, Mio,
let them look for us, whoever there is to
  look,
but we'll be away. (MIO *turns away toward
the tenement.*)

MIO. When I was four years old
we climbed through an iron gate, my mother
  and I,
to see my father in prison. He stood in the
  death-cell
and put his hand through the bars and said,
  My Mio,
I have only this to leave you, that I love you,
and will love you after I die. Love me then,
  Mio,

when this hard thing comes on you, that you
  must live
a man despised for your father. That night
  the guards,
walking in flood-lights brighter than high
  noon,
led him between them with his trousers slit
and a shaven head for the cathodes. This
  sleet and rain
that I feel cold here on my face and hands
will find him under thirteen years of clay
in prison ground. Lie still and rest, my
  father,
for I have not forgotten. When I forget
may I lie blind as you. No other love,
time passing, nor the spaced light-years of
  suns
shall blur your voice, or tempt me from the
  path
that clears your name—
till I have these rats in my grip
or sleep deep where you sleep. (*To* MIR-
IAMNE.)
I have no house,
nor home, nor love of life, nor fear of death,
nor care for what I eat, or who I sleep with,
or what color of calcimine the Government
will wash itself this year or next to lure
the sheep and feed the wolves. Love somewhere else,
and get your children in some other image
more acceptable to the State! This face of
  mine
is stamped for sewage! (*She steps back, sur-
mising.*)

MIRIAMNE. Mio—

MIO. My road is cut
in rock, and leads to one end. If I hurt you,
  I'm sorry.
One gets over hurts.

MIRIAMNE. What was his name—
your father's name?

MIO. Bartolomeo Romagna.
I'm not ashamed of it.

MIRIAMNE. Why are you here?

MIO. For the reason
I've never had a home. Because I'm a cry
out of a shallow grave, and all roads are
  mine
that might revenge him!

MIRIAMNE. But Mio—why here—why here?

MIO. I can't tell you that.

MIRIAMNE. No—but—there's someone
lives here—lives not far—and you mean to
see him—
you mean to ask him—(*She pauses.*)

MIO. Who told you that?

MIRIAMNE. His name
is Garth—Garth Esdras—

MIO (*after a pause, coming nearer*). Who are
you then? You seem
to know a good deal about me.—Were you
sent
to say this?

MIRIAMNE. You said there was death about
you! Yes,
but nearer than you think! Let it be as
it is—
let it all be as it is, never see this place
nor think of it—forget the streets you came
when you're away and safe! Go before
you're seen
or spoken to!

MIO. Will you tell me why?

MIRIAMNE. As I love you
I can't tell you—and I can never see you—

MIO. I walk where I please—

MIRIAMNE. Do you think it's easy for me
to send you away? (*She steps back as if to
go.*)

MIO. Where will I find you then
if I should want to see you?

MIRIAMNE. Never—I tell you
I'd bring you death! Even now. Listen!

(SHADOW *and* TROCK *enter between the
bridge and the tenement house.* MIRIAMNE
pulls MIO *back into the shadow of the rock
to avoid being seen.*)

TROCK. Why, fine.

SHADOW. You watch it now—just for the
record, Trock—
you're going to thank me for staying away
from it
and keeping you out. I've seen men get that
way,
thinking they had to plug a couple of guys
and then a few more to cover it up, and then
maybe a dozen more. You can't own all
and territory adjacent, and you can't
slough all the witnesses, because every man
you put away has friends—

TROCK. I said all right.
I said fine.

SHADOW. They're going to find this judge,
and if they find him dead it's just too bad,
and I don't want to know anything about
it—
and you don't either.

TROCK. You all through?

SHADOW. Why sure.

TROCK. All right.
We're through, too, you know.

SHADOW. Yeah? (*He becomes wary.*)

TROCK. Yeah, we're through.

SHADOW. I've heard that said before, and
afterwards
somebody died. (TROCK *is silent.*)
Is that what you mean?

TROCK. You can go.
I don't want to see you.

SHADOW. Sure, I'll go.
Maybe you won't mind if I just find out
what you've got on you. Before I turn my
back
I'd like to know. (*Silently and expertly he
touches* TROCK's *pockets, extracting a gun.*)
Not that I'd distrust you,
but you know how it is. (*He pockets the
gun.*)
So long, Trock.

TROCK. So long.

SHADOW. I won't talk.
You can be sure of that.

TROCK. I know you won't.

(SHADOW *turns and goes out right, past the
rock and along the bank. As he goes the*
TWO YOUNG MEN IN BLUE SERGE *enter from
the left and walk slowly after* SHADOW. *They
look toward* TROCK *as they enter and he
motions with his thumb in the direction
taken by* SHADOW. *They follow* SHADOW *out
without haste.* TROCK *watches them disappear, then slips out the way he came.* MIO
comes a step forward, looking after the TWO
MEN. *Two or three shots are heard, then
silence.* MIO *starts to run after* SHADOW.)

MIRIAMNE. Mio!

MIO. What do you know about this?

MIRIAMNE. The other way,
Mio—quick! (CARR *slips in from the right,
in haste.*)

CARR. Look, somebody's just been shot.
He fell in the river. The guys that did the
shooting
ran up the bank.

MIO. Come on.

(MIO *and* CARR *run out right.* MIRIAMNE
*watches uncertainly, then slowly turns and
walks to the rear door of the tenement. She
stands there a moment, looking after* MIO,
then goes in, closing the door. CARR *and* MIO
return.)

CARR. There's a rip tide past the point. You'd
never find him.

MIO. No.

CARR. You know a man ought to carry insurance living around here.—God, it's easy,
putting a fellow away. I never saw it done
before.

MIO (*looking at the place where* MIRIAMNE
stood). They have it all worked out.

CARR. What are you doing now?

MIO. I have a little business to transact in this
neighborhood.

CARR. You'd better forget it.

MIO. No.

CARR. Need any help?

MIO. Well, if I did I'd ask you first. But I
don't see how it would do any good. So
you keep out of it and take care of yourself.

CARR. So long, then.

MIO. So long, Carr.

CARR (*looking down-stream*). He was drifting face up. Must he halfway to the island
the way the tide runs. (*He shivers.*) Good,
it's cold here. Well—

(*He goes out to the left.* MIO *sits on the edge
of the rock.* LUCIA *comes stealthily back from
between the bridge and the tenement, goes
to the street-piano and wheels it away.* PINY
comes in. They take a look at MIO, *but say
nothing.* LUCIA *goes into his shelter and*
PINY *into hers.* MIO *rises, looks up at the
tenement, and goes out to the left.*)

CURTAIN

ACT TWO

SCENE: *The basement as in Scene 2 of Act One. The same evening.* ESDRAS *sits at the
table reading,* MIRIAMNE *is seated at the left, listening and intent. The door of the inner
room is half open and* GARTH's *violin is heard. He is playing the theme from the third
movement of Beethoven's Archduke Trio.* ESDRAS *looks up.*

ESDRAS. I remember when I came to the end
of all the Talmud said, and the commen-
taries,
then I was fifty years old—and it was time
to ask what I had learned. I asked this
question
and gave myself the answer. In all the Talmud
there was nothing to find but the names of
things,
set down that we might call them by those
names
and walk without fear among things known.
Since then
I have had twenty years to read on and on
and end with Ecclesiastes. Names of names,
evanid days, evanid nights and days

and words that shift their meaning. Space
is time,
that which was is now—the men of tomorrow
live, and this is their yesterday. All things
that were and are and will be, have their
being
then and now and to come. If this means
little
when you are young, remember it. It will
return
to mean more when you are old.

MIRIAMNE. I'm sorry—I
was listening for something.

ESDRAS. It doesn't matter.
It's a useless wisdom. It's all I have,

but useless. It may be there is no time,
but we grow old. Do you know his name?

MIRIAMNE. Whose name?

ESDRAS. Why, when we're young and listen
for a step
the step should have a name—(MIRIAMNE,
not hearing, rises and goes to the window.
GARTH *enters from within, carrying his
violin and carefully closing the door.*)

GARTH (*as* ESDRAS *looks at him*). Asleep.

ESDRAS. He may
sleep on through the whole night—then in
the morning
we can let them know.

GARTH. We'd be wiser to say nothing—
let him find his own way back.

ESDRAS. How did he come here?

GARTH. He's not too crazy for that. If he
wakes again
we'll keep him quiet and shift him off tomorrow.
Somebody'd pick him up.

ESDRAS. How have I come
to this sunken end of a street, at a life's
end—?

GARTH. It was cheaper here—not to be
transcendental—
So—we say nothing—?

ESDRAS. Nothing.

MIRIAMNE. Garth, there's no place
in this whole city—not one—
where you wouldn't be safer
than here—tonight—or tomorrow.

GARTH (*bitterly*). Well, that may be.
What of it?

MIRIAMNE. If you slipped away and took
a place somewhere where Trock couldn't
find you—

GARTH. Yes—
using what for money? and why do you
think
I've sat here so far—because I love my home
so much? No, but if I stepped round the
corner
it'd be my last corner and my last step.

MIRIAMNE. And yet—
if you're here—they'll find you here—
Trock will come again—
and there's worse to follow—

GARTH. Do you want to get me killed?

MIRIAMNE. No.

GARTH. There's no way out of it. We'll wait
and take what they send us.

ESDRAS. Hush! You'll wake him.

GARTH. I've done it.
I hear him stirring now. (*They wait quietly.*
JUDGE GAUNT *opens the door and enters.*)

GAUNT (*in the doorway*). I beg your
pardon—
no, no, be seated—keep your place—I've
made
your evening difficult enough, I fear;
and I must thank you doubly for your kindness,
for I've been ill—I know it.

ESDRAS. You're better, sir?

GAUNT. Quite recovered, thank you. Able,
I hope,
to manage nicely now. You'll be rewarded
for your hospitality—though at this moment
(*He smiles*)
I'm low in funds. (*He inspects his billfold.*)
Sir, my embarrassment
is great indeed—and more than monetary,
for I must own my recollection's vague
of how I came here—how we came together—
and what we may have said. My name is
Gaunt,
Judge Gaunt, a name long known in the
criminal courts,
and not unhonored there.

ESDRAS. My name is Esdras—
and this is Garth, my son. And Miriamne,
the daughter of my old age.

GAUNT. I'm glad to meet you.
Esdras. Garth Esdras. (*He passes a hand
over his eyes.*)
It's not a usual name.
Of late it's been connected with a case—
a case I knew. But this is hardly the man.
Though it's not a usual name. (*They are
silent.*)
Sir, how I came here,
as I have said, I don't well know. Such
things
are sometimes not quite accident.

ESDRAS. We found you
outside our door and brought you in.

GAUNT. The brain
can be overworked, and weary, even when
   the man
would swear to his good health. Sir, on my
   word
I don't know why I came here, nor how,
   nor when,
nor what would explain it. Shall we say the
   machine
begins to wear? I felt no twinge of it.—
You will imagine how much more than
   galling
I feel it, to ask my way home—and where
   I am—
but I do ask you that.

ESDRAS. This is New York City—
or part of it.

GAUNT. Not the best part, I presume? (*He
smiles grimly.*)
No, not the best.

ESDRAS. Not typical, no.

GAUNT. And you—(*To* GARTH.)
you are Garth Esdras?

GARTH. That's my name.

GAUNT. Well, sir, (*to* ESDRAS)
I shall lie under the deepest obligation
if you will set an old man on his path,
for I lack the homing instinct, if the truth
were known. North, east and south mean
   nothing to me
here in this room.

ESDRAS. I can put you in your way.

GARTH. Only you'd be wiser to wait a while—
if I'm any judge.—

GAUNT. It happens I'm the judge—(*with
stiff humor*)
in more ways than one. You'll forgive me
   if I say
I find this place and my predicament
somewhat distasteful. (*He looks round
him.*)

GARTH. I don't doubt you do;
but you're better off here.

GAUNT. Nor will you find it wise
to cross my word as lightly as you seem
inclined to do. You've seen me ill and
   shaken—
and you presume on that.

GARTH. Have it your way.

GAUNT. Doubtless what information is required
we'll find nearby.

ESDRAS. Yes, sir—the terminal,—
if you could walk so far.

GAUNT. I've done some walking—
to look at my shoes. (*He looks down, then
puts out a hand to steady himself.*)
That—that was why I came—
never mind—it was there—and it's gone.
(*To* GARTH.)
Professor Hobhouse—
that's the name—he wrote some trash about
   you
and printed it in a broadside.
—Since I'm here I can tell you
it's a pure fabrication—lacking facts
and legal import. Senseless and impudent,
written with bias—with malicious intent
to undermine the public confidence
in justice and the courts. I knew it then—
all he brings out about this testimony
you might have given. It's true I could have
   called you,
but the case was clear—Romagna was
   known guilty,
and there was nothing to add. If I've en-
   dured
some hours of torture over their attacks
upon my probity—and in this torture
have wandered from my place, wandered
   perhaps
in mind and body—and found my way to
   face you—
why, yes, it is so—I know it—I beg of you
say nothing. It's not easy to give up
a fair name after a full half century
of service to a state. It may well rock
the surest reason. Therefore I ask of you
say nothing of this visit.

GARTH. I'll say nothing.

ESDRAS. Nor any of us.

GAUNT. Why, no—for you'd lose, too.
You'd have nothing to gain.

ESDRAS. Indeed we know it.

GAUNT. I'll remember you kindly. When I've
   returned,
there may be some mystery made of where
   I was—
we'll leave it a mystery?

GARTH. Anything you say.

GAUNT. Why, now I go with much more
peace of mind—
if I can call you friends.

ESDRAS. We shall be grateful
for silence on your part, Your Honor.

GAUNT. Sir—
if there were any just end to be served
by speaking out, I'd speak! There is none.
No—
bear that in mind!

ESDRAS. We will, Your Honor.

GAUNT. Then—
I'm in some haste. If you can be my guide,
we'll set out now.

ESDRAS. Yes, surely. (*There is a knock at
the door. The four look at each other with
some apprehension.* MIRIAMNE *rises.*) I'll
answer it.

MIRIAMNE. Yes. (*She goes into the inner
room and closes the door.* ESDRAS *goes to the
outer door. The knock is repeated. He opens
the door.* MIO *is there.*)

ESDRAS. Yes, sir.

MIO. May I come in?

ESDRAS. Will you state your business, sir?
It's late—and I'm not at liberty—

MIO. Why, I might say
that I was trying to earn my tuition fees
by peddling magazines. I could say that,
or collecting old newspapers—paying cash—
highest rates—no questions asked—(*He
looks round sharply.*)

GARTH. We've nothing to sell.
What do you want?

MIO. Your pardon, gentlemen.
My business is not of an ordinary kind,
and I felt the need of this slight introduction
while I might get my bearings. Your name is
Esdras,
or they told me so outside.

GARTH. What do you want?

MIO. Is that the name?

GARTH. Yes.

MIO. I'll be quick and brief.
I'm the son of a man who died many years
ago
for a pay roll robbery in New England.
You

should be Garth Esdras, by what I've heard.
You have
some knowledge of the crime, if one can
believe
what he reads in the public prints, and it
might be
that your testimony, if given, would clear
my father
of any share in the murder. You may not
care
whether he was guilty or not. You may not
know.
But I do care—and care deeply, and I've
come
to ask you face to face.

GARTH. To ask me what?

MIO. What do you know of it?

ESDRAS. This man Romagna,
did he have a son?

MIO. Yes, sir, this man Romagna,
as you choose to call him, had a son, and I
am that son, and proud.

ESDRAS. Forgive me.

MIO. Had you known him,
and heard him speak, you'd know why I'm
proud, and why
he was no malefactor.

ESDRAS. I quite believe you.
If my son can help he will. But at this
moment,
as I told you—could you, I wonder, come
tomorrow,
at your own hour?

MIO. Yes.

ESDRAS. By coincidence
we too of late have had this thing in mind—
there have been comments printed, and
much discussion
which we could hardly avoid.

MIO. Could you tell me then
in a word?—What you know—
is it for him or against him?—
that's all I need.

ESDRAS. My son knows nothing.

GARTH. No.
The picture-papers lash themselves to a fury
over any rumor—make them up when
they're short
of bedroom slops.—This is what happened. I
had known a few members of a gang one
time

up there—and after the murder they picked
me up
because I looked like someone that was seen
in what they called the murder car. They
held me
a little while, but they couldn't identify me
for the most excellent reason I wasn't there
when the thing occurred. A dozen years
later now
a professor comes across this, and sees red
and asks why I wasn't called on as a witness
and yips so loud they syndicate his picture
in all the rotos. That's all I know about it.
I wish I could tell you more.

ESDRAS. Let me say too
that I have read some words your father said,
and you were a son fortunate in your father,
whatever the verdict of the world.

MIO. There are few
who think so, but it's true, and I thank you.
Then—
that's the whole story?

GARTH. All I know of it.

MIO. They cover their tracks well, the inner
ring
that distributes murder. I came three thousand miles
to this dead end.

ESDRAS. If he was innocent
and you know him so, believe it, and let
the others
believe as they like.

MIO. Will you tell me how a man's
to live, and face his life, if he can't believe
that truth's like a fire,
and will burn through and be seen
though it takes all the years there are?
While I stand up and have breath in my
lungs
I shall be one flame of that fire;
it's all the life I have.

ESDRAS. Then you must live so.
One must live as he can.

MIO. It's the only way
of life my father left me.

ESDRAS. Yes? Yet it's true.
the ground we walk on is impacted down
and hard with blood and bones of those who
died
unjustly. There's not one title to land or life,
even your own, but was built on rape and
murder,

back a few years. It would take a fire indeed
to burn out all this error.

MIO. Then let it burn down,
all of it!

ESDRAS. We ask a great deal of the world
at first—then less—and then less.
We ask for truth
and justice. But this truth's a thing unknown
in the lightest, smallest matter—and as for
justice,
who has once seen it done? You loved your
father,
and I could have loved him, for every word
he spoke
in his trial was sweet and tolerant, but the
weight
of what men are and have, rests heavy on
the graves of those who lost. They'll not
rise again,
and their causes lie there with them.

GAUNT. If you mean to say
that Bartolomeo Romagna was innocent,
you are wrong. He was guilty.
There may have been injustice
from time to time, by regrettable chance, in
our courts,
but not in that case, I assure you.

MIO. Oh, you assure me!
You lie in your scrag teeth, whoever you
are!
My father was murdered!

GAUNT. Romagna was found guilty
by all due process of law, and given his
chance
to prove his innocence.

MIO. What chance? When a court
panders to mob hysterics, and the jury
comes in loaded to soak an anarchist
and a foreigner, it may be due process of law
but it's also murder!

GAUNT. He should have thought of that
before he spilled blood.

MIO. He?

GAUNT. Sir, I know too well
that he was guilty.

MIO. Who are you? How do you know?
I've searched the records through, the trial
and what
came after, and in all that million words
I found not one unbiased argument
to fix the crime on him.

GAUNT. And you yourself,
were you unprejudiced?

MIO. Who are you?

ESDRAS. Sir,
this gentleman is here, as you are here,
to ask my son, as you have asked, what
    ground
there might be for this talk of new evidence
in your father's case. We gave him the same
    answer
we've given you.

MIO. I'm sorry. I'd supposed
his cause forgotten except by myself. There's
    still
a defense committee then?

GAUNT. There may be. I
am not connected with it.

ESDRAS. He is my guest,
and asks to remain unknown.

MIO (after a pause, looking at GAUNT). The
    judge at the trial
was younger, but he had your face. Can it be
that you're the man?—Yes—Yes.—The jury
    charge—
I sat there as a child and heard your voice,
and watched that Brahminical mouth. I
    knew even then
you meant no good to him. And now you're
    here
to winnow out truth and justice—the
    fountain-head
of the lies that slew him! Are you Judge
    Gaunt?

GAUNT. I am.

MIO. Then tell me what damnation to what
    inferno
would fit the toad that sat in robes and lied
when he gave the charge, and knew he lied!
    Judge that,
and then go to your place in that hell!

GAUNT. I know and have known
what bitterness can rise against a court
when it must say, putting aside all weakness,
that a man's to die. I can forgive you that,
for you are your father's son, and you think
    of him
as a son thinks of his father. Certain laws
seem cruel in their operation; it's necessary
that we be cruel to uphold them. This
    cruelty
is kindness to those I serve.

MIO. I don't doubt that.
I know who it is you serve.

GAUNT. Would I have chosen
to rack myself with other men's despairs,
stop my ears, harden my heart, and listen
    only
to the voice of law and light, if I had hoped
some private gain for serving? In all my
    years
on the bench of a long-established common-
    wealth
not once has my decision been in question
save in this case. Not once before or since.
For hope of heaven or place on earth, or
    power
or gold, no man has had my voice, nor will
while I still keep the trust that laid on me
to sentence and define.

MIO. Then why are you here?

GAUNT. My record's clean. I've kept it so.
    But suppose
with the best intent, among the myriad
    tongues
that come to testify, I had missed my way
and followed a perjured tale to a lethal end
till a man was forsworn to death? Could
    I rest or sleep
while there was doubt of this,
even while there was question in a layman's
    mind?
For always, night and day,
there lies on my brain like a weight, the
    admonition:
see truly, let nothing sway you; among all
    functions
there's but one godlike, to judge. Then see
    to it
you judge as a god would judge, with clarity,
with truth, with what mercy is found con-
    sonant
with order and law. Without law men are
    beasts,
and it's a judge's task to lift and hold them
above themselves. Let a judge be once
    mistaken
or step aside for a friend, and a gap is made
in the dykes that hold back anarchy and
    chaos,
and leave men bond but free.

MIO. Then the gap's been made,
and you made it.

GAUNT. I feared that too. May you be a judge
sometime, and know in what fear,

through what nights long
in fear, I scanned and verified and compared
the transcripts of the trial.

MIO. Without prejudice,
no doubt. It was never in your mind to prove
that you'd been right.

GAUNT. And conscious of that, too—
that that might be my purpose—watchful
   of that,
and jealous as his own lawyer of the rights
that should hedge the defendant!
And still I found no error,
shook not one staple of the bolts that linked
the door to the deed! Still following on
from step to step, I watched all modern
   comment,
and saw it centered finally on one fact—
Garth Esdras was not called. This is Garth
   Esdras,
and you have heard him. Would his deposi-
   tion
have justified a new trial?

MIO. No. It would not.

GAUNT. And there I come, myself. If the man
   were still
in his cell, and waiting, I'd have no faint
   excuse
for another hearing.

MIO. I've told you that I read
the trial from beginning to end. Every word
   you spoke
was balanced carefully to keep the letter
of the law and still convict—convict, by
   Christ,
if it tore the seven veils! You stand here now
running cascades of casuistry, to prove
to yourself and me that no judge of rank
   and breeding
could burn a man out of hate! But that's
   what you did
under all your varnish!

GAUNT. I've sought for evidence,
and you have sought. Have you found it?
   Can you cite
one fresh word in defence?

MIO. The trial itself
was shot full of legerdemain, prearranged
   to lead
the jury astray—

GAUNT. Could you prove that?

MIO. Yes!

GAUNT. And if
the jury were led astray, remember it's
the jury, by our Anglo-Saxon custom,
that finds for guilt or innocence. The judge
is powerless in that matter.

MIO. Not you! Your charge
misled the jury more than the evidence,
accepted every biased meaning, distilled
the poison for them!

GAUNT. But if that were so
I'd be the first, I swear it, to step down
among all men, and hold out both my hands
for manacles—yes, publish it in the streets,
that all I've held most sacred was defiled
by my own act. A judge's brain becomes
a delicate instrument to weigh men's lives
for good and ill—too delicate to bear
much tampering. If he should push aside
the weights and throw the beam, and say,
   this once
the man is guilty, and I will have it so
though his mouth cry out from the ground,
and all the world
revoke my word, he'd have a short way to go
to madness. I think you'd find him in the
   squares,
stopping the passers-by with arguments,—
see, I was right, the man was guilty there—
this was brought in against him, this— and
   this—
and I was left no choice! It's no light thing
when a long life's been dedicated to one end
to wrench the mind awry!

MIO. By your own thesis
you should be mad, and no doubt you are.

GAUNT. But my madness
is only this—that I would fain look back
on a life well spent—without one stain—
   one breath
of stain to flaw the glass—not in men's
   minds
nor in my own. I take my God as witness
I meant to earn that clearness, and believe
that I have earned it. Yet my name is
   clouded
with the blackest, fiercest scandal of our age
that's touched a judge. What I can do to
   wipe
that smutch from my fame I will. I think
   you know
how deeply I've been hated, for no cause
that I can find there. Can it not be—and I
   ask this
quite honestly—that the great injustice lies

on your side and not mine? Time and time
again
men have come before me perfect in their
lives,
loved by all who knew them, loved at home,
gentle, not vicious, yet caught so ripe red-
handed
in some dark violence there was no denying
where the onus lay.

MIO. That was not so with my father!

GAUNT. And yet it seemed so to me. To other
men
who sat in judgment on him. Can you be
sure—
I ask this in humility—that you,
who were touched closest by the tragedy,
may not have lost perspective—may have
brooded
day and night on one theme—till your eyes
are tranced
and show you one side only?

MIO. I see well enough.

GAUNT. And would that not be part of the
malady—
to look quite steadily at the drift of things
but see there what you wish—not what is
there—
not what another man to whom the story
was fresh would say is there?

MIO. You think I'm crazy.
Is that what you meant to say?

GAUNT. I've seen it happen
with the best and wisest men. I but ask the
question.
I can't speak for you. Is it not true wherever
you walk, through the little town where
you knew him well,
or flying from it, inland or by the sea,
still walking at your side, and sleeping only
when you too sleep, a shadow not your own
follows, pleading and holding out its hands
to be delivered from shame?

MIO. How you know that
by God I don't know.

GAUNT. Because one spectre haunted you and
me—
and haunts you still, but for me it's laid to
rest
now that my mind is satisfied. He died
justly and not by error. (A pause.)

MIO (stepping forward). Do you care to
know

you've come so near to death it's miracle
that pulse still beats in your splotchy throat?
Do you know
there's murder in me?

GAUNT. There was murder in your sire,
and it's to be expected! I say he died
justly, and he deserved it!

MIO. Yes, you'd like too well
to have me kill you! That would prove your
case
and clear your name, and dip my father's
name
in stench forever! You'll not get that from
me!
Go home and die in bed, get it under cover,
your lux-et-lex putrefaction of the right
thing,
you man that walks like a god!

GAUNT. Have I made you angry
by coming too near the truth?

MIO. This sets him up,
this venomous slug, this sets him up in a
gown,
deciding who's to walk above the earth
and who's to lie beneath! And giving
reasons!
The cobra giving reasons; I'm a god,
by Buddha, holy and worshipful my fang,
and can I sink it in! (He pauses, turns as if
to go, then sits.)
This is no good.
This won't help much. (The JUDGE and
ESDRAS look at each other.)

GAUNT. We should be going.

ESDRAS. Yes. (They prepare to go.)
I'll lend you my coat.

GAUNT (looking at it with distaste). No,
keep it. A little rain
shouldn't matter to me.

ESDRAS. It freezes as it falls,
and you've a long way to go.

GAUNT. I'll manage, thank you. (GAUNT and
ESDRAS go out, ESDRAS obsequious, closing the
door.)

GARTH (looking at MIO's back). Well?

MIO (not moving). Let me sit here a
moment.

(GARTH shrugs his shoulders and goes toward
the inner door. MIRIAMNE opens it and comes
out. GARTH looks at her, then at MIO, then

ays his fingers on his lips. She nods. GARTH
goes out. MIRIAMNE *sits and watches* MIO.
After a little he turns and sees her.)

MIO. How did you come here?

MIRIAMNE. I live here.

MIO. Here?

MIRIAMNE. My name is Esdras. Garth
is my brother. The walls are thin.
I heard what was said.

MIO (*stirring wearily*). I'm going. This is
no place for me.

MIRIAMNE. What place
would be better?

MIO. None. Only it's better to go.
Just to go. (*She comes over to him, puts her
arm round him and kisses his forehead.*)

MIRIAMNE. Mio.

MIO. What do you want?
Your kisses burn me—and your arms. Don't
offer
what I'm never to have! I can have nothing.
They say
they'll cross the void sometime to the other
planets
and men will breathe in that air.
Well, I could breathe there,
but not here now. Not on this ball of mud.
I don't want it.

MIRIAMNE. They can take away so little
with all their words. For you're a king
among them.
I heard you, and loved your voice.

MIO. I thought I'd fallen
so low there was no further, and now a pit
opens beneath. It was bad enough that he
should have died innocent, but if he were
guilty—
then what's my life—what have I left to
do—?
The son of a felon—and what they spat on
me
was earned—and I'm drenched with the
stuff.
Here on my hands
and cheeks, their spittle hanging! I liked
my hands
because they were like his. I tell you I've
lived
by his innocence, lived to see it flash
and blind them all—

MIRIAMNE. Never believe them, Mio,
never. (*She looks toward the inner door.*)

MIO. But it was truth I wanted, truth—
not the lies you'd tell yourself, or tell a
woman,
or a woman tells you! The judge with his
cobra mouth
may have spat truth—and I may be mad!
For me—
your hands are too clean to touch me. I'm
to have
the scraps from hotel kitchens—and instead
of love
those mottled bodies that hitch themselves
through alleys
to sell for dimes or nickels. Go, keep yourself chaste
for the baker bridegroom—baker and son
of a baker,
let him get his baker's dozen on you!

MIRIAMNE. No—
say once you love me—say it once; I'll never
ask to hear it twice, nor for any kindness,
and you shall take all I have! (GARTH *opens
the inner door and comes out.*)

GARTH. I interrupt
a love scene, I believe. We can do without
your adolescent mawkishness. (*To* MIRI-
AMNE)
You're a child.
You'll both remember that.

MIRIAMNE. I've said nothing to harm you—
and will say nothing.

GARTH. You're my sister, though,
and I take a certain interest in you. Where
have you two met?

MIRIAMNE. We danced together.

GARTH. Then
the dance is over, I think.

MIRIAMNE. I've always loved you
and tried to help you, Garth. And you've
been kind.
Don't spoil it now.

GARTH. Spoil it how?

MIRIAMNE. Because I love him.
I didn't know it would happen. We danced
together.
And the world's all changed. I see through
a mist,
and our father, too. If you brought this to
nothing
I'd want to die.

GARTH (*to* MIO). You'd better go.

MIO. Yes, I know. (*He rises. There is a trembling knock at the door.* MIRIAMNE *goes to it. The* HOBO *is there shivering.*)

HOBO. Miss, could I sleep under the pipes tonight, miss?
Could I, please?

MIRIAMNE. I think—not tonight.

HOBO. There won't be any more nights— if I don't get warm, miss.

MIRIAMNE. Come in. (*The* HOBO *comes in, looks round deprecatingly, then goes to a corner beneath a huge heating pipe, which he crawls under as if he's been there before.*)

HOBO. Yes, miss, thank you.

GARTH. Must we put up with that?

MIRIAMNE. Father let him sleep there— last winter.

GARTH. Yes, God, yes.

MIO. Well, good night.

MIRIAMNE. Where will you go?

MIO. Yes, where? As if it mattered.

GARTH. Oh, sleep here, too.
We'll have a row of you under the pipes.

MIO. No, thanks.

MIRIAMNE. Mio, I've saved a little money.
It's only
some pennies, but you must take it. (*She shakes some coins out of a box into her hand.*)

MIO. No, thanks.

MIRIAMNE. And I love you.
You've never said you love me.

MIO. Why wouldn't I love you
when you're clean and sweet,
and I've seen nothing sweet or clean
this last ten years? I love you. I leave you that
for what good it may do you. It's none to me.

MIRIAMNE. Then kiss me.

MIO (*looking at* GARTH). With that scowling over us? No.
When it rains, some spring

on the planet Mercury, where the spring comes often,
I'll meet you there, let's say. We'll wait for that.
It may be some time till then.
(*The outside door opens and* ESDRAS *enter with* JUDGE GAUNT, *then, after a slight inter val,* TROCK *follows.* TROCK *surveys the in terior and its occupants one by one, care fully.*)

TROCK. I wouldn't want to cause you in convenience,
any of you, and especially the Judge.
I think you know that. You've all got thing to do—
trains to catch, and so on. But trains ca wait.
Hell, nearly anything can wait, you'll find only I can't. I'm the only one that can't
because I've got no time. Who's all thi here?
Who's that? (*He points to the* HOBO.)

ESDRAS. He's a poor half-wit, sir,
that sometimes sleeps there.

TROCK. Come out. I say come out,
whoever you are. (*The* HOBO *stirs and look up.*)
Yes, I mean you. Come out. (*The* HOB emerges.*)
What's your name?

HOBO. They mostly call me Oke.

TROCK. What do you know?

HOBO. No, sir.

TROCK. Where are you from?

HOBO. I got a piece of bread. (*He brings out, trembling.*)

TROCK. Get back in there! (*The* HOBO *craw back into his corner.*)
Maybe you want to know why I'm doin this.
Well, I've been robbed, that's why— robbed five or six times;
the police can't find a thing—so I'm ou for myself—
if you want to know. (*To* MIO.)
Who are you?

MIO. Oh, I'm a half-wit,
came in here by mistake. The difference I've got no piece of bread.

ROCK. What's your name?

IO. My name?
Theophrastus Such. That's respectable.
You'll find it all the way from here to the
coast
in the best police blotters.
Only the truth is we're a little touched in
the head,
Ike and me. You'd better ask somebody
else.

ROCK. Who is he?

ESDRAS. His name's Romagna. He's the son.

ROCK. Then what's he doing here? You
said you were on the level.

GARTH. He just walked in. On account of
the stuff in the papers. We didn't ask him.

ROCK. God, we are a gathering. Now if
we had Shadow we'd be all here, huh?
Only I guess we won't see Shadow. No,
that's too much to ask.

IO. Who's Shadow?

ROCK. Now you're putting questions.
Shadow was just nobody, you see. He blew
away. It might happen to anybody. (*He
looks at* GARTH.) Yes, anyone at all.

IO. Why do you keep your hand in your
pocket, friend?

ROCK. Because I'm cold, punk. Because I've
been outside and it's cold as the tomb of
Christ. (*To* GARTH.) Listen, there's a car
waiting up at the street to take the Judge
home. We'll take him to the car.

GARTH. That's not necessary.

ESDRAS. No.

ROCK. I say it is, see? You wouldn't want
to let the Judge walk, would you? The Judge
going to ride where he's going, with a
couple of chauffeurs, and everything done
in style. Don't you worry about the Judge.
He'll be taken care of. For good.

GARTH. I want no hand in it.

ROCK. Anything happens to me happens
to you too, musician.

GARTH. I know that.

ROCK. Keep your mouth out of it then.
And you'd better keep the punk here tonight, just for luck. (*He turns toward the
door. There is a brilliant lightning flash
through the windows, followed slowly by
dying thunder.* TROCK *opens the door. The
rain begins to pour in sheets.*) Jesus, somebody tipped it over again! (*A cough racks
him.*) Wait till it's over. It takes ten days
off me every time I step into it. (*He closes
the door.*) Sit down and wait. (*Lightning
flashes again. The thunder is fainter.* ESDRAS,
GARTH *and the* JUDGE *sit down.*)

GAUNT. We were born too early. Even you
who are young
are not of the elect. In a hundred years
man will put his finger on life itself, and
then
he will live as long as he likes. For you and
me
we shall die soon—one day, one year more
or less,
when or where, it's no matter. It's what we
call
an indeterminate sentence. I'm hungry.
(GARTH *looks at* MIRIAMNE.)

MIRIAMNE. There was nothing left
tonight.

HOBO. I've got a piece of bread. (*He breaks
his bread in two and hands half to the
JUDGE.*)

GAUNT. I thank you, sir. (*He eats.*)
This is not good bread. (*He rises.*)
Sir, I am used
to other company. Not better, perhaps, but
their clothes
were different. These are what it's the
fashion to call
the underprivileged.

TROCK. Oh, hell! (*He turn toward the door.*)

MIO (*to* TROCK). It would seem that you and
the Judge know each other. (TROCK *faces
him.*)

TROCK. I've been around.

MIO. Maybe you've met before.

TROCK. Maybe we have.

MIO. Will you tell me where?

TROCK. How long do you want to live?

MIO. How long? Oh, I've got big ideas about
that.

TROCK. I thought so. Well, so far I've got nothing against you but your name, see? You keep it that way. (*He opens the door. The rain still falls in torrents. He closes the door. As he turns from it, it opens again, and* SHADOW, *white, bloodstained and dripping, stands in the doorway.* GARTH *rises.* TROCK *turns.*)

GAUNT (*to the* HOBO). Yet if one were careful of his health, ate sparingly, drank not at all, used himself wisely, it might be that even an old man could live to touch immortality. They may come on the secret sooner than we dare hope. You see? It does no harm to try.

TROCK (*backing away from* SHADOW). By God, he's out of his grave!

SHADOW (*leaning against the doorway, holding a gun in his hands*). Keep your hands where they belong, Trock.
You know me.

TROCK. Don't! Don't! I had nothing to do with it! (*He backs to the opposite wall.*)

SHADOW. You said the doctor gave you six months to live—
well, I don't give you that much. That's what you had,
six months, and so you start bumping off your friends
to make sure of your damn six months. I got it from you.
I know where I got it.
Because I wouldn't give it to the Judge.
So he wouldn't talk.

TROCK. Honest to God—

SHADOW. What God?
The one that let you put three holes in me when I was your friend? Well, He let me get up again
and walk till I could find you. That's as far as I get,
but I got there, by God! And I can hear you even if I can't see! (*He takes a staggering step forward.*)
A man needs blood
to keep going.—I got this far.—And now I can't see!
It runs out too fast—too fast—
when you've got three slugs
clean through you.
Show me where he is, you fools! He's here! I got here! (*He drops the gun.*)

Help me! Help me! Oh, God! Oh, God
I'm going to die! Where does a man lie
   down?
I want to lie down!

(MIRIAMNE *starts toward* SHADOW. GARTH *and* ESDRAS *help him into the next room,* MIRIAMNE *following.* TROCK *squats in his corner, breathing hard, looking at the door.* MIO *stands, watching* TROCK. GARTH *returns, wiping his hand with a handkerchief.* MIO *picks up and pockets the gun.* MIRIAMNE *comes back and leans against the door jamb.*)

GAUNT. You will hear it said that an old man makes a good judge, being calm, clear eyed, without passion. But this is not true.
Only the young love truth and justice. The old are savage, wary, violent, swayed by maniac desires, cynical of friendship or love, open to bribery and the temptations of lust, corrupt and dastardly to the heart. I know these old men. What have they left to believe, what have they left to lose? Whorers of daughters, lickers of girls' shoes, contrivers of nastiness in the night, purveyors of perversion, worshippers of possession. Death is the only radical. He comes late, but he comes at last to put away the old men and give the young their places. It was time. (*He leers.*) Here's one I heard yesterday:
   Marmaduke behind the barn
      got his sister in a fix;
   he says damn instead of darn;
      ain't he cute? He's only six!

THE HOBO. He, he, he!

GAUNT. And the hoot-owl hoots all night,
      and the cuckoo cooks all day,
   and what with a minimum grace of God
      we pass the time away.

THE HOBO. He, he, he—I got ya! (*He makes a sign with his thumb.*)

GAUNT (*sings*). And he led her all around
   and he laid her on the ground
   and he ruffled up the feathers of her
      cuckoo's nest!

HOBO. Ho, ho, ho!

GAUNT. I am not taken with the way you laugh. You should cultivate restraint. (ESDRA *reënters.*)

TROCK. Shut the door.

ESDRAS. He won't come back again.

TROCK. I want the door shut! He was dead,
tell you! (ESDRAS *closes the door.*) And
Romagna was dead, too, once! Can't they
keep a man under ground?

MIO. No. No more! They don't stay under
ground any more, and they don't stay under
water! Why did you have him killed?

TROCK. Stay away from me! I know you!

MIO. Who am I, then?

TROCK. I know you, damn you! Your name's
Romagna!

MIO. Yes! And Romagna was dead, too,
and Shadow was dead, but the time's come
when you can't keep them down, these dead
men! They won't stay down! They come in
with their heads shot off and their entrails
dragging! Hundreds of them! One by one—
all you ever had killed! Watch the door!
See!—It moves!

TROCK (*looking, fascinated, at the door*).
Let me out of here! (*He tries to rise.*)

MIO (*the gun in his hand*). Oh, no! You'll
sit there and wait for them! One by one
they'll come through that door, pulling their
heads out of the gunny-sacks where you
tied them—glauming over you with their
rotten hands! They'll see without eyes and
crawl over you—Shadow and the paymaster,
and all the rest of them—putrescent bones
without eyes! Now! Look! Look! For I'm
first among them!

TROCK. I've done for better men than you!
And I'll do for you!

GAUNT (*rapping on the table*). Order, gentlemen, order! The witness will remember
that a certain decorum is essential in the
court-room!

MIO. By God, he'll answer me!

GAUNT (*thundering*). Silence! Silence! Let
me remind you of courtesy toward the
witness! What case is this you try?

MIO. The case of the state against Bartolomeo Romagna for the murder of the paymaster!

GAUNT. Sir, that was disposed of long ago!

MIO. Never disposed of, never, not while I
live!

GAUNT. Then we'll have done with it now!
I deny the appeal! I have denied the appeal
before and I do so again!

HOBO. He, he!—He thinks he's in the moving pictures! (*A flash of lightning.*)

GAUNT. Who set that flash! Bailiff, clear the
court! This is not Flemington, gentlemen!
We are not conducting this case to make a
journalistic holiday! (*The thunder rumbles
faintly.* GARTH *opens the outside door and
faces a solid wall of rain.*) Stop that man!
He's one of the defendants! (GARTH *closes
the door.*)

MIO. Then put him on the stand!

GARTH. What do you think you're doing?

MIO. Have you any objection?

GAUNT. The objection is not sustained. We
will hear the new evidence. Call your witness.

MIO. Garth Esdras!

GAUNT. He will take the stand!

GARTH. If you want me to say what I said
before, I'll say it!

MIO. Call Trock Estrella then!

GAUNT. Trock Estrella to the stand!

TROCK. No, by God!

MIO. Call Shadow, then! He'll talk! You
thought he was dead, but he'll get up again
and talk!'

TROCK (*screaming*). What do you want of
me?

MIO. You killed the paymaster! You!

TROCK. You lie! It was Shadow killed him!

MIO. And now I know! Now I know!

GAUNT. Again I remind you of courtesy toward the witness!

MIO. I know them now!
Let me remind you of courtesy toward the
dead!
He says that Shadow killed him! If Shadow
were here
he'd say it was Trock! There were three
men involved
in the new version of the crime for which
my father died! Shadow and Trock Estrella

as principals in the murder—Garth as witness!—
Why are they here together?—and you—
the Judge—
why are you here? Why, because you were
all afraid
and you drew together out of that fear to
arrange
a story you could tell! And Trock killed
Shadow
and meant to kill the Judge out of that same
fear—
to keep them quiet! This is the thing I've
hunted
over the earth to find out, and I'd be blind
indeed if I missed it now! (*To* GAUNT.)
You heard what he said:
It was Shadow killed him! Now let the night
conspire
with the sperm of hell! It's plain beyond
denial
even to this fox of justice—and all his
words
are curses on the wind! You lied! You lied!
You knew this too!

GAUNT (*low*). Let me go. Let me go!

MIO. Then why
did you let my father die?

GAUNT. Suppose it known,
but there are things a judge must not believe
though they should head and fester underneath
and press in on his brain. Justice once rendered
in a clear burst of anger, righteously,
upon a very common laborer,
confessed an anarchist, the verdict found
and the precise machinery of law
invoked to know him guilty—think what
furor
would rock the state if the court then flatly
said;
all this was lies—must be reversed? It's
better,
as any judge can tell you, in such cases,
holding the common good to be worth more
than small injustice, to let the record stand,
let one man die. For justice, in the main,
is governed by opinion. Communities
will have what they will have, and it's quite
as well,
after all, to be rid of anarchists. Our rights
as citizens can be maintained as rights
only while we are held to be the peers

of those who live about us. A vendor of fish
is not protected as a man might be
who kept a market. I own I've sometimes
wished
this was not so, but it is. The man you
defend
was unfortunate—and his misfortune bore
almost as heavily on me.—I'm broken—
broken across. You're much too young to
know
how bitter it is when a worn connection
chars
and you can't remember—can't remember.
(*He steps forward.*)
You
will not repeat this? It will go no further?

MIO. No.
No further than the moon takes the tides—
no further
than the news went when he died—
when you found him guilty
and they flashed that round the earth. Wherever men
still breathe and think, and know what's
done to them
by the powers above, they'll know. That'
all I ask.
That'll be enough. (TROCK *has risen and
looks darkly at* MIO.)

GAUNT. Thank you. For I've said some
things
a judge should never say.

TROCK. Go right on talking.
Both of you. It won't get far, I guess.

MIO. Oh, you'll see to that?

TROCK. I'll see to it. Me and some others.
Maybe I lost my grip there just for a minute
That's all right.

MIO. Then see to it! Let it rain!
What can you do to me now when the
night's on fire
with this thing I know? Now I could almos
wish
there was a god somewhere—I could almos
think
there was a god—and he somehow brough
me here
and set you down before me here in the rain
where I could wring this out of you! For it'
said,
and I've heard it, and I'm free! He was as
thought him,
true and noble and upright, even when
he went

‣ a death contrived because he was as he
was
nd not your kind! Let it rain! Let the night
speak fire
nd the city go out with the tide, for he was
a man
nd I know you now, and I have my day!
There is a heavy knock at the outside door.
IRIAMNE opens it, at a glance from GARTH.
he POLICEMAN *is there in oilskins.*)

POLICEMAN. Evening. (*He steps in, followed
y a* SERGEANT, *similarly dressed.*) We're
looking for someone
ight be here. Seen an old man around
cting a little off? (*To* ESDRAS.)
ou know the one
mean. You saw him out there. Jeez! You've
got
funny crowd here! (*He looks round. The*
OBO *shrinks into his corner.*)
hat's the one I saw.
Vhat do you think?

ERGEANT. That's him. You mean to say
ou didn't know him by this pictures? (*He
oes to* GAUNT.)
Come on, old man.
ou're going home.

AUNT. Yes, sir. I've lost my way.
think I've lost my way.

ERGEANT. I'll say you have.
About three hundred miles. Now don't you
worry.
Ve'll get you back.

AUNT. I'm a person of some rank
a my own city.

RGEANT. We know that. One look at you
nd we'd know that.

AUNT. Yes, sir.

OLICEMAN. If it isn't Trock!
rock Estrella. How are you, Trock?

ROCK. Pretty good,
hanks.

OLICEMAN. Got out yesterday again, I hear?

ROCK. That's right.

RGEANT. Hi'ye, Trock?

ROCK. O.K.

RGEANT. You know we got orders
watch you pretty close. Be good now,
baby,

or back you go. Don't try to pull anything,
not in my district.

TROCK. No, sir.

SERGEANT. No bumping off.
If you want my advice quit carrying a gun.
Try earning your living for once.

TROCK. Yeah.

SERGEANT. That's an idea.
Because if we find any stiffs on the river
bank
we'll know who to look for.

MIO. Then look in the other room!
I accuse that man of murder! Trock Estrella!
He's a murderer!

POLICEMAN. Hello. I remember you.

SERGEANT. Well, what murder?

MIO. It was Trock Estrella
that robbed the pay roll thirteen years ago
and did the killing my father died for!
You know
the Romagna case! Romagna was innocent,
and Trock Estrella guilty!

SERGEANT (*disgusted*). Oh, what the hell!
That's old stuff—the Romagna case.

POLICEMAN. Hey, Sarge! (*The* SERGEANT *and*
POLICEMAN *come closer together.*)
The boy's a professional kidder. He took me
over
about half an hour ago. He kids the police
and then ducks out!

SERGEANT. Oh, yeah?

MIO. I'm not kidding now.
You'll find a dead man there in the next
room
and Estrella killed him!

SERGEANT. Thirteen years ago?
And nobody smelled him yet?

MIO (*pointing*). I accuse this man
of two murders! He killed the paymaster
long ago
and had Shadow killed tonight. Look, look
for yourself!
He's there all right!

POLICEMAN. Look boy. You stood out there
and put the booby sign on the dumb police
because they're fresh out of Ireland. Don't
try it twice.

SERGEANT (*to* GARTH). Any corpses here?

GARTH. Not that I know of.

SERGEANT. I thought so. (MIO *looks at* MIRI-AMNE.)

(*To* MIO.)
Think up a better one.

MIO. Have I got to drag him
out here where you can see him? (*He goes
toward the inner door.*)
Can't you scent a murder
when it's under your nose? Look in!

MIRIAMNE. No, no—there's no one—there's
no one there!

SERGEANT (*looking at* MIRIAMNE). Take a
look inside.

POLICEMAN. Yes, sir. (*He goes into the inside
room. The* SERGEANT *goes up to the door.
The* POLICEMAN *returns.*)
He's kidding, Sarge. If there's a cadaver
in here I don't see it.

MIO. You're blind then! (*He goes into the
room, the* SERGEANT *following him.*)

SERGEANT. What do you mean? (*He comes
out,* MIO *following him.*)
When you make a charge of murder it's
better to have
the corpus delicti, son. You're the kind puts
in
fire alarms to see the engine!

MIO. By God, he was there!
He went in there to die.

SERGEANT. I'll bet he did.
And I'm Haile Selassie's aunt! What's your
name?

MIO. Romagna. (*To* GARTH).
What have you done with him?

GARTH. I don't know what you mean.

SERGEANT (*to* GARTH). What's he talking
about?

GARTH. I wish I could tell you.
I don't know.

SERGEANT. He must have seen something.

POLICEMAN. He's got
the Romagna case on the brain. You watch
yourself,
chump, or you'll get run in.

MIO. Then they're in it together!
All of them! (*To* MIRIAMNE.)
Yes, and you!

GARTH. He's nuts, I say.

MIRIAMNE (*gently*). You have dreamed
something—isn't it true?
You've dreamed—
But truly, there was no one—(MIO *looks at
her comprehendingly.*)

MIO. You want me to say it. (*He pauses.*)
Yes, by God, I was dreaming.

SERGEANT (*to* POLICEMAN). I guess you're
right.
We'd better be going. Haven't you got a
coat?

GAUNT. No, sir.

SERGEANT. I guess I'll have to lend you mine.
(*He puts his oilskins on* GAUNT.)
Come on, now. It's getting late. (GAUNT, *the*
POLICEMAN *and the* SERGEANT *go out.*)

TROCK. They're welcome to him.
His fuse is damp. Where is that walking
fool
with the three slugs in him?

ESDRAS. He fell in the hall beyond
and we left him there.

TROCK. That's lucky for some of us. Is he
out this time
or is he still butting around?

ESDRAS. He's dead.

TROCK. That's perfect. (*To* MIO.)
Don't try using your firearms, amigo baby,
the Sarge is outside. (*He turns to go.*)
Better ship that carrion
back in the river! The one that walks when
he's dead;
maybe he'll walk the distance for you.

GARTH. Coming back?

TROCK. Well, if I come back,
you'll see me. If I don't, you won't. Let the
punk
go far as he likes. Turn him loose and let
him go.
And may you all rot in hell. (*He pulls his
coat around him and goes to the left.* MIR-
IAMNE *climbs up to look out a window.*)

RIAMNE. He's climbing up to the street,
ong the bridgehead. (*She turns.*)
uick, Mio! It's safe now! Quick!

RTH. Let him do as he likes.

RIAMNE. What do you mean? Garth! He
means to kill him!
ou know that!

RTH. I've no doubt Master Romagna
n run his own campaign.

RIAMNE. But he'll be killed!

o. Why did you lie about Shadow? (*There
a pause.* GARTH *shrugs, walks across the
om, and sits.*)
ou were one of the gang!

RTH. I can take a death if I have to! Go
tell your story,
ly watch your step, for I warn you,
Trock's out gunning
d you may not walk very far. Oh, I could
defend it
t it's hardly worth while.
they get Trock they get me too.
tell them. You owe me nothing.

RAS. This Trock you saw,
one defends him. He's earned his death
so often
re's nobody to regret it. But his crime,
same crime that has dogged you, dogged
us down
m what little we had, to live here among
the drains,
ere the waterbugs break out like a
scrofula
what we eat—and if there's lower to go
'll go there when you've told your story.
And more
t I haven't heart to speak—

o (*to* GARTH). My father died
your place. And you could have saved
him!
ou were one of the gang!

RTH. Why, there you are.
u certainly owe me nothing.

RIAMNE (*moaning*). I want to die.
want to go away.

o. Yes, and you lied!
d trapped me into it!

RIAMNE. But Mio, he's my brother.
ouldn't give them my brother.

MIO. No. You couldn't.
You were quite right. The gods were
damned ironic
tonight, and they've worked it out.

ESDRAS. What will be changed
if it comes to trial again? More blood poured
out
to a mythical justice, but your father lying
still
where he lies now.

MIO. The bright, ironical gods!
What fun they have in heaven! When a man
prays hard
for any gift, they give it, and then one more
to boot that makes it useless. (*To* MIR-
IAMNE.)
You might have picked
some other stranger to dance with!

MIRIAMNE. I know.

MIO. Or chosen
some other evening to sit outside in the rain.
But no, it had to be this. All my life long
I've wanted only one thing, to say to the
world
and prove it: the man you killed was clean
and true
and full of love as the twelve-year-old that
stood
and taught in the temple. I can say that now
and give my proofs—and now you stick a
girl's face
between me and the rites I've sworn the dead
shall have of me! You ask too much! Your
brother
can take his chance! He was ready enough
to let
an innocent man take certainty for him
to pay for the years he's had. That parts us,
then,
but we're parted anyway, by the same dark
wind
that blew us together. I shall say what I
have to say. (*He steps back.*)
And I'm not welcome here.

MIRIAMNE. But don't go now! You've stayed
too long! He'll be waiting!

MIO. Well, is this any safer?
Let the winds blow, the four winds of the
world,
and take us to the four winds.

(*The three are silent before him. He turns
and goes out.*)

CURTAIN

ACT THREE

SCENE: *The river bank outside the tenement, a little before the close of the previous act. The rain still falls through the street lamps. The* Two NATTY YOUNG MEN IN SERGE AND GRAY *are leaning against the masonry in a ray of light, concentrating on a game of chance. Each holds in his hand a packet of ten or fifteen crisp bills. They compare the numbers on the top notes and immediately a bill changes hands. This goes on with varying fortune until the tide begins to run toward the* FIRST GUNMAN, *who has accumulated nearly the whole supply. They play on in complete silence, evidently not wishing to make any noise. Occasionally they raise their heads slightly to look carefully about. Luck begins to favor the* SECOND GUNMAN, *and the notes come his way. Neither evinces the slightest interest in how the game goes. They merely play on, bored, half-absorbed. There is a slight noise at the tenement door. They put the bills away and watch.* TROCK *comes out, pulls the door shut and comes over to them. He says a few words too low to be heard, and without changing expression the* YOUNG MEN *saunter toward the right.* TROCK *goes out to the left, and the* SECOND PLAYER, *catching that out of the corner of his eye, lingers in a glimmer of light to go on with the game. The* FIRST, *with an eye on the tenement door, begins to play without ado, and the bills again shift back and forth, then concentrate in the hand of the* FIRST GUNMAN. *The* SECOND *shrugs his shoulders, searches his pockets, finds one bill, and playing with it begins to win·heavily. They hear the door opening, and putting the notes away, slip out in front of the rock.* MIO *emerges, closes the door, looks round him and walks to the left. Near the corner of the tenement he pauses, reaches out his hand to try the rain, looks up toward the street, and stands uncertainly a moment. He returns and leans against the tenement wall.* MIRIAMNE *comes out.* MIO *continues to look off into space as if unaware of her. She looks away.*

MIO. This rather takes one off his high horse.—What I mean, tough weather for a hegira. You see, this is my sleeping suit, and if I get it wet—basta!

MIRIAMNE. If you could only hide here.

MIO. Hide?

MIRIAMNE. Lucia would take you in. The street-piano man.

MIO. At the moment I'm afflicted with claustrophobia. I prefer to die in the open, seeking air.

MIRIAMNE. But you could stay there till daylight.

MIO. You're concerned about me.

MIRIAMNE. Shall I ask him?

MIO. No. On the other hand there's a certain reason in your concern. I looked up the street and our old friend Trock hunches patiently under the warehouse eaves.

MIRIAMNE. I was sure of that.

MIO. And here I am, a young man on a cold night, waiting the end of the rain.

Being read my lesson by a boy, a blind boy—you know the one I mean. Knee-deep in the salt-marsh, Miriam, bitten from within I fought.

MIRIAMNE. Wouldn't it be better if you came back in the house?

MIO. You forget my claustrophobia.

MIRIAMNE. Let me walk with you, the— Please. If I stay beside you he wouldn't dare—

MIO. And then again he might.—We don't speak the same language, Miriamne.

MIRIAMNE. I betrayed you. Forgive me.

MIO. I wish I knew this region. There's probably a path along the bank.

MIRIAMNE. Yes. Shadow went that way—

MIO. That's true, too. So here I am, a young man on a wet night, and blind in my weather eye. Stay and talk to me.

MIRIAMNE. If it happens—it's my fault.

MIO. Not at all, sweet. You warned me to keep away. But I would have it. Now I have to find a way out. It's like a chess game.

you think long enough there's always
way out.—For one or the other.—I wonder
hy white always wins and black always
ses in the problems. White to move and
ate in three moves. But what if white
re to lose—ah, what then? Why, in that
se, obviously black would be white and
hite would be black.—As it often it.—
s we often are.—Might makes white.
sers turn black. Do you think I'd have
ne to draw a gun?

RIAMNE. No.

o. I'm a fair shot. Also I'm fair game.
he door of the tenement opens and GARTH
*mes out to look about quickly. Seeing
ly* MIO *and* MIRIAMNE *he goes in and
mes out again almost immediately carry-
g one end of a door on which a body lies
vered with a cloth. The* HOBO *carries the
her end. They go out to the right with
ir burden.*)

is is the burial of Shadow, then;
t first he dips, and leaves the haunts of
men.
t us make mourn for Shadow, wetly
lying,
elegiac stanzas and sweet crying.
gentle with him, little cold waves and
fishes;
ble him not, respect his skin and tissues—

RIAMNE. Must you say such things?

o. My dear, some requiem is fitting over
the dead, even
Shadow. But the last rhyme was bad.
hittle him not, respect his dying wishes.
at's better. And then to conclude:
s aromatic virtues, slowly rising
ll circumnamb the isle, beyond disguising.
clung to life beyond the wont of men.
me and his silence drink us all. Amen.
w I hate these identicals. The French
ow them, but the French have no prin-
les anyway. You know, Miriamne, there's
lly nothing mysterious about human life.
purely mechanical, like an electric ap-
ance. Stop the engine that runs the
erator and the current's broken. When
think the brain gives off a small elec-
discharge—quite measurable, and con-
nt within limits. But that's not what
kes your hair stand up when frightened.

RIAMNE. I think it's a mystery.

o. Human life? We'll have to wear veils
we're to keep it a mystery much longer.
Now if Shadow and I were made up into
sausages we'd probably make very good
sausages.

MIRIAMNE. Don't—

MIO. I'm sorry. I speak from a high place,
far off, long ago, looking down. The
cortège returns. (GARTH *and the* HOBO *return, carrying the door, the cloth lying
loosely over it.*) I hoped you placed an obol
in his mouth to pay the ferry-man? Even
among the Greeks a little money was prerequisite to Elysium. (GARTH *and the* HOBO
go inside, silent.) No? It's grim to think
of Shadow lingering among lesser shades
on the hither side. For lack of a small
gratuity. (ESDRAS *comes out the open door
and closes it behind him.*)

ESDRAS. You must wait here, Mio, or go
inside. I know
you don't trust me, and I haven't earned
your trust.
You're young enough to seek truth—
and there is no truth;
and I know that—
but I shall call the police and see that you
get safely off.

MIO. It's a little late for that.

ESDRAS. I shall try.

MIO. And your terms? For I daresay you
make terms?

ESDRAS. No.

MIO. Then let me remind you what will
happen.
The police will ask some questions.
When they're answered
they'll ask more, and before they're done
with it
your son will be implicated.

ESDRAS. Must he be?

MIO. I shall not keep quiet. (*A pause.*)

ESDRAS. Still, I'll go.

MIO. I don't ask help, remember. I make no
truce.
He's not on my conscience, and I'm not
on yours.

ESDRAS. But you
could make it easier, so easily.
He's my only son. Let him live.

MIO. His chance of survival's
better than mine, I'd say.

ESDRAS. I'll go.

MIO. I don't urge it.

ESDRAS. No. I put my son's life in your hands.
When you're gone,
that may come to your mind.

MIO. Don't count on it.

ESDRAS. Oh,
I count on nothing. (*He turns to go.* MIRI-
AMNE *runs over to him and silently kisses
his hands.*)
Not mine, not mine, my daughter!
They're guilty hands. (*He goes out.* GARTH's
violin is heard within.)

MIO. There was a war in heaven
once, all the angels on one side, and all
the devils on the other, and since that time
disputes have raged among the learned,
   concerning
whether the demons won, or the angels.
  Maybe
the angels won, after all.

MIRIAMNE. And again, perhaps
there are no demons or angels.

MIO. Oh, there are none.
But I could love your father.

MIRIAMNE. I love him. You see,
he's afraid because he's old. The less one has
to lose the more he's afraid.

MIO. Suppose one had
only a short stub end of life, or held
a flashlight with the batteries run down
till the bulb was dim, and knew that he
  could live
while the glow lasted. Or suppose one knew
that while he stood in a little shelter of time
under a bridgehead, say, he could live, and
  then,
from then on, nothing. Then to lie and turn
with the earth and sun, and regard them not
  in the least
when the bulb was extinguished or he
  stepped beyond
his circle into the cold? How would he live
that last dim quarter-hour, before he went,
minus all recollection, to grow in grass
between cobblestones?

MIRIAMNE. Let me put my arms round y⌐
  Mio.
Then if anything comes, it's for me, t⌐
(*She puts both arms round him.*)

MIO. Only suppose
this circle's charmed! To be safe until
  steps
from this lighted space into dark! Ti⌐
  pauses here
and high eternity grows in one quarter-h⌐
in which to live.

MIRIAMNE. Let me see if anyone's there
there in the shadows. (*She looks towa⌐
the right.*)

MIO. It might blast our eternity—
blow it to bits. No, don't go. This is f⌐
  ever,
here where we stand. And I ask y⌐
  Miriamne,
how does one spend a forever?

MIRIAMNE. You're frightened?

MIO. Yes.
So much that time stands still.

MIRIAMNE. Why didn't I speak—
tell them—when the officers were here⌐
  failed you
in that one moment!

MIO. His life for mine? Oh, no.
I wouldn't want it, and you couldn't give⌐
And if I should go on living we're
  apart
by that brother of yours.

MIRIAMNE. Are we?

MIO. Well, think about it.
A body lies between us, buried in qui⌐
  lime.
Your allegiance is on the other side of t⌐
  grave
and not to me.

MIRIAMNE. No, Mio! Mio, I love you!

MIO. I love you, too, but in case my
  went on
beyond that barrier of dark—then Ga⌐
would run his risk of dying.

MIRIAMNE. He's punished, Mio.
His life's been torment to him. Let him
for my sake, Mio.

o. I wish I could. I wish
never seen him—or you. I've steeped too
long
this thing. It's in my teeth and bones. I
an't
go or forget. And I'll not add my lie
the lies that cumber his ground. We live
our days
a storm of lies that drifts the truth too
deep
path or shovel; but I've set my foot on
a truth
once, and I'll trail it down! (*A silence.*
RIAMNE *looks out to the right.*)

RIAMNE. There's someone there—
heard—(CARR *comes in from the right.*)

o. It's Carr.

RR. That's right. No doubt about it.
cuse me.

o. Glad to see you. This is Miriamne.
rr's a friend of mine.

RR. You're better employed
n when I saw you last.

o. Bow to the gentleman,
riamne. That's meant for you.

RIAMNE. Thank you, I'm sure.
ould I leave you, Mio? You want to talk?

o. Oh, no,
've done our talking.

RIAMNE. But—

R. I'm the one's out of place—
andered back because I got worried about
ou,
t's the truth.—Oh—those two fellows
with the hats
vn this way, you know, the ones that ran
er we heard the shooting—they're back
gain,
gering or malingering down the bank,
isiting the crime, I guess. They may
an well.

o. I'll try to avoid them.

R. I didn't care
the way they looked at me.—No luck, I
uppose,
h that case history? The investigation
had on hand?

MIO. I can't say. By the way,
the stiff that fell in the water and we saw
swirling
down the eddy, he came trudging up, later
on,
long enough to tell his name. His name was
Shadow,
but he's back in the water now. It's all in an
evening.
These things happen here.

CARR. Good God!

MIO. I know.
I wouldn't believe it if you told it.

CARR. But—
the man was alive?

MIO. Oh, not for long! He's dunked
for good this time. That's all that's happened.

CARR. Well,
if you don't need me—

MIRIAMNE. You had a message to send—
have you forgotten—?

MIO. I?—Yes, I had a message—
but I won't send it—not now.

MIRIAMNE. Then I will—!

MIO. No.
Let it go the way it is! It's all arranged
another way. You've been a good scout,
Carr,
the best I ever knew on the road.

CARR. That sounds
like making your will.

MIO. Not yet, but when I do
I've thought of something to leave you. It's
the view
of Mt. Rainier from the Seattle jail,
snow over cloud. And the rusty chain in my
pocket
from a pair of handcuffs my father wore.
That's all
the worldly goods I'm seized of.

CARR. Look, Mio—hell—
if you're in trouble—

MIO. I'm not. Not at all. I have
a genius that attends me where I go,
and guards me now. I'm fine.

CARR. Well, that's good news.
He'll have his work cut out.

MIO. Oh, he's a genius.

CARR. I'll see you then.
I'll be at the Grand Street place. I'm lucky tonight,
and I can pay. I could even pay for two.

MIO. Thanks, I may take you up.

CARR. Good night.

MIO. Right, Carr.

CARR (to MIRIAMNE). Good night.

MIRIAMNE (after a pause). Good night.
(CARR goes out to the left.)
Why did you do that? He's your genius, Mio,
and you let him go.

MIO. I couldn't help it.

MIRIAMNE. Call him.
Run after him and call him!

MIO. I tried to say it
and it strangled in my throat. I might have known
you'd win in the end.

MIRIAMNE. Is it for me?

MIO. For you?
It stuck in my throat, that's all I know.

MIRIAMNE. Oh, Mio,
I never asked for that! I only hoped
Garth could go clear.

MIO. Well, now he will.

MIRIAMNE. But you—
It was your chance!

MIO. I've lost
my taste for revenge if it falls on you. Oh, God,
deliver me from the body of this earth
I've dragged behind me all these years! Miriamne!
Miriamne!

MIRIAMNE. Yes!

MIO. Miriamne, if you love me
teach me a treason to what I am, and have been,
till I learn to live like a man! I think I'm waking
from a long trauma of hate and fear and death

that's hemmed me from my birth—a glimpse a life
to be lived in hope—but it's young in me y
I can't
get free, or forgive! But teach me how live
and forget to hate!

MIRIAMNE. He would have forgiven.

MIO. He?

MIRIAMNE. Your father. (A pause.)

MIO. Yes. (Another pause.)
You'll think it strange, but I've never remembered that.

MIRIAMNE. How can I help you?

MIO. You have.

MIRIAMNE. If I were a little older—if I kn
the things to say! I can only put out
hands
and give you back the faith you bring to
by being what you are. Because to me
you are all hope and beauty and brightn
drawn
across what's black and mean!

MIO. He'd have forgiven—
Then there's no more to say—I've gro
long enough
through this everglades of old revenge
here
the road ends.—Miriamne, Miriamne,
the iron I wore so long—it's eaten throu
and fallen from me. Let me have your ar
They'll say we're children—Well—th
world's made up
of children.

MIRIAMNE. Yes.

MIO. But it's too late for me.

MIRIAMNE. No. (She goes into his arms,
they kiss for the first time.)
Then we'll meet again?

MIO. Yes.

MIRIAMNE. Where?

MIO. I'll write—
or send Carr to you.

MIRIAMNE. You won't forget?

MIO. Forget?
Whatever streets I walk, you'll walk th
too,

m now on, and whatever roof or stars
ave to house me, you shall share my roof
d stars and morning. I shall not forget.

RIAMNE. God keep you!

o. And keep you. And this to remember!
I should die, Miriamne, this half-hour
our eternity. I came here seeking
ht in darkness, running from the dawn,
d stumbled on a morning.

ne of the YOUNG MEN IN SERGE *strolls in
ually from the right, looks up and down
thout expression, then, seemingly having
gotten something, retraces his steps and
es out.* ESDRAS *comes in slowly from the
t. He has lost his hat, and his face is bleed-
g from a slight cut on the temple. He
nds abjectly near the tenement.)*

RIAMNE. Father—what is it? (*She goes
vards* ESDRAS.)

RAS. Let me alone. (*He goes nearer to
o.*)
: wouldn't let me pass.
e street's so icy up along the bridge
had to crawl on my knees—he kicked
ne back
ee times—and then he held me there—
swear
at I could do I did! I swear to you
save you if I could.

o. What makes you think
t I need saving?

RAS. Child, save yourself if you can!
's waiting for you.

o. Well, we knew that before.

RAS. He won't wait much longer. He'll
ome here—
told me so. Those damned six months
f his—
wants them all—and you're to die—
ou'd spread
guilt—I had to listen to it—

o. Wait—(*He walks forward and looks
ually to the right, then returns.*)
ere must be some way up through the
ouse and out
oss the roof—

RAS. He's watching that. But come in—
let me look.—

MIO. I'll stay here, thanks. Once in
and I'm a rat in a deadfall—Ill stay here—
look for me if you don't mind.

ESDRAS. Then watch for me—
I'll be on the roof—(*He goes in hurriedly.*)

MIO (*looking up*). Now all you silent powers
that make the sleet and dark, and never yet
have spoken, give us a sign, let the throw
be ours
this once, on this longest night, when the
winter sets
his foot on the threshold leading up to spring
and enters with remembered cold—let fall
some mercy with the rain. We are two lovers
here in your night, and we wish to live.

MIRIAMNE. Oh, Mio—
if you pray that way, nothing good will
come!
You're bitter, Mio.

MIO. How many floors has this building?

MIRIAMNE. Five or six. It's not as high as
the bridge.

MIO. No, I thought not. How many pome-
granate seeds
did you eat, Persephone?

MIRIAMNE. Oh, darling, darling,
if you die, don't die alone.

MIO. I'm afraid I'm damned
to hell, and you're not damned at all. Good
God,
how long he takes to climb!

MIRIAMNE. The stairs are steep. (*A slight
pause.*)

MIO. I'll follow him.

MIRIAMNE. He's there—at the window—
now.
He waves you to go back, not to go in.
Mio, see, that path between the rocks—
they're not watching that—they're out at
the river—
I can see them there—they can't watch
both—
it leads to a street above.

MIO. I'll try it, then.
Kiss me. You'll hear. But if you never
hear—
then I'm the king of hell, Persephone,
and I'll expect you.

MIRIAMNE. Oh, lover, keep safe.

MIO. Good-bye. (*He slips quickly between the rocks. There is a quick machine gun rat-tat. The violin stops,* MIRIAMNE *runs toward the path.* MIO *comes back slowly, a hand pressed under his heart.*)
It seems you were mistaken.

MIRIAMNE. Oh, God, forgive me! (*She puts an arm round him. He sinks to his knees.*)
Where is it, Mio? Let me help you in!
  Quick, quick,
let me help you!

MIO. I hadn't thought to choose—this—
  ground—
but it will do. (*He slips down.*)

MIRIAMNE. Oh, God, forgive me!

MIO. Yes?
The king of hell was not forgiven then,
Dis is his name, and Hades is his home—
and he goes alone—

MIRIAMNE. Why does he bleed so? Mio, if you go
I shall go with you.

MIO. It's better to stay alive.
I wanted to stay alive—because of you—
I leave you that—and what he said to me
  dying:
I love you, and will love you after I die.
Tomorrow, I shall still love you, as I've
  loved
the stars I'll never see, and all the mornings
that might have been yours and mine. Oh,
  Miriamne,
you taught me this.

MIRIAMNE. If only I'd never seen you
then you could live—

MIO. That's blasphemy—Oh, God,
there might have been some easier way of it.
You didn't want me to die, did you,
  Miriamne—?
You didn't send me away—?

MIRIAMNE. Oh, never, never—

MIO. Forgive me—kiss me—I've got blood
  on your lips—
I'm sorry—it doesn't matter—I'm sorry—
(ESDRAS *and* GARTH *come out.*)

MIRIAMNE. Mio—
I'd have gone to die myself—you must hear
  this, Mio,

I'd have died to help you—you must liste
  sweet,
you must hear it—(*She rises.*)
I can die, too, see! You! There!
You in the shadows!—You killed him
  silence him! (*She walks toward the path*
But I'm not silenced! All that he knew
  know,
and I'll tell it tonight! Tonight—
tell it and scream it
through all the streets—that Trock's a mu
  derer
and he hired you for this murder!
Your work's not done—
and you won't live long! Do you hear?
You're murderers, and I know who you a
(*The machine gun speaks again. She sin
to her knees.* GARTH *runs to her.*)

GARTH. You little fool! (*He tries to lift her*

MIRIAMNE. Don't touch me! (*She craw
toward* MIO.)
Look, Mio! They killed me, too. Oh, y
  can believe me
now, Mio. You can believe I wouldn't h
  you,
because I'm dying! Why doesn't he answ
  me?
Oh, now he'll never know! (*She sinks dow
her hand over her mouth, choking.* GAR
kneels beside her, then rises, shudderin
The* HOBO *comes out.* LUCIA *and* PINY *lo
out.*)

ESDRAS. It lacked only this.

GARTH. Yes. (ESDRAS *bends over* MIRIAMI
then rises slowly.*)
Why was the bastard born? Why did
come here?

ESDRAS. Miriamne—Miriamne—yes, and
Mio,
one breath shall call you now—forgive
  both—
forgive the ancient evil of the earth
that brought you here—

GARTH. Why must she be a fool?

ESDRAS. Well, they were wiser than you a
I. To die
when you are young and untouched, tha
  beggary
to a miser of years, but the devils locked
synod
shake and are daunted when men set th
lives

t hazard for the heart's love, and lose. And
these,
vho were yet children, will weigh more
than all
. city's elders when the experiment
s reckoned up in the end. Oh, Miriamne,
nd Mio—Mio, my son—know this where
you lie,
his is the glory of earth-born men and
women,
iot to cringe, never to yield, but standing,
ake defeat implacable and defiant,
lie unsubmitting. I wish that I'd died so,
ong ago; before you're old you'll wish
hat you had died as they have. On this star,
n this hard star-adventure, knowing not
vhat the fires mean to right and left, nor
whether
i meaning was intended or presumed,

man can stand up, and look out blind, and
say:
in all these turning lights I find no clue,
only a masterless night, and in my blood
no certain answer, yet is my mind my own,
yet is my heart a cry toward something dim
in distance, which is higher than I am
and makes me emperor of the endless dark
even in seeking! What odds and ends of life
men may live otherwise, let them live, and
then
go out, as I shall go, and you. Our part
is only to bury them. Come, take her up.
They must not lie here.

(LUCIA *and* PINY *come near to help.* ESDRAS
and GARTH *stoop to carry* MIRIAMNE.)

CURTAIN

High Tor

BY MAXWELL ANDERSON

Guthrie McClintic presented Maxwell Anderson's HIGH TOR for the first time on any stage in the Hanna Theater, Cleveland, Ohio, Wednesday night, December 30, 1936, with this cast:

THE INDIAN	Harry Irvine	A SAILOR	William Casamo
VAN DORN	Burgess Meredith	DeWITT	Charles D. Brown
JUDITH	Mab Maynard	DOPE	Leslie Gorall
ART. J. BIGGS	Harold Moffet	ELKUS	Hume Cronyn
JUDGE SKIMMERHORN	Thomas W. Ross	BUDDY	John Drew Colt
LISE	Peggy Ashcroft	PATSY	Charles Forrester
CAPTAIN ASHER	Byron McGrath	A. B. SKIMMERHORN	John M. Kline
PIETER	John Philliber	BUDGE	Jackson Halliday

DUTCH CREW OF THE *ONRUST*

The play was staged by Mr. McClintic and the settings were designed by Jo Mielziner.

Copyright, 1937, by MAXWELL ANDERSON

NOTE

HIGH TOR

ACT ONE

SCENE I

SCENE: *A section of the broad flat trap-rock summit of High Tor, from which one looks out into sky and from which one might look down a sheer quarter mile to the Tappan Zee below. A cluster of hexagonal pillared rocks masks the view to the left and a wind-tortured small hemlock wedges into the rock floor at the right. Light from the setting sun pours in from the left, and an ancient* INDIAN, *wearing an old greatcoat thrown round him like a blanket, stands in the rays from a cleft, making his prayer to the sunset.*

THE INDIAN. I make my prayer to you, the
    falling fire,
bearing in mind the whisper in my ears
from the great spirit, talking on the wind,
whispering that a young race, in its morning,
should pray to the rising sun, but a race
    that's old
and dying, should invoke the dying flame
eaten and gulfed by the shark-toothed moun-
    tain-west,
a god that dies to live. As we have died,
my race of the red faces and old ways,
and as we hope to rise. I give you thanks
for light, for the coming summer that will
    warm
my snake's blood, cold and crawling; for
    the rain
that fed the ripe May apples in the woods
in secret for me; for the waterfall
where the trout climb and pause under my
    hand,
taken in silence; for quiet on the hills
where the loud races dare not walk for fear
lest they be lost, where their blind hunters
    pass
peering with caps and guns, but see no game,
and curse as they go down, while the raccoon
    waits,
the woodchuck stands erect to catch the
    wind,
the partridge steps so lightly over leaves
the listening fox hears nothing, the possum
    hangs
head down, looking through his hands, and
    takes no breath,
the gray squirrel turns to stone against the
    rock,
watching the owl, the rabbit holds his ears
steady above the trembling of his heart
and the crow mocks down the shellbark.
   I am fed
and sheltered on this mountain where their
    hands
are helpless. But I am old as my race is old;

my eyes hunt day and night along the
    ground
the grave where I shall lie; my ears have
    heard
dead women calling upward from the earth
mother and wife and child: "You are wel-
    come here;
you are no longer welcome where you walk,
but here you are most welcome." I shall go,
and lie and sleep, and I shall give you
    thanks,
O God that dies, that my last night is dark
and long, for I am tired, but yet I ask
one summer more, that I may be warm
    again
and watch the nestlings grown upon the
    crag,
and hear the wild geese honking south by
    night,
if this may be, but if it may not be
then is my prayer, that when I lie to sleep
I may lie long, sleep soundly, hear no step,
hear only through the earth your step in
    spring,
O God of the dying fire!
(VAN DORN *and* JUDITH *come in from the
right.*)

VAN DORN. Evening, John.

THE INDIAN. Evening.

VAN DORN. Had any luck so far?

THE INDIAN. Yes. Plenty of luck.

VAN DORN. Found it?

THE INDIAN. Yes.

VAN DORN. O.K., John, let me know.
Let me know in time.

THE INDIAN. I will. Good night.

VAN DORN. Good night. (*The* INDIAN *slips
away through the rocks to the left.*)

JUDITH. Who is it, Van?

VAN. Just an Indian.

JUDITH. Are there Indians?
didn't know there were any Indians left.

VAN. Well, there's one. There's not much
left of him,
and he's the last around here.

JUDITH. He's hunting something?
You asked him if he's found it.

VAN. Um—yes, you see,
he's looking for a place to make his grave,
and he's kind of captious about it—folks get
that way
along toward the end, wanting their bones
done up
in some particular fashion. Maybe because
that's all you've got to leave about that time
and you want it the way you want it.

JUDITH. Did he tell you this?

VAN. We've got an understanding. When he
feels it
coming over him he's going to die
he'll let me know, and I'll go dig him in
so the crows and foxes can't get at him. See,
he's all alone in the world. We fixed this up
a couple of years ago.

JUDITH. But you couldn't, Van,
without a permit. A burial permit.

VAN. Oh,
I guess you could. This getting old and
dying
and crawling into the ground, that was
invented
back before medical examiners
and taxes and all that. The old boy's clean.
He'll go right back to dirt.

JUDITH. But, Van, you can't!
People can't die that way!

VAN. I guess they can.
What the hell good's being wrapped in
cellophane?
You don't keep anyway.

JUDITH. You're impossible
to live with! Why do you say such things?
If I
should die—you'd get a pine box!—

VAN. If you should die
the old boy that drives the sun around up
there,

he'd unhitch, and put the cattle out
to grass, and give it up. He'd plumb lose
interest
if you should die. Maybe I would myself,
I don't say. Maybe I would.—Fetch out that
supper.
We want to see what we eat.

JUDITH (opening a lunch box). It's dinner,
Van,
not supper.

VAN. That's what I said. Fetch out that
dinner.
When it gets a little darker what's black's
pepper
and what's green's parsley; still you can't
be sure.
It might be ants.

JUDITH. Just the same we'll quarrel.
We'll always quarrel.

VAN. Oh, no, We've both got sense.
What's the sense fighting? (He looks at a
paper that was round the lunch.)

JUDITH. And you shouldn't read at table.

VAN. I never do. The Nanuet bank's been
robbed.
My God, there's not enough money in
Nanuet
to buy their gas for a get-away. One night
pap and me sat in on a poker game
in Nanuet and took twenty-seven dollars
out of town. Next day they couldn't do
business.
The place was clean.

JUDITH. There were troopers at the train
tonight, and sirens going through Haverstraw,
but the robbers got away.

VAN. They took twenty-five thousand.
How'd twenty-five thousand get to Nanuet?
It's against nature.

JUDITH. It didn't stay there long.

VAN. No—I understand that.
But just to have it there in passing, just
to look at, just to fool the customers,
how do they do it?

JUDITH. Maybe it wasn't real.

VAN. Federal money, that's it. Some of the
stuff

Jim Farley prints in Washington with the stamps
to pay you for voting straight. Only now you see it
and now you don't.

JUDITH. They say it buys as much
as if you earned it.

VAN. Bad for the stomach, though,
to live on humble pie.

JUDITH. I'd rather work.

VAN. Well, as I said, don't work if you don't feel like it.
Any time you want to move up in the hills
and sleep with me, it's a bargain.

JUDITH. Van!

VAN. Why not?
We'll get married if that's what you mean.

JUDITH. You haven't any job. And you make it sound
like animals.

VAN. I'm fond of animals.

JUDITH. You shoot them all the time.

VAN. Well, I get hungry.
Any man's liable to get hungry.

JUDITH. Van,
I want to talk to you seriously.

VAN. Can't be done.
Listen, things get serious enough
without setting out to do it.

JUDITH. Van, this spring
you had three weeks' work, laying dry wall.
You could have had more, but you didn't take it.
You're an expert mason—

VAN. I'm good at everything.

JUDITH. But you work three weeks in the year—

VAN. That's all I need—

JUDITH. And all the rest of the year you hunt or fish
or sleep, or God knows what—

VAN. Ain't it the truth?

JUDITH. Last fall I came looking for you once, and you

were gone—gone to Port Jervis hunting— deer,
you said on the postcard—

VAN. Sure, I was hunting deer—
didn't I bring you half a venison?

JUDITH. But not a word to me till I got the postcard
ten days later—

VAN. Didn't have a minute—

JUDITH. Then last winter there's a note nailed to a tree
and you're in Virginia, down in the Dismal Swamp
tracking bear. Now, for God's sake, Van,
it's no way to live.

VAN. Jeez, it's a lot of fun.

JUDITH. Maybe for you.

VAN. You want me to take that job.

JUDITH. Why don't you, Van?

VAN. Porter in a hotel, lugging up satchels,
opening windows, maybe you get a dime.
I'd choke to death.

JUDITH. I'd see you every day.

VAN. Yeah, I could see you on the mezzanine,
taking dictation from the drummer boys,
all about how they can't get home. You can stand it,
a woman stands that stuff, but if you're a man
I say it chokes you.

JUDITH. We can't live in your cabin
and have no money, like the Jackson Whites
over at Suffern.

VAN. Hell, you don't need money.
Pap worked that out. All you need's a place to sleep
and something to eat. I've never seen the time
I couldn't find a meal on the mountain here,
rainbow trout, jugged hare, something in season
right around the zodiac.

JUDITH. You didn't like
the Chevrolet factory, either?

VAN (*walking toward the cliff edge*). Look at it, Judy.
That's the Chevrolet factory, four miles down,

nd straight across, that's Sing Sing. Right
from here
you can't tell one from another; get inside,
nd what's the difference? You're in there,
and you work,
nd they've got you. If you're in the factory
you buy a car, and then you put in your time
o pay for the goddam thing. If you get in
a hurry
nd steal a car, they put you in Sing Sing
first,
nd then you work out your time. They
graduate
rom one to the other, back and forth, those
guys,
aying for cars both ways. But I was smart.
parked at a polis station and rung the bell
nd took to the woods. Not for your Uncle
Dudley.
They plugged the dice.

JUDITH. But one has to have a car.

VAN. Honest to God now, Judy, what's the
hurry?
Where in hell are we going?

JUDITH. If a man works hard,
and has ability, as you have, Van,
he takes a place among them, saves his
money,
works right out of the ruck and gets above
where he's safe and secure.

VAN. I wouldn't bet on it much.

JUDITH. But it's true.

VAN. All right, suppose it's true. Suppose
a man saves money all his life, and works
like hell about forty years, till he can say:
good-bye, I'm going, I'm on easy street
from now on. What's he do?

JUDITH. Takes a vacation.

VAN. Goes fishing, maybe? I'm on vacation
now.
Why should I work forty years to earn
time off when I've got it?

JUDITH. It's not always easy,
you know it's not. There was that time last
winter
when I helped you out.

VAN. Why, sure, you helped me out.
Why wouldn't you? But if you didn't help
me
I'd get along.

JUDITH. Yes, you would. I know you would.
But you don't even seem to want money.
You won't take it
when they bring it to you.

VAN. When did they bring me any?

JUDITH. And what if there was a child?

VAN. Why, he'd be fine—
the less they have the better they like it.—
Oh,
you mean the trap-rock company, wanting
to buy
High Tor? They offered seven hundred
dollars—
and they offered pap ten thousand before
he died,
and he wouldn't sell.

JUDITH. He wouldn't?

VAN. They wanted to chew
the back right off this mountain, the way
they did
across the clove there. Leave the old palisades
sticking up here like billboards, nothing left
but a false front facing the river. Not for
pap,
and not for me. I like this place.

JUDITH. But, Van Van Dorn!
Ten thousand dollars!

VAN. Well, it's Federal money.
Damn stuff evaporates. Put it in a sock
along with moth balls, and come back next
year,
and there's nothing left but the smell. Look,
Judy, its
a quarter mile straight down to the Tappan
Zee
from here.—You can see fifteen miles of
river
north and south. I grew up looking at it.
Hudson came up that river just about
three hundred years ago, and lost a ship
here in the Zee. They say the crew climbed
up
this Tor to keep a lookout for the fleet
that never came. Maybe the Indians got
them.
Anyway on dark nights before a storm,
they say you sometimes see them.

JUDITH. Have you seen them?

VAN. The Dutchmen? Maybe I have. You
can't be sure.
It's pretty wild around here when it storms.

That's when I like it best. But look at it now.
There was a Jaeger here from Switzerland
last year. He took one squint at this and said
they could keep their Alps, for all him.
   Look at the willows
along the far breakwater.

JUDITH. It's beautiful.

VAN. Every night I come back here like the
   Indian
to get a fill of it. Seven hundred dollars
and tear it down? Hell, no. (BIGGS and SKIM-
MERHORN *come in from the right, a bit bedraggled, and wiping their brows.* SKIMMER-
HORN *carries a brief-case. It is growing
darker.*)

BIGGS. Hey listen, Mac, any houses round
here?

VAN. Guess you're off the beat, buddy; never
heard of any houses on the mountain.

SKIMMERHORN. Come on, Art; we're doing
well if we're down at the road before dark.

BIGGS. Look, Mac, maybe you can help us
out. You familiar with this region, at all?

VAN. I've been around here some.

BIGGS. Well, we're all afternoon hunting a
cabin that's somewhere along the ridge. Ever
hear of it?

VAN. Anybody live in it?

BIGGS. Fellow named Van Dorn.

VAN. Oh, yes, sure.

BIGGS. You know where it is?

VAN. Sure. You climb down the face of the
cliff here and keep left along the ledge about
a hundred yards, then you turn sharp left
through a cleft up the ridge. Follow the trail
about half a mile and there you are.

SKIMMERHORN. Down the face of the cliff?

VAN. Down through the rocks there, then
turn left—

SKIMMERHORN. A monkey couldn't go down
there, hanging on with four hands and a
tail!

VAN. Well, you can always walk along back
toward Little Tor, and cut down from there
through the gulch. There's a slough at the
bottom of the ravine, but if you get through
that you can see the cabin up on the side
hill. About four miles that way.

SKIMMERHORN. Yeah, we'll set right out.
always did want to get lost up here an
spend a night in the hills.

VAN. Oh, you'll get lost, all right.

BIGGS. Any snakes?

VAN. No, you might see a copperhead, or
timber rattler.

SKIMMERHORN. Coming back down?

BIGGS. Yeah, we'd better go down. Thanks

VAN. Don't mention it. (BIGGS *and* SKIMMER
HORN *go out to the right.*)

JUDITH. But they were looking for you?

VAN. Yeah.

JUDITH. Why didn't you tell them?

VAN. What?

JUDITH. Who you were!

VAN. They didn't ask about that.

JUDITH. But out of common courtesy!

VAN. Well, you see, I know who they are

JUDITH. Who are they?

VAN. Art J. Biggs, Junior, and Skimmerhorn
Judge Skimmerhorn.

JUDITH. But why not talk to them?

VAN. Oh, we communicate by mail. I've go
a dozen letters stacked up from the firm
Skimmerhorn, Skimmerhorn, Biggs and
   Skimmerhorn,
and maybe two or three Skimmerhorns I lef
out
printed across the top. They're realtors
whatever that is, and they own the trap-rock
   company,
and one of the Skimmerhorns, he's probate
   judge,
and goes around condemning property
when they want to make a rake-off. Take
   a letter:
Dear Skimmerhorn—

JUDITH. But they're the trap-rock men!

VAN. That's what I said.

JUDITH. I'll call them!

VAN. Oh, no; oh, no!
I've got nothing to say to those two buzzards
except I hope they break their fat-back necks
on their own trap-rock.

JUDITH. You take a lot for granted.

VAN. Do I?

JUDITH. You think, because I said I loved
you once,
that's the end; I'm finished.

VAN. Oh, far from it.

JUDITH. Oh, yes—you think because a girl's
been kissed
she stays kissed, and after that the man
does her thinking for her.

VAN. Hell, it's all I can do
to handle my own thinking.

JUDITH. If we're married
I'll have to live the way you want to live.
You prefer being a pauper!

VAN. Get it straight!
I don't take money nor orders, and I live
as I damn well please.

JUDITH. But we'd live like paupers!
And you could have a fortune!

VAN. Seven hundred dollars?

JUDITH. You could get more!

VAN. I don't mean to sell at all.

JUDITH. You see; it's your place, and your
thinking! You decide,
but I'd have to stand it with you!

VAN. What do you want?

JUDITH. Something to start on; and now,
you see, we could have it,
only you won't!

VAN. I can't, Judy, that's the truth.
I just can't.

JUDITH. They'll get it anyway.
They've worked right up to where your land
begins,
and they won't stop for you. They'll just
condemn it
and take it.

VAN. They'll be in trouble.

JUDITH. You can't make trouble
for companies. They have a dozen lawyers
and ride right over you. I've worked for
them.
It's never any use.

VAN. Well, I won't sell.

JUDITH. We'll call it off then.

VAN. What?

JUDITH. Between you and me.

VAN. Only you don't mean it.

JUDITH. I know I do, though.
You haven't thought about it, and so you
think
I couldn't do it. But it's better now
than later.

VAN. You don't know what it means to me
if you can say it.

JUDITH. It means as much to me,
but I look ahead a little.

VAN. What do you see?

JUDITH. Two people growing old
and having children, running wild in the
woods
with nothing.

VAN. There's no better place to run.
But I've been counting on you. More than
you know.
More than—Judy, this is the kind of night
we've been in love most.

JUDITH. Yes, we could be in love,
but that's not everything.

VAN. Well, just about.
What else do we get?

JUDITH. I think I'd better go.
It's getting dark.

VAN. You could find your way by the beacon.

JUDITH. I'd better go. (BIGGS and SKIMMER-
HORN *come back from the right.*)

BIGGS. Listen, Mac, would you do something
for us?

VAN. I don't know.

BIGGS. Could you take a paper round to Van
Dorn and leave it with him?

VAN. A summons?

BIGGS. A sort of notice.

VAN. Yeah, a notice to appear. No, I couldn't.

BIGGS. It's worth a dollar to me.

VAN. I'd be cheating you.

SKIMMERHORN. Make it two dollars.

VAN. You'd be throwing away money.

SKIMMERHORN. Never mind that part of it. Will you do it?

VAN. You'll take a running jump over the edge of the cliff and think things over on the way down before I serve any papers for you.

BIGGS. What's the matter with us?

VAN. Might be hoof and mouth disease, for all I know. You certainly brought an awful stench up here with you.

SKIMMERHORN. Not much on manners, these natives.

VAN. My rule in life is keep away from skunks.

BIGGS. You'll get the tar kicked out of you one of these days.

VAN. Make it today.

JUDITH. If you gentlemen care to know, this is Mr. Van Dorn.

BIGGS. Say, are you Van Dorn?

VAN. Sure I am.

BIGGS (*extending a hand*). Oh, in that case, forget it—you're the fellow we want to see!— Boy, we apologize—(*He uncovers.*) and to the lady, too! Listen, I don't know what to say but you've got us all wrong. We want to buy this place!

VAN. You like the view, I suppose?

BIGGS. Certainly is a view.

VAN. You wouldn't spoil it, of course? You wouldn't move in with a million dollars' worth of machinery and cut the guts out of the mountain, would you?

SKIMMERHORN. We always leave the front— the part you see from the river.

VAN. But you take down all the law allows.

SKIMMERHORN. Well, we're in business.

VAN. Not with me.

JUDITH. Do you mind if I ask how much you're offering?

BIGGS. We said seven hundred, but I'll make it a thousand right here and now.

SKIMMERHORN. As a matter of fact, we'll make it two thousand.

BIGGS. Yeah, all right. Two thousand for the hundred and seven acres.

JUDITH. But you offered Mr. Van Dorn's father ten thousand before he died.

SKIMMERHORN. His father had a clear title, right down from the original Dutch patroon to the original Van Dorn. But unfortunately the present Mr. Van Dorn has a somewhat clouded claim to the acreage.

VAN. My father's title was clear, and he left it to me.

SKIMMERHORN. The truth is he should have employed a lawyer when he drew his will, because the instrument, as recorded, is faulty in many respects. It was brought before me in my capacity as probate judge at Leden-town.

VAN. And in your capacity as second vice-president of the trap-rock company you shot it full of holes.

SKIMMERHORN. Sir, I keep my duties entirely separate.

VAN. Sure, but when your left hand takes money your right hand finds out about it. And when there's too much to carry away in both hands you use a basket. You're also vice-president of the power company, and you stole right-of-ways clear across the country north and south—

SKIMMERHORN. We paid for every foot of land—

VAN. Yes, at your own price.

BIGGS. Let's not get in an argument, Mr. Van Dorn, because the fact that your father's will was improperly drawn means he died intestate and the land goes to his heirs. Now we've found twenty-seven Van Dorns living at Blauvelt, all claiming relationship and all willing to sign away their rights for a consideration.

VAN. The best you can do you'll need my name in your little paper, and you won't have it.

SKIMMERHORN. To put it straight, you'll take three thousand dollars, and I'll hold the will valid.

VAN. Oh, it's three thousand, now?

BIGGS. You'll say that's crooked, but it's not. It's perfectly legal—and it's what you get.

VAN. I'm still waiting to hear what you do about my signature.

KIMMERHORN. It's quite possible you'll be held incompetent by the court and a guardian appointed.

VAN. Me, incompetent.

KIMMERHORN. But I've got the validation in my pocket, naming you executor, if you'll sell.

BIGGS. And by God, anybody that won't take money when it's offered to him is incompetent! And you'll take it now or not at all! I don't go mountain-climbing every day with a blank check in my pocket! (*A pause.*) Come on: It's bad enough sliding down that trail by daylight.

VAN. Well, I wouldn't want to make you nervous,
a couple of eminent respectables
like you two—but a dog won't bite a Dutchman—
maybe you've heard that—and the reason is
Dutchman's poison when he don't like you. Now,
I'm Dutch and I don't like you.

KIMMERHORN. That's a threat?

VAN. Not at all. Only don't try to eat me
or you'll curl up. I'm poison to a hound-dog,
and you're both sons-of-bitches.

BIGGS. Come on. (*The daylight is now gone.
The airplane beacon lights the scene from
the right.*)

VAN. What's more
there's something funny about this mountain-top.
It draws fire. Every storm on the Tappan Zee
climbs up here and wraps itself around

High Tor, and blazes away at what you've got,
airplane beacon, steam-shovels, anything
newfangled. It smashed the beacon twice. It blew
the fuses on your shovel and killed a man
only last week. I've got a premonition
something might happen to you.

BIGGS. God, he's crazy.

SKIMMERHORN. Yeah, let him talk. (*There is
a sudden rumbling roar of falling rock.*)

BIGGS. What's that?

VAN. That's nothing much.
That's just a section of the cliff come down
across the trail. I've been expecting it
this last two years. You'd better go down this
way.

BIGGS. This way?

VAN. Yeah.

BIGGS. No, thanks.

VAN. Just as you say.
But there's something definitely hostile here
toward you two pirates. Don't try that trail
in the dark.
Not if you want to be buried in your vaults
in Mount Repose. Your grieving families
might have to move two thousand tons of rock
to locate your remains. You think High Tor's
just so much raw material, but you're wrong.
A lot of stubborn men have died up here
and some of them don't sleep well. They come back
and push things round, these dark nights. Don't blame me
if anything falls on you.

SKIMMERHORN. Oh, what the hell!
Let's get out of here. (*Another long rumble
of falling rock.*)

VAN. Another rock-fall.
Once they start there's likely to be more.
Something hanging round in the dark up here
doesn't like you boys. Not only me.
Better go down this way.

BIGGS. Thanks. (BIGGS *and* SKIMMERHORN *go
out to the right.*)

JUDITH. What do you mean?

VAN. I don't know.

JUDITH. They'll say you threatened them.
Good-bye, Van.

VAN. You'll be up tomorrow?

JUDITH. No. (*She steps down into a cleft.*)

VAN. You'd better let me see you down.

JUDITH. Oh, no.
I can climb. Stay here and guard your rock—
you think so much of it.

VAN. When will I see you?

JUDITH. Never.
We'll forget about it. You had a choice
and you chose High Tor. You're in love with
    your mountain.
Well, keep your mountain.

VAN. All right.

JUDITH. Good night.

VAN. Good night.
(*She disappears down the rocks.* VAN *sits in
the shadows, looking into darkness. After
a moment a barely perceptible* FIGURE *enters
from the gloom at the right and crosses the
stage toward the rocks at the left. At the foot
of the climb he pauses and his face is caught
in the light of the beacon. He is seen to be
young or middle-aged, bearded, and wearing
the costume of a Dutch sailor of the sixteen
hundreds. He climbs the rocks, and* ANOTHER
SAILOR, *a small cask strapped to his shoulders, follows.* THREE MORE *cross the stage
similarly, then the* CAPTAIN *and* HIS WIFE
*pause, like the others, in the light of the
beacon. The* CAPTAIN *is like his men, only
younger perhaps;* HIS WIFE *is a tiny figure,
with a delicate girlish face looking out from
under the Dutch bonnet. They too pass up
the rocks, and are followed by a rolling*
SILENUS *in the same garments. As they
vanish* VAN *rises, looking after them.*)
Uh—huh—going to rain.

CURTAIN

SCENE II

SCENE: *The curtain goes up on complete darkness enfolding the summit of the Tor.
There is a long cumbrous rolling, as of a ball going down a bowling alley, a flash of white
light, a crackling as of falling pins and a mutter dying into echo along the hills. The flash
reveals the outline of the Tor, black against the sky, and on it the figures of the* DUTCH
CREW. *Again the roll, the flash, the break and the dying away. The beam of the airplane
beacon steals into the scene sufficiently to suggest the bowlers, some of them standing,
some sitting about the keg, the* CAPTAIN'S WIFE *a little apart from the rest. Beyond the
peak is a moving floor, the upper side of blown cloud.*

THE CAPTAIN'S WIFE. I'm weary of it, Martin!
    When you drink
there should be one on guard to watch the
    river
lest the ship come, and pass, and we must
    haunt
the dark another year!

THE CAPTAIN. To humor her,
Pieter, old son, climb down and post the Zee,
and mind you keep good lookout.

PIETER. Ships, aye, ships—
when the ball's rolling and there's gin in
    hand
I go to post. My luck!

THE CAPTAIN. When you shipped with me
you signed the voyage.

PIETER. Is this sea or land?
I'm no foot soldier!

THE CAPTAIN. March!

PIETER. Aye, aye. I'm going. (PIETER *detach
himself from the group and goes down the
rocks.*)

THE CAPTAIN. Are you content?

THE CAPTAIN'S WIFE. When the *Half Moon*
    returns
and we have boarded her, and the wind
    scuds fair
into the east—yes, when we see the wharves
of Texel town across the Zuyder Zee,
with faces waiting for us, hands and cries
to welcome our returning, then perhaps
I shall be content.

SAILOR. Now God, for Texel town.

ANOTHER SOLDIER (*rising*). I'll drink no
more.

DEWITT (*the Silenus*). Drink up, lads, and
forget.
It's a long way to the Texel. Drink your
drink
and play your play.

THE CAPTAIN. Drink up and play it out.

THE CAPTAIN'S WIFE. Have you forgotten how
the cobbled street
comes down by cranks and turns upon the
quay,
where the *Onrust* set sail? The traders' doors
under the blowing signs, bright colors hung
to catch unwary eyes? The bakers' ovens
and the long, hot brown loaves? The red-
coal fires
and silver under candles? There your wives
wait for you, their sharp roofs in Amsterdam
cut on a rainy sky.

THE CAPTAIN. Be quiet, Lise.
You were so much in love you must come
with me;
you were so young that I was patient with
you,
but now day long, night long you carp and
quarrel,
a carping wife.

LISE. We stay so long—so long;
Asher, at first the days were years, but now
the years are days; the ship that set us down
to watch this river palisades becomes
alike with supper-stories round a hearth
when we were children. Was there this ship
at all,
was there a sailor-city, Amsterdam,
where the salt water washed the shallow
piers
and the wind went out to sea? Will the ship
return,
and shall I then see the Netherlands once
more,
with sabots clattering homeward from the
school
on winter evenings?

ASHER. Aye, there was a ship,
and we wait here for her, but she's long
away,
somewhere up-river.

LISE. And now you drink and drink,
distill your liquor on the mountain-top
and bowl against the light. But when you
break it
these new strange men come build it up
again;
and giant shovels spade the mountain down,
and when you break them still the new
strange men
rig them afresh and turn them on the rock,
eating the pillored stone. We must go back.
There's no safety here.

A SAILOR. We must go back.

ASHER. These muttering fools!

LISE. Oh, Asher, I'm afraid!
For one thing I have known, and never told
lest it be true, lest you be frightened, too,
lest we be woven of shadow! As the years
have gone, each year a century, they seem
less real, and all the boundaries of time,
our days and nights and hours, merge and
are one,
escaping me. Then sometimes in a morning
when all the crew come down the rocks together,
holding my breath, I see you in the light,
and back of you the gray rock bright and
hard,
seen through figures of air! And you, and
you,
and you were but cloud-drift walking,
pierced by the light,
translucent in the sun.

DEWITT. Now damn the woman!

LISE. Love, love, before our blood
be shadow only, in a dark fairyland
so far from home, we must go back, go back
where earth is earth, and we may live again
and one day be one day!

ASHER. Why, then, I knew it,
and I have known it, now that you know it,
too.
But the old Amsterdam of our farewells
lies in another world. The land and sea
about us on this dark side of the earth
is thick with demons, heavy with enchantment,
cutting us off from home.

LISE. Is it enchantment?
Yes, it may be. At home there were tulips
growing
along my bordered path, but here the flowers

are strange to me, not one I knew, no trace
of any flower I knew; no, seedling set
upon a darkened, alien outer rim
of sea, blown here as we were blown, enchanted,
drunken and blind with sorcery.

ASHER. And yet
what we're to have we shall have here.
Years past
the demons of this air palsied our hands,
fixed us upon one pinnacle of time,
and on this pinnacle of stone, and all
the world we knew slid backward to the
gulf,
stranding us here like seaweed on the
shingle,
remembering the sea. In Texel town
new houses have gone up, after new
fashions;
the children of the children of our days,
lying awake to think of what has been,
reach doubtfully beyond the clouds of years
back to our sailing out of Texel. Men
are like the gods, work miracles, have power
to pierce the walls with music. Their beacon
light
destroys us. You have seen us in the sun,
wraithlike, half-effaced, the print we make
upon the air thin tracery, permeable,
a web of wind. They have changed us. We
may take
the fire-balls of the lightning in our hands
and bowl them down the level floor of cloud
to wreck the beacon, yet there was a time
when these were death to touch. The life we
keep
is motionless as the center of a storm,
yet while we can we keep it; while we can
snuff out to darkness their bright sweeping
light,
melt down the harness of the slow machines
that hew the mountain from us. When it
goes
we shall go too. They leave us this place,
High Tor,
and we shall have no other. You learn it last.
A long while now we've known.

A SAILOR. Aye, aye, a long while.

ASHER. Come, we'll go down. (*The* CAPTAIN
and his MEN *go out, leaving only* DEWITT
with LISE.)

LISE. That's why they drink.

DEWITT. It's enough to drive a sailor-man
to drink, by the great jib boom, marooned

somewhere on the hinder parts of the earth
and degenerating hourly to the status of
a flying Dutchman, half-spook and half God-
knows-what. Maps and charts we have, compass and sextant, but the ship these days are
bewitched like ourselves, spanking up and
down the Mauritius with sails struck, against
wind and tide, and on fire from below.
Drink? Why wouldn't we drink? A pewter
flagon of Hollands gin puts manhood into
the remnants and gives a sailor courage to
look out on these fanciful new devils that
ride sea, land and air on a puff of blue
smoke. They're all witches and mermaids,
these new-world devils, dancing around on
bubbles, speaking a language God never
heard, and nothing human about them except when they fall they break like the rest
of us.

LISE. If I had known. It's too late. The sun
still rises in the east and lays a course
toward the old streets and days. These are
my hands
as when I was a child. Some great magician
binding a half-world in his wiles, has laid
a spell here. We must break it and go home.
I see this clearly.

DEWITT. Lise, little heart, the devils are too
much for us. God knows it's a hard thing
to say, and I'd help you if I could help myself, but all hell wouldn't know where we
are nor where we ought to go. The very
points of the compass grow doubtful these
latter years, partly because I'm none too
sober and partly because the great master
devil sits on top of the world stirring up
north and south with a long spoon to con-
fuse poor mariners. I've seen him at it, a
horned bull three times the size of Dunden-
berg and with more cloven feet than the
nine beasts in Revelations. Very clearly I saw
him, too, as clear as you see the east and a
path across the waters.

LISE. Are we to wait till all the color steal
from flower and cloud, before our eyes; till
a wind
out of the morning from the Tappan Zee
lifts us, we are so light, for all our crying
and takes us down the valleys toward the
west,
and all we are becomes a voiceless cry
heard on the wind?

DEWITT. We'll see the time, if they continue
to work on us, when we'll be apparent in a

trong light only by the gin contained in our
nterior piping. The odor itself, along with
hat of church-warden tobacco, should be
ufficient to convince a magistrate of our
existence.—You tremble, little Lise, and you
veep, but look now, there's a remedy I've
aad in mind. Fall in love with one of them.
Fall in love with one of these same strange
1ew-world magicians. I shall choose me out
one of their female mermaid witches, and
et my heart on her, and become a man
again. And for God's sake let her love me
strongly and hold on, lest I go down the
brook like a spring freshet in the next pound-
ng rain.

LISE. I gave my love long ago, and it's no
help.
I love enough.

DEWITT. Aye, but he's in a worse case than
you are, the Captain. Saving his captaincy,
here's not enough belief in him to produce
half a tear in a passion of sobbing. You'll
make me weep, little one, and what tears
I have I shall need, lest my protestation turns
out to be a dry rain.

LISE. Aye, we were warned before we came
away
against the cabalistic words and signs
of those who dwell along these unknown
waters;

never to watch them dance nor hear them
sing
nor draw their imprecations—lest their
powers
weave a weird medicine throughout the air,
chilling the blood, transfixing body and
mind
and we be chained invisibly, our eyes darkened,
our wrists and breasts pulseless, anchored in
time
like birds blown back in a wind. But we
have listened,
and we are stricken through with light and
sound,
empty as autumn leaves, empty as prayers
that drift in a godless heaven. Meaningless,
picked clean of meaning, stripped of bone
and will,
the chrysalids of locust staring here
at one another.

DEWITT. If it's true it's enough to make a
man weep for himself, Lise, and for all lost
mariners, wherever they are, and for us
more than any, here on these spellbound
rocks, drawing up water from time past—
the well growing deeper, and the water
lower, till there be none. (*He turns to go
down the path.*)

CURTAIN

SCENE III

SCENE: *Another section of the Tor, in darkness save for the airplane beacon. A large
steam shovel reaches in from an adjacent excavation and hangs over the rock, the control
cables dangling. VAN is alone on the stage looking at the machinery. He reaches up, catches
a cable, and swings the shovel a little. BIGGS and SKIMMERHORN enter from the right.*

BIGGS. Hey, what are you doing with that
shovel?

VAN. Did you know you're trespassing? Also
when a man owns land he owns the air
above it and the rock below. That means this
damn shovel of yours is also trespassing.

BIGGS. Oh, it's Van Dorn. We'll have that
moved tomorrow, Mr. Van Dorn. Somebody's made a miscue and left it hanging
over the line.

SKIMMERHORN. By the way, that trail's gone
out completely, Mr. Van Dorn; there's a fifty
foot sheer drop there now, where it was.

Now we've got to get off, if you can think
of any way to manage it.

VAN. I'm not worrying about it. Spend the
night. No charge.

SKIMMERHORN. The truth is I have to be in
court early tomorrow, and a man needs his
sleep.

VAN. Afraid you'd doze off on the bench
and somebody else might take a trick? Oh,
you'd wake up before they got far with anything. The Skimmerhorns are automatic
that way.

BIGGS. You don't know any other trail down?

VAN. I showed you the one I knew, and you both turned green looking at it. What am I supposed to do now? Pin wings on you? (*He goes out to the right.*)

SKIMMERHORN. I think I'll swear out a warrant for the squirt. He's too independent by half.

BIGGS. On what ground?

SKIMMERHORN. He threatened us, didn't he?

BIGGS. And where'll that get us?

SKIMMERHORN. He might be easier to talk to in jail.

BIGGS. That's true.

SKIMMERHORN (*sitting on a rock*). This is a hell of a mess.

BIGGS. You're explaining to me?

SKIMMERHORN. What did we ever come up here for?

BIGGS. Twenty-two thousand dollars.

SKIMMERHORN. Will we get it?

BIGGS. It'll look all right on the books.

SKIMMERHORN. It's not good enough, though.

BIGGS. What are you grousing about?

SKIMMERHORN. Because I want my dinner, damn it! And because I'm tired of taking forty per cent and giving you sixty on all the side bets! I want half!

BIGGS. You're a damn sight more likely to get your dinner. You're overpaid already.

SKIMMERHORN. The will's perfectly good. I could find holes in it, but I've probated plenty much the same.

BIGGS. What of it?

SKIMMERHORN. A judge has some conscience, you know. When he sets a precedent he likes to stick to it.

BIGGS. I never knew your conscience to operate except on a cash basis. You want half.

SKIMMERHORN. Yes, I want half.

BIGGS. Well, you don't get it. Any other judge I put in there'd work for nothing but the salary and glad of the job. You take a forty per cent cut and howl for more. The woods are full of shyster lawyers looking for probate judgeships and I'll slip one in at Ledentown· next election.

SKIMMERHORN. Oh, no, you won't, Art; oh, no, you won't. You wouldn't do that to an old friend like me; because if you did, think what I'd do to an old friend like you.

BIGGS. Well, maybe I wouldn't. Not if you're reasonable. Look, what's the difference between forty per cent and fifty per cent? Practically nothing!

SKIMMERHORN. Then why don't you give it to me?

BIGGS. Because, try and get it!—

SKIMMERHORN. Damn it, I'm hungry.—I ought to telephone my wife, too.

BIGGS. Why don't you?

SKIMMERHORN. Maybe it's fun for you— nothing to eat, no place to sleep, cold as hell, black as Tophet and a storm coming up! Only I'm not used to it!

BIGGS. You're pulling down forty per cent of twenty-two thousand dollars for the night's work. I say it's worth it.

SKIMMERHORN. Think we could slide down one of those cables?

BIGGS. Maybe you could, Humpty-Dumpty, but not me.

SKIMMERHORN. I'm going to look at it. (*He goes out left,* BIGGS *following. After a moment* THREE MEN *climb in through the rocks at the right, one of them carrying a small zipper satchel. They throw themselves down wearily on the rock. They are, in brief, the Nanuet bank robbers,* ELKUS, DOPE *and* BUDDY.)

DOPE. God, I got no wind. (*A siren is heard faintly, far down on the road.*)

ELKUS. Sons a' bitches a' troopers.

DOPE. What'd you want to wreck the car for?

ELKUS. Want to get caught with the stuff on you?

BUDDY. We'll get four hundred years for this.

ELKUS. Shut up!

PE. You didn't need to wreck the car,
)ugh.

KUS. Didn't you hear the trooper slam
the brakes when he went by? You'd be
aring bracelets right now if I hadn't
mped the old crate over the embankment!
e way it is he thinks he's following us,
d he'll blow that fire alarm all the way
Bear Mountain Bridge. Only hope he
ets something solid head-on at ninety
les an hour.

PE. What I want to know is where we go
m here.

KUS. Down the other side and pick up a
. (*The siren is heard receding.*)

)DY. We'll get four hundred years for
s.

KUS. What do you think you are, a chorus?
on back to St. Thomas's and sing it to
priest. You're about as much help as a
tire.

)DY. I never wanted to be in it. I was only
kout—you're both witness to that.

KUS. What good do you think that does
1, you poor fish? Brace up and take it like
1an. There's twenty-five thousand in that
r and some of it's yours.

PE. How do you know it's twenty-five
1usand?

KUS. It's the Orangeburg pay roll. (BUDDY
ks off left.)

)DY. Before God, it's Judge Skimmerhorn!

KUS. What? Where?

)DY. There. Coming round the rocks.
ge Skimmerhorn of Ledentown.

KUS. Does he know you?

)DY. Sure, he knows me.

US. We're out climbing, see? Hikers, see?
a picnic. (*They stand.* ELKUS *holds the
hel behind him casually.* BIGGS *and* SKIM-
RHORN *come in.*)

;S. Hello.

US. How are you?

;S. Out walking?

US. That's right. Climbed up on a bet.

SKIMMERHORN. Isn't that Buddy?

BUDDY. Yes, sir. Evening, Judge.

SKIMMERHORN. You're a long way from
home.

BUDDY. Yes, sir.

BIGGS. Think you could show us a way
down? We're stuck up here.

BUDDY. There's a path down the cliff. Yes,
sir.

SKIMMERHORN. No, thanks. I saw that one.
Going to camp here?

ELKUS. Might as well. Sure.

SKIMMERHORN. Bring anything to eat?

ELKUS. Matter of fact, we didn't. (*He sets the
satchel down behind the rock, unobtru-
sively.*)

SKIMMERHORN. Not a thing?

ELKUS. Not a thing.

SKIMMERHORN. That's funny. Camping wtih
nothing to eat.

ELKUS. Yeah, it is kinda funny.

DOPE. We ate before we started. (*He smiles
cunningly.*)

ELKUS. That's right. The Dope's right for
once. We ate before we started.

SKIMMERHORN. Wish I had.

BUDDY. You—you staying up here tonight,
sir?

SKIMMERHORN. Seems that way. We came
up looking for somebody.

ELKUS. Looking for somebody?

SKIMMERHORN. That's what I said.

ELKUS. Who was it?

BIGGS. That's our business.

ELKUS. I see.

SKIMMERHORN (*coming near the three*).
Listen, Buddy, you're young and ambitious.
Would you do something for me if you got
well paid?

BUDDY. I guess so, Judge.

SKIMMERHORN (*sitting on the rock and incidentally over the satchel*). We're done in, traipsing around the rocks. Would you climb down the Tor and get to Haverstraw and telephone my wife I can't come home?

BUDDY. I guess so, wouldn't I, Elkus?

ELKUS. Up to you.

SKIMMERHORN. And while you're there will you buy a dozen sandwiches and some beer?

BUDDY. Yes, sir.

SKIMMERHORN. There's another thing you could do. Call up the state troopers for me, and tell them I'm here and I want them to come up and make an arrest.

BUDDY. You—want to arrest somebody?

SKIMMERHORN. You get it. What do you say?

BUDDY. I—I guess so. Is it all right, Elkus?

DOPE. Oh—no. Oh—no.

ELKUS. Sure it's O.K. Why not?

BUDDY. It'd take about five hours—to get down and back.

SKIMMERHORN. Damn it—I'll starve to death.

DOPE. What do you want to make an arrest for?

BIGGS. That's our business.

BUDDY. All right. I'll go.

SKIMMERHORN. Here's five dollars for you. And another when you get back. And make it fast, will you?

BUDDY. Yes, sir. (*He starts out right.*)

ELKUS. Just a minute, Bud. (ELKUS *and* DOPE *follow* BUDDY *out to converse with him.*)

BIGGS. You might have made it two dozen sandwiches.

SKIMMERHORN. I guess I will. (*He starts to rise, places his hand on the satchel, and jumps.*) Christ, what's that? (*He kicks the satchel, then flips it up into the rocks.*)

BIGGS. Yeah?

SKIMMERHORN. I thought it was a snake. Somebody's mouldy luggage. People are always throwing truck around. (*He calls.*) Say, for God's sake, get started, will you?

BUDDY (*outside*). Yes, sir. Right away. (E[L]KUS *and* DOPE *return.*)

ELKUS. I guess we'll all go. (*He looks no[n]chalantly where the satchel was.*)

SKIMMERHORN. Fine. Will you make it tw[o] dozen sandwiches?

ELKUS. What the hell's going on here?

SKIMMERHORN. We're hungry, that's all.

ELKUS. Are you two finnegling with us? B[e]cause if you are—!

BIGGS. What are you looking for?

ELKUS. Nothing. Who said I was looki[ng] for anything?

DOPE. Hey, Elkus! They got the troopers [up] here!
(DEWITT's *broad Dutch hat appears abo[ve] the rocks in the rear, looking, for the m[o]ment, remarkably like that of a state troop[er.]* ELKUS *and* DOPE *freeze, looking at it.*)

ELKUS (*drawing a gun*). Why, you [?] pimps! (DEWITT *disappears.*)

DOPE. Beat it, you fool! (ELKUS *and* DO[PE] *scatter out to the right.*)

BIGGS (*looking at the rocks*). What was that about?

SKIMMERHORN. I hope they bring th[e] sandwiches. (*He also stares toward* [the] *rear.*)

BIGGS. Sandwiches? They're not bring[ing] sandwiches for anybody, those two. (*[He] calls.*) Hey! Hey, you! Anybody there[?] What did he mean by troopers?

SKIMMERHORN. Want to take a look?

BIGGS. I'm plenty unhappy, right wher[e I] am. (SKIMMERHORN *climbs up on the rock[.]*)

SKIMMERHORN. Wish to God I did se[e a] trooper.

BIGGS. Nobody there?

SKIMMERHORN. Not a thing. Hey! Hey, y[ou!] (*A silence.*) Nope. Nobody.

BIGGS. Looks to me as if we just missed be[ing] stuck up by a couple of lunatics.

SKIMMERHORN. If I can't eat I'm going [to] sleep.

GGS. Maybe you've never tried adjusting
urself to igneous limestone.

IMMERHORN. I'm about to try it now.

GGS. You have my sympathy. (SKIMMER-
RN *stretches out on the rock, takes off his
at for a pillow and lies down.*)

IMMERHORN. Thanks.

GS. Beautiful shape you have. A lot of slop
d up with a piece of string.

IMMERHORN (*sitting up*). God it's cold.
sten, we could use one coat for a pillow
d put the other one over us.

GS. What other one?

MMERHORN. Yours.

GS. A proposition, huh?

MMERHORN. You going to sit up all
ht?

GS. In some ways it might be preferable.

MMERHORN. You can't prop yourself on
forever, like a duck on a rock.

GS. Pull yourself together, then. You stick
behind like a bump on a duck. All right.
ve over.

MMERHORN. Your coat's bigger than mine.
hey pull BIGG's *coat around them and lie
wn.*)

GS. Just a couple of perfect forty-nines.
ere the hell am I supposed to put my
bone?

MMERHORN. You juggle your own hip
es. (DEWITT *appears on the rocks at the
, looking down.*)

GS. If you snore, you probate judge, I'll
e you disbarred.

MMERHORN. Go to sleep.

GS. Wish I thought I could. On bed rock.
ke me early, mother dear.

MMERHORN. Shut up.

WITT *meanwhile has opened the satchel
now brings it down into the light to
mine the contents. He sits down, takes
five packets of bills, shakes the satchel,
begins to go through the inner pockets.
finds a roll of pennies, which he breacks
into his hands.*)

DEWITT. Copper pieces, by the great jib boom, enough to purchase a new wig, if a man ever got back to a place where money was useful to him. A counting-house full of them wouldn't buy a ship from one of these semi-demi-demi-semi-devils, so that's no good. (*Two snores rise in concert from* BIGGS *and* SKIMMERHORN. DEWITT *goes over to them, dropping the money.*) What kind of demi-semi-devil do you think you are, with four legs and two faces, both looking the same direction? Jesu Maria, it's a kind of centaur, as big one way as another, no arms, and feet the size of dishpans.

BIGGS. What's that?

DEWITT (*backing away*). It's the rear end that talks, evidently, the front being fast asleep in the manner of a figure-head.

BIGGS. Who's there? Did somebody speak?

DEWITT. None too clear in the back thinker, I should say, which would be a natural result of lugging two sets of brains, fore and aft. I'd incline to communicate with the front end, but if necessary I'll converse with the posterior.

BIGGS (*sitting up, looking at* DEWITT). Skimmerhorn!

SKIMMERHORN. What's the matter?

BIGGS. I'm damned if I know.

SKIMMERHORN. Go to sleep, then.

BIGGS. Do you believe in apparitions?

SKIMMERHORN. No.

BIGGS. Well, there's a figure of fun sitting talking to me, right out of a masquerade ball.

SKIMMERHORN. You been drinking?

BIGGS. What would I find to drink?

DEWITT. If the forecastle wakes now I shall play both ends against the middle, like a marine auctioneer. I want to buy a boat.

BIGGS. You've come to the wrong shop, sailor. I'm in the real-estate business, and it's a long mile down to sea level. (SKIMMERHORN *sits up suddenly.*)

DEWITT. You have no boats?

BIGGS. No boats.

SKIMMERHORN. What in the hell?—

BIGGS. I told you I'm damned if I know.

DEWITT. And the front end has no boats?

BIGGS. You're the front end, see. He wants to know if you've got boats.

SKIMMERHORN. No, stranger, no boats.

DEWITT. Ah. (*He shakes his head mournfully, turns him about and goes to the right, still muttering.*) The great plague on them, the lying, two-headed fairies out of a witch's placket. What chance has an honest man against a two-faced double-tongued beast, telling the same tale — (*He disappears through the rocks.*)

BIGGS. Did you see what I saw?

SKIMMERHORN. Not if you saw what I saw. What I saw wasn't possible.—Did you fake that thing?

BIGGS. Fake it? I saw it.

SKIMMERHORN. Oh, no—! Nobody saw that —what I saw. I didn't either. I've got a family to support. They aren't going to put me away anywhere.

BIGGS. Whatever it was, it left a calling card. Looks as if he ate his lunch here, supposing a thing like that eats lunch. Maybe he left some for us.

SKIMMERHORN. I don't want any of that.

BIGGS (*rising and turning the package over with his foot*). There's something in it.

SKIMMERHORN. Help yourself.

BIGGS (*opening a package, tossing the cover away*). You know what this is?

SKIMMERHORN. Probably a sheaf of contracts with the devil, all ready to sign.

BIGGS. No, it's money.

SKIMMERHORN. Money! (*He leaps to his feet.*)

BIGGS. Fives and tens. (*He opens another package.* SKIMMERHORN *does the same.*)

SKIMMERHORN. Well, bless the poor little Dutchman's heart—after all we said about him, too!

BIGGS. Think he left it?

SKIMMERHORN. It wasn't there before.

BIGGS. No.

SKIMMERHORN. Were you born with a ca or anything?

BIGGS. Always before I had to work for or steal it. Never till tonight have I be waked up by a little man in a big h fetching it to me in packages.

SKIMMERHORN. Are you asleep?

SKIMMERHORN. If you're dreaming, you dreaming that I found money.

BIGGS. Oh, you found it now?

SKIMMERHORN. Fifty-fifty.

BIGGS. Wait a minute. You know wh money this is?

SKIMMERHORN. No. (BIGGS *picks up a a carded envelope.*)

BIGGS. It came out of the Nanuet ba (SKIMMERHORN *takes the envelope fr him.*)

SKIMMERHORN. If that little guy's a ba robber he's certainly careless with the p ceeds.

BIGGS. That's where it came from.

SKIMMERHORN. In that case we ought give it back. For the reward.

BIGGS. No reward offered yet.

SKIMMERHORN. Maybe we ought to giv back anyway.

BIGGS. Think so?

SKIMMERHORN. Might be marked bills.

BIGGS. No, it's not. I was talking with president of the bank on the 'phone. M up for a pay roll. No marks on any o

SKIMMERHORN. It ought to be retur though.

BIGGS. Sure, it should. Question is, wi be?

SKIMMERHORN. I think so, don't you?

BIGGS. I'm inclined to think so. Bank bing's away out of my line.

SKIMMERHORN. Mine, too, as a matter of The president of the bank's a frien yours?

GS. Yes, he is, in a way. Oh, he's gypped
: a couple of times, same as you would.

MMERHORN. He wouldn't lose anything.

GS. Oh, no, he's insured.

MMERHORN. Has it occurred to you the
le Dutchman that was here might not
an any good to us?

GS. Did you see a little Dutchman?

MMERHORN. I thought I did, there for
minute.

GS. I don't believe that any more.

MMERHORN. Certainly doesn't sound very
ely.

GS. We'd better count it. Man never ought
carry money around without knowing
w much it is.

MMERHORN. Yeah, let's count it. It said
enty-five thousand in the paper.

GS. You know, nobody in the world
uld ever know who had it?

MMERHORN. No, they wouldn't.

GS. What do you say?

MMERHORN. I say fifty-fifty.

GS. Damn you, Skimmerhorn, if I hadn't
n in business with you for twenty years
say you were a crook!

MMERHORN. If I wasn't a crook after
enty years with you I'd be slow in the
d and hard of hearing!

GS. What's fifty per cent of twenty-five
usand? Twelve thousand five hundred?
d what's forty per cent? Ten thousand!
: you going to hold up the deal for two
usand five hundred?

MMERHORN. I certainly am.

ss. All right, take it. Fifty-fifty on this
deal.

MMERHORN. And on the Van Dorn deal,

ss. Why, you fat louse—(VAN DORN *comes
rom the right out of the shadows.*)

. Sorry to bother you, gentlemen, but—

BIGGS (*as they stuff the bills into their
pockets*). Where the hell did you come
from?

VAN. Why, you're not friends of mine, but
there's a storm blowing in and it occurred
to me I might show you where you could
keep dry under a ledge.

BIGGS. Thanks. Much obliged.

VAN. Want me to go with you?

BIGGS. No, thanks—Let's get a little nearer
the light.

SKIMMERHORN. Good idea.
(BIGGS *and* SKIMMERHORN *go out right.* VAN
*looks after them, then picks up one of the
discarded envelopes and studies it. He sits.*
LISE *comes up the rocks in the rear and
stands looking out to the river, shading her
eyes from the beacon.*)

LISE. You who have watched this river in the
past
till your hope turned bitterness, pity me
now,
my hope gone, but no power to keep my eyes
from the mocking water. The hills come
down like sand,
and the long barges bear them off to town,
to what strange market in what stranger
town,
devouring mountains? but never, in all days,
never, though I should watch here without
rest,
will any ship come downward with the tide
flying the flag we knew. (VAN *rises.* LISE
*draws back an instant, then comes down a
step toward him.*)
Do you hear my voice?

VAN. Yes, lady.

LISE. Do you see me in the light,
as I see you?

VAN. Yes.

LISE. You are one of those
the earth bears now, the quick, fierce wizard
men
who plow the mountains down with steel,
and set
new mountains in their sky. You've come
to drive
machines through the white rock's heart.

VAN. Not I. I haven't.
I hate them all like poison.

LISE. You're against them—
the great machines?

VAN. I'd like to smash the lot,
and the men that own them.

LISE. Oh, if there were a friend
among so many enemies! I wish
I knew how to make you friend. But now
    my voice
shrinks back in me, reluctant, a cold thing,
fearing the void between us.—I have seen
    you.
I know you. You are kind.

VAN. How do you know?

LISE. When I have been most lonely in the
    spring,
the spring rain beating with my heart, I
    made
a wild flower garden; none of these I knew,
for none I knew are here, flowers of the
    woods,
little and lovely, nameless. One there was
like a pink moccasin, another low
with blotted leaves, wolf-toothed, and many
    more
rooted among the fern. I saw you then
come on this garden, secret as the tears
wept for lost days, and drew my breath in
    dread
that you should laugh and trample it. You
    smiled
and then went on. But when I came again
there was a new flower growing with the
    rest,
one I'd not seen. You brought and placed
    it there
only for love of gardens, ignorant whose
the garden you enriched. What was this
    flower?

VAN. Wild orchid. It was your garden?

LISE. Yes. You know
the names of all the flowers?

VAN. Yes.

LISE. But then
you'd teach them to me?

VAN. Yes.

LISE. Teach me the names.
What is the tall three-petaled one that's black
almost, the red's so dark?

VAN. That's trillium.
Speaking of flowers, tell me your name.

LISE. It's Lise,
or used to be.

VAN. Not now?

LISE. I'm weary of it,
and all things that I've been. You have
    lover?
She'll be angry?

VAN. She's angry now. She's off
and gone. She won't come back.

LISE. Love me a little,
enough to save me from the dark. But
you cannot give me love, find me a w
The seas lie black between your har
    town
and mine, but your ships are quick. I
    might see
the corner where the three streets come
    an end
on sundial windows, there, a child by
    fire—
no, but it's gone!

VAN. I've seen you on the hills
moving with shadows. But you're no
    shadow.

LISE. No.
Could one live and be shadow?

VAN. Take my hand.

LISE. I dare not.

VAN. Come, let me see your garden.

LISE. No.
I dare not. It is your race that thins
    blood
and gathers round, besieging us with cha
to stay the feet of years. But I know
    kind.—
Love me a little. Never put out your h
to touch me, lest some magic in your bl
reach me, and I be nothing. What I
I know not, under these spells, if I be cl
or dust. Nor whether you dream of me,
make you of light and sound. Between
    stone
and the near constellations of the stars
I go and come, doubting now when
    come
or when I go. Cling to me. Keep me
Be gentle. You were gentle with th
    orchid—

VAN. You're cold.

E. Yes.

N. Here on the Tor
 sun beats down like murder all day long
d the wind comes up like murder in the
ight.
a cold myself.

E. How have I slipped so far
m the things you have? I'm puzzled
ere and lost.
it so different for you? Keep my hand
d tell me. In these new times are all men
hadow?
men lost?

. Sometimes I stand here at night
d look out over the river when a fog
ers the light. Then if it's dark enough
d I can't see my hands or where the rock
ves off against the cloud, and I'm alone,
n, well I'm damned if I know who I am,
ing out into that black. Maybe I'm cloud
d maybe I'm dust. I might be old as time.
like to think I knew. A man gets that
ay
ding staring at darkness.

. Then—you do know.
better now.—Somewhere along a verge
ere your life dips in dusk and my gray
ays
to the light a moment, we walk there
our eyes meet.—Look, when the wizards
me
ear the mountain down, I'll have no
ace.
be gone then.

. Child, they won't get our mountain!
if I have to shoot them as they come
won't get our mountain! The moun-
in's mine,
you're to make your garden where you
ke;
r feet won't step across it! All their
orld's
e up of fat men doing tricks with laws
nanage tides and root up hills. The hills
afford to laugh at them. A race of grubs
down from men!

Is it the light I feel
e flooding back in me? Light or their
arms
en here, seeing your face?

Your hands are warm.

LISE. I'm not cold now; for an instant I'm not cold,
seeing your face. This is your wizardry. Let me stand here and see you.

ELKUS (*outside*). Somewhere around here it was. Over toward the crane.

DOPE (*outside*). What's you go and put down the satchel for?

ELKUS (*outside*). How did I know he'd sit on top of it? (VAN *and* LISE *slip out through the rocks at the rear.* ELKUS *and* DOPE *come in furtively from the right.*)

DOPE. That's where. Under that rock.

ELKUS. Keep your eye peeled. They're probably beating the woods for us.

DOPE. What's that? (*He picks up an envelope.*)

ELKUS. They got it.

DOPE. God damn the rotten business! Now we will get four hundred years.

ELKUS. Now you're saying it—

DOPE. What are we going to do?

ELKUS. I'm going to send Buddy back with sandwiches to see if the Judge got the money. If he did we'll stick him up.

DOPE. Hey, how about the troopers?

ELKUS. If that was troopers I'm Admiral Dewey. Troopers would a' used the artillery. Come on.

DOPE. O.K. Some pennies here.

ELKUS. To hell with 'em. (DOPE *flings the pennies to the left along the ledge.*)

DOPE. Get going. (ELKUS *and* DOPE *go out right.* BIGGS *and* SKIMMERHORN *come in along the ledge.*)

BIGGS. Now it's raining money. I got the price of a morning paper square in the eye.

SKIMMERHORN. I've got two thousand five hundred in a breast pocket, five thousand in a side pocket, and five thousand in the billfold. (*He slaps his rear.*) How do I look?

BIGGS. No different. Just a lot of slop tied up with string. I've got five thousand in each side pocket and two thousand five hundred in the back. How do I look?

SKIMMERHORN. You? All you need now's a pair of wings.

BIGGS. Wish I could find the little guy with the big heart that gave us the money. Maybe he'd help us down off this devil's belfry.

SKIMMERHORN. How about that shovel? Any possibility of making it pick us up and set us down below there?

BIGGS. Well—if anybody was running it, sure. If it swung us over on that dump we could slide the rest of the way. You might wear out that last five thousand of yours, the five thousand that's bringing up the rear there.

SKIMMERHORN. When do they come to work in the morning?

BIGGS. They won't come to work tomorrow. They can't do any more till we buy this land.

SKIMMERHORN. That's fine. That's just dandy.

BIGGS. Nice idea though. Somebody might come along that could run the engine.

SKIMMERHORN. You don't think that boy's coming back with the sandwiches?

BIGGS. No, I don't.

SKIMMERHORN. The way I feel inside I may never live to spend the money.

BIGGS. Who you going to leave it to?

SKIMMERHORN. Yeah?

BIGGS. Oh, all right. Nothing personal. (*They sit facing the audience. The* CAPTAIN *and his* CREW, *including* DEWITT, *seep in through the rocks about them and stand quietly looking on.*) There was something in that— what you said about needing a pair of wings.

SKIMMERHORN. I should say that wings was the last thing likely to grow on you. You might grow horns, or a cloven hoof, or a tail, but wings, no. Not unless somebody slipped up behind you and bashed you over the head.

BIGGS. You know, you'd murder me for what I've got in my pockets?

SKIMMERHORN. You thought of it first. Who am I going to leave it to, you said.

BIGGS. Just the same I wouldn't feel right you were standing behind me with a ro in your hand. (*The* CREW *move in a littl*

SKIMMERHORN. You wouldn't?

BIGGS. No. At the moment I wouldn't li to think anybody was creeping up behi me. (*He stiffens.*) And by God there somebody behind me.

SKIMMERHORN (*without turning*). W makes you think so?

BIGGS (*running a hand over his hair*). I j feel it. Turn around, will you? Take a lo

SKIMMERHORN (*shivering*). I will not.—N you've got me worried.—Or else I'm getti light-headed for lack of food.

(BIGGS *ducks suddenly, as if from an im inary blow.* SKIMMERHORN *dodges in sy pathy, and with their heads drawn in t turtles they creep forward on hands a knees.*)

BIGGS. See anything?

SKIMMERHORN. There's nothing there, ass! What are you dodging? Want to sc me to death? Go on, turn around and it like a man!

BIGGS. Now!

SKIMMERHORN. Now! (*They whirl in cert, on their knees, facing the* CREW. *T look at each other.*)

BIGGS. You're crazy!

SKIMMERHORN. I certainly am. And so you.

BIGGS. That isn't there at all. There's noth there.

SKIMMERHORN. All right, you go up and it. I'll stay right here, and you go punc in the nose. (BIGGS *stands up.*)

BIGGS. Uh—how do you do?—Maybe yc wanted to give us something, huh? DEWITT.) Uh—I see you brought your fri with you.—If you want the money back can have it, you know. We don't want money. (*He sticks a hand in his pock* How much was it now? (*The* CREW *loo each other gravely, tapping their foreh*

MMERHORN *rises.*) Anything we could
you know, we'd be glad to do. We're just
ing to get down off here.

MMERHORN. You know what it is, Art;
a moving picture company. And have
y got the laugh on us? Thinking they're
l. It's all right, boys, we're onto you.

GS. Is that so? Say, I guess that's so.
ls that moving picture money, you gave
you fellows? We thought that was real.
ha! That's a good one. I guess you must
ve thought we were pretty funny, back-
up that way and jumping around. You
l us scared stiff! (*The* CREW *shake their
ds at each other.*)

MMERHORN. Come on, now, you aren't
ffing us at all. We've seen the pictures
rk over at Suffern. We were right out on
ation there with actors and producers and
rything. Some of those girls didn't care
ether they wore clothes or not. You're
bably used to that where you come from,
I certainly got a kick out of pictures.
y chorus girls changing clothes in the
hes over there. (*A silence.* DEWITT *goes
r to the* CAPTAIN *and whispers in his ear.*)

ER. Lay a hand to it. (DEWITT *catches
d of the dangling cable.*)

ITT. Lay a hand to it, lads. Heave. (*The
w catch the rope and haul on it, sailor-
ion. The shovel begins to descend.*)

CREW (*pulling down*). Heave! Heave!
leave! Heave!
ning a blow, coming a blow;
runs black; glass runs low;
ve! Heave!
darm dips; foam's like snow!
ve! (*The shovel touches ground.*)

s. Say, that's an act if I ever saw one.
at kind of picture you putting on? (*The
*rAIN *points to the interior of the shovel,
ing at* BIGGS *and* SKIMMERHORN.) What's
anyway? Want us to go aboard? You
w, we were just saying if somebody
d run that thing we might get across to
dump and slide down out of here.
nk you could swing it across there?
e SAILORS *maneuver behind the two,
ng them into the machine.*) You might
us up there and not be able to get us
n, you know. It's mighty friendly of
to try it, but you'll have your work

cut out. Sure, I'll get in. I'll try anything
once. (*He steps in,* SKIMMERHORN *follows
reluctantly. The* CAPTAIN *and* DEWITT *guard
their retreat. The* SAILORS *catch hold of the
cable.*) Take it easy, now.

THE CREW. Hoist! Hoist! Hoist! Hoist!
Tar on a rope's end, man on a yard.
Wind through an eye-bolt, points on a card;
Hoist! Hoist!
Weevil in the biscuit, rats in the lard,
Hoist!

(*They haul the two up as far as seems
necessary, and swing the crane out over
the abyss. Then they stop to contemplate
their handiwork.*)

BIGGS. I'll tell you what—if you catch that
line over there some of you can hold back
while the rest pull and that'll swing it
around.—If that don't work you'd better
pull it down again and we'll just wait till
morning. (*The* CREW *continue to stare
silently.*)

SKIMMERHORN. I'm getting sick at my
stomach, boys; you better make it snappy.
It gives me the megrims to look down this
way. (*He draws his feet up suddenly.*)

BIGGS. Hey, don't rock the boat, you fool!
It's a thousand miles straight down!

SKIMMERHORN. I'm going to be sick.

BIGGS. You better take us down, fellows. It's
no good. You can't make it.

DEWITT. How about a game of bowls? (*The
*CAPTAIN *nods.*)

PIETER. Aye, a game of bowls. (*Led by the
*CAPTAIN, *the* CREW *begin to file out.*)

BIGGS. Hey, you wouldn't leave us up here,
would you? Hey, listen! You! You can have
that money back, you know! We don't want
the money! What in the name of time?—
Listen, what did we ever do to you?—
A joke's a joke, after all, but this thing
might let go any minute! What's more
you're responsible if anything happens to
us! There's such a thing as laws in this
country! (*But they have all gone.*)

SKIMMERHORN. I'm sick.

BIGGS. You'll be sicker before you're out of
this mess.—What do you think they meant
by that?

SKIMMERHORN. I don't know.—Quit kicking me, will you? I'm sick.

BIGGS. Well, keep it to yourself.

SKIMMERHORN. I wish I thought I could.

BIGGS. Help, somebody! Help! We're stuck up here!

SKIMMERHORN. What good's that going to do?

BIGGS. You don't think they'll leave us here, do you?

SKIMMERHORN. I don't know. I don't care. I wish I was dead!—Say, keep away from me, will you? What are you trying to do, pick my pocket?

BIGGS. Pick your pocket, you fish? All I ask is keep your feet out of my face.

SKIMMERHORN. Well, where in hell's my bill-fold?

BIGGS. How do I know? Do you think I took it?

SKIMMERHORN. Come on, now. Where is it? (*He searches his clothes frantically.*)

BIGGS. You're probably sitting on it.—You are sitting on it. There it is.

SKIMMERHORN (*finding it*). Jeez, I might have lost it.

BIGGS. Now you'd better count it. Just to make sure it's good.

SKIMMERHORN. I think I will. (*He begins to count the bills.*) It's good money, Art. Look at it.

BIGGS. Not a bad idea, either. (*He takes out money and counts it. There is a flash, a long roll and a crash of thunder. Then another and another.*) Isn't that coming pretty close?

SKIMMERHORN. What?

BIGGS. The lightning, you fool! Put your money away before you get it wet. You know what I think?

SKIMMERHORN. No.

BIGGS. There's something up there taking pot shots at us.

SKIMMERHORN. There's one thing about money you find. You don't have to pay income tax on it.

BIGGS. That's true. (*There is a terrific fla[sh] a crash, and the stage is in darkness.*) Th[at] one got the beacon! (*Another flash ru[ns] right down the crane.*) Good God, will y[ou] quit that? That's close enough!—Say, you know any prayers?

SKIMMERHORN. I know one.

BIGGS. Say it, will you?

SKIMMERHORN. Matthew, Mark, Luke a[nd] John,
Bless the bed that I lie on.

BIGGS. That's not much good, that one.

SKIMMERHORN. It's the only one I know Hey, catch it—hey!

BIGGS. What? (*The lightning is now almost perpetual illumination, the thun[der] a constant roll.*)

SKIMMERHORN. I dropped fourteen ten doll[ar] bills!

BIGGS. Do you know we're going to die he[re?]

SKIMMERHORN. We're going to what?

BIGGS. Will you quit counting money? W[e're] going to be killed! We're going to die ri[ght] here in our own steam shovel!

SKIMMERHORN. Oh, no. I can't die n[ow.] I'm not ready to die!

BIGGS. I wish you'd put up your money, th[en] and pray!

SKIMMERHORN. I don't know how to p[ray.] (*A crash.*)

BIGGS (*on his knees*). Oh, God, I never [did] this before, and I don't know how, but k[eep] me safe here and I'll be a better man! [I'll] put candles on the altar, yes, I'll get [the] Spring Valley church fixed up, the [one] that's falling down! I can do a lot for [you] if you let me live! Oh, God—(*A cra[sh.]*)

SKIMMERHORN (*on his knees, his hands [full] of money*). Oh, God, you wouldn't d[o a] thing like that, hang us up in our o[wn] steam shovel, wet through, and then st[ick] us with lightning! Oh, God, you've [been] kind to us tonight, and given us th[ings] we never expected to get so easy; don't s[poil] it now!—God damn it, there goes ano[ther] batch of bills! (*He snatches at the fal[ling] money, and is hauled back by* BIGGS.) I d[on't]

ow how to pray! What makes you think
re's anybody up there, anyway? (*Another
sh.*)

GS. Say the one you know then, for God's
e—say it!

MMERHORN. Matthew, Mark, Luke and
John,
ess the bed that I lie on!

GS. Matthew, Mark, Luke and John,
ss the bed—Oh, God, I've got an old

mother dependent on me; please let me live!
Why don't you tell him you'll give the
money back?

SKIMMERHORN. Because I won't! And you
won't, either! (*A crash.*)

BIGGS. Now you've done it! Can't you keep
anything to yourself? There's such a thing
as being politic, even when you're talking
to God Almighty! (*Thunder again.*)

CURTAIN

ACT TWO

SCENE I

SCENE: *The Tor and the steam shovel as before, only five or six hours later. It's still
ch dark, and* BIGGS *and* SKIMMERHORN *are still in the shovel. They are, however, fast
eep in much the same postures they took formerly on the ground. Under the shovel*
DEWITT, *picking up and smoothing on his knee a few bills which he has found
wing loose on the rock. The beacon light flashes into the scene.*

WITT. There comes on the light again, too,
sweeping light that withers a body's en-
ls. No sooner out than lit again.—(*Two
res rise from the sleeping pair.*) Aye,
e your ease and rest, you detachable
ppelgangers, swollen with lies, protected
the fiends, impervious to lightning, shed-
g rain like ducks—and why wouldn't
shed rain? your complexions being pure
ase and your insides blubber? You can
p, you can rest. You of the two-bottoms.
make nothing of the lightning playing
and down your backbones, or turning
on cold iron, but a poor sailor out of
land, what rest has he?—(*He smooths
l.*) These will be tokens and signs, these
, useful in magic, potent to ward off
or put a curse on your enemies. Devil's
k or not, I shall carry them on me, and
e myself a match for these fulminating
r-day spirits. (*He pouches the bills.*)
hanged if it's not noticeable at once, a
of Dutch courage infused into the joints
tissues from the mere pocketing up of
infernal numbered papers. (*He takes
a bill and looks at it.*) That's sorcery,
's witchcraft, that's black art for you—
's a trick after the old one's heart; why,
stuff would make a man out of a cocked
and a pair of crutches! (*He slaps his*

chest.) Now I shall face destiny and take it
like a pinch of snuff! Which reminds me
I could use a pinch of snuff. (*He takes out
his snuffbox.*) Snuff? When have I reached
for snuff? It would seem to me I haven't
gone after snuff in something like two
hundred years! (*He ladles into both nostrils
and sneezes violently.*) Aha, DeWitt! You're
a man and a devil! And what shall we wish
for now that we have wishing papers in the
pockets of our pantaloons? What but a
woman, one of these new female furies of
theirs, wearing pants like a man, and with
nothing to indicate her sex but the general
conformation! (*He draws out bills.*) Let
my woman appear, god of the numbered
papers, and let her wear what she likes, so
long as a man can make out how she's made.
Let her appear within this next three
minutes, for God knows how long this mood
will last in an old man! (*He takes another
pinch of snuff.*) Aha! Destiny, present occasions! (BUDDY *enters carrying beer and
sandwiches.*)

BUDDY. Hello.

DEWITT. What answer would a man make
to that now? That's a strange greeting.

BUDDY. Seen a couple of old fat men around
anywhere?

DEWITT. Boy, I have seen nothing else all night.

BUDDY. Where are they?

DEWITT. You wish to find a couple of old fat men?

BUDDY. That's right.

DEWITT. I begin to doubt the supernal powers of these new angel-demons. Here he stands in their presence and asks very foolishly if old DeWitt has seen them.

BUDDY. What's foolish about that?

DEWITT. A very cheap, witless little cabin boy unless all signs fail. One who carries packages and lives very badly by the day on half a skilling. A cabin boy.

BUDDY. What's the matter with you?

DEWITT. What do you carry in the bag?

BUDDY. That's my business.

DEWITT. He has a business then. He is not perhaps so witless as he appears.

BUDDY. Are you going to tell me where those two are or do you want me to blow your brains out?

DEWITT. Is my carcass so thin you think to puff my brains out with a breath? Look, 'prentice devil, I am one of you. I bear your signs and symbols. Here you see your own countersign, a cabalistic device of extreme rarity and force. What have you in the bag?

BUDDY. Nothing but sandwiches. What do you mean, you're one of us?

DEWITT (waving a sheaf of bills). You should recognize the insignium.

BUDDY. Where'd you get it?

DEWITT. It blew away from these same two fat men, 'prentice devil, but now I have it, and it's mine and I obtain power over you. Let me see these sandwiches.

BUDDY. It blew away from the fat men, huh? All right, that's what I want to know. It's mine, see? Hand it over.

DEWITT. You reveal yourself a very young and tender 'prentice.

BUDDY. Hand it over or I'll fill you full of holes. (He sets down his packages and draws

a gun, but DEWITT is beforehand with t￼ flintlock pistols.)

DEWITT. You will drop your child's armo￼ on the ground, cabin boy, or I shall pull bo￼ triggers at once and blast you halfway ￼ the water. (BUDDY drops the gun.) I tell y￼ I am now a great devil and violent. Wh￼ I wish merely I have my way.

(BUDDY suddenly takes to his heels. DEW￼ pulls the triggers one after another; t￼ hammers click but there is no explosio￼ Why, this new world is not so bad. I ￼ left in possession of the field. (He picks ￼ the automatic and the bag and retreat￼ his rock.) They fight with the weapons ￼ children. Why, this new world begins ￼ be mine, to do as I please with. Whate￼ kind of witch a sandwich may be come ￼ and let me interrogate you. (He takes ￼ sandwiches.) If it be food eaten by witc￼ and wizards so much the better, for I ￼ now a wizard myself, and by the great ￼ boom I haven't tasted food in God kn￼ when. (He eats.) A sweet and excell￼ morsel, very strong with garlic and sala￼ medical for the veins and bladder. (He lo￼ at his pistols.) A little glazed powder in ￼ priming now, and these two will speak w￼ more authority if it becomes necessary ￼ defend my position. (He opens his pow￼ horn and renews the priming.) We h￼ seen the time, these blunderbusses and ￼ self, when we could defend a crow's ￼ against a whole crew in mutiny. (He pus￼ away the beer bottles with his foot.) I ￼ eat your rations, cabin boy out of the ￼ age, and I will master you all, men ￼ maids, now that my strength comes b￼ but I will not drink your drink. As Pa￼ Van Dorf observed very wisely before ￼ sailed; you may eat the food of the salva￼ said he, when you have voyaged to the ￼ lands overseas; you may share their rati￼ you may even make up to their females ￼ the fashion of sailors when the flesh is w￼ but drink none of their drink, said he, ￼ it prove to be Circe's liquor and turn ￼ all to hogs. (He eats.) Now I have s￼ inclination to be a hog, but a man I wi￼ and a very good man, too, of the fie￼ model. (He hears JUDITH's step.) Take ￼ now, take care! I'm an armed man a￼ man of blood! (JUDITH enters.)

JUDITH (at some distance). I beg your ￼ don, sir—

WITT. A woman, by the great tropical
ss, a salvage woman, come in answer to
unspoken desires. (*He rises.*) Your
mblest servant, lady salvage; don't run
ay, please. I'm a poor lost little man,
uldn't hurt a fly.

DITH. Who are you?

WITT. I'm a poor bosun, ma'am, but
wn, God knows how, to something of a
son this last quarter hour.

DITH. Are you lost?

WITT. Completely adrift, ma'am, on my
a mountain.

DITH. I don't think I've seen you before.

WITT. That may be, though I'm by way
eing one of the earliest inhabitants, not
nting Indians and Patagonians.

DITH. You live on the mountain?

WITT. I maintain a residence here, though
situation eludes me at the moment.

DITH. Then you are acquainted with
—Van Dorn?

WITT. I have seen him about.

DITH. Have you seen him tonight? I want
nd him.

WITT. A mere blind, I should say, a maid-
defense, not to be too forthright; but
by the talisman she is.

DITH. You have seen him?

WITT. God help him, I have, and in none
sanctified an attitude, saving your lady-
, for the lad was obviously a bit taken
the captain's wife, and she a married
an of some years' standing, young
gh she appear.

DITH. Where was he? (*She takes a step
r to him.*)

WITT. I was never one to break in on a
ing romance, sweetheart, and out of
delicacy I looked the other way.

DITH. No, but where was he, please? I can
you the path.

WITT. If you hunt out a very pretty little
ess in a bonnet somewhat behind the
on, and look under the bonnet, you
chance to find him there.

JUDITH. Who are you?

DEWITT. Alpheus DeWitt, your most humble,
bosun in the King's navy.

JUDITH. Forgive me—I shall look elsewhere—

DEWITT. Oh, but I assure you the lad's head
over ears, ma'am, and loathe you'd be to
interrupt him. Now a pretty lass like yourself should have no trouble replacing one
sailor man with another in these stirring
times. They come and go like a run of
salmon.

JUDITH. Thank you.

DEWITT. I am myself a notionable lad. Salt
tears have been wept for me by one and
another.

JUDITH. No doubt.

DEWITT. I'm a blunt man, but constant and
of considerable substance on my own wharf.
Could you find it in your heart to love me?

JUDITH. I'm sorry, no.

DEWITT. To save a sad and desperate man
from such a death as the lines of frost on a
window? This is a kindly face, this of mine,
and a kindly heart under a worn jerkin.
These are real tears on my cheek, too, and
I weep them for you, lady.

JUDITH. I've never seen you till this moment.

DEWITT. Yet you could save me from their
sorcery, with one touch of your hand. I
waited here for you, and you came.

JUDITH. You're horrible. Your face is horrible!

DEWITT. Is it, truly?

JUDITH. Ancient and terrible and horrible!—
Tell me where he is. I must know.

DEWITT. I don't know where he is.—You
will think better of it. You need only pity
me a little at first, or even laugh at me—
so you do it kindly—

JUDITH. I'm in no mood for laughing,
though you're ridiculous enough in that
get-up.

DEWITT. It's not the latest, I know. And I'm
a sad and broken man, lady, lost here among
the lesser known peaks on the west side of

the world, and looking only for a hand to help me.

JUDITH. I don't think you're lost at all.

DEWITT. Yes, lady, quite lost.—Nevertheless they run from me! You should have seen the lad run when I snapped my pistols at him.

JUDITH (*stepping back*). I should think he would.—Isn't there someone coming there now? (*She points to the right.* DEWITT *faces about, reaching for his pistols.* JUDITH *slips away left.*)

DEWITT. If there be, watch what soldierly stand old DeWitt makes in defense of a lady! Come out, children of the new Satan, show yourselves in the light! (ELKUS *and* DOPE *appear at right.*)

ELKUS. Stick 'em up, bo! (*They train automatics on him.*)

DEWITT. More toys! Stand back, you cheap new devils!

ELKUS. Keep your hands down or I'll let you have it!

DEWITT. Watch now how a man holds off the fiends. (*He lifts his pistols.*)

ELKUS. Give it to him! (*They fire a fusillade at* DEWITT, *who stands unmoved.*)

DEWITT. Firecrackers! You think me a devil like yourselves, to be exorcised with firecrackers?

ELKUS. Give it to him! (*They fire once more.*)

DEWITT. Look, you puny devils, I'm a patient man, but in one moment I shall blow you both into the Tappan Zee!

ELKUS (*stepping up and pouring bullets into him*). Too bad about you! (*To* DOPE.) Take the money off him.

DOPE. There's something funny about this guy! I can see right through him!

ELKUS. No wonder. He's full of holes as a tennis racket.

DOPE. No, by God, I can see through him! Look! (*They step back together.*)

ELKUS. What kind of a thing are you?

DEWITT. I'm not a man to be daunted [by] loud noises and firecrackers, Beelzebub! [I] seek your place with the new father of h[ell] before I send you there! Wizards!

ELKUS. Where's the money?

DEWITT. I have a talisman and I ate a sa[nd]wich, devils!

DOPE. Look, he's a moving picture! He'[s a] regular church window! Look!

DEWITT. Disperse or I fire!

ELKUS. Keep out of the way of that saw[ed]-off shotgun! (DOPE *suddenly runs in* [and] *shoots* DEWITT *through the head, then* [re-]*treats.*)

DEWITT. I warn you I begin to be annoy[ed.]

DOPE. It's no use, chief. I blew his br[ains] out, and he's standing right there!

BIGGS (*looking over the side of the shot* [boat].) It's a war.

ELKUS. Who said that?

DOPE. Damned if I know.

ELKUS. Beat it.

DOPE. Yeah, beat it. Let the money hang. [Make] for Canada.

ELKUS. You said it. (*They turn tail. As* [they] *are going* DEWITT *fires his pistols in the* [air.])

DEWITT. Now am I master of the worl[d, of] things,
a buccaneer, a devil and a rake!
Women love mastery, and they ran from [me,]
they ran, these minor devils, ran from [De-]
    Witt!
Look where they go there, sweetheart! (*He* [
    turns.)
God, she's gone!
Lady! New-world lady! Are you lost? (*He* [
    follows her.)
Look now, I've dispersed them, brats [and]
    wizards,
spawn out of hell, they ran! I'm master [—]
I'm master of the world! Look, lady! (*He* [
    goes out left.)

SKIMMERHORN. Are you awake?

BIGGS. I hope not. I hope this is a night[mare] and I wake up at home in bed.

<table>
<tr><td>

MMERHORN. How did we get here?

GS. It must have been something we ate.

MMERHORN. I didn't eat anything.

GS. There's a bag of sandwiches down
re on the ground.

MMERHORN. That's a pleasant thought.

GS. Look for yourself.

MMERHORN. You're right. It's a bag of
dwiches.

GS. Didn't we send somebody for sand-
hes and beer, away back there before all
started?

MMERHORN. I don't know. I'm all wet,
I'm stuck to the shovel.

GS. You do seem to be kind of going to
es. What's the matter with your toupee?

MMERHORN. The glue must have melted.
takes off his wig.)Now I'll catch cold.

GS. If any of your constituency sees you
that condition you're out of office for
d.

MERHORN. I don't even care if I fall out.
el terrible.

s. Might be more comfortable for me if
did fall out. (*He shifts his weight.*)

MERHORN. Sit down! Quit rocking the
!

s. I've got a cramp. Ouch!

MERHORN. Don't shove me! (*He pushes
s.*)

s (*pushing back*). You want to pitch me
board?

MERHORN. Hey! You know I might have
out?

s. What do you care?

MERHORN. I'll show you what I care!
*ey lock in a deadly struggle on the
e.*)

s. Wait, Skimmer, look now! If one of
es down the other goes too. Look at the
You don't want to splash on those
s and I don't either.

MERHORN. Let go then.

</td><td>

BIGGS. I'll let go when you do. I'll count three
and we'll both let go.

SKIMMERHORN. All right.

BIGGS. One—two—three. (*They let go and
catch the ropes over the swinging basket.*)
That's better. Now take it easy, buddy. You
woke up feeling like poison this morning.
After this you count ten when you get an
impulse to push anybody.

SKIMMERHORN. Same to you.

BIGGS. Fine. (*They sit down cautiously.*)

SKIMMERHORN. How in hell did those sand-
wiches get there?

BIGGS. How in hell did we get here?

SKIMMERHORN. You haven't got a fishing
hook on you, have you?

BIGGS. No, I haven't. (*They sit gloomily look-
ing at the sandwiches.* LISE *and* VAN *come
in from the left.*)

VAN. Nothing in all the woods
is silent as the owl; you see his shadow
but never hear his wings. The partridge
    now,
every time he takes off he creaks and cranks
like an old Ford. You never heard such a
    fuss;
but he's quiet on the ground.

LISE. And is there a squirrel
that flies, bird-fashion?

VAN. Well, there's a flying squirrel,
but he's more the glider type. No engine,
    see,
but he'll do thirty yards. He's on the way
to be a bat if he's not careful.

LISE. How?

VAN. He'll leave off tail and put on wings
    until
he's mostly wing. No doubt the bat was once
some kind of flying mouse.

LISE. Some men have wings.
I've seen them overhead.

VAN. That's all put on.
They've no more wings than a goat. When
    they come down.

LISE. I've hoped that it was true that men
    had wings.

</td></tr>
</table>

van. Why?

lise. Oh, they've lived so long, and tried so hard,
and it all comes to nothing.

van. Having wings,
would that be something?

lise. Yes, it seems so. And yet
a bird has wings.

van. And he gets nowhere.

lise. Yes.
Nothing but just to be a bird, and fly,
and then come down. Always the thing itself
is less than when the seed of it in thought
came to a flower within, but such a flower
as never grows in gardens.

biggs. Eh—Van Dorn!

van (looking up). What are you doing on the roost, you birds?
Building a nest?

biggs. We can't get down.

van. I'd say
it ought to be just as easy to get down
as it was to get up there.

skimmerhorn. Will you help us out?

van. You look all right to me. What happened to you?

biggs. Everything.

van. How did you get there?

biggs. God,
it's a long story.

van. You've been there all night?

biggs. Yes, all night.

van. I wouldn't want to spoil it.
It's too good to be true. You see those two,
Lise, there in the scoop?

lise. They're pitiful.
Shouldn't you help them?

van. No. Since time began
there haven't been two fat-guts that deserved
a hoisting like those two. In their own machine—
that makes it perfect.

lise. What have they done?

van. They've been
themselves, that's all. Two thieves, a prob. judge
and a manipulator, hand and glove
to thieve what they can get. They've High Tor
among other things, and mean to carve down,
at three cents a square yard.

lise. These poor old men?

van. Yes, these poor old men.

lise. Let them hang there then!

van. They'll hang there for all me. (lise a
van turn to go.)

skimmerhorn. I'll tell you what,
Van Dorn, I'll let you have the validation
if you'll help me down.

van. That means I'd own the land?

skimmerhorn. Yes, you'd own it.

van. Only you'd cancel it,
once you got down.

skimmerhorn. To tell the truth I coul
not if you had the paper.

van. Toss it over;
I'd like to see it. (skimmerhorn gets ou
envelope and throws it to van.)

biggs. You're a simple judge!
Now the land's his.

van. There's a bond goes with this,
a bond signed by the court. Oh, I look
up.
I've read that much law.

skimmerhorn. Yes, I'll keep the bond
till we're on your level.

van. Then I'd advise you both
to make yourself a nest with two-three st
like a couple of crows, and settle down t
what you can hatch—or maybe lay an e
you'll have plenty of time.

biggs. Come now, Van Dorn,
we're in a bad way. It drops off str
down
a thousand feet here, and Judge Skim
horn

as vertigo. Why, just to save a life,
ıt of common humanity, lean on that cable
ıd pull us in.

ıN. This one? (*He pulls. The shovel dips.*)

ɢɢs. Oh, no, no! God,
ɔ you want to dump us out!

ıN. You said to pull it.

ɢɢs. Not that one! This! Pull up on that
again!
ʾe're sliding!

ıN. Sure. (*He rights the shovel.*)
ɔw you know how it feels
ʰen you kick out the props from under
 men
ıd slide 'em on the relief rolls. Ever think
ɔw that might feel?

ɢɢs. You don't know what we've both
ʾen through, Van Dorn. Rained on and
 struck by lightning,
 dinner; we're half-crazy; we've had nightmares,
ɔny people in hats; that's how we got
ʰere,
 e of those nightmares!

ı. You sound disconnected.
ɑybe you've lost your minds; still I'm not
 melting
ʷn in my shoes with compunction. The
 ʄact is
 s clinging to the bond, Judge Skimmer-
 ʰorn;
 ʾs not too sunk for that. Now here's my
 ɔargain:
 u're hanging onto life by one steel cable,
 ʈ that's much safer than the spider web
 ɔst men have to trust to. Toss me the bond,
 ɭge Skimmerhorn, or I'll give this line a
 ʲank
 ɗ you won't even hang.

ᴍᴍᴇʀʜᴏʀɴ. You wouldn't do it.

ɢ. Oh, wouldn't I? For a two-cent lollipop
 pull the chain right now!

ᴍᴍᴇʀʜᴏʀɴ. You wouldn't do it!

ɾ. Hang on, then! Just for a taste, how's
ʰe incline now?
ɪttle steep? (*He pulls the line. The shovel
 as before.*)

ɢs. Pull it up! Take the God damn
ɔnd!—
ɔw it to him!

SKIMMERHORN. I will not!

VAN. Try this then. (*He tips the shovel
further.*)

BIGGS. Give him his bond! I'm slipping!

SKIMMERHORN. I will not!

BIGGS. I say you will! What good's the money
 to you
if you're bologny?

SKIMMERHORN. What money?

BIGGS. You know what money!

SKIMMERHORN. Straighten it up.

VAN. Do I get the bond?

SKIMMERHORN. Hell, yes! (VAN *restores their
equilibrium.*)
You get the bond if you agree to accept
five thousand for your claim. (*He brings out
a paper.*)

VAN. Don't stall with me!
I'll never have a chance like this again,
and it's hard to resist!

SKIMMERHORN. I'm offering you five thousand!
Five thousand! Cash!

VAN (*leaping to the rope*). Keep it!

BIGGS. Give him his bond! (*He wrenches the
paper from* SKIMMERHORN *and sails it to*
VAN.)
And now you've got it how's five thousand
 sound?
You settle for it?

VAN. Bid against them, Lise. It's a game.
What would you say, Lise?
They offer me five thousand.

LISE. Pieces of silver?

VAN. Pieces of silver.

LISE (*smiling*). But I'll give you more!
Only five thousand for this crag at dawn
shedding its husk of cloud to face a sunrise
over the silver bay? For silver haze
wrapping the crag at noon, before a storm
cascading silver levin? For winter rains
that run in silver down the black rock's face
under a gray-sedge sky? For loneliness
here on this crag? I offer you nine thousand!
To be paid in silver!

VAN. You hear? I've got nine thousand;
what am I offered?

BIGGS. Make it ten thousand—
and let us down in the bargain!

VAN. Yes? Ten thousand?
A mountain for ten thousand? Hear them,
Lise,
In their despair they lift it by a grand!
Should it go for ten?

SKIMMERHORN. We'll never get it back—
but that's all right.

VAN. Yes, Lise?

LISE. Will they pay
no more then for the piling of this stone,
set in its tall hexagonals by fire
before men were? Searching a hundred king-
doms
men will not find a site for lodge or tower
more kingly! A hundred thousand, sir, in
silver,
this is my offer!

VAN. Come now, meet it boys—
I have a hundred thousand!

BIGGS. She's a fraud!
She's no dealer; she's a ringer, primed
to put the price up! What do you mean by
silver?
She won't pay silver!

VAN. Coinage of the moon,
but it's current here!

SIMMERHORN. Ten thousand, cash, and that's
the last. Five thousand out of my pocket, see,
and five from Biggs! (He pulls out a bundle
of bills. BIGGS does the same.)
Take a good look at cash,
see how that operates! (He tosses down the
roll. BIGGS follows suit.)

VAN. You go well-heeled
when you go mountain-climbing. Is it real?

SKIMMERHORN. Well, look it over. Count it.
(VAN takes up one packet, then another.)

VAN. Where did this come from?

SKIMMERHORN. Where would you think?

VAN. I'll say I got a shock. (He studies the
bills again.)
I don't want your money.

BIGGS. What's wrong with it?

VAN. Didn't I tell you I had a hundred tho[u]
sand?
Take the stuff back. We reckon in moo[n]
light here!
Put up your mitts! (He tosses the bund[le]
back.)

BIGGS. It's yours if you want it.

VAN. No,
oh, no, I thank you. It's no sale. What's mo[re]
I never meant to sell. The auctioneer's
about to take a walk.

BIGGS. Well, look, we're sitting
right where we were.

VAN. You sit there for your health,
and think it over.

SKIMMERHORN. You won't do that, V[an]
Dorn,
just leave us here.

VAN. Watch me, if you don't think so. ([He]
gives an arm to LISE.)
Let me tell you about those babes in t[he]
wood,
did I say they were thieves? (They st[art]
out.)

BIGGS. Make it fifteen!

VAN. Go to sleep.

SKIMMERHORN. Well, twenty! and let [us]
down!

VAN. Sweet dreams.

SKIMMERHORN. We'll run you out of t[he]
state, Van Dorn!

VAN. You'll have to get down first!

SKIMMERHORN. Is he going away
and leave us sitting?

BIGGS. Looks like it. (VAN and LISE m[ove]
off.)

SKIMMERHORN. Say, Van Dorn,
will you pitch us up a sandwich?

VAN. Sure; they're soggy,
lying out in the rain. (He returns and tos[ses]
sandwiches to them.)

BIGGS. Thanks.

VAN. Don't mention it. (He goes out ri[ght]
with LISE. BIGGS and SKIMMERHORN unw[rap]
sandwiches.)

SKIMMERHORN. He got away with that bond.

BIGGS. Yeah.

SKIMMERHORN. Looks as if we wouldn't make anything on Van Dorn.

BIGGS. That's what it looks like.

SKIMMERHORN. Christ.

BIGGS. Well, we've still got the windfall.

SKIMMERHORN. Yeah, we've got that.

BIGGS. And here he comes again.

SKIMMERHORN. Who?

BIGGS. Our mascot, little rabbit's foot, little good-luck token, little knee-high with the big heart.

(DEWITT comes in from the left, looks at the place where the sandwiches were and then at the two in the shovel. He mutters.)

DEWITT. Magic again! More devil's work! And the woman gone, slipped round a turn, and the scent was cold for an old dog like me. By the mizzen yards, it's wearing to the temper of a man even if he's not choleric!—And those two, those buzzards of evil omen, brooding there and how they'll cut the mountain like a pie and sell it off in slices! (He looks at his pistols.)

One apiece.
It should be just enough, and it's a wonder
I never thought of it. (He lifts his pistols, the two drop their sandwiches into the void, and cower down; he clicks the hammers.)
Damp again! Well, boys,
we'll fix that. (He sits down to freshen the priming.)
They'll brood over us no more,
those two sea-lions. Damn the rain and mist;
it penetrates the priming! Damn the flint,
and damn the spring! A brace of fine horse-pistols,
that's what the Jew said back in Amsterdam;
it takes a horse to cock 'em. Now then, damn you,
blow 'em off their perch! (As he rises his eye catches something out on the Zee. He stands transfixed for a moment, watching.)
It can't be there!
It's there! It's gone! I saw it! Captain Asher!
Captain! Captain! Captain! Captain Asher!
(BIGGS and SKIMMERHORN have ducked down again. DEWITT rushes out to the right, firing his pistols in the air in his excitement. BIGGS sits up, then SKIMMERHORN).

SKIMMERHORN. Am I hurt? Do you see blood anywhere?

BIGGS. It seems there was nothing there. (They contemplate the place where DEWITT stood.)

CURTAIN

SCENE II

SCENE: Another part of the Tor. LISE is sitting high up on a ledge, looking out over the Zee. VAN stands near her, looking at her as she speaks. She has his old felt hat in her and has woven a wreath of dandelions around the brim. The beacon light strikes thwart her face.

LISE. But nobody likes this flower?

VAN. I like it now.
I used to think it was a weed, but now, well, it's a flower now.

LISE. The dandelion.
Where will you find another prodigal
so merry or so golden or so wasteful,
pouring out treasure down the sides of hills
and cupping it in valleys?

VAN. Buttercups
and touch-me-nots. The touch-me-not's a shoe,

a tiny golden shoe, with a hair-spring latchet
for bees to loosen.

LISE. When did you part from Judith?

VAN. Judith?

LISE. When did she go away?

VAN. Last evening.
But it seems longer.

LISE. Why?

VAN. Why, a lot's happened.—
It's almost morning.

LISE. How do you know? (*He steps up to the ledge.*)

VAN. See that star,
that heavy red star back in the west? When that
goes down, then look for the morning star across
Long Island Sound, and after that the lights
dim down in the gray.

LISE. You loved her, very much?

VAN. Yes.

LISE. I loved someone too. I love him still.

VAN. No, you're mine now. (*He sits beside her.*)

LISE. See the great gulf that lies
between the heavy red star down the west
and the star that comes with morning? It's a
long way.
There's that much lies between us.

VAN. Not for me.

LISE. Even for you.—You're weary?

VAN. Well, the truth is
I sometimes sleep at night.

LISE. Put your head down.
I'll hold you. (*He lays his head on her knees
and stretches out.*)
Now I'll wish that I could sing
and make you sleep. Somehow they're all
forgotten,
the old songs. Over and over when the birds
begin at morning I try hard to catch
one tune of theirs. There's one that seems to
say:
　　　Merrily, merrily, chirr, chirr,
　　　Lueté, lueté, stee—
　　　Merrily, merrily, chirr, lueté,
　　　Chirr, lueté, stee.
That's only what it says; for what it sings
you'll have to ask the bird.

VAN. I know it, though.
That's the song sparrow.

LISE. Have I come so near?

VAN. Say it again.

LISE. I can't. May I ask you something?

VAN. Yes.

LISE. There's so much that's changed now
men can fly
and hear each other across seas, must me
still die—do they die still?

VAN. Oh yes, they die.
Why do you ask?

LISE. Because I'm still so young,
and yet I can't remember all the years
there must have been.—In a long nigh
sometimes
I try to count them, but they blow in cloud
across the sky, the dancing firefly years,
incredible numbers.—Tell me how old yo
are
before you go to sleep.

VAN. Lying here now
there's not much logic in arithmetic.
Five, or six, maybe. Five or six thousanc
maybe.
But when I'm awake I'm twenty-three.

LISE. No more?

VAN. No more.

LISE. Tell me why it is I am as I am
and not like you?

VAN. I don't know, Lise.

LISE. But tell me.
Have I been enchanted here? I've seen
the trap-rock men, there in the shovel, seen
ing
so stupid and so pitiful. Could these
use charms and rites to hold wrecked
mariners
forever in a deep cataleptic spell
high on a mountain-fringe?

VAN. The trap-rock men?
They're no more wizards than I am. The
buy
and sell, and when they've had their fi
of dust
they die like the rest of us.

LISE. But they laid spells
about us?

VAN. There are no wizards and no spell
Just men and women and money and th
earth
the way it always was. The trap-rock me
don't know you're here.

se. It's not sorcery then. If I had died
d left my bones here on the mountain-top
t had no memory of it, and lived on
    dreams, it might be as it is. As children
re we were told of living after death,
t there were angels there, and onyx stone
ving an angel city, and they sang
ernally, no darkness and no sun,
thing of earth. Now can it be men die
d carry thence no memory of death,
ly this curious lightness of the hands,
ly this curious darkness of the mind,
ly to be still changeless with the winters
ssing; not gray, not lined, not stricken
    down,
t stamped forever on the moving air,
echo and an image? Restless still
ith the old hungers, drifting among men,
l one by one forgotten, fading out
ke an old writing, undecipherable,
e lose our hold and go? Could it be true?
ould this be how men die?

n (half asleep). It may be, Lise.
love you when you speak.

se. And I love you.
t I am dead, and all the crew is dead;
l of the *Onrust* crew—and we have clung
yond our place and time, on into a world
real as sleep, unreal as this your sleep
at comes upon you now. Oh, you were
    cruel
love me and to tell me I am dead
d lie here warm and living! When you
    wake
e shall be parted—you will have a world
t I'll have none! There's a chill falls on
    me,
e night-dew gathering, or my mind's death
    chill—
owing at last I know.—You haven't
    heard.
ou told me this in a half-dream. You've
    been kind.
ou never thought to hurt me. Are you
    asleep?

n. I think I was.

se. Sleep, sleep. There was once a song,
only I could call back air and words,
out a king who watched a goblet rising
d falling in the sea. It came to land
d on the rim the king's name was inscribed
th a date many years before. Oh, many
    years,

a hundred or three hundred. Then he knew
that all his life was lived in an old time,
swept out, given to the waters. What remained
was but this goblet swimming in the sea,
touching his dust by chance.— But he's
    asleep.
And very well he might be with dull stories
out of old songs.—Sleep, sweet; let me have
your head here on my knees, only this night,
and your brown hair round my finger.
(*A girl's shadowy figure comes in from the
right, walking lightly, pauses, as if at seeing
them, and turns to go, the face still unre-
vealed.*)
Are you Judith?

JUDITH. Yes.

LISE. The lad's asleep, but when he wakes
you'll have him back.

JUDITH. Do you dispose of him
just as you please?

LISE. No. It's not what I please.
It's what will happen.

JUDITH. I don't know who you are.

LISE. I'm but a friend of his. You left him
    bitter
going away so lightly. I was bitter—
and so we tried to play at being lovers,
but it won't do. He'll wake, and he'll be
    yours,
all as it was. Only if I may hold him
while he lies here asleep, it helps a little
and I'll be happier.

JUDITH. You'll keep him then
after he wakes.

LISE. No.

JUDITH. Then why are you crying?

LISE. Am I crying?
Well, they're not for him, nor you, these
    tears;
something so far away, so long ago,
so hopeless, so fallen, so lost, so deep in dust
the names wash from the urns, summons
    my tears,
not love or longing. Only when you have
    him,
love him a little better for your sake,
for your sake, knowing how bitterly
I cried, for times past and things done.

JUDITH. You're strange—
the dress you wear's strange, too.—Who are
    you then?
I'm—afraid of you!

LISE. Afraid of tears
and a voice out of long ago? It's all I have.

JUDITH. No—no—I'm not afraid. Only for
    him.
I've done my crying, too.—Shall I come
    back?

LISE. Don't wake him now. Come back at
    dawn. You'll find him
here alone.
(TWO or THREE SAILORS appear on the rocks
at the rear, looking out over the Zee.)

PIETER. Look for yourself.

A SAILOR. Aye.

PIETER. Do you make her out?

THE SAILOR. She's the square top-yards.

ANOTHER SAILOR. Now, God, if it were she!

PIETER. It's the brigantine! The Onrust from
up-river
tacking this way!

ASHER (outside). Lise! Lise! Lise! (The
CAPTAIN comes in at the rear with DEWITT.)
Lise, the ship's on the river! Quick, there's
    haste!
She must catch the tide down-stream!

LISE. Hush! Hush! You'll wake him!

ASHER. But look across the Zee! The Onrust's
in
and waiting for us!

LISE. But you say it, Asher,
only to comfort me. There is no ship,
nor are we caught in spells here, or en-
    chanted,
but spectres of an old time. The life we live
is but a lingering, a clinging on,
our dust remembering. There is no ship,
only a phantom haunting down the Zee
as we still haunt the heights.

ASHER. Look! The Onrust!
Look, Lise!

LISE. Yes, I see it.

ASHER. Will you come?

LISE. Why would I stay? Why would I go
    For go
or stay we're phantoms still.

ASHER. But will you come?
Who is this lad?

LISE. Her lad. But he was hurt
and fell asleep. (VAN wakes and lifts h.
head.)

ASHER. Come quickly!

LISE. Yes, for his sake
it's better I should go.

VAN. Where must you go? (She rises.)

LISE. The Onrust's on the river
and we must catch the tide.

VAN. Would you leave me now?

LISE. Yes, I must leave you.

VAN. You'll go back with him?

LISE. Yes.

VAN. And was nothing meant of all we said

LISE. What could we mean, we two? You
    hurt's quite cured
and mine's past curing.

VAN. Let me go with you then.

LISE. I should have told you if I'd on
    known
how we stood at the tangent of two worl
that touched an instant like two wings
    storm
drawn out of night; touched and flew o
and, falling,
fall now asunder through a wide abyss,
not to touch again. (She steps back amor
the rocks.)

VAN. Let them go if they like!
What do I care about worlds? Any wor
    you have
I'll make it mine!

LISE. You told me in your sleep.
There is no witchcraft. Men are as th
    were;
we're parted now.

VAN. Give me your hand again!
They dare not take you from me, dare n
    touch you

o matter who they are, or where they come
from—
hey have no hold on us!

se. If I could stay!
I could stay with you. And tend my
garden
ly a little longer!

n. Put out your hand!

se. There were too many, many, many
years.

n. I'll be alone here—

se. No, not alone. When you must walk
the air,
all must walk it sometime, with a tread
at stirs no leaf, and breathe here with a
breath
at blows impalpable through smoke or
cloud,
hen you are as I am, a bending wind
ong the grain, think of me sometimes then
d how I clung to earth. The earth you
have
ems now so hard and firm, with all its
colors
arp for the eye, as a taste's sharp to the
tongue,
u'll hardly credit how its outlines blur
d wear out as you wear. Play now with fire
hile fire will burn, bend down the bough
and eat
fore the fruit falls. For there comes a time
hen the great sun-lit pattern of the earth
akes like an image under water, darkens,
ms, and the clearest voices that we knew
e sunken bells, dead sullen under sea,
ceding. Look in her eyes. (VAN *looks at*
DITH.)

her. Come!

se. See, the dawn
ints with one purple finger at a star
put it out. When it has quite gone out
en we'll be gone. (VAN *looks at the dawn,*
en turns back towards LISE.)

n. Lise! Lise! (*But even as he speaks* LISE
d *the* CREW *have disappeared.*)

se (*unseen*). This is your age, your dawn,
your life to live.
he morning light strikes through us, and
the wind
at follows after rain tugs at our sails—
d so we go.

DEWITT (*still half-seen*). And welcome you
are to the age, too, an age of witches
and sándwiches, an age of paper, an age of
paper money
and paper men, so that a poor Dutch wraith's
more man
than the thickest of you! (*He steps back and
vanishes. It is now dawn.*)

VAN. She never said good-bye.

JUDITH. There is a ship.

VAN. Yes?

JUDITH. Tiny, with black, square sails;
low and small.

VAN (*still looking after* LISE). She'll be a
phantom too
like all the rest. The canvas casts no shadow;
the light sifts through the spars. A moonlight
rig
no doubt they call it.

JUDITH. I think I hear their voices
as they go down the crag.

VAN. But you won't see them.
No matter what you hear.

THE SAILORS (*a wisp of chantey in the
distance*). Coming a blow, coming a blow,
sea runs black, glass runs low.

VAN. Just voices down the wind.
Why, then they were all mist, a fog that
hangs
along the crevices of hills, a kind
of memory of things you read in books,
things you thought you'd forgotten. She was
here,
and she was real, but she was cloud, and
gone,
and the hill's barren of her.

JUDITH. There are no ghosts.

VAN. I know—but these were ghosts or I'm
a ghost,
and all of us. God knows where we leave off
and ghosts begin. God knows where ghosts
leave off
and we begin.

JUDITH. You were in love with her.

VAN. She leaves the mountain barren now
she's gone.
And she was beautiful.

JUDITH. I came to tell you
that I was wrong—I mean about the land—
what you have here is better than one buys
down in the towns. But since I come too late
I'll say it and then go.—Your was was best.
I think it always would be.—So, good night,
    Van—
or, rather, it's good morning.

VAN. Yes, it's morning.—
Is it too late?

JUDITH. Oh, Van, I think it is.
It was for Lise you were calling, not
for Judith. I can't say I blame you much,
because she is more beautiful. And yet
you love her, and not me. You'll say they're
    ghosts
and won't come back. Perhaps. I'm not so
    certain
about the way of ghosts. She may come back.
And you still love her.

VAN. There's no ship at all.
It faded in the dawn. And all the mists
that hung about the Tor, look how they lift,
pouring downstream with the wind. What-
    ever it was,
was said, or came between us, it's all gone
now it's daylight again.

JUDITH. I came to say
if only I could keep you, you should keep
the Tor, or what you wished. I'r.1 sorry I
went.
I'm sorry this has happened. But it has.
And so—

VAN. Should I keep the Tor?

JUDITH. Yes, if you like.

VAN. God knows they haven't left me much
    of it.
Look, where the new road winds along the
    ledge.
Look at the jagged cut the quarries make
down to the south, and there's a boy scout
    trail
running along the ridge Mount Ivy way,

where they try out their hatchets. There
    the light,
and steps cut into stone the linesmen ble
for better climbing. The crusher underneat
dumps road rock into barges all day lor
and sometimes half the night. The We
    Shore tunnel
belches its trains above the dead lagoons
that line the brickyards. Their damne
    shovel hangs
across my line, ready to gouge the pe
we're standing on. Maybe I'm ghost myse
trying to hold an age back with my hand
maybe we're all the same, these ghosts
    Dutchmen
and one poor superannuated Indian
and one last hunter, clinging to his land
because he's always had it. Like a wa
that tries to build a nest above your door
and when you brush it down he builds aga
then when you brush it down he buil
    again—
but after a while you get him.

JUDITH. Then you'll sell?

VAN. I guess if you were with me then we
    sell
for what we could, and move out fart
    west
where a man's land's his own. But if I
    here
alone, I'll play the solitary wasp
and sting them till they get me.

JUDITH. If it's your way
then it's your way.

VAN. I'll sell it if you'll stay.
Won't you stay with me, Judith?

JUDITH. I think I'd always hear you calli
    Lise
while I was standing by. I took a wro
    turning
once, when I left you and went down
    hill,
and now it may not ever be the same.
(She turns.)

CURTAIN

ACT THREE

SCENE: *The shovel still hangs over the verge, and* BIGGS *and* SKIMMERHORN *still occupy*
The rising sun sends level rays across the rock, lighting their intent faces as they stare
inward. BIGGS *has torn a handkerchief into strips and tied them together into a string.*
appears to be fishing for something which lies below the ledge, out of view of the
ience. Over and over he tries his cast.

SKIMMERHORN. Little to the left.

BIGGS. You don't say?

SKIMMERHORN. Little to the right.

BIGGS. Put it to a tune and sing it, why don't
?

SKIMMERHORN. There! Almost!

BIGGS. I don't need any umpire.

SKIMMERHORN. Let me try it.

BIGGS. Oh, no. You always were a butter-
ers. (*The string tightens.*) By Golly!

SKIMMERHORN. It's on!

BIGGS. You're explaining to me? (*He pulls*
A bottle of beer emerges from below.)

SKIMMERHORN. Fifty per cent!

BIGGS. What? (*He pauses, the bottle in air.*)

SKIMMERHORN. You tore up my handker-
f! Fifty per cent. That's the natural di-
n between capital and labor.

BIGGS. Oh, now I'm labor and you're capital.
pulls up carefully.)

SKIMMERHORN. Fifty per cent!

BIGGS. I get the first pull at it. That's all I
(*The string parts, and the bottle*
ends silently into the void.) That's that.

SKIMMERHORN. You should 'a let me handle

BIGGS. Yeah. No doubt.

SKIMMERHORN. Am I thirsty?

BIGGS. Wait till the sun gets up a little. We'll
an-fried in this thing.

SKIMMERHORN. Look! (*He points down the*
s.)

BIGGS. If it's more of those little people I give
up.

SKIMMERHORN. It's a trooper.

BIGGS. What do you know? Up early for a
trooper, too. Listen, about that stuff in our
pockets?

SKIMMERHORN. Yeah?

BIGGS. Do we say anything about it?

SKIMMERHORN. Do you?

BIGGS. Do you?

SKIMMERHORN. No.

BIGGS. Neither do I, then.

SKIMMERHORN. Beautiful morning.

BIGGS. I always say it's worth while being up
early just to catch the sunrise. (*A* TROOPER
climbs in followed by SKIMMERHORN SENIOR.)

THE TROOPER. Hello!

BIGGS. Hello, Patsy.

PATSY. Say, you boys had the wives worried
down in Ledentown. Been looking for you
all night. There they are, Mr. Skimmerhorn.

SKIMMERHORN, SR. (*winded*). Good God!
(*He sits, a hand to his heart.*) And I climbed
up here. We thought you were under that
rock slide.

SKIMMERHORN. I guess you're disappointed.

SENIOR. The next time you two go on a bat
and spend a night up a tree you can stay
there and sober up.

SKIMMERHORN. We haven't been drinking.

SENIOR (*pointing to a bottle*). What's that?

SKIMMERHORN. Beer. But we didn't have a
drop to drink. I'd certainly appreciate a
swallow of that now.

PATSY (*tossing up bottle*). Here you are. Hair of the dog that bit you.

BIGGS. We're not drunk. We're dry. We didn't have a drop to drink nor a bite to eat.

PATSY. All right. All right. Only the ground's covered with beer and sandwiches.

BIGGS. You tell 'em how it was, Skimmer.

SKIMMERHORN. You tell 'em.

BIGGS. Well, you see, the whole thing's pretty complicated.

PATSY. I know. I've been through it. You wake up in the morning and you can't believe it yourself.

BIGGS. I don't mean that. I'm sober as a judge.

PATSY. Yeah, what judge? (*He hauls at a cable.*) Can you lend me a hand with this, A.B.?

SENIOR. Give me a minute. (*The shovel tips.*)

BIGGS. Hey, not that one! The other one!

PATSY. Sorry. Not much of a mechanic.

BIGGS. Straighten it up again. (PATSY *does so.*)

SKIMMERHORN. Are we never getting off this? My legs are paralyzed sitting here.

BIGGS. So are mine.

PATSY (*hauling down*). It's too much for me alone.

SKIMMERHORN. Got your wind yet, A.B.?

SENIOR. I don't know whether I want you down yet. You had your good time, now you can put in a few minutes paying for it.

SKIMMERHORN. Oh, we had a good time, did we?

SENIOR. What were you doing? You came up here to buy Van Dorn's property; you're gone all night, and the whole damn town's up all night hunting for you! And we find you up in a steam shovel enjoying a hangover!

PATSY. And now I know what a hang-over looks like.

BIGGS. I tell you we didn't even have a drink of water!

SENIOR. I believe that!

BIGGS. And we're thirsty! Have you got opener?

PATSY. No, I haven't.

SENIOR. Before you open anything tell what you were doing last night. Did y see Van Dorn?

SKIMMERHORN. Sure we saw him.

SENIOR. Well, what did he say?

SKIMMERHORN. He said no.

SENIOR. And I suppose that took all nigh

SKIMMERHORN. We had an argument.

SENIOR. And then he chased you up crane, I suppose?

SKIMMERHORN. No.

SENIOR. Well, how did you get up there?

SKIMMERHORN. We were hauled up.

SENIOR. All right. Who hauled you up?

SKIMMERHORN. You tell him, Art.

BIGGS. Oh, no. You tell him.

SKIMMERHORN. As a matter of fact, I do think it happened.

SENIOR. You're there, aren't you?

SKIMMERHORN. Yes, we're here.

SENIOR. Well, if you weren't drunk how you get there?

SKIMMERHORN. Well, you see, first we tr to negotiate with Van Dorn.

SENIOR. And he wouldn't take the money

SKIMMERHORN. That's right.

SENIOR. Did you tell him he didn't rea own the land? Till the will was validate

SKIMMERHORN. Yes, we told him that.

SENIOR. And he still wouldn't talk busine

SKIMMERHORN. He's stubborn. Stubborn a mule.

SENIOR. Did you tell him you could take land away from him?

SKIMMERHORN. Oh, yes.

NIOR. And you offered him the twenty-five ousand?

GS. We offered him a fair price.

NIOR. You were authorized to say twenty-e thousand.

GS. We didn't quite get to that. We ofed ten.

MMERHORN. You see, we thought we'd e the company some money.

NIOR. I'll bet you did. You thought you'd ke a little on the side, and I'd never know.

MMERHORN. Oh, no.

GS. Oh, no.

NIOR. All right, you offered ten and he uldn't take it. Then what happened?

MMERHORN. Well, we couldn't get down ause of the slide, so some sailors offered let us down in this thing.

NIOR. Sailors—up here?

MMERHORN. Little men, in big hats.

GS. Might have been a moving picture npany.

NIOR. Yeah? Any elephants? Or snakes?

MMERHORN. We're trying to tell you the th!

TSY. Certainly sounds like delirium mens, boys.

NIOR. Never mind, you were hauled up pink elephants, and then what?

MMERHORN. Van Dorn came along and rted to dump us down the cliff.

NIOR. What's Van Dorn look like? Kind an octopus, with long feelers?

MMERHORN. Are you going to let us down of this basket?

NIOR. No. Not till you come across with at's been going on.

MMERHORN. All right. I'll talk when I'm wn.

NIOR. Can a grown man get pie-eyed on er?

TSY. Must have been something stronger. AN DORN *comes in from the right.*)

SENIOR. Who are you?

VAN. Oh, I'm nobody. I just own the property.

SENIOR. What property?

VAN. This.

SENIOR. Are you Van Dorn?

VAN. I am.

SENIOR. I'm A. B. Skimmerhorn, Mr. Van Dorn, president of Igneous Trap rock, and I'm glad to meet you. (*He put out a hand.*)

VAN (*ignoring the hand*). Are these friends of yours?

SENIOR. One's a nephew and one's a partner. Why?

VAN. Because any friend of theirs is no friend of mine. (JUDITH *and* THE INDIAN *enter at the rear. She is leading him.*)

PATSY. Who do you think you're talking to?

VAN. A. B. Skimmerhorn, of Skimmerhorn, Skimmerhorn, Biggs and Skimmerhorn, small-time crooks and petty thieving done. Cheap.

SENIOR. Now, to be frank, there may have been some misunderstanding, Mr. Van Dorn. Those two were hardly in condition to negotiate. But I can offer you a fair price for your land, and if you don't take it we may have to push you a little, because we want this acreage and we intend to have it.

SKIMMERHORN. He's got the validation papers.

SENIOR. You gave him the validation papers?

BIGGS. We had to. He started to trip the machine.

SENIOR. That puts us in a sweet mess, that does. Will you take twenty-five thousand?

VAN. No.

SENIOR. Will you take fifty thousand?

VAN. No.

SENIOR. Then, we go home, and the machinery can rust here. That's the best I can do.

VAN. Fine. Let it rust.

JUDITH. Van?

VAN. Yes, Judith.

JUDITH. There's someone here to see you.

VAN. You want to see me, John?

THE INDIAN. But I can wait. I have time
enough.

VAN. I'll be right with you.

JUDITH. I had to bring him, Van, because
he said
his eyes were bad. He couldn't see the way.

VAN. Thanks, Judith.

SENIOR. Look, Van Dorn, you know the
saying,
every man has his price. I've heard it said
God has his price, if you'll go high enough.
Set a figure.

VAN. I'm not thinking of prices.
I don't want to sell. Hell, fifty thousand's
too much money for me.

SENIOR. We'll give you less.

VAN. I don't want less or more. It's not a
matter of money.

SENIOR. Will you take a partnership
in the company?

VAN. No.

SSENIOR. Good God, what do you want?

VAN. I want to have it back the way it was
before you came here. And I won't get that.
I know
what kind of fool I look to all of you,
all but old John there. But I'll be a fool
along with John, and keep my own, before
I let you have an inch. John, fifty thousand
or this old hill-top. Is it worth keeping?

THE INDIAN. No.

VAN. No?

THE INDIAN. It's gone already. Not worth
keeping.

VAN. I thought you'd say it was. I counted on
you
to be my friend in that.

THE INDIAN. It's an old question,
one I heard often talked of round the fire
when the hills and I were younger. Then as
now
the young braves were for keeping what was
ours

whatever it cost in blood. And they did tr
but when they'd paid their blood, and st
must sell,
the price was always less than what it w
before their blood was paid.

VAN. Well, that may be.

THE INDIAN. I wish now I had listened wh
they spoke
their prophecies, the sachems of the ten
they were wiser than I knew. Wisest of a
Iachim, had his camp here on this Tor
before the railroad came. I saw him sta
and look out toward the west, toward t
sun dying,
and say, "Our god is not the setting su
and we must follow it. For other races,
out of the east, will live here in their tim
one following another. Each will build
its cities and its monuments to gods
we dare not worship. Some will come wi
ships,
and some with wings, and each will c
secrate
the altars of the people overthrown,
but none will live forever. Each will li
its little time, and fly before the feet
of those who follow after." Let them cor
in
despoiling, for a time is but a time
and these will not endure. This little hill,
let them have the little hill, and find yo
peace
beyond, for there's no hill worth a mar
peace
while he may live and find it. But th
fought it out
and died, and sleep here.

SENIOR. Why, this is a wise Indian.
A little pessimistic about the aims
of civilization, but wise anyway.
What do you say, Van Dorn?

THE INDIAN. You too will go
like gnats on the wind. An evening and
day, but still you have your day. Bu
monuments
and worship at your temples. But you
will go.

SENIOR. You're on my side, so I don't mi
but you have a damned uncomfortable w
of speaking. I'm a Republican myself,
but I don't go that far! What do you s
Van Dorn?
Can we do business?

ʌ. Judith?

ᴅɪᴛʜ. I'm out of it.
, your decision. I'd say keep it though
you want to keep it.

ʌ. I'll sell it. Fifty thousand.
 one condition. There's a burying ground
vant to keep.

ᴠɪoʀ. Sure. That can be arranged.
 settled, then. Come down to Ledentown
morrow and get your money.

ʌ. Yes, I'll come.

ᴠɪoʀ. Why, three cheers, boys. We're out
of the woods. Take hold,
n Dorn, and swing these topers off the
imb.
ᴇn they can sign the pledge. (*A* ᴛʀooᴘᴇʀ
ᴘears with ᴇʟᴋᴜs *and* ᴅoᴘᴇ.)

ᴅɢᴇ (ᴛʜᴇ ᴛʀooᴘᴇʀ). Help me keep an eye
 these two, will you, Patsy? I've got a
ɴfession out of them on the Nanuet bank
bbery, and they say the money's up here.

ᴛsʏ. Up here? Whereabouts?

ᴅɢᴇ. They left it in a satchel.

ᴛsʏ. There's the satchel, all right. (*He
 ᴀmines it.*) Empty.

ᴅɢᴇ. Looks like a stall, you guys. You
ᴋied it.

ᴋᴜs. Didn't keep a cent, officer. Somebody
 here got it.

ᴅɢᴇ. Well, who?

ᴋᴜs. Last time I saw it one of those birds
 down on it. (*He points to* ʙɪɢɢs *and
 ᴀᴍᴍᴇʀʜoʀɴ.*)

ᴛsʏ. You know who they are? That's
ᴅlge Skimmerhorn of the Probate Court,
ᴅ Arthur Biggs of the Trap-rock Com-
ᴀy.

ᴋᴜs. Well, one of them sat down on it.

ᴅɢᴇ. Why didn't he pick it up?

ᴋᴜs. I don't know whether he saw it.

ᴘᴇ. And then there was a little guy in a
 hat that had some of it.

ᴛsʏ. Yeah? Who?

ʙᴜᴅɢᴇ. That's right. Buddy said something
about a little guy in a big hat.

ᴘᴀᴛsʏ. You think he got away with it?

ᴇʟᴋᴜs. He had some of it, and we haven't
got a cent.

ʙᴜᴅɢᴇ. So now we have to look for a little
guy in a big hat. Any other description?

ᴇʟᴋᴜs. Short and fat, had two sawed-off
shotguns, and wore knee-pants.

ᴅoᴘᴇ. And you could see right through him.
(ʙᴜᴅɢᴇ *is writing in a notebook.*)

ᴘᴀᴛsʏ. What?

ᴅoᴘᴇ. You could see right through him.

ʙᴜᴅɢᴇ. I'm beginning to think I can see
right through you.

ᴘᴀᴛsʏ. Check on that. Elkus, you saw him.
Could you see through him?

ᴇʟᴋᴜs. Certainly was a funny-looking guy.
Looked as if you could see right through
him.

ʙᴜᴅɢᴇ. You expect me to send that out
over the country: "Look for a short, fat man
with a big hat and two sawed-off shotguns.
Dangerous. You can see right through
him."?

ᴘᴀᴛsʏ. They buried the money, Budge. Or
else they're screwy.

ᴇʟᴋᴜs. I thought I was screwy. You couldn't
hurt him with a gun.

ʙᴜᴅɢᴇ. What do you mean?

ᴅoᴘᴇ. We bored him full of holes and he
wouldn't even sit down.

ʙᴜᴅɢᴇ. You mean he kept on running?

ᴅoᴘᴇ. Running? He just stood there and let
us shoot him. Like shooting through a window.

ʙᴜᴅɢᴇ. Must have been wearing a vest.

ᴅoᴘᴇ. I shot him through the head! Two feet
away! And it just made him mad!

ᴘᴀᴛsʏ. Take 'em away, Budge. They're nuts.

ᴇʟᴋᴜs. But he had the money! Buddy saw
him with the money!

PATSY. They're all three nuts.

BUDGE. I never heard a line like that before.

PATSY. Who lives around here?

VAN. I guess I'm the only one that lives nearby.

PATSY. Did you hear any shooting last night?

VAN. Plenty of it.

PATSY. Did you take a look round?

VAN. Yes, I did.

PATSY. Did you see a little guy in a big hat?

VAN. Six or seven of them.

BUDGE. What!

VAN. Six or seven of them.

BUDGE. I suppose you could see right through them?

VAN. Once in a while.

BUDGE. I'm going to quit writing this down. There's enough here to get me fired already.

PATSY. If you saw six or seven where did they go?

VAN. Down the river.

PATSY. In a car?

VAN. In a ship.

PATSY. Sounds like a motor-boat gang. Well, that's something. They went down the river.

VAN. But I can tell you where there's thirty dollars of the money.

BUDGE. Where?

VAN. On the ledge there below the shovel. (BUDGE *and* PATSY *step over to look*.)

BUDGE. There it is. Three ten dollar bills. How did it get there?

VAN. I don't know. I just happened to see it.

BUDGE. Did you try to get it?

VAN. No, I thought it probably belonged to the gentlemen up there in the scoop.

PATSY. Did one of you drop some money, Judge?

SKIMMERHORN. I don't think so. Not me.

BIGGS. Not me.

PATSY. Did either of you see a little man in big hat? (*The two look at each other.*)

SKIMMERHORN. Why, yes, we did. (PATSY *a* BUDGE *look at each other*.)

BUDGE. Well, if they say so he must ha been here.

PATSY. What was he doing?

SKIMMERHORN. He was fighting with the two. (*He points to* ELKUS *and* DOPE.)

BIGGS. A regular war.

PATSY. Say, listen to that.

BUDGE. Do you know if he took anythi out of the satchel?

SKIMMERHORN. Yes, I think he did. He h the satchel.

BUDGE. Now we're getting somewhere.

PATSY. You don't know where they wer

SKIMMERHORN. No.

PATSY. If you saw anything else that mi give us a clue—?

SKIMMERHORN. No, not a thing.

PATSY. It beats me.

VAN. Want me to suggest a question?

PATSY. What?

VAN. Ask the Judge if he gained any wei during the night.

PATSY. What's the matter with you?

VAN. Looks to me like he picked up a g deal.

PATSY. I'll think up my own questi thanks. Might as well trundle the yeggs b to pail, Budge. Whoever got the stuff gone.

BUDGE. That's what it looks like.

VAN. Aren't you going to help the Ju down before you go?

BIGGS. Oh, don't bother. We'll get down

SKIMMERHORN. No hurry. We're all ri You take care of your prisoners.

rsy. Might as well lend a hand while we're
re.

gs. Run along, boys. We're all right.
n't worry about us.

rsy (*to* BUDGE). Want to wait a minute?

oge. Well, I'm due back, if they can make
hemselves.

gs. Sure.

n. Oh, don't leave those poor fellows up
that crane! They've been there all night!

IMMERHORN. We're fine. You run along.

oge. Well, take a drag on the rope, Patsy.
. wait. (PATSY *and* VAN *haul the shovel*
wn.)

IMMERHORN. No need to go to all this
uble.

rsy. No trouble at all.

n. A pleasure. Why, you were asking me
night to get you out of this. (*The shovel*
iches ground. The two sit still.)

rsy. What's the matter?

IMMERHORN. Guess my legs are asleep.

gs. Mine too.

rsy. I'll help you up. (*They are pulled to*
ir feet, staggering. Their pockets are
y obvious.)

oge. How about it? O.K.?

rsy. All set. Say, you are loaded down.
rried plenty of lunch, I guess?

gs. Oh, we brought plenty.

n (*tapping* BIGG's *pocket*). I told you they
ned weight. Something in the air up here.

kus. Couldn't be money, could it?

gs. As a matter of fact, some of it is. We
re carrying cash to pay Van Dorn for his
m.

rsy. Cash?

gs. Yeah, cash.

rsy. How much?

gs. Just what we were authorized to pay.
venty-five thousand.

VAN. Funny thing, too. It's got the Orangeburg pay roll stamp on it.

BIGGS. Well, hardly.

PATSY. What makes you think so?

VAN. I saw it. They offered me ten thousand.

PATSY. Just for the record, I'd better look at
it, Judge.

SKIMMERHORN. I wouldn't if I were you. I'm
hardly under suspicion of bank robbery.

PATSY. I'll take a look at it. (*He holds out*
a hand. BIGGS *passes him a package.*)

SENIOR. I don't get this at all.

PATSY. It's got the Orangeburg stamp on it,
all right.

SKIMMERHORN. Must be some mistake. They
must have got the money mixed at the bank.

PATSY. Sure. Well, if that's all we can easy
check on that.

VAN. Sure. You'd better check on it.

SKIMMERHORN. Are you under the impression that we robbed the bank?

VAN. You explain it. I can't.

SENIOR. You say you drew the money to pay
Van Dorn?

SKIMMERHORN. That's right, A.B.

SENIOR. And it's got the Orangeburg label
on it?

SKIMMERHORN. That's what they say.

SENIOR. I'll have something to say to the
bank about that.

SKIMMERHORN. Oh, I'll take care of it. Just
a clerical error.

PATSY. I'm afraid I'll have to take the money,
though. Oh, you'll get your own money
back, but if this is the Orangeburg money—

BIGGS. Sure, take it. (*They unload.*)

PATSY. And I guess I really ought to put
you both under arrest.

BIGGS. What? Under arrest?

PATSY. Wouldn't you say so, Budge?

BUDGE. Don't see any way out of it. Doesn't mean anything. Just an examination.

SKIMMERHORN. I'd like to keep it out of the papers, if possible, of course. An examination might be very embarrassing—you see, I have political enemies.

BIGGS. Always ready to think the worst of a man, and print it, too.

PATSY. Still, I guess we'll have to have an examination. Just for the record.

SKIMMERHORN. You know who we are, of course?

PATSY. Yes, sir.

SKIMMERHORN. I won't submit to an examinaton! It's preposterous!

PATSY. I don't see how we can get out of it, though. Because we had a robbery, and here's the money, and we've got to explain it somehow.

SKIMMERHORN. I won't submit to it!

PATSY. You got an extra pair of handcuffs there, Budge?

BUDGE. Yeah.

SKIMMERHORN. All right. I'll go.

BIGGS. Sure. We'll go. And we'll make a lot of people sorry!

PATSY. Go on ahead, Budge. (BUDGE *starts out with his prisoners.*)

DOPE. But how about the little guy with the big hat? How about him?

BUDGE. I'll tell you about him. It's entirely possible there wasn't any little guy in a big hat.

DOPE. But we all saw him!

BUDGE. Oh, no, you didn't see him. You saw right through him. And the reason was he wasn't there. (BUDGE, ELKUS *and* DOPE *go out.*)

BIGGS. You don't think we made that up, about the man in the big hat?

PATSY. Well, you have to admit it doesn't sound exactly plausible. (PATSY, BIGGS *and* SKIMMERHORN *go out.*)

SENIOR (*as he goes*). It shakes a man's fait in evidence. (*To* VAN.) See you tomorrow

VAN. I'll be there. (SKIMMERHORN SENIOR goe out.) So now—I've sold the Tor.

THE INDIAN. Yes, but it's better.

VAN. Better than living on a grudge, I gues It might come down to that.

THE INDIAN. There's wilder land,
and there are higher mountains, in the wes

VAN. Out Port Jervis way.

THE INDIAN. Perhaps. You'll find them.

JUDITH. He came to tell you, Van—this his death-day.
I'll go now.

VAN. All right, John.

THE INDIAN. Could I keep it?
The hand I held? It's a new thing, bein blind,
when you've had an Indian's eyes. (JUDIT *returns and gives him her hand again*

JUDITH. I'll stay a while.

THE INDIAN. When I had lost the path
halfway along the ridge, there at my feet
I heard a woman crying. We came on
together, for she led me. There'll be tim
for crying later. Take her west with yo
She'll forget the mountain.

VAN. Will you come?

JUDITH. I'd remember Lise!

VAN. Was there a Lise?
I think she was my dream of you and n
and how you left the mountain barren on
when you were gone. She was my dream you
and how you left the Tor. Say you'll con with me.

JUDITH. Yes.

THE INDIAN. It's a long day's work to d a grave
in stony ground. But you're young and ha good shoulders.
It should be done tonight.

VAN. I'll have it done
even if you don't need it. Tell me the plac

THE INDIAN. There's still an Indian burying ground that lies
behind the northern slope. Beneath it runs
a line of square brown stones the white men used
to mark their dead. Below still, in a ring,
the seven graves, a woman and six men,
the Indians killed and laid there. In the freshet,
after the rain last night, the leaf-mould washed,
and the seven looked uncovered at the sky,
white skeletons with flintlocks by their sides,
and on the woman's hand a heavy ring
made out of gold. I laid them in again.

VAN. Seven graves—a woman and six men—
maybe they'll rest now.

THE INDIAN. Dig them in deeper, then.
They're covered only lightly.

VAN. I'll dig them deeper.

THE INDIAN. But you must make my grave with my own people,
higher, beneath the ledge, and dig it straight,
and narrow. And you must place me in the fashion
used by the Indians, sitting at a game,
not fallen, not asleep, And set beside me
water and food. If this is strange to you,
think only I'm an Indian with strange ways,
but I shall need them.

VAN. Don't worry. You shall have it
but the way you want it.

THE INDIAN. Shall we go?

VAN. One last look at the rock. It's too late
to hold out on the bargain. Think of the gouge
they'll make across these hills.

JUDITH. If it's for me
you sell, we'll have enough without it, Van.
We'll have each other.

VAN. Oh, but you were right.
When they wash over you, you either swim
or drown. We won't be here.

THE INDIAN. And there's one comfort.
I heard the wise Iachim, looking down
when the railroad cut was fresh, and the bleeding earth
offended us. There is nothing made, he said,
and will be nothing made by these new men,
high tower, or cut, or buildings by a lake
that will not make good ruins.

JUDITH. Ruins? This?

THE INDIAN. Why, when the race is gone, or looks aside
only a little while, the white stone darkens,
the wounds close, and the roofs fall, and the walls
give way to rains. Nothing is made by men
but makes, in the end, good ruins.

VAN. Well, that's something.
But I can hardly wait.

CURTAIN

Idiot's Delight

BY ROBERT EMMET SHERWOOD

THIS PLAY IS LOVINGLY DEDICATED TO
LYNN FONTANNE
AND
ALFRED LUNT

IDIOT'S DELIGHT

Presented by the Theatre Guild, at the National Theatre, Washington, D. C., March 9th, '36, with the following cast:

JMPTSY	George Meader	ELAINE	Marjorie Baglin
RCHESTRA LEADER	Stephen Sandes	EDNA	Frances Foley
)NALD NAVADEL .	Barry Thompson	MAJOR	George Greenberg
TTALUGA	S. Thomas Gomez	FIRST OFFICER	Alan Hewitt
JGUSTE	Edgar Barrier	SECOND OFFICER ...	Winston Ross
APTAIN LOCICERO	Edward Raquello	THIRD OFFICER	Gilmore Bush
R. WALDERSEE	Sydney Greenstreet	FOURTH OFFICER ...	Tomasso Tittoni
R. CHERRY	Bretaigne Windust	QUILLERY	Richard Whorf
RS. CHERRY	Jean Macintyre	SIGNOR ROSSI	Le Roi Operti
ARRY VAN	Alfred Lunt	SIGNORA ROSSI	Ernestine de Becker
IRLEY	Jacqueline Paige	MAID	Una Val
ULAH	Connie Crowell	ACHILLE WEBER	Francis Compton
BE	Ruth Timmons	IRENE	Lynn Fontanne
ANCINE	Etna Ross		

The scene of the play, designed by Lee Simonson, is the cocktail lounge in the Hotel ꞏnte Gabriele, in the Italian Alps, near the frontiers of Switzerland and Austria.

———

ACT I

Afternoon of a winter day in any imminent year.

ACT II

Scene I. Eight o'clock that evening.
Scene II. Eleven o'clock that evening.
Scene III. After midnight.

ACT III

The following afternoon.

———

IDIOT'S DELIGHT

ACT ONE

The cocktail lounge of the Hotel Monte Gabriele.

The hotel is a small one, which would like to consider itself a first-class resort. It wa originally an Austrian sanatorium. Its Italian management has refurnished it and adde this cocktail lounge and a few modern bedrooms with baths, in the hope that some do Monte Gabriele may become a rival for St. Moritz. So far, this is still a hope. Although th weather is fine, the supply of winter sports enthusiasts at Monte Gabriele is negligible, an the hotel is relying for its trade upon those itinerants who, because of the current politic situation, are desirous of leaving Italy.

Near at hand are a railway line into Switzerland, highways into Switzerland and Austr and an Italian army airport.

At the left, up-stage, is a large doorway, leading to the lobby, in which we can just s the Reception Desk.

At the upper right is a staircase. A few steps up is a landing, above which is a hig window with a fine view of the Alpine scenery to the North and West. The panes a fringed with frost. From the landing, the stairs continue up to a gallery which leads bedrooms off to the upper left.

Downstairs left is a swinging door marked with the word "BAR."

Over this bar entrance are crossed skis and the head of a mountain goat. On the wall the right is a Fascist emblem with crossed Italian flags. About the Reception Desk, off the left, are signs assuring the guest that this hotel has been approved by all the automob associations of Europe and that Travellers' Cheques may be cashed here. Somewhere the walls are pictures of the Coliseum and the S.S. "Conte di Savoia."

There are small tables and chairs about, with perhaps a couch or two. At the left i piano, and when the first curtain rises a dismal little four-piece orchestra is playi "June in January."

Note a line in the dialogue along toward the end of Act One: there is something ab this place that suggests "a vague kind of horror." This is nothing definite, or identifia or even, immediately, apparent. Just an intimation.

Behind the Reception Desk, PITTALUGA *is occasionally visible. He is the proprietor the hotel—a fussy, worried little Italian in the conventional morning coat and striped pa*

On the landing at the upper right, looking dolefully out the window, is DONALD NAVAD *a rather precious, youngish American, suitably costumed for winter sports by Saks F Avenue. Experienced in the resort business, he was imported this year to organize sport and social life at Monte Gabriele with a view to making it a Mecca for American touri He is not pleased with the way things have turned out.*

DUMPTSY *comes in from the left. He is an humble, gentle little bell-boy, aged about fo born in this district when it was part of Austria, but now a subject of the Fascist Emp He has come in to clean the ash-trays. He listens to the music.*

DUMPTSY. Come si chiama questa musica che suonate?

ORCHESTRA LEADER. Il pezzo si chiama: "Giugno in Gennaio."

DUMPTSY. Oh, com'e bello! Mi piace! (*To* DON.) It's good.

DON. Will you please for God's sake stop playing that same damned tiresome thing?

DUMPTSY. You don't like it, Mr. Navadel?

DON. I'm so sick of it, I could scream!

DUMPTSY. I like it. To me, it's good.

DON. Go on, and clean the ash-trays.

DUMPTSY. But they're not dirty, sir. Beca there's nobody using them.

DON. There's no need to remind me of t Do as you're told!

DUMPTSY. If you please, sir. (*He whis the tune and goes out.*)

DON (*to the* LEADER). You've played enou Get out!

94

ADER. But it is not yet three o'clock.

N. Never mind what time it is. There's
body here to listen to you, is there? You
n just save the wear and tear on your
rpsichord and go grab yourselves a smoke.

ADER. Very good, Mr. Navadel. (*To the
er musicians*) E inutile continuare a suo-
re. La gente non ascolta più. Si potrà
ece far quattro chiachiere e fumare una
aretta. (*They put away instruments and
sic and start to go out, as* PITTALUGA *ap-
rs bristling.*)

TALUGA (*to* LEADER). Eh, professori?
rchè avete cessato di suonare? Non sono
cora le tre.

ADER. Il Signor Navadel ci ha detta di
dare a fumare egli ne ha avuto abbastanza
la nostra musica. (*The* MUSICIANS *have
e.*)

TALUGA (*going to* DON). You told my
hestra it would stop?

(*untroubled*). I did.

TALUGA. My orders to them are they play
here until three o'clock. Why do you
e it to yourself to countermand my or-
s?

. Because their performance was just a
e too macabre to be bearable.

ALUGA. So! You have made yourself the
nager of this hotel, have you? You give
ers to the musicians. Next you will be
ng orders to me—and to the guests themes, I have no doubt. . . .

. The guests! (*He laughs drily.*) That's
ly very funny. Consult your room chart,
dear Signor Pittaluga, and let me know
many guests there are that I can give
rs to. The number when last I count-
. .

ALUGA. And you stop being insolent, you
nimale fetente. I pay you my money,
n I am plunging myself into bank-
cy. . . .

. Yes, yes, Signor—we know all about
. You pay me your money. And you
a right to know that I'm fed to the
with this little pension that you eu-
nistically call a high-grade resort hotel.

Indeed, I'm fed to the teeth with you personally.

PITTALUGA (*in a much friendlier tone*). Ah!
So you wish to leave us! I'm very sorry, my
dear Donald. We shall miss you.

DON. My contract expires on March the first.
I shall bear it until then.

PITTALUGA. You insult me by saying you
are fed with me, but you go on taking my
money?

DON. Yes!

PITTALUGA. Pezzo mascalzone farabutto pre-
potente canaglia . . .

DON. And it will do you no good to call me
names in your native tongue. I've had a
conspicuously successful career in this business, all the way from Santa Barbara to St.
Moritz. And you lured me away from a
superb job . . .

PITTALUGA (*as* DON *continues*). Lazzarone,
briccone, bestione. Perdio.

DON. . . . with your glowing descriptions of
this handsome place, and the crowds of
sportlovers, gay, mad, desperately chic, who
were flocking here from London, Paris, New
York. . . .

PITTALUGA. Did *I* know what was going to
happen? Am *I* the king of Europe?

DON. You are the proprietor of this obscure
tavern. You're presumably responsible for
the fact that it's a deadly, boring dump!

PITTALUGA. Yes! And I engaged you because
I thought you had friends—rich friends—
and they would come here after you instead
of St. Moritz, and Muerren, and Chamonix.
And where are your friends? What am I
paying for you? To countermand my orders
and tell me you are fed . . . (*Wails from
warning sirens are heard from off-stage
right.* PITTALUGA *stops short. Both listen.*)
Che cosa succede?

DON. That's from down on the flying field.

PITTALUGA. It is the warning for the air
raids! (AUGUSTE, *the barman, is heard in bar
off-stage, left.*)

AUGUSTE'S VOICE. Che cosa? (PITTALUGA *and*
DON *rush to the window.*)

PITTALUGA. Segnali d'incursione. La guerra e incominiciata e il nemico viene. (*Airplane motors are heard off right.*)

DON (*looking through window*). Look! The planes are taking off. They're the little ones —the combat planes. (CAPTAIN LOCICERO *enters from the lobby. He is the officer in charge of the frontier station. He is tired, quiet, nice.* AUGUSTE *enters from the bar.* DUMPTSY *follows the* CAPTAIN.)

AUGUSTE. Signor Capitano!

CAPTAIN. Buona sera! (AUGUSTE *helps him take off his coat.*)

DUMPTSY. Che cosa succede, Signor Capitano? È la guerra?

CAPTAIN. No—no—datemi cognac. (DUMPTSY *puts coat on chair right of table and goes up and exits through arch center.* CAPTAIN *sits chair left of table.*)

AUGUSTE (*as he goes out*). Si, signor Capitano. (*The* CAPTAIN *sits down at a table.* PITTALUGA *and* DON *cross to him.* DUMPTSY *goes.*)

PITTALUGA. Che cosa significano quei terribili segnali? È, forse, il nemico che arriva?

DON. What's happened, Captain? Is there an air raid? Has the war started?

CAPTAIN (*smiling*). Who knows? But there is no raid. (*The porter's hand-bell in the lobby is heard.*) They're only testing the sirens, to see how fast the combat planes can go into action. You understand—it's like lifeboat drill on a ship. (DUMPTSY *enters.*)

DUMPTSY. Scusi, padrone. Due Inglesi arrivati. (*He hurries out.*)

PITTALUGA. Scusi. Vengo subito. Presto, presto! (*He goes.*)

CAPTAIN. Have a drink, Mr. Navadel?

DON. Thank you very much—but some guests are actually arriving. I must go and be very affable. (*He goes.* DR. WALDERSEE *appears on the gallery above and comes down the stairs as* AUGUSTE *enters from the bar and serves the* CAPTAIN *with brandy and soda. The* DOCTOR *is an elderly, stout, crotchetty, sad German.*)

CAPTAIN. Good afternoon, Doctor. Have a drink?

DOCTOR. Thank you very much—no. What is all that aeroplanes? (AUGUSTE *goes.*)

CAPTAIN. This is a crucial spot, Dr. Walder see. We must be prepared for visits from th enemy.

DOCTOR. Enemy, eh? And who is that?

CAPTAIN. I don't quite know, yet. The ma of Europe supplies us with a wide choice opponents. I suppose, in due time, our go ernment will announce its selection—and w shall know just whom we are to shoot at.

DOCTOR. Nonsense! Obscene nonsense!

CAPTAIN. Yes—yes. But the taste for obsce ity is incurable, isn't it?

DOCTOR. When will you let me go into Sw zerland?

CAPTAIN. Again I am powerless to answ you. My orders are that no one for the tir being shall cross the frontiers, either in Switzerland or Austria.

DOCTOR. And when will this "time bein end?

CAPTAIN. When Rome makes its decision tween friend and foe.

DOCTOR. I am a German subject. I am your foe.

CAPTAIN. I am sure of that, Dr. Walders The two great Fascist states stand togeth against the world.

DOCTOR (*passionately*). Fascism has noth to do with it! I am a scientist. I am a serv of the whole damn stupid human race. (*crosses toward the* CAPTAIN.) If you delay any longer here, my experiments will ruined. Can't you appreciate that? I must my rats at once to the laboratory in Zur or all my months and years of research have gone for nothing. (DON *enters, follo by* MR. *and* MRS. CHERRY—*a pleasant yo English couple in the first flush of t honeymoon.*)

DON. This is our cocktail lounge. Ther the American bar. We have a thé dan here every afternoon at 4:30—supper d ing in the evening.

CHERRY. Charming.

N. All this part of the hotel is new. Your
oms are up there. (*He crosses to the win-
w.*) I think you'll concede that the view
om here is unparalleled. We can look into
ur countries. (*The* CHERRYS *follow him to
e window.*) Here in the foreground, of
urse, is Italy. This was formerly Austrian
rritory, transferred by the treaty of Ver-
illes. It's called Monte Gabriele in honor
D'Annunzio, Italian poet and patriot. Off
ere is Switzerland and there is Austria.
nd far off, you can just see the tip of a
ountain peak that is in the Bavarian Tyrol.
ather gorgeous, isn't it?

ERRY. Yes.

S. CHERRY. Darling—*look* at that sky!

ERRY. I say, it *is* rather good.

N. Do you go in for winter sports, Mrs.
erry?

S. CHERRY. Oh, yes—I—we're very keen
them.

N. Splendid! We have everything here.

ERRY. I've usually gone to Kitzbuhel.
TTALUGA *and* DUMPTSY *appear up-stage
d speak in Italian through the dialogue.*)

TALUGA. Dumptsy, il bagaglio è stato por-
o su?

MPTSY. Si, signore, è già sopra.

TALUGA. Sta bene, vattene.

N. It's lovely there, too.

ERRY. But I hear it has become much too
wded there now. I—my wife and I hoped
vould be quieter here.

N. Well—at the moment—it is rather
et here.

TALUGA (*coming down*). Your luggage
been sent up, Signor. Would you care
see your room now?

ERRY. Yes. Thank you.

TALUGA. If you will have the goodness to
this way. (*He goes up the stairs.*)
use me.

ERRY (*pauses at the window on the way
. What's that big bare patch down there?

DON (*casually*). Oh, that's the airport. (PIT-
TALUGA *coughs discreetly.*) We have a great
deal of flying here.

PITTALUGA. Right this way, please.

CHERRY. Oh—I see. (*They continue on up,
preceded by* PITTALUGA.)

DON. And do come down for the dansant.

MRS. CHERRY. We should love to.

PITTALUGA. Right straight ahead, please.
(*They exit through gallery.*)

DON (*standing on first step*). Honeymooners.

CAPTAIN. Yes—poor creatures.

DON. They wanted quiet.

DOCTOR (*rises*). Ach Gott! When will you
know when I can cross into Switzerland?

CAPTAIN. The instant that word comes
through from Rome. (*The hand-bell is
heard.*) You understand that I am only an
obscure frontier official. And here in Italy, as
in your own Germany, authority is central-
ized.

DOCTOR. But you can send a telegram to
Rome, explaining the urgency of my position. (DUMPTSY *appears, greatly excited.*)

DUMPTSY. More guests from the bus, Mr.
Navadel. Seven of them! (*He goes.*)

DON. *Good* God! (*He goes out.*)

DOCTOR. Ach, es gibt kein Ruhe hier.

CAPTAIN. I assure you, Dr. Waldersee, I shall
do all in my power.

DOCTOR. They must be made to understand
that time is of vital importance.

CAPTAIN. Yes, I know.

DOCTOR. I have no equipment here to exam-
ine them properly—no assistant for the constant observation that is essential if my experiments are to succeed . . .

CAPTAIN (*a trifle wearily*). I'm so sorry . . .

DOCTOR. Yes! You say you are so sorry. But
what do you *do*? You have no comprehension of what is at stake. You are a soldier
and indifferent to death. You say you are
sorry, but it is nothing to you that hundreds
of thousands, *millions,* are dying from a disease that it is within my power to cure!

CAPTAIN. Again, I assure you, Dr. Waldersee, that I . . .

DON'S VOICE. Our Mr. Pittaluga will be down in a moment. In the meantime, perhaps you and the—the others . . . (*He comes in, followed by* HARRY VAN, *a wan, thoughtful, lonely American vaudevillian promoter, press agent, book-agent, crooner, hoofer, barker or shill, who has undertaken all sorts of jobs in his time, all of them capitalizing his powers of salesmanship, and none of them entirely honest. He wears a snappy, belted, polo coat and a brown felt hat with brim turned down on all sides*) . . . would care to sit here in the cocktail lounge. We have a thé dansant here at 4:30 . . . supper dancing in the evening . . .

HARRY. Do you run this hotel?

DON. I'm the Social Manager.

HARRY. What?

DON. The Social Manager.

HARRY. Oh! American, aren't you?

DON. I am. Santa Barbara's my home, and Donald Navadel is my name.

HARRY. Happy to know you. My name's Harry Van. (*They shake hands.*)

DON. Glad to have you here, Mr. Van. Are you—staying with us long?

DOCTOR (*rising*). I shall myself send a telegram to Rome, to the German Embassy.

CAPTAIN. They might well be able to expedite matters. (*The* DOCTOR *goes.*)

HARRY. I've got to get over that border. When I came in on the train from Fiume, they told me the border is closed, and the train is stuck here for to-night and maybe longer. I asked them why, but they either didn't know or they refused to divulge their secrets to me. What seems to be the trouble?

DON. Perhaps Captain Locicero can help you. He's the commander of Italian Headquarters here. This is Mr. Van, Captain.

CAPTAIN (*rising*). Mr. Van, my compliments.

HARRY. And mine to you, Captain. We're trying to get to Geneva.

CAPTAIN. You have an American passport?

HARRY. I have. Several of them. (*He reach in his pocket and takes out seven passpor bound together with elastic. He fans the like a deck of cards and hands them to th* CAPTAIN.)

CAPTAIN. You have your family with you

HARRY. Well—it isn't exactly a family. (*H goes to the right.*) Come in here, girls!

SHIRLEY (*from off-stage*). Come on in, kic Harry wants us. (*Six blonde chorus gi come in. They are named:* SHIRLEY, BEULA BEBE, FRANCINE, EDNA *and* ELAINE. *Of thes* SHIRLEY *is the principal, a frank, knowi fan dancer.* BEULAH *is a bubble dancer, ar therefore ethereal.* BEBE *is a hard, harsh lit number who shimmies.* DON *doesn't kno quite how to take this surprising troupe, b the* CAPTAIN *is impressed, favorably.*)

HARRY. Allow me to introduce the girls, Ca tain. We call them "Les Blondes." We' been playing the Balkan circuit—Budape Bucharest, Sofia, Belgrade, and Zagreb. (*h turns to* DON.) Back home, that would the equivalent of "Pan Time." (*He laug nervously, to indicate that the foregoing u a gag.*)

CAPTAIN (*bowing*). How do you do?

HARRY. The Captain is head man, girls.

GIRLS. How do you do? . . . Pleased to m you. . . . Etc.

HARRY. The situation in brief is this, Capta We've got very attractive bookings at night spot in Geneva. Undoubtedly they f that the League of Nations needs us. (*A other laugh.*) It's important that we there at once. So, Captain, I'll be grate for prompt action.

CAPTAIN (*looking at the first passport*). M Shirley Laughlin.

HARRY. Laughlin. This is Shirley. Step honey. (SHIRLEY *steps forward.*)

CAPTAIN (*pleased with* SHIRLEY). How you do?

SHIRLEY. Pleased to meet you.

CAPTAIN. This photograph hardly does y justice.

SHIRLEY. I know. It's terrible, isn't it!

RY (*interrupting*). Who's next, Captain?

TAIN. Miss Beulah Tremoyne.

RY. Come on, Beulah. (*She comes for-*
d in a wide sweep, as SHIRLEY *goes up*
joins the group.) Beulah is our bubble
cer, a product of the æsthetic school, and
efore more of a dreamer.

TAIN. Exquisite!

LAH. Thank you *ever* so much. (*She*
ts to sit down by the CAPTAIN. *She is*
ing it on.*)

RY. That'll be all, Beulah.

TAIN. Miss Elaine Messiger—

RY. Come on, babe.

TAIN. Miss Francine Merle—

RY. No tricks, Francine. This is just iden-
ation.

TAIN. Miss Edna Creesh—

RY. Turn it off, honey.

TAIN. And Miss Bebe Gould.

RY. You'll find Bebe a very, very lovely

(*remonstrating*). Harry!

RY. A shimmy artiste, and incorrigibly
phisticated.

AIN (*summing up*). Very beautiful.
, very beautiful. Mr. Van, I congratulate

Y. That's nice of you, Captain. Now,
we . . .

AIN. And I wish I, too, were going to
eva. (*He hands back the passports to*
Y.*)

Y. Then it's O.K. for us to pass?

AIN. But won't you young ladies sit
n?

EY. Thanks, Captain.

AH. We'd love to.

CINE. He's cute.

. I'll say. (*They all sit.*)

Y. I don't want to seem oblivious of
courtesy, Captain, but the fact is we
can't afford to hang around here any longer.
That train may pull out and leave us.

CAPTAIN. I give you my word, that train will
not move to-night, and maybe not to-morrow
night, and maybe never. (*He bows deeply.*)
It is a matter of the deepest personal regret
to me, Mr. Van, but—

HARRY. Listen, pal. Could you stop being polite for just a moment, and tell us how do we
get to Geneva?

CAPTAIN. That is not for me to say. I am as
powerless as you are, Mr. Van. I, too, am a
pawn. (*He picks up his coat and hat.*) But,
speaking for myself, I shall not be sorry if
you and your beautiful companions are
forced to remain here indefinitely. (*He sa-*
lutes the girls, smiles and goes out.)

HARRY. Did you hear that? He says he's a
pawn.

BEBE. He's a Wop.

BEULAH. But he's cute!

SHIRLEY. Personally, I'd just as soon stay
here. I'm sick of the slats on those stinking
day coaches.

HARRY. After the way we've been betrayed in
the Balkans, we can't afford to stay any
place. (*He turns to* DON.) What's the matter,
anyway? Why can't decent respectable people be allowed to go about their legitimate
business?

DON. Evidently you're not fully aware of the
international situation.

HARRY. I'm fully aware that the international
situation is always regrettable. But what's
wrong now?

DON. Haven't you been reading the papers?

HARRY. In Bulgaria and Jugo-Slavia? (*He*
looks around at the girls, who laugh.) No.

DON. It may be difficult for you to understand, Mr. Van, but we happen to be on the
brink of a frightful calamity.

HARRY. What?

DON. We're on the verge of **War.**

SHIRLEY. War?

BEBE. What about?

HARRY. You mean—that business in Africa?

DON. Far more serious than that! *World* war! All of them!

HARRY. No lie! You mean—it'll be started by people like that? (*Points after the* CAPTAIN.) Italians?

DON. Yes. They've reached the breaking point.

HARRY. I don't believe it. I don't believe that people like that would take on the job of licking the world. They're too romantic. (PITTALUGA *steps forward.*)

PITTALUGA. Do you wish rooms, Signor?

HARRY. What have you got?

PITTALUGA. We can give you grande luxe accommodations, rooms with baths. . . .

HARRY. What's your scale of prices?

PITTALUGA. From fifty lira up.

DON. That's about five dollars a day.

HARRY (*wincing*). What?

DON. Meals included.

HARRY. I take it there's the usual professional discount.

PITTALUGA (*to* DON). Che cosa significa?

DON. Mr. Van and the young ladies are artists.

PITTALUGA. Ebbene?

DON (*scornfully*). In America we give special rates to artists.

PITTALUGA (*grimly*). Non posso, non posso. (*The* CHERRYS *appear on the balcony above.*)

DON. I'm sure Mr. Pittaluga will take care of you nicely, Mr. Van. He will show you attractive rooms on the *other* side of the hotel. They're delightful.

HARRY. No doubt. But I want to see the accommodations.

PITTALUGA. Step this way, please.

HARRY. Come on, girls. Now—I want two girls to a room, and a single room for me adjoining. I promised their mothers I'd always be within earshot. Put on your shoes, Beulah. (*He goes out right, followed by the* GIRLS *and* DON.)

BEULAH (*as they go*). Why's he kicking think this place is *attractive!*

SHIRLEY. Oh—you know Harry. He's alw got to have something to worry ab (*They have gone.*)

MRS. CHERRY (*coming down*). What an traordinary gathering!

CHERRY. There's something I've never b able to understand—the tendency of An icans to travel en masse. (*They pause admire the view and each other. He to her in his arms and kisses her.*) Darling

MRS. CHERRY. What?

CHERRY. Nothing. I just said, "Darlin (*He kisses her again.*) My sweet. I love y

MRS. CHERRY. That's right. (*She kisses hi*

CHERRY. I think we're going to like it h aren't we, darling?

MRS. CHERRY. Yes. You'll find a lot to pa

CHERRY. No doubt. But I'm not goin waste any time painting.

MRS. CHERRY. Why not, Jimmy? You've to work and—

CHERRY. Don't ask "why not" in that la iously girlish tone! You know damned why not!

MRS. CHERRY (*laughing*). Now really ling. We don't have to be maudlin. W old enough to be sensible about it, aren't

CHERRY. God forbid that we should everything by being sensible! This is an sion for pure and beautiful foolishness don't irritate me by any further mentic work.

MRS. CHERRY. Very well, darling. If yo going to be stinking about it . . . (*He k her again.*) (*The* DOCTOR *comes in fron right and regards their love-making scant enthusiasm. They look up and him. They aren't embarrassed.*)

CHERRY. How do you do?

·DOCTOR. Don't let me interrupt you. *rings a bell and sits down.*)

CHERRY. It's quite all right. We were starting out for a walk.

, CHERRY. The air is so marvellous up
, isn't it?

OR (*doubtfully*). Yes. (DUMPTSY *comes
rom the right.*)

RRY. Yes—we think so. Come on, dar-
. (*They go out at the back.*)

OR. Mineral water.

PTSY. Yes, sir. (QUILLERY *comes in and
at the left. He is small, dark, brooding
French—an extreme-radical-socialist, but
French.*)

OR. Not iced—warm.

PTSY. If you please, sir. (*He goes out,
*) (*A group of five Italian flying corps
ers come in, talking gaily in Italian.
y cross to the bar entrance and go out.*)

OFFICER. Sono Americane.

ND OFFICER. Sono belle, proprio da far
iliare.

D OFFICER. Forse sarrano stelle cinemato-
che di Hollyvood.

ND OFFICER. E forse ora non ci rincres-
che abbiano cancellato la nostra licenza.
y go into the bar.)

Y (*coming in*). Good afternoon.

OR. Good afternoon.

Y. Have a drink?

OR. I am about to have one.

Y. Mind if I join you? (*He sits down
the* DOCTOR.)

OR. This is a public room.

Y (*whistles a snatch of a tune*). It's a
y kind of situation, isn't it?

OR. To what situation do you refer?

Y. All this stopping of trains . . .
PTSY *enters from the bar and serves the
OR with a glass of mineral water*) and
s from Rome and we are on the thres-
of calamity.

OR. To me it is not funny. (*He rises
his mineral water.*)

Y. Get me a Scotch.

TSY. With soda, sir?

HARRY. Yes.

DUMPTSY. If you please, sir.

QUILLERY. I will have a beer.

DUMPTSY. We have native or imported, sir.

QUILLERY. Native will do.

DUMPTSY. If you please, sir. (*He goes out.*)

DOCTOR. I repeat—to me it is *not* funny! (*He
bows.*) You will excuse me.

HARRY. Certainly. . . . See you later, pal.
(*The* DOCTOR *goes.* HARRY *turns to* QUIL-
LERY.) Friendly old bastard!

QUILLERY. Quite! But you were right. The
situation *is* funny. There is always something essentially laughable in the thought of
a lunatic asylum. Although, it may perhaps
seem less funny when you are inside.

HARRY. I guess so. I guess it isn't easy for
Germans to see the comical side of things
these days. Do you mind if I join you? (*He
rises and crosses to the left.*)

QUILLERY. I beg of you to do so, my comrade.

HARRY. I don't like to thrust myself forward—(*He sits down*)—but, you see, I travel with a group of blondes, and it's always
a relief to find somebody to talk to. Have
you seen the girls?

QUILLERY. Oh, yes.

HARRY. Alluring, aren't they?

QUILLERY. Very alluring. (DUMPTSY *comes in
with the drinks and goes.*) (HARRY *takes out
his chewing gum, wraps it in paper, places
it in a silver snuff box, which he shows to*
QUILLERY.)

HARRY. That's a genuine antique snuff box
of the period of Louis Quinze.

QUILLERY. Very interesting.

HARRY. It's a museum piece. (*Puts the box
in his pocket.*) You've got to hoard your
gum here in Europe.

QUILLERY. You've travelled far?

HARRY. Yeah—I've been a long way with
that gorgeous array of beautiful girls. I took
'em from New York to Monte Carlo. To say
we were a sensation in Monte Carlo would
be to state a simple incontrovertible fact. But

then I made the mistake of accepting an offer from the manager of the Club Arizona
in Budapest. I found that conditions in the
South-East are not so good.

QUILLERY. I travelled on the train with you
from Zagreb.

HARRY. Zagreb! A plague spot! What were
you doing there?

QUILLERY. I was attending the Labor Congress.

HARRY. Yeah—I heard about that. The night
club people thought that the congress would
bring in a lot of business. They were wrong.
But—excuse me—(*Rises.*) My name is Harry Van.

QUILLERY (*rises*). Quillery is my name.

HARRY. Glad to know you, Mr.—?

QUILLERY. Quillery.

HARRY. Quillery. (*Sits.*) I'm an American.
What's your nationality?

QUILLERY. I have no nationality. (*Sits.*) I
drink to your good health.

HARRY. And to your lack of nationality, of
which I approve. (*They drink.* SIGNOR *and*
SIGNORI ROSSI *come in and cross to the bar.*
ROSSI *is a consumptive.*)

ROSSI. Abbiamo trascorso una bella giornata,
Nina. Beviamo un po'?

SIGNORA ROSSI. Dopo tutto quell' esercizio ti
farebbe male. Meglio che tu ti riposi per un'-
oretta.

ROSSI. Ma, no mi sento proprio bene. Andiamo. Mi riposerò più tardi. (*They go into the
bar.*)

HARRY. I get an awful kick hearing Italian.
It's beautiful. Do you speak it?

QUILLERY. Only a little. I was born in France.
And I love my home. Perhaps if I had
raised pigs—like my father, and all his fathers, back to the time when Cæsar's Roman
legions came—perhaps, if I had done that,
I should have been a Frenchman, as they
were. But I went to work in a factory—and
machinery is international.

HARRY. And I suppose pigs are exclusively
French?

QUILLERY. My father's pigs are! (H[...]
laughs.) The factory where I have wo[...]
made artificial limbs—an industry that [...]
been prosperous the last twenty years. [...]
sometimes—in the evening—after my w[...]
—I would go out into the fields and help [...]
father. And then, for a little while, I w[...]
become again a Frenchman.

HARRY (*takes out his cigarette case*). T[...]
a nice thought, pal. (*Offers* QUILLERY *a* [...]
rette.) Have a smoke?

QUILLERY. No, thank you.

HARRY. I don't blame you. These Jugo-
cigarettes are not made of the same [...]
grade quality of manure to which I gre[...]
customed in Bulgaria.

QUILLERY. You know, my comrade [...]
seem to have a long view of things.

HARRY. So long that it gets very tireson[...]

QUILLERY. The long view is not easy to [...]
tain in this short-sighted world.

HARRY. You're right about that, pal.

QUILLERY. Let me give you an inst[...]
There we were—gathered in Zagreb, r[...]
sentatives of the workers of all Europe[...]
brothers, collaborating harmoniously fo[...]
United Front! And now—we are rushi[...]
our homes to prevent our people from p[...]
ing into mass murder—mass suicide!

HARRY. You're going to try to stop the [...]

QUILLERY. Yes.

HARRY. Do you think you'll succeed?

QUILLERY. Unquestionably! This is not [...]
remember! Since then, some new [...]
have been heard in this world—loud v[...]
I need mention only one of them—Le[...]
Nikolai Lenin! (*A ferocious looking* N[...]
of the Italian flying corps comes in and [...]
quickly to the bar. As he opens the do[...]
calls "Attention!" He goes into the ba[...]
door swinging to behind him.)

HARRY. Yes—but what are you going [...]
about people like *that*?

QUILLERY. Expose them! That's all we [...]
to do. Expose them—for what they [...]
atavistic children! Occupying their un[...]
oped minds playing with outmoded to[...]

RY. Have you *seen* any of those toys?

LLERY. Yes! France is full of them. But e is a force more potent than all the bing planes and submarines and tanks. I that is the mature intelligence of the kers of the world! There is one antidote war—Revolution! And the cause of Revion gains steadily in strength. Even here taly, despite all the repressive power of ism, sanity has survived, and it bees more and more articulate. . . .

RY. Well, pal—you've got a fine point e. And I hope you stick to it.

LLERY. I'm afraid you think it is all futile lism!

RY. No—I don't. And what if I did? I an idealist myself.

LERY. You too believe in the revolution?

RY. Not necessarily in *the* revolution. I'm in favor of any revolution. Anything will make people wake up, and get selves some convictions. Have you ever n cocaine?

LERY. Why—I imagine that I have—at dentist's.

Y. No—I mean, for pleasure. You know ice.

LERY. No! I've never indulged in that

Y. I have—during a stage of my career luck was bad and confusion prevailed.

ERY. Ah, yes. You needed delusions of eur.

Y. That's just what they were.

ERY. It must have been an interesting ience.

Y. It was illuminating. It taught me is the precise trouble with the world . We have become a race of drug ad--hopped up with false beliefs—false -false enthusiasms. . . . (*The four* OF- *emerge from the bar, talking excit-*

D OFFICER. Ma, è state fatta la dichiara-li guerra attuale?

OFFICER. Caricheremo delle bombe es-e?

THIRD OFFICER. Se la guerra è in cominciata, allora vuol dire che noi. . . .

FOURTH OFFICER. La guerra è in cominciata

MAJOR. Silenzio! Solo il vostro commandante conosce gli ordini. Andiamo! (*All five go out hurriedly.*)

QUILLERY (*jumps up*). Mother of God! Did you hear what they were saying?

HARRY (*rises*). I heard, but I couldn't understand.

QUILLERY. It was about war. I know only a little Italian—but I thought they were saying that war has already been declared. (*He grabs his hat.*) I *must* go and demand that they let me cross the border! At once! (*He starts to go.*)

HARRY. That's right, pal. There's no time to lose.

QUILLERY. Wait—I haven't paid. . . . (*He is fumbling for money.*)

HARRY. No, no. This was my drink. You've got to hurry!

QUILLERY. Thank you, my comrade. (*He goes out quickly. Airplane motors are heard, off at the right.* HARRY *crosses to the window.* DUMPTSY *comes in to remove the empty glasses.*)

DUMPTSY. Fine view, isn't it, sir?

HARRY. I've seen worse.

DUMPTSY. Nothing quite like it, sir. From here, we look into four nations. Where you see that little village, at the far end of the valley—that is Austria. Isn't that beautiful over there?

HARRY. Are you Italian?

DUMPTSY. Well, yes, sir. That is to say, I didn't used to be.

HARRY. What did you used to be?

DUMPTSY. Austrian. All this part was Austria, until after the big war, when they decided these mountains must go to Italy, and I went with them. In one day, I became a foreigner. So now, my children learn only Italian in school, and when I and my wife talk our own language they can't understand us. (*He gets* HARRY'S *drink and brings it over to him.*) They changed the name of this mountain. Monte Gabriele—that's what it is now. They named it after an Italian who dropped poems on Vienna. Even my old father—he's dead—but all the writing on the gravestones was in German, so they rubbed it out and translated it. So now he's Italian, too. But they didn't get my sister. She married a Swiss. She lives over there, in Schleins.

HARRY. She's lucky.

DUMPTSY. Yes—those Swiss are smart.

HARRY. Yeah, they had sense enough to get over there in the first place.

DUMPTSY (*laughs*). But it doesn't make much difference who your masters are. When you get used to them, they're all the same. (*The Porter's bell rings.* PITTALUGA *appears.*)

PITTALUGA. Dumptsy! Dumptsy! Una gentildonna arriva. Prendi i suoi bagagli. Affretati!

DUMPTSY. Si, Signore. Vengo subito. (*He goes.*)

PITTALUGA (*claps his hands*). Sciocco! Anna, Per Dio! Dove sei stata, va sopra a preparare la stanza. (ANNA, *the maid, enters with towels.*) Presto, presto! (ANNA *runs up the steps, exits.* PITTALUGA *goes back into the lobby.*)

IRENE'S VOICE. Vieni, Achille.

DON (*coming in*). This is our cocktail lounge, madame. (IRENE *enters. She is somewhere between thirty and forty, beautiful, heavily and smartly furred in the Russian manner. Her hair is blonde and quite straight. She is a model of worldly wisdom, chic, and carefully applied graciousness. Her name is pronounced* "EAR-RAY-NA." . . . *She surveys the room with polite appreciation, glancing briefly at* HARRY.)

DON. Your suite is up there, madame. All this part of the hotel is quite new.

IRENE. How very nice!

DON. We have our best view from this side of the hotel. (*He goes to the window.* IRENE *follows slowly.*) You can see four countries—Italy, Switzerland, Austria and Bavaria

IRENE. Magnificent!

DON. Yes—we're very proud of it.

IRENE. All those countries. And they all [so very much alike, don't they!

DON. Yes—they do really—from this [tance.

IRENE. All covered with the beautiful s[I think the whole world should be al[covered with snow. It would be so n[more clean, wouldn't it?

DON. By all means!

IRENE. Like in my Russia. White Ru[(*Sighs, and goes up to the next land[*) Oh, and—how exciting! A flying field. L[They're bringing out the big bombers.

DON. Madame is interested in aviation?

IRENE. No, no. Just ordinary flying bore[But there is no experience in life qui[thrilling as a parachute jump, is there!

DON. I've never had that thrill, I'm asha[to say.

IRENE. Once I had to jump when I wa[ing over the jungle in Indo-China. It[indescribable. Drifting down, sinking[that great green sea of enchantment[hidden danger. (DUMPTSY *comes in.*)

DON. And you weren't afraid?

IRENE. No—no—I was not afraid. In [ments like that, one is given the sen[eternity.

HARRY (*viciously*). Dumptsy! Get m[other Scotch.

DUMPTSY. Yes, sir.

HARRY. And put ice in it, this time. I[haven't got any ice, go out and scoo[some snow.

DUMPTSY. If you please, sir. (*He goe[the bar.*)

IRENE (*her gaze wandering about the r[*) But your place is really charming.

DON. You're very kind.

IRENE. I must tell every one in Paris [it. There's something about this desig[suggests a—an amusing kind of horr[

DON (*not knowing quite how to int[that*). Madame is a student of decora[

E. No, no. Only an amateur, my friend.
amateur, I'm afraid, in everything. (*The*
sounds from off at the right. IRENE,
the top of the staircase, stops to listen.)

E. What is that?

Oh—it's merely some kind of warning.
y've been testing it.

E. Warning? Warning against what?

I believe it's for use in case of war.

E. War? But there will be no war. (PIT-
GA *enters from the lobby, escorting*
LLE WEBER—*which is pronounced "VAY-*
." *He is a thin, keen executive, wearing*
at little mustache and excellent clothes.
is lapel is the rosette of the Legion of
or. He carries a brief case.)

ALUGA (*as they come in*). Par ici, Mon-
Weber. Vous trouverez Madame ici . . .

E (*leaning over the railing*). Achille!

R (*pausing and looking up*). Yes, my
?

E. Achille—there will be no war, will
?

R (*amused*). No, no—Irene. There will
o war. They're all much too well pre-
d for it. (*He turns to* PITTALUGA.)
re are our rooms?

LUGA. Votre suite est par ici, Monsieur.
lus belle de la maison! La vue est su-
!

(*to* DON). There, you see! They will
ght. They are all much too much afraid
ch other. (WEBER *is going up the stair-*
ignoring the view. PITTALUGA *is fol-*
g.)

(*to* WEBER). Achille—I am mad about
lace! Je rafolle de cette place!

R (*calmly*). Yes, my dear.

. We must be sure to tell the Maha-
of Rajpipla, Achille. Can't you ima-
how dear little "Pip" would love this?
y go out on the landing above.*)

. Who was that?

(*impressed*). That was Achille Weber.
of the biggest men in France. I used to

see him a lot at St. Moritz. (*There is a
sound of airplane motors off at the right.*)

HARRY. And the dame? Do you assume that
is his wife?

DON (*curtly*). Are you implying that she's
not?

HARRY. No, no—I'm not implying a thing.
(*He wanders to the piano.*) I'm just kind of
—kind of baffled.

DON. Evidently. (*He goes out.*) (HARRY *at
the piano strikes a chord of the Russian
song, "Kak Stranna."* DUMPTSY *enters from
the bar and serves* HARRY *with Scotch. The
off-stage noise increases as more planes take
the air.*)

DUMPTSY (*at the window*). Do you see them
—those aeroplanes—flying up from the field
down there?

HARRY (*glances toward window, without interest*). Yes—I see them.

DUMPTSY. Those are the big ones. They're
full of bombs, to drop on people. Look!
They're going north. Maybe Berlin. Maybe
Paris. (HARRY *strikes a few chords.*)

HARRY. Did you ever jump with a parachute?

DUMPTSY. Why, no—sir. (*He looks questioningly at* HARRY.)

HARRY. Well, I have—a couple of times. And
it's nothing. But—I didn't land in any jungle. I landed where I was supposed to—in
the Fair Grounds.

DUMPTSY (*seriously*). That's interesting, sir.
(*The* ROSSIS *enter from the bar: He is holding a handkerchief to his mouth. She is
supporting him as they cross.*)

SIGNORA ROSSI. Non t'ho detto che dovevi fare
attenzione? Te l'ho detto, te l'ho detto che
sarebbe accaduto ciò. Vedi, ora ti piglia un
accesso di tosse.

ROSSI. 'Scusatemi, Mina. (*Another coughing
fit.*)

SIGNORA ROSSI. Va a sdraiarti. Dovresti ripo-
sarti a lungo. E adopera il termometro. Sco-
metto che t'è aumentata la temperatura.
(*They go out.*)

DUMPTSY. That Signor Rossi—he has tuber-
culosis.

HARRY. Is he getting cured up here? (*The* DOCTOR *appears on the landing above.*)

DUMPTSY. Ja. This used to be a sanatorium, in the old days. But the Fascisti—they don't like to admit that any one can be sick! (*He starts to go.*)

DOCTOR. Dumptsy!

DUMPTSY. Herr Doctor.

DOCTOR (*coming down*). Mineral water.

DUMPTSY. Ja wohl, Herr Doctor. (DUMPTSY *goes out, left. The* DOCTOR *sits down.* HARRY *takes one more look toward the gallery, where* IRENE *had been. He then looks at the* DOCTOR, *and decides not to suggest joining him. He starts to play* "Kak Stranna." *The* DOCTOR *turns and looks at him, with some surprise. The uproar of planes is now terrific, but it starts to dwindle as the planes depart.*)

DOCTOR. What is that you are playing?

HARRY. A Russian song, entitled "Kak Stranna," meaning "how strange!" One of those morose ballads about how once we met, for one immortal moment, like ships that pass in the night. Or maybe like a couple of trucks, side-swiping each other. And now we meet again! How strange!

DOCTOR. You are a musician?

HARRY. Certainly. I used to play the piano in picture theatres—when that was the only kind of sound they had—except the peanuts. (DUMPTSY *brings the mineral water and stops to listen, admiringly.*)

DOCTOR. Do you know Bach?

HARRY. With pleasure. (*He shifts into something or other by Bach.*)

DOCTOR (*after a moment*). You have good appreciation, but not much skill.

HARRY. What do you mean, not much skill? Listen to this. (*He goes into a trick arrangement of* "The Waters of the Minnetonka.") "The Waters of the Minnetonka"—Cadman. (*He goes on playing.*) Suitable for Scenics— Niagara Falls by moonlight. Or—if you play it this way—it goes fine with the scene where the young Indian chief turns out to be a Yale man, so it's O.K. for him to marry Lillian ("Dimples") Walker. (*Starts playing* "Boola Boola.")

DOCTOR. Will you have a drink?

HARRY. Oh! So you want me to stop playi[ng]

DOCTOR. No, no! I like your music [so] much.

HARRY. Then, in that case, I'd be delig[hted] to drink with you. Another Scotch, Du[mp]tsy.

DUMPTSY. If you please, sir. (*He goes o[ut.]*)

DOCTOR. I'm afraid I was rude to you.

HARRY. That's all right, pal. I've been r[ude] to lots of people, and never regretted it. [He] *plays on, shifting back into* "Kak Strann[a.]"

DOCTOR. The fact is, I am a man who is [very] gravely distressed.

HARRY. I can see that, Doctor. And I s[ym-] pathize with you.

DOCTOR (*fiercely*). You cannot sympat[hize] with me, because you do not know!

HARRY. No—I guess I don't know—ex[cept] in a general way.

DOCTOR. You are familiar with the writ[ings] of Thomas Mann. (*It is a challenge, ra[ther] than a question.*)

HARRY. I'm afraid not, pal. (*The* DO[CTOR] *opens* "The Magic Mountain," *which h[e has] been reading.*)

DOCTOR. "Backsliding"—he said—"spir[itual] backsliding to that dark and tortured [time] —that, believe me, is disease! A degrad[ation] of mankind—a degradation painful an[d of-] fensive to conceive." True words, eh?

HARRY. Absolutely! (DUMPTSY *comes in [with] the Scotch.* HARRY *gets up from the [piano] and crosses.* DUMPTSY *goes.* HARRY *sits [down] with the* DOCTOR.)

DOCTOR. Have you had any experience [with] cancer?

HARRY. Certainly. I once sold a remedy [for it.]

DOCTOR (*exploding*). There *is* no remed[y for] it, so far!

HARRY. Well—this was kind of a remed[y for] everything.

DOCTOR. I am within *that* of finding the [cure] for cancer! You probably have not hea[rd of] Fibiger, I suppose?

RRY. I may have. I'm not sure.

TOR. He was a Dane—experimented with s. He did good work, but he died before ould be completed. I carry it on. I have n working with Oriental rats, in Bolog- But because of this war scare, I must to neutral territory. You see, nothing st be allowed to interfere with my experi- nts. Nothing!

RRY. No. They're important.

TOR. The laboratory of the University of ⁻ich has been placed at my disposal—and Switzerland, I can work, undisturbed. I e twenty-eight rats with me, all in var- s carefully tabulated stages of the disease. s the disease of civilization—and I can e it. And now they say I must not cross border.

RRY. You know, Doctor, it *is* funny.

TOR. What's funny? To you, everything unny!

RRY. No—it's just that you and I are in the ıe fix. Both trying to get across that line. ı with rats—me with girls. Of course—I ⁻reciate the fact that civilization at large n't suffer much if *we* get stuck in the war e. Whereas with you, there's a lot at ⁻e . . .

TOR. It is for me to win one of the great- victories of all time. And the victory be- ɡs to Germany.

RY. Sure it does!

TOR. Unfortunately, just now the situa- ı in Germany is not good for research. ⁻y are infected with the same virus as ⁻. Chauvinistic nationalism! They expect bacteriologists to work on germs to put bombs to drop from airplanes. To fill ple with death! When we've given our s to *save* people. Oh—God in heaven— ⁻ don't they let me do what is good? ⁻d for the whole world? Forgive me. I ⁻me excited.

RY. I know just how you feel, Doctor. ⁻k in 1918, I was a shill with a carnival w, and I was doing fine. The boss thought ⁻ highly of me. He offered to give me a ⁻e of the show, and I had a chance to get ⁻ewhere. And then what do you think ⁻pened? Along comes the United States ⁻ernment and they drafted me! You're in

the army now! They slapped me into a uni- form and for three whole months before the Armistice, I was parading up and down guarding the Ashokan Reservoir. They were afraid your people might poison it. I've al- ways figured that that little interruption ruined my career. But I've remained an op- timist, Doctor.

DOCTOR. *You* can afford to.

HARRY. I've remained an optimist because I'm essentially a student of human nature. You dissect corpses and rats and similar un- pleasant things. Well,—it has been my job to dissect suckers! I've probed into the souls of some of the God-damnedest specimens. And what have I found? Now, don't sneer at me, Doctor—but above everything else I've found Faith. Faith in peace on earth and good will to men—and faith that "Muma," "Muma" the three-legged girl, really has got three legs. All my life, Doctor, I've been selling phoney goods to people of meagre intelligence and great faith. You'd think that would make me contemptuous of the human race, wouldn't you? But—on the contrary— it has given *me* Faith. It has made me sure that no matter how much the meek may be bulldozed or gypped they *will* eventually inherit the earth. (SHIRLEY *and* BEBE *come in from the lobby.*)

SHIRLEY. Harry!

HARRY. What is it, honey? (SHIRLEY *goes to* HARRY *and hands him a printed notice.*)

SHIRLEY (*excited*). Did you see this?

HARRY. Doctor—let me introduce, Miss Shir- ley Laughlin and Miss Bebe Gould.

SHIRLEY. How do you do?

DOCTOR (*grunts*). How do you do.

BEBE. Pleased to know you, Doctor. (HARRY *looks at the notice.*)

SHIRLEY. They got one of those put up in every one of our rooms.

HARRY (*showing it to the* DOCTOR). Look— "What to do in case of air-raids"—in all languages.

DOCTOR. Ja—I saw that.

SHIRLEY. Give it back to me, Harry. I'm going to send it to Mama.

HARRY (*handing it to her*). Souvenir of Europe.

SHIRLEY. It'll scare the hell out of her.

BEBE. What's the matter with these people over here? Are they all screwy?

HARRY. Bebe—you hit it right on the nose! (*Turns to the* DOCTOR.) I tell you, Doctor —these are very wonderful, profound girls. The mothers of tomorrow! (*He beams on them.* BEULAH *comes in.*)

SHIRLEY. Oh—shut up!

BEULAH. Say—Harry . . .

HARRY. What is it, honey?

BEULAH. Is it all right if I go out with Mr. Navadel and try to learn how to do this ski-ing? (WEBER *comes out on the gallery and starts down.*)

HARRY. What? And risk those pretty legs? Emphatically—no!

BEULAH. But it's healthy.

HARRY. Not for me, dear. Those gams of yours are my bread and butter. (WEBER *crosses. They look at him. He glances briefly at them.*) Sit down, girls, and amuse yourselves with your own thoughts. (*The* GIRLS *sit.* WEBER, *at the left, lights his cigar. The* CAPTAIN *comes in, quickly, obviously worried.*)

CAPTAIN. I have been trying to get through to headquarters, Monsieur Weber.

WEBER. And when can we leave?

CAPTAIN. Not before to-morrow, I regret to say. (IRENE *appears on the gallery.*)

WEBER. Signor Lanza in Venice assured me there would be no delay.

CAPTAIN. There would be none, if only I could get into communication with the proper authorities. But—the wires are crowded. The whole nation is in a state of uproar.

WEBER. It's absurd lack of organization. (*The* PIANIST *and* DRUMMER *come in from the lobby. The* VIOLINIST *and* SAXOPHONIST *follow.*)

CAPTAIN (*with tense solemnity*). There is good excuse for the excitement now, Monsieur Weber. The report has just come to us that a state of war exists between It and France.

HARRY. What?

CAPTAIN. There is a rumor of war betw Italy and France!

HARRY. Rumors—rumors—everything's r ors! When are we going to *know*?

CAPTAIN. Soon enough, my friend.

DOCTOR. And what of Germany?

CAPTAIN. Germany has mobilized. (IR *pauses to listen.*) But I don't know if any cision has been reached. Nor do I know a thing of the situation anywhere else. Bu God help us—it will be serious enough everyone on this earth. (IRENE *joins* WE *who has sat down at the left.*)

IRENE (*to* WEBER, *and straight at him*). I thought they were all too well prepa Achille. Has there been some mistake so where?

WEBER (*confidentially*). We can only a bute it to spontaneous combustion of dictatorial ego.

IRENE (*grimly*). I can imagine how thril it must be in Paris at this moment. Just 1914. All the lovely soldiers—singin marching! We must go at once to P Achille.

HARRY (*rises*). What's the matter with music, professor? Us young folks wan dance. (ELAINE *and* FRANCINE *come in*

ELAINE. Can we have a drink now, Ha

HARRY. Sure. Sit down. (DON *enters, exu gratification at the sight of this gay, throng. The* ORCHESTRA *starts to play* lencia.")

WEBER. Will you have a drink, Irene?

IRENE. No, thank you.

WEBER. Will you, Captain Locicero?

CAPTAIN. Thank you. Brandy and s Dumptsy.

DUMPTSY. Si, Signor.

BEBE (*yells*). Edna! We're going to ha drink! (EDNA *comes in.*)

WEBER. For me, Cinzano.

ᴘᴛꜱʏ. Oui, Monsieur. (*He goes into the*

ᴏʀ. It is all incredible.

ʏ. Nevertheless, Doctor, I remain an
ᴍist. (*He looks at* ɪʀᴇɴᴇ.) Let doubt
ᴀil throughout this night—with dawn
ᴄome again the light of truth! (*He turns*

to ꜱʜɪʀʟᴇʏ.) Come on, honey—let's dance.
(*They dance.* ᴅᴏɴ *dances with* ʙᴇᴜʟᴀʜ. *The*
ᴏʀᴄʜᴇꜱᴛʀᴀ *continues with its spirited but*
frail performance of "Valencia." *There are*
probably "border incidents" *in Lorraine, the*
Riviera, Poland, Czecho-Slovakia and Mon-
golia.)

ᴄᴜʀᴛᴀɪɴ

ACT TWO

SCENE I

is about 7:30 *in the evening of the same day.*
ᴴe ᴄʜᴇʀʀʏꜱ *are seated, both of them dressed for dinner.* ᴀᴜɢᴜꜱᴛᴇ *is serving them*
ᴛails.

ʀʏ. Thank you.

ᴜꜱᴛᴇ. Thank you, Signor.

ʟʀʏ. Has any more news come through?

ꜱᴛᴇ. No, Signor. They permit the wire-
ᴛo say nothing.

ʟʀʏ. I suppose nothing really will hap-

ꜱᴛᴇ. Let us pray that is so, Signor. (ᴀᴜ-
ᴇ *goes into the bar.* ᴄʜᴇʀʀʏ *leans over*
ᴋisses his wife.)

ʟʀʏ. My sweet . . . you're really very
ʏ.

ᴄʜᴇʀʀʏ. Yes. (*He kisses her again, then*
his glass.)

ʀʏ. Here's to us, darling.

ᴄʜᴇʀʀʏ. And to hell with all the rest.

ʟʀʏ. And to hell with all the rest. (*They*
ᴋ, solemnly.)

ᴄʜᴇʀʀʏ. Jimmy—

ʟʀʏ. What is it, darling?

ᴄʜᴇʀʀʏ. Were you just saying that—or
ᴏu believe it?

ʟʀʏ. That you're lovely? I can give you
ᴍost solemn assurance. . . .

ᴄʜᴇʀʀʏ. No—that nothing is going to
ᴇn.

ᴄʜᴇʀʀʏ. Oh.

ᴍʀꜱ. ᴄʜᴇʀʀʏ. Do you believe that?

ᴄʜᴇʀʀʏ. I know this much: they can't start
any real war without England. And no matter how stupid and blundering our government may be, our people simply won't stand
for it.

ᴍʀꜱ. ᴄʜᴇʀʀʏ. But people can be such complete fools.

ᴄʜᴇʀʀʏ. I know it, darling. Why can't they
all be like us?

ᴍʀꜱ. ᴄʜᴇʀʀʏ. You mean—nice.

ᴄʜᴇʀʀʏ. Yes—nice—and intelligent—and
happy.

ᴍʀꜱ. ᴄʜᴇʀʀʏ. We're very conceited, aren't
we?

ᴄʜᴇʀʀʏ. Of course. And for good and sufficient reason.

ᴍʀꜱ. ᴄʜᴇʀʀʏ. I'm glad we're so superior,
darling. It's comforting. (ʜᴀʀʀʏ *comes in*
from bar.)

ᴄʜᴇʀʀʏ. Oh—good evening, Mr. Van.

ʜᴀʀʀʏ. Good evening. Pardon me— (*He*
starts to go.)

ᴄʜᴇʀʀʏ. Oh—don't run away, Mr. Van.
Let's have some music.

ᴍʀꜱ. ᴄʜᴇʀʀʏ. Won't you have a drink with
ᴜꜱ?

HARRY. No, thanks, Mrs. Cherry—if you don't mind. (*Sits down at the piano.*) I'm afraid I put down too many Scotches this afternoon. As a result of which, I've just had to treat myself to a bicarbonate of soda. (*Starts playing* "Some of these days.")

MRS. CHERRY. I love that.

HARRY. Thanks, pal—always grateful for applause from the discriminating. (*Finishes the chorus and stops.*)

CHERRY. Do play some more.

HARRY. No. The mood isn't right.

MRS. CHERRY. I can't tell you what a relief it is to have you here in this hotel.

HARRY. It's kind of you to say that, Mrs. Cherry. But I don't deserve your handsome tribute. Frequently, I can be an asset to any gathering — contributing humorous anecdotes and bits of homely philosophy. But here and now, I'm far from my best.

CHERRY. You're the only one here who seems to have retained any degree of sanity.

MRS. CHERRY. You and your young ladies.

HARRY. The girls are lucky. They don't know anything. And the trouble with me is that I just don't give a damn.

MRS. CHERRY. We've been trying hard not to know anything—or not to give a damn. But it isn't easy.

HARRY. You haven't been married very long, have you? I hope you don't mind my asking. . . .

CHERRY. We were married the day before yesterday.

HARRY. Let me offer my congratulations.

CHERRY. Thank you very much.

HARRY. It's my purely intuitive hunch that you two ought to get along fine.

CHERRY. That's our intention, Mr. Van.

MRS. CHERRY. And we'll do it, what's more. You see—we have one supreme thing in common:

HARRY. Yeah?

MRS. CHERRY. We're both independent.

CHERRY. We're like you Americans, in that respect.

HARRY. You flatter us.

MRS. CHERRY. Jimmy's a painter.

HARRY. You don't say!

MRS. CHERRY. He's been out in Australia, ing colossal murals for some governm building. He won't show me the ph graphs of them, but I'm sure they're sim awful. (*She laughs fondly.*)

CHERRY. They're allegorical. (*He lau too.*)

HARRY. I'll bet they're good, at that. W do you do, Mrs. Cherry?

MRS. CHERRY. Oh, I work in the gift dep ment at Fortnum's—

HARRY. Behind a counter, eh!

MRS. CHERRY. Yes—wearing a smock, disgracing my family.

HARRY. Well, what d'ye know!

MRS. CHERRY. Both our families hoped w be married in some nice little church, settle down in a nice little cottage, in a little state of decay. But when I heard Jim was on the way home I just dropped ev thing and rushed down here to meet him and we were married, in Florence.

CHERRY. We hadn't seen each other for n ly a year—so, you can imagine, it was rather exciting.

HARRY. I can imagine.

MRS. CHERRY. Florence is the most per place in the world to be married in.

HARRY. I guess that's true of any place.

CHERRY. We both happen to love Italy. —I suppose—we're both rather on the mantic side.

HARRY. You stay on that side, no ma what happens.

MRS. CHERRY (*quickly*). What do you th is going to happen?

HARRY. Me? I haven't the slightest idea

CHERRY. We've looked forward so muc being here with no one bothering us, plenty of winter sports. We're both keen

-ing. And now—we may have to go dash-
: back to England at any moment.

s. CHERRY. It's rotten luck, isn't it?

RRY. Yes, Mrs. Cherry. That's what it is
t's rotten. (QUILLERY *enters from the bar,*
ding a newspaper.) So they wouldn't let
1 cross?

LLERY. No!

RRY. Is there any news?

LLERY (*glaring*). News! Not in this pa-
tic journal! "Unconfirmed rumors"—
m Vienna, London, Berlin, Moscow, To-
). And a lot of confirmed lies from Fascist
dquarters in Rome. (*He slaps the paper
vn and sits.*) If you want to know what
eally happening, ask *him*—up there! (*In-
tes the rooms above.*)

RRY. Who?

LLERY. Weber! The great Monsieur
ille Weber, of the Comité des Forges!
can give you all the war news. Because
made it. You don't know who he is, eh?
what he has been doing here in Italy?
tell you. (*He rises and comes close to
m.*) He has been organizing the arms in-
try. Munitions. To kill French babies.
d English babies. France and Italy are at
. England joins France. Germany joins
y. And that will drag in the Soviet Union
l the Japanese Empire and the United
es. In every part of the world, the good
re of men for peace and decency is un-
mined by the dynamite of jingoism. And
eeds only one spark, set off anywhere
one egomaniac, to send it all up in one
l, fatal explosion. Then love becomes ha-
, courage becomes terror, hope becomes
air. (*The* DOCTOR *appears on the gallery
ve.*) But—it will all be very nice for
ille Weber. Because he is a master of the
real League of Nations—(*The* DOCTOR
ly comes down steps.*) The League of
neider-Creusot, and Krupp, and Skoda,
Vickers and Dupont. The League of
th! And the workers of the world are
ected to pay him for it, with their sweat,
their life's blood.

TOR. Marxian nonsense!

LLERY. Ah! Who speaks?

TOR. *I* speak.

QUILLERY. Yes! The eminent Dr. Hugo Waldersee. A wearer of the sacred swastika.
Down with the Communists! Off with their
heads! So that the world may be safe for
the Nazi murderers.

DOCTOR. So that Germany may be safe from
its oppressors! It is the same with all of you
—Englishmen, Frenchmen, Marxists—you
manage to forget that Germany, too, has a
right to live! (*Rings handbell on the table.*)

QUILLERY. If you love Germany so much,
why aren't you there, now—with your rats?
DOCTOR (*sitting.*) I am not concerned with
politics. (AUGUSTE *enters from the bar.*) I am
a scientist. (*To* AUGUSTE.) Mineral water!
(AUGUSTE *bows and exits into the bar.*)

QUILLERY. That's it, Herr Doctor! A scientist—a servant of humanity! And you know
that if you were in your dear Fatherland,
the Nazis would make you abandon your
cure of cancer. It might benefit too many
people outside of Germany—even maybe
some Jews. They would force you to devote
yourself to breeding malignant bacteria—
millions of little germs, each one trained to
give the Nazi salute and then go out and
poison the enemy. You—a fighter against
disease and death—you would come a Judas
goat in a slaughter house. (DON *has appeared during this.*)

CHERRY. I say, Quillery, old chap—do we
have to have so much blood and sweat just
before dinner?

QUILLERY (*turning on him*). Just before dinner! And now we hear the voice of England!
The great, well-fed, pious hypocrite! The
grabber — the exploiter — the immaculate
butcher! It was *you* forced this war, because
miserable little Italy dared to drag its black
shirt across your trail of Europe. What do
you care if civilization goes to pieces—as
long as you have your dinner—and your
dinner jacket!

CHERRY (*rising*). I'm sorry, Quillery—but I
think we'd better conclude this discussion
out on the terrace.

MRS. CHERRY. Don't be a damned fool, Jimmy. You'll prove nothing by thrashing him.

QUILLERY. It's the Anglo-Saxon method of
proving everything! Very well—I am at your
disposal.

DON. No! I beg of you, Mr. Cherry. We

mustn't have any of that sort of thing. (*He turns to* QUILLERY.) I must ask you to leave. If you're unable to conduct yourself as a gentleman, then . . .

QUILLERY. Don't say any more. Evidently I cannot conduct myself properly! I offer my apologies, Mr. Cherry.

CHERRY. That's quite all right, old man. Have a drink. (*He extends his hand. They shake.*)

QUILLERY. No, thank you. And my apologies to you, Herr Doctor.

DOCTOR. There is no need for apologizing. I am accustomed to all that.

QUILLERY. If I let my speech run away with me, it is because I have hatred for certain things. And you should hate them, too. They are the things that make us blind—and ignorant—and—and dirty. (*He turns and goes out quickly.* DON *goes with him.*)

MRS. CHERRY. He's so right about everything.

CHERRY. I know, poor chap. Will you have another cocktail, darling?

MRS. CHERRY. I don't think so. Will you, Doctor? (*He shakes his head, indicates the mineral water. She rises.*) Let's dine.

CHERRY. It will be a bit difficult to summon up much relish. (*They go out, hand in hand.*)

HARRY. I find them very appealing, don't you, Doctor? (*The* DOCTOR *doesn't announce his findings.*) Did you know they were married only the day before yesterday? Yeah— they got themselves sealed in Florence—because they love Italy. And they came here hoping to spend their honeymoon on skis. . . . Kind of pathetic, isn't it?

DOCTOR. What did you say?

HARRY. Nothing, pal. (DON *comes in.*) Only making conversation.

DOCTOR (*rising*). That Communist! Making me a criminal because I am a German!

DON. I'm dreadfully sorry, Dr. Waldersee. We never should have allowed the ill-bred little cad to come in here.

DOCTOR. Oh— It's no matter. I have heard too many Hymns of Hate before this. To be a German is to be used to insults, and in-

juries. (*He goes out.* DON *starts to go ‹ left.*)

HARRY. Just a minute, Don.

DON. Well?

HARRY. Have you found out yet who t dame is?

DON. What "dame"?

HARRY. That Russian number with Wel

DON. I have not enquired as to her identi

HARRY. But did he register her as his wi

DON. They registered separately! And if not too much to ask, might I suggest t you mind your own damned business?

HARRY. You might suggest just that. An should still be troubled by one of the m tantalizing of questions—namely, "Wh have I seen that face before?" Generally turns out to be someone who was in second row one night, yawning.

DON. I'm sure that such is the case now. (starts again to go.)

HARRY. One moment, Don. There's so thing else.

DON (*impatiently*). What is it?

HARRY. I take it that your job here is so thing like that of a professional greeter

DON. You're at liberty to call it that, if choose.

HARRY. You're a sort of Y.M.C.A. secret —who sees to it that all the guests get gether and have a good time.

DON. Well?

HARRY. Well—do you think you're doin very good job of it right now?

DON (*simply furious*). Have you any sug; tions for improving the performance of duties?

HARRY. Yes, Don—I have.

DON. And I'd very much like to know exactly who the hell do you think you to be offering criticism of my work?

HARRY. Please, please! You needn't scr at me. I'm merely trying to be helpful. making you an offer.

ᴠ. What is it?

ʀʀʏ (*looking around*). I see you've got a
or wheel here. (*Referring to the light.*)

ᴠ. We use it during the supper dance.
ᴛ—if you don't mind, I—

ʀʀʏ. I see—well—how would it be if I
ᴅ the girls put on part of our act here, to-
ʜt? For purposes of wholesome merri-
ᴇnt and relieving the general tension?

ᴠ. What kind of an act is it?

ʀʀʏ. And don't say, "What kind of an
," in that tone of voice. It's good enough
this place. Those girls have played before
King of Rumania. And if some of my
picions are correct—but I won't pursue
t subject. All that need concern you is
t we can adjust ourselves to our audience,
ᴅ to-night we'll omit the bubble dance
ᴅ the number in which little Bebe does a
ᴍmy in a costume composed of detach-
ᴇ gardenias, unless there's a special re-
ᴇst for it.

ᴛ. Do you expect to be paid for this?

ʀʏ. Certainly not. I'm making this offer
of the goodness of my heart. Of course,
ou want to make any appropriate adjust-
ᴛ on our hotel bill . . .

ᴛ. And you'll give me your guarantee that
ᴇ'll be no vulgarity? (ɪʀᴇɴᴇ *appears on*
gallery *and starts to come down. She is*
ᴇring *a dinner dress.*)

ʀʏ. Now be careful, Don. One more
ᴅd like that and the offer is withdrawn . . .
ᴎ *cautions him to silence.*)

. It's a splendid idea, Mr. Van. We'll all
ᴀtly appreciate your little entertainment,
sure. (*To* ɪʀᴇɴᴇ.) Good evening, Ma-
ᴇ.

ᴎᴇ (*with the utmost graciousness*). Good
ᴎing, Mr. Navadel. (*She pauses at the*
ᴅow.) It *is* a lovely view. It's like a land-
ᴇ on the moon.

. Yes—yes. That's exactly what it's like.
ᴇ *comes down.*)

ʀʏ. You understand, we'll have to re-
ᴇse with the orchestra.

ᴅᴏɴ. Oh, yes—Mr. Van. Our staff will be
glad to co-operate in every way. . . . Do sit
down, Madame.

ɪᴋᴇɴᴇ (*sitting*). What became of those
planes that flew off this afternoon? I haven't
heard them come back. (*Takes out a cigarette.*)

ᴅᴏɴ. I imagine they were moving to some
base farther from the frontier. I hope so.
They always made the most appalling racket.
(*Lights her cigarette for her.*)

ʜᴀʀʀʏ. About eleven o'clock? (ᴡᴇʙᴇʀ *appears on the gallery.*)

ᴅᴏɴ. Yes, Mr. Van. Eleven will do nicely.
You'll have a cocktail, Madame? (ʜᴀʀʀʏ
goes into the lobby.)

ɪʀᴇɴᴇ. No, no. Vodka, if you please.

ᴅᴏɴ. I shall have it sent right in. (*He goes
off at the left into bar.* ɪʀᴇɴᴇ *looks slowly off,
after* ʜᴀʀʀʏ. *She smiles slightly.* ᴡᴇʙᴇʀ
*comes down the stairs quickly. He is not in
evening dress. He too pauses at the window.*)

ᴡᴇʙᴇʀ. A perfectly cloudless night! They're
very lucky. (*He comes on down.*)

ɪʀᴇɴᴇ. Did you get your call?

ᴡᴇʙᴇʀ. Yes. I talked to Lanza.

ɪʀᴇɴᴇ. I gather the news is, as usual, good.

ᴡᴇʙᴇʀ. It is extremely serious! You saw
those bombers that left here this afternoon?

ɪʀᴇɴᴇ. Yes.

ᴡᴇʙᴇʀ. They were headed for Paris. Italy is
evidently in a great hurry to deliver the first
blow.

ɪʀᴇɴᴇ. How soon may we leave here?

ᴡᴇʙᴇʀ. None too soon, I can assure you. The
French high command will know that the
bombers come from this field. There will be
reprisals—probably within the next twenty-
four hours.

ɪʀᴇɴᴇ. That will be exciting to see.

ᴡᴇʙᴇʀ. An air raid?

ɪʀᴇɴᴇ. Yes—with bombs bursting in the
snow. Sending up great geysers of diamonds.

WEBER. Or perhaps great geysers of us.

IRENE (*after a moment*). I suppose many people in Paris are being killed now.

WEBER. I'm afraid so. Unless the Italians bungle it.

IRENE. Perhaps your sister—Madame d'Hilaire—perhaps she and her darling little children are now dying.

WEBER (*sharply*). My sister and her family are in Montbeliard.

IRENE. But you said the Italians might bungle it. They might drop their bombs on the wrong place.

WEBER. I appreciate your solicitude, my dear. But you can save your condolences until they are needed. (DUMPTSY *comes in from the bar and serves the vodka.* WEBER *rises.*) I must telegraph to Joseph to have the house ready. It will be rather cold in Biarritz now—but far healthier than Paris. You are going in to dinner now?

IRENE. Yes.

WEBER. I shall join you later. (*He goes out.* DUMPTSY *picks up the* CHERRYS' *glasses.*)

DUMPTSY. We will have a great treat to-night, Madame.

IRENE. Really?

DUMPTSY. That American impresario, that Mr. Harry Van—he will give us an entertainment with his dancing girls.

IRENE. Is he employed here regularly?

DUMPSTY. Oh, no, Madame. He is just passing, like you. This is a special treat. It will be very fine.

IRENE. Let us hope so. (*She downs the vodka.*)

DUMPTSY. Madame is Russian, if I may say so.

IRENE (*pleased*). How did you know that I am Russian? Just because I am having vodka?

DUMPTSY. No, Madame. Many people try to drink vodka. But only true Russians can do it gracefully. You see—I was a prisoner with your people in the war. I liked them.

IRENE. You're very charming. What is yo[ur] name?

DUMPTSY. I am called Dumptsy, Madam[e].

IRENE. Are you going again to the w[ar,] Dumptsy?

DUMPTSY. If they tell me to, Madame.

IRENE. You will enjoy being a soldier?

DUMPTSY. Yes—if I'm taken prisoner so[on] enough.

IRENE. And who do you think will win?

DUMPTSY. I can't think, Madame. It is [a] very doubtful. But one thing I can tell y[ou,] whoever wins, it will be the same as last ti[me] —Austria will lose.

IRENE. They will all lose, Dumptsy. (*T[he]* CHERRYS *come in. She greets them pleasa[nt]ly.*) Good evening.

CHERRY. Good evening, Madame. (*The* CH[ER]RYS *start to sit, across from* IRENE.)

IRENE. Bring some more vodka, Dump[tsy.] Perhaps Mr. and Mrs. Cherry will h[ave] some, too.

CHERRY. Why, thank you—we . . .

MRS. CHERRY. I'd love to. I've never tas[ted] vodka.

IRENE. Ah—then it's high time. Bring in [a] bottle, Dumptsy.

DUMPTSY. Yes, Madame. (*He goes in to [the] bar.*)

IRENE. Come, sit down here. (*The* CHE[RRYS] *sit by her.*) You will find vodka a per[fect] stimulant to the appetite. So much be[tter] than that hybrid atrocity, the Ame[rican] cocktail!

CHERRY. To tell you the truth, Mada[me,] we've already dined.

IRENE. It is no matter. It is just as goo[d as] a liqueur.

MRS. CHERRY. We didn't really dine at all. [We] merely looked at the minestrone and [the] Parmesan cheese—and we felt too depre[ssed] to eat anything.

IRENE. It's the altitude. After the first [wild] hilaration there comes a depressive react[ion.]

ecially for you, who are accustomed to the
vy, Pigwiggian atmosphere of England.

ERRY. Pigwiggian?

NE. Yes, Pigwig—Oliver Twist—you
ow, your Dickens? (DUMPTSY *enters from*
with a bottle of vodka and two more
sses, *which he places on the table. He re-*
ns *to the bar.*)

ERRY. You know England, Madame?

NE (*fondly*). Of course I know England!
governess was a sweet old ogre from
r north country—and when I was a lit-
girl I used to visit often at Sandringham.

ERRY (*impressed*). Sandringham?

s. CHERRY. The palace?

NE. Yes. That was before your time. It
s in the reign of dear, gay King Edward,
l the beautiful Alexandra. (*She sighs a*
le for those days.) I used to have such fun
ying with my cousin David. He used to
to teach me to play cricket, and when I
ldn't swing the bat properly, he said,
h, you Russians will never be civilized!"
ughs.) When I went home to Petersburg
ld my uncle, the Tsar, what David had
l, and he was so amused! But now—you
st drink your vodka. (*They rise, and lift*
ir *glasses.*) A toast! To his most gracious
jesty the King. (*They clink glasses.*) God
ss him.

ERRY. Thank you, Madame. (*All three*
nk *and* MRS. CHERRY *coughs violently.*)

NE (*to* MRS. CHERRY). No—no! Drink it
ht down. Like this. (*She swallows it in a*
p.) So! (*Refills the glasses from the bot-*
) The second glass will go more easily.
hey sit.) I used to laugh so at your funny
tish Tommies in Archangel. They all
ed vodka until one of them thought of
king it with beer.

s. CHERRY. How loathsome!

NE. It was! But I shall be forever grateful
them—those Tommies. They saved my
when I escaped from the Soviets. For
s and nights—I don't know how many—
vas driving through the snow—snow—
w—snow—, in a little sleigh, with the
ly of my father beside me, and the wolves
ning along like an escort of dragoons.

You know—you always think of wolves as
howling constantly, don't you?

CHERRY. Why, yes—I suppose one does.

IRENE. Well, they don't. No, these wolves
didn't howl! They were horribly, confidently
silent. I think silence is much more terrify-
ing, don't you!

CHERRY. You must have been dreadfully
afraid.

IRENE. No, I was not afraid for myself. It
was the thought of my father. . . .

MRS. CHERRY. Please! I know you don't want
to talk about it any more.

IRENE. Oh, no—it is so far away now. I shall
never forget the moment when I came
through the haze of delirium, and saw the
faces of those Tommies. Those simple,
friendly faces. And the snow—and the
wolves—and the terrible cold—they were all
gone—and I was looking at Kew Gardens
on a Sunday afternoon, and the sea of golden
daffodils—"fluttering and dancing in the
breezes." (WEBER *has come in with the daf-*
fodils.)

WEBER. Shall we go in to dinner now, Irene?

IRENE. Yes, yes, Achille. In a minute. I am
coming. (WEBER *goes.* IRENE *rises.*) Now—
we must finish our vodka. (CHERRY *rises.*)
And you must make another try to eat something.

CHERRY. Thank you so much, Madame.
(*They drink.*)

IRENE. And later on, we must all be here for
Mr. Van's entertainment—and we must all
applaud vigorously.

MRS. CHERRY. We shall, Madame.

CHERRY. He's such a nice chap, isn't he?

IRENE (*going*). Yes—and a real artist, too.

CHERRY. Oh—you've seen him?

IRENE. Why—yes—I've seen him, in some
café chantant, somewhere. I forget just
where it was. (*The three of them have gone*
out together. The light is dimmed to extinc-
tion. The curtain falls.)

END OF SCENE ONE

SCENE II

About two hours later.
WEBER *is drinking brandy. The* CAPTAIN *is standing.*

CAPTAIN. I have been listening to the radio. Utter bedlam! Of course, every government has imposed the strictest censorship—but it is very frightening—like one of those films where ghostly hands suddenly reach in and switch off all the lights.

WEBER. Any suggestions of air raids?

CAPTAIN. None. But there is ominous quiet from Paris. Think of it—Paris—utterly silent! Only one station there is sending messages, and they are in code.

WEBER. Probably instructions to the frontier.

CAPTAIN. I heard a man in Prague saying something that sounded interesting, but him I could not understand. Then I turned to London, hopefully, and listened to a gentleman describing the disastrous effects of ivy upon that traditional institution, the oak.

WEBER. Well—we shall soon know. . . . There'll be no trouble about crossing the frontier to-morrow?

CAPTAIN. Oh, no. Except that I am still a little worried about madame's passport.

WEBER. We'll arrange about that. Have a cigar, Captain?

CAPTAIN. Thank you. (IRENE *comes in as the* CAPTAIN *starts to light the cigar.*)

IRENE. Do you hear the sound of airplanes? (*All stop to listen, intently. The sound becomes audible. The* CAPTAIN *shakes out the match, throws the unlit cigar on the table, and dashes to the window and looks upward.*)

CAPTAIN. It is our bombers. One—two—three. Seven of them. Seven out of eighteen. You will excuse me? (*He salutes and dashes out.*)

WEBER. Seven out of eighteen! Not bad, for Italians. (IRENE *has gone to the window to look out.*)

IRENE. I'm so happy for you, Achille.

WEBER. What was that, my dear?

IRENE. I said—I'm so happy for you.

WEBER. But—just why am I an object of congratulation?

IRENE. All this great, wonderful death and destruction, everywhere. And you promote it!

WEBER. Don't give me too much credit, Irene.

IRENE. But I *know* what you've done.

WEBER. Yes, my dear. You know a great deal. But don't forget to do honor to Him—up there—who put fear into man. I am but the humble instrument of His divine will.

IRENE (*looking upward, sympathetically*). Yes—that's quite true. We don't do half enough justice to Him. Poor, lonely old soul. Sitting up in heaven, with nothing to do, but play solitaire. Poor, dear God. Playing Idiot's Delight. The game that never means anything, and never ends.

WEBER. You have an engaging fancy, my dear.

IRENE. Yes.

WEBER. It's the quality in you that fascinates me most. Limitless imagination! It is what has made you such an admirable, brilliant liar. And so very helpful to me! Am I right?

IRENE. Of course you are right, Achille. Had I been bound by any stuffy respect for the truth, I should never have escaped from the Soviets.

WEBER. I'm sure of it.

IRENE. Did I ever tell you of my escape from the Soviets?

WEBER. You have told me about it at least eleven times. And each time it was different.

IRENE. Well, I made several escapes. I am always making escapes, Achille. When I am worrying about you, and your career. I have to run away from the terror of my own thoughts. So I amuse myself by studying the faces of the people I see. Just ordinary

ual, dull people. (*She is speaking in a
e that is sweetly sadistic.*) That young
glish couple, for instance. I was watching
m during dinner, sitting there, close to-
her, holding hands, and rubbing their
es together under the table. And I saw
a in his nice, smart, British uniform,
oting a little pistol at a huge tank. And
tank rolls over him. And his fine strong
ly, that was so full of the capacity for ec-
y, is a mass of mashed flesh and bones—
near of purple blood—like a stepped-on
il. But before the moment of death, he
soles himself by thinking, "Thank God
is safe! She is bearing the child I gave
, and he will live to see a better world."
e walks behind* WEBER *and leans over his
ulder.*) But I know where she is. She is
g in a cellar that has been wrecked by
air raid, and her firm young breasts are
nixed up with the bowels of a dismem-
d policeman, and the embryo from her
nb is splattered against the face of a dead
op. That is the kind of thought with
ch I amuse myself, Achille. And it makes
so proud to think that I am so close to
—who make all this possible. (WEBER
*and walks about the room. At length
urns to her.*)

ER. Do you talk in this whimsical vein
nany people?

E. No. I betray my thoughts to no one
you. You know that I am shut off from
world. I am a contented prisoner in your
y tower.

ER. I'm beginning to wonder about that.

E. What? You think I could interest
elf in some one else—?

ER. No—no, my dear. I am merely won-
ng whether the time has come for you to
commonplace, like all the others?

E. The others?

ER. All those who have shared my life.
ormer wife, for instance. She now boasts
she abandoned me because part of my
ne is derived from the sale of poison
Revolvers and rifles and bullets she
't mind—because they are also used by
smen. Battleships too are permissible;
look so splendid in the news films. But
couldn't stomach poison gas. So now
s married to an anemic Duke, and the

large fortune that she obtained from me enables the Duke to indulge his principal passion, which is the slaughtering of wild animals, like rabbits, and pigeons and rather
small deer. My wife is presumably happy
with him. I have always been glad you are
not a fool as she was, Irene.

IRENE. No. I don't care even for battleships.
And I shall not marry an anemic Duke.

WEBER. But—there was something unpleasantly reminiscent in that gaudy picture you
painted. I gather that this silly young couple
has touched a tender spot, eh?

IRENE. Perhaps, Achille. Perhaps I am soft-
ening.

WEBER. Then apply your intelligence, my
dear. Ask yourself: why shouldn't they die?
And who are the greater criminals—those
who sell the instruments of death, or those
who buy them, and use them? You know
there is no logical reply to that. But all these
little people—like your new friends—all of
them consider me an arch-villain because I
furnish them with what they want, which is
the illusion of power. That is what they vote
for in their frightened governments—what
they cheer for on their national holidays—
what they glorify in their anthems, and their
monuments, and their waving flags! Yes—
they shout bravely about something they call
"national honor." And what does it amount
to? Mistrust of the motives of every one else!
Dog in the manger defense of what they've
got, and greed for the other fellow's possessions! Honor among thieves! I assure you,
Irene—for such little people the deadliest
weapons are the most merciful. (*The* CHER-
RYS *enter. He is whistling* "Minnie the
Moocher.")

IRENE. Ah! Mr. and Mrs. Cherry!

CHERRY. Hello there. (*They come down.*)

IRENE. You have dined well!

MRS. CHERRY. Superbly!

CHERRY. We ate everything—up to and including the zabaglione.

IRENE. You can thank the vodka for that.
Vodka never fails in an emergency.

CHERRY. And we can thank you, Madame,
and do so.

IRENE. But—permit me to introduce Monsieur Weber. (WEBER *rises.*) Mrs. Cherry—Mr. Cherry. (*They are exchanging greetings as* DON *comes in.*)

DON. We're going to have a little cabaret show for you now, Madame.

WEBER. I don't think I shall wait for it, my dear.

IRENE. But you must—

WEBER. I really should look over Lanza's estimates—

IRENE. Please, Achille—Mr. Van is an artist. You will be so amused.

WEBER (*resuming seat*). Very well, Irene.

DON (*his tone blandly confidential*). Between ourselves, I don't vouch for the quality of it. But it may be unintentionally amusing.

IRENE. I shall love it.

CHERRY. This is the most marvellous idea, Mr. Navadel.

DON. Oh, thank you. We try to contrive some novelty each evening. If you'll be good enough to sit here— (DON *goes up to usher in the* ROSSIS *and direct them to their seats. The musicians come in and take their places. The* DOCTOR *comes in.* DUMPTSY *is busily moving chairs about, clearing a space for the act.* IRENE *and the* CHERRYS *chat pleasantly.* ANNA, *the maid, appears on the gallery above to watch the entertainment.*) (HARRY *comes in. He is wearing a tight-fitting dinner jacket, and carries a cane and a straw hat.*)

HARRY. All set, Don?

DON. Quite ready, whenever you are.

HARRY. Okey-doke. Give us a fanfare, professor. (*He goes out. The band obliges with a fanfare.* HARRY *returns, all smiles.*) Before we start, folks, I just want to explain that we haven't had much chance to rehearse with my good friend, Signor Palota, and his talented little team here. (*He indicates the orchestra with a handsome gesture.*) So we must crave your indulgence and beg you to give us a break if the rhythm isn't all kosher. (*He waits for his laugh.*) All we ask of you, kind friends, is "The Christian pearl of Charity," to quote our great American poet, John Greenleaf Whittier. We thank you. Take it away! (*He bows. All applaud. He*

then sings a song—*The girls come on in c tume and dance.*)

(*During the latter part of the act, the* C TAIN, *the* MAJOR, *and four flying corps of* CERS *come in. The latter are dirty and i fever of heroically restrained exciteme They survey the scene with wonderment a then with delight, saying, in Italian, "Wh all this?" and "What brought these blon bambinos to Monte Gabriele?" etc.* HARRY *terrupts the act and orders the orchestra play the Fascist anthem, "Giovinezza." T officers acknowledge this graceful gestu with the Fascist salute. The* GIRLS *wave ba The* CAPTAIN *gets the* OFFICERS *seated a then goes to order drinks.* HARRY *and* GIRLS *resume.*)

(*At the end of the act, all applaud and* OFFICERS *shout "Brava—Bravissima" a stamp their feet with enthusiasm. The* GI *take several bows and go.* HARRY *returns a solo bow, waving his straw hat. One of* OFFICERS *shouts, in Italian, "We want young ladies!"*)

CAPTAIN (*to* HARRY). My friends wish know respectfully if the young ladies care to join them in a little drink?

HARRY. Certainly! Come back in, girls. over there and join the army! (*The* GIRLS so.) Now, folks—with your kind permiss —I shall give the girls an interlude of and refreshment and treat you to a li piano specialty of my own. Your strict att tion is not obligatory. (*He starts his spec ty, assisted by* SHIRLEY *and* EDNA. *The* o CERS *don't pay much attention. Bottles champagne are brought for them and GIRLS.*)

(WEBER *goes and speaks to the* CAPTAIN. *beckons him up to the landing of the st where they converse in low tones, the* TAIN *telling him about the air-raid.*)

(HARRY's *act is interrupted by the entr of* QUILLERY.)

QUILLERY (*to* HARRY). Do you know w has happened?

DON. I told you we didn't want you her

PITTALUGA. We're having an entertainm here.

QUILLER. Yes! An entertainment!

HARRY. If you'll just sit down, pal. . . . *and the* GIRLS *continue with their singi*

ILLERY. An entertainment—while Paris is ruins!

ERRY (*rises*). What?

CTOR. What are you saying?

ILLERY. They have bombed Paris! The scisti have bombed Paris!

N. What? But it can't be possible—

RRY. Go on, Shirley. Keep on singing.

ILLERY. I tell you—to-night their planes w over and—

ERRY. But how do you know this?

ILLERY. It is on the wireless—everywhere. d I have just talked to one of their me nics, who was on the flight, and saw, th his own eyes—

RRY. Won't you please sit down, pal? e're trying to give you a little entertain nt— (*Stops playing.*)

ILLERY. For the love of God—listen to me! hile you sit here eating and drinking, to ht, Italian planes dropped twenty thou d kilos of bombs on Paris. God knows w many they killed. God knows how ch of life and beauty is forever destroyed! d you sit here, drinking, laughing, with m—the murderers. (*Points to the flyers, o ask each other, in Italian, what the hell he talking about.*) They did it! It was ir planes, from that field down there. ssins! (*The* OFFICERS *make a move to d* QUILLERY—*one of them arming himself h a champagne bottle.*)

RRY (*comes down from the piano*). We 't have any skull-cracking in this club. y, Captain, speak to your men before any ng starts. (*The* CAPTAIN *comes down to* OFFICERS *and pacifies them.* CHERRY nes down to stand by QUILLERY.)

s. CHERRY. Jimmy! . . . You keep out of !

OR *and* FIRST *and* THIRD OFFICERS (*jump* . Assassini!

RRY. Now listen, pal. . . .

RLEY. Harry! Don't get yourself mixed in this mess!

LLERY. You see, we stand together! nce—England—America! Allies!

HARRY. Shut up, France! It's O.K., Captain. We can handle this—

QUILLERY. They don't dare fight against the power of England and France! The free democracies against the Fascist tyranny!

HARRY. Now, for God's sake stop fluctuating!

QUILLERY. England and France are fighting for the hopes of mankind!

HARRY. A minute ago, England was a butcher in a dress suit. Now we're Allies!

QUILLERY. We stand together. We stand together forever. (*Turns to* OFFICERS.) I say God damn you. God damn the villains that sent you on this errand of death.

CAPTAIN (*takes a few steps toward* QUILLERY). If you don't close your mouth, Frenchman, we shall be forced to arrest you.

QUILLERY. Go on, Fascisti! Commit national suicide. That's the last gesture left to you toy soldiers.

HARRY. It's all right, Captain. Mr. Quillery is for peace. He's going back to France to stop the war.

QUILLERY (*turns on* HARRY). You're not authorized to speak for me. I am competent to say what I feel. And what I say is "Down with Fascism! Abbasso Fascismo!" (*There is an uproar from the* OFFICERS.)

CAPTAIN (*ordinarily gentle, is now white hot with rage*). Attenzione!

QUILLERY. Vive la France! Viv—

CAPTAIN. E agli arresti.

QUILLERY. Call out the firing squad! Shoot me dead! But do not think you can silence the truth that's in me.

CAPTAIN (*grabs* QUILLERY *from the left and calls the* FIRST OFFICER). Molinari! (FIRST OFFICER *grabs* QUILLERY *from the right. They start to take him out.*)

QUILLERY (*as he is being led out*). The Empire of the Fascisti will join the Empire of the Cæsars in smoking ruins. Vive la France! Vive la France! (WEBER *goes upstairs and exits. They have gone.*)

CHERRY (*to* HARRY). You'd better carry on with your turn, old boy.

HARRY. No, pal. The act is cold. (*To the orchestra leader.*) Give us some music, Signor. (*The orchestra starts playing.*) Let dancing become general.

CHERRY. Let's dance, my sweet.

MRS. CHERRY. I can't bear to, Jimmy.

CHERRY. I think we should.

MRS. CHERRY. Very well, darling. (*They dance. The* OFFICERS *dance with the* GIRLS.)

HARRY (*goes over to* IRENE). Would y[ou] care to dance?

IRENE. Why—why, thank you. (*She star[ts] up, and they join the slowly moving m[ass.]*)

SHIRLEY *is singing as loud as she can. T[he] color wheel turns so that the dancers [are] bathed in blue, then amber, then red.*)

CURTAIN

END OF SCENE TWO

SCENE III

Later that night.
IRENE *and* HARRY *are alone. She is sitting, telling the story of her life. He is listening w[ith] fascination and doubt.*

IRENE. My father was old. The hardships of that terrible journey had broken his body. But his spirit was strong—the spirit that is Russia. He lay there, in that little boat, and he looked up at me. Never can I forget his face, so thin, so white, so beautiful, in the starlight. And he said to me, "Irene—little daughter," and then—he died. For four days I was alone, with his body, sailing through the storms of the Black Sea. I had no food—no water—I was in agony from the bayonet wounds of the Bolsheviki. I knew I must die. But then—an American cruiser rescued me. May God bless those good men! (*She sighs.*) I've talked too much about myself. What about you, my friend?

HARRY. Oh—I'm not very interesting. I'm just what I seem to be.

IRENE. C'est impossible!

HARRY. C'est possible! The facts of my case are eloquent. I'm a potential genius—reduced to piloting six blondes through the Balkans.

IRENE. But there is something that you hide from the world—even, I suspect, from yourself. Where did you acquire your superior education?

HARRY. I worked my way through college selling encyclopædias.

IRENE. I knew you had culture! What college was it?

HARRY. Oh—just any college. But my s[ales] talk was so good that I fell for it mysel[f. I] bought the God-damned encyclopædia. A[nd] I read it all, travelling around, in d[ay] coaches, and depot hotels, and Fox-t[rot] dressing rooms. It was worth the money.

IRENE. And how much of all this have y[ou] retained?

HARRY (*significantly*). I? I—never fo[rget] anything.

IRENE. How unfortunate for you! Does y[our] encyclopædia help you in your dealings w[ith] the girls?

HARRY. Yes, Mrs. Weber. . . . I got consi[der] able benefit from studying the lives of [the] great courtesans, and getting to underst[and] their technique. . . .

IRENE. Forgive me for interrupting you— that is not my name.

HARRY. Oh—pardon me; I thought . . .

IRENE. I know what you thought. Mons[ieur] Weber and I are associated in a sort [of] business way.

HARRY. I see.

IRENE. He does me the honor to consult [me] in matters of policy.

HARRY. That's quite an honor! Busine[ss] pretty good, isn't it!

NE. I gather that you are one of those
le souls who does not entirely approve
he munitions industry?

RY. Oh, no—I'm not noble. Your friend
ust another salesman. And I make it a
nt never to criticize anybody else's racket.

NE. Monsieur Weber is a very distin-
shed man. He has rendered very distin-
shed services to all the governments of
world. He is decorated with the Legion
Ionor, the Order of the White Eagle, the
ler of St. James of the Sword, and the
itary Order of Christ!

RY. The Military Order of Christ. I never
rd of that one.

NE. It is from Portugal. He has many or-
s.

RY. Have you ever been in America?

NE. Oh, yes—I've seen it all—New York,
shington, Palm Beach . . .

RY. I said America. Have you ever been
he West?

NE. Certainly I have. I flew across your
tinent. There are many White Russians
California.

RY. Did you ever happen to make any
chute landings in any places like Kan-
or Iowa, or Nebraska?

NE (laughing). I have seen enough of
r countrymen to know that you are typi-

RY. Me? I'm not typical of anything.

NE. Oh, yes, you are. You are just like
of them—an ingenuous, sentimental
list. You believe in the goodness of hu-
n nature, don't you?

RY. And what if I do? I've known mil-
s of people, intimately—and I never
nd more than one out of a hundred that
dn't like, once you got to know them.

NE. That is very charming—but it is
ve.

RY. Maybe so. But experience prevents
from working up much enthusiasm over
one who considers the human race as
so many clay pigeons, even if he does
ong to the Military Order of Christ.

IRENE. If you came from an older culture,
you would realize that men like Monsieur
Weber are necessary to civilization.

HARRY. You don't say.

IRENE. I mean, of course, the sort of civilization that we have got. (*She smiles upon him
benevolently. It is as though she were explaining patiently but with secret enjoyment
the facts of life to a backward nephew.*)
Stupid people consider him an arch-villain
because it is his duty to stir up a little trouble
here and there to stimulate the sale of his
products. Do you understand me, my friend?

HARRY. I shouldn't wonder.

IRENE. Monsieur Weber is a true man of the
world. He is above petty nationalism; he
can be a Frenchman in France—a German
in Germany—a Greek—a Turk—whatever
the occasion demands.

HARRY. Yes—that little Quillery was an In-
ternationalist, too. He believed in brother-
hood, but the moment he got a whiff of
gunpowder he began to spout hate and revenge. And now those nice, polite Wops
will probably have to shut him up with a
firing squad.

IRENE (*takes out a cigarette from her case*).
It is a painful necessity.

HARRY. And it demonstrates the sort of little
trouble that your friend stirs up. (*He takes
out his lighter and lights her cigarette.*)

IRENE. Do you know that you can be extremely rude?

HARRY. I'm sorry if I've hurt your feelings
about Mr. Weber, but he just happens to
be a specimen of the one per cent that I *don't*
like.

IRENE. I was not referring to that. Why do
you stare at me so?

HARRY. Have I been staring?

IRENE. Steadily. Ever since we arrived here
this afternoon. Why do you do it?

HARRY. I've been thinking I could notice a
funny resemblance to some one I used to
know.

IRENE. You should know better than to tell
any woman that she resembles somebody
else. We none of us like to think that our
appearance is commonplace.

HARRY. The one you look like wasn't commonplace.

IRENE. Oh! She was some one near and dear to you?

HARRY. It was somebody that occupies a unique shrine in the temple of my memory.

IRENE. That *is* a glowing tribute. The temple of your memory must be so crowded! But I am keeping you from your duties.

HARRY. What duties?

IRENE. Shouldn't you be worrying about your young ladies?

HARRY. They're all right; they've gone to bed.

IRENE. Yes—but there are several Italian officers about. Aren't you supposed to be the chaperone?

HARRY. I leave the girls to their own resources, of which they have plenty. (*He stares hard at her.*) Have you always been a blonde?

IRENE. Yes—as far as I can remember.

HARRY. You don't mind my asking?

IRENE. Not at all. And now, may I ask you something?

HARRY. Please do so.

IRENE. Why do you waste yourself in this degraded work? Touring about with those obvious little harlots?

HARRY. You mean you think I'm fitted for something that requires a little more mentality?

IRENE. Yes.

HARRY. How do you know so much about me? (*It should be remembered that all through this scene HARRY is studying her, trying to fit together the pieces of the jigsaw puzzle of his memory.*)

IRENE. For one thing, I saw your performance to-night.

HARRY. You thought it was punk?

IRENE. I thought it was unworthy.

HARRY. It was unfortunately interrupted. You should have seen . . .

IRENE. I saw enough. You are a very b dancer.

HARRY. The King of Rumania thought I v pretty good.

IRENE. He is entitled to his opinion—and mine.

HARRY. I'll admit that I've done better thi in my time. Would it surprise you to kn that I was once with a mind-reading act?

IRENE. Really?

HARRY. Yeah.

IRENE. Now you're staring at me again.

HARRY. Have you ever been in Omaha?

IRENE. Omaha? Where is that? Persia?

HARRY. No. Nebraska. That's one of states. I played there once with the grea act of my career. I was a stooge for Zule the Mind Reader. At least she called me stooge. But I was the one who had to do the brain work.

IRENE. And she read people's minds?

HARRY. I did it for her. I passed through audience and fed her the cues. We w sensational, playing the finest picture ho in all the key cities. Zuleika sat up on stage, blindfolded—and usually blind dru

IRENE. Oh, dear. And was *she* the one t I resemble?

HARRY. No! There was another act on same bill. A troupe of Russians . . .

IRENE. Russians?

HARRY. Singers, mandolin players, and sc dancers. One of them was a red-headed g She was fascinated by our act, and she k pestering me to teach her the code. She s she could do it better than Zuleika.

IRENE. Those poor Russians. There are many of them all over the world. Anc many of them completely counterfeit!

HARRY. This dame was counterfeit all ri In fact, she was the God-damnedest li ever saw. She lied just for the sheer arti of it. She kept after me so much that I her finally to come up to my hotel room night, and we'd talk it over.

IRENE. I hope you didn't tell her the co

HARRY. No. After the week in Omaha the
ll split. The Russians went to Sioux Falls
d we went on the Interstate Time. I played
ith Zuleika for another year and then the
ink got her and she couldn't retain. So the
t busted up. I've always hoped I'd catch
with that red-headed Russian again some-
me. She might have been good. She had
e voice for it, and a kind of overtone of
ystery.

IRENE. It's a characteristic Gypsy quality.
d you never saw her again?

HARRY. No.

IRENE. Perhaps it is just as well. She couldn't
ve been so clever—being duped so easily
o going to your room.

HARRY. She wasn't being duped! She knew
at she was doing. If there was any duping
ing on, she was the one that did it.

IRENE. She *did* make an impression!

HARRY (*looking straight at her*). I was crazy
out her. She was womanhood at its most
irable—and most unreliable.

IRENE. And you such a connoisseur. But—it's
ting late.

HARRY (*rises*). Do you know any Russian
sic? (*He crosses to the piano.*)

IRENE (*rises*). Oh, yes. When I was a little
my father used to engage Chaliapin to
e often to our house. He taught me
ny songs.

HARRY. Chaliapin, eh? Your father spared no
ense. (*He sits at the piano.*)

IRENE. That was in *old* Russia. (*He plays a
bars of "Kak Stranna."*) Kak Stranna!

HARRY. Yeah! How strange! (*He starts to
"Prostchai."*) Do you know this one?
IRENE *sings some of it in Russian.*) How do
spell that name—Irene?

IRENE. I-R-E-N-E. (HARRY *pounds the piano
jumps up.*) What's the matter?

HARRY. That's it! Irene! (*He pronounces it
EN.*)

IRENE. But what—?

HARRY. I knew it! You're the one!

IRENE. What one?

HARRY. That red-headed liar! Irene! I knew
I could never be mistaken. . . .

IRENE. Irene is a very usual name in Russia.
(*She laughs heartily.*)

HARRY. I don't care how usual it is. Everything fits together perfectly now. The name
—the face—the voice—Chaliapin for a teacher! Certainly it's you! And it's no good shaking your head and looking amazed! No matter how much you may lie, you can't deny
the fact that you slept with me in the Governor Bryan Hotel in Omaha in the fall of
1925. (IRENE *laughs heartily again.*) All
right—go ahead and laugh. That blonde
hair had me fooled for a while—but now
I know it's just as phoney as the bayonet
wounds, and the parachute jumps into the
jungle. . . .

IRENE (*still laughing*). Oh—you amuse me.

HARRY. It's a pleasure to be entertaining.
But you can't get away with it.

IRENE. You amuse me very much indeed.
Here we are—on a mountain peak in Bedlam. To-night, the Italians are bombing
Paris. At this moment, the French may be
bombing Rome, and the English bombing
Germany—and the Soviets bombing Tokyo,
and all you worry about is whether I am a
girl you once met casually in Omaha.

HARRY. Did I say it was casual?

IRENE (*laughing*). Oh—it *is* amusing!

HARRY (*angrily*). I know you're amused. I
admit it's all very funny. I've admitted
everything. I told you I was crazy about you.
Now when are you going to give me a break
and tell me—

IRENE. You! You are so troubled—so—so uncertain about everything.

HARRY. I'm not uncertain about it any more,
Babe. I had you tagged from the start.
There was something about you that was in-
delible . . . something I couldn't forget all
these years. (WEBER *appears on the gallery,
wearing his Sulka dressing gown.*)

WEBER. Forgive me for intruding, my dear.
But I suggest that it's time for you to go
to bed.

IRENE. Yes, Achille. At once. (WEBER *treats
HARRY to a rather disparaging glance and*

exits. IRENE *starts upstairs*.) Poor Achille! He suffers with the most dreadful insomnia —it is something on his mind. (*She goes up a few more steps*.) He is like Macbeth. Good night, my friend—my funny friend.

HARRY. Good night.

IRENE. And thank you for making me laugh so much—to-night.

HARRY. I could still teach you that code.

IRENE. Perhaps—we shall meet again in—what was the name of the hotel?

HARRY. It was the Governor Bryan.

IRENE. Oh, yes! The Governor Bryan! (*Laughing heartily, she exits.* HARRY *goes to the piano, sits down and starts to play* "Kak Stranna." DUMPTSY *enters from the bar*.)

DUMPSTY. That was wonderful—that sing ing and dancing.

HARRY (*still playing*). Thanks, pal. Glad yc enjoyed it.

DUMPTSY. Oh, yes, Mr. Van—that was goo

HARRY (*bangs a chord*). Chaliapin—f God's *sake*!

DUMPSTY. I beg your pardon, sir?

HARRY (*rises*). It's nothing. Good nig Dumptsy. (*He goes out into the lobby.*)

DUMPTSY. Good night, sir. (*He starts for t bar*.)

CURTAIN

ACT THREE

The following afternoon.

HARRY *is at the piano, idly playing the "Caprice Viennoise," or something similar. F thoughts are elsewhere.*

SHIRLEY *is darning some stockings and humming the tune.* BEBE *is plucking her e brows.*

BEULAH, ELAINE, FRANCINE *and* EDNA *are seated at a table.* BEULAH *is telling* ELAIN *fortune with cards. The others are watching. All are intensely serious, and all chewing gu*

SHIRLEY. What's that number, Harry?

HARRY. The "Caprice Viennoise"—Kreisler.

SHIRLEY. It's pretty.

HARRY. You think so? (*He shifts to something jazzier*.)

BEULAH. You are going to marry.

ELAINE. Again?

BEULAH. The cards indicate dis*tinctly* two marriages, and maybe a third.

ELAINE (*chewing furiously*). For *God's* sake!

SHIRLEY (*to* HARRY). We certainly need some new stockings.

HARRY. We'll renovate the wardrobe in Geneva.

BEULAH. Now—let's see what the fates tell us next.

BEBE. Say, Harry—when do we lam it of here?

HARRY. Ask Beulah. Maybe she can get it of the cards.

BEBE. I hate this place. It's spooky.

BEULAH (*to* HARRY). What'd you say, hon

ELAINE. Ah—don't pay any attention him. What else do they say about me?

BEULAH. Well . . . you'll enter upon a per of very poor health.

ELAINE. When?

BEULAH. Along about your thirty-seve year.

SHIRLEY. That means any day now. (*winks broadly at* BEBE, *who laughs*.)

HARRY (*vehemently*). Listen to me, nymphs! We can't be wasting our time card tricks. We've got to do a little rehe ing.

SHIRLEY. Why, Harry—what are you mad about now?

HARRY. Who said I was mad about anything?

SHIRLEY. Well—every time you get yourself into a peeve, you take it out on us. You start in hollering, "Listen, girls—we got to rehearse."

HARRY. I am not peeved. Merely a little disgusted. The act needs brushing up.

BEBE. Honestly, Harry—don't you think we know the routine by now?

HARRY. I'm not saying you don't know it. I'm just saying that your performance last night grieved me and shocked me. You had your eyes on those officers and not on your work. That kind of attitude went big in Rumania, but now we're going to a town where artistry counts. Some day, I'll take the whole bunch of you to watch the Russian ballet, just to give you an idea of what dancing is. (CAPTAIN LOCICERO comes in.)

CAPTAIN. Your pardon, Mr. Van.

HARRY. Ah, Captain. Good afternoon. . . . Rest, girls.

CAPTAIN (to the GIRLS). Good afternoon.

GIRLS. Good afternoon, Captain.

HARRY. You bring us news?

CAPTAIN. Good news, I hope. May I have your passports?

HARRY. Certainly. (He gets them out of his coat and hands them to the CAPTAIN.)

CAPTAIN. Thank you. I hope to have definite word for you very shortly. (He salutes and starts to go.)

HARRY. What about Mr. Quillery, Captain? What's happened to him?

CAPTAIN. Mr. Quillery was very injudicious. Very injudicious. I am glad that you are so much more intelligent. (He goes out.)

SHIRLEY. I don't think they could have done anything cruel to him. They're awfully sweet, those Wops.

HARRY. So I observed. . . . Now listen to me, girls. Geneva's a key spot, and we've got to be good. Your audiences there won't be a lot of hunkies, who don't care what you do as long as you don't wear practically any pants. These people are accustomed to the best. They're mains—big people, like prime ministers, and maharajahs and archbishops. If we click with them, we'll be set for London and Paris. We may even make enough money to get us home.

BEBE. Oh—don't speak of such a thing! Home!

EDNA. To get a real decent henna wash again!

HARRY. The trouble with all of you is, you're thinking too much about your own specialties. You're trying to steal the act, and wreck it. Remember what the late Knute Rockne said: "Somebody else can have the all-star, all-American aggregations. All *I* want is a team!" Now, you—Beulah. You've got plenty of chance to score individually in the bubble number. But when we're doing the chorus routine, you've got to submerge your genius in the mass.

BEULAH. What do I do wrong, honey?

HARRY. Your Maxie Ford is lacklustre. Here —I'll show you. . . . (HARRY gets up to demonstrate the Maxie Ford.)

SHIRLEY (laughs). If you do it that way, Beulah, you'll go flat on your face. Here— I'll show you.

HARRY. Just a minute, Miss Laughlin. Who's the director of this act, you or me?

SHIRLEY (amiably). You are, you old poop. But you just don't know the steps.

ELAINE. Don't let her get fresh, Harry.

BEBE. Slap her down!

SHIRLEY. Give us the music, Harry.

BEULAH. Please, Harry. Shirley just wants to be helpful.

HARRY. I feel I should resent this—but— (He returns to the piano.) Go ahead, Miss Laughlin. Carry on. (He plays. SHIRLEY demonstrates. BEULAH tries it.)

BEULAH. Have I got it right?

SHIRLEY. Sure! He's just shooting his face off! (During this, the following conversation goes on:)

ELAINE. You know that Wop that was giving me a play last night?

FRANCINE. You mean the one with the bent nose?

BEBE. I thought he was terrible. But that boy I had is a Count.

ELAINE. Well, look what he gave me.

EDNA. What is it?

BEBE. Let me see it.

ELAINE. I don't know what it is.

BEBE. Looks like money. What kind of money is that, Harry?

HARRY. It's an old Roman coin.

SHIRLEY. How much is it worth?

HARRY. I haven't looked up the latest rate of exchange on dinars. But I think, dear, you've been betrayed. Now, pay attention, girls. . . . As I said, we've got to improve the act, and with that in view, I'm going to retire from all the dance routine.

BEBE. What?

BEULAH. Why, *Harry*—we couldn't. . . .

SHIRLEY. Oh! I hurt you, didn't I! (*She rushes to him, coos over him.*) Yes, I did, you poor baby. I hurt his feelings—and I'm sorry—I'm very, very sorry.

HARRY. All right, Shirley. We can dispense with the regrets. Save your lipstick. (*He thrusts her away.*)

SHIRLEY. But why . . . ?

HARRY. I've decided that I'm a thinker, rather than a performer. From now on, I shall devote myself to the purely creative end of the act, and, of course, the negotiation of contracts.

BEULAH. But when did you make up your mind to this, honey?

HARRY. I've been considering it for a long time.

SHIRLEY. Say! What were you talking about to that Russian dame?

HARRY. We discussed world politics.

FRANCINE. Oh!

SHIRLEY. And how are politics these days?

BEBE. Did you get anywheres near to fir base, Harry?

HARRY. I find it impossible to explain certa things to you girls. You're children of n ture.

SHIRLEY. We're *what*?

BEULAH. He means we're natural.

HARRY. Never mind, sweetheart. You'll si the number, Shirley.

SHIRLEY. Me?

BEBE. With that terrible voice?

HARRY. She handled it fine that time I h bronchitis in Belgrade. And with a little hearsal, you'll have the whole League Nations rooting for you. Now—let's have (*He plays,* SHIRLEY *sings,* BEBE *disapprove* (DON *comes in, dressed for travelling.*)

DON. Captain Locicero has got the orders let us through and the train is due to le about four o'clock. What a relief to be of this foul place!

HARRY. You going too, Don?

DON. Yes. There's nothing for me here. fact, I'm sick and tired of Europe as a wh I was in town this morning when they s Quillery.

BEBE. Who?

SHIRLEY. It was that little guy that baw out the Wops.

BEULAH. They *shot* him? Why did they h to do that?

DON. Of course, he asked for it. But even it's pretty sickening to see one of your low human beings crumpled up in horri violent death. Well—there'll be plenty m like him, and right here, too. The Fre know all about this air base, and they'l over any minute with their bombs. So— California here I come!

HARRY. And run right into the Japs? B stop off at Wichita.

DON. I'll see you all on the train. (*He up the stairs.*)

HARRY. You girls go get yourselves re (*The* CHERRYS *appear on the gallery. speaks to them, then goes out. The* CHE *come down.*)

INE. O.K., Harry.

A (*going*). I'm surprised at those Wops.
ey seemed like such sweet boys.

E. Sure—when they talk they sound like
ra. But they're awful excitable. (BEBE,
INE, EDNA and FRANCINE *have gone out.*)

LAH. But I can't understand—why did
y have to shoot that poor boy?

RY. It's hard to explain, Beulah. But it
ns there's some kind of argument going
over here, and the only way they can
e it is by murdering a lot of people.

E. You don't need to tell *me* what it's
. I was in the Club Grotto the night the
ple Gang shot it out with the G's. And
that terrible! Blood all over everything!
e and SHIRLEY and BEULAH *have gone*
)

RY. You heard what they did to Quillery?

RRY. Yes. It seems that he died like a
patriot, shouting "Vive La France."

RY. Better if he died like a man—sticking
vhat he knew was right.

RRY. He was a nice little chap.

. CHERRY. The Italians are swine! (DON
pears on the balcony and comes down.)

RRY. Oh, they had a perfect right to do it.

. CHERRY. But to kill a man for saying
t he thinks!

RRY. Many people will be killed for less
a that.

RY. I'll have to be saying good-bye pretty
. Did you say the train goes at four,
?

, Four o'clock. Correct! (*He goes.*)

RY. I hope all this unpleasantness won't
your winter sports.

RRY. Oh, that's all washed up. We're go-
too—if they'll let us cross the border.

RY. So the honeymoon has ended al-
y?

CHERRY. Yes—I suppose so.

RRY. England is coming into this busi-
. We have to stand by France, of course.
so there's nothing for it but . . .

MRS. CHERRY. And so Jimmy will have to
do his bit, manning the guns, for civilization. Perhaps he'll join in the bombardment
of Florence, where we were married.

CHERRY. You know—after the ceremony we
went into the Baptistery and prayed to the
soul of Leonardo da Vinci that we might
never fail in our devotion to that which is
beautiful and true. I told you we were a
bit on the romantic side. We forgot what
Leonardo said about war. Bestial frenzy, he
called it. And bestial frenzy it is.

MRS. CHERRY. But we mustn't think about
that now. We have to stand by France. We
have to make the world a decent place for
heroes to live in. Oh, Christ! (*She starts to
sob.* CHERRY *rushes to her.*)

CHERRY. Now, now, darling. We've got to
make a pretense of being sporting about it.
Please, darling. Don't cry.

HARRY. Let her cry, the poor kid. Let her
sob her heart out—for all the God-damned
good it will do her. You know what I often
think? (*He is trying to be tactful.*) I often
think we ought to get together and elect
somebody else God. Me, for instance. I'll bet
I'd do a much better job.

MRS. CHERRY. You'd be fine, Mr. Van.

HARRY. I believe I would. There'd be a lot of
people who would object to my methods.
That Mr. Weber, for instance. I'd certainly
begin my administration by beating the can
off him.

CHERRY. Let's start the campaign now! Vote
for good old Harry Van, and his Six Angels!
(*The* CAPTAIN *comes in with a brief-case full
of papers and passports. He takes these out
and puts them on a table.*)

CAPTAIN. Good afternoon, Mrs. Cherry. Gentlemen.

HARRY. Do we get across?

CAPTAIN. Here is your passport, Mr. Van—
and the young ladies, with my compliments.
They have been duly stamped. (*He hands
them over.*)

HARRY. Thanks, Captain. And how about
Mr. Weber and his—friend? Are they going,
too?

CAPTAIN. I have their passports here. I advise
you to make ready, Mr. Van. The train will
leave in about forty-five minutes.

HARRY. O.K., Captain. See you later, Mr. and Mrs. Cherry. (*He goes.*)

CHERRY. O.K., Harry.

MRS. CHERRY. And what about us, Captain?

CAPTAIN. Due to a slight technicality, you will be permitted to cross the frontier. Here are your passports.

CHERRY. I can't tell you how grateful we are. (WEBER *appears on the gallery.*)

CAPTAIN. You needn't be grateful to me, Mr. Cherry. The fact that you are allowed to pass is due to the superb centralization of authority in my country. The telegram authorizing your release was filed at 11:43 today, just seventeen minutes before a state of war was declared between Great Britain and Italy. I must obey the order of Rome, even though I know it's out of date. Is your luggage ready?

CHERRY. It's all out here in the hall. We're off now, Captain. Well, good-bye and good luck!

CAPTAIN. And good luck to you—both of you.

CHERRY. I need hardly say that I'm sorry about all this. It's really a damned rotten shame.

CAPTAIN. It is. All of that. Good-bye, my friend. (*He extends his hand and* CHERRY *shakes it.*) Madame. . . . (*He extends his hand to* MRS. CHERRY.)

MRS. CHERRY. Don't call *me* your friend, because I say what Quillery said—damn you —damn your whole country of mad dogs for having started this horror.

CAPTAIN (*bows*). It is not my fault, Mrs. Cherry.

CHERRY. It's utterly unfair to talk that way, darling. The Captain is doing his miserable duty as decently as he possibly can.

CAPTAIN (*tactfully*). In this unhappy situation, we are all in danger of losing our heads.

MRS. CHERRY. I know . . . I know. Forgive me for the outburst. (*She extends her hand to the* CAPTAIN *and they shake.*) I should have remembered that it's everybody's fault.

CHERRY. That's right, my sweet. Come along. (*They go out.*)

CAPTAIN (*to* WEBER). Frankly, my he bleeds for them.

WEBER. They're young. They'll live throu it, and be happy.

CAPTAIN. Will they? I was their age, and their situation, twenty years ago, when I w sent to the Isonzo front. And people s. just that to me: "Never mind, you are you —and youth will survive and come to umph." And I believed it. That is why couldn't say such deceiving words to th now.

WEBER. The cultivation of hope never d any immediate harm. Is everything in ord

CAPTAIN (*rises*). Quite, Monsieur Web Here it is. (*He hands over* WEBER's p port.)

WEBER. And Madame's? (*The* CAPTAIN pi up a document on foolscap.*)

CAPTAIN. This is an unusual kind of passp It has given us some worry.

WEBER. The League of Nations issues do ments like that to those whose nationality uncertain.

CAPTAIN. I understand—but the attitude Italy toward the League of Nations is no the moment cordial.

WEBER. Then you refuse to honor Madan passport?

CAPTAIN. My instructions are to accord every consideration, Monsieur Weber. view of the fact that Madame is travell with you, I shall be glad to approve her v

WEBER. Madame is not travelling with She has her own passport.

CAPTAIN. But it is understood that you vo for her, and that is enough to satisfy authorities.

WEBER (*with cold authority*). Vouch her? It is not necessary for anyone to vo for Madame! She is entirely capable of ing care of herself. If her passport is entirely in order, it is no affair of min

CAPTAIN (*genuinely distressed*). But—I r tell you, Monsieur Weber—this is somet I do not like. This places me in a most barrassing position. I shall be forced to tain her.

BER. You are a soldier, my dear Captain, l you should be used to embarrassing po- ons. Undoubtedly you were embarrassed ; morning, when you had to shoot that fused pacifist, Quillery. But this is war, l unpleasant responsibilities descend upon : and on me as well. However . . . (*He* · HARRY, *who is coming in.*) I shall at- d to my luggage. Thank you, Captain. *e goes out.*)

TAIN. Don't mention it. (*To* HARRY) The ng ladies are ready?

RY. Yes—they're ready. And some of r aviators are out there trying to talk n into staying here permanently.

TAIN (*smiling*). And I add my entreaties heirs.

RY. We won't have any more trouble, we? (*The* DOCTOR *appears on the gallery ı coat, hat, books done in a bundle, and rella. He comes downstairs.*)

TAIN. Oh, no, Mr. Van. Geneva is a love- ot. All of Switzerland is beautiful, these . I envy you going there, in such charm- company.

Y. Hi, Doctor. Have you got the rats all ed?

OR. Good afternoon. I am privileged to ow? (*He puts down all of his belong- and crosses.*)

AIN. Yes, Dr. Waldersee. Here is your ort.

OR. Thank you. (*He examines the pass- carefully.*)

Y. I can tell you, Doctor—I'm going to roud to have known you. When I read e papers that you've wiped out cancer won the Nobel prize, and you're the est hero on earth, I'll be able to say, s a personal friend of mine. He once red my music."

OR (*solemnly*). Thank you very much. *the* CAPTAIN.) This visa is good for ing the Austrian border?

AIN. Certainly. But you are going to h?

OR (*rises*). I have changed my plans. going back into Germany. Germany is at war. Perhaps I am needed. (*He crosses to pick up his coat.*)

HARRY. Needed for what?

DOCTOR. I shall offer my services for what they are worth. (HARRY *goes to help him on with his coat.*)

HARRY. But what about the rats?

DOCTOR (*fiercely*). Why should I save people who don't want to be saved—so that they can go out and exterminate each other? Obscene maniacs! (*Starts to put on his gloves.*) Then I'll be a maniac, too. Only I'll be more dangerous than most of them. For I know all the tricks of death! And—as for my rats, maybe they'll be useful. Britain will put down the blockade again, and we shall be starving—and maybe I'll cut my rats into filets and eat them. (*He laughs, not pleasantly, and picks up his umbrella and books.*)

HARRY. Wait a minute, Doctor. You're doing this without thinking. . . .

DOCTOR. I'm thinking probably that remedy you sold is better than mine. Hasten to apply it. We are all diseased. . . .

HARRY. But you can't change around like this! Have you forgotten all the things you told me? All that about backsliding?

DOCTOR. No, I have not forgotten the degradation of mankind—that is painful and offensive to conceive. (*He is going out.*) I am sorry to disappoint you about the Nobel prize. (*He has gone.*)

HARRY. Good-bye, Doctor. (*He sits down, wearily.*) Why in the name of God can't somebody answer the question that everybody asks? Why? Why? Oh—I know the obvious answers, but they aren't good enough. Weber—and a million like him—they can't take the credit for *all* of this! Who is it that did this dirty trick on a lot of decent people? And why do you let them get away with it? That's the thing that I'd like to know!

CAPTAIN. We have avalanches up here, my friend. They are disastrous. They start with a little crack in the ice, so tiny that one cannot see it, until, suddenly, it bursts wide open. And then it is too late.

HARRY. That's very effective, Captain. But it don't satisfy me, because this avalanche isn't made out of ice. It's made out of flesh and blood—and—and *brains*. . . . It's Goddamned bad management—that's what it is! (*This last is half to himself.*)

(IRENE *has appeared on the gallery and started to come down.*)

IRENE. Still upset about the situation, Mr. Van? Ah—good afternoon, my dear Captain Locicero.

CAPTAIN. Good afternoon, Madame.

IRENE. I have had the most superb rest here. The atmosphere is so calm, and impersonal, and soothing. I can't bear to think that we're going to Biarritz, with the dull, dismal old sea pounding in my ears. (WEBER *comes in.*)

IRENE. We are leaving now, Achille?

WEBER. I believe that some difficulties have arisen. (*He looks toward the* CAPTAIN.)

IRENE. Difficulties?

CAPTAIN. I regret, Madame, that there must be some further delay.

IRENE. Oh! Then the train is not going through, after all?

CAPTAIN. The train is going, Madame. But this passport of yours presents problems which, under the circumstances—

IRENE. Monsieur Weber will settle the problems, whatever they are. Won't you, Achille?

WEBER. There is some question about your nationality, Irene.

CAPTAIN (*referring to the passport*). It states here, Madame, that your birthplace is uncertain, but assumed to be Armenia.

IRENE. That is a province of Russia!

CAPTAIN. You subsequently became a resident of England, then of the United States, and then of France.

IRENE (*angrily*). Yes—it's all there—clearly stated. I have never before had the slightest difficulty about my passport. It was issued by the League of Nations.

WEBER. I'm afraid the standing of the League of Nations is not very high in Italy at this moment.

CAPTAIN. The fact is, Madame, the very existence of the League is no longer recognized by our government. For that reason, we ca not permit you to cross the frontier at th time. (*She looks at him and then at* WEBE The CAPTAIN *hands her the passport.*) I' sure you will appreciate the delicacy of m position. Perhaps we shall be able to adju the matter to-morrow. (*He salutes and go out, glad to escape.* HARRY *goes with hi asking, "What's the trouble, Captain? Ca something be done about it?"*)

WEBER. I should of course wait over, Irer But you know how dangerous it is for me delay my return to France by so much as o day. I have been in touch with our agen The premier is demanding that producti be doubled—trebled—at once.

IRENE. Of course.

WEBER. Here—(*He takes out an envel containing money.*) This will cover all p sible expenses. (*He gives her the envelop* There is a train for Venice this evening. Y must go there and see Lanza. I have alrea sent him full instructions.

IRENE. Yes, Achille. And I thank you having managed this very, very tactfully.

WEBER (*smiles*). You are a genuinely su rior person, my dear. It is a privilege to h known you.

IRENE. Thank you again, Achille. Good-l

WEBER. Good-bye, Irene. (*He kisses hand.* HARRY *returns.*) Coming, Mr. Van

HARRY. In a minute. (WEBER *goes.* IRENE *the money in her handbag.*) Tough l babe.

IRENE. It's no matter.

HARRY. I just talked to the Captain and isn't going to be as brutal as the Bolshe were. I mean, you won't suffer any bay wounds. He'll fix it for you to get thro to-morrow.

IRENE. You want to be encouraging, my friend. But it's no use. The Italian gov ment has too many reasons for wishin detain me. They'll see to it that I disap —quietly—and completely.

HARRY. Yes—I know all about that.

IRENE. All about what?

HARRY. You're a person of tremendous sig-ficance. You always were. (SHIRLEY appears at the left.)

SHIRLEY. Hey, Harry! It's time for us to go.

HARRY. I'll be right out. (SHIRLEY goes.)

IRENE. Go away—go away with your friends. I am to die, it is no concern of yours!

HARRY. Listen, babe—I haven't any wish ...

IRENE (flaming). And please don't call me babe! (She stands up and walks away from him. He follows her.)

HARRY. My apologies, Madame. I just call everybody "babe."

IRENE. Perhaps that's why I do not like it!

HARRY. Even if I don't believe anything you, I can see pretty plainly that you're in a tough spot. And considering what we were each other in the old Governor Bryan Ho—

IRENE. Must you always be in Omaha?

HARRY. I'd like to help you, Irene. Isn't there something I can do?

IRENE. I thank you, from my heart, I thank for that offer. But it's useless. . . .

HARRY. You don't have to thank me. Tell —what can I do?

IRENE. You're very kind, and very gallant. , unfortunately, you're no match for mille Weber. He has decided that I shall ain here and his decision is final!

HARRY. Is he responsible for them stopping?

IRENE. Of course he is. I knew it the moment I saw that ashamed look on Captain Cicero's face, when he refused to permit ...

HARRY. So Weber double-crossed you, did he! What has the son of a bitch got against you?

IRENE. He's afraid of me. I know too much about his methods of promoting his own business.

HARRY. Everybody knows about his methods. le Quillery was talking about them last it. . . .

IRENE. Yes—and what happened to Quillery? That's what happens to every one who dares to criticize him. Last night I did the one thing he could never forgive. I told him the truth! At last I told him just what I think. And now—you see how quickly he strikes back! (SHIRLEY and BEBE appear.)

SHIRLEY. Harry! The bus is going to leave.

HARRY. All right—all right!

BEBE. But we got to go this minute!

HARRY. I'll be with you. Get out!

SHIRLEY (as they go). Can you imagine? He stops everything to make another pass at that Russian. (They have gone.)

IRENE. Go ahead—go ahead! You can't help me! No one can! (He picks up his coat and hat.) But—if it will make you any happier in your future travels with Les Blondes, I'll tell you, yes—I did know you, slightly, in Omaha!

HARRY (peering at her). Are you lying again?

IRENE. It was Room 974. Does that convince you?

HARRY (ferociously). How can I remember what room it was?

IRENE (smiling). Well, then—you'll never be sure, Mr. Van.

BEBE'S VOICE. Harry!

SHIRLEY'S VOICE. For God's sake, Harry!

DON (appearing). We can't wait another instant! (DON goes.)

SHIRLEY'S VOICE. Come on!

HARRY (He turns and starts for the door, addressing the GIRLS en route). All right, God damn it! (He goes out.)

(IRENE takes out her vanity case, and does something to her face. She takes off her hat and cloak. DUMPTSY comes in from the back. He is wearing the uniform of a private in the Italian army, with gas mask at the alert, and a full pack on his back.)

DUMPTSY. Good afternoon, Madame.

IRENE (turning). Why, Dumptsy—what is that costume?

DUMPTSY. They called me up. Look! I'm an Italian soldier.

IRENE. You look splendid!

DUMPTSY. If you please, Madame. But why didn't you go on that bus?

IRENE. I've decided to stay and enjoy the winter sports.

DUMPTSY. I don't think this is a good place any more, Madame. They say the war is very big—bigger than last time.

IRENE. Yes—I hear that on all sides.

DUMPTSY. The French will be here to drop bombs on everybody.

IRENE. It will be thrilling for us if they do. Won't it, Dumptsy?

DUMPTSY. Maybe it will, Madame. But—I came to say good-bye to Auguste, the barman, and Anna, the maid. They're both cousins of mine. They'll laugh when they see me in these clothes. (*He goes to the left.*) Can I get you anything, Madame?

IRENE. Yes, Dumptsy. I'll have a bottle of champagne. Bring two glasses. We'll have a drink together.

DUMPTSY. If you please, Madame. (DUMPTSY *goes into the bar.* IRENE *lights a cigarette and goes up to the window to look out.* PITTALUGA *comes in.*)

PITTALUGA. Your luggage is in the hall, Madame. Will you wish it taken to the same suite?

IRENE. No—I didn't really care much for those rooms. Have you anything smaller?

PITTALUGA (*in a less deferential tone*). We have smaller rooms on the other side of the hotel.

IRENE. I'll have the smallest. It will be cozier.

PITTALUGA. You wish to go to it now?

IRENE. No. You can send up the luggage. I'll look at it later. (PITTALUGA *bows and goes.* DUMPTSY *returns with the champagne.*)

DUMPTSY. I was right, Madame. Auguste laughed very much.

IRENE (*coming down*). What will happen to your wife and children, Dumptsy?

DUMPTSY. Oh—I suppose the Fascisti w feed them. They promised to feed all families with a man who is out fighting their country. (*He has filled her glass. : sits down.*)

IRENE. Go ahead and pour yourself o Dumptsy.

DUMPTSY. Thank you so much, Madame wasn't sure I heard correctly.

IRENE. Here's to you, Dumptsy—and to A tria.

DUMPTSY. And to you, Madame, if y please.

IRENE. Thank you. (*They drink.*)

DUMPTSY. And may you soon be restored your home in Petersburg.

IRENE. Petersburg?

DUMPTSY. Yes, Madame. Your home.

IRENE (*with a slight smile*). Ah, yes. home! (*They drink again.*) And have fear for the future, Dumptsy. Whate happens—have no fear!

DUMPTSY. If you please, Madame. (*He ishes his drink.*) And now I must go Anna, if you will excuse me.

IRENE. Here, Dumptsy. (*She hands hi note of money.*) Good-bye, and God b you.

DUMPTSY. Thank you so much, Mada (DUMPTSY *leans over and kisses her ha Kiss die hand, Madame.* (*The* CAPTAIN MAJOR *come in from the lobby.* DUMPTSY lutes, strenuously, and goes out. The MA goes across and into the bar. The* CAPT is following him.*)

IRENE. Some champagne, Captain?

CAPTAIN. No, thank you very much.

IRENE. You needn't be anxious to avoid Captain. I know perfectly well that it w your fault.

CAPTAIN. You are very understanding, dame.

IRENE. Yes—that's true. I am one of the remarkably understanding people on e (*She swallows her drink.*) I understan damned much that I am here, alone, on

d mountain, and I have no one to turn
nowhere to go . . .

TAIN. If I can be of service to you in any
y . . .

NE. I know you'll be kind, Captain Loci-
o. And faultlessly polite.

TAIN (*with genuine sympathy*). I realize,
dame, that politeness means nothing
v. But—under these tragic circumstances
vhat else can I do?

NE (*deliberately*). What else can you do?
tell you what else you can do in these
ʒic circumstances. You can refuse to
it! Have you ever thought of that possi-
ty? You can refuse to use those weapons
t they have sold you! But—you were go-
into the bar. Please don't let me detain
.

TAIN. You will forgive me, Madame?

ʏE. Fully, my dear Captain. . . . Fully.

ʏAIN. Thank you. (*He salutes and goes
the bar.*)

NE *pours herself another drink. Then
picks it up, goes to the piano, and starts
lay a sketchy accompaniment for "Kak
ɪnna." She seems to be pretty close to
. Perhaps she does cry a little, thorough-
njoying the emotion.* HARRY *comes in
ʻring his snappy overcoat and his hat. He
ʻ no attention to her, as he takes off his
and hat and throws them down some-
ʻe.*)

ʏE. Did you have some trouble?

ʏʏ. No. Whose is that champagne?

ʏE. Mine. Won't you have some?

ʏʏ. Thanks.

ʏE. Dumptsy used that glass.

ʏʏ. That's all right. (*He fills the glass
drinks.*)

ʏE. What happened? Didn't the train

ʏʏ. Yes—the train went. . . . I got the
on board. Mr. and Mrs. Cherry prom-
to look out for them. They'll be O.K.

ʏE. And you came back—to me?

ʏʏ (*curtly*). It seems fairly obvious that
come back. (*He refills his glass.*)

IRENE. You meant it when you said that you
wanted to help me.

HARRY. You said I'd never be sure. Well—I
came back to tell you I *am* sure! I got thinking back, in the bus, and I came to the conclusion that it *was* Room 974 or close to it,
anyway. And somehow or other, I couldn't
help feeling rather flattered, and touched, to
think that with all the sordid hotel rooms
you've been in, you should have remembered
that one. (*He has some more champagne.*)

IRENE (*after a moment*). Bayard is not dead!

HARRY. Who?

IRENE. The Chevalier Bayard.

HARRY. Oh?

IRENE. Somewhere in that funny, music-hall
soul of yours is the spirit of Leander, and
Abelard, and Galahad. You give up everything—risk your life—walk unafraid into
the valley of the shadow—to aid and comfort a damsel in distress. Isn't that the truth?

HARRY. Yes—it's the truth—plainly and simply put. (*He pours himself more champagne
and drinks it quickly.*) Listen to me, babe
—when are you going to break down and
tell me who the hell are you?

IRENE. Does it matter so very much who I
am?

HARRY. No.

IRENE. Give me some more champagne.
(HARRY *goes to her and pours.*) My father
was not one of the Romanoffs. But for many
years, he was their guest—in Siberia. From
him I learned that it is no use telling the
truth to people whose whole life is a lie.
But you—Harry—you are different. You are
an honest man.

HARRY (*after a short pause*). I am—am I?
(*He crosses to the bar.*) Another bottle of
champagne. . . . Hi, Captain.

CAPTAIN'S VOICE (*offstage in bar*). What has
happened, Mr. Van? Did you miss the train?

HARRY. No—just a God-damned fool. (*He
closes the bar door.* IRENE *is gazing at him.
He goes to her and kisses her.*)

IRENE. All these years—you've been surrounded by blondes—and you've loved only
me!

HARRY. Now listen—we don't want to have any misunderstanding. If you're hooking up with me, it's only for professional reasons—see?

IRENE. Yes—I see.

HARRY. And what's more, I'm the manager. I'll fix it with the Captain for us to cross the border tomorrow, or the next day, or soon. We'll join up with the girls in Geneva —and that's as good a place as any to rehearse the code.

IRENE. The code! Of *course*—the code! I shall learn it easily.

HARRY. It's a very deep complicated scientific problem.

IRENE. You must tell it to me at once.

HARRY. At once! If you're unusually smart and apply yourself you'll have a fairly good idea of it after six months of study and rehearsal.

IRENE. A mind reader! Yes—you're quite right. I shall be able to do that very well! (AUGUSTE *enters from the bar with a bottle of champagne. He refills their glasses, then refills* HARRY's *glass, gives* HARRY *the bottle and goes back in to the bar.*)

HARRY. And, another thing, if you're going to qualify for this act with me, you've got to lay off liquor. I mean, after we finish this. It's a well-known fact that booze and science don't mix. (*He has another drink.* IRENE *is as one in a trance.*)

IRENE. I don't think I shall use my own name. No—Americans would mispronounce it horribly. No, I shall call myself—Namoura . . . Namoura the Great—assisted by Harry Van.

HARRY. You've got nice billing there.

IRENE. I shall wear a black velvet dress— very plain—My skin, ivory white. I must have something to hold. One white flower. No! A little white prayer book. That's it. A little white . . . (*The warning siren is heard.*) What's that?

HARRY. Sounds like a fire. (*The* CAPTAIN *and* MAJOR *burst out of the bar and rush to the big window, talking excitedly in Italian and pointing to the northwestern sky. The siren shrieks continue. The* MAJOR *then rushes*

out, *the* CAPTAIN *about to follow hi* What's up, Captain?

CAPTAIN. French aeroplanes. It is reprisal last night. They are coming to destroy base here.

HARRY. I see.

CAPTAIN. They have no reason to attack hotel. But—there may easily be accident advise the cellar. (AUGUSTE *rushes in fr the bar,* PITTALUGA *from the lobby. The ter orders* AUGUSTE *to lower the Vene blinds.*)

IRENE. Oh, no, Captain. We must stay and watch the spectacle.

CAPTAIN. I entreat you not to be reckl Madame. I have enough on my conscie now, without adding to it your inno life!

IRENE. Don't worry, Captain. Death ar are old friends.

CAPTAIN. God be with you, Madame. goes out. HARRY *and* IRENE *empty t glasses.* HARRY *refills them. Airplane mc are heard, increasing. Then the soun machine guns.*)

(*Bombs are heard bursting at some dista* AUGUSTE *and* PITTALUGA *go.*)

IRENE. Those are bombs.

HARRY. I guess so.

IRENE. We're in the war, Harry.

HARRY. What do you think we ought t about it? Go out and say "Boo"?

IRENE. Let them be idiotic if they wish. are sane. Why don't you try singing s thing?

HARRY. The voice don't feel appropriate. bad we haven't got Chaliapin here. *laughs.*) You know, babe—you look b blonde.

IRENE. Thank you. (PITTALUGA *runs in*

PITTALUGA. The French beasts are bom us! Every one goes into the cellar.

HARRY. Thanks very much, Signor.

PITTALUGA. You have been warned! *rushes out.*)

NE. Ridiculous! Here we are, on top of world—and he asks us to go down into cellar. . . . Do you want to go into cellar?

RY. Do you?

NE. No. If a bomb hits, it will be worse the cellar. (*He holds her close to him. kisses him.*) I love you, Harry.

RY. You do, eh!

NE. Ever since that night—in the Gov-or Bryan Hotel—I've loved you. Because new that you have a heart that I can trust. that whatever I would say to you, I ld never—*never* be misunderstood.

RY. That's right, babe. I told you I had tagged, right from the beginning.

NE. And you adore me, don't you dar-?

RY. No! Now lay off—

NE. No—of course not—you mustn't ad-it!

RY. Will you please stop pawing me? *e laughs and lets go of him.*)

RRY *pours more champagne, as she ses to the window, opens the slats of the ds, and looks out. There is now great e of planes, machine guns and bombs.*)

NE. Oh, you must see this! It's superb! *crosses to the window with his glass looks out. The light on the stage is ving dimmer, but a weird light comes the window. The scream of many gas bs is heard.*) It's positively Wagnerian 't it?

RY. It looks to me exactly like "Hell's els." Did you ever see that picture, babe?

NE. No. I don't care for films.

RY. I *do*. I love 'em—every one of them. *is dragging her to the piano—a com-ively safe retreat.*) Did you know I to play the piano in picture theatres? sure—I know all the music there is. *y are now at the piano—*HARRY *sitting,*

IRENE *standing close by him. She is looking toward the window. He starts to accompany the air-raid with the* "Ride of the Walkyries." *There is a loud expulosion.*)

IRENE. Harry . . .

HARRY. Yes, babe?

IRENE. Harry—do you realize that the whole world has gone to war? The *whole world!*

HARRY. I realize it. But don't ask me why. Because I've stopped trying to figure it out.

IRENE. I know why it is. It's just for the purpose of killing *us* . . . you and me. (*There is another loud explosion.* HARRY *stops playing.*) Because we are the little people—and for us the deadliest weapons are the most merciful. . . . (*Another loud explosion.* HARRY *drinks.*)

HARRY. They're getting closer.

IRENE. Play some more. (*He resumes the* "Walkyrie.") Harry—do you know any hymns?

HARRY. What?

IRENE. Do you know any hymns?

HARRY. Certainly. (*He starts to play* "Onward, Christian Soldiers" *in furious jazz time, working in strains of* "Dixie." *There is another fearful crash, shattering the pane of the big window. He drags her down beside him at the piano.* HARRY *resumes* "Onward, Christian Soldiers" *in a slow, solemn tempo.*)

HARRY (*sings*). Onward, Christian Soldiers —(IRENE *joins the loud singing.*)

BOTH (*singing*)
Marching as to war—
With the Cross of Jesus
Going on before. . . .

(*The din is now terrific. Demolition— bombs, gas-bombs, airplanes, shrapnel, machine guns.*)

CURTAIN

Johnny Johnson

The Biography of a Common Man

BY PAUL GREEN

Music by Kurt Weill

SCENES

ACT I

ACT II

ACT III

The cast of the play as presented by The Group Theatre at the Forty-Fourth Street Theatre, w York City, Thursday, November 19, 1936.

Johnny Johnson

PLAY BY	MUSIC BY
PAUL GREEN	KURT WEILL

Staged by Lee Strasberg	Musical direction, Lehman Engel
Settings by Donald Oenslager	Costumes by Paul Du Pont

CAST

(In order of their speech)

HONOR, the Mayor .... *Played by* Bob Lewis
E VILLAGE EDITOR .... " " Tony Kraber
NNY BELLE TOMPKINS, the sweetheart of Johnny Johnson .... " " Phoebe Brand
ANDPA JOE, her grandfather .... " " Roman Bohnen
HOTOGRAPHER .... " " Will Lee
ICYCLE MESSENGER .... " " Curt Conway
NNY JOHNSON, a tombstone cutter and private citizen ...... " " Russell Collins
GUISH HOWINGTON, rival to Johnny in business and love and owner
 of the Crystal Mineral Springs .... " " Grover Burgess
GIE TOMPKINS, Minny Belle's mother .... " " Susanna Senior
TAIN VALENTINE, a U. S. Army officer and formerly a movie stand-in " " Sanford Meisner
TOR McBRAY, a major in the medical corps, formerly a veterinary
 surgeon and county health officer .... " " Lee J. Cobb
VATE JESSEL, a stenographer at the recruiting office .... " " Curt Conway
GEANT JACKSON, the Captain's aide, an old army man and top-sergeant " " Art Smith
AMP DOLL .... " " Eunice Stoddard
PORAL GEORGE, formerly a waiter at Child's .... ⎫ " " Albert Van Dekker
VATE FAIRFAX, formerly a gangster .... ⎪ " " William Challee
VATE GOLDBERGER, a junkman's apprentice ..... *All* ⎪ " " Will Lee
VATE HARWOOD, a Texas cowpuncher .... *Members* ⎬ " " Tony Kraber
VATE KEARNS, a baseball pitcher .... *of* ⎪ " " Elia Kazan
VATE O'DAY, a life-insurance salesman ...... *Johnny* ⎪ " " Curt Conway
VATE SVENSON, a Swedish farm-hand .... *Johnson's* ⎭ " " Herbert Ratner
 Squad
ESTPOINT LIEUTENANT .... " " Joseph Pevney
ENGLISH SERGEANT .... " " Jules Garfield
RENCH NURSE .... " " Paula Miller
ORDERLY .... " " Paul Mann
OCTOR .... " " Art Smith
STER, from the organization for the Delight of Soldiers Disabled in Line
 of Duty (ODSDLD) .... " " Ruth Nelson
 CHIEF OF THE ALLIED HIGH COMMAND .... " " Morris Carnovsky
 MAJESTY, A KING .... " " Orrin Jannings
ELGIAN MAJOR-GENERAL .... " " Luther Adler
 BRITISH COMMANDER-IN-CHIEF .... " " John Most
RENCH MAJOR-GENERAL .... " " Lee J. Cobb
 FRENCH PREMIER .... " " Bob Lewis
 AMERICAN COMMANDER-IN-CHIEF .... " " Roman Bohnen
COTTISH COLONEL .... " " Thomas C. Kennedy
IAISON OFFICER .... " " Jack Saltzman
ECOND LIAISON OFFICER .... " " Joseph Pevney
AMERICAN PRIEST .... " " Alfred Saxe
ERMAN PRIEST .... " " Paul Mann
ILITARY POLICEMAN .... " " Herbert Ratner
TOR MAHODAN, a phychiatrist .... " " Morris Carnovsky
 SECRETARY .... " " Kate Allen
 FREWD .... " " Elia Kazan
THER THOMAS .... ⎫ " " Art Smith
THER CLAUDE .... *Inmates* ⎪ " " Roman Bohnen
THER GEORGE .... *of the* ⎪ " " Lee J. Cobb
THER WILLIAM .... *forensic* ⎬ " " Curt Conway
THER HIRAM .... *arena in* ⎪ " " Albert Van Dekker
THER JIM .... *a house* ⎪ " " Robert Joseph
THER THEODORE .... *of* ⎪ " " Tony Kraber
THER HENRY .... *balm* ⎭ " " Luther Adler
OCTOR .... " " William Challee
UISH HOWINGTON'S SECRETARY .... " " Alfred Saxe
ATTENDANT .... " " Herbert Ratner
UISH HOWINGTON, Jr. .... " " Eddie Ryan, Jr.
 ⎧ " " Peter Ainsley
OIERS .... ⎨ " " James Blake
 ⎩ " " Judson Hall

GHBORS, men and women, young and old; A SQUAD OF ENGLISH SOLDIERS, A SQUAD OF GERMAN SOLDIERS, THE ENGLISH PREMIER, AN ITALIAN BRIGADIER-GENERAL, A POLISH COLONEL, THREE FIELD CLERKS, SEVERAL ORDERLIES, HOSPITAL DIRECTORS, A GUARD, and ATTEND-ANTS.

TIME

A few years ago as well as now.

PLACE

Somewhere in America, somewhere in France, and somewhere in a house of balm.

ACT ONE

SCENE I

"How sweetly friendship binds."

The curtain rises on the level and clean-swept top of a little hill. The ground is covered with a carpet of green grass, and at the right front a quaint young arbor-vitae tree is growing. In the middle background is a funereal obelisk-like monument about ten feet high and draped in a dark low-hanging cloth. At the left is a naïve and homemade example of the Star-spangled Banner hanging down from a hoe-handle staff which stands stuck in the ground. It is a beautiful day in spring, and far beyond the obelisk and far beyond the scene stretches the blue and light-filled sky with here and there a tiny billowy cloud hanging motionless in it.

At the conclusion of the slightly mock-heroic overture the curtain goes up revealing a group of villagers assembled on the little hilltop. They have just marched in and are taking their places around the monument. On the left are some eight or ten women, young and old. They are garbed in dark dresses and wear brown slat bonnets which shadow their faces, and each one holds a little United States flag in her hand. Some eight or ten men, young and old, stand on the right. They are dressed in ordinary sober clothes; and each holds his dark hat against his heart with one hand and in the other like the women a little flag. At the right front stands a little bow-legged swarthy man with a camera, and at the left front a young girl with a large wreath of flowers. To the right front and opposite the girl stands ANGUISH HOW-INGTON *with a bottle of water in his hand. He is a long gangling young man resembling the stage undertaker type. To the rear and at the left of the monuments stands* MINERVA TOMPKINS, *or* MINNY BELLE *to us. She is a vision of loveliness with her golden hair, baby limpid eyes, and doll-like face, and is dressed like a village May Queen. Her filmy white dress comes down to the ground to hide all except the toes of her tiny white shoes. Her shoulders are draped with a light blue scarf, and her golden hair is set off by a chaplet of pasture daisies. Clasped against her girlish bosom*

in her two white cotton-gloved hands is object that looks like a small picture fra
MINNY BELLE *is about twenty years Opposite to her and to the right of obelisk stands* JOHNNY JOHNSON, *a qu mannered young fellow of twenty-five six. He is dressed in a well-worn p beach suit, soft checked shirt, blue tie, topped straw hat, and square-toed ru shoes. He is of medium height, his roundish and clean-shaven, his nose s and snubby, his eyes blue and mild, whole appearance denoting a gentle complacent attitude towards both his ne bors and the world in which he l Between* MINNY BELLE *and the monum stands* GRANDPA JOE, *an old man wi scraggly graying mustache, dressed i shrunk-up faded blue-and-gray uniform 1865, on the breast of which is pinne marksman's badge and some sort of medal about the size of an alarm c dial. He wears an old dark felt hat tu up at one side, and around his neck a red handkerchief as large as a towel, holds a bloodthirsty looking sabre in hand. Between* JOHNNY JOHNSON *and obelisk stands the* EDITOR *of The Co Argus, a nondescript middle-aged ma a dark shiny-sleeved seersucker suit, spectacles, a grimy collar and shoestrin Several huge carpenter's pencils an fountain pen resembling a small fire tinguisher show in his upper outside po Standing on a little platform directly be the* EDITOR *is the* MAYOR. *He is an el fellow with a violet red nose, and dr in an antediluvian swallow-tailed coat, collar, swollen black tie, baggy st trousers and button shoes. In his lap wears a big red rose. His old top hat a big day ledger rest on a little stand b him.*

As the music in the orchestra stop holds up one lean hand in a gesture looks like a combination raspberry Fascist salute, and begins his speech.

MAYOR. Friends and fellow-citizens,
We are met this April sixth,
In the year of our Lord nineteen hu
   and seventeen,

1 an occasion most auspicious—
lt the pompous dignity in the MAYOR's
ice, JOHNNY *removes his hat, and* GRAND-
JOE *salutes sharply with his sabre.*)
r we are gathered to commemorate
1e anniversary of the founding of our
    town—
esturing off to the left.)
vo hundred years ago today.
was on this hilltop here—
1is very site—
1at our forefathers met to arbitrate
1d sign a treaty with the Indians
hich ended strife and war.
ith this eternal stone we mark that fact.
1d at this moment let me pay respect
› Johnny Johnson here,
r gentle-hearted friend and artisan
1d tombstone carver of the skilful hand—
was through his kindly zeal
1at we at this late date
ect this monument of peace—
r thanks to Johnny Johnson.
he villagers applaud warmly.)

1NNY. (*With shy awkward acceptance
as* MINNY BELLE *looks admiringly over at
1.*) Thanks, folks, thanky.
*eaching out and shaking hands with a
le old lady in a black dress and bonnet.*)
›wdy, Miz Smith.

SMITH. Howdy, Johnny.

'OR. (*Continuing as* JOHNNY *turns
k respectfully.*) And now
l meet it is that I speak forth my
    thoughts
on this vital subject—peace.
aning forward.)
2se are parlous times—
› *the* EDITOR.)
lous times.
war clouds belch and thunder over
Europe's sky
if to swallow up the solid earth—
1ere Germany and France and half the
world
battle unto death.
: question now before th' American
2eople is
ll we take part or not—
ter an emphatic pause.)
›int you to our glorious president—
*points in a general direction towards
shington.*)
0 stands unshaken like a rock

And tells us nay—
We are too proud to fight—
For peace it is that's made our nation great
And peace that's made our village likewise
    what she is
Where each man loves his neighbor as him-
    self
And puts his money in the bank on Mon-
    day morn.
(*Cutting a sudden spasmodic step and be-
ginning to sing, his slightly cracked and
nasal voice filling the air as the orchestra
strikes up a soft and teasing accompani-
ment.*)
    Over in Europe things are bad,
    A great big war is going on,
    And every day somebody's dad
    Has shot and killed somebody's son.
       —Turr-uble—turr-uble,
    It's awful to think about,
    Oh frightful, oh shameful,
    America will stay out.

VILLAGERS. —Turr-uble—turr-uble,
    It's awful to think about.

MAYOR. They say in France a million odd
    Of souls have yielded up their lives,
    In Germany th' elect of God
    Have widowed more'n a million wives.
       —Turr-uble—turr-uble,
    The woe and ruin and rout—
    Oh monstrous, oh horrible,
    America must stay out.

VILLAGERS. —Turr-uble—turr-uble,
    The woe and ruin and rout—
    Oh monstrous, oh horrible,
    America *must* stay out.
(*With the exception of* JOHNNY *everybody
has joined in with the singing.*)

MAYOR. (*Continuing his speech.*) America
    must stay out.
(*Some of the villagers nod agreement, and*
JOHNNY *reaches gravely out and takes the
wreath from the girl and places it at the
foot of the monument. The* MAYOR *con-
tinues with deepening oratory.*)
What said th' immortal Washington?
No entangling alliances.
And James Monroe?
People of Europe stay over on your side,
You heard me.
(*He looks around to see if the* EDITOR *is on
the job with his pencil. He is.*)
And what does the great President of the

United States say today—
Than whom there is none whom—ahem—?
He says that neutral we must be to the
   last ditch.
And what do I your mayor say?
I say the same.
(*Pointing to* MINNY BELLE.)
You all do well recall the matchless verse
Which lately in *The Argus* said—
(*Pulling out his handkerchief, he violently
blows his flaming red nose.*)

EDITOR. (*Intoning to his pad as he writes.*)
"Democracy Advancing"—Minerva Tompkins.

MINNY BELLE. (*Beginning to sing from
her framed verses as the orchestra strikes
up and the others join in.*) Though Wash-
      ington did fighting stand
      Embattled in the fray,
   My children, 'twas that this great land
      Should know a happier day
   Of peace—peace—peace—
   And then his flag was furled,
      Washington—Washington,
      The leader of the world.
(*The* MAYOR *now joins in with his nasal
bleating.*)

MAYOR and the VILLAGERS. And then when
      frightful carnage swept
      With red and direful gleam
   Across our land 'twas Lincoln kept
      The vision and the dream
   Of peace—peace—peace,
   And then his flag was furled,
      Lincoln, Abe Lincoln,
      The leader of the world.

MAYOR. (*With great feeling.*) And now
      today a mighty third
      Proclaims that men are free,
   'Tis Wilson with the golden word
      Of peace and liberty—

MAYOR and the VILLAGERS. (*With* MINNY
BELLE's *voice fresh and clear above.*) Of
      peace—peace—peace,
   And thus his flag is furled—
      Wilson, great Wilson,
      The leader of the world.
(GRANDPA JOE *suddenly stands by the monu-
ment.*)

GRANDPA JOE. (*His eyes closed with intense
reminiscence as he babbles.*) Up Chicka-
mauga Hill we rode,

The bullets whizzed, and loud the she[ll]
      they screamed—
Hold, hold, they cried, enough!
But on we sped and straight we flew
And never stopped until
We reached the parapet and grasped the fl[ag]
And brought the victory home.
This leg was crushed that day,
(*Indicating his leg.*)
This ear was sorely hacked,
(*Indicating his ear.*)
But praises to Almighty God,
Behind us came the riding fools
Of Barlow's cavalry—
(*Letting out a sudden bloodthirsty yell.*)
Yay-eh! Yay-eh! Yay-eh!
It's victory or die!

VILLAGERS. (*Including the* MAYOR.) Yay-e[h!]
      Yay-eh! Yay-eh!
It's victory or die!
(JOHNNY *touches the* MAYOR *on the arm.*)

JOHNNY. (*Quietly.*) Say, your honor, a[re]
we for peace or war?

VILLAGERS. Peace, Johnny!

MAYOR. (*Recovering himself.*) Why, yes[, of]
course—
Our hero of the Civil War
Always enthuses us—ahem—
And now before we unveil the monum[ent]
and have our pictures made, I think [we]
ought to hear a few words from the you[ng]
man who carved this work of art—John[ny]
Johnson.

VILLAGERS. Speech, Johnny! Hooray [for]
Johnny!

JOHNNY. (*In hesitating embarrassmen[t.]*)
Aw shucks—I can't make a speech. I mi[ght]
say though, I think we've done a migh[ty]
good thing in putting up this monume[nt.]
It's the biggest job I've ever done.—[And]
then peace and arbitration's a big ide[a. I]
side with Woodrow Wilson on that. ([He]
stops.)

MAYOR. He'll be glad to hear of it, John[ny.]

JOHNNY. I reckon he's already heard o[f it.]
I wrote him a letter— (*The villagers* [ap-]
plaud.*)—inviting him down to the unv[eil-]
ing—(*The applause is louder.*) But [he]
hasn't come—not yet—(*Helplessly he tu[rns]
his hat about in his hands.*) Well, th[at's]
about all. I am better at working with

ands than my tongue. (*Looking up
dmiringly.*) But the Mayor now—(*The
AYOR starts slightly.*)

AYOR. And now we'll gather round the
onument and have our picture made—

HOTOGRAPHER. (*Hopping out in front of
is camera.*) One moment, please. (*Every-
ody looks toward the camera and stiffens
imself as the little guy runs around and
icks his head under the cloth. Immediately
e bounds out again, grasps the shutter bulb
nd quavers.*) Here's the little bir-dee-ee!
He presses the bulb and there is a flash,
ollowed by a sharp explosion. A nervous
hock goes through the crowd, and MINNY
ELLE lets out a low scream. JOHNNY looks
ver at her paternally and smiles. The little
uy jerks out the plate, reverses it, and
rasps his bulb again.*) Once more, please.
The villagers with the exception of JOHNNY
l get set again. The PHOTOGRAPHER presses
e bulb but nothing happens. He hops
ound in front of the camera and begins
orking hurriedly at one of his gadgets.
nd now beginning softly in the orchestra
d coming rapidly nearer is the tuh-blickety-
ickety-blickety-blick of a galloping horse.
he villagers gradually take their eyes from
e camera and begin looking at one an-
her. The sound of the galloping horse
rows louder in the orchestra. They all
rn to look off at the left. Now the thun-
ring hoofs are upon them, for it seems
e scudding horse is coming into the
ene. It does—a lanky bare-foot boy with
tangle of grimy hair under a coca-cola
p, riding slowly on a ramshackle bicycle
d gnawing the remnant of an ice-cream
ne. He skids the machine a few inches
dragging his heel on the ground, lets it
ll out from under him, and then wanders
er to the MAYOR and hands him up a big
velope, sealed with authoritative devices,
ich he pulls from his blouse.*)

Y. (*In a gosling voice.*) Extry for his
erence the Mayor. (*The MAYOR grabs the
ter and rips open the envelope. Pulling
wn his spectacles he peers at the unwind-
 sheet of paper. Back and forth he runs
 eyes and then suddenly flings up his
nd.*)

YOR. (*Bellowing.*) War is declared!
or a moment he holds his hand so and

then lets it fall with heavy finality. A low
murmur runs through the villagers.*)

FIRST VILLAGER. War—war.

SECOND VILLAGER. What war? (*The MAYOR
is peering at the paper and mumbling to
himself as he tries to decipher it.*)

THIRD VILLAGER. Who're we fighting
against?

MAYOR. (*Now straightens up again, his
shoulders squared in the grip of a sudden
military feeling.*) And in this fateful hour,
  my friends,
America expects that every man shall do
  his duty.

GRANDPA JOE. (*Giving his sabre a trembling swish through the air.*) Forward
  against the enemy—
Lead on.
(*He begins hacking at an imaginary adversary before him, and JOHNNY steps nimbly out of the way.*)

JOHNNY. (*Looking around in dolorous
amazement, at the growing excitement.*)
Heigh, folks, we got to unveil the monument!

MAYOR. (*Holding up his hand again in
his raspberry and Fascist gesture.*) Silence!
(*Now beginning to read, his words running
out in a low, voluble roll.*) Now therefore I,
Woodrow Wilson, by virtue of—and so on
—so on—do hereby proclaim to all whom it
may concern that a state of war exists—
ahem—exists—between the United States
and the Imperial German government, and
I do specially direct all officers, civil or military, of the United States that they exercise
vigilance and zeal in the discharge of duties
incident to such a state of war— (*Looking
over at GRANDPA JOE.*) Our police force will
take cognizance of these orders. (*GRANDPA
JOE pulls out a whistle and blows a sharp
and sudden blast.*)

GRANDPA JOE. (*Gazing searchingly about
him, his voice hoarse with sudden ominous-
ness.*) Be careful of what you say,
Be watchful of everyone,
All spies will be shot or hanged without
  mercy—
At the rising of the sun.

MAYOR. (*Rolling up the long paper.*) In
  such an hour as this, my friends,

'Tis not for us to question why,
'Tis but for us to do and die—
I command each and every one of you to
meet me at the courthouse for a public
reading.

EDITOR. (*Again talking to his pad as he
writes.*) The president has called to arms—
the nation answers to a man.

MAYOR. (*Calling out again.*) Our democratic institutions stand endangered. (*Shaking his fist at the* BOY.) Go ring the courthouse bell!

BOY. Sure. (*He turns and gets on his bicycle and goes rolling off.*)

MAYOR. Volunteers, hold up your hands!
(*The hands of the men and women go up,
with,* GRANDPA JOE'S *sabre showing above
them all. And even* ANGUISH *gets his hand
slowly hoisted, for he like Johnny is under
the watchful eye of* MINNY BELLE. *But*
JOHNNY *does not raise his hand. The*
MAYOR *peers over at him an instant.*)
Johnny Johnson, where's your good right
hand?

JOHNNY. (*Hesitating.*) Why — why — I
thought we were all for peace.

MAYOR. (*Bawling out.*) These exercises
are adjourned! (MINNY BELLE *stares at*
JOHNNY *in querying reproachment.*)

JOHNNY. But folks—heigh, people—we've
got to unveil the monument! Your Honor
—heigh!— (*The* MAYOR *makes no answer,
for by this time he has hopped down from
his perch and hurried over to the flag,
pulled it up and begun waving it in the
air.*)

MAYOR. Follow me to the courthouse!
War! War!

MINNY BELLE. (*Starting to sing as she and
the* MAYOR *begin marching at the head of
the rout.*) And now the fateful hour has
come— (ANGUISH, *who has been watching
his chance, steps to* MINNY BELLE'S *side,
bows and smiles, waves his bottle and begins singing in a loud flat voice. Now they
all sing, waving their little flags and swirling about the stage.*)

PEOPLE. (*With the exception of* JOHNNY.)
And now the fateful hour has come
And millions strong we rise

To fight for France and Belgium
And crush their enemies!—
—War! War! War!
Our banner flies unfurled—
(*The* MAYOR *waves the flag aloft.*)
America—America,
The leader of the world!

(*They go milling around, shouting an[d]
singing out at the right front, the litt[le]
guy caught helplessly in the maelstrom an[d]
knocked this way and that as he and h[is]
camera are swept along. In an instant t[he]
scene is deserted save for* JOHNNY *wh[o]
stares mournfully before him.*

*And now the orchestra begins softly pla[y]-
ing* JOHNNY'S *theme melody. In the distan[ce]
the singing and the shouting die away. [A]
moment passes, and then* MINNY BELL[E'S]
voice is heard off at the right—"Johnny!"[—]
JOHNNY *turns quickly around as* MIN[NY]
BELLE *comes running in. The orchestra, o[ut]
of deference to her, suddenly stops.*)

MINNY BELLE. (*In sharp petulance.*) Wh[at]
ever is the matter with you, Johnn[y]
(*Hurrying over and getting him by t[he]
hand.*) Come on, come on!

JOHNNY. But, Minny Belle—

MINNY BELLE. (*Wiggling her childli[ke]
form up and down in a panic of nervo[us]
haste.*) Please—please—listen to the b[ell]
ringing— (ANGUISH'S *long lean figu[re]
comes hurrying in.*)

ANGUISH. The Mayor needs his ledg[er.]
(*He goes over to the monument, picks [up]
the volume, and then turns back and slo[ws]
up by* MINNY BELLE'S *side.*)

MINNY BELLE. (*Taking hold of* JOHNN[Y'S]
arm with one hand and* ANGUISH'S *arm w[ith]
the other.*) Forward march— One—tw[o—]
three—four— (*But* JOHNNY *balks.*)

JOHNNY. I can't go just now. (*Calling [off]
to the left.*) Heigh you, Mr. Fink[—I]
want our pictures took!

MINNY BELLE. (*Staring at him.*) [Oh,]
Johnny, surely you'll be the first to fly [to]
the defense of your flag.

JOHNNY. But—why, I got all my work [to]
attend to (*Softly.*) and— (*He touches [her]
shyly and lovingly on the arm.*) I've [got]
other things to arrange for—for you a[nd]
me. I'll tell you Wednesday night.

MINNY BELLE. (*Hiding her face in her hands.*) He can't mean it. His country needs him, and now he talks of personal happiness.

JOHNNY. Good gracious, Minny Belle, you don't expect me to do that—go off and enlist—and we don't even know what it's all about.

MINNY BELLE. We've declared war on Germany, that's what.

JOHNNY. And it ain't like Woodrow Wilson to do that. Why, he's been our first leader for peace. And now— (*Shaking his head.*) I bet it's a false alarm.

ANGUISH. (*Swallowing manfully and then speaking out boldly, as he raises his clenched fist.*) I'll go—I'll be in No-Man's Land in a fortnight. Yes, that I will! (*His valor mounting.*) They'll get a taste of my smoke—them Huns and Boches that rape—mistreat French ladies. Let me at 'em.

MINNY BELLE. Ah, listen!

ANGUISH. Yeh, dod-rot their souls!

MINNY BELLE. Yes, Anguish, yes.

ANGUISH. Dod-dum 'em, I say. (*Letting out a bloodthirsty gr-r-r.*) Give me a gun and a bayonet—a gun and a bayonet is all I want.

MINNY BELLE. (*Rapturously.*) Hurrah!

JOHNNY. (*Growling.*) Yeh, hurrah! Anguish Howington won't ever see the sight of a German. He can run too fast.

ANGUISH. Here, now—

MINNY BELLE. (*Stamping her tiny foot.*) Stop it—stop it!

JOHNNY. Oh, Minny Belle, I'm sorry, but this buzzard here— (*Snapping at ANGUISH.*) Take your hand off her arm. (ANGUISH *instinctively jerks away from* MINNY BELLE, *and then reaches out to take her hand, but she denies him that. In the distance a trumpet begins blowing "The Star Spangled Banner."* JOHNNY *calls out.*) All right, Mr. Fink, we're ready for the pictures! (*Reaching out and taking* MINNY BELLE's *hand.*) You and me, Minny Belle, one on either side of the tombstone.

MINNY BELLE. (*Pulling her hand away.*) No—most emphatically no.

JOHNNY. But I need the pictures for advertising the business.

MINNY BELLE. (*Almost ready to weep with vexation.*) Business — business — and our country called to war.

ANGUISH. (*Taking his cue from* MINNY BELLE.) Yes, he talks of business—and at such an hour!

JOHNNY. (*Angrily again.*) Yeh? You may not be talking it right now but you're thinking it. (*Scornfully.*) And such a business!

ANGUISH. (*Likewise angry again.*) Well, selling mineral water is just as elevated as putting up tombstones. And there's a sight more money in it.

MINNY BELLE. Stop it! You boys promised not to quarrel over me again. (*She starts away at the right and then turns back.*) I'm not engaged to either of you. Remember that. (*She hurries tearfully away at the right.* ANGUISH *starts to follow after when* JOHNNY *darts in front of him.*)

JOHNNY. Now you listen to me, Anguish Howington, I want you to stay away from my girl.

ANGUISH. (*Edging back.*) Well, she's no more yours than mine.

JOHNNY. But she's gonna be.

ANGUISH. (*With weak determination.*) Not if I can help it.

JOHNNY. You — heard me — you — (*He springs at* ANGUISH *who darts around behind the monument.*)

ANGUISH. (*Defensively.*) I got a right to love her.

JOHNNY. The hell you have! I love her myself. (*He doubles up his left fist and starts towards him.*)

ANGUISH. (*Pleadingly, as he peeps out from behind the monument.*) Why—I—I thought you believed in settling things by arbitration, Johnny.

JOHNNY. This here's a different matter. (*He starts on towards* ANGUISH *and then stops and stares queryingly at the ground a moment as if suddenly confronted with a tough problem.* ANGUISH *flies out at the left front.* JOHNNY *gazes quizzically after him, and then turning in vexation, pulls the*

draw-string hanging down from the mon‚‚ ment. The drape rolls up and reveals th‚ single word "peace" engraved in large le‚ ters on the stone.)

BLACK OUT.

SCENE II

"Keep the home fires burning."

The living-room of MINNY BELLE'S *house a few days after Scene I. The interior is a simple one and rather typical of the American rural village home of the year 1917. At the right center is a fireplace, with a window on each side set off by clean muslin curtains. At the right rear is a door that opens into the hall, at the left rear a combination day-bed and sofa, the kind that can be got from a cheap mail-order house on the instalment plan, and at the right and left front are doors that open into other rooms. In the center is an oval table of the same style as the sofa, and placed here and there about the room are several heavy imitation oak chairs of the same suite. Between the center-table and the sofa is a sewing machine. The floor is covered with clean straw matting and the walls with a bright flower-patterned wall paper. But though the room is typical and ordinary, the arrangement of the three framed poster portraits on the rear wall is not. For here we see the touch of an individual and patriotic hand. In the center of the wall hangs a large picture of Woodrow Wilson, on the right is a smaller picture of George Washington, and on the left likewise a picture of Abraham Lincoln. Under the Washington picture is a semi-circular pasteboard slogan with these words—"He saved the colonies," under Lincoln's a second slogan—"He saved a nation," and under Wilson's portrait in larger letters—"Make the world safe for democracy." Further emphasis upon Wilson is given by a United States flag which drapes his portrait from above.*

It is early evening, and the light that comes into the scene from the windows reveals GRANDPA JOE *sitting just beyond the fireplace. He is working at some sort of contraption about two feet high which resembles a small Ferris wheel, and is dressed in a not too clean collarless white shirt, galluses and sleeve holders, a pair of dark trousers and old carpet slippers. His thin*

graying hair is pushed raggedly back fro‚ his smooth dome-like forehead, and h‚ high ridged nose is set off with a pair ‚ steel-rimmed spectacles which somewh‚ hide his dead dreamy eyes and give a home‚ comic touch to his face. In brief his who‚ get-up and personality are now no long‚ that of the bloodthirsty warrior but rath‚ that of the quiet local inventor who ‚ always on the verge of perfecting a ne‚ patent window-shade or a perpetual motio‚ machine. In the case of GRANDPA JOE, *it ‚ the latter mysterious device which has hi‚ in thrall.*

When the curtain rises he is hypnotical‚ engaged with his machine, hovering ov‚ it and fiddling with some screw, gadg‚ tooth or cog. AGGIE TOMPKINS, *with the r‚ sponsible and somewhat harassed appea‚ ance of a housewife and bread earner, ‚ sitting at the sewing machine. She is ‚ stoutish middle-aged woman with a stro‚ jowled face, a thundering ample boso‚ and a pair of capable arms.*

AGGIE. (*Belching and looking angrily ou‚ at the bent back of the old man as she sto‚ her sewing.*) Father, how you can sit the‚ working at that old perpetual motion m‚ chine and my Minny Belle running arou‚ town stark raving mad with the war fev‚ is more than I can see. I want you to ta‚ to her. (GRANDPA JOE *makes no answe‚* You know what she did when she came ‚ a while ago? (*Grimly biting off a threa‚* Why, she stood up on her tip-toes a‚ kissed that picture. Now anybody tha‚ kiss Woodrow Wilson—

GRANDPA JOE. I'd rather kiss him than t‚ bearded fellow—er—Charles Evans Hugh‚

AGGIE. I hadn't.

GRANDPA JOE. That's because you're ‚ Republican.

AGGIE. It's not— If that low-down Joh‚ Johnson didn't like Wilson so much ma‚ I wouldn't mind. (*With a loud belch.*) ‚

rd, why don't Anguish come on with
y mineral water.

ANDPA JOE. Yeh, and if you don't quit
inking them slops you're going to rot out
ur insides, Aggie.

GIE. It's not slops. Anguish had his
ring tested by experts. It says so in *The
gus*.

ANDPA JOE. Yeh, and Johnny says that
ter's plumb poison to both man, bird,
d beast. I'd believe him.

GIE. (*Scornfully.*) Of course he'd say
t. He hates the very ground Anguish
lks on.

ANDPA JOE. And I don't blame him
her—in a manner of speaking.

GIE. You listen to me, Father Joe. An-
ish Howington is going somewhere in
world. Johnny Johnson won't ever
ount to a row of pins. (*Grimacing.*) Too
od—wishy-washy—no backbone.

ANDPA JOE. That's what you think. Any-
w *I* like Johnny. A lot of people do.

GIE. You may like him, but you all
gh at him. Now you don't catch folks
ghing at Anguish.

ANDPA JOE. That's right, they don't get
ch fun out of him. (*He begins ham-
ring on his machine.*)

GIE. (*Singing defensively to herself as
sews, her voice suddenly grown melli-
ous and free.*) My husband is dead,
God rest the poor man,
And I in his stead
Do all that I can,
Keeping body and soul
And the house from the dole—
   —Sing treddle, trid-treddle,
   The wheel it goes around.
I wash and I cook,
I sweep and I clean,
I once dreamt a dook
Had made me his queen,
But oh weary me,
Such things cannot be
   —Sing treddle, trid-treddle,
   The wheel it goes round.

*he stands up and begins fitting her corset
und her.* JOHNNY *appears at the rear
or with a package in his hand.*)

JOHNNY. Howdy, you all.

AGGIE. (*Dropping her corset from around
her and glaring at him.*) Oh, it's you!

GRANDPA JOE. Come in, Johnny. (JOHNNY
*comes on into the room. He is dressed in
the same clothes as before.* AGGIE *now busily
begins folding up her mending and piling
it on top of the machine.*)

AGGIE. (*With a scissors snip in her voice.*)
And how is your tombstone business?
Guess this war will kill it off.

JOHNNY. Well, can't be fair weather all
the time—as the cuckoo said. (*With
finality.*) That's the way I've figured it out,
Miz Tompkins. Still things are not so bad.
(*Nodding gravely.*) Miz Esther Smith has
just ordered a nice piece of stone work.

AGGIE. Well, I'm glad to hear that. Her
poor husband has been lying there in the
graveyard these ten years with nothing but
a plank headboard to mark his resting
place.

JOHNNY. She only wanted to put out
twenty dollars for him. Then she decided
to let her husband's headboard stand and
take a sixty-dollar job for the cow.

AGGIE. (*Throwing up her hands.*) The
cow!

JOHNNY. Yes'm, the one that used to give
four gallons of milk a day, year in, year
out. I had a mighty lot of respect for that
cow. There's nothing like good milk for
humanity, you know. (*With a genial
pointed touch.*) Better'n mineral water.
(*Slapping his thigh as* AGGIE *stares at him.*)
Daggone, I was forgetting. I've got a little
present for your birthday, Miz Tompkins.
(AGGIE, *who has started out of the room at
the left front, with her arms full of the
clothes, turns back.*)

AGGIE. (*Somewhat mollified.*) For me?

JOHNNY. Yes ma'am. (*He is busy un-
wrapping the package.* AGGIE, *showing she
is a bit touched by his thoughtfulness as
well as curious, comes over nearer* JOHNNY.)

AGGIE. That's real nice of you, Johnny.

JOHNNY. Shucks, I was glad to do it. It's
a jim-dandy piece of work, too. (*He now
lifts out a small white tombstone and sets*

it on the center table. AGGIE *stares at it in speechless horror.* JOHNNY *runs his hand lovingly over the carving.*) You see there's two hands a-shaking. Below that the word "Friendship." (*Looking around at her.*) What's the matter, Miz Tompkins, don't you—?

AGGIE. (*Her voice almost breaking with anger and chagrin.*) So—you're already making a tombstone for me, are you? (*Fiercely.*) Well, let me tell you, I'm not ready to die yet!

JOHNNY. Why Miz Tompkins, I didn't mean it that way—

AGGIE. (*Yelling.*) Don't Miz Tompkins me, you—you fool! (*She turns and goes storming out at the left front, carrying the clothes with her.* JOHNNY *stares forlornly after her a moment, sighs, and begins wrapping up the tombstone again. A low chuckle breaks from* GRANDPA JOE *where he works.*)

GRANDPA JOE. She don't like you, Johnny.

JOHNNY. (*Giving his shoulders a doleful shrug.*) Well, everybody to his own taste, as the goat said to the skunk.

GRANDPA JOE. It's Anguish she likes, the rising young business man. (JOHNNY *sits down with the tombstone in his lap and stares abstractedly at the floor.* GRANDPA JOE *looks over at his glum face.*) Come on now, don't worry about Aggie.

JOHNNY. I'm not worrying about her— especially. It's the war, Mr. Joe. I still can't make heads or tails of it.

GRANDPA JOE. I didn't understand the Civil War but I fought in it—just the same.

JOHNNY. Yeh, and suppose you had been killed—

GRANDPA JOE. Then they'd a-raised me up a fine tombstone the way you did to peace.

JOHNNY. But what good would it do you and you dead as a door-nail?

GRANDPA JOE. Whew—no good, that's certain. Say, you ain't afraid are you, Johnny?

JOHNNY. No, but if I had to die I'd like to know what I was dying for— (*Emphatically.* You're durn right I would.

GRANDPA JOE. You're getting sort of strong in your language, ain't you, Johnny?

JOHNNY. Yeh—I feel strong about it a Mr. Joe. I tell you it's plain as the no on your—my face—war is about the lo downest thing the human race could i dulge in. Add up all the good in it and i still a total loss. There ought to be son way of settling it by discussion—the w we do over in the Adelphi Debating S ciety, and not by killing. The more y fight and kill the worse it gets. You m conquer your enemy for a while but he his friends only wait to grow strong aga to come back at you. That's human natu And what I can't understand about Wils is—why all of a sudden he's willing to out and kill a lot of people for some id about freedom of the seas.

GRANDPA JOE. The sea has got to be fr Johnny—it's got to be free.

JOHNNY. Well, maybe it has, though af all you could look on it as nothing but big pond. Now if I was out in a pond a Anguish passed by—

GRANDPA JOE. Anguish?

JOHNNY. Well, take anybody you do like. And he tried to come in and c taminate the water, I'd raise a little d turbance all right, but I wouldn't try kill him. No, we'd get out on the ba and—

GRANDPA JOE. Arbitrate, Johnny?

JOHNNY. Anyhow there would'nt be a killing, at least I don't think so. (*Glum* There must be some other idea in Wilso mind—for him and me's been seeing to eye all along. Maybe when *The Arg* comes out—

GRANDPA JOE. Well, you needn't worry You don't *have* to go fight, not yet y don't.

JOHNNY. Uh, that's just the trouble, I Joe. I'm for peace and Minny Belle's war. That's the long and short of it.

GRANDPA JOE. (*Thoughtfully.*) Uhm, y are in a kind of a jam, ain't you—in manner of speaking? On the one han your principle, on the other—your—e love?

JOHNNY. (*Fervently.*) Yes sir.

GRANDPA JOE. I'd drop principle,

JOHNNY. But I can't do what I don't believe in.

GRANDPA JOE. Then you're sunk—like the *Titania*.

JOHNNY. (*Going heavily on.*) If I could see some honest-to-God reason in this war then I'd go quick as scat. Like if by going I could help — well — (*Deep in thought.*) put an end to—sort of like the idea of—say, a war to put down war. You know what I mean. Sometimes you have to meet fire with fire. Then I'd feel the cause was worth it. For when it was over the democratic nations maybe could league up and unite for peace and— (*His voice dies out and for a moment he is silent. Then he turns to the old man.*) What is democracy, Grandpa Joe?

GRANDPA JOE. (*Hesitating and then speaking thoughtfully.*) Democracy?—Well—

JOHNNY. I asked the Mayor and he said democracy is the principle of freedom—self-government—whatever that is.

GRANDPA JOE. He's right—that's what it is—the principle of liberty—to follow your own business like I do my perpetual motion machine and—be happy.

JOHNNY. (*Staring at the portrait of Wilson.*) Yes, but suppose in order to be happy, you want something and somebody else wants— (*He suddenly sets the package on the floor by the table and rises out of his seat as MINNY BELLE enters at the right front. It is almost as if he were so sensitive to her presence that he can feel her near—without even seeing or hearing her. She comes on into the room and JOHNNY pulls a chair ready for her to sit down. MINNY BELLE is dressed in a trim blue coat—the lace collar of which is fastened with a little pin, and her golden hair is combed back into a becoming bob. She comes over and sits down in the chair which he holds for her.*)

GRANDPA JOE. (*Suddenly beginning to sing in his flat cracked voice.*) When two are alone in a parlor at eve,
And a manly young arm waits inside of its sleeve
So anxious its duty to do and receive—
Then, Grandpa, it's skidoo for you—
For you—

(*With a fond glance at the two, he goes nimbly out at the left front.* JOHNNY *in great glee, suddenly stands up, dusts off his chair, and then sits down again and begins fumbling sheepishly with his hat.*)

JOHNNY. (*Presently.*) You're—you're looking purty as a pink tonight, Minny Belle.

MINNY BELLE. (*With a slight touch of coldness.*) Thank you.

JOHNNY. (*Furtively taking a small trinket from his pocket.*) That locket come in the mail today. (*He reaches out and quickly lays it in her lap.*) When you open it—see—it's got a picture of me inside.

MINNY BELLE. (*Examining it after a moment.*) It's nice, Johnny—nice. (*She hesitates and then puts it on.*)

JOHNNY. (*Joyously.*) I knew you'd like it. (*He stares at her in speechless love and stammers.*) You—you ain't mad at me for quarrelling with that rapscallion Anguish?

MINNY BELLE. (*As she pulls a tiny snow-white handkerchief from her sleeve and puts it demurely against her lips.*) Please, Johnny—you know I can't ever stay mad with you.

JOHNNY. (*Haltingly getting out a few more words.*) You remember that night when I was here—two weeks ago?

MINNY BELLE. I remember.

JOHNNY. And I pointed out that verse in the song book. (*Looking about him.*) Where is that book? It was here on the table.

MINNY BELLE. It's up in my room.

JOHNNY. (*Gazing at her fondly, his face wreathed in a sudden beatific smile.*) In your room, Minny Belle—where you sleep at night? (*His chair moves a bit nearer.*) You must remember what the song said. Something about—about how one person feels when separated from the other. (*Pulling out a pencil he writes in the palm of his hand and holds it out to her. She reads it and drops her eyes.*) You see—see what I mean— (*Spelling.*) "L-o-n-g-ing." (*Helplessly.*) Oh, Minny Belle!

MINNY BELLE. (*Looking off before her and beginning to sing softly.*) Oh heart of love,
The soul of all my yearning,

Come back to me,
My days are filled with pain,

JOHNNY. (*Sliding his chair still nearer.*)
You sing it—almost like—like you meant it.

MINNY BELLE. My fondest thoughts
To you are ever turning—
Wild foolish hopes
To have you back again.

JOHNNY. Why, you know it all by heart.

MINNY BELLE. Every sound along the street,
Every voice I chance to hear,
Every note of music sweet
Sets me longing for you, dear.
—Come back to me,
Oh, can't you hear me calling!
Lost is my life,
Alas, what can I do?
Shadows of night
Across my path are falling,
Frightened and lone
I die apart from you.

JOHNNY. (*Rapturously.*) Minny Belle,
Minny Belle! (*By this time his chair is
alongside of hers. He reaches over and
takes her hand.*) Minny Belle — oh — you
know what I want to say.

MINNY BELLE. (*Singing again as she looks
around at him with bright eyes and pink
cheeks.*) Every footfall on the floor,
Every tip-tap on the stair—
Open wide I fling the door,
You are never standing there.
—Come back to me,
Oh, can't you hear me calling!
Lost is my life,
Alas, what can I do?
Shadows of night
Across my path are falling,
Frightened and lone
I die apart from you.

JOHNNY. (*His words pouring out as he
stands up, his hat falling unnoticed to the
floor.*) Like the song says, Minny Belle, you
are the— (*He stutters, swallows the lump
in his throat and struggles on.*) From that
first day I saw you down there in the meat
market—yes, my heart thumps like it will
hurt when I think of you. When I'm carving my tombstones—my hammer going
whick-whack — whick-whack — it's all in
time to my heart beating out what I want
to say— (*Pulling out his handkerchief and
wiping his forehead.*) And I can't say it—

MINNY BELLE. (*Murmuring and likew*
standing up.) Beautiful—beautiful how y
talk so. (*She leans against him, and he p*
his arms suddenly around her and star
stupefied with joy.)

JOHNNY. (*Brokenly.*) My little—er—bi
(*Holding her from him he stares do*
into her averted face, and then bends o
and kisses her tenderly on top of the hea

MINNY BELLE. (*Clinging to him an*
stant.) Oh, Johnny—

JOHNNY. (*In hushed wonder.*) We're
gaged. (*Spinning drunkenly about*
room.) We're engaged. I'm the happ
man in all the world. Yay-eh! (*Turn*
ecstatically back to her.) And now ca
ask you—ask you that other question?
tiny nod of her bright head says he ma
When are we to be— (*His voice trembl*
over the word.) be married? What do
say to next week? We'll get his honor
Mayor to—to do it.

MINNY BELLE. (*With ever the sligh*
movement away from him.) But we c
do that.

JOHNNY. Why not, Precious?

MINNY BELLE. It's the war—you've go
enlist.

JOHNNY. (*His arms dropping down f*
her with a thud.) Great guns, I'd fo
all about the war! (*He stands gaz*
moodily at the floor.)

MINNY BELLE. (*Her handkerchief to*
lips.) It will be hard to be separated f
you—hard. But we both must endure it
our country's sake.

JOHNNY. (*Wretchedly.*) But, Mi
Belle—

MINNY BELLE. At night I'll think of
there on the battlefield—under the vast
starry sky—think of you standing t
with your rifle, a bulwark of strength.

JOHNNY. (*Murmuring.*) A bulwark
strength.—But, Minny Belle—

MINNY BELLE. (*Her face already tou*
with the pain of woman's renunciatio
she stares off into the air.) Like that
song says— (*Beginning to recite.*)
Alone I'll wait

Steadfast and true,
My every thought
A thought of you—
Of you.

alf-singing as JOHNNY *gazes yearningly*
her.)

So go, my dear, and quickly now,
And then the cruel deed is done,
For parting is a sharper blow
Than absence, my beloved one.

er voice now rising into a plaintive
lody.)

Farewell, goodbye,
Goodbye, farewell,
No tears, no words
My love can tell—
Farewell.

he buries her face tearfully against his
ulder.)

NNY. (*Pulling her tightly to him.*)
n't cry, Minny Belle. It breaks my heart
h, don't—

NNY BELLE. (*Gulping.*) Be careful won't
? Do be careful, Johnny, and come back
e.

NNY. Sure—sure.—Oh—but look here,
nny Belle, you see I'm not really gone
.—

NNY BELLE. (*Mournfully.*) I know,
nny, but what is one day, or two days?
r then you are gone. It comes so quick.

NNY. No, I just as well tell you, Minny
lle, I've not been able to make up my
nd about this war yet. I've got some
re thinking to do.

NNY BELLE. (*Starting to speak and then*
ing at him in sudden and pained sur-
se.) You mean—you mean you still hesi-
?—(*His unhappy face betraying him.*)
er all I've promised? (*With a wail.*) Oh,
nny, you can't!

NNY. (*Pleadingly.*) But, Minny Belle,
en. You know how it is. I've got to have
eason before I—

NNY BELLE. Reason? (*Her voice almost*
aking in a sob.) And I thought you—
, Johnny, you don't love me—no you
't.

NNY. (*With a groan.*) My Lord! (*He*
ks helplessly about him as if seeking aid
m the empty air.) Maybe I can figure

things out—maybe—

MINNY BELLE. Figure—figure— (*With a*
sob.) Then we're not engaged, we're not.
I take it all back. (*With heaving shoulders,*
her handkerchief stuffed against her mouth,
she hurries into the room at the right and
closes the door behind her.)

JOHNNY. (*Calling piteously after her.*)
Minny Belle! Minny Belle! (*But there is no*
answer. For a while he stands in the mid-
dle of the room crushed and desolate. Pres-
ently he picks up his tombstone and goes
slowly out at the rear. A moment passes and
the door at the left front opens and AN-
GUISH HOWINGTON, *carrying a large glass*
jug full of water, stick his head in. He
looks inquiringly about him and then
knocks on the side of the wall.)

ANGUISH. (*Calling.*) Mis' Agnes! Mis'
Agnes! (MINNY BELLE's *grieving face looks*
out from the room at the right.)

MINNY BELLE. Oh, it's you! (*She slams the*
door shut.)

ANGUISH. (*Knocking and calling.*) Mis'
Agnes! I've brung your mineral water at
last! Mis' Agnes! (*The door at the rear*
opens and AGGIE *enters. She is looking be-*
hind her.)

AGGIE. (*Reaching out a supplicating hand*
as she comes across the room.) Quick—
quick—Anguish. (ANGUISH *hurries over to*
her with the jug. She seizes it and, like a
mighty toper drinking from the bung, holds
it aloft and lets the life-giving fluid trickle
down her throat. Then she sets the jug
down, wipes her lips with her apron, and
looks over at him, the anger and grief
gradually passing from her face.)

ANGUISH. I'm sorry to be so late, but I'm
trying to wind up my business before I
enlist.

AGGIE. (*Sitting.*) Uh-huh, and that's what
I want to talk to you about. (*She gazes at*
him a moment and then continues.) You're
not going to enlist, Anguish.

ANGUISH. (*With a questioning look, and*
then shaking his head glumly.) Don't see
any way out of it. Minny Belle's determined that I—

AGGIE. (*Leaning forward and speaking*
with deep confidentiality.) In the Civil War

my Uncle Heck didn't enlist. Why? He melted down a whole beeswax candle, got himself a hollow reed, and blew the stuff into a hole he'd cut into his arm. From then until Grant captured Lee at Appomattox he had a bad case of St. Vitus Dance. He shook so bad that bringing the milk from the cowbarn he'd make the butter come. Yes, and Cousin Melchisidec, he hamstrung his left leg with a butcher knife.

ANGUISH. (*Staring at her in fearful amazement as he drops down in a chair.*) Lord upon me, you mean they done damage to theirselves with knives!

AGGIE. And Bud Lauderdale, an old sweetheart of Ma's, cut off his big toe with a grass hook. He limped bad the rest of his life and wore a special made shoe.

ANGUISH. (*Aghast.*) Merciful heavens!

AGGIE. (*Shaking her head reminiscently.*) Ah, they had nerve—Uncle Heck and Cousin Melchisidec, and Bud Lauderdale. Brave men all, they were. (*Consolingly.*) But you don't have to do damage to yourself to keep out of this war, Anguish. It's your eyes. Cataracts and scales—Anguish.

ANGUISH. Huh, Mis' Agnes?

AGGIE. You can hardly see from here to the door— Almost blind. I'll swear an affidavid for you. (*She gazes at him in silence.*)

ANGUISH. (*A great ragged smile sliding around his slit of a mouth.*) I see—I see (*Suddenly rising and grasping her hand in thankfulness.*) You've saved my life— Ever since last Sunday when that English hero

preached in church I haven't slept a wink (*Stiffening sharply and croaking in a hy notic, sepulchral voice.*)
"In Flanders Fields the poppies blow Between the crosses row and row That mark *my* place—"

AGGIE. (*Rising.*) I got a pair of cross-ey glasses I used when the flues settled in eyes. You wear 'em and if you're not bli now you will be shortly. Come on into kitchen. (*She starts out at the left fro ANGUISH following; then suddenly she tu back, picks up the jug, and goes off dri ing from it. For a moment the scene empty except for a low note that scurr around in the orchestra like a mouse the floor. Then there is a noise of thumpi footsteps in the hall at the rear. The d is opened and JOHNNY comes running with a newspaper in his hand.*)

JOHNNY. (*Calling out wildly.*) Min Belle! Minny Belle, say, I've got some w derful news for you! (MINNY BELLE com in at the right front, with her hair hang down. Her eyes are red from weepi JOHNNY runs over to her.) Minny Belle, going to enlist. Listen, it's all here in Argus. Wilson's proclamation. And n I'm ready to go. (*Reading enthusiasticall* "We have no quarrel with the Germ people. It's their leaders who are to blar Drunk with military power and glory, tl are leading the democratic people of G many as well as the whole world shameless slaughter." (*With deep finali* "This is a war to end war." Daggone, n 'bout my own words! (*He sweeps MIN BELLE into his arms and kisses her on lips.*)

BLACK OUT.

SCENE III

"Your Country needs another man—and that means you."

Interior of the recruiting office—a medium-sized room. At the right front is a door opening to the street outside, and at the left rear a door opening into an inner room. On the wall at the back is a wide flamboyant poster with the sign—"Recruiting Office 18,659." Plastered all around the walls are other flaming signs and posters calling upon American manhood to go and fight for its country. At the left front,

diagonally placed, is a bare-topped of desk, and farther back towards the rea another and smaller desk with a typewri behind which PRIVATE JESSEL, the sten rapher, sits. Just to the right of him tall white weighing and measuring sc and still farther over at the right is a s table with a phonograph, the horn of wh disappears through the wall toward street. At the right front is a bench which CAPTAIN VALENTINE and SERGE JACKSON sit, and in the exact center of

ge near the foot-lights a chair is placed
ing outwards.

hen the curtain rises, PRIVATE JESSEL *is*
sily typewriting, his keys going in a
irring clatter of sound somewhat like a
all mowing machine, for his typewriter
of ancient model. CAPTAIN VALENTINE *and*
GEANT JACKSON, facing the front, are
ding a lurid magazine which carries the
ture of a male movie star on its cover.
VATE JESSEL *is a slender, nervous fellow*
h a pale burning eye, and is about twenty
rs old; CAPTAIN VALENTINE *is a handsome*
n, some thirty years old, with a dark
tinee-idol face, and is dressed in a spick
d span uniform of the United States In-
try; SERGEANT JACKSON *is shorter, with*
crubby bull-dog face and stubby upturned
se, and is about forty years old.
a moment after the curtain goes up
VATE JESSEL *clatters away at his work,*
d the CAPTAIN *and the* SERGEANT *read*
ir magazine, the CAPTAIN's *fingers going*
tap on the bench. Then suddenly from
room at the left rear comes a low moan-
cry. No one pays any attention to it.
GEANT JACKSON *bends closer to the*
gazine, snickers lewdly, and points to
page with extended forefinger. The
TAIN smiles and nods a languorous
eement to the joke. The SERGEANT *now*
tes the CAPTAIN, stretching his snaggle-
thed mouth in a grin, and drops his
d. He turns the page and the two of
m read on. The CAPTAIN's *voice rises out*
his tapping into a low croon.)

TAIN VALENTINE. (*Singing abstractedly*
he reads.) What are you coming for
Into my private boudoir
turbing the sleep of a lady, an innocent
    one?
So sorry, the soldier replied,
I'll honorably step outside,
eant no offense in the least and 'twas
    only in fun.
nd now the scene is suddenly split by
lood-curdling scream from the room at
left rear. PRIVATE JESSEL *abruptly stops*
ng, and sits listening. The CAPTAIN *con-*
es his reading and singing.)

Up spake the lady demure,
If fun and not robbery, sir,
what you intend then perchance and
    perhaps you may stay.
Nay, nay I confess on my oath

Most stiffly inclined to them both
Was my will, and they say with a will like
    my will there's a way.
(*And now* PRIVATE JESSEL *leans over and
sets the phonograph playing, and we can
hear the air in the street outside being
flooded with the brassy band notes of the
"Democracy March." The record has played
only part way through when the door at
the left rear opens and* DOCTOR MC BRAY, *a
middle-aged, pot-gutted fellow wearing a
medical corps major's uniform comes in,
carrying a stethoscope in his hand and mopping his face exhaustedly. He gestures to
the stenographer—who cuts off the record,
steps swiftly back to his little desk, takes
up his dictation pad and waits. The* MAJOR
*stands mopping and scouring his hand
around down in his coat collar. Again the
door at the left rear opens and two giant
private soldiers of the regular U. S. army
come in bringing* ANGUISH HOWINGTON *between them. They are stripped to the waist
and their great muscular torsos are tattooed
most horribly, mainly with voluptuous women's figures. As for* ANGUISH, *or what there
is left of him, he is stark naked except for
a scanty hand-towel tied around his middle,
and his bony shaking form is on the verge
of collapse. His swollen red eyes are almost
closed, his face is bathed in cold sweat, and
he is panting hoarsely for breath. The soldiers drag him over to the chair and drop
him into it, and step one to the left and
one to the right and stand waiting, the
while they pinch and wiggle the women's
figures on their fore-arms.* ANGUISH *sits
shivering and mumbling incoherently to
himself.*)

DOCTOR MC BRAY. (*Barking out to the
stenographer as the* CAPTAIN *and the* SER-
GEANT *continue to read their magazine in
unconcern.*) Examination findings. (*Dictating rapidly, with a mixed jargon of veterinary and medical learning, and now and
then shooting out a word of advice to* AN-
GUISH.) Venereal diseases—none—candidate
claims virginity. Claim sustained. General
diseases—none—needs feeding, short on his
fodder and corn— (*Snapping his fingers.*)
—Chook—nutritious food, I mean. Nervous
diseases—characteristic hysteria during use
of pump. Nose and throat—foul. (*To* AN-
GUISH.) Drench with turpentine and linseed
oil. (ANGUISH *bends his head over on his
arms and begins to weep softly.*) Teeth

show candidate to be about twenty-eight. (*Snapping his fingers again.*) Sight—moon-eyed, almost blind. Combination diseases—leucoma, incipient cataract, granular conjunctivitis and God knows what. (*Yelling at* ANGUISH.) Get out! (ANGUISH *springs to his feet and stands cowering in terror. At a gesture from the doctor, the two giants seize him and hurl him through the door at the left rear.* MC BRAY *sits down at the desk at the left and sprawls himself forward exhaustedly on it. And now the handsome* CAPTAIN VALENTINE *is interested. He turns towards* MC BRAY *and speaks in a polite stage voice, his manner that of a cross-mixture of Sherlock Holmes and Rudolph Valentino.*)

CAPTAIN. It's all very well for you to turn down that fellow, Major, but I need another man to fill out my company.

MC BRAY. And pursuant thereof to General Order thirty-four thousand oh—oh—six, we've got to have him today. (*Grimly.*) And let me tell you—the next fellow comes in here better be a man. (*He gestures to* PRIVATE JESSEL *who sets the phonograph playing again. The two giant privates come back into the room and take up the same position and business as before.*)

PRIVATE JESSEL. (*Leaning out the door at the right and calling high above the music.*) Next man! Next man! (*Everybody waits, the record plays, but no one comes in. With a low wheezy growl, the phonograph stops.*)

MC BRAY. (*Savagely.*) Don't they love their country in this lousy dump! Only three enlistments today.

PRIVATE JESSEL. There's that same fellow walking up and down.

SERGEANT. (*Turning and looking back through the door.*) He was there an hour ago.

MC BRAY. Get the—(*Clearing his throat.*) —get him in here.

SERGEANT. That music hooked him. Here he comes. (*The* MAJOR *rubs his hands gleefully and fits his stethoscope into his ears.*)

CAPTAIN. (*Languidly, as he sits down to his magazine again.*) Pass him if you possibly can, Major.

MC BRAY. If he lives, I will. (JOHNNY JOH[N]-SON *enters and stops just inside the do[or]. He is in smiling good humor and wears [a] new blue serge suit all pressed for the occ[a]-sion. A red poppy blooms in his lapel an[d] a little United States flag is tucked into t[he] band of his flat-topped straw hat.* MC BR[AY] *grunts with anticipated joy.*) Unh.—

JOHNNY. (*Removing his hat, giving the[m] a benign smile, and beginning to sha[ke] hands around.*) Well, folks, I've decided [to] do what Minny Belle said and enli[st]. Where's the paper I sign?

MC BRAY. (*Motioning* JOHNNY *to a ch[air] in the manner of a headwaiter welcomi[ng] an honored guest to a table.*) Come rig[ht] in, sir, and make yourself at home.

SERGEANT JACKSON. We're tickled to dea[th] to see you.

JOHNNY. And I'm real glad to see you [too.] (*Turning towards the chair.*) I came h[ere] last night, but the office was closed.

MC BRAY. Now ain't that too bad?

JOHNNY. Yes sir. But if you don't succe[ed] at first—you know. And so—since this [is] war to end war, I'm in it a hundred p[er] cent strong.

MC BRAY. You are?

JOHNNY. You bet your tintype. But [I'm] not against the common man I'm going [to] fight. No-siree. It's the German leaders. [As] Wilson says, drunk with military pow[er] and—

MC BRAY. (*Chortling.*) Good, goo[d.] (*Growling.*) Sit down. (*The two priva[tes] step forward and, lifting him suddenly fr[om] the floor, slam him down in the ch[air.] JOHNNY *looks up at them in pained s[ur]-prise.*)

JOHNNY. Heigh, you fellows are kin[d of] rough, ain't you?

MC BRAY. (*Chuckling in low malevolen[ce.]* Don't mind them, son, it's just their li[ttle] way.

JOHNNY. (*Sharply.*) Well, I don't like i[t.]

SERGEANT JACKSON. (*To the* CAPTAIN.) [He] don't like it.

CAPTAIN VALENTINE. (*Crooning.*) Says [he] don't like it, but he will—

NNY. Still if that's the way you initiate
s into the army, then I suppose I'll have
stand it. It's all in the cause.

TAIN VALENTINE. (*Languorous as al-
ys.*) And what cause is that, my friend?

NNY. Why, democracy—world democ-
y—the biggest idea of modern times, in-
ding electricity. (*They all stare at him
h some show of interest.* PRIVATE JESSEL
s a sort of tripod easel from the corner
sets it between JOHNNY and MC BRAY
slightly towards the rear, then stands
ting with his notebook in his hand.*)

BRAY. (*In his barking manner again.*)
at's your name?

NNY. Johnny Johnson.

BRAY. (*As* PRIVATE JESSEL *writes.*)
cupation?

NNY. I'm an artist.

BRAY. Artist?

NNY. At least that's what the Mayor
ed me. Artists in stone—I make tomb-
es—tombstones for both people and
mals. You know we don't properly ap-
ciate our pets. They are about the best
nds man ever—

BRAY. (*Snapping.*) Place of birth?

NNY. I don't know.

BRAY. Don't know?

NNY. You see, my daddy and mammy
e sort of worthless and wandered around
over—from one poorhouse to another.
n't know where I was born. I was drag-
from pillar to post—

BRAY. (*To* PRIVATE JESSEL.) Born—be-
en pillar and post.

NNY. (*With a wide breaking laugh as
slaps his knee.*) Daggone my hide, that's
d!

BRAY. How old are you?

NNY. Well, let me see.—According to
way my pappy figured it I ought to be
ut twenty-six come pumpkin time. He
embered there was a big frost on the
und—

BRAY. (*Wagging his tired shaggy head
speaking in a soft query to the* CAP-
N.) My God, don't tell me he's crazy!

CAPTAIN VALENTINE. (*Bored.*) Let science
decide it.

MC BRAY. (*Loudly to* PRIVATE JESSEL.)
Army intelligence test number one—lowest grade. (PRIVATE JESSEL *now throws
back a wide sheet of paper from the easel
and reveals the illustrated example in test
number one.*)

PRIVATE JESSEL. Look this way, Mr. Johnson. (JOHNNY *shifts himself around and
stares at the easel. As* MC BRAY *calls off the
questions,* PRIVATE JESSEL'S *pencil points
them out.*) First question—

MC BRAY. Cats are useful animals because
—one, they catch mice; two, they are gentle; and three, because they are afraid of
dogs. (*Whirling on him.*) Quick, Mr. Johnson, which is correct—one, two or three?

PRIVATE JESSEL. (*Looking at his wrist
watch and counting off the seconds.*) One
—two—three—four—

SERGEANT JACKSON and CAPTAIN VALENTINE.
(*In unison.*) Make it snappy, Mr. Johnson.

JOHNNY. Well, as a matter of fact, cats
ain't useful. They're the worst pests in the
world. Once I had a mocking-bird—

MC BRAY. (*Controlling himself by grim
will.*) Mr. Johnson, I want you to understand that we are trying to find out whether
you've got sense enough to be a soldier.

JOHNNY. Sure I have. You ain't blind.

MC BRAY. (*Loudly—as he strikes the table
with his fist.*) Problem number two! (PRI-
VATE JESSEL *turns another sheet.*) If you
fell into a river and couldn't swim, would
you—one, yell for help and try to scramble
out; two, dive to the bottom and crawl out;
or three, lie on your back and float until
help came?

JOHNNY. How deep is the river? (MC BRAY
wipes his dripping forehead with his sleeve.
PRIVATE JESSEL *turns over another leaf.*)

MC BRAY. (*Hoarsely and with suppressed
but withering scorn.*) Maybe you forget,
Mr. Johnson, that these tests are prepared
by the psychological experts of the United
States government and you're either crazy
or you're not.

CAPTAIN VALENTINE. (*Sweetly.*) Yes, Mr.
Johnson, we need another man immediately.
Please tell us whether you're a lunatic.

JOHNNY. (*Flaring up.*) Now look here, you folks—

MC BRAY. (*Intoning heavily.*) Why is wheat better for food than corn?—Is it, one,—because it—Chook—is it because, one —is it more nutritious, two, more expensive than nutrinsive—or because in a miller you can flound it gri-ner?—Ha-ha— (*A sickly look spreads over his face.*)

JOHNNY. I catch your drift, neighbor. It all depends. Now take a mule—he likes corn better for his food than he does wheat. Of course I like wheat better—that is, flour. But take a sheep now—he—likes grass. And a hog'll eat anything.

MC BRAY. (*Flinging up his hands.*) Po-leece! Po-leece!

JOHNNY. (*Looking about him and grinning with sudden comprehension.*) I know what you all are doing. You're playing riddles, ain't you? I'm good at that. Me and my daddy used to play 'em. (*His words snapping out with stern authority.*) Everybody get set— (*He pops his fingers dramatically, and with the exception of the two giant watchdogs everybody looks up with sudden attention. Even the exhausted MC BRAY raises his drooping head.*) If a hen and a half lays an egg and a half in a day and a half, how many eggs will three hens lay in one day? (*Pulling out a big brass watch and staring at it.*) Quick—one —two— (*They look at one another and then almost simultaneously all jerk out their pencils and set to figuring.*) —three, four, five— You give up?—Sure you do, takes a quick mind to answer that. Well, a hen lays only one egg a day anyhow, so the answer is three eggs, that is, if they're three good hens. (*Popping his fingers.*) Here's another one. On your toes— If two snakes got hold of each other's tail and started swallowing and kept on swallowing how would they wind up?

MC BRAY. (*In a spinning rhythm.*) How would they wind-up?—How· would they wind up?— (*Suddenly waked out of* JOHNNY'S *spell by his pencil breaking under his great figuring, and gasping.*) Nuts, that's how! (*Yelling.*) Throw him out!

(*The two privates start toward* JOHNNY but he darts around behind the easel.*)

JOHNNY. (*Staring about him.*) What y folks mean? I come here to enlist, I you. (*Running over to* MC BRAY, *his vo almost frantic.*) You can't turn me dow you can't. (*Aghast.*) Lord, Minny B wouldn't ever speak to me again. No, I got to go fight— I want to help end t war. I got to go—I— (*At a gesture fr* MC BRAY *the guards seize* JOHNNY *and d him through the door at the left.* MC BF *staggers to his feet, feels blindly about h and goes in after them.* SERGEANT JACKS *shrugs his shoulders hopelessly.*)

SERGEANT JACKSON. Looks like we got spend another night in this burg.

CAPTAIN VALENTINE. (*Beginning to cr again as he looks off into space.*) The d
went happy by,
And the nights more merrily,
But alas like my ditty most every g
thing has an end.
The Colonel came home from
wars—
(*He breaks off.*)

SERGEANT JACKSON. (*Staring at his fig ing.*) Say what *would* happen to them t snakes? (*A loud guttural cry comes fr the left rear.*) That old horse doctor's ing him the works—ha-ha! (*Suddenly door flies open and one of the tatto giants pitches headlong into the scene lies groaning on the floor, with his ha over his face.* JOHNNY *springs in after h bareheaded and his torn blue serge in his hand.*)

JOHNNY. (*Shaking his left fist at the p trate figure and roaring.*) So you'd tear blue serge, would you? Well, let me you, I'm planning to get married in coat—at least I was. (*They all stare at in amazement. The giant moans and on the floor.* JOHNNY *now looks dow him somewhat in sorrow.*) I got a mig hard fist from chiseling tombstones, an didn't mean to hit you such a blow in face.

CAPTAIN VALENTINE. (*With a courtly and sweet smile.*) Crazy or not crazy, our man!

BLACK OUT.

SCENE IV

"A light that lighteth men their way."

*is night. A prospect looking seaward
m the entrance to the harbor of New
rk. The tips of a few dark branches
me the scene of an infinite ocean and
less sky. Far in the background stands
* STATUE OF LIBERTY, *the upper part of
figure illuminated from a hidden light,
l in her hand a brightly glowing beacon.
ll and majestic she stands, immovable,
d brooding over the scene like some
led apocalyptic figure.
en the curtain rises, the orchestra is
cluding a soft, harmonious arrangement
a lullaby. And then sliding across the
kground from right to left, a painted
ng upon a painted ocean, comes the gray
stly shape of a great warship with its
eatening guns stuck forward like the
ennae of some strange, primeval crus-
an. It disappears at the left ,and now
from the right and almost close enough
he ledge to be touched by an onlooker's
d come the curved rail and part of the
k of a passenger ship. Stretched out on
floor one after the other lie the sleeping
ns of soldiers, their pale upturned faces
hed in the radiance of the moon, and
king like recumbent figures on a great
y-moving catafalque. Standing by the
and partly obscured by his hanging
ket is* JOHNNY JOHNSON, *dressed in an
y union suit, and his rumpled hair
ly caressed by a little breeze. He has just
n from his sleep and is staring in dreamy
silent awe at the faraway* STATUE.*

NNY. (*After a moment, his words ris-
at first broken and almost indistinct.*)
nk of it—
e motion of the rail and deck stops.*)
re you stand,
a picture in that history book I read.
ny Belle said I'd see you so,
now at last I have—
r hand uplifted with a torch
ng goodbye to us,
d luck and bless you every one.
th hushed fervency.*)
God bless you,
Iother of Liberty—
t's what you are,
rt of mother to us all,
uting sharply.*)
we your sons.
here tonight as we set forth

To fight the German Lords,
I raise my hand
(*He does so.*)
And swear a Bible oath
That Johnny Johnson—
That's my name,
You maybe haven't heard of me,
But some day soon you will—
I swear that neither by a look, a thought,
   or word,
Will I fail either you or Minny Belle.
And I will keep my character clean
And come back as I went—
Without a smirch.
(*More sternly and emphatically.*)
And furthermore I swear
That I will never see your light again
Until I've helped to bring back peace—
And win this war which ends all wars.
And yet I'm not just sure
How it will come to pass,
But I will find a way,
And if the generals and the kings don't
   know
I'll show them how it's done,
For never yet has Johnny Johnson failed
To get an answer when he hunted for it.
I swear!
I swear!
And once an oath is made with me,
It's same as sealed and bound.
(*Murmuring.*)
Farewell, Mother,
And peaceful be thy dreams.
(*With his hand still at salute, he pulls his
blanket around him and slowly sinks back
to his rest. And only when he is stretched
out like the other figures does he let his
hand fall. A murmurous groan seems to
run among the sleepers; they turn in their
hard beds and lie still again.* JOHNNY's *voice
rises once more in falling drowsy syllables.*)
Starlight, star-bright—
Goodbye, Minny Belle, my darling,
I sleep with your dear—picture—'gainst—
   my—heart.
(*The rail and the deck slowly move away
at the left and disappear in a great engulfing shadow. The illuminated* STATUE *remains alone in the depths of the night,
lonely and aloof as she holds her beacon
up, and following with her sightless, stony
stare the progress of the boat that carries*
JOHNNY JOHNSON *out to sea:*)

CURTAIN.

ACT TWO

SCENE I

"Lead, Kindly Light."

The scene is a shadowy road somewhere in France behind the front lines. It is night. A slow cortege of dark twisted and anguished French soldiers is moving like a small funeral procession across the foreground of the scene from right to left. These are the wounded men returning from the front. A few black trees show against the dim light of the sky in the background. As the figures go limping and moving painfully by, a file of American soldiers in full war gear, including gas masks at the alert, are discerned moving along the upper level of the roadbank from left to right. They are going up to the front lines as the Frenchmen are coming out. The wounded men—some blinded, some walking with the aid of crutches, some helped along by their more fortunate fellows—are chanting a low, mournful hymn of pain.

WOUNDED SOLDIERS.   Nous sommes blessés,
    Ayez pitié,

    Aidez, aidez,
    Nous sommes blessés.
(*The last of the file of American soldie stops on the roadbank and stands lookin sympathetically down as the end of t cortege moves slowly out at the left. In t dim light of approaching dawn and s houetted as he is against the sky we reco nize the form of* JOHNNY JOHNSON. *stands there in an attitude of great sorro and sympathy as the orchestra plays out Marche Dolorosa and the little bleati cries and mumbling words of pain bre forth from the lips of the wounded m When the last Frenchman has disappeare* JOHNNY *straightens himself up, looks before him, and raises his clenched fist if making another covenant.*)

JOHNNY. (*With grim and stern emphasi* Lafayette, we are here! (*He turns, and u his bayoneted rifle held on left-handed gu before him, sets off running to the righ*

           BLACK OUT.

SCENE II

"There is one spot forever England."

The scene represents the front line trench, with its parapet and kneeling ledge running zig-zag across the stage at the rear. Beyond the trench and leaning awkwardly against the sky the tops of a few scattered and broken wooden crosses show themselves. On one of them a little bird is sitting.

When the curtain rises, CORPORAL GEORGE *and his squad of six men are standing on guard at an interval of a step apart with their backs to the audience, their rifles resting on the parapet and pointing out into No Man's Land. Sitting on the ledge in each of the intervals is a sleepy English soldier in full marching equipment. Standing to the front and in profile to the audience is an English* SERGEANT.
The time is late afternoon of an early autumn day.

SERGEANT. (*Showing a mouth gapped with snaggled teeth, as he continues his speech.*) It's the big push, the big push you Yanks will be facing and me risking my life in

the traffic of London. Gawd help yo Some of you'll come out of it alive. (hoists one foot up on a broken box, s in his palm and begins polishing his sho

CORPORAL GEORGE. (*Looking around.*) Y

SERGEANT. Things is quiet up here, quiet. You can see the little larks sitt on the crosses out there. (*He gestu towards the rear. A noise is heard of the left like the sound of a breaking bo* PERCY FAIRFAX *at the right rear sudd fires off his rifle into the vastness of Man's Land, his body recoiling backw from the kick of the gun. The little disappears from the cross, and the Eng* SERGEANT *bounds around and stares at angrily.*) Oh, it's Percival Fairfax, the cago bad man.

FAIRFAX. (*Reloading his rifle and still ing straight ahead of him his voice t ulous and frightened.*) Yes sir, I— nervous, I guess. If it—this was killing I wouldn't mind it, but this silenc can't stand it.

ᵥATE SVENSON. (*A long horse-faced*
ᵈe.) You scare our little bird away.

ᴘORAL GEORGE. (*Softly.*) The waiting
ᵉe waiting—that's what unnerves a man.

ᵥATE GOLDBERGER. (*A little squabby*
ᵛ.) Yeh, it says so in the books—the
ᵗing. (*And now the musical whing of*
ᵘllet is heard flying towards the men.
ᵉ Americans duck their heads down, but
English sit as they are. The bullet strikes
parapet with a plop.)

ᴿFAX. O-ooh, and that sniper, he keeps
oting at us!

ᴰBERGER. (*Mannishly.*) Aw, what the
! (*He whirls around and begins grub-*
g in the bank, then holds up a little
ᵉct triumphantly and jiggles it.) Look-
ᵉere—that bullet's hot enough to burn
ᵛ hand. (*Going over to his place at the*
ᵃpet he lifts the lid of an old box and
ᵖs the bullet in.)

ᵥATE KEARNS. (*A huge square shoul-*
ᵈ fellow about twenty years old, chew-
ᵗobacco.) Abie here likes this war. He
a junk man back home.

ᵥATE GOLDBERGER. Yeh, and let me tell
there's plenty of junk up here. Beats
flats of Jersey all hollow.

ᵥATE O'DAY. (*A short red-faced Irish-*
.) And prowling around some of these
ᵗs you're gonna get your head blowed

ᵃTE HARWOOD. (*Sandy-haired and blue-*
ᵈ, about twenty-one, singing softly to
self.) Keep your head down, Allemand,
ᴸate last night, by the pale moonlight—
saw you—
ᵍh, Swede, how's your corn crop com-
on?

ᵃTE SVENSON. (*Gazing dolefully down*
little potted plant on the ledge beside
) It can't grow—gas—too much in the
ᴵ tank.

ᴱANT. (*Staring around.*) Is it m'ize
got here?

ᵃTE O'DAY. (*Sarcastically.*) No, corn.
ᵒund it growing back there in a shell-
Reminds him of Iowa.

ᴱANT. (*Resuming his spitting and*
polishing.*) Bless me, what queer birds—
you Americans!

PRIVATE O'DAY. (*Belligerently.*) Yeh? That's
like an Englishman—everybody's queer
but himself.

CORPORAL GEORGE. (*Sternly.*) Keep your
shirt on, Pat.

SERGEANT. (*With a sharp grunt.*) Uhck—
"Pat"—Irish be Gawd! (*The other English*
soldiers snicker.)

PRIVATE O'DAY. Yes, from Boston.

SERGEANT. (*Calling loudly off at the left.*)
Private Johnson!—Where is that bloody
skivvy?

PRIVATE KEARNS. (*Spitting.*) He'll be back.

PRIVATE FAIRFAX. He always comes back.

SERGEANT. Queer?—Anyway me lads, England never produced a specimen like your
Johnny Johnson.

PRIVATE KEARNS. You're right about that.

SERGEANT. Yesterday he offered to set me
up with a nice tombstone for a shilling.

CORPORAL GEORGE. With epitaph?

SERGEANT. Cripes, that too.

PRIVATE HARWOOD. He's got epitaphs writ
for everybody in the company, including
the Captain and the Colonel.

PRIVATE GOLDBERGER. (*Teasingly, as he*
indicates PRIVATE FAIRFAX.) Sold him one.

PRIVATE FAIRFAX. (*With timid bragga-*
docio.) Johnny says—he says—be prepared
for the worst is the way to keep it from
happening.

PRIVATE KEARNS. (*Gloomily.*) I wish there
was some way of being prepared for that
big battle the Sergeant talks about.

PRIVATE SVENSON. Yohnny Yohnson, he say
maybe the war be over soon. (*He bends*
down, peers at his corn and then dipping
a handful of water up out of the bottom
of the trench pours it around its roots.)

SERGEANT. (*With genial cruelty.*) This
war will last ten years.

PRIVATE FAIRFAX. (*With a groan.*) We
might as well be dead then.

SERGEANT. The big blighters back home don't want it to end. Who'd they sell their munitions to if we have peace? Ten years? It might last twenty.

PRIVATE O'DAY. (*Still anxious to put salt in the split tail.*) It would if you English had to win it. (*Defiantly.*) Yeh, it's me talking.

SERGEANT. (*Scornfully.*) Yeh, and if talking meant anything, the Irish would rule the world—not England.

PRIVATE O'DAY. (*Now doubling up his fists.*) Is it a fight you want? Come on!

CORPORAL GEORGE. (*Shouting.*) Can it! Can it! (*He jerks down his gun and steps between* O'DAY *and the* SERGEANT. *The* SERGEANT *tries to push by* CORPORAL GEORGE *as* JOHNNY *comes in from the left, staggering under a heavy load. In one hand he carries a huge battered tin bucket full of hot steaming tea, and over his shoulder a tow sack of provisions. Like the other soldiers he wears a helmet and gas mask at the ready, but he is stripped to the waist, grimed and muddy, and in general is a poor specimen of democracy's champion. A big hole has been torn in the top of his helmet. But though he looks somewhat dirty he seems to be the same cheerful* JOHNNY *as before.*)

JOHNNY. Old England and Ireland fighting again?—Here's something to stop it— your tea! (*At the word "tea" the English soldiers spring to their feet and along with the* SERGEANT *snap their drinking cups from their belts.* JOHNNY *drops the bag of provisions, and with a dipper in one hand and the can in the other pours each man a drink.*)

SERGEANT. (*Joyously.*) Ha-ha-ha—here's to everybody. Cheer up, Yanks, cheer up.

ENGLISH SOLDIERS. Ha-ha-ha-ha-ha—tea— tea!

SERGEANT. (*Suddenly, beginning to sing.*)
Now, England is, as we all know,
A great and mighty nation
With power big as half the world
And colonies galore.
Her army and her navy too
They quite befit her station,
The watchdogs of her flag unfurled
From Bath to Singapore.
(*The English Soldiers join in the chorus.*)
Then hail—hail—hail!

All hail Britannia and her crown!
We lift our cups to thee—
(*They do so.*)
And drink thy health in bumpers do[w]
Of tea, strong tea.
(*They all drink.*)
'Twas tea that raised her in her mig[ht]
At least that's our opinion.
And tea that made America—
Go read your history—
And fit it is that we unite
To further the dominion
Of freedom's laws and lead the way
For England and her tea.

ALL. (*With the exception of* JOHNNY *[and]*
PRIVATE O'DAY—*singing.*)
Then hail! hail! hail!
All hail Britannia and her crown!
We lift our cups to thee
And drink thy health in bumpers do[wn]
Of tea—strong tea.
(*Their song ended, they drain down [the] last drop, snap their cups back in t[heir] belts, and stand ready to march a[way]. Suddenly as if coming from undergro[und] at the back a faint and faraway chorus [of] foreign voices is heard answering like [an] echo.*)

VOICES. "Then hail! hail! hail!
All hail Britannia and her crown!
We lift our cups to thee!—"

CORPORAL GEORGE. (*Softly, as they listen.*) Golly, them Heinies are answe[ring] us.

SERGEANT. (*With quiet and forlorn re[mi]niscence.*) Last Christmas up here we w[as] singing "Holy Night," and they done [the] same.

JOHNNY. (*Snapping his fingers and t[urn]ing inclusively around.*) See there—[good] scouts like us, I been telling you.

SERGEANT. Well, good or bad, our [busi]ness is to lick 'em. (*Shaking his shoul[ders] mournfully.*) Everything shipshape, m[en?]

ENGLISH SOLDIERS. (*Loudly as they [slap] their bellies.*) Aye, sir.

SERGEANT. Right-face! (*They obey.*) [Hip,] hip— (*They start marching off. The* [SER]GEANT *salutes.*) Cheerio, Yanks—we [leave] this war over to you. And Johnson, if [you] capture old Hindenburg, let me know. [(] JOHNNY *makes no reply, for he has al[ready]*

ne over and sat down on a box to the
ht of the can of tea and begun figuring
a sheet of paper. The SERGEANT goes on
after his squad singing.)
Then hail! hail! hail!
All hail Britannia and her crown!
We lift—
he American soldiers turn and watch
m leave regretfully.)

VATE KEARNS. God, it's lonesome al-
dy!

VATE O'DAY. (Furiously.) Just like the
y English. As soon as they think a real
t's coming on they march out and leave
holding the bag.

NNY. (Still figuring.) Well, every jug's
to stand on its own bottom sometime—
ny mammy said.

PORAL GEORGE. (Snapping.) Don't start
n old sayings again, Johnson, I'm sick
em.

NNY. All right, sir, you're the boss,
he ox said to the yoke—

PORAL GEORGE. (Yelling.) You heard

NNY. (Humbly.) Sorry, sir. (And now
men come over and get their food out
he bag—a hunk of bread to each man
a can of bully beef. Then they turn
nd from their rifles and sit down on
ledge and begin eating.)

ATE KEARNS. (Scratching himself with
lbows.) Where did you learn them old
ngs, Johnson— "As the minnow said
he whale" and "If smell was all the
would win," and all the rest of it?

NNY. Huh? Oh, just picked 'em up.

ATE SVENSON. (Throwing crumbs over
parapet.) Chick-chick-chick!

PORAL GEORGE. That little bird won't
e back around here, Slim. He's got too
h sense. (Yawning.) I feel like I've
d watch forty hours. What time is it,
son? (JOHNNY pulls out his big watch
looks at it, then begins to chuckle
v.) What you laughing at?

NNY. Back home there was a teamster
en you asked him what time it was
say— (He stops.)

CORPORAL GEORGE. Yeh, and what would
he say?

JOHNNY. He'd say—Time all dogs was
dead, ain't you sick? (The soldiers laugh
and CORPORAL GEORGE springs angrily to his
feet.)

CORPORAL GEORGE. Damm it, I told you
not to pull any more of them cracks. (Wagging his head, he sinks back on the parapet.)
For six years I was a head waiter in Childs',
I thought I'd met every kind of a crumb—

JOHNNY. (Now springing up.) I won't
take any more of that. I'm not a crumb.
(He seizes his bayoneted rifle which has
been leaning against the bank and starts
towards CORPORAL GEORGE.) You keep picking on me—

CORPORAL GEORGE. (With a shriek.) Stop
that left-handed fool! (PRIVATE KEARNS and
HARWOOD jump up and get in front of
him.)

JOHNNY. (In a low hard voice.) Take it
back, Corporal—

PRIVATE KEARNS. (Eyeing JOHNNY.) You
better, Corp, you better.

CORPORAL GEORGE. (Muttering.) All right,
I take it back. And put that gun down,
Johnson. You're breaking orders by touching it anyhow. (JOHNNY waits a moment
and then with a chuckle replaces the gun
against the parapet, after which he sits
down and sets to figuring again.)

PRIVATE O'DAY. (After a moment's silence.)
What you figuring on now, Old-end-the-
war?

CORPORAL GEORGE. (Satirically.) He's writing a letter to the general, again . . . I
guess . . . or is it Minny Belle this time?

JOHNNY. (Quietly.) I'm figuring on a sort
of document addressed to the German enlisted men.

CORPORAL GEORGE. Ho-ho! Will wonders
never cease as the Rabbi said to the— (With
sour distaste.) Bah!

JOHNNY. Well, you'll never end this war
if you don't try to.

CORPORAL GEORGE. And you think you can
do that by writing letters. Wonderful, wonderful.

JOHNNY. Well we don't seem to be able to end it with guns. (PRIVATE HARWOOD *suddenly pushes his food away from him and picking up a rope from the ledge sits spinning it aimlessly.*)

PRIVATE HARWOOD. (*Twirling his rope.*) What I'd like to do would be to slip up on the Kaiser standing somewhere and lasso the crook. That'd stop the whole crazy business. (*He throws his lariat backward over his shoulder, jerks it, and begins pulling it in.*)

PRIVATE KEARNS. (*Scratching himself savagely.*) And what I wish is old Kaiser Bill had my cooties.

PRIVATE HARWOOD. (*Springing up from the ledge and pulling on his lariat.*) Heigh, I've hung something. (*He sticks his head quickly up and jerks it down again.*) God, it's a German soldier's leg—with a boot on! (*He drops the rope and sits staring before him. With the exception of* JOHNNY *the others shoot their heads up, then jerk them down and sit in grim silence.* PRIVATE FAIRFAX *starts to whimper and pulls a little book from his pocket and begins to read.*)

JOHNNY. Yeah, there's legs and arms scattered all around. Down there where you cross that gully you can see 'em. Young arms and legs that used to throw rocks and walk about. (*Now once more comes the musical whing of the sniper's bullet. They all, except* JOHNNY, *duck their heads and then sit a moment in silence.*)

PRIVATE FAIRFAX. (*As if to himself.*) It says here in the Bible to love your enemies. How can a man do that? (*And now off at the right the voice of* CAPTAIN VALENTINE *is heard humming. He comes drifting slowly in, immaculately dressed as ever.*)

CAPTAIN VALENTINE. (*Continuing his ballad as he gives the scene a thorough inspection.*) Woe, woe, cried the lady so fair
The while she disrupted her hair—
Ha-ha laughed the colonel, you're guilty,
I knew I'd unearth it.
And the sergeant he too had his say
Ere the rope took his brave life away—
(*He breaks off his humming as they all stand to attention.*) At ease. (*They all relax. He continues in a fast sharp flow of words, unlike his former drawling.*) We've got orders to get this sniper. You can draw lots.

JOHNNY. (*Stepping forward.*) Is he leader—a big man, sir?

CAPTAIN VALENTINE. Right now he's m[ore] important to us than Hindenburg hims[elf.] He's got the provision train scared off that road down there.

JOHNNY. (*Saluting.*) I volunteer, sir.

CAPTAIN VALENTINE. (*Turning and lo[ok]ing at him with a smile.*) That's very [nice] of you, Johnson, but you're too valuabl[e a] man to risk. (*He takes a box of mat[ches] from his pocket and strikes one of th[em,] then reverses the ends of several mat[ches] and holds them out.*) The fellow [who] draws the burnt match goes for the sn[iper] at dawn.

JOHNNY. Can I draw, sir?

CAPTAIN VALENTINE. Yes—last. (*He tu[rns] and holds out his hand to* PRIVATE FAIR[FAX] who draws and lets out a glad cry.*)

PRIVATE FAIRFAX. I didn't get it! (*CAP[TAIN]* VALENTINE *holds out his hand to* PRI[VATE] GOLDBERGER. *He draws. From the loo[k of] relief he too is saved.*)

JOHNNY. (*Crowding up.*) I'm always lu[cky] at such things. (*CAPTAIN VALENTINE h[olds] his hand out to* PRIVATE HARWOOD.*)

PRIVATE HARWOOD. (*Drawing.*) Ha-h[a, I] don't go. (*Then* PRIVATE KEARNS *draws,[and] strikes the match joyously on his he[el] and flings it down. And now* PRIVATE S[VEN]SON *stands up trembling. He draws.*)

PRIVATE SVENSON. (*In a nervous titte[r] of relief.*) Ha-ha—hee-hee—

CAPTAIN VALENTINE. (*With an i[rate]* groan.*) I see what's coming.

JOHNNY. (*Grinning.*) I told you so. [He] draws the last match and the CA[PTAIN] shakes his head disgustedly.*)

CAPTAIN VALENTINE. I'll say this for [you,] Johnson, whatever your drawbacks, cow[ard]ice is not one of them. (*Angrily.*) To[mor]row night I'm going to send some o[ther] fellows out too.

JOHNNY. Aw, you won't need to do [that,] sir.

CAPTAIN VALENTINE. Lie down now [and] get some sleep—all of you. There's [a]

be a patrol directly in front of you. (*He gestures to the rear.*) Johnson, you can use your own judgment about the sniper.

JOHNNY. Yes, sir.

CORPORAL GEORGE. Attenshun. (*They all stand up, salute, and* CAPTAIN VALENTINE *starts away at the left. And now once more we hear the musical whinging of the sniper's bullet, followed by a loud yell off to the left. Everybody ducks, then straightens up again.* CAPTAIN VALENTINE *looks off and hurries away. They all resume their seats.*) I wonder who got hit that time? Well, Johnson, I suppose you'd better begin to wind up your earthly business.

JOHNNY. (*Now sitting down and cleaning the mud from his shoe with a stick.*) I will be about forty or fifty years from now, I hope.

PRIVATE FAIRFAX. (*Staring at him.*) You mean you're not scared?

PRIVATE KEARNS. Ever notice these nuts?— They ain't scared. (*By this time the shades of evening have begun to fall. The soldiers sit a moment in silence and then begin to make themselves comfortable on the ground and on the parapet ledge.* JOHNNY *gets his coat, brings it over and spreads it out close beside the can of tea. With the exception of* PRIVATE FAIRFAX *and* PRIVATE HARWOOD, *they all stretch themselves out.* PRIVATE HARWOOD *pulls off his shirt and sits musing before him.*)

PRIVATE FAIRFAX. (*Beginning to read aloud from his Bible.*) "For God so loved the world that he gave his only begotten Son that whosoever believeth on Him should not perish but have everlasting life." (*He drops down on his knees in an attitude of prayer.* JOHNNY *looks around and breaks into a low chuckle.*)

CORPORAL GEORGE. (*Muttering as he lies down.*) I'll tell you this, Johnson, if I were in your shoes, I'd be praying too.

JOHNNY. Human beings are funny, ain't they?—I was just thinking how the Germans are praying to the same God on their side too. (CORPORAL GEORGE *lies down again, and with the exception of* PRIVATE HARWOOD *all settle themselves for sleep.*)

PRIVATE HARWOOD (*Mournfully.*) Getting on towards dark—just about this time the boys are rounding up the calves back home.

CORPORAL GEORGE. Yeh, back home— Good-night everybody.

JOHNNY. (*Kissing a photograph and putting it in his shirt.*) Good-night, Minny Belle—good-night.

PRIVATE KEARNS. (*With a mock-smacking sound.*) Good-night, Minny Belle, the mighty hero is thinking of you.

JOHNNY. Thank you, Private Kearns.

PRIVATE HARWOOD. (*Beginning to unwrap his leggings and singing with wistful remembrance.*) Oh the Rio Grande—where
the wind blows free
And the sun shines so clear and bright,
Where the trail is long, o'er the wide prairie
And the cowboy travels light.
Well it's saddle and boots
In sun and rain
And away, and watch me ride
Up along the canyon and over the plain.
Myself and my horse are one and the same
And one shadow runs beside.

(*The men stir and murmur sleepily to themselves.*)

Oh life was dull but it happened so
A rodeo came one day.
I took my gal to see the show—
There stood my little bay.
I jumped in the saddle and grabbed the
horn
And yelled to all around,
I'm the best damn cowpuncher ever was
born,
And for Texas I am bound.

(*A foggy twilight begins to envelop the scene.*)

Oh the Rio Grande—where the wind blows
free—
(*He lies down on the parapet. The lights slowly die out, and the scene is gradually enveloped in the gloom of night, with the sightless eyelid of the world slowly shutting out the sky. Far away as if under the rim of the earth the low growling of the mighty guns is heard. A moment passes. The muffled forms of the soldiers are dimly discerned as they sleep. Only the smiling*

blissful face of JOHNNY *is visible. In the orchestra the low melody of* MINNY BELLE'S *love song is playing, and far away from out of No Man's Land comes the faint indistinguishable whisper of her tender voice.*)

JOHNNY. (*Murmuring.*) Minny Belle— My honey-love! (*And now the gray illumination of* JOHNNY'S *face begins to die out, and* MINNY BELLE'S *song fades in air. As it fades the other sleepers are heard moaning and twisting in the grip of an uneasy dream. And on their now tortured faces appears the same gray illumination, but* JOHNNY'S *face remains in shadow. As if embodied forth by the restless sleepers' nightmare, the round muzzles of three great cannon push themselves slowly up over the parapet and then out and out until their long threatening necks stretch above the recumbent figures.* MINNY BELLE'S *song has now died out from the orchestra and is supplanted by the growling croompy notes of the guns. They begin to sing in a queer outlandish trio harmony.*)

GUNS. Soldiers, soldiers—
Sleep softly now beneath the sky,
　　Soldiers, soldiers—
Tomorrow under earth you lie.
We are the guns that you have meant
For blood and death. — Our strength is
　　spent
Obedient to your stern intent—
　　Soldiers, masters, men.

　Masters, masters,
Deep dark in earth as iron we slept,
　　Masters, masters,
Till at your word to light we leapt.
We might have served a better will—
Ploughs for the field, wheels for the mill,
But you decreed that we must kill—
　　Masters, soldiers, men.

　Soldiers, soldiers,
Sleep darkly now beneath the sky,
　　Soldiers, soldiers—
No sound shall wake you where you lie,
No foe disturb your quiet bed
Where we stand watching overhead—
We are your tools—and you the dead!—
　　Soldiers, masters, men!

(*As the cannon song begins to die, the air is split by the musical tinkling of an alarm clock. As it continues to ring, the guns*

withdraw behind the parapet, their gre muzzles slowly and sullenly sinking out sight. The ringing of the clock stops. a JOHNNY *sits up looking about him. Jerki his arms above his head, he yawns a gapes and then gets to his feet.*)

CORPORAL GEORGE. (*Mumbling.*) Wh time is it, Johnson?

JOHNNY. (*Looking up at the sky.*) Abo three-thirty—by the ell and the yard. (on and get your sleep. (*He takes an o sock from his knapsack and begins to fit over his face like a mask. Suddenly* PRIVA FAIRFAX *lets out a scream, sits up and gins to beat wildly about him.*)

PRIVATE FAIRFAX. Catch him, catch hi (*The other soldiers sit up and beat at son thing in the trenches.*)

PRIVATE GOLDBERGER. (*Lunging off to t left.*) There he goes.

PRIVATE O'DAY. Whoo!—that bugger v big as a hog!

JOHNNY. (*Still working with his mas Yeah, the rats get plenty to eat up he I saw one yesterday squatted on a de Australian's face. (*For a while they all in disconsolate silence.*)

CORPORAL GEORGE. What in the devil you doing now, Johnson?

JOHNNY. Camouflage. (*Now pulling old poncho over his shoulders, he picks the bread knife and begins whetting it his palm. Then he goes over to the para pulls in part of the lariat and cuts it The soldiers stare at him.*)

CORPORAL GEORGE. Don't tell me yo going after that sniper without a gun.

JOHNNY. This piece of rope and br knife ought to do.

PRIVATE GOLDBERGER. Do you know wh he hangs out?

JOHNNY. I've got an idea.

PRIVATE KEARNS. He's got ideas. (PRIV SVENSON *clambers up and comes over* JOHNNY.)

PRIVATE SVENSON. (*Grabbing his hand, voice choked with emotion.*) Good Yohnny. Be careful—uh— (*He gulps*

NY. I will, Slim. (*Jauntily*.) So long.
be back about sun-up. (*Stopping and
ng back*.) Better have some breakfast
that sniper, he'll be hungry. (*He goes
at the left*.)

PRIVATE SVENSON. (*Blubbering*.) He'll be
killed!—

CORPORAL GEORGE. I hope so. Go to sleep.
(*They all lie down again*.)

BLACK OUT.

SCENE III

"A new way to pay old debts."

near dawn, and the scene represents
ell-battered churchyard with a few
en tombstones about and a piece of
ed church tower distant in the back-
nd. The earth is covered with a thick
e of grass about knee high. In the
ediate center rear of the scene stands
ge black wooden statue of the Christ,
ng a bit awry and showing in its
re something of the beaten and agon-
torture of an El Greco figure. While
orchestra continues to play the music
he stricken Redeemer, JOHNNY crawls
om the right front and secretes him-
in the tall rank grass. A moment
s, the music continues, and then from
left rear the SNIPER enters, dodging
d tombstones and any bit of covering
h in the manner of the Big Bad Wolf
ing upon the house of the three little
He comes to the base of the statue
looks appraisingly about him. He is a
er fellow with a rather large Kaiser
elm mustache and an evil-looking hel-
pulled low down over his forehead.
bing up on a little platform built be-
the statue, he opens a panel in the
of the Christ, crawls in and secretes
elf, the door closing after him. And
as he worms his way further up in-
the dolorous figure, like an animal
zing along inside a hollow tree, the
e shakes and wriggles with his weight.
it grows still, the orchestra stops
ng, and a moment of silence passes.
now through a great wounded hole in
reast of Christ where the heart should
he ugly muzzle of a telescopic rifle
a silencer attached is pushed through.
muzzle comes to rest on the out-
hed hand of the Redeemer. It seems
ow tense and the eye of the SNIPER can
n shining out of the heart as he takes
ght. Suddenly the air is stricken with
ffled explosion and the bullet goes

whinging on its musical way. JOHNNY
bounds up out of the grass and rushing
forward, flings his rope around the statue
and draws it tight. Immediately a tremendous drumming sets up inside, and the
wooden figure totters and sways and gestic-
ulates like a live thing.

JOHNNY. Ha-ha— I got the dead wood on
you this time— (*He ties the rope as the
statue continues to shake and the drumming keeps up*.)

SNIPER. (*In a high piteous voice as the
figure bobs about*.) Kamerad! Kamerad!

JOHNNY. Yeah, and I'll Kamerad you, you
Proosian devil! Drop that gun. (*The statue
gives a final buck and lunge*.) Drop it, I
tell you. (*And now the rifle is pushed
through the hole and falls to the ground*.)
Pistol too! You've got one. (*A moment
passes. And now a mean-looking Luger
with belt attached is disgorged from the
heart and falls to the ground. JOHNNY un-
winds his rope and stands aside as he
flings open the door*.) Come on out. (*The
SNIPER comes gingerly down, and as he
steps to the earth JOHNNY lays his knife
against the back of his neck*.)

SNIPER. (*In a high treble cry*.) Ooh, um
Gottes willen, tun Sie das nicht!

JOHNNY. (*Cuffing him about the head*.)
You dirty stinking rascal! I've a good mind
to cut your throat. Ain't you ashamed—
using Jesus Christ like that!—and he a good
man! (*He slaps his face again. The SNIPER
drops down on the ground and buries his
face in his hands. JOHNNY steps over, picks
up the gun and the pistol and throws them
out of reach towards the front and then
stands over the SNIPER looking angrily down
at him, wiping his sweaty face with his
sleeve*.)

SNIPER. (*Looking up as JOHNNY takes off
his mask*.) Du lieber Himmel!

JOHNNY. (*Suddenly kicking him in the shins as he pulls off his helmet.*) Look-a-there—that hole. You shot at me yesterday!

SNIPER. (*Howling.*) Ow! Ow!

JOHNNY. (*Stamping down on one of his feet and mocking him.*) Ow! Ow! I ought to get me a switch and beat the lard out of you.

SNIPER. (*With piteous pleading.*) Bitte, bitte— (*He begins sobbing.*)

JOHNNY. (*Staring at him malevolently.*) Stop that crying! (*The* SNIPER's *sobs stop.*)

SNIPER. Yes—yes, sir.

JOHNNY. Why, you speak English.

SNIPER. Yes, sir.

JOHNNY. Smart, mean and smart, you big guys.—What's happened to your mustache? (*The* SNIPER *pushes his hanging lip piece quickly back but it comes off in his hand, revealing the lips and face of a beardless boy.*)

JOHNNY. (*Throwing up his hands.*) Great Jehosaphat! You're just a boy!

BOY. (*Pushing back his helmet and wiping his forehead with his hand, disclosing his close-cropped boyish head.*) Yes, sir. (JOHNNY *suddenly turns away and stands looking off deep in thought. The* BOY *watches him apprehensively.*)

JOHNNY. (*In anger and disgust.*) That knocks me for a row of stumps—it does! (*Turning back to him.*) Come over here by this pile of dirt. (*He goes over and sits down. The* BOY *crawls along the ground and sits a few feet away from him.*) Of all the ungodly things! How old are you?

BOY. Sixteen, sir.

JOHNNY. Sixteen— Hardly weaned. (*After a pause.*) Is your mother living?

BOY. Yes—sir. (*He bows his bare head over in his hands and begins to weep again.*)

JOHNNY. Aw, don't do that— Aw—quit it. (*He moves over a bit and puts his hand on the* BOY's *shoulder. With the back of his other hand he furtively wipes his own eyes. Turning to him again.*) Why in devil did you get into this war—youn you are?

BOY. (*His voice suddenly stronger.*) Faterland and Kaiser, sir. (*He salutes air.*)

JOHNNY. (*With an exclamation of patience.*) Nuts, as the monkey said! never mind that— Don't you know it' his own power and glory that the K sends such little boys as you out to (*As the* BOY *makes no answer.*) Don't believe that?

BOY. (*Lowering his voice.*) That's Sergeant Mueller says. (*Quickly.*) Bu only talks it among the soldiers— (muring.*) Sergeant Mueller.

JOHNNY. And he's right. (*After a ment's silence.*) Who is this Serg Miller?

BOY. (*Fervently.*) He is kind and go The best man in the world. He was English teacher.

JOHNNY. He is—huh?

BOY. Yes, sir.

JOHNNY. And how does he feel about war?

BOY. (*Reluctantly.*) Yes—yes, sir, hates it.

JOHNNY. Like you and me—huh?

BOY. May-bee.

JOHNNY. Hmn-n. (*After a moment.*) some chewing gum? (*He hands the a piece which he has drawn from pocket.*) Put it in your mouth and ch like me— Don't swallow it. (*The* BOY so. JOHNNY *watches him with a so paternal geniality.*) Good? (*A tiny frightened smile breaks for an instant the* BOY's *white drawn face.* JOHNNY him on the shoulder.*) What's your son?

BOY. Johann—Johann Lang. It means —in English.

JOHNNY. I be jim-swingled! Why my name too—John. (*He reaches ove shakes the* BOY's *limp hand.*) Don afraid. I'm not going to hurt you.

NN. (*Now staring at him.*) But the als tell us you Americans cut and kill scalp and chop the German soldiers eces with knives.

NY. Ha-ha, they do!

NN. Yes, sir, they all do— (*Hesitat-.*) The generals and the colonels in speeches—the newspapers too.

NY. That's because the Kaiser's crowd 'em what to say.

NN. (*More confidingly as he chews.*) Herr Mueller says he don't believe it us he says so. (*Eagerly.*) He says he s you soldiers are like us—in the heart But he don't know—he think so. NNY *sits looking off. Suddenly he slaps nee.*)

NY. Say—it looks like me and this r fellow ought to get together on the (*He begins tapping his lip with his nger in deep thought. Young* JOHANN *es him constantly, though now some- of his first fright has disappeared.*)

JN. Pardon me, sir, but the sun will rise. Then it will be very dangerous ou here.

NY. (*Turning to the* BOY.) Suppose friend Miller knew we American sol- wanted to end this war the way he what do you think he'd do?

JN. (*Mournfully.*) Aber, he cannot that.

NY. Suppose he knew that we Amer- deep down are the German people's s—what do you think he'd want to

JN. Stop fighting.

NY. He's a sensible man. (*Dumping letters and folded papers from his ts, he suddenly begins writing with a f a pencil, reading off some of the as he does so.*) "Friend Miller, John who brings this letter to you was ed by me, but I am sending him -"

JN. (*With a cry.*) You let me go! springs forward and hugs JOHNNY's and then lies weeping on the ground, his hands touching JOHNNY's *foot.*)

JOHNNY. (*Smiling.*) Yeah, that's right— (*Looking around towards the flaming horizon.*) and we got to hurry. (*Reading aloud again as he writes.*) "—sending him back with these messages—um—um— See the enclosed speeches of Woodrow Wilson, also some by me which come quicker to the point. You and me have the same ideas about being friends and ending this war. John will tell you more. I must close on account of the sun coming up—
　　　　　　　Yours in friendship,
　　　　　　　　Johnny Johnson,
　　　　　　　　Private soldier."
(*Touching* JOHANN *on the shoulder.*) Get up, son. (JOHANN *rises and stands wiping the tears of happiness from his eyes.*)

JOHANN. You—you really let me go?

JOHNNY. (*Shoving several papers in an envelope and sticking them into* JOHANN's *pocket.*) I'm sending you back, son, and I hope we end the war before it ends you.

(JOHANN *grabs his hand and kisses it with wild joy.*)

JOHANN. Forgive me—the Colonel, he made me do it—

JOHNNY. (*Pulling his hand sheepishly away.*) Do what?

JOHANN. (*With a gesture towards the figure of Christ.*) Hide in there and shoot at you Americans. All the time after this I shoot in the air.

JOHNNY. (*Quickly.*) That's the idea. Tell friend Miller to spread the news among his soldiers—his friends—make copies of the speeches, distribute them everywhere. You'll hear from me again—somehow. Now quick—run—we're going to save a lot of lives. (*He pushes him along.* JOHANN *grabs* JOHNNY's *hand once more, then embraces him and dashes away at the left rear.* JOHNNY *stares after him, waves his hand, and then picks up the rifle and the pistol and stands looking at the statue of Christ. He pulls off his helmet in humility and respect.* CAPTAIN VALENTINE *comes crawling in on his all-fours at the right front. He is humming softly to himself.* JOHNNY *gives a last look at the statue, gazes at the rifle and pistol in his hands, then shrugs his shoulders in a vague comment on the world*

and comes towards the front. CAPTAIN VAL-
ENTINE *calls out in a low admiring voice.*)

CAPTAIN VALENTINE. You killed him!

JOHNNY. (*In good humor.*) No.

CAPTAIN VALENTINE. (*Standing quickly
up.*) What! (*Looking off and then jerking
out his pistol.*) Yonder—look out! (*Raging.*)
Oh, you fool!

JOHNNY. (*Springing in front of him.*)
Don't you shoot him! (CAPTAIN VALENTINE
tries to dodge this way and that around
JOHNNY, *and finally gets in a shot over his
shoulder.*)

CAPTAIN VALENTINE. (*Raising his pistol as
if to strike* JOHNNY *with the butt of it.*)
I missed him. (*Suddenly a burst of machine*

gun fire rattles out from the directio⟨n⟩
the German trenches. The air is filled ⟨with⟩
a medley of whinging sounds and the ⟨noise⟩
of bullets striking against the earth.
CAPTAIN *throws himself flat on his* ⟨face⟩
JOHNNY *darts forward to drop down b⟨y⟩*
him, then suddenly slaps his hand t⟨o⟩
rump with a howl. CAPTAIN VALEN⟨TINE⟩
laughs hysterically as JOHNNY *sprawls* ⟨down⟩
by him.) Ha-ha-ha, got you, did t⟨hey?⟩
There is a just God after all!

JOHNNY. (*Half-sobbing with anger* ⟨and⟩
vexation, one hand still on his r⟨ump.⟩
Ain't that a hell of a place to get ⟨it?⟩
(*The* CAPTAIN *starts crawling off a⟨nd⟩
right front,* JOHNNY *crawling painfully* ⟨after⟩
him.)

                  BLACK OUT.

SCENE IV

" 'Tis not so deep as a well—but 'tis enough.
              'Twill serve.''

The hospital. JOHNNY's *bed is in the foreground with an infinite row of beds painted
on the backdrop and diminishing in the
distance.* JOHNNY *is lying restless · on his
side with his face towards the audience.
A young French* NURSE, *very chic and attractive in her French uniform, is trying to
make him comfortable.*

NURSE. (*Sitting down by him and beginning to sing.*) My Madelon of Paree
      She laugh and dance and sing
      To cheer the weary soldier
         At his homecoming.
      A little room together,
      An hour of love to spend,
      Comme-ça, your arm around me,
         Oh—mon ami, my friend.

(JOHNNY *stirs and closes his eyes.*)
      But she—ah—she remembers
      That other love and joy,
      The first, the best, the dearest,
         Tired soldier boy—
      A narrow room alone now,
      Rain on the roof above,
      And he will sleep forever,
         Oh—mon ami, my love.
      My Madelon of Paree
      She does not sit and grieve,
      But sings away her sorrow
      To cheer the soldier's leave.

      For life is short and funny,
      And love must have an end.
      An hour may be forever—
         Oh—mon ami, my friend.
(*A fat middle-aged hospital* ORDERLY ⟨comes⟩
in from the right and starts on acros⟨s the⟩
scene.)

JOHNNY. (*Jerking up his head and c⟨alling⟩
out.*) Any mail for me?

ORDERLY. (*Chuckling.*) Not even a ⟨card⟩
from General Pershing. (*Laughing s⟨oftly.⟩*
Hee-hee—how's the wound this mor⟨ning?⟩

JOHNNY. (*Irately.*) I've told you to l⟨ay off⟩
that subject.

ORDERLY. The doctor's coming to ha⟨ve an⟩
other look at it in a minute.

JOHNNY. (*Irritably.*) Yeh—and I w⟨ant to⟩
have a look at him. He's got to let m⟨e out⟩
of here.

ORDERLY. Why in blazes you want ⟨to get⟩
back to the front is more than I ca⟨n see.⟩
(*Wagging his head he goes on out at* ⟨left.⟩

NURSE. (*Putting her hand on his* ⟨fore-
head.*) Forty times a day I say take i⟨t easy,⟩
bébé, you last longer.

JOHNNY. And how can I take it eas⟨y with⟩
me with work to do in the trenches⟨?⟩ ⟨He⟩
pulls a letter from under his pillo⟨w and⟩
begins reading it.)

E. (*Presently.*) Johnny.

NY. Yeh.

E. (*Softly.*) Don't you love me a—
say—little bit?

NY. There you go—back on that sub—
Now look here—you know I'm an
ged man.

E. Oui, but your Minny Belle—she is
away—

NY. (*Pressing the letter to his breast.*)
s here—close by— (*Reading his letter
l to himself perhaps for the twentieth
) "Every night when we meet in the
h I think of you and pray for victory.
sure the despicable Hun will soon be
ght to their knees." (*The warmth
out of his voice.*) "Anguish has just
with his new motor truck to take me
e office— How many of the enemy
you killed? Goodbye till next time."

E. I don't like Anguish.

NY. Nobody does.

E. Maybe Minny Belle likes him?

NY. (*Rearing up in bed.*) I should
ot. (*Grimacing he lies down again.*)

E. (*In a flutter of sympathy.*) You
sleep—your fever will be worse.

NY. (*Gruffly.*) Fever or no fever, I
go, I tell you. (*He turns over on his

. (*After a moment timidly.*) Johnny?

NY. Unh-hunh.

. You don't mind—me loving you—
e? Comprenez-vous?

NY. I comprenez, all right, but it
do me no good.—You go try one of
fellows with boots and spurs (*A
e-aged DOCTOR wearing a goatee and
ng a black satchel in his hand enters
the left. Close behind him comes the
LY with a little cylinder-tank, about
inches long and three inches in di-
r in his hand. They stop by JOHNNY's

R. (*Gesturing with an inclination of
ad towards the orderly.*) Better give
whiff, I guess.

JOHNNY. (*As the* ORDERLY *steps to the
head of his bed.*) What for?

ORDERLY. It's laughing gas—make you feel
good.

JOHNNY. I don't need any gas, or whatever it is. Go ahead. And then I want you
to tell me when you're going to turn me
loose.

DOCTOR. (*Opening his satchel.*) Hm—m—
At the proper time.

JOHNNY. (*Vexatiously.*) What time is that
—as the owl said?

DOCTOR. (*Sourly.*) Maybe sooner than you
expect, as the pill said—ah-oom— Turn
over. (*The* ORDERLY *lays his cylinder down
on the bed and rolls up his sleeve. He and
the* DOCTOR *now step behind the bed, bend
down and begin deftly dressing* JOHNNY's
wound. The little NURSE *pulls a waist-high
screen from under the bed and sets it up
in front of* JOHNNY; *after which she moves
over to the right and stands looking off.
And now entering from the right comes
the* SISTER *of the Organization for the Delight of Disabled Soldiers. She is a tall,
rawboned, breezy woman of middle-age,
over-dressed and slightly over-enthusiastic
in her manner.*)

SISTER. (*Gazing about her.*) I vow! This
will be bully for our show. The acoustics
look good. (*Trying them.*) Tra-la-la. (*To
the* NURSE.) How many brave buddies have
we got here?

NURSE. Four thousand and sixty-four soldiers this morning, madame.

SISTER. That's a real break. There's nothing like a big audience to cheer the actor—
I mean the soldier. I wish to speak to the
head doctor.

NURSE. (*Gesturing towards the screen.*)
He is busy.

SISTER. (*Looking behind the* NURSE *at the
bed, her voice filling with sudden sympathy.*) Hello, how are you buddy! (*Then
springing back in confusion.*) Oh—it's not
decent— And I was mistaken. One of our
brave buddies is a coward.

NURSE. (*Stoutly.*) Johnny Johnson is not a
coward.

SISTER. Then how did he get shot where he did? (*The* DOCTOR *finishes with* JOHNNY, *straightens up and sees the* SISTER.)

DOCTOR. (*Hurrying over and shaking her hand.*) Delighted, delighted. (*To the* ORDERLY *who is covering* JOHNNY *with the sheet.*) Run—notify the Colonel. We will have entertainment this evening. The Sister from the Organization for the Delight of Soldiers Disabled in the Line of Duty is here. (*At the rigmarole of words,* JOHNNY *raises himself up. The* ORDERLY *hurries away to do the* DOCTOR's *bidding leaving the little gas cylinder behind.*)

SISTER. You got my message—

DOCTOR. Yes-yes-yes.

SISTER. The piano and the stage?

DOCTOR. All arranged.

SISTER. Good. (*Looking approvingly about.*) Wonderful hospital, doctor. Best I've seen on my tour.

DOCTOR. (*Bowing low.*) Thank you, thank you. They tell me so in higher quarters.

SISTER. Hmn-n. Everything so spick and span—so many beds. (*Sleepily.*) I could lie right down. (JOHNNY *looks up watchfully.*)

DOCTOR. (*Stiffly, as a military manner creeps over him.*) Extra facilities are being provided for the great oncoming battle, madam.

JOHNNY. (*Calling out.*) Battle?—when is it to start, sir?

DOCTOR. (*Turning to him.*) My man, the exact hour is known only to the Allied High Command, but it will doubtless be soon—perhaps tomorrow.

JOHNNY. (*Aghast.*) Tomorrow? — And here I lie. (*His face full of pain.*) And there will be thousands killed—thousands of boys killed. (*He begins fingering the little cylinder abstractedly.*)

DOCTOR. But we must be prepared to offer these sacrifices on the altar of freedom.

JOHNNY. (*Starting violently up.*) The more I hear of this freedom the less I like it.

SISTER. (*Loudly.*) I was right. He *is* a coward!

JOHNNY. (*Angrily.*) And old lady, y full of prunes.

DOCTOR. (*Sternly.*) Lie down, young You do not know to whom you are tal

JOHNNY. (*Wagging his head in pa the* NURSE *comes over and lays her on his shoulder.*) When I think of the running this world it near'bout sets m tracted. (*Frantically.*) Can't somebod something to put off this fight?

DOCTOR. This is the most opportune (*To the* SISTER.) From yesterday's pris we learn that a spirit of rebellion has b to spread among the German soldiers

JOHNNY. (*Crying out.*) What! Say again.

DOCTOR. And we must strike while th is hot. (*Taking the* SISTER's *arm.*) Le show you around.

JOHNNY. (*Wildly.*) Hooray! Hooray working! Good for you, Sergeant Mil (*Gazing out at them in happy innoce He's a German friend of mine on the side—thinks the same way I do. He Johann. (*The* SISTER *looks at him in ho*

SISTER. (*Bending down and glari him.*) Not only a coward, but a—tr (JOHNNY *in fingering the gas cylinde denly lets loose a spray in her face.*)

DOCTOR. Heigh! (*He starts toward jo then he turns and steadies the* SISTER *seems about to fall.*)

JOHNNY. (*As he cuts off the hiss of ing gas.*) Excuse me—I'm excited— (*A vacant look passes over the s countenance, and then she begins to with a low infectious gurgle of fun. jo stares at her in amazement.*)

SISTER. (*With a sudden whoop.*) good! I love everybody. I love you brave suffering hero!

DOCTOR. Never mind, it's only the (*She suddenly grabs* JOHNNY *and beg manhandle him in an affectionate en The* DOCTOR *and the young French spring forward and pull her off. The now begins cavorting about and fl her long shanks shamelessly before gaze.*)

R. I feel wonderful! I feel like flying.
begins a clattering tap dance, and then
vs her arms around the DOCTOR.) Come
loctor, the show's ready to start.

OR. Young man, I'll attend to you
! (*The* SISTER *goes dancing off at the
pulling the* DOCTOR *with her.* JOHNNY
the NURSE *sit looking off at the left as
sound of the dancing dies out. Then
NY's gaze comes back to the cylinder
he stares at it.*)

NY. You see what happened? One
te she wanted to shoot me and the
minute eat me with love. Wonderful
this laughing gas.

E. (*As* JOHNNY *keeps staring before
) You sleep now.

NY. Pity they don't use laughing gas
e war instead of poison gas. (*Snapping
ngers.*) Bring me my britches.

NURSE. (*Alarmed, as she bends over him
and tries to push him back.*) No, Johnny!
Mon Dieu!

JOHNNY. (*He looks at the* NURSE, *then
suddenly lays himself back.*) All right—
(*The* NURSE *pulls the cover up and tucks
him in.*)

NURSE. (*Kissing him on the forehead.*)
'S'right—a good boy. Good-night, Johnny.

JOHNNY. (*Dreamily.*) Good-night—(*She
blows him a kiss from her fingers and goes
softly away at the right. A moment passes,
JOHNNY cautiously raises his head, looks
around and then slides his legs out of the
bed. He pulls the sheet off and the gas
tank falls to the floor.*) Guess I better take
you along—might meet another fool. (*He
picks it up, then crawls out, pajamas and
all, through the open window at the right.*)

BLACK OUT.

SCENE V

the multitude of counsellors there is
safety."

scene is a meeting of the Allied High
*mand in the Chateau de Cent Fon-
somewhere behind the lines. The
g is one of magnificence, mainly con-
g of glass, red plush, and a flight of
le-columned stairs in the right rear.
ing along the back is a glassed hall
potted palms and decorative flowers,
vith a door opening inward.

a the curtain rises, the Allied High
*mand is sitting around a long table
e middle of the room. At the center,
of the table, sits the* CHIEF OF THE
INED ALLIED FORCES. *He bears a strik-
esemblance to Marshal Foch. And at
ight sits an* AMERICAN GENERAL, *the
mander of the American Expeditionary
s, who just as obviously resembles
al Pershing; and on his left sits the
ANDER-IN-CHIEF of the British Expedi-
y Forces, an almost exact replica of
al Sir Douglas Haig. On the* BRITISH
ANDER'S *left sits a* BRITISH MAJOR-GEN-
who resembles General Rawlinson,
n the* AMERICAN COMMANDER'S *right a
H* MAJOR-GENERAL *who looks much
eneral Petain. At the left end of the*

*table in profile to the audience sits a man
in civilian clothes somewhat resembling the
British Premier Lloyd George. At the other
end of the table also in profile is another
man in civilian clothes much like Clemen-
ceau, the Tiger Premier of France. On the
side of the table next to the audience sits
a single lone figure in uniform somewhat
resembling Albert, King of the Belgians,
who throughout most of the military proceedings remains with bowed head, as if
taking no interest in what goes on around
him. At the left in the rear stand several
staff officers—a* BELGIAN MAJOR-GENERAL, *a*
BRITISH BRIGADIER-GENERAL, *a* SCOTTISH COLO-
NEL *and a* POLISH COLONEL. *Behind each of
the three central figures—the* CHIEF OF THE
ALLIED FORCES, *the* BRITISH COMMANDER, *and
the* AMERICAN COMMANDER—*stands a* FIELD
CLERK *with a stenographic pad in his hand.
All of the officers are dressed in most elite
uniforms and are plentifully decorated with
medals, crosses and orders of merit. Their
field coats and caps are placed on a sofa
near the stairway. Spread out on the table
is a huge war map which the three military
leaders are considering.*

*As these mighty keepers of men's destiny
speak forth their arguments and plans with
puppet pomp and solemn precision, the*

orchestra *keeps up an accompaniment of wide-spaced chords with now and then an ironic figure played by the flute or oboe in between.*

CHIEF OF THE ALLIED HIGH COMMAND. (*Continuing with a slight accent as he gestures with his baton of Maréchal de France.*)
The Flanders group of armies—hmmn—
Will march as we have said
Towards Brussels on the left,
The right towards Hal—
(*Saluting and addressing the* KING.)
Your Majesty.
(*The* KING *without replying gestures with a long finger towards the* BELGIAN MAJOR-GENERAL *at the left rear.*)

BELGIAN MAJOR-GENERAL. (*With his wooden salute.*) Poor Belgium understands and quite agrees—
What little part is left of her I mean—

BRITISH COMMANDER-IN-CHIEF. (*With a low mutter.*) And plenty of her's left, I'm shuah—
Such as it is.

BELGIAN MAJOR-GENERAL. (*With his hand on his sword.*) I did not catch the gentleman's remarks—

CHIEF. (*Sternly.*) We're not concerned with private quarrels here.
The question is not reparations now,
Nor yet division of the spoils.

BRITISH COMMANDER. My speech was purely topographical. (*The* BELGIAN MAJOR-GENERAL *bows.*)

CHIEF. (*Looking around at the* BRITISH COMMANDER.) The mission of the British army, sir,
Will be to hurl th'invader forces back
Towards Froidchapelle and Philippeville.
(*The* BRITISH-COMMANDER *looks confusedly around and then turns to the* ENGLISH MAJOR-GENERAL *at his side. The* MAJOR-GENERAL *looks uncertainly about him and then turns towards the* ENGLISH BRIGADIER-GENERAL *at the left.*)

BRIGADIER-GENERAL (*Vacuously.*) Ha-ha—
quite so—
To hurl th'invader's forces back.

CHIEF. (*Briskly.*) It seems that everything goes well in hand.

(*The* FIELD CLERKS *continue writing rap*
The one behind the CHIEF *bends down*
whispers in his ear. The CHIEF *nods*
continues.)
—Right—goes well in hand—
Though we were much remiss in lea
out
Our allied friends—les braves Améric

AMERICAN COMMANDER-IN-CHIEF. (*Gru*
Mistakes in such small matters will o

CHIEF. (*Consulting his map again.*)
American forces will move south
Co-operating with the French armies—
The first, the fourth, the fifth, the tent
Maneuvring on both wings
To catch the Boches by surprise.
(*He looks questioningly at the* AMER
COMMANDER *who nods his head in slo*
agreement. Then as the CHIEF *gazes*
the room for confirmation, everybody
with the exception of the KING*. The*
now picks up a huge stamp and with
swift and sudden blows puts the fina
upon the orders before him. Then he
and in even more puppet dignity
before addresses the assembly, while
orchestra keeps up its mock solemn a
paniment.)
And so, Messieurs,
The disposition of the Allied arms
Is—all—arranged,
And each man knows his task,
N'est-ce-pas?
(*They all nod.*)
And now the saddest subject possible
The necessary loss of life
In this oncoming drive—
Are we prepared to suffer it—
As we have done so many times befo

THE ASSEMBLY. (*Like one man wit*
exception of the KING *and the* AME
COMMANDER.) Oui!
We are!

CHIEF. Your majesty? (*The* KING
points his finger towards the B
MAJOR-GENERAL *at the left.*)

BELGIAN MAJOR-GENERAL. (*In a crisp*
matical voice.) The rivers, mud, co
and wire,
Which Belgium's sons must struggle th
Force us to allow for heavy loss—
Some thirty thousand dead perhaps,

me hundred and ten thousand wounded
too.
he CHIEF *stamps an order with his seal.*)

IEF. Your excellency of the British Isles?
he BRITISH COMMANDER *leans towards the*
GLISH MAJOR-GENERAL, *who turns once*
re and looks to the left at the ENGLISH
GADIER-GENERAL.)

GADIER-GENERAL. More than a hundred
thousand killed
d thrice as many wounded, sir.

IEF. (*Hollowly.*) Vive, vive!
ud England's glory never shall grow
dim
e while her sons can die so easily.
nce more he stamps an order.)

GIAN MAJOR-GENERAL. (*Piteously.*) But
Belgium, sir, is such a little land,
tiny and so small—
eginning to figure on a piece of paper.)
t tiny though she is, who knows?
e may enlarge that figure some—to say—
—fifty thousand dead.

EF. Bravo!

HERS. Bravo! (*The* BELGIAN MAJOR-GEN-
L *bows and looks at the* BRIGADIER-GEN-
L.)

EF. (*Continuing as he addresses the*
NCH MAJOR-GENERAL *at the left.*) Et vous,
mon cher brave camarade?

NCH MAJOR-GENERAL. (*Rising and glanc-*
about him.) We bow before the mighty
English nation.
unding the table with his knuckles, his
n face working with pent-up emotion.)
ve lose more than eighty thousand dead
volt will spread and anarchy break out in
France!
e sits down.)

EF. (*Stamping another order with a*
g.) Vraiment!
t now the PREMIER OF FRANCE *stands*
his white mustache quivering with
ation and rage.)

NCH PREMIER. Non, non, I say and
still say non!
England gives her hundred thousand
dead,
Belle France, my native France,

Can give her hundred thousand so the
same.
(*He collapses suddenly in his chair.*)

VOICES. Vive la France!

FRENCH MAJOR-GENERAL. But England has
more men to lose—
(*Loudly.*)
—and why?—
(*Now on his feet again.*)
Because the sons of France fell with their
guns
The while the English let them fall—
At Ypres, Vimy Ridge and Mons they did.

ENGLISH PREMIER. (*Springing up.*) The
English soldiers are no fools.
They know well when to die—
(*Scornfully.*)
Unlike the French who at Verdun
Lost half a million wasteful dead—
Perhaps a million if the truth were known.
(*And now the French and Belgian staff*
officers are on their feet and the FRENCH
PREMIER *sputters like a fire cracker in his*
chair.)

OFFICERS. We protest!

BRITISH PREMIER. I see that's still a hornet's
nest—
So let it lie—
I only wanted to make clear my point,
And no offense was meant.
(*He sits down. The* CHIEF *bangs on the*
table with his baton.)

CHIEF. As allies in a sacred cause
I ask you to forget what's past—
(*To the French and Belgian officers.*)
Please have no worry, mes amis,
The course of tactics and control
Is safely in French hands.
Be seated.
(*They all sit down, and the* CHIEF *now*
turns to the AMERICAN COMMANDER.)
Your estimated losses, sir?

AMERICAN COMMANDER. (*Curtly.*) Very few,
I hope.
(*Bending over the spread-out map.*)
It seems we have right many trees
Along the sector where we fight—
I don't expect so many killed—
I say expect.
(*The generals and officers look at him in*
querying displeasure. The BRITISH PREMIER

suddenly applauds, then stares morosely at the floor.)
There's nothing better than a tree
Between you and machine gun fire—
Especially if it's big.

CHIEF. (*Airily.*) Much so the poor benighted Indians used to fight.
(*With a shrug.*)
Where are they now?

AMERICAN COMMANDER. I hear they're living peaceful in the West
And doing well with copper mines and oil.

CHIEF. (*With a more violent shrug.*)
Tant pis!
(*His voice suddenly stern and authoritative.*)
Messieurs,
At this high moment and historic hour
We all stand up—stand up—stand up—
(*Everybody does so including the unhurrying* AMERICAN COMMANDER.)
Salute—
(*They all lift their hands and salute, staring straight towards the front.*)
Salute the coming of the early dawn
That marks the zero hour of doom,
The end of Germany.

VOICES. The end of Germany! (*For a moment they all stand in silence while the orchestra continues its commenting chords. Suddenly the* CHIEF *barks out.*)

CHIEF. We meet upon the battlefield—
The Council is adjourned—
For breakfast—
(*They all rise and, with the exception of the* AMERICAN COMMANDER, *begin shaking one another's hand solemnly.* JOHNNY *appears on the stairway at the right rear. He is still dressed in his pajamas which are now muddy-legged. And under his arm he carries the little gas tank bundled up in the hospital sheet.*)

JOHNNY. (*Calling out.*) Say—say, you folks, don't break up just yet. (*He comes on down into the scene and stops at the right front. Everybody has whirled around and is staring at the bizarre newcomer in speechless amazement.*)

AMERICAN COMMANDER. (*Blinking.*) How did you get in here?

JOHNNY. (*With a tired disarming smile*)
Oh, but I didn't hurt your guards. They[...]
down there in the bushes, all feeling fi[...]
(*He chuckles and looks around at them[...]*
I know most of you. I've seen your pictu[...]
in the papers.

CHIEF. Arrest that man. (*The* FIELD CLER[...]
start around the table towards him. JOHN[...]
*steps toward the footlights, his hand on t[...]
concealed cylinder.*)

JOHNNY. Say—wait a minute.

AMERICAN COMMANDER. Gentlemen, he[...]
one of my countrymen. I know him by[...]
accent. (*He addresses* JOHNNY.) You[...]
man, I ask you quietly to leave the roo[...]
otherwise these gentlemen here will ha[...]
the pleasant duty of hanging you.

JOHNNY. No, they won't hang me, G[...]
eral. They'll thank me—all of you wil[...]
when I tell you what I've come for.

AMERICAN COMMANDER. (*With a placat[...]
gesture around him.*) And what have y[...]
come for?

JOHNNY. To help you end this war. (*N[...]
edging closer to the footlights as the s[...]
officers at the right and left rear take a s[...]
towards him.*) Yes sir, I've been in comr[...]
nication with some of the German sold[...]
and they're about ready to stop this fighti[...]
(*Triumphantly.*) A rebellion is spreadi[...]

CHIEF. (*In a low voice to the* AMERI[...]
COMMANDER.) Rebellion?—How did[...]
know that?

JOHNNY. I know it all right.

AMERICAN COMMANDER. (*With a smile[...]
he gazes around him as much as to[...]
"He is harmless. We can spare him a [...]
ment or two."*) You do?

JOHNNY. Yes sir, I got direct news fr[...]
the German sniper I captured. (*The* CH[...]
and the AMERICAN COMMANDER *look at e[...]
other.*)

AMERICAN COMMANDER. So you captu[...]
a German?

JOHNNY. Yes sir. He said the common [...]
diers wanted to be friends with us, an[...]
sent him back with all kinds of messa[...]
saying we want to be friends too. An[...]

l you it's beginning to work. They're
elling against their German war lords—
eady. What we got to do now is get
llions of articles and speeches printed
d—

ERICAN COMMANDER. (*Abruptly.*) Is your
me by any chance — Johnson — Johnny
nson?

HNNY. (*With a sudden pleased grin.*)
s sir, that's me, and you never did an-
er my letters.

ERICAN COMMANDER. (*To the assembly.*)
ere's nothing to fear, gentlemen, he's
rmless.

IEF. The meeting is adjourned.

HNNY. (*Springing frantically towards
m.*) But it's the truth, the truth I'm tell-
g you. You've got to hold up this battle.
make my way into the German lines—
prove it—I'll do anything! You and the
er generals can sign an order right now
pping the offensive. Then we get busy
th prop—propaganda—words—words.—
ssir, they're a lot more powerful than
llets if you speak them at the right time.
d this is the right time. For the more
Germans read, the more they'll see the
th of what we say. And right now when
y're worn out and sick of war they'll be
d to come to terms, and there won't be
ozen people killed. (*Turning vehemently
the* SCOTTISH COLONEL.) Ain't there some
th in what I'm saying, ma'am?

ONEL. (*Blinking and hesitating.*) Aye,
re is. (*Then wadding up his kilt nerv-
ly as his confreres stare around at him.*)
er—mean—ha-ha-ha.

NNY. That's right, you can always de-
d on the women folks. Now, come on,
s use our heads—that's what they're for.
's—

EF. (*Sternly to the staff officers.*) Take
away!

NNY. (*Incredulously.*) You mean—you
't believe what I'm saying? (*Crying
warningly as the staff officers move
ards him.*) Heigh, better not! (*Suddenly
shoots his gas cylinder out and holds it
tectively in front of him.*)

KING. (*In a low horror-struck voice as he
points a quivering fore-finger.*) A bomb!

VOICES. (*Softly.*) A bomb.

JOHNNY. (*Eyeing them.*) Well— (*Then
quickly.*) Ho-ho, then suppose I have got
a bomb. (*He takes a quick step forward
and they all draw back from him and stand
frightened and awed, and even the* AMERI-
CAN COMMANDER *is stopped in his tracks.*
JOHNNY *watches them in silence a moment
and then continues with suppressed emotion.*) Now then maybe you'll listen to me.
(*Anger creeping into his voice.*) I was
standing there listening to you all right and
you were speaking of a pile of dead men in
tomorrow's battle higher'n that big tower
in Paris—poor dumb guys like me you're
sending out to die—to be blown to pieces!
(*With sudden rage.*) All right, suppose I
blow you to pieces with this—er—bomb.
(*Yelling.*) Sit down, King! (*He lifts his
bundle menacingly.*)

KING. (*Collapsing into his chair and calling piteously.*) Gendarmes! Gendarmes!
(*And now all the others, with the exception of the* AMERICAN COMMANDER *who never
takes his eyes off* JOHNNY, *sink down into
their chairs and stare about them with fearful faces.*)

JOHNNY. So here you sit on your hind
ends holy as God and make your plans—
marking up your thousands of dead and
dying like cold figures on a blackboard.
Know what that means? I ask you—know
what it means?—all these boys—young fellows like me—like what you used to be—
going out to die—shot down—killed—murdered—to be dead and stiff and rotten in
a trench with rats and mud? We were
meant for something better, I tell you!
(*Vehemently.*) We want to live, and you
could let us live! We want to be let alone
to do our work in peace—to have our
homes—to raise our families— We want to
look back someday and say our life has
meant something—we have been happy and
it was good to be born into this world.
(*Pleadingly to the* AMERICAN COMMANDER
who has approached close to him.) You see
what I mean don't you—don't you? (*More
quietly as he controls the trembling in his
voice.*) When you come right down to it
what sense is there in human beings trying

to cut and tear and destroy one another like wild beasts in a jungle? There's no sense in it, is there? Is there! (*Stretching out his hands to all of them.*) You're our leaders— you're all-powerful over us—you tell us to die for freedom or a flag or our country or whatever crazy ideal it is—and we have to die. (*Half-sobbing as they look at him with cold authority-set faces.*) You'd rather live too, hadn't you? You'd rather be at home with your wives and children, hadn't you —living in peace the way men were meant to live? Then end this killing—end it now— (*Brokenly.*) Only a second's time— a movement of your hand—a written word —and you could stop this war. Do it! Do it! (*Staring at them aghast as they look at him with dull baleful eyes.*) But you don't listen. That Englishman was right. You don't want to end this war. (*A queer baffled grieving in his voice.*) There's something black and evil got into you—something blinded you—something— (*He drops his head. Suddenly at a gesture from the* AMERICAN COMMANDER *several of the staff officers spring upon him. He turns quick as a flash and starts toward the stairway at the right rear, but the* FIELD CLERKS *head him off. And now as several of the officers close in upon him he suddenly unscrews the tank of gas and sends it hissing and spraying into their faces. The officers gradually stop their pursuit, look at one another, and the expression of their faces changes. And now they begin to laugh.* JOHNNY *stares at them in astonishment, as do the great generals. Then as the latter rise and move towards him, he rushes around among them releasing the gas in their faces, taking time to squirt the* KING *a full dose.*)

KING. (*Throwing up his hands in a loud clapping.*) Ho-ho-ho!

OTHERS. Whoops!—Wonnerful!—Merveil-leux! (*And now the* AMERICAN COMMANDER *breaks into a roar and slaps his side. The orchestra begins to play a sprightly tune, and the scene changes from one of solemn dignity into one of humor and gaiety. Several of the officers begin dancing their native dances—the* POLISH COLONEL *at the right doing a Polonaise, the* SCOTTISH COLO-NEL *at the left a Highland Fling, and the American, English, and French officers tap*

dancing, waltzing, and minuetting. JOHN[NY] *with the sheet wadded over his nose a[nd] mouth, stands gazing at them with qu[es-] tioning, puckered eyes. And now the* BR[IT-] ISH PREMIER *and the* FRENCH PREMIER *h[urry] out into the middle of the room, and hoo[k-] ing their arms together cut a few steps li[ke] old men at a country dance.* HIS MAJES[TY] THE KING *bows his head over on the ta[ble] like a great ungainly puppet and begins [to] laugh at some secret and mysterious jok[e.]*

KING. Ho-ho-ho-ho!

OTHERS. Heh-heh-heh-heh| (*And now th[ere] is a general chorus of merry laughter, a[nd] even* JOHNNY *giggles a bit.*)

THE WHOLE ASSEMBLY. (*With the exc[ep-] tion of* JOHNNY. Ha-ha-ha-ho-ho-ho-
Haw-haw-haw-
Hey-hey-hey-hey-hey-hey-
Hy-hy-hy-hee-hee-hee-
Hi-hi-hi-iiiiiiiiiii-ay!
(*The Frenchmen now kiss the Americ[ans] and the Americans kiss the Frenchmen, a[nd] then they all take hands and dance arou[nd] the table in a circle like children aroun[d a] may-pole. As they whirl by, the* AMERIC[AN] COMMANDER *grabs* JOHNNY'S *hand and p[ulls] him into the dance. He moves with the[m] holding his sheet around him. The* AM[ERI-] CAN COMMANDER *in a benevolent outb[urst] of feeling picks up his great-coat with [its] insignia and puts it around* JOHNNY [and] then follows by placing his cap on [his] head.*)

AMERICAN COMMANDER. (*With a loud v[oice] as he salutes.*) General Johnny Johns[on!] (*The dance suddenly stops, and the offi[cers] all crowd towards* JOHNNY, *click their h[eels] and salute likewise, as they repress t[heir] laughter into bubbling giggles.*)

VOICES. Vive General Johnny Johnson[!] Hooray General Johnny Johnson! Hip, hip General Johnny Johnson!

CHIEF. What can we do for you, Gene[ral?]

JOHNNY. (*Shaking his head groggily [and] returning their salute with his left ha[nd] and then after a moment's hesitation b[awl-] ing out.*) Stop this war!

AMERICAN COMMANDER. Just as you [say], General. Tee-hee-hee—so you want

hting stopped? (*Turning around and
'ing to everybody.*) General Johnson's
ht. This war is foolish, there's nothing
it but blood and murder.

ces. War is foolish! Let's stop it!

ERICAN COMMANDER. (*Embracing the
EF. Old boy, we're going to stop this
r. What you say?

IEF. (*Clapping his hands.*) Stop the
r! (*A great burst of applause and cheer-
follows.*)

ERICAN COMMANDER. We'll sign the or-
right now. (*He hurries over to the
le, writes something, signs it and hands
pen to the CHIEF who also signs and
mps it. Then he gives the paper to
INNY, and calls out in a loud voice.*)
nce! (*The laughter dies down once more
suppressed giggles.*) We have signed an
er stopping the offensive! General John-
, see that it is carried out!

: ASSEMBLY. Vive Johnny Johnson!
oray Johnny Johnson!
b, hip Johnny Johnson!
nd now the orchestra resumes playing.
e officers lift JOHNNY on their shoulders
l march around the room, then place
t on the table and stand applauding
.)

ces. Speech, speech!

INNY. (*Blinking and passing his hand
oss his forehead as if to clear his mind.*)

There's not much to say, friends. Now that
we're going to stop the war, we'll all be
home in time for Christmas to see old
Santa Claus. Ain't that fine?

VOICES. Christmas! Christmas! Merry
Christmas! (*And now they all start marching around the table again and singing,
with the exception of JOHNNY, who hops
down and disappears up the stairs the way
he came.*)

ALL. (*Singing as in a round.*) We'll all be
home for Christmas—a merry, merry Christmas! (*A moment passes while the singing
continues. The orchestra rises to a loud fortissimo and suddenly stops. Gradually the
noise subsides, the generals and the others
sink down in their seats and gaze about
them in amazement. The AMERICAN COM-
MANDER looks at the CHIEF's scattered and
windblown hair and the CHIEF looks at his
disarray.*)

CHIEF. (*In a hollow dazed voice.*) What
time is it?

AMERICAN COMMANDER. (*Staring at his
wrist watch.*) Ten minutes till five.

CHIEF. (*With a cry.*) The offensive!

AMERICAN COMMANDER. (*Springing out of
his chair with a yell.*) My God!—We gave
him an order stopping the offensive! Catch
that man! (*He and the CHIEF tear out
through the door at the rear followed by
the mad scramble of the others.*)

BLACK OUT.

SCENE VI

"Still stands thine ancient sacrifice."

e scene is the edge of a great battlefield
r dawn. In the foreground is a small
gout opening into a raised eyebrow of
earth. By a shaded lantern light two
son officers are discerned, one a CAPTAIN,
king into a field telephone, and the other
oung LIEUTENANT, squatted by him, tak-
notes in a book. The orchestra accom-
iment has continued.

TAIN. (*Chanting into the phone.*)
th—first British army;
th—British six, two, one, three, four.

LIEUTENANT. Check.

CAPTAIN. French army toward Saint-Quen-
tin.

LIEUTENANT. Check.

CAPTAIN. On the right the American army.
Code—L E, Prefix three, six S M.

LIEUTENANT. Check.

CAPTAIN. Zero hour—0 1 5 1 0.

LIEUTENANT. Check.

CAPTAIN. Three minutes now—
Three minutes—

Three minutes and the western front
From Calais to Sedan will go—
Over the top—
The zero hour falls.

LIEUTENANT. (*Half-sobbing.*) Check.

CAPTAIN. May heaven help our enemies—
In such an hour!

LIEUTENANT. Check.—And help us all!
(*And now off at the left we hear the singing command "Attention," then nearer at
hand the command repeated, and then still
nearer the command repeated. The* CAPTAIN
and the LIEUTENANT *look around and suddenly spring to their feet as* JOHNNY JOHN-
son enters wrapped in the AMERICAN COM-
MANDER'S *overcoat, and cap.*)

CAPTAIN. (*Saluting and clicking his heels.*)
Attenshun! (*The* LIEUTENANT *quickly salutes, clicks his heels likewise.* JOHNNY'S
*hand is pushed into his coat in an attitude
somewhat resembling the popular picture
of Napoleon.*)

JOHNNY. (*In a slightly disguised voice.*)
At ease.

CAPTAIN. (*Gasping.*) General—General—
General—
The danger is too great—
Oh General!

JOHNNY. (*In a still heavy voice.*) The
General has no fear when his own men
are involved.
Are you in touch with the different com-
manders?

CAPTAIN. Everything's in order, sir—in
order, sir—
(*Jerking his wrist watch by his eyes.*)
Two minutes now—two minutes—
The barrage will begin—

LIEUTENANT. (*With a moan.*) Check.

JOHNNY. There'll be no barrage—no bom-
bardment either.
(*With a bark.*)
The war is called off!

CAPTAIN. (*With a shout.*) What!

JOHNNY. Suspended until further orders—
(*Authoritatively.*)
In the name of the Allied High Command.
Here!
(*He hands him the signed order.*)

LIEUTENANT. (*With a broken cry.*) Thank
God, thank God.
(*Slightly hysterical.*)
We'll live to get back home again!
(*Wildly.*)
We'll live!
(*He runs over and kisses* JOHNNY'S hand,
then whirls and embraces the CAPTAIN.)

JOHNNY. Quick—get the news on the
wire.

CAPTAIN. (*Now down on his knees and
grinding the telephone.*) Hello, hello! Sec-
ond Army Corps, Second Army Corps—
Ypres section, General Godby— Hell!
This is Varner—Varner—L-two-V-O-seven.
(*Reading from the order.*) Order urgent.
Special invoice—Allied High Command.
Cancellation. Eight - four - three - two - one.
Code— Acceptive. G. O.

JOHNNY. (*From the shadow where he
stands.*) Talk sense!

CAPTAIN. General offensive will not take
place. Indefinite suspension of hostilities.

LIEUTENANT. (*Running about and clapping his hands.*) Shall we send up the
signals?

JOHNNY. (*Shouting.*) Send 'em up! Send
'em up!

LIEUTENANT. (*Rushing off at the right.*)
Flares! Flares! (BLACK OUT. *The orchestra
plays the "Democracy March." fortissimo.
The lights come up again.* JOHNNY *is at the
back looking off and waving his sheet in
the air. And now at the left the sound
of cheering is heard, coming nearer as if
underground. From a flare somewhere at
stage the scene of No Man's Land at the
rear is lighted up. The subterranean cheering seems to pass across the stage. And now
at the back as if popping out of the ground
several American soldiers spring up on the
parapet yelling and waving their caps.*)

A SOLDIER. Hooray, the war is over! War
is over! (*Shouting across No Man's Land.*)
Heigh, Heinie, where are you?

ANOTHER SOLDIER. Come on out, you boys!
We've quit fighting!

ANOTHER SOLDIER. Kommt d'raus! Kein
Krieg mehr! (*And now as the orches-*

*ays, the figures of several German sol-
rs, muddy and begrimed, appear at the
t and right rear. The Americans run
ward and shake hands with them. They
p one another on the back and embrace
ectionately, weeping with happiness. Sud-
nly off at the left a siren blows. The
PTAIN and the LIEUTENANT look off.
HNNY hops across the trench and joins
e German and American soldiers at the
ar. They salute him and he goes among
em shaking hands. And now rushing in
m the left come three or four brigadier-
nerals and colonels with drawn pistols.)*

RST BRIGADIER. (*Yelling and pointing
wards* JOHNNY.) Catch that man!

HNNY. (*Coming over to the trench and
eaking sternly to the staff officers.*) Get
ck to headquarters, you fellows, or I'll
p you under arrest.

COND BRIGADIER. (*Raising his pistol.*)
y! Spy! Kill him!

EUTENANT. (*Stepping in front of him.*)
y God, would you shoot the Commander-
-Chief? (*The soldiers spring protectively
und* JOHNNY.)

COND BRIGADIER. Commander-in-Chief!

HNNY. (*Pushing his way through the
diers and turning towards them.*) Boys,
you want to stop this war?

DIERS. (*With some of the Germans
ing "Ja, Ja!"*) Yes, General, great God,
we say so!

d it right now. And let's go home.
Home—let's go home.

COLONEL *springs suddenly over, jerks*
INNY'S *coat from him and at the same
e another officer knocks off his cap.*)

COLONEL. Look at him! (*The soldiers
stare at him in silent astonishment.*)

FIRST BRIGADIER. (*To the liaison* CAPTAIN.)
Command the offensive to begin at once!
(*He sticks an order into his hand. The*
CAPTAIN *stares at the order, then springs to
the telephone and begins cranking.* JOHNNY
*whirls about as the officers and soldiers
start towards him, jumps down into the
trench and disappears. The* FIRST BRIGADIER
yells to the soldiers.) Back into your
trenches! The battle is beginning! (*The
American soldiers look helplessly about.
Both brigadiers now have their pistols
drawn.*)

SECOND BRIGADIER. At "three" we fire.
One—two— (*He raises his pistol. The
American soldiers jump down into the
trenches.*)

CAPTAIN. (*At the telephone.*) G-O-eight-
four-three-two-one cancelled. Forged orders.
Work of spies.

LIEUTENANT. (*Now weeping as he squats
with his pad and pencil.*) Check. (*The
German soldiers at the back turn and flee
toward their trenches. But some of them
never reach there, for the American machine guns now begin their rat-tat-tat-tat-
tat-tat, and they are seen falling. The* CAP-
TAIN *continues yelling into the telephone.*)

CAPTAIN. *At once! At once!* (*As he looks
at his watch.*) It is now exactly hours—
0 5 1 0— Open fire!—Fire! (*Somewhere
far away and as if beneath the earth, a
great gun is fired. There is an instant of
pause, and then the battle begins, with the
music in the orchestra portraying its fury
and violence.*)

BLACK OUT.

SCENE VII

here's many a mangled body, a blanket
for their shroud."
*SERIES OF FLASHES—by the light of
rsting shells. The orchestra is now an
an playing the stately chant music of a
urch prayer, while in a nebulous circle
light at the extreme right front of the
ge an* AMERICAN PRIEST *is seen standing
ve the members of his congregation who
bowed in prayer, and while at the left*

front a GERMAN PRIEST *likewise stands above
his praying flock. As the battle goes on and
the organ plays, the two priests repeat in
unison, the one in English, the other in
German, the prayer "In Time of War and
Tumults"—*
Almighty God, the supreme Governor of
all things, whose power no creature is able
to resist, to whom it belongeth justly to
punish sinners, and to be merciful to those

who truly repent; save and deliver us, we humbly beseech thee, from the hands of our enemies; that we, being armed with thy defense, may be preserved evermore from all perils, to glorify thee, who art the only giver of all victory; through the merit of thy Son, Jesus Christ our Lord. *Amen.*

FLASH 1

Two squads of horrible creatures in gas masks, German and American, flying to meet each other and fighting hand to hand.

BLACK OUT

FLASH 2

Two men fighting, a German and an American, with bare fists choking and strangling each other, towering up over the footlights.

BLACK OUT

FLASH 3

Two soldiers—an American and a German —tangled in a roll of barbed wire, gasping and frothing from burning gas, clasping the hand of friendship as they die.

BLACK OUT

FLASH 4

A squad of Germans holding up their hands in surrender. An American on his belly in the foreground with a machine gun mowing them down.

BLACK OUT

FLASH 5

A squad of American soldiers holding their hands in surrender. A German m chine-gunner in the foreground mowi them down.

BLACK OUT

FLASH 6

JOHNNY JOHNSON, fleeing around in Man's Land, bare-headed, his pajamas tatters.

BLACK OUT

FLASH 7

A young German praying at the foot of black wooden statue of Christ. He rises meet an American who enters with dra bayonet. They fight and the German is through. An exploding shell kills the An ican. The statue totters and falls with crash.

BLACK OUT

FLASH 8

JOHNNY JOHNSON, holding the head o dying man in his lap and giving him drink of water. (*And now the organ m and the entire scene gradually fade out u the long breathing word of the two priest "Amen."*)

BLACK OUT

SCENE VIII

"Dulce et decorum est pro patria mori."
It is dawn over No Man's Land. In the dim light that showers a faint gray in the east we can discern the forms of dead men scattered about us as far as the eye can see, and in the background the mutilated and shattered figure of the Christ. And ever and anon from somewhere out of that vast stretch of ruined world come the feeble and begging cries of those who have not yet died. The music in the orchestra now is that of the wounded French soldiers in Scene I, Act Two, "Nous Sommes Blessés." In the middle foreground, sitting on the edge of the raised lip of a torn shell hole is JOHNNY JOHNSON. *Stretched out at his feet is the form of a soldier, his pale face upturned in the gray light. The face is that of* JOHANN *the young sniper.* JOHNNY *is naked save for a torn piece of cloth around his middle. His body is mar with sweat and powder burns. For a w he sits staring down at the pale face, t reaching out he lays his hand on the dier's forehead, moving the German hel back from his head to do so.*

JOHNNY. (*In a low voice.*) Feel be now? (*There is no reply. He bends clo puts his hand on the soldier's mouth, then sits with his head and shoulders bo and his hands clasped around his kn His voice rises through his burnt swo lips in a hoarse broken monologue.*) hundred thousand dead, five hundred th sand dead, a million dead.—And they h had their way, Johann. And all for w And why? What for? (*Wagging his he*

ody knows—nobody! (*Far off in the
kground a voice calls piteously.*)

ce. Mother, mother. (JOHNNY con-
es to stare before him.*)

nny. He'll quit calling soon, he'll quit
ing and lie still—like you, Johann, lie
. And they killed you. I saw it happen.
e of my own squad did it. He stuck
ayonet through you. (*Gasping.*) I had

 war stopped once. Maybe there's no
se in that. They said so. But you
uldn't say so—no, you wouldn't would
? (*Stretching out his hands over the
figure with a loud cry.*) Would you!

(*And now two tall military police loom up
in the darkness at the left. With their hands
on their pistols they approach* JOHNNY.)

FIRST MILITARY POLICE. Are you Johnny
Johnson?

JOHNNY. (*Without looking around.*) He's
dead.

SECOND MILITARY POLICE. Are you Johnny
Johnson? (*His head sags down on his
breast.*)

FIRST MILITARY POLICE. In the name of the
armies of Europe and America we arrest
you!

BLACK OUT.

SCENE IX

"Hail, Mary full of grace."

prospect looking out upon the entrance
New York harbor. In the distance the
TUE OF LIBERTY stands against the eve-
g sky, but this time she is not illumi-
ed. And now the same gray ghostly
ship slides across the back of the scene
from left to right, and from the left
es the rail and the deck of the passenger
again. JOHNNY is sitting at the rail

with his back to the STATUE and staring
straight before him. A uniformed GUARD is
standing at his side. The GUARD salutes and
then touches JOHNNY on the shoulder and
points to the STATUE. But JOHNNY keeps
staring ahead of him. The rail and the
deck pass out at the right and disappear into
a great engulfing shadow without stopping.

CURTAIN.

ACT THREE

SCENE I

there no balm in Gilead? Is there no
physician there?"

psychiatrist's office in the State Hospital.
the left front is a heavy door opening
 a corridor. At the left a typewriter
k and to the right of that a larger desk
h telephones, papers, and so on. At the
ter rear another door opens to an inner
m. At the right rear are several filing
es, and to the right front a third door
ning towards the entrance hall.
en the curtain rises DR. MAHODAN, a
ancholy middle-aged man is seated at
 desk looking through several folders of
spaper clippings, letters and reports.
 telephone rings. He picks up the re-
er.

MAHODAN. Hello. (*Wearily.*) Yes, this
he bureau of psychiatry— (*Listening a*

moment and then bawling out at the unknown speaker.*) You're crazy! (*He hangs
up the receiver and sits staring before him.
Presently he begins to sing to himself, to
a low tom-tom accompaniment in the orchestra.*)

Back in the ages primitive
When souls with devils were possess't,
The witch man came and did his best
With yell and blow and expletive
    And loudly beaten drum.
And up and down and round about
He whirled with fearful fetish rout
    And wild delirium.
But rarely did the patient live
Back in the ages primitive.
(*Continuing with organ accompaniment.*)

Back when the priests had things their
    way

They viewed insanity the same,
Though now they would invoke the
     name
Of heaven's hosts, and sing and pray
   In accents dolorous.
And if they failed to ease his pains,
They bound the poor soul down in
     chains,
   Condemned and infamous.
And there in dungeon cell he lay,
Back when the priests had things their
     way.

(*And now the orchestra is jazzing a bit.*)

Today psychologists agree
The insane man is only sick,
The problem is psy-chi-a-trick,
See Jung and Adler, Freud and me,
   And we will analyze.
And though it hurts, we probe the ruts
Of mental pain that drives men nuts
And heal their lunacies.
And from their devils being free,
They all take up Psychiatry.

(*The telephone rings again as a spinsterish
looking stenographer appears from the
rear with a glass of yellow liquid in her
hand. She sets the glass down and picks up
the receiver.*)

STENOGRAPHER. Dr. Mahodan's office— Yes,
we're expecting him. (*Sitting down and
holding her stenographic pad in readiness.*)
Take your medicine.

DR. MAHODAN. Yes—yes— (*He gulps down
some of the liquid and shudders.*)

STENOGRAPHER. Better this morning?

DR. MAHODAN. No, worse— (*Sadly.*) Well,
my business is to cure others, and not
myself. (*Picking up a photograph and staring at it.*) And this Johnny Johnson looks
like a difficult case to cure. (*As the STEN-
OGRAPHER writes.*) Rare, very, very rare.
Only once in a generation does such a diseased personality occur. According to his
record, he appears to be one of those nat-
urals born into the world at rare intervals.
You recall my monograph on Jesus, the
rural prophet and will-less egocentric.—
Same type, same type. (*Tapping the photograph with his finger.*) You will notice one
significant fact. He holds his rifle left-
handed—the others do not. (*Musingly.*)

Also notice the discrepancy between h
forehead and his chin. (*The telephone
the desk rings again. The* STENOGRAPH
picks it up.)

STENOGRAPHER. Dr. Mahodan.—Good—y
send him right in.

DR. MAHODAN. You'd better fetch the
derlies.

STENOGRAPHER. Yes, sir. (*She rises a
goes to the heavy door at the left, unloc
it with a loud click and disappears beyon
DR. MAHODAN picks up a hand mirror a
begins studying the interior of his mou
The door at the right opens and* JOHNN
JOHNSON *is escorted in by his former guar
He wears his old over-sized soldier's u
form, though now it is clean, and in ge
eral his whole appearance denotes his usu
cheerfulness and complacency. He loo
about the scene with interest as* DR. MAH
DAN *rises and receives a large envelope fr
the guard.*)

DR. MAHODAN. Mr.—er—? (*He consults
clipping.*)

JOHNNY JOHNSON. Howdy, sir.

DR. MAHODAN. Have a seat, Mr.—er—Jo
son. (JOHNNY *sits down and the gua
retires towards the door at the right a
stands waiting.*)

JOHNNY. (*With a gentle disarming smil
Yes sir, I don't mind sitting down. I h
to give my seat to a lady on the train, a
my feet hurt. (*The* STENOGRAPHER *re-ente
She looks keenly at* JOHNNY *and he ri
out of his seat.*) Have my chair, ma'am.

STENOGRAPHER. (*Startled.*) Oh—no, tha
you. (*She sits at her desk again and ta
up a writing pad.*)

DR. MAHODAN. (*As the* STENOGRAPH
writes.) Were you seasick on the oce
Mr. Johnson?

JOHNNY. Oh no, sir. Funny, I didn't
seasick either way.

DR. MAHODAN. (*With a slight inclinati
of his head toward the* STENOGRAPHE
Perfect adjustment of sense organs as
pected.

JOHNNY. Sir?

MAHODAN. I was just speaking to the ung lady.

JHNNY. Excuse me. Could I ask you a estion, Mr.—Mr.?

MAHODAN. (*Bowing slightly.*) My me? Er—? (*Blankly and then getting answer.*) —Ah—Mahodan, Dr. Ma-dan.

HNNY. Glad to know you, sir. Has nny Belle come yet?

ARD. (*Taking a step forward.*) That's fiancée, Doctor. He wanted her to know was home from the war so I let him d her a telegram.

MAHODAN. Hum—hum. Question of ocedure. (*To* JOHNNY *soothingly.*) No, hasn't come yet.

HNNY. (*Dolefully.*) That's funny. I nder if she'll be able to locate me here. such a big place.

MAHODAN. Yes, it's quite large.

HNNY. (*Looking around him.*) It's one the nicest jails I ever saw.

MAHODAN. (*As the* STENOGRAPHER ites away.) This is not a jail, Mr.—er— nson. It's a hospital. (*And now several sky orderlies enter from the left in white iforms. They take up their position by door.* JOHNNY *looks at them with in-est.*)

HNNY. Why it is a jail too. I saw some s beyond that door. (*He stares around h quizzical eyes.*) And why is he lock-up?

MAHODAN. That's all right. We do that a matter of habit. (JOHNNY *stares at the or now, saying nothing.* DR. MAHODAN's ice changes to a more professional curt-s as he sits down and hands the* STEN-RAPHER *the envelope he has received from guard.*) Usual six copies of these, please. *hen turning to* JOHNNY.) We've looked ward with interest to seeing you. You quite a famous man in military circles.

HNNY. (*Looking up now with a grin.*) the man that stopped the war if that's at you mean. (*Shaking his head glumly, the smile dying from his face.*) But they wouldn't let it stay stopped. They're still killing each other and shooting over there right on. They've got everything bassack-wards!

DR. MAHODAN. (*With the faintest touch of amusement beginning to show in his eyes.*) Bass what?

JOHNNY. (*Chuckling.*) Oh, shucks, that's just a word means the front part behind— (DR. MAHODAN *stares at him and gradually the dour hardness of his face begins to break up into a wrinkly smile. As if in-fected by* JOHNNY's *chuckle, he throws back his head and laughs and then goes off into a paroxysm of sputtering and coughing. The astonished* STENOGRAPHER *hurries to him with the remainder of the medicine which he drains off.*)

DR. MAHODAN. (*Dabbing his lips with a large white handkerchief.*) Excuse me, I am not accustomed to laughter. (*Leaning forward eagerly.*) Tell us more about your wonderful experiences.

JOHNNY. (*Humbly.*) I didn't have any ex-periences. I didn't even shoot my gun once.

DR. MAHODAN. (*To the* STENOGRAPHER *who jumps to her pad and starts writing rapidly.*) The superman complex through the technique of humility, which— (*Stop-ping and eyeing* JOHNNY *closely.*) No— Cancel that.

JOHNNY. Sir?

DR. MAHODAN. I was addressing the young lady.

JOHNNY. I know you were. But it was about me.

DR. MAHODAN. Yes, and very complimen-tary. (*And now the door at the right opens and* MINNY BELLE *comes in. She is dressed in a little blue coat suit and cute' hat and looks adorable, though somewhat pale and worn.*)

MINNY BELLE. Johnny— (*Springing up, he whirls around and grabs her.*)

JOHNNY. (*Brokenly.*) Minny Belle, Minny Belle! (*His lips quiver with emotion, and tears come into his eyes. And now he pulls her into his arms and hugs her tight to him. Then he pushes her from him and stares at her with hungry, devouring eyes. For a moment he stands looking at her so, and then kisses her on the forehead.)

MINNY BELLE. No—Johnny—please—these people!

JOHNNY. (Manfully.) Oh, it's all right. They already know we're engaged. (Taking MINNY BELLE by the hand and turning towards the doctor.) This is Minny Belle, Dr. Mahodan. Yes, that's his name, Minny Belle. He says it is. And he seems like a fine man.

MINNY BELLE. I'm sorry I'm late, sir, but we had a puncture on the way.

JOHNNY. A puncture?

MINNY BELLE. Yes, Anguish was good enough to bring me over in his new car.

JOHNNY. Oh—

MINNY BELLE. You're all dressed out in your uniform. (Gazing at him queryingly.) But why are you back? The war's not over yet.

JOHNNY. They decided to send me back here. (Then quickly.) But it weren't because I wasn't a good soldier. Maybe I was too good.

MINNY BELLE. (Stiffly.) But why did you come back so soon? (JOHNNY says nothing.) And how many Germans did you kill, Johnny?

JOHNNY. None, Minny Belle—not a single one.

MINNY BELLE. Oh, Johnny!

DR. MAHODAN. We are sorry to interrupt you, Mr.—er—

STENOGRAPHER. (Prompting.) —Johnson.

DR. MAHODAN. Yes—I'd like to have a word with the young lady in private. Will you kindly go with these gentlemen—to another room for a moment?

JOHNNY. (Looking about him.) All right, sir. I'll be right back, Minny Belle. (The orderlies come forward and escort JOHNNY

out at the rear and close the door behi them.)

DR. MAHODAN. (Gesturing MINNY BELLE a seat.) My dear young lady, I have a ve sorrowful duty to perform. (Curtly, to t STENOGRAPHER.) You needn't write dow everything I say. (The STENOGRAPHER sto writing.) Your fiancé will not be able go home with you.

MINNY BELLE. What's the matter?

DR. MAHODAN. This is a home for men cases. Does that mean anything to you?

MINNY BELLE. I—I thought it was strar —Johnny's being here but— (With a su den cry.) You don't mean there's som thing wrong—wrong with his mind?

DR. MAHODAN. (Gravely.) The psychol ical experts of the United States army so. I have their reports here.

MINNY BELLE. (Crying out.) No, Johnny—he's a little peculiar in his w but— (Her words die out and she staring horrified at the doctor.)

DR. MAHODAN. To you it may not app that anything is wrong. But to one skil in the science of mental diseases it is parent that— (The door at the rear s denly opens and JOHNNY dashes in. has been stripped of his army coat a wears in its place the blue denim jacket an inmate of the house of balm. He is lowed by the orderlies.)

JOHNNY. (Hotly to DR. MAHODAN as tears off his jacket and throws it dow What's the meaning of this sir? (He sta from the doctor to MINNY BELLE's grie face. She suddenly drops her head in hands and begins sobbing. JOHNNY hur over to her.) Has this—this queer dick a doctor done anything to you, Mi Belle?

MINNY BELLE. Oh—oh—oh!

DR. MAHODAN. Unfortunately I had to her about your condition.

JOHNNY. What condition?

DR. MAHODAN. That you are sick.

JOHNNY. Sick? Why I never felt in be

lth—at least I did till I came into this
ce. (*Grabbing* MINNY BELLE's *hand.*)
me on, we're going out of here!

NNY BELLE. (*With a wail.*) Oh, Johnny!
u can't.

INNY. We'll see about that! (*The door
the right opens and* ANGUISH *sticks his
d in. He is sportingly dressed, like the
ng young business man he is.*)

GUISH. Did you call me, Minny Belle?

NNY BELLE. (*Looking at* JOHNNY, *wav-
ng a moment and then pulling away
m him and running over to* ANGUISH.)
ey're going to keep Johnny here, An-
sh.

GUISH. (*As he takes hold of her arm.*)
ll, an asylum is where he belongs.

INNY. Asylum! (*Whirling around.*)
ke your hand off her arm.

GUISH. (*As* MINNY BELLE *clings to him.*)
n't you let him get at me, folks.

DR. MAHODAN. (*Raising a gently teasing
finger.*) Now, Mr.—er— Now, now—

JOHNNY. (*Stopping as the orderlies take a
step towards him.*) I see. They think I'm
crazy. They're going to shut me up. (*Then
turning to* MINNY BELLE. *Pleadingly.*) You
can't—you can't think— (MINNY BELLE
drops her head and begins to sob again.
ANGUISH *puts his arm protectingly around
her. At a gesture from the doctor, he leads
her away at the right and closes the door.*
JOHNNY *stands staring at the floor like a
man in a dream.* DR. MAHODAN *comes over
and puts his hand kindly on his shoulder.
Then he picks up the jacket from the floor,
and* JOHNNY *slowly holds out his arm for
the sleeve.*)

DR. MAHODAN. I think you'll make a very
interesting patient, Mr.—er— (*Blankly,
then getting the answer.*) Mr. Mahodan.

BLACK OUT.

SCENE II

ut of the mouths of babes and sucklings."

e forensic arena in the house of balm—
sort of ordinary reading or club room
h several rows of chairs at the center
ht and a little speaker's stand facing
gonally outward from the left rear. Above
speaker's stand hangs a beflagged pic-
e of Woodrow Wilson and above that
big placard with the words "Adelphi
bating Society" on it. When the curtain
es some dozen or more elderly men are
nding by their seats as they face the
trum. Some of them have pencils and
eap writing tablets in their hands. They
emble the ordinary type of American
siness men—railroad, bank, or insurance
npany directors. On the rostrum sits
OTHER THOMAS, a man who resembles a
tain late Vice-President of the United
ttes, and to his left a pale-faced clerk
pe of man about thirty years old. Sitting
a lower level and to the right of the
trum is JOHNNY JOHNSON. JOHNNY has
ed much since we saw him last. He is
essed in an old collarless white shirt and
dark sack coat much too large for him,
d his hair with suspicious signs of gray-*

ness at the temples is still unruly though
brushed somewhat to one side. Like the portrait above him he wears spectacles though
his are of the plain steel-rimmed kind, and
in an indefinite way he seems to resemble
the portrait. With a small brush he is painting a wooden toy which he holds in his
hand.

The scene is somewhat cut off from the
footlights by a low railing which crosses
the front of the stage and in the center of
which is a little gate. Two uniformed hospital guards stand one on either side of
the scene at the front looking straight ahead
of them and with their arms folded akimbo.
It is ten years after the preceding scene.
As the curtain rises, the Brethren are concluding a song. With the exception of
JOHNNY everybody is singing.*

BRETHREN. (*As* BROTHER THOMAS *beats
time with his rubber gavel.*) How sweetly
friendship binds—
Our hearts in brother love
With kindness of forgiving minds—
Life's sweetest pleasures prove.

For fled are hate and harm,

No foe seeks us to kill—
To all we stretch the open arm
Of welcome and good will.
(*Ending with a churchly long-drawn chant.*)
—Amen.
(*Then all sit down.* DR. FREWD, *an old bearded gentleman wearing a linen duster, springs up in the front row.*)

DR. FREWD. (*Piping out gently.*) Hurrah for the President of the United States! (*And now several of the other Brethren join in likewise, while* BROTHER THOMAS *thumps on the table with his soft gavel.*)

BRETHREN. Hurrah for Johnny Johnson! (*They begin a gentle clapping.* JOHNNY *smiling kindly at them, shushes them with downward gestures of his hands.*)

THOMAS. (*Bowing to the old bearded brother.*) I'm sorry, Dr. Frewd, but you keep making the same mistake. Johnny is not the President of the United States. (*Turning to* JOHNNY.) Are you, Johnny?

JOHNNY. (*Looking up at the portrait.*) No. (*The* SECRETARY *begins writing in a huge ledger.*)

DR. FREWD. (*Sitting down.*) I stand corrected, sir. (*Then rising again.*) If Johnny Johnson's not the President of these United States, he ought to be. (*The old gentlemen nod an enthusiastic agreement.*)

ANOTHER VOICE. That's true. As chairman of the ways and means committee I say we ought to elect him.

ANOTHER VOICE. As ex-secretary of war, I say so.

JOHNNY. (*With kindly firmness.*) You all honor me a lot but— Maybe you'd better get on with the business. (*He resumes his painting.*)

ANOTHER VOICE. That's right—asylum rules —get on with the business.

THOMAS. Call the roll, sir.

SECRETARY. (*Intoning above the ledger.*) Brother Claude—

CLAUDE. Present.

SECRETARY. Brother George—

GEORGE. Present.

SECRETARY. Brother Henry— (*There is answer, and the members look about the A man resembling a well-known Sena. from the Northwest rises.*)

WILLIAM. The gentleman from Mas chusetts is working on his speech. He w be here at any moment. (*He sits dow*

A VOICE. I thought he'd lost his voice that filibuster.

THOMAS. (*Chuckling as he holds up gavel.*) As Johnny says—who ever heard a politician losing his voice?

VOICES. That's right. Johnny knows.

ANOTHER VOICE. But I thought Mas chusetts had finished speaking. (*A m resembling a certain Senator from the u coast rises in pompous importance.*)

HIRAM. Like California the old Bay St is never finished. Thar she blows—I m stands. (*He sits down as* WILLIAM plauds.*)

SECRETARY. (*With a questioning look* JOHNNY *which* JOHNNY *answers with nod.*) Brother Hiram—

HIRAM. Present.

SECRETARY. Brother Jim—

JIM. Present.

SECRETARY. (*With a slight change of tor* Brother Theodore— (*A man resemblin certain late President of the United Sta ·with his square teeth and mustache, ri He has an inflated rubber stick in hand.*)

THEODORE. (*Waving his stick.*) Both p ent—me and my stick. (*He bows and down.*)

THOMAS. Read the minutes of the meeting.

SECRETARY. (*Beginning to intone m sonorously.*) On December the twelfth Adelphi Debating Society met in wee session assembled, same being the five h dred and fifteenth meeting of the or and proceeded to the business of vot upon their final draft of the League

orld Republics. This League was passed
an overwhelming majority—overwhelm-
g majority— (*The door at the left rear
ens and a little man resembling a certain
e Senator from Massachusetts comes
stling in. Under one arm he carries a
d of books and in his hand several sheets
paper.*)

NRY. (*In a voice hoarse from too much
e.*) One moment, gentlemen. (*He comes
rward in front of the rostrum and drops
s books with a bang. The old gentlemen
ring out of their seats with a squeal, and
HNNY looks out at them nodding and
iling, and under his influence they sit
wn again.*) This infamous league cuts at
e very base of our democratic institutions.
omeone makes a loud raspberry noise and
NRY glares about him.*) I am first and
remost an American. I love the American
g, a flag devoted to the principles of
erty, and the pursuit of happiness.

VOICE. And in this asylum we're all
ppy.

NRY. Not only did the great Washing-
 tell us to keep ourselves aloof and in-
lable in the service of—

CRETARY. (*Spontaneously.*) —Liberty.
le looks about him abashed and begins
iting hurriedly in the ledger.*)

NRY. I challenge these interruptions.
icking up a book, opening it and read-
.*) "If this damnable document is foisted
on the American people it will mark
e beginning and end of our nation."
ho said that?

EODORE. (*Rising again and bowing all
und.*) I said it, and you all know me.

NRY. (*Continuing.*) Gentlemen, if we
owed the sentimentality and romanticism
our President ex-officio—and he is the
l author of this covenant— (*Reaching
und and shaking hands.*) Hello,
nny— (*Continuing.*) —allow him to
olve us in responsibility for any and
ry unimportant quarrel in Europe, we
uld find our strength wasted and the
at principles of—

CES. (*In unison.*) —Liberty! Sit down!

HENRY. (*Turning towards the members,
and stretching out his hands emphatically.*)
Under the rules governing this floor I have
a right to speak—and I exercise that right
in a last appeal to you to use your reason
as—as— (*Croaking.*) My voice is failing—
I have given my all in the service of my
country. (*He staggers and sits down.*)

WILLIAM. Look at this martyr. (*Rising to
applaud.*) In his name I move the vote be
retaken.

THEODORE. (*Rising.*) Second the motion.

SEVERAL VOICES. No! No!

WILLIAM. The motion's before the house.

THOMAS. Let me speak! (*The SECRETARY
nods. HIRAM, THEODORE and WILLIAM murmur to one another in disgruntlement.*)
Gentlemen, we've passed this covenant once
and let's let it stay passed. As Johnny says,
don't chew your tobacco twice.

VOICES. That's right.

WILLIAM. (*Springing up under HENRY's
urging.*) But under the Constitution we
have a right to ask for a recount. (*He sits
down.*)

THOMAS. Brethren, it is obvious that a
majority of people everywhere want some
sort of world co-operation which will bring
peace and happiness to mankind—in place
of wars and misery which we have had so
long.

VOICES. Hear, hear!

THOMAS. The disorganized nations of the
earth—frightened, suspicious, hating one
another—are waiting for someone to show
them the way out of their dilemma. (*Gesturing towards the ledger.*) And in this
covenant we show them.

VOICES. We show them.

THOMAS. Every day the need for great
statesmanship increases — (*Bowing to
JOHNNY.*)—while the terrors of war hang
in the air. Remember the pictures Johnny
showed us yesterday?—horrible pictures—
(*Some of the old gentlemen shudder.*)
—Little children all over the world are
leaving their toys and their playthings, their

marbles and their maypoles, to learn to wear gas masks and sleep in shell- and gas-proof dungeons. In this very town they're doing it.

SEVERAL BRETHREN. (*Covering their faces with their hands.*) Horrible! Horrible!

THEODORE. (*Waving his rubber stick.*) In time of peace prepare for war.

JOHNNY. (*Chuckling.*) Same old argument, Theodore. We answered that the other day, I thought.

SECRETARY. (*Intoning.*) Article nineteen, Section six—inviolability of noncombatants.

THOMAS. Silence, Johnny's going to speak.

VOICES. (*Eagerly.*) That's right, Johnny, tell us a story.

JOHNNY. (*As they listen attentively.*) I'm no speaker. (*Lifting his hand as* THEODORE *starts to interrupt.*) And I've already said what I believe on the subject. But Brother Theodore's old argument about every country having to have a big show-off army and navy to keep peace reminds me of old Mr. Zollicoff's dog. Now that was a good dog—until one day Mr. Zollicoff dressed him up in a brass spiked collar. First thing you know that dog was showing off his spikes and fighting every other dog in the neighborhood. They finally had to kill him with a baseball bat. Now our constitution shows—

VOICES. (*With gentle laughter.*) That's right, Johnny. He speaks straight to the point, don't he?

WILLIAM. We are not talking about dogs, but civilized men. (*JOHNNY smiles, shrugs his shoulders and resumes his work.*)

THOMAS. The Chair feels that men are same as dogs—when they start fighting one another. (*He looks at* JOHNNY *for confirmation.*) History shows it.

DR. FREWD. I beg to report that in this asylum we are civilized men. Put it in the minutes. (*He sits down amid applause.*)

THEODORE. (*Doggedly.*) Let's vote.

THOMAS. (*Bowing in resignation.*) All in favor of the League of World Republics

as laid down— (*Gesturing towards th ledger.*) —in our Constitution please signif the same by rising. (*The majority of th brethren rise.* JOHNNY *keeps his seat.*)

SECRETARY. (*Beginning to count.*) One— two — three — four — five — six — seven — (JOHNNY *leans over and whispers t* THOMAS.)

THOMAS. Will the gentleman from Cal fornia there in the rear kindly make hi vote clear? He seems to be in a crouchin position.

HIRAM. (*Straightening up.*) I—I—all righ I'll vote for it, but I'll have a hard tim explaining it to the folks back home.

THEODORE. (*Staring at him.*) You—you'v sold Brother Henry out.

HIRAM. (*Now rising in recovered dignity.* I was offered a price but I didn't sell.

HENRY. (*Springing up and croaking.*) A Abe Lincoln said—let the American peop speak. And they won't accept your verdic I've got a hundred postal cards— (*Feelin in his pocket.*) —and I'm going to floo the country—

VOICES. Sit down! (*He stands wavering a instant and then collapses in his chair.*)

JOHNNY. (*Gently but firmly as he stan up.*) I think now we ought to make it unan mous, boys. What do you say, Henry (HENRY *makes no answer.*) You'd feel be ter if you joined in. We've done a lot good work here, and we've got a lot mo to do. We all need to pull together.

SECRETARY. Section forty-three—pull gether.

JOHNNY. And you need to do it too— your own good. Think how much happi all of us are since we started to work something that interested us. We've forg our own troubles and we eat better, sle better. And besides if we don't take these big problems, who will? In the o side world they don't seem to be interest any more. (*He looks smilingly at* HENRY Come on now.

HENRY. (*Croaking gruffly.*) No, no.

OMAS. Dr. Frewd will just have to
lyze him some more—I reckon. (HENRY
vers in his seat as DR. FREWD steps nim-
to his side and begins a crouching down
l lifting up pantomime. The brethren,
h the exception of THOMAS and JOHNNY,
d around.)

NRY. (In a pleading mumble.) No—no
'm a free individual—I'm— (But as if
inst his will he is finally lifted to his
. He receives their plaudits and hand-
kings with bowed head and deep emo-
.)

OMAS. (Happily.) The League of World
ublics is passed unanimously. This is
historic hour. (Loud applause.)

FREWD. (Crying out.) Hurrah for the
gue!

GENTLEMEN. (Loudly.) Hurrah!
OMAS thumps with his rubber gavel.)

MAS. We're making a little too much
e, brethren.

ES. All right.

MAS. The new chairman of the board
specting the hospital this morning and
want everything quiet.

ETARY. And he's a millionaire too.

E. (From the rear.) We don't like
ionaires.

THER VOICE. No, we don't.

NNY. Millionaires ain't so bad, fellows.
y have their troubles too as the lap
said.

FREWD. Hurrah for peace.

THER VOICE. Hurrah for peace! (DR.
VD stands up and lifting his arms begins
ad them in a song.)

HREN. (Singing as in a round, with
MAS and the clerk joining in.) Come let
s hymn a hymn to peace,
y, merrily we will sing—
lly proclaiming wars shall cease,
ye, how the bells go ting-ling-ling—
guard at the right front reaches out
he wall and turns on a radio. A gentle
sleepy requiem is heard playing.

Gradually the brethren stop their singing
and sit down in their seats as if feeling the
drowsy spell of some opiate.)

JOHNNY. (Resuming his work.) That's
right—rest a while—listen to the soft music
—listen and rest a while—

THOMAS. (Mumbling.) The next question
before the house is—Capital and Labor—
Section one— (He sinks down into his
seat.) —the man who works must share
in—share in— (He bows his head over on
the table. And now all the old men likewise bow their heads over and go to sleep.
JOHNNY sits working at his toy as the scene
of the Adelphi Debating Society begins to
dim out. The soft music continues to play
for a moment and then it too dies gradually away.
Now entering slowly and dreamily from
the right come the group of hospital directors on their tour of inspection. In front
walks ANGUISH HOWINGTON, carrying a cane
and wearing a top silk hat, and by his side
walks a young clinical-faced DOCTOR. Behind
ANGUISH and the DOCTOR come five or six
stout and well-dressed business men, a few
orderlies, and a young man secretary
dressed in a Crystal Mineral Water uniform.)

DOCTOR. (Gesturing to the rear where only
JOHNNY now is visible.) —And here we
have developed a little debating society
where some of our elderly patients engage
in harmless talk.

ANGUISH. (Softly, mechanically, and almost
dreamily.) Interesting idea.

DOCTOR. Owing to our limited means the
equipment is poor, as you see.

ANGUISH. (To his secretary.) Make a note
of that. (The young man writes on his
pad.)

DOCTOR. Thank you, sir, thank you, sir.
You have already been very generous.

ANGUISH. And Mrs. Howington and I will
continue to be so. She has a deep interest
in this institution.

DOCTOR. For which we are very grateful.
I may mention that all of our staff use
Crystal Mineral Water nightly— Before

retiring we do so. (*Slightly bowing.*) We find it very helpful.

ANGUISH. (*Stiffening with a sense of greatness.*) Millions find it helpful in these disordered times. (*Staring towards the rear.*) Adelphi Debating Society—I used to belong to a society with the same name—in the old days. It wasn't very peaceful though. There was a fellow—Johnson— He was always creating friction. (*His voice dies out.*)

DOCTOR. But the founder of this society—you see him there—seems to be able to keep peace. In fact we have finally diagnosed his disease as peace monomania.

ANGUISH. Is it dangerous?

DOCTOR. (*Gravely.*) Oh no—I shouldn't say so.

ANGUISH. (*Still gazing towards the rear.*) That fellow's face looks familiar.

DOCTOR. His name is Johnson too—Johnny Johnson.

ANGUISH. Oh yes. Yes, I remember now.

DOCTOR. We are thinking of letting him out in a few days.

ANGUISH. (*Quickly.*) Do you think it is safe?

DOCTOR. Oh quite, quite. It will be a loss to us too. He has a way with the patients—(*Hurriedly.*) I mean everybody likes him. (*Far off in the distance a musical gong begins to sound. The light comes up on the scene in the rear as if in time to the notes, and the old gentlemen rise sleepily from their chairs. The two attendants step over and stand by the little gate that opens in the railing and* JOHNNY, *carrying his basket of toys and accompanied by the* SECRETARY *with the great ledger, leads them out.* ANGUISH *and the directors move slowly on across the foreground to the left.*)

ANGUISH. (*Pointing off down the hall.*) Those bars seem rather frail and old.

DOCTOR. They are, sir.

ANGUISH. (*To the young fellow behind him with the pad.*) Make a note of that.

DOCTOR. Thank you, sir. (*At the sound* ANGUISH's *voice* JOHNNY *stops, and t. SECRETARY and the old gentlemen mo away at the right with the two attendan leaving him behind. Suddenly he runs f ward and pulls* ANGUISH *by the arm.*)

JOHNNY. (*As* ANGUISH *turns coldly a puppetlike around.*) Why, I hardly kn you, Anguish, in all them duds. (*The derlies spring back and surround* ANGUISH

ANGUISH. (*Manfully.*) Never mind, men—

JOHNNY. (*Hesitating.*) Tell me—have got any news—about Minny Belle, I mea

ANGUISH. (*Pondering a moment gravel* She's—er—well—very well.

JOHNNY. Golly, I'm glad to hear that. been so long since—I heard. (*Staring off instant as if caught in a vague worry then smiling around at* ANGUISH.) She m be awful busy—yeh—tell her I will seeing her—I hope—soon.

ANGUISH. (*After a cruel and genteel pau* You don't keep up with what is going do you?

JOHNNY. Well, we get the *Internatio Digest* and that gives us the world ne

ANGUISH. (*Coldly.*) Miss Tompkins me the honor some years ago of accep my hand in marriage. (*He bows and n: on accompanied by the* DOCTOR, *the direc and attendants. As he goes out he p quietly towards Wilson's portrait with cane.*) That picture there should be moved.

DOCTOR. It shall be sir, at once. (*The disappear at the left.* JOHNNY *stands bent head looking at the floor. A mor passes and an* ATTENDANT *comes hurr in from the right.*)

ATTENDANT. Say, it's against the ru even for you, Johnny—to fall out like Lunch is ready. (*He takes* JOHNNY *b arm and then stares at him.*) You kind of sick—anything wrong? (*Joi makes no answer but continues lookin the floor. The* ATTENDANT, *touched by s thing in his face, speaks kindly to h* Can I get a doctor? (*Gazing carefully him.*) You can trust me.

HNNY. (*Murmuring.*) No, thanks.

TENDANT. (*A little more confidentially.*) e got some good news for you, Johnny. u're going to be let out of here next eek. It's a secret, but we know it. Don't make you feel better?

HNNY. (*Shaking his head.*) No, I guess —I'll stay here—now.

TENDANT. What!

JOHNNY. All—my friends—are here—my work too.

ATTENDANT. Yeh, but when they say you're ready to leave you got to leave. That's the law. (JOHNNY *says nothing, and the* ATTENDANT, *taking him by the arm, leads him away at the right.*)

BLACK OUT

SCENE III

"Whither have ye made a road?"

e scene is a street corner—projecting gonally in at the right front. Stretching ng the right towards the rear is an rgreen hedge with an imposing iron gate rked "Private." Behind the hedge in the tance and showing through the leafless nter trees is the high rim of a great ananated stadium cutting horizontally oss the sky. It is viewed from the rear, d from over this rim now and then comes muted trumpet sound of a high hoarse terical voice haranguing a multitude. e words are cacophonous and are ap-uded now and then by a burst of martial d music, beaten drum, or the husky ay-sounding cheers of thousands. Over he left front is the corner of a red brick ory-like building.

en the curtain rises, JOHNNY JOHNSON— *a man of forty-five or fifty but looking ch older, though his face and manner still cheery—is standing by a lightless lamp-post looking out before him. He ressed in non-descript clothes, an old eless gray felt hat, a work shirt, dark and trousers, and heavy well-worn king shoes. Hung by a string around neck and held in front of him is a e tray like that with which street hawk-pursue their calling. Stray passersby on r way to the stadium go down the street he right every now and then.*

NNY. (*Keeping a watchful eye for any pective customer as he sends his voice ss the scene in a quavering call.*) Toy-Toy-ees for sale! (*He waits a moment, ing about him and wiggling his feet to them warm. Then he calls again.*) ees! (*And now coming down through the great iron gate is a little* BOY *about twelve years old, dressed in the new uniform of a boy scout. He stops and looks behind him.*)

BOY. (*Calling.*) Can I give the old man a nickel, Mother?

A WOMAN'S VOICE. (*Beyond the gate.*) Remember, nickels make dollars—as daddy says.

BOY. But I haven't done my scout's good deed for today. (MINNY BELLE *comes suddenly out through the gate. She is wrapped in furs and somewhat stout.*) May I, Mother?

MINNY BELLE. We're already late for the parade. (*She starts on down the street at the left rear.*)

JOHNNY. (*Calling.*) Nice little toy-ees for nice little girls and boy-ees! (*As if touched by some faint and far-off remembrance* MINNY BELLE *stops. She slowly and abstractedly opens her purse.*)

MINNY BELLE. All right, give him a nickel— He looks cold. (*The* BOY *takes the nickel and comes over to* JOHNNY.)

BOY. (*Touching* JOHNNY *on the arm.*) Here's the nickel, sir.

JOHNNY. What do you want?—A monkey or a dove?—Maybe this little terrapin. See —he can wiggle his legs when you pull the string. Look.

BOY. (*Appraisingly.*) Hmn— Maybe I might take a toy soldier.

JOHNNY. (*Sternly.*) No—no—I don't make soldiers.

BOY. Then I don't want anything.

JOHNNY. Here's your nickel.

BOY. Oh no, you must keep the nickel anyway. My daddy's rich.

JOHNNY. (*Smiling.*) Is he?—That's nice. What's your name, son?

BOY. Anguish Howington, Junior.

JOHNNY. (*After a moment's silence.*) That's a nice name. (*And now as if conscious that* MINNY BELLE *is there in the distance he pulls up his coat collar and turns his face slightly away.*)

ANGUISH, JR. I'm named after my father. He's mayor of the town, you know.

JOHNNY. Is he? That's wonderful. I'm a sort of stranger here— So he's mayor of the town? And you're a boy scout?

ANGUISH, JR. Yes sir. And some day I'm going to be a soldier.

JOHNNY. (*Quickly.*) No, I wouldn't be that.

ANGUISH, JR. Why not?

JOHNNY. You could be—well, you could make things—or be a great doctor—or a good farmer—do something that would be of use to the world.

ANGUISH, JR. But daddy says that we're in for a terrible war and all the people have got to be ready to keep the enemy from destroying us.

JOHNNY. (*Staring out before him.*) Ah—

MINNY BELLE. (*Calling.*) Come on!

JOHNNY. And—and how is your mother, son?

ANGUISH, JR. Why, she's all right. She's standing right over there. (*But* JOHNNY *keeps looking before him.*) Goodbye.

JOHNNY. (*In a muffled voice.*) Goodbye, son. (*Little* ANGUISH *turns and runs back to his mother, elated by his charitable act.*

MINNY BELLE *takes him by the hand an they go away at the left rear.* JOHNNY *gaz at the nickel in his hand and then rais his voice again in a call.*) Toy-ees for sal Nice little— (*His voice dies out and stands staring before him. And now blari suddenly in the air nearby, comes a sour of a brass band playing the "Democra March."* JOHNNY *still stands gazing befo him. The rat-tat-tat-tat of the drums com near him, and crossing the scene at t extreme left rear is the American Legi Drum Corps with a few bugles and piec of brass. Two boy scout flag-bearers go fore, and behind them, several young m and women carrying banners and placar —"America First," "Be Prepared," and forth. The parade passes on like a visi in a dream, but* JOHNNY *still looks befo him with his old man's face and unblir ing eyes. He shivers a bit, and his should seem to sag. By this time the gloom of proaching twilight has spread over scene. The street lamp above his he gradually lights up, casting its nebul halo over his shabby figure standing tionless as stone. Suddenly he begins whistle low and aimlessly to himself— theme melody of the play. For a mom he continues whistling; then giving shoulders the faintest touch of a shrug, turns and starts down the long street. looks up now and then at the row of sil houses on his right.*) Toy-ees! Toy-ee for nice little girls and boys! (*But nob answers, no windows are opened, no s ing youthful faces appear, for all are g ered into the great stadium in the dista where the drear outlandish haranguer v can still be heard continuing its q clamor to the sky—"Gog-a-gog—Mago gog." Yet even so,* JOHNNY JOHNSON *is hushed by this strange voice boom through the world. As he disappears d the long street that leads from the g city into the country and beyond, he be whistling his song again—a little clearly now, a little more bravely.*)

CURTAIN.

The Green Pastures

A Fable

SUGGESTED BY ROARK BRADFORD'S SOUTHERN
SKETCHES, "OL' MAN ADAM AN' HIS CHILLUN"
BY MARC CONNELLY

———

TO MY MOTHER

———

Produced by Lawrence Rivers at the Mansfield Theatre, New York, February
, 1930.

CHARACTERS

₹. DESHEE, the Preacher	ZEBA	FIRST MAN
¹RTLE	CAIN THE SIXTH	FLATFOOT
₹ST BOY	BOY GAMBLER	HAM
COND BOY	GENERAL	JAPHETH
₹ST COOK	HEAD MAGICIAN	FIRST CLEANER
VOICE	FIRST WIZARD	SECOND CLEANER
COND COOK	SECOND WIZARD	ABRAHAM
₹ST MAN ANGEL	JOSHUA	ISAAC
₹ST MAMMY ANGEL	FIRST SCOUT	JACOB
STOUT ANGEL	MASTER OF CEREMONIES	MOSES
SLENDER ANGEL	FIRST GAMBLER	ZIPPORAH
₹CHANGEL	SECOND GAMBLER	AARON
₹BRIEL	VOICE IN SHANTY	A CANDIDATE MAGICIAN
₯D	NOAH	PHARAOH
₹OIR LEADER	NOAH'S WIFE	KING OF BABYLON
₹STARD MAKER	SHEM	PROPHET
₯AM	FIRST WOMAN	HIGH PRIEST
₯E	SECOND WOMAN	CORPORAL
₹IN	THIRD WOMAN	HEZDREL
₹IN'S GIRL		SECOND OFFICER

———

SCENES
Part I

1. The Sunday School
2. A Fish Fry
3. A Garden
4. Outside the Garden
5. A Roadside
6. A Private Office
7. Another Roadside and a House
8. A House
9. A Hillside
10. A Mountain Top

Part II

1. The Private Office
2. The Mouth of a Cave
3. A Throne Room
4. The Foot of a Mountain
5. A Cabaret
6. The Private Office
7. Outside a Temple
8. Another Fish Fry

———

Copyright, 1929, by Marc Connelly
ALL RIGHTS RESERVED

———

PART ONE

SCENE I

A corner in a Negro church.

Ten children and an elderly preacher.

The costumes are those that might be seen in any lower Louisiana town at Sunday-School time. As the curtain rises, MR. DESHEE, *the preacher, is reading from a Bible. The* CHILDREN *are listening with varied degrees of interest. Three or four are wide-eyed in their attention. Two or three are obviously puzzled, but interested, and the smallest ones are engaged in more physical concerns. One is playing with a little doll, and another runs his fingers on all the angles of his chair.*

DESHEE. "An' Adam lived a hundred and thirty years, an' begat a son in his own likeness, after his image; an' called his name Seth. An' de days of Adam, after he had begotten Seth, were eight hundred years; an' he begat sons an' daughters; an' all de days dat Adam lived were nine hundred an' thirty years; an' he died. An' Seth lived a hundred an' five years an' begat Enos; an' Seth lived after he begat Enos eight hundred an' seven years and begat sons and daughters. An' all de days of Seth were nine hundred and twelve years; an' he died." An' it go on like dat till we come to Enoch an' de book say: "An' Enoch lived sixty an' five years and begat Methuselah." Den it say: "An' all de days of Methuselah were nine hundred an' sixty an' nine years an' he died." An' dat was de oldest man dat ever was. Dat's why we call ol' Mr. Gurney's mammy ol' Mrs. Methuselah, caize she's so ol'. Den a little later it tell about another member of de fam'ly. His name was Noah. Maybe some of you know about him already. I'm gon-ter tell you all about him next Sunday. Anyway dat's de meat an' substance of de first five chapters of Genesis. Now, how you think you gonter like de Bible?

MYRTLE. I think it's jest wonderful, Mr. Deshee. I cain't understand any of it.

FIRST BOY. Why did dey live so long, Mr. Deshee?

DESHEE. Why? Caize dat was de way God felt.

SECOND BOY. Dat made Adam a way ba[ck]

DESHEE. Yes, he certainly 'way back [in] de time Noah come along. Want to [ask] me any mo' questions?

SECOND BOY. What de worl' look l[ike] when de Lawd begin, Mr. Deshee.

DESHEE. How yo' mean what it look li[ke]

MYRTLE. Carlisle mean who was [in] N'Orleans den.

DESHEE. Dey wasn't nobody in N'Orl[eans] on 'count dey wasn't any N'Orleans. [In] de whole idea I tol' you at de end of [de] first Chapter. Yo' got to git yo' m[inds] fixed. Dey wasn't any Rampart Street. [Dey] wasn't any Canal Street. Dey wasn't [any] Louisiana. Dey wasn't nothin' on de e[arth] at all caize fo' de reason dey wasn't [any] earth.

MYRTLE. Yes, but what Carlisle wa[nt to] know is—

DESHEE.....(*Interrupting and addres[sing a] little boy who has been playing with [his] chair and paying no attention.*) Now [Ran]dolph, if you don't listen, how yo' g[onter] grow up and be a good man? Yo' wa[nt to] grow up an' be a transgressor?

LITTLE BOY. (*Frightened.*) No.

DESHEE. You tell yo' mammy yo' [jest] got to come wid you next time. She[can] git de things done in time to bring [you] to de school. You content yo'self. (*The little boy straightens up in his ch[air.*] Now, what do Carlisle want to kno[w?]

CARLISLE. How he decide he wan[t de] worl' to be right yere and how he g[it de] idea he wanted it?

MYRTLE. Caize de Book say, don't it[, Mr.] Deshee?

DESHEE. De Book say, but at de [same] time dat's a good question. I reme[mber] when I was a little boy de same [thing] recurred to me. An ol' Mr. Dubois, h[e was] a wonderful preacher at New Hope C[hurch] over in East Gretna, he said: "De a[nswer] is dat de Book ain't got time to go[

de details." And he was right. You
~w sometimes I think de Lawd expects
:o figure out a few things for ourselves.
. know that at one time dey wasn't any-
~g except Heaven, we don't know jest
~ere it was but we know it was dere.
~be it was everywhere. Den one day de
~d got the idea he'd like to make some
~es. He made de sun and de moon,
~tars. An' he made de earth.

~TLE. Who was aroun' den, nothin'
~ angels?

~EE. I suppose so.

~ BOY. What was de angels doin' up
~ ?

~EE. I suppose dey jest flew aroun'
~ had a good time. Dey wasn't no sin,
~ey musta had a good time.

~ BOY. Did dey have picnics?

~EE. Sho, dey had the nicest kind of
~cs. Dey probably had fish frys, wid
~ custard and ten cent seegars for de
~ts. God gives us humans lotsa ideas
~t havin' good times. Maybe dey were
~gs he'd seen de angels do. Yes, sir, I
~ey had a fish fry every week.

~TLE. Did dey have Sunday School,

~EE. Yes, dey musta had Sunday
~ol for de cherubs.

MYRTLE. What did God look like, Mr.
Deshee?

DESHEE. Well, nobody knows exactly what
God looked like. But when I was a little
boy I used to imagine dat he looked like
de Reverend Dubois. He was de finest
looking ol' man I ever knew. Yes, I used
to bet de Lawd looked exactly like Mr.
Dubois in de days when he walked de
earth in de shape of a natchel man.

MYRTLE. When was dat, Mr. Deshee?

DESHEE. Why, when He was gettin' things
started down heah. When He talked to
Adam and Eve and Noah and Moses and
all dem. He made mighty men in dem
days. But aldo they was awful mighty dey
always knew dat He was beyond dem all.
Pretty near one o'clock, time fo' you chillun to go home to dinner, but before I
let you go I wan' you to go over wid me
de main facts of de first lesson. What's
de name of de book?

CHILDREN. Genesis.

DESHEE. Dat's right. And what's de other
name?

CHILDREN. First Book of Moses.

DESHEE. Dat's right. And dis yere's Chapter One. (*The lights begin to dim.*) "In
de beginnin' God created de heaven an'
de earth. An' de earth was widout form
an' void. An' de darkness was upon de
face of de deep."

SCENE II

~he darkness many voices are heard
~ng "Rise, Shine, Give God The
~y." They sing it gayly and rapidly.
~lights go up as the second verse ends.
~ chorus is being sung diminuendo by
~xed company of angels. That is they
~ngels in that they wear brightly col-
~ robes and have wings protruding
~ their backs. Otherwise they look and
~ke a company of happy negroes at a
~ry. The scene itself is a pre-Creation
~en with compromises. In the distance
~ unbroken stretch of blue sky. Com-
~nable varicolored clouds billow down
~ floor of the stage and roll overhead
~ branches of a live oak tree which is
~ft. The tree is leafy and dripping

with Spanish moss and with the clouds
makes a frame for the scene. In
the cool shade of the tree are the
usual appurtenances of a fish fry a large
kettle of hot fat set on two small parallel
logs, with a fire going underneath, and a
large rustic table formed by driving four
stakes into the ground and placing planks
on top of the small connecting boards. On
the table are piles of biscuits and corn
bread and the cooked fish in dish pans.
There are one or two fairly large cedar
or crock "churns" containing boiled custard, which looks like milk. There is a
gourd dipper beside the churns and several glasses and cups of various sizes and
shapes from which the custard is drunk.

The principal singers are marching two by two in a small area at the R. *of the stage. Two* MAMMY ANGELS *are attending to the frying beside the kettle. Behind the table a* MAN ANGEL *is skinning fish and passing them to the cooks. Another is ladling out the custard. A* MAMMY ANGEL *is putting fish on bread for a brood of cherubs, and during the first scene they seat themselves on a grassy bank upstage. Another* MAMMY ANGEL *is clapping her hands disapprovingly and beckoning a laughing* BOY CHERUB *down from a cloud a little out of her reach. Another* MAMMY ANGEL *is solicitously slapping the back of a girl cherub who has a large fish sandwich in her hand and a bone in her throat. There is much movement about the table, and during the first few minutes several individuals go up to the table to help themselves to the food and drink. Many of the women angels wear hats and a few of the men are smoking cigars. A large boxful is on the table. There is much laughter and chatter as the music softens, but continues, during the early part of the action. The following short scenes are played almost simultaneously.*

FIRST COOK. (*At Kettle*) (*Calling off*) Hurry up, Cajey. Dis yere fat's cryin' fo' mo' feesh.

A VOICE. (*Off stage.*) We comin', fas' we kin. Dey got to be ketched, ain't dey? We cain't say. "C'm'on little fish. C'm'on an' git fried," kin we?

SECOND COOK. (*At Table.*) De trouble is de mens is all worm fishin'.

FIRST MAN ANGEL. (*At Table*) Whut dif'runce do it make? Yo' all de time got to make out like somebody's doin' somethin' de wrong way.

SECOND COOK. (*Near Table*) I s'pose you got de per'fec' way fo' makin' bait.

FIRST MAN ANGEL. I ain't sayin' dat. I is sayin' whut's wrong wid worm fishin'.

SECOND COOK. Whut's wrong wid worm fishin'? Ever'thing, dat's all. Dey's only one good way fo' catfishin', an' dat's minny fishin'. Anybody know dat.

FIRST MAN ANGEL. Well, it jest so happen dat minny fishin' is de doggondest fool way

of fishin' dey is. You kin try minny fishi[n'] to de cows come home an' all you catch[ ] be de backache. De trouble wid you, s[is]ter, is you jest got minny fishin' on [de] brain.

SECOND COOK. Go right on, loud mo[uth] You tell me de news. My, my! You j[est] de wisest person in de worl'. First y[ou] den de Lawd God.

FIRST MAN ANGEL. (*To the custard la[d]ler.*) You cain't tell dem nothin'. (*Wa[lks] away to the custard churn.*) Does you [got] to 'splain some simple fac' dey git m[ad] deaf.

FIRST MAMMY ANGEL. (*To* CHERUB *on [the] cloud.*) Now, you heerd me. (*The* CHER[UB] *assumes several mocking poses, as [she] speaks.*) You fly down yere. You wan[t to] be put down in de sin book? (*She g[oes] to the table, gets a drink for herself a[nd] points out the cherub to one of the m[en] behind the table.*) Dat baby must got i[n his] blood in him he so vexin'. (*She returns [to] her position under the cloud.*) You w[ant] me to fly up dere an' slap you dow[n?] Now, I tol' you. (*The* CHERUB *starts [to] come down.*)

STOUT ANGEL. (*To the* CHERUB *with [a] bone in her throat.*) I tol' you you was [too] little fo' cat fish. What you wanter g[it a] bone in yo' froat fo'? (*She slaps the* CH[ER]UB'S *back.*)

SLENDER ANGEL. (*Leisurely eating a s[and]wich as she watches the back-slappi[ng.]*) What de trouble wid Leonetta?

STOUT ANGEL. She got a catfish b[one] down her froat. (*To the* CHERUB.) [It's] gone, I tol' you to eat grinnel instea[d.]

SLENDER ANGEL. Ef'n she do git all da[t] she gonter have de bellyache.

STOUT ANGEL. Ain't I tol' her dat? (*To the* CHERUB.) Come on now; let go dat [bone.] (*She slaps* CHERUB'S *back again. The [bone] is dislodged and the* CHERUB *grins he[r re]lief.*) Dat's good.

SLENDER ANGEL. (*Comfortingly.*) Now [she's] all right.

STOUT ANGEL. Go on an' play wid [yo'] cousins. (*The* CHERUB *joins the* CHE[RUBS]

ing on the embankment. The concur-
cy of scenes ends here.) I ain't see you
ely, Lily. How you been?

ENDER ANGEL. Me, I'm fine. I been
itin' my mammy. She waitin' on de
lcome table over by de throne of grace.

UT ANGEL. She always was pretty holy.

NDER ANGEL. Yes, ma'am. She like it
e. I guess de Lawd's took quite a fancy
her.

UT ANGEL. Well, dat's natural. I dere yo' mammy one of de finest lady
gels I know.

NDER ANGEL. She claim you de best
she know.

UT ANGEL. Well, when you come right
vn to it, I suppose we is all pretty near
fec'.

NDER ANGEL. Yes, ma'am. Why is dat,
' Jenny?

UT ANGEL. I s'pose it's caize de Lawd
don' 'low us 'sociatin' wid de devil
mo' so dat dey cain' be no mo' sin-
.

NDER ANGEL. Po' ol' Satan. Whutevah
ome of him?

UT ANGEL. De Lawd put him some
e I s'pose.

NDER ANGEL. But dey ain't any place
Heaven, is dey?

UT ANGEL. De Lawd could make a
e, couldn't he?

NDER ANGEL. Dat's de truth. Dey's one
g confuses me though.

T ANGEL. What's dat?

DER ANGEL. I do a great deal of trav-
an' I ain't never come across any place
Heaven anywhere. So if de Lawd kick
n out of Heaven jest whereat did he
Dat's my question.

T ANGEL. You bettah let de Lawd
his own secrets, Lily. De way things
oin' now dey ain't' been no sinnin'
dey give dat scamp a kick in de
s. Nowadays Heaven's free of sin an'
lady wants a little constitutional she

kin fly 'til she wing-weary widout gittin'
insulted.

SLENDER ANGEL. I was jest a baby when
Satan lef'. I don't even 'member what he
look like.

STOUT ANGEL. He was jest right fo' a devil.
(*An* ARCHANGEL *enters. He is older than
the others and wears a white beard. His
clothing is much darker than that of the
others and his wings a trifle more imposing.*) Good mo'nin', Archangel. (*Others
say good morning.*)

ARCHANGEL. Good mo'nin'', folks. I wonder kin I interrup' de fish fry an' give out
de Sunday school cyards? (*Cries of "Sut-
tingly!" "Mah goodness, yes"—etc. The
marching* CHOIR *stops.*) You kin keep singin' if you want to. Why don' you sing
"When de Saints Come Marchin' In?"
Seem to me I ain' heard dat lately. (*The*
CHOIR *begins "When the Saints Come
Marching In", rather softly, but does not
resume marching. The* ARCHANGEL *looks
off left.*) All right, bring 'em yere. (*A
prim looking* WOMAN TEACHER-ANGEL *enters, shepherding ten* BOY *and* GIRL CHER-
UBS. *The* TEACHER *carries ten beribboned
diplomas, which she gives to the* ARCH-
ANGEL. *The* CHERUBS *are dressed in stiffly
starched white suits and dresses, the little
girls having enormous ribbons at the backs
of their dresses and smaller ones in their
hair and on the tips of their wings. They
line up in front of the archangel and receive the attention of the rest of the company. The* CHOIR *sings through the ceremony.*) Now den cherubs, why is you
yere?

CHILDREN. Because we so good.

ARCHANGEL. Dat's right. Now who de big
boss?

CHILDREN. Our dear Lawd.

ARCHANGEL. Dat's right. When you all
grow up what you gonter be?

CHILDREN. Holy angels at de throne of
grace.

ARCHANGEL. Dat's right. Now, you passed
yo' 'xaminations and it gives me great
pleasure to hand out de cyards for de whole
class. Gineeva Chaproe. (*The* FIRST GIRL

CHERUB *goes to him and gets her diploma.
The* CHOIR *sings loudly and resumes
marching, as the* ARCHANGEL *calls out another name—and presents diplomas.)* Cor-
ey Moulter. (SECOND GIRL CHERUB *gets her
diploma.)* Nootzie Winebush. (THIRD GIRL
CHERUB.) Harriet Prancy. (FOURTH GIRL
CHERUB.) I guess you is Brozain Stew't.
(*He gives the* FIFTH GIRL CHERUB *the
paper. Each of the presentations has been
accompanied by hand-clapping from the by-
standers.)* Now you boys know yo' own
names. Suppose you come yere and help
me git dese 'sorted right? (BOY CHERUBS
*gather about him and receive their diplo-
mas. The little* GIRLS *have scattered about
the stage, joining groups of the adult angels. The angel* GABRIEL *enters. He is bigger and more elaborately winged than
even the* ARCHANGEL, *but he is also much
younger and beardless. His costume is less
conventional than that of the other men,
resembling more the* GABRIEL *of the Doré
drawings. His appearance causes a flutter
among the others. They stop their chattering with the children. The* CHOIR *stops
as three or four audible whispers of "GAB-
RIEL!" are heard. In a moment the heavenly company is all attention.)*

GABRIEL. (*Lifting his hand.*) Gangway!
Gangway for de Lawd God Jehovah!
(*There is a reverent hush and* GOD *enters.
He is the tallest and biggest of them all.
He wears a white shirt with a white bow
tie, a long Prince Albert coat of black
alpaca, black trousers and congress gaiters.
He looks at the assemblage. There is a
pause. He speaks in a rich, bass voice.*)

GOD. Is you been baptized?

OTHERS. (*Chanting.*) Certainly, Lawd.

GOD. Is you been baptized?

OTHERS. Certainly, Lawd.

GOD. (*With the beginning of musical
notation.*) Is you been baptized?

OTHERS. (*Now half-singing.*) Certainly,
Lawd. Certainly, certainly, certainly, Lawd.
(*They sing the last two verses with equiv-
alent part division.*)
    Is you been redeemed?
        Certainly, Lawd.
    Is you been redeemed?

Certainly, Lawd.
Is you been redeemed?
    Certainly, Lawd. Certainly, certai[n]
        certainly, Lawd.
Do you bow mighty low?
    Certainly, Lawd.
Do you bow mighty low?
    Certainly, Lawd.
Do you bow mighty low?
    Certainly, Law'd. Certainly, certai[n]
        certainly, Lawd.
(*As the last response ends all heads
bowed.* GOD *looks at them for a mom[ent]
then lifts His hand.*)

GOD. Let de fish fry proceed. (EVERY[ONE]
rises. The ANGELS *relax and resume t[he]
inaudible conversations. The activity be[hind]
the table and about the cauldron is [re-]
sumed. Some of the choir members [go]
to the table and get sandwiches and [some]
of the boiled custard. Three or four of [the]
children in the Sunday School class [and]
the little girl who had the bone in [her]
throat affectionately group themselves a[bout]
GOD as he speaks with the ARCHANGEL.[He]
pats their heads, they hang to his coat-[tails,]
etc.)*

ARCHANGEL. Good mo'nin', Lawd.

GOD. Good mo'nin', Deacon. You lo[ok]
pretty spry.

ARCHANGEL. I cain' complain. We [been]
been givin' our cyards to de chillun.

GOD. Dat's good. (*A small* CHERUB,[*its*]
feet braced against one of GOD's *sho[es,]
using* GOD's *coat tail as a trapeze. On[e of]
the* COOKS *offers a fish sandwich w[hich]
GOD politely declines.*)

FIRST MAMMY ANGEL. Now, you leav[e]
de Lawd's coat, Herman. You heah[?]

GOD. Dat's all right, sister. He jest pla[yin']

FIRST MAMMY ANGEL. He playin' [too]
rough. (GOD *picks up the* CHERUB [*and*]
spanks him good-naturedly. The CH[ILD]
*squeals with delight and runs to [its]
mother.* GABRIEL *advances to* GOD w[ith a]
glass of the custard.*)

GABRIEL. Little b'iled custud, Lawd?

GOD. Thank you very kindly. Dis [is]
nice.

TARD MAKER. (*Offering a box.*) Ten
t seegar, Lawd?

.....(*Taking it.*) Thank you, thank you.
w de fish fry goin'? (*Ad lib. cries of
K. Lawd," "Fine an' dandy, Lawd,"
best one yit, Lawd," etc. To the
IR.*) How you shouters gittin' on?

IR LEADER. We been marchin' and
in' de whole mo'nin'.

I heerd you. You gittin' better all de
. You gittin' as good as de one at de
ne. Why don' you give us one dem
ime jump-ups?

R LEADER. Anythin' you say, Lawd.
the others.) "So High!" (*The* CHOIR
ns to sing "So High You Can't Get
r It." They sing softly, but do not
ch. An ANGEL offers his cigar to GOD
which He can light His own.*)

No, thanks. I'm gonter save dis a
(*He puts the cigar in his pocket and
s to the singers a moment. Then he
his custard. After the second sip, a
of displeasure comes on his face.*)

IEL. What's de matter, Lawd?

(*Sipping again.*) I ain't jest sure,
Dey's something 'bout dis custahd.
es another sip.*)

ARD MAKER. Ain't it all right, Lawd?

It don't seem seasoned jest right.
make it?

ARD MAKER. Yes, Lawd. I put every-
in it like I allus do. It's' supposed
e perfec'.

Yeah. I kin taste de eggs and de
n and de sugar. (*Suddenly.*) I know
it is. It needs jest a little bit mo'
ment.

ARD MAKER. Dey's firmament in it,
l.

Maybe, but it ain' enough.

ARD MAKER. It's all we had, Lawd.
ain't a drap in de jug.

Dat's all right. I'll jest r'ar back an'
a miracle. (CHOIR *stops singing.*) Let
some firmament! An' when I say

let it be some firmament, I don't want jest
a little bitty dab o' firmament caize I'm
sick an' tired of runnin' out of it when
we need it. Let it be a whole mess of
firmament! (*The stage has become misty
until* GOD *and the heavenly company are
obscured. As he finishes the speech there
is a burst of thunder. As the stage grows
darker.*) Dat's de way I like it. (*Murmurs
from the others;* "Dat's a lot of firmament." "My, dat is firmament!" "Look to
me like he's created rain," etc.)

FIRST MAMMY ANGEL. (*When the stage is
dark.*) Now, look Lawd, dat's too much
firmament. De cherubs is gettin' all wet.

SECOND MAMMY ANGEL. Look at my Car-
lotta, Lawd. She's soaked to de skin. Dat's
plenty too much firmament.

GOD. Well, 'co'se we don't want de chillun
to ketch cold. Can't you dreen it off?

GABRIEL. Dey's no place to dreen it,
Lawd.

FIRST MAMMY ANGEL. Why don't we jest
take de babies home, Lawd?

GOD. No, I don' wanta bust up de fish
fry. You angels keep quiet an I'll pass
another miracle. Dat's always de trouble
wid miracles. When you pass one you always gotta r'ar back an' pass another.
(*There is a hush.*) Let dere be a place to
dreen off dis firmament. Let dere be mountains and valleys an' let dere be oceans an'
lakes. An' let dere be rivers and bayous
to dreen it off in, too. As a matter of fac'
let dere be de earth. An' when dat's done
let dere be de sun, an' let it come out and
dry my Cherubs' wings. (*The lights go up
until the stage is bathed in sunlight. On
the embankment upstage there is now a
waist-high wrought iron railing such as
one sees on the galleries of houses in the
French quarter of New Orleans. The
CHERUBS are being examined by their parents and there is an ad lib. murmur of,
"You all right, honey?" "You feel better
now, Albert?" "Now you all dry, Vangy?"
until the ARCHANGEL, who has been gazing
in awe at the railing, drowns them out.*)

ARCHANGEL. Look yere! (*There is a rush
to the embankment accompanied by exclamations, "My goodness!" "What's dis?"*

"I declah!" etc. GABRIEL *towers above the group on the middle of the embankment* GOD *is wrapped in thought, facing the audience. The* CHOIR *resumes singing "So High You Can't Get Over It" softly. The babbling at the balustrade dies away as the people lean over the railing.* GABRIEL *turns and faces* GOD *indicating the earth below the railing with his left hand.)*

GABRIEL. Do you see it, Lawd?

GOD. *(Quietly, without turning his head upstage.)* Yes, Gabriel.

GABRIEL. Looks mighty nice, Lawd.

GOD. Yes. (GABRIEL *turns and looks over the railing.)*

GABRIEL. *(Gazing down.)* Yes, suh. Dat'd make mighty nice farming country. Jest look at dat South forty over dere. You ain't going to let dat go to waste is you, Lawd? Dat would be a pity an' a shame.

GOD. *(Not turning.)* It's a good earth. (GOD *turns, room is made for him beside* GABRIEL *on the embankment.)* Yes. I ought to have somebody to enjoy it. *(He turns, facing the audience. The others, save for the choir who are lined up in two rows of six on an angle upright, continue to look over the embankment.)* Gabriel! (GOD *steps down from the embankment two paces.)*

GABRIEL. *(Joining him.)* Yes, Lawd.

GOD. Gabriel, I'm goin' down dere.

GABRIEL. Yes, Lawd.

GOD. I want you to be my working b⟨oss⟩ yere while I'm gone.

GABRIEL. Yes, Lawd.

GOD. You know dat matter of dem t⟨wo⟩ stars?

GABRIEL. Yes, Lawd.

GOD. Git dat fixed up! You know ⟨dat⟩ sparrow dat fell a little while ago? 'Te⟨nd⟩ to dat, too.

GABRIEL. Yes, Lawd.

GOD. I guess dat's about all. I'll be b⟨ack⟩ Saddy. *(To the* CHOIR.*) Quiet, ang⟨els⟩ (The* CHOIR *stops singing. Those on ⟨the⟩ embankment circle down stage.* GOD *g⟨oes⟩ to embankment. Turns and faces the c⟨om⟩pany.)* I'm gonter pass one more mira⟨cle⟩ You all gonter help me an' not mak⟨e a⟩ soun' caize it's one of de most impo't⟨ant⟩ miracles of all. *(Nobody moves.* GOD *tu⟨rns⟩ facing the sky and raises his arms ab⟨ove⟩ his head.)* Let there be man. *(There ⟨is a⟩ growing roll of thunder as stage gr⟨ows⟩ dark. The* CHOIR *bursts into "Halleluj⟨ah"⟩ and continues until the lights go up on ⟨the⟩ next scene.)*

SCENE III

(Enclosing the stage is a heterogeneous cluster of cottonwood, camphor, live oak and sycamore trees, youpon and turkey berry bushes, with their purple and red berries, sprays of fern-like indigo fiera and splashes of various Louisiana flowers. In the middle of the stage, disclosed when the mistiness at rise grows into warm sunlight, stands ADAM. *He is a puzzled man of 30, of medium height, dressed in the clothing of the average field hand. He is bare-headed. In the distance can be heard the choir continuing. "Bright Mansions Above." A bird begins to sing.* ADAM *smiles and turns to look at the source of this novel sound. He senses his strength and raises his forearms, his fists clenched. With his left hand he carefully touches the muscles of his upper right arm. He smiles*

again, realizing his power. He looks at ⟨his⟩ feet which are stretched wide apart⟨. He⟩ stamps once or twice and now al⟨so⟩ laughs in his enjoyment. Other birds b⟨egin⟩ trilling and ADAM *glances up joyfully ⟨to⟩ ward the foliage.* GOD *enters.*

GOD. Good mo'nin', Son.

ADAM. *(With a little awe.)* Good mo'⟨n',⟩ Lawd.

GOD. What's yo name, Son?

ADAM. Adam.

GOD. Adam which?

ADAM. *(Frankly, after a moment's puz⟨zled⟩ groping.)* Jest Adam, Lawd.

GOD. Well, Adam, how dey treatin' ⟨you?⟩ How things goin?

M. Well, Lawd, you know it's kind
a new line of wukk.

. You'll soon get de hang of it. You
ow yo' kind of a new style with me.

M. Oh, I guess I'm gonter make out
right soon as I learn de ropes.

. Yes, I guess you will. Yo' a nice job.

M. Yes, Lawd.

. Dey's jest one little thing de matter
h you. Did you notice it?

M. Well, now you mentioned it, Lawd,
kind of thought dey was somethin'
ong.

. Yes suh, you ain't quite right. Adam,
need a family. De reason for dat is in
heart you is a family man. (*Flicking
ash off his cigar.*) *I'd say dat was de
n trouble at de moment.*

M. (*Smiling.*) *Yes sir.* (*His smile
es and he is puzzled again.*) *At de
e time—dey's one thing puzzlin' me,
vd. Could I ask you a question?*

. Why, certainly, Adam.

M. Lawd, jest what *is* a family?

. I'm gonter show you. (*Indicates a
.*) Jest lie down dere, Adam. Make out
you was goin' to slumber.

M. (*Gently.*) Yes, Lawd. (*He lies
n. GOD stands beside him and as he
es his arms above his head the lights
down. In the darkness GOD speaks.*)

Eve. (*Lights go up. EVE is standing
de ADAM. She is about twenty-six, and
e pretty. She is dressed like a country
Her gingham dress is quite new and
n. GOD is now at the other side of the
e, looking at them critically. EVE looks
DAM in timid wonder and slowly turns
head until she meets the glance of
ADAM stands beside EVE. They gaze
ch other for a moment. GOD smiles.*)
you all right, Eve. (ADAM *and* EVE
him.*) Now I'll tell you what I'm
er do. I'm gonter put you in charge
. I'm gonter give you de run of dis
e garden. Eve, you take care of dis
an' Adam you take care of dis woman.

You belong to each other. I don' want you
to try to do too much caize yo' both kind
of experiment wid me an' I ain't sho'
whether you could make it. You two jest
enjoy yo'self. Drink de water from de little
brooks an' de wine from de grapes an' de
berries, an' eat de food dat's hangin' for
you in de trees. (*He pauses, startled by a
painful thought.*) Dat is, in all but one
tree. (*He pauses. Then, not looking at
them.*) You know what I mean, my children?

ADAM AND EVE. Yes, Lawd. (*They slowly
turn their heads left, toward the branches
of an offstage tree. Then they look back
at GOD.*)

ADAM. Thank you, Lawd.

EVE. Thank you, Lawd.

GOD. I gotter be gittin' along now. I got
a hund'ed thousan' things to do fo' you
take yo' nex' breath. Enjoy yo'selves—
(GOD *exits.*) (ADAM *and* EVE *stand looking
after Him for a moment, then each looks
down and watches their hands meet and
clasp.*) (*After a moment they lift their heads
slowly until they are again gazing at the
tree.*)

EVE. Adam.

ADAM. (*Looking at the tree, almost in
terror.*) What?

EVE. (*Softly as she too continues to look
at the tree.*) Adam. (*The* CHOIR *begins
singing "Turn You Round" and as the
lights go down the* CHOIR *continues until
there is blackness. The* CHOIR *suddenly
stops. The following scene is played in the
darkness.*)

MR. DESHEE'S VOICE. Now, I s'pose you
chillun know what happened after God
made Adam 'n' Eve. Do you?

FIRST GIRL'S VOICE. I know, Mr. Deshee.

MR. DESHEE'S VOICE. Jest a minute, Ran-
dolph. Didn't I tell you you gotta tell yo'
mammy let yo' sister bring you. Carlisle,
take way dat truck he's eatin'. You sit by
him, see kin you keep him quiet. Now,
den, Myrtle what happened?

FIRST GIRL'S VOICE. Why, den dey ate de
fo'bidden fruit and den dey got driv' out
de garden.

MR. DESHEE'S VOICE. An' den what happened?

FIRST GIRL'S VOICE. Den dey felt ver bad.

MR. DESHEE'S VOICE. I don' mean how dey feel, I mean how dey do. Do dey have any children or anything like dat?

FIRST GIRL'S VOICE. Oh, yes, suh, dey have Cain 'n' Abel.

MR. DESHEE'S VOICE. Dat's right, dey have Cain an' Abel.

BOY'S VOICE. Dat was a long time after dey got married, wasn't it, Mr. Deshee? My mammy say it was a hund'ed years.

MR. DESHEE'S VOICE. Well, nobody kin so sure. As I tol' you befo' dey was beginnin' to be able to tell de time nobody was any too sure 'bout anyth even den. So de bes' thing to do is realize dat de thing happened an' de bother 'bout how many years it was. remember what I told you about it git dark when you go to sleep an' it b light when you wake up. Dat's de time went by in dem days. One thing do know an' dat was dis boy Cain w mean rascal. (*The lights go up on next scene.*)

SCENE IV

A roadside.

CAIN, *a husky young Negro, stands over the body of the dead* ABEL. *Both are dressed as laborers.* CAIN *is looking at the body in awe, a rock in his right hand.* GOD *enters.*

GOD. Cain, look what you done to Abel.

CAIN. Lawd, I was min'in' my own business and he come monkeyin' aroun' wit' me. I was wukkin' in de fiel' an' he was sittin' in de shade of de tree. He say "Me, I'd be skeered to git out in dis hot sun. I be 'fraid my brains git cooked. Co'se you ain't got no brains so you ain' in no danger." An' so I up and flang de rock. If it miss im all right, an' if it hit 'im, all right. Dat's de way I feel.

GOD. All right, but I'm yere to tell you dat's called a crime. When de new Judge is done talkin' to you you'll be draggin' a ball and chain de rest of yo' life.

CAIN. Well, what'd he want to come n keyin' aroun' me fo' den? I was plowin', min'in' my own business, not payin him no min', and yere he c makin' me de fool. I'd bust anybody v make me de fool.

GOD. Well,, I ain't sayin' you right a ain't sayin' you wrong. But I do say I you I'd jest git myself down de road I was clean out of de county. An' you ter take an' git married an' settle d an' raise some chillun. Dey ain't no to make a man fo'git his troubles raisin' a family. Now, you better git.

CAIN. Yessuh. (CAIN *walks off.*) watches him from the forestage and a lights begin to dim looks off. The c begins "Run, Sinner, Run."*)

GOD. Adam an' Eve you better try a You better have Seth an' a lot mo' ch (*There is darkness. The* CHOIR *cont until the lights go up on the next sc*

SCENE V

CAIN *is discovered walking on an unseen treadmill. A middle distance of trees, hillsides and shrubbery passes him on an upper treadmill. Behind is the blue sky. He stops under the branches of a tree to look at a sign on a fence railing. Only half the tree is visible on the stage. The sign reads,* "NOD PARISH. COUNTY LINE."

CAIN. (*Sitting down with a sigh of relief under the tree.*) At las'. Phew! (*Wipes his forehead with a handkerchief.*) Feels like

I been walkin' fo'ty years. (*He looks b Well, dey cain' git me now. Now raise a fam'ly. (*An idea occurs to him suddenly he begins looking right and Well, I'll be hit by a mule! Knocl down for a trustin' baby! Where I g git dat fam'ly? Dat preacher foolee (*He is quite dejected.*) Doggone!

CAIN'S GIRL. (*Off stage.*) Hello, C Boy! (CAIN *glances up to the o branches of the tree.*)

N. Hey-ho, Good lookin'! Which way it to town?

N's GIRL. (*Off stage.*) What you tryin' do? You tryin' to mash me? I be dog-e if it ain' gittin' so a gal cain't hardly e de house 'out some of dese fast men passin' remarks at her.

N. I ain' passin' remarks.

N's GIRL. (*Off stage.*) If I thought you tryin' to mash me, I'd call de police git you tooken to de first precinct.

N. Look yere, gal, I ast you a question, if you don' answer me I'm gonter d you 'cross my pants an' burn you up.

N's GIRL. (*Off stage.*) I'm comin' n. (CAIN *takes his eyes from the tree.*)

N. Yes, an' you better hurry. (CAIN's enters. *She is as large as* CAIN, *wick-pretty, and somewhat flashily dressed. smiles at* CAIN.)

's GIRL. I bet you kin handle a gal n wid dem big stout arms of your'n. o' would hate to git you mad at me, ntry Boy.

. (*Smiling.*) Come yere. (*She goes a closer to him.*) Don't be 'fraid, I ain' ean.

's GIRL. You got two bad lookin' eyes. yo' hot coffee 'mong de women folks.

. I ain' never find out. What was doin' in dat tree?

's GIRL. Jest coolin' myself in de ele-
.

Is you a Nod Parish gal?

's GIRL. Bo'n an' bred.

You know yo' kinda pretty.

s GIRL. Who tol' you dat?

Dese yere two bad eyes of mine.

s GIRL. I bet you say dat to every-all de way down de road.

Comin' down dat road I didn't talk body.

CAIN'S GIRL. Where you boun' for, Beautiful?

CAIN. I'm jest seein' de country. I thought I might settle down yere fo' a spell. You live wit' yo' people?

CAIN'S GIRL. Co'se I does.

CAIN. 'Spose dey'd like to take in a boarder?

CAIN'S GIRL. Be nice if dey would, wouldn' it?

CAIN. I think so. You got a beau?

CAIN'S GIRL. Huh-uh!

CAIN. (*Smiling.*) You has *now*.

CAIN'S GIRL. I guess—I guess if you wanted to kiss me an' I tried to stop you, you could pretty nearly crush me wit' dem stout arms.

CAIN. You wouldn't try too much, would you?

CAIN'S GIRL. Maybe for a little while.

CAIN. An' den what?

CAIN'S GIRL. Why don' we wait an' see?

CAIN. When would dat be?

CAIN'S GIRL. Tonight. After supper. Think you kin walk a little further now, City Boy?

CAIN. Yeh, I ain' so weary now. (*She takes his hand.*)

CAIN'S GIRL. What yo' name? (*Takes his arm.*)

CAIN. Cain.

CAIN'S GIRL. Then I'm Cain's Gal. Come on, honey, an' meet de folks. (*They exit.*) (*The* CHOIR *is heard singing "You Better Mind," as* GOD *enters.* GOD *watches the vanished* CAIN *and his girl.*)

GOD. (*After shaking his head.*) Bad business. I don' like de way things is goin' atall. (*The stage is darkened.*) (*The* CHOIR *continues singing until the lights go up on the next scene.*)

SCENE VI

GOD's *private office in Heaven. It is a small room, framed by tableau curtains. A large window up center looks out on the sky. There is a battered roll-top desk. On the wall next to the window is a framed religious oleograph with a calendar attached to it underneath. A door is at the left. A hat rack is on the wall above the door. There are two or three cheap pine chairs beside the window, and beyond the door. In front of the desk is an old swivel armchair which creaks every time GOD leans back in it. The desk is open and various papers are stuck in the pigeonholes. Writing implements, etc. are on the desk. On a shelf above the desk is a row of law books. A cuspidor is near the desk and a waste basket by it. The general atmosphere is that of the office of a Negro lawyer in a Louisiana town. As the lights go up GOD takes a fresh cigar from a box on the desk and begins puffing it without bothering to light it. There is no comment on this minor miracle from* GABRIEL *who is sitting in one of the chairs with a pencil and' several papers in his hand. The singing becomes pianissimo.*

GABRIEL. (*Looking at the papers.*) Well, I guess dat's about all de impo'tant business this mornin', Lawd.

GOD. How 'bout dat Cherub over to Archangel Montgomery's house?

GABRIEL. Where do dey live, Lawd? (*The singing stops.*)

GOD. Dat little two story gold house, over by de pearly gates.

GABRIEL. Oh, *dat* Montgomery. I thought you was referrin' to de ol' gentleman. Oh, yeh. (*He sorts through the papers and finds one he is looking for.*) Yere it 'tis. (*Reads.*) "Cherub Christina Montgomery; wings is moltin' out of season an' nobody knows what to do."

GOD. Well, now, take keer of dat. You gotter be more careful, Gabe.

GABRIEL. Yes, Lawd. (*Folds the papers and puts them in a pocket.* GOD *turns to his desk, takes another puff or two of the cigar, and with a pencil, begins checking off items on a sheet of paper before him.*

His back is turned toward GABRIEL. GABR... *takes his trumpet from the hat rack ... burnishes it with his robe. He then u... his lips and puts the mouthpiece to ... mouth.*)

GOD. (*Without turning around.*) N... watch yo'self, Gabriel.

GABRIEL. I wasn't goin' to blow, Law... jest do dat every now an' den so I ... keep de feel of it. (*He leans trum... against the wall.* GOD *picks up the pa... and swings his chair around tou... * GABRIEL.)

GOD. What's dis yere about de moon?

GABRIEL. (*Suddenly remembering.*) De moon people say it's beginnin' to ... a little, on 'count caize de sun's so hot...

GOD. It's goin' 'round 'cordin' to sched... aint it?

GABRIEL. Yes, Lawd.

GOD. Well, tell 'em to stop groanin'. D... nothin' de matter wid dat moon. Tro... is so many angels is flyin' over dere... Saddy night. Dey git to beatin' dere w... when dey dancin' an' dat makes de ... Tell them dat from now on dancin' '... de moon is sinnin'. Dey got to sto... Dat'll cool off de moon. (*He swings ... and puts the paper on the desk. He ... back in the chair comfortably, his h... clasped behind his head.*) Is dere any... else you ought to remin' me of?

GABRIEL. De prayers, Lawd.

GOD. (*Puzzled, slowly swinging cha... round again.*) De prayers?

GABRIEL. From mankind. You know, ... on de earth.

GOD. Oh, yeh, de poor little earth. ... my soul, I almos' forgot about dat. ... be three or four hund'ed years since I ... down dere. I wasn't any too pleased ... dat job.

GABRIEL. (*Laughing.*) You know you... make mistakes, Lawd.

GOD. (*Soberly, with introspective d...* ment.) So dey tell me. (*He looks at* GA... *then through the window again.*) S...

l me. I fin' I kin be displeased though,
' I was displeased wid de mankind I
' seen. Maybe I ought to go down dere
in—I need a little holiday.

BRIEL. Might do you good, Lawd.

D. I think I will. I'll go down an' walk
earth agin an' see how dem poor hu-
ans is makin' out. What time is it, by
sun an' de stars?

GABRIÈL. (*Glancing out of the window.*) Jest exactly half-past, Lawd. (GOD *is taking his hat and stick from the hat rack.*)

GOD. (*Opening the door.*) Well, take keer o' yo'self. I'll be back Saddy. (*He exits.*) (*The stage is darkened. The* CHOIR *begins* "Dere's No Hidin' Place," *and continues until the lights go up on the next scene.*)

SCENE VII

D *is walking along a country road. He
ps to listen. Church bells are heard in
e distance.*

D. Dat's nice. Nice an' quiet. Dat's de
y I like Sunday to be. (*The sound is
oken by a shrill voice of a girl. It is
BA singing a "blues.") Now, dat ain't
good. (GOD *resumes his walk and the
er treadmill brings on a tree stump on
ich* ZEBA *is sitting. She is accompanying
song with a ukulele.* GOD *and the tread-
lls stop. When the stump reaches the
ter of the stage, it is seen that* ZEBA *is
rouged and extremely flashily dressed
ppy of about eighteen.*) Stop dat!

A. What's de matter wid you, Country
y? Pull up yo' pants. (*She resumes
ging.*)

. Stop dat!

A. (*Stops again.*) Say, listen to me,
jo Eyes. What right you got to stop
ady enjoyin' herself?

. Don't you know dis is de Sabbath?
s no kin' o' song to sing on de Lawd's

A. Who care 'bout de Lawd's day any-
? People jest use Sunday now to git
r Saddy.

. You a awful sassy little girl.

A. I come fum sassy people! We even
k mean of de dead.

. What's yo' name?

A. (*Flirtatiously.*) "What's my name?"
't you de ol'-time gal hunter! Fust,
hat's my name?" den I s'pose, what
e like if you tried to kiss me? You
chers' is de debbils.

GOD. I ain't aimin' to touch you daughter. (*A sudden sternness frightens* ZEBA. *She looks at him sharply.*) What is yo' name?

ZEBA. Zeba.

GOD. Who's yo' fam'ly?

ZEBA. I'm de great-great gran' daughter of Seth.

GOD. Of Seth? But Seth was a good man.

ZEBA. Yeh, he too good, he die of holiness.

GOD. An' yere's his little gran' daughter reekin' wid cologne. Ain't nobody ever tol' you yo' on de road to Hell?

ZEBA. (*Smiling.*) Sho' dat's what de preacher say. Exceptin' of course, I happens to know dat I'm on de road to de picnic groun's, an' at de present time I'm waitin' to keep an engagement wid my sweet papa. He don' like people talkin' to me. (CAIN THE SIXTH *enters. He is a young buck, wearing a "box" coat and the other flashy garments of a Rampart Street swell.*)

CAIN THE SIXTH. Hello sugah! (*He crosses in front of* GOD *and faces* ZEBA.) Hello, mamma! Sorry I'm late baby, but de gals in de barrel-house jest wouldn't let me go. Doggone, one little wirehead swore she'd tear me down. (ZEBA *smiles and takes his hand.*)

GOD. What's yo' name, son?

CAIN THE SIXTH. (*Contemptuously; without turning.*) Soap 'n water, Country Boy.

GOD. (*Sternly.*) What's yo' name, son? (CAIN *slowly turns and for a moment his manner is civil.*)

CAIN THE SIXTH. Cain the Sixth.

GOD. I was afraid so.

CAIN THE SIXTH. (*His impudence returning.*) You a new preacher?

GOD. Where you live?

CAIN THE SIXTH. Me, I live mos' any piace.

GOD. Yes, an' you gonter see dem all. Is de udder young men all like you?

CAIN THE SIXTH. (*Smiling.*) De gals don' think so. (*He turns towards* ZEBA *again, picks her up and sits on the stump with the laughing* ZEBA *on his lap.*)

ZEBA. Dey ain't nobody in de worl' like my honey-cake. (CAIN *kisses her and she resumes her song.*) (GOD *watches them.* ZEBA *finishes a verse of the song and begins another softly.* CAIN THE SIXTH's *eyes have been closed during the singing.*)

CAIN THE SIXTH. (*His eyes closed.*) Is de preacher gone? (ZEBA *looks quickly at* GOD *without seeing him, and then looks off. She stops the song.*)

ZEBA. Yeh, I guess he walks fast. (CAIN *pushes her off his lap and rises.*)

CAIN THE SIXTH. (*With acid sweetness.*) Dey tell me las' night you was talkin' to a creeper man, baby.

ZEBA. Why, you know dey ain't nobody in de worl' fo' me but you.

CAIN THE SIXTH. (*Smiling.*) I know dey ain't. I even got dat guaranteed. (*Takes a revolver from his pocket.*) See dat, baby?

ZEBA. Sho' I see it, honey.

CAIN THE SIXTH. Dat jest makes me positive. (*Puts the gun back.*)

ZEBA. (*Pushing him back on the stump.*) You don' wanter believe dem stories, papa.

CAIN THE SIXTH. (*With sinister lightness.*) No, I didn't believe dem, baby. Co'se dat big gorilla, Flatfoot, from de other side of de river *is* in town ag'in.

ZEBA. Dat don' mean nothin'. Flatfoot ain't nothin' to me.

CAIN THE SIXTH. (*Sitting again.*) Co'se he ain't. Go 'head, sing some mo', baby. (ZEBA *resumes singing.*)

GOD. Bad business. (*The treadmills sta* turning. GOD *resumes his walk.* ZEBA, *st* singing, and CAIN THE SIXTH *recede wi* the landscape. GOD *is again alone on th* country road. There is a twitter of bird* GOD *looks up and smiles.*) De birds is goi 'bout dere business, all right. (*A patch* flowers goes by, black-eyed Susans, co* spicuously.*) How you flowers makin' ou* (CHILDREN's' *voices answer,* "We O. K LAWD.") Yes, an' you looks very prett (CHILDREN's *voices:* "Thank you, Lawd The flowers pass out of sight.) It's only* human bein's makes me downhearte Yere's as nice a Sunday as dey is turni out anywhere, an' nobody makin' de rig use of it. (*Something ahead of him attra* his attention.*) (*His face brightens.*) We now dis is mo' like it. Now dat's nice see people prayin'. It's a wonder dey do do it in de church. But I fin' I don' mi it if dey do it outdoors. (*A group of fi adult Negroes and a boy on their kne in a semicircle, appears. The treadmi stop. The* BOY, *his head bent, swings* hands rhythmically up to his head three four times. There is a hush.*)

GAMBLER. Oh, Lawd, de smoke-house empty. Oh, Lawd, lemme git dem groceri Oh, Lawd, lemme see dat little *six*. (*I casts the dice.*) Wham! Dere she is, frier (*Exclamations from t h e others:* "W damn my eyes!" "Doggone, dat's de eigh pass he make." "For God's sake, can't y ever crap?" etc. The BOY *is picking the money.*)

GOD. Gamblin' (*Looks over the grou shoulders.*) An' wid frozen dice!

BOY GAMBLER. Dey's a dolla' 'n' a h talkin' fo' me. How much you want of Riney?

FIRST GAMBLER. I take fo bits. Wait minute. Mebbe I take a little mo'. (*counts some money in his hand.*)

SECOND GAMBLER.. (*Glancing up at GO* Hello, Liver Lips. (*To the others.*) Loo ol' Liver Lips. (*The others look up a laugh good-naturedly, repeating* "Li Lips.")

FIRST GAMBLER. Ain't his pockets h from de groun? Ol' High-Pockets. (*T*

thers keep saying "Ole Liver Lips." "Ol'
iver Lips don't like to see people dicin'."
Dats a good name, 'High Pockets'.")

OY GAMBLER. (To others.) Come on, you
onter fade me or not? (GOD seizes the
oy's ears and drags him to his feet. The
thers do not move, but watch, amused.)

OD. Come yere, son. Why, yo' jest a
tle boy. Gamblin' an' sinnin'. (GOD looks
the boy's face.) You been chewin' to-
cco, too, like you was yo' daddy. (GOD
iffs.) An' you been drinkin' sonny-kick-
ammy-wine. You oughta be 'shamed.
To the others.) An' you gamblers oughta
'shamed, leadin' dis boy to sin.

RST GAMBLER. He de bes' crap shooter in
wn, mister.

D. I'm gonter tell his mammy. I bet
e don' know 'bout dis.

ST GAMBLER. No, she don' know. (The
hers laugh.) She don' know anythin'.

COND GAMBLER. Das de God's truth.

ST GAMBLER. See kin you beat 'im, High
ckets. Dey's a dolla' open yere.

O. I ain't gonter beat 'im. I'm gonter
ch 'im. I may have to teach you all.
e starts walking from them. The BOY
cks out his tongue the moment GOD's
ck is turned.)

GAMBLER. If you fin' my mammy you
mo'n I kin. Come on, gamblers, see kin
gimme a little action. Who wants any
t of dat dollar? (The treadmill carries
m off. The FIRST GAMBLER is heard say-
: "I'll take anoder two bits," and the
ers, "Gimme a dime's wo'th," "I ain't
ly got fifteen cents left," etc. as they
appear.)

. (Walking.) Where's dat little boy's
me? (The front of a shanty appears and
stops in front of the door.) Yere's de
ce. It ain't any too clean, either. (Knocks
the door with his cane.)

CE IN SHANTY. Who dar?

. Never you min' who's yere. Open
door.

CE IN SHANTY. You gotta search war-
t?

GOD. I don' need one.

VOICE IN SHANTY. Who you wanter see?

GOD. I wanter see da mammy of de little gamblin' boy.

VOICE IN SHANTY. You mean little Johnny Rucker?

GOD. Dat may be his name.

VOICE IN SHANTY. Well, Mrs. Rucker ain't home.

GOD. Where's she at?

VOICE IN SHANTY. Who, Mrs. Rucker?

GOD. You heerd me.

VOICE IN SHANTY. Oh, she run away las' night wid a railroad man. She's eloped.

GOD. Where's Rucker?

VOICE IN SHANTY. He's flat under de table. He so drunk he cain't move.

GOD. Who are you?

VOICE IN SHANTY. I'se jest a fren' an' neighbor. I come in las' night to de party, an' everybody in yere's dead drunk but me. De only reason I kin talk is I drank some new white mule I made myself, an' it burn my throat so I cain't drink no mo'. You got any mo' questions?

GOD. Not for you. (The shanty begins to move off as GOD starts walking again.)

VOICE IN SHANTY. Good riddance, I say. (Shanty disappears.)

GOD. Dis ain't gittin' me nowheres. All I gotta say dis yere mankind I been peoplin' my earth wid sho' ain't much. (He stops and looks back.) I got good min' to wipe 'em all off an' people de earth wid angels. No. Angels is all right, singin, an' playin' an' flyin' around, but dey ain't much on workin' de crops and buildin' de levees. No, suh, mankind's jest right for my earth, if he wasn't so doggone sinful. I'd rather have my earth peopled wit' a bunch of channel catfish, dan I would mankin' an' his sin. I jest cain't stan' sin. (He is about to resume his walk when NOAH enters. NOAH is dressed like a country preacher. His coat is of the "hammer-tail" variety. He carries a prayer book under his arm.)

NOAH. Mo'nin', brother.

GOD. Mo'nin', brother. I declare you look like a good man.

NOAH. I try to be, brother. I'm de preacher yere. I don't think I seen you to de meetin'. (*They resume walking.*)

GOD. I jest come to town a little while ago an' I been pretty busy.

NOAH. Yeh, mos' everybody say dey's pretty busy dese days. Dey so busy dey cain't come to meetin'. It seem like de mo' I preaches de mo' people ain't got time to come to church. I ain't hardly got enough members to fill up de choir. I gotta do de preachin' an' de bassin' too.

GOD. Is dat a fac'?

NOAH. Yes, suh, brother. Everybody is mighty busy, gamblin', good-timin', an' goin' on. You jest wait, though. When Gabriel blow de horn you gonter fin' dey got plenty of time to punch chunks down in Hell. Yes, suh.

GOD. Seems a pity. Dey all perfec'ly healthy?

NOAH. Oh, dey healthy, all right. Dey jest all lazy, and mean, and full of sin. You look like a preacher, too, brother.

GOD. Well, I am, in a way.

NOAH. You jest passin' through de neigh borhood?

GOD. Yes, I wanted to see how thing was goin' in yo' part of de country, an I been feelin' jest 'bout de way you do It's enough to discourage you.

NOAH. Yes, but I gotta keep wres'lin' wi 'em. Where you boun' for right now brother?

GOD. I was jest walkin' along. I though I might stroll on to de nex' town.

NOAH. Well, dat's a pretty good distance I live right yere. (*He stops walking.*) Wh don' you stop an' give us de pleasure o yo' comp'ny for dinner? I believe my o woman has kilt a chicken.

GOD. Why, dat's mighty nice of yo brother. I don' believe I caught yo' name

NOAH. Noah, jest brother Noah. Dis my home, brother. Come right in. (GO and NOAH *start walking towards* NOAH house *which is just coming into view o the treadmill.*) (*The stage darkens, th* CHOIR *sings "Feastin' Table," and whe the lights go up again, the next scene disclosed.*)

SCENE VIII

Interior of NOAH'*s house. The ensemble suggests the combination living-dining room in a fairly prosperous Negro's cabin. Clean white curtains hang at the window. A table and chairs are in the center of the room. There is a cheerful checked table-cloth on the table, and on the wall, a framed, highly colored picture reading "God Bless Our Home."* (NOAH'S WIFE, *an elderly Negress, simply and neatly dressed,* GOD *and* NOAH *are discovered grouped about the table.*)

NOAH. Company, darlin'. (NOAH'S *wife takes* NOAH'S *and* GOD'S *hats.*) Dis gem-man's a preacher, too. He's jest passin' through de country.

GOD. Good mo'nin', sister.

NOAH'S WIFE. Good mo'nin'. You jest ketch me when I'm gittin' dinner ready. You gonter stay with us?

GOD. If I ain't intrudin'. Brother No suggested—

NOAH'S WIFE. You set right down ye I got a chicken in de pot an' it'll be rea in 'bout five minutes. I'll go out de ba an' call Shem, Ham 'n' Japheth. (*To* GO Dey's our sons. Dey live right acrost de w but always have Sunday dinner wid You mens make yo'selves comf'table.

GOD. Thank you, thank you very kind

NOAH. You run along, we all right. (G and NOAH *seat themselves.* NOAH'S W exits.)

GOD. You got a fine wife, Brother No

NOAH. She pretty good woman.

GOD. Yes, suh, an' you got a nice li home. Have a ten cent seegar? (GOD *of him one.*)

NOAH. Thank you, much obliged. (*Both en lean back restfully in their chairs.*)

GOD. Jest what seems to be de main rouble 'mong mankind, Noah?

NOAH. Well, it seems to me de main rouble is dat de whol' distric' is wide pen. Now you know dat makes fo' loose vin'. Men folks spen's all dere time ghtin', loafin' an' gamblin', an' makin' id likker.

GOD. What about de women?

NOAH. De women is worse dan de men. dey ain't makin' love powder dey out g, borrow an' stealin' money for policy kets. Doggone, I come in de church unday 'fo' las' 'bout an' hour befo' de eetin' was to start, and dere was a woman alin' de altar cloth. She was goin' to ck it. Dey ain't got no moral sense. ow you take dat case las' month, over East Putney. Case of dat young Willy back.

GOD. What about him?

NOAH. Dere is a boy sebenteen years old. ggone, if he didn't elope with his aunt. ow, you know, dat kin of goin' on is d fo' a neighborhood.

GOD. Terrible, terrible.

NOAH. Yes, suh. Dis use' to be a nice, cent community. I been doin' my best preach de Word, but seems like every ue I preach de place jest goes a little ' to de dogs. De good Lawd only knows at's gonter happen.

GOD. Dat is de truth. (*There is a pause. ch puffs his cigar.*) (*Suddenly* NOAH sps his knee, as if it were paining him, d twists his foot.*)

NOAH. Huh!

GOD. What's de matter?

NOAH. I jest got a twitch. My buck-auger uess. Every now and den I gets a twitch de knee. Might be a sign of rain.

GOD. That's just what it is. Noah, what's mos' rain you ever had 'round dese ts?

NOAH. Well, de water come down fo' six rs steady last April an' de ribber got so

swole it bust down de levee up 'bove Freeport. Raise cain all de way down to de delta.

GOD. What would you say was it to rain for forty days and forty nights?

NOAH. I'd say dat was a *complete* rain!

GOD. Noah, you don't know who I is, do you?

NOAH. (*Puzzled.*) Yo' face looks easy, but I don' think I recall de name. (GOD *rises slowly, and as he reaches his full height there is a crash of lightning, a moment's darkness, and a roll of thunder. It grows light again.* NOAH *is on his knees in front of* GOD.) I should have known you. I should have seen de glory.

GOD. Dat's all right, Noah. You didn't know who I was.

NOAH. I'm jes' ol' preacher Noah, Lawd, an' I'm yo' servant. I ain' very much, but I'se all I got.

GOD. Sit down, Noah. Don' let me hear you shamin' yo'se'f, caize yo' a good man. (*Timidly* NOAH *waits until* GOD *is seated, and then sits, himself.*) I jest wanted to fin' out if you was good, Noah. Dat's why I'm walkin' de earth in de shape of a natchel man. I wish dey was mo' people like you. But, far as I kin see you and yo' fam'ly is de only respectable people in de worl'.

NOAH. Dey jest all poor sinners, Lawd.

GOD. I know. I am your Lawd. I am a god of wrath and vengeance n' dat's why I'm gonter destroy dis worl'.

NOAH. (*Almost in a whisper. Drawing back.*) Jest as you say, Lawd.

GOD. I ain't gonter destroy you, Noah. You and yo' fam'ly, yo' sheep an' cattle, an' all de udder things dat ain't human I'm gonter preserve. But de rest is gotta go. (*Takes a pencil and a sheet of paper from his pocket.*) Look yere, Noah. (NOAH *comes over and looks over his shoulder.*) I want you to build me a boat. I want you to call it de "Ark," and I want it to look like dis. (*He is drawing on the paper. Continues to write as he speaks.*) I want you to take two of every kind of animal and bird dat's in de country. I want you to take seeds an' sprouts an' everythin' like dat an' put dem on dat Ark, because dere is gonter be all dat rain. Dey's gonter to be a deluge, Noah, an' dey's goin' to be a flood. De levees is gonter bust an' everythin' dat's fastened down is comin' loose, but it ain't gonter float long, caize I'm gonter make a storm dat'll sink everythin' from a hencoop to a barn. Dey ain't a ship on de sea dat'll be able to fight dat tempest. Dey all got to go. Everythin'. Everythin' in dis pretty worl' I made, ex cept one thing, Noah. You an' yo' fam'ly an' de things I said are going to ride dat storm in de Ark. Yere's de way it's to be. (*He hands* NOAH *the paper.* NOAH *takes it and reads.*)

NOAH. (*Pause. Looks at paper again.*) Yes, suh, dis seems to be complete. Now 'bout the animals, Lawd, you say you want everythin'?

GOD. Two of everythin'.

NOAH. Dat would include jayraffes an' hippopotamusses?

GOD. Everythin' dat is.

NOAH. Dey was a circus in town las' week. I guess I kin fin' dem. Co'se I kin git all de rabbits an' possums an' wil' turkeys easy. I'll sen' de boys out. Hum, I'm jest wonderin'—

GOD. 'Bout what?

NOAH. 'Bout snakes? Think you'd like snakes, too?

GOD. Certainly, I want snakes.

NOAH. Oh, I kin git snakes, lots of 'em Co'se, some of 'em's a little dangerous Maybe I better take a kag of likker, too

GOD. You kin have a kag of likker.

NOAH. (*Musingly.*) Yes, suh, dey's a aw ful lot of differ'nt kin's of snakes, com to think about it. Dey's water moccasin cotton-moufs, rattlers—mus' be a hund'e kin's of other snakes down in de swamp Maybe I better take two kags of likke

GOD. (*Mildly.*) I think de one kag enough.

NOAH. No. I better take two kags. B sides I kin put one on each side of boat, an' balance de ship wid dem as we as havin' dem fo' medicinal use.

GOD. You kin put one kag in de midd of de ship.

NOAH. (*Buoyantly.*) Jest as easy to ta de two kags, Lawd.

GOD. I think one kag's enough.

NOAH. Yes, Lawd, but you see forty da an' forty nights—(*There is a distant r of thunder.*)

GOD. (*Firmly.*) One kag, Noah.

NOAH. Yes, Lawd. One kag. (*The door the back opens and* NOAH'S WIFE ent with a tray of dishes and food.*)

NOAH'S WIFE. Now, den, gen'lemen, you'll jest draw up cheers. (*The stage darkened. The* CHOIR *is heard singing Want to Be Ready." They continue in darkness until the lights go up on the n scene.*)

SCENE IX

In the middle of the stage is the Ark. On the hillside, below the Ark, a dozen or more men and women, townspeople, are watching NOAH, SHEM, HAM *and* JAPHETH *on the deck of the Ark. The three sons are busily nailing boards on the cabin.* NOAH *is smoking a pipe. He wears a silk hat, captain's uniform and a "slicker."*

NOAH. (*To* SHEM.) You, Shem, tote up some ol' rough lumber, don' bring up any

planed up lumber, caize dat ain't fo' main deck.

SHEM. Pretty near supper time, daddy

NOAH. Maybe 'tis, but I got de feelin' ought to keep goin'.

FIRST WOMAN. You gonter work all ni Noah, maybe, huh?

NOAH. (*Without looking at her.*) If sperrit move me.

SECOND WOMAN. Look yere, Noah, whyn't you give up all dis damn foolishness? Don' you know people sayin' yo' crazy? What you think you doin' anyway?

NOAH. I'se buildin' a Ark. (*Other men and women join those in the foreground.*) Ham, you better stop for a while 'n see whether dey bringin' de animals up all right. (*He looks at his watch.*) Dey ought be pretty near de foot o' de hill by dis time; if dey ain't you wait fo' dem and bring 'em yo'se'f. (HAM *goes down a ladder at the side of the ship and exits during the following scene. The newcomers in group have been speaking to some of the early arrivals.*)

SECOND WOMAN. (*To* THIRD WOMAN, *one of the newcomers.*) No, you don't mean

THIRD WOMAN. I do so. Dat's what de talk is in de town.

FIRST MAN. You hear dat, Noah? Dey say yo' ol' lady is tellin' everybody it's gonter rain fo' fo'ty days and fo'ty nights. You know people soon gonter git de idea you *all* crazy.

NOAH. Lot I keer what you think. (*To* JAPHETH.) Straighten up dem boards down here, Japheth. (*Indicates floor of deck.*)

FIRST MAN. (*To* THIRD WOMAN) Was I you, I wouldn' go 'roun with Mrs. Noah anymore, lady. Fust thing you know you'll be gittin' a hard name, too.

THIRD WOMAN. Don' I know?

SECOND WOMAN. A lady cain't be too par-ticlar dese days. (ZEBA *and* FLATFOOT, *a tall, black, wicked-looking buck, enter, their arms around each other's waist.*)

ZEBA. Dere it is baby. Was I lyin'?

FLATFOOT. Well, I'll be split in two!

FIRST MAN. What you think of it Flatfoot?

FLATFOOT. I must say! Look like a house o' a warpin' cellar.

NOAH. Dis yere vessel is a boat.

FLATFOOT. When I was a little boy dey used to build boats down near de ribber, where de water was. (*The others laugh.*)

NOAH. Dis time it's been arranged to have de water come up to de boat. (JAPHETH *looks belligerently over the rail of the Ark at* FLATFOOT. *To* JAPHETH.) Keep yo' shirt on, son.

SECOND WOMAN. (*To* THIRD WOMAN.) Now, you see de whole fam'ly's crazy.

THIRD WOMAN. Listen, dey ain't gonter 'taminate me. It was me dat started resolvin' dem both out o' de buryin' society.

ZEBA. When all dis water due up yere, Noah?

NOAH. You won't know when it gits yere, daughter.

ZEBA. Is she goin' to be a side-wheeler, like de Bessy-Belle?

FLATFOOT. No! If she was a side-wheeler she'd get her wheels all clogged wid sharks. She gonter have jus' one great big stern wheel, like de Commodore. Den if dey ain't 'nuf water why de big wheel kin stir some up. (*General laughter. Two or three of the* GAMBLERS *enter and join the group, followed by* CAIN THE SIXTH.)

CAIN THE SIXTH. Dere's de fool an' his monument, jest like I said! (*The* GAMBLERS *and* CAIN THE SIXTH *roar with laughter, slap their legs, etc., the members of the main group talk sotto voce to each other as* CAIN THE SIXTH *catches* ZEBA'S *eye.* FLATFOOT *is on her right and is not aware of* CAIN *the* SIXTH'S *presence.*)

NOAH. See how dey makin' out inside, son. (*Stops hammering.*) (JAPHETH *exits into Ark.*) (NOAH *turns and gazes towards the east.*)

CAIN THE SIXTH. Hello, honey.

ZEBA. (*Frightened but smiling.*) Hello, sugah.

CAIN THE SIXTH. (*Pleasantly.*) Ain' dat my ol' frien' Flatfoot wid you?

ZEBA. Why, so 'tis! (FLATFOOT *is now listening.*) (*To* FLATFOOT.) He's got a gun.

CAIN THE SIXTH. No, I ain't. (*He lifts his hands over his head.* ZEBA *quickly advances and runs her hands lightly over his pockets.*)

ZEBA. (*Relieved.*) I guess he ain't.

CAIN THE SIXTH. No, I ain't got no gun for my ol' friend, Flatfoot. (*He walks up to him.*)

FLATFOOT. (*Smiling.*) Hi, Cain. How's de boy? (CAIN *quickly presses his chest against* FLATFOOT's, *his downstage arm sweeps around* FLATFOOT's *body and his hand goes up to the small of* FLATFOOT's *back.*)

CAIN THE SIXTH. (*Quietly, but triumphantly.*) I got a little knife fo' him. (FLATFOOT *falls dead.*) (*The laughter of the others stops and they look at the scene.* ZEBA *for a moment is terrified, her clenched hand pressed to her mouth. She looks at* CAIN THE SIXTH, *who is smiling at her. He tosses the knife on the ground and holds his hands out to her. She goes to him, smiling.*)

ZEBA. You sho' take keer of me, honey.

CAIN THE SIXTH. Dat's caize I think yo' wo'th takin' keer of. (*To the others.*) It's all right, folks. I jest had to do a little cleanin' up.

FIRST WOMAN. (*Smiling.*) You is de quickes' scoundrel.

FIRST GAMBLER. It was a nice quick killin'. Who was he?

SECOND WOMAN. (*Casually.*) Dey called him Flatfoot. From over de river. He wa'nt any good. He owed me for washin' for over a year.

THIRD WOMAN. Used to peddle muggles. Said it had a kick like reg'lar snow. Wasn't no good.

SECOND GAMBLER. Think we ought to bury him?

FIRST MAN. No, just leave him dere. Nobody comes up yere, 'cept ol' Manatee. (*Indicates* NOAH. *Cries of "Ol' Manatee! Ol' Manatee, dat's good!"*)

NOAH. (*Still looking off.*) You bettah pray, you po' chillun. (*They all laugh.*)

FIRST WOMAN. We bettah pray? You bettah pray, Ol' Manatee?

ZEBA. You bettah pray for rain. (*Laughter again.*)

NOAH. Dat's what I ain't doin', sinner Shem! Japheth! (*To others, as he poin off. Patter of rain.*) Listen!

CAIN THE SIXTH. (*Casually.*) Doggone, believe it *is* gonter shower a little.

FIRST GAMBLER. It do looks like rain.

FIRST WOMAN. I think I'll git on home. got a new dress on.

ZEBA. Me, too. I wants to keep looki nice fo' my sweet papa. (*She pats* CAIN T SIXTH's *cheek.* CAIN THE SIXTH *hugs her*)

NOAH. (*Almost frantically.*) Ham! Is animals dere?

HAM. (*Off stage.*) Yes, sir, dere ye We're comin'.

NOAH. Den bring 'em on. (SHEM a JAPHETH *come on deck with their ha mers. The stage begins to darken.*)

THIRD WOMAN. I guess we all might home 'till de shower's over. Come on, pa

SECOND GAMBLER. See you after supp Noah. (*Crowd starts moving off* R.)

NOAH. God's gittin' ready to start, sons. Let's git dis plankin' done.

ZEBA. Put a bix Texas on it, Noah, a we'll use fo' excursions. (*There is a a tant roll of thunder, there are cries "Good night, Admiral." "See you late "So long, Manatee," as the crowd goes The thunder rumbles again. There is sound of increasing rain. The hammers* SHEM *and* JAPHETH *sound louder and joined by the sounds of other hammere There is a flash of lightning. The* CH *begins "Dey Ol' Ark's a-Movering," sounds on the Ark become faster a louder. The rush of rain grows heavie*

NOAH. Hurry! Hurry! Where are y Ham?

HAM. (*Just off stage.*) Yere, I am, fath wid de animals.

NOAH. God's give us his sign. Send up de gangplank. (*An inclined plane thrown against the Ark from the side the stage by* HAM, *who cracks a whip.*

ı. Get on dere. (*The heads of two
ohants are seen.*)

ıH. Bring 'em on board! De Lawd is
kin' down de worl'! (*The singing and

...en the lights go up on scene, the Ark
...t sea. Stationary waves run in front of
...The hillside has disappeared. The Ark
...n the only lighted area.
...M is smoking a pipe on the deck, lean
...on the rail. A steamboat whistle blows
...e short and one long blast.* SHEM *is
...prised. In a moment* HAM *appears, also
...h a pipe, and joins* SHEM *at the rail.*

ıM. Who'd you think you was signal-
?

ı. Dat wasn't me, dat was daddy.

ıM. He think he gonter git a reply?

ı. I don' know. He's been gittin' a
...of comfort out of dat likker.

ıM. De kag's nearly empty, ain't it?

ı. Pretty nearly almos'. (*They look
... the rail. A pause.*) Seen anythin'?

ıM. Dis mornin' I seen somethin' over
...migh'a' been a fish.

ı. Dat's de big news of de week.

ıM. How long you think dis trip's gon-
...las'?

ı. I don' know! Rain fo'ty days 'n'
...nights an' when dat stop' I thought
...we'd come up ag'inst a san' bar o'
...ethin'. Looks now like all dat rain was
...a little incident of de trip. (*The
...stle blows again.*) Doggone! I wish
...wouldn't do dat. Fust thing we know
...wake up dem animals ag'in. (JAPHETH
...ars.)

ıM. What de matter wit' de ol' man,
?

...ETH. Doggone, he say he had a
...m dat we're nearly dere. Dat's why
...ullin de whistle cord. See kin he git
...iswer. (*He looks over the rail.*) Look
...ne like de same ol' territory. (MRS.
...appears on deck.)

the noises reach fortissimo as HAM *cracks
his whip again, and the rain falls on the
stage.*) (*The stage is darkened. The* CHOIR
continues singing in the darkness.)

SCENE X

NOAH'S WIFE. You boys go stop yo' paw
pullin' dat cord. He so full of likker he
think he's in a race.

JAPHETH. He claim he know what he's
doin'.

NOAH'S WIFE. I claim he gittin' to be a
perfec' nuisance. Me an' yo' wives cain't
hardly heah ou'sel'es think. (NOAH *appears,
his hat rakishly tilted on his head. He goes
to the railing and looks out.*) You 'spectin'
company?

NOAH. Leave me be, woman. De watah
don' look so rough today. De ol' boat's
ridin' easier.

NOAH'S WIFE. Ridin' like a ol' mule!

NOAH. Yes suh, de air don' feel so wet.
Shem! 'Spose you sen' out 'nother dove.
(SHEM *goes into the Ark.*) Ham, go git
de soundin' line. Jape, keep yo' eye on de
East. (JAPHETH *goes to the end of the
boat.*)

NOAH'S WIFE. As fo' you, I s'pose you'll
help things along by takin' a little drink.

NOAH. Look yere, who's de pilot of dis
vessel?

NOAH'S WIFE. Ol' Mister Dumb Luck.

NOAH. Well, see dat's where you don'
know anythin'.

NOAH'S WIFE. I s'pose you ain't drunk as
a fool?

NOAH. (*Cordially.*) I feel congenial.

NOAH'S WIFE. An' you look it. You look
jest wonderful. I wonder if you'd feel so
congenial if de Lawd was to show up?

NOAH. De Lawd knows what I'm doin',
don' you worry 'bout dat.

NOAH'S WIFE. I wouldn't say anythin'
ag'inst de Lawd. He suttinly let us know
dey'd be a change in de weather. But I

bet even de Lawd wonders sometimes why he ever put you in charge.

NOAH. Well, you let de Lawd worry 'bout dat. (SHEM *appears with the dove.*)

SHEM. Will I leave her go, Paw?

NOAH. Leave 'er go. (*There is a chorus of "Good Luck, Dove," from the group as the dove flies off stage.* HAM *appears with the sounding line.*) Throw 'er over, Boy. (HAM *proceeds to do so.*)

NOAH'S WIFE. An' another thing—

HAM. Hey!

NOAH. (*Rushing to his side.*) What is it?

HAM. Only 'bout a inch! Look! (*They lean over.*)

JAPHETH. It's gettin' light in de East. (*As* HAM *works the cord up and down,* NOAH *and* NOAH'S WIFE *turn toward* JAPHETH. *The* CHOIR *begins "My Soul Is a Witness for the Lord."*)

NOAH. Praise de Lawd, so it is.

NOAH'S WIFE. Oh, dat's pretty.

NOAH. (*To* HAM.) An' de boat's stopped. We've landed. Shem, go down n' drag de fires an' dreen de boiler. Yo go help 'im, Ham.

JAPHETH. Look, Paw. (*The dove wings back to the Ark with an olive branch in its mouth.*)

NOAH. 'N' yere's de little dove wid greenery in its mouth! Take 'er down, Jape, so she kin tel de animals. (JAPHETH *exits after* SHEM *and* HAM *carrying the dove. To* MRS. NOAH.) Now, maybe you feel little different.

NOAH'S WIFE. (*Contritely.*) It was jes' gittin' to be so tiresome. I'm sorry, Noah.

NOAH. Dat's all right, ol' woman. (NOAH'S WIFE *exits.* NOAH *looks about him. The lights have changed and the water piece is gone and the ark is again on the hillside. Two mountains can be seen in the distance and a rainbow slowly appears over the Ark. The singing has grown louder.*) Thank you, Lawd. thank you very much

indeed. Amen. (*The singing stops with t* "Amen." GOD *appears on the deck.*)

GOD. Yo' welcome, Noah. (NOAH *tur and sees him.*)

NOAH. O, Lawd, it's wonderful.

GOD. (*Looking about him.*) I sort of li it. I like de way you handled de ship, t Noah.

NOAH. Was you watchin', Lawd?

GOD. Every minute. (*He smiles.*) Did de ol' lady light into you?

NOAH. (*Apologetically.*) She was kin restless.

GOD. That's all right. I ain't blamin' body. I don' even min' you' cussin' drinkin'. I figure a steamboat cap'n on long trip like you had has a right to little redeye, jest so he don' go crazy.

NOAH. Thank you, Lawd. What's de ders now?

GOD. All de animals safe?

NOAH. Dey all fin'n' dandy, Lawd.

GOD. Den I want you to open dat st board door, an' leave 'em all out. Let ' go down de hill. Den you an' de fam take all de seeds 'n de sprouts an' be plantin' ag'in. I'm startin' all over, No (NOAH *exits.* GOD *looks around.*)

GOD. Well, now we'll see what happe (GOD *listens with a smile, as noises acc panying the debarking of the animals heard. There are the cracks of whips, voices of the men on the Ark, shouti "Git along dere." "Whoa, take it ea "Duck yo' head." "Keep in line dere," Over the Ark there is a burst of centrifu shadows, and the sound of a myriad wings.* GOD *smiles at the shadows.*) D right, birds, fin' yo' new homes. (E twitters are heard again.* GOD *listens a ment and rests an arm on the railing. speaks softly.*) Gabriel, kin you spar minute?" (GABRIEL *appears.*)

GABRIEL. Yes, Lawd? (*The sounds f the other side of the Ark are by now most hushed. The* LORD *indicates the world with a wave of the hand.*)

. Well, it's did.

RIEL. (*Respectfully, but with no en-*
siasm.) So I take notice.

. Yes, suh, startin' all over again.

RIEL. So I see.

. (*Looking at him suddenly.*) Don'
m to set you up much.

RIEL. Well, Lawd, you see— (*He hes-*
es.) 'Tain't none of my business.

. What?

RIEL. I say, I don' know very much
ut it.

. I know you don'. I jest wanted you

to see it. (*A thought strikes him.*) Co'se,
it ain' yo' business, Gabe. It's my business.
'Twas my idea. De whole thing was my
idea. An' every bit of it's my business 'n nobody else's. De whole thing rests on my
shoulders. I declare, I guess *dat's* why I
feel so solemn an' serious, at dis particklar
time. You know *dis* thing's turned into
quite a proposition.

GABRIEL. (*Tenderly.*) But, it's all right,
Lawd, as you say, it's did.

GOD. Yes, suh, it's did. (*Sighs deeply.*
Looks slowly to the right and the left.
Then softly.) I only hope it's goin' to
work out all right.

CURTAIN

PART TWO

SCENE I

's *Office again.*
newhere the CHOIR *is singing: "A City*
led Heaven." In the office 'are TWO
MEN CLEANERS. *One is scrubbing the*
r, the other dusting the furniture. The
dusting stops and looks out the win-
. There is a whirr and a distant faint
m. The CHOIR *stops.*

T CLEANER. Dat was a long way off.

OND CLEANER. (*At window.*) Yes,
am. An' dat must a' been a big one.
gone, de Lawd mus' be mad fo' sho',
mo'nin'. Dat's de fo'ty-six' thunde'-bolt
e breakfast.

T CLEANER. I wonder where at He's
hin' dem.

OND CLEANER. My goodness, don' you
w?

T CLEANER. (*A little hurt.*) Did I
w I wouldn't ask de question.

OND CLEANER. Every one of dem's
nd fo' de earth.

T CLEANER. De earth? You mean dat
e ol' dreenin' place?

OND CLEANER. Dat's de planet. (*An-*
r faint whirr and boom.) Dere goes
ther.

FIRST CLEANER. Well, bless me. I didn't
know dey was thunde'bolts.

SECOND CLEANER. Wha'd you think dey
was?

FIRST CLEANER. (*Above desk.*) I wasn't
sho', but I thought maybe He might be
whittlin' a new star o' two, an' de noise
was jest de chips fallin'.

SECOND CLEANER. Carrie, where you been?
Don' you know de earth is de new scandal?
Ever'body's talkin' 'bout it.

FIRST CLEANER. Dey kep' it from me.

SECOND CLEANER. Ain't you noticed de
Lawd's been unhappy lately?

FIRST CLEANER. (*Thoughtfully.*) Yeah, He
ain't been his old self.

SECOND CLEANER. What did you think was
de matteh? Lumbago?

FIRST CLEANER. (*Petulantly.*) I didn't
know I didn't think it was fo' me
t'inquieh..

SECOND CLEANER. Well, it jest so happens
dat de Lawd is riled as kin be by dat
measly little earth. Or I should say de scum
dat's on it.

FIRST CLEANER. Dat's mankind down dere.

SECOND CLEANER. Dey mus' be scum, too, to git de Lawd so wukked up.

FIRST CLEANER. I s'pose so. (*Another whirr and boom.*) Looks like He's lettin' dem feel de wrath. Ain' dat a shame to plague de Lawd dat way?

SECOND CLEANER. From what I hear dey been beggin' fo' what dey're gittin'. My brother flew down to bring up a saint de other day and he say from what he see mos' of de population down dere has made de debbil king an' dey wukkin' in three shifts fo' him.

FIRST CLEANER. You cain't blame de Lawd.

SECOND CLEANER. Co'se you cain't. Dem human bein's 'd make anybody bile oveh. Ev'rytime de Lawd try to do sompin' fo' dem, doggone if dey don't staht some new ruckus.

FIRST CLEANER. I take notice He's been wukkin' in yere mo' dan usual.

SECOND CLEANER. I wish He'd let us ladies fix it up. Wouldn't take a minute to make dis desk gold-plated.

FIRST CLEANER. I s'pose He likes it dis way. De Lawd's kind o' ol' fashioned in some ways. I s'pose He keeps dis office plain an' simple on purpose.

SECOND CLEANER. (*Finishing her work.*) I don' see why.

FIRST CLEANER. (*Looking off.*) Well, it's kind of a nice place to come to when He's studyin' somethin' impo'tant. 'Most evah-thin' else in heaven's so fin' 'n' gran', may-be ev'ry now an den He jest gits sick an' tired of de glory. (*She is also collecting her utensils.*)

SECOND CLEANER. Maybe so. Jest de same I'd like to have a free hand wid dis place for a while, so's I could gold it up. (GOD *appears in the doorway.*)

GOD. Good mo'nin', daughters.

FIRST AND SECOND CLEANERS. Good mo'-nin', Lawd. We was jest finishin'.

GOD. Go ahead den, daughters. (*Goes to the window.*)

FIRST AND SECOND CLEANERS. Yes, Law (*They exeunt. Off stage.*) Good mo'ni Gabriel (*Off stage* GABRIEL *says*, "Go mo'nin', sisters," *and enters immediate He stands in the doorway for a mom watching* GOD—*a notebook and pencil his hand.*)

GOD. What's de total?

GABRIEL. (*Consulting the book.*) Eight thousand nine hund'ed an' sixty for mo'nin'. Dat's includin' de village wid fo'tune tellers. Dey certainly kin breed f

GOD. (*Solemnly.*) Dey displease me. I displease me greatly.

GABRIEL. Want some more bolts, Law

GOD. (*Looking through window.*) Look 'em dere. Squirmin' an' fightin' an' be in' false witness. Listen to dat liar, dere. don' intend to marry dat little gal. don' even love her. What did you say

GABRIEL. Should I git mo' bolts?

GOD. Wait a minute. (*He carefully po his finger down through the window.*) goin' to git dat wicked man myself. (*Fr a great distance comes an agonized "Oh, Lawd!"* GOD *turns from the windo* No use gittin' mo' thunde'bolts. Dey d do de trick. (*He goes to the swivel c and sits.*) It's' got to be somethin' else

GABRIEL. How would it be if you was doom 'em all ag'in, like dat time you s down de flood? I bet dat would make d mind.

GOD. You see how much good de fl did. Dere dey is, jest as bad as ever.

GABRIEL. How about cleanin' up de w mess of 'em and sta'tin' all over ag'in some new kind of animal?

GOD An' admit I'm licked?

GABRIEL. (*Ashamedly.*) No, of co'se Lawd.

GOD. No, suh No, suh. Man is a kin pet of mine and it ain't right fo' me to up tryin' to do somethin' wid him. L gone, mankin' *mus'* be all right at de or else why did I ever bother wid him de first place? (*Sits at desk.*)

RIEL. It's jest dat I hates to see you
rryin' about it, Lawd.

. Gabe, dere ain't anythin' worth
ile anywheres dat didn't 'cause some-
ly some worryin'. I ain't never tol' you
trouble I had gittin' things started up
e. Dat's a story in itself. No, suh, de
re I keep on bein' de Lawd de more I
ow I got to keep improvin' things. An'
takes time and worry. De main trouble
l mankin' is he takes up so much of
time. He ought to be able to help
elf a little. (*He stops suddenly and
itates.*) Hey, dere! I think I got it!

RIEL. (*Eagerly.*) What's de news?

. (*Still cogitating.*) Yes, suh, dat seems
: an awful good idea.

RIEL. Tell me, Lawd.

. Gabriel, have you noticed dat every
v an' den, mankin' turns out some
:ty good specimens?

RIEL. Dat's de truth.

. Yes, suh. Dey's ol' Abraham and
c an' Jacob an' all dat family.

RIEL. Dat's so, Lawd.

. An' everyone of dem boys was a
l wukker an' a good citizen. We got
.dmit dat.

RIEL. Dey wouldn't be up yere flyin'
us if dey hadn't been.

. No, suh. An' I don' know but what
answer to de whole trouble is right
:.

RIEL. How you mean, Lawd?

. Why, doggone it, de good man is
man dat keeps busy. I mean I been
a' along on de principle dat he was
ething like you angels—dat you ought
oe able to give him somethin' an' den
let him sit back an' enjoy it. Dat ain't
Now dat I recollec' I put de first one
'n dere to take keer o' dat garden an'
I let him go ahead an' do nothin' but
into michief. (*He rises.*) Sure, *dat's* it.
ain't' *built* jest to fool 'roun' an' not do
hin'. Gabe, I'm gonter try a new
eme.

GABRIEL. (*Eagerly.*) What's de scheme,
Lawd?

GOD. I'll tell you later. Send in Abraham,
Isaac an' Jacob. (*A voice outside calls:
Right away, Lawd."*) You go tell dem to
put dem bolts back in de boxes. I ain'
gonter use dem a'gin a while.

GABRIEL. O. K., Lawd.

GOD. Was you goin' anywhere near de
Big Pit?

GABRIEL. I could go.

GOD. Lean over de brink and tell Satan
he's jest a plain fool if he thinks he kin
beat anybody as big as me.

GABRIEL. Yes, suh, Lawd. Den I'll spit
right in his eye. (GABRIEL *exits.*) (GOD *looks
down through the window again to the
earth below.*)

GOD. Dat new polish on de sun makes
it powerful hot. (*He "r'ar back."*) Let it
be jest a little bit cooler. (*He feels the
air.*) Dat's nice. (*Goes to His desk. A
knock on the door.*) Come in. (ABRAHAM
ISAAC *and* JACOB *enter. All are very old
men, but the beard of* ABRAHAM *is the longest and whitest, and they suggest their
three generations. They have wings that
are not quite so big as those of the native
angels.*)

ISAAC. Sorry we so long comin', Lawd.
But Pappy and me had to take de boy
(*Pointing to* JACOB) over to git him a can
of wing ointment.

GOD. What was de matter, son?

JACOB. Dey was chafin' me a little. Dey
fine now, thank you, Lawd.

GOD. Dat's good. Sit down an' make yo'-
selves comf'table. (*The three sit.* MEN:
"*Thank you, Lawd.*") Men, I'm goin' to
talk about a little scheme I got. It's one
dat's goin' to affec' yo' fam'lies an' dat's why
I 'cided I'd talk it over wid you, fo' it
goes into ee-fect. I don' know whether you
boys know it or not, but you is about de
three best men of one fam'ly dat's' come
up yere since I made little apples. Now I
tell you what I'm gonter do. Seein' 'dat
you human bein's cain't 'preciate anythin'

lessen you fust wukk to git it and den keep strugglin' to hold it, why I'm gonter turn over a very valuable piece of property to yo' fam'ly, and den see what kin dey do with it. De rest of de worl' kin go jump in de river fo' all I keer. I'm gonter be lookin' out fo' yo' descendants only. Now den, seein' dat you boys know de country pretty tho'ly' where at does you think is de choice piece of property in de whole worl'? Think it over for a minute. I'm gonter let you make de s'lection.

ABRAHAM. If you was to ask me, Lawd, I don't think dey come any better dan de Land of Canaan.

GOD. (To ISAAC and JACOB.) What's yo' feelin' in de matter?

JACOB. (After a nod from ISAAC.) Pappy an' me think do we get a pick, dat would be it.

GOD. (Goes to window again; looks out.) De Land of Canaan. Yes, I guess dat's a likely neighborhood. It's all run over wid Philistines and things right now, but we kin clean dat up. (He turns from the window and resumes his seat.) All right. Now who do you boys think is de best of yo' men to put in charge down dere? You see I ain't been payin' much attention to anybody in partic'lar lately.

ISAAC. Does you want de brainiest or de holiest, Lawd? (MEN look up.)

GOD. I want de holiest. I'll make him brainy. (MEN appreciate the miracle.)

ISAAC. (As ABRAHAM and ISAAC nod to him.) Well, if you want A Number One, goodness, Lawd, I don't know where you'll git more satisfaction dan in a great- great-great-great grandson of mine.

GOD. Where's he at?

ISAAC. At de moment I b'lieve he's in sheep business over in Midian County. got in a little trouble down in Egypt, t'wan't his doin'. He killed a man was abusin' one of our boys in de bri works. Of co'se you know old King Ph aoh's got all our people in bondage.

GOD. I heard of it. (With some ire.) W did you think put them dere? (The visit lower their heads.) It's all right, bo (All rise.) I'm gonter take dem out of An' I'm gonter turn over de whole La of Canaan to dem. An' do you know wh gonter lead dem dere? Yo' great, gre great, great grandson. Moses, ain't it?

ISAAC. Yes, Lawd.

GOD. (Smiling.) Yes. I been noticin' h

ABRAHAM. It's quite a favor fo' de fa 'ly, Lawd.

GOD. Dat's why I tol' you. You see, it happens I love yo' fam'ly, an' I delight honor it. Dat's all, gen'lemen. (The th others rise and cross to the door, m muring, "Yes, Lawd," "Thank y Lawd," "Much obliged, Lawd." etc. T CHOIR begins, "My Lord's A-Writin' De Time" pianissimo. GOD stands watch the men leave.) Enjoy yo'selves. (He g to the window. The singing grows sof He speaks through the window to earth.) I'm comin' down to see you Mo an' dis time my scheme's got to wukk

(The stage is darkened. The singing gr louder and continues until the lights go on the next scene.)

SCENE II

The tableau curtains frame the opening of a cave, which is dimly lighted. A large turkey-berry bush is somewhere near the foreground. MOSES is seated on the grass eating his lunch from a basket in his lap. ZIPPORAH, his wife, stands watching him. He is about forty, ZIPPORAH somewhat younger. They are dressed inconspicuously. MOSES stutters slightly when he speaks. He looks up to see ZIPPORAH smiling.

MOSES. What you smilin' at, Zippora

ZIPPORAH. Caize you enjoyin' yo'self.

MOSES. You is a good wife, Zipporah.

ZIPPORAH. You is a good husband, Mo (MOSES wipes his mouth with a hand chief and begins putting into the ba the various implements of the meal wh had been on the ground about him.) W

u suppose it's so dark yere today? Dey's
rain in de air.

)SES. Seems like it's jest aroun' dis cave.
' father's house is got de sun on it. (*He
ks in another direction.*) Looks all clear
wn toward Egypt.

PPORAH. Co'se it *would* be fine weather
Egypt. De sky looks all right. Maybe
s gonter rain jest right yere. Why don't
u move de sheep over to de other pas-
re?

)SES. (*A bit puzzled.*) I don' know. It
t dark like dis befo' you come along
d de dinner an' I was gonter stop you
de top of de hill. Den somethin' kep'
yere.

PPORAH. S'pose it could be de Lawd
rnin' you dat dey's 'Gyptians hangin'
un'?

)SES. Dey may have fo'gotten all about
t killin' by now. Dey got a new Pharoah
wn dere.

PPORAH. An' I hear he's' jest as mean
yo' people as his pappy was. I wouldn't
t it pas' him to send soljahs all the way
yere fo' you.

)SES. Dat's all right. De Lawd's looked
er me so far, I don't 'spect him to fall
wn on me now. You better be gittin'
me.

PPORAH. (*Taking the basket.*) I'll be
rryin' about you.

)SES. (*Kissing her and then smiling.*)
rently de Lawd ain't. He knows I'm
e as kin be. Lemme see you feel dat way.

PPORAH. You is a good man, Moses.

)SES. I's a lucky man. (ZIPPORAH *exits
th the basket.* MOSES *looks up at the
y.*) Dat's funny. De sun seems to be
nin' everyplace but right yere. It's shinin'
de sheep. Why ain't dey no cloud dere?

). (*Off stage.*) Caize I want it to be
e dat, Moses.

)SES. (*Looking about him.*) Who's dat?

). (*Off stage again.*) I'm de Lawd,
)ses.

MOSES. (*Smiling.*) Dat's what you say.
Dis yere shadow may be de Lawd's wukk,
but dat voice soun' pretty much to me like
my ol' brother Aaron.

GOD. (*Off stage.*) Den keep yo' eyes open,
son. (*The turkey-berry bush begins to glow
and then turns completely red.* MOSES *looks
at it fascinated.*) Maybe you notice de bush
ain't burnin' up.

MOSES. Dat's de truth. (MOSES *is full of
awe but not frightened.*)

GOD. (*Off stage.*) Now you believe me?

MOSES. Co'se I does. It's wonderful. (*The
light in the bush dies and* GOD *appears
from behind it.*)

GOD. No, it ain't, Moses. It was jest a
trick.

MOSES. 'Scuse me doubtin' you, Lawd. I
always had de feelin' you wuz takin' keer
of me, but I never 'spected you'd fin' de
time to talk wid me pussunly. (*He
laughs.*) Dat was a good trick, Lawd. I'se
seen some good ones, but dat was de beat-
enest.

GOD. Yo' gonter see lots bigger tricks dan
dat, Moses. In fac', yo' gonter perfo'm dem.

MOSES. (*Incredulously.*) Me? I'm gonter
be a tricker?

GOD. Yes, suh.

MOSES. An' do magic? Lawd, my mouth
ain't got de quick talk to go wid it.

GOD. It'll come to you now.

MOSES. (*Now cured of stuttering.*) Is I
goin' wid a circus?

GOD. (*Slowly and solemnly.*) Yo' is goin'
down into Egypt, Moses, and lead my
people out of bondage. To do dat I'm gonter make you de bes' tricker in de worl'.

MOSES. (*A little frightened.*) Egypt! You
know I killed a man dere, Lawd. Won't
dey kill me?

GOD. Not when dey see yo' tricks. You
ain't skeered, is you?

MOSES. (*Simply and bravely.*) No, suh,
Lawd.

GOD. Den yere's what I"m gonter do. Yo' people is my chillun, Moses. I"m sick and tired o' de way ol' King Pharoah 'is treatin' dem, so I'se gonter take dem away, and yo' gonter lead dem. You gonter lead 'em out of Egypt an' 'across de river Jordan. It's gonter take a long time, and you ain't goin' on no excursion train. Yo' gonter wukk awful hard for somethin' yo' goin' to fin' when de trip's over.

MOSES. What's dat, Lawd?

GOD. It's de Land of Canaan. It's de bes' land I got. I've promised it to yo' people, an' I'm gonter give it to dem.

MOSES. Co'se, ol' King Pharaoh will do everything he kin to stop it.

GOD. Yes, an' dat's where de tricks come in. Dey tell me he's awful fond of tricks.

MOSES. I hear dat's all he's fon' of. Dey say if you can't take a rabbit out of a hat you cain't git in to see him.

GOD. Wait'll you see de tricks you an' me's goin to show him.

MOSES. (Delightedly.) Doggone! Huh, Lawd?

GOD. Yes, suh. Now de first trick—(GOD is lifting a stick which he carries.)

MOSES. Jest a minute, Lawd. (GOD halts the demonstration.) I'm gonter learn de tricks and do just like you tell me, but I know it's gonter take me a little time to learn all dat quick talkin'. Cain't I h[ave] my brother Aaron go wid me? He's [a] good man.

GOD. I was gonter have him help you w[ith] de Exodus. I guess he can watch, too.

MOSES. I'll call 'im. (He turns as if shout.)

GOD. Wait. (MOSES turns and looks GOD.) I'll bring him. (Softly.) Aar[on] (AARON appears between GOD and MOSES the mouth of the cave. He is a little tal than MOSES and slightly older. He, too, dressed like a field hand.)

AARON. (Blankly.) Hey! (MOSES goes him, takes his hand and leads him, wildered, down to where MOSES had be standing alone. AARON then sees GOD.)

MOSES. (Almost in a whisper.) It's right.

GOD. Don't worry, son, I'm jest show some tricks. Bringin' you yere was one dem. (AARON stares at GOD as if hyp tized.) Now den, you see dis yere r Looks like a ordinary walking stick, d it?

MOSES. Yes, Lawd.

GOD. Well, it ain't no ordinary walk stick, caize look. (MOSES leans forwar when I lays it down on de groun'—(T stage is darkened. The CHOIR begins, " Down, Moses," and continues until lights go up on the next scene.)

SCENE III

The throne room of PHARAOH. It suggests a Negro lodge room. The plain board walls are colored by several large parade banners of varying sizes, colors and materials, bordered with gold fringe and tassels on them. Some of the inscriptions on them read:

SUBLIME ORDER OF THE HOUSE OF PHARAOH
HOME CHAPTER

MYSTIC BROTHERS OF THE EGYPTIAN HOME
GUARD

LADIES AUXILIARY, NO. I

SUPREME MAGICIANS AND WIZARDS OF THE
UNIVERSE

PRIVATE FLAG OF HIS HONOR OLD K[ING]
PHARAOH

ROYAL YOUNG PEOPLE'S PLEASURE CL[UB]

ENCHANTED AND INVISIBLE CADETS OF EG
BOYS' BRIGADE

There is one door up right and a wind The throne, an ordinary armchair wit drapery over its back, is on a dais. PHAR is seated on the throne. His crown garments might be those worn by a h officer in a Negro lodge during a rit About the throne itself are high offic several of them with plumed hats, cloth that suggests military uniforms, and ra

*borate sword belts, swords and scab-
*rds. A few soldiers carrying spears are
*o in his neighborhood and one or two
*rded ancients in brightly colored robes
*th the word "Wizard" on their conical
*ts. In the general group of men and
*men scattered elsewhere in the room
*nday finery is noticeable everywhere.
*st of the civilians have bright "parade"
*bons and wear medals. In a cleared
*ace immediately before the throne a
*NDIDATE MAGICIAN is performing a
*ight-of-hand trick with cards. PHARAOH
*tches him apathetically. He is receiving
*nest attention from a few of the others,
*t the majority of the men and women
*talking quietly among themselves. Be-
*e the CANDIDATE MAGICIAN are several
*raphernalia of previously demonstrated
cks.

*NDIDATE MAGICIAN. (Holding up some
ds.) Now den, ol' King Pharaoh, watch
. *(He completes a trick. There is a
*rmur of "Not Bad." "Pretty Good,"
. from a few of the watchers. PHARAOH
kes no comment.) Now, I believe de
*rd I ast you to keep sittin' on was de
*y of diamonds, wasn't it?

ARAOH. Yeah.

NDIDATE MAGICIAN. Den kin I trouble
*1 to take a look at it now? (PHARAOH
*f rises to pick up a card he has been
ing on, and looks at it.) I believe you'll
*w notice dat it's de King of Clubs?

*IARAOH nods and shows the card to
*se nearest him. The CANDIDATE MAGI-
*N waits for an audible approval and gets
ctically none.) An' dat, ol' King Phar-
*a, completes de puffohmance. (An eld-
y man in a uniform steps forward.)

NERAL. On behalf of my nephew I beg
*' Honor to let him jine de ranks of de
*al trickers and magicians.

ARAOH. (To the two WIZARDS.) What
*de committee think? (The WIZARDS
ke their heads.) Dat's what I thought.
*ain't good enough. I'd like to help you
*, General, but you know a man's got
*be a awful good tricker to git in de
*al society dese days. You better go back
*steddy some mo', son. (He lifts his

*voice and directs two soldiers guarding the
door.)* Is de head magician reached de
royal waitin' room yit? *(One of the soldiers opens the door to look out.)* If he is,
send him in. *(The soldier beckons to some
one off stage, throws the door open, and
announces to the court.)*

SOLDIER. De Head Magician of de land
of Egypt. *(A very old and villainous man
enters. His costume is covered with cabalistic and zodiacal signs. He advances to
the KING, the other magician and his uncle
making way for him. He bows curtly to
PHARAOH.)*

HEAD MAGICIAN. Good mo'nin', ol' King
Pharaoh.

PHARAOH. Mo'nin', Professor. What's de
news?

HEAD MAGICIAN. Evahthing's carried out
like you said.

PHARAOH. How's de killin' of de babies
'mongst de Hebrews comin' 'long?

HEAD MAGICIAN. Jes' like you ordered.

PHARAOH. *(Genially.)* Dey killed all of
'em, huh?

HEAD MAGICIAN. Do dey see one, dey kill
'im. You teachin' 'em a great lesson. Dey
don' like it a-tall.

PHARAOH. *(Smilingly.)* What do dey say?

HEAD MAGICIAN. *(Pawing the air inartic-
ulately.)* I hates to tell in front of de ladies.

PHARAOH. Dey feels pretty bad, huh?

HEAD MAGICIAN. Dat's jest de beginnin' of
it. Betwixt de poleece and de soljahs we
killed about a thousan' of 'em las' night.
Dat's purty good.

PHARAOH. *(Thoughtfully.)* Yeh, it's fair.
I guess you boys is doin' all you kin. But
I fin' I ain't satisfied, though.

HEAD MAGICIAN. How you mean, Yo'
Honor?

PHARAOH. I mean I'd like to make dose
Hebrew chillun realize dat I kin be even
mo' of a pest. I mean I hates dem chillun.
An' I'm gonter think of a way of makin'
'em even mo' mizzable.

HEAD MAGICIAN. But dey *ain't* anythin' meaner dan killin' de babies, King.

PHARAOH. Dey must be sump'n. Doggone, you is my head tricker, you put yo' brains on it. (*To the others.*) Quiet, whilst de Head Magician go into de silence.

HEAD MAGICIAN. (*After turning completely around twice, and a moment's cogitation.*) I tell you what I kin do. All de Hebrews dat ain't out to de buryin' grounds or in de hospitals is laborin' in de brick wukks.

PHARAOH. Yeh?

HEAD MAGICIAN. (*After a cackling laugh.*) How would it be to take de straw away from 'em and tell 'em dey's got to turn out jest as many bricks as usual? Ain't dat nasty?

PHARAOH. Purty triflin', but I s'pose it'll have to do for de time bein'. Where's de extreme inner guard? (*One of the military attendants comes forward.*) Go on out an' tell de sup'intendent to put dat into eeffect. (*The attendant bows and starts for the door. He stops as* PHARAOH *calls to him.*) Wait a minute! Tell 'im to chop off de hands of anybody dat say he cain't make de bricks dat way. (*The attendant salutes and exits, the door being opened and closed by one of the soldiers.*) Now what's de news in de magic line?

HEAD MAGICIAN. I ain't got very many novelties today, King, I bin wukkin' too hard on de killin's. I'm so tired I don' believe I could lift a wand. (*There are murmurs of protest from the assemblage.*)

PHARAOH. Doggone, you was to 'a been de chief feature o' de meetin' dis mawnin'. Look at de turn-out you got account of me tellin' 'em you was comin'.

HEAD MAGICIAN. Well, dat's de way it is, King. Why don' you git de wizards to do some spell castin'?

PHARAOH. Dey say it's in de cyards dat dey cain't wukk till high noon. (*He glances at the* WIZARDS.) Think mebbe you kin cheat a little?

FIRST WIZARD. Oh dat cain't be done, King.

PHARAOH. Well, we might as well a journ, den. Looks to me like de wh program's shot to pieces. (*He starts to r when there is a furious banging on door.*) What's de idea, dere? See who is. (*The soldiers open the door.* MOSES a AARON *enter, pushing the two soldiers as and coming down in front of* PHARA *The soldiers are bewildered and* PHARA *is angry.*) Say, who tol' you two babo you could come in yere?

MOSES. Is you ol' King Pharaoh?

PHARAOH. Dat's me. Did you heah w I asked you?

MOSES. My name is Moses, and dis is brother Aaron. (*Murmur of "Hebre spreads through the room.*)

PHARAOH. (*In a rage.*) Is you Hebrew

MOSES. Yes, suh.

PHARAOH. (*Almost screaming.*) Put to de sword! (*As the courtiers approa* AARON *suddenly discloses the rod, which swings once over his head. The court draw back as if their hands had b stung. Cries of "Hey!" "Lookout," e*

MOSES. Keep outside dat circle. (*The c tiers nearest* MOSES *and* AARON *look at e other, exclaiming ad lib., "Did you dat?" "What is dat?" "What's goin' heah?" "My hands is stingin'!" etc.*)

PHARAOH. (*Puzzled but threatenin* What's de idea yere?

MOSES. We is magicians, ol' King P aoh.

PHARAOH. (*To the* HEAD MAGICIAN.) a spell on 'em. (*The* HEAD MAGICIAN *sta looking at them bewildered. To* MOSE got some magicians, too. We'll see w got de bes' magic. (*MOSES and* AA *laugh. Most of the courtiers are cower To the* HEAD MAGICIAN.) Go ahead, 'em gri-gri.

MOSES. Sure, go ahead.

PHARAOH. Hurry up, dey's laughin' you. What's de matter?

HEAD MAGICIAN. I cain't think of de r spell.

PHARAOH. (*Now frightened himself.*) You mean dey got even *you* whupped?

HEAD MAGICIAN. Dey's got a new kind of magic.

PHARAOH. (*Gazes at* HEAD MAGICIAN *a moment, bewildered. To the* WIZARDS.) I 'pose if de Professor cain't, you cain't.

FIRST WIZARD. Dat's a new trick, King.

HEAD MAGICIAN. (*Rubbing his fingers 'long his palms.*) It's got 'lectricity in it!

PHARAOH. H'm, well dat may make it a little diff'rent. So you boys is magicians, is?

MOSES. Yes, suh.

PHARAOH. Well, we's always glad to see some new trickers in de co't, dat is if dey good. (*He glances about him.*) You look like you is O. K.

MOSES. Dat's what we claims, ol' King Pharaoh. We think we's de best in de worl'.

PHARAOH. You certainly kin talk big. Jest what is it you boys would like?

MOSES. We came to show you some tricks. Den we's goin' to ask you to do somethin' for us.

PHARAOH. Well, I s'pose you know I'm fool for conjurin'. If a man kin show me some tricks I ain't seen, I goes out of my way to do him a favor.

MOSES. Dat's good. Want to see de first trick?

PHARAOH. It ain't goin' 'to hurt nobody?

MOSES. Dis one won't.

PHARAOH. Go ahead.

MOSES. Dis yere rod my brother has looks like a walkin' stick, don't it? (*The courtiers now join the King in interest.*)

PHARAOH. Uh huh. Le's see. (AARON *hands rod, which* PHARAOH *inspects and returns.*)

MOSES. Well, look what happens when he puts it on de groun'. (AARON *places the rod on the second step of the throne. It turns into a lifelike snake. There are exclamations from the assemblage.*)

PHARAOH. Dat's a good trick! Now turn it back into a walkin' stick again. (AARON *picks is up and it is again a rod. Exclamations of* "Purty good!" "Dat's all right!" "What do you think of that!" *etc.*) Say, you is good trickers!

MOSES. You ain't never seen de beat of us. Now I'm goin' to ask de favor.

PHARAOH. Sure, what is it?

MOSES. (*Solemnly.*) Let de Hebrew chillun go!

PHARAOH. (*Rises and stares at them. There is a murmur of* "Listen to 'im!" "He's got nerve!" "I never in my life!" "My goodness!" *etc.*) What did you say?

MOSES. Let de Hebrew chillun go. (PHARAOH *seats himself again.*)

PHARAOH. (*Slowly.*) Don' you know de Hebrews is my slaves?

MOSES. Yes, suh.

PHARAOH. Yes, suh, my slaves. (*There is a distant groaning.*) Listen, and you kin hear 'em bein' treated like slaves. (*He calls toward the window.*) What was dey doin' den?

MAN NEAR THE WINDOW. Dey's jest gettin' de news down in de brick-yard.

PHARAOH. I won't let them go. (*He snorts contemptuously.*) Let's see another trick.

MOSES. Yes, suh, yere's a better one.(*He lowers his head.*) Let's have a plague of de flies. (AARON *raises the rod. The room grows dark and a great buzzing of flies is heard. The courtiers break out in cries of* "Get away fum me!" "Take 'em away!" "De place is filled with flies!" "Dis is terrible!" "Do sump'n, PHARAOH!")

PHARAOH. (*Topping the others.*) All right —stop de trick!

MOSES. Will you let de Hebrews go?

PHARAOH. Sho' I will. Go ahead stop it!

MOSES. (*Also above the others.*) Begone! (*The buzzing stops and the room is filled* with light again, as AARON *lowers the rod. All except* MOSES *and* AARON *are brushing the flies from their persons.*)

PHARAOH. (*Laughing.*) Doggone, dat was a good trick! (*The others, seeing they are uninjured, join in the laughter, with exclamations of* "Doggone!" "You all right?" "Sho' I'm all right." "Didn' hurt me," *etc.*) You is good trickers.

MOSES. Will you let de Hebrew chillun go?

PHARAOH. (*Sitting down again.*) Well, I'll tell you, boys. I'll tell you sump'n you didn' know. You take me, *I'm* a pretty good tricker, an' I jest outtricked you. So, bein' de bes' tricker, I don' think I will let 'em go. You got any mo' tricks yo'self?

MOSES. Yes, suh. Dis is a little harder one. (AARON *lifts the rod.*) Gnats in de mill pon', gnats in de clover, gnats in de tater patch, stingin' all over. (*The stage grows dark again. There is the humming of gnats and the slapping of hands against faces and arms, and the same protests as were heard with the flies, but with more feeling,* "I'm gittin' stung to death!" "I'm all stung!" "Dey're like hornets!" "Dey's on my face!" *etc.*)

PHARAOH. Take 'em away, Moses!

MOSES. (*His voice drowning the others.*) If I do, will you let 'em go?

PHARAOH. Sho' I will, dis time.

MOSES. Do you mean it?

PHARAOH. Co'se I mean it! Doggone, one just stang me on de nose.

MOSES. Begone! (*Lights come up as* AARON *lowers the rod. There is a moment of general recovery again.* PHARAOH *rubs his nose, looks at his hands, etc., as do the others.*) Now, how about it?

PHARAOH. (*Smiling.*) Well, I'll tell you, Moses. Now dat de trick's over—(MOSES *takes a step toward* PHARAOH.)

MOSES. Listen, Pharaoh. You been lyin' to me, and I'm gittin' tired of it.

PHARAOH. I ain't lyin', I'm trickin', too. You been trickin' me and I been tricki[n'] you.

MOSES. I see. Well, I got one mo' tri[ck] up my sleeve which I didn't aim to wu[k] unless I had to. Caize when I does it, [I] cain't undo it.

PHARAOH. Wukk it an' I'll trick you ri[ght] back. I don' say you ain't a good trick[er,] Moses. You is one of de best I ever se[en.] But I kin outtrick you. Dat's all.

MOSES. It ain't only me dat's goin' [to] wukk dis trick. It's me an' de Lawd.

PHARAOH. Who?

MOSES. De Lawd God of Israel.

PHARAOH. I kin outtrick you an' de La[wd] too!

MOSES. (*Angrily.*) Now you done it, [King] King Pharaoh. You been mean to [de] Lawd's people, and de Lawd's been e[asy] on you caize you didn't know no bet[ter.] You been givin' me a lot of say-so-a[nd] no do-so, and I didn' min' dat. But n[ow] you've got to braggin' dat you's better [dan] de Lawd, and dat's too many.

PHARAOH. You talk like a preacher, a[n' I] never did like to hear preachers talk.

MOSES. You ain't goin' to like it any [bet]ter, when I strikes down de oldes' bo[y in] every one of yo' people's houses.

PHARAOH. Now you've given up tric[kin'] and is jest lyin'. (*He rises.*) Listen, [King] Pharaoh. I do de strikin' down yere[. I] strike down my enemies, and dere's [no] one in all Egypt kin kill who he w[ant] to, 'ceptin' me.

MOSES. I'm sorry, Pharaoh. Will you [let] de Hebrews go?

PHARAOH. You heard my word. (AARO[N is] *lifting his rod again at a signal f[rom]* MOSES.) Now, no more tricks or I'll—

MOSES. Oh, Lawd, you'll have to do [de] guess. Aaron, lift de rod. (*There [is a] thunderclap, darkness and screams. [As] lights go up. Several of the younger [men] on the stage have fallen to the groun[d and] are being held in the arms of the horr[ified] elders.*)

ARAOH. What have you done yere? here's my boy? (*Through the door come ur men bearing a young man's body.*)

ST OF THE FOUR MEN. King Pharaoh. HARAOH *drops into his chair, stunned, the dead boy is brought to the throne.*)

ARAOH. (*Grief-stricken.*) Oh, my son, fine son. (*The courtiers look at him h mute appeal.*)

MOSES. I'm sorry, Pharaoh, but you cain't fight de Lawd. Will you let his people go?

PHARAOH. Let them go. (*The lights go out. The* CHOIR *begins, "Mary Don't You Weep," and continues until it is broken by the strains of "I'm Noways Weary and I'm Noways Tired." The latter is sung by many more voices than the former, and the cacophony ends as the latter grows in volume and the lights go up on the next scene.*)

SCENE IV

e CHILDREN of ISRAEL *are marching on treadmill and now singing fortissimo. ey are of all ages and most of them ragged. The men have packs on their ulders, one or two have hand carts. e line stretches across the stage. It is ring twilight, and the faces of the as- blage are illumined by the rays of the afternoon sun. The upper treadmill ies a gradually rising and falling mid- distance past the marchers. The foot a mountain appears: a trumpet call is rd as the foot of the mountain reaches e center. The marchers halt. The pic- now shows the mountain running up of sight off right. The singing stops. abel of "What's de matter?" "Why we stop?" "Tain't sundown yet!" hat's happened?" "What's goin' on?" hat are they blowin' for?" etc. Those ing ahead begin to murmur. "It's es," "Moses." "What's happened to ?" The others take up the repetition "Moses," and Moses enters, on the arm AARON. He is now an old man, as is brother, and he totters toward the cen- of the stage. Cries of "What's de mat- MOSES?" "You ain't hurt, is you?" n't that too bad?" etc. He slowly seats self on the rock at the foot of the ntain.*

N. How you feelin' now, brother?

ES. I'm so weary, Aaron. Seems like s took all of a sudden.

N. Do we camp yere?

ES. (*Pathetically.*) No, you got to goin'.

N. But you cain't go no further to- t, brother.

MOSES. Dis never happened to me befo'.

A YOUNG WOMAN. But you's a ol' man, now, Father Moses. You cain't expect to go as fas' as we kin.

MOSES. But de Lawd said I'd do it. He said I was to show you de Promised Land. Fo'ty years, I bin leadin' you. I led you out o' Egypt. I led you past Sinai, and through de wilderness. Oh, I cain't fall down on you now!

AARON. Le's res' yere fo' de night. Den we'll see how you feel in de mo'nin'.

MOSES. We tol' de scouts we'd meet 'em three miles furder on. I hate fo' 'em to come back all dis way to report. 'Tis gettin' a little dark, ain't it?

AARON. It ain't dark, Brother.

MOSES. No, it's my eyes.

AARON. Maybe it's de dust.

MOSES. No, I jest cain't seem to see. Oh, Lawd, dey cain't have a blind man leadin' 'em! Where is you Aaron?

AARON. I'se right yere, Moses.

MOSES. Do you think—(*Pause.*) Oh! Do you think it's de time He said?

AARON. How do you mean, Moses? (*Crowd look from one to another in wonder.*)

MOSES. He said I could lead 'em to de Jordan, dat I'd *see* de Promised Land, and dat's all de further I could go, on account I broke de laws. Little while back I thought I *did* see a river ahead, and a pretty land on de other side. (*Distant shouts "Hoo-*

ray!" "Yere dey are!" "Dey travelled quick." etc.) Where's de young leader of de troops? Where's Joshua? (*The call "JOSHUA" is taken up by those on the right of the stage, followed almost immediately by "Yere he is!" "MOSES wants you!" etc.*) (*JOSHUA enters. He is a fine looking Negro of about thirty.*)

JOSHUA. (*Going to MOSES' side.*) Yes, suh.

MOSES. What's de shoutin' 'bout, Joshua?

JOSHUA. De scouts is back wid de news. De Jordan is right ahead of us, and Jericho is jest on de other side. Moses, we're dere! (*There are cries of "Hallelujah!" "De Lawd be praised!" "Hooray!" "De Kingdom's comin'!" etc. With a considerable stir among the marchers, several new arrivals crowd in from right, shouting "MOSES, we're dere!" JOSHUA seeing the newcomers.*) Yere's de scouts! (*Three very ragged and dusty young men advance to MOSES.*)

MOSES. (*As the shouting dies.*) So it's de River Jordan?

FIRST SCOUT. Yes, suh.

MOSES. All we got to take is de city of Jericho.

FIRST SCOUT. Yes, suh.

MOSES. Joshua, you got to take charge of de fightin' men, an' Aaron's gotta stay by de priests.

JOSHUA. What about you?

MOSES. You are leavin' me behind. Joshua, you gonter get de fightin' men together and take dat city befo' sundown.

JOSHUA. It's a big city, Moses, wid walls all 'round it. We ain't got enough men.

MOSES. You'll take it, Joshua.

JOSHUA. Yes, suh, but how?

MOSES. Move up to de walls wid our people. Tell de priests to go wid you with de rams' horns. You start marchin' 'roun' dem walls, and den—

JOSHUA. Yes, suh.

MOSES. De Lawd'll take charge, jest as he's' took charge ev'y time I've led you

against a city. He ain't never failed, h he?

SEVERAL VOICES. No, Moses. (*All rai their heads.*)

MOSES. And he ain't goin' to fail us no (*He prays. All bow.*) Oh, Lawd, I'm tu in' over our brave young men to yo caize I know you don' want me to le 'em any further. (*Rises.*) Jest like y said, I've got to de Jordan but I cain't over it. An' yere dey goin' now to ta de city of Jericho. In a little while dey be marchin' 'roun' it. An' would you ple: be so good as to tell 'em what to d Amen. (*To JOSHUA.*) Go ahead. Ev'ybo follows Joshua now. Give de signal move on wid e'ything. (*A trumpet heard.*) You camp fo' de night in de C of Jericho. (*MOSES seats himself on rock.*)

JOSHUA. Cain't we help you, Moses?

MOSES. You go ahead. De Lawd's got plans fo' me. Soun' de signal to mar (*Another trumpet call is heard. The co pany starts marching off. AARON linger moment.*) Take care of de Ark of Covenant, Aaron.

AARON. Yes, Brother. Good-bye.

MOSES. Good-bye, Aaron. (*The singing resumed softly and dies away. The last the marchers has disappeared.*) Yere I Lawd. De chillun is goin' into de Pr ised Land. (*GOD enters from behind hill. He walks to MOSES, puts his hands his shoulders.*) You's with me, ain't y Lawd?

GOD. Co'se I is.

MOSES. Guess I'm through, Lawd. like you said I'd be, when I broke tablets of de law. De ol" machine's b down.

GOD. Jest what was it I said to y Moses? Do you remember?

MOSES. You said I couldn't go into Promised Land.

GOD. Dat's so. But dat ain't all dey to it.

MOSES. How do you mean, Lawd?

. Moses, you been a good man. You
n a good leader of my people. You
me angry once, dat's true. And when
anger me I'm a God of Wrath. But
ever meant you wasn't gonter have what
s comin' to you. An' I ain't goin' to
you out of it, Moses. It's jest de country
ost de River dat you ain't gonter enter.
u gonter have a Promised Land. I been
tin' it ready fo' you, fo' a long time.
a you stand up?

SES. (*Rising, with* GOD's *help.*) Yes,
, Lawd.

. Come on, I'm goin' to show it to
. We goin' up dis hill to see it. Moses,
a million times nicer dan de Land of
aan. (*They start up the hill.*)

SES. I cain't hardly see.

. Don't worry. Dat's jest caize you so
(*They take a step or two up the hill,*
n MOSES *stops suddenly.*)

SES. Oh!

. What's de matter?

ES. We cain't be doin' dis!

. Co'se we kin!

ES. But I fo'got! I fo'got about Joshua
de fightin' men!

How about 'em?

ES. Dey're marchin' on Jericho. I tol'

'em to march aroun' 'de walls and den de
Lawd would be dere to tell 'em what to
do.

GOD. Dat's all right. He's dere.

MOSES. Den who's dis helpin' me up de
hill?

GOD. Yo' faith, yo' God.

MOSES. And is you over dere helpin' them
too, Lawd? Is you goin' to tell dem poor
chillun what to do?

GOD. Co'se I is. Listen Moses. I'll show
you how I'm helpin' dem. (*From the distance comes the blast of the rams' horns,
the sound of crumbling walls, a roar, and
a moment's silence. The* CHOIR *begins
"Joshua Fit De Battle of Jericho" and continues through the rest of the scene.*)

MOSES. You did it, Lawd! You've tooken
it! Listen to de chillun'—dey's in de Land
of Canaan at last! You's de only God dey
ever was, ain't you, Lawd?

GOD. (*Quietly.*) Come on, ol' 'man. (*They
continue up the hill.*) (*The stage is darkened.*)

MR. DESHEE. (*In the dark.*) But even dat
scheme didn't work. Caize after dey got
into the Land of Canaan dey went to de
dogs again. And dey went into bondage
again. Only dis time it was in de City of
Babylon. (*The* CHOIR, *which has been singing "Cain't Stay Away," stops as the next
scene begins.*)

SCENE V

er a low ceiling is a room vaguely
mbling a Negro night club in New
ans. Two or three long tables run
ss the room, and on the left is a table
a dais with a gaudy canopy above it.
table bears a card marked "Reserved
King and guests."
hy young men and women are seated
he tables. About a dozen couples are
ing in the foreground to the tune of
zz orchestra. The costumes are what
ld be worn at a Negro masquerade
present the debauchees of Babylon.

MAN. When did yuh git to Babylon?

ND MAN. I jes' got in yesterday.

THIRD MAN. (*Dancing.*) How do you like
dis baby, Joe?

FOURTH MAN. Hot damn! She could be de
King's pet!

A WOMAN. Anybody seen my papa?

THIRD MAN. Don' fo'git de dance at de
High Priest's house tomorrow. (*The dance
stops as a bugle call is heard. Enter* MASTER
OF CEREMONIES.)

MASTER OF CEREMONIES. Stop! Tonight's
guest of honor, de King of Babylon an'
party of five. (*Enter the* KING *and five
girls. The* KING *has on an imitation ermine cloak over his conventional evening*

clothes and wears a diamond tiara.' All rise as the KING *enters, and sing, "Hail, de King of Bab—Bab—Babylon."*

KING. Wait till you see de swell table I got. (*He crosses the stage to his table. The girls are jabbering.*) Remind me to send you a peck of rubies in de mo'nin'.

MASTER OF CEREMONIES. Ev'nin', King!

KING. Good ev'nin'. How's de party goin'?

MASTER OF CEREMONIES. Bes' one we ever had in Babylon, King.

KING. Any Jew boys yere?

MASTER OF CEREMONIES. (*Indicating some of the others.*) Lot o' dem yere. I kin go git mo' if you want 'em.

KING. I was really referrin' to de High Priest. He's a 'ticlar frien' o' mine an' he might drop in. You know what he look like?

MASTER OF CEREMONIES. No, suh, but I'll be on de look-out fo' him.

KING. O. K. Now le's have a li'l good time.

MASTER OF CEREMONIES. Yes, suh. (*To the orchestra.*) Let 'er go, boys. (*The music begins, waiters appear with food and great urns painted gold and silver, from which they pour out wine for the guests. The* MASTER OF CEREMONIES *exits. The* KING'S *dancing-girls go to the middle of the floor, and start to dance. The* KING *puts his arms about the waists of two girls, and draws them to him.*)

KING. Hot damn! Da's de way! Let de Jew boys see our gals kin dance better'n dere's. (*There is an ad lib. babel of "Da's de truth,* KING!" "I don' know—we got some good gals, too!" etc.*) Dey ain' no-body in de worl' like de Babylon gals. (*The dancing grows faster, the watchers keep time with hand-claps. The door at the left opens suddenly, and the* PROPHET, *a patriarchal, ragged figure enters. He looks belligerently about the room, and is followed almost immediately by the* MASTER OF CEREMONIES.)

PROPHET. Stop! (*The music and the da[ncers halt.*)

KING. What's the idea, bustin' up [my] party?

MASTER OF CEREMONIES. He said he w[as] expected, King. I thought mebbe he w[as] de—

KING. Did you think he was de Hi[gh] Priest of de Hebrews? Why, he's jest [a] ol' bum! De High Priest is a fashion pla[te]. T'row dis ole bum out o' yere!

PROPHET. Stop! (*Those who have be[en] advancing to seize him stop, somew[hat] amused.*)

KING. Wait a minute. Don't throw h[im] out. Let's see what he has to say.

PROPHET. Listen to me, King of Babyl[on]. I've been sent yere by de Lawd God J[eh]ovah. Don't you dare lay a hand on [de] Prophet!

KING. Oh, you're a prophet, is yuh? W[ell] you know we don' keer muh fo' proph[ets] in dis part of de country.

PROPHET. Listen to me, sons and daught[ers] of Babylon! Listen, you children of Is[rael] dat's given yo'selves over to de evil ways [of] yo' oppressors! You're all wallowin' [like] hogs in sin, an' de wrath of Gawd [is] goin' to be held back much longer! [I'm] tellin' you, repent befo' it's too late. [Re]pent befo' Jehovah casts down de sa[me] fire dat burned up Sodom and Gomor[rah]. Repent befo' de— (*During this scene y[?] increase as the* PROPHET *continues.*) (*The* HIGH PRIEST *enters left. He is a [?] voluptuary elaborately clothed in brig[ht] colored robes. He walks in hand in h[and] with a gaudily dressed "chippy."*)

HIGH PRIEST. (*Noise stops.*) Whoa, d[?] What you botherin' the King fo'?

PROPHET. (*Wheeling.*) And you, de H[igh] Priest of all Israel, walkin' de town wi[th a] dirty li'l tramp.

KING. Seems to be a frien' o' yours, J[?]

HIGH PRIEST. (*Crossing to the* KING [and] his girl.*) Aw, he's one of dem wild m[en] like Jeremiah and Isaiah. Don' let [?] bother you none. (*Pushes* PROPHET *aside[, and] goes to* KING'S *table.*)

PHET. You consort with harlots, an' yo'
ution in the sight of de Lawd. De
'd God's goin' to smite you down, jest
.e's goin' to smite down all dis wicked
ld! (*Grabs* HIGH PRIEST *and turns him
nd.*)

. (*Angrily against the last part of
preceding speech.*) Wait a minute. I'm
ng tired of this. Don' throw him out.
kill him! (*There is the sound of a
The* PROPHET *falls*)

HET. Smite 'em down, Lawd, like you
Dey ain't a decent person left in de
le world. (*He dies.* MASTER OF CERE-
IES, *revolver in hand, looks down at
PROPHET.)

'ER OF CEREMONIES. He's dead, King.

. Some of you boys take him out.
couple of young men come from the
ground and walk off with the body.*)

PRIEST. Don' know whether you
ld'a done that, King.

. Why not?

PRIEST. I don' know whether de
d would like it.

. Now, listen, Jake. You know yo'
d ain't payin' much attention to dis
s town. Except fo' you boys, it's tho'ly
cted by de Gods o' Babylon.

PRIEST. I know, but jest de same—

. Look yere, s'pose I give you a
e hund'ed pieces of silver. Don' you
e you kin arrange to persuade yo'
d to keep his hands off?

PRIEST. (*Oilily.*) Well of co'se we
l try. I dunno how well it would
. (*As the* HIGH PRIEST *speaks, The*

KING *claps his hands.* MASTER OF CEREMON-
IES *enters with bag of money.*)

KING. Yere it is.

HIGH PRIEST. (*Smiling.*) I guess we kin
square things up. (*He prays—whiningly.*)
Oh Lawd, please forgive my po' frien' de
King o' Babylon. He didn't know what he
was doin' an'—(*There is a clap of thunder, darkness for a second. The lights go
up and* GOD *is standing in the center of
the room.*)

GOD. (*In a voice of doom.*) Dat's about
enough. (*The guests are horrified.*) I's
stood all I kin from you. I tried to make
dis a good earth. I helped Adam, I helped
Noah, I helped Moses, an' I helped David.
What's de grain dat grew out of de seed?
Sin! Nothin' but sin throughout de whole
world. I've given you ev'y chance. I sent
you warriors and prophets. I've given you
laws and commandments, an' you betrayed my trust. Ev'ything I've given you,
you've defiled. Ev'y time I've fo'given you,
you've mocked me. An' now de High
Priest of Israel tries to trifle wid my name.
Listen, you chillun of darkness, yo' Lawd
is tired. I'm tired of de struggle to make
you worthy of de breath I gave you. I
put you in bondage ag'in to cure you an'
yo' worse dan you was amongst de flesh
pots of Egypt. So I renounce you. Listen
to the words of yo' lawd God Jehovah, for
dey is de last words yo' ever hear from me.
I repent of dese people dat I have made
and I will deliver dem no more. (*There is
darkness and cries of "Mercy!" "Have
pity, Lawd!" "We didn' mean it, Lawd!"
"Forgive us, Lawd!" etc. The* CHOIR *sings
"Death's Gwinter Lay His Cold Icy Hands
On Me" until the lights go up on the next
scene.*)

SCENE VI

s writing at his desk. Outside, past
oor, goes HOSEA, *a dignified old man,
wings like* JACOB's. GOD, *sensing his
nce, looks up from the paper he is
ining, and follows him out of the
r of his eye. Angrily he resumes his
as soon as* HOSEA *is out of sight.
e is a knock on the door.*

Who is it? (GABRIEL *enters.*)

GABRIEL. It's de delegation, Lawd.

GOD. (*Wearily.*) Tell 'em to come in.
(ABRAHAM, ISAAC, JACOB, *and* MOSES *enter.*)
Good mo'nin', gen'lemen.

THE VISITORS. Good mo'nin', Lawd.

GOD. What kin I do for you?

MOSES. You know, Lawd. Go back to our
people.

GOD. (*Shaking his head.*) Ev'ry day fo' hund'ed's of years you boys have come in to ask dat same thing. De answer is still de same. I repented of de people I made. I said I would deliver dem no more. Good mo'nin', gen'lemen. (*The four visitors rise and exeunt.* GABRIEL *remains.*) Gabe, why do dey do it?

GABRIEL. I 'spect dey think you gonter change yo' mind.

GOD. (*Sadly.*) Dey don' know me. (HOSEA *again passes the door. His shadow shows on the wall.* GABRIEL *is perplexed, as he watches.* GOD *again looks surreptitiously over His shoulder at the passing figure.*) I don' like dat, either.

GABRIEL. What Lawd?

GOD. Dat man.

GABRIEL. He's jest a prophet, Lawd. Dat's jest old Hosea. He jest come up the other day.

GOD. I know. He's one of de few dat's come up yere since I was on de earth last time.

GABRIEL. Ain' been annoyin' you, has he?

GOD. I don' like him walkin' past de door.

GABRIEL. All you got to do is tell him to stop, Lawd.

GOD. Yes, I know. I don' want to tell him. He's got a right up yere or he wouldn' be yere.

GABRIEL. You needn' be bothered by him hangin' aroun' de office all de time. I'll tell 'im. Who's he think he—

GOD. No, Gabe. I find it ain't in me to stop him. I sometimes jest wonder why he don' come in and say hello.

GABRIEL. You want him to do dat? (*He moves as if to go to the door.*)

GOD. He never has spoke to me, and if he don' wanta come in, I ain't gonter make him. But dat ain't de worst of it, Gabriel.

GABRIEL. What is, Lawd?

GOD. Ev'y time he goes past de door I hears a voice.

GABRIEL. One of de angels?

GOD. (*Shaking his head.*) It's from earth. It's a man.

GABRIEL. You mean he's prayin'?

GOD. No, he ain't exactly prayin'. jest talkin' in such a way dat I got to sen. His name is Hezdrel.

GABRIEL. Is he on de books?

GOD. No, not yet. But ev'y time dat H goes past I hear dat voice.

GABRIEL. Den tell *it* to stop.

GOD. I find I don' want to do that, ei Dey's gettin' ready to take Jerusalem d dere. Dat was my big fine city. Dis drel, he's jest one of de defenders. (*denly and passionately, almost wildl* ain' comin' down. You hear me? I comin' down. (*He looks at* GABRIEL.) ahead, Gabriel. 'Tend to yo' chores. gonter keep wukkin' yere.

GABRIEL. I hates to see you feelin' lik Lawd.

GOD. Dat's all right. Even bein' G ain't a bed of roses. (GABRIEL *exits. H shadow is on the wall. For a second hesitates.* GOD *looks at the wall. Go window.*) I hear you. I know yo' fig bravely, but I ain't comin' down. Oh, don' you leave me alone? You know ain' talkin' to me. *Is* you talkin' to I cain't stand yo' talkin' dat way. only hear part of what you' sayin', a puzzles me. Don' you know you puzzle God? (*A pause. Then tend* Do you want me to come down dere much? You know I said I wouldn't down? (*Fiercely.*) Why don' he a me a little? (*With clenched fists, down through the window.*) Listen tell you what I'll do. I ain't goi promise you anythin', and I ain't go do nothin' to help you. I'm jest fee little low, an' I'm only comin' dow make myself feel a little better, dat (*The stage is darkened.* CHOIR *begi Blind Man Stood In De Middle Road," and continues until the ligh up on the next scene.*)

SCENE VII

*a shadowed corner beside the walls
[th]e temple in Jerusalem. The light of
[the] fires flickers on the figure of HEZ-
[drel] who was* ADAM *in Part I. He stands
[in th]e same position* ADAM *held when first
[disco]vered but in his right hand is a sword,
[and] his left is in a sling. Around him are
[sever]al prostrate bodies. Pistol and cannon
[shots], then a trumpet call. Six young men
[enter] from left in command of a* CORPORAL.
[They] are all armed.*

[CORPO]RAL. De fightin's stopped fo' de
[night], Hezdrel.

[HEZD]REL. Yes?

[CORPO]RAL. Dey're goin' to begin ag'in at
[sun]row. (*Man enters, crosses the stage
[and e]xits.*) Herod say he's goin' to take
[de te]mple tomorrow, burn de books and
[a]rk of de Covenant, and put us all to
[de s]word.

[HEZD]REL. Yo' ready, ain't you?

[EVERY]BODY. Yes, Hezdrel.

[HEZD]REL. Did de food get in through de
[hole] in de city wall? (*Two soldiers enter,
[cross] the stage and exit.*)

[CORPO]RAL. Yessuh, we's goin' back to
[git] it out now.

[HEZD]REL. Good. Any mo' of our people
[come] today?

[CORPO]RAL. Ol' Herod's got de ol' hole
[clos]ed up now, but fifteen of our people
[come in thr]u a new one we made. (*Other sol-
[diers] enter, cross the stage and exit.*)

[HEZDR]EL. Good. Take dese yere wounded
[boys] back and git 'em took care of.

[CORPO]RAL. Yes, suh. (*They pick up the
[bodies] on the ground and carry them off
[just] as* HEZDREL *speaks.*)

[HEZD]REL. So dey gonter take de temple
[in de] mo'nin'? We'll be waitin' for 'em.
[R]emember, boys, when dey kill us we
[go] out of our skins, right into de lap
[of G]od. (*The men disappear with the
[woun]ded; from the deep shadow upstage
[enters] GOD.*)

Hello, Hezdrel—Adam.

HEZDREL. (*Rubbing his forehead.*) Who
is you?

GOD. Me? I'm jest an ol' preacher, from
back in de hills.

HEZDREL. What you doin' yere?

GOD. I heard you boys was fightin'. I jest
wanted to see how it was goin'.

HEZDREL. Well, it ain't goin' so well.

GOD. Dey got you skeered, huh?

HEZDREL. Look yere, who is you, a spy
in my brain?

GOD. Cain't you see I's one of yo' people?

HEZDREL. Listen, Preacher, we ain't skeered. We's gonter be killed, but we ain't
skeered.

GOD. I's glad to hear dat. Kin I ask you a
question, Hezdrel?

HEZDREL. What is it?

GOD. How is it you is so brave?

HEZDREL. Caize we got faith, dat's why!

GOD. Faith? In who?

HEZDREL. In our dear Lawd God.

GOD. But God say he abandoned ev' one
down yere.

HEZDREL. Who say dat? Who dare say dat
of de Lawd God of Hosea?

GOD. De God of Hosea?

HEZDREL. You heard me. Look yere, you
is a spy in my brain!

GOD. No, I ain't, Hezdrel. I'm jest puzzled. You ought to know dat.

HEZDREL. How come you so puzzled 'bout
de God of Hosea?

GOD. I don' know. Maybe I jest don' hear
things. You see, I live 'way back in de hills.

HEZDREL. What you wanter find out?

GOD. Ain't de God of Hosea de same
Jehovah dat was de God of Moses?

HEZDREL. (*Contemptuously.*) No. Dat ol'
God of wrath and vengeance? We have de

God dat Hosea preached to us. He's de one God.

GOD. Who's he?

HEZDREL. (*Reverently.*) De God of mercy.

GOD. Hezdrel, don' you think dey must be de same God?

HEZDREL. I don' know. I ain't bothered to think much about it. Maybe dey is. Maybe our God is de same ol' God. I guess we jest got tired of his appearance dat ol' way.

GOD. What you mean, Hezdrel?

HEZDREL. Oh, dat ol' God dat walked de earth in de shape of a man. I guess he lived wid man so much dat all he seen was de sins in man. Dat's what made him de God of wrath and vengeance. Co'se he made Hosea. An' Hosea never would a found what mercy was unless dere was a little of it in God, too. Anyway, he ain't a fearsome God no mo'. Hosea showed us dat.

GOD. How you s'pose Hosea found dat mercy?

HEZDREL. De only way he could find it. De only way I found it. De only way anyone kin find it.

GOD. How's dat?

HEZDREL. Through sufferin'.

GOD. (*After a pause.*) What if dey kill you in de mo'nin', Hezdrel.

HEZDREL. If dey do, dey do. Dat's all.

GOD. Herod say he's goin' to burn de temple—

HEZDREL. So he say.

GOD. And burn de Ark an' de books. Den dat's de end of de books, ain't it?

HEZDREL. (*Buoyantly.*) What you mean? If he burns dem things in dere? Naw. Dem's jest copies.

GOD. Where is de others?

HEZDREL. (*Tapping his head.*) Dey's a set in yere. Fifteen got out through de hole

in the city wall today. A hundred fifty got out durin' de week. Each of is a set of de books. Dey's scattered all over de countryside now, jest wa to git pen and paper fo' to put 'em d agin.

GOD. (*Proudly.*) Dey cain't lick you, dey Hezdrel?

HEZDREL. (*Smiling.*) I know dey ca (*Trumpet.*) You better get out o' Preacher, if you wanter carry de to yo' people. It'll soon be daylight.

GOD. I'm goin'. (*He takes a step up and stops.*) Want me to take any mess

HEZDREL. Tell de people in de hills ain't nobody like de Lawd God of H

GOD. I will. If dey kill you tomorro bet dat God of Hosea'll be waitin' for

HEZDREL. I *know* he will.

GOD. (*Quietly.*) Thank you, Hezdre

HEZDREL. Fo' what?

GOD. Fo' tellin' me so much. You been so far away I guess I was jest behin' de times. (*He exits. Pause, trumpet sounds.*) (HEZDREL *paces back forth once or twice. Another young s appears. Other men enter and stand g ed about* HEZDREL.)

SECOND OFFICER. (*Excitedly.*) De jest crowed, Hezdrel. Dey started fightin' ag'in.

HEZDREL. We's ready for 'em. Com boys. (*From the darkness upstage another group of soldiers.*) Dis is de da say dey'll git us. Le's fight till de last goes. What d'you say?

CORPORAL. Le's go, Hezdrel!

HEZDREL. (*Calling left.*) Give 'em thing, boys! (*There is a movement t the left, a bugle call and the sou distant battle. The lights go out.* CHOIR *is heard singing, "March On umphantly. They continue to sing the lights go up on the next scene.*)

SCENE VIII

the same setting as the Fish Fry Scene
art I. The same angels are present
the CHOIR, *instead of marching, is*
'ing in a double row on an angle up-
right. GOD *is seated in an armchair*
center. He faces the audience. As the
continues to sing, GABRIEL *enters,*
ticed by the chattering angels. He
at GOD *who is staring thoughtfully*
'd the audience.

EL. You look a little pensive, Lawd.
nods his head.) Have a seegar,
?

No thanks, Gabriel. (GABRIEL *goes*
table, accepts a cup of custard; chats
the angel behind the table for a mo-
as he sips, puts the cup down and
's to the side of GOD.)

EL. You look awful pensive, Lawd.
been sittin' yere, lookin' dis way, an
long time. Is it somethin' serious,
?

Very serious, Gabriel.

EL. (*Awed by His tone.*) Lawd, is
ne come for me to blow?

Not yet, Gabriel. I'm just thinkin'.

EL. What about, Lawd? (*Puts up*
Singing stops.)

GOD. 'Bout somethin' de boy tol' me. Somethin' 'bout Hosea, and himself. How dey foun' somethin'.

GABRIEL. What, Lawd?

GOD. Mercy. (*A pause.*) Through *sufferin'*, he said.

GABRIEL. Yes, Lawd.

GOD. I'm tryin' to find it, too. It's awful impo'tant. It's awful impo'tant to all de people on my earth. Did he mean dat even God must suffer? (GOD *continues to look out over the audience for a moment and then a look of surprise comes into his face. He sighs. In the distance a voice cries.*)

THE VOICE. Oh, look at him! Oh, look, dey goin' to make him carry it up dat hill! Dey goin' to nail him to it! Oh, dat's a terrible burden for one man to carry! (GOD *rises and murmurs "Yes!" as if in recognition. The heavenly beings have been watching him closely, and now, seeing him smile gently, draw back, relieved. All the angels burst into "Hallelujah, King Jesus."* GOD *continues to smile as the lights fade away. The singing becomes fortissimo.*

CURTAIN

ou Can't Take It With You

BY MOSS HART AND GEORGE S. KAUFMAN

"You Can't Take It With You" was produced at the Booth Theatre, New City, Monday night, December 14th, 1936, by Sam H. Harris, with the foling cast:

PENELOPE SYCAMORE	Josephine Hull
ESSIE	Paula Trueman
RHEBA	Ruth Attaway
PAUL SYCAMORE	Frank Wilcox
MR. DE PINNA	Frank Conlan
ED	George Heller
DONALD	Oscar Polk
MARTIN VANDERHOF	Henry Travers
ALICE	Margot Stevenson
HENDERSON	Hugh Rennie
TONY KIRBY	Jess Barker
BORIS KOLENKHOV	George Tobias
GAY WELLINGTON	Mitzi Hajos
MR. KIRBY	William J. Kelly
MRS. KIRBY	Virginia Hammond
THREE MEN	George Leach / Ralph Holmes / Franklin Heller
OLGA	Anna Lubowe

The Scene Is the Home of Martin Vanderhof, New York.

ACT I

A Wednesday Evening

During this act the curtain is lowered to
denote the passing of several hours.

ACT II

A Week Later

ACT III

The Next Day

YOU CAN'T TAKE IT WITH YOU

ACT ONE

SCENE I

The home of MARTIN VANDERHOF—*just around the corner from Columbia Univer*
but don't go looking for it. The room we see is what is customarily described as a li
room, but in this house the term is something of an understatement. The every-man
himself room would be more like it. For here meals are eaten, plays are written, snakes
lected, ballet steps practiced, xylophones played, printing presses operated—if there i
room enough there would probably be ice skating. In short, the brood presided ove
MARTIN VANDERHOF *goes on about the business of living in the fullest sense of the u*
This is a house where you do as you like, and no questions asked.

At the moment, GRANDPA VANDERHOF'*s daughter,* MRS. PENELOPE SYCAMORE, *is d*
what she likes more than anything else in the world. She is writing a play—her eleve
Comfortably ensconced in what is affectionately known as Mother's Corner, she is poun
away on a typewriter perched precariously on a rickety card table. Also on the table is
of those plaster-paris skulls ordinarily used as an ash tray, but which serves PENELOP
a candy jar. And, because PENNY *likes companionship, there are two kittens on the t*
busily lapping at a saucer of milk.

PENELOPE VANDERHOF SYCAMORE *is a round little woman in her early fifties, comfor*
looking, gentle, homey. One would not suspect that under that placid exterior there su
the Divine Urge—but it does, it does.

After a moment her fingers lag on the keys; a thoughtful expression comes over her
Abstractedly she takes a piece of candy out of the skull, pops it into her mouth. As alu
it furnishes the needed inspiration—with a furious burst of speed she finishes a page
whips it out of the machine. Quite mechanically, she picks up one of the kittens, add.
sheet of paper to the pile underneath, replaces the kitten.

As she goes back to work, ESSIE CARMICHAEL, MRS. SYCAMORE'*s eldest daughter, c*
in from the kitchen. A girl of about twenty-nine, very slight, a curious air of the pixie a
her. She is wearing ballet slippers—in fact, she wears them throughout the play.

ESSIE (*fanning herself*). My, that kitchen's
hot.

PENNY (*finishing a bit of typing*). What, Essie?

ESSIE. I say the kitchen's awful hot. That
new candy I'm making—it just won't ever
get cool.

PENNY. Do you have to make candy today,
Essie? It's such a hot day.

ESSIE. Well, I got all those new orders. Ed
went out and got a bunch of new orders.

PENNY. My, if it keeps on I suppose you'll be
opening up a store.

ESSIE. That's what Ed was saying last night,
but I said No, I want to be a dancer. (*Brac-
ing herself against the table, she manipulates
her legs, ballet fashion.*)

PENNY. The only trouble with dancing is, it
takes so long. You've been studying such a
long time.

ESSIE (*slowly drawing a leg up behind h*
she talks). Only—eight—years. After
mother, you've been writing plays for
years. We started about the same time, d
we?

PENNY. Yes, but you shouldn't count my
two years, because I was learning to
(*From the kitchen comes a colored*
named RHEBA—*a very black girl somet*
in her thirties. She carries a white table
and presently starts to spread it over t
ble.)

RHEBA (*as she enters*). I think the ca
hardening up now, Miss Essie.

ESSIE. Oh, thanks, Rheba. I'll bring son
mother—I want you to try it. (*She goe*
the kitchen.)

(PENNY *returns to her work as* RHEBA
herself with the table.)

RHEBA. Finish the second act, Mrs.
more?

234

NY. Oh, no, Rheba. I've just got Cynthia ring the monastery.

BA. Monastery? How'd she get there? was at the El Morocco, wasn't she?

NY. Well, she gets tired of the El Moroc- and there's this monastery, so she goes e.

BA. Do they let her in?

NY. Yes, I made it Visitors' Day, so of se anybody can come.

BA. Oh.

NY. So she arrives on Visitors' Day, and st stays.

BA. All night?

NY. Oh, yes. She stays six years.

BA (*as she goes into the kitchen*). Six s? My, I bet she busts that monastery e open.

NY (*half to herself, as she types.*) "Six rs Later." . . . (PAUL SYCAMORE *comes up the cellar. Mid-fifties, but with a kind outhful air. His quiet charm and mild ner are distinctly engaging.*)

. (*turning back as he comes through the .*) Mr. De Pinna! (*A voice from below. ?"*) Mr. De Pinna, will you bring up of those new sky rockets, please? I want how them to Mrs. Sycamore. (*An an- ing monosyllable from the cellar as he s toward* PENNY.) Look, Penny—what ou think of these little fire crackers? strings for a nickel. Listen. (*He puts down on the center table and lights it. es off with a good bang.*) Nice, huh?

NY. Paul, dear, were you ever in a mon- y?

. (*quite calmly*). No, I wasn't. . . . Wait ou see the new rockets. Gold stars, then stars, then some bombs, and then a bal- , Mr. De Pinna thought of the balloon.

NY. Sounds lovely. Did you do all that y?

. Sure. We made up—oh, here we are. DE PINNA *comes up from the cellar. A -headed little man with a serious man- and carrying two good-sized sky rock- Look, Penny. Cost us eighteen cents to

make and we sell 'em for fifty. How many do you figure we can make before the Fourth, Mr. De Pinna?

DE PINNA. Well, we've got two weeks yet— what day you going to take the stuff up to Mount Vernon?

PAUL. Oh, I don't know—about a week. You know, we're going to need a larger booth this year—got a lot of stuff made up.

DE PINNA (*examining the rocket in his hand*). Look, Mr. Sycamore, the only thing that bothers me is, I'm afraid the powder chamber is just a little bit close to the bal- loon.

PAUL. Well, we've got the stars and the bombs in between.

DE PINNA. But that don't give the balloon time enough. A balloon needs plenty of time.

PAUL. Want to go down in the cellar and try it?

DE PINNA. All right.

PAUL (*as he disappears through the cellar door*). That's the only way you'll really tell.

PENNY (*halting* DE PINNA *in the cellar door- way*). Mr. De Pinna, if a girl you loved en- tered a monastery, what would you do?

DE PINNA (*he wasn't expecting that one*). Oh, I don't know, Mrs. Sycamore—it's been so long. (*He goes.*)
(RHEBA *returns from the kitchen, bringing a pile of plates.*)

RHEBA. Miss Alice going to be home to din- ner tonight, Mrs. Sycamore?

PENNY (*deep in her thinking*). What? I don't know, Rheba. Maybe.

RHEBA. Well, I'll set a place for her, but she's only been home one night this week. (*She puts down a plate or two.*) Miss Essie's making some mighty good candy today. She's doing something new with cocoanuts. (*More plates.*) Let's see—six, and Mr. De Pinna, and if Mr. Kolenkhov comes that makes eight, don't it? (*At which point a muffled crack, reminiscent of the Battle of the Marne, comes up from the cellar. It is the sky rocket, of course. The great prelim- inary hiss, followed by a series of explosions. PENNY and RHEBA, however, don't even no-*)

tice it. RHEBA *goes right on.*) Yes, I'd better set for eight.

PENNY. I think I'll put this play away for a while, Rheba, and go back to the war play.

RHEBA. Oh, I always liked that one—the war play. (ESSIE *returns from the kitchen, carrying a plate of freshly made candy.*)

ESSIE. They'll be better when they're harder, mother, but try one—I want to know what you think.

PENNY. Oh, they look awfully good. (*She takes one.*) What do you call them?

ESSIE. I think I'll call 'em Love Dreams.

PENNY. Oh, that's nice. . . . I'm going back to my war play, Essie. What do you think?

ESSIE. Oh, are you, mother?

PENNY. Yes, I sort of got myself into a monastery and I can't get out.

ESSIE. Oh, well, it'll come to you, mother. Remember how you got out of that brothel. . . . Hello, boys. (*This little greeting is idly tossed toward the snake solarium, a glass structure looking something like a goldfish aquarium, but containing, believe it or not, snakes.*) The snakes look hungry. Did Rheba feed them?

PENNY (*as* RHEBA *re-enters*). I don't know. Rheba, did you feed the snakes yet?

RHEBA. No, Donald's coming and he always brings flies with him.

PENNY. Well, try to feed them before Grandpa gets home. You know how fussy he is about them.

RHEBA. Yes'm.

PENNY (*handing her the kittens*). And take Groucho and Harpo into the kitchen with you. . . . I think I'll have another Love Dream. (MR. SYCAMORE *emerges from the cellar again.*)

PAUL. Mr. De Pinna was right about the balloon. It was too close to the powder.

ESSIE (*practicing a dance step*). Want a Love Dream, father? They're on the table.

PAUL. No, thanks. I gotta wash.

PENNY. I'm going back to the war play, Paul.

PAUL. Oh, that's nice. We're putting so red stars after the blue stars, then come bombs and *then* the balloon. That ought do it. (*He goes up the stairs.*)

ESSIE (*another dance step.*) Mr. Kolenkh says I'm his most promising pupil.

PENNY (*absorbed in her own troubles*). Y know, with forty monks and one girl, sor thing ought to happen. (ED CARMICH comes down the stairs. A nondescript you man in his mid-thirties. In shirtsleeves the moment.)

ED. Listen! (*He hums a snatch of melody he heads for the far corner of the room— xylophone corner. Arriving there, he pi up the sticks and continues the melody the xylophone. Immediately* ESSIE *is up her toes, performing intricate ballet steps* ED's *accompaniment.*)

ESSIE (*dancing*). I like that, Ed. Yours?

ED (*shakes his head*). Beethoven.

ESSIE (*never coming down off her toe* Lovely. Got a lot of *you* in it. . . . I m those new candies this afternoon, Ed.

ED (*playing away*). Yah?

ESSIE. You can take 'em around tonight.

ED. All right. . . . Now, here's the fin This is me. (*He works up to an elabo crescendo, but* ESSIE *keeps pace with* right to the finish.)

ESSIE. That's fine. Remember it when K lenkhov comes, will you?

PENNY (*who has been busy with her pape* Ed, dear, why don't you and Essie hav baby? I was thinking about it just the ot day.

ED. I don't know—we could have one if wanted us to. What about it, Essie? Do want to have a baby?

ESSIE. Oh, I don't care. I'm willing if Gra pa is.

ED. Let's ask him. (ESSIE *goes into the ki en as* PENNY *goes back to her manuscrip*

PENNY (*running through the pile*). La play . . . religious play . . . sex play. I k it's here some place. (ED, *meanwhile, transferred his attention from the xyloph to a printing press that stands handily*

d now gives it a preliminary workout.)
R. DE PINNA comes out of the cellar, bound
the kitchen to wash up.)

PINNA. I was right about the balloon. It
s too close to the powder.

, Anything you want printed, Mr. De
na? How about some more calling
ds?

PINNA (as he passes into the kitchen).
, thanks. I've still got the first thousand.

(calling after him). Well, call on some-
ly, will you? (He then gives his attention
RHEBA, who is busy with the table again.)
at have we got for dinner, Rheba? I'm
dy to print the menu.

EBA. Cornflakes, watermelon, some of
se candies Miss Essie made, and some
d of meat—I forget.

I think I'll set it up in boldface Cheltena
n tonight. (He starts to pick out the let-
.) If I'm going to take those new candies
und I'd better print up some descriptive
tter after dinner.

NY. Do you think anybody reads those
gs, Ed—that you put in the candy
es? . . . Oh, here it is. (She pulls a
nuscript out of a pile.) "Poison Gas."
he door bell sounds.) I guess that's Don-
(As RHEBA breaks into a broad grin.)
k at Rheba smile.

The boy friend, eh, Rheba?

NY (as RHEBA disappears into the hall-
). Donald and Rheba are awfully cute
ther. Sort of like Porgy and Bess. (RHE-
having opened the door, the gentleman
ed DONALD now looms up in the door-
—darkly. He is a colored man of no un-
ain hue.)

ALD. Good evening, everybody!

Hi, Donald! How've you been?

ALD. I'm pretty good, Mr. Ed. How you
, Mrs. Sycamore?

NY. Very well, thank you. (She looks at
appraisingly.) Donald, were you ever in
onastery?

ALD. No-o. I don't go no place much. I'm
elief.

PENNY. Oh, yes, of course.

DONALD (pulling a bottle out of each side
pocket). Here's the flies, Rheba. Caught a
big mess of them today.

RHEBA (taking the jars). You sure did.

DONALD. I see you've been working, Mrs. Sycamore.

PENNY. Yes, indeed, Donald.

DONALD. How's Grandpa?

PENNY. Just fine. He's over at Columbia this
afternoon. The Commencement exercises.

DONALD. My, the years certainly do roll
'round.

ED (with his typesetting). M — E — A — T.
. . . What's he go there for all the time,
Penny?

PENNY. I don't know. It's so handy—just
around the corner. (PAUL comes downstairs.)

PAUL. Oh, Donald! Mr. De Pinna and I are
going to take the fireworks up to Mount
Vernon next week. Do you think you could
give us a hand?

DONALD. Yes, sir, only I can't take no money
for it this year, because if the Government
finds out I'm working they'll get sore.

PAUL. Oh! . . . Ed, I got a wonderful idea
in the bathroom just now. I was reading
Trotzky. (He produces a book from under
his arm.) It's yours, isn't it?

ED. Yah, I left it there.

PENNY. Who is it?

PAUL. You know, Trotzky. The Russian
Revolution.

PENNY. Oh.

PAUL. Anyhow, it struck me it was a great
fireworks idea. Remember "The Last Days
of Pompeii"?

PENNY. Oh, yes. Palisades Park. (With a
gesture of her arms she loosely describes a
couple of arcs, indicative of the eruption of
Mt. Vesuvius.) That's where we met.

PAUL. Well, I'm going to do the Revolution!
A full hour display.

DONALD. Say!

PENNY. Paul, that's wonderful!

ED. The red fire is the flag, huh?

PAUL. Sure! And the Czar, and the Cossacks!

DONALD. And the freeing of the slaves?

PAUL. No, no, Donald— (*The sound of the front door slamming. A second's pause, and then* GRANDPA *enters the living room.* GRANDPA *is about 75, a wiry little man whom the years have treated kindly. His face is youthful, despite the lines that sear it; his eyes are very much alive. He is a man who made his peace with the world long, long ago, and his whole attitude and manner are quietly persuasive of this.*)

GRANDPA (*surveying the group*). Well, sir, you should have been there. That's all I can say—you should have been there.

PENNY. Was it a nice Commencement, Grandpa?

GRANDPA. Wonderful. They get better every year. (*He peers into the snake solarium.*) You don't know how lucky you are you're snakes.

ED. Big class this year, Grandpa? How many were there?

GRANDPA. Oh, must have been two acres. *Everybody* graduated. And much funnier speeches than they had last year.

DONALD. You want to listen to a good speech you go up and hear Father Divine.

GRANDPA. I'll wait—they'll have him at Columbia.

PENNY. Donald, will you tell Rheba Grandpa's home now and we won't wait for Miss Alice.

DONALD. Yes'm. . . . (*As he goes through the kitchen door.*) Rheba, Grandpa's home—we can have dinner.

PAUL. Got a new sky rocket today, Grandpa. Wait till you see it. . . . Wonder why they don't have fireworks at Commencements.

GRANDPA. Don't make enough noise. You take a good Commencement orator and he'll drown out a whole carload of fireworks. And say just as much, too.

PENNY. Don't the graduates ever say anything?

GRANDPA. No, they just sit there in cap a nightgown, get their diplomas, and th along about forty years from now they s denly say, "Where am I?" (ESSIE *comes from the kitchen, bringing a plate of to toes for the evening meal.*)

ESSIE. Hello, Grandpa. Have a nice day

GRANDPA (*watching* ESSIE *as she puts tomatoes on the table*). Hello-have-a-n day. (*Suddenly he roars at the top of voice.*) Don't I even get kissed?

ESSIE (*kissing him*). Excuse me, Grandpa

GRANDPA. I'll take a tomato, too. (E *passes the plate;* GRANDPA *takes one and with it in his hand, solemnly weighing* You know, I could have used a couple these this afternoon. . . . Play something,

(ED *at once obliges on the xylophone—so thing on the dreamy side. Immediately* E *is up on her toes again, drifting through mazes of a toe dance.*)

ESSIE (*after a moment*). There was a le came for you, Grandpa. Did you get it

GRANDPA. Letter for me? I don't know a body.

ESSIE. It was for you, though. Had y name on it.

GRANDPA. That's funny. Where is it?

ESSIE. I don't know. Where's Grandpa's ter, mother?

PENNY (*who has been deep in her wo* What, dear?

ESSIE (*dancing dreamily away*). Whe that letter that came for Grandpa last we

PENNY. I don't know. (*Then, brightly.*) member seeing the kittens on it.

GRANDPA. Who was it from? Did you not

ESSIE. Yes, it was on the outside.

GRANDPA. Well, who was it?

ESSIE (*first finishing the graceful flutter of the Dying Swan*). United States Gov ment.

GRANDPA. Really? Wonder what *they* war

ESSIE. There was one before that, too, f the same people. There was a couple them.

ANDPA. Well, if any more come I wish 'd give them to me.

E. Yes, Grandpa. (*A fresh flurry of danc-; the xylophone grows a little louder.*)

ANDPA. I think I'll go out to Westchester morrow and do a little snake-hunting.

UL (*who has settled down with his book me time before this*). "God is the State; State is God."

ANDPA. What's that?

UL. "God is the State; the State is God."

NDPA. Who says that?

UL. Trotzky.

NDPA. Well, that's all right—I thought said it.

It's nice for printing, you know. Good short. (*He reaches into the type case.*) — O — D — space — I — S — space — — H — E (*The sound of the outer door ing, and* ALICE SYCAMORE *enters the room. ovely, fresh young girl of about twenty-. She is plainly* GRANDPA's *grand-daugh- but there is something that sets her rt from the rest of the family. For one g, she is in daily contact with the world; ddition, she seems to have escaped the e of mild insanity that pervades the rest hem. But she is a Sycamore for all that, her devotion and love for them are plain-apparent. At the moment she is in a ll nervous flutter, but she is doing her to conceal it.*)

E (*as she makes the rounds, kissing her dfather, her father, her mother*). And he beautiful princess came into the pal- and kissed her mother, and her father, her grandfather—hi, Grandpa—and t do you think? They turned into the more family. Surprised?

E (*examining* ALICE's *dress*). Oh, Alice, e it. It's new, isn't it?

NY. Looks nice and summery.

E. Where'd you get it?

E. Oh, I took a walk during lunch hour.

NDPA. You've been taking a lot of walks y. That's the second new dress this k.

ALICE. Oh, I just like to brighten up the office once in a while. I'm known as the Kay Francis of Kirby & Co.... Well, what's new around here? In the way of plays, snakes, ballet dancing or fireworks. Dad, I'll bet you've been down in that cellar all day.

PAUL. Huh?

PENNY. I'm going back to the war play, Alice.

ESSIE. Ed, play Alice that Beethoven thing you wrote. Listen, Alice. (*Like a shot* ED *is at the xylophone again,* ESSIE *up on her toes.*)
(GRANDPA, *meanwhile, has unearthed his stamp album from under a pile of oddments in the corner, and is now busy with his magnifying glass.*)

GRANDPA. Do you know that you can mail a letter all the way from Nicaragua for two pesetos?

PENNY (*meanwhile dramatically reading one of her own deathless lines*). "Kenneth, my virginity is a priceless thing to me."

ALICE (*finding it hard to break through all this*). Listen, people. . . . Listen. (*A break in the music; she gets a scattered sort of attention.*) I'm not home to dinner. A young gentleman is calling for me.

ESSIE. Really? Who is it?

PENNY. Well, isn't that nice?

ALICE (*with quiet humor*). I did everything possible to keep him from coming here, but he's calling for me.

PENNY. Why don't you both stay to dinner?

ALICE. No, I want him to take you in easy doses. I've tried to prepare him a little, but don't make it any worse than you can help. Don't read him any plays, mother, and don't let a snake bite him, Grandpa, because I like him. And I wouldn't dance for him, Essie, because we're going to the Monte Carlo ballet tonight.

GRANDPA. Can't do *anything*. Who *is* he—President of the United States?

ALICE. No, he's vice-president of Kirby & Co. Mr. Anthony Kirby, Jr.

ESSIE. The Boss' son?

PENNY. Well!

ALICE. The Boss' son. Just like the movies.

ESSIE. That explains the new dresses.

ED. And not being home to dinner for three weeks.

ALICE. Why, you're wonderful!

PENNY (all aglow). Are you going to marry him?

ALICE. Oh, of course. Tonight! Meanwhile I have to go up and put on my wedding dress.

ESSIE. Is he good-looking?

ALICE (vainly consulting her watch). Yes, in a word. Oh, dear! What time is it?

PENNY. I don't know. Anybody know what time it is?

PAUL. Mr. De Pinna might know.

ED. It was about five o'clock a couple of hours ago.

ALICE. Oh, I ought to know better than to ask you people. . . . Will you let me know the minute he comes, please?

PENNY. Of course, Alice.

ALICE. Yes, I know, but I mean the *minute* he comes.

PENNY. Why, of course. (ALICE looks apprehensively from one to the other; then disappears up the stairs.) Well, what do you think of that?

GRANDPA. She seems to like him, if you ask me.

ESSIE. I should say so. She's got it bad.

PENNY. Wouldn't it be wonderful if she married him? We could have the wedding right in this room.

PAUL. Now, wait a minute, Penny. This is the first time he's ever called for the girl.

PENNY. You only called for me once.

PAUL. Young people are different nowadays.

ESSIE. Oh, I don't know. Look at Ed and me. He came to dinner *once* and just stayed.

PENNY. Anyhow, I think it's wonderful. I'll bet he's crazy about her. It must be he that's been taking her out every night. (The door bell rings.) There he is! Never mind, Rheba, I'll answer it. (She is fluttering to the door.)

Now remember what Alice said, and be ve[ry] nice to him.

GRANDPA (rising). All right—let's take a lo[ok] at him.

PENNY (at the front door; milk and hon[ey] in her voice). Well! Welcome to our lit[tle] home! I'm Alice's mother. Do come rig[ht] in! Here we are! (She reappears in the ar[ch]way, piloting the stranger.) This is Grand[pa,] and that's Alice's father, and Alice's sist[er] and her husband, Ed Carmichael. (The fa[m]ily all give courteous little nods and smi[les] as they are introduced.) Well Now give [me] your hat and make yourself right at ho[me.]

THE MAN. I'm afraid you must be makin[g a] mistake.

PENNY. How's that?

THE MAN. My card.

PENNY (reading). "Wilbur C. Henders[on,] Internal Revenue Department."

HENDERSON. That's right.

GRANDPA. What can we do for you?

HENDERSON. Does a Mr. Martin Vander[hof] live here?

GRANDPA. Yes, sir. That's me.

HENDERSON (all milk and honey). Well, [Mr.] Vanderhof, the Government wants to t[alk] to you about a little matter of income t[ax.]

PENNY. Income tax?

HENDERSON. Do you mind if I sit down?

GRANDPA. No, no. Just go right ahead.

HENDERSON (settling himself). Thank y[ou.] (From above stairs the voice of ALICE flo[ats] down.)

ALICE. Mother! Is that Mr. Kirby?

PENNY (going to the stairs). No. No, it i[sn't,] darling. It's—an internal something or ot[her.] (To Mr. Henderson.) Pardon me.

HENDERSON (pulling a sheaf of papers fr[om] his pocket). We've written you several let[ters] about this, Mr. Vanderhof, but have not [had] any reply.

GRANDPA. Oh, that's what those letters w[ere.]
ESSIE. I told you they were from the Gove[rn]ment. (MR. DE PINNA comes up from the [cellar.])

, *bearing a couple of giant firecrackers.*
pauses as he sees a stranger.)

PINNA. Oh, pardon me.

UL. Yes, Mr. De Pinna?

PINNA. These things are not going off,
. Sycamore. Look. (*He prepares to apply
 match to one of them, as a startled income
 man nearly has a conniption fit. But PAUL
 too quick for him.*)

UL. Ah—not here, Mr. De Pinna. Grand-
 s busy.

PINNA. Oh. (MR. DE PINNA *and* PAUL
 rry into the hall with their firecrackers.)

NDERSON (*now that order has been reed*). According to our records, Mr. Van-
hof, you have never paid an income tax.

NDPA. That's right.

NDERSON. Why not?

NDPA. I don't believe in it.

DERSON. Well—you own property, don't
 ?

NDPA. Yes, sir.

DERSON. And you receive a yearly income
 n it?

NDPA. I do.

DERSON. Of— (*He consults his records.*)
 etween three and four thousand dollars.

NDPA. About that.

DERSON. You've been receiving it for
 s.

NDPA. I have. 1901, if you want the exact
 .

DERSON. Well, the Government is only
 cerned from 1914 on. That's when the
 me tax started.

NDPA. Well?

DERSON. Well—it seems, Mr. Vanderhof,
 you owe the Government twenty-two
 s' back income tax.

Wait a minute! You can't go back that
 —that's outlawed.

DERSON (*calmly regarding him*). What's
 name?

ED. What difference does that make?

HENDERSON. Ever file an income tax return?

ED. No, sir.

HENDERSON. What was your income last
year?

ED. Ah—twenty-eight dollars and fifty cents,
wasn't it, Essie? (ESSIE *gives quick assent;
the income tax man dismisses the whole matter with an impatient wave of the hand and
returns to bigger game.*)

HENDERSON. Now, Mr. Vanderhof, you know
there's quite a penalty for not filing an income tax return.

PENNY. Penalty?

GRANDPA. Look, Mr. Henderson, let me ask
you something.

HENDERSON. Well?

GRANDPA. Suppose I pay you this money—
mind you, I don't say I'm going to do it—
but just for the sake of argument—what's
the Government going to do with it?

HENDERSON. How do you mean?

GRANDPA. Well, what do I get for my money?
If I go into Macy's and buy something, there
it *is*—I see it. What's the Government give
me?

HENDERSON. Why, the Government gives
you everything. It protects you.

GRANDPA. What from?

HENDERSON. Well—invasion. Foreigners that
might come over here and take everything
you've got.

GRANDPA. Oh, I don't think they're going to
do that.

HENDERSON. If you didn't pay an income tax,
they would. How do you think the Government keeps up the Army and Navy? All
those battleships . . .

GRANDPA. Last time we used battleships was
in the Spanish-American War, and what
did we get out of it? Cuba—and we gave
that back. I wouldn't mind paying if it were
something sensible.

HENDERSON (*beginning to get annoyed*).
Well, what about Congress, and the Supreme

Court, and the President? We've got to pay *them,* don't we?

GRANDPA (*ever so calmly*). Not with my money—no, sir.

HENDERSON (*furious*). Now wait a minute! I'm not here to argue with you. All I know is that you haven't paid an income tax and you've got to pay it!

GRANDPA. They've got to show me.

HENDERSON (*yelling*). We *don't* have to show you! I just told you! All those buildings down in Washington, and Interstate Commerce, and the Constitution!

GRANDPA. The Constitution was paid for long ago. And Interstate Commerce—what *is* Interstate Commerce, anyhow?

HENDERSON (*with murderous calm*). There are forty-eight states—see? And if there weren't Interstate Commerce, nothing could go from one state to another. See?

GRANDPA. Why not? They got fences?

HENDERSON. No, they haven't got fences! They've got *laws!* . . . My God, I never came across anything like this before!

GRANDPA. Well, I might pay about seventy-five dollars, but that's all it's worth.

HENDERSON. You'll pay every cent of it, like everybody else!

ED (*who has lost interest*). Listen, Essie—listen to this a minute. (*The xylophone again;* ESSIE *goes into her dance.*)

HENDERSON (*going right ahead, battling against the music*). And let me tell you something else! You'll go to jail if you don't pay, do you hear that? There's a law, and if you think you're bigger than the law, you've got another think coming! You'll hear from the United States Government, that's all I can say! (*He is backing out of the room.*)

GRANDPA (*quietly*). Look out for those snakes

HENDERSON (*jumping*). Jesus! (*Out in the hall, and not more than a foot or two behind* MR. HENDERSON, *the firecracker boys are now ready to test that little bomber. It goes off with a terrific detonation, and* MR. HENDERSON *jumps a full foot. He wastes no time at all in getting out of there.*)

PAUL (*coming back into the room*). H did that sound to you folks?

GRANDPA (*quite judicially*). I liked it.

PENNY. My goodness, he was mad, was he?

GRANDPA. Oh, it wasn't his fault. It's j that the whole thing is so silly.

PENNY (*suddenly finding herself with a p fectly good Panama in her hand*). He for his hat.

GRANDPA. What size is it?

PENNY (*peering into its insides*). Seven a an eighth.

GRANDPA. Just right for me.

DE PINNA. Who was that fellow, anyho (*Again the door bell.*)

PENNY. This *must* be Mr. Kirby.

PAUL. Better make sure this time.

PENNY. Yes, I will. (*She disappears.*)

ESSIE. I hope he's good-looking.

PENNY (*heard at the door*). How do you

A MAN'S VOICE. Good evening.

PENNY (*taking no chances*). Is this Mr. thony Kirby, Jr.?

TONY. Yes.

PENNY (*giving her all*). Well, Mr. Ki come right in! We've been expecting y Come right in! (*They come into si* PENNY *expansively addresses the fami* This is *really* Mr. Kirby! Now, I'm Ali mother, and that's *Mr.* Sycamore, and Ali grandfather, and her sister Essie, and Es husband. (*There are a few mumbled gr ings.*) There! Now you know *all* of us, Kirby. Give me your hat and make you right at home. (TONY KIRBY *comes a steps into the room. He is a person young man, not long out of Yale, and, as will presently learn, even more recently of Cambridge. Although he fits all the ph cal requirements of a Boss' son, his face something of the idealist in it. All in a very nice young man.*)

TONY. How do you do? (*Again the voic the vigilant* ALICE *floats down from upst "Is that Mr. Kirby, mother?"*)

NNY (*shouting up the stairs*). Yes, Alice.
e's lovely!

ICE (*aware of storm signals*). I'll be right
wn.

NNY. Do sit down, Mr. Kirby.

NY. Thank you. (*A glance at the dinner
le.*) I hope I'm not keeping you from
ner?

NDPA. No, no. Have a tomato?

NY. No, thank you.

NNY (*producing the candy-filled skull*).
w about a piece of candy?

Y (*eyeing the container*). Ah—no,
nks.

NNY. Oh, I forgot to introduce Mr. De
na. This is Mr. De Pinna, Mr. Kirby.
n exchange of "How do you do's?"*)

PINNA. Wasn't I reading about your father
the newspaper the other day? Didn't he
indicted or something?

Y (*smiling*). Hardly that. He just testi-
before the Securities Commission.

PINNA. Oh.

NY (*sharply*). Yes, of course. I'm sure
re was nothing crooked about it, Mr. De
na. As a matter of fact— (*She is now
dressing* TONY.)—Alice has often told us
at a lovely man your father is.

Y. Well, I know father couldn't get along
hout Alice. She knows more about the
iness than any of us.

E. You're awful young, Mr. Kirby, aren't
, to be vice-president of a big place like

Y. Well, you know what that means,
-president. All I have is a desk with my
le on it.

NY. Is that all? Don't you get any salary?

Y (*with a laugh*). Well, a little. More
I'm worth, I'm afraid.

NY. Now you're just being modest.

NDPA. Sounds kind of dull to me—Wall
et. Do you like it?

Y. Well, the hours are short. And I
n't been there very long.

GRANDPA. Just out of college, huh?

TONY. Well, I knocked around for a while
first. Just sort of had fun.

GRANDPA. What did you do? Travel?

TONY. For a while. Then I went to Cambridge for a year.

GRANDPA (*nodding*). England.

TONY. That's right.

GRANDPA. Say, what's an English commencement like? Did you see any?

TONY. Oh, very impressive.

GRANDPA. They are, huh?

TONY. Anyhow, now the fun's over, and—
I'm facing the world.

PENNY. You've certainly got a good start, Mr.
Kirby. Vice-president, and a rich father.

TONY. Well, that's hardly my fault.

PENNY (*brightly*). So now I suppose you're
all ready to settle down and—get married.

PAUL. Come now, Penny, I'm sure Mr. Kirby
knows his own mind.

PENNY. I wasn't making up his mind for
him—was I, Mr. Kirby?

TONY. That's quite all right, Mrs. Sycamore.

PENNY (*to the others*). You see?

ESSIE. You mustn't rush him, mother.

PENNY. Well, all I meant was he's bound to
get married, and suppose the wrong girl
gets him? (*The descending* ALICE *mercifully
comes to* TONY's *rescue at this moment. Her
voice is heard from the stairs.*)

ALICE. Well, here I am, a vision in white.
(*She comes into the room—and very lovely
indeed.*) Apparently you've had time to get
acquainted.

PENNY. Oh, yes, indeed. We were just having
a delightful talk about love and marriage.

ALICE. Oh, dear. (*She turns to* TONY.) I'm
sorry. I came down as fast as I could.

RHEBA (*bringing a platter of sliced water-
melon*). God damn those flies in the kitchen.
. . . Oh, Miss Alice, you look beautiful.
Where you going?

ALICE (*making the best of it*). I'm going out,
Rheba.

RHEBA (*noticing* TONY). Stepping, huh? (*The door bell sounds.*)

ESSIE. That must be Kolenkhov.

ALICE (*uneasily*). I think we'd better go, Tony.

TONY. All right. (*Before they can escape, however,* DONALD *emerges from the kitchen, bearing a tray.*)

DONALD. Grandpa, you take cream on your cornflakes? I forget.

GRANDPA. Half and half, Donald. (*The voice of* BORIS KOLENKHOV *booms from the outer door.*)

KOLENKHOV. Ah, my little Rhebishka!

RHEBA (*with a scream of laughter*). Yassuh, Mr. Kolenkhov!

KOLENKHOV. I am so hungry I could even eat my little Rhebishka! (*He appears in the archway, his great arm completely encircling the delighted* RHEBA. MR. KOLENKHOV *is one of* RHEBA'S *pets, and if you like Russians he might be one of yours. He is enormous, hairy, loud, and very, very Russian. His appearance in the archway still further traps* ALICE *and* TONY.) Grandpa, what do you think? I have had a letter from Russia! The Second Five Year Plan is a failure! (*He lets out a laugh that shakes the rafters.*)

ESSIE. I practiced today, Mr. Kolenkhov!

KOLENKHOV (*with a deep Russian bow*). My Pavlowa! (*Another bow.*) Madame Sycamore! . . . My little Alice! (*He kisses her hand.*) Never have I seen you look so magnificent.

ALICE. Thank you, Mr. Kolenkhov. Tony, this is Mr. Kolenkhov, Essie's dancing teacher. Mr. Kirby.

TONY. How do you do? (*A click of the heels and a bow from* KOLENKHOV.)

ALICE (*determined, this time*). And now we really *must* go. Excuse us, Mr. Kolenkhov— we're going to the Monte Carlo ballet.

KOLENKHOV (*at the top of his tremendous voice*). The Monte Carlo ballet! It *stinks!*

ALICE (*panicky now*). Yes. . . . Well—goodbye, everybody. Goodbye.

TONY. Goodbye. I'm so glad to have met you all. (*A chorus of answering "Good-byes" from the family. The young people ar gone.*)

KOLENKHOV (*still furious*). The Monte Carl ballet!

PENNY. Isn't Mr. Kirby lovely? . . . Come or everybody! Dinner's ready!

ED (*pulling up a chair*). I thought he wa a nice fellow, didn't you?

ESSIE. Mm. And so good-looking.

PENNY. And he had such nice manners. Di you notice, Paul? Did you notice his man ners?

PAUL. I certainly did. You were getting pret personal with him.

PENNY. Oh, now Paul . . . Anyhow, he's very nice young man . . .

DE PINNA (*as he seats himself*). He look kind of like a cousin of mine.

KOLENKHOV. Bakst! Diaghlieff! *Then* yo had the *ballet!*

PENNY. I think if they get married here I' put the altar right where the snakes ar You wouldn't mind, Grandpa, would you

ESSIE. Oh, they'll want to get married in church. His family and everything.

GRANDPA (*tapping on a plate for silence* Quiet, everybody! Quiet! (*They are imm diately silent—Grace is about to be pr nounced.* GRANDPA *pauses a moment f heads to bow, then raises his eyes heave ward. He clears his throat and proceeds say Grace.*) Well, Sir, we've been getti along pretty good for quite a while now, a we're certainly much obliged. Remembe all we ask is just to go along and be hap in our own sort of way. Of course we wa to keep our health, but as far as anythi else is concerned, we'll leave it to Yo Thank You. (*The heads come up as* RHE *comes through the door with a steami platter.*) So the Second Five Year Plan i failure, eh, Kolenkhov?

KOLENKHOV (*booming*). Catastrophic! (*reaches across the table and spears a pi of bread. The family, too, is busily plungi in.*)

THE CURTAIN IS DOWN

SCENE II

Late the same night. The house is in darkness save for a light in the hall.
Somewhere in the back regions an accordion is being played. Then quiet. Then the still-
ess of the night is suddenly broken again by a good loud BANG! from the cellar. Some-
here in the nether regions, one of the Sycamores is still at work.
Once more all is quiet, then the sound of a key in the outer door. The voices of ALICE
d TONY *drift through.*

.ICE. I could see them dance every night of
e week. I think they're marvelous.

NY. They are, aren't they? But of course
st walking inside *any* theatre gives *me* a
rill.

ICE (*as they come into sight in the hall-*
y). It's been *so* lovely, Tony. I hate to
ve it over.

NY. Oh, is it over? Do I have to go right
ay?

ICE. Not if you don't want to.

NY. I don't.

ICE. Would you like a cold drink?

NY. Wonderful.

ICE (*pausing to switch on the light*). "I'll
: what's in the ice-box. Want to come
ng?

NY. I'd follow you to the ends of the earth.

ICE. Oh, just the kitchen is enough. (*They*
out. *A pause, a ripple of gay laughter*
m *the kitchen, then they return.* ALICE *is*
rying a couple of glasses, TONY *brings two*
tles *of ginger ale and an opener.*) Lucky
're not hungry, Mr. K. An ice-box full
cornflakes. That gives you a rough idea
the Sycamores.

NY (*working away with the opener*). Of
rse, why they make these bottle openers
Singer midgets I never *was* able to—ah!
s *the bottle opens.*) All over my coat.

CE. I'll take mine in a glass, if you don't
d.

Y (*pouring*). There you are. A foaming
ker.

CE. Anyhow, it's cold.

TONY (*pouring his own*). Now if you'll
please be seated, I'd like to offer a toast.

ALICE (*settling herself*). We are seated.

TONY. Miss Sycamore— (*He raises his glass*
on high.)—to you.

ALICE. Thank you, Mr. Kirby. (*Lifting her*
own glass.) To you. (*They both drink.*)

TONY (*happily*). I wouldn't trade one minute
of this evening for—all the rice in China.

ALICE. Really?

TONY. Cross my heart.

ALICE (*a little sigh of contentment. Then*
shyly). Is there much rice in China?

TONY. Terrific. Didn't you read "The Good
Earth?" (*She laughs. They are silent for a*
moment.) I suppose I ought to go.

ALICE. Is it very late?

TONY (*looks at his watch*). Very. (ALICE
gives a little nod. Time doesn't matter.)
I don't want to go.

ALICE. I don't want you to.

TONY. All right, I won't. (*Silence again.*)
When do you get your vacation?

ALICE. Last two weeks in August.

TONY. I might take mine then, too.

ALICE. Really?

TONY. What are you going to do?

ALICE. I don't know. I hadn't thought much
about it.

TONY. Going away, do you think?

ALICE. I might not. I like the city in the summer time.

TONY. I do too.

ALICE. But you always go up to Maine, don't you?

TONY. Why—yes, but I'm sure I *would* like the city in the summer time. That is, I'd like it if—Oh, you know what I mean, Alice. I'd love it if *you* were here.

ALICE. Well—it'd be nice if you were here, Tony.

TONY. You know what you're saying, don't you?

ALICE. What?

TONY. That you'd rather spend the summer with me than anybody else.

ALICE. It looks that way, doesn't it?

TONY. Well, if it's true about the summer, how would you feel about—the winter?

ALICE (*seeming to weigh the matter*). Yes. I'd—like that, too.

TONY (*tremulous*). Then comes spring—and autumn. If you could—see your way clear about those, Miss Sycamore. . . .

ALICE (*again a little pause*). Yes.

TONY. I guess that's the whole year. We haven't forgotten anything, have we?

ALICE. No.

TONY. Well, then— (*Another pause; their eyes meet. And at this moment,* PENNY *is heard from the stairway.*)

PENNY. Is that you, Alice? What time is it? (*She comes into the room, wrapped in a bathrobe.*) Oh! (*In sudden embarrassment.*) Excuse me, Mr. Kirby. I had no idea— that is, I—(*She senses the situation.*)—I didn't mean to interrupt anything.

TONY. Not at all, Mrs. Sycamore.

ALICE (*quietly*). No, mother.

PENNY. I just came down for a manuscript— (*Fumbling at her table.*)—then you can go right ahead. Ah, here it is. "Sex Takes a Holiday." Well—good-night, Mr. Kirby.

TONY. Good-night, Mrs. Sycamore.

PENNY. Oh, I think you can call me Penny, don't you, Alice? At least I hope so. (*With*

a little laugh she vanishes up the stairs.) (*Before* PENNY's *rippling laugh quite die* BANG! *from the cellar.* TONY *jumps.*)

ALICE (*quietly*). It's all right, Tony. That father.

TONY. This time of night?

ALICE (*ominously*). Any time of night. An time of *day.* (*She stands silent. In the paus* TONY *gazes at her fondly.*)

TONY. You're more beautiful, more lovel more adorable than anyone else in the who world.

ALICE (*as he starts to embrace her*). Don Tony. I can't.

TONY. What?

ALICE. I can't, Tony.

TONY. My dear, just because your mother all mothers are like that, Alice, and Penn a darling. You see, I'm even calling h Penny.

ALICE. I don't mean that. (*She faces h squarely.*) Look, Tony. This is somethi I should have said a long time ago, but didn't have the courage. I let myself swept away because—because I loved you

TONY. Darling!

ALICE. No, wait, Tony. I want to make clear to you. You're of a different world whole different kind of people. Oh, I do mean money or socially—that's too silly. P your family and mine—it just would work, Tony. It just wouldn't work. (*Ag an interruption. This time it is* ED *and* ESS *returning from the neighborhood movie.* hear their voices at the door, deep in argument.* ED: "*All right, have it your w She can't dance. That's why they pay her that money—because she can't dance.*" *A then* ESSIE: "*Well, I don't call that danci what she does.*") (*They come into sight.*)

ESSIE. Oh, hello. (*There is an exchange greetings, a note of constraint in* ALI *voice. But* ESSIE *goes right ahead.*) Lo What do *you* think? Ed and I just saw F Astaire and Ginger Rogers. Do you th she can dance, Mr. Kirby?

ɔNY (*mildly taken aback by this*). Why,
ᵉs—I always thought so.

SIE. What does she do, anyhow? Now,
ok—you're Fred Astaire and I'm Ginger
ᵒgers. (*She drapes herself against* TONY, *a
Ginger Rogers.*)

ɪCE. Essie, please.

SIE. I just want to use him for a minute.
. Look, Mr. Kirby— (*Her arms go round
s neck, her cheek against his.*)

ɪCE (*feeling that it's time to take action*).
ᵴsie, you're just as good as Ginger Rogers.
ᵉ all agree.

SIE (*triumphantly*). You see, Ed?

. Yeh. . . . Come on, Essie—we're butting
here.

SIE. Oh, they've been together all evening.
. Good night, Mr. Kirby. (*An exchange
good-nights—it looks as though the* CAR-
ᵻCHAELS *are really going upstairs before
ᵉ whole thing gets too embarrassing. Then
turns casually to* ESSIE *in the doorway.*)

. Essie, did you ask Grandpa about us
ving a baby?

SIE (*as they ascend the stairs*). Yes—he
d go right ahead.

ᵻCE (*when they are gone*). You see? That's
ᵼat it would be like, always.

NY. But I didn't mind that. Besides, dar-
g, we're not going to live with our fami-
ᵴ. It's just you and I.

ᵻCE. No, it isn't—it's never quite that. I
ᵉ them, Tony—I love them deeply. Some
ᵒple could cut away, but I couldn't. I
ᵒw they do rather strange things—I never
ᵒw what to expect next—but they're gay,
d they're fun, and—I don't know—there's
ᵻind of nobility about them. That may
ᵼnd silly, but I mean—the way they just
ᵼ't care about things that other people
ᵉ their whole lives to. They're—really
ᵼnderful, Tony.

ᵼY. Alice, you talk as though only you
ᵼld understand them. That's not true.
ᵼy, I fell in love with them tonight.

ᵼCE. But your family, Tony. I'd want *you*,
l everything about you, everything about

me, to be—one. I couldn't start out with a
part of me that you didn't share, and part
of you that I didn't share. Unless we were
all one—you, and *your* mother and father—
I'd be miserable. And they never can be,
Tony—I know it. They couldn't be.

TONY. Alice, every family has got curious little traits. What of it? My father raises orchids at ten thousand dollars a bulb. Is that
sensible? My mother believes in spiritualism. That's just as bad as your mother writing plays, isn't it?

ALICE. It goes deeper, Tony. Your mother
believes in spiritualism because it's fashionable. And your father raises orchids because
he can afford to. My mother writes plays because eight years ago a typewriter was delivered here by mistake.

TONY. Darling, what *of* it?

ALICE. And look at Grandpa. Thirty-five
years ago he just quit business one day. He
started up to his office in the elevator and
came right down again. He just stopped. He
could have been a rich man, but he said it
took too much time. So for thirty-five years
he's just collected snakes and gone to circuses and commencements. It never occurs
to any of them— (*As if to prove her point,
they are suddenly interrupted at this moment by the entrance of* DONALD *from the
kitchen. It is a* DONALD *who has plainly not
expected to encounter midnight visitors, for
he is simply dressed in a long white nightgown and a somewhat shorter bathrobe—a
costume that permits a generous expanse of
white nightshirt down around the legs, and,
below that, a couple of very black shins. His
appearance, incidentally, explains where all
that music had been coming from, for an
accordion is slung over his shoulder.*)

DONALD (*surprised, but not taken aback*).
Oh, excuse me. I didn't know you folks was
in here.

ALICE (*resigned*). It's all right, Donald.

DONALD. Rheba kind of fancied some candy,
and—(*His gaze is roaming the room.*)—oh,
there it is. (*He picks up* ENNY's *skull, if
you know what we mean.*) You-all don't
want it, do you?

ALICE. No, Donald Go right ahead.

DONALD. Thanks. (*He feels that the occasion calls for certain amenities.*) Have a nice evening?

ALICE. Yes, Donald.

DONALD. Nice dinner?

ALICE (*restraining herself*). Yes, Donald.

DONALD. The ballet nice?

ALICE (*entirely too quietly*). Yes, Donald.

DONALD (*summing it all up*). That's nice. (*He goes—and* ALICE *bursts forth.*)

ALICE. Now! Now do you see what I mean? Could you explain Donald to your father? Could you explain Grandpa? You couldn't, Tony, you couldn't! I should have known! I did know! I love you, Tony, but I love them too! And it's no use, Tony! It's no use! (*She is weeping now in spite of herself.*)

TONY (*quietly*). There's only one thing you've said that matters—that makes any sense at all. You love me.

ALICE. But, Tony, I know so well . . .

TONY. My darling, don't you think other people have had the same problem? Everybody's got a family.

ALICE (*through her tears*). But not like mine.

TONY. That doesn't stop people who love each other. . . . Darling! Darling, won't you trust me, and go on loving me, and forget everything else?

ALICE. How can I?

TONY. Because nothing can keep us apart. You know that. You must know it. Just as I know it. (*He takes her in his arms.*) They want you to be happy, don't they? They *must.*

ALICE. Of course they do. But they can't change, Tony. I wouldn't want them to change.

TONY. They won't have to change. They're charming, lovable people, just as they are. You're worrying about something that may never come up.

ALICE. Oh, Tony, am I?

TONY. All that matters right now is that we love each other. That's right, isn't it?

ALICE (*whispering*). Yes.

TONY. Well, then!

ALICE (*in his arms*). Tony, Tony!

TONY. Now! I'd like to see a little gayet around here. Young gentleman calling, an getting engaged and everything.

ALICE (*smiling up into his face*). What d I say?

TONY. Well, first you thank the young ma for getting engaged to you.

ALICE. Thank you, Mr. Kirby, for getting e gaged to me.

TONY. And then you tell him what it wa about him that first took your girlish hear

ALICE. The back of your head.

TONY. Huh?

ALICE. Uh-huh. It wasn't your charm, and wasn't your money—it was the back of you head. I just happened to like it.

TONY. What happened when I turne around?

ALICE. Oh, I got used to it after a while.

TONY. I see . . . Oh, Alice, think of it. We' pretty lucky, aren't we?

ALICE. I know that *I* am. The luckiest g in the world.

TONY. I'm not exactly unlucky myself.

ALICE. It's wonderful, isn't it?

TONY. Yes . . . Lord, but I'm happy.

ALICE. Are you, Tony?

TONY. Terribly . . . And now—good-nig my dear. Until tomorrow.

ALICE. Good-night.

TONY. Isn't it wonderful we work in t same office? Otherwise I'd be hangi around *here* all day.

ALICE. Won't it be funny in the office tom row—seeing each other and just going as thought nothing had happened?

TONY. Thank God I'm vice-president. I dictate to you all day. "Dear Miss Sy more: I love you, I love you, I love you."

ᴀLICE. Oh, darling! You're such a fool.

ᴛONY (*an arm about her as he starts toward the hallway*). Why don't you meet me in the drugstore in the morning—before you go up to the office? I'll have millions of things to say to you by then.

ᴀLICE. All right.

ᴛONY. And then lunch, and then dinner to-morrow night.

ᴀLICE. Oh, Tony! What will people say?

ᴛONY. It's got to come out some time. In fact, if you know a good housetop, I'd like to do a little shouting. (*She laughs—a happy little ripple. They are out of sight in the hallway by this time; their voices become inaudible.*)

ᴘAUL, *at this point, decides to call it a day down in the cellar. He comes through the door, followed by* ᴍR. ᴅE ᴘINNA. *He is carrying a small metal container, filled with powder.*)

ᴘAUL. Yes, sir, Mr. De Pinna, we did a good day's work.

ᴅE ᴘINNA. That's what. Five hundred Black Panthers, three hundred Willow Trees, and eight dozen Junior Kiddie Bombers. (ᴀLICE *comes back from the hallway, still under the spell of her love.*)

ᴘAUL. Why, hello, Alice. You just come in?

ᴀLICE (*softly*). No. No, I've been home quite a while.

ᴘAUL. Have a nice evening? Say, I'd like you to take a look at this new red fire we've got.

ᴀLICE (*almost singing it*). I had a beautiful evening, father.

ᴘAUL. Will you turn out the lights, Mr. De Pinna? I want Alice to get the full effect.

ᴀLICE (*who hasn't heard a word*). What, father?

ᴘAUL. Take a look at this new red fire. It's beautiful. (ᴍR. ᴅE ᴘINNA *switches the lights out;* ᴘAUL *touches a match to the powder. The red fire blazes, shedding a soft glow over the room.*) There! What do you think of it? Isn't it beautiful?

ᴀLICE (*radiant; her face aglow, her voice soft*). Yes, father. Everything is beautiful. It's the most beautiful red fire in the world! (*She rushes to him and throws her arms about him, almost unable to bear her own happiness.*)

ᴄURTAIN

ACT TWO

A week later, and the family has just risen from the dinner table. Two or three of them have drifted out of the room, but GRANDPA *and* PAUL *still sit over their coffee cups. There is, however, a newcomer in the room. Her name is* GAY WELLINGTON, *and, as we will presently guess, she is an actress, a nymphomaniac, and a terrible souse. At the moment she sits with a gin bottle in one hand and a glass in the other, and is having a darned good time. Hovering over her, script in hand, is a slightly worried* PENNY. ED *is watching the proceedings from somewhere in the vicinage of the printing press, and* DONALD, *leisurely clearing the table, has paused to see if* MISS WELLINGTON *can really swallow that one more drink of gin that she is about to tackle. She does, and another besides.* PENNY *finally decides to make a try.*

ᴘENNY. I'm ready to read the play now, Miss Wellington, if you are.

ᴡELLINTON. Just a minute, dearie—just a minute. (*The gin again.*)

ᴘENNY. The only thing is—I hope you won't mind my mentioning this, but—you don't drink when you're acting, do you, Miss Wellington? I'm just asking, of course.

ᴄAY. I'm glad you brought it up. Once a play opens, I never touch a drop. Minute I enter a stage door, this bottle gets put away till intermission.

ᴄRANDPA (*who plainly has his doubts*). Have you been on the stage a long time, Miss Wellington?

ᴄAY. All my life. I've played everything. Ever see "Peg o' My Heart"?

GRANDPA. Yes, indeed.

GAY (*with that fine logic for which the inebriated brain is celebrated*). I saw it too. Great show. (*She staggers backwards a bit, but recovers herself just in time.*) My! Hot night, ain't it?

DONALD (*ever helpful*). Want me to open a window, Miss Wellington?

GAY. No, the hell with the weather. (*She takes a second look at the dusky* DONALD.) Say, he's cute. (RHEBA, *who has entered just in time to overhear this, gives* GAY *a look that tells her in no uncertain terms to keep out of Harlem on dark nights. Then she stalks back into the kitchen,* DONALD *close on her heels.*)

DONALD (*trying to explain it all*). She's just acting, Rheba. She don't mean anything.

PENNY. Well, any time you're ready, we can go up to my room and start. I thought I'd read the play up in my room.

GAY. All right, dearie, just a minute. (*She starts to pour one more drink, then suddenly her gaze becomes transfixed. She shakes her head as though to dislodge the image, then looks again, receives verification, and starts to pour the gin back into the bottle.*) When I see snakes it's time to lay down. (*She makes for a couch in the corner, and passes right out—cold.*)

PENNY. Oh, but those are real, Miss Wellington. They're Grandpa's. . . . Oh, dear! I hope she's not going to— (*Shaking her.*) Miss Wellington! Miss Wellington!

ED. She's out like a light.

PAUL. Better let her sleep it off.

DONALD (*carrying the news into the kitchen*). Rheba, Miss Wellington just passed out. (*From the nether recesses we hear* RHEBA's *reaction—an emphatic "Good!"*)

PENNY. Do you think she'll be all right?

GRANDPA. Yes, but I wouldn't cast her in the religious play.

PENNY. Well, I suppose I'll just have to wait. I wonder if I shouldn't cover her up.

GRANDPA. Next time you meet an actress on the top of a bus, Penny, I think I'd *send*

her the play, instead of bringing her hom to read it.

ESSIE (*as* ED *starts in with the printin press*). Ed, I wish you'd stop printing an take those Love Dreams around. They'r out in the kitchen.

ED. I will. I just want to finish up these ci culars.

ESSIE. Well, do that later, can't you? You' got to get back in time to play for me whe Kolenkhov comes.

GRANDPA. Kolenkhov coming tonight?

ESSIE. Yes, tomorrow night's his night, b I had to change it on account of Alice.

GRANDPA. Oh! . . . Big doings around he tomorrow night, huh?

PENNY. Isn't it exciting? You know, I'm nervous—you'd think it was me he w engaged to, instead of Alice.

ESSIE. What do you think they'll *be* like— mother and father? . . . Ed, what are y doing *now*?

ED. Penny, did you see the new mask I ma last night? (*He reveals a new side of character by suddenly holding a homema mask before his face.*) Guess who it is.

PENNY. Don't tell me now, Ed. Wait a m ute . . . Cleopatra.

ED (*furious*). It's Mrs. Roosevelt. (*He g into the kitchen.*)

(PAUL, *meanwhile, has gone to a table in corner of the room, from which he brings a steel-like boat model, two or th feet high, puts it down on the floor, proceeds to sit down beside it. From a la cardboard box, which he has also brou with him, he proceeds to take out additio pieces of steel and fit them into the mod*

PAUL. You know, the nice thing about th Erector Sets, you can make so many differ thinks with them. Last week it was the pire State Building.

GRANDPA. What is it this week?

PAUL. The Queen Mary.

PENNY (*looking it over*). Hasn't got right hat on. (ED *comes in from the kitc*

nging a pile of about a dozen candy boxes,
tly wrapped, and tied together for pur-
es of delivery.)

(as MR. DE PINNA comes in from the hall).
ok. Mr. De Pinna, would you open the
r and see if there's a man standing in
nt of the house?

E. Why, what for?

Well, the last two days, when I've been
delivering, I think a man's been follow-
me.

E. Ed, you're crazy.

No, I'm not. He follows me, and he
ds and watches the house.

PINNA. Really? (Striding out.) I'll take
ok and see.

NDPA. I don't see what anybody would
ow *you* for, Ed.

NY. Well, there's a lot of kidnapping go-
on, Grandpa.

NDPA. Yes, but not of Ed.

(as MR. DE PINNA returns from the hall).
l? Did you see him?

PINNA. There's nobody out there at all.

You're sure?

PINNA. Positive. I just saw him walk
y.

You see? I told you.

E. Oh, it might have been anybody, walk-
along the street. Ed, will you hurry and
back?

(picking up his boxes). Oh, all right.

PINNA. Want to go down now, Mr. Syca-
e, and finish packing up the fireworks?

L (putting the Queen Mary back on the
). Yeh, we've got to take the stuff up
Mt. Vernon in the morning. (They go
the cellar. Simultaneously the voice of
E, happily singing, is heard as she de-
ds the stairs.)

E. Mother, may I borrow some paper?
making out a list for Rheba tomorrow
t.

PENNY. Yes, dear. Here's some.

ALICE (as she sights MISS WELLINGTON).
Why, what happened to your actress friend?
Is she giving a performance?

PENNY. No, she's not acting, Alice. She's
really drunk.

ALICE. Essie, you're going to give Rheba the
kitchen all day tomorrow, aren't you? Because she'll need it.

ESSIE. Of course, Alice. I'm going to start
some Love Dreams now, so I'll be 'way
ahead. (She goes into the kitchen.)

ALICE. Thanks, dear . . . Look, mother, I'm
coming home at three o'clock tomorrow.
Will you have everything down in the cellar
by that time? The typewriter, and the
snakes, and the xylophone, and the printing
press . . .

GRANDPA. And Miss Wellington.

ALICE. And Miss Wellington. That'll give
me time to arrange the table, and fix the
flowers.

GRANDPA. The Kirbys are certainly going to
get the wrong impression of this house.

ALICE. You'll *do* all that, won't you, mother?

PENNY. Of course, dear.

ALICE. And I think we'd better have cocktails ready by seven-fifteen, in case they happen to come a little early. . . . I wonder if
I ought to let Rheba cook the dinner. What
do you think, Grandpa?

GRANDPA. Now, Alice, I wouldn't worry.
From what I've seen of the boy I'm sure
the Kirbys are very nice people, and if
everything isn't so elaborate tomorrow night,
it's all right too.

ALICE. Darling, I'm not trying to impress
them, or pretend we're anything that we
aren't. I just want everything to—to go
off well.

GRANDPA. No reason why it shouldn't, Alice.

PENNY. We're all going to do everything we
can to make it a nice party.

ALICE. Oh, my darlings, I love you. You're
the most wonderful family in the world,

and I'm the happiest girl in the world. I didn't know anyone could *be* so happy. He's so wonderful, Grandpa. Why, just seeing him—you don't know what it does to me.

GRANDPA. Just seeing him. Just seeing him for lunch, and dinner, and until four o'clock in the morning, and at nine o'clock *next* morning you're at the office again and there he is. You just see him, huh?

ALICE. I don't care! I'm in love. (*She swings open the kitchen door.*) Rheba! Rheba! (*She goes into the kitchen.*)

GRANDPA. Nice, isn't it? Nice to see her so happy.

PENNY. I remember when I was engaged to Paul—how happy I was. And you know, I still feel that way.

GRANDPA. I know . . . Nice the way Ed and Essie get along too, isn't it?

PENNY. And Donald and Rheba, even though they're *not* married. . . . Do you suppose Mr. De Pinna will ever marry anyone, Grandpa?

GRANDPA (*a gesture toward the couch*). Well, there's Miss Wellington.

PENNY. Oh, dear, I *wish* she'd wake up. If we're going to read the play tonight— (MR. DE PINNA *comes up from the cellar, bringing along a rather large-sized unframed painting.*)

DE PINNA. Mrs. Sycamore, look what I found! (*He turns the canvas around, revealing a portrait of a somewhat lumpy discus thrower, in Roman costume—or was it Greek?*) Remember?

PENNY. Why, of course. It's my painting of you as The Discus Thrower. Look, Grandpa.

GRANDPA. I remember it. Say, you've gotten a little bald, haven't you, Mr. De Pinna?

DE PINNA (*running a hand over his completely hairless head*). Is it very noticeable?

PENNY. Well, it was a long time ago—just before I stopped painting. Let me see—that's eight years.

DE PINNA. Too bad you never finished it, Mrs. Sycamore.

PENNY. I always meant to finish it, Mr. [De] Pinna, but I just started to write a play o[ne] day and that was that. I never painted aga[in.]

GRANDPA. Just as well, too. *I* was going [to] have to strip next.

DE PINNA (*meditatively*). Who would ha[ve] thought, that day I came to deliver the i[ce] that I was going to stay here for eight year[s.]

GRANDPA. The milkman was here for fi[ve,] just ahead of you.

DE PINNA. Why did he leave, anyhow? I f[or]get.

GRANDPA. He didn't leave. He died.

PENNY. He was such a nice man. Rememb[er] the funeral, Grandpa? We never knew [his] name and it was kind of hard to get a c[er]tificate.

GRANDPA. What was the name we fina[lly] made up for him?

PENNY. Martin Vanderhof. We gave h[im] *your* name.

GRANDPA. Oh, yes, I remember.

PENNY. It was a lovely thought, beca[use] otherwise he never would have got all th[ose] flowers.

GRANDPA. Certainly was. And it didn't h[urt] me any. Not bothered with mail any m[ore,] and I haven't had a telephone call from t[hat] day to this. (*He catches an unwary fly [and] drops it casually into the snake solariu[m.]*)

PENNY. Yes, it was really a wonderful id[ea.]

DE PINNA (*with the picture*). I wish yo[u'd] finish this sometime, Mrs. Sycamore. [I] kind of like to have it.

PENNY. You know what, Mr. De Pinna[? I] think I'll do some work on it. Right [to]night.

DE PINNA. Say! Will you? (*The door [bell] rings.*)

PENNY (*peering at the prostrate* GAY). [I] don't think she's going to wake up anyh[ow] . . . Look, Mr. De Pinna! You go d[own] in the cellar and bring up the easel and [get] into your costume. Is it still down there[?]

DE PINNA (*excited*). I think so! (*He [goes] into the cellar.*)

NY. Now, where did I put my palette brushes? (*She dashes up the stairs as voice of* KOLENKHOV *is heard at the door, ming, of course.*)

ENKHOV. Rhebishka! My little Rhebish-

BA (*delighted, as usual*). Yassuh, Mr. enkhov!

NY (*as she goes up the stairs*). Hello, Kolenkhov. Essie's in the kitchen.

ENKHOV. Madame Sycamore, I greet you! s great arm again encircling RHEBA, he s her protestingly into the room.) Tell Grandpa—what should I do about Rhe-ka! I keep telling her she would make eat toe dancer, but she laughs only!

BA (*breaking away*). No, suh! I couldn't up on my toes, Mr. Kolenkhov! I got s! (*She goes into the kitchen.*)

ENKHOV (*calling after her*). Rhebishka, could wear diamonds! (*Suddenly he ts the portrait of* MR. DE PINNA.) What hat?

IDPA (*who has taken up his stamp album n*). It's a picture of Mr. De Pinna. ny painted it.

ENKHOV (*summing it up*). It stinks.

IDPA. I know. (*He indicates the figure he couch.*) How do you like that?

ENKHOV (*peering over*). What is *that*?

IDPA. She's an actress. Friend of Penny's.

ENKHOV. She is drunk—no?

IDPA. She is drunk—yes. . . . How are Kolenkhov?

ENKHOV. Magnificent! Life is chasing nd inside of me, like a squirrel.

IDPA. 'Tis, huh? . . . What's new in Rus- Any more letters from your friend in cow?

ENKHOV. I have just heard from him. I d for you the stamp. (*He hands it over.*)

IDPA (*receiving it with delight*). Thanks, nkhov.

ENKHOV. They have sent him to Siberia.

GRANDPA. That so? How's he like it?

KOLENKHOV. He has escaped and gone back to Moscow. He will get them yet, if they do not get him. The Soviet Government! I could take the whole Soviet Government and—grrah! (*He crushes Stalin and all in one great paw, just as* ESSIE *comes in from the kitchen.*)

ESSIE. I'm sorry I'm late, Mr. Kolenkhov. I'll get into my dancing clothes right away.

KOLENKHOV. Tonight you will really work, Pavlowa. (*As* ESSIE *goes up the stairs.*) To-night we will take something new.

GRANDPA. Essie making any progress, Kolen-khov?

KOLENKHOV (*first making elaborately sure that* ESSIE *is gone.*) Confidentially, she stinks.

GRANDPA. Well, as long as she's having fun. . . . (DONALD *ambles in from the kitchen, chuckling.*)

DONALD. You sure do tickle Rheba, Mr. Kolenkhov. She's laughing her head off out there.

KOLENKHOV. She is a great woman. . . . Donald, what do you think of the Soviet Government?

DONALD. The what, Mr. Kolenkhov?

KOLENKHOV. I withdraw the question. What do you think of *this* Government?

DONALD. Oh, I like it fine. I'm on relief, you know.

KOLENKHOV. Oh, yes. And you like it?

DONALD. Yassuh, it's fine. Only thing is you got to go round to the place every week and collect it, and sometimes you got to stand in line pretty near half an hour. Gov-ernment ought to be run better than that —don't you think, Grandpa?

GRANDPA (*as he fishes an envelope out of his pocket*). Government ought to stop sending me letters. Want me to be at the United States Marshal's office Tuesday morning at ten o'clock.

KOLENKHOV (*peering at the letter*). Ah! In-come tax! They have got you, Grandpa.

GRANDPA. Mm. I'm supposed to give 'em a lot of money so as to keep Donald on relief.

DONALD. You don't say, Grandpa? You going to pay it now?

GRANDPA. That's what they want.

DONALD. You mean I can come right *here* and get it instead of standing in that line?

GRANDPA. No, Donald. You will have to waste a full half hour of your time every week.

DONALD. Well, I don't like it. It breaks up my week. (*He goes into the kitchen.*)

KOLENKHOV. He should have been in Russia when the Revolution came. Then he would have stood in line—a bread line. (*He turns to* GRANDPA.) Ah, Grandpa, what they have done to Russia. Think of it! The Grand Duchess Olga Katrina, a cousin of the Czar, she is a waitress in Childs' restaurant! I ordered baked beans from her only yesterday. It broke my heart. A crazy world, Grandpa.

GRANDPA. Oh, the world's not so crazy, Kolenkhov. It's the people *in* it. Life's pretty simple if you just relax.

KOLENKHOV. How can you relax in times like these?

GRANDPA. Well, if they'd relaxed there wouldn't *be* times like these. That's just my point. Life is simple and kind of beautiful if you let it come to you. But the trouble is, people forget that. I know I did. I was right in the thick of it—fighting, and scratching, and clawing. Regular jungle. One day it just kind of struck me. I wasn't having any fun.

KOLENKHOV. So you did what?

GRANDPA. Just relaxed. Thirty-five years ago, that was. And I've been a happy man ever since. (*From somewhere or other* GRANDPA *has brought one of those colored targets that one buys at Schwartz's. He now hangs it up on the cellar door, picks up a handful of feathered darts, and carefully throws one at the target.*)
(*At the same time* ALICE *passes through the room, en route from kitchen to the upstairs region.*)

ALICE. Good evening, Mr. Kolenkhov.

KOLENKHOV (*bowing low over her han*... Ah, Miss Alice! I have not seen you to p... sent my congratulations. May you be v... happy and have many children. That is prayer for you.

ALICE. Thank you, Mr. Kolenkhov. Th... quite a thought. (*Singing gayly, she g... up the stairs.*)

KOLENKHOV (*looking after her*). Ah, l... That is all that is left in the world, Gran...

GRANDPA. Yes, but there's plenty of that.

KOLENKHOV. And soon Stalin will take t... away, too. I tell you, Grandpa— (*He stop*... PENNY *comes down the stairs—a living*... *ample of what the well-dressed artist sho*... *wear. She has on an artist's smock over*... *dress, a flowing black tie, and a large bl*... *velvet tam-o'-shanter, worn at a rakish an*... *She carries a palette and an assortmen*... *paints and brushes.*)

PENNY. Seems so nice to get into my things again. They still look all right, d... they, Grandpa?

GRANDPA. Yes, indeed.

KOLENKHOV. You are a breath of Paris, ... dame Sycamore.

PENNY. Oh, thank you, Mr. Kolenkhov...

DONALD (*coming in from the kitchen*... didn't know you was working for the W...

PENNY. Oh, no, Donald. You see, I used... paint all the time, and then one day— (... *outer door slams and* ED *comes in.*)

ED (*in considerable excitement*). It happe... again! There was a fellow following every place I went!

PENNY. Nonsense, Ed. It's your imaginat...

ED. No, it isn't. It happens every time I... out to deliver candy.

GRANDPA. Maybe he wants a piece of ca...

ED. It's all right for you to laugh, Gran... but he keeps following me.

KOLENKHOV (*somberly*). You do not k... what following is. In Russia *everybod*... followed. I was followed right out of Ru...

PENNY. Of course. You see, Ed—the w... thing is just imagination. (MR. DE PI...

…es up from the cellar, ready for posing. … wears the traditional Roman costume, … he certainly cuts a figure. He is carrying NY's easel, a discus, and a small plat-… for posing purposes.) Ah, here we are! … Right here, Mr. De Pinna.

…ALD (*suddenly getting it*). Oh, is that …ure supposed to be Mr. De Pinna?

…NY (*sharply*). Of course it is, Donald. …at's it look like—me?

…ALD (*studying the portrait*). Yes, it does … little bit.

…NY. Nonsense! What would I be doing … a discus?

…ENKHOV. Ed, for tonight's lesson we use … first movement of Scheherazade.

…Okay.

…INNA (*about to mount the platform*). I … I haven't forgotten how to pose. (*He …s up the discus and strikes the classic … of the Discus Thrower. Somehow, it …t quite convincing.*)

…ALD. What's he going to do with that …g? Throw it?

…NY. No, no, Donald. He's just posing. … Mr. De Pinna, has something happened …our figure during these eight years?

…INNA (*pulling in his stomach*). No, I …t think it's any different. (*With a sud-…snort,* GAY WELLINGTON *comes to.*)

…NY (*immediately alert*). Yes, Miss Well-…on? (*For answer,* GAY *peers first at* …NY, *then at* MR. DE PINNA. *Then, with a* …ge snort, she just passes right out …n.*)

…NY. Oh, dear. (ESSIE *comes tripping* …n the stairs—very much the ballet dan-… She is in full costume—ballet skirt, tight … satin bodice, a garland of roses in her …*)

…. Sorry, Mr. Kolenkhov, I couldn't find … slippers.

…NKHOV (*having previously removed his* … he now takes off his shirt, displaying …normous hairy chest beneath his under-…*). We have a hot night for it, my …owa, but art is only achieved through …iration.

PENNY. Why, that's wonderful, Mr. Kolen-khov. Did you hear that, Grandpa—art is only achieved through perspiration.

GRANDPA. Yes, but it helps if you've got a little talent with it. (*He returns to his dart throwing.*) Only made two bull's-eyes last night. Got to do better than that. (*He hurls a dart at the board, then his eye travels to* MISS WELLINGTON, *whose posterior offers an even easier target.*) Mind if I use Miss Well-ington, Penny?

PENNY. What, Grandpa?

GRANDPA (*shakes his head*). Never mind. . . . Too easy. (GRANDPA *throws another dart at the target.*)

KOLENKHOV. You are ready? We begin! (*With a gesture he orders the music started; under* KOLENKHOV's *critical eye* ESSIE *begins the mazes of the dance.*) Foutte temp el levee. (ESSIE *obliges with her own idea of foutte temp el levee.*) Pirouette! . . . Come, come! You can do that! It's eight years now. Pirouette! . . . At last . . . Entre chat . . . Entre chat! (ESSIE *leaps into the air, her feet twirling.*) No, Grandpa, you cannot relax with Stalin in Russia. The Czar relaxed, and what happened to *him?*

GRANDPA. He was too late.

ESSIE (*still leaping away*). Mr. Kolenkhov! Mr. Kolenkhov!

KOLENKHOV. If he had not relaxed the Grand Duchess Olga Katrina would not be selling baked beans today.

ESSIE (*imploringly*). Mr. Kolenkhov!

KOLENKHOV. I am sorry. (*The door bell rings.*) We go back to the pirouette.

PENNY. Could you pull in your stomach, Mr. De Pinna? . . . That's right.

KOLENKHOV. A little freer. A little freer with the hands. The whole body must work. Ed, help us with the music. The music must be free, too. (*By way of guiding* ED, KOLEN-KHOV *hums the music at the pace that it should go. He is even pirouetting a bit him-self.*)
(*From the front door comes the murmur of voices, not quite audible over the music. Then the stunned figure of* RHEBA *comes into the archway, her eyes popping.*)

RHEBA. Mrs. Sycamore. . . . Mrs. Sycamore. (*With a gesture that has a grim foreboding in it, she motions toward the still invisible reason for her panic.*)

(*There is a second's pause, and then the reason is revealed in all its horror. The* KIRBYS *in full evening dress, stand in the archway. All three of them.* MR. and MRS. KIRBY, *and* TONY.)

(PENNY *utters a stifled gasp; the others are too stunned even to do that. Their surprise at seeing the* KIRBYS, *however, is no greater than that of the* KIRBYS *at the sight that is spread before them.*)

(GRANDPA, *alone of them all, rises to the situation. With a kind of old world grace, he puts away his darts and makes the guests welcome.*)

GRANDPA. How do you do?

KIRBY (*uncertainly*). How do you do? (*Not that it helps any, but* MR. DE PINNA *is squirming into his bathrobe,* KOLENKHOV *is thrusting his shirt into his trousers, and* ED *is hastily getting into his coat.*)

TONY. Are we too early?

GRANDPA. No, no. It's perfectly all right— we're glad to see you.

PENNY (*getting rid of the smock and tam*). Why—yes. Only—we thought it was to be tomorrow night.

MRS. KIRBY. Tomorrow night!

KIRBY. What!

GRANDPA. Now, it's perfectly all right. Please sit right down and make yourselves at home. (*His eyes still on the* KIRBYS, *he gives* DONALD *a good push toward the kitchen, by way of a hint.* DONALD *goes, promptly, with a quick little stunned whistle that sums up HIS feelings.*)

KIRBY. Tony, how could you possibly—

TONY. I—I don't know. I thought—

MRS. KIRBY. Really, Tony! This is most embarrassing.

GRANDPA. Not at all. Why, we weren't doing a thing.

PENNY. Just spending the evening at home.

GRANDPA. That's all. . . . Now don't let it bother you. This is Alice's mother, Mrs.

Sycamore . . . Alice's sister, Mrs. Carmicha[el] . . . Mr. Carmichael. . . . Mr. Kolenkhov. . (*At this point* MR. DE PINNA *takes an ant[ici]patory step forward, and* GRANDPA *is prac[ti]cally compelled to perform the introdu[c]tion.*) And—Mr. De Pinna. Mr. De Pin[na] would you tell Mr. Sycamore to come ri[ght] up? Tell him that Mr. and Mrs. Kirby [are] here.

PENNY (*her voice a heavy whisper*). And [be] sure to put his pants on.

DE PINNA (*whispering right back*). [All] right. . . . Excuse me. (*He vanishes—di[s]* and all.*)

GRANDPA. Won't you sit down?

PENNY (*first frantically trying to cover [the] prostrate* GAY WELLINGTON). I'll tell Al[ice] that you're— (*She is at the foot of [the] stairs.*) —Alice! Alice, dear! (*The voice [of]* ALICE *from above, "What is it?"*) Al[ice] will you come down, dear? We've go[t a] surprise for you. (*She comes back into [the] room, summoning all her charm.*) Well!

GRANDPA. Mrs. Kirby, may I take your wra[p?]

MRS. KIRBY. Well—thank you. If you're [per]fectly sure that we're not— (*Suddenly [she] sees the snakes and lets out a scream.*)

GRANDPA. Oh, don't be alarmed, Mrs. Ki[rby.] They're perfectly harmless.

MRS. KIRBY (*edging away from the so[lar]ium*). Thank you. (*She sinks into a ch[air] weakly.*)

GRANDPA. Ed, take 'em into the kitc[hen.] (*Ed at once obeys.*)

PENNY. Of course we're so used to t[hem] around the house—

MRS. KIRBY. I'm sorry to trouble you, [but] snakes happen to be the one thing—

KIRBY. I feel very uncomfortable ab[out] this. Tony, how could you have done su[ch a] thing?

TONY. I'm sorry, Dad. I thought it was [to]night.

KIRBY. It was very careless of you. *Ver[y]*

GRANDPA. Now, now Mr. Kirby—we're [de]lighted.

NY. Oh, now, anybody can get mixed up,
, Kirby.

NDPA. Penny, how about some dinner for
se folks? They've come for dinner, you
w.

. KIRBY. Oh, please don't bother. We're
ly not hungry at all.

NY. But it's not a bit of bother. Ed!—
r voice drops to a loud whisper.) Ed,
Donald to run down to the A. and P.
get half a dozen bottles of beer, and—
—some canned salmon— (*Her voice
es up again.*) —do you like canned sal-
, Mr. Kirby?

BY. Please don't trouble, Mrs. Sycamore.
ave a little indigestion, anyway.

NY. Oh, I'm sorry . . . How about you,
. Kirby? Do you like canned salmon?

. KIRBY (*you just know that she hates*
Oh, I'm very fond of it.

NY. You can have frankfurters if you'd
er.

. KIRBY (*regally*). Either one will do.

NY (*to* ED *again*). Well, make it frank-
rs, and some canned corn, and Camp-
s Soup.

going out the kitchen door). Okay!

NY (*calling after him*). And tell him to
ry! (PENNY *again addresses the* KIRBYS.)
 A. and P. is just at the corner, and
kfurters don't take *any* time to boil.

NDPA (*as* PAUL *comes through the cellar
*). And this is Alice's father, *Mr. Syca-
e. Mr. and Mrs. Kirby.

KIRBYS. How do you do?

. I hope you'll forgive my appearance.

NY. This is Mr. Sycamore's busiest time
e year. Just before the Fourth of July—
d then ALICE *comes down. She is a step
the room before she realizes what has
ened; then she fairly freezes in her
s.*)

. Oh!

. Darling, will you ever forgive me? I'm
most dull-witted person in the world. I
ght it was tonight.

ALICE (*staggered*). Why, Tony, I thought
you— (*To the* KIRBYS.) —I'm so sorry—I
can't imagine—why, I wasn't—have you all
met each other?

KIRBY. Yes, Indeed.

MRS. KIRBY. How do you do, Alice?

ALICE (*not even yet in control of herself*).
How do you do, Mrs. Kirby? I'm afraid
I'm not very—presentable.

TONY. Darling, you look lovely.

KIRBY. Of course she does. Don't let this upset you, my dear—we've all just met each
other a night sooner, that's all.

MRS. KIRBY. Of course.

ALICE. But I was planning such a nice party
tomorrow night . . .

KIRBY (*being the good fellow*). Well, we'll
come again tomorrow night.

TONY. There you are, Alice. Am I forgiven?

ALICE. I guess so. It's just that I—we'd better
see about getting you some dinner.

PENNY. Oh, that's all done, Alice. That's all
been attended to. (DONALD, *hat in hand,
comes through the kitchen door; hurries
across the room and out the front way. The
KIRBYS graciously pretend not to see.*)

ALICE. But mother—what are you—what did
you send out for? Because Mr. Kirby suffers
from indigestion—he can only eat certain
things.

KIRBY. Now, it's quite all right.

TONY. Of course it is, darling.

PENNY. I asked him what he wanted, Alice.

ALICE (*doubtfully*). Yes, but—

KIRBY. Now, now, it's not as serious as all
that. Just because I have a little indigestion.

KOLENKHOV (*helping things along*). Perhaps
it is not indigestion at all, Mr. Kirby. Perhaps you have stomach ulcers.

ALICE. Don't be absurd, Mr. Kolenkhov!

GRANDPA. You mustn't mind Mr. Kolenkhov,
Mr. Kirby. He's a Russian, and Russians are
inclined to look on the dark side.

KOLENKHOV. All right, I am a Russian. But a friend of mine, a Russian, *died* from stomach ulcers.

KIRBY. Really, I—

ALICE (*desperately*). Please, Mr. Kolenkhov! Mr. Kirby has indigestion and that's all.

KOLENKHOV (*with a Russian shrug of the shoulders*). All right. Let him wait.

GRANDPA (*leaping into the breach*). Tell me, Mr. Kirby, how do you find business conditions? Are we pretty well out of the depression?

KIRBY. What? . . . Yes, yes, I think so. Of course, it all depends.

GRANDPA. But you figure that things are going to keep on improving?

KIRBY. Broadly speaking, yes. As a matter of fact, industry is now operating at sixty-four per cent. of full capacity, as against eighty-two per cent. in 1925. Of course in 1929, a peak year— (*Peak year or no peak year,* GAY WELLINGTON *chooses this moment to come to life. With a series of assorted snorts, she throws the cover back and pulls herself to a sitting position, blinking uncertainly at the assemblage. Then she rises, and weaves unsteadily across the room. The imposing figure of* MR. KIRBY *intrigues her.*)

GAY (*playfully rumpling* MR. KIRBY's *hair as she passes him.*) Hello, Cutie. (*And with that she lunges on her way—up the stairs.*) (*The* KIRBYS, *of course, are considerably astounded by this exhibition; the* SYCAMORES *have watched it with varying degrees of frozen horror.* ALICE, *in particular, is speechless; it is* GRANDPA *who comes to her rescue.*)

GRANDPA. That may seem a little strange to you, but she's not quite accountable for her actions. A friend of Mrs. Sycamore's. She came to dinner and was overcome by the heat.

PENNY. Yes, some people feel it, you know, more than others. Perhaps I'd better see if she's all right. Excuse me, please. (*She goes hastily up the stairs.*)

ALICE. It *is* awfully hot. (*A fractional pause.*) You usually escape all this hot weather, don't you, Mrs. Kirby? Up in Maine?

MRS. KIRBY (*on the frigid side*). As a ru I had to come down this week, howev for the Flower Show.

TONY. Mother wouldn't miss that for world. That blue ribbon is the high spot her year.

ESSIE. I won a ribbon at a Flower Show on For raising onions. Remember?

ALICE (*quickly*). That was a Garden Sho Essie.

ESSIE. Oh, yes. (PENNY *comes bustling do the stairs again.*)

PENNY. I'm so sorry, but I think she'll right now. . . . Has Donald come back y

ALICE. No, he hasn't.

PENNY. Well, he'll be right back, and won't take any time at all. I'm afraid must be starved.

KIRBY. Oh, no. Quite all right. (*Pacing room, he suddenly comes upon* PAUL's *E tor Set.*) Hello! What's this? I didn't kn there were little children in the house.

PAUL. Oh, no. That's mine.

KIRBY. Really? Well, I suppose every n has his hobby. Or do you use this as a m of some kind?

PAUL. No, I just play with it.

KIRBY. I see.

TONY. Maybe you'd be better off if *you* a hobby like that, Dad. Instead of rai orchids.

KIRBY (*indulgently*). Yes, I wouldn't be prised.

ALICE (*leaping on this as a safe topic*). do tell us about your orchids, Mr. Ki (*She addresses the others.*) You know, take six years before they blossom. Thin that!

KIRBY (*warming to his subject*). Oh, s of them take longer than that. I've got coming along now that I've waited ten y for.

PENNY (*making a joke*). Believe it or n was waiting for an orchid.

KIRBY. Ah—yes. Of course during that time
they require the most scrupulous care. I
remember a bulb that I was very fond of—

(DONALD *suddenly bulges through the archway, his arms full. The tops of beer bottles
and two or three large cucumbers peep over
the edge of the huge paper bags.*)

PENNY. Ah, here we are! Did you get everything, Donald?

DONALD. Yes'm. Only the frankfurters didn't
look very good, so I got pickled pigs' feet.
(MR. KIRBY *blanches at the very idea.*)

ALICE (*taking command*). Never mind,
Donald—just bring everything into the
kitchen. (*She turns at the kitchen door.*)
Mr. Kirby, please tell them *all* about the
orchids—I know they'd love to hear it. And
excuse me. (*She goes.*)

GRANDPA. Kind of an expensive hobby, isn't
it, Mr. Kirby—raising orchids?

KIRBY. Yes, it is, but I feel that if a hobby
gives one sufficient pleasure, it's never expensive.

GRANDPA. That's very true.

KIRBY. You see, I need something to relieve
the daily nerve strain. After a week in Wall
Street I'd go crazy if I didn't have something
like that. Lot of men I know have yachts—
just for that very reason.

GRANDPA (*mildly*). Why don't they give up
Wall Street?

KIRBY. How's that?

GRANDPA. I was just joking.

MRS. KIRBY. I think it's necessary for everyone to have a hobby. Of course it's more to
me than a hobby, but my great solace is—
spiritualism.

PENNY. Now, Mrs. Kirby, don't tell me you
fall for that. Why, everybody knows it's a
fake.

MRS. KIRBY (*freezing*). To me, Mrs. Sycamore, spiritualism is—I would rather not
discuss it, Mrs. Sycamore.

PAUL. Remember, Penny, you've got one or
two hobbies of your own.

PENNY. Yes, but not silly ones.

GRANDPA (*with a little cough*). I don't think
it matters what the hobby is—the important
thing. is to have one.

KOLENKHOV. To be ideal, a hobby should
improve the body as well as the mind. The
Romans were a great people! Why! What
was their hobby? Wrestling. In wrestling
you have to think quick with the mind and
act quick with the body.

KIRBY. Yes, but I'm afraid wrestling is not
very practical for most of us. (*He gives a
deprecating little laugh.*) I wouldn't make
a very good showing as a wrestler.

KOLENKHOV. You could be a *great* wrestler.
You are built for it. Look! (*With a startling-
ly quick movement* KOLENKHOV *grabs* MR.
KIRBY's *arms, knocks his legs from under
him with a quick movement of a foot, and
presto!* MR. KIRBY *is flat on his whatsis. Not
only that, but instantaneously* KOLENKHOV
is on top of him.)

(*Just at this moment* ALICE *re-enters the
room—naturally, she stands petrified. Several people, of course, rush immediately to
the rescue,* TONY *and* PAUL *arriving at the
scene of battle first. Amidst the general confusion they help* MR. KIRBY *to his feet.*)

ALICE. Mr. Kirby! Are you—hurt?

TONY. Are you all right, father?

KIRBY (*pulling himself together*). I—I—
uh— (*He blinks, uncertainly.*) —where are
my glasses?

ALICE. Here they are, Mr. Kirby. . . . Oh, Mr.
Kirby, they're broken.

KOLENKHOV (*full of apology*). Oh, I am
sorry. But when you wrestle again, Mr. Kirby, you will of course not wear glasses.

KIRBY (*coldly furious*). I do not intend to
wrestle again, Mr. Kolenkhov. (*He draws
himself up, stiffly, and in return gets a sharp
pain in the back. He gives a little gasp.*)

TONY. Better sit down, father.

ALICE. Mr. Kolenkhov, how could you do
such a thing? Why didn't somebody stop
him?

MRS. KIRBY. I think, if you don't mind, perhaps we had better be going.

TONY. Mother!

ALICE (*close to tears*). Oh, Mrs. Kirby—please! Please don't go! Mr. Kirby—please! I—I've ordered some scrambled eggs for you, and—plain salad—Oh, please don't go!

KOLENKHOV. I am sorry if I did something wrong. And I apologize.

ALICE. I can't tell you how sorry I am, Mr. Kirby. If I'd been here—

KIRBY (*from a great height*). That's quite all right.

TONY. Of course it is. It's all right, Alice. We're not going. (*The* KIRBYS *reluctantly sit down again.*)
(*A moment's silence—no one knows quite what to say.*)

PENNY (*brightly*). Well! That was exciting for a minute, wasn't it?

GRANDPA (*quickly*). You were talking about your orchids, Mr. Kirby. Do you raise many different varieties?

KIRBY (*still unbending*). I'm afraid I've quite forgotten about my orchids. (*More silence, and everyone very uncomfortable.*)

ALICE. I'm—awfully sorry, Mr. Kirby.

KOLENKHOV (*exploding*). What did I do that was so terrible? I threw him on the floor! Did it kill him?

ALICE. Please, Mr. Kolenkhov. (*An annoyed gesture from* KOLENKHOV; *another general pause.*)

PENNY. I'm sure dinner won't be any time at all now. (*A pained smile from* MRS. KIRBY.)

ESSIE. Would you like some candy while you're waiting? I've got some freshly made.

KIRBY. My doctor does not permit me to eat candy. Thank you.

ESSIE. But these are nothing, Mr. Kirby. Just cocoanut and marshmallow fudge.

ALICE. Don't, Essie. (RHEBA *appears in the kitchen doorway, beckoning violently to* ALICE.)

RHEBA (*in a loud whisper*). Miss Alice! Miss Alice! (ALICE *quickly flies to* RHEBA's *side.*) The eggs fell down the sink.

ALICE (*desperately*). Make some mo[re]. Quick!

RHEBA. I ain't got any.

ALICE. Send Donald out for some!

RHEBA (*disappearing*). All right.

ALICE (*calling after her*). Tell him to ru[n]. (*She turns back to the* KIRBYS.) I'm so sor[ry]. There'll be a little delay, but everything w[ill] be ready in just a minute. (*At this mom[ent]* DONALD *fairly shoots out of the kitchen d[oor] and across the living room, beating [the] Olympic record for all time.*)
(PENNY *tries to ease the situation with a g[ay] little laugh. It doesn't quite come off, h[ow]ever.*)

TONY. I've certainly put you people to a [lot] of trouble, with my stupidity.

GRANDPA. Not at all, Tony.

PENNY. Look! Why don't we play a game [of] some sort while we're waiting?

TONY. Oh, that'd be fine.

ALICE. Mother, I don't think Mr. and M[rs.] Kirby—

KOLENKHOV. *I* have an idea. I know a w[on]derful trick with a glass of water. (*[He] reaches for a full glass that stands on [the] table.*)

ALICE (*quickly*). No, Mr. Kolenkhov.

GRANDPA (*shaking his head*). No-o.

PENNY. But I'm sure Mr. and Mrs. Ki[rby] would love this game. It's perfectly harml[ess].

ALICE. Please, mother. . . .

KIRBY. I'm not very good at games, M[rs.] Sycamore.

PENNY. Oh, but *any* fool could play [this] game, Mr. Kirby. (*She is bustling arou[nd] getting paper and pencil.*) All you d[o is] write your name on a piece of paper—

ALICE. But mother, Mr. Kirby doesn't wa[nt]—

PENNY. Oh, he'll love it! (*Goes right [on.]* Here you are, Mr. Kirby. Write your n[ame] on this piece of paper. And Mrs. Kirby, [you] do the same on this one.

ALICE. Mother, what *is* this game?

NY. I used to play it at school. It's called
get-Me-Not. Now, I'm going to call out
words—just anything at all—and as I
each word, you're to put down the first
ng that comes into your mind. Is that
r? For instance, if I say "grass," you
ght put down "green"—just whatever you
k of, see? Or if I call out "chair," you
ght put down "table." It shows the reac-
s people have to different things. You
how simple it is, Mr. Kirby?

Y. Come on, father! Be a sport!

BY (*stiffly*). Very well. I shall be happy
lay it.

NY. You see, Alice? He *does* want to
.

CE (*uneasily*). Well—

NY. Now, then! Are we ready?

ENKHOV. Ready!

NY. Now, remember—you must play
Put down the first thing that comes into
r mind.

Y (*pencil poised*). I understand.

NY. Everybody ready? ... The first word
potatoes." (*She repeats it.*) "Potatoes."
Ready for the next one? ... "Bathroom."
CE *shifts rather uneasily, but seeing that
one else seems to mind, she relaxes
n.*) Got that?

ENKHOV. Go ahead.

NY. All ready? ... "Lust."

E. Mother, this is not exactly what you—

NY. Nonsense, Alice—that word's all
t.

E. Mother, it's *not* all right.

KIRBY (*unexpectedly*). Oh, I don't
. It seems to me that's a perfectly fair
.

Y (*to* ALICE). You see? Now, you
n't interrupt the game.

. May I have that last word again,
e?

Y. "Lust," Mr. Kirby.

(*writing*). I've got it.

PA. This is quite a game.

PENNY. Sssh, Grandpa. ... All ready? ...
"Honeymoon." (ESSIE *snickers a little, which
is all it takes to start* PENNY *off. Then she
suddenly remembers herself.*) Now, Essie!
... All right. The last word is "sex."

ALICE (*under her breath*). Mother!

PENNY. Everybody got "sex?" ... All right
—now give me all the papers.

GRANDPA. What happens now?

PENNY. Oh, this is the best part. Now I read
out your reactions.

KIRBY. I see. It's really quite an interesting
game.

PENNY. I knew you'd like it. I'll read your
paper first, Mr. Kirby. (*To the others.*) I'm
going to read Mr. Kirby's paper first. Listen,
everybody! This is Mr. Kirby. ... "Potatoes
—steak." That's very good. See how they
go together? Steak and potatoes?

KIRBY (*modestly, but obviously pleased with
himself*). I just happened to think of it.

PENNY. It's *very* good. ... "Bathroom—
toothpaste." Uh-huh. "Lust—unlawful."
Isn't that nice? "Honeymoon—trip." Yes.
And "sex—male." Yes, of course ... That's
really a wonderful paper, Mr. Kirby.

KIRBY (*taking a curtain call*). Thank you
... it's more than just a game, you know.
It's sort of an experiment in psychology,
isn't it?

PENNY. Yes, it is—it shows just how your
mind works. Now we'll see how *Mrs.* Kirby's mind works. ... Ready? ... This is
Mrs. Kirby. ... "Potatoes—starch." I
know just what you mean, Mrs. Kirby. ...
"Bathroom—Mr. Kirby."

KIRBY. What's that?

PENNY. "Bathroom—Mr. Kirby."

KIRBY (*turning to his wife*). I don't quite
follow that, my dear.

MRS. KIRBY. I don't know—I just thought
of you in connection with it. After all, you
are in there a good deal, Anthony. Bathing,
and shaving—well, you *do* take a long time.

KIRBY. Indeed? I hadn't realized that I was
being selfish in the matter. ... Go on, Mrs.
Sycamore.

ALICE (*worried*). I think it's a very silly game and we ought to stop it.

KIRBY. No, no. Please go on, Mrs. Sycamore.

PENNY. Where was I . . . Oh, yes. . . . "Lust —human."

KIRBY. 'Human? (*Thin-lipped.*) Really!

MRS. KIRBY. I just meant, Anthony, that lust is after all a—human emotion.

KIRBY. I don't agree with you, Miriam. Lust is not a human emotion. It is depraved.

MRS. KIRBY. Very well, Anthony. I'm wrong.

ALICE. Really, it's the most pointless game. Suppose we play Twenty Questions?

KIRBY. No, I find this game rather interesting. Will you go on, Mrs. Sycamore? What was the next word?

PENNY (*reluctantly*). Honeymoon.

KIRBY. Oh, yes. And what was Mrs. Kirby's answer?

PENNY. Ah—"Honeymoon—dull."

KIRBY (*murderously calm*). Did you say— dull?

MRS. KIRBY. What I meant, Anthony, was that Hot Springs was not very gay that season. All those old people sitting on the porch all afternoon, and—nothing to do at night.

KIRBY. That was not your reaction at the time, as I recall it.

TONY. Father, this is only a *game.*

KIRBY. A very illuminating game. Go on, Mrs. Sycamore!

PENNY (*brightly, having taken a look ahead*). This one's all right, Mr. Kirby. "Sex—Wall Street."

KIRBY. Wall Street? What do you mean by that, Miriam?

MRS. KLRBY (*nervously*). I don't know what I meant, Anthony. Nothing.

KIRBY. But you must have meant something, Miriam, or you wouldn't have put it down.

MRS. KIRBY. It was just the first thing that came into my head, that's all.

KIRBY. But what does it mean? Sex—Wall Street.

MRS. KIRBY (*annoyed*). Oh, I don't kno what it means, Anthony. It's just that you always talking about Wall Street, ev when— (*She catches herself.*) I don't kno what I meant . . . Would you mind terrib Alice, if we didn't stay for dinner? I' afraid this game has given me a headac

ALICE (*quietly*). I understand, Mrs. Kir

KIRBY (*clearing his throat*). Yes, possi we'd better postpone the dinner, if you do mind.

PENNY. But you're coming tomorrow nig aren't you?

MRS. KIRBY (*quickly*). I'm afraid we have engagement tomorrow night.

KIRBY. Perhaps we'd better postpone whole affair a little while. This hot weath and—ah—

TONY (*smoldering*). I think we're being v ungracious, father. Of *course* we'll stay dinner—tonight.

MRS. KIRBY (*unyielding*). I have a very headache, Tony.

KIRBY. Come, come, Tony, I'm sure ev one understands.

TONY (*flaring*). Well, I don't. I think ought to stay to dinner.

ALICE .(*very low*). No, Tony.

TONY. What?

ALICE. We were fools, Tony, ever to th it would work. It won't. Mr. Kirby, I w be at the office tomorrow. I—won't be t at all any more.

TONY. Alice, what are you talking abo

KIRBY (*to* ALICE). I'm sorry, my dear— sorry . . . Are you ready, Miriam?

MRS. KIRBY (*with enormous dignity*). Anthony.

KIRBY. It's been very nice to have met you Are you coming, Anthony?

TONY. No, father. I'm not.

KIRBY. I see. . . . Your mother and I wi waiting for you at home. . . . Good-nig (*With* MRS. KIRBY *on his arm, he sweep ward the outer door.*)

(*Before the* KIRBYS *can take more th step toward the door, however, a new* FI

ms up in the archway. *It is a quiet and
npetent-looking individual with a steely
, and two more just like him loom up
ind him.)*

E MAN (*very quietly*). Stay right where
are, everybody. (*There is a little scream
m* MRS. KIRBY, *an exclamation from* PEN-
.) Don't move.

NY. Oh, good heavens!

BY. How dare you? Why, what does this
an?

NDPA. What *is* all this?

BY. I demand an explanation!

MAN. Keep your mouth shut, you! (*He
ances slowly into the room, looking the
up over. Then he turns to one of his
n.*) Which one is it?

THER MAN (*goes over and puts a hand
ED's shoulder.*) This is him.

E. Ed!

(*terrified*). Why, what do you mean?

CE. Grandpa, what is it?

BY. This is an outrage!

MAN. Shut up! (*He turns to* ED.) What's
r name?

Edward—Carmichael. I haven't done
thing.

MAN. You haven't, huh?

NDPA (*not at all scared*). This seems
er high-handed to me. What's it all
It?

MAN. Department of Justice.

NY. Oh, my goodness! J-men!

. Ed, what have you done?

haven't done anything.

NDPA. What's the boy done, Officer?

E. What is it? What's it all about?

MAN (*taking his time, and surveying the
*). That door lead to the cellar?

Y. Yes, it does.

. Yes.

THE MAN (*ordering a man to investigate*).
Mac . . . (MAC *goes into the cellar.*) . . . Jim!

JIM. Yes, sir.

THE MAN. Take a look upstairs and see what
you find.

JIM. Okay. (JIM *goes upstairs.*)

ED (*panicky*). I haven't done anything!

THE MAN. Come here, you! (*He takes some
slips of paper out of his pocket.*) Ever see
these before?

ED (*gulping*). They're my—circulars.

THE MAN. You print this stuff, huh?

ED. Yes, sir.

THE MAN. And you put 'em into boxes of
candy to get 'em into people's homes.

ESSIE. The Love Dreams!

ED. But I didn't mean anything!

THE MAN. You didn't, huh? (*He reads the
circulars.*) "Dynamite the Capitol!" "Dynamite the White House!" "Dynamite the Supreme Court!" "God is the State; the State
is God!"

ED. But I didn't mean that. I just like to
print. Don't I, Grandpa? (DONALD *returns
with the eggs at this point, and stands quietly
watching the proceedings.*)

GRANDPA. Now, Officer, the government's in
no danger from Ed. Printing is just his hobby, that's all. He prints anything.

THE MAN. He does, eh?

PENNY. I never heard of such nonsense.

KIRBY. I refuse to stay here and— (MR. DE
PINNA, *at this point, is shoved through the
cellar door by* MAC, *protesting as he comes.*)

DE PINNA. Hey, let me get my pipe, will you?
Let me get my pipe!

MAC. Shut up, you! . . . We were right,
Chief. They've got enough gunpowder down
there to blow up the whole city.

PAUL. But we only use that—

THE MAN. Keep still! . . . Everybody in this
house is under arrest.

KIRBY. What's that?

MRS. KIRBY. Oh, good heavens!

GRANDPA. Now look here, Officer—this is all nonsense.

DE PINNA. You'd better let me get my pipe. I left it—

THE MAN. Shut up, all of you!

KOLENKHOV. It seems to me, Officer—

THE MAN. Shut up! (*From the stairs comes the sound of drunken singing—"There was a young lady," etc.* GAY WELLINGTON, *wrapped in* PENNY's *negligee, is being carried down the stairway by a somewhat bewildered* G-MAN.)

THE G-MAN. Keep still, you! Stop that! Stop it!

THE LEADER (*after* GAY *has been persuaded to quiet down*). Who's that?

GRANDPA (*pretty tired of the whole business*). That—is my mother. (*And then, sud-* denly, we hear from the cellar. MR. DE PIN seems to have been right about his pipe, judge from the sounds below. It is a wh year's supply of fireworks—bombs, crackers, little crackers, sky rockets, wheels, everything. The house is fa rocked by the explosion.*)

(*In the room, of course, pandemoni reigns.* MRS. KIRBY *screams; the* G-MAN *dr* GAY *right where he stands and dashes the cellar, closely followed by* MR. DE PIN *and* PAUL; PENNY *dashes for her manuscr and* ED *rushes to save his xylophone.* KOL KHOV *waves his arms wildly and dashes all directions at once; everyone is rush this way and that.*)

(*All except one. The exception, of course* GRANDPA, *who takes all things as they co* GRANDPA *just says "Well, well, well!"—sits down. If a lot of people weren't in way, in fact, you feel he'd like to thro few darts.*)

CURTAIN

ACT THREE

The following day.
    RHEBA *is in the midst of setting the table for dinner, pausing occasionally in her lat to listen to the Edwin C. Hill of the moment—*DONALD. *With intense interest and con tration, he is reading aloud from a newspaper.*

DONALD. " . . . for appearance in the West Side Court this morning. After spending the night in jail, the defendants, thirteen in all, were brought before Judge Callahan and given suspended sentences for manufacturing fireworks without a permit."

RHEBA. Yah. Kept me in the same cell with a strip teaser from a burlesque show.

DONALD. I was in the cell with Mr. Kirby. My, he was mad!

RHEBA. Mrs. Kirby and the strip teaser—they were fighting all night.

DONALD. Whole lot about *Mr.* Kirby here. (*Reading again.*) "Anthony W. Kirby, head of Kirby & Co., 62 Wall Street, who was among those apprehended, declared he was in no way interested in the manufacture of fireworks, but refused to state why he was on the premises at the time of the raid. Mr. Kirby is a member of the Union Club, the Racquet Club, the Harvard Club, and National Geographic Society." My, he tainly is a joiner!

RHEBA. All those rich men are Elks or s thing.

DONALD (*looking up from his paper*). I pose, after all this, Mr. Tony ain't ever ing to marry Miss Alice, huh?

RHEBA. No, suh, and it's too bad, too. Alice sure loves that boy.

DONALD. Ever notice how white folks al getting themselves in trouble?

RHEBA. Yassuh, I'm glad I'm colored. sighs, heavily.*) I don't know what I'm g to do with all that food out in the kit Ain't going to be no party tonight, t sure.

DONALD. Ain't we going to eat it anyl

EBA. Well, I'm cooking it, but I don't
nk anybody going to have an appetite.

ALD. *I'm* hungry.

EBA. Well, *they* ain't. They're all so broke
about Miss Alice.

ALD. What's she want to go 'way for?
ere's she going?

BA. I don't know—mountains some place.
d she's *going,* all right, no matter what
say. I know Miss Alice when she gets
look in her eye.

ALD. Too bad, ain't it?

BA. Sure is. (MR. DE PINNA *comes up
the cellar, bearing the earmarks of the
ious day's catastrophe. There is a small
dage around his head and over one eye,
another around his right hand. He also
s slightly.*)

PINNA. Not even a balloon left. (*He
bits a handful of exploded firecrackers.*)
k.

BA. How's your hand, Mr. De Pinna?
er?

INNA. Yes, it's better. (*A step toward
kitchen.*) Is there some more olive oil
there?

BA (*nods*). It's in the salad bowl.

INNA. Thanks. (*He goes out the kitchen
as* PENNY *comes down the stairs. It is
w and rather subdued* PENNY.)

NY (*with a sigh*). Well, she's going.
ing anybody said could change her.

A. She ain't going to stay away long, is
Mrs. Sycamore?

Y. I don't know, Rheba. She won't say.

A. My, going to be lonesome around
without her. (*She goes into the kitch-*

LD. How *you* feel, Mrs. Sycamore?

Y. Oh, I'm all right, Donald. Just kind
set. (*She is at her desk.*) Perhaps if I
me work maybe I'll feel better.

LD. Well, I won't bother you then, Mrs.
more. (*He goes into the kitchen.*)
NY *puts a sheet of paper into the type-
; stares at it blankly for a moment;*

types in desultory fashion, gives it up. She
leans back and sits staring straight ahead.*)
(PAUL *comes slowly down the stairs; stands
surveying the room a moment; sighs. He
goes over to the Erector Set; absentmind-
edly pulls out the flag. Then, with another
sigh, he drops into a chair.*)

PAUL. She's going, Penny.

PENNY. Yes. (*She is quiet for a moment;
then she starts to weep, softly.*)

PAUL (*going to her*). Now, now, Penny.

PENNY. I can't help it, Paul. Somehow I feel
it's our fault.

PAUL. It's mine more than yours, Penny.
All these years I've just been—going along,
enjoying myself, when maybe I should have
been thinking more about Alice.

PENNY. Don't say that, Paul. You've been
a wonderful father. And husband, too.

PAUL. No, I haven't. Maybe if I'd gone
ahead and been an architect—I don't know
—something Alice could have been proud of.
I felt that all last night, looking at Mr.
Kirby.

PENNY. But we've been so happy, Paul.

PAUL. I know, but maybe that's not enough.
I used to think it was, but—I'm kind of
all mixed up now.

PENNY (*after a pause*). What time is she
going?

PAUL. Pretty soon. Train leaves at half past
seven.

PENNY. Oh, if only she'd see Tony. I'm sure
he could persuade her.

PAUL. But she won't, Penny. He's been trying all day.

PENNY. Where is he now?

PAUL. I don't know—I suppose walking
around the block again. Anyhow, she won't
talk to him.

PENNY. Maybe Tony can catch her as she's
leaving.

PAUL. It won't help, Penny.

PENNY. No, I don't suppose so. . . . I feel so
sorry for Tony, too. (GRANDPA *comes down
the stairs—unsmiling, but not too depressed*

by the situation.) (*Anxiously.*) Well?

GRANDPA. Now, Penny, let the girl alone.

PENNY. But, Grandpa—

GRANDPA. Suppose she *goes* to the Adirondacks? She'll be back. You can take just so much Adirondacks, and then you come home.

PENNY. Oh, but it's all so terrible, Grandpa.

GRANDPA. In a way, but it has its bright side, too.

PAUL. How do you mean?

GRANDPA. Well, Mr. Kirby getting into the patrol wagon, for one thing, and the expression on his face when he and Donald had to take a bath together. I'll never forget that if I live to be a hundred, and I warn you people I intend to. If I can have things like that going on.

PENNY. Oh, it was even worse with Mrs. Kirby. When the matron stripped her. There was a burlesque dancer there and she kept singing a strip song while Mrs. Kirby undressed.

GRANDPA. I'll bet you Bar Harbor is going to seem pretty dull to the Kirbys for the rest of the summer. (*With a determined step,* ALICE *comes swiftly down the stairs. Over her arm she carries a couple of dresses. Looking neither to right nor left, she heads for the kitchen.*)

GRANDPA. Need any help, Alice?

ALICE (*in a strained voice*). No, thanks, Grandpa. Ed is helping with the bags. I'm just going to press these.

PENNY. Alice, dear—

GRANDPA. Now, Penny. (ED *has appeared in the hallway with a couple of hatboxes,* ESSIE *behind him.*)

ED. I'll bring the big bag down as soon as you're ready, Alice.

ESSIE. Do you want to take some candy along for the train, Alice?

ALICE. No, thanks, Essie.

PENNY. Really, Alice, you could be just as alone here as you could in the mountains. You could stay right in your room all th time.

ALICE (*quietly*). No, mother, I want to by myself—away from everybody. I love y all—you know that. But I just have to away for a while. I'll be all right. . . . Fath did you 'phone for a cab?

PAUL. No, I didn't know you wanted o

PENNY. Oh, I told Mr. De Pinna to tell y Paul. Didn't he tell you?

ED. Oh, he told *me,* but I forgot.

ALICE (*the final straw*). Oh, I wish I liv in a family that didn't always forget eve thing. That—that behaved the way ot people's families do. I'm sick of cornflak and—Donald, and— (*Unconsciously, in impatience, she has picked up one of* GRA PA'S *darts; is surprised to find it suddenly her hand.*) —everything! (*She dashes dart to the floor.*) Why can't we be 1 other people? Roast beef, and two gr vegetables, and—doilies on the table, and place you could bring your friends to—w out— (*unable to control herself further, bursts out of the room, into the kitchen.*)

ESSIE. I'll—see if I can do anything. (*goes into the kitchen.*)
(*The others look at each other for a ment, helplessly.* PENNY, *with a sigh, d into her chair again.* PAUL *also sits.* GRA *mechanically picks up the dart from floor; smooths out the feathers.* ED, *wit futile gesture, runs his fingers idly over xylophone keys. He stops quickly as e head turns to look at him.*)
(*The sound of the door opening and* T *appears in the archway. A worried an sheveled* TONY.)

PENNY (*quickly*). Tony, talk to her! S in the kitchen!

TONY. Thanks. (*He goes immediately the kitchen.*)
(*The family, galvanized, listen inten (Almost immediately,* ALICE *emerges the kitchen again, followed by* TONY. *crosses the living room and starts qu up the stairs.*) Alice, won't you listen to Please!

ALICE (*not stopping*). Tony, it's no use

NY (*following her*). Alice, you're not be-
g fair. At least let me talk to you. (*They
both gone—up the stairs.*)

NNY. Perhaps if I went upstairs with
m . . .

ANDPA. Now, Penny. Let them alone. (*ES
comes out of the kitchen.*)

IE. Where'd they go? (ED, *with a gesture,
indicates the upstairs region.*) She walked
ght out the minute he came in. (MR. DE
INA *also emerges from the kitchen.*)

. DE PINNA. Knocked the olive oil right
of my hand. I'm going to smell kind
fishy.

NDPA. How're you feeling, Mr. De Pinna?
nd still hurting you?

PINNA. No, it's better.

L. Everything burnt up, huh? Down-
rs?

PINNA (*nodding, sadly*). Everything. And
Roman costume, too.

NDPA (*to* PENNY). I told you there was
right side to everything. All except my
nty-two years back income tax. (*He pulls
envelope out of his pocket.*) I get an-
er letter every day.

PINNA. Say, what are you going to do
ut that, Grandpa?

NDPA. Well, I had a kind of idea yester-
. It may not work, but I'm trying it, any-
.

PINNA (*eagerly*). What is it? (*Suddenly
ENKHOV appears in the doorway.*)

ENKHOV (*even he is subdued*). Good
ing, everybody!

NY. Why, Mr. Kolenkhov!

NDPA. Hello, Kolenkhov.

ENKHOV. Forgive me. The door was
.

NDPA. Come on in.

ENKHOV. You will excuse my coming to-
I realize you are—upset.

NY. That's all right, Mr. Kolenkhov.

. I don't think I can take a lesson, Mr.
nkhov. I don't feel up to it.

KOLENKHOV (*uncertainly*). Well, I—ah—

PENNY. Oh, but do stay to dinner, Mr. Kolenkhov. We've got all that food out there, and
somebody's got to eat it.

KOLENKHOV. I will be happy to, Madame
Sycamore.

PENNY. Fine.

KOLENKHOV. Thank you. . . . Now, I wonder if I know you well enough to ask of
you a great favor.

PENNY. Why, of course, Mr. Kolenkhov.
What is it?

KOLENKHOV. You have heard me talk about
my friend the Grand Duchess Olga Katrina.

PENNY. Yes?

KOLENKHOV. She is a great woman, the
Grand Duchess. Her cousin was the Czar of
Russia, and today she is a waitress in Childs'
Restaurant. Columbus Circle.

PENNY. Yes, I know. If there's anything at
all that we can do, Mr. Kolenkhov . . .

KOLENKHOV. I tell you. The Grand Duchess
Olga Katrina has not had a good meal since
before the Revolution.

GRANDPA. She must be hungry.

KOLENKHOV. And today the Grand Duchess
not only has her day off—Thursday—but it
is also the anniversary of Peter the Great.
A remarkable man!

PENNY. Mr. Kolenkhov, if you mean you'd
like the Grand Duchess to come to dinner,
why, we'd be honored.

ESSIE. Oh, yes!

KOLENKHOV (*with a bow*). In the name of
the Grand Duchess, I thank you.

PENNY. I can hardly wait to meet her. When
will she be here?

KOLENKHOV. She is outside in the street,
waiting. I bring her in. (*And he goes out.*)

GRANDPA. You know, if this keeps on I want
to live to be a hundred and *fifty*.

PENNY (*feverishly*). Ed, straighten your tie.
Essie, look at your dress. How do *I* look?
All right? (KOLENKHOV *appears in the hall-
way and stands at rigid attention.*)

KOLENKHOV (*his voice booming*). The Grand Duchess Olga Katrina! (*And the* GRAND DUCHESS OLGA KATRINA, *wheat cakes and maple syrup out of her life for a few hours, sweeps into the room. She wears a dinner gown that has seen better days, and the whole is surmounted by an extremely tacky-looking evening wrap, trimmed with bits of ancient and moth-eaten fur. But once a Grand Duchess, always a Grand Duchess. She rises above everything—Childs', evening wrap, and all.*) Your Highness, permit me to present Madame Sycamore— (PENNY, *having seen a movie or two in her time, knows just what to do. She curtsies right to the floor, and catches hold of a chair just in time.*) Madame Carmichael— (ESSIE *does a curtsey that begins where all others leave off. Starting on her toes, she merges the Dying Swan with an extremely elaborate genuflection.*) Grandpa—

GRANDPA (*with a little bow*). Madame.

KOLENKHOV. Mr. Sycamore, Mr. Carmichael, and Mr. De Pinna. (PAUL *and* ED *content themselves with courteous little bows, but not so the social-minded* MR. DE PINNA. *He bows to the floor—and stays there for a moment.*)

GRANDPA. All right now, Mr. De Pinna. (MR. DE PINNA *gets to his feet again.*)

PENNY. Will you be seated, Your Highness?

THE GRAND DUCHESS. Thank you. You are most kind.

PENNY. We are honored to receive you, Your Highness.

THE GRAND DUCHESS. I am most happy to be here. What time is dinner?

PENNY (*a little startled*). Oh, it'll be quite soon, Your Highness—very soon.

THE GRAND DUCHESS. I do not mean to be rude, but I must be back at the restaurant by eight o'clock. I am substituting for another waitress.

KOLENKHOV. I will make sure you are on time, Your Highness.

DE PINNA. You know, Highness, I think you waited on me in Childs' once. The Seventy-Second Street place?

THE GRAND DUCHESS. No, no. That was m sister.

KOLENKHOV. The Grand Duchess Natash

THE GRAND DUCHESS. I work in Columbu Circle.

GRANDPA. Quite a lot of your family livin over here now, aren't there?

THE GRAND DUCHESS. Oh, yes—many. My u cle, the Grand Duke Sergei—he is an elev tor man at Macy's. A very nice man. The there is my cousin, Prince Alexis. He wi not speak to the rest of us because he worl at Hattie Carnegie's. He has cards printed Prince Alexis of Hattie Carnegie. Bah!

KOLENKHOV. When he was selling Eskim Pies at Luna Park he was willing to talk you.

THE GRAND DUCHESS. Ah, Kolenkhov, o time is coming. My sister Natasha is stud ing to be a manicure, Uncle Sergei the have promised to make floor-walker, a next month I get transferred to the Fif Avenue Childs'. From there it is only a st to Schrafft's, and *then* we will see wh Prince Alexis says!

GRANDPA (*nodding*). I think you've got hi

THE GRAND DUCHESS. You are telling m (*She laughs a triumphant Russian laugh, which* KOLENKHOV *joins.*)

PENNY. Your Highness—did you know t Czar? Personally, I mean.

THE GRAND DUCHESS. Of course—he was cousin. It was terrible, what happened, b perhaps it was for the best. Where could get a job now?

KOLENKHOV. That is true.

THE GRAND DUCHESS (*philosophically*). Y And poor relations are poor relations. It the same in every family. My cousin, King of Sweden—he was very nice to us about ten years, but then he said, I just c not go on. I am not doing so well, eith ... I do not blame him.

PENNY. No, of course not. . . . Would y excuse me for just a moment? (*She goes the foot of the stairs and stands peering anxiously, hoping for news of* ALICE.)

E PINNA (*the historian at heart*). Tell me, Grand Duchess, is it true what they say bout Rasputin?

HE GRAND DUCHESS. Everyone wants to know bout Rasputin. . . . Yes, my dear sir, it is rue. In spades.

E PINNA. You don't say?

OLENKHOV. Your Highness, we have to vatch the time.

HE GRAND DUCHESS. Yes, I must not be late. The manager does not like me. He is a Communist.

ENNY. We'll hurry things up. Essie, why on't you go out in the kitchen and give heba a hand?

HE GRAND DUCHESS (*rising*). I will help, oo. I am a very good cook.

ENNY. Oh, but Your Highness! Not on our day off!

HE GRAND DUCHESS. I do not mind. Where your kitchen?

SSIE. Right through here, but you're the uest of honor, Your Highness.

HE GRAND DUCHESS. But I love to cook! ome, Kolenkhov! If they have got sour ream and pot cheese I will make you some lintzes!

OLENKHOV. Ah! Blintzes! . . . Come, Pav-wa! We show you something! (*With* ESSIE, e goes into the kitchen.*)

E PINNA. Say! The Duchess is all right, n't she? Hey, Duchess! Can I help? (*And to the kitchen.*)

ENNY. Really, she's a very nice woman, you now. Considering she's a Grand Duchess.

RANDPA. Wonderful what people go rough, isn't it? And still keep kind of gay, o.

ENNY. Mm. She made me forget about erything for a minute. (*She returns to the airs and stands listening.*)

UL. I'd better call that cab, I suppose.

NNY. No, wait, Paul. I think I hear them. aybe Tony has— (*She stops as* ALICE'S p is heard on the stair. She enters—dressed r traveling.* TONY *looms up behind her.*)

ALICE. Ed, will you go up and bring my bag down?

TONY (*quickly*). Don't you do it, Ed! (ED *hesitates, uncertain.*)

ALICE. Ed, please!

TONY (*a moment's pause; then he gives up*). All right, Ed. Bring it down. (ED *goes up the stairs as* TONY *disconsolately stalks across the room. Then he faces the Sycamores.*) Do you know that you've got the stubbornest daughter in all forty-eight states? (*The door bell rings.*)

ALICE. That must be the cab. (*She goes to the door.*)

GRANDPA. If it is, it's certainly wonderful service. (*To the considerable surprise of everyone, the voice of* MR. KIRBY *is heard at the front door.*)

KIRBY. Is Tony here, Alice?

ALICE. Yes. Yes, he is. (MR. KIRBY *comes in.*)

KIRBY (*uncomfortably*). Ah—good afternoon. Forgive my intruding . . . Tony, I want you to come home with me. Your mother is very upset.

TONY (*he looks at* ALICE). Very well, father . . . Good-bye, Alice.

ALICE (*very low*). Good-bye, Tony.

KIRBY (*trying to ease the situation*). I need hardly say that this is as painful to Mrs. Kirby and myself as it is to you people. I—I'm sorry, but I'm sure you understand.

GRANDPA. Well, yes—and in a way, no. Now, I'm not the kind of person tries to run other people's lives, but the fact is, Mr. Kirby, I don't think these two young people have got as much sense as—ah—you and I have.

ALICE (*tense*). Grandpa, will you please not do this?

GRANDPA (*disarmingly*). I'm just talking to Mr. Kirby. A cat can look at a king, can't he? (ALICE, *with no further words, takes up the telephone and dials a number. There is finality in her every movement.*)

PENNY. You—you want me to do that for you, Alice?

ALICE. No, thanks, mother.

PAUL. You've got quite a while before the train goes, Alice.

ALICE (*into the phone*). Will you send a cab to 761 Claremont, right away, please? . . . That's right, thank you. (*She hangs up.*)

KIRBY. And now if you'll excuse us . . . are you ready, Tony?

GRANDPA. Mr. Kirby, I suppose after last night you think this family is crazy, don't you?

KIRBY. No, I would not say that, although I am not accustomed to going out to dinner and spending the night in jail.

GRANDPA. Well, you've got to remember, Mr. Kirby, you came on the wrong night. Now tonight, I'll bet you, nothing'll happen at all. (*There is a great burst of Russian laughter from the kitchen—the mingled voices of* KOLENKHOV *and the* GRAND DUCHESS. GRANDPA *looks off in the direction of the laughter, then decides to play safe.*) Maybe.

KIRBY. Mr. Vanderhof, it was not merely last night that convinced Mrs. Kirby and myself that this engagement would be unwise.

TONY. Father, I can handle my own affairs. (*He turns to* ALICE.) Alice, for the last time, will you marry me?

ALICE. No, Tony. I know exactly what your father means, and he's right.

TONY. No, he's *not,* Alice.

GRANDPA. Alice, you're in love with this boy, and you're not marrying him because we're the kind of people we are.

ALICE. Grandpa—

GRANDPA. I know. You think the two families wouldn't get along. Well, maybe they wouldn't—but who says they're right and we're wrong?

ALICE. I didn't say that, Grandpa. I only feel—

GRANDPA. Well, what *I* feel is that Tony's too nice a boy to wake up twenty years from now with nothing in his life but stocks and bonds.

KIRBY. How's that?

GRANDPA (*turning to* MR. KIRBY). Yes. Mixed up and unhappy, the way you are.

KIRBY (*outraged*). I beg your pardon, M Vanderhof, I am a very happy man.

GRANDPA. Are you?

KIRBY. Certainly I am.

GRANDPA. I don't think so. What do you think you get your indigestion from? Hap piness? No, sir. You get it because most your time is spent in doing things you don want to do.

KIRBY. I don't do anything I don't want do.

GRANDPA. Yes, you do. You said last nig that at the end of a week in Wall Stre you're pretty near crazy. Why do you ke on doing it?

KIRBY. Why do I keep on—why, that's n business. A man can't give up his busine

GRANDPA. Why not? You've got all t money you need. You can't take it with yo

KIRBY. That's a very easy thing to say, M Vanderhof. But I have spent my entire l building up my business.

GRANDPA. And what's it got you? Same ki of mail every morning, same kind of dea same kind of meetings, same dinners night, same indigestion. Where does the f come in? Don't you think there ought to something *more,* Mr. Kirby? You must ha wanted more than that when you started o We haven't got too much time, you know any of us.

KIRBY. What do you expect me to do? L the way *you* do? Do nothing?

GRANDPA. Well, I have a lot of fun. Ti enough for everything—read, talk, visit zoo now and then, practice my darts, e have time to notice when spring con around. Don't see anybody I don't want don't have six hours of things I *have* to every day before I get *one* hour to do w I like in—and I haven't taken bicarbon of soda in thirty-five years. What's the m ter with that?

KIRBY. The matter with that? But supp we *all* did it? A fine world we'd ha everybody going to zoos. Don't be ridicul Mr. Vanderhof. Who would do the wo

ᴳᴿᴬNDPA. There's always people that like to
ᵂᵒrk—you can't *stop* them. Inventions, and
ʸy fly the ocean. There're always people
ᵗᵒ go down to Wall Street, too—because
ᵗʰᵉy *like* it. But from what I've seen of you,
ᴵ ᵈon't think you're one of them. I think
ʸᵒu're missing something.

ᴷᴵᴿBY. I am not aware of missing anything.

ᴳᴿᴬNDPA. I wasn't either, till I quit. I used
ᵗᵒ get down to that office nine o'clock sharp,
ᴺᵒ matter how I felt. Lay awake nights for
ᶠᵉᵃr I wouldn't get that contract. Used to
ʷᵒrry about the world, too. Got *all* worked
ᵘᵖ about whether Cleveland or Blaine was
ᵍᵒing to be elected President—seemed awful
ᶦᵐportant at the time, but who cares now?
ᵂʰat I'm trying to say, Mr. Kirby, is that
ᴵᵛᵉ had thirty-five years that nobody can
ᵗᵃᵏe away from me, no matter what they
ᵈᵒ to the world. See?

ᴷᴵᴿBY. Yes, I do see. And it's a very danger-
ᵒᵘˢ philosophy, Mr. Vanderhof. It's—it's un-
ᴬmerican. And it's exactly why I'm opposed
ᵗᵒ this marriage. I don't want Tony to come
ᵘⁿᵈᵉr its influence.

ᵀONY (*a gleam in his eye*). What's the mat-
ᵗᵉr with it, father?

ᴷᴵᴿBY. Matter with it? Why, it's—it's down-
ᵗ᷇ght Communism, that's what it is.

ᵀONY. You didn't always think so.

ᴷᴵᴿBY. I most certainly did. What are you
ᵗᵃˡᵏing about?

ᵀONY. I'll tell you what I'm talking about.
ᵞᵒu didn't always think so, because there
ʷᵃˢ a time when you wanted to be a trapeze
ᵃrtist.

ᴷᴵᴿBY. Why—why, don't be an idiot, Tony.

ᵀONY. Oh, yes, you did. I came across those
ˡᵉᵗᵗers you wrote to grandfather. Do you
ʳᵉmember those?

ᴷᴵᴿBY. NO! . . . How dared you read those
ˡᵉᵗᵗers? How dared you?

ᵀONY. Why, isn't that wonderful? Did you
ʷᵉᵃr tights, Mr. Kirby?

ᴷᴵᴿBY. Certainly not! The whole thing is ab-
ˢᵘʳᵈ. I was fourteen years old at the time.

TONY. Yes, but at *eighteen* you wanted to
be a saxophone player, didn't you?

KIRBY. Tony!

TONY. And at twenty-one you ran away from
home because grandfather wanted you to go
into the business. It's all down there in black
and white. You didn't *always* think so.

GRANDPA. Well, well, well!

KIRBY. I may have had silly notions in my
youth, but thank God my father knocked
them out of me. I went into the business
and forgot about them.

TONY. Not altogether, father. There's still
a saxophone in the back of your clothes
closet.

GRANDPA. There is?

KIRBY (*quietly*). That's enough, Tony. We'll
discuss this later.

TONY. No, I want to talk about it *now*. I
think Mr. Vanderhof is right—dead right.
I'm never going back to that office. I've always hated it, and I'm not going on with it.
And I'll tell you something else. I didn't
make a mistake last night. I knew it was the
wrong night. I brought you here on purpose.

ALICE. Tony!

PENNY. Well, for heaven's—

TONY. Because I wanted to wake you up. I
wanted you to see a real family—as they
really *were*. A family that loved and understood each other. You don't understand *me*.
You've never had time. Well, I'm not going
to make *your* mistake. I'm clearing out.

KIRBY. Clearing out? What do you mean?

TONY. I mean I'm not going to be pushed
into the business just because I'm your son.
I'm getting out while there's still time.

KIRBY (*stunned*). Tony, what are you going
to do?

TONY. I don't know. Maybe I'll be a brick-
layer, but at least I'll be doing something
I want to do. (*Whereupon the door bell
rings.*)

PENNY. That must be the cab.

GRANDPA. Ask him to wait a minute, Ed.

ALICE. Grandpa!

GRANDPA. Do you mind, Alice? . . . You know, Mr. Kirby, Tony is going through just what you and I did when we were his age. I think, if you listen hard enough, you can hear yourself saying the same things to *your* father twenty-five years ago. We all did it. And we were right. How many of us would be willing to settle when we're young for what we eventually get? All those plans we make . . . what happens to them? It's only a handful of the lucky ones that can look back and say that they even came close. (GRANDPA *has hit home.* MR. KIRBY *turns slowly and looks at his son, as though seeing him for the first time.* GRANDPA *continues.*) So . . . before they clean out that closet, Mr. Kirby, I think I'd get in a few good hours on that saxophone. (*A slight pause, then* THE GRAND DUCHESS, *an apron over her evening dress, comes in from the kitchen.*)

THE GRAND DUCHESS. I beg your pardon, but before I make the blintzes, how many will there be for dinner?

PENNY. Why, I don't know—ah—

GRANDPA. Your Highness, may I present Mr. Anthony Kirby, and Mr. Kirby, Junior? The Grand Duchess Olga Katrina.

KIRBY. How's that?

THE GRAND DUCHESS. How do you do? Before I make the blintzes, how many will there be to dinner?

GRANDPA. Oh, I'd make quite a stack of them, Your Highness. Can't ever tell.

THE GRAND DUCHESS. Good! The Czar always said to me, Olga, do not be stingy with the blintzes. (*She returns to the kitchen, leaving a somewhat stunned* MR. KIRBY *behind her.*)

KIRBY. Ah—who did you say that was, Mr. Vanderhof?

GRANDPA (*very offhand*). The Grand Duchess Olga Katrina, of Russia. She's cooking the dinner.

KIRBY. Oh!

GRANDPA. And speaking of dinner, Mr. Kirby, why don't you and Tony both stay?

PENNY. Oh, please do, Mr. Kirby. We've g[ot] all that stuff we were going to have la[st] night. I mean tonight.

GRANDPA. Looks like a pretty good dinne[r], Mr. Kirby, and'll kind of give us a chan[ce] to get acquainted. Why not stay?

KIRBY. Why—I'd like to very much. (*H[e] turns to* TONY, *with some trepidation.*) Wh[at] do you say, Tony? Shall we stay to dinne[r]?

TONY. Yes, father. I think that would [be] fine. If— (*His eyes go to* ALICE.) —if Al[ice] will send away that cab.

GRANDPA. How about it, Alice? Going to [be] a nice crowd. Don't you think you oug[ht] to stay for dinner?

ALICE. Mr. Kirby—Tony—oh, Tony! (*A[nd] she is in his arms.*)

TONY. Darling!

ALICE. Grandpa, you're wonderful!

GRANDPA. I've been telling you that for yea[rs.] (*He kisses her.*)
(ESSIE *enters from the kitchen, laden w[ith] dishes.*)

ESSIE. Grandpa, here's a letter for you. It w[as] in the ice-box.

GRANDPA (*looks at the envelope*). The G[ov]ernment again.

TONY (*happily*). Won't you step into the [of]fice, Miss Sycamore? I'd like to do a li[ttle] dictating.

GRANDPA (*with his letter*). Well, well, w[ell—]

PENNY. What is it, Grandpa?

GRANDPA. The United States Governm[ent] apologizes. I don't owe 'em a nickel[. It] seems I died eight years ago.

ESSIE. Why, what do they mean, Grand[pa?]

GRANDPA. Remember Charlie, the milkm[an?] Buried under my name?

PENNY. Yes.

GRANDPA. Well, I just told them they m[ade] a mistake and I was Martin Vanderhof[.] So they're very sorry and I may even [get] a refund.

ALICE. Why, Grandpa, you're an old cr[ook.]

GRANDPA. Sure!

KIRBY (*interested*). Pardon me, how did you say you escaped the income tax, Mr. Vander-of?

KOLENKHOV (*bursting through the kitchen door, bringing a chair with him*). Tonight, my friends, you are going to eat. . . . (*He stops short as he catches sight of* KIRBY.)

KIRBY (*heartily*). Hello, there!

KOLENKHOV (*stunned*). How do you do?

KIRBY. Fine! Fine! Never was better.

KOLENKHOV (*to* GRANDPA). What has happened?

GRANDPA. He's relaxing. (ED *strikes the keys of the xylophone.*) That's right. Play something, Ed. (*He starts to play.* ESSIE *is immediately up on her toes.*)

THE GRAND DUCHESS (*entering from the kitchen*). Everything will be ready in a minute. You can sit down.

PENNY. Come on, everybody. Dinner! (*They start to pull up chairs.*) Come on, Mr. Kirby!

KIRBY (*still interested in the xylophone*). Yes, yes, I'm coming.

PENNY. Essie, stop dancing and come to dinner.

KOLENKHOV. You will like Russian food, Mr. Kirby.

PENNY. But you must be careful of your indigestion.

KIRBY. Nonsense! I haven't any indigestion.

TONY. Well, Miss Sycamore, how was your trip to the Adirondacks?

ALICE. Shut your face, Mr. Kirby!

KOLENKHOV. In Russia, when they sit down to dinner . . .

GRANDPA (*tapping on his plate*). Quiet! Everybody! Quiet! (*Immediately the talk ceases. All heads are lowered as* GRANDPA *starts to say Grace.*) Well, Sir, here we are again. We want to say thanks once more for everything You've done for us. Things seem to be going fine. Alice is going to marry Tony, and it looks as if they're going to be very happy. Of course the fireworks blew up, but that was Mr. De Pinna's fault, not Yours. We've all got our health and as far as anything else is concerned, we'll leave it to You. Thank You. (*The heads come up again.* RHEBA *and* DONALD *come through the kitchen door with stacks and stacks of blintzes. Even the Czar would have thought there were enough.*)

CURTAIN

End Of Summer

BY S. N. BEHRMAN

For

MAY AND HAROLD FREEDMAN

————

END OF SUMMER was produced by the Theatre Guild, Inc., at the Guild Theatre,
ew York, on Monday night, February 17, 1936, with the following cast:

(in the order of their appearance)

WILL DEXTER	Shepperd Strudwick
MRS. WYLER	Mildred Natwick
PAULA FROTHINGHAM	Doris Dudley
ROBERT	Kendall Clark
LEONIE FROTHINGHAM	Ina Claire
SAM FROTHINGHAM	Minor Watson
DR. KENNETH RICE	Osgood Perkins
DENNIS McCARTHY	Van Heflin
DR. DEXTER	Herbert Yost
BORIS, COUNT MIRSKY	Tom Powers

————

CHARACTERS

WILL DEXTER	SAM FROTHINGHAM
MRS. WYLER	DR. KENNETH RICE
PAULA FROTHINGHAM	DENNIS McCARTHY
ROBERT	DR. DEXTER
LEONIE FROTHINGHAM	BORIS, COUNT MIRSKY

SCENE

The action of the play takes place in the living room of
Bay Cottage, the Frothinghams' summer place in Northern
Maine.

TIME

The present

COPYRIGHT, 1936, BY S. N. BEHRMAN

ACT ONE

SCENE: *The verandah-living room of the Frothingham estate. Bay Cottage in Northern Maine. It is a charmingly furnished room with beautiful old distinguished pieces. A chintz couch and chairs give the room an air of informality. Beyond the door back you see a spacious, more formal room. Through the series of glass windows over the curving window seat on the right wall you see the early budding lilac and sumach. Woodbine and Virginia creeper are sprawling over the fence of native stone. Silver birch and maple are beginning to put out their leaves. The tops of red pine and cedar are visible over the rocks which fall away to the sea.*

Time: The present. A lovely afternoon in May.

At Rise: MRS. WYLER, *a very old lady and* WILL DEXTER, *an attractive, serious boy, are engaged in conversation.* MRS. WYLER *is knitting.*

WILL. When you were a young girl in Cleveland, did you see much of Mr. Rockefeller?

MRS. WYLER. Not much. Of course my husband saw him every day at the office. But he never came to our house. We were young and worldly. He was strict and religious.

WILL. Did you suspect, in those days, how rich you were going to be?

MRS. WYLER. Mercy no! We debated a long time before we moved up to Cleveland from Oil City. My mother thought Oil City was no place to bring up a young girl. She finally persuaded my father to let us move up to Cleveland. But there was a lot of talk about the expense.

WILL. Was Oil City lively?

MRS. WYLER. (*Demurely.*) It was pretty rough! I remember the celebration when they ran the first pipe-line through to Pittsburgh. That was a celebration!

WILL. The oil just poured, didn't it? Gushed out of the ground in great jets, and the people swarmed from everywhere to scoop it up.

MRS. WYLER. I remember we had a gusher in our backyard. We put a fence around it to keep the cows from lapping up the oil.

WILL. Were you excited?

MRS. WYLER. Not by the oil.

WILL. I should think you would have been!

MRS. WYLER. (*Dryly.*) We weren't. O was smelly. We wanted to get away from it. We discovered bath-salts.

WILL. You didn't know it was the tr fountain of your—dynasty?

MRS. WYLER. We left it to the men— I look back over my life the principal citement came from houses—buying a building houses. The shack in Oil City the mansion on Fifth Avenue. We h houses everywhere—houses in Londo houses in Paris, Newport and this—a yet, it seemed to me, we were alwa checking in and out of hotels.

WILL. It seems strange to think—

MRS. WYLER. What?

WILL. This golden stream — that y stumbled on so accidentally—it's flowi still—quenchless—and you on it—all y dynastic families—floating along in it— luxurious barges!

MRS. WYLER. When I read these boo about the early days of oil—these debu ing books, you call them—they make smile.

WILL. Do they? Why? I'd like to kn that.

MRS. WYLER. They're so far from the tru

WILL. Are they?

MRS. WYLER. Of course they are!

WILL. Why?

MRS. WYLER. Because they're written fr a foreign point of view—not *our* point view. We did as well as anybody co have done according to our lights.

ILL. Yes, but what sort of lights were
ey?

RS. WYLER. (*Tolerantly.*) There you are!

ILL. How lucky you were!

RS. WYLER. (*Teasing him.*) Our young
en didn't moon about. They made op-
ortunities for themselves!

ILL. Or did the opportunities make
em? All you had to do was pack your
eek-end bag and pioneer.

RS. WYLER. Is the world quite exhausted
en?

ILL. Possibly not, but our pioneering
ight take a form you would find—un-
latable.

RS. WYLER. Yes yes. (*Benevolently.*) I
ppose you're one of those young radicals
r colleges are said to be full of noways. Tell me, what do you young radicals
nd for?

ILL. I haven't decided exactly what I'm
r, but I'm pretty certain what I'm
ainst.

RS. WYLER. (*Pumping him.*) Most young
ople are bored by the past. You're full
curiosity. Why is that?

LL. (*Not committing himself.*) I'm in-
ested.

S. WYLER. At my age to be permitted
talk of one's youth is an indulgence.
k me anything you like. At my age
o one has no reason for restraint. I have
d the bad judgment to survive most of
contemporaries.

LL. I love talking to you, Mrs Wyler.
think you're very wise.

RS. WYLER. (*With a sigh.*) Go on
nking so—I'll try not to disillusion you!
moment's pause.) Are you staying on
re at Bay Cottage?

LL. Oh, no, I have to go back to Am-
st to get my degree.

S. WYLER. And after that?

LL. (*Humorously.*) The dole! (*The old
y laughs.*)

MRS. WYLER. My daughter tells me she's
invited your father here.

WILL. Yes.

MRS. WYLER. I shall be so glad to meet
him. He's an inventor, isn't he?

WILL. He's a physicist. Specializes in—

MRS. WYLER. Don't tell me—in spite of
my great wisdom I can't keep up with
science. Whenever anybody makes a scientific explanation to me I find there are
two things I don't know instead of just
one.

WILL. (*Cheerfully.*) Anyway, Dad's been
fired.

MRS. WYLER. I am very sorry to hear that.

WILL. He's been working on a method
for improving high-speed steel.

MRS. WYLER. Did he fail?

WILL. He succeeded. (MRS. WYLER *is surprised.*) They decided that his discovery,
if perfected and marketed, might increase
the technological unemployment. They
have decided therefore to call a halt on
scientific discovery — especially in those
branches where it might have practical results. That is one of the differences, Mrs.
Wyler, between my day—and yours—in
your day, you put a premium on invention
—we declare a moratorium on it. (*The
old lady gives him a shrewd look.*)

MRS. WYLER. Yes, yes. I am perfectly sure
that you're in for a hard time, Will.

WILL. (*Lightly, shrugging his shoulders.*)
As I have been elected by my class as
the one most likely to succeed, I am not
worrying, Mrs. Wyler. All I have to do is
bide my time.

MRS. WYLER. (*Amused.*) I am perfectly
certain you'll come out! Paula tells me
you and your friend, Dennis McCarthy,
want to start some kind of magazine.

WILL. Yes. A national magazine for undergraduate America. You see, Mrs. Wyler,
before the rift in our so-called system, college men were supposed to live exclusively
in a world of ukuleles, football slogans,
and petting-parties—*College Humor* sort

of thing. But it was never entirely true. Now it is less true than ever. This magazine—if we can get it going—would be a forum for intercollegiate thought. It would be the organ of critical youth as opposed—to the other.

MRS. WYLER. What other?

WILL. The R.O.T.C., the Vigilantes and the Fascists—the Youth Movement of guns and sabres—

MRS. WYLER. I see. Well, I wish you luck, Will.

WILL. Thank you. (PAULA FROTHINGHAM *comes in, a lovely young girl in gay summer slacks.*)

PAULA. (*To* WILL.) Aren't you swimming? Hello, Granny.

WILL. Your grandmother and I have been discussing life.

PAULA. With a capital L, I suppose?

WILL. Enormous! I've been getting data on the pioneer age. Your grandmother thinks the reason we're in the condition we're in is because we're lazy.

MRS. WYLER. (*Mildly.*) Lazy? Did I say that?

WILL. In a way

MRS. WYLER. If I said it, it must be so. Everybody over seventy is infallible!

PAULA. (*Nestling to her.*) Darling.

MRS. WYLER. Survival is quite a knack. You children don't realize it.

WILL. Oh, don't we though! It's getting harder every day.

MRS. WYLER. Nonsense! At your age you can't help it.

WILL. In your stately opulence that's what you think, Mrs. Wyler. You just don't know!

MRS. WYLER. Nonsense! Do you think your generation has a monopoly on hard times?

WILL. Now please don't tell me we've had depressions before?

MRS. WYLER. (*Rising to go.*) Paula, yo[ur] young man is impertinent. Don't have a[ny]thing to do with him. (*She goes out.*)

PAULA. What a conquest you've made[,] Granny! Way and ahead of all my bea[ux]

WILL. That undistinguished mob! W[hy] couldn't?

PAULA. As long as you admit there is[a] mob . . .

WILL. Why wouldn't there be? Ever[y]body loves you for your money!

PAULA. (*Confidently.*) I know it! And all the fortune-hunters I've had dangli[ng] after me you're easily the most . . .

WILL. Blatant!

PAULA. That's it! Blatant! Like my n[ew] slacks?

WILL. Love 'em.

PAULA. Love me?

WILL. Loathe you.

PAULA. Good! Kiss? (*They kiss quickl[y.]*)

WILL. Funny thing about your gra[nd]mother . . .

PAULA. Now I won't have you criticisi[ng] Granny . . .

WILL. I'm crazy about her. You feel sh[e's] been through everything and that she [un]derstands everything. Not this though. [It's] the essential difference between her ti[me] and ours.

PAULA. Oh dear! Is it the end of the wo[rld] then?

WILL. The end of this world.

PAULA. (*Goes to window seat right, w[ith] a sigh.*) Such a pretty world. (*She po[ints] through windows at the garden and [the] beyond.*) Look at it! Too bad it has to [go.] Meantime before it quite dissolves let's [go] for a swim. (*She starts for door.*)

WILL. (*Abstracted.*) All right . . . (*[fol]lowing her to window seat.*)

PAULA. (*She turns back.*) What's on y[our] mind?

LL. Wanted to speak to you about
nething. . . .

ULA. What?

LL. (*Embarrassed slightly.*) Er—your
ther. . . .

JLA. What's Mother gone and done
w? Out with it. Or is it you? My boy-
ends are always in love with Mother.
e had to contend with that all my life.
if it's that you needn't even mention
. . . come on.

LL. No, but really, Paula. . . .

JLA. Well then, out with it! What is

LL. This. (*He gives her note.*) Found
on my breakfast tray this morning in a
led envelope marked "Confidential."

JLA. (*Reading note aloud, rather be-
dered.*) "To give my little girl a good
e with. Leonie Frothingham."

LL. And this! (*He hands her check.
JLA takes it and looks at it.*)

JLA. A hundred dollars. Does Mother
nk her little girl can have a good time
h *that*? She doesn't know her little girl!

LL. But what'll I do with it? How'll
et it back to her?

JLA. Over my dead body you'll get it
k to her! You'll spend it on Mother's
e girl. Now come on swimming!

LL. Does your mother put one of these
every breakfast tray?

JLA. Argue it out with her.

LL. I can't. It would seem ungracious.
u must give it back to her for me.

JLA. Catch me! Don't take it too ser-
sly. She slips all the kids something
ry once in a while. She knows my friends
all stony. You overestimate the impor-
ce of money, Will—it's a convenience,
t's all. You've got a complex on it.

LL. I have! I've got to have. It's all
it to be dainty about money when you've
of it as you have. . . .

JLA. Rotten with it is the expression,
elieve. . . .

WILL. I repudiate that expression. It is
genteel and moralistic. You can't be rotten
with money—you can only be *alive* with it.

PAULA. You and the rest of our crowd
make me feel it's bad taste to be rich. But
what can I do? I didn't ask for it!

WILL. I know. But look here . . . I've got
a brother out of college two years who's
worked six weeks in that time and is broke
and here I am in an atmosphere with
hundred-dollar bills floating around!

PAULA. (*With check.*) Send him that!

WILL. Misapplication of funds!

PAULA. (*Warmly.*) Mother would be only
too . . .

WILL. I know she would—but that isn't
the point. . . . You know, Paula—

PAULA. What?

WILL. Sometimes I think if we weren't
in love with each other we should be ir-
reconcilable enemies—

PAULA. Nothing but sex, eh?

WILL. That's all.

PAULA. In that case—(*They kiss.*)

WILL. That's forgiving. But seriously,
Paula—

PAULA. Seriously what?

WILL. I can't help feeling I'm here on
false pretenses. What am I doing with a
millionaire family — with you? If your
mother knew what I think, and what
I've let you in for in college—she wouldn't
touch me with a ten-foot pole. And you
too—I'm troubled about the superficiality
of your new opinions. Isn't your radicalism—acquired coloring?

PAULA. I hope not. But—so is all education.

WILL. I know but—!

PAULA. What are you bleating about?
Didn't I join you on that expedition to
Kentucky to be treated by that sovereign
state as an offensive foreigner? My back
aches yet when I remember that terrible
bus ride. Didn't I get my name in the

papers picketing? Didn't I give up my holiday to go with you to the Chicago Peace Congress? Didn't I?

WILL. (*Doubtfully.*) Yes, you did.

PAULA. But you're not convinced. Will darling, don't you realize that since knowing you and your friends, since I've, as you say, acquired your point of view about things, my life has had an excitement and a sense of reality it's never had before. I've simply come alive—that's all! Before then I was bored—terribly bored without knowing why. I wanted something more—fundamental — without knowing what. You've made me see. I'm terribly grateful to you, Will darling. I always shall be.

WILL. You are a dear, Paula, and I adore you—but—

PAULA. Still unconvinced?

WILL. This money of yours. What'll it do to us?

PAULA. I'll turn it over to you. Then you can give me an allowance—and save your pride.

WILL. I warn you, Paula—

PAULA. What?

WILL. If you turn it over to me, I'll use it in every way I can to make it impossible for anyone to have so much again.

PAULA. That's all right with me, Will.

WILL. Sometimes you make me feel I'm taking candy from babies.

PAULA. The candy is no good for the baby, anyway. Besides, let's cross that bridge when we come to it. (ROBERT, *the butler, enters.*)

ROBERT. I beg your pardon, Miss Frothingham.

PAULA. Yes, Robert?

ROBERT. Telephone for you.

PAULA. Thank you, Robert. (*She crosses to table back of sofa for telephone.*) (*At phone.*) Yes—this is Paula—Dad!—Darling!—Where are you? . . . but how wonderful . . . I thought you were in New

York . . . well, come right over this minute. . . . Will you stay the night? . . Oh, too bad! . . . I'll wait right here for you. Hurry, darling! Bye! (*She hangs up.*) Imagine, dad! He's motoring up to Selena Bryant's at Murray Bay—I'm dying to have you meet him. He's the lamb of the world.

WILL. Not staying long, is he?

PAULA. No. He wants to see Mother he says. I wonder . . . oh, dear!

WILL. What?

PAULA. I was so excited I forgot to tell him. . . .

WILL. What?

PAULA. That a new friend of Mother's is coming.

WILL. The Russian?

PAULA. The Russian's here. He dates from last winter. You're behind the times, Will.

WILL. Who's the new friend?

PAULA. I'm not sure about it all yet. Maybe Mother isn't either. But I've had some experience in watching them come and go and my instinct tells me Dr. Rice is elected.

WILL. Who is Dr. Rice?

PAULA. Psychoanalyst from New York. (*Burlesquing slightly.*) The last word, my dear—(*At this point the object of PAULA's maternal impulse comes in, running a little and breathless, like a young girl.* LEONIE FROTHINGHAM, *as she has a daughter nearly twenty, must be herself forty, but at this moment, she might be sixteen. She is slim, girlish, in a young and quivering ecstasy of living and anticipation. For* LEONIE, *her daughter is an agreeable phenomenon whom she does not specially relate to herself biologically—a lovely apparition who hovers intermittently, in the wild garden of her life. There is something, for her gaiety, heartbreaking about* LEONIE, *something childish and child-like—an acceptance of people instantly and uncritically at the best of their own valuation. She is impulsive and warm-hearted and generous to a fault. Her own fragile and exquisite loveliness she offers to the world h* hyly, tentatively, bearing it like a cup ntaining a precious liquid of which not drop must be spilled. A spirituelle moureuse she is repelled by the gross or e voluptuary; this is not hypocrisy—it is, LEONIE, a more serious defect than that. the world· in which she moves hypocrisy merely a social lubricant but this myopia —alas for LEONIE!—springs from a con enital and temperamental inability to face nything but the pleasantest and the most mmediately appealing and the most flat ring aspects of things—in life and in her wn nature.· At this moment, though, she the loveliest fabrication of Nature, hap y in the summer sun and loving all the orld.)*

EONIE. My darlings, did you ever know ch a day?

ILL. (*He is a shy boy with her.*) It's ice!

EONIE. Nice! It's . . . (*Her gesture con eys her utter inadequacy to express the eauties of the day.*) It's—radiant! It knows 's radiant! The world is pleased with erself today. Is the world a woman? To ay she is—a lovely young girl in blue nd white.

ILL. In green and white.

EONIE. (*Agreeing—warmly.*) In green nd white!—It depends where you look, oesn't it? I'm just off to the station to eet Dr. Rice. Will, you'll be fascinated y him.

AULA. (*Cutting in—crisply.*) Sam tele honed.

EONIE. Sam!

AULA. Your husband. My father. Think ack, Leonie.

EONIE. Darling! Where is he?

AULA. He's on his way here. He tele honed from Miller's Point.

EONIE. Is he staying?

AULA. No.

EONIE. Why not?

AULA. He's going on to Selena Bryant's.

LEONIE. What is this deep friendship be tween Sam and Selena Bryant?

PAULA. Now, Leonie, don't be prudish!

LEONIE. (*Appealing for protection to* WILL.) She's always teasing me. She's al ways teasing everybody about everything. Developed quite a vein. I must warn you, Paula—sarcasm isn't feminine. In their hearts men don't like it. Do you like it, Will? Do you really like it?

WILL. I hate it!

LEONIE. (*In triumph to* PAULA.) There you see! He hates it!

PAULA. (*Tersely.*) He doesn't always hate it!

LEONIE. (*Her most winning smile on* WILL.) Does she bully you, Will? Don't let her bully you. The sad thing is, Paula, you're so charming. Why aren't you con tent to be charming? Are you as serious as Paula, Will? I hope not.

WILL. Much more.

LEONIE. I'm sorry to hear that. Still, for a man, it's all right, I suppose. But why are the girls nowadays so determined not to be feminine? Why? It's coming back you know—I'm sure of it—femininity is due for a revival.

PAULA. So are Herbert Hoover and paint ing on china.

LEONIE. Well I read that even in Russia . . . the women . . . (*She turns again to* WILL *whom she feels sympathetic.*) It isn't as if women had done such marvels with their—masculinity! Have they? Are things better because women vote? Not that I can see. They're worse. As far as I can see the women simply reinforce the men in their —mistakes.

WILL. (*To* PAULA.) She has you there!

LEONIE. (*With this encouragement warm ing to her theme.*) When I was a girl the calamities of the world were on a much smaller scale. It's because the women, who, after all, are half of the human race, stay ed at home and didn't bother. Now they do bother—and look at us!

PAULA. Well, that's as Victorian as anything I ever—

LEONIE. I'd love to have been a Victorian. They were much happier than we are, weren't they? Of course they were.

PAULA. (*Defending herself to* WILL.) It's only Mother that brings out the crusader in me—(*To* LEONIE.) When you're not around I'm not like that at all. Am I, Will? (*But* WILL *is given no chance to answer because* LEONIE *is holding a sprig of lilac to his nostrils.*)

LEONIE. Smell. (WILL *smells.*) Isn't it delicious?

WILL. It's lovely.

LEONIE. Here . . . . (*She breaks off a sprig and pins it into his lapel. While she is doing it she broaches a delicate subject quite casually to* PAULA.) Oh, by the way, Paula . . .

PAULA. Yes, Mother?

LEONIE. Did you mention to Sam that— that Boris—

PAULA. I didn't, no. It slipped my mind.

LEONIE. It doesn't matter in the least.

PAULA. Father isn't staying anyway . . .

LEONIE. Well, why shouldn't he? You must make him. I want him to meet Dr. Rice. He's really a most extraordinary man.

PAULA. Where'd you *find him?*

LEONIE. I met him at a party at Sissy Drake's. He *saved* Sissy.

PAULA. From what?

LEONIE. From that awful eye-condition.

PAULA. Is he an oculist too?

LEONIE. (*To* WILL.) She went to every oculist in the world—she went to Baltimore and she went to Vienna. Nobody could do a thing for her—her eyes kept blinking—twitching really in the most unaccountable way. It was an ordeal to talk to her—and of course she must have undergone agonies of embarrassment. But Dr. Rice psychoanalyzed her and com-

pletely cured her. How do you suppos[e?] Well, he found that the seat of the troub[le] lay in her unconscious. It was too simp[le.] She blinked in that awful way becau[se] actually she couldn't bear to look at h[er] husband. So she divorced Drake and sin[ce] she's married to Bill Wilmerding she's [as] normal as you or me. Now I'll take y[ou] into a little secret. I'm having Dr. Rice [up] to see Boris. Of course Boris mustn't kn[ow] it's for him.

PAULA. What's the matter with Boris[?]

LEONIE. I'm not sure. I think he's wo[rk]ing too hard.

WILL. What's he working at?

LEONIE. Don't you know? Didn't you [tell] him, Paula? His father's memoirs. H[e's] the son, you know, of the great Co[unt] Mirsky!

WILL. I know.

LEONIE. I must show you the photogra[ph] of his father—wonderful old man with [a] great white beard like a snow-storm—lo[oks] like Moses—a Russian Moses—and B[oris] is sitting on his knees—couldn't be o[ver] ten years old and wearing a fur cap a[nd] boots—boots!—and they drank tea out [of] tall glasses with raspberry jelly in—peo[ple] came from all over the world, you kn[ow] to see his father . . . !

WILL. Isn't it strange that Count Mirsk[y's] son should find himself in this stran[ge] house on this odd headland of Maine[—] Maine of all places!—writing his fath[er's] life? It's fantastic!

PAULA. (*With some malice.*) Is Dr. R[ice] going to help you acclimate him?

LEONIE. I hope so. You and Paula w[ill] have to entertain him—you young in[tel]lectuals. Isn't it a pity I have no mi[nd?] (*She rises and crosses to table right to* [ar]*range lily-of-the-valley sprigs in a vase.*)

PAULA. (*To* WILL.) She knows it's [her] greatest asset. Besides she's a fake.

WILL. (*Gallantly.*) I'm sure she is.

LEONIE. Thank you, my dears. It's [gal]lant of you. (*She crosses to* PAULA [*and em*]*braces her from behind.*) But I'm not [

ved. I know what Paula thinks of me—
 looks down on me because I won't
 interested in sociology. There never
re any such things about when I was a
l. The trouble is one generation never
 any perspective about another genera-
n.

LL. That's what your mother was say-
 to me just a little while ago.

NIE. Was she? (*She sits left of* WILL.)
 sure though Mother and I are much
ser—that is, we understand each other
ter than Paula and I. Don't you think
 Paula?

LA. (*Considering it.*) Yes. I do think

NIE. I knew you'd agree. Something's
pened between my generation and
la's. New concepts. I don't know what
y are exactly but I'm very proud that
la's got them.

LA. (*Laughing helplessly.*) Oh, Moth-
You reduce everything to absurdity!

NIE. (*Innocently.*) Do I? I don't
an to. At any rate it's a heavenly day
 I adore you and I don't care about
thing so long as you're happy. I want
 to be happy.

LA. (*Helplessly.*) Oh dear!

NIE. What's the matter?

LA. You're saying that!

NIE. Is that wrong? Will—did I say
ething wrong?

LA. You want me to be happy. It's
 saying you want me to be eight feet
 and to sing like Lily Pons.

NIE. Is it like that? Why? Will . . .

L. (*Gravely feeling he must stand up
 PAULA, but hating to.*) Paula means . . .
use.)

NIE. Yes . . . ?

L. (*Miserable.*) She means—suppose
 isn't any happiness to be had? Sup-
 the supply's run out?

NIE. But, Will, really . . . ! On a day
 this! Why don't you go swimming?

(*Rises.*) Nothing like sea-water for—mor-
bidity! Run out indeed! And today of all
days! Really! (*Gets gloves.*) I'm disappointed in you, Will. I counted on you
especially . . .

WILL. (*Abjectly.*) I was only fooling!

LEONIE. Of course he was. (*Sits on arm
of sofa beside* WILL.) Will, I rely on you.
Don't let Paula brood. Can't she drop the
sociology in the summer? I think in the
fall you're much better—braced—for things
like that. Keep her happy, Will.

WILL. I'll do my best now that—thanks
to you—I have the means.

LEONIE. Oh . . . . (*Remembering.*) Oh,
you didn't mind, did you? I hope you
didn't mind.

WILL. (*Embarrassed.*) Very generous of
you.

LEONIE. Generous! Please don't say that.
After all—we who are in the embarrassing
position nowadays of being rich must do
something with our money, mustn't we?
That's why I'm helping Boris to write this
book. *Noblesse oblige.* Don't you think so,
Will? Boris tells me that the Russians—the
present Russians—

WILL. You mean the Bolsheviks?

LEONIE. Yes, I suppose I do. He says they
don't like his father at all any more and
won't read his works because in his novels
he occasionally went on the assumption
that rich people had souls and spirits too.
You don't think like that too, do you,
Will—that because I'm rich I'm just not
worth bothering about at all— No, you
couldn't! (*The appeal is tremulous.* WILL
succumbs entirely.)

WILL. (*Bluntly.*) Mrs. Frothingham, I
love you!

LEONIE. (*Rises from arm of sofa and sits
in sofa beside* WILL. *To* PAULA.) Isn't he
sweet? (*To* WILL.) And I love you, Will.
Please call me Leonie. Do you know how
Mother happened to name me Leonie? I
was born in Paris, you know, and I was
to be called Ruhama after my father's sister. But Mother said no. No child of mine,
she said, shall be called Ruhama. She shall

have a French name. And where do you think she got Leonie?

WILL. From the French version of one of those Gideon Bibles.

LEONIE, (*As breathless as if it happened yesterday.*) Not at all. From a novel the nurse was reading. She asked the nurse what she was reading and the nurse gave her the paper book and Mother opened it and found Leonie!

WILL. What was the book?

LEONIE. Everyone wants to know that . . . But I don't know. Mother didn't know. She kept the book to give to me when I grew up. But one day she met M. Jusserand on a train—he was the French Ambassador to Washington, you know—and he picked up the book in Mother's compartment and he read a page of it and threw it out of the window because it was trash! You see what I've had to live down.

WILL. Heroic!

LEONIE. I hope you stay all summer, Will. I won't hear of your going anywhere else.

WILL. Don't worry. I have nowhere else to go!

LEONIE. Tell me—that magazine you and Dennis want to start—will it be gay?

WILL. Not exactly.

LEONIE. Oh, dear! I know. Columns and columns of reading matter and no pictures. Tell me—your father is coming to dine, isn't he? I am so looking forward to meeting him. I love scientific men. They're usually so nice and understanding. Now, I've really got to go. (*Rises and starts out.*)

PAULA. Dennis will be on that train.

LEONIE. Oh, good! I like Dennis. He makes me laugh and I like people around who make me laugh, but I do wish he'd dress better. Why can't radicals be chic? I saw a picture of Karl Marx the other day and he looks like one of those advertisements before you take something. I'll look after Dennis, Will—save you going to the station— (*To* PAULA.) And Paula, tell Sam—

PAULA. Yes?

LEONIE. (*Forgetting the message to* Sa) You know, I asked Dr. Rice if he wo treat me professionally and he said I uninteresting to him because I was q normal. Isn't that discouraging? Reall must cultivate something. Good-bye, lings. (*She runs out.*)

WILL. But what was the message to Sa (*He sits.*)

PAULA. (*Helplessly.*) I'll never kn Neither will she. (WILL *laughs.*) W can you do with her? She makes me like an opinionated old woman. An worry about her.

WILL. Do you?

PAULA. Yes. She arouses my maternal pulse.

WILL. (*Who feels he can be casual a* LEONIE *now that she is gone.*) She r rather too much on charm!

PAULA. (*Turning on him bitterly.*) she does, does she! (*Goes over to sofa sits right of* WILL.) You renegade. You all my discipline with Mother. You're a blushing schoolboy in front of her .

WILL. (*Protesting sheepishly.*) N Paula, don't exaggerate!

PAULA. You are! I thought in an minute you were going to ask her to frat dance. And where was all that derful indignation about her leaving the check? Where was the insult to pride? Where was your starving bro in Seattle? Where? Where?

WILL. I don't know but somehow can't face your mother with things that. It seems cruel to face her with ities. She seems outside of all that.

PAULA. (*Conceding that.*) Well, y going to be no help to me in han Mother, I can see that!

WILL. (*Changing subject—a bit sen about having yielded so flagrantly to* ie.) This Russian—

PAULA. What about him?

WILL. (*Gauche.*) Platonic, do you pose?

LA. Don't be naïve! (*Enter* SAM FROTH-
IAM, PAULA's *father, a very pleasant-
d, attractive man between forty-five
fifty.*)

Oh, hello. (WILL *rises*.)

LA. (*Flying to him.*) Darling!—

(*They meet center and embrace.*)
o, Paula. Delighted to see you.

LA. This is Will Dexter.

(*Shaking hands with* WILL.) How
ou do?

. I'm delighted to meet you.

LA. (*To* WILL.) Wait for me at the
h, will you, Will?

.. No, I'll run down to the station
ride back with the others.

LA. Okay. (SAM *nods to him.* WILL
out.)

(*Crosses to front of sofa.*) Nice boy.
lows her.)

A. Like him?

Do you?

A. I think so.

Special?

A. Sort of.

Very special?

A. (*Sits right end of sofa.*) Well—
sure.

Wait till you are. You've lots of

A. Oh, he's not exactly impulsive.

Then he's just a fool.

A. How are you, darling?

Uneasy.

A. With me!

Especially.

A. Darling, why?

I'll tell you. That's why I've come.

A. Everything all right?

SAM. Oh, fine.

PAULA. (*Mystified.*) Then . . . ?

SAM. (*Switching off.*) How's Leonie?

PAULA Fine. Delighted you were coming.

SAM. Was she?

PAULA. She really was. She's off to Ellsworth to meet a doctor.

SAM. Doctor?

PAULA. Psychoanalyst she's having up to
massage her Russian's complexes.

SAM. (*Laughing.*) Oh— (*With a sigh.*)
What's going to happen to Leonie?

PAULA. Why? She's on the crest!

SAM. She needs that elevation. Otherwise
she sinks.

PAULA. Well—you know Mother . . .

SAM. Yes. (*A moment's pause.*) Paula?

PAULA. Yes, dad.

SAM. The fact is—it's ridiculous I should
feel so nervous about telling you—but the
fact is . . .

PAULA. What?

SAM. I've fallen in love. I want to get
married. There! Well, thank God that's
out! (*He wipes his forehead, quite an ordeal.*) Romance at my age. It's absurd,
isn't it?

PAULA. Selena Bryant?

SAM. Yes.

PAULA. She has a grown son.

SAM. (*Smiling at her.*) So have I — a
grown daughter.

PAULA. You'll have to divorce Mother.

SAM. Yes.

PAULA. Poor Leonie!

SAM. Well, after all—Leonie—you know
how we've lived for years.

PAULA. Has Leonie hurt you?

SAM. Not for a long time. If this with
Selena hadn't happened we'd have gone on
forever, I suppose. But it has.

PAULA. You know, I have a feeling that, in spite of everything, this is going to be a shock to Leonie.

SAM. Paula?

PAULA. Yes.

SAM. Do you feel I'm deserting you? (*She turns her head away. She is very moved.*)

PAULA. No—you know how fond I am of you—I want you to be . . .

SAM. (*Deeply affected.*) Paula . . . !

PAULA. Happy. (*A silence. She is on the verge of tears.*)

SAM. I must make you see my side, Paula.

PAULA. (*Vehemently.*) I do!

SAM. It isn't only that—you're so young—but somehow—we decided very soon after you were born, Leonie and I, that our marriage could only continue on this sort of basis. For your sake we've kept it up. I thought I was content to be an—appendage—to Leonie's entourage. But I'm not—do you know what Selena—being with Selena and planning with Selena for ourselves has made me see—that I've never had a home. Does that sound mawkish?

PAULA. I thought you loved Bay Cottage.

SAM. Of our various menages this is my favorite—it's the simplest. And I've had fun here with you—watching you grow up. But very soon after I married Leonie I found this out—that when you marry a very rich woman it's always *her* house you live in. (*A moment's pause.*)

PAULA. I'm awfully happy for you, Sam, really I am. You deserve everything but I can't help it I . . .

SAM. I know. (*A pause.*) Paula . . .

PAULA. Yes, dad?

SAM You and I get on so well together—always have—Selena adores you and really —when you get to know her . . .

PAULA. I like Selena enormously. She's a dear. Couldn't be nicer.

SAM. I'm sure you and she would get on wonderfully together. Of course, Leonie

will marry again. She's bound to. W[ ] don't you come to live with us? Wh[ ] you want to . . .

PAULA. Want to!

SAM. All the time then. Leonie has su[ ] a busy life.

PAULA. It's awfully sweet of you.

SAM. Sweet of me! Paula!

PAULA. Where are you going to live?

SAM. New York. Selena has her job to [ ]

PAULA. She's terribly clever, isn't she?

SAM. She's good at her job.

PAULA. It must be wonderful to be in[ ] pendent. I hope I shall be. I hope I c[ ] make myself.

SAM. No reason you can't.

PAULA. It seems to take so much—

SAM. What sort of independence?

PAULA. Leonie's independent, but that dependence doesn't mean anything so[ ] how. She's always been able to do w[ ] she likes.

SAM. So will you be.

PAULA. That doesn't count somehow. independence in a vacuum. No, it doe[ ] count.

SAM. Maybe it isn't independence [ ] want then?

PAULA. Yes, it is. I want to be able [ ] stand on my own feet. I want to be—ju[ ] fied.

SAM. (*Understandingly.*) Ah! Tha[ ] something else. (*A little amused.*) Th[ ] harder!

PAULA. I mean it, really I do—(*Pau[ ]* It's curious—how—adrift—this makes [ ] feel. As if something vital, something [ ] damental had smashed. I wonder [ ] Mother'll take it. I think—unconscious[ ] she depends on you much more than [ ] realizes. You were a stabilizing force, S[ ] in spite of everything and now . . .

SAM. (*Seriously.*) *You* are the stabili[ ] force, if you ask me, Paula . . .

ULA. I don't know.

I. What's worrying you, Paula? Is it s Russian?

ULA. Oh, I think he's harmless really.

I. What then?

ULA. That one of these days—

I. What?

ULA. That one of these days—now that 're going—somebody will come along— o won't be harmless.—You know, I ly love Leonie. (LEONIE *comes running ust ahead of* DR. KENNETH RICE, DENNIS WILL. LEONIE *is in the gayest spirits.* RICE *is handsome, dark, magnetic, t, masterful. He is conscious of author- and gives one the sense of a strange, ius-like intuition.* DENNIS *is a flamboy- Irishman, a little older than* WILL, *ky, black-haired, slovenly, infinitely h.* SAM *and* PAULA *rise.* LEONIE *comes n to center with* KENNETH *at her left.* L *remains back of sofa.* DENNIS *follows n to right center.*)

NIE. Oh, Sam, how perfectly . . . This Dr. Rice—my husband Sam Frothing- —and my daughter Paula! Sam, Den- McCarthy.

NIS. How do you do? (*No one pays attention to him.* DR. RICE *shakes hands* SAM *and* PAULA. LEONIE *keeps bub- , her little laugh tinkling through her ter.*)

IE. It's courageous of me, don't you , Dr. Rice, to display such a daugh- Does she look like me? I'll be very ed if you tell me that she does. Sit 1, sit down, everybody.

IS. (*Holding up his pipe.*) You mind if I—?

IE. No, no, not at all—(*She sits cen- hair,* PAULA *sits on right end sofa,* IS *sinks into chair, right, by table.*) How well you're looking! Are you ig at Selena's? How is Selena?

She's very well.

IE. Dr. Rice knows Selena.

ETH. Yes, indeed!

LEONIE. I envy Selena, you know, above all women. So brilliant, so attractive and so self-sufficient. That is what I envy in her most of all. I have no resources—I depend so much on other people. (*Turns to* RICE.) Do you think, Dr. Rice, you could make me self-sufficient?

KENNETH. I think I could.

LEONIE. How perfectly marvelous!

KENNETH. But I shouldn't dream of doing it!

LEONIE. But if I beg you to?

KENNETH. Not even if you beg me to.

LEONIE. But why?

KENNETH. It would deprive your friends of their most delightful avocation.

LEONIE. Now that's very grateful. You see, Sam, there are men who still pay me compliments.

SAM. I can't believe it!

LEONIE. You must keep it up, Dr. Rice, please. So good for my morale. (*To* PAULA.) Oh, my dear, we've been having the most wonderful argument — (*To* DENNIS.) Haven't we?

DENNIS. Yes.

LEONIE. All the way in from Ellsworth— (*To* RICE.) Really, Doctor, it's given me new courage . . .

PAULA. New courage for what?

LEONIE. I've always been afraid to say it for fear of being old-fashioned—but Dr. Rice isn't afraid.

KENNETH. (*Explaining to* SAM.) It takes great courage, Mr. Frothingham, to dis- agree with the younger generation.

SAM. It does indeed.

PAULA. Well, what is it about?

LEONIE. Yes—what *was* it about, Dennis?

DENNIS. Statistics and theology. Some metaphysics thrown in.

SAM. Good heavens! (*Sits.*)

DENNIS. Statistics as a symbol.

WILL. Dr. Rice still believes in the individual career.

KENNETH. I hang my head in shame!

DENNIS. He doesn't know that as a high officer of the National Student Federation, I have at my fingers' ends the statistics which rule our future, the statistics which constitute our horizon. Not your future, Paula, because you are living parasitically on the stored pioneerism of your ancestors.

PAULA. Forgive me, Reverend Father!

DENNIS. I represent, Doctor, the Unattached Youth of America—

KENNETH. Well, that's a career in itself! (*They laugh.*)

DENNIS. (*Imperturbable.*) When we presently commit the folly of graduating from a benevolent institution at Amherst, Massachusetts, there will be in this Republic two million like us. Two million helots. (*Leaning over* LEONIE.) But Dr. Rice poohpoohs statistics.

LEONIE. (*Arranging his tie.*) Does he Dennis?

DENNIS. He says the individual can surmount statistics, violate the graphs. Superman!

WILL. Evidently Dr. Rice got in just under the wire.

KENNETH. I'd never submit to statistics, Mr. Dexter—I'd submit to many things but not to statistics.

LEONIE. Such dull things to submit to—

DENNIS. You must be an atheist, Dr. Rice.

KENNETH. Because I don't believe in statistics?—the new God?

LEONIE. Well, *I'm* a Protestant and I don't believe in them either.

DENNIS. Well, Protestant is a loose synonym for atheist—and I, as an Irishman—and a—

KENNETH. Young man—

DENNIS. Yes?

KENNETH. Have you ever heard Bismarck's solution of the Irish problem?

DENNIS. No. What?

KENNETH. Oh, it's entirely irrelevant.

LEONIE. Please tell us. I adore irrelev cies.

KENNETH. Well, he thought the Irish the Dutch should exchange countries. Dutch, he thought, would very soon m a garden out of Ireland, and the I would forget to mend the dikes. (*T laugh.*)

LEONIE. That's not irrelevant—

DENNIS. It is an irrelevance, but par able in an adversary losing an argume

KENNETH. (*To* PAULA.) Miss Froth ham, you seem very gracious. Will get me out of this?

PAULA. No, I'm enjoying it.

LEONIE. Whatever you may say, De it's an exciting time to be alive.

DENNIS. That is because your abno situation renders you free of its major citement—

LEONIE. And what's that, Dennis?

DENNIS. The race with malnutrition.

KENNETH. But that race, Mr.—?

DENNIS. McCarthy.

KENNETH. Is the eternal condition of kind. Perhaps mankind won't surviv solution of that problem.

WILL. (*With heat.*) It's easy to sit in living room—and be smug about the vival of the fittest—especially when y convinced you're one of the fittest. there are millions who won't conceded that superiority, Dr. Rice. There are lions who are so outrageously dema that they actually insist on the rig live! They may demand it one day a cost of your complacency.

LEONIE. Will! We were just chattin

WILL. I'm sorry! The next thing Rice'll be telling us is that war is essary also—to keep us stimulated— letting for the other fellow.

NNETH. Well, as a matter of fact, there's
nething to be said for that too. If you
ven't settled on a career yet, Mr. Dex-
, may I suggest evangelism?

NNIS. But Dr. Rice—!

NNETH. And now, Mrs. Frothingham,
ore these young people heckle me too
ectively, may I escape to my room?

NIE. (*Rising.*) Of course. Though I
n't think you need be afraid of their
kling, Doctor. You say things which
e always believed but never dared say.

NNETH. (*As they walk out.*) Why not?

NIE. I don't know—somehow—I lack-
the—the authority. I want to show you
r rooms myself. (*Leaving the room, fol-
ed by* RICE.) I'll be right back, Sam—
CE *nods to them and follows her out.
they go out she keeps talking to him.*)
m giving you my father's rooms—he
lt the wing especially so that when he
nted to work he'd be away from the
of the house—you have the sea *and*
garden—(*They are off. A moment's
se.*)

LA. Well, that's a new type for Leonie!

NIS. There's something Rasputinish
ut him. What's he doing in Maine?

L. What, for the matter of that, are
and I doing in Maine? We should be
New York, jockeying for position on
bread-line. Let's go to the beach, Den-
Pep us up for the struggle.

NIS. In that surf? It looks angry. I
t face life today.

LA. Swim'll do you good.

NIS. (*Starting for garden.*) It's not a
m I want exactly but a float—a vigor-
float. Lead me to the pool, Adonais—

L. All right. (*As he starts to follow,
NIS, DR. DEXTER, WILL's father, comes
ishered by* ROBERT. *He is a dusty little
with a bleached yellow Panama hat.
keeps wiping his perspiring face with
ld handkerchief. He doesn't hear very
-*)

NIS. Ah, the enemy—! (PAULA *and* SAM
)

WILL. Hello, dad. You remember Paula.

DEXTER. Yes . . . yes, I do.

WILL. (*Introducing* SAM.) My father—Mr.
Frothingham.

SAM. Very glad to see you.

DEXTER. (*Shaking hands.*) Thank you.

DENNIS. (*Pointing dramatically at* DEX-
TER.) Nevertheless I repeat—the enemy!'

PAULA. Dennis!

WILL. Oh, he's used to Dennis!

DEXTER. (*Wipes his forehead.*) Yes, and
besides it was very dusty on the road.

PAULA. Won't you sit down? (DEXTER *does
so, in center chair. The others remain
standing.*)

WILL. How long did it take you to drive
over, dad?

DEXTER. Let's see—left New Brunswick
at two. . . .

WILL. (*Looks at watch.*) Three and one
half hours—pretty good—the old tin Lizzie's got life in her yet.

DEXTER. You young folks having a good
time, I suppose? (*He looks around him
absent-mindedly.*)

PAULA. Dennis has been bullying us.

DEXTER. He still talking? (*Mildly.*) It's
the Irish in him.

DENNIS. (*Nettled.*) You forgot to say
shanty!

DEXTER. (*Surprised.*) Eh? Why should I
say that?

WILL. Dennis is a snob. Wants all his
titles.

DENNIS. You misguided children don't realize it—but here—in the guise of this
dusty, innocent-seeming man—sits the
enemy.

DEXTER. (*Turning as if stung by a fly—
cupping his hand to his ear.*) What? What
did he say?

DENNIS. The ultimate enemy, the true be-
getter of the fatal statistics—Science. You

betray us, Paula, by having him in the house; *you* betray us, Will, by acknowledging him as a father.

DEXTER. (*Wiping his forehead.*) Gosh, it's hot!

SAM. (*Sensing a fight and urging it on—solemnly.*) Can all this be true, Dr. Dexter?

DEXTER. What be true?

SAM. Dennis's accusation.

DEXTER. I am slightly deaf and McCarthy's presence always fills me with gratitude for that affliction.

DENNIS. It's perfectly obvious. You've heard of technological unemployment. Well, here it sits, embodied in Will's father. Day and night with diabolical ingenuity and cunning he works out devices to unemploy us. All over the world, millions of us are being starved and broken on the altar of Science. We Catholics understand that. We Catholics repudiate the new Moloch that has us by the throat.

WILL. Do you want us to sit in mediaeval taverns with Chesterton and drink beer? (DEXTER *turns to* DENNIS; *as if emerging suddenly from an absent-minded daze, he speaks with great authority, casually but with clarity and precision.*)

DEXTER. The fact is, my voluble young friend, I am not the Moloch who is destroying you but that you and the hordes of the imprecise and the vaguely trained—are destroying me! I have, you will probably be pleased to learn, just lost my job. I have been interrupted in my work. And why? Because I am successful. Because I have found what, with infinite patience and concentration, I have been seeking to discover. From the elusive and the indeterminate and the invisible, I have crystallized a principle which is visible and tangible and—predictable. From the illimitable icebergs of the unknown I have chipped off a fragment of knowledge, a truth which so-called practical men may put to a use which will make some of your numbers unnecessary in the workaday world. Well—what of it, I say?—who decrees that you shall be supported? Of what importance are your lives and futures and

your meandering aspirations compared the firmness and the beauty and cohesion of the principles I seek, the tr I seek? None—none whatever! Whet you prattle on an empty stomach whether you prattle on a full stomach make no difference to anybody that I see. (*To* PAULA *abruptly, rising.*) And n young woman, as I have been invited h to spend the night, I'd like to see my roo

PAULA. (*Crossing to him.*) Certai Come with me. I'll have Robert show your room. (*They go to door back. calls.*) Robert! (ROBERT *enters.*) Will take Dr. Dexter to his room? (DEXTER *lows* ROBERT *out.*)

SAM. Gosh! I thought he was deaf!

WILL. He can hear when he wants (*To* DENNIS.) Now will you be good!

DENNIS. I'm sorry—I didn't know l lost his job or I wouldn't have . . .

WILL. Oh, that's all right. Well, Den how does it feel to be superfluous?

DENNIS. (*Sourly.*) The man's child (*He goes out, door right through garde*

PAULA. Isn't he marvelous? Don't love Will's father?

SAM. Crazy about him. He's swell.

WILL. He's a pretty good feller. He se absent-minded but actually he's extren present-minded. If you'll excuse me, I'm ing out to soothe Dennis. (*He follows* NIS *out.*) (*A pause.*)

SAM. That young man appears to h sound antecedents.

PAULA. Oh, yes—Will's all right, but— Sam—!

SAM. What?

PAULA. With you gone—I'm terrified Leonie. I really am! When I think of foolish marriages Leonie would have n if not for you!

SAM. It's a useful function, but I'm af I'll have to give it up!

PAULA. (*With new determinati* Sam . . .

ɪ. Yes, Paula.

ʟᴀ. If Leonie goes Russian—

. Well?

ʟᴀ. Or if she goes Freudian—?

. In any case you and this boy'll bably be getting married.

ʟᴀ. That's far from settled yet.

. Why?

ʟᴀ. Will's scared.

. Is he?

ʟᴀ. Of getting caught in Leonie's sil- web.

. That's sensible of him. (LEONIE *es back, half running, breathless.*)

ɴɪᴇ. Well! Isn't Dr. Rice attractive?

. (*Rising.*) Very.

ʟᴀ. (*Rising.*) And so depressed about self! (*She goes out—door right.*)

ɴɪᴇ. Isn't it extraordinary, Dr. Rice ng achieved the position he has—at age? He's amazing. And think of it, —not yet forty.

Anybody under forty is young to me!

ɴɪᴇ. How old are you, Sam?

Forbidden ground, Leonie.

ɴɪᴇ. I should know, shouldn't I, but n't. I know your birthday—I always mber your birthday . . .

You do indeed!

ɴɪᴇ. It's June 14. But I don't know old you are.

Knowledge in the right place—ig-nce in the right place!

ɴɪᴇ. (*Meaning it.*) You're more at-ive and charming than ever.

You're a great comfort.

ɴɪᴇ. It's so nice to see you!

And you too! (*He is not entirely ortable—not as unself-conscious and al as she is.*)

LEONIE. Sometimes I think Paula should see more of you. I think it would be very good for her. What do you think of her new friends?

SAM. They seem nice.

LEONIE. They're all poor and they're very radical. They look on me—my dear, they have the most extraordinary opinion of me . . .

SAM. What is that?

LEONIE. I'm fascinated by them. They think of me as a hopeless kind of spoiled Bourbon living away in a never-never land —a kind of Marie Antoinette . . . (*She laughs.*) It's delicious!

SAM. Is Paula radical too?

LEONIE. I think she's trying to be. She's a strange child.

SAM. How do you mean?

LEONIE. Well, when I was a child I was brought up to care only if people were charming or attractive or . . .

SAM. Well-connected . . .

LEONIE. Yes . . . These kids don't care a hoot about that.

SAM. I think the difference between their generation and ours is that we were ro-mantic and they're realistic.

LEONIE. Is that it?

SAM. I think so.

LEONIE. What makes that?

SAM. Changes in the world—the war—the depression. . . .

LEONIE. What did people blame things on before—the war?

SAM. (*Smiling.*) Oh, on the tariff and on the Republicans—and on the Democrats! Leonie—

LEONIE. Yes, Sam.

SAM. I—I really have something to tell you.

LEONIE. (*Looks up at him curiously.*) What? (*Pause.*)

SAM. I am in love with Selena Bryant. We want to get married.

LEONIE. (*Pause—after a moment.*) Human nature is funny! Mine is!

SAM. Why?

LEONIE. I know I ought to be delighted to release you. Probably I should have spoken to you about it myself before long—separating. And yet—when you tell me—I feel—a pang . . .

SAM. That's very sweet of you.

LEONIE. One's so possessive—one doesn't want to give up anything.

SAM. For so many years our marriage has been at its best—a friendship. Need that end?

LEONIE. No, Sam. It needn't. I hope truly that it won't.

SAM. What about Paula?

LEONIE. Did you tell Paula?

SAM. Yes. . . .

LEONIE. Did she . . . ?

SAM. (*Rising.*) Leonie . . .

LEONIE. (*Pauses.*) Yes, Sam.

SAM. A little while ago you said—you thought Paula ought to see more of me.

LEONIE. Yes . . . I did. . . . (*She is quite agitated suddenly. The thought has crossed her mind that perhaps* PAULA *has told* SAM *that she would prefer to go with him. This hurts her deeply, not only for the loss of* PAULA *but because, from the bottom of her being, she cannot bear not to be loved.*)

SAM. Don't you think then . . . for a time at least . . .

LEONIE. (*Defeatist in a crisis.*) Paula doesn't like me! (*It is a sudden and completely accepted conviction.*)

SAM. Leonie!

LEONIE. She'd rather go with you!

SAM. Not at all—it's only that . . .

LEONIE. I know what Paula thinks of me. . . .

SAM. Paula adores you. It's only that .

LEONIE. It's only that what—

SAM. Well, for instance— if you sho[uld] get married—

LEONIE. What if I did?

SAM. (*Coming to stand close to her le[ft.]*) It would mean a considerable readjustm[ent] for Paula—wouldn't it? You can see th[at]

LEONIE. (*Rising.*) But it would too w[ith] you and Selena.

SAM. (*Taking step toward her.*) [She] knows Selena. She admires Selena.

LEONIE. (*Rising and walking down [in] front of sofa.*) What makes you think [she] wouldn't admire—whomever I married[?]

SAM. (*After a moment, completely seri[ous] now.*) There's another aspect of it wh[ich] I think for Paula's sake you should c[on]sider most carefully.

LEONIE. What aspect?

SAM. (*Coming down to her.*) Paula's [cur]ious. You know that yourself. She's in[ter]ested in things. She's not content to b[e a] Sunday-supplement heiress—floating a[bout] —she wants to do things. Selena's a w[ork]ing woman. Selena can help her.

LEONIE. I know. I'm useless.

SAM. I think you ought to be unse[lfish] about this.

LEONIE. Paula can do what she likes[, of] course. If she doesn't love me . . .

SAM. Of course she loves you.

LEONIE. If she prefers to live with [you] and Selena I shan't stand in her way. (*Her martyrish resignation irritates* SAM *[pro]foundly. He feels that really* LEONIE *sh[ould] not be allowed to get away with it.*)

SAM. You're so vain, Leonie.

LEONIE. (*Refusing to argue.*) I'm s[ick] (*This makes it worse.* SAM *goes dee[per]*)

SAM. After all, you're Paula's mo[ther] Can't you look at her problem—objecti[vely]

LEONIE. Where my emotions are inv[olved] I'm afraid I never know what words [like] that mean. (*He blunders in worse, fa[rther] than he really means to go.*)

. (*Flatly.*) Well, this sort of thing isn't
d for Paula.

NIE. (*Very cold, very hurt.*) What sort
thing? (*A moment's pause. He is an-
ed with himself at the ineptitude of his
roach.*) Be perfectly frank. You can be
 me. What sort of thing?

, Well—Leonie—(*With a kind of des-
te bluntness.*) You've made a career of
ation. Obviously Paula isn't going to.
 know you and Paula belong to differ-
worlds. (*With some heat.*) And the
n Paula is the way she is is because
 lives in an atmosphere of perpetual
lict.

NIE. Conflict? Paula?

 With herself. About you.

NIE. (*Rising.*) That's too subtle for
 I'm afraid.

 Paula's unaware of it herself.

IE. Where did you acquire this amaz-
psychological insight? You never used
ave it. Of course! From Selena. Of
se!

 I've never discussed this with Selena.

IE. No?

 She's told me she'd be happy to
Paula but . . .

IE. That's extremely generous of her
offer without discussion. . . .

 (*She has him there; he loses his
er.*) It's impossible for you to consider
hing without being personal.

IE. I am afraid it is. I don't live on
wonderful rarefied, intellectual plane
ited by Selena and yourself—and
e you want to take Paula. I'm sorry
e made Paula serious, I'm sorry she's
perpetual conflict about me. I'm sorry
let her in for—this sort of thing! I'm
! (*She is on the verge of tears. She
out.*)

 Leonie . . . ! (*He follows her to
back, calling.*) Leonie! (*But it is too
 She is gone. He turns back into
.*) Damn! (*PAULA comes in—from
, door right.*)

PAULA. Where's Leonie?

SAM. She just went upstairs.

PAULA. I've been showing Dr. Rice our
rock-bound coast.

SAM. What's he like?

PAULA. Hard to say. He's almost too sympathetic. At the same time—

SAM. What?

PAULA. At the same time—he is inscrut-
able! I can't tell whether I like him or
dislike him. You say Selena knows him.
What does she say about him?

SAM. Selena isn't crazy about him.

PAULA. Why not?

SAM. Brilliant charlatan, she says—also a
charmer.

PAULA. I gather that, and I resent him.
How'd you come out with Leonie?

SAM. I've made a mess of it. I'm a fool!

PAULA. My going with you, you mean?

SAM. Yes.

PAULA. Sam . . .

SAM. Yes?

PAULA. Will you mind very much . . .

SAM. What?

PAULA. If I don't go with Selena and you?

SAM. But I thought you said—and especially if she marries somebody—

PAULA. (*Slowly.*) That's just what I'm
thinking of—

SAM. What's happened?

PAULA. There's no way out of it, Sam—
I've got to stay.

SAM. But why?

PAULA. (*Simply, looking up at him.*)
Somebody's got to look after Leonie. . . .
(KENNETH *enters.*)

KENNETH. My first glimpse of Maine. A
masculine Riviera.

PAULA. It's mild now. If you want to see
it really virile—come in the late fall.

KENNETH. You've only to crook your little finger. I'll be glad to look at more of Maine whenever you have the time. (*Sits, facing her.*)

PAULA. Of course. Tomorrow?

KENNETH. Yes. Tomorrow. (*To* SAM.) You know, from Mrs. Frothingham's description— (*Looking back at* PAULA, *intently.*) I never could have imagined her. Not remotely. (ROBERT *enters.*)

SAM. What is it, Robert?

ROBERT. Mrs. Frothingham would like [to] see Dr. Rice in her study.

KENNETH. (*Rising.*) Oh, thank you. (*He walks to door back.*) Excuse me. (*He g[oes] upstairs.* PAULA *and* SAM *have contin[ued] looking front. As* KENNETH *starts upst[airs] they slowly turn and look at one anot[her]. The same thought has crossed both t[heir] minds—they both find themselves look[ing] suddenly into a new and dubious vista.*)

Curtain

ACT TWO

SCENE I

SCENE: *The same.*

Time: *Midsummer—late afternoon.*

At Rise: KENNETH *is at a bridge table working out a chess problem. He hears voices and footsteps approaching. Gets up, unhurried, and looks off into garden. Sees* BORIS *and* LEONIE *approaching. As they come in he strolls off—they do not see him.* LEONIE's *arms are full of flowers. She is looking for* KENNETH. COUNT MIRSKY *follows her in.*

COUNT MIRSKY, *a Russian, is very good-looking, mongoloid about the eyes. His English is beautiful, with a slight and attractive accent. He is tense, jittery—a mass of jangled nerves—his fingers tremble as he lights one cigarette after another. He is very pale—his pallor accentuated by a dark scarf he wears around his neck.*

BORIS. (*Stopping center.*) It appears he is not here either.

LEONIE. He? Who? (*Crossing to table behind sofa to put some flowers in vase.*)

BORIS. When you're in the garden with me you think—perhaps he is in the house. When you are in the house you think perhaps he is in the garden.

LEONIE. Boris, darling, you have the odd habit of referring to mysterious characters without giving me any hint who they are. Is that Russian symbolism? There will be a long silence; then you will say: He would not approve, or they can't hear us. It's a bit mystifying.

BORIS. (*Crossing to stand near her.*) [You] know who I mean.

LEONIE. (*Going to table right to [put] flowers in vase.*) Really, you flatter [me.] I'm not a mystic, you know, Boris. [I'm] a simple extrovert. When you say "[he]" why can't it refer to someone defini[te] and, if possible, to someone I know.

BORIS. (*Crossing to back of table, fa[cing] her across it.*) You know him, all right[.]

LEONIE. There you go again! *Really, B[oris]*

BORIS. (*Moving closer to her are[und] table.*) You've been divorced now for [sev]eral weeks. You're free. We were [all] waiting for you to be free—

LEONIE. (*Moving away, sitting in c[hair] right.*) Now that I am free you wan[t to] coerce me. It's a bit unreasonable, [don't] you think? (BORIS *walks to end of win[dow] seat and sits.*) (*Enter* KENNETH, *back.*)

KENNETH. (*Strolling across stage to[ward] LEONIE.) Hello, Leonie. Count Mirsk[y.]

LEONIE. Kenneth—I haven't seen yo[u all] day.

KENNETH. I've been in my room sl[aving] away at a scientific paper.

LEONIE. My house hums with cre[ative] activity. I love it. It gives me a sen[se of] vicarious importance. What's your[s] on?

KENNETH. Shadow-neurosis.

NIE. Shadow-neurosis. How marvel-
What does it mean?

NETH (*Looking at* BORIS.) It is a sen-
on of non-existence.

NIE. Is it common?

NETH. Quite. The victim knows that
xists and yet he feels that he does not!

NIE. In a curious way I can imagine
nsation like that—do you know I ac-
y can. Isn't it amusing?

s. The doctor is so eloquent. Once he
ribes a sensation it becomes very easy
el it.

IE. That's an entrancing gift. Why
you so antagonistic to Kenneth? He
ts to help you but you won't let him.
ked him here to help you.

NETH. (*To* BORIS.) Your skepticism
t this particular disease is interesting,
it Mirsky, because, as it happens, you
r from it.

s. (*Bearing down on* KENNETH.) Has
ver occurred to you that you are a
ed novelist?

NETH. Though I have not mentioned
in my article I have described you.

IE. (*Rising and crossing left to table
d sofa.*) You should be flattered,
.

. I am!

IE. Another case history! I've been
ng some of Kenneth's scientific text-
s. Most fascinating form of biography.
was that wonderful fellow who did
odd things—Mr. X.? You'd never
you could get so interested in anony-
people. I'd have given anything to
Mr. X.—though I must say I'd feel
nervous about having him in the
.

ETH. How is your book getting
, Count Mirsky?

Very well. Oh—so—

ETH. Far along in it?

Quite.

LEONIE. I'm crazy to see it. He's dedicat-
ing it to me but he hasn't let me see a
word of it!

KENNETH. For a very good reason.

LEONIE. What do you mean?

KENNETH. Because there is no book. There
never has been a book.

LEONIE. (*She lets flowers drop.*) Kenneth!

KENNETH. Isn't that true, Count Mirsky?

BORIS. It is not!

KENNETH. Then why don't you let us see
a bit of it?

LEONIE. Oh, do! At least the dedication
page.

KENNETH. A chapter—

BORIS. Because it isn't finished yet.

LEONIE. Well, it doesn't have to be finished. We know the end, don't we? The end
belongs to the world.

KENNETH. Let us see it, Count.

BORIS. I can't.

KENNETH. What are you calling the book?

BORIS. I haven't decided yet.

KENNETH. May I suggest a title to you—?

LEONIE. Oh, do! What shall we call it,
Kenneth?

KENNETH. "The Memoirs of a Boy Who
Wanted to Murder His Father."

LEONIE. What!

BORIS. (*Gripping arms of chair.*) I am not
a hysterical woman, Doctor—and I'm not
your patient!

LEONIE. But Kenneth—Boris worshipped
his father.

KENNETH. No, he hated him. He hated
him when he was alive and he hates him
still. He grew up under the overwhelming shadow of this world-genius whom,
in spite of an immense desire to emulate
and even surpass—he felt he could never
emulate and never surpass—nor even equal
— Did you worship your father, Count
Mirsky?

BORIS. It's true! I hated him!

LEONIE. Boris!

BORIS. I hated him!

KENNETH. Now you can let us see the book, can't you—now that we know the point of view—just a bit of it?

LEONIE. I'm more crazy than ever to see it now. I can tell you a little secret now, Boris. I was afraid—I was rather afraid—that your book would be a little like one of those statues of an ancestor in a frock-coat. Now it sounds really exciting. You hated him. But how perfectly marvelous! I can't wait to see it now. Do run up to your study and bring it down, Boris—do!

BORIS. No.

LEONIE. That's very unpleasant of you.

BORIS. You might as well know it then. There isn't any book. There never will be. Not by me.

LEONIE. But I don't understand—every day—in your room working—all these months!

BORIS. (Facing her.) One wants privacy! Possibly you can't realize that. You who always have to have a house full of people.

LEONIE. (Goes back to flowers at table.) Boris!

KENNETH. (Rising.) Why don't you write the book anyway, Count Mirsky? There is a vogue these days for vituperative biography.

BORIS. I am not interested in the vogue.

KENNETH. We are quite used nowadays to children who dislike their fathers. The public—

BORIS. To titillate the public would not compensate me for forcing myself to recall the atmosphere of saintly sadism in which my childhood was spent—I can still smell that living room, I can still smell those stinking, sexless pilgrims who used to come from all over the world to get my saintly father's blessing. I used to sit with my mother in a room no bigger than a closet to get away from the odor of that nauseating humanitarianism. There was no

privacy in the Villa Mirskovitch. Oh, it was a Mecca—do you understan Mecca!

KENNETH. Yes, I think I understanc

BORIS. Well, I have been paying haloed one back. I have been getting vacy at his expense at last.

LEONIE. Why have you never told m fore that you felt this way about father?

BORIS. I never said anything about It was you who did the talking. Yo ways raved about the great man with characteristic American enthusiasm what you don't know.

LEONIE. Nevertheless, the world r nizes your father as a great man. books are there to prove it. There are. You can't write books like that out greatness—no matter what you You are a petulant child. Your fathe a great man.

BORIS. It makes no difference how he was—those pilgrims stank! (L turns away.)

KENNETH. I suggest that to write book, even if no one ever sees the script but you, might amuse you—a of revenge which, when you were you were in no position to take.

BORIS. Are you trying to cure me, tor? Please don't trouble. I don't your particular species of profession I do not need any help from you goes to door back, turns to LEONIE. looks bewilderedly at KENNETH. BORI out.)

LEONIE. How did you know? You canny!

KENNETH. All in the day's work.

LEONIE. Why is it I always get my volved with men weaker than my certainly am no tower of strength.

KENNETH. Possibly not—but you a erous and impulsive. You have a te to accept people at the best of the valuation.

E. I want to help them. I do help
. After they get used to my help, af-
hey get to count on my help, I get
tient with them. Why, I ask myself,
people help themselves?

ETH. And very natural.

E. I seem to attract people like that!

ETH. Leonie—you are the last wo-
on earth Count Mirsky should marry.
vould only transfer his hatred of his
r to you.

E. I don't think I understand you,
eth—really I don't—and I do so want
derstand things.

ETH. Well—your charm, your gaiety,
position, your wealth, your beauty—
would oppress him. Again, he cannot
mself.—Or, if he is himself, it is to
his nonentity, his inferiority—again
econdary rôle—Leonie Frothingham's
nd—the son of Count Mirsky—the
nd of Leonie Frothingham. Again the
w—again, eternally and always—non-
nce. Poor fellow. (*Pause.*)

E. I'm so grateful to you, Kenneth.

ETH. Nonsense. You mustn't be grate-
me because I—exercise my profession.

E. I want to express my gratitude—
ne tangible form. I've been thinking
thing else lately. I can't sleep for
ng of it.

ETH. Well, if it gives you insomnia,
better tell me about it.

E. I want to make it possible for
o realize your ambition.

ETH. Ambition? What ambition?

E. Ah! You've forgotten, haven't
But you let it slip out one day—you
me professionally—but I do the
to you—non-professionally.

ETH. You terrify me!

E. That night last winter when we
to dinner in that little restaurant
you go with your doctor friends...
old me your dream.

ETH. My censor must have been nap-

LEONIE. He was. Or she was. What sex
is your censor?

KENNETH. That's none of your business.

LEONIE. I'm sorry.

KENNETH. Which of my dreams was I so
reckless as to reveal to you?

LEONIE. To have a sanatorium of your
own one day—so you can carry out your
own ideas of curing patients.

KENNETH. Oh, that! Out of the question.

LEONIE. Why?

KENNETH. To do it on the scale I visu-
alize, would cost more than I'm ever likely
to save out of my practice.

LEONIE. I'll give you the sanatorium. I've
never given anyone anything like that before. What fun!

KENNETH. Will I find it all wrapped up
in silver foil on Christmas morning?

LEONIE. Yes. You will! You will! We'll
have a suite in it for Mr. X.—for all your
anonymous friends—we'll entertain the
whole alphabet!

KENNETH. You see, Leonie!

LEONIE. What do you mean? I thought
you'd be—

KENNETH. Of course, it's terribly generous of you. I'm deeply touched. But . . .

LEONIE. But . . . ?

KENNETH. I'm a stranger to you.

LEONIE. Kenneth!

KENNETH. Outside of my professional relation—such as I have with scores of
patients—little more than that.

LEONIE. I thought—

KENNETH. And yet you are willing to
back me in a venture that would cost a
sizeable fortune—just on that. Leonie!
Leonie!

LEONIE. It would be the best investment
I've ever made. Paula's always telling me
I have no social consciousness. Well, this
would be.—It would keep me from feeling
so useless. I do feel useless, Kenneth. Please!

KENNETH. I'm sorry. I couldn't hear of it. Of course, it's out of the question.

LEONIE. It isn't. I can afford it. Why shouldn't I? It would be helping so many people—you have no right to refuse. It's selfish of you to refuse.

KENNETH. I distrust impulsive altruism. You will forgive me, Leonie, but it may often do harm.

LEONIE. How do you mean, Kenneth?

KENNETH. I gather you are about to endow a radical magazine for the *boys*—

LEONIE. Will and Dennis! I thought it would be nice to give them something to do!

KENNETH. Yes. You are prepared tc back them in a publication which, if it attained any influence, would undermine the system which makes you and your people like you possible.

LEONIE. But it never occurred to me anyone would read it.

KENNETH. There is a deplorably high literacy in this country. Unfortunately it is much easier to learn to read than it is to learn to think.

LEONIE. Well, if you don't think it's a good idea, Kenneth, I won't do it. But this sanatorium is different.

KENNETH. Why?

LEONIE. Because, if you must know it, it would be helping you—and that means everything in the world to me. There, I've said it. It's true! Kenneth—are you terrified?

KENNETH. You adorable child!

LEONIE. It's extraordinary, Kenneth—but you are the first strong man who's ever come into my life—(*Enter* PAULA, DENNIS, WILL, *door back*.) Oh, I'm very glad to see you! Will! Hullo, Dennis. You all know Dr. Rice. Mr. Dexter, Mr. McCarthy. Sit down, everybody. Well, children, how is New York? (DENNIS *crosses down front of them to chair left by sofa and sits*.)

WILL. Stifling, thank you.

LEONIE. Any luck yet?

WILL. I am available, but New York dead to its chief opportunity.

LEONIE. Then you can stay here for a You can both stay here.

DENNIS. That was all right when we w in college, Mrs. Frothingham. Can't d now.

LEONIE. Oh, you're working. I'm so g

DENNIS. I beg your pardon. Did you working?

LEONIE. Well, then! I don't see why can't stay here and take a holiday.

WILL. From what?

LEONIE. Since none of you are doing thing in town, you might as well stay and do nothing and be comfortable.

DENNIS. Yes, but it's an ethical quest When we're in New York doing noth we belong to the most respectable ve group going! The unemployed. As we have a status, position, authority. if we stay here doing nothing—what we? Low-down parasites.

KENNETH. No jobs about anywhere, e

WILL. Extinct commodity.

DENNIS. I did pretty well last week.

LEONIE. Really?

DENNIS. I was rejected by seven n papers—including the *Bronx Home* and the *Yonkers Herald*—six magaz and trade papers—a total of twenty-e rejections in all, representing a net over the previous week of seven solic jections. I submit to you, gentlemen, t progress—pass the cigars, Will.

LEONIE. Couldn't you stay here and rejected by mail?

DENNIS. Doesn't give you that same ing somehow—that good, rich, dark-br sensation of not being wanted!

LEONIE. You know, Kenneth, in a ious way, Dennis reminds me a bi Mr. X.

DENNIS. And who's X.?

LEONIE. A sporting acquaintance.

NIS. There's one thing I'd like to ask Rice. . . . Do you mind?

NETH. At your service

NIS. (*Turning chair and facing KEN-* I *upstage.*) In the psychoanalytic hier- y Freud is the god, isn't he?

NETH. Of one sect, yes.

NIS. Well, the original sect—

NETH. Yes. . . .

NIS. Now, every psychoanalyst has to himself analyzed. That's true, isn't Doctor?

NETH. Generally speaking—yes.

NIS. As I understand it, the highest es go to those nearest the Master him-

NETH. This boy is irreverent . . .

NIS. I know whereof I speak. I pre- d an article on the subject for *Fortune.*

L. Rejection number three hundred.

NIS. I am afraid, Will, that you are a ess worshipper!

NIE. Dennis is an *enfant terrible,* and exhausts himself keeping it up!

NIS. I have examined the racket with microscopic patience and this I find to rue: at the top of the hierarchy is the at Pan Sexualist of Vienna. To be an odox and accepted Freudian, you must been analyzed by another of the e. Now what I am burning to know his: Who analyzed Sig Freud himself? om does he tell his repressions to? Why, poor guy must be lonely as hell!

NIE. What would you do with him, neth? He has no repressions whatever!

NETH. He needs some badly.

NIE. I wonder what Dennis would con- to his psychoanalyst that he isn't al- s shouting to the world?

NIS. I'd make the psychoanalyst talk. KENNETH. *Beckoning.*) Tell me, Doc- what did you dream last night?

NETH. (*Behind his cupped hand.*) Not public.

DENNIS. (*Rises and crosses straight right.*) You see—he's repressed! I tell you these psychoanalysts are repressed. They've got nobody to talk to! I'm going swimming. It's pathetic! (*He goes out.*)

LEONIE. I'm going too. He makes me laugh. How about you, Kenneth?

KENNETH. Oh, I'll watch.

LEONIE. (*To others.*) Come along with us. There's plenty of time for a swim be- fore dinner. (KENNETH *starts out with* LEONIE.....*stops on the way.*)

KENNETH. I suppose you and your Irish friend edited the comic paper at college?

WILL. No, we edited the serious paper.

KENNETH. Just the same it must have been very funny. (*He goes out after* LEONIE.)

WILL. Don't think that feller likes me much.

PAULA. You're psychic.

WILL. Well, for the matter of that I'm not crazy about him either.

PAULA. Don't bother about him. Concen- trate on me!

WILL. How are you, darling?

PAULA. Missed you.

WILL. (*Pulls her to sofa and sits with her.* PAULA *left end sofa.*) And I you. Pretty lousy in town without you.

PAULA. Oh, poor darling!

WILL. Although my star is rising. I did some book-reviews for the New York *Times* and the *New Masses.*

PAULA. What a gamut!

WILL. I made, in fact, a total of eleven dollars. The student most likely to succeed in the first four months since graduation has made eleven dollars.

PAULA. Wonderful!

WILL. My classmates were certainly clair- voyant. As a matter of fact, I shouldn't have told you. Now I'll be tortured think- ing you're after me for my money.

PAULA. You'll never know!

WILL. (*Putting arm around her shoulders and drawing her to him.*) What've you been doing?

PAULA. Lying in the sun mostly.

WILL. Poor little Ritz girl.

PAULA. Wondering what you do every night.

WILL. Forty-second Street Library mostly. Great fun! Voluptuary atmosphere!

PAULA. Is your life altogether so austere?

WILL. Well, frankly, no. Not altogether.

PAULA. Cad!

WILL. What do you expect?

PAULA. Loyalty.

WILL. I am loyal. But you go around all day job-hunting. You find you're not wanted. It's reassuring after that to find a shoulder to lean on, sort of haven where you *are* wanted. Even the public library closes at ten. You have to go somewhere. If I'm ever Mayor of New York, I'll have the public libraries kept open all night ... the flop-houses of the intellectuals!

PAULA. Is it anyone special . . . ?

WILL. Just a generalized shoulder.

PAULA. Well, you're going to have a special one from now on—mine! You know, the way you're avoiding the issue is all nonsense.

WILL. You mean my gallant fight against you?

PAULA. I've decided that you are conventional and bourgeois. You're money-ridden.

WILL. Eleven dollars. They say a big income makes you conservative.

PAULA. I don't mean your money. I mean —my money. It's childish to let an artificial barrier like that stand between us. It's also childish to ignore it.

WILL. (*Rising.*) I don't ignore it. That's what worries me. I count on it. Already I find myself counting on it. I can't help it. Sitting and waiting in an office for some bigwig who won't see me or for

some underling who won't see me I thi "Why the Hell should I wait all day this stuffed shirt?" I don't wait. Is it cause of you I feel in a special catego Do I count on your money? Is that I don't wait as long as the other felle There's one consolation: the other fel doesn't get the job either. But the p is disquieting!

PAULA. What a Puritan you are!

WILL. (*Sitting beside her again.*) Wi become an appendage to you—like y mother's men?

PAULA. You're bound to—money or money.

WILL. (*Taking her into his arms.*) I pose I might as well go on the lai dole—

PAULA. What?

WILL. Once you are paid merely for isting—you are on the dole. I rather ho you know—

PAULA. What?

WILL. It's extraordinary the difference one's thinking when you're in college when you're out—

PAULA. How do you mean?

WILL. Well, when I was in college, interest in the—"movement"—was re impersonal. I imagined myself giving energies to the poor and the downtrod in my spare time. I didn't really bel I'd be one of the poor and downtrod myself. In my heart of hearts I was s I'd break through the iron law of Denr statistics and land a job somewhere. I can't—and it's given a tremendous to my self-esteem.

PAULA. But you'll come through. I'm s of it. I wish you could learn to look at money as a means rather than an enc

WILL. I'd rather use my own.

PAULA. You're proud.

WILL. I am.

PAULA. It's humiliating but I'm afraid got to ask you to marry me, Will.

L. It's humiliating but considering my
ngs I see no way out of accepting you.

LA. You submit?

L. (*Kissing her hand.*) I submit.

LA. After a hard campaign—victory!

L. You *are* a darling.

LA. (*Getting up and crossing to cen-*
) I can't tell you what a relief it'll be
get away from this house.

L. Why?

LA. I don't know. It's getting very
plicated.

L. Leonie?

LA. *And* Boris. *And* Dr. Rice. Funny
g how that man . . .

L. What?

LA. Makes you insecure somehow.

L. Supposed to do just the opposite.

LA. He answers every question—and
he's secretive. I've never met a man
—who—

L. Who what?

LA. Really, I can't stand Dr. Rice.

L. I believe he fascinates •you.

LA. He does. I don't deny that. And
n't tell you how I resent it. Isn't it
? (*The old lady* WYLER *in a wheel*
r is propelled in by a nurse. The old
is much wasted since the preceding
mer; she is touched with mortality.)
nny!

. WYLER. Paula! How are you, my
-?

LA. I came up to see you before, but
were asleep.

. WYLER. Nurse told me. (*Exit* NURSE,
left.)

LA. You remember Will?

L. How do you do, Mrs. Wyler?

. WYLER. Of course. How do you do,
ng man?

PAULA. Well, this is quite an adventure
for you, isn't it, Granny?

MRS. WYLER. You're the boy who was always so curious about my youth.

WILL. Yes.

MRS. WYLER. I've forgotten most of it.
Now I just live from day to day. The
past is just this morning. (*A moment's
pause.*) And I don't always remember that
very well. Aren't there insects who live
only one day? The morning is their youth
and the afternoon their middle age. . . .

PAULA. You don't seem yourself today.
Not as cheerful as usual.

MRS. WYLER. Can't I have my moods,
Paula? I am pleased to be reflective today.
People are always sending me funny books
to read. I've been reading one and it depressed me.

PAULA. Well, I'll tell you something to
cheer you up, Granny—Will and I are going to be married.

MRS. WYLER. Have you told your mother?

PAULA. Not yet. It's a secret. (*Enter* KEN-
NETH.)

KENNETH. Well, Mrs. Wyler! Wanderlust
today?

MRS. WYLER. Yes! Wanderlust!

KENNETH. Paula, if you're not swimming,
what about our walk, and our daily argument?

MRS. WYLER. What argument?

KENNETH. Paula is interested in my subject. She hovers between skepticism and
fascination.

PAULA. No chance to hover today, Kenneth. Will's improving his tennis. Sorry.

KENNETH. So am I.

MRS. WYLER. I've a surprise for you, Paula.

PAULA. What?

MRS. WYLER. Your father's coming.

PAULA. No!

MRS. WYLER. Yes.

PAULA. But how—! How do you know?

MRS. WYLER. Because I've sent for him, and he wired me he's coming. He's driving from Blue Hill. He should be here now.

PAULA. That's too—! Oh, Granny, that's marvelous! Will, let's drive out to meet him, shall we? Does Mother know?

MRS. WYLER. I only had Sam's wire an hour ago.

PAULA. Granny, you're an angel.

MRS. WYLER. Not quite yet. Don't hurry me, child.

PAULA. Come on, Will. (*Exit* PAULA *and* WILL.)

MRS. WYLER. I can see you are interested in Paula. You are, aren't you, Dr. Rice?

KENNETH. Yes. She's an extraordinary child. Adores her father, doesn't she?

MRS. WYLER. How would you cure that, Doctor?

KENNETH It's quite healthy.

MRS. WYLER. Really? I was hoping for something juicy in the way of interpretation.

KENNETH. Sorry!

MRS. WYLER. What an interesting profession yours is, Dr. Rice.

KENNETH. Why particularly?

MRS. WYLER. Your province is the soul. Strange region.

KENNETH. People's souls, I find are, on the whole, infinitely more interesting than their bodies. I have been a general practitioner and I know.

MRS. WYLER. These young 'people—don't they frighten you?

KENNETH. Frighten!

MRS. WYLER. They are so radical—prepared to throw everything overboard—every tradition—

KENNETH. Paula's friends have nothing to lose, any change would be—in the nature of velvet for them.

MRS. WYLER. What do you think of W

KENNETH. I'm afraid I've formed strongly defined opinion on Will.

MRS. WYLER. Oh, I see— That is a c ment in itself.

KENNETH. He's nondescript.

MRS. WYLER. Do you mean to point out to Paula?

KENNETH. I don't think so. That won' necessary.

MRS. WYLER. Why not?

KENNETH. Blood will tell.

MRS. WYLER. That's very gracious of Doctor. (*Pause.*) And what do you t of Leonie?

KENNETH. Very endearing—and very pulsive.

MRS. WYLER. For example—I mean of latter—

KENNETH. She offered to build me a atorium—a fully equipped modern s torium.

MRS. WYLER. Did she? Convenient you.

KENNETH. Except that I refused.

MRS. WYLER. Wasn't that quixotic?

KENNETH. Not necessarily. (PAULA SAM *enter, door back.*)

PAULA. Here he is!

MRS. WYLER. Sam!

SAM. Louise!

PAULA. He wouldn't come if I'd ask He said so shamelessly. You know Rice?

SAM. Of course.

KENNETH. Excuse me. (KENNETH *out*)

SAM. Well, Louise!

MRS. WYLER. Hello, Sam. (SAM *k her.*)

SAM. How's she behaving?

ʟᴀ. Incorrigible. Dr. Prentiss tells her
ᴇst in her room You see how she obeys
ᴀ. She'll obey you though.

. Well, I'll sneak her away from Dr.
ɴtiss and take her abroad.

�. ᴡʏʟᴇʀ. I want to go to Ethiopia.
ᴀ along, dear. I want to talk to Sam.

ʟᴀ. Keep him here, Granny. Pretend
're not feeling well.

. ᴡʏʟᴇʀ. I'll try. (*Exit* ᴘᴀᴜʟᴀ *door
ᵗ.*) Well, Sam—

. I got your wire last night. Here I

. ᴡʏʟᴇʀ. It's nice of you.

. Oh, now, Louise. You know you're
love of my life.

. ᴡʏʟᴇʀ. Yes, Sam, I know—but how
ᴇlena?

. Flourishing.

. ᴡʏʟᴇʀ. You're all right then?

. Unbelievably.

. ᴡʏʟᴇʀ. I knew you would be.

. And you?

. ᴡʏʟᴇʀ. I'm dying, Sam.

. Not you—

. ᴡʏʟᴇʀ. Don't contradict me. Besides,
rather looking forward to it.

. Is Dr. Prentiss—?

. ᴡʏʟᴇʀ. Dr. Prentiss soft-soaps me. I
ᴀim. It relieves his mind. But that's why
sent for you.

. You know, my dear—

. ᴡʏʟᴇʀ. Yes, Sam. I know I can
ᴀt on you. I'm dying. And I'm dying
ᴇ. I have to talk to somebody. You're
only one.

. Is anything worrying you?

. ᴡʏʟᴇʀ. Plenty.

. What, dear?

. ᴡʏʟᴇʀ. The future. Not my own.
ᵗ's fixed or soon will be. But Leonie's—
ᴀ's—

ꜱᴀᴍ. Aren't they all right?

ᴍʀꜱ. ᴡʏʟᴇʀ. I am surrounded by aliens.
The house is full of strangers. That Russian upstairs; this doctor.

ꜱᴀᴍ. Rice? Are you worried about him?

ᴍʀꜱ. ᴡʏʟᴇʀ. What is he after? What does
he want? He told me Leonie offered to
build him a sanatorium—

ꜱᴀᴍ. Did he accept it?

ᴍʀꜱ. ᴡʏʟᴇʀ. No. He refused. But something tells me he will allow himself to be
persuaded.

ꜱᴀᴍ. I don't think Rice is a bad feller
really. Seems pretty sensible. Are you worried about this boy—Dexter, and Paula?

ᴍʀꜱ. ᴡʏʟᴇʀ. Not in the same way. I like
the boy. But Paula—I'm worried about
what the money'll do to her. We know
what it's done to Leonie. You know, Sam,
in spite of all her romantic dreams Leonie
has a kind of integrity. But I often wonder if she's ever been really happy.

ꜱᴀᴍ. Oh, now, Louise, this pessimism's
unlike you—

ᴍʀꜱ. ᴡʏʟᴇʀ. This money we've built our
lives on—it used to symbolize security—
but there's no security in it any more.

ꜱᴀᴍ. Paul'll be all right. I count on Paula.

ᴍʀꜱ. ᴡʏʟᴇʀ. In the long run. But that
may be too late. One can't let go of everything, Sam. It isn't in nature. That's why
I've asked you to come. I want you to remain as executor under my will.

ꜱᴀᴍ. Well, I only resigned because—since
I'm no longer married to Leonie—

ᴍʀꜱ. ᴡʏʟᴇʀ. What has that got to do
with it?

ꜱᴀᴍ. All right.

ᴍʀꜱ. ᴡʏʟᴇʀ. Promise?

ꜱᴀᴍ. Certainly.

ᴍʀꜱ. ᴡʏʟᴇʀ. I feel something dark ahead,
a terror—

ꜱᴀᴍ. Now, now, you've been brooding.

ᴍʀꜱ. ᴡʏʟᴇʀ. Outside of you—Will is the
soundest person I'll leave behind me, the

healthiest—but in him too I feel a reckless-
ness that's just kept in—I see a vista of the
unknown—to us the unknown was the
West, land—physical hardship—but he's
hard and bitter underneath his jocularity—
he isn't sure, he says, what he is— Once
he is sure, what will he do?—I want you
to watch him, Sam, for Paula's sake.

SAM. I will.

MRS. WYLER. They're all strange and dark
. . . And this doctor. A soul doctor. We
didn't have such things—I am sure that
behind all this is a profound and healing
truth. But sometimes truths may be perverted, and this particular doctor—how are
we to know where his knowledge ends and
his pretension begins? Now that I am dying, for the first time in my life I know
fear. Death seems easy and simple, Sam—
a self-indulgence—but can I afford it? (*She
smiles up at him. He squeezes her hand.*)

SAM. Everything will be all right. Trust
me.

MRS. WYLER. I do. (*A pause.*) You'll stay
the night?

SAM. Of course.

MRS. WYLER. Now I feel better.

SAM. That's right. (*Pause.*)

MRS. WYLER. I'd like to live till autu

SAM. Of course you will. Many autum

MRS. WYLER. Heaven forbid. But this
tumn. The color— the leaves turn. (*L
ing out window.* SAM *looks too.*) The
pression seems strange. What do they t
to?

SAM. (*Softly, helping her mood.*) T
mother. The earth.

MRS. WYLER. I'm happy now. I'm at pe

SAM. (*Puts arm around her and dr
her to him.*) That's better.

MRS. WYLER. (*Smiling up at him.*)
very clever of me to have sent for y
Sam. I'm pleased with myself. Now, S
let 'em do their worst—

SAM. (*Smiling back at her and patt
her hand.*) Just let 'em . . . !

Curtain

SCENE II

SCENE: *The same.*

Time: *A few hours later—before dinner.*
LEONIE *is standing in doorway looking out.*
BORIS *center; he is fatalistically quiet at
first.*

BORIS. What it comes to is this then!
You're through with me. You want me
to go!

LEONIE. I'm no good to you! I can no
longer help you.

BORIS. Frustrated altruist!

LEONIE. You hate me!

BORIS. That would be encouraging!

LEONIE. We have nothing more for each
other.

BORIS. Less than we had in the beginning!

LEONIE. Less than I thought we had.

BORIS. (*Walking toward her.*) And the
man of science?

LEONIE. What?

BORIS. (*Still bearing down on her.*) T
intricate man of science. You fluctuate
Leonie. (*Facing her.*)

LEONIE. Please, Boris. I've failed. C
we part—beautifully?

BORIS. What do you want to do? Go
on the bay and say farewell before
villagers in a barge drawn by a flock
swans? Shall we have a little orchestra
play—with the strings sobbing—and
bassoon off key?

LEONIE. You are bitter and cruel. W
I've tried to help you. Why are you bitt

BORIS. (*Moving close to her.*) At l
I'm honest. Can you say the same?

LEONIE. (*Breaking away from him.*)
don't know what you mean by that.

BORIS. (*Getting in front of her.*) Yes,
do.

NIE. You're eating yourself up. You're
ng yourself. There's the great lovely
ld outside and you sit in your room
ng—

.s. What do you recommend? Cold
vers and Swedish massage? What does
man of science prescribe for me?

NIE. Why do you hate Kenneth so?

s. I'm jealous, my dear!

NIE. Poor Boris. You're beyond a
le emotion like that, aren't you?

s. I envy you, Leonie. All like you.

NIE. Do you?

s. I envy all sentimental liars who
fy their desires on high principle. It
.es all your diversions an exercise in
y. You're sick of me and want to sleep
the man of science. (LEONIE *turns*
y. *He seizes her arms and turns her*
im.) Does this suffice for you? No. It
t be that you can no longer help me.
tle silent laugh.) My sainted father
like that! God!

NIE. This is the end, Boris.

s. Of course it is. I tell you this
gh: Beware of him, Leonie. Beware
im.

NIE. Your hatred of Kenneth—like all
hatreds—they're unnatural, frighten-
I'm frightened of you. (*Turning from*
)

s. (*Crossing before her, closing door*
he can't escape.) Much better to be
tened of him. You know what I
k. What does he think? Does he tell
Do you know?

NIE. Yes, I know.

s. You know what he tells you. This
voyant who gets rich profoundly aning the transparent. (*Enter* KENNETH,
back.*)

NETH. Your mother would like to see
Leonie.

NIE. Is she all right? (BORIS *goes up-*
e to small table. Gets cigarette.)

KENNETH. Oh, very chipper. Mr. Frothingham is with her.

LEONIE. She sent for Sam, didn't she? I
wonder why.

BORIS. Perhaps she felt the situation too
complicated—even for *you,* Dr. Rice.

KENNETH. I don't think so.

BORIS. You are so Olympian, Dr. Rice.
Would it be possible to anger you?

KENNETH. Symptoms, my dear Count,
never anger me. I study them.

BORIS. Really, you are in a superb position. I quite envy you. One might cut
oneself open in front of you—and it would
be a symptom. Wouldn't it?

LEONIE. Boris, please—what's the good?

BORIS. (*Crossing slowly to* LEONIE.) You
are quite right, my dear, no good—no good
in the world. Give your mother this message for me. Tell her that under the circumstances I shall simplify the situation by
withdrawing.

LEONIE. You make me very unhappy,
Boris.

BORIS. How agreeable then that you have
Dr. Rice here—to resolve your unhappiness.
(*Crosses quickly to table behind sofa and
puts out cigarette.*)

LEONIE. (*Following him.*) Where will you
be in case I—in case you—Boris?

BORIS. Don't worry about me. A magazine
syndicate has offered me a great deal for
sentimental reminiscences of my father.
Imagine that, sentimental! They have
offered me—charming Americanism—a
ghost-writer. It will be quaint—one ghost
collaborating with another ghost. (*Raising
hand like Greek priest.*) My blessings,
Leonie. (*Kisses her hand.*) You have been
charming. Dr. Rice— (*He bows formally.
Exit* BORIS.)

LEONIE. Poor Boris— (*She sinks into a
chair, overcome.*)

KENNETH. He's part of the past. You
must forget him.

LEONIE. Poor Boris!

KENNETH. You will forget him.

LEONIE. I'll try.

KENNETH. Exorcised!

LEONIE. You know, Kenneth, I feel you are the only one in the world I can count on.

KENNETH. Not me.

LEONIE. Whom else?

KENNETH. Yourself!

LEONIE. Light reed! Fragile! Fragile!

KENNETH. Pliant but unbreakable.

LEONIE. No. Don't think much of myself, Kenneth. Really I don't. My judgment seems to be at fault somehow. Paula thinks so too. She's always lecturing me. (*Sits right end of sofa.*)

KENNETH. Paula can't abide me.

LEONIE. It's not true!

KENNETH. You know, Leonie, I have an instinct in these matters—so, also, has your daughter.

LEONIE. Don't you like Paula?

KENNETH. I love her. Everyone connected with you.

LEONIE. Kenneth! How dear of you! Of course Paula and I are poles apart. Look at her friends!

KENNETH. Raffish!

LEONIE. (*A little taken aback by this.*) Oh, do you think so? All of them? Don't you like Will?

KENNETH. Nice enough. Clever in his way. With an eye to the main chance.

LEONIE. Really?

KENNETH. Naturally—penniless boy.

LEONIE. I've always encouraged Paula to be independent. I've never tried to impose my ideals or my standards on her. Have I done wrong to give her her own head this way? She's such a darling, really. She's killing, you know. So superior, so knowing. The other day—the other day, Ken-

neth . . . I took her to lunch in town she criticized me—now what do you th about?

KENNETH. (*Sitting on arm of chair.*) once my intuition fails me.

LEONIE. About my technique with m She said it was lousy. Isn't it delicious

KENNETH. Not more specific than sim lousy?

LEONIE. She said I threw myself at r instead of reversing the process.

KENNETH. But I should think she wo have approved of that. She makes suc fetish of being candid!

LEONIE. That's just what I said—exac I said I couldn't pretend—that I coul descend to—technique. I said that when feelings were involved I saw no point not letting the other person see it. I proached her for deviousness. Strange i that child has—strange!

KENNETH. I'm afraid her generation theory-ridden! (*Pause.*)

LEONIE. Kenneth?

KENNETH. Yes, Leonie?

LEONIE. It's true of course.

KENNETH. What?

LEONIE. Paula's—criticism. I can't con my feelings. Least of all—from you. (*Sl pause.*)

KENNETH. Why should you?

LEONIE. Oh, Kenneth, I'm so useless! know how useless I am!

KENNETH. I know only that you are cious and lovely—and that you have gift of innocence.

LEONIE. I hate my life. It's been so tered—emotionally.

KENNETH. Whose isn't?

LEONIE. You are such a comfort. R it's too much now to expect me to without you. Kenneth?

KENNETH. Yes . . . Leonie.

ONIE Will you be a darling—and marry ?

NNETH. Leonie?

ONIE. (*Returning his gaze.*) Yes, Kenth.

NNETH. Have you thought this over?

ONIE. It's the first time—the very first ne—that I've ever been sure.

NNETH. You are so impulsive, Leonie.

ONIE. Kenneth, don't you think we'd ve a chance—you and I—don't you nk? (*Enter* PAULA, *door back.*)

ULA. (*Realizes she has interrupted a e-à-tête.*) Oh, sorry—!

ONIE. Paula dear, have you been with other?

ULA. Yes. Granny wants to see you, as matter of fact.

ONIE. Oh, I forgot! Is she all right? eerful?

ULA. Oh, very.

ONIE. I'll be right there. Stay and talk Kenneth, Paula. He thinks you don't e him. Prove to him it isn't true. Do u think you could be gracious, Paula? is that too old-fashioned? (*Exit* LEONIE or back. *In the following scene* PAULA termines to get rid of the tantalizing and itating mixed feelings she has about NNETH, her sense of distrusting, dislik- g and simultaneously being fascinated by m—she feels he has something up his eve; she is playing a game to discover at it is and yet she becomes increasingly nscious that game is not unpleasant to r because of her interest in her victim.*)

ULA. Leonie's all a-flutter. What is it?

NNETH. She was just telling me—she vies you your poise.

ULA. Your intentions are honorable, I pe.

NNETH. Old hat, Paula.

ULA. I beg your pardon.

NNETH. Undergraduate audacity. Scott tzgerald. Old hat.

PAULA. We don't like each other much, do we?

KENNETH. That's regrettable.

PAULA. And yet—I'm very curious about you.

KENNETH. What would you like to know?

PAULA. Your motive.

KENNETH. Ah!

PAULA. And yet even if you told me—

KENNETH. You wouldn't believe it?

PAULA. (*Facing him.*) No. Now why is that? Even when you are perfectly frank, your frankness seems to me—a device. Now why is that?

KENNETH. I'll tell you.

PAULA. Why?

KENNETH. Because you yourself are confused, muddled, unsure, contradictory. I am simple and co-ordinated. You resent that. You dislike it. You envy it. You would like such simplicity for yourself. But, as you are unlikely to achieve it, you soothe yourself by distrusting me.

PAULA. You say I'm muddled. Why am I muddled?

KENNETH. You've accepted a set of premises without examining them or thinking about them. You keep them like jewels in a box and dangle them. Then you put them back in the box, confident that they belong to you. But as they don't you feel an occasional twinge of insecurity—

PAULA. Do you mind dropping the parables—?

KENNETH. Not at all—

PAULA. Why am I muddled? For example—

KENNETH. You're a walking contradiction in terms—

PAULA. For example?

KENNETH. For example—for example— your radicalism. Your friends. Your point of view. Borrowed. Unexamined. Insincere.

PAULA. Go on.

KENNETH. You are rich and you are exquisite. Why are you rich and exquisite? (*Walking back to face her.*) Because your forbears were not moralistic but ruthless. Had they been moralistic, had they been concerned, as you pretend to be, with the "predatory system"—this awful terminology—you'd be working in a store somewhere wrapping packages or waiting on querulous housewives with bad skins or teaching school. Your own origins won't bear a moralistic investigation. You must know that. Your sociology and economics must teach you that.

PAULA. Suppose I repudiate my origins?

KENNETH. That takes more courage than you have.

PAULA. Don't be so sure.

KENNETH. But why should you? If you had a special talent or were a crusader there might be some sense in it. But you have no special talent and you are not a crusader. Much better to be decorative. Much better for a world starving for beauty. Instead of repudiating your origins you should exult in them and in that same predatory system that made you possible. (*Crossing to table behind sofa for cigarette.*) (*Pause.*)

PAULA. What were your origins?

KENNETH. (*Lighting cigarette.*) Anonymous.

PAULA. What do you mean?

KENNETH. I was discovered on a doorstep.

PAULA. Really?

KENNETH. Like Moses.

PAULA. Where were you brought up?

KENNETH. In a foundling asylum in New England. The place lacked charm. This sounds like an unpromising beginning but actually it was more stimulating than you might imagine. I remember as a kid of twelve going to the library in Springfield and getting down the *Dictionary of National Biography* and hunting out the bastards. Surprising how many distinguished ones there were and are. I allied myself early with the brilliant and variegated company of the illegitimate.

PAULA. You don't know who your pare[nts] were?

KENNETH. No.

PAULA. Did you get yourself through c[ol]lege?

KENNETH. *And* medical school.

PAULA. Did you practice medicine?

KENNETH. For a bit. I devoted mysel[f] when the victims would let me—to th[e] noses and throats. It was a starveling [oc]cupation. But I gave up tonsilectomy [for] the soul. The poor have tonsils but o[nly] the rich have souls. My instinct was j[us]tified—as you see.

PAULA. You've gone pretty far.

KENNETH. Incredible journey!

PAULA. Having come from—from—

KENNETH. The mud—?

PAULA. Well—I should think you'd [be] more sympathetic to the under-dogs.

KENNETH. No, why should I? The he[rd] bores me. It interests me only as an in[di]cation of the distance I've travelled.

PAULA. Will would say that you are [a] lucky individual who—

KENNETH. Yes, that is what Will wo[uld] say. It always satisfies the mediocrity [to] call the exceptional individual lucky.

PAULA. You don't like Will?

KENNETH. I despise him.

PAULA. Why?

KENNETH. I detest these young firebra[nds] whose incandescence will be extinguish[ed] by the first job! I detest radicals w[ho] lounge about in country-houses.

PAULA. You're unfair to Will.

KENNETH. I have no interest in being f[air] to him. We were discussing you.

PAULA. You are too persuasive. I don't [be]lieve you.

KENNETH. My advice to you is to fi[nd] out what you want before you comm[it] yourself to young Mr. Dexter.

ULA. But I have committed myself.

KENNETH. Too bad.

ULA. For him or for me?

KENNETH. For both of you; but for him particularly.

ULA. Why?

KENNETH. I see precisely the effect your money will have on him. He will take it and the feeling will grow in him that in having given it you have destroyed what he calls his integrity. He will even come to believe that if not for this quenching initiative he might have become a shining leader of the people. At the same time he will be aware that both these comforting alibis are delusions—because he has no integrity to speak of nor any initiative to speak of. Knowing they are lies he will simply proclaim them the louder, cling to them the harder. He will hate you as the thief of his character—petty larceny, I must say.

ULA. (*Jumping up, taking several steps away from him.*) That's a lie.

KENNETH. Will is an American Puritan. A foreigner—Boris, for example—marries money, feeling that he gives value received. Very often he does. But young Dexter will never feel that—and maybe he'll be right.

ULA. You hate Will.

KENNETH. You flatter him.

ULA. How did you get to know so much about people? About what they feel and what they will do?

KENNETH. I began by knowing myself—by not lying to myself. (*A silence. He looks at her. He takes in her loveliness. He speaks her name, in a new voice, softly.*) Paula—

ULA. (*She looks at him fixedly.*) What?

KENNETH. Paula—

ULA. What?

KENNETH. Do you know me any better now? Do you trust me any better now?

ULA. I don't know. (*Enter* WILL.)

KENNETH. Paula, Paula, Paula— (PAULA *starts toward door back.*) Don't go, Paula!

WILL. Oughtn't you to be changing for dinner? (PAULA *stops upstage.*) Hello, Doctor. What's the matter?

KENNETH. May I congratulate him?

WILL. What's he been saying?

KENNETH. Paula told me she is going to marry you.

PAULA. The doctor is a cynic.

KENNETH. We were discussing the European and American points of view toward money marriages—There's a great difference. The European fortune-hunter, once he has landed the bag, has no more twinge of conscience than a big-game hunter when he has made his kill. The American—

WILL. Is that what you think I am, Doctor?

KENNETH. (*To* PAULA *amiably.*) You see. He resents the mere phrase. But my dear boy, that is no disgrace. We are all fortune-hunters—

PAULA. (*Pointedly.*) Not all, Kenneth—!

KENNETH. But I see no difference at all between the man who makes a profession of being charming to rich ladies—or any other—specialist. The former is more arduous.

PAULA. Are you defending Will or yourself?

KENNETH. I am generalizing. (*To* WILL.) Congratulations! I admit that to scatter congratulations in this way is glib, but we live in a convention of glibness. Good God, we congratulate people when they marry and when they produce children— we skim lightly over these tremendous hazards— Excuse me. (*Exit* KENNETH.)

WILL. God damn that man!

PAULA. Will!

WILL. I can't stand him—not from the moment I saw him—because he's incapable of disinterestedness himself, h e c a n ' t imagine it in others. He's the kind of cynical, sneering— He's a marauder. The adventurer with the cure-all. This is just the moment for him. And this is just the place!

PAULA. I've never seen you lose your temper before, Will.

WILL. You know why, don't you?

PAULA. Why?

WILL. Because he's right! While he was talking I felt like hitting him. At the same time a voice inside me said: Can you deny it? When I came in here he was saying your name. He was looking at you —it seems he hasn't quite decided, has he?

PAULA. I'm worried about him and Leonie—

WILL. He's got Leonie hook, line and sinker. That's obvious.

PAULA. She mustn't! Will, she mustn't!

WILL. You can't stop it—you can't do anything for Leonie. Nobody can do anything for anybody. Nobody should try.

PAULA. Will—you mustn't go back to New York. You must stay and help me.

WILL. Sorry. Nothing doing.

PAULA. Will!

WILL. I have a feeling you'll rather enjoy saving Leonie from the doctor.

PAULA. Will! That's not fair, Will!

WILL. It may not be fair but it is obvious. Also, it is obvious that the doctor won't mind being saved.

PAULA. It's lucky for both of us that one of us has some self-control.

WILL. No, I won't stay here. I hate the place, I hate Dr. Rice, I hate myself for being here!

PAULA. Don't let me down, Will—I need you terribly just now—

WILL. (At white heat.) I haven't quite the technique of fortune hunting yet—in the European manner. Which of the two is he after—you or Leonie? Will he flip a coin?

PAULA. I hate you! I hate you!

WILL. Well, we know where we are any rate.

PAULA. Yes. We do! (LEONIE comes ru[n]ning in. She wears an exquisite summ[er] evening frock. She is breathless with h[ap]piness.)

LEONIE. Paula! Why aren't you dresse[d] I want you to wear something especia[lly] lovely tonight! Do you like this? It's ne[w] I haven't worn it before. (She twirls [for] them.) I've a surprise for you, Will. You[']ll know what it is in a minute. I was thi[nk]ing of you and it popped into my mi[nd] You know, Will, I'm very, very fond [of] you. And I think you are equally fond [of] me. I can't help liking people who li[ke] me. I suppose you think I'm horribly va[in] But then, everybody's vain about som[e]thing. (BUTLER comes in with cocktails a[nd] sandwiches, to table right of fireplace.) [If] they're not, they're vain about their la[ck] of vanity. I believe that's a mot! Pre[tty] good for a brainless— Here, Will, have [a] cocktail— (WILL takes cocktail.) Paula what's your pet vanity? She thinks min[e is] my looks but it's not. If I had my w[ay] I shouldn't look at all the way I look. (E[n]ter DR. DEXTER, door back. He wears [a] sea-green baggy dinner-suit; he looks "hicky" and uncertain as ever.)

DEXTER. Good evening, Mrs. Frothingha[m]

LEONIE. Dr. Dexter—how good of you [to] come. Delighted to see you.

DEXTER. Good evening. Hello, Will.

WILL. Dad!

DEXTER. Mrs. Frothingham invited [me.] Didn't you know?

LEONIE. (Takes DEXTER's arm and goes [to] WILL.) You told me you had to leave [to]morrow to visit your father in Brunsw[ick] so I just called him up in Brunswick—

DEXTER. She sent the car all the way [for] me. Nice car. Great springs.

LEONIE (To WILL.) Now you won't ha[ve] to leave tomorrow. You can both spe[nd] the week-end here.

WILL. (Walking away a little righ[t.]) Awfully nice of you, Leonie.

NIE. (*Following him.*) (DEXTER *sits on* a.) You see, Will, I leave the big issues the professional altruists. I just do what can toward making those around me ppy. And that's *my* vanity! (*Enter* DEN-, *door back.*)

NNIS. Well! Well! **Fancy** that now, dda!

ONIE. Oh, hello, Dennis, just in time a cocktail. (LEONIE *leads him over to* a. WILL *is isolated down right center.*)

NNIS. (*To* DEXTER.) How are you?

XTER. (*Not friendly.*) I'm all right.

NNIS. Complicated week-end! You and Healer! Faraday and Cagliostro. That'll something.

ONIE. (*Takes* DENNIS's *arm.*) Everybody s me to like you, Dennis. I'm in such a od that I'm going to make the effort.

NNIS. I've been waiting for this. I'm illed!

ONIE. (*Strolling with him across stage* nt.) Something tells me you could be y charming if you wanted to. Tell me, nnis, have you ever tried being lovable l sweet?

NNIS. For you, Mrs. Frothingham, I uld willingly revive the age of chivalry!

ONIE. But there's no need of that. I t want you to be nice. Here, have a ktail. Give you courage.

NNIS. Just watch me from now on, Mrs. othingham.

ONIE. I will. Passionately. (*Hands him* ktail.) I'll be doing nothing else. (BUT- crosses back of sofa, *offers* DEXTER *and* ULA *cocktails.* DR. RICE *comes in.*)

NNIS. (*Stage sigh.*) A-h-h! The doctor! t in time to look at my tongue, Doctor.

NNETH. That won't be necessary, young n. I can tell— It's excessive.

ONIE. (*Crossing to* KENNETH.) Kenneth ou remember Will's father—Dr. Dexter.

NNETH. How do you do? (*They shake* ds. *A second* BUTLER *has come in and* and ROBERT *are passing cocktails and*

hors d'oeuvres. LEONIE *keeps circulating among her guests.* KENNETH *and* DEXTER *are in the center—*DENNIS, *obeying a malicious impulse, presides over them. Announces a theme on which he eggs them on to utter variations.*)

DENNIS. A significant moment, ladies and gentlemen—the magician of Science meets the magician of Sex—The floating libido bumps the absolute! What happens?

DEXTER. (*Cupping his hand to his ear.*) What? (WILL *crosses to door and looks out moodily.*)

DENNIS. The absolute hasn't got a chance. Isn't that right, Dr. Rice?

KENNETH. I shouldn't venture to contradict a young intellectual. Especially a very young intellectual.

LEONIE. (*Crosses front of* KENNETH, *to* DENNIS.) There, you see, I'm afraid, after all, I'll have to give you up, Dennis. You can't be lovable. You can't be sweet.

DENNIS. But I didn't promise to be winsome to everybody, only to you.

LEONIE. You really must treat him, Kenneth. He has no censor at all.

DENNIS. My censor is the Catholic tradition. We Catholics anticipated both Marx and Freud by a little matter of nineteen centuries. Spiritually, we have a Communion in the Holy Ghost—Communion. As for Dr. Rice, he offers confession without absolution. He is inadequate. (LEONIE *returns with tray of canapes.*)

LEONIE. It seems such bad taste to discuss religion at cocktail time. Try a stuffed olive.

DEXTER. By the time you got your beautiful new world, true science will have perished.

LEONIE. Aren't you too pessimistic, Dr. Dexter? Too much science has made you gloomy. Kenneth, the depression hasn't stopped your work, has it? Depression or no depression— (WILL *springs up.*)

WILL. (*Tensely.*) That's right, Leonie. (*Everyone faces* WILL.) Depression or no depression—war or peace—revolution or reaction—Kenneth will reign supreme! (KENNETH *stares at him.* WILL *confronts him.*)

LEONIE. Will!

WILL. Yes, Leonie. His is the power and the glory!

LEONIE. Dennis, this is your influence—

WILL. I admire you unreservedly, Doctor. Of your kind you are the best. You are the essence.

KENNETH. You embarrass me.

WILL. Some men are born ahead of their time, some behind, but you are made pat for the instant. Now is the time for you— when people are unemployed and distrust their own capacities—when people suffer and may be tempted—when integrity yields to despair—now is the moment for you!

KENNETH. (*Strolling closer to him so they are face to face.*) When, may I ask, is the moment for you—when if ever?

WILL. After your victory. When you are stuffed and inert with everything you want, then will be the time for me. (*He goes out.*)

PAULA. (*Running after* WILL.) Will . . . Will . . . Will . . . (*She follows him out.*)

LEONIE. (*Devastated by this strange behavior.*) What is it? I don't like it when people stand in the middle of the floor and make speeches. What's the matter with him? Dennis, do you know?

DENNIS. (*With a look at* KENNETH.) can guess.

LEONIE. Has he quarreled with Paul Paula is so inept. She doesn't know ho to . . . At the same time, if he had grievance, why couldn't he have kept until after dinner? (*Enter* ROBERT.)

ROBERT. Dinner is served. (*Exit* ROBERT

LEONIE. Well, we'll do what we can. Sa is dining with Mother in her room, Bo has a headache. Dennis, you and D Dexter—

DENNIS. You've picked me, Dr. Dexter. congratulate you.

DEXTER. Thank God, I can't hear a wo you say. (*Exit* DEXTER, *door back.*)

DENNIS. (S*adistically.*) Oh, yes, he ca And we'll fight it out on these lines if takes all dinner. (*He follows* DEXTER ou

LEONIE. What extraordinary behavi What do you suppose, Kenneth—shall go after them?

KENNETH. I wouldn't. It's their proble Give them time.

LEONIE. (*Reassured.*) You are so wi Kenneth. How did I ever get on witho you? I have that secure feeling that y are going to be my last indiscretion. Wh I think how neatly I've captured you— feel quite proud. I guess my techniq isn't so lousy after all. (*She takes his a and swings along beside him as th waltz in to dinner.*)

Curtain

ACT THREE

SCENE: *The same.*
Time: *Late that fall. The trees have turn-ed. The sumach have put out the brilliant red flowers of autumn.*

At Rise: WILL *and* DENNIS *have just arrived, and are standing at fireplace, back.* LEONIE *comes in to greet them.* SAM *strolls in with her.*

LEONIE. I'm so glad to see you! (*She shakes hands with each of them warmly.*) Will! How are you? (*To* DENNIS.) It's so good of you to come.

SAM. (*Shaking hands with* WILL.) V glad to see you.

WILL. Thanks. (SAM *shakes hands w* DENNIS.)

LEONIE. Sam drove over for a few ho from Blue Hill to talk business to me. hasn't had much luck so far. It's sim wonderful having you boys here—it's l old times. I didn't tell Paula. (*To* SA I did all this on my own. It's a' surprise Paula.

NNIS. She'll be overcome when she sees
_. Maybe you should prepare her.

LL. Where is Paula?

ONIE. Isn't it provoking! She and Kenth went for a walk. They should have
_n back long before this. (*Turning back
_them.*) Paula hasn't been at all herself,
ill. I thought you would cheer her up.

NNIS. I will be glad to do what I can,
course. Several very stubborn cases have
_lded to my charm.

ONIE. I'm sure! Do sit down. (*She sits.*)

NNIS. (*Taking out his pipe.*) Do you
_nd? (WILL *sits.*)

ONIE. Oh, please—I can't tell you how
_appreciate your coming—

NNIS. (*The harassed business man.*)
_ll, as a matter of fact, Leonie, it wasn't
_y to get away from the office—

ONIE. Are you in an office?

NNIS. Sometimes as many as fifteen in
_day. (LEONIE *laughs.*) But when I got
_ur appealing letter — *and* the return
_kets—I'm chivalrous at heart, you know,
_onie—

ONIE. I know you are!

_. How's town?

_LL. Very hot.

_. I'm just on my way down. Stopped
_to go over several things with Leonie—

ONIE. Poor Sam's been having an awful
_e with me. He keeps putting things in
_row. Where is escrow?

NNIS. It's where squirrels put nuts in
_ winter-time.

ONIE. I see! Dennis is much more lucid
_n you, Sam.

NNIS. I have a knack for making the
_truse translucent. Especially in eco-
_mics. Now, would you like to know why
_gland went off gold?

ONIE. No, I wouldn't.

NNIS. I shall yield to your subconscious
_nand and tell you.

LEONIE. (*To others.*) Help!

DENNIS. I see that there is no audience
for my peculiar gift.

LEONIE. You know, Will, I've thought
perhaps you were angry with us.

WILL. Why?

LEONIE. You haven't been here for so long.
(*To* SAM.) Since Granny died—none of
them have been here. Did Paula write you
about Granny's funeral?

WILL. No. She didn't.

LEONIE. Of course I hate funerals—I can't
bear them—but this was so—natural.
Mother wanted to live till the fall and she
did. It was a dreaming blue sky and there
was that poignant haze over the hills and
over the bay, and the smell of burning
wood from somewhere. Burning wood
never smells at any other time the way it
does in Indian summer. And the colors
that day! Did you ever, Sam, see such a
day?

SAM. It was beautiful.

LEONIE. They say the colors of autumn
are the colors of death, but I don't believe
that. They were in such strength that day.
I cried—but not on account of Mother—
that kind of day always makes me cry a
little bit anyway. You couldn't cry over
consigning anyone you loved to an earth
like that—on a day like that. I put some
blazing leaves over her, but when I passed
there the other day, they were withered
and brown—

SAM. (*Chiding her.*) Now Leonie—

LEONIE. Sam thinks I shouldn't talk about
Mother. But I don't see why. She doesn't
depress me. I think of her with joy. She
had a wonderful life.

SAM. She was a wonderful woman.

LEONIE. (*To* WILL.) Imagine, Will—when
Sam was here last time—you were here
that week-end—she *knew*. She asked Sam
to be executor of her will.

SAM. (*Very annoyed at her for bringing
this up.*) Leonie—

LEONIE. Why didn't you tell me, Sam,
then?

SAM. Seemed no point.

LEONIE. She didn't want me to know, did she?

SAM. No. She didn't want to distress you. (*A moment's pause.*)

LEONIE. What can be keeping Paula? (*She glances out of the window.*) Sam, do you want to talk business to me some more?

SAM. I'd like to talk to Will a minute.

LEONIE. Oh—yes. Well, Dennis, wouldn't you like me to show you to your room? (*She rises, goes to door into hallway.* DENNIS *follows.*)

DENNIS. Thanks. I've got to answer a chain letter.

LEONIE. I've given you a room you've never had. The tower room.

DENNIS. Is it ivory? I won't be comfortable if it isn't ivory.

LEONIE. Well just this once you're going to be uncomfortable — and like it! (*She goes out.*)

DENNIS. (*Tragically.*) And for this I gave up a superb view of the gas-house on 149th Street. (*He goes out.*)

SAM. (*Rises and goes up toward fireplace.*) Will—

WILL. Yes, Mr. Frothingham.

SAM. Oh—call me Sam.

WILL. All right.

SAM. I'll have to be pushing off in an hour or so. I rather wanted to talk to you.

WILL. Yes—

SAM. (*Wipes his forehead.*) Gosh, Leonie's a difficult woman to talk business to. (*Sits.*)

WILL. I can imagine that. She's not interested in business

SAM. She —is—not!!!

WILL. What do you want to speak to me about?

SAM. Paula.

WILL. What about Paula?

SAM. As I'm her father—I hope you wo[n]t think me—

WILL. Of course not—

SAM. It's not altogether easy—

WILL. Do you want me to help you?

SAM. Yes. I wish you would!

WILL. You're worried about Paula and m[e] aren't you? So was her grandmother. Y[ou] think me irresponsible. Less responsible f[or] example—(*As if making a random co[m]parison*) than Dr. Rice?

SAM. Well, as a matter of fact, I've rath[er] gotten to know Dr. Rice, and in ma[ny] respects, he's a pretty sound feller. (*Risi[ng] and going to stand above* WILL.) Hang [it] all, Will, I like you, and I don't like [to] preach to you, you know.

WILL. Go on.

SAM. Well, there are—from my point [of] view at least—a lot of nonsensical id[eas] knocking about. I'd like to point out j[ust] one thing to you. Your radicalism a[nd] all that— Well, the point is this—if y[ou] marry Paula—and I hope you do, becau[se] I like you—and, what is more importa[nt] Paula likes you—you'll have responsib[ili]ties. Paula will be rich. Very rich. Mo[ney] means responsibility. Now, I shouldn't, [for] example, like you to start radical ma[ga]zines with it. I shouldn't like you to [let] money drift through your fingers in [all] sorts of aimless, millennial directions t[hat] won't get anywhere.

WILL. Who told you that was my int[en]tion?

SAM. A little bird.

WILL. With a black moustache?

SAM. Does that matter?

WILL. No.

SAM. (*Putting hand on* WILL's *should[er].* As a matter of fact, I'm not worried ab[out] you at all. Money, I expect, will do to [you] what getting power does to radical [op]position, once it gets office—

WILL. Emasculate me, you mean?

SAM. Well, hardly. Mature you. O[nce]

're rich yourself, I have no doubt you'll
—

L. Sound.

. Yes. Sound. But your friends—this
Carthy boy—

L. Well, I can easily cut Dennis—all
poor and unsound friends—

. (*Quietly.*) I'm sorry you're taking
tone with me, Will. I'm the last person
he world to ask you to drop anybody.
be ashamed of you if you did. Only—

L. Only?

. I must tell you that I am in posi-
—by virtue of the will left by Mrs.
er—to keep Paula's money from being
for any purpose that might be con-
ed as—subversive.

L. From whose point of view?

. (*Quietly.*) From mine.

. I see.

Possibly you may not believe this—
I trust you, Will. Mrs. Wyler trusted

. You needn't worry. Paula seems to
other interests apparently.

What do you mean?

. Sounder interests— (DENNIS *enters,*
ugh door back.)

IS. The tower room lets in light on
sides, but nothing to look at. Just the
and the landscape.

What did you do with Leonie?

IS. She's gone to her mother's room
otter around.

Maybe I can get her attention while
pottering. Excuse me. (SAM *goes out.*)

IS. Poor Leonie—she's the last of the
y ladies. The inheritance taxes'll get
soon. You know we were by way of
ng our magazine from Leonie when
Rice spiked our guns. So I'm leaving.
time is too valuable. But the Healer
t last forever, and when he goes, I
return. Take heart, my good man. I

know you feel a little tender about this,
but remember, my lad, it's the Cause that
counts. Remember what Shaw says: "There
is no money but the devil's money. It is
all tainted and it might as well be used
in the service of God." (*A moment—*WILL
is obviously thinking of something else.)
What's the matter?

WILL. Nothing.

DENNIS. (*Bringing down chair to sit left
of* WILL *he imitates* RICE's *manner.*) Now
you must speak, young man—how can I
sublimate your subconscious troubles, if
you won't speak? Are you unhappy about
Paula, my lad? (*No answer.*) Tell me
what's happened between you—relieve your
soul, and, as a reward, I may make you
co-editor of our magazine. (*No response.
He rises and walks to opposite side of
table.*) No? Assistant editor you remain. I
may even fire you. Yes, I think I will fire
you. (*Crossing in front of* WILL *to fireplace.*) Dexter—you're through. Go upstairs and get your check. (*Rubs his hands
together in glee.*) God, it gives me a sense
of power to fire a man—especially an old
friend! (PAULA *and* KENNETH *come in door
right from the garden.*)

PAULA. (*Amazed to see them.*) Will! But
how—! Dennis!

WILL. (*Rather coolly.*) Hello, Paula.

DENNIS. We came to surprise you. Now
that we have surprised you, we can go
home.

WILL. Leonie asked me to come.

PAULA. Oh. Well, it's very nice to see you.

WILL. Thanks.

PAULA. When I wired you to come a few
weeks ago, you were too busy. It takes
Leonie, doesn't it?

DENNIS. You should have tried me, Paula.
Hello, Dr. Rice. How's business? Any sup-
pressions today?

KENNETH. (*Significantly.*) Apparently not.

DENNIS. Well, come on up to my room,
Doctor, and we'll play Twenty Questions.
(*He goes out.*)

WILL. Hello, Dr. Rice.

KENNETH. How are you?

PAULA. Will—I'm awfully glad to see you. I was just going to write you to thank you for the sweet letter you sent me after Granny died.

KENNETH. I'm afraid it's my fault, Dexter. I do my best to keep Paula so busy that she finds no time to write letters.

WILL. I was sure I could count on you, Doctor. (WILL goes out.)

PAULA. You enjoy hurting Will, don't you?

KENNETH. When there is an obstacle in my path, I do my best to remove it.

PAULA. What makes you think it is only Will that stands between us— That if left to myself I—

KENNETH. Because it is true. Were it not for the squids of idealistic drivel spouted around you by Will and his friends, there would be no issue at all between us. I resent even an imputed rivalry with someone I despise.

PAULA. Rivalry?

KENNETH. Paula— There's no reason any longer why I shouldn't tell you the truth.

PAULA. What is it, Kenneth?

KENNETH. (After a moment—slowly.) Do you know what I feel like? I feel like a man on a great height, irresistibly tempted to jump over. Do you want the truth really? (She says nothing. Somehow his words, his voice, his attitude make her feel that really now he may reveal something which before he wouldn't have revealed. He is in a trance-like state almost; she feels it; she is rather horribly fascinated—somehow, though she distrusts him utterly, some instinct tells her that, at this moment actually he is tempted by a force, disruptive to himself, to tell her the truth.) Don't you know it? Don't you feel it? (Pause.) Haven't you known it? Haven't you felt it? (A moment's pause.) I love you.

PAULA. What?

KENNETH. I love you. (A pause. She too stupefied to speak. She too is unde spell. She is fascinated by him—by enormity of this. She rises, walks a from him to stand by sofa.)

PAULA. I suppose I should be afraid you. I'm not afraid of you.

KENNETH. I am afraid of you. You te me to venture the impossible. That is practical. And I have always been e nently practical.

PAULA. I'm sure you have. (She f herself talking automatically, as if ou a hypnotic state—at the same time s vanity and shrewdness keeps pounding side her: "See how far he will go— how far he will go!")

KENNETH. I have lived by a plan. plan has matured. But I have yearned a face that would give me joy, for voice that would soothe me. It is your It is your voice. (PAULA is fighting no scream; at the same time she is caugh a nightmarish fascination.)

PAULA. (Very faintly.) Don't you Mother?

KENNETH. No. (A moment's pause.) are the youth I have never had, the s ity I have never had—you are the h I have hungered for. (Moves toward h stands over her and a little back.) Th am standing near you now, that I achieved a share in your life, that you listening to me, that you are thinkin me and of what I am, to the exclu of everything else in the whirling uni —this is a miracle so devastating, th makes any future possible—Paula—

PAULA. What?

KENNETH. Paula?

PAULA. What is it!

KENNETH. (Bending over her.) Paul (It is as if he got a sexual joy from s her name.) I love your name. I lov say your name.

PAULA. I am afraid of you. I'm sorr you.

KENNETH. Do you think me insane?

LA. Yes.

NETH. Because I am ambitious, be-
se I am forthright, because I deal scien-
ally with the human stuff around me—
think me insane. Because I am ruthless
romantic, you think me insane. This
you think you love—who spends his
e sniveling about a system he is not
ng enough to dominate—is he sane?

LA. I don't expect you to—

NETH. When I hear the chatter of
r friends, it makes me sick. While they
their kind prate of co-operative com-
wealths, the strong man takes power,
rides over their backs—which is all
r backs are fit for. Never has the op-
unity for the individual career been
xalted, so infinite in its scope, so hori-
al. House-painters and minor journal-
become dictators of great nations.
*th puckish humor—leaning on arm of
chair.*) Imagine what a really clever
could do! See what he has done! (*He
es, makes a gesture of modest self-
tion, indicating the room as part of
conquest. She laughs, rather choked
embarrassed. He goes on.*) And this
ve done alone. From an impossible dis-
e—I have come to you, so that when
eak, you can hear. What might we not
ogether, Paula—you and I—(*To her
rise,* PAULA *finds herself arguing an
ceivable point. She loathes the strange
nation she feels in this man, and yet
vare that it might turn to her advan-
*)

A. We don't want the same things.

ETH. You want what everyone wants
has vitality and imagination—new
s of power—new domains of knowl-
—the ultimate sensations.

A. You *are* romantic, aren't you?

ETH. Endlessly. And endlessly—re-
c. (*Staring at her.*) What are you
ing?

A. (*Shrewd against him—against her-
I keep thinking—what you want now
at you're after now?

ETH. (*Moving toward her.*) You
believe then—that I love you?

PAULA. (*Leaning back in chair—not looking at him.*) You are a very strange man.

KENNETH. I am simple really. I want
everything. That's all!

PAULA. And you don't care how you get
it.

KENNETH. Don't be moralistic, Paula—I
beg you. I am directly in the tradition of
your own marauding ancestors. They pass
now for pioneers—actually they fell on the
true pioneers, and wrested what they had
found away from them, by sheer brutal
strength. I am doing the same thing—but
more adroitly.

PAULA. Why are you so honest with me?

KENNETH. (*With his most charming
smile.*) Perhaps because I feel that, in your
heart, you too are an adventurer. (*A pause.
During these half-spell-bound instants a
thought has been forming slowly in* PAULA's
*mind that crystallizes now. This man is
the enemy. This man is infinitely cunning,
infinitely resourceful. Perhaps—just the
possibility—he really feels this passion for
her. If so, why not use this weakness in an
antagonist so ruthless? She will try.*)

PAULA. I shouldn't listen to you— (*A moment. He senses her cunning. He looks at
her.*)

KENNETH. You don't trust me?

PAULA. Have I reason to trust you?

KENNETH. What reason would you like?
What proof would you like?

PAULA. Aren't you going to marry Mother?

KENNETH. Only as an alternative.

PAULA. Will you—tell her so? Will you
give up the alternative?

KENNETH. And if I do?

PAULA. What shall I promise you?

KENNETH. Yourself.

PAULA. (*Looks at him—speaks.*) And if
I do?

KENNETH. Then . . .

PAULA. (*Taking fire.*) You say you love
me! If you feel it—really feel it— You

haven't been very adventurous for all your talk! Taking in Mother and Sam! Give up those conquests. Tell her! Tell Mother! Then perhaps I will believe you.

KENNETH. And then?

PAULA. Take your chances!

KENNETH. (*Quietly.*) Very well.

PAULA. You will?

KENNETH. I will.

PAULA. You'll tell Mother—you love me?

KENNETH. Yes.

PAULA. (*Going to the foot of the stairs, calls:*) Mother! Mother!

LEONIE. (*Offstage.*) Yes, Paula. I'm coming right down! I've the most marvelous surprise for you! Wait and see! (PAULA *walks to end of sofa—looking at* KENNETH. LEONIE *comes in. She is wearing an exquisite old-fashioned silk wedding-dress which billows around her in an immense shimmering circle. She is a vision of enchantment.*)

LEONIE. (*In a great flurry of excitement.*) Children, look what I found! It's Mother's. It's the dress she was married in. I was poking around in Granny's room while Sam was talking to me about bonds, and I came upon it. Do you like it, Kenneth? Isn't it adorable? Have you ever . . . What's the matter? Don't you like it?

PAULA. It's very pretty.

LEONIE. (*Overwhelmed by the inadequacy of this word.*) Pretty! Pretty! (*She hopes for more from* KENNETH.) Kenneth. . . ?

KENNETH. It's exquisite.

LEONIE. Isn't it? (*She whirls around in the dress.*) Isn't it? Yes. Exquisite. Can you imagine the scene? Can you imagine Granny walking down the aisle—and all the august spectators in mutton-chop whiskers and Prince Alberts? We've lost something these days—a good deal—oh, I don't miss the mutton-chops—but in ceremony, I mean—in punctilio and grace. . . .

PAULA. (*Cutting ruthlessly through the nostalgia.*) Mother!

LEONIE. What is it, Paula?

PAULA. Kenneth has something to tell y

LEONIE. Kenneth?

PAULA. Yes. He has something to tell y

LEONIE. Have you, Kenneth?

KENNETH. Yes.

LEONIE. What is it?

KENNETH. (*Quietly.*) I love Paula. I w to marry Paula. (*A pause. Granny's u ding dress droops.*)

LEONIE. Do you mean that, Kenneth?

KENNETH. Yes.

LEONIE. (*Piteously.*) This isn't very of you, Paula.

PAULA. I had nothing to do with i loathe Kenneth. But I wanted you know him. Now you see him, Mo your precious Lothario—there he is! I at him!

LEONIE. These clothes are picturesque, I think our modern ones are more fortable. I think—I feel quite faint— it ridiculous? (*She sways.*)

PAULA. I'm sorry, Mother. I had to. I love you. I really do.

LEONIE (*Very faint.*) Thank you, Pa

PAULA. You'd better go up and lie d I'll come to you in a moment.

LEONIE. Yes. I think I'd better. Yes. begins to sob; she goes out, hiding face in the lace folds of her dress. P having gone with her to the door, bell for ROBERT, turns to KENNETH.)

PAULA. I suppose you're going to te this isn't cricket. Well, don't, becau will only make me laugh. To live a code with people like you is only weak and absurd.

KENNETH. (*His voice is low and eve tense with hate.*) You, Miss Frothing are my *last* miscalculation. I might say my first. Fortunately, not irrepa (ROBERT *enters.*)

PAULA. Robert.

RT. Yes, Miss Frothingham.

LA. (*Still staring fixedly at* KENNETH.) Rice is leaving. Will you see that his are packed, please?

RT. Yes, Miss. (*He goes out.*)

NETH. Forgive me—for having over-ated you. (*He goes out door right.* LA *comes slowly down and sits on sofa. gets a reaction herself now from all has been through; this game hasn't natural to her; she is trembling phy- y; she is on the verge of tears.* WILL *es in.*)

LA. Will—Will darling— (*She clings* ILL.)

.. (*Worried.*) Paula!

LA. Put your arms around me, Will— me close— (WILL *obeys.*)

.. What's happened?

LA. I've tricked him. I made him say ront of Mother that he loved me, that vanted to marry me. Poor Leonie! But d to be done! And do you know, Will the end I felt—gosh, one has so many s, Will. I must tell you—for the—well, he completeness of the record—

.. (*Curious.*) What?

LA. At the end I felt I had to do it— only to save Leonie—but to save my-Can you understand that? I felt hor-drawn to him, and by the sordid g I was doing— But it's over. Thank it's over. Will, darling, these six weeks been hell without you. When I got letter about Granny, I sat down and l. I wanted to go right to New York e with you. And yet I couldn't. How l I? But now, Will—I don't want to for you any longer. I've done what n. It's cost me almost— Will—l need terribly—

.. And I you, Paula. But listen, dar--I've decided during the weeks I've away from you— I can't marry you — I can't face what I'd become—

A. But Will, I— (*Springing up.*) Will, I'll give up the money. I'll live you anywhere.

WILL. I know that, Paula. But I mustn't. You mustn't let me. I've thought it all out. You say you'd live with me anywhere. But what would happen? Supposing I didn't get a job? Would we starve? We'd take fifty dollars a week from your grandmother's estate. It would be foolish not to. Taking fifty, why not seventy-five? Why not two hundred? I can't let myself in for it, Paula. (*A long pause.*) Paula, darling— do you hate me?

PAULA. No.

WILL. Supposing you weren't rich? Is it a world in which, but for this, I'd have to sink? If it is, I'm going to damn well do what I can to change it. I don't have to scrabble for the inheritance of dead men. That's for Kenneth—one robber baron— after the lapse of several generations—succeeding another. I don't want this damn fortune to give me an unfair advantage over people as good as I am who haven't got it. (*Torn with pity for her.*) Paula— my dearest—what can I do?

PAULA. I see that you can't do anything. I quite see. Still—

WILL. I love you, Paula, and I'll be longing for you terribly, but I can't marry you—not till there's somebody for you to marry. When I've struck my stride, I won't care about Sam, or the money, or anything, because I'll be on my own. If you feel the way I do, you'll wait.

PAULA. (*Very still voice.*) Of course, Will. I'll wait.

WILL. (*Overcome with gratitude and emotion—seizes her in his arms passionately.*) Darling—darling— (LEONIE *comes in.* WILL, *overcome with emotion, goes out.*)

LEONIE. It's easy to say "lie down." But what happens then? Thoughts assail you. Thoughts . . .

PAULA. Mother . . .

LEONIE. Kenneth's going. He's leaving. I suppose you're happy. It's the end—the end of summer.

PAULA. (*Herself shaken with emotion.*) Mother— (*She wants to talk to* LEONIE, *to tell her what has happened, but* LEONIE *is lost in her own maze.*)

LEONIE. It's cold here. I hate this place. I'm going to sell it. (*She sits, in chair, right of fireplace.*) I've always wanted things around me to be gay and warm and happy. I've done my best. I must be wrong. Why do I find myself this way? With nothing. With nothing.

PAULA. (*Running to her mother and throwing herself on her knees beside her.*) Mother—Mother darling—

LEONIE. (*Not responding, reflectively.*) I suppose the thing about me that is wrong is that love is really all I care about. (*A moment's pause.*) I suppose I should have been interested in other things. Good works. Do they sustain you? But I couldn't somehow. I think when you're not in love—you're dead. Yes, that must be why I'm ... (*Her voice trails off rather.* PAULA *drops her head in her mother's lap and begins to cry.*)

LEONIE. (*Surprised.*) Paula—what is it? What's the matter? Are you sorry? It's all right, child.

PAULA. (*Through her tears.*) It's Will—

LEONIE. Will?

PAULA. He's going away.

LEONIE. Why don't you go with him?

PAULA. He doesn't want me.

LEONIE. That's not true. It must be something else.

PAULA. The money.

LEONIE Oh, the money. Yes, the money. The money won't do anything for you. It'll work against you. It's worked against me. It gives you the illusion of escape—but always you have to come back to yourself. At the end of every journey—you find yourself.

PAULA. What shall I do, Mother?

LEONIE. You and Will want the same things. In the end you will find them. But don't let him find them with so[me] one else. Follow him. Be near h[im]. When he is depressed and discouraged, it be your hand that he touches, your f[ace] that he sees.

PAULA. (*Breathless.*) Mother—you're ri[ght] —he told me last summer—"you m[ust] have a shoulder to lean on"—

LEONIE. Let it be your shoulder, Pa[ula,] follow him. Be near him.

PAULA. Thank you, Mother.

LEONIE. (*Ruefully.*) I am telling you w[hat] I should do. It must be bad advice.

PAULA. (*Gratefully.*) Darling! (DENNIS WILL *come in.*)

DENNIS. Here you are! We're off to [the] boat! Thirty minutes! Why don't you [let] Paula come too? What do you say, Leo[nie?]

LEONIE. You know, all these years [I've] been coming up here, and I've never b[een] on the Bar Harbor boat.

DENNIS. It may be said, Mrs. Froth[ing]ham, if you have never been on the [Bar] Harbor boat, that you have not lived!

LEONIE. Really! I'd always heard it [was] poky.

DENNIS. Poky! The *Normandie* of [the] Kennebec poky! Mrs. Frothingham!

LEONIE. It's fun, is it? But doesn't it [get] into New York at some impossible h[our.]

DENNIS. At seven A.M.

LEONIE. Seven! (*She shudders.*)

DENNIS. (*The brisk executive.*) Se[ven!] Yes, sir! At my desk at nine! All refre[shed] and co-ordinated and ready to attack [the] South American correspondence.

LEONIE. I must learn not to believe [you,] mustn't I?

DENNIS. I am my own master, Le[onie!] All day for nine mortal hours I grin[d out] escape fiction for the pulp magazines. [But] one day I shall become famous and em[...]

the slicks and then I doubt very much
ther I shall come here.

NIE. I shall miss you.

NIS. **Then I'll come.**

NIE. I hate to have you go, Dennis.
cheer me up. Why don't you stay?

NIS. Impossible, Leonie. I must go to
York to launch the magazine. But for
moment, good-bye, Leonie. As a re-
d for your hospitality I shall send you
original copy of one of my stories.
ld you like to escape from something?

IE. (*Smiling wanly.*) I would indeed!

NIS. Think no more about it. You're
ood as free. The story is yours, typed
onally on my Underwood. Those mis-
d keys—those inaccuracies—how they
bemuse posterity! (*He goes out.*)

.. (*Awkwardly.*) Good-bye, Leonie.

IE. Good-bye, Will. (*He goes out
out looking at* PAULA. *In pantomime,*
IE *urges* PAULA *to go after him.* PAULA
s her quickly and runs out after WILL.
alone, LEONIE *walks to the chair in*
h her mother sat so often—she looks
ugh the glowing autumn at the dark-
g sea. KENNETH *comes in. There is a*
e.)

ETH. Leonie—

IE. Yes, Kenneth.

ETH. I don't expect you to under-
this. I shall not try to make you un-
and it.

E. Perhaps I'd better not.

ETH. Really I am amused at myself
hly entertained. That I should have
st had to practice on myself what
to I have reserved for my patients—
who have made such a fetish of dis-
e and restraint so nearly succumbed
inconsistency. I must revise my no-
of myself.

E. And I too.

KENNETH. Why? Why **you?**

LEONIE. I seem to be a survival—Paula's
directness—and your calculations—they are
beyond me.

KENNETH. Nevertheless, it's curious how
you and Paula are alike—no wonder that,
for a moment at least, you seemed to me—
interchangeable.

LEONIE. Did you know it from the beginning—that it was Paula?

KENNETH. I was attracted by her resemblance to you—for exercising this attraction I hated her. She felt it too—from the
beginning and she must have hated me
from the beginning. Between us there grew
up this strange, unnatural antagonism—

LEONIE. What?

KENNETH. This fused emotion of love and
hate. It had to be brought out into the
open. It's a familiar psychosis—the unconscious desire of the daughter to triumph over the mother.

LEONIE. But I don't understand—

KENNETH. There is so much in these intricate relationships that the layman can't
understand—

LEONIE. You mean that you—felt nothing
for Paula?

KENNETH. No, I don't mean that at all.
But I saw that what I felt for her was
some twisted reflection of what I felt for
you. And I saw there was only one way
out of it—to let her triumph over you. I
told her that I loved her. But this was not
enough. I must repeat it in front of you.
You must witness her triumph. I made it
possible. I gave her her great moment.
Well, you see what it's done. It freed her
so beautifully that she was able to go to
Will. They've gone away together. Perfect
cure for her as well as for myself. (*A moment's pause.*)

LEONIE. It all sounds almost too perfect,
Kenneth.

KENNETH. I said I didn't expect you to
understand it—you have lived always on

your emotions You have never bothered to delve beneath them. You are afraid to, aren't you?

LEONIE. I know this, Kenneth. I heard you say that you loved Paula. I heard your voice. No, I can't accept this, Kenneth! It's not good enough. I've never done that before. I'd only think now that everything you did, everything you said, was to cover what you felt. And I'd end by telling myself that I believed you. I'd end by taking second best from you. No, I must guard myself from that. I felt this a month ago —that's why I sent for Will.

KENNETH. Some day, Leonie, you will learn that feeling is not enough.

LEONIE. But I trust my instinct, Kenneth.

KENNETH. That, Leonie, is your most adorable trait—

LEONIE. What?

KENNETH. That trust—that innocence. If it weren't for that, you wouldn't be you— and everyone wouldn't love you—

LEONIE. Oh, no, Kenneth— (DENNIS comes in.)

DENNIS. Oh, excuse me. But I left my brief-case. Oh, here it is. (He picks it up.) Without my brief-case I am a man without a Destiny. With it I am—

KENNETH. A man with a brief-case.

LEONIE. (Crossing rather desperately to DENNIS—this straw in the current.) What's in it—your stories?

DENNIS. Stories—no, that wouldn't matter. I am fertile; I can spawn stories. But the plans for the magazine are in here—the future of Young America is here—

LEONIE. Will you stay and have a whiskey and soda?

DENNIS. Thanks, but if I do, I shall miss the boat.

LEONIE. Suppose you do?

KENNETH. Leonie—that would delay the millennium one day.

DENNIS. The doctor's right. That w⟨ be selfish.

LEONIE. Be selfish. Please stay.

DENNIS. No. Once you are enlisted ⟨ cause, you can't live a personal life. ⟨ a dedication.

LEONIE. Kenneth is leaving. I shall lonely, Dennis. I can't bear to be alone

KENNETH. Your need for people is ⟨ nant, isn't it, Leonie?

LEONIE. Stay for dinner. After dinner can talk about your magazine.

DENNIS. Oh, well—that makes it pos for me to stay. Thank you, Kenneth. goes to sofa, sits, busying himself ⟨ brief-case.) (She goes to console to ⟨ highball.)

KENNETH. Send me your magazine, ⟨ nis. I shall be honored to be the first scriber.

DENNIS. I'll be glad to. Your patients read it in the waiting-room instead o⟨ National Geographic.

KENNETH. Your first subscriber—and possibly your last. (He crosses to door turns back.) Good-bye, Leonie. Good Dennis. We who are about to re⟨ salute you. (She does not look at him bows formally to DENNIS's back, ma⟨ gesture of "good luck" and exits.)

DENNIS. Trouble with that fellow i⟨ lives for himself. No larger interest. ⟨ what dignifies human beings, Leon⟨ dedication to something greater than ⟨ selves.

LEONIE. (Coming down to hand hi⟨ highball.) Yes? Here's your whiskey soda. I envy you, Dennis. I wish I dedicate myself to something—som⟨ outside myself.

DENNIS. (Rising to sit beside her.) here's your opportunity, Leonie—it's identical. You couldn't do better tha magazine. It would give you a new i⟨ —impersonal. It would emancipate

onie. It would be a perpetual dedication
Youth—to the hope of the world. The
rld is middle-aged and tired. But we—

NIE. (*Wistfully.*) Can you refresh us,
nnis?

NNIS. Refresh you? Leonie, we can re-
enate you!

NIE. (*Grateful there is some one there
nother human being she can laugh
h.*) That's an awfully amusing idea.
u make me laugh.

NIS. (*Eagerly selling the idea.*) In the
th of any country, there is an immense
entiality—

NIE. You're awfully serious about it,
n't you, Dennis?

DENNIS. Where the magazine is concerned,
Leonie, I am a fanatic.

LEONIE. I suppose if it's really successful—
it'll result in my losing everything I have—

DENNIS. It'll be taken from you anyway.
You'll only be anticipating the inevitable.

LEONIE. Why—how clever of me!

DENNIS. Not only clever but grateful.

LEONIE. Will you leave me just a little to
live on—?

DENNIS. Don't worry about that—come the
Revolution—you'll have a friend in high
office. (LEONIE *accepts gratefully this earnest of security. They touch glasses in a
toast as the curtain falls.*)

The Animal Kingdom

BY PHILIP BARRY

———

TO GILBERT MILLER AND LESLIE HOWARD

———

"THE ANIMAL KINGDOM" was first produced by Gilbert Miller and Leslie How-
d at the Broadhurst Theatre in New York City on January 12, 1932. It was
ected by Gilbert Miller and the settings were designed by Aline Bernstein.

———

CHARACTERS

RUFUS COLLIER   JOE FISK
TOM COLLIER   FRANC SCHMIDT
CECELIA HENRY   OWEN ARTHUR
DAISY SAGE   GRACE MACOMBER
RICHARD REGAN

ACTION AND SCENE

The action of the Play takes place in the course of about eighteen months, last
r and this. The Scenes are as follows:

ACT ONE

Scene 1. At Tom Collier's, in Connecticut. An evening in April.
Scene 2. At Daisy Sage's, on Thirty-eighth Street.
         Later the same evening.

ACT TWO

Scene 1. At Tom Collier's. An evening in January.
Scene 2. At Daisy Sage's. An afternoon in May.

ACT THREE

Scene 1. At Tom Collier's. A Sunday morning in October.
Scene 2. At Tom Collier's. Later the same evening.

ACT ONE

SCENE I

The library of TOM COLLIER's *house in the country near New York. About seven o'clock on an April evening, two years ago. The library is a fair-sized, comfortable room in a small, partially converted farmhouse, situated in a countryside which is neither fashionable nor suburban. There is an entrance from the hall at left and one into the dining-room through another hall at back right. In the center wall at back, there is a fine old fire place, framed with pine panelling. The side walls are of white plaster, windows in the one at right, with bookshelves around them. At left, a small staircase leads to the upper floor. The furniture, of no particular period, is well chosen and, in the case of chairs and sofa, invitingly comfortable. It is a cheerful room, now filled with the late evening sun.*

Upon the sofa, sits OWEN ARTHUR. *In an easy chair, turned away from him, is* RUFUS COLLIER. CECELIA HENRY *is seated in a straight chair beside a table at right center.* OWEN *is about thirty-five, well built, well dressed, agreeable looking.* RUFUS *is in his early fifties, small, slight and gray. He wears silver-rimmed spectacles, which add to his picture of himself as the man of decision.* CECELIA *is twenty-eight, lovely of figure, lovely of face, beautifully cared for, beautifully presented.*
For some moments, all sit staring in front of them, saying nothing. Finally OWEN *clears his throat, waits a moment, and without turning, ventures:*

OWEN. There's quite a fine view from the hill behind the house. (*A silence.*) —Or did I tell you that?

RUFUS. Yes.

OWEN. Sorry. (*Another silence. Then* CECELIA *speaks.*)

CECELIA. You've really never been here before?

RUFUS. I?

CECELIA. Yes.

RUFUS. Never.

CECELIA. It seems a little strange.

RUFUS. I've never been asked before. (*H glances about him.*) What anyone wa[n]t with a place at the end of the world li[ke] this, is beyond me anyhow.

OWEN. I make it in less than an hour, a rule.

RUFUS. Oh, you come often, do you?

OWEN. Fairly. I find there's nothing li[ke] it after a stiff week in Court. I'm a n[ew] man since Friday.

RUFUS. You seem to be a fixture with hi[m.] I'm surprised he hasn't given you the go-[by] as well.

OWEN. I'm too fond of him. I won't al[low] it.

RUFUS. But you're well-off, you work ha[rd,] you live like a gentleman—his nat[ural] enemy, I should say.

OWEN. We make few demands on e[ach] other. And he knows how I love this pl[ace.]

RUFUS. But there's nothing *here!* No so[cial] life, no—

OWEN. Exactly.

CECELIA. His press is in the Village, i[sn't] it?

RUFUS. Press? What press?

CECELIA. The Bantam Press. (*He star[es.]* You know—for books.

RUFUS. Oh, so it's publishing now, is [it?]

CECELIA. I think it has been, for s[ome] time.

RUFUS. (*To* OWEN.) How's it going, [do] you know?

OWEN. Very well. Last year he only [made] something like—

RUFUS. —Don't tell me! (*He rises [and] goes to the window.*)

CECELIA. You're not awfully fond of [your] son, are you, Mr. Collier? (RUFUS *tur[ns to]* her.)

326

FUS. Miss—I beg your pardon—you said ur name was—?

CELIA. Henry. Cecelia Henry.

FUS. Miss Henry, if you had spent the ne and money and effort I have to make t young man realize who he is and what ought to be doing in the world—how g have you known him?

ELIA. I'm comparatively new, I'm afraid.

US. (*To* OWEN.) Perhaps, from longer erience, you might enlighten her.

EN. I presume what Mr. Collier means hat on ordinary terms, Tom doesn't seem have got very far.

ELIA. There's still time, isn't there?

US. Thirty-one—thirty-two in October nd he's wasted his life from the cradle.

ELIA. It must have been pathetic to see wasting it at three.

US. I assure you, his genius for it ved even then. I send him to Harvard, he lasts two years there. I send him to ord, and he commutes from Paris. I him in the Bank, and he— (*He sighs oundly.*) —The world at the feet of boy, the whole world. And all he's done is to run from it.

N. Tom has his own ideas about what wants to do with his life. (RICHARD N *has come into the room. He is about y-two, with the figure of an athlete, hair, and a genial, ugly Irish face that ars at some time to have been thor- ly mauled. He wears dark trousers a white linen jacket, and carries a slip aper in his hand.*) —Yes, Regan?

N. There's· a radio-message came by e for him.

N. You can leave it here. I'll tell him. AN *folds the message and places it upon table.*)

N. Right. (*He turns and beams upon .*)—Everything satisfactory?

. Yes, thanks.

N. Comfortable, Miss?

LIA. Quite, thank you.

REGAN. Like a drink, anyone?

RUFUS. (*Exasperated.*) No, no! Nothing! We were talking!

REGAN. (*With a wave of his hand.*) Go right ahead. Make yourselves to home. He'll be along. (*He goes out.* CECELIA *laughs.*)

CECELIA. —The butler? But he's charm-ing!

RUFUS. He looks like a prize-fighter.

OWEN. He was. (RUFUS *begins to hover curiously about the radio-message, wanting to read it, not quite able to bring himself to.*)

RUFUS. Why did he send me word to come out here tonight? Exceedingly important? Don't let anything interfere?

OWEN. I don't know. I found a message asking me to get Miss Henry at my Aunt's in New Canaan, and come back on the run. He had to go to town for something.

RUFUS. Well, I'll tell you what's in my mind—God knows I don't want it there.— That girl he's been living with for the last three years— (OWEN *glances quickly at* CECELIA.)

OWEN. Just a minute, Sir.

CECELIA. It's all right, Owen.

RUFUS. Good Lord, it's no secret, is it? (*To* CECELIA.) —You're not her are you?

CECELIA. Not that I know of.

RUFUS. (*To* OWEN.) Who is she, anyhow? What is she?

OWEN. —An extremely nice girl—hard-working, talented. She draws for the fash-ion magazines, and very successfully.

RUFUS. Admirable.—We'll, I believe he's got me out here to tell me he wants to marry her—or has already.—I've no doubt he'll bring her with him.

OWEN. Seriously—can you see Tom marry-ing anyone?

RUFUS. I can see her marrying him. It has happened before, and to better men. (*Again he hovers about the radio-message.*)

OWEN. If it was going to them, it would have long before this. Besides, she left for her magazine's Paris office three months ago, for an indefinite stay.

RUFUS. Maybe she's coming back.—In fact, I'm certain that she's why we're here. It offers the perfect opportunity to cut himself off finally and completely from the life he was born to. I'm surprised he has missed it as long as he has. Well—I've stood for his rowdy friendships, I've put up with his idleness, his ill-mannered insolence, his— (CECELIA *rises and faces him.*)

CECELIA. I'm sorry, Mr. Collier, but I'll have to ask you to let it go at that.

RUFUS. Ah? Why so?

CECELIA. —Because it so happens that *I'm* why we're here.

RUFUS. How's that?

CECELIA. It's me Tom's going to marry, and I've heard enough against him to last me quite a while. (RUFUS *stares.* OWEN *starts forward.*)

OWEN. —You that Tom's—?!—Good Lord, C, what are you talking about?

CECELIA. Marrying. On May first, to be exact. (*To* RUFUS.) He asked you out here to tell you, and, I imagine, to receive your good wishes. (RUFUS *still stares.*) —Thanks so much. (*She reseats herself,* OWEN *continues to gaze at her, speechless.*)

RUFUS. What did you say your name was? I'm sorry, but I—

CECELIA. Cecelia Henry. My mother was Cecelia Bond, of Baltimore. She married Stephen Henry, also of Baltimore. Except for a few distant cousins, such as Owen here, I'm alone now—poor, but quite respectable. Will it do?

RUFUS. Tom has very little of his own, you know.

CECELIA. It will be ample, thank you.

RUFUS. (*After a moment.*) Miss Henry, I'm inclined to like you. I think you have what I call "character."

CECELIA. Really? You're too kind.

RUFUS. You'll need it with him.

CECELIA. I don't agree wih you. Tom the most interesting, most attractive m I've ever known. I consider myself sh with luck. And you make me a little tir with your abuse of him.

RUFUS. —Very loyal.

CECELIA. Not at all. I simply believe him.—Not in his so-called "past" perhaps I'm not quite a fool—but certainly in wha to be.

RUFUS. Faith is a beautiful thing.

CECELIA. *I* think so.

RUFUS. Well, if you can make a respecta citizen of Tom Collier at this date, yo have nothing but praise from me, my de (*He picks up the radio-message and dra it through his fingers.*)

CECELIA. It seems not to occur to you t when Tom has someone who really un stands him to work and care for—

OWEN. Understands him!

CECELIA. Yes. Completely. (*Again* RUFUS.) —He'll make what you call citizen" of himself. (RUFUS *adjusts spectacles and reads the message.*)

RUFUS. You think?

CECELIA. I know.—And if what you la ingly refer to as my "faith" is of any to him—

RUFUS. "Love will conquer all." Yes, y of course— (*He sighs and refolds the* sage.) —But forgive me a few do (OWEN *leans forward.*)

OWEN. Oh? How's that, Sir?

RUFUS. "Darling. Am coming back. A on 'Paris' at eight tonight. Much Daisy." (*He looks at* CECELIA. *There slight pause. Then:*)

CECELIA. Well? (RUFUS *rises, and re her intently.*)

RUFUS. —Yes, you seem to be a firs girl.

CECELIA. I've heard some rather agre things about *you,* now and then. It v be pleasant sometime to—

FUS. (*Smiling.*) —To see one or two of
m? Well, my dear, perhaps some day
shall.—And now if you'll let me have
.—er—Mr. Arthur to myself for a mont— (*He moves toward the doorway.*)
There are a few dull but practical facts
ut—er—about your fiancé, I should like
– (*He turns to* OWEN.) —Would you
d? (OWEN *moves to follow him.* RUFUS
s *out.*)

ELIA. Wait a minute, Owen, will you
se? (OWEN *stops and turns.*)

EN. Well?

ELIA. I'm sorry you had to learn about
o—abruptly.

EN. It doesn't matter much, does it?

ELIA. I don't know.

N. Perhaps I was supposed to hear it
little cries of pleasure.

ELIA. The point is, that I intended to
you on the way over, but somehow
dn't.

N. I'm touched by your reluctance to
ver the blow.

LIA. Don't be nasty, Owen.

N. It was kind of me to bring you
ther, wasn't it?

LIA. In inspiration. I'm sure I'm most
ful.

N. I can't make it out. You aren't in
east the sort of girl I'd expect Tom to
terested in. (*She laughs.*)

LIA. Thanks!

. You know what I mean.

LIA. Perhaps it's the artist in him. You
he has the charming illusion that I'm
beauty.

. —And I can't make *you* out, either.

IA. It's quite simple: I'm in love at

. Have you the remotest idea of
you're letting yourself in for?

IA. I think so.

OWEN. I'm the one friend you and Tom
have in common.

CECELIA. —But such a lovely friend, Owen.
Don't ever leave me—us.

OWEN. There's not a taste, not an attitude—

CECELIA. Perhaps there will be. Give us
time.

OWEN. C—how on earth did it happen?

CECELIA. Very suddenly, very sweetly.—
Yesterday. (*He turns away.*) I'm sorry. You
asked. (*A moment. Then:*)

OWEN. —I'll see what it is Mr. Collier
wants, if you don't mind. (OWEN *goes out.*
CECELIA *looks after him for a moment,
then removes her hat, seats herself in a
large chair, hidden from the doorway, and
thoughtfully lights a cigarette. A moment,
then* TOM COLLIER *appears in the doorway,*
REGAN *close behind him.* TOM *is in his early
thirties, slim, youthful, with a fine, sensitive, humorous face. He carries several packages in his arms.*)

TOM. Where are they?

REGAN. Well—they were. (CECELIA *rises
and turns.*)

CECELIA.....Hello, Tom.

TOM. (*To* REGAN.) Take my hat. (REGAN
removes it from his head.) Thanks. Now
get out.

REGAN. I just wanted to tell you that—

TOM. Later. (*He is gazing fondly at* CE-
CELIA.)

REGAN. But there's a—

TOM. Get, will you, Red? (REGAN *goes out,
murmuring.*)

REGAN. —Radio-message come for you.
(*But* TOM *scarcely hears him. Suddenly he
drops his parcels upon the table, goes to*
CECELIA *and takes her in his arms.*)

TOM. Darling, darling— (*He is about to
kiss her, but she averts her head.*)

CECELIA. No. You're late. I'm furious with
you.

TOM. (*Blankly.*) Late? (*She looks at him for a moment, then smiles and kisses him lightly.*)

CECELIA. There.—All right?

TOM. Terrible. I've taken up with a thrifty spinster.

CECELIA. It's all you deserve. (*He laughs.*)

TOM. How do you like it?—I mean the place.

CECELIA. I love it.

TOM. I call it "the house in bad taste."— Look out for taste, C. There's too much of it in the world. (*He goes to the packages on the table.*) See here—what I fetched from town for you.

CECELIA. What are they?

TOM. A celebration: good things to eat and drink.—Where are they? Father? Owen?

CECELIA. In the other room.

TOM. What do you think of Father?

CECELIA. Well—

TOM. Keep a civil tongue in your head.

CECELIA. It may take a little time.

TOM. You can learn to like him and beer together. Mother was the prize: you missed something, there. Father means well, but you have to stand him off. Give him an inch, and he takes you home in his pocket. Did you really say you'd marry me? (*He slips her arm through his and leads her to a chair.*)

CECELIA. I'm afraid I did.

TOM. Heaven help us both.—Just this one marriage please, darling. I haven't been very good about marriage. I was exposed to a very bad case of it as a baby. We must make a grand go of it.

CECELIA. We shall, never you fear. (TOM smiles. CECELIA *seats herself in the chair,* TOM *upon the arm of it.*)

TOM. —Just do everything I say, and it will be all right.

CECELIA. —With pleasure. (*He gazes* her.)

TOM. C, what a marvellous object you a (*He picks up her hand, looks at it.*) Lo at those fine small bones in your wrist

CECELIA. What about them?

TOM. This— (*He kisses the wri* —You're so cunningly contrived.

CECELIA. What?

TOM. I say, you're put together on very best principles.

CECELIA. I don't see so many blunders you either, Thomas.

TOM. No, mine is entirely beauty of s Shall I tell you about my soul, C?—W lantern-slides?

CECELIA. (*Softly.*) Put your arms aro me, Tom. (*He draws her to him and k her. Then:*)

TOM. —Oh God, I feel good!

CECELIA. (*In a breath.*) —So do I.

TOM. —Let's have all our good th together. (*He turns and calls loudly:*) Oh, Red! (*Then turns again to* CECE That's a very good rule of life, dar all one's good things together.

CECELIA. Is it, dear? (REGAN *appears b ing.* TOM *rises from the chair.*)

REGAN. Hello. Not so loud.

TOM. —Glasses with ice, Red, and all the way.

REGAN. O.K. (*He goes out.* TOM again:*)

TOM. Owen? Father! *Then turns an gards* CECELIA *once more.*) Oh, my l C— you lovely thing, you.

CECELIA. Stop it, Tom. You're really barrassing me. I feel quite naked.

TOM. That's fine. (*He goes to her draws two fingers gently across her ch* It's such a fine binding, darling—s good book. (RUFUS *re-enters, followe* OWEN.) Hello, Father, hello, Owen—te nice you're here. You've met Miss I Father?

ꜰus. I've had that pleasure, yes.

ᴍ. It *is* a pleasure.—How are the
ses?

ꜰus. Do you care? (ᴛᴏᴍ *laughs.*)

ᴍ. Not a bit.

ꜰus. Then why ask?

ᴍ. Politeness.

ꜰus. You said five o'clock. It's seven.

ᴍ. Did I? Is it?—Listen,—you and
ᴇn—I want to tell you what this is all
ᴜt.

ꜰus. We know. We've heard. (ᴛᴏᴍ
ꜱ to ᴄᴇᴄᴇʟɪᴀ.)

ᴇʟɪᴀ. He was abusing you so, I had
ᴛell him. (ᴛᴏᴍ *laughs delightedly.*)

ᴍ. And it didn't discourage you?

ᴇʟɪᴀ. On the contrary.

ᴍ. Stout heart. (*Then, gravely, to*
ᴜs.) Why, thank you very much, Sir,
I think *I'm* the one to be congratulated.
, indeed we are. Yes, I'm sure we shall
(ᴿᴇɢᴀɴ *comes in with a tray of glasses*
d with ice.) Oh—er—this is my father,
ᴅ.

ᴀɴ. Glad to meet you, Sir. (ᴿᴜꜰᴜꜱ
ꜱ *slightly.* ᴿᴇɢᴀɴ *undoes one of the*
ᴋages and produces a bottle of cham-
ne.)

ᴍ. —And my fiancée, Miss Henry.
ttle in hand, ᴿᴇɢᴀɴ *stares at him,*
zled.)

ᴀɴ. Your—? (*Then goes to* ᴄᴇᴄᴇʟɪᴀ,
es her hand, shakes it warmly and goes
ᴄᴇᴄᴇʟɪᴀ *laughs.*)

ᴇʟɪᴀ. He is priceless!

ᴍ. A magnificent fellow, Red. We box
ᴿy morning. I gave him that ear—but
watch, I'll pay for it. (*To* ᴿᴜꜰᴜꜱ.) *You*
ᴘ pretty fit, don't you, Father?

ᴜs. Quite. Do you mind?

ᴍ. I'm delighted. My only wonder is
some designing woman doesn't snap
up. Look how C got me. (*To* ᴄᴇᴄᴇʟɪᴀ.)
ᴋike rolling off a log, wasn't it?

ᴄᴇᴄᴇʟɪᴀ. Easier, much.

ᴿᴜꜰᴜꜱ. I keep my defenses well in line.
(ᴛᴏᴍ *laughs, and turns to* ᴏᴡᴇɴ.)

ᴛᴏᴍ. Did you hear what he said? (*To*
ᴿᴜꜰᴜꜱ.) —Millions for defense, eh, Sir?—
But not one cent for cab-fare. (ᴿᴇɢᴀɴ *has*
come in again with the bottle, now opened,
and is filling the glasses.) That's the boy,
Red. Pass them, will you? Then get dinner
going. I could eat an ox. (ᴿᴇɢᴀɴ *passes the*
glasses. ᴛᴏᴍ *turns to* ᴄᴇᴄᴇʟɪᴀ.) Are you
hungry too, Angel?

ᴄᴇᴄᴇʟɪᴀ. Simply famished.

ᴛᴏᴍ. Good. I like a girl who likes her
food. Once I said to Daisy— (*He stops,*
waits a moment, then smiles and raises his
glass.) Well—here's how and why and
wherefore—and you know where marriages
are made. (*All drink.* ᴿᴇɢᴀɴ *has a glass of*
his own, which he downs at a gulp.)
—Speaking of eating, I ran into Jim Winter
—you know Jim, Owen—in town today.
He wants me to go salmon-fishing in Canada in June. I think I'll take him up on it.
I've never done it.—It sounds like great
sport, eh, Red?

ᴿᴇɢᴀɴ. (*Putting down his glass.*) Did you
get your radio, Tom?

ᴛᴏᴍ. What radio's that?

ᴿᴇɢᴀɴ. There on the table. (*He goes out.*)

ᴄᴇᴄᴇʟɪᴀ. In June, did you say?

ᴛᴏᴍ. Yes. It won't be for long. (*He takes*
a swallow from his glass and puts it down.)
My, what a noble wine. (*He picks up the*
radio-message.)—I'll be back in three weeks
at the outside.

ᴄᴇᴄᴇʟɪᴀ. Then we'll be married in July.

ᴛᴏᴍ. (*Turning.*) July! You said May.

ᴄᴇᴄᴇʟɪᴀ. Not if you're going straight off
on a trip. (*There is a silence. He regards*
her soberly.)

ᴛᴏᴍ. —That's easy, then. I won't go.

ᴄᴇᴄᴇʟɪᴀ. Perhaps you'd better think it
over.

ᴛᴏᴍ. No, darling. I don't have to.

CECELIA. All right, Tom. (*She smiles and raises her glass to him.*) —To May first. (*All drink.* TOM *opens the radio-message, reads it and refolds it carefully. All are watching him. He thinks a moment, frowning, then turns to* OWEN.)

TOM. Owen—would you like to show Father the new bantam-cock? (OWEN *rises and moves toward* RUFUS.)

OWEN. The red one?—Right.—Will you come along, Sir? (OWEN *goes out.* RUFUS *does not stir.* TOM *goes to him, and slips his arm through his.*)

TOM. You must see him, Father. He's a beauty, that bird. He fights at the drop of a hat. (*He draws him toward the door,* OWEN *following.*) —Even if you don't drop it, he fights. I'm sure he'll be interested to meet you, too, Sir. (*He withdraws his arm, and* RUFUS *goes out.* TOM *closes the door after him, hesitates a moment, then returns slowly to* CECELIA.)

CECELIA. Don't tell me if you don't want to, Tom.

TOM. But I do. I intended to at the first opportunity anyhow, and— (*He glances at the radio-message once again.*) —And it seems that suddenly here it is. (*And puts it in his pocket.*)

CECELIA. Am I to be a good soldier?

TOM. No. There's no need to be.—Though I'm sure you would be, if there were.

CECELIA. Thanks, dear.

TOM. C, for quite a long time I've known —known intimately—a girl who's been very important to me—

CECELIA. Yes.

TOM. —Who always ·will be very important to me.

CECELIA. (*Smiling.*) —That's harder.

TOM. It shouldn't be. Because it has nothing to do with you and me, not possibly.

CECELIA. I'm relieved to hear that.

TOM. In fact, as it stands, I think she'll be glad for us.

CECELIA. I hope she will.

TOM. I'm sure of it.—C, Daisy has d[one] more for me than anyone in this wor[ld] She's the best friend I've got. I believe [she] always will be. I'd hate terribly to lose h[er] It's been a queer sort of arrangement— arrangement at all, really. There's ne[ver] been any idea of marriage between us. [It's] hard to explain what there has been betwe[en] us. I don't believe it's ever existed bef[ore] on land or on sea. Well— (*He hesita[tes] again.*)

CECELIA. Is she attractive, Tom?

TOM. To me, she is. She's about so hi[gh] and made of platinum wire and sand[...] You wouldn't like me half so well, if Da[isy] hadn't knocked some good sense into [me]

CECELIA. Well, someone's done a good j[ob] (TOM *laughs.*)

TOM. I'll tell her that. (*Then serious[ly]* I sent her a long cable about us this mo[rn]ing. She couldn't have got it, because th[is] (*He taps his pocket.*) this is from the b[oat] She lands tonight.

CECELIA. I see.

TOM. I want to be sure that you un[der]stand it—understand it both ways. I'd ra[ther] not go—terribly deeply into it if you d[on't] mind.

CECELIA. I don't, Tom.

TOM. We've been—everything possible [to] each other of course, and—

CECELIA. Yes, Tom.

TOM. But at the same time, free as [air] There's never been any responsibility [to] each other involved in it—

CECELIA. I can understand that.

TOM. Can you, C? Because I never co[uld] —Anyhow, that's the way it's been.—[I] haven't been what you'd call "in love," [for] quite a long time, now, so—

CECELIA. (*Smiling.*) Does she know th[at?]

TOM. She knew it first. Well— I d[on't] know what more there is to say abou[t it] except that there's no reason at all for [you] to worry, and—you won't, will you?

CECELIA. No, Tom. Not if you tell m[e]

dn't.

1. I do.—And finally, that I think she
ght to know the—news about us, pretty
mptly.

ELIA. Yes. Probably.

1. Is whatever I do about it all right
h you?

ELIA. Absolutely.

1. Thanks, C.

ELIA. There's just one thing I'd like to
. May I?

1. Why of course, darling. What?

ELIA. Are you quite sure that—? (*She
s* OWEN *and* RUFUS *coming in.*) —Poor
. Collier. I'm sure you loathe chickens.
uite agree with you.

us. —Vicious little beast. (REGAN
es *in beaming.*)

AN. Come on, everyone! Dinner!

1. You haven't put the car away, have
?

AN. Say, how many hands have I got?

1. Don't. I'll need it. (REGAN *goes out.*
turns to his father.)

1. Father, I'm afraid I'll have to ask
to do the honors at dinner.

us. The—? Why? How's that?

1. I find I've got to go straight back
own. (*A silence. Then:*)

EN. But I thought this was to be a
bration.

us. I had the same impression.

1. I'm sorry: it can't be helped.

OWEN. Is it so important to go in just this
minute, Tom?

TOM. Yes—unfortunately. (RUFUS *is eyeing
him shrewdly.*)

RUFUS. Why? What's wrong?

TOM. Nothing at all. It's simply that someone's arriving from Europe. I've missed the
landing, as it is.— (*To* OWEN.) —Someone
I've known a long time, and am fond of.

OWEN. Oh, I see.

TOM. (*To* RUFUS.) I must—well, the fact
is, I must tell her my—my— good news.

RUFUS. Now you listen to me— (TOM *confronts him.*)

TOM. —And it seems to me extremely important that I should do it at once. In fact,
I can't do otherwise. (RUFUS *bursts out:*)

RUFUS. —You have the effrontery, the
colossal bad taste, on the night of celebrating your engagement to a fine trusting,
loyal girl, to go from her—your fiancée—
to your—to your— (TOM *smiles.*)

TOM. —The same old difficulty with
words, eh, Sir?—Never mind. None of
them would apply to Daisy.

RUFUS. It's beyond me. It's the confound-
est impertinence I've ever known.

TOM. (*Smiling.*) But you see, for all your
splendid moral judgments, you know so
very little, Sir.

RUFUS. I suppose you know better.—If you
leave here tonight— (TOM's *smile vanishes.*)

TOM. —Yes. Much better. (*He returns to*
CECELIA, *lifts her hand and kisses it lightly.*)
—Until tomorrow, my Angel. (*He nods
good-night to* OWEN *and* RUFUS, *and goes
out.*)

CURTAIN.

SCENE II

e sitting-room of DAISY SAGE's *flat, later
same night.*

*y's flat occupies the top floor of an old
se in the Murray Hill section of New
k. The sitting-room also serves as a
kroom for* DAISY. *Victorian in atmos-
re, it is light and cheerful and has been
rated and furnished with an original*

*and unerring feeling for the period. There
is a fire place of simple design at left and
above it, a door opening into the bedroom.
The entrance from the hall is up right, and
into the pantry, down right. The sofa and
chairs are fine old Victorian pieces, but
comfortable in spite of it. There are three
large windows in the back wall. Below*

them stands DAISY's *work-table, piled with old magazines and sketches, drawing-boards, crayons, pens and pencils.*

Opposite TOM, JOE FISK *is seated. Between them stands* FRANC SCHMIDT, *violin under her chin, playing, and playing well, the concluding measures of a César Franck sonata. She is thirty, hard, rugged—in appearance more of a handsome farm-girl than musician.* JOE *is twenty-eight, fine Irish, nervous, intense, attractive.* FRANC *concludes the piece.*

JOE. Good!—You'll get there, Franc, if you work. (*She returns the violin to its case and seats herself near them. She speaks with a slight German accent.*)

FRANC. —Only I played it much better, much.

TOM. He just wasn't impressed, eh?

FRANC. Oh, yes.—He could book me on the Big Time, he said.

JOE. (*Incredulous.*) Vaudeville?

FRANC. —That is, if I would learn to roller-skate.

TOM. He wanted you to play on skates?

FRANC. —A sensation, he said. (JOE *and* TOM *laugh with delight.* JOE *goes to her, takes her face between his hands and kisses her resoundingly upon the brow.*)

JOE. My darling. My Dutch darling. (*She brushes him aside.*)

FRANC. Get away. (JOE *calls in the direction of the bedroom:*)

JOE. Daisy!—Did you hear about Franc and the booking-agent? (*He turns to* FRANC.) Where is she?

FRANC. —Probably taking another bath. It will be her third in six hours. That's what Europe does for you.

TOM. (*Indicating the pantry.*) —No. She's in there, I think.

JOE. (*Incredulously.*) Six hours! Two o'clock—?

FRANC. It's past it.

TOM. Will you two never go home?

JOE. (*Calling in the direction of* pantry.) Daisy! We're going! (*To* TOM *a* FRANC.) —And I promised myself tom row I'd do a chapter or die.

TOM. How's it coming?

JOE. All right. At least it's begun to mo

TOM. What are you calling it?

JOE. "Easy Rider."

TOM. I like that.

FRANC. But what does it mean?

JOE. Good God, must it mean somethin (*Again he calls.*) Daisy!

FRANC. Yes. Your eyes have got smal You should get to bed.

TOM. Both of you should—go on, you?

JOE. Why?

TOM. I want to talk to Daisy.

JOE. Look here, Tom, what *is* on y mind?

TOM. I've got something to tell her.

JOE. News?

TOM. Yes.

JOE. Good news?

TOM. Very.

FRANC. Will she cheer?

TOM. I think so.

FRANC. Tell *us*, Tom!

TOM. No.

JOE. Why not?

TOM. I want to tell Daisy first. (FRANC.) You know, I've been thinki Johnny Bristed might get a concert for y

FRANC. I don't want it yet. I'm not re yet. (*Again* JOE *calls.*)

JOE. (Daisy! (DAISY SAGE *comes in fr the pantry. She is twenty-six, slim, li a stripling, but with dignity beyond years and a rare grace to accompany it. contrast to* CECELIA's *lush beauty, she plain, but there is a certain style of*

*n, a presence, a manner that defies de-
...iption. Instantly and lastingly attractive,*
...e no one else one knows; in short "a
...rson," an "original." She wears white
...jamas that might as well be a dress, and
...ries a tray containing coffee and sand-
...ches.

...SY. —And furthermore, I don't believe
...ike France as much as I say I do. (*She*
...ts down the tray.) —And I don't for a
...nute believe that you're leaving.

...NC. Joe must. So must I.

...SY. —You stay the night, if you like,
...m. You can have my room. I've got all
...work in the world to do before morning.

...M. Why, thanks. Daisy, but—

...SY. As you like. (*She seats herself, and*
...es them coffee and sandwiches.) I had
...rty sketches to get through on the boat.
...Oh, what lovely intentions.

...NC. Was it rough?

...SY. No, but Pilard was on board and
...spent hours on end in the smoking-
...m—talk, talk, and more talk.

... He's a fine painter, Pilard.

...1. He's a good painter.

... Fine, I said.

...1. —And last week Henry Collins
...uld write. Hold on to your standards,

... You teach me, will you, Master?

...1. Collins' life shows in his work. He
...'t make up his mind whether he wants
...oe a writer or a man-about-town.

... Why not both?

...1. —Because, little Joe, his work is the
...y true mistress a real artist ever had.
...en he takes on the world he takes on a
...ore.

...NC. That goes for all good men, not
...y artists.

...SY. —But all good men are, aren't they?
...ook at Tom.—You don't have to put
...ks on paper or dents in stone to qualify,
...you?

TOM. (*To* JOE.) —Yes, and pays for her
favors with something a lot more precious
than twenty dollars left on the mantel-piece.
(JOE *reflects.*)

JOE. I had twenty dollars once. Now,
when was it?

DAISY. There's a statue in Florence that
made me think of you, Tom. (TOM *laughs.*)

TOM. Me! How?

DAISY. It's a David by Donatello.

TOM. You mean with the curls and the
derby hat?

DAISY. That's right! (TOM *shakes his head.*)

TOM. —No David, me. I'm just the no-
account-boy. Ask Father—he'll tell you.—
Hand me another sandwich, Joe. (JOE *gives*
him one.)

JOE. No-account, is it?—You've done more
for people than any one man I know.

TOM. Why thanks, Joe.—It's not true, of
course, but thanks.

JOE. And done it in the damndest, most
unassuming way I've ever heard of.

TOM. Oh, go to hell, will you?

JOE. (*To* FRANC.) I could name a dozen
first-class talents that, if *he* hadn't nosed 'em
out, would have—

TOM. Say, are you two going to hang
around here all night?

JOE. We haven't seen her either you know.
(FRANC *puts down her cup.*)

FRANC. I must teach you again how to
make coffee, darling.

DAISY. Your country's the one, Franc.

FRANC. Ach! There is no more new music
in Germany today than there is here.

JOE. I thought there was plenty here.

FRANC. Like what?—If someone goes—
(*She hums the opening bar of the "Rhap-*
sody in Blue.") —at me again, I shall
become mad. (DAISY *gazes at the bulging*
brief-case on the floor beside the work-table.
Her smile fades.)

DAISY. Oh, that work!—Look at it.

TOM. Is there much of it?

DAISY. At least eight hours.

JOE. I wish we could help.

TOM. —You can. Good-night, Joe.

DAISY. —And Briggs was at the dock.

TOM. I didn't get your radio till seven.

DAISY. That didn't matter. Anyhow I hate being met. Anyhow, I tell myself I do. Briggs was frantic. Apparently they've held the presses for two days.

TOM. You're a bad girl.

DAISY. I'm a scoundrel. I swore it would be on his desk at nine. I'll be lucky if I'm through by noon. (JOE laughs, and rises.)

JOE. Urge us to stay once more and we may give in.—Come along, Franc. I'll see you across the hall. (FRANC rises and takes up her violin-case.)

FRANC. —It is good to have you back, too, Tom. You are better than all of us, but Daisy. She is better than best. Between you, you stir up our lazy bones, you hold us together, you bind our wounds. You two are the—ach!—my blood is turned to beer.—Auf wiedersehen. Good-night. (She goes out.)

JOE. I'll drop in tomorrow afternoon about five, if I can.

DAISY. Fine. I ought to be up by then. (She follows FRANC into the hall.)

JOE. (To TOM.) Will you be here?

TOM. I'm afraid I'll have to go to the country.

JOE. Shun the country. Things come out of the ground there in Spring. (He goes out. TOM is alone for a moment Then DAISY re-enters.)

DAISY. —Love them as I do, I thought they'd never go.

TOM. So did I. (She puts her arms around him and looks up at him.)

DAISY. Hello, you dear Tom.

TOM. Hello, Daisy. (She kisses him lightly.)

DAISY. Now it seems I haven't been aw at all. (And leaves his arms.) Oh, it's gra to be back!

TOM. It's grand having you.—Was t trip really all that you hoped it would b

DAISY. It was better.—If only you'd be along. Oh Tom—the pictures! I got dru on them every day, twice a day.

TOM. I was sure you would.

DAISY. And at night when the galler were closed I sat around and dreamed them.—The silly contempt I always p tended to have for painting—self-protecti of course—the stuff I draw.

TOM. But some of it's good.

DAISY. You're right, my boy. Some of it (She goes to the table and picks up a po folio.) Look—full—sketches.—And not dress, a hat, a pajama among them. market-wagon—the angle of a doorway— open trunk. A melon cut in half—th glasses and a corkscrew—all manner funny objects. Oh Tom, two of the m exciting things have happened to me! N one—two! (She moves toward the sof Come—sit down—

TOM. What are they?

DAISY. I'm bursting with them. (She ma room for him beside her on the sofa, lo at him lovingly, smiles contentedly, touc his arm.) Good, this—isn't it?

TOM. But what, Daisy? Did you fall love with Pilard?

DAISY. Well I should say not! (She laug Pilard! (Then.) What's that? (From distance the strains of a violin are he playing variations on the scales.) O Franc. Still working.—Guess what I fo in my room when I came in? (He lo at her questioningly. She laughs.) seems the Swede maid Franc got me doe approve of you:—Four shirts, three so five ties and a razor, all done up in a g big white handkerchief.

TOM. You'd better go back to colored o —Maids, I mean.—

DAISY. —Remember Gladys?

TOM. Remember Hannah?

sy. Remember Marietta? (*They laugh zether happily. She slips her arm through ⸳, and for a moment drops her head upon ⸳ shoulder.*) Oh Tom, God love you.

м. God love you, my dear. (*For a ⸳ment there is silence, except for the ⸳nd of* FRANC's *violin. Then she raises ⸳ head and they speak simultaneously.*) ⸳isy—

⸳sy. Darling— (*She laughs.*) What?

м. No—you tell me—

⸳sy. Well, my heavy sledding ought to ⸳ over in a few weeks—by the first of ⸳y, anyway. What have you got on the ⸳—much?

м. Yes. A great deal. The fact is—

⸳sy. (*In a rush.*) —Work night and ⸳ until May. Then come to Mexico for a ⸳nth with Daisy. I'm dying to go. Pilard ⸳s full of it. I know it's what I need for ⸳hile, because—well, first—oh, I feel like ⸳ool. You mustn't breathe a word of it. *⸳e shakes his head.*)—Tom, I think I ⸳ paint.

м. But that's no surprise. I've always ⸳ught if only you'd—

⸳sy. (*Quickly.*) Then you've always ⸳n wrong!—It's new. It's since these two ⸳nths.—I believe that if I work my eyes ⸳, and my fingers to the bone, someday ⸳ay paint.—You must be hard with me— ⸳ parties—no hell-raising—*work.*—And ⸳ mustn't let me show until you know ⸳ ready to. Is that agreed?

м. All right.

⸳sy. You have a funny instinct about ⸳h things. I count on you.—As for the ⸳nd thing—(*She hesitates.*)—You know ⸳uddenly I feel shy with you. (*She rises.*) ⸳on't like it. I don't like it a bit.

м. We've—it's been a long time. (DAISY ⸳s again to the work-table.*)

⸳sy. Too long.—Perhaps I'd better wait ⸳ell you the second thing.

⸳. No. Tell me now.

⸳sy. Oh, my dear—what's wrong with ⸳ Come here to me. (*He goes to her,*

takes her hands in his.) That's better. Now I don't feel it so much. (*But still she looks at him anxiously. Finally she releases her hands, turns and fumbles among her work-materials, picks up a pencil.*)—These are German pencils. They can't touch ours. You'd think they could, but they can't. Give me a "Venus-6B," every time. (*She stares fixedly at the pencil for another moment, then puts it down and turns to him.*) You're a free man, Tommy. You always have been, with me. No questions asked. But please, Mexico in May together, because listen—No! Don't look at me. Look the other way— (*He averts his head. She goes on, rapidly.*) —I stayed three days with the Allens at Vevey and they've got the sweetest small boy about two and I got crazy about him and I want one, I want one like the devil. I'm crazy for one, and would you please be good enough to marry me, and—

TOM. Daisy, I—!

DAISY. Oh, it needn't be terribly serious!— It's not a life-sentence—just for a short while, if you like—it'd be such a dirty trick on him, if we didn't.—After I get my stuff through for the June issue—then Mexico for a month—I love you so much, I was a fool ever to think I didn't, and— ah, come on, Tom—be a sport—. (*She is breathless.*) —Give me a cigarette—(*But he does not.*)

TOM. Daisy—

DAISY. (*Quickly.*) All right. No go. Let's forget about it. What a foul necktie that is. The colors are awful.

TOM. Daisy, I—Oh God, God Almighty—

DAISY. Well, what is it? (*He covers her hand with his.*) —You're going to tell me something terrible.—What is it?

TOM. I'm going to be married.

DAISY. (*Incredulously.*) To be—?! (*Then silence. She averts her head.*)

TOM. Listen to me, darling, listen: you don't really care so much. You can't. It's simply that we—you and I—after all this time, naturally we'd feel—

DAISY. It must have happened pretty quickly.

TOM. It did. A month ago we hadn't even met. It was—

DAISY. You can spare me the details, please. I don't even want to know who she is. (*He moves away from her.* FRANC's *violin begins to be heard again.*)

TOM. —Her name is Cecelia Henry.

DAISY. It sounds familiar. I've heard or read that somewhere. Where?—Well, well, will wonders never cease? —If I'd thought you were in a marrying mood, I might have thrown my own— (*She picks up a small limp hat from the table.*) —could you call it a hat?—in the ring a bit sooner. (*She drops the hat upon the table.*) —Behold, the Bridegroom cometh—and no oil for my lamp, as usual.—A foolish virgin, me—well, foolish, anyway.—When's it to be? Soon?

TOM. —About the first of May, we planned.

DAISY. I see.—Of course, in that event Mexico *would* be out, wouldn't it?

TOM. —But I never dreamed you'd—oh God, I feel so awful.

DAISY. Does she know about us?

TOM. Yes.

DAISY. Honest Tom.

TOM. Oh, shut up.

DAISY. Remember me, Tom.

TOM. Oh my dear—as if ever in this world I— (*Suddenly, fearfully.*) Daisy!—There's to be no nonsense about not seeing each other as friends again, or any of that, you know—

DAISY. No?

TOM. No. We're grown-up human beings. We're decent and we're civilized. We—

DAISY. But there *will* be that nonsense. Oh yes—there'll be that, all right.—"Cecelia Henry"—Now I know where it was! (*She picks up a magazine and begins to run through it.*)

TOM. —But I don't understand it. I don't see why we shouldn't. I thought for a long time we'd been out of danger so far as well, so far as— (*He cannot finish it, b* DAISY *can.*)

DAISY. —Wanting each other goes?

TOM. But haven't we?

TOM. Speak for yourself, Tom. (*He loo at her, waits a moment, then speaks.*)

TOM. —You too, Daisy.—You first, thought.

DAISY. (*Slowly, thoughtfully.*) It's tr that side of it was never so much to was it? Not in comparison—not after th first crazy months. But I thought that v natural. I was even glad of it—glad to f it was—other needs that held us togeth (*She looks away.*)—Closely—without clai —not a claim—but so closely. (*A mome Then suddenly, sharply.*) Tom—do y have to marry her?

TOM. I want to marry her.

DAISY. (*Into the magazine.*) I was j thinking—perhaps you simply want he want her most awfully.

TOM. It's more than that, much more.

DAISY. I don't see how you can tell q yet.—For all our big talk, we still belc to the animal kingd— (*She stops and lo closely at a photograph in the magazin Here she is!—Oh, these neat, protec women. I've drawn so many of th dressed so many more.

TOM. If you knew her—

DAISY. But I don't, you see.— (*She h the magazine at arm's length, gazing at photograph.*) Such a pretty face—lov eyes, Tom. She's a prize, my boy. (closes the magazine and replaces it u the table.*) —But look out for that chi

TOM. Why?

DAISY. Just look out for it. (*She goe him.*) —Does she love you? *Will* she you, head over heels, regardless, as shall I say "as I once did"? Would rather?

TOM. Daisy—don't—

DAISY. I hold you dear, Tom—*you* what you are— just *as* you are. I thou

was my special gift. But maybe she has
too. I hope, I hope— (*He gropes for her
hand, raises it to his lips kisses it.*)

M. There's no one like you—never will
I know that.—But this—it's the damn-
est thing—I can't tell you—

SY. Don't try. I'll pray for you every
night, Tom. I really shall, you know I do
it.

M. Oh, my sweet dear—

SY. Yes—be good enough to remember
kindly, if you will. (*She returns to the
ble.*)

M. (*Wretchedly.*) Oh, don't *talk* that
ff! (*He goes to the fire place. She takes
her work-board.*)

SY. Now just stand like that a minute,
ll you? Erect!—Will you stand erect,
ease? (*He turns. She looks at him
enly.*)

M. What's all this about "remember-
g"? You sound as if we were— (*She
aws one strong line upon the paper and
s the work-board drop.*)

SY. There! That's all I want of you,
I shall keep of you. So goodbye, you
om Collier. (*He looks at her, puzzled.*)

M. "Goodbye"?—Until when—?

SY. (*So lightly.*) Doomsday, my darling.

M. Daisy, what *are* you talking about!

SY. Just that. (*He advances to her, takes
r shoulders in his hands.*)

M. Now you listen to me: If you think
I going to allow two people as important
each other as you and I are, to be sepa-
ed by any such false, ridiculous notion
this, you're mistaken. Just you try it.

SY. Tell me goodbye!

M. I'll do nothing of the sort.

SY. Yes! You have to.—Sharp, decent,
an—no loose ends between *us* two!

M. But it's not decent!—It's soft. It's
timental. It's the sort of thing you've
ver had any use for—taught *me* never to.

DAISY. Goodbye!

TOM. I will not say it

DAISY. Goodbye!

TOM. No.

DAISY. You must!

TOM. You'll never get me to. So give up.
(DAISY *throws back her head and closes
her eyes in pain.*)

DAISY. Oh, sweet heaven, what a world!
I could do better by people than this—

TOM. Daisy dear—listen to me—

DAISY. —And I want you to take those
things of yours—you hear? I don't want
them hanging around the place, not me.—
That new maid had a very fine hunch
about us, didn't she?—Packed you all up,
yes. Second sight—well, she gets the gate
for it, the big Swede. (*He stands gazing at
her.*)

TOM. I don't believe in this. I don't believe in any of it. (*She indicates the bedroom.*)

DAISY. —Go in and get them, will you?
Fetch, Thomas. It's quite a neat, tidy little
bundle. You won't be ashamed of it.—But
if it stays around—well, I don't quite see
myself crying into an old shirt, do you?—
I have work to do, my son—a great deal
of it. (*He does not move.*) No? Won't
fetch?—Then kindly permit me to— (*She
moves toward the bedroom.*) —And then
you must say goodbye to me—you will,
won't you? You've said it so many times,
so brightly—Say it this time sadly.—We'll
make it an *un*-marriage ceremony, to keep
it all quite regular. You must grasp my
hand in yours—one splendid gesture—and
murmur "Goodbye, my Daisy. Thanks very
much. A charming association." (*She goes
into the bedroom.*) —And may we never,
never meet again so long as we two shall
live.—You will, won't you? (*He has been
staring fixedly after her. Suddenly he
straightens.*)

TOM. —No. (*He moves swiftly to the hall
doorway, picks up his hat and goes out.
A moment. Then* DAISY *comes in again,
with a small bundle tied up in a large white
handkerchief.*)

DAISY. —See?—The wash is back.—Now do as Daisy says, and say— (*She sees that he has gone. She moves toward the door, stops against the work-table. The bundle*

droops in her hand, drops upon the tab There she stands, staring at the door. Aga FRANC's *violin is heard, playing the scale.*
CURTAIN.

ACT TWO

SCENE I

At TOM COLLIER'S. *About half-past seven on a Saturday night the following January. The living-room has undergone a certain change. Small, feminine touches, such as new lamps, cretonne curtains at the windows and slip-covers of the same material on chairs and sofa, have made a woman's room of it.*

CECELIA *and* GRACE MACOMBER *are seated near the fire place having after-dinner coffee. Grace is just over thirty. Without a single feature to remark upon except a slim and well-kept body, she manages, with the aid of coiffeurs, dressmakers and manicurists, to impress one as an attractive woman. She puts down her coffee cup and moves closer to the fire.*

GRACE. My dear, I'm congealed. I can't say I envy you the trip into town.

CECELIA. It's not my idea. (*She takes up a piece of needlepoint and begins to work upon it.*)

GRACE. But why do you do it? It's so grim.

CECELIA. Tom wants to.

GRACE. Such devotion.

CECELIA. It's her first big concert and he thinks for some reason we ought to be there.

GRACE. Who is she, anyway?

CECELIA. Schmidt, her name is. (GRACE *laughs.*)

GRACE. My dear! Not really!

CECELIA. Franc Schmidt, at that.—Tom says she's supreme.

GRACE. Oh—she's a friend, then.

CECELIA. She used to be.

GRACE. (*With meaning.*) I see. (CECELIA *smiles.*)

CECELIA. No, Grace. I doubt if you do.

GRACE. I suppose publishers have to h nob with all sorts of queer people.

CECELIA. We see very few people of a description any more.

GRACE. Don't tell me about the hermit l you live! I think the least you could would be to come to my Sunday breakfa now and then. Tomorrow's will be su fun. Do, C.

CECELIA. Perhaps we shall.

GRACE. —Not if you go in tonight.

CECELIA. Perhaps we shan't go in.

GRACE. (*Knowingly.*) Ah-ha! (*She loo about her.*) —You know, you could do much with this house.

CECELIA. —If we weren't so poor.

GRACE. Don't be funny. Your name's C lier, isn't it?

CECELIA. Somehow that doesn't seem make the difference it might.

GRACE. Well, I think it's brutal the w old Rufus K. hangs onto it.

CECELIA. We seem to manage somehow.

GRACE. I'd take *knives*, my dear, a gouge it out. (*A moment. Then*) —Wl would he be doing now, for instance? To I mean.

CECELIA. Didn't he say he had letters write? (GRACE *seats herself again.*)

GRACE. He's really extraordinary. He feats me. (CECELIA *laughs.*)

CECELIA. What's so extraordinary ab writing letters?

GRACE. The minute dinner's finished? fore coffee, even?—I guess I'm just miliar with publishers' eccentricities. (*Again* CECELIA *laughs.*)

CELIA. He's a little worried tonight, or dear.—Some more coffee?— (*She gives* ACE *a second cup.*) —He has a rather fficult ordeal to face.

ACE. The concert?

CELIA. No. Discharging Regan.

ACE. Reg—?

CELIA. —When, as and if he gets back om his weekly bat in town.

ACE. You mean that desperate butler? my dear, I'm so glad! He must have barrassed you to death,—But how did u manage to persuade Tom to let him ?

CELIA. I had nothing to do with it.

ACE. No? (*She laughs gaily.*) I believe t! (TOM *comes in from the other room,* th two or three magazines, which he is wrapping.) Ah! With us again.

M. With you again. (*He looks at his* tch.) Look here, C—hadn't we better be tting under way?

CELIA. We've got hours. Let's not sit d wait in a stuffy theater. (*A silence.* en:)

ACE. (*Brightly.*) I read the new book u published last week, Tom.

M. (*Without interest.*) Yes? What did u think of it?

ACE. Superlative, my dear. I was simply ished!

M. Well, that's something, isn't it? RACE *laughs.*)

ACE. —Isn't he beyond words? (*To* M.) You're the world's funniest man. u couldn't possibly be funnier.

M. You don't know me.

ACE. Oh yes I do! Don't *you* adore it, The book, I mean—

ELIA. I like it very much. (*She glances* TOM.) In fact I'm afraid it was I who de Tom do it.

TOM. And I'm afraid I still think it's the worst tripe The Bantam ever published.

GRACE. —But my dear! Everyone's simply devouring it!

TOM. There'll be a lot of sickness this winter.

CECELIA. You're so foolish about it, Tom. (*To* GRACE.) —He'll make enough on that one book to bring out ten he really cares for. (TOM *unwraps a second magazine.*)

TOM. I suppose that's the way it works.

CECELIA. Of course it is. It's simply common sense.

TOM. I suppose so.

CECELIA. Besides, I don't care what you say, it really is amusing.

TOM. It's tripe.

GRACE. Isn't there such a thing as having too high a standard?

TOM. No, there's not. (*She looks at him, startled.*)

CECELIA. What Grace means—

TOM. (*More emphatically still.*) No, C. There is not.

CECELIA. All right, darling. (*He looks over one of the magazines. A moment. Then.*) Oh—I meant to tell you: your father wants us to dine with him Wednesday and spend the night. (GRACE *pricks up her ears.*)

TOM. Get us out of it, won't you?

CECELIA. Again? How can I?

TOM. Oh, say I'm up to my ears in work, or something else he won't believe. Say the old boat is frozen stiff.

GRACE. I could easily send you in, in the closed car. Sammy and I might even join you.

TOM. Thanks. We cannot accept your sacrifice.

GRACE. But this weather—in that *racer!* It couldn't be more sobbing.

TOM. Oh yes it could! (GRACE *rises.*)

GRACE. Well, I guess I'd better be "barging along," as they say. I'm sure it's getting colder by the minute.

TOM. Yes—I think we'd best bring the brass monkeys in tonight. (*He returns to his magazine.*)

GRACE. The—? Oh, by the way, do you happen to know a stage-director named Prentice Frith?

TOM. You know, I'm awfully afraid I don't?

GRACE. He's supposed to be the absolute top in amateur dramatics.

TOM. I can't imagine how I've missed him.

GRACE. He's coming out especially for my Sunday breakfast tomorrow—

TOM. That's perfectly fine. That's just what Sunday breakfast needs, isn't it?—Of course the coffee must be very hot, as well. (GRACE *stares.* CECELIA *rises quickly. Finally* GRACE *turns to her.*)

GRACE. Good-night, C.

CECELIA. Good-night, Grace. Must you really?

GRACE. (*Moving toward the hall door.*) Yes. I'm afraid I must. (*She goes out, followed by* CECELIA. TOM *lights a cigarette, seats himself upon the stairs and continues to glance through the magazine. A door is heard to close in the hall. A moment, then* REGAN *comes in and makes his way quietly, but only fairly steadily, toward the dining-room door. He has almost reached it, when* TOM *turns.*)

TOM. Hi, Red.
REGAN. 'Evening.

TOM. Did you have a good day in town?

REGAN. Fine, thanks.

TOM. Lots of beer?

REGAN. No.

TOM. No?

REGAN. —Ale.

TOM. Why ale?

REGAN. It's quicker.

TOM. It's bitter.

REGAN. It's bitter and quicker.

TOM. You don't seem to be in very go[od] shape.

REGAN. I'm in awful shape.

TOM. You'd better get to bed.

REGAN. —Just where I'm headed. (*[He] moves toward the door again.*)

TOM. —See here a minute first, Red— (*[He] turns.* TOM *goes to him and confronts h[im] sternly.*)

REGAN. Yes? (*Tom hesitates. Then.*)

TOM. The fact is, that— (*He stops, a[nd] concludes.*) —Bring a couple of bottles [of] beer, will you?

REGAN. Right. (*He goes out.* TOM dra[ws] *a deep breath of smoke, sinks down up[on] the sofa, and exhales it slowly.* CECE[LIA] *comes in from the hall.*)

CECELIA. You ought to be ashamed, To[m].

TOM. Why?

CECELIA. You were terrible to Grace.

TOM. Why we should be exposed to [a] woman like that at all, is more than I [can] make out.

CECELIA. She's perfectly kind and frien[dly].

TOM. She's a silly, idle, empty, destruct[ive] woman. And the woods are full of her.

CECELIA. Grace destructive?—She does[n't] know enough to be.

TOM. It's pure instinct with her. If [she] were malicious, that might be interesting[.] Come on—it's nearly eight.

CECELIA. She thought you were trying [to] insult her.

TOM. Do you have to change or are y[ou] ready?

CECELIA. It seemed to *me* you were [un]necessarily rude.—I have to change.

TOM. (*Rising.*) I'll warm up the car.

CECELIA. Now we've simply got to go [to] her breakfast in the morning.

TOM. Not me.

CECELIA. But you'll have to make *some* gesture toward her.

TOM. I only know one.

CECELIA. Tom—please be serious.

TOM. Darling, I've spent my life trying to get away from her kind of people.

CECELIA. Just what do you call her kind?

TOM. Well—people utterly without stature, without nobility of any sort.

CECELIA. It takes all kinds to make a world, doesn't it?

TOM. Yes—and then what have you got? (*He laughs, takes her face between his hands, and kisses her.*) Go get dressed.

CECELIA. All the same, I insist that if—. What did you say to Regan?

TOM. Why, I— (*He stops and smiles.*) —I told him to bring some beer, but I expect he's forgotten it.

CECELIA. Oh, I see.

TOM. —Anyhow, I've been thinking: He never drinks on duty. Why shouldn't he have a right to get slightly mellow on his one day off?

CECELIA. "Slightly mellow"!—When he came back last week, he could hardly stand. When I said "Good evening" to him he didn't even answer.

TOM. Maybe he couldn't speak.

CECELIA. Probably not.—I said "Don't forget the furnace, Regan," and all he did was to bow like this, with a foolish grin— so low he nearly toppled over.

TOM. It's pretty hard to gauge a bow under those conditions.

CECELIA. Of course *I* think it's selfish of us to keep him.

TOM. Selfish?

CECELIA. We're certainly depriving him of any chance he ever had to make anything of himself.

TOM. But hang it, C—he broke his hand. He'll never fight again.

CECELIA. I don't mean fighting.

TOM. These are hard times: I don't know what else there is for him. (CECELIA *shrugs and rises*)

CECELIA. All right. Do as you like about him. I'll leave it to you.

TOM. —And anyhow, I feel for some reason that Red's good luck for me. He's—I don't know—we understand each other. I'm awfully fond of him.

CECELIA. You must be, to ruin whatever chance in life he might have. (*A moment. Then:*)

TOM. I wouldn't do that, C. You know I wouldn't.

CECELIA. You're doing it, though. What possibly could be more degrading to a man than housework?

TOM. You're making a regular Simon Legree of me. Where's my whip?

CECELIA. No, it's simply that in your delightful, casual way, you've never thought of his side of it.

TOM. (*Thoughtfully.*) —I wouldn't do that to Red. I really wouldn't. (*A moment. Then:*) Ring for him, will you?

CECELIA. Not me. I have nothing to do with it. (TOM *stares in front of him for a moment, then goes to a bell in the wall, presses it and returns to the fire place.*)

TOM. I don't know how I'll tell him. (*A silence. He ponders it. Then:*)

CECELIA. I suppose you feel we really must go into town tonight—

TOM. Why, yes. Why?

CECELIA. She'll play again, won't she?

TOM. I hope so—and often. But the first concert's an occasion, you know.

CECELIA. I suppose all your old friends will be there, en masse.

TOM. Without a doubt. (*Then, to himself.*) —All week long I've been trying to tell Red—

CECELIA. —The one you were so fond of— the Daisy something—

TOM. —Daisy Sage.

CECELIA. What's *she* doing now?

TOM. Painting, I believe.

CECELIA. Well?

TOM. I don't know. But I should imagine so.—I haven't seen her.

CECELIA. Don't you see any of them anymore?

TOM. No.

CECELIA. But why not, dearest? (*A moment. Then:*)

TOM. They won't see me.

CECELIA. —Won't see *you!*

TOM. No.—Go on now, please, like a good girl, and get ready. (*She turns, passing her hand over her eyes, and moves toward the stairs.*) What's the matter?

CECELIA. Nothing.

TOM. But dear—what is it?

CECELIA. Just this blasted headache, that's all. I've had it all day.

TOM. What a shame.—The cold air will fix you up.

CECELIA. It's that that gave it to me. I'm—honestly, Tom, I don't think I can face it. Why not telegraph, instead? Best wishes, and all that.

TOM. It wouldn't do.

CECELIA. I'm sure she'd be every bit as glad to have a telegram.

TOM. You don't understand, C. Franc has been working for years for this. She— (*REGAN comes in with bottles of beer and two glasses on a tray.*) —Just put them there, will you? (*He does so, and turns to go.*) —And wait a minute. What's the rush? Stick around.

REGAN. Certainly. (*He waits, steadying himself in the doorway.* TOM *turns again to* CECELIA.)

TOM. —Sorry, darling, a telegram wouldn't do. I've got to be there. But there's no particular reason why you should come. I can go alone.

CECELIA. I'll come.

TOM. No, you hop into bed with a flo⟨ of aspirin. I'll be out again bright ar early.

CECELIA. —I'll come, too. (*She goes o⟨ up the stairs.* TOM *waits a moment, th⟨ turns to* REGAN.)

TOM. —Drag up a chair. (REGAN *brings chair to the table.*)

REGAN. One more's about all I need. (*To opens the beer and fills the glasses.*) Th morning if all the bad heads in the world been put together in a row, my he⟨ would've got up and sneered at the rest them. (TOM *laughs and raises his glass*)

TOM. Here's how. (REGAN *raises his.*)

REGAN. How. (*He drinks, and beam*⟨ That's the stuff.

TOM. It builds you up.

REGAN. Yo! (*He takes an old pack of car⟨ from his pocket.*) —Seen this one?

TOM. I don't think so. (REGAN *holds t pack before him and releases one card af⟨ another with his thumb.*)

REGAN. —Tell me where to stop, and ⟨ member the card.

TOM. All right.

REGAN. Got it?

TOM. I've got it. (REGAN *makes a conceal⟨ "pass," shuffles the pack rapidly and han⟨ it to him.*)

REGAN. Where is it? (TOM *looks throu⟨ the pack.*)

TOM. Gone, of course.

REGAN. Feel in your pocket. (TOM *fe⟨ in his breast-pocket.*)

TOM. Not this time.

REGAN. No? (*He reaches into the pock⟨ draws out a card and shows it to him⟨* That it?

TOM. Marvellous. (REGAN *gloomily retu⟨ the pack to his pocket.*)

REGAN. I paid five dollars for that one. ⟨ let it go for two ninety-eight.

M. Not interested. (*A moment.*) —Was cold in town, today?

GAN. —I don't envy those guys selling ples on the corners.

M. (*Soberly.*) No.—Not much of a job, at.

GAN. Women's work.

M Pretty tough times, all right.

GAN. —Some of 'em, by God, are down selling those white flowers that stink so. *Again he raises his glass.*) Two hundred r steel! (*They drink.*)

M. I'm feeling the pinch a bit myself.

GAN. —Say, look here, Tom—

M. What?

GAN. If I— (*But he thinks better of it d concludes.*) —nothing. (*They finish eir glasses.* TOM *refills them.*)

M. (*Suddenly.*) Red, I might as well l you straight off—

GAN. What?

M. (*After a moment.*) —Nothing. (*They ink.*)

GAN. —All goes to show you ought to t something by.

M. It certainly does.

GAN. —Clean up while you're young d close your mitts on it.

M. That's it. (*A silence. Then:*)

GAN. How's your father these days?

M. Never better. (REGAN *shakes his ad.*)

GAN. Tsch-tsch-tsch.

M. Red, do you ever think of your ture?

GAN. (*Ruefully.*) I guess I'll go to hell, right. (TOM *laughs.*) Oh—you mean re.—Now that's a funny thing, because ten, Tom—

M. What?

GAN. I've been thinking: maybe I— *Ie falters, and cannot go on.*) —Oh, what e hell—

TOM. But what? (REGAN *holds out his glass.*)

REGAN. Fill her up, will you? (TOM *refills both glasses.*)

TOM. Not much future in buttling, eh, Red?

REGAN. (*With a deprecatory gesture.*) Oh, well—

TOM. I'm—I'm certainly very grateful for all you've done.

REGAN. (*Uncomfortably.*) Ah!—Be still, will you?

TOM. I am, though.

REGAN. That's fine, from you.—I'll never forget, when I was—and you— (*He gulps.*) I'll never forget it. (*He sniffs, and drinks.*)

TOM. Put it there, old man. (*They clasp hands across the table.*) You're a fine fellow.

REGAN. You're the top, boy. I don't know what you'll think of me, when I— (*Again, he is unable to continue.*)

TOM. When you what?

REGAN. When I—well, what would you say, for instance, if I— (*He looks at him, then looks away.*) Nope, it's no good—

TOM. (*Anxiously.*) You're not in trouble, are you?

REGAN. Trouble? Me? What trouble? (TOM *once more refills the glasses. Then, steeling himself:*)

TOM. —Then look here, Regan—

REGAN. Well, Chief? (TOM *looks at him. The steel melts.*)

TOM. —Good old Red. (REGAN *raises his glass.*)

REGAN. Tom Collier for President. The People's Choice.

TOM. Listen a minute—

REGAN. Wait! (*He takes another deep draught.*) Tom, I've just got to tell you. I've—I've— (*He grasps for* TOM's *hand and misses it.*) —Don't hold it against me, Tom, but I'm quitting you. I've took another job.

(TOM *half-rises in astonishment.*)

TOM. You've—?!

REGAN. Oh, I know what you'll say! (TOM *drops into his chair again, and stares.*)

TOM. Holy cats, Red—

REGAN. I couldn't stand it any longer. She don't like my ways. I mean the Missus. I get on her nerves.—Last week Moe Winters told me he wanted to open a country gym and would I run it with him, on the order of Muldoon's, but with a little bar attached and, well, God help me, I give him my word.

TOM. What's there in it for you?

REGAN. Don't put it that way, Tom.

TOM. But I really want to know.

REGAN. Two hundred a month, and a smell at the gate, if any.

TOM. It sounds like a good deal.

REGAN. Ah, the hell with it!—Let's let it go. I'll phone him.

TOM. (*Alarmed.*) No! (REGAN *looks at him.*) When do you start?

REGAN. He wanted me last Wednesday. I've been trying all week to get up the nerve to tell you. But—

TOM. How long will it take you to pack? (REGAN *grins.*)

REGAN. Well, there's my hat-trunk and my shoe-trunk, and the trunk for my fancy-dress ball-clothes—

TOM. (*Firmly.*) You leave by noon tomorrow, you hear? Not a minute later. (REGAN's *grin fades.*)

REGAN. O.K., Chief.—I'm sorry you had to take it this way.

TOM. Don't be a fool. I'm overjoyed for you.

REGAN. (*Uncertainly.*) Fact?

TOM. Absolute. (*He raises his glass.*) Here's to the new job.

REGAN. —Take it from me, boy, you're the goods.

TOM. You've got your points, too, you know. (REGAN *rises, swaying slightly, an* raises his glass.)

REGAN. Anyhow— (TOM *rises and rais* his.)

TOM. Anyhow. (*They drain their glasse* put them down and again clasp hands.)

REGAN. You'll explain to the Missus?

TOM. Of course.

REGAN. Tell her I'm sorry—hope no inco venience—but—

TOM. I'll explain.

REGAN. So long, Tom.

TOM. Good-bye, Red.

REGAN. So long, Tom.

TOM. Good-bye, Red.

REGAN. I'll give you a ring how it goes.

TOM. Do that.

REGAN. Keep your bib clean.

TOM. I will, old boy. (*Suddenly* REGA *sobers, looks at him intently for a lo* moment, then touches him on the should and says:*)

REGAN. Good luck, Tom. (*Turns abrupt* and swiftly and steadily goes to the do and out. TOM *takes a deep breath and se* himself at the table, with his back to t stairs, in utter dejection. He picks REGAN's *pack of cards and moodily glanc* through it. CECELIA *comes down the sta* in a lovely negligee. A moment, then s speaks lowly.*)

CECELIA. Tom—

TOM. (*Without turning.*) Hello. Ready

CECELIA. Did you tell him?

TOM. I'll miss that guy. I'll miss havi him around. (*She goes to him.*)

CECELIA. I know, dear. But it's for t best. I'm sure of it. (TOM *puts down t cards.*)

TOM. I've got a feeling that my luc going with him.

CECELIA. No, no!—I'm your luck. (*S*

ws him into her arms and takes his
d against her breast. A moment. Then:)

1. You feel good, C.

ELIA. Do I, dear?

1. You haven't any clothes on. Go on
ress—dress quickly—we've got to run.
e moves from him toward the stairs,
ere she turns again.)

ELIA. —Come and help me? (He looks
er for an instant, then goes to her. She
as into his arms. He holds her to him
a moment, then she leans away from
, provocatively.) No, you'd better not.
e glances down at the negligee, arms
) Look—I came across it in the bottom
wer, and my spine simply melted.—Do
remember it? (He picks up the edge
he loose sleeve and kisses it.)

. —Quebec.

ELIA. Then you do!—That funny little
nch hotel—

. (Gazing at her.) Yes.

ELIA. —Darling place.—Wasn't it cold
morning?—Frost on the windows an
thick.—Remember?

. —We couldn't see out—

ELIA. We didn't want to.

. No one else could see in.

ELIA. Breakfast before the fire—shiver-
—Remember—?

. I remember.

ELIA. We didn't finish it—

. No.

ELIA. (With a little laugh.) There was
one way to keep warm. (He moves
ard her.)

TOM. Oh C, darling— (She retreats, up one step of the stairs.)

CECELIA. No.—You'll make us late.

TOM. What of it?

CECELIA. It's late already. It's—we might miss the concert altogether.

TOM. What if we do?

CECELIA. Tom, you're the limit! Ten minutes ago you said—. (A moment. Then, in another voice.) Tom—

TOM. Oh yes, darling. What—

CECELIA. You go in alone. I've decided to stay here.

TOM. You've—?

CECELIA. Yes. It's too cold. I'm going to tuck myself into my warm bed, and—you'll need your heavy coat, won't you? It's here— (She goes into the hall, returning with an overcoat which she leaves upon a chair.) Good-night, love. I'll miss you— (He is about to take her in his arms, but she retreats, with the same provocative smile and an admonitory gesture.) No, no!—Good-night, dear. Keep warm. (He turns from her. She mounts the stairs, turns once, smiles down upon him curiously, and goes out leaving the door open. A moment. Then he takes up his coat, crosses the room, puts out the lights, and is returning to the hall doorway, when he hears CECELIA singing lowly to herself from upstairs. He stops, listens a moment, then moves slowly to the side table, where he leaves his coat upon a chair and takes up the telephone.)

TOM. Western Union, please. (A moment.) Western Union? (The curtain begins to fall.) I want to send a telegram.

CURTAIN.

SCENE II

DAISY SAGE'S. Late afternoon on a fine
ht day the following May. The sitting-
is as before, excepting for the painting-
erials upon the work-table, and a large
, turned away from the front, at the
dow.

is seated upon the sofa, smoking. FRANC

stands at the window, looking out. A moment, then she turns abruptly to JOE.

FRANC. —But what if she doesn't come?

JOE. She'll come. (FRANC leaves the window and seats herself, tense, upon a chair near him.)

FRANC. My nerves are like that.

JOE. Have a cigarette?

FRANC. No.

JOE. It ought to be quite a meeting. Only that once, months ago—think of it.

FRANC. And in a speakeasy!

JOE. —Like old times, though, like a reunion. That is, until *they* came for him.—You know, I think the last thing he wanted to do was to go on to that party with them.

FRANC. She is a pretty, the wife.—But did you notice? In his top hat, when he put it on, suddenly he looked like only anybody.

JOE. Domestication works fast, when it works.

FRANC. —Well, Daisy has not spoke of him one time since. Never, never will she forgive us this.—Give me a cigarette. What did he say to you? (*He gives her a cigarette and lights it for her.*)

JOE. He just telephoned that he wanted to see me, said it seemed years.—Your hand's shaking.

FRANC. I know it.—What did you tell him?—Why shouldn't it shake?

JOE. I said I'd be back at five. Then I left a note on the door: "Had to go to Daisy's. Come there."—It wouldn't if you smoked less.

FRANC. At five. (*She looks at her watch.*) Ach, Gott!

JOE. You're getting emotional in your old age, Frankie.

FRANC. —But why did you do it? It was well enough left alone.

JOE. I like Tom, and he sounded pathetic. I imagine he saw her exhibition, and—

FRANC. What makes you think he did?

JOE. He said he was telephoning from the Overton Gallery.—I wonder what he thought of it.

FRANC. What did you?

JOE. I know so damn little about painting.

FRANC. I know less.—But it all seemed me so fresh—done with such spirit.

JOE. That's it!

FRANC. —Bold—what-you-call it—un——without compromising.

JOE. Yes.—And the real stuff. No fakin

FRANC. —Every one of them Daisy. little Matisses or Picassos. (*A moment.*)

JOE. But Franc—

FRANC. (*Nerves again.*) Yes? All rig What?

JOE. What really did you think of the (*She shrugs.*)

FRANC. I tell you I am not—what-you—competent to judge.

JOE. What did they do to you, Fra (*She looks at him sharply, hesitates. The*

FRANC. —Nothing. I am sorry. But n ing—

JOE. Nor to me. (*She grasps his arm.*

FRANC. —But we must believe in her,

JOE (*In pain.*) We do, don't we? Lord, if only all my friends made s for a living.

FRANC. Yes. You could say "That is a good shirt" quite easily.

JOE. This afternoon—after a few min we duck out on them, understand?

FRANC. Joe, I don't like it. I am afrai this. I think it is not wise.

JOE. —If only they'd have one of good old-time rows. I'll bet he and wife of his never had a decent scra their lives.

FRANC. (*Thoughtfully.*) —And still, be seeing him, Daisy finds it is all ov finished—cold. Sometimes that is so. I for her it will be so.

JOE. Listen, child: it's May, and the are in bloom.

FRANC. (*Scornfully.*) You should wr German.

JOE. Poor Tom. Poor guy. He's up ag it for fair now, Franc.

NC. Why now more than usual?

Well, I ran into Hal Foster today,
—

NC. Foster—?—The one who did those
es?

That's the boy. He's finished a new
el that's even better, they say. Appar-
y Tom thinks he can grab it for The
tam, and stage a comeback on the
ngth of it. A sort of a last straw. He's
neet him this afternoon.

NC. Oh, good! (JOE *shakes his head.*)

No, not so: Foster told me that hard
as he is, he'd be damned before he'd
with a house that was responsible for
ung Ecstasy" and—

NC. But you should have talked to
Joe!

I did, till I was blue in the face. He
kept saying "Then how about *you?*"
as no use explaining how Tom thought
do better with— (JOE *glances quickly*
e door, and rises.) Look out!

rc. Him?

Yes, or— (DAISY *comes in.*) Oh,
, Daisy! (DAISY *pulls off her hat and*
es and looks at them.)

c. My, you're hearty. (*To* FRANC.)
t's the matter?

c. With me?

. Yes. You look queer.

c. I don't like the Spring. I don't
May and the trees in bloom.

. No? Nor do I. I say it's maple-
, and I say the hell with it. (*She*
herself near them.) Well, the show's
It's been a fine week. I've learned a
bout new painters, the so-called Public
the so-called Press.

c. There are no judges of one's work
oneself, Daisy.

. Then you don't by any chance agree
them?

c. I would sooner sleep with an art
than agree with him.

DAISY. It's touching the way my friends
have rallied round. Stout hearts. Thanks,
thanks.—But oh heaven!—If only someone I love and trust would be honest with
me!

JOE. And what do you call what we've
been?

DAISY. Friendly, Joe, very friendly.

JOE. *I* tell you: let's all get drunk.

DAISY. No thanks. (*For a brief moment*
she covers her face with her hands, then
looks up again.) It's all right. It's over.
Let's talk about something. Who knows
anything? (*A silence.* DAISY's *head sinks*
again. Finally FRANC *ventures:*)

FRANC. Jim and Nancy Peters are going
to have a baby.

DAISY. (*Absently.*) A boy?

FRANC. I think so.

DAISY. Good for them. (*Another silence.*
Then:)

JOE. —Er—Tom Collier rang me up this
afternoon. (*A moment. Then:*)

DAISY. Oh? How is he?

JOE. He sounded sunk.

DAISY. That's too bad. (*She cools her*
wrists. Then, to FRANC.) —You know, it's
hot.

FRANC. It *is* hot.—Don't be bitter, Daisy.

DAISY. I heard grand things about Nova
Scotia yesterday.—Why should I be bitter?

FRANC. You shouldn't. — About what?
Where is it?

DAISY. North, way north.—Bitter! Me!—
They say it's beautiful beyond words, and
you can live there on oh, so little.

JOE. He said—I mean Tom did—that—

DAISY. Joe, you seem to have an idea that
I might be interested in what he'd say—

JOE. Well—

DAISY. But as it happens, I'm not. (*To*
FRANC.) There are miles of green meadows
and a seacoast that's nobody's business.

Woods, as well. (*To* JOE.) —I suppose he was full of explanations about those choice eggs The Bantam Press has been laying lately.

JOE. No, he didn't mention them. He only said—

DAISY. Why tell me? (*To* FRANC.) The only out's the swimming. It's too cold. But other things make up for it. (*To* JOE.) —He always gets colds in the Spring—I suppose his voice was gone entirely—

JOE. It didn't seem to be.

DAISY. (*To* FRANC.) It's like Maine, they say. Only better, much.

FRANC. Not too many people? (DAISY *closes her eyes.*)

DAISY. No people. Gloriously, happily, mercifully, no people. (*The buzzer at the door sounds.*) Joe—will you? (*To* FRANC.) —Speaking of no people. (JOE *presses a button to open the door.* DAISY *continues to* FRANC.) Imagine Joe thinking that at this date *I* should give a damn what— (TOM *comes in with a brief-case in his hand.*)

TOM. Joey! How are you? (*He drops the brief-case upon the work-table.*) Franc!

FRANC. Tom, you look fine. (*He turns to* DAISY.)

TOM. Hello, Daisy.

DAISY. (*So coolly.*) Hello. How have you been?

TOM. In rude health, thanks.—And you?

DAISY. Never better.

TOM. Oh, it's fine to see you! I've been starving for you—all of you.

DAISY. Thanks.

TOM. How's the job?

DAISY. The magazine job?

TOM. Yes.

DAISY. I gave it up last winter.—A trifle— shall we say "quixotic"?—of me?

TOM. Shall we? (*He looks from one to the other of them.*) Listen: I love you three, I love you. (*He takes* FRANC's *head in his*

hands and kisses her brow.) Oh L⟨⟩ (*Gives* JOE *a friendly shove.*) Lord mighty— (*Laughs joyfully, seats him⟨⟩ and gazes fondly at them. There is a l⟨⟩ silence. Finally:*) Holy cats! Talk to will you?—Am I a leper? (*Silence. leans forward.*) Now listen, the lot of y⟨⟩ I've had enough of this nonsense. months you've been avoiding me like plague and I won't stand for it. Yo⟨⟩ important to me and by heaven, I'm g⟨⟩ to hang onto your coat-tails, dog y⟨⟩ footsteps, sit on your doorsteps, until yo⟨⟩ ready to grant that a man can marry, go on being a friend.—Is that underst⟨⟩ —Well, then: who's seen Sandy Pa⟨⟩ (*Then, in a rush:*)

JOE. I have.

FRANC. So have I.

DAISY. We all have.

TOM. What's he doing?

JOE. A war group in bronze for ⟨⟩ town in Texas. He's making them like sheep.

TOM. Good boy!

DAISY. —Except that they'll probably t⟨⟩ it back at him.

JOE. He'll get paid, though. Sam F⟨⟩ sees to that for him now.

TOM. How's your book doing?

JOE. Fair.—Of course nothing like Bantam's "Indian Summer" or "Y⟨⟩ Ecstasy."

TOM. Ouch.

JOE. What the devil made you take ⟨⟩ on?

TOM. Money.—Ah, but Joey, I'm re⟨⟩ ing! Did you know it?

JOE. In time, I hope.—How?

TOM. Williamson, Warren can have bright boys now, and welcome.

JOE. It's about where they belong.

TOM. Wait till you see The Bantam'⟨⟩ list.

JOE. I'm waiting.

. —That was certainly a foul format
ndon gave your book.

The words are there.

. If you can read them. What's the
k they printed it on—paper-towelling?
hear you're a hit, Franc.

NC. It has gone well enough. (*He looks
AISY, hesitates. Then:*)

. I—I saw your exhibition today.

Y. Oh really?—Funny I missed you.
at did you think of it?

. Well—

. (*Suddenly, eagerly.*) Tell me!

I don't think you were ready to show
How did it happen?

. Saunders and Munn arranged it.

Your old editors? The fashion boys?

. What about it? (TOM *shakes his*
.)

Daisy, Daisy.—How were the no-

. Appalling.

I suppose their reasons were all
g—

. Of course.—What are yours? (*A
ent. Then:*)

Well, you've been painting less than
ar—

. Yes.

—And yet you had about thirty
ases to show. (*Now* DAISY *is well on
nettle.*)

. Thirty-two.

It's a lot, Daisy.

. So you didn't care for any of them.

Oh yes!—One I loved particularly:
ne of the doorstep, with the milk-
s. I'd like to own that one.

. —Number Seven.—Sorry, it's not
le.

Two hundred—?

DAISY. Nope?

TOM. Two-fifty!

DAISY. Nope.

TOM. Seventy-five—

DAISY. Nope.

TOM. Four hundred and one—

DAISY. Nope.

TOM. I wouldn't take it as a gift.

DAISY. That's all right, then.

TOM. Of course your drawing's a marvel.
Lord, how that's come along!

DAISY. —Only what?

TOM. Good draughtsmanship's not to be
sneezed at, is it?

DAISY. Certainly not. Look at Belcher.

TOM. No—at Goya.

DAISY. Thanks so much.

TOM. Of course it depends on what you
want to be. I thought it was a painter.
(FRANC *rises.*)

DAISY. So did I.—Goya painted pretty well,
too, I thought.

TOM. In the first year? I doubt it.

DAISY. I wasn't aware it took a definite
length of time.

TOM. —And living in cities all your life,
you know.

DAISY. Perhaps I'd better hie me to some
sylvan dell.

TOM. I don't think it would hurt a bit.

DAISY. —Listen, you: if you can show me
a purer cobalt than the winter sky over the
East River any afternoon at four—

TOM. That's not the point. (DAISY's *voice
is higher.*)

DAISY. What is?

TOM. Fever—rush—hysteria—all day, every
day. (DAISY *turns away.*)

DAISY. Oh, go to hell, will you? (FRANC
moves toward the door.)

TOM. Sure. When do we start?

FRANC. Come along, Joe. (JOE *follows her*.)

DAISY. —And leave me with this moss-back? This— (*Again she turns upon* TOM.) —So I'm to sit under a parasol and paint tight little cows in streams, am I?

TOM. That's not what I said. (*Unnoticed by* DAISY, JOE *and* FRANC *have gone out*.)

DAISY. —Something suitable as an over-mantel for the Home of Her Dreams, I suppose.

TOM. Now you're being bull-headed.

DAISY. (*Turning*.) Bull-headed!—He calls *me* bull— (*She sees that* FRANC *and* JOE *are no longer there*.) Oh, you snakes—

TOM. (*With a gesture*.) Well—

DAISY. Well? What more, Teacher?

TOM. All I said and all I'm saying is, you can't expect, the first crack out of the box, to—*you've* got to *work*, Daisy.

DAISY. Sweet heaven! What else have I been doing? What have I done but?

TOM. —But differently—with such pains. You're turning out too much, you know it. (*Suddenly the fight goes out of her*.)

DAISY. Maybe, maybe.—Anything's too much.

TOM. Ah, darling—

DAISY. No!—Don't soften on me. Stay tough!

TOM. I do believe that's it, though. I be-lieve it's the whole story: still hung over from the old job. Pressure, pressure all the time. Still rushing countless sketches through against a magazine's deadline. (*She looks away from him. Her hand gropes blindly for his and finds it*.)

DAISY. —Anyway, against some deadline—

TOM. Daisy—darling—

DAISY. You're cruel, inhuman. You're a brute.

TOM. Oh Daisy—

DAISY. Thanks for being.

TOM. If you mean it—

DAISY. From my heart— (*She looks him, smiling now*.) Oh, you skunk— *laughs, relieved*.)

TOM. Worse. Much worse.

DAISY. (*Serious again*.) Who but Tom? (*She points her finger at hi Look: only you and strangers honest me ever. (*He draws her down beside on the sofa*.)

TOM. —The country's the place to w Daisy. Listen: There's a grand little h about six miles from us. Woods, meadows — you can get it for al nothing.

DAISY. That's about my price.

TOM. It could easily be painted up. W about a white roof for it?

DAISY. Oh, lovely idea!

TOM. C discovered it. She can find ou about it. I'll tell her who it's for. (*B this*, DAISY's *mood changes*.)

DAISY. Don't dream of it.

TOM. Why not?

DAISY. I've got other places in mind.

TOM. Anyhow, go somewhere.

DAISY. Sure—somewhere.

TOM. You're going to be good, D don't think I don't think you're good.

DAISY. I won't. I won't think anyt

TOM. This is a big day for me, do know it?

DAISY. How?

TOM. Well, I've been seeing the fol my ways here lately. Poor C—I must been sweet to live with this past She's been grand about it, though.

DAISY. I'm sure she has.

TOM. I—suddenly, for some reason, I that I'd got off the track—my trac was pretty painful— But I'm getting on, I think.

DAISY. I'm glad, Tom. You must, know.

. Did you ever hear of a fellow named Foster?

r. No. What does he do?

. Writes. My God, how he writes!— nobody knows it—not yet—

y. Have you got him?

. I'm getting him. He's done a fine, onous short novel that makes Candide sick. (*In growing excitement.*) I'm g to make a grand type-job of it, ad- se it all over the place, and sell it at bucks. I don't care if I lose my shirt t.—I'm to meet him at six this after- , to make arrangements.

. It must be nearly that now. You'd r go.

. —Daisy.—Have you missed me, y?

. You? Well, I'll tell you, it's this I— (*But she stops and looks at him, s her bantering tone, and nods, bly.*)

Much? (*Again she nods, and adds, r her breath:*)

. —Skunk, skunk.

Oh, and I you!—It's a lot of non- , this. It's ridiculous. (*She looks at her h.*)

. It *is* six.

Hell.

. You'd better run.

We need each other, we two do.

. You think?

Most terribly. I'm convinced of it. e never were such friends as you and t's wicked to give that up, to lose any- so fine for no good reason.—Why of all people, for a shabby, lowdown ion of convention, fit only to be con- d by shabby, lowdown—

. Wait a minute!

A hundred times I'd given my eyes you, to talk to you—

. Well—here I am—

TOM. (*Eagerly.*) Daisy—may I come again?—Just now and then, you know?

DAISY. (*After a moment.*) —If you like— just now and then.

TOM. Oh my sweet dear—thanks!

DAISY. But don't say "sweet dear." That belongs to another life, years ago.

TOM. Oh—there are to be rules, are there?

DAISY. One or two. One strict one— (*She hesitates.*)

TOM. What?

DAISY. Never secret. Never hidden.

TOM. No, no!

DAISY. —Always open, as before.

TOM. But of course, of course!

DAISY. I couldn't go it otherwise.

TOM. Why should a friendship be hidden? What's there to hide?

DAISY. It gets misunderstood.

TOM. It won't, it can't, or the whole world's rotten.

DAISY. It's been pretty ripe for a long time, Tommy.

TOM. "Tommy"! (*He laughs exultantly and draws her into his arms. They stand rocking back and forth, laughing in de- light.*) Oh my darling, how grand this is!

DAISY. I see you run to tweeds this season.

TOM. I even have a horse now—practically a county squire.

DAISY. Look out for it.

TOM. Oh, it's tame.

DAISY. I mean going county.

TOM. Never you fear! I wouldn't be let. I'm a terribly queer duck to them.

DAISY. "Lit'ry," I suppose.

TOM. "Very artistic."

DAISY. Are they good and dull?

TOM. Crashing.

DAISY. —And respectable.

TOM. My God, how!

DAISY. *We* aren't respectable.

TOM. Not a bit. Never shall be.

DAISY. For which, praise heaven.

TOM. Heaven, I praise you that Daisy and I are not—. Kiss the boy, Daisy.

DAISY. No.—You've got to go.

TOM. Why? Would it take long? (*She laughs, and pecks his cheek.*)

DAISY. There.

TOM. Ask me am I happy—

DAISY. It's all right, isn't it?

TOM. Magnificent.—All as before.

DAISY. Yes.—But for one thing.

TOM. What? (*She leaves his arms.*)

DAISY. We aren't in love any more.—Now run. You might miss what's-his-name.

TOM. How about lunch tomorrow?

DAISY. It's fine with me.

TOM. The old place?

DAISY. I'd love it.

TOM. One o'clock?

DAISY. One o'clock.

TOM. —And we'll dine at John Donovan's. He's opened a new place on Forty-eighth Street.

DAISY. Dine?

TOM. Why not?

DAISY. All right.

TOM. The next day's Wednesday, isn't it? I said I'd drive out in the morning to see Pat Atkins. He's been sick again.

DAISY. Poor dear. I'm sorry.

TOM. He's better now.—Come along with me, Daisy.

DAISY. Wednesday? No— Wednesday, I—

TOM. If it's a good day we'll take a picnic. What do you say?

DAISY. I—I guess so.

TOM. Fine!—We'll get back in time [t]o let's see, can I stay in town Wednes[day] night? Yes, of course, I can. I want to [see] that black woman dance.

DAISY. Which one?

TOM. Down on Grand Street.

DAISY. Oh yes, I've heard about her!

TOM. We can look in, anyway.—Thurs[day] I'm at the Press all day. But Friday—

DAISY. Wait a minute, Tom.—You [came] only now and—

TOM. I'll bring Hal Foster in about [five] on Friday. Will you be here?

DAISY. I—I think so.

TOM. Good-bye then, darling. Till to[mor]row!

DAISY. Good-bye, Tom. (*He takes her* [hand] *in his hands, kisses it several times,* [then] *her mouth, briefly:*)

TOM. Sweet dear, sweet dear—. (*He re*[leases her.*) One o'clock?

DAISY. One o'clock. (*He goes swiftly t[o the] door, where he turns once more.*)

TOM. —Ten minutes to one! (*He is g[one,] his footsteps heard upon the stairs. [She] stands rigid, exalted, her eyes shining. [Then] she sees his brief-case, left behind him [on] the work-table. She stares at it for a [long] time, apprehension growing in her [eyes.] Then she murmurs "Franc," runs to [the] door, flings it open and calls in terro[r:])

DAISY. Franc! (*Then returns, puts [the] brief-case upon a chair, then places a w[ooden] box upon her table and begins filli[ng it] with tools and materials.* FRANC *comes [in.*)

FRANC. Daisy?—What is it? Your [cry] frightened me.

DAISY. Franc, you're the one wom[an I] know who can hold her tongue. ([She] shrugs.)

FRANC. What is not my business— ([She] sees what DAISY is doing, and her c[asual] air is replaced by a real anxiety.) Pack[ing?] What's this? What for? You and—? [No,] Daisy, hold on a minute. Wait, Lieb[chen.] Think, are you wise, Daisy—

Y. I'm going alone—a long way, for ng time.

NC. To that place you said?

Y. (*A sudden idea.*) Yes!

NC. Wait! I come with you—

Y. No, I don't want anyone now. Later, be.

NC. But what is it, dear?

Y. I guess I'm running for my life, nc.

NC. —Tom again.

Y. —Still.

NC. It's no better—

Y. (*Packing furiously.*) —It's worse.

NC. Poor child.

Y. No, no! I'm glad.—But I've got to out.

C. Yes, that is wise.

Y. No one's to know where I've gone

C. No.

Y. No mess—it's to avoid one I'm g.

C. —But compose yourself, Daisy. Be n.

Y. I can't! Look— (*She points to the -case.*) He went without it. He'll come for it. And if I see him again for one ute I'll die.

C. He loves you, Daisy?

Y. I don't know. I don't believe *he* ws. But— (*She looks up from her ing.*) Oh Franc—he's so young!—Did notice how young he looked?

C. Yes, like a child.

Y. All slim and brown and sandy.

C. Quick, Daisy!

. (*Far away.*) He'll always be like —even when he's old. I know!—And way he stands—that funny way—stiff— his feet out—

FRANC. —What they call duck-footed, eh?

DAISY. (*Indignantly.*) Not at all. It's a perfectly natural way to stand. It's a fine, strong way to stand.

FRANC. Hurry, darling. Run quick!

DAISY. Yes, yes, I must. (*She resumes her packing.*)

FRANC. Will you take a trunk?

DAISY. The small one.

FRANC. How do you go—by train?

DAISY. I don't know. Boat, I think.

FRANC. But when? From where?

DAISY. I guess Boston. (*A moment.*) Perhaps I'd better see him just once more. Maybe if I can explain to him how impossible it is for us to—

FRANC. No!—And you go to Boston tonight.

DAISY. Yes. Yes, that's right. (FRANC *goes into the bedroom.* DAISY *continues to pack for a moment, then calls:*) Franc!

FRANC. What now?

DAISY. When those things come back from the Gallery, cover them, will you?

FRANC. Yes, dear.

DAISY. —Number Seven—do you hear me, Franc?

FRANC. I hear.

DAISY. Pack Number Seven and send it to him at the Press. (FRANC *re-enters.*)

FRANC. All right, dear.

DAISY. You're lunching with him tomorrow.

FRANC. So?

DAISY. At the old place, at one o'clock.

FRANC. One o'clock.

DAISY. Franc—

FRANC. Yes, darling? (DAISY *gathers up some paint-tubes.*)

DAISY. When you see him—

FRANC. Yes, darling—

DAISY. Kiss him for me. (*She realizes what she has said, and murmurs:*) Kiss him for me— (*Then hurls a tube into the box, in fury.*) Kiss him for me! (*The buzzer sounds imperatively.* DAISY *starts in alarm.* FRANC *takes her arm.*)

FRANC. Come—and don't speak— (*She leads her toward the bedroom, stopping to press the button at the fire place. They go out.* TOM *is heard running up the stairs. He hurries in, calling:*)

TOM. Daisy—? (*There is no answer. He goes to the table, and calls again:*) Daisy!

(*A moment. Then* DAISY's *voice is he faintly from the next room.*)

DAISY. Hello—

TOM. I forgot my case. (*He finds it u the chair and picks it up.*) It's all ri I've got it. (*At the door he turns more and calls:*) Don't be late tomorr Remember! Twelve-thirty! (*And goes Again footsteps are heard upon the st and a door slams below.*)

CURTAIN.

ACT THREE

SCENE I

At TOM COLLIER's, *six months later. Ten o'clock of a bright Sunday morning. Alterations have been made, and the old library has become a chaste dining-room. Now, at last,* TOM's *house is* CECELIA's *house, which is to say, The House in Good Taste.*
The door beside the fire place at right opens, through the hall, upon a large new living-room. The library furniture has been replaced with a dining-room table, sideboard, serving-table and chairs. The large table is set for breakfast and there are various breakfast dishes being kept hot upon the serving-table.

CECELIA *and* OWEN *are at breakfast,* CECELIA *seated and* OWEN *standing, napkin in hand, half turned in the direction of the serving-table, toward which* GRACE *is moving with a coffee-cup.*

GRACE. Oh no, thanks! I love to serve myself. It's so English. (OWEN *reseats himself.* GRACE *refills her cup and returns to the table with it.* CECELIA *presses a button upon the table.*)

CECELIA. I'll order some more hot. (OWEN *takes a swallow of water, puts down his napkin and pushes back his chair.*)

OWEN. Well, for the morning after a party, I feel pretty good. Where's the birthday-boy?

CECELIA. Still recovering upstairs.

GRACE. He was never more amusing. Honestly, when he did that skit from his

new magazine, I thought I couldn't s it. I was in stitches.

OWEN. —What's happened to the ar element? Still asleep?

CECELIA. Miss Sage and Fisk insisted walking to the station with La Schr It turned out that she had to take an train.

GRACE. I've never known a musicia make such difficulties about playing.

CECELIA. She's used to her own violi

GRACE. But is there any differ—? (*T thoughtfully.*) Yes—I suppose there The Sage is rather a number, isn't Do you know she actually spent six mc in Tierra del Fuego?

OWEN. Nova Scotia.

GRACE. I mean Nova Scotia.

CECELIA. Yes, I'd heard.

GRACE. The places they go!—C, I w knew how you get hold of such intere people.

CECELIA. I asked them as a parti favor, for Tom's birthday. I insisted It was part of the surprise party. (*sighs.*)

GRACE. —They invariably *say* they'll to me, and then at the last minute thing always happens.

ELIA. —Besides they're very old friends
…is. I said he was longing to see them.—
…ink he really has missed them a little.

EN. Clever Cecelia.

ELIA. Why?

EN. Real security at last, eh?

ELIA. Do you object (GRACE *looks at*
…n *suspiciously.*)

CE. What are you talking about?
…*ere is no answer. She rises.*) Oh, you
…le people! I wish I were subtle. (CECELIA
…*ses the bell again.*)

ELIA. I wish someone would answer
…bell. (GRACE *looks about her.*)

CE. Darling, you *have* done wonders
…this house. It's all in such perfect
…, now.

ELIA. I wish Tom was as enthusiastic
…it about it as you are.

CE. Oh, men never like changes.

LIA. Unless they think of them them-
…s.—We're having a charming time
…t the roof.

EN. The roof?

ELIA. It's got to be fixed—and ever
…e he came back from Bermuda last
…er he's been saying he wanted a white
…—been wanting to whitewash it white.

E. What!?

EN. (*Simultaneously.*) The roof here?

LIA. Yes. They're all white in Ber-
…a.

EN. But this isn't Bermuda.

LIA. I've tried to explain that to him.

EN. (*To* GRACE.) But I don't think I've
…seen a white roof around here, have

E. Let me think. (*She thinks, pain-
Then:*) —No.

IA. He says, What does that matter?
…wants one. He thinks they're pretty.
…inks— (*In sudden irritation.*) Oh, he
…e exasperating! (*To* OWEN.) His father

sent him a check for his birthday: he may accept it, he may not.

GRACE. Not accept a *check?*

CECELIA. —Because it's from him.

GRACE. Well, I'm amazed.—A whopper, too, I'll bet.

CECELIA. I don't know. I didn't see it.

OWEN. I thought he'd got over the nonsense about his father.

CECELIA. So did I. Everything has been simply beautiful for months. He's been so pleased with Tom, and the way business has been going. Apparently someone told him about it.

OWEN. Williamson, probably.

CECELIA. —Or Warren. I don't know which.

GRACE. Are they the ones that want to buy The Bantam Press?

CECELIA. —To buy into it, yes.

GRACE. How does Tom feel about that? (CECELIA *shrugs.*)

OWEN. He's made the price so high they'll have to refuse it.

CECELIA. Not if *you* tell them not to, Owen!

OWEN. I thought I'd explained all that to you. (*A moment. Then:*)

CECELIA. —I suppose I'll have to get the coffee myself. (*She rings again.*) I told Tom that with *him* back, the maids would do nothing.

OWEN. It does seem funny, seeing him around again.

GRACE. I was overcome last night.—How did it happen, C?

CECELIA. The new job didn't pan out. Tom ran into him somewhere and telephoned to ask if he could bring him out for a day or two, he'd been ill. There was nothing to do but say yes. Now, of course, he wants to keep him.

GRACE. Why not—you know—just give him something, and—?

CECELIA. He won't take anything without earning it. Tom swears he'll teach him manners—at least to the extent of calling us "Sir" and "Madam." He said it was the one birthday-present he really— (*She sees* REGAN *standing, beaming, in the doorway.*) Oh.

REGAN. Did someone ring?

CECELIA. Several times. Will you bring some hot coffee, please?

REGAN. Sure thing. (*He takes the coffeepot and goes out with it.* GRACE *laughs.*)

GRACE. Manners!

CECELIA. I'm afraid he's hopeless.

GRACE. You know, I can't get over old Rufus K. actually sending checks. He can be nice, can't he?

CECELIA. Extremely. Did I tell you? He's invited us to spend the winter with him in town.

GRACE. Not in the big house?

CECELIA. Yes.

GRACE. But it's the most unheard-of thing I've ever heard of!

CECELIA. We may not go. Tom's not too keen for that, either.

GRACE. He's mad!—Of course you can persuade him. It will *be such*— (TOM *comes down the stairs, a trifle white and wan.*) Ah! Good morning, host!

TOM. Is it?—How are you, Grace? Hello, Owen. (*He seats himself and eyes the food distrustfully.*) Did Franc get her train?

CECELIA. I imagine so.

TOM. I meant to get up. Where are Joe and Daisy?

CECELIA. They went walking. (TOM *settles back painfully in his chair.*)

GRACE. Oh come now! It's not as bad as that.

TOM. Lady, you don't know. (*To* CECELIA.) Was I dreadful?

CECELIA. You were delightful.

TOM. Oh, don't say that!—That mean put on an act.

GRACE. You were the life of the pa (TOM *cringes.*)

TOM. Good Grace. (REGAN *comes in u the coffee-pot and a glass of what app to be milk.*)

REGAN. (*Heartily.*) How're ye, Tom, boy!

TOM. —'Morning, Red. (REGAN *puts coffee-pot upon the serving-table.* TOM *lo guiltily at* CECELIA, *who turns away.* RE *comes beaming from the serving-table, glass in hand.*)

REGAN. Look what Baby brought yo (TOM *rises and goes to him.*)

TOM. —Just a minute. (*He puts his through his, turns him away from others and low enough to be heard by one but him, murmurs:*) Look, Red you don't mind, I think you'd bette "Regan" from now on, and us "Sir" "Madam."—You're a pretty good a (REGAN *stiffens into the Perfect Butler.*)

REGAN. (*Audibly.*) Right, Sir. H'I kr me place, Sir. (TOM *laughs, and return the table.*)

TOM. Don't lay it on.

REGAN. Oh no, Sir. (*He offers the obsequiously.* TOM *takes it.*)

GRACE. Milk?!

TOM. —Punch. (*He makes a face ou and returns it to* REGAN.) Could you sibly brush the nutmeg off?

REGAN. I think so, Sir.

TOM. Try. Move heaven and earth. (R *returns to the serving-table with the and removes the nutmeg.* DAISY *come from the hall.*)

GRACE. Oh, hello!

DAISY. Good morning.

CECELIA. How was the walk?

DAISY. Very pleasant, thanks. We miles. It's a lovely village.

CECELIA. It is nice.

y. Whose house is the pretty white
on the Square?

LIA. Near the Post Office? (*To*
E.) Isn't that Judge Evans's?

E. Yes.

·. (*To* TOM.) I hope you remembered
nd the new magazine-proofs for me.
ɪ *takes some folded proof-sheets from
pocket.*)

Right here. (DAISY *extends her*
.)

·. Please—

If you'd really like to—

·. I should, very much. (*She takes
proofs and goes to the stairs, where she
herself upon the bottom step.* REGAN
ns *the glass of punch to* TOM.)

That's better. (JOE *comes in from
hall.* REGAN *coughs discreetly behind
and.*)

N. (*Not presuming to look directly
s master.*) Beg pardon, Sir—

Yes?

N. —If I may so, Sir—it has always
ed to me that life is like a sailboat—

(*Smiling.*) Ah?

N. In good weather, no better ridin'
here—but the very deuce, Sir, in a
, Sir. (TOM *laughs and waves him
.*)

Get out! (REGAN *bows gravely.*)

N. Very good, Sir. (*And goes out.
ɪA's fixed smile leaves her face. She
a deep breath.* DAISY *laughs softly,* JOE
y. GRACE *turns to* JOE.)

. Oh hello! (JOE *recovers himself
advances into the room.*)

How are you?

. Pleasant walk?

If you like the country.

. I'll bet you made a good plot, too.

A good—?

. I know you writer-men!

DAISY. (*From the stairs.*) —Remember
your prescription for me, Tom?

TOM. Prescription?

DAISY. "The country's the place to work,"
you said.

JOE. Something did it for you, Daisy.

TOM. —Daisy herself.—You can spend the
night, can't you, Joe?

JOE. It's up to Daisy.

DAISY. I'm not certain, yet. Must we say
straight off?

CECELIA. Of course not.—Do, though.
We'd so love having you.

TOM. I've got to run over to Greenwich
to see one C. B. Williamson, but I'll be
back this evening.

JOE. The publisher?

TOM. Yes. Why?

JOE. What have *you* got to do with that
old pirate? (TOM *smiles.*)

TOM. Shh?—It's a secret. (JOE *stares.*)

JOE. My God!

GRACE. You're coming to my house for
Sunday breakfast, you know.

JOE. Thanks, we've had it.

GRACE. Oh, but mine is a very special
breakfast!—

JOE. (*To* TOM.) —I liked the old Press
building better.

TOM. We needed more room.

CECELIA. (*To* TOM.) Don't you want some
coffee or something?

TOM. This is fine. Will you join me in a
milk-punch, Daisy?

DAISY. Would you mind awfully if I
didn't?

TOM. I'm not sure.

GRACE. Not disapproving, is she? (DAISY
laughs pleasantly.)

DAISY. Not in the least.

TOM. (*To* JOE.) —You couldn't publish a magazine in that old shack.

JOE. Don't tell me it's that smart.

GRACE. *I* think it's going to be a sensation. I'm practically a collaborator, aren't I, Tom? (TOM *laughs.*)

TOM. Grace is my reaction-agent. She submits to tests. (DAISY *stares at the proofs.*)

DAISY. Is this all of it?

TOM. —The dummy for the first number.

DAISY. No name yet—

TOM. No.

JOE. —Any Sunday papers, by any chance?

TOM. —In the living-room. I'll send for them.

JOE. It's all right. I'll read them there. (*He goes out.* TOM *looks after him.* GRACE *rises.*)

TOM. Extraordinary fellow, Fisk.

GRACE. My people will be arriving. Who's going to run me home? (*She holds out her hand to* TOM. *He takes it and rises.*)

TOM. We'll go in Joe's Ford, and shock the village.

GRACE. Divine!

DAISY. Bring it back, Tom.

TOM. You bet.—How about your coming with us? (DAISY *rises upon the stairs.*)

DAISY. Thanks, but I want to finish this.

TOM. Be sure to like it.

DAISY. I'm afraid I'm no judge.

GRACE. Tom, I've got to tell you: *I* think the idea of a white roof in this country is idiotic. (*She tucks his hand under her arm and they move toward the door.*)

TOM. (*As they go out.*) So do I. It's insane. Whatever made you think of it? (DAISY *mounts the stairs and goes out,* CECELIA *watching her.* OWEN *moves toward the living-room.* CECELIA'S *low voice stops him.*)

CECELIA. Owen—

OWEN. What, C?

CECELIA. Why did she come?

OWEN. Daisy? I thought you wanted [her?] for all those highly special reasons.

CECELIA. —First she said she could[n't.] Then she telephoned back she would.

OWEN. Well?

CECELIA. I believe she came for some [spe]cial reason of her own.

OWEN. Quite possibly.

CECELIA. What, though?

OWEN. Search me.

CECELIA. Twice last night I caught [her] watching me in the most curious way. [Once] when I was with Fisk, once with yo[u.] But you know, I'm not the least bit jea[lous] any more. I'm even inclined to like he[r.]

OWEN. That's big of you.

CECELIA. I suppose Fisk is one of hers,

OWEN. (*Frowning.*) How do you me[an?]

CECELIA. Sweet innocent!

OWEN. How's that?

CECELIA. I should think by this time y[ou'd] know a promiscuous little— (*She see[s his] frown deepen, and with a gesture, [con]cludes:*) —Oh, well—

OWEN. You're a strange girl, C.—A[nd a] pretty cruel one.

CECELIA. —Not at all. I tell you I [don't] mind in the least. In fact I really don'[t see] why Tom and she shouldn't be as [good] friends now as—well, as you and I are.

OWEN. Their history is a little differe[nt.]

CECELIA. Why? Don't you like our hist[ory?]

OWEN. What there is of it.—A trifle [un]eventful, don't you think?—Or shal[l we] simply call it lacking in excitement? [(A moment. Then:)]

CECELIA. —You've been so strange, l[ately.] So remote, Owen.

OWEN. I wasn't aware of it.

ELIA. —Refusing to help us one bit
Mr. Williamson.

N. But Tom doesn't want to be
ed!

LIA. I do.

N. C, I've told you. I simply can't do
(CECELIA *turns from him coldly.*)

LIA. Very well.

N. Certainly, you must realize—

LIA. Of course. (*She moves toward*
iving-room.) Come on—shall we?

N. I've told you a dozen times, I'm
sel for Williamson's, and— (CECELIA
and turns to him.)

LIA. Exactly.—And so they do what-
you tell them to.

N. Tom's price is out of all reason.

LIA. Not if they really want it.

N. But hang it, he made it that to
them off! He doesn't want them to
it.

LIA. Tom doesn't know what he
s. (*Coaxing.*) —Just one little word to
from you—on the telephone—before
oes over this afternoon—now—before
ets back from Grace's.

N. There's something called legal
s you seem not to understand, C.

LIA. And something called friendship?
turns away. A moment. Then she looks
im sideways.) Owen— (*He gestures*
at?) "Lacking in excitement," you
—For you?

J. For you, I meant.

LIA. I suppose you're the judge of
too.

. I don't know who else.

LIA. Of course you couldn't possibly
rong.

. Could I?

LIA. (*Softly.*) —And I'm not a hu-
being at all, of course. (*He advances*
d her.*)

OWEN. C—!

CECELIA. (*Quickly.*) Do one thing for me:
just tell them it *might* be a good thing for
them.—It might, mightn't it?

OWEN. But even so, I—don't think I can.

CECELIA. —That it *is* high—admit that—
but it might be a good thing. (*He ponders*
it, frowning.) —Owen—telephone him—
just one little word, Owen— (*He is about*
to protest again, but is stopped by her even
gaze and her hand upon his arm. Finally
he nods assent. She breathes:) You darling—
(*He inclines toward her, but she leans*
away from him. Suddenly he glances up at
the staircase. She senses that someone is
coming, and begins to talk rapidly, in a
different voice:) —And of course it will
be the most marvellous thing for Tom if
Williamson agrees. You can imagine what
it will mean to him.

OWEN. Yes, of course. (DAISY *comes down*
the stairs, the magazine-proofs still in
hand.)

CECELIA. His father will be pleased as
Punch, too, but the main thing is— (*She*
looks at DAISY *in pretended surprise.*) Oh,
hello! Owen and I were just talking about
The Bantam Press combining with Williamson's. Owen engineered it.

OWEN. Oh no, C. If there's any credit
due— (CECELIA *laughs, and exclaims:*)

CECELIA. Never mind! (*Then again to*
DAISY.) —I'm so excited about it, I can
hardly speak. (*Then, to* OWEN.) —Why,
Owen—do you realize?—But you wanted
to telephone, didn't you?

OWEN. Why, er—why—yes, yes, I did.
(CECELIA *moves toward the living-room.*)

CECELIA. It's in here, now. (*He follows.*
She speaks over her shoulder to DAISY.)
Coming along?

DAISY. In just a moment. (OWEN *and* CE-
CELIA *go out, encountering* JOE *coming in.*
DAISY *gazes after them.*)

JOE. (*To* CECELIA.) I thought I'd get ready
for breakfast—lunch—whatever it is.

CECELIA. But you look lovely! (*She follows*

OWEN *out, into the living-room.* DAISY *moves to the table, where she sits, staring in front of her, slowly comprehending.* JOE *approaches her, as* REGAN *comes in.)*

JOE. (*To* DAISY.) What do you say we— (REGAN *clears his throat portentously.*) —God, Red, get that fixed, will you? (REGAN *lifts a lemon in two fingers.*)

REGAN. Have you seen this one?

JOE. I had grapefruit.

REGAN. Give me a five-dollar bill. (JOE *finds one for him.* REGAN *folds it and closes his hand upon it.*) Which hand?

JOE. That one. (REGAN *opens both hands.* DAISY *is still staring, wrapt in thought.*) Good!—Only where does the lemon come in? (REGAN *beckons him nearer, cuts the lemon with a fruit-knife, extracts a five-dollar bill from it, shows it to him, picks up a tray, and moves toward the door.*)

REGAN. Thank you, sir. (*He goes out with the tray and* JOE's *five dollars.* JOE *turns to* DAISY *about to speak, but she speaks first.*)

DAISY. Are you packed, Joe?

JOE. Not yet. Why?

DAISY. I want to go.

JOE. What's the rush?

DAISY. I want to get out of this house.

JOE. But why all of a sudden?

DAISY. I want to get out, that's all.

JOE. Tom?

DAISY. Yes.

JOE. Poor devil—

DAISY. Yes.

JOE. Of course he's terribly on the defensive: you can see that.

DAISY. (*Dully.*) Can you?

JOE. Of course. He felt us disapproving, and simply gave us the works.

DAISY. Maybe.

JOE. He was awful last night, all right.

DAISY. Go and pack, Joe.

JOE. And what an outfit they were give you Grace Macomber in your Ch mas stocking.

DAISY. Thanks.

JOE. I'll even throw her husband in, good measure.

DAISY. That would be too divine.

JOE. And all those pitiful second-h opinions of Tom's! What's happened him? What do you suppose has don for God's sake—

DAISY. That's what I came to find out

JOE. Have you?

DAISY. Yes.

JOE. What?

DAISY. The most pitiful thing that happen to any man.

JOE. But what?

DAISY. Go and pack, Joe.

JOE. It won't take a minute.—It cert can't be C. I think she's a fine girl, you? I talked with her for quite aw last night. She made great sense. I t she's a damned nice, attractive wo (DAISY *moves away from him.*)

DAISY. So was Delilah.

JOE. Deli—? Oh come on, Daisy!

DAISY. —And bring my bag down yours.

JOE. But I don't get you at all.

DAISY. (*Turning.*) Will you go and p

JOE. Honestly, Daisy, you're the dam girl. (TOM *comes in from the pant whisky-and-soda in hand.*)

TOM. A drink anyone?

JOE. At this hour? I should say not. *seats himself at the end of the table, f them.*)

TOM. Too bad.

JOE. Besides, we've got to go.

TOM. So soon? Too bad. (*He takes a low of his drink, and smiles at t* Godspeed—

. (*After a moment.*) —There was a
ow once told me drink was in a way
ecoming my own personal Hollywood—

. Really? How amusing.

, You, by a strange coincidence.

. Oh not possibly!

—And it was you, incidentally, who
ght me how to drink moderately.

. No mean feat, I'm sure.

(*With a gesture.*) Well, physician—
M *raises his glass again, still smiling.*)

. Similia similibus curantur. Trans-
d, the hair of the dog that—

Y. Go get ready, will you, Joe? (*JOE*
es at TOM *a moment, then mounts the*
s and goes out.)

. —So solemn—all so solemn. (*He*
down his glass, unfinished.) I'm sorry
don't like my friends.

Y. Your—?

. They are, however.—Did you read
magazine?

Y. Most of it.

. Couldn't finish it, eh?

Y. No. I didn't care for it.

. Why not?

Y. It seemed to me that one oh-so-
ht weekly was enough, without more
he same.

. —Not sufficiently solemn. I see.

Y. Not half!—And so *cheap,* Tom!
how can you? (*A moment. Then:*)

. You can't please everybody.

Y. Never mind. It doesn't matter.
M *drops his cynical tone and speaks*
uinely:)

. Doesn't it, Daisy?

Y. Tom, ever since I got home I've
rd from all sides how you've changed.
me here to find out if it was true, and
o why.

. Well, is it?

DAISY. Tom—

TOM. And if so why? Why?

DAISY. (*A sudden cry.*) Oh, Tom—I pity
you with all my heart! (*He is at her side
in an instant, her wrists in his hands.*)

TOM. Pity me! What are you talking
about?

DAISY. I came to find out. I've found out.
Now I'm going. (*She calls.*) Joe!

TOM. Found out what? Pity me why?
(DAISY *looks down at her wrists.*)

DAISY. Would you mind? (*He releases her.
A moment. They gaze at each other. Her
eyes soften.*) —And love you, Tom—love
you with all my heart, as well. Remember
that.

TOM. (*Brokenly.*) Daisy, I— (*He recovers
himself, and with the recovery the cynical
smile returns. He advances, one hand out,
his voice coaxing.*) Give us a kiss, Daisy.
(*She takes a step back from him, in horror.
Her call is almost a scream:*)

DAISY. Joe! Are you ready? (JOE'S *voice
is heard from the stairs.*)

JOE. Coming! (JOE *comes down the stairs
with the bags.* CECELIA *comes in from the
living-room.*)

CECELIA. Did someone call? (*She sees the
bags.*) Why, what's all this?

DAISY. I'm sorry, but we've got to leave.

CECELIA. But what's happened?

DAISY. I suddenly remembered something.
Please don't bother—

CECELIA. But I never heard of such a—

DAISY. I'm terribly sorry, but it can't be
helped.

CECELIA. But can't you at least wait until
after luncheon?

DAISY. I'm afraid not. (*She turns to* JOE.)

JOE. (*To* CECELIA.) Good-bye. Thanks
very much.

CECELIA. Good-bye. I must say it all seems
very strange. (*Then to* DAISY.) —And when
we've so loved having you.

DAISY. You were kind to ask us.

CECELIA. Well, if you insist, I suppose there's no help for it. Good-bye. Do come again when you can really stay.—Your coat's here, isn't it? (*She goes out into the hall.*)

JOE. Give me a ring sometime, Tom.

TOM. Right. (JOE *looks at* DAISY. *She nods her head in the direction of the door. He goes out.*)

DAISY. Good-bye, Tom.

TOM. —Once I wouldn't say it, would I?

DAISY. Once you wouldn't—

TOM. Well, good-bye.

DAISY. —This time you do.—

TOM. Good-bye. (*She gestures helples[s] turns and goes out. For a moment h[e] alone. A door is heard to close, then* CEC[E] *re-enters.*)

CECELIA. Honestly! If that wasn't rudest thing! (*He is silent.*) —I presu[me] you agree, don't you?

TOM. I don't know what it was. (*He st[ares] in front of him, unseeing. She looks at [him] intently for a moment. Then:*)

CECELIA. Well—if we're going to Grace'[s]

TOM. I'll get my hat. (*He moves tow[ard] the hall. She follows.*)

CURTAIN.

SCENE II

At TOM COLLIER's. *Ten o'clock the same night.*
The dining-room is dimly lighted from the hall and living-room. There is a small fire burning in the fire place. Leaves have been removed from the table, which is now at its smallest. Two chairs are at the table, the others against the wall.

REGAN *comes in from the hall with an armful of wood, some of which he places upon the fire, making it burn brighter. This done, he lights a small candle-lamp upon the table. Two places have been set and a light supper prepared: a platter of cold meat, a bowl of salad, sandwiches, fruit. There is a champagne glass at each place. A moment, then* CECELIA *calls from upstairs:*

CECELIA. Regan?

REGAN. —Right here, Ma'am.

CECELIA. I thought I heard a car.

REGAN. Yes, Madam.

CECELIA. Is Mr. Collier's supper ready?

REGAN. Yes, Madam. (*He lights a small lamp on the serving-table, pokes the fire again, and goes out into the hall. A moment, then* CECELIA *comes down the stairs, in another charming negligee, this time more severe in cut and somber in color. She examines the table, rearranges a few things*

and puts out the lamp upon the serv[ing] table. Now the room is lit only by [the] candle-lamp and the fire upon the hea[rth]. A door closes in the hall. She turns tow[ard] it, calling:)

CECELIA. Tom? (TOM *comes in.*)

TOM. Hello. (*He looks at the tab[le.]* What's all this?

CECELIA. I thought you might be hung[ry,] I know what you think of Williams[on] food. (*He looks at the fire, then arou[nd] him, curiously.*) What's the matter?

TOM. —Lighted this way, it reminds [me] of some place.

CECELIA. Where?

TOM. I don't know. (*His voice is stra[nge,] as if speaking from a distance.*)

CECELIA. Do eat something, dear. (*A[s] he looks about him, puzzled.*)

TOM. —I came back the long way, [by] the Pound Ridge road, through Mi[ddle] Patent.

CECELIA. What made you do that, Sill[y?]

TOM. I don't know, I wanted to d[rive.] (*Now it is her he looks at curiously.*)

CECELIA. Tom—what *is* the matter? [He] shakes his head, as if to shake somet[hing] out of it, and laughs shortly.*)

. Sorry!

ELIA. (*Anxiously.*) Everything went right, didn't it?

. Oh yes, perfectly. (*A moment. n:*) In fact, it's settled.

ELIA. Not already!

. Yes. They've signed. All I have to s to dig up a notary in the Village and e my name under theirs.

ELIA. Oh, Tom!

. Are you pleased?

ELIA. Aren't you?

. I think something's happened to my ous system. I feel awfully light.

ELIA. You're famished. Come and sit n and eat— (*She draws him to the e. He seats himself there, and for a nent drops his head in his hands.*) nd tired, too, poor darling.

. No—just light. So awfully light.— nking too much. (*She puts meat and d upon a plate and sets it before him.*)

ELIA. Here.

. C—

ELIA. Yes, dear?

. I think it's time we had a child or , C. (*A moment. Then:*)

ELIA. We'll talk about that.

. Yes. We must. (*Another moment.*) he trees along the road stood out like— rubs his eyes and looks up again.*) ke whatever it is trees stand out like.

ELIA. You've been going much too l, you know.

. It's good for me. I'm having visions. ain he looks around him.*) —What *is* reminds me of? (*She seats herself near at the table.*)

ELIA. —Nothing. You're just tired and gry.

. Please let me have my visions. GAN *comes in with a pint of cham- ne.*) Good evening, Mr. Regan.

REGAN. Good evening, Sir.

TOM. —Those buttons on your coat—you know, they're terribly bright.

REGAN. I'll try to bring 'em down.

TOM. Do. It's essential.—Champagne, is it?

CECELIA. I thought you might feel like celebrating.

TOM. Well—

CECELIA. A little wine won't hurt you, Tom.

TOM. (*To himself.*) —The little more, and how much it is— (*Rousing himself.*) —Fill them, Mr. Regan. (REGAN *looks at him oddly, then fills the glasses.* TOM *raises his and squints at it.*) —Infinite riches, in a little room. (CECELIA *laughs.*)

CECELIA. You've got the quotes badly.

TOM. Little lamb, who made thee?—Regan —dost thou know who made thee? (*He holds out the glass to him.*) —And a little more, old son. (REGAN *refills the glass and goes out.* TOM *watches him, curiously.*) The discreet withdrawal—I've seen that before, too. (*Looks around him again, then cries, suddenly:*) I know! The Florentine! —A private room at the Florentine.

CECELIA. What's that?

TOM. A kind of a hotel. Flora Conover's place.

CECELIA. It sounds wicked.

TOM. It used to be the best twenty-guinea house in London.

CECELIA. Twenty-guinea? What are you talking about?

TOM. In advance, at that. (CECELIA *glances at him.*)

CECELIA. Rather expensive, wasn't it?

TOM. But one went to Flora's to celebrate. —And the food was good, the waiter discreet, the wines excellent, the lady most artful.

CECELIA. Tom! How revolting—

TOM. But we must send the boys back happy, you know.

CECELIA. I don't care to hear about it, thank you.

TOM. Very well, my dear. (*A moment. He stares at his glass. Then:*)

CECELIA. Weren't they difficult at all, Tom?

TOM. Who? Williamson's?—Easy.

CECELIA. And you actually got your own terms?

TOM. Except for their right to pass on my selections.

CECELIA. That's probably just a form.

TOM. Probably.

CECELIA. They want to feel they have *some* say.

TOM. That's all.—C, What have you done to your hair?

CECELIA. Why, nothing, why?

TOM. It looks lighter.

CECELIA. It isn't. (*He gazes at it for a moment longer, then eats a little, disinterestedly.*)

TOM. I quashed the announcement they'd prepared for the papers.

CECELIA. Why? What was it?

TOM. "Williamson, Warren and Company have absorbed The Bantam Press, formerly owned by—"

CECELIA. "Absorbed"!

TOM. Yes. Like a sponge. I quashed it. For "absorbed" read "bought a controlling interest in."

CECELIA. Well—that's more like it.

TOM. —Poor little Bantam.—For "Bantam" read small little, plucked little capon.

CECELIA. Oh, don't Tom! You know it's a good thing for you—it's a grand thing for you.

TOM. —Increased scope.

CECELIA. Of course.

TOM. —Perfect distribution facilities.

CECELIA. But aren't they?

TOM. Williamson, Warren Books Gir the Globe. Hear the eagle scream.—P₁ little Bantam—peep, peep—

CECELIA. —And I thought you'd be bes yourself for joy. (*He gazes at her. She* ₁

TOM. C, your eyes are so bright. (*S laughs shortly.*)

CECELIA. Eat, you. You're seeing thin (*He looks at his plate.*)

TOM. C—

CECELIA. Yes, dear?

TOM. —Little love is no love.

CECELIA. —Meaning what, precisely?

TOM. It wasn't necessary to lock your d₁ against me last night. (*A moment. The₁*)

CECELIA. But I didn't.—I mean—₁ against—

TOM. Then why?

CECELIA. I'm—it's just that sometimes I afraid, alone at night. (*He is watchi₁ her.*)

TOM. I don't believe you. (*She laug nervously.*)

CECELIA. Well, really!

TOM. I don't believe you, C. (*She ave her head.*) —Only I'd like you to know t₁ that isn't necessary, ever.

CECELIA. Very well. (*Suddenly he reac₁ for her hand and takes it.*)

TOM. Why was it? Tell me instantly w it was.

CECELIA. Is that an order?

TOM. Tell me. (*She tries to meet his ga₁ but cannot.*)

CECELIA. (*With difficulty.*) You mear why I—why I didn't want you near me

TOM. Yes.

CECELIA. —And you don't know—

TOM. No.

CECELIA. Well, if you don't, you ought

ɪ. Tell me, I say.

ELIA. You'd been so—consistently dis-
eeable, that's all.

ɪ. About what? — Wanting Regan
k?

ELIA. No.

ɪ. What, then?

ELIA. Your father, chiefly. (*She rises
goes to the serving-table.*) He tele-
ned this afternoon. (*A moment.*) He
ted to know if you'd got the birthday-
ck. (*Another moment.*) I told him that
had, and had tried to call him. (*He
is away.*) Well, I had to say something!
*e reseats herself at the table with a
e for herself.*)

ɪ. I don't know whether to send it
k, or just not to cash it. (*He finds a
ck among the letters in his pocket, and
s at it frowning.*)

ELIA. —Of course, you simply can't
w yourself to show any kind of gra-
sness toward him.

ɪ. No.

ELIA. —As a way of telling you how
sed with you he is, he sends you a
ll check,—and you have the extraordi-
y bad taste to— (*He holds the check
for her to see. Her eyes widen.*) What!
ood heavens—I don't believe it!

ɪ. There it is.

ELIA. But there isn't that much money
he world!

ɪ. In Father's world there is. He feels
can afford it, to get us to come and
with him.

ELIA. Of course, I don't understand
r attitude about that, either.

ɪ. Don't you, C?

ELIA. He knows how inconvenient it is
in winter,—and having that great,
e, lovely house in town, it's perfectly
et and natural of him to—to, well to
—

ɪ. Yes—you, to preside night after
ht at his deadly dinners, me to listen
eternally to his delphic advice on what to do and how to live—in short, to allow him to own us. Of course, he's willing to pay. He always is.

CECELIA. Oh, how ridiculous you are, really!—His whole life long he's tried to help you, to do things for you—

TOM. —In order to own me. I tell you I know him.

CECELIA. You're the only child he's got, and he's an old man and a very lonely man. I think it's horrible beyond belief, the way you treat him. How you can be so hard, I don't know.

TOM. Hard!—I'm not hard enough. All my life I've been trying to harden. I was born soft, that's the trouble with me.

CECELIA. You soft!

TOM. Yes. Born it.—And then brought up to refuse to face any truth that was an unpleasant truth, in myself or anyone else—always be the little gentleman, Tommy—charming and agreeable at all costs—give no pain, Tommy.

CECELIA. You seem to have outgrown it nicely.

TOM. Not yet, I haven't. No, not by a long shot. The inclination's still there, all right. Still going strong.

CECELIA. Don't be discouraged.

TOM. (*Wearily.*) All right, C.

CECELIA. —It's nothing but your old self-consciousness about money, again. It simply defeats me.—Honestly, has everyone who lives well sold his soul to the devil?

TOM. (*Rising.*) "Lives well"!—I'd give my eyes to live well. That's all I want for us. (*He goes to a chair at the window.*)

CECELIA. Oh—definitions again.—We being so weak, of course, that a little luxury would completely ruin us.

TOM. —Little—little—everything's so little. Add it up, though. (*His head sinks upon his breast.*) —Add it up.

CECELIA. To my way of thinking, if a person can't stand—

TOM. Let's drop it.

CECELIA. (*Coldly.*) Very well. We shall. (*He looks up again.*)

TOM. —Now you've gone from me again—

CECELIA. A lot you care.

TOM. Oh C—my lovely C— Where are you? What's become of you?

CECELIA. There's something you call your damned integrity— (TOM *rises from his chair.*)

TOM. (*Suddenly, sharply.*) That's the word! (CECELIA *rises also.*)

CECELIA. I see it's no use talking. (*A silence. He looks at her intently.*)

TOM. —This is what you call "being disagreeable."

CECELIA. Yes. Very. (*He returns to her.*)

TOM. —But how to be otherwise, when—

CECELIA. (*In a burst.*) Possibly by being the fine, kind, generous man you ought to be!

TOM. To Father?

CECELIA. You might begin there.

TOM. —Accept the check with thanks— and go to live with him—

CECELIA. It's only for a few months—and I think to refuse his present would be extremely bad manners—just about in a class with those of your little lady of easy virtue, this morning. If— (*She sees she has gone too far.*) I'm sorry to have said that about her. I didn't mean—

TOM. Never mind. (*A long moment. Then:*) —Suppose I should do as you say about Father—

CECELIA. Oh, Tom—do be the darling I know you are!

TOM. Would you like me better?

CECELIA. Much.

TOM. How much?

CECELIA. Oh—very much. (*He leans forward, watching her, hardly believing it possible.*)

TOM. No locked doors, anymore?

CECELIA. (*Lowly.*) Not one—ever—

TOM. That sounds—most inviting. (smiles.)

CECELIA. Does it? (*Again he seats h self at the table.*)

TOM. —And suddenly I'm beginning see with an awful clearness— (*He sto*

CECELIA. (*Smiling.*) What? How stu you've been?—And what I am to you?

TOM. (*After a moment.*) Yes.

CECELIA. —And so you *are* going to nice again?

TOM. You'll see. (*Again* CECELIA's smi

CECELIA. —But how am I to be sure?

TOM. You've told me ways to convi you.

CECELIA. I do so hate us not to ag Tom.

TOM. I know. (*She brings her chair cl and sits at his side.*)

CECELIA. I want so to feel—I don't kn —together again, as we used to be. (O more, TOM *looks incredulously around h at the room. Then:*)

TOM. You're very pretty, you know—

CECELIA. Why, thank you, Sir.

TOM. —Very exciting, too. (*His man has changed. From now on, he is no lor the husband sitting before the fire with wife, but a host at supper with a pr girl, whom later he will know better.*)

CECELIA. I don't know whether it's or the wine speaking.

TOM. —Me.

CECELIA. Shall we have a little more?

TOM. Why not? (*She presses the butt*

CECELIA. It's a party, then.

TOM. It's a party.

CECELIA. Sometimes you're so thrilli Tom.

TOM. You think? (*A moment. Then:*

ELIA. Put your arms around me,
n-- (*He inclines toward her, does not
ch her, but looks full into her eyes,
ching for something he still cannot be-
e he will find.*)

ᴛ. Are they around?

ELIA. (*In a breath.*) Oh—yes—yes—
ɢᴀɴ *comes in.*)

ᴛ. Another small bottle. (ʀᴇɢᴀɴ *goes
, ᴄᴇᴄᴇʟɪᴀ laughs a little throaty, excited
ʒh.*)

ELIA. We shouldn't. You know we
uldn't.

ᴛ. But we seem to be—

ELIA. I feel—all at once I feel terribly
ghty, somehow—

ᴛ. I suppose you're the prettiest girl
ever seen—

ELIA. (*Archly.*) So nice of you to think
Sir.

ᴛ. —So very attractive—

ELIA. I like to be attractive.

ᴛ. So very seductive—

ELIA. There, there! That's enough! (*He
found it. Coldly he salutes it:*)

ᴛ. You're a strange woman. Your lips
p honeycomb, your mouth is smoother
ı oil.

ELIA. Now what are you quoting?
ɢᴀɴ *comes in with the wine.*)

ᴛ. —Give the lady some, waiter. (ʀᴇɢᴀɴ
ᴄᴇᴄᴇʟɪᴀ's *glass, then* ᴛᴏᴍ's *without a
d.*) You can leave the bottle. (ʀᴇɢᴀɴ
ᴇs it upon the table, near him.*) —And
 will be all. (ʀᴇɢᴀɴ *bows and goes out.
ELIA raises her glass and smiles invit-
ly. He raises his, murmuring:*) —To the
asant ways of life. (*She drinks. He does
)*)

ELIA. —Such pleasant ways. (*She
ᴇs at her glass.*)

ᴛ. Is it good?

ELIA. So good.—I'm feeling it a little.

ᴛ. That's what it's for, eh?

CECELIA. It must be.

TOM. "Champagne, the friend of lovers"—
(*Her face inclines to him, then she averts
her head.*)

CECELIA. (*Softly.*) No—not yet—

TOM. Artful child.

CECELIA. You think?

TOM. —Lovely, alluring thing—

CECELIA. I like you too, now.

TOM. Pleasant here, isn't it?

CECELIA. So pleasant. (*She refills her glass
and finds that his is still full.*) —But you
aren't taking any—

TOM. It makes me see almost too clearly.

CECELIA. Take a little more, and everything will get so—lovely and vague and—
the way I feel now.

TOM. —A good feeling, is it?

CECELIA. (*A whisper.*) Delicious— (*She
gropes for his hand, holds it against her
breast.*) Oh—Tom— (*He looks at her. She
smiles again.*) —One last toast? (*He draws
her to her feet, glass in hand.*) But to what
—what to?

TOM. You name it. (*A moment. Then:*)

CECELIA. To love— (*She comes against
him, steadies her glass in both hands against
his breast, bends her head and takes it. He
raises his glass, holds it for a moment near
his lips, then sets it down, untouched, upon
the table. She replaces hers beside it, and
murmurs:*) And darling—

TOM. Yes?

CECELIA. You—you *are* going to be an
angel about—about things, aren't you?

TOM. You'll see.

CECELIA. Oh, I knew you would!—I'm so
happy— (*She smiles, moves slowly toward
the stairs, and mounts them, opening the
door at the top. There she turns and whispers.*) Don't be long— (*And goes out.
ᴛᴏᴍ's eyes following her. Then he turns
and stares down at the table. Finally his
hand finds the bell and presses it. A moment then ʀᴇɢᴀɴ enters, in a business suit.*)

TOM. See here, Red, I—

REGAN. (*Sharply.*) Never mind! (TOM *looks up.* REGAN *gestures.*) All I mean is— well, I'm out for good, this time.

TOM. Why?

REGAN. I just don't like it here, that's all.

TOM. When do you want to go?

REGAN. As soon as I can.

TOM. To-night, then.

REGAN. That's all right with me. I'm packed.

TOM. Look in and say good-bye as you're leaving.

REGAN. I'm leaving now.

TOM. Look in, anyhow. (REGAN *turns to go.*) —Have you got a fountain-pen? (REGAN *finds a pen and gives it to him.*) —Don't let me forget to return it. (REGAN *goes out. Slowly, methodically,* TOM *opens the pen, shakes it, spreads the check upon the table and writes upon its back. Then, as carefully, he replaces the top of the pen, picks up the check and waves it back and forth, to dry it.* REGAN *re-enters with a traveling-bag.* TOM *returns the pen to him.*) —Here you are. Thanks.

REGAN. Well—good-bye—

TOM. Get into the car.

REGAN. I can walk to the train all ri

TOM. Bring my coat and hat, will y (REGAN *does not stir.*) —Will you bring coat and hat, please? (REGAN *puts d his bag and goes into the hall for th* TOM *folds the check carefully, goes to fire place and places it upon the ma piece, one corner under a vase.* REGAN enters with his overcoat and hat. TOM on the hat. REGAN *holds the coat for* TOM *gets into it. He takes a cigarette f the pocket and puts it in his mouth.*)

REGAN. What's the idea?

TOM. —Light, please— (REGAN *hold match for him.* TOM *pulls on his glov* Now, then—

REGAN. I can walk, I tell you.

TOM. Not at all. We'll drive in.

REGAN. *We will*—?

TOM. (*Very gently.*) I'm going back my wife, Red.

REGAN. To your—? (*Puzzled,* REGAN l toward the lighted doorway at the to the stairs.)

TOM. —To my wife, I said. (REGAN p up his bag, and goes out, into the TOM *looks once around him, draws a breath of smoke, exhales it slowly, turns and follows him.*)

CURTAIN.

Boy Meets Girl

BY BELLA AND SAMUEL SPEWACK

To
JO DAVIDSON
WHOSE HOSPITALITY AND
ENCOURAGEMENT DELAYED THE COMPLETION OF
THIS PLAY THREE MONTHS

BOY MEETS GIRL was produced by George Abbott at the Cort Theatre,
ew York City, Wednesday evening, November 27, 1935. The production was
rected by Mr. Abbott; the settings designed by Arne Lundborg.

THE CAST

)BERT LAW ......Allyn Joslyn		SUSIE ....Joyce Arling
RRY TOMS ......Charles McClelland		A NURSE ....Helen Gardner
CARLYLE BENSON Jerome Cowan		DOCTOR ....Perry Ivins
)SETTI ....Everett H. Sloane		CHAUFFEUR ....Edison Rice
R. FRIDAY (C.F.)...Royal Beal		YOUNG MAN ....Philip Faversham
GGY ....Peggy Hart		STUDIO OFFICER ...George W. Smith
ISS CREWS ....Lea Penman		CUTTER ....Robert Foulk
)DNEY BEVAN .....James MacColl		ANOTHER NURSE ...Marjorie Lytell
REEN ....Garson Kanin		MAJOR THOMPSON ..John Clarke
ADE ....Maurice Sommers		

SCENES

ACT ONE
Mr. Friday's Office, the Royal Studios in Hollywood.

ACT TWO
Scene   I. A Neighborhood Theatre. Seven months later.
Scene   II. Mr. Friday's Office.
Scene III. The same. Several hours later.

ACT THREE
Scene   I. A hospital corridor. Three weeks later.
Scene   II. In your home.
Scene III. Mr. Friday's office.

COPYRIGHT, 1936, BY BELLA AND SAMUEL SPEWACK

BOY MEETS GIRL

ACT ONE

The room we see is one of a suite of three, comprising the sanctum of MR. C. ELIOT
FRIDAY, *a supervisor, sometimes called a producer, who is engaged in manufacturing
motion pictures in Hollywood, California.*

*In its present state the room is a happy combination of the Regency and Russell Wright
periods—given over to pale green, mauve and canary yellow, with Rodier-cloth-covered
easy chairs and couch. A magnificent, be-French-phoned desk is at one end of the room.
On it rests the inner-office dictograph, over which in the course of the play we hear the
voice of the great B.K., chief executive of the studio. Beside it, appropriately, stands an
amiable photograph of Mrs. C. Eliot Friday, a cultured if fatuous lady; a copy of "Swann's
Way" (leaves uncut), a bronze nude astride an ash tray, a bottle of Pyramidon and a copy
of "Variety." In the trash basket is a copy of "Hollywood Reporter." (It was very unkind
to* MR. FRIDAY.) *On the wall back of the desk are bookshelves with pots of hanging ivy
on the top shelf, the rest given over, curiously enough, to books—and occasional bric-a-brac.
There are a few end tables with ash trays and boxes of cigarettes, for it is the unwritten law
in Hollywood that supervisors must provide cigarettes for writers during conferences and
other times of stress. The two windows, although of the old-fashioned, non-casement kind,
are framed by tasteful, expensive drapes and are partially concealed by half-drawn Venetian
blinds. (A supervisor would lose caste without Venetian blinds.) The door left leads
an anteroom where sits* MISS CREWS, *secretary to* MR. FRIDAY. *The door at right rear leads
to a smaller office where* MR. FRIDAY *sometimes thinks in solitude. This room contains
MR. FRIDAY's Commencement Day photograph (Harvard '19), snapshots of B.K.'s wedding, at which* MR. FRIDAY *served as an usher, and a huge picture of Pola Negri inscribed
"Sincerely yours." There are other photographs with more florid inscriptions upon faces
once famous and since vanished in film dust. The room is also memorable for the fact
that* MR. FRIDAY—*a bit of a diplomat in his way—sometimes keeps earnest writers here
while he submits their scripts to other writers in his inner office. At times as many as
fifteen bright minds are thus let loose upon a C. Elliot Friday production, with sometimes
startling results.*

*All this, however, is very much by the by. It is really more important to note that
through those Venetian blinds you can feel the sweet sterility of the desert that is so essentially Southern California. The sun is bright, of course, and it pours endlessly through
the windows. The time is two o'clock, and the boys have been at it since noon.*

One of the boys is BENSON—J. CARLYLE BENSON, *whom we discover prone on a couch.
He is in his thirties and in his flannels. Years ago, as he will tell you, he worked as a scene
painter and a property boy. He became a writer because he learned how bricks were made
and laid. He knows every cliché, every formula, and in his heart of hearts he really believes
the fairy tale is a credo of life. And he's a damned nice guy; handicapped somewhat by
the fact that he married a beautiful but extravagant young woman who obviously doesn't
love him. They live in a gorgeous home, have four dogs, two cars and, as* MR. FRIDAY
would put it, "a menage."

The other member of the writing team is ROBERT LAW *whom you will find listed in
O'Brien's "Best Short Stories" of five years ago. He came to Hollywood to make a little
money and run right back to Vermont where he could really write. He is rather handsome,
a little round-shouldered; smokes incessantly. He's a damned nice guy, too.*

There is a deep and abiding affection between the two men, even though LAW's *nostalgia
for realism and sincerity and substance finds no echoing response in* MR. BENSON. *They have
one great thing in common—their mutual love of a great gag, a practical joke to enliven
the monotony of the writing factory.*

*For we are dealing here with a factory that manufactures entertainment in approved
sizes; that puts the seven arts right on the belt. And it is this very quality that makes* MR.
FRIDAY's *office as fascinating as a power house and a good deal more entertaining.*

The other inmates of the room are LARRY TOMS—*you know* LARRY TOMS—*a Western
star, and one* ROSETTI, *an agent. It is* MR. ROSETTI's *business to see to it that* MR. TOMS

ofitably employed, for MR. ROSETTI *collects ten per cent of* MR. TOM's *weekly salary which, [de]spite the star's fading popularity, is still a respectable sum.* MR. TOMS *is handsome, of [co]urse. He is also parsimonious. He leads a completely righteous life, and if you don't like [hi]m it isn't our fault; in all respects he is an extremely admirable character.*
As the curtain goes up we see that LAW *is on his feet and obviously he has been telling [a] story to* MR. TOMS—*a story that* MR. TOMS *is expected to re-enact before the camera.*

LAW. And this bozo comes up to you and [yo]u look him straight in the eye and you say, "[W]hy, damn your soul, I loved her before [yo]u ever married her." And then in walks [th]e bitch, and she cries, "Larry, I heard [ev]erything you said." And you just look at [he]r, and there's a long pause—a *long* pause. [An]d then finally you say, "Did you?" That's [it]. Just a plain, quiet, simple "Did you?" [Bo]y, what a moment! (*He lies down on the [co]uch beside* BENSON.)

LARRY. But what's the story about?

BENSON (*rolling over*). Love!

LAW (*singing*). "Love is the sweetest [thi]ng—"

LARRY. Now, come on, boys—get off the [co]uch. This ain't fair. I got a lot at stake [in] this picture. It's the last one in my con-[tra]ct. If I get a poor story I'm out in the [col]d.

LAW. Shivering with a million dollar annuity.

ROSETTI. Now, gentlemen, don't let's get per-[son]al.

LARRY (*rises and crosses to couch*). When [the]y told me I was getting the star team [of] writers on the lot, I was all for it. But [yo]u've done nothing but clown around, and [the] shooting date's only two weeks off. I've [got] to play this picture.

LAW. Why?

LARRY (*swallowing*). Tell me the story in a [few] simple words.

LAW. Mr. Benson, what's our story?

BENSON. How the hell do I know?

LAW (*sits up*). Didn't you listen?

BENSON. No. We ought to have a stenogra-[ph]er.

LAW. But they won't wear tights. And I can't dictate to a stenographer who won't wear tights.

LARRY. Now listen, boys—

LAW. Don't speak to me. You don't like our story.

LARRY. I didn't say I didn't like it. I couldn't follow it. (*He slumps in disgust.*)

BENSON (*indignantly*). You couldn't follow it? Listen, I've been writing stories for eleven years. Boy meets girl. Boy loses girl. Boy gets girl.

LAW. Or—girl meets boy. Girl loses boy. Girl gets boy. Love will find a way. Love never loses. Put your money on love. You can't lose. (*Rises and saunters to window.*) I'm getting hungry.

BENSON. It's a sorry state of affairs when an actor insists on following a story. Do you think this is a golf tournament?

ROSETTI (*earnestly*). If I may make a point, I don't think you're showing the proper respect to one of the biggest stars in this studio. A man who's not only captivated millions of people but is going to captivate millions more—

BENSON (*wearily*). With his little lasso—

LARRY. Just because I don't get Gable's fan mail don't mean I ain't got his following. A lot of those that want to write me ain't never learned how.

LAW. Benson, injustice has been done. We've been lacking in respect for the idol of illiteracy.

BENSON. Do we apologize?

LAW. No!

ROSETTI. Well, let me tell you something. Before I became an agent I taught diction for years, and Larry Toms is potentially the greatest actor I've ever met. And I can prove it with X-rays. I was just taking them up to show B.K. He's got the Barrymore larynx. I'll put his larynx against John Barrymore's and I defy you to tell me which is which. (*Takes X-rays from brief-case. Gives one to* BENSON, *one to* LAW.)

LARRY. I couldn't tell it myself and it's my own larynx.

BENSON (*drawling*). Say—are you sure this is his *larynx?*

ROSETTI (*the diplomat; retrieving X-rays*). Gentlemen, I wouldn't be surprised with the proper training if Larry couldn't sing. That opens up the whole field of musicals. (*Puts brief-case on chair.*)

BENSON (*to* LAW). What are we waiting for?

LAW. Lunch.

LARRY (*angrily rising*). I'm getting fed up with this. I got writers who are just plain crazy—a producer who can't concentrate— and ain't even here—and—(*Throws hat on floor and starts for* BENSON *and* LAW. LAW *moves to back of couch and* BENSON *goes up to door.*)

ROSETTI (*crossing down on* LARRY'S *left*). Now . . . now . . . Larry . . . don't lose your temper.

LARRY (*righteously*). The idea of writers getting fifteen hundred a week for acting like hoodlums.

LAW. I agree with you.

LARRY. Huh?

LAW. We're not writers. We're hacks. If we weren't would I be sitting here listening to your inarticulate grunts?

LARRY. Huh?

LAW. That's exactly what I mean. For two cents, Benson, I'd take the next train back to Vermont.

LARRY. That's all right with me.

BENSON. Will you forget Vermont?

LAW. At least I wouldn't have to sit around with *that* in Vermont. I'd write—really write. My God, I wrote once. I wrote a book.

A darn good book. I was a promising youn[g] novelist. O'Brien reprinted three of my sto[r]ies. 1928-1929-1930. And in 1935 I'm writin[g] dialogue for a horse!

LARRY (*enraged*). Now, listen—

ROSETTI (*pleading*). Larry—Larry, take [a] deep breath. The boys mean no harm. . . [.] Exhale!

LAW (*sniffing*). I smell carbon monoxide.

LARRY. One more crack, that's all—just o[ne] more crack! (*Phone rings.*)

ROSETTI (*at phone*). Hello . . . oh, yes . [. .] just a minute. For you, Benson.

BENSON (*taking up phone*). Yes, speakin[g.] Who? Of course, Mrs. Benson's check [is] good! How much is it for? Thirty-five hu[n]dred? Oh! I hope it was real ermine. . . [.] Certainly it's all right. You put the che[ck] through tomorrow. (*Hangs up; dia[ls] phone.*)

ROSETTI (*with a feline purr*). Ermine is [a] nice fur. (MISS CREWS *enters regally; pu[ts] letters on desk.*)

LARRY (*grumbling*). Miss Crews, wha[t's] keeping C.F.?

MISS CREWS. He's still up with B.K. (*S[he] exits regally.*)

BENSON (*into phone*). Jim? Benson. Liste[n,] sell three of my Municipal Fives this afte[r]noon, will you? And put it in my joi[nt] account in the Security. I've got a check [to] meet. Never mind about that. I'll talk [to] her. Right. (*Hangs up.*)

LAW. Pearl is certainly spreading prosperit[y.]

BENSON. What the hell? She's only a ki[d.] She's having a good time. What's mon[ey] for? (C.F. *enters.* C.F. *is, of course,* C. ELLI[S] FRIDAY.)

C.F. (*briskly*). Good morning.

ROSETTI (*rises*). Good morning, C.F.

LARRY (*rises and sits*). Hello, C.F. (BENS[ON] lies on sofa. LAW *rises and salaams Hin[du] fashion, as popularized by Mr. De Mille.*)

C.F. Boys, no antics, please. We've go[t a] heavy day ahead of us. (*Sits at desk; pic[ks] p phone. Into phone*) I don't won't to be isturbed by anybody—understand? And rder some lunch. A plate of raw carrots, nd a bottle of certified, raw milk. See that 's raw. Bring enough for everybody. *About to hang up.*)

AW (*rises*). Just a moment. (*Takes phone.*) Ir. Benson and Mr. Law want two cups f chicken broth—some ham hocks—cab- age—lemon meringue pie—and some bi- arbonate of soda. (*Hangs up; returns to* ouch.)

F. You're slaughtering yourselves, boys. ou won't be able to think with that poison n your stomachs, and we've got to think. ve just seen the front office. Boys, we're acing a crisis.

OSETTI (*eagerly*). Any truth in the report, .F., that Gaumont British wants to buy he studio?

F. You know as much about it as I do, osetti.

AW. Why sell? I thought we were sitting retty. We're in receivership.

OSETTI. Well, I'm going up to see B.K. hope you boys get a good story for Larry.

F. (*ignoring him;* C.F. *can ignore beauti- lly*). As a matter of fact, you may as well now it. There may be a reorganization.

ENSON. Again?

F. And you know my position. I'm the nly college-bred man in the studio. They sent me.

AW. The big snobs.

F. Just because I've always tried to do omething fine, something dignified, some- ing worth while, I'm being hammered on l sides. Boys, if my next picture fails, I'm ut. And you're out, Larry. And it won't o you boys any good either. Of course you n always write plays.

AW. I don't see why not. We never wrote y.

F. I have an idea for a play I want to dis- ss with you some time. You'll be wild out it. Just one set, too—simple to produce, d practically anybody can play it. Katha- ne Cornell would be marvelous for the rl. She dies in the first act.

LARRY. Listen here, C.F., I ain't in the thea- tre. What about my picture?

C.F. Boys, we need a big picture. Not just a good story. I want to do something fine— with sweep, with scope—stark, honest, grip- ping, adult, but with plenty of laughs and a little hokum.

LARRY (*bitterly*). And no "Did you?" scenes.

C.F. Something we'll be proud of. Not just another picture, but the picture of the year. A sort of Bengal Lancer, but as Kipling would have done it. Maybe we could wire Kipling and get him to write a few scenes. It would be darned good publicity. (PEGGY *enters;* PEGGY *is the manicurist on the lot.*) Oh, come in . . . come in, Peggy. (PEGGY *puts tray of manicurist's paraphernalia on desk; moves small chair at* C.F.'s *side; takes bowl and exits for water.*)

BENSON (*in astonishment*). He doesn't think we're as good as Kipling.

C.F. (*quickly*). Mind you, not that I think Kipling is a great writer. A story-teller, yes. But greatness? Give me Proust any time. Now, boys, how about a story?

LAW. Nestling on your desk for two weeks there's a script we wrote for Larry Toms.

BENSON. A beautiful script. That one with my fingerprints on the cover.

C.F. (*picking up script, holding it in his hands as if weighing it*). This? This won't do.

LAW. That's where you're wrong. I had it weighed at the A. & P. and the manager went wild over it. (C.F. *puts script on top of dictograph.* MISS CREWS *enters.*)

MISS CREWS. Excuse me, Mr. Friday, but Casting wants to know how many midgets you'll need.

C.F. (*irritably*). Midgets? I don't need any midgets.

MISS CREWS. Casting says you ordered midg- ets and they've got them.

C.F. They're crazy. I'm not doing a horror story. (*Phone rings; at phone.*) Hello. . . . It's for you, Benson.

BENSON. For me?

C.F. I think it's Mrs. Benson. Listen, Miss Crews, we're in conference. Please don't disturb us again.

MISS CREWS. Yes, Mr. Friday. (*She exits.*)

BENSON (*into telephone*). Oh, hello, darling. . . . Yes, I know you've been shopping. . . . Why don't you try Woolworth's? . . . No, I'm not mad. . . . Oh, you're taking the dogs for a walk? That's good. . . . Oh, no, I can't take you to lunch. I'm in a story conference. . . . But look, darling, I'm in a story conference. . . . Hello . . . (*He mops his brow and tries to shake off his gloom.*)

C.F. How is Mrs. Benson?

BENSON. Swell.

C.F. I must get Mrs. Friday to invite her over to her French class. All the wives are taking it up very seriously. Gives them something to do, and as I said to Mrs. Friday: I'm a linguist—why shouldn't you be? That's the great thing in marriage—mutual interests. (BENSON *crosses to couch.*) Of course, Mrs. Benson isn't the studious type, is she? Beautiful girl, though. . . . Where were we? What was I saying?

BENSON (*crosses back to desk; sighs; indicates script*). You were saying that this is one of the greatest picture scripts ever written.

C.F. (*with a superior smile*). Now, just a minute—

LAW (*quickly*). And do you know why? Because it's the same story Larry Toms has been doing for years.

BENSON. We *know* it's good.

LAW. Griffith used it. Lubitsch used it. And Eisenstein's coming around to it.

BENSON. Boy meets girl. Boy loses girl. Boy gets girl.

LAW. The great American fairy tale. Sends the audience back to the relief rolls in a happy frame of mind.

BENSON. And why not?

LAW. The greatest escape formula ever worked out in the history of civilization. . . .

C.F. Of course, if you put it that way . . but, boys, it's hackneyed.

LAW. You mean classic.

C.F. (*triumphantly*). *Hamlet* is a classic—but it isn't hackneyed!

LAW. *Hamlet* isn't hackneyed? Why, I'd b ashamed to use that poison gag. He lifte that right out of the Italians. (PEGGY *enter and crosses to her chair and sits.*) Ask Pegg (PEGGY *puts the bowl now half-filled wit water down on the desk.*)

BENSON. Yes, let's ask Peggy . . . if she wan to see Larry Toms in a different story. She your audience.

PEGGY. Don't ask me anything, Mr. Benso I've got the damnedest toothache. (*S takes* C.F.'s *hand and looks up at him su denly.*) Relax! (*She begins filing.*)

BENSON (*wheedling*). But, Peggy, you go pictures, don't you?

PEGGY. No.

BENSON. But you've seen Larry's pictur and enjoyed them?

PEGGY. No.

BENSON. . . . As millions of others have .

LAW. Why, one man sent him a rope all t way from Manila—with instructions.

C.F. Boys. this isn't getting us anywhere.

BENSON (*assuming the manner of a distr attorney; barking at* PEGGY). Peggy, do y mean to sit there and tell me you have seen *one* Larry Toms picture?

PEGGY. I saw one.

BENSON. Ah!

PEGGY. *Night in Death Valley.*

BENSON. This isn't getting us anywhere, e How would you like to see *Night in Dea Valley* again—with a new title?

PEGGY. I wouldn't.

BENSON. That's all. Step down. (*Crosses couch; slaps* LAW *on shoulder.*) May I po out to this court that the body was fou only two feet away, in an open field, w every door and window shut? (*To* LA Your witness. (*He exits.*)

w (*rises*). I've got to see a man about a
oman. (*He exits. Our writers have van-
ed. They love to vanish from story con-
ences.*)

. (*rises*). Come back here! (*Picks up
one.*)

RRY. That's what I mean—clowning.

. (*at phone*). Miss Crews, leave word at
e gate Benson and Law are not to be al-
ved off the lot. They're to come right back
my office. (*Hangs up.*)

RRY. Why do you stand for it?

. Larry, those boys are crazy, but they've
t something.

RRY. They've been fired off every other lot.

. I'll fire them off this one, after they've
oduced a story. I've made up my mind to
at. Meanwhile, patience.

RRY. That's easy to say.

. You can't quibble with the artistic tem-
rament when it produces.

RRY (*grumbling*). They've been produc-
; nothing but trouble around here. (YOUNG
TOR *enters in the resplendent uniform of
 Coldstream Guards. His name is* RODNEY.
th *uniform and actor explain themselves
 the play proceeds.*)

SS CREWS. Right in here.

DNEY. How do you do.

. What do *you* want?

DNEY. Why, Wardrobe sent me. Do you
prove the uniform?

. Uniform for what?

DNEY. *Young England.*

. You see, Larry—three pictures in pro-
ction—all going on at the same time—I'm
nding on my head—and then they won-
· what's wrong with the industry. (*Rises;
·ks at* RODNEY.) Stand over there. (MISS
ws *exits.* C.F. *surveys the actor judicially.*)
an't say I like the hat. (*He is referring,
course, to the awe-inspiring busby.*)

DNEY (*mildly*). The hat is authentic, sir.

. I still don't like it. You can't photograph
(*Phone rings.*) Yes?—What midgets? I

didn't send out any call for midgets. Get
rid of them. (*Hangs up. He jiggles the
phone.*) Get me Wardrobe. (*Hubbub is
heard outside window.*) Who's making all
that noise? (PEGGY *goes to the window.*)
This is C.F.—I don't like the hat.—I don't
care if it's authentic or not— Who's making
all that noise?

PEGGY (*at window*). Midgets.

C.F. (*into phone*). Change the hat. . . . You
can't photograph it. . . . We want to see
faces, not hats. (*Hangs up. Stone crashes
through the window left.*) Good God!
Somebody's thrown a rock through my window. (*To* RODNEY.) Here, you—pull down
those blinds.

RODNEY (*always the little gentleman*). Yes,
sir.

C.F. (*in phone*). Get me Casting. . . . This
is C.F. . . . Somebody's thrown a rock
through my window. One of the midgets.
Of course they're indignant! Sour grapes!
I'm telling you to get rid of them. (*Hangs
up.*)

RODNEY. What shall I tell Wardrobe, sir?

C.F. Tell them I don't like the hat.

RODNEY (*smiles diffidently*). Well, it's very
peculiar that you should take umbrage at
the hat as it happens to be the only correct
item in the entire outfit.

C.F. What's that?

RODNEY. This coat doesn't hang properly—
these buttons are far too large. These shoulder straps are absurd, of course. And the
boots . . . if I may say so . . . are too
utterly fantastic. Any Guardsman would
swoon away at the sight of them.

C.F. So!

RODNEY. The hat, however, *is* authentic.

C.F. It is, eh? What's your salary?

RODNEY. As I understand it, I'm to receive
seven dollars a day Monday and Tuesday,
when I speak no lines, and fifteen dollars a
day Thursday, Friday and Saturday, when
I propose a toast.

C.F. And you're telling a fifty-thousand-dol-
lar-a-year man how to run his picture. Look

here—I spent two weeks in London, my man, at the Savoy, and I watched them change the Guards, personally.

RODNEY. At the Savoy?

C.F. Young man, we have a technical adviser on this picture. And it doesn't happen to be you.

RODNEY. Quite. He's a splendid fellow, but he's a third generation Canadian. He's never even been to London.

C.F. So you don't like the uniform and you don't like the technical expert. (*Smoothly*) What's your name?

RODNEY. Rodney Bevan. Of course, it's a sort of nom de plume, or nom de guerre—

C.F. Rodney Bevan. (*Picks up phone.*) Give me Casting. . . . This is C.F. . . . Extra here by the name of Rodney Bevan doesn't like his uniform. Fire him.

RODNEY (*aghast*). Fire? Have you given me the sack?

C.F. I've enough trouble without extras telling me how to make pictures. That's the trouble with this business. A man spends his life at it, and anybody can walk in and tell him how to run it.

RODNEY. But I merely suggested— (MISS CREWS *enters.*)

MISS CREWS. Mr. Green and Mr. Slade are outside, Mr. Friday. They want you to hear the song.

RODNEY. I've waited a long time for this opening—

C.F. Get out! (*To* MISS CREWS) I'm in no mood for *music.* (GREEN *and* SLADE *enter.*)

GREEN. We've got it, and you're going to listen. If you don't like it, Schulberg's nuts about it. (SLADE *crosses to piano and starts playing the song.*) We wrote it for *Young England,* but it's flexible— Flexible as hell. (MISS CREWS *exits.* RODNEY *turns forlornly and fades out through the door. What else can he do?*)

C.F. Boys, I'm in no mood for—

GREEN. It's a touching little thing, but, boy, what power! There's a "Pain in My Heart, and My Heart's on My Sleeve." Like the

title? (SLADE *is one of those who glues him self to a piano. He's all pasted together now and his fingers fly.* GREEN *sings with all th fervid sincerity of Georgie Jessel with cold.*)

You promised love undying,
And begged me to believe;
Then you left, and left me crying
With a pain in my heart, and my heart
    on my sleeve.

It isn't right to show it,
To flaunt the way I grieve;
But the world will quickly know it,
For the pain's in my heart and my heart
    on my sleeve.

I confess that I'm a mess—
The way I lived my life,
But what does it matter?
Yes, I guess that happiness
Is only for a wife;
Sorrow isn't served on a silver platter.

I really shouldn't blame you
Because you chose to leave;
But one thing forever will shame you—
It's the pain in my heart, and my heart
    on my sleeve.

(*During the song* MISS CREWS *enters wi glass of orange juice. She crosses arour desk, puts glass in front of* C.F., *gets bo from lower drawer.*)

C.F. (*as* GREEN *finishes song*). Miss Crew get hold of Benson and Law! (MISS CREW *exits.*)

LARRY (*as the din grows*). I've worked f Biograph. . . . I've worked for Monogra . . . I've worked for Columbia. . . . I' worked for Warners. . . . I've worked f Metro . . . but a screwier outfit I never d see! (BENSON *and* LAW *enter in costume beefeaters. They, too, wear busbies.*)

C.F. (*whose nails are being buffed*). Wh do you want? (*At the musicians.*) Qui (*At the busbies, for* C.F. *doesn't deign look at actors' faces.*) I told Wardrobe don't like the hats.

BENSON. He doesn't like the hats.

LAW. Call Jock Whitney. We want to in color.

C.F. (*exasperated*). For God's sake! This a fine time to be masquerading.

<table>
<tr><td>

ₛON (*leaping into character; picking up*
ₑ). Wait! What a pretty stone! I won-
where that came from.

(*in his own big scene*). I wonder.

ₛON (*transporting himself to the desert*).
ink we've found gold, partner.

(*grabbing for it*). Gold!

ₛON. Stand back—you desert rat!

. Gold—after all these years! I'm going
⌐ ... mad ... mad ...

Oh, stop it, boys.

ᵧ (*suddenly inspired. To* C.F.) I
ldn't be surprised if they threw that
ₑ rock through the window.

ON. What an innuendo!

You didn't do that, did you, boys? Smash
Vita-glass?

. To think—after all these years of loyal,
ſul service— Larry Toms, you ought
ₑ ashamed!

ON. The man with the poison-pen mind.
re going to tell Louella Parsons on you.

(*impatiently*). *Very* well ... *very* well.
But I still have my suspicions. (*Snaps.*)
⌐ what about our story?

ON. Right here. (*Indicating script on*
.)

(*takes a statuette from top of desk*).
Benson, for the most brilliant script
ₑ year, the Academy takes great pleasure
resenting to you this little gargoyle—

ON. Wrap it up, please. (LAW *drops it*
ARRY's *hat and stands back of couch.*
ic *plays.*)

ᵧ (*rising in a dither*). Now, listen—
crosses below desk, retrieves statue,
ₑs *it back on desk.*)

N (*to* SLADE *at piano*). What do you say
is, Otto, for the second chorus:
    Yes, I've been kissed,
    But like Oliver Twist,
    I'm still crying for more.
ſhout *waiting for an answer, to* C.F.)
⌐ did you like the song, C.F.?

Darn good. Can you play *Over the*
ₑs?

</td><td>

C.F. Boys, can't you be sensible for a mo-
ment? You're trying my patience. What
about our story?

LAW. What about it? It's a rich, protean part
for Larry.

LARRY. It just don't make sense.

LAW. I resent that as a gentleman and a
grammarian.

C.F. Now really, boys, I'm tolerant, but I've
got to see results. I'm not one to put the
creative urge in a strait-jacket. But you've
been fired off every other lot in this industry
for your pranks. Perhaps you've forgotten,
Benson, but when I hired you for this job
you promised me to behave in no uncertain
terms. And you promised me Law would
toe the line. Now, I'm warning you, boys.
Let's get to work. Let's concentrate. (*Crosses
above desk to chair back of desk.*) Do you
realize you boys are making more than the
President of the United States?

LAW. But look at the fun he's having!

LARRY (*angrily*). Now looka here—

GREEN. How do you like the song, C.F.?

C.F. It lacks body.

LAW. No breasts.

C.F. That's exactly it— Pallid.

GREEN. Come on, Otto.

SLADE (*starts for door*). This isn't my idea
of a fair audition.

GREEN. Wait'll they hear it at the Cocoanut
Grove. They'll be sorry. (GREEN *and* SLADE
exit. PEGGY *enters and* LAW, *humming "Mer-
ry Widow," intercepts her, dances a few
measures with her.*)

C.F. Listen, boys—we've had enough of this.
(SUSIE *enters carrying a tray.* SUSIE *is a
waitress. We worship* SUSIE. *Why describe
her? We'll tell you what she wears—the full-
blown costume of a Hollywood waitress.
Of her blonde fragility, her intricate but
blameless sex life, and the ineffable charm
of her touching naïveté we won't say a
word.*)

LAW. *Lunch!*

BENSON. Grub! Susie, I love you. (PEGGY
*exits. She never comes back. Why should
she?*)

</td></tr>
</table>

c.f. Wait a minute—wait a minute— (LAW *gets end table and places it in front of couch.* BENSON *takes tray from* SUSIE.)

SUSIE (*weakly*). Please, Mr. Benson, be careful.

LAW. Put that tray right down here.

SUSIE (*quavering*). Thanks. . . . It's not very heavy . . . (*She then collapses neatly on the floor.*)

c.f. Good Lord!

LAW (*bending over her*). Susie—Susie—

BENSON (*grabbing phone*). Get the doctor over here—right away——

LAW. Somebody give me water. (BENSON *takes glass from tray on table.*)

c.f. (*disapprovingly*). This is a nice thing to happen in my office. . . . Who is this girl, anyway?

LAW (*putting water to her as he kneels beside her*). Come on, Susie. (*Lifting her head up to glass.*)

LARRY (*whose father wrote letters to the papers*). That commissary shouldn't employ people with epilepsy.

c.f. (*bitter, still*). I had an actor who did that to me once. Held up my shooting schedule fourteen days.

LAW. She's all right. Here.

SUSIE. Did you all get napkins? (*Opens her eyes for the first time.*)

BENSON. Now, Susie—get into this chair.

SUSIE. Thanks. (*She sits.*)

c.f. (*sharply*). What's wrong with you, young woman?

SUSIE (*still quavering*). Nothing. . . . I'm much better now. . . . Thanks.

c.f. Where's that doctor?

SUSIE. Did you call for a doctor? You didn't have to.

c.f. Do you get these epileptic fits often?

SUSIE. I didn't have an epileptic fit.

c.f. Then what's wrong with you?

SUSIE. There's nothing wrong . . . it's o natural.

c.f. Only natural for you to come into office and collapse on the floor.

SUSIE. Oh, no, sir . . . it's only natural you to feel sick when you're going to h a baby.

LAW. A baby!

BENSON. Susie, you're not going to hav baby!

SUSIE. That's what they told me. . . .

BENSON. Susie's going to have a baby!

LAW. Let's get drunk!

c.f. (*into phone*). Tell that doctor no come. You heard me. I don't want him. (*hangs up.*) I won't have my office conve into a maternity ward! (*He turns on* sus I don't think much of your husband— ting you work at a time like this!

SUSIE. Oh, but I haven't got a husband.

c.f. Huh?

SUSIE (*rises*). You'd better eat your lu before it gets cold. Have you all got kins?

LAW (*humbly*). The new generation! F the facts of nature without squeamish without subterfuge. "I haven't got a band," she says. "It's only natural," she "I'm going to have a baby." . . . Susie, yo magnificent.

SUSIE. I'm quitting at the end of the v so I thought I'd tell everybody wh wouldn't want them to think I was dis tented.

LAW. Our little mother!

SUSIE. Oh, don't make fun of me.

LAW (*rises*). Fun? I've never been touched in my life. Susie, I feel puri

BENSON. Susie—can we be godfather?

SUSIE. Do you mean it?

BENSON. Do we mean it? We haven't a baby. And we've been collaborating years.

E. Oh, I think that would be wonderful
Happy to have writers for a godfather.

ꜱON Happy?

E. I'm going to call him Happy—even
ꞁe's a girl. Because I want him to be
ꝑy—even if he's a girl.

ꜱON. Beautiful! A beautiful thought!
ꞓere are you going to have this baby,
ꞓe?

E. In the County Hospital. It's all fixed.
ꞵas very lucky because I've only lived
ꞓhe county three months and I'm not
ꞵble.

Now, listen, boys—enough of this.

(into phone). Give me the Cedars of
ꞁanon Hospital—and make it snappy.

ꜱON (jubilant). We've got a baby!

Just a minute. Hang up that phone.
ꞀꜱON good-naturedly brushes his arm
ꞁn.)

. Dr. Marx, please. . . . Willy, this is
ꞏ of Benson and Law. Reserve the best
ꞏ in the house for us. I'm serious. Dead
ꞏus. A little friend of ours is going to
ꞏ a baby and we want the goddamnedest
ꞓnement you've got in stock. . . .

ON. Day and night nurse.

(to BENSON). And not the one with the
ꞏ teeth either. She's dynamite. (Into
ꞏe) We want everything that Gloria
Ꞁson had—only double. What's that?
Bill the studio, of course. (He hangs

You'll do no such thing! What kind
gag is this? (MISS CREWS enters.)

CREWS. Do you want to hear the trum-
ꞏall? The men are here. Music Depart-
ꞏ wants your O.K.

Trumpets?

CREWS. For Young England.

Look here—I haven't time to listen to
now. Come back here at two o'clock.
give it to me from out there. I don't
them blasting in my ear. (Meanwhile
ꞁN and LAW have been in whispered
rencꞏ.)

MISS CREWS. Yes, Mr. Friday. (Exits.)

C.F. Now, boys—let's get together on this.
(Turns on SUSIE from below desk.) And
you—what are you sitting here for? Get out!
(SUSIE tries to rise.)

LAW. Sit right where you are. (Crosses to
front of desk.) Don't you bark at our in-
spration! We've got it!

C.F. What?

LAW (with mounting excitement). A baby!

C.F. Boys, I'm a patient man, but you're
trying me.

BENSON (awed). Larry Toms and a baby!

LAW (to C.F.). Do you see it?

LARRY (bellowing). Wait a minute—wait a
minute!

LAW (quickly). He finds a baby—in the
Rockies—

BENSON (inspired; quickly to C.F.). Girl with
a no good gambler—out of Los Vegas—has
a baby . . . gambler is killed. Girl leaves
baby on the ranger's door step. Larry is the
ranger.

LAW (dramatizing it all). My God, he says—
a baby!

BENSON (awed). A baby!

LAW. The most precious thing in life. The
cutest, goddam little bastard you ever saw.

BENSON. Tugging at every mother's heart.
And every potential mother.

LAW. And who isn't!

BENSON. A love story between Larry and
the baby—

LAW. The two outcasts! Get it?

BENSON. And then he meets the mother!

LAW. She wants her baby back.

BENSON. She's been through the fires of hell.

LAW. The man she loved . . . let her
down. . . .

BENSON. She hates men . . . all men. . . .

LAW. She won't look at Larry.

BENSON (to LARRY). No. There she sits . . . bitter, brooding, cynical, but underneath— a mother's heart.

LAW. Out on the Rockies—

BENSON. The hell with the Rockies—back to the Foreign Legion!

LAW. Right! Larry's joined to forget. He's out on the march. We can use all that stock stuff—and he finds a baby!

BENSON. He's gone off to fight the Riffs.

LAW. The hell with the Riffs! Ethiopians!

BENSON. Stick to the Riffs. We don't want any race problem.

LAW. Right! She doesn't know if he's coming back.

BENSON. She's waiting—waiting!

LAW. We cut to the Riffs—

BENSON. Cut back—

LAW (to BENSON). Right into the battle.

BENSON (really inspired now). His father's the Colonel!

LAW. Talk about Kipling—

BENSON. Talk about scope—sweep—what a set-up!

LAW. A love story!

BENSON. A great love story!

LAW. Mary Magdalen of the Foreign Legion and the West Point man who wanted to forget!

BENSON (rises). The baby brings them together, splits them apart, brings them together—

LAW. Boy meets girl—

BENSON. Boy loses girl—

LAW. Boy gets girl!

C.F. (rising in excitement). Boys, I think you've got something! Let's go up and try it on B.K. while it's hot.

LAW. Let's go! (They move forward.)

LARRY (crosses to behind couch). Wait a minute—you can't act with a baby. They steal every scene— Look what happened to Chevalier.

LAW. Are you selling motherhood sh (LAW, BENSON and C.F. exit through speech.)

LARRY. They'll be looking at the baby they should be looking at me. I tell yo won't play it. (Follows off. SUSIE tries to now she is left alone. She sits down a RODNEY, in the Coldstream Guards uni enters. SUSIE turns.)

RODNEY. Oh, I'm sorry. I hope I didn't s you.

SUSIE. Oh, no. (Then, as he looks at desk) They all stepped out—and they d even touch their lunch.

RODNEY (licking his lips involunta Lunch?—You don't happen to know Mr. Friday is coming back?

SUSIE. No, I don't.

RODNEY. I did want to see him. It's r urgent. Do you mind if I wait here?

SUSIE. No, of course not. (He seats hi on couch, near a tray. There is an awk silence. SUSIE stares straight ahead. RO plays with a cracker. Finally SUSIE b the silence.) What are you supposed t

RODNEY. Eh? Oh! That's just it. . . . I'm posed to be a Buckingham Palace G sergeant major—(He pops the cracke his mouth and swallows it. SUSIE loo him rather intently.) Good Lord! Wh: I doing?

SUSIE. You're eating Mr. Friday's cra

RODNEY. I'm awfully sorry. I don't u stand how I—

SUSIE. You must be very hungry.

RODNEY. Not a bit. Not at all.

SUSIE. You look hungry.

RODNEY. Do I?

SUSIE. Why don't you have somet! They'll never eat it. They're always se things back they order—never even tou

RODNEY. Really?

SUSIE. You'll only be doing me a favo

RODNEY. Oh?

SUSIE. I won't have so much to carry b the commissary. Sometimes I think I back more than I bring.

EY. You're pulling my leg, of course.

. What did you say?

EY. You're not really a waitress.

. Sure I am.

EY (*triumphantly*). Waitresses don't ly sit in producer's offices.

. They do when they don't feel well.

EY. You don't feel well? Oh, I'm sorry. ere anything I can do?

. No, thanks.

EY. But what's wrong?

. Oh, there's no use telling you. I told Friday and he made such a fuss about guess I better keep it to myself.

EY. I'm afraid I don't quite understand.

. Try the chicken soup. It's very good.

EY. Are you seriously suggesting that I some of this broth?

. We make it special for B.K. with nine ens.

EY. Well, dash it, I will eat it. Just to the joke good! (*He laughs weakly and up the bowl and puts it to his lips, ips it.*)

(*warningly*). It's hot!

EY (*now quite gay*). So I've learned.

When did you eat last?

EY (*lying, of course*). I had my lunch our ago.

Have some crackers with it.

Y. Thanks.

You're English, aren't you?

Y. Yes, of course.

So is Ronald Colman.

Y (*bolting his food*). So he is.

I like the way the English talk.

Y. Do you?

It's very soothing.

RODNEY. What an idea!

SUSIE. Of course, that's only *my* idea. I'm very ignorant.

RODNEY. Oh, please don't say that. I think you're very intelligent.

SUSIE. Oh, I'm intelligent. But I don't know anything.

RODNEY. You're an extraordinary girl.

SUSIE. I've never been to high school.

RODNEY (*gallantly*). May I say that's the high school's loss?

SUSIE. But some day I'll go to high school. That's my secret ambition. Try the ham hocks. The cook eats them himself. He comes from Czechoslovakia.

RODNEY. Does he really? Look here—I feel an awful swine guzzling by myself. Won't you join me?

SUSIE. Well, I'm not very hungry, but I can eat.

RODNEY. Good! (*He rises and adjusts a chair for her.*)

SUSIE. It's funny how I keep on eating.

RODNEY. Some ham hocks?

SUSIE. No. Happy doesn't like ham. He likes milk.

RODNEY (*mystified*). I beg your pardon? (*But he doesn't press the point.*) Did you say milk?

SUSIE. Yes. Milk.

RODNEY (*as he pours*). There you are.

SUSIE. Thanks.

RODNEY. Cozy, this—what?

SUSIE. It's good milk. Have some.

RODNEY. Do you know, I think you're the most extraordinary girl I ever met.

SUSIE. Why?

RODNEY. You're so kind. You're so direct, so sincere. Most girls one meets play about with words so. They're so infernally smart. They make one feel like a worm.

SUSIE. Of course, I'm different on account of my condition. Most girls aren't in my condition.

RODNEY. Your condition?

SUSIE. The minute I found out about Happy I said to myself: I'm going to be very good and very sincere, because then Happy will be very good and very sincere.

RODNEY. I'm afraid I don't quite follow.

SUSIE (sighing). Nobody does.

RODNEY. Eh? Oh, yes. . . . As I was saying— What was I saying?

SUSIE (looking into his eyes and feeling strangely stirred). Have some mustard.

RODNEY. Do you know, I must confess. I was hungry. As a matter of fact, I was close to wiring home for funds today. But I didn't. (Looks very determined, righteous.)

SUSIE. You mean you need money, and you can get it—and you won't wire for it?

RODNEY. I can't—and keep my pride. I told them I was on my own. You see, my family didn't want me to act. Not that they've any prejudices against the stage—or the films. Not at all. In fact, one of my aunts was a Gaiety girl. Quite all right. But they don't think I can act. That's what hurts.

SUSIE. Can you act?

RODNEY. No.

SUSIE. Not at all?

RODNEY. Not at all. I'm awful!

SUSIE. Oh, that's too bad.

RODNEY. But I only realized it in the stock company . . . out in Pasadena. I was the worst member of the company. At first I thought it was because they were always giving me character parts—American gangsters—and that sort of thing. And then one week I played a Cambridge undergraduate. And, mind you, I've been a Cambridge undergraduate. And do you know that I was utterly unconvincing?

SUSIE. Then why don't you give it up?

RODNEY. Pride.

SUSIE. I can understand that— Pride.

RODNEY. Can you really?

SUSIE. Sure I can.

RODNEY. That's why I simply must see [Mr.] Friday. (Suddenly) Look here— (He ta[kes] a book from couch and opens it.) Look [at] this color plate. Does this uniform remo[tely] resemble the one I'm wearing? (He cro[sses] down right.)

SUSIE (looks at book; then at RODNEY). [Yes,] I think so.

RODNEY (crosses to her left). But, my [dear] girl, look at the coat and the buttons— the boots—note the heels—and look at m[e.] (Steps back.)

SUSIE. Well, come to think of it. I guess [it's] different.

RODNEY. Of course. And I've taken this b[ook] right out of their own research departm[ent.] When I show this to Mr. Friday he's bo[und] to be sporting enough to admit an err[or.]

SUSIE. Oh, sure.

RODNEY (leaning over her). You see, [all I] want is to appear in one picture—and [then] I can tell the family: "I've done it." Bu[t it's] not good enough. I'm chucking it. But [I] have my pride.

SUSIE (gazing at him). I see.

RODNEY. Oh . . . I say . . . I'm not bo[ring] you?

SUSIE. Oh, no. Finish your ham.

RODNEY. Eh? Oh! Don't mind if I do. [A bit] of pie for you? (He extends plate [and] fork.)

SUSIE (brightly. Almost flirting). Wel[l, I'll] try. (She smiles at him and he at her, [forks] poised in mid-air.)

RODNEY. Do you know, I've never en[joyed] a lunch quite as much as this one—th[anks] to you. (Suddenly) Would it bore yo[u if I] tried out my lines—in Young Englan[d, you] know.

SUSIE. Oh, no.

RODNEY. Very well. (He rises, holding [glass] of milk.) Gentlemen, the Queen— [she] waits.)

SUSIE. Is that all?

EY. That's all. But of course I could
"Gentlemen, I give you the Queen."
en up the part a bit, what? . . . Gen-
en, I give you the Queen! . . . Sounds
er better, doesn't it? (*Then with pro-
d bass*) Gentlemen, I give you the
en! (LARRY *enters followed by* C.F. C.F.
s.)

Y. I don't cotton to the whole idea, and
K.'s got any sense, he won't listen to
e maniacs.

What's going on here?

EY. How'd you do. . . . I . . . I . . .
s glass of milk back on tray.)

What is this? A tete-à-tete in my office!
d Gad! You've been drinking my milk!

. It's all right, Mr. Friday. I told him
ould have it.

You told him?

EY. I'm awfully sorry. I owe you an
gy, and money, of course. Will you
ot my I.O.U.? And I have the book—
Research. I can show you the really
entic uniform. I'm sure if you study
— (SUSIE *finds the page and hands book*
DNEY.)

've a good mind to call the studio police.

(*rises*). Oh, please don't do that, Mr.
y.

x. That's what you get for having for-
actors around. Take the food right out
ur mouth!

EY. I'm terrible sorry, of course.

Get out!

EY. I realize there's nothing I can say—
turns to SUSIE) except—my eternal
ude. (He grabs her by the hand and
s it. Exits.)

. Oh, you shouldn't have done that.
been having a terrible time.

glaring at SUSIE). Get these dishes out
re.

(*meekly*). Yes, sir. (*She begins piling
shes on tray.*)

. The idea of a baby! The more I think
the less I like it.

C.F. (*crosses to chair at desk*). Larry, you're
driving me into a nervous breakdown. I had
to take you out of B.K.'s office so you'd
stop arguing before he could make a decision.

LARRY. There's nothing to decision. I won't
play it.

C.F. If B.K. likes the idea, you'll play it.

LARRY. Maybe—and maybe not. I'm willing
to bet ten to one right now B.K. kicks the
whole story in the ash can. He's no fool.
(BENSON *and* LAW *enter in shirt sleeves.
They've obviously had a hot session with*
B.K.)

BENSON. Sold! Lock, stock and baby! B.K.
says it's the best mother-love story he's heard
in years.

LARRY. What? What's that?

LAW (*magnificently*). Susie, put that tray
down!

SUSIE. Please, Mr. Law, I've got to get back
to the commissary.

LARRY. You sold him that story, huh?

BENSON. Lie down, actor!

LARRY. I'll see about this. (*He exits.*)

BENSON. Now listen, Susie—and listen carefully.

LAW. Let me tell her, will you? (*He faces
her.*) Susie, nature meant you for a sucker.
You were designed to get the short end of
the stick. The girl who gets slapped.

BENSON (*quickly*). But we're changing all
that.

LAW. Susie, in real life, you'd have your baby
in the County Hospital . . . get yourself a
job, if lucky, with a philanthropic Iowa
family of fourteen adults and twelve minors
for twenty bucks a month. And when your
grateful son grew up he'd squirt tobacco
juice in your eye and join the Navy.

BENSON. There you go with your goddamn
realism. (*Turns to* SUSIE *with paper and
pencil.*) Sign, please—

SUSIE. Here? (*She signs; and then turns,
brightly.*) What is it?

BENSON. Just a power of attorney authorizing us to deal for you in all matters with this studio.

C.F. What power of attorney? What are you boys up to?

LAW. We said to ourselves upstairs—why shouldn't Susie have the good things of life?

BENSON. After all, we're godfathers.

SUSIE. I—don't feel very good.

LAW. Get this, Susie. We've just sold a story about a baby.

BENSON. Sweetest story ever told!

LAW. A new-born baby.

BENSON. Brand new.

LAW. We're going to watch that baby—the first hair—the first tooth—the first smile—

BENSON. The same baby. No switching—first time in the history of pictures. That baby's going to grow before your eyes.

LAW. Open up like a flower. . . . Just like the Dionne quintuplets.

BENSON. Minute he's born we set the camera on him. We stay with him—

LAW. That baby's going to gurgle and google and drool his way to stardom!

SUSIE. But—

LAW. And that baby, Susie, is Happy. stairs in B.K.'s office we put your unb child into pictures.

SUSIE (transported). Happy—in pictures! —that's wonderful— (Then, with a sud gasp.) Oh!

LAW (quickly). Susie! What's the matter

SUSIE. I don't know . . . I . . . I . . don't feel so good . . . I think . . . . . (In these broken words, SUSIE tells BENSON helps SUSIE to lie on couch. looks over SUSIE's shoulder; whistles; to phone.)

LAW (into phone). Emergency! Get the bulance over to Mr. Friday's office away—get the doctor—get the nurse.

C.F. (staring). What is it? In my office. Gad! Miss Crews! (Door opens.)

MISS CREWS (at door). The trumpets here! (Trumpets sound their triump clarion call.)

LAW (through the Wagnerian brass, to SON, awed). Happy's on his way!

CURTAIN

ACT TWO

SCENE I

We are in your neighborhood theatre, seven months later.

As the curtain rises we face a motion picture screen, and to the sound-track accom ment of "Home on the Range," these glaring titles pop out at us:

IF YOU LIKED HAPPY
IN
"WANDERING HEARTS"
YOU'LL ADORE HIM
IN
"GOLDEN NUGGET"

This is what is known as a trailer, in technical terms. It is shown at neighbor theatres prior to the release of the picture so that the customers will be teased into re ing the following week.

There are, of course, beautifully composed shots of horses, men and open spaces finally we come upon a series of close-ups of HAPPY, over which these titles dance

HAPPY!
HAPPY!
HAPPY!

e sound track blares forth "Ride of the Valkyries."

CROWN PRINCE OF COMEDY!
KING OF TRAGEDY!
EMPEROR OF EMOTION!

*t prior to these titles we have seen a Chinese, who has emerged from God knows
ere, but what is a ranch without a Chinese? The general idea is that the Chinese
ds* HAPPY *on the doorstep and communicates his discovery to* LARRY TOMS. *There fol-
vs a title which explains all:*

THE DESERT WAIF WHO MADE
A SOFTIE OF A BAD MAN

e picture is further described as:

THE BIG GOLD STRIKE
OF MOTHER LOVE

see horses galloping, men falling, revolvers barking, and nice, big, wavy

THRILLS
CHILLS

credit card is as follows:

FROM A STORY BY H. G. WELLS
ADAPTED BY J. CARLYLE BENSON AND ROBERT LAW
DIRECTED BY SERGE BORODOKOV

, appropriately enough, in solitary grandeur:

PRODUCED BY C. ELLIOT FRIDAY

SCENE II

*he screen lifts, and once more we are in Mr. Friday's office.
.F. is at his desk,* MISS CREWS *is seated upstage and at desk;* BENSON *is on the couch
de* LARRY. ROSETTI *is seated on the piano bench.*

SON. Read those figures, Miss Crews.

CREWS. Eighty-two thousand at the Mu-
Iall. Forty-eight thousand five hundred
thirty-eight in Des Moines.

SON. Without a stage show.

Y. I always went big in Des Moines.

CREWS. Twenty-eight thousand in New-

Y. That's one of my big towns.

CREWS. Forty-two thousand three hun-
and eighty-four in San Francisco.

Y. I'm big there, too.

CREWS. Twenty-six thousand eight hun-
and seventy-five in Detroit.

BENSON (*to* C.F.). And you sit there and tell
me Happy isn't worth thirty-five hundred
a week?

C.F. But, Benson, be reasonable. I can't go to
B.K. with any such fantastic figure.

BENSON (*sighing*). Read that list again, Miss
Crews.

C.F. Never mind, Miss Crews.

LARRY. What about me? *Wandering Hearts*
was my picture, wasn't it? Folks came to
see me. They didn't come to see Happy.

BENSON (*taking "Variety" from his pocket*).
Let me read "Variety" to the assembled multitude. *Wandering Hearts* socko in Minne-
apolis despite Larry Toms . . .

LARRY. Huh?

BENSON. Mexico nuts about Happy but no like Larry Toms—

LARRY. Where? Where does it say that? (*He takes paper.* ROSETTI *rises and looks over* LARRY'S *shoulder.*)

BENSON. This is an accidental business in an accidental world. Happy is going to get it while it's hot.

C.F. Benson, you owe me something.

BENSON. What?

C.F. Gratitude. . . . After all, the idea of a baby was mine—more or less.

BENSON. More or less.

C.F. I made that baby act.

BENSON. All right, Svengali.

C.F. Shall we say three hundred a week for Happy?

BENSON. Shall we say thirty-five hundred a week for Happy?

C.F. I've a good mind to have you thrown out of this studio.

BENSON. All right. Happy goes with us. We've still got that power of attorney.

C.F. Of course, I didn't mean that literally.

BENSON. I did. (*Telephone rings.*)

C.F. Hello. . . . Yes, Miss Goodwin. . . . What? You can't write about Brussels because you've never been there? My dear girl, why do you think we have a research department? After all, Bernard Shaw wrote *Don Juan* and he never went to Bulgaria. Imagination, my dear girl—imagination. (*Hangs up.*) Look here, Benson, I knew I couldn't deal with Law. I thought I could with you. After all, you're in no position to antagonize this studio. Some day you may need my friendship.

BENSON. I'm supposed to be working with our Mr. Law on a story. To wit: *Tiger Tamer.* Do you mind if I join my partner in a little English composition?

C.F. Some day you may be very sorry for this, Benson.

BENSON. What do you think, Miss Crews?

MISS CREWS. I think Happy ought to ge while it's hot.

C.F. Get back to your desk.

MISS CREWS. Yes, Mr. Friday. (*She exits.*

LARRY (*waving "Variety"*). I said that bat ruin me! Well, he ain't going to steal more pictures! I won't play that new sce

C.F. (*irritably*). What new scene?

LARRY. I'm supposed to wash Happy.

C.F. That's a cute scene. I read it.

LARRY. Am I the type that washes babies

C.F. Why not?

LARRY. 'Tain't manly!

BENSON. No. You want the baby to w you!

LARRY. Listen!

BENSON. Any further business before house? (*Turns to* LARRY.) By the way, I you with Susie at the Trocadero last ni We don't approve of you as an escort. mind me to speak to her about that.

C.F. Benson, I'm asking you once more fair—be reasonable.

BENSON. I am. We're asking thirty-five dred a week. We'll consider three thou and settle for twenty-five hundred. But a penny less. Incidentally, Fox'll pay tw five hundred for Happy. We promise let them know by Saturday. No hurry course. (*Exits.*)

C.F. Have you ever seen anything damnably unfair? Imagine *writers* hol up this studio at the point of a gun nothing but blackmail.

ROSETTI (*rises*). I've got a hunch, C.F. V did you sign Happy? Do you remembe

C.F. Of course I remember . . . July teenth . . . Fall of the Bastille. I reme my wife pointing out the coincidence a time. Why?

ROSETTI (*crosses to desk*). I've got a h that power of attorney expires pretty I want to be prepared.

Rosetti, I'm not interested in the future. interested in signing Happy right now— ore we lose him to Fox. (*Phone rings.*)

ETTI. You've got to have vision in this iness, C.F. (*He reaches for other phone, nges his mind, and then exits.*)

(*into phone*). Hello. . . . Yes, listen, gg. . . . I ran the sound track on *Young land* last night. I don't like the trumpets. y're sour. They spoil the whole mood. What? . . . What's that? You can't walk on a picture like that. What kind of a ctor are you if you can't take construc- criticism . . . hello . . . hello . . . ngs up.) Gregg is walking out on ng England, I can't sign Happy—

ıY. What about me?

Ten thousand feet of film sick—and he ks out. I'll have to run the picture all the rnoon and sit up all night cutting it. ss CREWS *enters.*)

CREWS. Happy's through for the day.

SE (*wheeling in a stream-lined baby car- e*). Through for the day.

'OR (*as he enters*). Through for the day. is mother here?

CREWS. No, Doctor, but she should be very soon.

SE (*backing carriage in front of desk*). da-da to Mr. Friday.

(*waving obediently*). Da-da, Happy.

OR. Nurse, take the little trouper out the garden and keep him in the sun-

Y. He's through for the day and I'm king until eight. He's sure got it soft. SE *exits with* HAPPY. ROSETTI *enters.*)

OR. They've been overworking you, have

Y. I ain't feeling so hearty, doc. I wish l look me over.

'rises and goes below desk*). Just your ination. I wish I had your constitution. ;ot to see B.K. (*He exits.*)

OR. All you picture people are hypo- lriacs. However, come up to my office 'll look you over. (*He exits.*)

LARRY. I'm a star. I've been a star for ten years. I've worked hard to get where I'm at— (*He rises. Phone rings.*)

ROSETTI (*at phone*). Hello. . . . Yes . . . speaking—

LARRY. I don't drink. I don't smoke. I don't swear. I don't get into no scandal. And the girls I passed up!

ROSETTI (*into phone*). Oh, you've got that, Mr. Williams? Fine. When does it expire? . . . It *did* expire? Last week? . . . No, don't do that. I'll tell the boys. . . . You see, I may be handling Happy's new contract. Right. (*He hangs up.*)

LARRY. They ain't making pictures here no more. They're shooting nothing but close- ups of babies. Happy laughing! Happy cry- ing! Happy! . . . Happy! . . .

ROSETTI. Larry, I've just checked with the Legal Department. The boys' power of at- torney expired last week. And they don't even know it.

LARRY. What's that got to do with me?

ROSETTI. Larry, there's been something de- veloping in the back of my mind for some weeks. Why do you think I asked you to take Susie to the Trocadero?

LARRY. She talked me deaf, dumb, and blind about going to high school. She set me back fourteen bucks. Lucky she don't drink.

ROSETTI (*the dreamer*). I wanted you to get friendly with her because I visualized a way for you and me to get Happy—for life.

LARRY. Huh?

ROSETTI (*with Napoleonic intensity*). Larry, here's the tactical move. You marry Susie.

LARRY. Marry her?

ROSETTI. That's what I said.

LARRY. I won't do it.

ROSETTI (*who knows his client*). All right, suit yourself.

LARRY. We got community property in Cali- fornia. If there's a bust-up the woman gets half.

ROSETTI. Larry, I don't want to hurt your feelings, but I can't get you a new contract

the way things are now. B.K. is dickering to borrow Clark Gable or Gary Cooper for Happy's next picture.

LARRY (*touched to the quick*). What?

ROSETTI. I'd marry her myself if I was free. Show me a girl with a better heart—with more culture—

LARRY. You don't expect me to believe what the studio hands out—her husband was a prominent portrait painter who went down on the *Morro Castle?*

ROSETTI (*indignantly*). Who are you to cast the first stone?

LARRY. I don't want to marry nobody. Anyways, there's no sense to it.

ROSETTI (*patiently*). If you marry her, you're Happy's legal guardian and we control the situation. A father and son team off the screen as well as on! Is that practical or am I just an idealist? Look at Guy Lathrop! He argued with me when I told him to marry Betty Bird. But he finally had the sense to play along with me and we've been drawing top money ever since.

LARRY. I don't want to marry nobody.

ROSETTI. Larry, you're at the crossroads right now. One road leads to stardom and big pictures, with Happy and me. The other leads to Poverty Row and cheap Westerns. Will you put your hand in mine and let me guide you? (MISS CREWS *enters.*)

MISS CREWS. Mr. Toms, you're wanted on the set.

LARRY (*growling.*) All right.

MISS CREWS. Oh, hello, Mrs. Seabrook . . . how nice you look. (*For* SUSIE *enters. She wears a white middy-blouse and a navy blue, pleated skirt.*)

SUSIE. We had gym today. . . . Hello, Larry. . . . Hello, Mr. Rosetti. . . . I hope I didn't interrupt anything important.

ROSETTI. Not at all. . . . (*Significantly*) I'll be in the Legal Department, Larry. (*He exits.*)

SUSIE. Where's Happy?

MISS CREWS. Happy's in the garden with his nurse. He's all through for the day.

SUSIE. Oh, that's wonderful. I don't get see him very much. He's working and going to high school. (CHAUFFEUR *ente*

CHAUFFEUR. Excuse me, Miss.

SUSIE. What is it, Simpson?

CHAUFFEUR. You forgot your algebra bo Miss.

SUSIE. Oh, thank you, Simpson. That very thoughtful. (CHAUFFEUR *exits.*)

MISS CREWS. And I have a new batch of mail for you and Happy. (*Exits.*)

SUSIE. It's wonderful to get mail. Nob used to write me before. Now I even letters from Japan. (MISS CREWS *enters letters.*) All those letters? Thank you, N Crews.

LARRY (*sighs*). Miss Crews, call the set tell 'em I may be a little late.

MISS CREWS. Very well. (*She exits.*)

SUSIE (*sitting on desk, poring over her h written, moronic literature*). Here's one f North Carolina. Oh, the poor thing! Th so much sadness in this world. (LARRY *si she looks up at him.*) You look sad, Larry. What's the matter?

LARRY. Well—(*He rises and crosses to* SIE.)—uh—I been waiting a long tim talk to you, Susie. I couldn't go to the school. All those girls would mob me autographs, especially when I tell them I am.

SUSIE. All the girls are crazy about C Gable.

LARRY (*clears his throat*). Susie—I ca two tickets for the opening at the Chin the De Mille picture.

SUSIE. Can you?

LARRY. I knew that'd knock you over.

SUSIE. Oh, it'll be wonderful!

LARRY. I'm always thinkin' of little t to make life wonderful—for you.

SUSIE (*nods*). Everybody is.

LARRY (*bridling*). What do you me everybody?

ᴇ. Only the other day Mr. Benson said
ᴇthing very true. He said: "Susie, you're
ᴅerella." And that's just what I feel like.
░ you know what else he said? He said:
░ you need now is a Prince Charming."

ʀʏ. He did, huh? Who did he have in
ᴅ?

ᴇ. Oh, nobody.

ʀʏ. He didn't mention me, did he?

ᴇ. Oh, no. (ʟᴀʀʀʏ *grunts*.) Of course I've
ᴇr met a Prince Charming. I wouldn't
ᴡ what he looks like. Although, one day
ᴡful nice boy came in here.

ʏ. Who?

ᴇ. I don't even know his name. He was
ᴎiform and I was in my condition—I've
ᴇr seen him since.

ʏ. You shouldn't be thinking of him.
░ should be thinking of Happy.

ᴇ. But I do . . . only sometimes it gets
ᴇome for me, especially at night. And
ᴏurse, Mr. Benson and Mr. Law are
░ all the time. Happy used to say good
░ to them every night on the telephone.
░really good night—just goo-n'—just like
░ But they're so busy they won't come
ᴎe telephone any more.

ʏ. Happy needs a father.

ᴇ. Do you think so?

ʏ. Well, you want him to be able to
░the whole world in the face, don't you?

ᴇ (*twinkling*). He does!

ᴋ. I mean when he grows up. He's gon-
ᴇ ashamed when he finds out he never
░ father.

ᴇ. Of course he had a father.

ᴋ. I mean—a married father.

ᴇ. He was married—but I didn't know
ᴀʀʀʏ *winces*.)

ᴋ. Uh—listen, Susie—I'm mighty fond
ᴜu and Happy. (*He tries playing the
ᴜl Western hero*.) Mighty fond.

ᴇ. Are you really, Larry?

LARRY. Mighty fond.

SUSIE. Who would have thought six months
ago that I'd be sitting in the same room with
Larry Toms and he'd be saying to me he
was—

LARRY. Mighty fond.

SUSIE. Do you know something very odd?
When I first came to California, it was raining very hard—oh, it rained for three weeks
—it was very unusual—and I was looking
for a job, and I couldn't find one—and I had
fifteen cents—and I just had to get out of the
rain—and I went into a theatre and there
you were—on the screen—

LARRY. Mighty fond—

SUSIE (*awed*). That's just what you were saying to Mary Brian—and now you're saying
it to me.

LARRY. What was the picture?

SUSIE. *Thunder over Arizona*. It was a beautiful picture. I don't remember what it was
about, but I saw it four times. Until I got
dry.

LARRY. Susie, soon's this picture's over, how'd
you like to come up to my ranch? You and
Happy—

SUSIE (*rises*). Ranch? Oh, that would be
lovely! Maybe Mr. Benson and Mr. Law
could come, too?

LARRY. Maybe they could, but they won't.

SUSIE. But I couldn't go alone—without a
chaperon.

LARRY. Susie—you and Happy'll love that
ranch. I got a mighty nice house, big and
rambling. I got plenty of barns and a corral
and plenty of live stock. But no baby.

SUSIE. I know Happy'll just love it.

LARRY. Susie—I know you don't expect this,
and I don't want you to get too excited—but,
Susie, I been thinkin' about you and Happy
—thinkin' a lot. Ever since the day you
come into this office and fell on that there
floor, I said to myself: Larry, there's your
leadin' lady—for life.

SUSIE. Me?

LARRY. Nobody else.

SUSIE. But I don't—you won't get mad?— but I'm not in love with you.

LARRY. You shouldn't be thinking of yourself —I'm not thinking of myself—you should be thinking of Happy.

SUSIE. I guess you're right. I don't know what to say. (*Pauses.*) I'll ask Mr. Benson and Mr. Law—

LARRY. Huh?

SUSIE. They've been so good to me.

LARRY. I'm not proposing to them!

SUSIE. I know, but—

LARRY. You don't mean nothing to them. Before you came along they had a Spanish snake charmer until they got tired of her. And before that they had a broken-down pug who wiggled his ears. They was groomin' him for my place. There ain't nothin' holy to them!

SUSIE. But they've done everything for me.

LARRY (*crosses to* SUSIE). I'm offering you my ranch—my name—and a father Happy'll be proud of!

SUSIE. I know, but—

LARRY. Don't give me your answer now. Think it over. (*Pats her arm.*) Only don't think too long. I'll be waiting for your answer in the Legal Department. You know where that is?

SUSIE. Oh, yes. (MISS CREWS *opens the door.*)

LARRY. I'll be there. (*He exits.* SUSIE *looks a little dazed.*)

MISS CREWS. Oh, Mrs. Seabrook—I've located that young man you were looking for. He's outside.

SUSIE. Oh, you have? Really?

MISS CREWS (*at door*). Come in. (SUSIE *tenses herself. A strange* YOUNG MAN *enters and stops.*)

SUSIE (*staring at him*). Oh! Oh, no, that's not him—I mean—he.

YOUNG MAN (*earnestly*). Won't I do? I've just finished a short for Hal Roach—I'm making a test for Metro tomorrow, and—

MISS CREWS (*firmly escorting him ou* Thank you for coming! (YOUNG MAN *shru and exits, and* MISS CREWS *closes the doo*

SUSIE. He's not English.

MISS CREWS. English? We didn't have English actors in *Young England.*

SUSIE. This boy was an extra.

MISS CREWS. Does he owe you a lot of mon

SUSIE. Oh, no. It was nothing like tha

MISS CREWS (*as it dawns on her*). Oh, I A personal matter! Well, I'll try ag (*Brightly.*)

SUSIE. I guess it's no use, Miss Cr (*Sighs.*) He probably swallowed his p and went back to England. (BENSON LAW *enter.* BENSON *carries paper and pe* BENSON *sits upstage end of desk.* LAW *cro to front of couch.*)

LAW. Hi, Susie! How's the little mot Clear out. We're trying to work and a dred chorus boys are practicing fencing derneath our windows. (*Turns to* CREWS.) Miss Crews, leave a note for He's got to change our office. We can't with fencing fairies! (*Sits on couch.*)

MISS CREWS. Yes, Mr. Law. (*She exits.*)

SUSIE. Are you very busy?

BENSON. We still need an opening.

LAW. Fade-in. . . . A zoo!

SUSIE (*crossing to* BENSON). I just wa to thank you, Mr. Benson, for the bea white teddy bear.

BENSON. What teddy bear?

SUSIE. Mrs. Benson brought it herself.

BENSON (*looking up from typewriter*) she did?

SUSIE. She played with Happy, too. And after he went for his nap, she stayed looked at him.

BENSON (*to* LAW—*covering*). Where we?

SUSIE. When she left, she was cryi think she ought to have a baby of her

SON (*angered*). Come on, Law—come
—fade-in on the zoo.

. I've got it! Larry's carrying a hunk of
t for his pet tiger. He's crossing the road.
g! The dame comes tearing down ninety
s an hour.

SON. Give her a little character.

. She's a high-handed rich bitch. Bang!
almost runs the bastard down. . . .
ere the hell do you think you're going?
. She burns. . . . Society girl. . . .
s never been talked to like that before.
Why, you lousy bum, she snarls. . . .
en, here's a cute piece of business. She
ds the hell out of him and he throws the
k of meat right in her puss!

SON (*enthusiastically*). That's charming!

. Listen, Susie, what are you standing
e for? Go home and write in your diary.

E. Boys, I wanted to ask you some-
g . . .

SON. Fade-out!

. Fade-in!

E. . . . and then I'll go.

(*wearily*). What is it?

E. Do you think I should marry Larry
ms?

. Who?

E. Larry Toms.

(*rises, crosses below couch*). No. . . .
-in. . . .

ON. Better get a different background.
ve been staying in the zoo too long.

. Right! Girl's home—a Pan shot—fif-
hundred butlers with white socks. . . .
ns to SUSIE.) Did he ask you to marry

. Yes.

. Did you spit in his face?

. He's taking me to the opening tonight.
ays he's mighty fond of Happy and

(*crosses to back of couch*). Why
dn't he be? His contract depends on it.

Even Wilkes Barre doesn't want him and
they're still calling for Theda Bara—

SUSIE. Don't you think he'd be good for
Happy? He's an outdoor man.

LAW. So is the fellow who collects my garbage.

BENSON. Listen, let's get on with this. Introducing the fiancé. A pale anemic louse. A
business man!

LAW. Right! The minute the audience sees
him they yell: Don't marry that heel.

SUSIE. I know you're very busy. . . .

LAW. Go away, Susie.

SUSIE. You boys were so sweet to me. I felt
I had somebody. But lately I've been awfully
alone. . . .

LAW. Sure! Everybody's alone. What do you
think life is? Why do you have crowds?
Because everybody's alone. (*Stops; crosses
above couch to front.*) That's a thought.
That's what I should be writing instead of
this titivating drivel. Life as it is. People
as they are.

SUSIE. But that would be terrible. You don't
know, Mr. Law; you don't know how awful
life can be.

BENSON. When you philosophers are through
I'd like to get on with this story.

SUSIE (*eagerly, to* BENSON). You wouldn't
like to come out and say hello to Happy?
He's in the garden. (LAW *waves her away;
crosses and sits on couch.* SUSIE *is quite defeated now.*)

BENSON (*ignoring her*). I've got it. (*To*
SUSIE) Don't bother me! (SUSIE *crosses to
desk, gets mail, and fades from the scene.*)
I've got it! Introducing Happy! Back to the
zoo—Larry gets up in the morning and
there, curled up with his pet tiger cub, is a
baby! Happy!

LAW. Not bad!

BENSON. Larry looks at him. "How'd you get
here?" (*He mimics* LARRY's *voice.*)

LAW. The baby can't answer. The tiger begins to growl. Happy cries. Larry takes the
baby to his hut.

BENSON. We meet Larry's drunken pal, the comic. (*Rises and crosses to* LAW.) That's where we have swell business. Two clumsy men pinning up his diapers—

LAW (*his enthusiasm gone*). Formula 284 . . . Diapers gag.

BENSON (*exulting*). Ah, yes, but the tiger runs away with the diapers! Fade-out! Now we need excitement. The tigers are loose—

LAW. How did they get loose?

BENSON (*crosses to* LAW). The comic's drunk. He opens the cages by accident. Christ! I see it! The city in uproar—the police—National Guard—the girl's come down to the zoo—she's trapped with Larry—and the baby. Fifty tigers snapping at Happy's throat.

LAW. And where does my priceless dialogue come in? (*Rises and crosses to chair back of desk.*) That's the worst of hack writing. It's hard work.

BENSON. Suppose—Larry—thinks—it's—the girl's baby?

LAW. Society girls go around leaving foundlings in the zoo? (*Drinking.*) Prostitution of a God-given talent! (*Sits.*) Pasteboard pictures of pasteboard people.

BENSON. Will you shut up? I've got to get this line-up today. Pearl expects me to take her to the opening.

LAW (*fiddling with the dictograph*). Eenie . . . Meenie . . . Mina . . . Mo . . . (*Dictograph buzzes.*) Music Department?

GREEN'S VOICE. Yes, this is the Music Department. This is Mr. Green.

LAW (*mimics* C.F.'s *voice*). Not Mr. Green! This is C.F. . . . Can you write me a roundelay with a symphonic undertone in about fifteen minutes? . . . Do it! (*Dictograph buzzes.*) Yes?

GREEN'S VOICE. Look, Mr. Friday, did you say a lullaby?

LAW. No, I didn't say a lullaby. I said a roundelay. The sort of thing Beethoven dashes off. (*He clicks the dictograph off.* ROSETTI *enters.*)

ROSETTI (*genially*). Hello, boys . . . have a cigar.

LAW. Hello, buzzard. What's the occasi[on]

BENSON. Fade-out, stooge, we're busy.

ROSETTI. Same old boys! Anything for a g[ag] Well, I'm feeling pretty good myself. just set Larry to a long-term contract. A he didn't have to take a cut, either. I him a nice little set-up. A joint contract v Happy!

BENSON. With Happy?

LAW (*rises*). Huh? You're crazy!

ROSETTI. Well, the mother came to me now and said you two were tired of her. I happened to look up your power of a[ttor]ney, and it seems you didn't even car[e to] get a new one when it expired.

BENSON. Is this on the level?

LAW. Where's that power of attorney?

BENSON. I thought you had it.

LAW (*aghast*). What'd you get for Hap[py?]

ROSETTI. Three hundred!

LAW. Why, we turned down fifteen hun[dred] from Fox!

ROSETTI. You should have taken it. But t[hree] hundred's a lot of money. Anyway, w[hat's] the difference? It's all in the family—

LAW. Where's Susie?

ROSETTI. She went out with Larry. Th[ey're] going to the opening tonight. They're [cele]brating.

LAW. Who thought this up—you?

ROSETTI. Sure.

LAW. Why, you scavenging son of a—

ROSETTI. You better be careful how you [talk] to me. And you'd better be careful how [you] talk to Larry from now on. He's fe[d up] with your gags and insults. You got a[way] with a lot of stuff around here because [you] had Happy. Well, Larry's got him now [and] he's going to have plenty to say around [here.] I'm warning you. He'd like to see you [kicked] off this lot. And he's in a position to do [it] now. So be careful. If you want to keep [your] jobs. (*Turns away to door.*) And if I [

wife who was throwing my money away
fore I even made it, I'd be plenty care-
l.

NSON. Why, you— (ROSETTI *exits quickly.*
NSON *crosses to door, then turns to* LAW.)
hy the hell didn't you keep track of that
wer of attorney?

w. Why didn't *I*?

NSON. Why the hell didn't you talk to
sie? She was in here.

w. Yeah.

NSON. I see it—I see it now. Larry—Ro-
ti—and we let her walk right into it.
you realize what this means? We're
our way out. (*Crosses to piano.*)

w. That's fine.

NSON. Fine?

w. Now I'll have to go back to Vermont.
ow I'll have to write.

NSON. Pearl doesn't like Vermont.

w. The whims of your wife don't interest
. I've got a book—all planned.

NSON. Listen—I want to stay in pictures.
love pictures. I'm knee-deep in debts.
e've got to bust this Larry thing wide
en. We've got to get Happy back.

w. But it's closed.

NSON. Well, what of it? We'll open it.
e've got to get Happy back.

w. How?

NSON. Suppose we get Larry Toms to
ak that joint contract.

w. All right—but how?

NSON. He's scared green of scandal. Sup-
e we show up at the opening tonight
h a drunken dame. *Larry's deserted wife!*

w. Has he got one?

NSON. We'll get one of your tarts.

w. That's too damned obvious.

NSON. Can you top it?

w. Let me think.

SON. How about a poor deserted mother?
bet he's got one.

LAW (*rises, carried away*). I know! *Happy's
father!*

BENSON. Huh?

LAW. We're going to produce Happy's father
on the air—tonight. (*Crosses to phone.*)

BENSON. Happy's father! That's swell! That's
marvellous. . . . (*Pause.*) But where'll we
get a father?

LAW (*into phone*). *Central Casting, please.*
. . . Hello. I want a handsome young extra,
a gentleman, a little down at the heel, not
too well fed, neat business suit—shiny but
well pressed; quiet manner . . . (*Door opens
and* RODNEY *enters.*)

BENSON. What do you want?

RODNEY. I received a message from Miss
Crews but apparently she's stepped out. Is
Mr. Friday here? I assume I've been called
for a part.

LAW (*into phone, as his eyes refuse to leave*
RODNEY). Never mind—cancel it. (*Hangs
up.*)

BENSON. Will you shut the door, please?
(RODNEY *complies.*) So you're an actor, my
boy? (*Paternally.*)

RODNEY. Of course, I haven't had much experience. As a matter of fact, I never appeared in a picture. I almost did. Since then
I've been out of the profession, so to speak.
Odd jobs—barbecue stand, and when that
closed I offered to show tourists homes of
the movie stars. Unfortunately I haven't a
motor car and they won't walk. . . . I don't
mind saying this call was an extremely pleasant surprise.

LAW. He's perfect!

RODNEY. Do you really think I'll do?

LAW (*inspired*). Benson, take these lines.
. . . (BENSON *goes to chair.*)

RODNEY. Oh, are there lines? Then the fee
will be fifteen dollars, I assume?

LAW. Fifteen? One hundred for you.

RODNEY. I'm afraid I'm not worth that.

LAW. This is a trailer we're making tonight.
We pay more for trailers.

RODNEY. Oh, I say!

BENSON (*at desk, with paper and pencil.*) We're going to shoot this at Grauman's Chinese in the lobby. There'll be a girl at the microphone. Her name is Susie. You come running up . . . you say . . .

LAW (*at downstage end of desk*). "Susie, why did you leave me?" . . . Say it.

RODNEY. Susie, why did you leave me?

BENSON. With feeling.

RODNEY (*with feeling*). Susie, why did you leave me?

LAW. I'm Happy's father.

RODNEY. I'm Happy's father.

BENSON. Louder.

RODNEY. *I'm Happy's father.*

LAW. I did not go down on the *Morro C* tle. . . . Susie, I've searched for you in four corners of the earth. . . . *Susie, why you leave me?*

RODNEY (*who has been repeating the e of the phrases in* LAW's *speech.*) Susie, u did you leave me?

BENSON (*jubilant*). Right!

BLACKOUT *and* CURTAIN

SCENE III

A radio voice is heard in the theatre before the rise of the curtain. We're right in Gr man's Chinese Theatre in Hollywood.

RADIO ANNOUNCER. Folks, this is the première of Cecil B. DeMille's super-spectacle of Egyptian life—*King Saul*—at Grauman's Chinese. Your favorite stars, folks, in person—and the *crowds*. They're pushing and shoving and yelling for autographs, but it's all in good-natured fun. Only two hurt and they've refused medical treatment. There's Constance Bennett, folks, with her husband, the Marquise de la Falaise. No, I'm wrong. Sorry. It's not the Marquis . . . it's not Constance Bennett. It's Mary Pickford. By the way, I've been reading our Mary's book, folks. She's selling God, folks, and that's something we all ought to be in the market for. Give a thought to God and He'll give a thought to you. That's the big lesson in *King Saul*, folks. Oh, there's Leotta Marvin. . . .
As the curtain rises, the booming voice softens to the normal tone of a radio.
Again we are in MR. FRIDAY's *office, later in the evening. At the rise of the curtain,* C.F. *is seated with* A CUTTER, *and* BENSON *sits a little apart from him, in chair back of couch, near the radio, which is on.*

RADIO ANNOUNCER. . . . And if you've seen her on the screen, I don't have to tell you she's blonde, beautiful and gorgeous. Folks, I want to tell you that this is the most thrilling première it's been my privilege to cover. *King Saul*, de Mille's super-spectacle of Egyptian life at Grauman's Chinese—

C.F. Benson, turn down that radio. We've to get three thousand feet of *Young Engla* It's a sick picture, Benson. Where's Law left word at his hotel.

BENSON. He'll be here. I'm inside man night. He's outside.

C.F. (*to* CUTTER). Cut the coronation scen it drags. And give me an underlying so thing that means something. I want a ring Britannic quality. (BENSON *turns the radio.*)

RADIO ANNOUNCER. . . . And that, folks, Mr. Stanley Oswald, veteran of old si films. . . . This is the première of *King S* Cecil B. de Mille's super-spectacle at G man's Chinese . . .

C.F. Benson, turn to page 94 and read scene. I want to lap dissolve through Qu Victoria. Simmons, you're supposed to b cutter. Give me some ideas.

RADIO ANNOUNCER. . . . And now, folks, told that none other than Larry Tom with us tonight. And he's not altogether his lonesome for hanging on his manly is none other than Mrs. Susan Seabro mother of America's Crown Prince—Ha

BENSON. Hooray!

CUTTER. I got a way of cutting all that War stuff so you won't even miss it.

RADIO ANNOUNCER. . . . And now I have the honor to present Mrs. Seabrook, the mother Happy . . .

C.F. Will you turn that infernal thing off? (*To* CUTTER) I can't cut the Boer War. It's historically valuable.

RADIO ANNOUNCER. . . . And now I have the honor to present Mrs. Seabrook, the mother Happy—

SUSIE'S VOICE. But I don't know what to say!

BENSON. Susie's on the air.

RADIO ANNOUNCER. Is it true, Mrs. Seabrook, that you and Larry have been window shopping?

SUSIE'S VOICE (*and it's very nervous indeed*). Well—

RADIO ANNOUNCER. The microphone is yours.

SUSIE'S VOICE. I would like to thank all of you for the thousands of letters and gifts that you've sent my baby Happy. I read all your letters and some of them make me cry they're so pathetic. I would like to send of you money only I haven't got that much and the studio won't let me. I'd like say a few words about the letters asking about Happy's diet. You read a lot of advertisements of what he eats but if Happy everything they said he ate I guess he'd a giant, and he's really got a very little stomach.

BENSON. Good for Susie! Truth in advertising!

C.F. (*struck by appalling thought*). Benson, is Queen Victoria alive during the Boer War?

BENSON. If she's alive in the picture, she was.

RADIO ANNOUNCER (*through this*). Folks, this the première of Cecil B. De Mille's super-spectacle of Egyptian life, *King Saul,* at Grauman's Chinese—

SUSIE'S VOICE. Can I say hello to all my girl friends at the Julia Marshall High School? Hello!

C.F. Benson—

BENSON. Sssh . . . Susie's talking.

SUSIE'S VOICE. A lot of you wonder in your letters how a grown woman can go to high

school. Well, it's not easy. I'm a mother, and the other girls aren't . . .

BENSON. Let's hope not.

SUSIE'S VOICE (*brightly*). . . . although some of the girls are very developed.

RADIO ANNOUNCER (*quickly*). Folks, this is the première of *King Saul,* Cecil B. De Mille's super-spectacle of Egyptian life. . . .

C.F. Shut that infernal thing off. (BENSON *lifts hand like traffic signal "Stop."*)

SUSIE'S VOICE. I didn't finish. I wanted to explain that I'm going to high school so I can keep up with Happy when he goes to college. Because I'm the only one Happy can go to. He hasn't got a father, and—

RADIO ANNOUNCER (*very, very firmly*). That was Happy's mother, folks. . . . She was wearing a white evening gown. And folks, meet Larry Toms, the lucky man.

C.F. Benson, can we lap-dissolve through, do you think, on page 94?

LARRY'S VOICE. I know this is going to be a wonderful picture.

RADIO ANNOUNCER. A little bird has whispered to me that you and Mrs. Seabrook are contemplating marriage, Larry.

BENSON. Well, what do you know about that!

C.F. Will you come here, Benson, with that script?

LARRY'S VOICE. Well, to tell you the truth—

BENSON. He's blushing.

LARRY'S VOICE. I kinda missed the little fella after the day's work was done. So I guess pretty soon I'll be Happy's father off the screen as well as on—

BENSON. Who wrote his speech? You or Rosetti?

RODNEY'S VOICE. Stop! I'm Happy's father!

C.F. (*rises*). What's that?

RODNEY'S VOICE. I did not go down on the *Morro Castle.* I've searched for you in the four corners of the earth. Susie, why did you leave me?

C.F. (*excitedly*). Did you hear that?

BENSON (*softly*). Yes. I wonder what that was . . . (*Cries are heard of "Here, Officer" —inarticulate shouts—a siren.*)

RADIO ANNOUNCER. Folks, there was a slight interruption. That voice you heard was a young man . . . he . . . well, he threw his arms about Mrs. Seabrook and kissed her. There's some confusion—a police officer is making his way through—they've got the young man . . . no, they haven't got him. . . . Folks, this is the opening of Cecil B. De Mille's super-spectacle of Egyptian life, *King Saul,* at Grauman's Chinese . . . (BENSON *turns it off.*)

C.F. (*stunned*). Good Gad! (*Phone rings. He moves to it.*)

BENSON (*shakes his head*). Strangest thing I ever heard.

C.F. Oh, hello, B.K. . . . Yes, I've just heard it over the radio . . . (*Miserable*) I'm sitting here trying to cut *Young England* . . . what? . . . But, B.K., . . . yes, of course, it's a serious situation . . . I agree with you . . . yes, . . . yes . . . of course . . . I'll get hold of the mother immediately. (*He rises; hangs up, still dazed. To* BENSON) B.K.'s coming down to the studio! (*Phone rings*) Yes . . . Look here, I've nothing to say to the press. It's a canard. (*He hangs up.*) (*Phone rings again.*) I won't answer it. (MISS CREWS *enters.*)

MISS CREWS. Doctor Tompkins is calling you, Mr. Friday. He says it's important.

C.F. What's he want? I'm not in. Call Mrs. Seabrook's house and have her ring me the minute she comes in.

MISS CREWS. Yes, Mr. Friday. (*She exits.*)

C.F. Benson, do you think that young man was genuine?

BENSON (*rises, crosses around downstage end of couch*). Search me.

C.F. Well, we'll soon find out. B.K.'s set the police after him.

BENSON (*a little disturbed*). Why do that? Best thing the studio can do is ignore it.

C.F. We can't ignore it. This has brought up the whole paternity issue.

BENSON. What of it?

C.F. Suppose Happy has a skeleton in [his] closet?

BENSON (*lies on couch*). I don't even kn[ow] if he's got a closet.

C.F. Save your gags for your pictures. Th[ey'll] need them. I've never heard B.K. so excite[d.] (*Crosses to window.*) What do you thi[nk] the reaction will be in the sticks—in t[he] provinces? An illegitimate baby!

BENSON. This is 1935.

C.F. To me, yes. But how many intellectu[als] have we in America?

BENSON. One.

C.F. You don't seem to realize—

BENSON. Why, this is going to send Happ[y's] stock up one hundred per cent. From n[ow] on he's not only cute, he's romantic.

C.F. He's illegitimate! I know America!

CUTTER (*studying the script*). What ab[out] Prince Albert? I can cut him out of [the] picture and you won't even miss him.

C.F. (*crossing below desk*). Yes, yes, Si[m]mons. You go to the cutting room and [do] the best you know how. (SIMMONS *rises a[nd] puts chair up against wall.*) I've someth[ing] more urgent right now. (*Crosses to* S[IM]MONS.) And, for God's sake, Simmons, [get] me some trumpets that sound like trump[ets.]

CUTTER (*not gruffly, but politely*). You s[ure] you don't mean a trombone, C.F.?

C.F. No. I mean trumpets. I'm not a music[ian] but I know what I mean. Trumpets—t[he] slide. (*He pantomimes a trombone, [of] course.*)

BENSON (*to* CUTTER). He wants a slide tru[m]pet. (CUTTER *exits.*) (*Simultaneously through other door* GR[EEN] *and* SLADE *appear.*)

GREEN. Well, we've got that roundelay.

C.F. What do you want? What roundel[ay?] (*Phone rings.*)

GREEN. Park it, Otto. (*Both go to piano.*)

C.F. (*at phone*). Yes—yes—no, Mr. Fri[day] is not here. He has nothing to say to [the] press. (*He hangs up.*)

EEN. You're going to be enthusiastic about
s. We've been up all night working on it.
ADE *starts playing Beethoven's Turkish
rch. As* C.F. *starts toward the piano, the
one rings*). Smooth, ain't it?

. (*at phone*). Miss Crews? Where's Mrs.
abrook? Why haven't you got her? (*To*
EEN) I will not listen to any more music.

EEN. Get a load of this. It's the real McCoy.

. (*at phone*). Yes—I'm holding the line—
right, never mind. Call me. (*Hangs up.*
SLADE *and* GREEN) I'll call the studio
ards if you don't stop that infernal din.
report you to B.K. for insubordination.
have your contracts torn up!

EEN. Are you kidding, or is this on the
el?

. Get out!

EEN. O.K. Don't get tough! Come on,
to. (*Crosses back of couch to door.*) But
a fine how-do-you-do when you call up
ouple of artists late at night and put 'em
work going through Beethoven's sym-
onies for a little inspiration and then give
m the bum's rush just because you ain't
the mood. (GREEN *and* SLADE *exit.*)

ARRY *and* ROSETTI *enter, both in tails and
pers.*)

SETTI. Now calm down, Larry, calm
wn—

RRY. I'm not saying a word.

. Where's Mrs. Seabrook? What did you
with her?

RRY. I don't know, and I don't care.

NSON (*mockingly*). "I kinda missed the
le fella after the day's work was done—"

. (*quickly*). Look here, Larry, I want to
ow what Susie said. Did she know the
ung man? What did she say?

RRY. You listen to what *I* gotta say. I ain't
in' to go through with no contract to play
th no unbaptized baby!

SETTI (*placatingly*). Just a moment, Lar-
—

RRY. I'm through! (*Overwhelmed with the
mory.*) On the air—with all my fans
ening in! I'm serving you notice now.

I ain't marrying her. I ain't doing no more
pictures with Happy.

ROSETTI. Larry, will you listen to reason?

LARRY. There's only one thing you can do for
me, Rosetti. Get me a doctor. I'm going up
to my dressing room. I need a sedative.
(LAW *enters quietly.*)

BENSON. Don't stand there. Get him a doctor—

LAW. Take me. I'm a qualified veterinary.
(ROSETTI *exits with* LARRY.)

C.F. Law— (BENSON *sits up.*)

LAW. Hello, C.F. I just got your message
at the hotel. *Young England* in trouble?
Well, the old salvaging crew will pitch in.
(*Takes off his coat.*)

C.F. Were you there?

LAW. Where? At the opening? Yes. Extraordinary, wasn't it?

BENSON (*significantly*). *We* heard it over
the radio.

LAW (*casually*). How'd it come over?

BENSON (*admiringly*). Clear as a bell!

LAW. It certainly broke Larry up. You
should have seen our chivalrous hero running from the rescue. Why, the wind whistled right past me!

C.F. Law, do you think that fellow was a
crank, or do you think he was really—

LAW (*judicially*). Hard to say. He had a
sinister underlip.

C.F. (*into phone*). Miss Crews, did you get
Mrs. Seabrook's house? No one answers?
Someone *must* answer—she has a ménage!
(*Hangs up. Dictograph buzzes.*) Hello?

B.K.'s VOICE. Look here, Friday . . .

C.F. Yes, B.K.

B.K.'s VOICE. Did you get any dope on that
young man?

C.F. No. I can't get any information. No one
seems to know.

B.K.'s VOICE. Why not? I ask you to do the
simplest little thing and, as usual, you fall
down on me.

c.f. (*piteously*). Why blame me? I was sitting here cutting *Young England*.

b.k.'s voice. Don't bother me with *Young England*. You come up here—I want to talk with you.

c.f. Yes, B.K. I'll be right up. (*He moves to the door; sighs.*) Sometimes I wonder if this industry is worth the sacrifice. (*He exits.*)

benson (*smiles*). What'd you do with him?

law. Put him in an office across the hall.

benson (*aghast*). What? Why here?

law. They won't look for him here.

benson. Why didn't you dump him somewhere else?

law. And leave him free to roam—and blab? Listen, Benson, B.K.'s called the Chief personally and the whole damn police department is scouring the town for Rodney. (*Crosses to liquor cabinet; pours a drink.*) And you don't know what I've been up against with Rodney. (*He drinks.*) In his own peculiar English fashion, he's not entirely nitwitted. I had to shove him at the mike, and he's been demanding explanations ever since.

benson. One question: What'll we do with him?

law (*crossing back to couch; sits*). Frankly, I planned everything but Rodney's disposal. I don't know. But given a little time we'll work this problem out.

benson (*really aghast now*). Time?

law. Rodney's all right. He doesn't know it, but I've locked him in.

benson. Listen: I've got a wife to support! I've got a job to keep! I haven't got Vermont on my mind! I *like* writing pictures! I'm no goddamn realist!

law (*soothingly*). Easy, there, easy—

benson. If B.K. even dreamed we had anything to do with this we'd be blacklisted in the industry.

law (*rising*). Give me a chance to think, will you? Why the panic? I'll admit I've overlooked a few details.

benson. Get that guy out of the studio. P__ him on a plane to Mexico. Strangle him I don't care what you do.

law. No—no. Murder leads to theft an__ theft leads to deceit. Haven't you read D__ Quincey?

benson. C.F. may breeze in here any minut__ Will you get going!

law. Very well, my sweet—I go. (*He star__ for door, remembers that he had a coa__ looks around room and finally locates__ on couch. Gets it and exits. Phone rings__*)

benson (*into phone*). Hello . . . Yes. Rig__ here. Oh, hello, darling. How are you fee__ ing? (*Tenderly*) Of course I recognize__ your voice . . . Pearl, I'll be home in half a__ hour. . . . Less . . . Well, what are you cr__ ing about? . . . But I told you I couldn__ take you to the opening. Well, if Loui__ was going why didn't you go with them__ They'd be tickled to have you . . . Liste__ darling . . . I know . . . I know . . . Ye__ I'm listening . . . (law *re-enters—a chang__* law. *He goes right to the second telephone__*

law (*picking up the second telephone__*) Give me the front gate!

benson (*into phone*). Yes, darling . . . y__ . . . (*Sincerely*) Darling, please—please do__ say that.

law. Smitty, this is Mr. Law. Any strang__ go through the gate in the last ten minute__ . . . No?

benson (*sighs*). Yes, darling. . . .

law. Well, listen. The fellow that was __ the air tonight—Happy's father—yes! H__ loose in the studio . . . Yeah. . . .

benson (*turns to* law, *still holding t__ phone*). What?

law. Grab him and hold him. Don't __ anyone come near him. Report to me p__ sonally . . . yeah . . .

benson. Darling, I'll call you back. (*Sla__ down the phone.*)

law (*hangs up*). The damn cleaning __ man let him out!

benson (*apoplectic*). I told you, didn't __ I told you you shouldn't have brought h__ here! (susie *enters. She has been magn__*

*atly decked out for the opening, but
spite her splendor she seems extremely
happy.*)

SIE. Oh, Mr. Benson . . . I tried to get
u at your house but Mrs. Benson said
u were here. I tried to get you, too, Mr.
w, at the hotel.

w. Now, now, Susie—I know—I know.

SIE. Oh, I should never have gone to that
ening. I didn't want to go. When I was
essing I put my slip on the wrong side.
new something terrible was going to hap-
n. And then in the nursery when I went
say good night to Happy, he wouldn't
his formula. And he wouldn't say good
ght to me. He was so cross. I told Larry I
dn't want to leave Happy—but he insisted
and then the way Larry ran out on me—

w (*consolingly*). Now, now—

SIE. Why should he do that? Oh, I was
ashamed . . . I didn't even see the pic-
e. And then when I got home—I knew I
uldn't have gone—I should never have
t Happy. When I went to the hospital. . . .

w. Hospital?

NSON. Hospital?

SIE. They won't let me in . . . not for two
eks.

NSON (*crosses to* SUSIE). Happy's in the
spital?

SIE (*puzzled*). Happy's got the measles.

w. What?

IE. And they won't let me come near him.

NSON. Measles!

w. He certainly picked the right time for

SIE. That's why he wouldn't eat his for-
la.

.'s VOICE (*off-stage; grimly*). Well, we'll
— (*As he opens the door*) I brought you
ne visitors, boys. Come in. (RODNEY *enters
h* STUDIO OFFICER. *To* RODNEY) Are these
men?

NEY. They most certainly are.

IE (*crosses to* RODNEY). You know you're
Happy's father.

RODNEY. Of course not, but—

SUSIE. You couldn't be!

RODNEY. Of course not! My dear, I'm very
sorry. Look here, we always seem to meet
under extraordinary circumstances . . . I
never dreamt . . . I'd no idea . . . It was
all so spectacular . . . And to do this to
you— You were so kind to me . . . They
said it was a trailer . . . I didn't realize until
I was in the midst of it . . . And then I
found myself in a car . . . with him . . .
(*Indicates* LAW.) I asked him to bring me
to you at once. Instead, he locked me in a
dusty office.

C.F. So you boys put him up to it!

LAW. Before you say anything you'll be sorry
for, C.F. . . . (*Turns to officer*) Smitty, who
called you tonight to tell you this unfortunate young man was loose in the studio?

OFFICER. *You* did, Mr. Law.

LAW (*grandly*). That's all.

BENSON. Take him away.

LAW. It's an obvious psychiatric case, C.F.

BENSON (*to* C.F.). I wouldn't be surprised if
he's the boy that's been springing out of
bushes.

LAW. Certainly. Look at the way he kissed
Susie!

RODNEY (*appalled*). But you coached me for
hours. Both of you. Wait—here are my lines.
(*He fumbles in his pocket.*) I know I have
them—unless I've lost them.

LAW. So you're an author, too! And I thought
it was extemporaneous.

RODNEY. Here—here they are! My dear, will
you please read these lines? (*He hands the
paper to* SUSIE.) They're the very words I
spoke over the radio.

SUSIE (*reads and backs away from* RODNEY).
You never said *these* lines. You *must* be a
crank. Maybe you do spring out of bushes.

RODNEY (*stares*). Oh, I beg your pardon. My
lines are on the other side.

LAW (*grabs for paper*). I'll take that! Susie—

C.F. (*taking paper out of* SUSIE's *hand,
brushes* LAW *aside*). Just a minute. (*Reads*)

"She's a high-handed rich bitch."—*Tiger Tamer!*—There it is in the corner. *Tiger Tamer* by J. Carlyle Benson and Robert Law!

LAW (*hurt to the quick*). It's a forgery. Benson, we've been framed!

C.F. (*grimly*). This is the last prank you'll ever play. (*Clicks the dictograph.*)

MISS CREWS (*enters*). The new trumpets are here. (*For once, c.f. is not interested. The trumpets blare out.*)

C.F. (*into dictograph*). B.K.? I just found out—Benson and Law put that young man on the radio.

B.K.'s VOICE. Are you sure of that?

C.F. I have the proof. The young man is in my office.

B.K.'s VOICE. All right, fire them. I don't want them on this lot. If they think they can get away with that—

C.F. Fire them? Of course I'll fire the (LARRY'S VOICE *is heard as he enters.*)

LARRY. Don't tell me nothing—let go of n (DOCTOR *and* ROSETTI *enter, following* LAR *and struggling with him.*)

C.F. Quiet there—

LARRY. Let go of me!

C.F. Larry, I have neither the time nor t patience to pander to actors!

LARRY (*bellowing with the hurt roar of wounded bull*). No? Babies, huh . . . (*Tur on* SUSIE) You—you—

SUSIE (*frightened; runs to* BENSON). What you want?

LARRY. What do I want? That goddar baby of yours has given me the measles!

CURTAIN

ACT THREE

A hospital corridor. Several weeks later. Facing us are several doors, punctuated by little white cards identifying the patients within.

As the curtain rises, a white-clad NURSE *is walking down the corridor bearing a cover tray. Before she disappears,* BENSON *enters. He knocks on the door of the room wh* HAPPY *is ensconced.* SUSIE *opens the door.*

SUSIE. Oh, hello, Mr. Benson. I'd ask you to come in but Happy's still sleeping. The doctor says he can be discharged tomorrow or the day after, he's getting along so fine. Where's Mr. Law?

BENSON. I don't know. We haven't been patronizing the same bar-rooms.

SUSIE. You look as if you didn't get much sleep.

BENSON (*slumping into a wheel chair*). I didn't.

SUSIE (*pityingly*). Why don't you go home?

BENSON. Home?

SUSIE. Is there anything wrong?

BENSON. Not a thing! Everything's fine.

SUSIE. How's Mrs. Benson?

BENSON. She's fine.

SUSIE. That's good. I called your house thank her for the radio for Happy but t said you moved.

BENSON. We *were* moved.

SUSIE. You mean you were thrown out?

BENSON. If you want to be technical ab it, yes.

SUSIE. Oh, I'm sorry.

BENSON (*broodingly*). What hurts is Agg fino Jesus.

SUSIE. Who?

BENSON. My favorite Filipino butler. slapped a lien on my brand-new Packa

SUSIE. Oh!

BENSON. That's what the missionaries tau *him!*

SIE. You boys shouldn't have played that ...e on me. You only hurt yourselves. Please ...n't drink any more, Mr. Benson.

...NSON. So it's come to that! You're going ... reform me.

SIE. Well, I feel just like a sister to you ...ys. That's why I couldn't stay mad at you. ...ase, Mr. Benson, if you need money— ...can give you some. I mean—when the ...dio sends Happy's checks. They haven't ...t them yet.

...NSON (*looking up*). They haven't? How ...ny do they owe you?

...SIE. Two. I called Mr. Friday but he ...uldn't talk to me. Do you think they're ...cking Happy?

...NSON. They can't do that. Measles are an ... of God. (NURSE *enters with box of flow-* ...)

...RSE. Some flowers for you, Mrs. Seabrook.

...IE (*extending her hand for it*). Oh, ...nk you.

...RSE. And he'd like to know if he can ...me up to see you. He's downstairs.

...IE (*embarrassed*). Oh . . .

...SON. Who's downstairs? Who's sending ... flowers?

...IE (*reluctantly*). It's Mr. Bevan. You ...ow—

...SON. You haven't been seeing our Neme-...

...IE. Oh, no. But he's been writing me ...ry day and sending me flowers. I didn't ... you. I didn't want to get you excited.

...SON (*to* NURSE; *sweetly*). Tell him to ...me up, Nurse. And stand by.

...IE (*quickly*). Oh, no, Nurse. He's not ... come up. I don't want to see him. Ever. ... give him back his flowers. (*She hands* ... *back to* NURSE.)

...RSE (*taking it*). Very well. (*She exits.*)

...SON. Why deprive me of the pleasure ...kicking an actor?

...IE. It wasn't his fault. After all, you put ... up to it.

BENSON (*outraged*). Are you defending him?

SUSIE. Oh, no, I'm just as disappointed in him as you are. But I'm trying to be fair. (*She pauses.*) He writes very nice letters. (*A far-away look comes into her eyes.*)

BENSON (*suspiciously*). What kind of letters do you write him?

SUSIE (*hastily*). Oh, I don't write *any* letters.

BENSON. Good!

SUSIE. I'm afraid of my spelling. (LAW *enters. There's an air of on-my-way about him.*)

LAW. Hello, Susie. . . . And good-bye, Susie.

SUSIE. Hello, Mr. Law. Are you going away?

LAW. I am.

SUSIE. Where?

LAW. Where I belong. Vermont. Where you can touch life and feel life, and write it! (*Glares at* BENSON.)

BENSON. When does the great exodus begin?

LAW. In exactly thirty-five minutes. I'm flying back to my native hills, like a homing pigeon. No stopping in New York for me! I've chartered a plane—right to Vermont.

BENSON. Chartered a plane! Where'd you get the money?

LAW (*grudgingly*). Well, there are twelve Rotarians coming along.

BENSON. You'll be back in a week.

SUSIE (*eagerly*). Will you, Mr. Law?

LAW (*scornfully*). Back to what? Sunshine and psyllium seed? Listen, I've got me a little shack overlooking the valley . . . I'm going to cook my own food, chop my own wood, and *write*—

BENSON (*sardonically*). At twenty below?

LAW (*rapturously*). Snow! . . . God, how I love snow! (*He raises his eyes to Heaven.*)
　　And since to look at things in bloom
　　Fifty springs are little room,
　　About the woodlands, I will go
　　To see the cherry—hung with snow!

SUSIE. That's poetry.

LAW. A. E. Housman! *Shropshire Lad*. (*He pats the book in his pocket*.)

BENSON. There's plenty of snow in Arrowhead.

LAW. Yeah; they deliver it in trucks. And even when it's real you think it's cornflakes.

SUSIE. You won't drink too much in Vermont, will you, Mr. Law?

LAW. Only the heady wine air that has no dregs!

SUSIE. Because you're crazy enough without drinking.

LAW (*defensively*). I drank for escape . . . escape from myself . . . but now I'm free! I've found peace!

SUSIE. You'll say good-bye to Happy before you go? I want him to remember you.

LAW. Right now!

SUSIE. Wait! I'll see if he's awake. (*She enters* HAPPY's *room*.)

BENSON. Will you send me a copy of the book—autographed?

LAW. You get copy number one—first edition.

BENSON. What's the book about?

LAW. I'm going to bare my soul . . . I'm going to write life in the raw. I've got the opening all planned—two rats in a sewer!

BENSON. Sounds delightful.

LAW (*scornfully*). You wouldn't appreciate real writing. You've been poisoned. On second thought, I won't send you a book.

BENSON. Tell me more about the rats. What's your story?

LAW (*slightly patronizing*). This isn't a picture that you paste together, Mr. Benson. I'm going to write Life. Life isn't a story . . . it's a discordant overture to death!

BENSON. Well, if you want people to read it, the boy had better meet the girl.

LAW. There is no girl. There is no boy. These are people—real, live people—listen! I'm not even going to use a typewriter! I'm going to weigh every word—with a pencil!

BENSON. Well, maybe you're on the rig[ht] track. You've got something to say—and th[e] talent to say it with.

LAW. It's finally penetrated!

BENSON. You're probably doing the rig[ht] thing.

LAW. The only thing. It's different with yo[u] —you've got a wife.

BENSON. I had.

LAW. Huh?

BENSON. Oh—uh—Pearl left last night.

LAW. No! I'm sorry.

BENSON (*shrugs*). You can't blame her. Sh[e] wasn't wild about marrying me in the fi[rst] place. I coaxed her into it. I painted som[e] pretty pictures for her. It just didn't pan ou[t].

LAW. You still want her?

BENSON (*almost to himself*). I guess I do.

LAW. Personally, I'd say the hell with her.

BENSON (*smiles bitterly*). The trouble is [I] don't mean it when I say it. (ROSETTI e[n]ters.)

ROSETTI. Hello, boys.

LAW (*cheerily*). Hello, louse. Get Benson [a] job, will you? He wants to stay in th[is] God-forsaken hole.

ROSETTI. Listen! I'm not handling secon[d] hand writers. Chicken feed! Right now I [am] immersed in a three million dollar deal.

LAW (*interested*). Yeah?

ROSETTI. Yeah. With Gaumont British, a[nd] I'm underestimating when I say three m[il]lion because B.K.'s turned down three m[il]lion. Why should I bother with writers [on] the blacklist? So don't go calling me [a] louse! (SUSIE *enters*.)

SUSIE (*gaily*). Happy has his eyes open. Y[ou] want to come in now, Mr. Law?

LAW. Coming, Susie. (*He follows* SUSIE i[nto] HAPPY's *room*.)

BENSON. Rosetti—(*going to him, whisp*[er]*ing*)—Law wants to leave. He's flying [in] half an hour. Can you call up the studi[o] an you get us a one-picture contract? 'e'll make you our agent for life. *He's ιving!*

ιSETTI. Sure, he's leaving. Nobody wants m.

NSON. How do you know? You haven't ed.

ιSETTI. I've tried. I don't let my personal elings interfere with commissions.

NSON. Listen, I've been a scene painter, op boy, camera man, director, producer . I even sold film in Australia . . . they n't throw me out of this business!

SETTI (*crosses to a door and throws it ck*). They won't touch you with a ten- ot pole. You, Law, or Happy.

NSON. Or Happy?

ιSETTI. I gave B.K. a swell angle. Listen on KNX this afternoon.

NSON. Huh?

ιSETTI. The world is full of babies. You n get them two for a nickel. (*He opens ner door and meets* LARRY *coming out*.) ello, Larry. I was just coming in to see u. (NURSE *pushes* LARRY *in wheel chair to corridor*.)

w's VOICE. Good-bye, Happy. (*He enters th* SUSIE.) Good-bye, Susie.

SIE. Good-bye, Mr. Law.

w. Hello, Larry. How's every little spot?

RRY. What's the idea?

w. What idea?

RRY. What's the idea of sending me a box dead spiders?

w. Didn't you like the box?

RRY. You wait until I'm through con- escing!

RSE. Now, don't excite yourself. You heard hat the doctor said. You're going for your n bath now. (*She wheels him out*.)

ιSETTI. I'll go along with you, Larry. I've t some great news for you. B.K.'s lending u out to Mascot! (*He exits*.)

RRY (*as he goes out*). What?

LAW. Well, Susie, take good care of Happy.

SUSIE. Oh, I will.

LAW. Continue your education.

SUSIE. I'm doing that.

LAW (*quickly*). What's the capital of Ne-braska?

SUSIE. Lincoln.

LAW. Who hit Sir Isaac Newton on the bean with an apple?

SUSIE. The law of gravity.

LAW. Who said, "Don't give up the ship?"

SUSIE. Captain James Lawrence in the bat-tle of Lake Erie, 1813.

LAW. Don't give up the ship, Susie. I'll write you. (*He kisses her on the forehead*.)

SUSIE. Good-bye, Mr. Law. I've got to go back to Happy. (*Her voice breaks*.) I feel awful funny—your going away. (*Exits*.)

BENSON (*finally*). Well, you bastard—get out of here.

LAW. I'm going, stinker. (*Crosses to* BENSON. *They look at each other. A pause. Then* LAW *extends hand. They shake.* LAW *moves to go*.)

BENSON (*without turning*). Say— (LAW *stops*.) I don't suppose you'll be interested —Rosetti finally admitted Paramount wants us. Two thousand bucks a week to save Dietrich. We can close the deal in three or four days.

LAW (*turns slowly*). My plane leaves in twenty-five minutes. And you're a liar!

BENSON. I'm not trying to hold you back. But I figured this time you might *save* your money and—

LAW. I can live on twelve dollars a week in Vermont—in luxury!

BENSON. It would kind of help *me* out— If I could lay my hands on some ready dough Pearl might listen to reason.

LAW (*casually*). Well, we loaned out a lot of money in our time. Collect it. And send me my share.

BENSON. I thought of that. The trouble is I don't remember just who it was—and how much. The only one I remember is Jascha Simkovitch.

LAW. Who?

BENSON. Jascha Simkovitch. The fellow that came over with Eisenstein. Don't you remember? You made a wonderful crack about him. He said "There's a price on my head in Russia." And you said, "Yeah—two rubles." (*Laughs. He is flattering* LAW *smoothly.*)

LAW (*laughs with him*). Sure, I remember him. Why, we gave that bed-bug three thousand bucks! Get hold of him and collect it.

BENSON. He's in Paris. What's-his-name came over and said Jascha was living at the Ritz bar.

LAW. Then you can't collect it. Well, I'm off. (*He moves to exit once more.*)

BENSON (*as if struck with sudden thought*). Wait a minute! I've got a great gag for you! Let's call Jascha up in Paris—on Larry's phone! (*Chuckles, throws arms around* LAW. *Both laugh.*) Can you imagine Larry's face when he gets the bill? A farewell rib!

LAW (*hesitates*). Have I got time?

BENSON (*reassuringly; looks at his watch*). You've got plenty of time.

LAW. I'll work fast. Stand guard, Benson. (*He enters* LARRY'S *room.* BENSON *follows and partly closes door.*)

LAW'S VOICE. I'm talking for Mr. Toms. I want to put a call through to Paris, France. . . . I want Jascha Simkovitch . . . Hotel Ritz, Paris. . . . Listen, don't worry about the charges . . . That's right—Jascha, as in Heifetz . . . S-i-m-k-o-v-i-t-c-h. (BENSON *closes door on* LAW. NURSE *enters with registered letter, knocks on* SUSIE'S *door.* BENSON *looks at his watch.* SUSIE *appears.*)

NURSE. Registered letter for you, Mrs. Seabrook.

SUSIE. For me?

NURSE. You'll have to sign for it. There's a return receipt on it. (SUSIE *signs.*)

SUSIE. Now what do I do?

NURSE. Now you give me the receipt back and I'll give it to the postman. He's waiting

for it. Here's your letter. (NURSE *exits.* SUS opens letter.*)

SUSIE (*cheerily*). Why—it's from Mr. F day. (LAW *emerges, as she opens the letter*)

LAW. The service had better be good there'll be no farewell rib. I haven't g much time.

SUSIE. Oh, didn't you go yet, Mr. Law?

LAW. I'm on my way!

SUSIE (*reading letter*). What does Mr. Frid mean when he says they're taking advanta of Clause 5A?

LAW. What? Let me see that. (*He rea the letter.* BENSON *looks over his shoulder* Well, this is the goddamest . . .

SUSIE. You mustn't swear so much. I do mind—I'm used to it—but Happy mig hear you. What does it mean?

LAW (*reading*). Clause 5A—when an art through illness—for a period of more th fourteen days—

BENSON. They're just using that for an cuse. It's the paternity issue!

SUSIE. What paternity issue?

BENSON. They're crazy! That kid's going be as good as he ever was—better.

SUSIE. What does it mean?

LAW. It means, Susie—Happy is out.

SUSIE. Out?

BENSON. Yeah. Finished—done. At the a of eight months—In his prime!

SUSIE. Out of pictures?

BENSON (*turning on* LAW). And there's man who did it. It was your brilliant id

SUSIE (*such a nice girl!*). Oh, no. After it was just like a dream. I had to wake some time.

LAW (*as phone rings*). I guess that's Pa

SUSIE. What's Paris? (*Phone still rings.*)

BENSON. Go ahead and have your farew rib, and get out, author! (*Phone still rin* LAW *enters room.*)

SUSIE. What's Paris?

son (*going to door of* LARRY's *room*). A
y in France.

w (*in room*). Hello—right here.—Yes—
—I'm ready. Hello! . . . Hello—Jascha?
cha Simkovitch? This is Bobby Law. Is
aining in Paris? . . . well, it's not raining
e!

son. Wonderful age we're living in!

w (*in room*). Listen, Jascha, are you so-
-? . . . How come? . . . Oh, you just
there! . . . You're going to London?
. Today? . . . Hold the wire. (LAW
ers.) I've got an idea! *Let's buy the stu-*
!

son. What?

w. You heard Rosetti. Gaumont British
offering three million. Let's get Jascha to
d a cable—sign it Gaumont British—of-
ing four!

son. Why be petty? Offer five!

LAW (*judicially*). Right! (*Exits into room.*)

SUSIE. You boys are very peculiar.

LAW (*in room*). Jascha—got a pencil and
paper? Fine. Listen, Jascha, we want you
to send a cable from London as follows:
Quote. . . . (LARRY *enters in his wheel chair.*
BENSON *closes the door hurriedly.*)

LARRY. Hey, that's my room!

BENSON (*firmly shutting the door*). A private conversation should be private.

LARRY. What's the idea of using my phone?

BENSON. Do you object?

LARRY. Certainly I object. I ain't gonna pay
for your calls.

BENSON. All right, if that's the way you feel
about it—here's your nickel!

BLACKOUT *and* CURTAIN

SCENE II

In Your Own Home. That is, if you have one, and if you listen to the radio.

DIO ANNOUNCER. Ladies and Gentlemen,
s is Station KNX—the Voice of Holly-
od. At this time we take great pleasure in
nouncing the winner of the Royal Studios'
by Star Contest to find the successor to
ppy who retired from the screen after
illness. Ladies and Gentlemen, the lucky
by is Baby Sylvester Burnett, infant son

of Mr. and Mrs. Oliver Burnett of Glendale,
California. Congratulations, Mr. and Mrs.
Burnett. Contracts for your baby are waiting
in Mr. C. Elliot Friday's office at the Royal
Studios. Incidentally, Mr. Friday asks that
you bring your baby's birth certificate and
your marriage licence. This is KNX, the
Voice of Hollywood. (*Chimes are heard.*)

SCENE III

MR. FRIDAY's *office, the following day.* MR. FRIDAY *is sitting at his desk, dictating to*
SS CREWS.

. My dear Mr. Pirandello. . . . On second
ught, you'd better make that Signor Pir-
dello. . . . I am writing to ascertain if
ssibly you have something in your trunk
every author has—which would be suit-
e as a vehicle for our new baby star,
by Sylvester Burnett. It can be either a
rt story or sketch or a few lines which
can jot down at your leisure and which
can whip up into suitable material. I am
iting of my own volition as both Mrs.
day and I are great admirers of you.

Very truly yours. . . . Now take a letter to
Stark Young. (*Dictograph buzzes.*) Yes?

B.K.'s VOICE. Listen, Friday—

C.F. What, B.K.?

B.K.'s VOICE. Come right up here. I want to
see you. We've got a new cable from Gaumont British.

C.F. Gaumont British? Yes, sir, I'll be right
up. (*He rises.*) Miss Crews, have you the
contracts for the Burnett baby?

MISS CREWS. Right on your desk, Mr. Friday. And the parents are in the commissary.

C.F. Good. I've got to go up and see B.K. (*Exits.*)

GREEN (*who enters almost simultaneously, followed by* SLADE.) Where is he? Where's C.F.?

MISS CREWS. You can't shoot him today.

GREEN. It's a wonder we don't. We're walking up and down in front of the projection room developing an idea when we hear a number—our number— We go in, and it's in *Young England!* Our song! They don't even tell us about it—they murdered it! They run dialogue over it. You got to spot a song—we ask for Guy Lombardo and they give us a six-piece symphony orchestra!

MISS CREWS. If you buy me a handkerchief I promise to cry. Lace, if you don't mind.

GREEN. Lissen—play her the number the way it should be.

MISS CREWS. Must you?

SLADE. Oh, what's the use?

GREEN. Give her the chorus.

SLADE. I'm losing my pep.

GREEN. You might as well hear it. Nobody else will. (SLADE *plays.*) Will you listen to that? Ain't it a shame?

> You promised love undying,
> And begged me to believe;
> Then you left, and left me crying
> With pain in my heart, and my heart
>   on my sleeve.
>
> I really shouldn't blame you
> Because you chose to leave;
> But one thing forever will shame you—
> It's the pain in my heart, and my heart
>   on my sleeve.

(C.F. *has entered.*)

C.F. Miss Crews!

MISS CREWS. Yes, Mr. Friday?

C.F. Miss Crews, get hold of Benson and Law right away!

MISS CREWS. Who?

C.F. Have Benson and Law come here—immediately.

MISS CREWS. Yes, Mr. Friday.

GREEN (*as* SLADE *pounds away*). That's tł chorus! That's the chorus that you mu[r]dered!

C.F. Wait a minute, Miss Crews! Get m the hospital. I want to talk to Happy mother.

MISS CREWS. Yes, Mr. Friday. (*She exits.*)

C.F. Miss Crews! Call my florist and tell hi[m] to send Happy a bouquet of roses. An[d] some orchids for his mother, right awa[y] (*He turns to* GREEN.) Will you stop th noise! (*He picks up telephone.*)

GREEN. Noise? The song that you murdere[d] We just wanna see if you got a conscienc[e]

C.F. (*into phone*). Miss Crews, call up Ma[r]nin's and tell them to send a radio to tł hospital for Happy. One of those slick, mo[d]ernistic sets in white. And don't forget have my card put in with the flowers. D you get Benson and Law? . . . Well, did y[ou] get Happy's mother? . . . Well, get ther (*Hangs up.*)

GREEN. Is that a song that you run dialog over, C.F.?

C.F. What are you babbling about, Gree[n] I haven't used any of your songs in *You[ng] England!*

GREEN (*outraged*). How about *Westmins[ter] Abbey in the Moonlight*? They wasn't o lyrics, but it was our tune!

C.F. I used an old Jerome Kern numb[er] we've had for years, out of the library.

GREEN (*crestfallen*). You did? (*To* SLAD[E] I thought you said it came to you in the m[i]d[dle] of the night. Where? In the library?

C.F. Will you get out of my office?

GREEN (*with sudden enthusiasm*). We [got] a new number you'll be crazy about.

C.F. I've got too much on my mind to list[en] to your tinny effusions. I told the studio hire Richard Strauss and no one else. O[ne] great composer is worth twenty of your il (ROSETTI *enters with* LARRY.)

LARRY. Looka here, C.F., I just got out o[f] sick bed to see you.

. What do you want, Larry? (SLADE *plays*
.) What do you want? I'm very busy.
urns to GREEN.) Will you please go? I
ll not listen!

EEN (*as the worm turns*).... O.K., music
er! (GREEN *and* SLADE *exit*.)

RRY. I shouldn't be here. I should be on
ranch convalescing. I'm weak.

. Come to the point, Larry. Come to the
nt.

RRY (*bitterly*). What's the idea of lending
out to Mascot? I'm a star! I ain't goin'
degrade myself by playing in no undig-
ed thirty-thousand-dollar feature.

. Larry, face the facts—you're through.

RRY. That's a nice thing to tell a sick man.

ETTI. Now, Larry, I told you. Your atti-
e is all wrong.

RRY. Never mind about my attitude.

. (*at the phone*). Miss Crews, have you
Benson and Law? . . . Who's gone to
mont? . . . What about Susie? . . .
at? They left the hospital? (*He hangs*
)

ETTI (*eagerly*). What's up, C.F.?

. (*finally*). This is confidential, Rosetti.
owers his voice.) Gaumont British wants
buy the company intact.

RRY. Gaumont British?

. They want all our stars, including Hap-
Naturally they want him. He's the sen-
on of London.

ETTI. But B.K. turned down three mil-
n. I've been handling that deal myself.

. They've raised it. They've just cabled
offer of five million.

ETTI. They did? Say, that's marvellous.
in on that!

RRY. Well, you better get me back from
scot quick. Gaumont British wants *me*.
hy, they made me an offer a year ago,
ly I was tied up.

. They make no mention of you.

RRY. What?

C.F. Rosetti, we've got to sign Happy immediately. Get hold of Susie and let's close.

ROSETTI. You can sign the three of 'em for a
hundred a week. They're broke. And they're
low. I'm going right after it. (*He starts
for door*.)

LARRY. Come back here. You're supposed to
be *my* agent! What are you going to do
about *me*?

ROSETTI. You're all right where you are—
with Mascot. I'll call you later, C.F. (*Exits*.)

LARRY (*to* C.F.). My agent! I been distrustin'
that guy for years. (*Exits*.)

C.F. (*who can balance a budget, picks up
phone*). Miss Crews, you didn't send those
flowers off, did you? . . . What? . . . But
they've left the hospital. What about the
radio? . . . Well, call them up right away
and cancel it. . . . Who? . . . She's here?
Send her right in! (*He crosses to greet*
SUSIE. *He is now cordial; hearty, a thing of
beauty and a joy forever*.) Well, Susie, I'm
delighted to see you. You're looking well. I
must say we've missed you. I hear the boys
are in Vermont.

SUSIE (*stands in door*). Mr. Law was going
but he missed the plane.

C.F. (*taken aback*). Well, where are they?

SUSIE. They're in B.K.'s office, getting the
contracts.

C.F. Without consulting me?

SUSIE. They said they don't trust you, Mr.
Friday.

C.F. Gad! After all I've done for them!

SUSIE (*seating herself on the couch*). Do you
mind if I sit here and do my homework?
I'm way behind and I don't want to be left
back. I'm supposed to wait here until they
get B.K.'s signature, and then I'm going to
sign.

C.F. I'm going right up to see B.K. (MISS
CREWS *enters*.)

MISS CREWS. Mr. and Mrs. Burnett have had
their coffee and now they want their contracts.

C.F. What contracts?

MISS CREWS. The parents of the other infant.

C.F. What other infant? What other infant is there except Happy?

MISS CREWS. But what'll I do with them?

C.F. Send them away. (*Now he sees* RODNEY *looking in through door.* RODNEY *has a large box of flowers.*) What do you want?

RODNEY. Here's the check for the milk—and other odd items.

C.F. Check.

RODNEY. I think you'll find it correct. I verified it at the commissary. And of course I included a service charge—and interest at six per cent. The total is two dollars and eighty-four cents. Thank you. (*Dictograph buzzes.*)

C.F. (*into dictograph*). Hello—

B.K.'s VOICE. Listen, Friday, you might as well be here. I'm settling the Happy contract with Benson and Law.

C.F. Yes, B.K. I'm coming right up. (*Phone rings; into phone*) What? . . . I never asked for trumpets in the first place. I don't want any trumpets. I want a period of utter silence. See that I get it. (*Hangs up. To* RODNEY) *You* get out!

RODNEY (*firmly*). I've something to say to Mrs. Seabrook. (SUSIE *turns away. Softly*) I brought you some flowers.

C.F. Give her her flowers, and get out. And don't let me find you here when I come back. Miss Crews, I'll be up in B.K.'s office. (*He exits.*)

RODNEY. I know you don't want to see me. (*Extends flowers.*) Won't you take them? (MISS CREWS *exits.*) I wrote, you know. I explained everything.

SUSIE (*still not facing him*). Happy's not allowed to have flowers.

RODNEY. Oh, but they're for Happy's mother —from Happy's father.

SUSIE (*turning; aghast*). Are you joking about what you did?

RODNEY. I'm not joking. Lord, no. I mean it. Look here—will you marry me? (SUSIE *stares*

at him.) I've thought it all out. I owe it you. Shall we consider it settled?

SUSIE. Did Mr. Law and Mr. Benson p you up to this, too?

RODNEY. Good Lord, no. I haven't seen the and, what's more, I don't intend to.

SUSIE. Then why do you want to marry m

RODNEY. I owe it to you.

SUSIE (*angrily*). That's no reason.

RODNEY. My visa's expired—I've two day grace. I must get a train this afternoon. A you coming with me?

SUSIE. I don't think you'd make a ve sensible father for Happy. I don't think at all.

RODNEY. I'm not at all sensible. I'm frigh fully stupid — impulsive — emotional — b I'm not really at my best these days. Mo people aren't when they're infatuated.

SUSIE. You couldn't be infatuated with m

RODNEY. But I am. Look here, it's no goo debating. My mind's made up. I don't fi quently make it up, but when I do, I sti to the end.

SUSIE. But you don't know about my pa

RODNEY. I've been through all that, in r mind. It doesn't matter.

SUSIE. But it does. I'm ashamed to tell yo

RODNEY. Please don't, then.

SUSIE. Happy's father was a bigamist.

RODNEY. Eh?

SUSIE. He married twice.

RODNEY. Is that it?

SUSIE. What did you think?

RODNEY. It doesn't really matter.

SUSIE. I didn't know he was married befc

RODNEY. But, good Lord, nobody can bla you.

SUSIE. His wife did.

RODNEY. Naturally.

E. How was I to know? And it wasn't
fault, either. He got a Mexican divorce
he didn't know it wasn't good.

NEY. Oh!

E (*drawing herself up à la Fairfax*). So
id to him, "Your duty is to your first
." And I ran away. I didn't know I
going to have Happy, then.

NEY. Have you—heard from him?

E. Oh, no. Of course, he should have
me in the first place. But he was in-
ated, too, and I didn't know any better.

NEY. Well, have you divorced him?

E. No.

NEY. You'll have to clear that matter up,
ink—immediately.

E. I can't clear it up. He's dead.

NEY. Oh!

E. She shot him.

NEY. His wife?

E. Yes.

NEY. Good Lord!

E. I hear from her sometimes. She's aw-
sorry.

EY (*brightly*). Well then, you're free to
y, aren't you?

E. Oh, I'm free, but the point is—do I
to? After all, I don't know you very
and every time we meet something
le happens. I didn't know Jack very
either, and look what happened to him.
got to be careful.

EY. But I'm not a bigamist.

E. Maybe not. You may be something

EY. But the British Consul'll vouch for
He knows my family. I haven't had
a of a life, but it's an open book.

E. Oh, I believe you. But I can't listen
y heart. I've got to listen to my head.

EY. Of course, I haven't much to offer
I've just come into a little money, and
y thirtieth birthday I come into a great
nore. We can have a flat in London and

one of my aunts is going to leave me a place
in the country.

SUSIE. That's in Europe, isn't it?

RODNEY. Yes, of course.

SUSIE. Oh, I couldn't go to Europe.

RODNEY. But why not?

SUSIE. The boys want to put Happy back
in pictures.

RODNEY. I wouldn't hear of it. That's no life
for a baby. Thoroughly abnormal. And,
furthermore, I don't like the California climate. Now in England we have the four
seasons.

SUSIE. You have?

RODNEY (*ardently*). Summer, winter, spring
and fall.

SUSIE (*finally*). I want to ask you something.

RODNEY. Certainly.

SUSIE. When I come into a room—does something happen to you?

RODNEY. Eh? Of course—very much so.

SUSIE (*rises and turns away*). Well, I'll
think it over.

RODNEY (*rises and takes* SUSIE's *arm*). Look
here, I couldn't possibly take no for an answer.

SUSIE. Of course, when you come into a
room, something happens to me, too.

RODNEY. Does it really? (SUSIE *nods. He takes
her in his arms. They kiss. Door opens and*
LAW *enters with* BENSON.)

LAW. Susie, did my eyes deceive me? Were
you kissing an actor?

BENSON. What's that?

LAW (*to* BENSON). An English actor!

BENSON. What? Didn't I tell you—?

SUSIE. Boys, I've been thinking it over—

BENSON (*wearily drops down to piano;* LAW
down to end of couch). With what?

SUSIE. I'm going to marry Rodney and I'm
going to Europe. They've got the four seasons over there, and Happy'll be normal.

RODNEY. Well put, my dear. (C.F. *enters*.)

SUSIE. So I don't think I'd better sign the contract.

RODNEY. Most certainly not!

C.F. You're not going to sign Happy?

LAW. Susie, I've just given up Vermont for a whole year—for you. A whole year out of my life—because B.K. begged me to stay and handle Happy. I've sacrificed a great book—for what? A paltry fifteen hundred dollars a week? I didn't want it!

C.F. If she doesn't sign, we'll break that contract with you, Law.

LAW. Try and do it.

SUSIE. I'm going to Europe with Rodney.

LAW. Do you want to tell Happy he's out of pictures? Do you want to break his little heart?

SUSIE. He'll understand!

BENSON (*suddenly*). Do you know who Rodney is? English Jack! Confidence man.

LAW (*quickly*). Yes! Ship's gambler, petty racketeer and heart-breaker. (RODNEY *tries to speak*.)

BENSON. Served two terms for bigamy!

SUSIE. Bigamy?

RODNEY. But that's absurd.

BENSON (*bitterly*). I've seen hundreds of your kind in Limehouse.

C.F. So have I!

BENSON (*quietly*). Listen, C.F., stay off our side!

RODNEY (*to* SUSIE). You don't believe this, of course. They can't possibly believe it themselves.

LAW. Brazening it out, eh? As sure as God made little green apples—and He did— you're not coming near Susie. We'll have you in the can and out of the country by morning.

BENSON. No sooner said— (*into phone*) Get me the Department of Justice.

SUSIE (*to* RODNEY). You see? Something terrible always happens when you come.

LAW (*to* SUSIE). And you—sign that c[ontract] tract immediately.

RODNEY. She'll do nothing of the sort. Yo[u] not to intimidate her. Do you hear? (*D[oor] opens and* LARRY *enters, accompanied middle-aged English gentleman*.)

LARRY. Come on in here, Major.

C.F. What do you want, Larry? I'm bus[y]

BENSON (*into telephone*). Department Justice? I want two of your best operati[ves] to come down to the Royal Studios im[me-] diately. Report to Mr. Friday's office.

SUSIE. Oh, but you can't do that—

LARRY (*angrily*). Just a minute. M[r.] Thompson is the representative here Gaumont British.

C.F. Oh! I'm sorry. We've been rather up[set] How do you do, Major. I'm Mr. Frida[y.]

MAJOR. How do you do, sir. I won't b[e a] moment. Mr. Toms suggested I come d[own] here. He told me you'd received a cable fr[om] my home office.

C.F. Yes—yes—

MAJOR. He was rather upset because name wasn't mentioned.

C.F. Yes, yes—

MAJOR. I called my home office, and assure me they never sent such a cabl[e.]

C.F. What?

LARRY. That's what! It was a phony.

RODNEY (*who has been trying to attrac[t] tention for some time*). Major!

MAJOR. Well! Aren't you— Why, how you do. I thought I recognized you. you with your brother. By the way, I him a few weeks ago just before I sa[w] Particularly asked me to look you up.

RODNEY. Is my name English Jack? A[m I a] ship's gambler? Have I served sente[nce] for bigamy?

MAJOR. Good Gad, no!

RODNEY. Will you vouch for me?

MAJOR (*a bore of bores*). Vouch for [you,] Bevan? Delighted! His brother—sple[ndid] chap— I met him first in India—h[e]

ain in the Coldstream Guards. His father
ᴏrd Severingham. His sister is Lady
sley—lectures, I believe. Now, let me
—

(*interrupting*). Did you say—Lord Sev-
gham?

ᴏʀ. Yes.

sᴏɴ. I beg your pardon, sir—*his* father?
indicates ʀᴏᴅɴᴇʏ.)

ᴏʀ. Yes. (ʙᴇɴsᴏɴ *shakes his head in
der.*)

ᴇ. Is your father a lord?

ᴋᴇʏ. It doesn't matter, does it?

ᴇ. If you don't care, I don't care.

ᴏʀ. If I can be of any further service—

ᴋᴇʏ. No. I think we'll sail along beauti-
now. Thanks.

ᴏʀ. Good afternoon. (*Shakes hands with
ᴋᴇʏ.*)

Who sent that cable? That's all I want
ɪow! Who sent that cable! (ᴍᴀᴊᴏʀ *and
ʏ exit.*) Who perpetrated this hoax?
's responsible for this outrage? By Gad,
ɪnd out. (*Exits.*)

ᴇʏ (*turns to* sᴜsɪᴇ). Shall we go?

. Good-bye, boys. Take care of your-
s.

(*bows; bitterly*). Thank you, milady.

. Don't drink too much.

Thank you, milady.

. You were awful good to me. Yes,
were, Rodney. They were awful good
ᴇ sometimes.

ʀᴏᴅɴᴇʏ. In that case, I don't mind shaking
hands with you. (*Starts toward* ʟᴀᴡ.)

ʟᴀᴡ (*quickly*). Don't shake hands. Just go.
Dissolve—*slow fade-out!*

ʙᴇɴsᴏɴ (*pantomiming*). Shimmer away!

ʀᴏᴅɴᴇʏ. Eh? (*Shrugs.*) Well—come, Susie.

sᴜsɪᴇ (*waving a delicate little hand*). Good-
bye, boys. (*Pause. They exit in silence.*)

ʟᴀᴡ (*tense*). I wonder what C.F.'s up to?

ʙᴇɴsᴏɴ (*struck all of a heap*). The hell
with that. Look at it—it checks! Cinderella
—Prince Charming—Boy meets girl. . . . Boy
loses girl. . . . Boy gets girl! Where's your
damned realism now? (ᴄ.ғ. *enters. He looks
grimly at the boys.*)

ᴄ.ғ. (*firmly*). Well—it's a good thing you
boys are not mixed up in this! (*He goes to
desk.*)

ʙᴇɴsᴏɴ (*slowly*). What?

ʟᴀᴡ (*slowly*). What happened, C.F.?

ᴄ.ғ. I don't understand it at all. The cable
was sent from London all right. But B.K.
should have known it was a fake. It was
sent collect. (*He picks up phone.*)

ʟᴀᴡ. Jascha always sends collect.

ᴄ.ғ. Huh? (*Into phone.*) Miss Crews, get
hold of the Burnett baby immediately. . . .
Who? . . . the *what* is here? (*Puzzled. The
answer comes in the clarion call of the
trumpets, blaring their gay, lilting notes
through the windows. Ta-ra-ta-ta-ta-ta-tata-
tata-tata! So much pleasanter than a factory
whistle, don't you think?*)

ᴄᴜʀᴛᴀɪɴ

The Women

BY CLARE BOOTHE

To BUFF COBB *with Love*

THE WOMEN

Produced by Max Gordon at the Ethel Barrymore Theatre, New York City,
ember 26, 1936, with the following cast:

(IN ORDER OF THEIR APPEARANCE)

JE	Anne Teeman	HEAD SALESWOMAN ..	Lucille Fenton
VIA (Mrs. Howard Fowler)	Ilka Chase	FIRST MODEL	Beryl Wallace
NCY BLAKE	Jane Seymour	THIRD SALESWOMAN ..	Martina Thomas
GY (Mrs. John Day)	Adrienne Marden	CRYSTAL ALLEN	Betty Lawford
TH (Mrs. Phelps Potter) ..	Phyllis Povah	A FITTER	Joy Hathaway
RY (Mrs. Stephen Haines)	Margalo Gillmore	SECOND MODEL	Beatrice Cole
S. WAGSTAFF	Ethel Jackson	PRINCESS TAMARA	Arlene Francis
GA	Ruth Hammond	EXERCISE INSTRUCTRESS	Anne Hunter
ST HAIRDRESSER	Mary Stuart	MAGGIE	Mary Cecil
OND HAIRDRESSER ..	Jane Moore	MISS WATTS	Virgilia Chew
ICURIST	Ann Watson	MISS TRIMMERBACK ..	Mary Murray
HIE	Eloise Bennett	A NURSE	Lucille Fenton
S FORDYCE	Eileen Burns	LUCY	Marjorie Main
TLE MARY	Charita Bauer	COUNTESS DE LAGE....	Margaret Douglass
S. MOREHEAD	Jessie Busley	MIRIAM AARONS	Audrey Christie
ST SALESWOMAN	Doris Day	HELENE	Arlene Francis
OND SALESWOMAN ...	Jean Rodney	SADIE	Marjorie Wood
		CIGARETTE GIRL	Lillian Norton

Directed by ROBERT B. SINCLAIR   Settings designed by JO MIELZINER
Costumes supervised by JOHN HAMBLETON

SYNOPSIS OF SCENES

ACT ONE

Scene 1.   Mary Haines' living room. A winter afternoon.
Scene 2.   A hairdresser's. An afternoon, a few days later.
Scene 3.   Mary's boudoir, an hour later.
Scene 4.   A fitting room. An afternoon, two months later.

ACT TWO

Scene 1.   An exercise room, two weeks later.
Scene 2.   Mary's kitchen, midnight, a few days later.
Scene 3.   Mary's living room, a month later.
Scene 4.   A hospital room, a month later.
Scene 5.   A Reno hotel room, a few weeks later.

ACT THREE

Scene 1.   Crystal's bathroom, early evening, two years later.
Scene 2.   Mary's bedroom, eleven-thirty, the same night.
Scene 3.   The Powder Room at the Casino Roof, near midnight, the same night.

THE WOMEN

ACT ONE

SCENE I

Mary Haines' living room. Today, Park Avenue living rooms are decorated with a sig[nifi]cant indifference to the fact that ours is still a bi-sexual society. Period peacock al[cove,] crystal-hung prima-donna roosts, they reflect the good taste of their mistresses in everyt[hing] but a consideration of the master's pardonable right to fit in his own home decor. M[ary] Haines' living room is not like that. It would be thought a comfortable room by a [man.] This, without sacrificing its own subtle, feminine charm. Above the fireplace, the[re is] a charming portrait of Mary's children—a girl of 11, a boy of 5 or 6. Right, a door to [the] living quarters. Left, another to the hall. Center, a sofa, armchair, tea-table group; [and,] in the good light from the window, a bridge-table group.

As the curtain rises, JANE, *a pretty, and quite correct little Irish-American mai[d, is] arranging the tea-table.* FOUR WOMEN *are playing bridge in a smoking-car cloud of sm[oke.] They are:*

NANCY, *who is sharp, but not acid; sleek but not smart; a worldly and yet virgina[l 35.] And her partner—*

PEGGY, *who is pretty, sweet, 25.* PEGGY's *character has not, will never quite "jell." A[nd]* SYLVIA, *who is glassy, elegant, feline, 34. And her partner—*

EDITH, *who is a sloppy, expensively dressed (currently, by Lane Bryant) matro[n of] 33 or 34. Indifferent to everything but self,* EDITH *is incapable of either deliberate malic[ious]ness or spontaneous generosity.*

SYLVIA. So I said to Howard, "What do you expect me to do? Stay home and darn your socks? What do we all have money for? Why do we keep servants?"

NANCY. You don't keep them long, God knows— (*Placing the pack of cards.*) Yours, Peggy.

PEGGY. Isn't it Mrs. Potter's? I opened with four spades. (SYLVIA *firmly places the pack before* PEGGY. PEGGY *wrong again, deals.*)

SYLVIA. Second hand, you did. And went down a thousand. (*Patronizingly.*) Peggy, my pet, you can't afford it.

PEGGY. I can too, Sylvia. I'm not a pauper.

SYLVIA. If your bridge doesn't improve, you soon will be.

NANCY. Oh, shut up, Sylvia. She's only playing till Mary comes down.

SYLVIA (*querulously*). Jane, what's Mrs. Haines doing up there?

JANE (*reproachfully*). It's that lingerie woman *you* sent her, Mrs. Fowler.

SYLVIA. I didn't expect Mrs. Haines to buy anything. I was just trying to get rid of the creature. (JANE *exits.*) Peggy, bid.

PEGGY. Oh, mine? By.

SYLVIA (*looking at* PEGGY). She won't [con]centrate.

NANCY. She's in love, bless her. After[a] child's been married as long as you [—]she may be able to concentrate on vital [mat]ters like bridge.

SYLVIA (*bored*). Another lecture on the [Mod]ern Woman?

NANCY. At the drop of a hat. By.

SYLVIA. I consider myself a perfectly [good] wife. I've sacrificed a lot for Howard Fo[wler] —two spades. I devote as much time t[o my] children as any of my friends.

NANCY. Except Mary.

SYLVIA. Oh, Mary, of course. Mary is a[n ex]ception to all of us.

NANCY. Quite right. (*They are waitin[g on]* PEGGY *again*). Peggy?

PEGGY (*uncertainly*). Two no tru[mp.] (EDITH *rises suddenly. Plainly, she [is]* squeamish.)

SYLVIA (*wearily*). Edith, not *again?*

ᴴ. I shouldn't have eaten that alligator
Morning sickness! I heave the whole
day. This is positively the last time I go
ᴵgh this lousy business for any man!
spades. If men had to bear babies,
'd never be—

ᴇʏ. —more than one child in a family.
he'd be a boy. By. (ᴇᴅɪᴛʜ *sinks on the
of her chair, lays down her cards.*)

ʏ. I wish *I* were having a baby. We
afford one now.

ᴀ. And you'll never be able to, until
know Culbertson. (*Arranging* ᴇᴅɪᴛʜ's
.) Honestly, Edith! Why didn't you
a slam?

ᴵ (*rising hurriedly*). Oh, I *have* got to
allow. Wait till you've had three, Peg-
ᴼu'd wish you'd never gotten past the
and flowers. (*Exits precipitously.*)

ʏ (*disgusted*). Poor, frightened, bewil-
madonna!

ᴀ. I'm devoted to Edith Potter. But she
gets me down. You'd think she had a
time. Dr. Briggs says she's like shelling
She ought to go through what *I* went
gh. Nobody *knows!*

ʏ. No clubs, partner?

ᴀ. So when Cynthia came, I had a Cæ-
ᴵ. You should see my stomach— It's a

ʏ. Are you sure?

ᴀ. Got the king, Peggy? (ᴘᴇɢɢʏ *oblig-
plays the king.*) Thanks, dear, it's a
And the rubber. (*Rises, lights a fresh
ᴿᵗte, goes to armchair and perches.*) But
ᴇpt my figure. I must say, I don't blame
s Potter for playing around.

'. Oh, does her husband . . . ?

ᴀ. Oh, Phelps has made passes at all us
I do think it's bad taste for a man
to make his wife's friends, *especially*
he's bald and fat. I told him once,
ᴘs Potter," I said, "the next time you
ᵃt me, I'm going straight to Edith."

'. And did you?

. Certainly not. I wouldn't say any-
to hurt Edith for the world. Well, you
ᵇlame the men. But I'll say one thing

for Edith. She's not as dumb as *some* of my
friends. She's on to her husband.

ᴘᴇɢɢʏ· (*bravely*). Do you think *he* is on to
her?

sʏʟᴠɪᴀ. What do you mean?

ᴘᴇɢɢʏ. If he could only hear her talk about
him!

sʏʟᴠɪᴀ. Listen, Peggy, do we know how men
talk about us when we're not around?

ɴᴀɴᴄʏ. I've heard rumors.

sʏʟᴠɪᴀ. Exactly. Peggy, you haven't been
married long enough to form a private opinion of your husband.

ᴘᴇɢɢʏ. Well, if I had one, I'd keep it to myself. Do you think I'd tell anybody in the
world about the quarrels John and I have
over money? I'd be too proud! (*Enter* ᴇᴅɪᴛʜ.
*Goes to tea-table, and gathers a handful of
sandwiches.*)

sʏʟᴠɪᴀ. All over, dear?

ᴇᴅɪᴛʜ. Oh, that was a false alarm. What happened?

sʏʟᴠɪᴀ. Only a slam, dear. You do underbid.

ᴇᴅɪᴛʜ. I'll bet you had me on the pan.

sʏʟᴠɪᴀ. I never say behind my friends' backs
what I won't say to their faces. I said you
ought to diet.

ᴇᴅɪᴛʜ. There's no use dieting in my condition. I've got to wait until I can begin from
scratch. Besides, I've got the most wonderful
cook. She was with Mary. She said Mary
let her go because she was too extravagant.
I think this cook Mary has is too, too
homey. (*Examines sandwich.*) Water cress.
I'd just as soon eat my way across a front
lawn.

sʏʟᴠɪᴀ. I think Mary's gone off terribly
this winter. Have you noticed those deep
lines, here? (*Draws her finger around her
mouth.*)

ɴᴀɴᴄʏ. Smiling lines. Tragic, aren't they?

sʏʟᴠɪᴀ. Perhaps they *are*. Maybe a woman's
headed for trouble when she begins to get
too—smug.

ɴᴀɴᴄʏ. Smug? Don't you mean, happy?

·ᴘᴇɢɢʏ. Mr. Haines adores her so!

SYLVIA (*snickering and flashing* EDITH *a significant glance*). Yes, doesn't he?

NANCY (*coldly*). You just can't bear it, Sylvia, can you?

SYLVIA. Bear what?

NANCY. Mary's happiness. It gets you down.

SYLVIA. Nancy Blake, if there's one thing I can say for myself, I've never been jealous of another woman. Why should I be jealous of Mary?

NANCY. Because she's contented. Contented to be what she is.

SYLVIA. Which is what?

NANCY. A woman.

EDITH. And what, in the name of my revolting condition, are we?

NANCY. Females.

SYLVIA. Really. And what are you, pet?

NANCY. What nature abhors, I'm—a virgin —a frozen asset.

EDITH. I wish I were a virgin again. The only fun I ever had was holding out on Phelps. Nancy, you ought to thank God every night you don't have to make sacrifices for some man.

PEGGY. I wish I could make a little money, writing the way you do, Miss Blake.

NANCY. If you wrote the way I do, that's just what you'd make.

SYLVIA. You're not exactly a popular author, are you, dear?

NANCY. Not with you. Well, good news, Sylvia. My book is finished and once again I'm about to leave your midst.

PEGGY. Oh, I wish we could afford to travel. Where do you go this time, Miss Blake?

NANCY. Africa, shooting.

SYLVIA. Well, darling, I don't blame you. I'd rather face a tiger any day than the sort of things the critics said about your last book. (*Enter* MARY. *She is a lovely woman in her middle thirties. She is what most of us think our happily married daughters are like. She is carrying several white boxes.*)

MARY. Sorry, girls. (*Teasing.*) Sylvia, ſ you always send me woe-begone creatų like that lingerie woman? It's been a expensive half hour for me.

PEGGY (*looking at* SYLVIA). For me too, N Haines.

MARY (*laughing*). Nonsense, Peggy, were playing for me. Here. (*Hands* PE *a box.*) Don't open it now. It's a bed-jac Or a tea cozy. Or something padde wouldn't know. I was crying so hard.

SYLVIA. You didn't believe that wom sob story?

MARY. Of course I did. (*She really didí Anyway, she's a lot worse off than you I. (*Putting down another box.*) Edith, garments—

EDITH. Darling, how sweet! (*It comes ℓ her again.*) Oh, my God! I'm sick as a (*Sits.*)

SYLVIA. It's a girl. Girls always make sicker.

NANCY. Even before they're born?

EDITH. I don't care what it is. I've lost ev thing including my curiosity. Why did ℓ make it take nine months?

NANCY (*helpfully*). It takes an elepl seven years.

EDITH. I wish I were an elephant. I'll l like one anyway before I'm finished. An would be heaven not to worry for sℓ years.

MARY (*laughing*). Oh, Edith, it is ra trying. But when it's all over, isn't it grandest thing in the world to have thℓ

EDITH. Well, I'd love mine just as muℓ they came out of cabbages.

NANCY. And I dare say your husband wℓ hardly notice the difference.

JANE (*entering with tea-kettle*). Ma'am, Haines would like to speak to you oɩ phone.

MARY. Oh, I can feel what it is in my bℓ Jane. (*To the others.*) Stephen's going ℓ kept at the office again tonight. (*Exits.*)

SYLVIA. Give him my love, pet.

MARY (*offstage*). I will.

ιΑ (*she never lets anything pass*). Nancy,
couldn't be more wrong about me and
y.

cy. Still rankling?

ιΑ. Jealous? As a matter of fact, I'm
y for her.

cy. Oh-ho? Why?

ιΑ (*mysteriously*). Well, for all *we*
w she may be living in a fool's paradise
Stephen.

cy. Let's check that one for a moment,
ia. Jane, are the children in?

₂. Yes, Miss. Just back from the Park.
τΗ *rises*—SYLVIA, *in pantomime, signals
not to leave room. This is not lost on
cy. For a moment she hesitates at the
.*)

y. Oh, I'd love to see Mrs. Haines' little
Miss Blake—

cy (*following* PEGGY). Come along,
ι. Anyway, it's our turn to go on the
But we don't have to worry. You've
poor man. I've got no man at all. (*They
)*

ι (*goes to tea-table—pours two cups.
: empties ash-trays*). This is positively
ast time I play bridge with Nancy. She
r misses a chance to get in a dig. What
creature like her got but her friends?
Ε *exits, closing door, left.* SYLVIA *stealth-
'oses door, right.*) The way she kept at
about Mary made me so nervous, I
ght I'd scream. And in my condition—

ιΑ. Edith, I've got to tell you! I'll burst
wait!

ι. I *knew* you had something! (*She
ιs her well-laden plate and tea-cup and
s herself happily beside* SYLVIA *on the
)*

ιΑ. You'll die!

ι. Mary?

ιΑ. No, Stephen. Guess!

ι. You couldn't mean . . . ?

ιΑ (*nodding*). Stephen Haines is cheat-
ιn Mary!

ι. I don't believe you; is it true?

SYLVIA. Wait till you hear. (*Now she is into
it.*) You know I go to Michael's for my hair.
You ought to go, pet. I despise whoever does
yours. Well, there's the most wonderful new
manicurist there. (*Shows her scarlet nails.*)
Isn't that divine? Jungle Red—

EDITH. Simply divine. Go on.

SELVIA. It all came out in the most extraordinary way, this morning. I tried to get you
on the phone—

EDITH. I was in the tub. Go on.

SYLVIA. This manicurist, she's marvelous,
was doing my nails. I was looking through
Vogue, the one with Mary in the Beaux
Arts Ball costume—

EDITH. —in that white wig that flattered her
so much?

SYLVIA (*nodding*). Well, this manicurist:
"Oh, Mrs. Fowler," she said, "is that that
Mrs. Haines who's so awfully rich?"

EDITH. Funny how people like that think
people like us are awfully rich.

SYLVIA. I forget what she said next. You
know how those creatures are, babble, babble, babble, babble, and never let up for a
minute! When suddenly she said: "I know
the girl who's being *kept* by Mr. Haines!"

EDITH. No!

SYLVIA. I swear!

EDITH (*thrilled*). Someone *we* know?

SYLVIA. No! That's what's so awful about
it. She's a friend of this manicurist. Oh, it
wouldn't be so bad if Stephen had picked
someone in his own class. But a blonde
floosie!

EDITH. But how did Stephen ever meet a
girl like that?

SYLVIA. How do men ever meet girls like
that? That's what they live for, the rats!

EDITH. But—

SYLVIA. I can't go into all the details, now.
They're utterly fantastic—

EDITH. You suppose Mary knows?

SYLVIA. Mary's the kind who couldn't help
showing it.

EDITH (*nodding, her mouth full of her third cake*). No self-control. Well, she's bound to find out. If a woman's got any instincts, she feels when her husband's off the reservation. I know *I would.*

SYLVIA. Of course you do, darling. Not Mary— (*Rises, and walks about the room, wrestling with* MARY's *sad problem.*) If only there were some way to *warn* her!

EDITH (*horrified, following her*). Sylvia! You're not going to tell her?

SYLVIA. Certainly not. I'd *die* before I'd be the one to hurt her like that!

EDITH. Couldn't someone shut that manicurist up?

SYLVIA. A good story like that? A lot those girls care whose life they ruin.

EDITH. *Isn't* it a dirty trick?

SYLVIA. Isn't it *foul?* It's not as though only Mary's friends knew. We could keep our mouths shut.

EDITH. I know plenty that I never *breathe* about my friends' husbands!

SYLVIA. So do I? (*They exchange a sudden glance of sharp suspicion.*) Anyway, the whole thing's disgustingly unfair to Mary. I feel like a disloyal skunk, just knowing abut it—

EDITH. I adore her—

SYLVIA. I *worship* her. She's my dearest friend in all the world— (*Voices, off-stage. They sit down at the card-table and begin to play solitaire hastily. Enter* NANCY *and* PEGGY.)

NANCY. Well, Sylvia, feeling better?

SYLVIA (*innocently*). Meaning what?

NANCY. Must've been choice. You both look so *relaxed.*

SYLVIA. Nancy, were you listening at that door?

PEGGY. Oh, Mrs. Fowler, we were in the nursery. (MARY *enters.*)

SYLVIA (*quickly*). Well, darling, how is Stephen, the old dear? And did you give him my love?

MARY. I did. Stephen's not so well, Sylvia.

SYLVIA. Oh? What's the trouble?

MARY. Nervous indigestion. That's w have such a plain cook now.

EDITH. Phelps has had indigestion for y You should hear that man rumble ir night. Like a truck on cobblestones.

SYLVIA. There's nothing—worrying Step

MARY. Oh, no, he's just been working He's not coming home tonight. Oh, I wi (*Abruptly, with an indulgent laugh.*) 'man's love is of man's life a thing apar woman's whole—et cetera.

SYLVIA. Are you sure it's *work,* darling not a beautiful blonde?

MARY. Stephen? (*Laughing, and perh little smugly, too.*) Oh, Sylvia.

EDITH (*afraid that* SYLVIA *will go too* Sylvia, let's play!

SYLVIA. Stephen's a very attractive m

MARY. Isn't he? I can't imagine wh hasn't deserted me for some glamorous ture long ago.

NANCY (*alarmed*). Mary, you *do* s smug.

MARY. Oh, let me be, Nancy. How car be too sure of what you believe in mo

SYLVIA. I wouldn't be sure of the A Paul. I always tell Howard, "If you manage to make a fool of me, I'll de what I get."

NANCY. You certainly will. (*Faces s squarely.*) Now, Sylvia, let's have it.

SYLVIA. Have what?

NANCY. Just what did you mean whe said Mary was living in a fool's paradi

MARY. What?

SYLVIA (*angrily*). Nancy, don't be al (*A pause. Then, wriggling out of it.* Mary, I was just trying to make a t Nancy Blake wisecrack about marri said, "A woman's paradise is always a paradise!"

MARY. That's not bad, is it, Nancy? Sylvia, whatever I'm living in, I li Nancy, cut.

A (SYLVIA *examines her nails minutely,*
nly shows them to MARY). Mary, how
u like that?

Y (*not looking*). Too, too adorable.

A. You can't imagine how it stays on.
it at Michael's—you ought to go,
!

(*protestingly*). Oh, Sylvia—

A. A wonderful new manicurist. Olga's
ame. She's marvelous.

. Will you cut, Sylvia?

A. Look, Jungle Red.

Y. Looks as if you'd been tearing at
ody's throat.

SYLVIA. I'll be damned, Nancy, if I'll let you
ride me any more!

MARY. Now, Sylvia, Nancy's just being
clever, too.

SYLVIA. She takes a crack at everything about
me. Even my nails!

MARY (*laughing*). Well, I like it. I really do!
It's new and smart. (*Pats her hand.*) Michael's, Olga, Jungle Red? I'll remember
that. (*Cuts cards.*) You and I, Sylvia. I feel
lucky today.

SYLVIA (*with a sweet, pitying smile.*) *Do*
you, darling? Well, you know what they
say, "Lucky in cards"—

CURTAIN

SCENE II

afternoon, a few days later. A hairdressing booth in Michael's. An elegantly func-
cubby-hole. Right, a recessed mirror in the wall. Left, from the high partition pole,
ain to the floor. The rear wall is a plain partition. Center, a swivel hairdressing chair.
e it, from an aluminum tree, the hanging thicket of a permanent-wave machine.
e wall, gadgets for curling irons, electric outlets which connect with wires to the
g machines, the hand drier, the manicurists' table-light, stools for the pedicurist,
anicurist, OLGA.
the curtain rises, the booth is, to put it mildly, full.
s. WAGSTAFF, *a fat, elderly woman is in the chair, undergoing the punishment of a*
nent. Wires and clamps, Medusa-like, rise from her head, to the cap of the machine.
GA, *at her right, is doing her nails. Her fat bare feet rest in the lap of the* PEDICURIST.
FIRST HAIRDRESSER *cools her steaming locks with a hand-drier. The* SECOND HAIR-
R, *watch in hand, fiddles with the wires, times the operation. When the machine*
king, *a small red, light glows among the wires.*
s. WAGSTAFF, *apparently inured to public execution, smokes, reads a magazine on*
p, *occasionally nibbles a sandwich which the* MANICURIST *passes her from a tray*
her instruments. The drier, whenever it is on, makes a loud noise, drowning out
, *which must be harshly raised above it. Now the drier is on, the voices loud.*

WAGSTAFF. It's burning my neck!

D HAIRDRESSER. Be brave! One minute

WAGSTAFF (*in pain*). O-o-oo!

HAIRDRESSER. It's going to be so worth
s. Wagstaff.

WAGSTAFF. My ears!

D HAIRDRESSER. Be brave!

MRS. WAGSTAFF. O-o-o-o! My nerves— Oo—
my God! (*To* PEDICURIST) My sandwich—
(OLGA *hands her sandwich.*)

SECOND HAIRDRESSER. Ten seconds. We must
suffer to be beautiful. (*The curtain parts;* A
FIGURE *in flowing white half-enters. It is,*
judging by the voice, a woman, but its face
is completely obliterated by a mud-mask.)

MUD-MASK. Oh, pardon—I thought I was in
here. Why, hello, Mrs. Wagstaff. (*Coyly.*)
Guess who I am? (*A second* FACE *appears*

over this intruder's shoulder. At first, it looks like another mud-mask. It's not. It's the COLORED MAID, EUPHIE. *She clutches the shoulder of the mud-mask.*)

EUPHIE. Mustn't talk, ma'am. You'll crack yo'self. (*Exit* MUD-MASK *followed by* EUPHIE.)

MRS. WAGSTAFF. Who was it?

FIRST HAIRDRESSER. Mrs. Phipps— (*Switches off the drier. Now they all lower their voices to a normal pitch.*) There, dear, the agony's over. (*They take the permanent clamps off* MRS. WAGSTAFF's *hair. A drier is on in the next booth. A voice is heard off-stage, screaming above it.*)

VOICE. —so I feel awful. I ate a lobster at the opening of the Ritz— (*The drier goes off.*)

OLGA (*To* MRS. WAGSTAFF). Mrs. Mordie Barnes. She's been in the hospital. It wasn't ptomaine at all. It was a mis—

SECOND HAIRDRESSER. Olga! She'll hear you—

MRS. WAGSTAFF (*thoughtfully*). I think I'll have a mud-mask.

SECOND HAIRDRESSER (*calling outside*). Euphie! Tell the desk Mrs. Wagstaff's working in a mud!

MRS. WAGSTAFF (*enviously*). Mrs. Phipps has such a lovely skin.

FIRST HAIRDRESSER. Not lovelier than yours, Mrs. Wagstaff.

CHORUS (SECOND HAIRDRESSER, OLGA, PEDICURIST). Oh, yours is lovely! Why, not nearly as lovely! Lovelier than yours?

MRS. WAGSTAFF (*coyly*). I do think it's rather good for a woman my age.

FIRST HAIRDRESSER. You talk as if you were an old woman, dear.

MRS. WAGSTAFF (*lying*). I'm 42.

SECOND HAIRDRESSER. Mustn't tell anyone. You don't look a day over 35!

CHORUS (SECOND HAIRDRESSER, PEDICURIST, OLGA). Why, no one would believe it! Why, not a day! Oh, you don't look it!

SECOND HAIRDRESSER. —now you've gotten so much slimmer!

MRS. WAGSTAFF. I have slimmed down, haven't I?

CHORUS (PEDICURIST, OLGA, FIRST HAIR[DRES]SER). Oh, thin as a shadow! Why, ter[ribly] thin! Oh, just right, now!

MRS. WAGSTAFF (*admiring her nail pol[ish]*). That's lovely.

OLGA. Jungle Red. Everybody loves it. [Do] you know Mrs. Howard Fowler?

PEDICURIST (*rising, gathering up her thin[gs]*). Don't put your stockings on yet, Mrs. W[ag]staff, you'll smear your beautiful big t[oe.] (*Exits.*)

OLGA. They say Mr. Fowler made a for[tune] in some stock. But one of the ladies [Mrs.] Fowler sent in was telling me Mr. Fo[wler] does like to drink! Only the other day—

FIRST HAIRDRESSER (*sharply*). We're r[eady] now, Mrs. Wagstaff. (*Gets* MRS. WAGS[TAFF] *up.*) We'll unwind you in the sham[poo.] (*Calling.*) Euphie!

SECOND HAIRDRESSER (*taking* MRS. WAGS[TAFF] *to door*). This way, dear. How does [the] permanent feel? And it's going to look [love]ly, too— (SECOND HAIRDRESSER *herds* [MRS.] WAGSTAFF *out of the booth,* MRS. WAGS[TAFF] *walking on her heels, her toes still wa[dded] with cotton. Enter* EUPHIE, *who, durin[g the] ensuing dialogue, cleans up the debris o[n the] floor of the booth*).

OLGA. That old gasoline truck! Fifty-tw[o] she's a day!

FIRST HAIRDRESSER. One more permanen[t and] she won't have a hair left on her head.

OLGA. There's plenty on her upper li[p.]

EUPHIE. She sho' does shed, don't she?

OLGA. Any woman who's fool enoug[h to] marry a man ten years younger! Know [what] a client told me? Her husband's a p[erfect] (HAIRDRESSER *exits followed by* OLGA.)

SECOND HAIRDRESSER (*entering*). Ready[.]

EUPHIE. Yes, ma'am. (*The* SECOND [HAIR]DRESSER *holds back the curtain.*)

MARY (*off-stage*). So I woke up this mo[rning] and decided for no reason at all to ch[ange] the way— (*She enters, followed by* NA[NCY]. I do my hair. (*Exit* EUPHIE.)

ND HAIRDRESSER. Mr. Michaels will be
minutes, ma'am. Anyone in particular
our manicure?

. Who does Mrs. Fowler's nails?

DRESSER. Olga. I'll see. (*Exits.*)

Y. God, I'd love to do Mrs. Fowler's
, right down to the wrist, with a nice
uzz saw.

. Sylvia's all right. She's a good friend
rneath.

Y. Underneath what?

. Nancy, you don't humor your friends
gh.

Y. So that's the big idea coming here?
re humoring Sylvia?

. Oh, you did hurt her. I had it all
again at lunch. (*She catches a glimpse
rself in the mirror.*) Nancy, am I get-
old?

Y. Who put that in your head? Sylvia?

. Tell me the truth.

Y. Beauty is in the eye of the beholder,
waddle to that effect.

. But it's such a scary feeling when
see those little wrinkles creeping in.

Y. Time's little mice.

. And that first gleam of white in your
It's the way you'd feel about autumn
u knew there'd never be another
g—

Y (*abruptly*). There's only one tragedy
woman.

. Growing old?

Y. Losing her man.

. That's why we're all so afraid of
ng old.

Y. Are you afraid?

. Well, I was very pretty when I was
. I never thought about it twice then.
I know it's why Stephen loved me.

Y. Smart girl.

. Now I think about it all the time.

NANCY. Love is not love which alters when
it alteration finds. Shakespeare.

MARY. Well, he told me, on my birthday,
I'd always look the same to him.

NANCY. Nice present. No jewels?

MARY. It rained that day. He brought me a
bottle of perfume called "Summer Rain."

NANCY. How many ounces?

MARY. Nancy, you've never been in love.

NANCY. Says who?

MARY (*surprised*). Have you?

NANCY. Yes.

MARY. You never told me.

NANCY. You never asked— (*Wistfully.*)
Neither did *he.* (OLGA *enters with fresh bowl
of water.*) Here, innocent. (*Gives a book to
MARY.*) The book my readers everywhere
have been waiting for with such marked
apathy.

MARY. "All the Dead Ladies"?

NANCY. Originally called, "From the Silence
of the Womb." My publisher thought that
would make too much noise.

MARY. What's it about? (OLGA *begins to file
MARY's nails.*)

NANCY. Women I dislike: "Ladies"—

MARY. Oh, Nancy!

OLGA. Don't soak it yet. (*Taking MARY's
hand out of the water.*)

NANCY. No good? Too bad. It's a parting
shot. I'm off.

MARY. Off?

NANCY. Africa.

MARY. But not today?

NANCY. I knew if I told you you'd scurry
around and do things. A party. Steamer
baskets of sour fruit. Not nearly as sour as
the witty cables your girl friends would send
me— So don't move. No tears. For my sake
—just soak it? Good-bye, Mary—

MARY. Good-bye, Nancy. I'll miss you.

NANCY. I doubt it. Practically nobody ever misses a clever woman. (*Exits.*)

OLGA. Funny, isn't she?

MARY. She's a darling.

OLGA (*filing* MARY's *nails*). She's a writer? How do those writers think up those plots? I guess the plot part's not so hard to think up as the end. I guess anybody's life'd make a interesting plot if it had a interesting end— Mrs. Fowler sent you in? (MARY, *absorbed in her book, nods.*) She's sent me three clients this week. Know Mrs. Herbert Parrish that was Mrs. Malcolm Leeds? Well, Mrs. Parrish was telling me herself about her divorce. Seems Mr. Parrish came home one night with lipstick on his undershirt. Said he always explained everything before. But *that* was something he just wasn't going to try to explain. Know Mrs. Potter? She's awful pregnant—

MARY (*she wants to read*). I know.

OLGA. Soak it, please. (*Puts* MARY's *hand in water. Begins on other hand.*) Know Mrs. Stephen Haines?

MARY. What? Why, yes, I—

OLGA. I guess Mrs. Fowler's told you about that! Mrs. Fowler feels awfully sorry for her.

MARY (*laughing*). Oh, she does! Well, I don't. I—

OLGA. You would if you knew this girl.

MARY. What girl?

OLGA. This Crystal Allen.

MARY. Crystal Allen?

OLGA. Yes, you know. The girl who's living with Mr. Haines. (MARY *starts violently.*) Don't you like the file? Mrs. Potter says it sets her unborn child's teeth on edge.

MARY (*indignant*). Whoever told you such a thing?

OLGA. Oh, I thought you knew. Didn't Mrs. Fowler—?

MARY. No—

OLGA. Then you will be interested. You Crystal Allen is a friend of mine. S really a terrible man-trap. Soak it, ple (MARY, *dazed, puts her hand in the di* She's behind the perfume counter at S. So was I before I got fi—left. That's she met him.

MARY. Stephen Haines?

OLGA. Yeah. It was a couple a months Us girls wasn't busy. It was an awful r day, I remember. So this gentleman w up to the counter. He was the serious t nice-looking, but kind of thin on top. \ Crystal nabs him. "I want some perfu he says. "May I awsk what type of wo for?" Crystal says, very Ritzy. That d mean a thing. She was going to sell Summer Rain, our feature anyway. "Is young?" Crystal says. "No," he says, of embarrassed. "Is she the glamorous ty Crystal says. "No, thank God," he "Thank God?" Crystal says and bats eyes. She's got those eyes which run up down a man like a searchlight. Well, puts perfume on her palm and in the c of her arm for him to smell. So he g smelling around and I guess he liked it cause we heard him tell her his name, w one of the girls recognized from C Knickerbocker's column—Gee, you're vous—Well, it was after that I le wouldn't of thought no more about it. I couple of weeks ago I stopped by w Crystal lives to say hello. And the lan says she'd moved to the kind of house w she could entertain her gentleman frie "What gentleman friend?" I says. " that Mr. Haines that she's had up i room all hours of the night," the lan says—Did I hurt? (MARY *draws her away.*) One coat, or two? (*Picks up bottle.*)

MARY. None. (*Rises and goes to the where she has left her purse.*)

OLGA. But I thought that's what you for? All Mrs. Fowler's friends—

MARY. I think I've gotten what all Fowler's friends came for. (*Puts coin c table.*)

OLGA (*picks up coin*). Oh, thanks— good-bye. I'll tell her you were in, Mr

MARY. Mrs. Stephen Haines.

ѕA. Mrs. —? Oh, gee, gee! Gee, Mrs.
ines—I'm sorry! Oh, isn't there some-
ng I can do?

RY. Stop telling that story!

ѕA. Oh, sure, sure, I will!

RY. And please, don't tell anyone— (Her
ce breaks) that you told it to me—

ѕA. Oh, I won't, gee, I promise! Gee, that
uld be kind of humiliating for you! (De-
sively.) But in a way, Mrs. Haines, I'm
da glad you know. Crystal's a terrible
—I mean, she's terribly clever. And she's
ibly pretty, Mrs. Haines—I mean, if I
ѕ you I wouldn't waste no time getting

Mr. Haines away from her— (MARY turns
abruptly away.) I mean, now you know,
Mrs. Haines!

(OLGA eyes the coin in her hand distaste-
fully, suddenly puts it down on the table
and exits. MARY, alone, stares blankly in
the mirror, then suddenly focusing on her
image, leans forward, searching her face between her trembling hands. A drier goes on
in the next booth. A shrill voice rises above
its drone.)

VOICE. —Not too hot! My sinus! So she
said: "I wouldn't want anybody in the
world to know," and I said: "My dear, you
know you can trust me!"

CURTAIN

SCENE III

n hour later. MARY's boudoir. Charming, of course. A door to bedroom, right. A door
he hall, left. A chaise-longue; next to it, a table with books, flowers, a telephone. A
sing table.

s the curtain rises, MARY is discovered on the chaise-longue, trying to read. JANE enters
ᵻ the hall. She is upset about something. She keeps daubing at her eyes.

ʏ. Tea, Jane?

ᴇ. It's coming, ma'am.

ʏ. My mother will be here in a few
utes. A cup for her.

ᴇ. Yes, ma'am. (Sniffling.) Ma'am—

ʏ. And tell Cook please, dinner on time.
ᴿe going to the theatre. Mr. Haines likes
ᵉ there for the curtain. I'll wear my old
ᵏ, Jane.

ᵋ (looking nervously at the door behind
, Yes, ma'am.

ʏ. No, I'll wear my new blue, Jane.

ᵋ. Ma'am, it's Cook. She wants to see
(Defensively.) It's about me. She says

ᵉ. Later, Jane.

, Don't you believe a word she says,
n. It's all his fault.

(aware of JANE's distress for the first
. Whose fault?

Her husband's. Ford's.

MARY (surprised). What's the matter with
Ford? He's a very good butler.

JANE. Oh, he does his work, ma'am. But
you don't know how he is in the pantry.
Always kidding around with us girls. He
don't mean any harm, but Cook— (Enter
COOK abruptly with MARY's tea tray. She is
a fat, kind woman, with a strong Scandinav-
ian accent. At the moment she is very mad.)

COOK. Afternoon, ma'am. (Glaring at JANE.)
I'd like to talk to you alone, ma'am.

JANE. I told you, it isn't my fault.

COOK. You led him on!

JANE. I didn't. (Bursting into tears.) I've
been with Mrs. Haines seven years. She
knows I never make trouble downstairs.
(Exits to hall.)

MARY. Yes, Ingrid?

COOK. Ma'am, you're the nicest I ever had.
But I go. I got to get Ford away from that
bad girl.

MARY (very firmly). Jane is not a bad girl.

COOK (*bursts into tears*). Oh, course she ain't. He was always like that! Sometimes I could die, for the shame!

MARY (*kindly*). I'll send him away. You can stay.

COOK (*more soberly*). No, I don't do that, ma'am.

MARY. I'll give you a hundred dollars. That's more than half of what you make together.

COOK. Thank you, ma'am. We both go.

MARY. Is that sensible?

COOK. No. It's plain dumb.

MARY. Then why?

COOK (*she pauses, rocking from foot to foot*). I guess nobody understand. Sure it was no good to marry him. My mother told me he's a lady-killer. Don't marry them, she said. His wife is the lady he kills. Oh, he's terrible. But except for women he's a good man. He always says, "Ingrid, you take the money. You manage good." Oh, he don't want nobody but me for his wife! That's an awful big thing, ma'am.

MARY. Is that the thing that really matters?

COOK. With women like us, yes, ma'am— You give us references? (MARY *nods*.) And don't say nothing about his ways?

MARY. I won't.

COOK (*moving to the door*). Black bean soup, a fricassee, fried sweets and apple pie for dinner, ma'am—(*She opens the door.* JANE *has been eavesdropping.*)

COOK (*in a low, fierce voice*). Slut! (*Exit* COOK.)

JANE (*entering with extra cup on tray*). Did you hear what she called me, Mrs. Haines?

MARY. Please, Jane.

JANE (*cheerfully*). I'd rather be that any day than have some man make a fool of me! (*Enter* MISS FORDYCE. *She is a raw-boned, capable English spinster of 32.*)

MISS FORDYCE. May I see you, Mrs. Haines?

MARY. Of course, Miss Fordyce.

MISS FORDYCE. It's about little Mary—Re Mrs. Haines, you'll have to talk to child. She's just smacked her little bro hard. Pure temper.

MARY. What did little Stevie do to her, Fordyce?

MISS FORDYCE. Well, you see, it happ while I was down getting my tea. Wh came up, she'd had such a tantrum, s made herself ill. She positively refuse discuss the incident with me. But I'm sure the dear boy hadn't done a thing.

MARY. You're very apt to take the boy's Miss Fordyce.

MISS FORDYCE. Not at all. But in Engl Mrs. Haines, our girls are not so wretcl spoiled. After all, this *is* a man's w The sooner our girls are taught to a the fact *graciously*—

MARY (*gently*). Send her in to me, Miss dyce. (*Exit* MISS FORDYCE.) Oh, Jane, I understand it. Miss Fordyce really pi Mary, but she insists we all make a god of Stevie. (*Exits to bedroom, lea the door open.*)

JANE. Them English ones always hol for the boys. But they say since the ma'am, there's six women over ther every man. Competition is something f Over here, you can treat the men the they deserve—Men aren't so scarce. (LITTLE MARY. *She is a broad-bro thoughtful, healthy, little girl, phys well developed for her age.*)

LITTLE MARY. Where's Mother?

JANE. You're going to catch it. Sma your little brother. (*Mimicking* MISS DYCE.) Such a dear, sweet little lad—s (LITTLE MARY *does not answer.*) I'll be wish you were Mother's girl, inste Daddy's girl today, don't you? (LITTLE *doesn't answer.*) What's the matter, t got your tongue? (*Enter* MARY, *wear negligée.*)

MARY. Hello, darling—Aren't you go kiss me? (LITTLE MARY *doesn't move.*) red eyes!

LITTLE MARY. I was mad. I threw up. you throw up, doesn't it make you c

RY (*smiling*). Stevie tease you? (LITTLE
RY, *embarrassed, looks at* JANE. JANE
~kers, takes the hint and goes out.*) Well,
ling?

TLE MARY. Mother, I don't know how to
in.

RY (*sitting on the chaise-longue, and put-
g out her hand*). Come here. (LITTLE
RY *doesn't budge.*) Would you rather
t until tonight and tell Dad?

TLE MARY (*horrified*). Oh, Mother, I
ldn't tell him! (*Fiercely.*) And I'd be
ed to death before I'd tell skinny old
s Fordyce—

RY. That's not the way for my dear little
to talk.

TLE MARY (*setting her jaw*). I don't want
e a dear little girl. (*She suddenly rushes
her mother's outstretched arms in tears.*)
, Mother dear, Mother dear!

RY. Baby, what?

TLE MARY. What brother said!

RY. What did he say, the wretched boy?

TLE MARY (*disentangling herself*). He
I I had bumps!

RY. Bumps? You don't mean mumps?

TLE MARY. No, bumps. He said I was
ered with disgusting bumps!

RY (*alarmed*). Mary, *where*?

TLE MARY (*touching her hips and breasts
h delicate, ashamed finger tips*). Here
here!

RY. Oh— (*Controlling her relieved laugh-
and drawing her daughter to her side.*)
course you have bumps, darling. Very
ty little bumps. And you have them
ause—you're a little girl.

TLE MARY (*wailing*). But, Mother dear, I
't want to be a little girl. I hate girls! I
y're so silly, and they tattle, tattle—

RY. Not really, Mary.

TLE MARY. Yes, Mother, I know. Oh,
ther, what *fun* is there to be a lady?
at can a lady do?

MARY (*cheerfully*). These days, darling, ladies do all the things men do. They fly aeroplanes across the ocean, they go into politics
and business—

LITTLE MARY. You don't, Mother.

MARY. Perhaps I'm happier doing just what
I do.

LITTLE MARY. What do you do, Mother?

MARY. Take care of you and Stevie and Dad.

LITTLE MARY. You don't, Mother. Miss Fordyce and the servants do.

MARY (*teasing*). I see. I'm not needed around
here.

LITTLE MARY (*hugging her*). Oh, Mother, I
don't mean that. It wouldn't be any fun
at all without *you*. But, Mother, even when
the ladies *do* do things, they stop it when
they get the lovie-dovies.

MARY. The what?

LITTLE MARY. Like in the movies, Mother.
Ladies always end up so *silly*. (*Disgusted.*)
Lovey-dovey, lovey-dovey all the time!

MARY. Darling, you're too young to understand—

LITTLE MARY. But, Mother—

MARY. "But Mother, but Mother!" There's
one thing a woman can do, no man can do.

LITTLE MARY (*eagerly*). What?

MARY. Have a child. (*Tenderly.*) Like you.

LITTLE MARY. Oh, that! Everybody knows
that. But is that any fun, Mother dear?

MARY. Fun? No. But it is—joy. (*Hugging
her.*) Of a very special kind.

LITTLE MARY (*squirming away*). Well, it's
never sounded specially exciting to me—I
love you, Mother. But I bet you anything you
like, Daddy has more *fun* than you! (*She
slips away from* MARY. *Then sees her
mother's dispirited face, turns and kisses her
warmly.*) Oh, I'm sorry, Mother. But you
just *don't understand!* (*A pause.*) Am I to
be punished, Mother?

MARY (*she is thinking about something
else*). What do you think?

LITTLE MARY. I smacked him awful hard—
Shall I punish myself?

MARY. It will have to be pretty bad.

LITTLE MARY (*solemnly*). Then I won't go down to breakfast with Daddy tomorrow, or the next day—O.K., Mother?

MARY. O.K. (LITTLE MARY *walks, crestfallen, to the door as* JANE *enters.* LITTLE MARY *sticks out her tongue.*)

LITTLE MARY. There's my tongue! So what? (*Exits skipping.*)

JANE (*laughing*). She never lets anybody get the best of her, does she, Mrs. Haines?

MARY. My poor baby. She doesn't want to be a woman, Jane.

JANE. Who does?

MARY. Somehow, I've never minded it, Jane. (*Enter* MRS. MOREHEAD. *She is a bourgeois aristocrat of 55.* MARY *rises, kisses her.*)

MRS. MOREHEAD. Hello, child. Afternoon, Jane.

JANE. Afternoon, Mrs. Morehead. (*Exits to bedroom.*)

MARY. Mother, dear! (*She walks slowly to the dressing-table.*)

MRS. MOREHEAD (*cheerfully*). Well, what's wrong? (*Sits.*)

MARY (*turning*). How did you know something's wrong?

MRS. MOREHEAD. Your voice on the phone. Is it Stephen?

MARY. How did you know?

MRS. MOREHEAD. You sent for *Mother*. So it must be he. (*A pause.*)

MARY. I don't know how to begin, Mother.

MRS. MOREHEAD (*delighted to find that her instincts were correct*). It's a woman! Who is she?

MARY. Her name is Crystal Allen. She—she's a salesgirl at Saks'. (*Her mother's cheerful and practical manner discourages tears, so she begins to cream and tonic her face instead.*)

MRS. MOREHEAD. She's young and pretty, I suppose.

MARY. Well, yes. (*Defensively.*) But co mon.

MRS. MOREHEAD (*soothingly*). Of cours Stephen told you?

MARY. No. I—I found out—this afterno

MRS. MOREHEAD. How far has it gone?

MARY. He's known her about three mon

MRS. MOREHEAD. Does Stephen know know?

MARY (*shaking her head*). I—I wanted speak to you first. (*The tears come a way.*) Oh, Mother dear, what am I go to say to him?

MRS. MOREHEAD. *Nothing.*

MARY. Nothing? (*Enter* JANE *with the n dress.*)

JANE. I'll give it a touch with the iron.

MARY. Look, Schiaparelli—(JANE *holds dr up.*) It's rather trying, though, one of th tight skirts with a flared tunic—

MRS. MOREHEAD. Personally, I always thou you looked best in things not too extrem (*Exit* JANE.)

MARY. But, Mother, you don't really mea should say nothing?

MRS. MOREHEAD. I do.

MARY. Oh, but Mother—

MRS. MOREHEAD. My dear, I felt the sa way twenty years ago.

MARY. Not Father?

MRS. MOREHEAD. Mary, in many ways y father was an exceptional man. (*Philoso cally.*) That, unfortunately, was not one them.

MARY. Did you say nothing?

MRS. MOREHEAD. Nothing. I had a w mother, too. Listen, dear, this is not a story. It comes to most wives.

MARY. But Stephen—

MRS. MOREHEAD. Stephen is a man. He's b married twelve years—

MARY. You mean, he's tired of me!

s. MOREHEAD. Stop crying. You'll make
ir nose red.

RY. I'm not crying. (*Patting tonic on her
e.*) This stuff stings.

s. MOREHEAD (*going to her*). Stephen's
d of himself. Tired of feeling the same
ngs in himself year after year. Time comes
en every man's got to feel something new
vhen he's got to feel young again, just be-
ise he's growing old. Women are just the
ne. But when *we* get that way we change
hair dress. Or get a new cook. Or re-
orate the house from stem to stern. But
nan can't do over his office, or fire his
retary. Not even change the style of his
r. And the urge usually hits him hardest
t when he's beginning to lose his hair.
, dear, a man has only one escape from
old self: to see a different self—in the
ror of some woman's eyes.

RY. But, Mother—

s. MOREHEAD. This girl probably means
more to him than that new dress means
you.

RY. But, Mother—

s. MOREHEAD. "But Mother, but Mother!"
's not giving anything to her that be-
gs to you, or you would have felt that
irself long ago.

RY (*bewildered*). Oh, I always thought
vould. I love him so much.

s. MOREHEAD. And he loves you, baby.
rawing MARY *beside her on the chaise-
gue.*) Now listen to me: Go away some-
ere for a month or two. There's nothing
e a good dose of another woman to make
nan appreciate his wife. Mother knows!

RY. But, there's never been a lie between
before.

s. MOREHEAD. You mean, there's never
n a *silence* between you before. Well, it's
ut time. Keeping still, when you *ache* to
k, is about the only sacrifice spoiled wo-
n like us ever have to make.

RY. But, I'd forgive him—

MRS. MOREHEAD. Forgive him? (*Impatiently.*) For what? For being a man? Accuse
him, and you'll never get a chance to forgive him. He'd have to justify himself—

MARY. How can he!

MRS. MOREHEAD (*sighing*). He can't and he
can. Don't make him try. Either way you'd
lose him. And remember, dear, it's being
together at the *end* that really matters. (*Rising.*) One more piece of motherly advice:
Don't confide in your girl friends!

MARY. I think they all know.

MRS. MOREHEAD. They think you don't?
(MARY *nods.*) Leave it that way. If you let
them advise you, they'll see to it, in the name
of friendship, that you lose your husband
and your home. I'm an old woman, dear,
and I know my sex. (*Moving to the door.*)
I'm going right down this minute and get
our tickets.

MARY. Our—tickets?

MRS. MOREHEAD. You're taking me to Bermuda, dear. My throat's been awfully bad. I
haven't wanted to worry you, but my doctor
says—

MARY. Oh, Mother darling! Thank you!

MRS. MOREHEAD. Don't thank me, dear. It's
rather—*nice* to have you need Mother again.
(*Exits. The telephone rings.* MARY *answers
it.*)

MARY. Yes?—Oh, Stephen—Yes, dear?—
(*Distressed.*) Oh, Stephen! Oh, no—I'm not
angry. It's—it's just that I wanted to see the
play. Yes, I can get Mother. Stephen, will
you be very—late? (*It's a bit of a struggle,
but she manages a cheerful voice.*) Oh, it's—
all right. Have a good time. Of course, I
know it's just business—No, dear—I won't
wait up—Stephen. I love— (*A click. The
other end has hung up.* JANE *enters.* MARY
*turns her back. Her face would belie the
calmness of her voice.*) Jane—The children
and I will have dinner alone—

CURTAIN

SCENE IV

Two months later. A dressmaker's shop. We see two fitting booths, the same in appo. ment: triplex pier glasses, dress-racks, smoking stands, two small chairs. They are divi. by a mirrored partition. At the rear of each booth, a curtain and a door, off a corria. which leads to "the floor."

As the curtain rises the booth on the left is empty. The other booth is cluttered u. dresses. Two SALESGIRLS *are loading them over their arms.*

FIRST GIRL (*with vivid resentment against a customer who has just departed*). Well, now we can put them all back again. Makes you drag out everything in the damn store, and doesn't even buy a brassiere!

SECOND GIRL. And that's the kind who always needs one.

FIRST GIRL. This isn't her type. That isn't her type. I'd like to tell her what her type is.

SECOND GIRL. I'd like to know.

FIRST GIRL. It's the type that nobody gives a damn about! Gee, I'd like to work in a men's shop once. What can a man try on?

SECOND GIRL. Ever see a man try on hats? What they go through, you'd think a head was something peculiar. (*Both* GIRLS *exit.* FIRST SALESWOMAN *enters the booth on the right, hereafter called "Mary's Booth."*)

FIRST SALESWOMAN. Miss Myrtle, step in here a moment. (*A handsome wench, in a slinky negligée, enters.*)

MODEL. Yes, Miss Shapiro.

FIRST SALESWOMAN. If I've told you once, I've told you a thousand times, when you're modelling that dress, your stomach must lead. If you walk like this (*Pantomimes.*) you take away all the seduction. *This* is seduction! (*Shows* MISS MYRTLE *her rather unconvincing conception of a seductive walk.*)
MODEL. I'll try, Miss Shapiro. (*Tearfully.*) But if you had my appendix!

FIRST SALESWOMAN. Well, Miss Myrtle, you can take your choice: You will either lose your job or lose your appendix! (*Exit* MODEL. *In right booth, hereafter called "Crystal's Booth," enter* SECOND SALESWOMAN.)

SECOND SALESWOMAN (*to the* FIRST *and* SECOND GIRLS *who have returned for another load of dresses*). Quickly, please. I have a client waiting. (SECOND GIRL *exits with last*

of clothes as enter CRYSTAL, followed SALESWOMAN. THIRD SALESWOMAN *is s. crossing corridor from right to left.*) (*Mary's Booth.*)

FIRST SALESWOMAN (*giving little white . to the* SALESWOMAN *who passes*). Bring do Mrs. Haines' fittings. (*Exits, leaving bo empty.*)
(*Crystal's Booth.*)

SECOND SALESWOMAN. Will you open charge?

CRYSTAL (*taking off her gloves and h. Please.

SECOND SALESWOMAN. May I have the nam

CRYSTAL (*she is quite self-assured*). Al Miss Crystal Allen. The Hotel Waverly.

SECOND SALESWOMAN. May I have your ot charges? Saks, Bergdorf, Cartier—?

CRYSTAL (*putting it on*). Oh, I'll be open those, in the next few days—

SECOND SALESWOMAN. Then may I have y bank?

CRYSTAL. I've no checking account eit at the moment. (*Enter* MARY *in her bo with* FITTER *and* FIRST SALESWOMAN, *t carries her try-on gown. During the foll ing scene* MARY *undresses, gets into gay ning gown, fits.*)

FIRST SALESWOMAN (*to* MARY, *as they ent. Shall we show the things that came in w. you were away?

MARY. Please. But I'd like to see some you er things than I usually wear.
(*Crystal's Booth.*)

SECOND SALESWOMAN. I'm sorry, Miss Al But we *must* ask for one business re ence—

CRYSTAL (*lightly; she was prepared for th Oh, of course. Mr. Stephen Haines, 40 W He's an old friend of my family.

ND SALESWOMAN (*writing*). That will do. . Haines is a very good client of ours.

TAL (*unprepared for that*). Oh?

ND SALESWOMAN. Will you try on now, nish seeing the collection?

TAL. By the way, I've never met Mrs. 1es.

ND SALESWOMAN. She's lovely.

TAL. So—I'd rather you didn't mention er, that I gave her husband as reference. *zuiling.*) Do you mind?

ND SALESWOMAN (*with a faint smile*). of course not, Miss Allen. (*Indulgently.*) understand.

TAL (*angrily*). Do you! What do you erstand?

ND SALESWOMAN (*flustered*). I mean—

TAL (*very injured*). Never mind.

ND SALESWOMAN. Please, I hope you t think I meant—

TAL (*laughing and very charming n*). Of course not. Oh, it's dreadful, g in a strange city alone. You have to careful not to do anything people can onstrue. You see, I don't know Mrs. 1es yet. So I'd hate to get off on the g foot, before I've met her *socially.*

ND SALESWOMAN (*she sounds convinced*). rally. Women are funny about little gs like that.

ry's Booth—Enter SYLVIA.)

IA. Yoo-hoo! May I come in?

x (*not at all pleased to see her*). Hello, a.

Crystal's Booth.)

ND SALESWOMAN. What are you most in-ted in, Miss Allen, evening gowns?

TAL. Until I—I organize my social life von't have much use for evening gowns.

ND SALESWOMAN. I'll show you some t daytime things. (*Deliberately tone-* And we have very *exciting* negligées— *y exit.*)

ry's Booth.)

IA *circles around* MARY, *appraising her g with a critical eye.*)

MARY. Oh, sit down, Sylvia.

SYLVIA (*to the fitter*). I don't like that under-slung line. (*Demonstrating on* MARY.) It cuts her across the fanny. Makes her look posi-tively duck-bottomed.

MARY (*pulling away*). It's so tight, Mrs. Fow-ler can't sit down.

FIRST SALESWOMAN. Mrs. Fowler, shall I see if your fittings are ready?

SYLVIA. They'll call me.

MARY (*pointing to dress* FIRST SALESWOMAN *has over her arm*). Have you seen that?

FIRST SALESWOMAN (*holding up dress*). It's a lovely shape on. It doesn't look like a thing in the hand. (*Hands dress to someone outside and calls.*) Show this model, girls.

SYLVIA (*settling in a chair and smoking a cigarette*). So you had a marvelous time in Bermuda.

MARY. I had a good rest.

SYLVIA (*with unconscious humor*). Howard wants *me* to take a world cruise. By the way, dear, how is Stephen.

MARY. Splendid. (*Smiling, and very glad to be able to tell* SYLVIA *this*). He's not nearly so busy. He hasn't spent an evening—in the office, since I've come home. (*Enter* FIRST MODEL *in an elaborate negligée.* MARY *shakes her head, very practical.*) Pretty, but I never need a thing like that—

SYLVIA. Of course *you* don't. A hot little number, for intimate afternoons. (*Exit* FIRST MODEL.) Howard says nobody's seen Stephen in the Club, in the afternoon, for months—

MARY (*the thought flashes across her mind that* STEPHEN *could, of course, have revised his extra-marital schedule, from an evening to an afternoon one, but she quickly dis-misses it;* STEPHEN *has never let anything in-terfere with his hours downtown*). Don't worry so much about Stephen, Sylvia. He's my concern. (*Enter* SECOND MODEL *in a cor-set. She is prettily fashioned from head to toe. She does a great deal for the wisp of lace she wears. It does nothing that nature didn't do better for her.*)

SECOND MODEL. This is our new one-piece lace foundation garment. (*Pirouettes.*) Zips up the back, and no bones. (*She exits.*)

SYLVIA. Just that uplift, Mary, you need. I always said you'd regret nursing. Look at me. I don't think there's another girl our age who has bazooms like mine. I've taken care of them. Ice water every morning, camphor at night.

MARY. Doesn't it smell like an old fur coat? (PRINCESS TAMARA *passes in the corridor*.)

SYLVIA. Who cares?

MARY. Howard?

SYLVIA (*laughing harshly*). Howard!

FIRST SALESWOMAN (*calling out door*). Princess Tamara, show here. (*Enter* PRINCESS TAMARA *in a very extreme evening gown. She is Russian, regal, soignée*.)

MARY. Oh, Tamara, how lovely!

TAMARA. You must have it. Stephen would be amazed.

MARY. He certainly would. It's too extreme for me.

SYLVIA (*rises*). And you really haven't the figure. (*Yanks at gown*.) Tamara, you wear it wrong. I saw it in *Vogue*. (*Jerks*.) Off here, and down there.

TAMARA (*slapping* SYLVIA's *hand down*). Stop mauling me!

FIRST SALESWOMAN. Princess!

TAMARA. What do you know how to wear clothes?

SYLVIA. *I* am not a model, Tamara, but no one disputes how *I* wear clothes!

TAMARA. No one has mistaken you for Mrs. Harrison Williams yet!

FIRST SALESWOMAN. Princess Tamara, you'd better apologize.

MARY (*to* SALESWOMAN). It's just professional jealousy. They're really good friends!

SYLVIA (*maliciously*). You mean Tamara and *Howard* are friends.

TAMARA (*disgusted at the thought*). Do you accuse me of flirting with *your* husband?

SYLVIA (*pleasantly*). Go as far as you can, Tamara! If I know Howard, you're wasting valuable time.

TAMARA (*very angry*). Perhaps I am. F perhaps somebody else is not! (*The* SAL WOMAN *gives her an angry shove*.) You riding for a fall-off, Sylvia dear! (*Exit* MARA *angrily, followed by* SALESWOMAN.)

SYLVIA. Did you get that innuendo? I'd l to see Howard Fowler put anything ov on me. Oh, I've always hated that girl, ploiting her title the way she does! (CRYST *and* SECOND SALESWOMAN *enter* Cryst Booth.)

SECOND SALESWOMAN (*calling down the c ridor*). Princess Tamara, show in here, Miss Allen. (MARY's SALESWOMAN ent Mary's Booth, *picking up the call*.)

FIRST SALESWOMAN. Girls, show in Numl 3 to Miss Allen.

SYLVIA (*alert*). Did you say Miss Allen?

FIRST SALESWOMAN. Yes.

SYLVIA. Not—Crystal Allen?

FIRST SALESWOMAN. Why, yes—I just saw l on the floor. She's so attractive I asked l name.

SYLVIA (*watching* MARY *closely*). Oh, Crystal Allen gets her things here? (MA *sits down suddenly*.)

FIRST SALESWOMAN. She's a new client Why, Mrs. Haines, are you ill? (MARY caught SYLVIA's *eye in the mirror*. SYL knows now that MARY knows.)

MARY. No, no. I'm just tired. (TAMARA ent Crystal's Booth.)

FITTER. We've kept you standing too long

FIRST SALESWOMAN. I'll get you a glass sherry. (*Exit* MARY's FITTER *and* SALESW MAN. SYLVIA *closes door*.) (Crystal's Booth.)

CRYSTAL (*admiring* TAMARA's *extreme e ning gown*). I'm going to have that, i have to wear it for breakfast.

SECOND SALESWOMAN. Send it in here, Pr cess. (TAMARA *exits*.) (Mary's Booth.)

SYLVIA. Mary, you do know! (*Deeply sy pathetic*.) Why didn't you confide in n

MARY. Sylvia, go away.

VIA (*fiercely*). Stephen is a louse. Spend-
ng your money on a girl like that.

RY. Sylvia, please mind your own affairs.

VIA. She's already made a fool of you
fore all your friends. And don't you think
e salesgirls know who gets the bills?

RY (*distraught*). I don't care, I tell you.
don't care!

VIA. Oh, yes, you do. (*Pointing to* MARY'S
icken *face in the mirror.*) Don't be an
rich, Mary. (*A pause.*) Go in there.

RY. Go in there? I'm going home. (*She
es and begins to dress.*)

ST SALESWOMAN (*half enters*). Mrs.
ines' sherry—

VIA (*taking it from her, and closing the
or in her face*). All right.

VIA. You've caught her cold. It's *your*
ince to humiliate her. Just say a few
iet words. Tell her you'll make Stephen's
e *hell* until he gives her up.

RY. Stephen will give her up when he's
ed of her.

VIA. When he's tired of her? Look where
e was six months ago. Look where she is
w.

RY. Stephen's not in love with that girl.

VIA. Maybe not. But you don't know wo-
n like that when they get hold of a man.

RY. Sylvia, please let me decide what is
t for me, and my home. (CRYSTAL, *in her
oth, has been undressing, admiring herself
she does so in the mirror. Now she slips
o a "really exciting" negligée.*)

VIA. Well, she may be a perfectly marvel-
influence for Stephen, but she's not go-
to do your children any good.

RY (*turning to her*). What do you mean?

VIA (*mysteriously*). Never mind.

RY (*going to her*). Tell me!

VIA. Far be it from *me* to tell you things
a don't care to hear. I've known this all
ng. (*Nobly.*) Have I *uttered?*

RY (*violently*). What have my children
do with this?

SYLVIA (*after all,* MARY's *asking for it*). It
was while you were away. Edith saw them.
Stephen, and that tramp, and your children
—together, lunching in the Park.

MARY. It's not true!

SYLVIA. Why would Edith lie? She said
they were having a hilarious time. Little
Stevie was eating his lunch sitting on that
woman's lap. She was kissing him between
every bite. When I heard that, I was positively *heart-sick,* dear! (*Sees she has scored.
Celebrates by tossing down* MARY's *sherry.*)
(*Crystal's Booth.*)

CRYSTAL. Oh, go get that evening gown.
This thing bores me.

SECOND SALESWOMAN. Right away, Miss Allen. (*Exits.*)
(*Mary's Booth.*)

SYLVIA. But, as you say, dear, it's your affair,
not mine. (*Goes to the door, looking very
hurt that* MARY *has refused her good advice.*) No doubt that girl will make a perfectly good *step-mamma* for your children!
(*Exits.* MARY, *now dressed, is alone. She
stares at the partition which separates her
from that still unmeasured enemy to her
well-ordered domesticity, "the other woman." Her common sense dictates she should
go home, but now she violently experiences
the ache to talk. She struggles against it,
then goes, bitterly determined, to the door.
Exits. A second later, there is a knock on*
CRYSTAL's *door.* CRYSTAL *is alone.*)

CRYSTAL. Come in! (*Enter* MARY. *She closes
door.*) I beg your pardon?

MARY. I am—Mrs. Stephen Haines.

CRYSTAL (*her poise is admirable*). Sorry—I
don't think I know you!

MARY. Please don't pretend.

CRYSTAL. So Stephen finally told you?

MARY. No. I found out. (SECOND SALESWO-
MAN *half enters.*)

CRYSTAL. Stay out of here! (*Exit* SALESWO-
MAN.)

MARY. I've known about you from the beginning.

CRYSTAL. Well, that's news.

MARY. I kept still.

CRYSTAL. Very smart of you. (SECOND SALES-WOMAN *pantomimes down the corridor, to another girl to join her. Enters* MARY's *booth. One by one, during the rest of this scene, the* FITTERS, SALESWOMEN *and* MODELS *tip-toe into* MARY's *booth and plaster their ears against the partition.*)

MARY. No, not smart. I wanted to spare Stephen. But you've gone a little too far— You've been seeing my children. I won't have you touching my children!

CRYSTAL. For God's sake, don't get hysterical. What do I care about your children? I'm sick of hearing about them.

MARY. You won't have to hear about them any more. When Stephen realizes how humiliating all this has been to me, he'll give you up instantly.

CRYSTAL. Says who? The dog in the manger?

MARY. That's all I have to say.

CRYSTAL. That's plenty.

MARY (*more calmly*). Stephen would have grown tired of you anyway.

CRYSTAL (*nastily*). Speaking from your *own* experience? Well, he's not tired of me yet, Mrs. Haines.

MARY (*contemptuous*). Stephen is just amusing himself with you.

CRYSTAL. And he's amusing himself plenty.

MARY. You're very hard.

CRYSTAL. I can be soft—on the *right* occasions. What do you expect me to do? Burst into tears and beg you to forgive me?

MARY. I found exactly what I expected!

CRYSTAL. That goes double!

MARY (*turning to the door*). You'll have to make other plans, Miss Allen.

CRYSTAL (*going to her*). Listen, I'm taking my marching orders from Stephen.

MARY. Stephen doesn't love you.

CRYSTAL. He's doing the best he can in the circumstances.

MARY. He couldn't love a girl like you.

CRYSTAL. What do you think we've be doing for the past six months? Crossw puzzles? What have you got to kick abo You've got everything that matters. name, the position, the money—

MARY (*losing control of herself again*). No ing matters to me but Stephen—!

CRYSTAL. Oh, can the sob-stuff, Mrs. Hai You don't think this is the first time phen's ever cheated? Listen, I'd break your smug little roost if I could. I h just as much right as you have to sit in a of butter. But I don't stand a chance!

MARY. I'm glad you know it.

CRYSTAL. Well, don't think it's just beca he's *fond* of you—

MARY. *Fond?*

CRYSTAL. You're not what's stopping hin You're just an old *habit* with him. It's those brats he's afraid of losing. If he wer such a sentimental fool about those k he'd have walked out on *you* years ago.

MARY (*fiercely*). That's not true!

CRYSTAL. Oh, yes, it is. I'm telling you a plain truths you won't get from Stephen.

MARY. Stephen's always told me the truth

CRYSTAL (*maliciously*). Well, look at the ord. (*A pause.*) Listen, Stephen's satis with this arrangement. So don't force issues, unless you want plenty of trouble

MARY. You've made it impossible for m do anything else—!

CRYSTAL (*rather pleased*). Have I?

MARY. You haven't played fair—!

CRYSTAL. Where would any of us get if played fair?

MARY. Where do you hope to get?

CRYSTAL. Right where *you* are, Mrs. Hai

MARY. You're very confident.

CRYSTAL. The longer you stay in here, more confident I get. Saint or no saint, M Haines, you are a hell of a *dull woma*

MARY (MARY *stares at her wide-eyed at horrid thought that this may be the tr She refuses to meet the challenge. She e ocates*). By your standards, I probably am. — (*Suddenly ashamed that she has allowed erself to be put so pathetically on the de-nsive.*) Oh, why am I standing here talk-ig to you? This is something for Stephen id me to settle! (*Exits.*)

RYSTAL (*slamming the door after her*). Oh, hat the hell!

Mary's Booth.)

COND SALESWOMAN. So that's what she lls meeting Mrs. Haines *socially.*

RST SALESGIRL. Gee, I feel sorry for Mrs. aines. She's so nice.

EGLIGEE MODEL. She should have kept her outh shut. Now she's in the soup.

FIRST SALESWOMAN. It's a terrible mistake to lay down ultimatums to a man.

FIRST MODEL. Allen's smart. She's fixed it so anything Mr. Haines says is going to sound wrong.

FIRST SALESGIRL. She'll get him sure.

FIRST FITTER. Look at that body. She's got him now.

SECOND SALESGIRL. You can't trust any man. *That's* all they want.

CORSET MODEL (*plaintively, her hands on her lovely hips*). What else have we got to give?

CURTAIN

ACT TWO

SCENE I

Two weeks later. A small exercise room in Elizabeth Arden's beauty-salon. Right, a mir-red wall. Rear, a door. Left, a cabinet victrola beneath an open window. On the floor, wadded pink satin mat. As the curtain rises, SYLVIA, *in a pair of shorts, is prone on the at, describing lackadaisical arcs with her legs, to the sensuous rhythm of a tango record. ne* INSTRUCTRESS, *a bright, pretty girl, in a pink silk bathing suit, stands above her, drilling r in a carefully cultured voice. Until the cue "stretch," the* INSTRUCTRESS' *lines are spoken rough* SYLVIA'S *prattle, which she is determined, for the honor of the salon, to ignore, d, if possible, to discourage. From the word "up," this is a hopeless task.*

STRUCTRESS. Up—over—up—down. Up— etch—up—together. Up—stretch—up—

LVIA. Of course, my sympathies are for rs. Haines. They always are for a woman ainst a man—

STRUCTRESS (*louder*). Up—over—up— wn. Up—stretch—up—together. Up—

LVIA. But she did behave like an awful ot—

TRUCTRESS. Stretch—up—together. Please n't try to talk, Mrs. Fowler.

LVIA. But you know how some women are en they lose their heads—

TRUCTRESS (*grimly*). Stretch—up—toge-r—up—

VIA. They do things they regret all their es—

INSTRUCTRESS (*grabs* SYLVIA'S *languid limb and gives it a corrective yank*). Ster-retch!

SYLVIA. Ouch, my scars!

INSTRUCTRESS (*callously*). This is very good for adhesions. Up—

SYLVIA (*resolutely inert*). It's got me down.

INSTRUCTRESS. Rest. (SYLVIA *groans her re-lief*). And relax your diaphragm muscles, Mrs. Fowler, (*bitterly*) if you can. (*Goes to the victrola, changes the record for a fox-trot*).

SYLVIA. Of course, I do wish Mrs. Haines would make up her mind if she's going to get a divorce. It's terrible on all her friends, not knowing. Naturally, you can't ask them anywhere—

INSTRUCTRESS. Of course not. Now, on your side. (SYLVIA *rolls to her side, reclining on her elbow.*) Ready? Up—down—up—down —(*Snaps her fingers.* SYLVIA *flaps a limp leg up, down—*) Don't bend the knee—

SYLVIA (*thoughtfully*). Of course, for the children's sake, I think Mrs. Haines ought to stay. (*Piously*) I know I would. (*Her knees look bent, not to say broken.*)

INSTRUCTRESS (*imploring*). Don't crook it, please.

SYLVIA. And she ought not to have faced Mr. Haines with the issue. When a man's got himself in that deep he has to have time to taper it off—

INSTRUCTRESS (*straightening out* SYLVIA's *offending member with considerable force*). Thigh in, not out.

SYLVIA (*pained, but undaunted*). But Mrs. Haines never listens to any of her friends. She is a very peculiar woman.

INSTRUCTRESS. She must be. Now, please— up—down—up—down—

SYLVIA (*redoubling her efforts, and her errors*). Oh, I tell everybody whatever she wants to do is the right thing. I've got to be loyal to Mrs. Haines, you know . . . Oh, I'm simply exhausted. (*Flops over, flat on her stomach, panting.*)

INSTRUCTRESS. Then suppose you try something simple—like crawling up the wall? (SYLVIA *lifts a martyred face. The* INSTRUCTRESS *changes the record for a waltz.*)

SYLVIA (*scrambling to her feet*). What I go through to keep my figure! Lord, it infuriates me at dinner parties when some fat lazy man asks, "What do you do with yourself all day, Mrs. Fowler?" (*Sits alongside the rear wall.*)

INSTRUCTRESS. You rotate on your buttocks. (SYLVIA *rotates, then lies back, her knees drawn up to her chin, the soles of her feet against the wall*). Arms flat. Now you crawl slowly up the wall.

SYLVIA (*crawling*). I wish you wouldn't say that. It makes me feel like vermin—

INSTRUCTRESS (*kneeling beside her*). Don't talk.

SYLVIA. There's a couple of people I'd like to exterminate, too—

INSTRUCTRESS. Let's reverse the action. (SYL VIA *crawls down, as* PEGGY *enters in an exer cise suit. The* INSTRUCTRESS *brightens.*)

INSTRUCTRESS. How do you do, Mrs. Day (*To* SYLVIA.) Down slowly—

PEGGY (*gaily*). How do you do? Hello, Syl via.

SYLVIA. You're late again, Peggy.

PEGGY (*crestfallen*). I'm sorry.

SYLVIA (*sitting up*). After all, dear, I an paying for this course.

PEGGY. You know I'm grateful, Sylvia—

SYLVIA. Well, don't cry about it. It's onl fifty dollars.

PEGGY. That's a lot to me—

SYLVIA (*sweetly*). To you, or just to you husband, dear?

INSTRUCTRESS. Please, ladies. Let us begi with posture. (SYLVIA *rises*). A lady alway enters a room erect.

SYLVIA. Lots of my friends exit horizontall (PEGGY *and* SYLVIA *go to the mirrored wa stand with their backs to it.*)

INSTRUCTRESS. Now—knees apart. Sit on th wall. (*They sit on imaginary seats.*) Rela (*They bend forward from the waist, finge tips brushing the floor.*) Now, roll slow up the wall . . . pressing each little verteb against the wall as hard as you can . . shoulders back, and where they belon Heads back. Mrs. Fowler, lift yourself b hind the ears. Pretend you're just a silly litt puppet dangling on a string. Chin up. (S places her hand at the level of PEGGY's strai ing chin.) No, Mrs. Day, your chin is re ing comfortably on a little table. Elbo bent—up on your toes—arms out—sho with the small of your back—you're o (SYLVIA *and* PEGGY, *side by side, mince acr the room.*)

PEGGY (*whispering*). Oh, Sylvia, why you always insinuate that John is practica a—miser?

INSTRUCTRESS (*she refers to* PEGGY's *swayi hips*). Tuck under!

SYLVIA. You have your own little incom Peggy. And what do you do with it? Y give it to John—

INSTRUCTRESS. Now, back, please! (*They ince backwards across the room.*)

PEGGY (*staunchly*). John makes so little—

INSTRUCTRESS (*she refers to* SYLVIA's *relaxed mmy*). Steady center control!

SYLVIA. Peggy, you're robbing John of his .anly sense of responsibility. You're turn-g him into a gigolo. A little money of her vn she lets no man touch is the only pro-ction a woman has. (*They are against the irror again.*)

INSTRUCTRESS. Now, are you both the way u were when you left the wall?

SYLVIA (*brightly*). Well, I am.

INSTRUCTRESS. No, Mrs. Fowler, you're not. *She imitates* SYLVIA's *posture, showing how* *LVIA's posterior protrudes, against the dic- tes of fashion, if not of nature.*) Not *this,* Mrs. Fowler—("*Bumps*") That! (*She leads* LVIA *forward.*) Try it, please. (*Facing one* aother, *they do an elegant pair of* "umps.") Now, relax on the mat.

This piece of business defies description, ut to do the best one can: the GIRLS *stand de by side, arms straight above their heads. t the* INSTRUCTRESS' *count of "one," each rops a hand, limp, from the wrist. At* "wo," *the other hand drops, then their eads fall upon their breasts, their arms flap their sides, their waists cave in, their knees uckle under, and they swoon, or crumble ke boneless things, to the mat.*)

INSTRUCTRESS (*she has changed the record*). ow, ready? Bend—stretch, you know. Be-n— (*They do another leg exercise on the at.*) Bend—stretch—bend—down—plenty : pull on the hamstrings, please! Bend—retch—bend—down— (*Enter* EDITH. *She draped in a white sheet. Her head is bound a white towel. Her face is undergoing a ie-up," that is, she wears broad white raps under her chin and across her fore-ead. She appears very distressed.*)

EDITH. Oh, Sylvia! Hello, Peggy—

SYLVIA (*sitting up*). Why, Edith, what are u doing up here?

EDITH. Having a facial, downstairs. Oh, Syl-a. I'm so glad you're here. I've done the ost *awful* thing, I—

INSTRUCTRESS. We're right in the middle of our exercises, Mrs. Potter—

SYLVIA (*To* INSTRUCTRESS). Will you tell them outside—I want my paraffine bath now? There's a dear.

INSTRUCTRESS. But, Mrs. Fowler—

SYLVIA (*cajoling*). I'm simply exhausted.

INSTRUCTRESS. You've hardly moved a mus-cle.

SYLVIA (*with elaborate patience*). Look, whose carcass is this? Yours or mine?

INSTRUCTRESS. It's yours, Mrs. Fowler, but I'm paid to exercise it.

SYLVIA. You talk like a horse-trainer.

INSTRUCTRESS. Well, Mrs. Fowler, you're get-ting warm. (*Exits.*)

EDITH. I've done the most *ghastly* thing. Move over. (PEGGY *and* SYLVIA *move over;* EDITH *plumps between them on the mat.*) But it wasn't until I got here, in the middle of my facial, that I realized it—I could bite my tongue off when I think of it—

SYLVIA. Well, what is it, Edith?

EDITH. I was lunching with Frances Jones, and—

SYLVIA. Edith Potter, I know exactly what you're going to say!

EDITH. I forgot she—

SYLVIA. You forgot she's Dolly de Peyster.

EDITH. But I never read her awful column—

SYLVIA (*fiercely*). You told her something about me? What did you tell her?

EDITH. Oh, darling, you know I never give *you* away. (*Remorsefully.*) I—I—told her all about Stephen and Mary—

SYLVIA (*relieved*). Oh! That!

EDITH. It wasn't until the middle of my fa-cial—

PEGGY. Oh, Edith! It will be in all those dreadful tabloids!

EDITH. I know—I've been racking my brains to recall what I said—I think I told her that when Mary walked into the fitting room, she yanked the ermine coat off the Allen girl—

SYLVIA. You didn't!

EDITH. Well, I don't know whether I said ermine or *sable*—but I know I told her that Mary *smacked* the Allen girl!

PEGGY. Edith!

EDITH. Well, that's what Sylvia told me!

SYLVIA. I didn't!

EDITH. You did, too!

SYLVIA (*hurt*). Anyway, I didn't expect you to tell it to a cheap reporter—

EDITH. Well, it doesn't really make much difference. The divorce is practically settled—

SYLVIA (*eagerly*). Who says so?

EDITH. You did!

SYLVIA (*patiently*). I said, Mary couldn't broadcast her domestic difficulties, and not expect them to wind up in a scandal.

PEGGY. Mary didn't broadcast them!

SYLVIA. Who did?

PEGGY. *You* did. You—you're all making it impossible for her to do anything now but get a divorce!

SYLVIA. You flatter us. We didn't realize how much influence we had on our friends' lives!

PEGGY. Everybody calling her up, telling her how badly she's been treated—

SYLVIA. As a matter of fact, I told her she'd make a great mistake. What has any woman got to gain by a divorce? No matter how much he gives her, she won't have what they have together. And you know as well as I do, he'd marry that girl. What he's spent on her, he'd have to, to protect his investment. (*Sorrowfully.*) But, I have as much influence on Mary as I have on *you*, Peggy. (*The* INSTRUCTRESS *re-enters.*)

INSTRUCTRESS. The paraffine bath is ready, Mrs. Fowler.

SYLVIA (*rises*). Well, don't worry, Edith, I'll give de Peyster a ring. I can fix it.

EDITH. How?

SYLVIA (*graciously*). Oh, I'll tell her ⟨ were lying.

EDITH. You'll do no such thing!

SYLVIA (*shrugging*). Then let the story ri⟨ It will be forgotten tomorrow. You kn⟨ the awful things they printed about—wh⟨ her name?—before she jumped out the w⟨ dow? Why, I can't even remember ⟨ name, so who cares, Edith? (*Exits.*)

INSTRUCTRESS. Mrs. Potter, you come ri⟨ back where you belong.

EDITH. Why, you'd think this was a board⟨ school!

INSTRUCTRESS. But, Mrs. Potter, it's suc⟨ foolish waste of money—

EDITH. Listen, relaxing is part of my fac⟨

INSTRUCTRESS (*coolly*). Then you should⟨ lax completely, Mrs. Potter, from the c⟨ up. (*Exits.*)

EDITH. Honestly, the class feeling you ⟨ into these days! (*Struggles to her feet.*) ⟨ so tired of paying creatures like that to in⟨ me—

PEGGY (*going to her*). Edith! Let's call M⟨ up and warn her!

EDITH. About what?

PEGGY. The newspapers!

EDITH. My dear, how could we do t⟨ without involving Sylvia—

PEGGY. But it's *her* fault— Oh, she's su⟨ dreadful woman!

EDITH. Oh, she can't help it, Peggy. It's ⟨ her tough luck she wasn't born deaf ⟨ dumb. But what can we do about it? S⟨ always gotten away with murder. Why, s⟨ been having an affair for a year with ⟨ young customers' man in Howard's of⟨

PEGGY (*shocked*). Edith!

EDITH. Right under Howard's nose! ⟨ Howard doesn't care! So what business ⟨ of yours or mine? (*Earnestly.*) Peggy, ⟨ a tip from me—keep out of other wom⟨ troubles. I've never had a fight with a ⟨ friend in all my life. Why? I hear no ⟨ I see no evil, I speak no evil!

CURTAIN

SCENE II

A few days later.

Mary's pantry, midnight. Left, a swinging door, to the kitchen. Rear, a sink under a ~~r~~*tained window. A small, built-in refrigerator. Center, a table, two chairs.*
As the curtain rises, JANE, *the maid, and* MAGGIE, *the new cook, are having a midnight* ~~sn~~*ck.* MAGGIE, *a buxom, middle-aged woman, wears a wrapper and felt bedroom slippers.*

~~JA~~NE (*folding a tabloid newspaper which* ~~she~~ *has been reading to* MAGGIE.) So *he* says, ~~"A~~ll you can do with a story like that, is live ~~it~~ down, Mary."

~~M~~AGGIE. I told you they'd begin all over. ~~On~~ce a thing like that is out between a mar~~rie~~d couple, they've got to fight it out. De~~pe~~nds which they get sick of first, each ~~oth~~er, or the argument.

~~JA~~NE. It's enough to make you lose your faith ~~in~~ marriage.

~~M~~AGGIE. Whose faith in marriage?

~~JA~~NE. You don't believe in marriage?

~~M~~AGGIE. Sure I do. For women. (*Sighs.*) But ~~it'~~s the sons of Adam they got to marry. ~~Go~~ on.

~~JA~~NE. Well, finally he said to the madam, ~~"I~~ gave her up, didn't I? And I was a swine, ~~ab~~out the way I did it." How do you suppose ~~he~~ did it, Maggie?

~~M~~AGGIE. Maybe he just said, "Scram, the ~~wi~~fe is onto us."

~~JA~~NE. Well, the madam didn't believe him. ~~Sh~~e says, "Stephen, you really ain't seen ~~he~~r?"

~~M~~AGGIE. He lied in his teeth—

~~JA~~NE. Oh, the way he said it, I kind of be~~lie~~ved him. But the madam says, "Oh, but ~~ca~~n I ever trust you again?"

~~M~~AGGIE. You can't trust none of 'em no fur~~th~~er than I can kick this lemon pie.

~~JA~~NE. Oh, it was terrible sad. He said, "Mary, ~~de~~ar Mary, Mary, dear Mary, Mary—"

~~M~~AGGIE. Dear Mary. But it ain't exactly con~~vi~~ncing.

~~JA~~NE. Then, I guess he tried to kiss her. ~~Be~~cause she says, "Please don't. I'll never be ~~ab~~le to kiss you again, without thinking of ~~he~~r in your arms."

MAGGIE (*appreciatively*). Just like in the movies— Imagine him taking up with a girl like that.

JANE. He was telling the madam: She's a virgin.

MAGGIE. She *is*? Then what's all the rumpus about?

JANE. Oh, she ain't a virgin now. She was.

MAGGIE. So was Mae West—once.

JANE. He told the madam he'd been faithful for twelve years.

MAGGIE. Well, that's something these days, that beats flying the Atlantic. Did the madam believe him?

JANE. She said, "How do I know you've been faithful?"

MAGGIE. She don't.

JANE. But the way he said it—

MAGGIE. Listen, if they lay off six months, they feel themselves busting out all over with haloes.

JANE. Anyway, he says this girl was really a nice girl. So sweet and interested in him and all. And how it happened one night, unexpected, in her room—

MAGGIE. Did he think it was going to happen in Roxy's?

JANE. He said she wouldn't take nothing from him for months—

MAGGIE. Only her education. Oh, that one knew her onions. She certainly played him for a sucker.

JANE. That's what the madam said. She said, "Stephen, can't you see that girl's only interested in you for your money?"

MAGGIE. Tch, tch, tch. I'll bet that made him sore. A man don't like to be told no woman but his wife is fool enough to love him. It drives 'em nutty.

JANE. Did it! "Mary, I told you what kind of girl she is," he says. You know—I just told you—

MAGGIE. I had her number. You didn't convey no information.

JANE. Well, then they both got sore.

MAGGIE (*rises, goes out for coffee*). I knew it.

JANE. So, he began to tell her all over, what a good husband he'd been. And how hard he'd worked for her and the kids. And she kept interrupting with what a good wife she'd been and how proud she was of him. Then they began to exaggerate themselves—

MAGGIE (*enters with coffee pot*). Listen, anybody that's ever been married knows that line backwards and forwards. What happened?

JANE. Well, somewhere in there the madam says, "Stephen, you do want a divorce. Only you ain't got the courage to ask it." And he says, "Oh, my God, no I don't, Mary. Haven't I told you?" And she says, "But you don't love me!" And he says, "But oh, my God, Mary, I'm awful *fond* of you." And she says, very icy, "Fond, fond? Is that all?" And he says, "No Mary, there's the children." Maggie, that's the thing I don't understand. Why does she get so mad every time he says they've got to consider the children? If children ain't the point of being married, what is?

MAGGIE. A woman don't want to be told she's being kept on just to run a kindergarten. (*Goes to the ice box for a bottle of cream.*)

JANE. Well, the madam says, "Stephen, I want to keep the children out of this. I haven't used the children. I ain't asked you to sacrifice yourself for the children." Maggie, that's where he got so terrible mad. He says, "But why, in God's name, Mary? You knew about us all along. Why did you wait until now to make a fool of me?"

MAGGIE. As if he needed her help.

JANE. So, then, suddenly she says, in a awful low voice, "Stephen, oh, Stephen, we can't go on like this. It ain't worthy of what we been to each other!" And he says, "Oh, no, it's not, Mary!"

MAGGIE. Quite a actress, ain't you?

JANE. My boy friend says I got eyes li[ke] Claudette Colbert's.

MAGGIE. Did he ever say anything about yo[ur] legs? Have a cup of coffee. (*Pours coffee*)

JANE. That's when the madam says wh[at] you could have knocked me down with [a] feather! The madam says, "Stephen, I wa[nt] a divorce. Yes, Stephen, *I* want a divorc[e]."

MAGGIE. Tch. Tch. Abdicating!

JANE. Well, Maggie, you could have knock[ed] him down with a feather!

MAGGIE (*waving coffee pot*). I'd like to kno[ck] him down with this.

JANE. "My God! Mary," he says, "you do[n't] mean it!" So she says, in a funny voi[ce], "Yes, I do. You've killed my love for yo[u], Stephen."

MAGGIE. He's just simple-minded enough [to] believe that.

JANE. So he says, "I don't blame you. [My] God, how can I blame you?"

MAGGIE. My God, he can't!

JANE. So then she said it was all over, [be]cause it was only the children he minded l[os]ing. She said that made their marriage [a] mockery.

MAGGIE. A mockery?

JANE. Something funny.

MAGGIE. I ain't going to die laughing.

JANE. He said she was talking nonsense. [He] said she was just upset on account of t[he] story in the papers. He said what else cou[ld] she expect if she was going to spill her tr[ou]bles to a lot of gabby women? He said s[he] should go to bed until she could thi[nk] things over. He was going out for a breath [of] fresh air.

MAGGIE. The old hat trick.

JANE. So the madam says, "You're going [to] see that girl." And he says, "Oh, for Go[d's] sake, Mary, one minute you never want [to] see me again, the next I can't even go o[ut] for a airing!"

MAGGIE. You oughtn't to let none of '[em] out except on a leash.

NE. And she says, "Are you going to see r, or ain't you?" And he says, "Well, what fference does it make, if you're going to vorce me?" And she says, "It don't make difference to *you,* I guess. Please go, ephen. And don't come back *ever.*" (*Be-ns to cry.*)

AGGIE (*impatiently*). Yes?

NE. I didn't hear his last words. Because aturally, when he said he was going, I ooted down the hall. But I heard her call, tephen?" And he stops on the landing d says, "Yes, Mary?" and she says, "Noth-g. Just don't slam the front door— The rvants will hear you!" So I came down re. Oh, Maggie, what's going to happen?

AGGIE. She's going to get a divorce.

NE. Oh, dear. I'm so sad for her.

AGGIE. I ain't.

NE. What?

AGGIE. She's indulging a pride she ain't titled to. Marriage is a business of taking re of a man and rearing his children. It n't meant to be no perpetual honeymoon. ow long would any husband last if he was pposed to go on acting forever like a red-t Clark Gable? What's the difference if don't love her?

JANE. How can you say that, Maggie!

MAGGIE. That don't let her off her obligation to keep him from making a fool of himself, does it?

JANE. Do you think he'll marry that girl?

MAGGIE. When a man's got the habit of supporting some woman, he just don't feel natural unless he's doing it.

JANE. But he told the madam marrying her was the furthest thing from his mind.

MAGGIE. It don't matter what he's got in his mind. It's what those two women got in theirs will settle the matter.

JANE. But the madam says it's up to *him.* She said, "You love her, or you love me, Stephen."

MAGGIE. So what did he say to that?

JANE. Nothing for a long time. Just walked up and down—up and down—up and—

MAGGIE. He was thinking. Tch—tch. The first man who can think up a good explanation how he can be in love with his wife *and* another woman, is going to win that prize they're always giving out in Sweden!

CURTAIN

SCENE III

A month later.
MARY's *living room. The room is now denuded of pictures, books, vases, etc. The rug rolled up. The curtains and chairs are covered with slips.*
As the curtain rises, MARY, *dressed for traveling, is pacing up and down.* MRS. MORE-AD, *dressed for the street, watches her from the sofa.*

RS. MOREHEAD. What time does your train ?

ARY (*looking at her wrist watch*). An hour. s secretary ought to be here. I never knew ere could be so many papers to sign.

RS. MOREHEAD. You showed everything to ur lawyers—

ARY. They always say the same thing! I'm tting a "raw deal"—

RS. MOREHEAD (*alarmed*). But, Mary—

ARY. Oh, I know it's not true. Stephen's en very generous.

MRS. MOREHEAD. Oh, I wouldn't say that. If Stephen is a rich man now, he owes it largely to you.

MARY. Stephen would have gotten where he is, with or without me.

MRS. MOREHEAD. He didn't have a penny when you married him.

MARY. Mother, are you trying to make me bitter, too?

MRS. MOREHEAD (*helplessly*). I'm sure I don't know what to say. If I sympathize with Stephen, you accuse me of taking his side.

And when I sympathize with you, I'm making you bitter. The thing for me to do is keep still. (*There is a pause. Then, emphatically.*) You're both making a terrible mistake!

MARY. Mother, please!

MRS. MOREHEAD. But the children, Mary. The children—

MARY. What good will it do them to be brought up in a home full of quarrelling and suspicion? They'll be better off just with me.

MRS. MOREHEAD. No, they won't. A child needs both its parents in one home.

MARY. A home without love?

MRS. MOREHEAD. He's terribly fond of you—

MARY. Mother, don't use that word! Oh, Mother, please. Every argument goes round in circles. And, it's too late now—

MRS. MOREHEAD. It's never too late when you love. Mary, why don't you call this thing off? I'm sure that's what Stephen's waiting for.

MARY (*bitterly*). Is it? He hasn't made any sign of it to me. Isn't he the one to come to me?

MRS. MOREHEAD. You're the one, Mary, who insisted on the divorce.

MARY. But don't you see; if he hadn't wanted it, he'd have fought me—

MRS. MOREHEAD. Stephen's not the fighting kind.

MARY. Neither am I.

MRS. MOREHEAD. Damn these modern laws!

MARY. Mother!

MRS. MOREHEAD. Damn them, I say! Fifty years ago, when women couldn't get divorces, they made the best of situations like this. And sometimes, out of situations like this they made very good things indeed! (*Enter JANE, right.*)

JANE. Mr. Haines' secretary, ma'am.

MRS. MOREHEAD. Tell her to come in. (*Exit JANE.*) Now, go bathe your eyes. Don't let that adding-machine see you like this. And don't be long. Remember, you have one more unpleasant task.

MARY. Mary?

MRS. MOREHEAD. The child must be told.

MARY (*miserably, and a little guiltily*). have been putting it off. Because—

MRS. MOREHEAD. Because you hope at the la minute a miracle will keep you from makir a mess of your life. Have you thought: St phen might marry that girl?

MARY (*very confident*). He won't do that.

MRS. MOREHEAD. What makes you so sure

MARY. Because, deep down, Stephen do love me— But he won't find it out, un I've—really gone away— (*At the door* You'll take good care of the childre Mother? And make them write to me Reno, once a week? And please, Moth don't spoil them so. (*Exits left.*)

MRS. MOREHEAD. Gracious! You'd think I never raised children of my own! (*Ent MISS WATTS and MISS TRIMMERBACK, rig They are very tailored, plain girls. M WATTS, the older and the plainer of the tu carries a brief-case.*) How do you do, M Watts?

MISS WATTS. How do you do, Mrs. Mo head? This is Miss Trimmerback from o office.

MISS TRIMMERBACK. How do you do?

MISS WATTS. She's a notary. We have so papers for Mrs. Haines to sign.

MRS. MOREHEAD. Anything I can do?

MISS WATTS. The children will be with yo (MRS. MOREHEAD *nods.*) Any incidental bi Mrs. Morehead, send to the office. But y understand, bills arriving after the divo will be assumed by Mrs. Haines under t terms of the settlement.

MRS. MOREHEAD. Mrs. Haines will be w you in a minute. Please don't bother with unnecessary details. She's—she's press for time. (*Exits right.*)

MISS TRIMMERBACK. Gee, don't you feel so for Mrs. Haines?

MISS WATTS (*bitterly*). I don't feel sorry any woman who thinks the world owes breakfast in bed.

MISS TRIMMERBACK. You don't like her.

WATTS. Oh, she never interfered at the
e.

TRIMMERBACK. Maybe that's why he's
a success.

WATTS. He'd have gotten further with-
her. Everything big that came up, he was
cautious, because of her and the kids.
*ens the brief-case, takes out papers and
arranges the papers, for signing, on
table.*) Well, thank heaven it's almost
. He and I can go back to work. (*Sits.*)

TRIMMERBACK. What about Allen?

WATTS (*guardedly.*) What about her?

TRIMMERBACK. Is he going to marry

WATTS. I don't butt into his private af-
. Oh, I hold no brief for Allen. But I
t say knowing *her* gave him a new inst in his work. Before her, he was cer-
ly going stale. That had me worried.

TRIMMERBACK (*sinking on the sofa*).
, she's lucky, I'll say.

WATTS. Oh?

TRIMMERBACK. I wish I could get a
to foot my bills. I'm sick and tired,
ing my own breakfast, sloshing through
rain at 8 A.M., working like a dog. For
t? Independence? A lot of indepen-
e you have on a woman's wages. I'd
k it like that for a decent, or an inde-
, home.

WATTS. I'm sure you would.

TRIMMERBACK. Wouldn't you?

WATTS. I have a home.

TRIMMERBACK. You mean Plattsburgh,
re you were born?

WATTS. The office. That's my home.

TRIMMERBACK. Some home! I see. The
-wife?

WATTS (*defiantly*). He could get along
r without Mrs. Haines or Allen than
ould without me.

TRIMMERBACK. Oh, you're very efficient,
. But what makes you think you're in-
nsable?

WATTS. I relieve him of a thousand fool-
etails. I remind him of things he forgets,

including, very often these days, his good
opinion of himself. I never cry and I don't
nag. I guess I *am* the office-wife. And a lot
better off than Mrs. Haines. He'll never divorce me!

MISS TRIMMERBACK (*astonished*). Why,
you're in love with him! (*They both rise,
face each other angrily.*)

MISS WATTS. What if I am? I'd rather work
for him than marry the kind of a dumb
cluck I could get— (*Almost tearful*) just
because he's a *man*— (*Enter* MARY, *left.*)

MARY. Yes, Miss Watts.

MISS WATTS (*collecting herself quickly*). Here
are the inventories of the furniture, Mrs.
Haines. I had the golf cups, the books, etch-
ings, and the ash stands sent to Mr. Haines'
club. (*Pauses.*) Mr. Haines asked if he could
also have the portrait of the two children.

MARY (*looking at the blank space over the
mantel*). Oh, but—

MISS WATTS. He said it wouldn't matter, if
you really didn't *care* for him to have it.

MARY. It's in storage.

MISS WATTS (*laying a paper on the table*).
This will get it out. Sign there. The cook's
letter of reference. Sign here. (MARY *sits,
signs.*) The insurance papers. You sign here.
(MISS TRIMMERBACK *signs each paper after*
MARY.) The transfer papers on the car. What
do you want done with it?

MARY. Well, I—

MISS WATTS. I'll find a garage. Sign here.
What do you want done if someone meets
your price on this apartment?

MARY. Well, I thought—

MISS WATTS. This gives us power of attorney
until you get back. Sign here.

MARY. But—I—

MISS WATTS. Oh, it's quite in order, Mrs.
Haines. Now, Mr. Haines took the liberty
of drawing you a new will. (*Places a blue,
legal-looking document before* MARY.)

MARY (*indignantly*). But—really—

MISS WATTS. If anything were to happen to
you in Reno, half your property would re-
vert to him. A detail your lawyers over-

looked. Mr. Haines drew up a codicil cutting himself out—

MARY. But, I don't understand legal language, Miss Watts. I—I must have my lawyer—

MISS WATTS. As you please. (*Stiffly.*) Mr. Haines suggested this for *your* sake, not his. I'm sure you realize, he has nothing but your interests at heart. (*A pause.*) Sign here. (MARY *signs,* MISS WATTS *signs.*) We need three witnesses. (*Enter* JANE, *right, with a box of flowers.*) Your maid will do.

MARY. Jane, please witness this. It's my will.

JANE (*in tears*). Oh, Mrs. Haines! (*Signs.*)

MISS WATTS (*gathering all the papers*). You can always make changes, in the event of your remarriage. (MARY *rises.*) And don't hesitate to let me know at the office, if there is anything *I* can ever do for you.

MARY (*coldly*). There will be nothing, Miss Watts.

MISS WATTS (*cheerfully*). Oh, there are always tag ends to a divorce, Mrs. Haines. And you know how Mr. Haines hates to be bothered with inconsequential details. Good day, Mrs. Haines, and pleasant journey to you! (*Exit* MISS WATTS *right, followed by* MISS TRIMMERBACK.)

JANE (*sniveling as she places the box on the table*). Mr. Haines said I was to give you these to wear on the train. (*Exits abruptly.* MARY *slowly opens the box, takes out a corsage of orchids and a card. Reads aloud: "What can I say? Stephen." Then throws them violently in the corner. Enter* MRS. MOREHEAD, LITTLE MARY, *dressed for street.*)

MRS. MOREHEAD. All set, dear?

MARY (*grimly*). All set—Mary, Mother wants to talk to you before she goes away.

MRS. MOREHEAD. Brother and I will wait for you downstairs. (*Exit* MRS. MOREHEAD.)

MARY. Mary, sit down, dear. (LITTLE MARY *skips to the sofa, sits down. A pause.* MARY *discovers that it's going to be even more painful and difficult than she imagined.*) Mary—

LITTLE MARY. Yes, Mother?

MARY. Mary—

LITTLE MARY (*perplexed by her moth[er's] tone, which she feels bodes no good to h[er]*). Have I done something wrong, Mother[?]

MARY. Oh, no, darling, no. (*She sits be[side] her daughter, and takes her two han[ds].*) Mary, you know Daddy's been gone [for] some time.

LITTLE MARY (*sadly*). A whole month[.]

MARY. Shall I tell you why?

LITTLE MARY (*eagerly*). Why?

MARY (*plunging in*). You know, dar[ling,] when a man and woman fall in love [—] they do, don't you?

LITTLE MARY. They kiss a lot—

MARY. They get married—

LITTLE MARY. Oh, yes. And then they [have] those children.

MARY. Well, sometimes, married pe[ople] don't stay in love.

LITTLE MARY. What, Mother?

MARY. The husband and the wife—fall [out] of love.

LITTLE MARY. Why do they do that?

MARY. Well, they do, that's all. And w[hen] they do, they get unmarried. You see?

LITTLE MARY. No.

MARY. Well, they do. They—they get w[hat] is called a divorce.

LITTLE MARY (*very matter of fact*). Oh[, do] they?

MARY. You don't know what a divor[ce is,] but—

LITTLE MARY. Yes, I do. I go to the mo[vies,] don't I? And lots of my friends have m[om]mies and daddies who are divorced.

MARY (*relieved, kisses her*). You kno[w I] love you very much, don't you, Mary?

LITTLE MARY (*a pause*). Of course, Mo[ther.]

MARY. Your father and I are going to [get a] divorce. That's why I'm going away. T[he] why— Oh, darling, I can't explain to [you] quite. But I promise you, when you are [older] you will understand. And you'll forgi[ve me.] You really will! Look at me, baby, plea[se.]

TLE MARY (*her lips begin to tremble*). looking at you, Mother—Doesn't Daddy : you any more?

Y. No, he doesn't.

LE MARY. Don't you love him?

Y. I—I—no, Mary.

LE MARY. Oh, Mother, why?

Y. I—I don't know—But it isn't either Idy's or Mother's fault.

LE MARY. But, Mother, when you love ebody I thought you loved them until day you die!

Y. With children, yes. But grown-ups different. They can fall out of love.

LE MARY. I won't fall out of love with and Daddy when I grow up. Will you out of love with me?

Y. Oh, no, darling, that's different, too.

LE MARY (*miserable*). I don't see *how*.

Y. You'll have to take my word for it, , it is. This divorce has nothing to do our love for you.

LE MARY. But if you and Daddy—

Y (*rising and drawing her daughter up er*). Darling, I'll explain it better to you

in the taxi. We'll go alone in the taxi, shall we?

LITTLE MARY. But, Mother, if you and Daddy are getting a divorce, which one won't I see again? Daddy or you?

MARY. You and Brother will live with me. That's what happens when—when people get divorced. Children must go with their mothers. But you'll see Daddy—sometimes. Now, darling, come along.

LITTLE MARY. Please, Mother, wait for me downstairs.

MARY. Why?

LITTLE MARY. I have to go to the bathroom.

MARY. Then hurry along, dear— (*Sees the orchids on the floor, and as she moves to the door stoops, picks them up, goes out. LITTLE MARY stands looking after her, stricken. Suddenly she goes to the back of the chair, hugs it, as if for comfort. Then she begins to cry and beat the back of the chair with her fists.*)

LITTLE MARY. Oh, please, please, Mother dear— Oh! Daddy, Daddy darling! Oh, why don't you do something—*do something* —Mother dear!

CURTAIN

SCENE IV

month later.

room in a lying-in hospital. Left, a door to the corridor. Right, a window banked to sill with expensive flowers. Center, a hospital bed, in which EDITH, propped up in a of lace pillows, lies with a small bundle at her breast. A white-uniformed nurse sits he window. The droop of her shoulders is eloquent: EDITH is a trying patient. As the ain rises, EDITH reaches across the bundle to the bedside table for a cigarette. She t make it.

H (*whining*). Nurse!

SE (*rising wearily*). Yes, Mrs. Potter.

H. Throw me a cigarette.

SE. Can't you wait, at least until you're ugh nursing?

H. How many children have you nursed? nursed four. (NURSE *lights her cigarette;* H *shifts the bundle slightly.*) Ouch! n it! It's got jaws like a dinosaur. (*En- PEGGY with a box of flowers.*)

PEGGY. Hello, Edith.

EDITH (*in a faint voice*). Hello, Peggy.

PEGGY (*putting flowers on bed*). Here—

EDITH. How thoughtful! Nurse, will you ask this damn hospital if they're equipped with a decent vase? (NURSE, *takes the box, opens flowers and arranges them, with others, in the window.*)

PEGGY (*leans over baby*). Oh, let me see. Oh, Edith, isn't he divine!

EDITH. I hate that milky smell.

PEGGY (*alarmed*). What's that on his nose?

EDITH. What nose? Oh, that's an ash. (*Blows away the ash. Hands* PEGGY *a letter from bedside table.*)

PEGGY. Mary?

EDITH (*nodding*). All about how healthy Reno is. Not a word about how she feels. I thought she cared more about Stephen than that. She sends her love to you and John. (PEGGY *reads. The wail of a new-born is heard outside.*)

EDITH. Nurse, close that door. (*The* NURSE *closes the door.*) I can't tell you what that new-born yodel does to my nerves. (*To* PEGGY.) What're you so down in the mouth about? I feel as badly about it as you do, but it was the thing Mary wanted to do, or she wouldn't have done it. Judging by that, she's reconciled to the whole idea.

PEGGY. She's just being brave!

EDITH. Brave? Why should she bother to be brave with her friends? Here, Nurse, he's through. (*The* NURSE *takes the bundle from her.*) I told Phelps to be sure to tell Stephen that Mary's perfectly happy. It will cheer Stephen up. He's been going around like a whipped dog.

PEGGY. Oh, Edith, please let me hold him! (*The* NURSE *gives* PEGGY *the baby.*)

NURSE (*smiling*). Careful of his back. Mrs. Day.

PEGGY (*goes to the window, hugging the bundle*). Oh, I *like* the feeling so!

EDITH. You wouldn't like it so much if you'd just had it. (*Whimpering.*) I had a terrible time, didn't I, Nurse?

NURSE. Oh, no, Mrs. Potter. You had a very easy time. (*She is suddenly angry.*) Why, women like you don't know what a terrible time is. Try bearing a baby and scrubbing floors. Try having one in a cold filthy kitchen, without ether, without a change of linen, without decent food, without a cent to bring it up—and try getting up the next day with your insides falling out, to cook your husband's—! (*Controls herself.*) No, Mrs. Potter, you didn't have a terrible time at all— I'll take the baby, please. (*Sees the reluctant expression on* PEGGY's *face.*) I hope

some day you'll have one of your own, M Day. (*The* NURSE *exits with the baby.* PE breaks into tears.*)

EDITH. Well, for God's sake, Peggy, that battle-axe didn't hurt my feelings a They're all the same. If you don't get p tonitis or have quintuplets, they th you've had a picnic—(PEGGY *sits beside bed, crying.*) What's the matter?

PEGGY. Oh, Edith—John and I are gett a divorce!

EDITH (*patting her hand*). Well, darl that's what I heard!

PEGGY (*surprised*). But—but we didn't cide to until last night.

EDITH (*cheerfully*). Oh, darling, everyb could see it was in the cards. Money, I pose?

PEGGY (*nodding*). Oh, dear! I wish M were here—

EDITH. Well, she'll be there. (*Laughs.*) forgive me, dear. I do feel sorry for But it is funny.

PEGGY. What's funny?

EDITH. It's going to be quite a gatherin; the clan. (*Sitting up in bed, full of en to break the news.*) Howard Fow bounced Sylvia out right on her ear! threatened to divorce her right here in I York if she doesn't go to Reno. And n her young customer's man—

PEGGY. But—Howard's always known—

EDITH. Certainly. He hired him, so have plenty of time for his own aff Howard's got some girl he wants to m; But nobody, not even Winchell, knows she is! Howard's a coony cuss. (*Laughi I do think it's screaming. When you member how Sylvia always thought she putting something over on us girls! laughs so hard, she gives herself a s: She falls back among her pillows, limp martyred.*)

PEGGY (*bitterly*). Life's awfully unattrac isn't it?

EDITH (*yawning*). Oh, I wouldn't comp if that damned stork would take the In sign off me.

CURTAIN

SCENE V

A few weeks later. Mary's living room in a Reno hotel. In the rear wall, a bay window ~wing a view of Reno's squat roof-tops and distant Nevada ranges. Left, doors to the *chenette, the bedroom. Right, a door to the corridor. A plush armchair, a sofa. In corner,* MARY'S *half-packed trunks and bags. It is all very drab and ugly. As the* tain rises, LUCY, a slatternly middle-aged, husky woman in a house-dress, is packing *clothes that are strewn on the armchair and the table. She is singing in a nasal falsetto.*

Y.
wn on ole Smokey, all covered with snow,
st my true lov-ver, from courtin' too slow.
irtin' is pul-leasure, partin' is grief,
na false-hearted lov-ver is worse thanna
iief—

GGY *enter, right. She wears a polo-coat* a wool tam. She is on the verge of *s.)*

GY. Lucy, where's Mrs. Haines?

Y. Down waiting for the mail. You'll s her a lot when she goes tomorrow? GGY *nods, sinks, dejected, on the sofa.)* . Haines is about the nicest ever came e.

GY. I hate Reno.

Y. You didn't come for fun. (*Goes on* h her packing and singing.) grave'll de-cay you, an' change you tuh ust, 't one boy outta twenty, a poor gal kin ust—

GY. You've seen lots of divorcees, haven't , Lucy?

Y. Been cookin' for 'em for ten years.

GY. You feel sorry for us?

. Well, ma'am, I don't. You feel plenty enough for yourselves. (*Kindly.*) Lord, ain't got much else to do.

Y (*resentfully*). You've never been mar- Lucy.

(*indignant*). I've had three—

Y. Husbands?

. Kids!

Y. Oh, then, you're probably very hap-

LUCY. Lord, ma'am, I stopped thinking about being happy years ago.

PEGGY. You don't think about being happy?

LUCY. Ain't had the time. With the kids and all. And the old man such a demon when he's drinking— Them big, strong, red-head-ed men. They're fierce.

PEGGY. Oh, Lucy, he beats you? How ter-rible!

LUCY. Ain't it? When you think what a lot of women in this hotel need a beating worse than me.

PEGGY. But you live in Reno. You could get a divorce overnight.

LUCY. Lord, a woman can't get herself worked up to a thing like that overnight. I had a mind to do it once. I had the money, too. But I had to call it off.

PEGGY. Why?

LUCY. I found out I was in a family way. (*There is a rap on the door.*)

PEGGY (*going to her*). Lucy, tell Mrs. Haines I must talk to her—alone—before supper— (*Enter* COUNTESS DE LAGE, *left. She is a silly, amiable, middle-aged woman, with carefully waved, bleached hair. She wears a gaudily checked riding habit, carries an enormous new sombrero and a jug of corn liquor.*)

COUNTESS. Ah, Peggy, how are you, dear child?

PEGGY. All right, Countess de Lage.

COUNTESS. I've been galloping madly over the desert all day. Lucy, here's a wee juggie. We must celebrate Mrs. Haines' divorce.

PEGGY. Oh, Countess de Lage, I don't think a divorce is anything to celebrate.

COUNTESS. Wait till you've lost as many husbands as I have, Peggy. (*Wistfully.*) Married, divorced, married, divorced! But where Love leads I always follow. So here I am, in Reno.

PEGGY. Oh, I wish I were anywhere else on earth.

COUNTESS. My dear, you've got the Reno jumpy-wumpies. Did you go to the doctor? What did he say?

PEGGY. He said it was—the altitude.

COUNTESS. Well, la, la, you'll get used to that. My third husband was a Swiss. If one lives in Switzerland, Peggy, one has simply got to accept the Alps. As I used to say to myself, Flora, there those damn Alps are, and there's very little even you can do about it.

PEGGY. Yes, Countess de Lage. (*Exits, hurriedly, left.*)

COUNTESS. Oh, I wish she hadn't brought up the Alps, Lucy. It always reminds me of that nasty moment I had the day Gustav made me climb to the top of one of them. (*Sits in armchair.*) Lucy, pull off my boots. (LUCY *kneels, tugs at her boots.*) Anyhow, there we were. And suddenly it struck me that Gustav had pushed me. (*Tragically.*) I slid halfway down the mountain before I realized that Gustav didn't love me any more. (*Gaily.*) But Love takes care of its own, Lucy. I slid right into the arms of my fourth husband, the Count.

LUCY (*rises, with boots.*) Ain't that the one you're divorcing now?

COUNTESS. But, of course, Lucy. (*Plaintively.*) What could I do when I found out he was putting arsenic in my headache powders. Ah! L'amour! L'amour! Lucy, were you ever in love?

LUCY. Yes, ma'am.

COUNTESS. Tell me about it, Lucy.

LUCY. Well, ma'am, ain't much to tell. I was kinda enjoyin' the courtin' time. It was as purty a sight as you ever saw, to see him come lopin' across them hills. The sky so big and blue and that hair of his, blazing like the be-jesuss in the sun. Then we'd sit on my back fence and spark. But, ma'am,

you know how them big, strong, red-hea[d] men are. They just got to get to the po[int] So we got married, ma'am. And natch[e] I ain't had no chanct to think about [love] since—

COUNTESS (*she has not been listening*). [The] trouble with me, Lucy, is I've been marry[ing] too many foreigners. I think I'll go bac[k] marrying Americans. (*Enter* MIRIAM, *r[ight] She is a breezy, flashy red-head, about [30] years old. She is wearing a theatrical pa[ir of] lounging pajamas.*)

MIRIAM. Hya, Lucy?

LUCY. Evening, Mrs. Aarons. (*Exits, rig[ht]*)

MIRIAM. Hya, Countess, how's rhythm o[n the] range? (*Sees the jug on the table, pour[s for] * COUNTESS *and herself drinks.*)

COUNTESS. Gallop, gallop, gallop, madly [over] the sagebrush! But now, Miriam, I'm [hav]ing an emotional relapse. In two week[s I'll] be free, free as a bird from that little Fr[ench] bastard. But whither, oh, whither sh[all I] fly?

MIRIAM. To the arms of that cowboy [at] the dude ranch?

COUNTESS (*modestly*). Miriam Aarons!

MIRIAM. Why, he's nuts for you, Cou[ntess.] He likes you better than his horse, an[d it's] such a damn big horse.

COUNTESS (*rises, and pads in her stoc[kinged] feet to the sofa*). Well, Buck Winston is [big.] So young. So strong. Have you notice[d the] play of his muscles? (*Reclining.*) Mu[scle]-Musical.

MIRIAM. He could crack a coconut with [his] knees. If he could get them together. [But,] Countess, that guy hasn't been aro[und to] your honorable intentions, has he?

COUNTESS. Yes, Miriam, but I'm dif[ferent] from the rest of you. I've always pu[t my] faith in love. Still, I've had four div[orces.] Dare I risk a fifth?

MIRIAM. What are you risking, Cou[ntess,] or maybe I shouldn't ask?

COUNTESS. I mean, Miriam, I could [still] make a success of Buck at Newport.

MIRIAM. Even Mrs. Astor would have [to ad]mit Buck's handsome. If I had your d[ough] ake him to Hollywood first, then New-

NTESS. Hollywood? Why *not*? I might
him into a picture star. After all, my
nd husband was a gondolier, and a
th after I married him, a Duchess
ed with him. Ah! L'amour! (*Enter* SYL-
right. She is wearing a smart dinner
s. *Her trip to Reno has embittered her,*
it has not subdued her.)

AM. Hya, Sylvia? Going to a ball?

IA (*pours a drink*). Doing the town
a boy friend.

AM. Where'd you pick him up?

IA. The Silver State Bar. I'm not going
t around, moping, like Mary.

TESS. Poor Mary. If her husband gave
the flimsiest excuse, she'd take him

IA. She has no pride. I'd roast in hell
re I'd take Howard Fowler back. Kick
me out like that! After all I sacrificed!

AM. Such as what?

IA. I gave him my *youth!*

TESS (*dreamily*). Hélas, what can a
an do with her youth, but give it to a
?

AM. Hélas, she can't preserve it in alco-

TESS (*practical*). But, Sylvia, how could
husband kick you out, if you were a
ne fidèle.

IA. Of course, I was a faithful wife.
IAM *snorts*.) What are you laughing at?

AM. Two kinds of women, Sylvia, owls
ostriches. (*Raises her glass.*) To the
ered sisterhood! To the girls who *get*
and paid. (*Parenthetically.*) And you
aid *plenty!*

IA. You bet I got plenty! The skunk!

TESS. I never got a sou from any of my
ands, except my first husband, Mr.
s. He said the most touching thing in
ill. I remember every word of it. "To
eloved wife, Flora, I leave all my estate

in trust to be administered by executors,
because she is an A No. 1 *schlemeil."*
(*Touched anew.*) Wasn't that sweet?

MIRIAM (*Enter* MARY, *right. She is subdued.
She is carrying some letters*). Hya, queen?

MARY. Fine.

MIRIAM. Ya lie.

COUNTESS. Mary, I'm starved. (LUCY *enters,
left, takes* MARY's *hat.*)

MARY. Supper's nearly ready. As my last official act in Reno, I cooked the whole thing
with my hands, didn't I, Lucy?

LUCY. All but the steak and tomatoes and
dessert, Mrs. Haines. (*Exits, left.*)

MARY (*gives a letter to* SYLVIA, *glancing as
she does so, at the inscription*). For you,
Sylvia. From Edith?

SYLVIA. You couldn't miss that infantile
handwriting. (*Pointedly.*) You didn't hear
from anyone?

MARY. No.

SYLVIA. Well, darling, Stephen's hardly worth
a broken heart.

MARY. The less you have to say about me
and Stephen the better I like it!

SYLVIA. I'm only trying to cheer you up.
That's more than you do for me.

MARY. I'm doing enough, just being pleasant
to you.

SYLVIA. My, you have got the jitters, dear.

MIRIAM. Hey, Sylvia, we're all out here in
the same boat. Mary's laid off you. Why
don't you lay off her?

SYLVIA. Oh, I'm just trying to make her see
life isn't over just because Stephen let her
down. (*Opens her letter. A batch of press-
clippings falls out. The* COUNTESS *picks them
up, reads them idly, as* SYLVIA *goes on with
the letter.*)

COUNTESS. You see, Miriam? What else is
there for a woman but l'amour?

MIRIAM. There's a little corn whiskey left.
(*She pours another drink.*)

COUNTESS. Cynic, you don't believe in Cupid.

MIRIAM. That double-crossing little squirt! Give me Donald Duck. (*To* MARY.) Have a drink? (MARY *shakes her head.*) Listen, Babe, why not—give out? You'd feel better—

MARY (*laughing*). Miriam, you're not very chatty about your own affairs.

COUNTESS (*suddenly engrossed by the clippings from* SYLVIA'S *letter*). Miriam, you sly puss, you never told us you even knew Sylvia's husband.

SYLVIA (*looking up from her letter*). What?

COUNTESS (*rises*). Sylvia, listen to this: "Miriam Vanities Aaron is being Renovated. Three guesses, Mrs. Fowler, for whose Ostermoor?" (SYLVIA *snatches the clippings from her.*)

MIRIAM. Why can't those lousy rags leave a successful divorce alone?

COUNTESS (*reading another clipping*). "Prominent stockbroker and ex-chorine to marry."

SYLVIA (*To* MIRIAM). Why, you little hypocrite! (*During this,* PEGGY *has entered and goes back of the sofa. She listens but does not join the group.*)

MARY (*going to her*). Now, Sylvia—

SYLVIA. Did you know this?

MARY. Oh, Sylvia, why do you care? You don't love Howard—

SYLVIA (*brushing her aside*). That has nothing to do with it. (*To* MIRIAM, *fiercely.*) How much did he settle on you?

MIRIAM. I made Howard pay for what he wants; you made him pay for what he doesn't want.

SYLVIA. You want him for his money.

MIRIAM. So what do you want him for? I'll stay bought. That's more than you did, Sylvia.

SYLVIA. Why, you dirty little trollop!

MIRIAM. Don't start calling names, you Park Avenue push-over! (SYLVIA *gives* MIRIAM *a terrific smack. In the twinkling of an eye, they are pulling hair.* MARY *seizes* SYLVIA'S

arm; SYLVIA *breaks loose. The* COUNTESS t[...] at MIRIAM'S *belt, as* LUCY *comes in, looks [...] the fight with a rather professional eye, [...] exits for the smelling-salts.*)

COUNTESS. Tiens! Miriam. Don't be vulg[...] (*Her interference enables* SYLVIA *to s[...]* MIRIAM *unimpeded.*)

MIRIAM (*shoving the* COUNTESS *on the so[...]* Out of the way, you fat old—! (SYL[...] *grabs* MIRIAM'S *hair.*) Ouch, let go! (SYL[...] *is about to use her nails.* MARY *takes a han[...]*

MARY. I won't have this, you hear! (MA[...] *interference allows* MIRIAM *to give* SYLVI[...] *terrific kick in the shins.*)

SYLVIA (*routed, in sobs*). Oh, you hurt [...] you bitch, you! (*As she turns away,* MIR[...] *gives her another well-placed kick, wh[...] straightens* SYLVIA *up.*)

MIRIAM. Take that! (SYLVIA, *shrieking [...] rage and humiliation, grabs* MIRIAM *ag[...] sinks her white teeth into* MIRIAM'S *arm[...] this mayhem,* MARY *seizes her, shakes [...] violently, pushes her sobbing into the [...] chair.*)

MARY (*to* MIRIAM). That's enough.

MIRIAM. Where's the iodine? (MARY *po[...] to bedroom.*) Gotta be careful of hydrop[...] bia, you know. (*Exits, right.*)

SYLVIA (*blubbering, nursing her woun[...]* Oh, Mary, how could you let her do [...] to me!

MARY (*coldly*). I'm terribly sorry, Sylvi[...]

SYLVIA. The humiliation! You're on her s[...] After all I've done for you!

MARY. What have you done for me?

SYLVIA. I warned *you!*

MARY (*bitterly*). I'm not exactly gratefu[...] that.

SYLVIA (*hysterical*). Oh, aren't you? Li[...] to me, you ball of conceit. You're not [...] object of pity you suppose. Plenty of [...] girls are tickled to death you got what [...] coming to you. You deserved to lose Step[...] the stupid way you acted. But I always s[...] up for you, like a loyal friend. What th[...] do I get? You knew about that woman, [...] you stood by, gloating, while she—

ARY. Get out of here! (LUCY *enters from
e bedroom, with a bottle of spirits of am-
onia, as* SYLVIA *gives way completely to
·steria, and, screaming with rage, picks
· ash-trays, glasses, and cigarette boxes,
d hurls them violently against the wall.*)

·LVIA (*at the top of her lungs*). I hate you!
·ate you! I hate *everybody*—

·CY (*takes* SYLVIA *firmly by the shoulders,
·ces the bottle under her nose*). Listen,
·s. Fowler! You got the hy-strikes! (*Rushes
· gasping, sobbing, to the door.*)

·VIA. You wait. Some day you'll need a
·man friend. Then you'll think of me—
·xit LUCY *and* SYLVIA, *struggling helplessly,
·ht.*)

·UNTESS (*rising from the sofa*). Poor crea-
·es. They've lost their equilibrium because
·y've lost their faith in love. (*Philosophi-
·ly.*) L'amour. Remember the song Buck
·de up, just for me? (*Pours herself a
·nk, sings.*) "Oh, a man can ride a horse
·the range above, But a woman's got to
·e on the wings of love, Coma a ti-yi-yip-
·" (*Throws the jug over her shoulder, and
·s right, still singing, as* MIRIAM *enters,
·ravages of her fight repaired.*)

·IAM. The coast clear?

·GY. Oh, that was the most disgusting
·ng I ever saw.

·IAM. Right, kid, we're a pair of alley
·—

·RY. You should not be here, Peggy, to
·it at all. (*She picks up the ash-trays,
·*)

·IAM. What the hell are you doing here?

·Y. Peggy wanted to buy a car.

·GY. With my own money!

·Y. John said they couldn't afford a car.

·GY. He couldn't. I could.

·Y. What was his—is yours. What is
·s—is your own. Very fair.

·GY. A woman's best protection is a little
·ey of her own.

·Y. A woman's best protection is—the
·: man. (*With gentle sarcasm.*) Obvious-

ly, John isn't the right man and Peggy will
forget all about him in another month.

PEGGY. No, I won't. I can't. Because—because— (*Bursts into tears.*) Oh, Mary, I'm
going to have a baby. Oh, Mary, what shall
I do?

MARY. Peggy, what's his telephone number?

PEGGY (*quickly*). Eldorado 5-2075. (MIRIAM
*goes at once to the phone. Gets the operator,
gives the number.*) But, oh, Mary, I can't
tell him!

MIRIAM. Why? Isn't it his?

PEGGY. Oh, of course!

MIRIAM. And make it snappy, operator.

PEGGY. I always wanted it. But what can I
do with it now?

MIRIAM. Land it with the Marines—

MARY. Peggy, you've shared your love with
him. Your baby will share your blood, your
eyes, your hair, your virtues—and your
faults— But your little pin-money, that, of
course, you could not share.

PEGGY. Oh, Mary, I know I'm wrong. But,
it's no use—you don't know the things he
said to me. I have my pride.

MARY (*bitterly*). Reno's full of women who
all have their pride.

PEGGY. You think I'm like them.

MIRIAM. You've got the makings, dear.

MARY. Love has pride in nothing—but its
own humility.

MIRIAM (*at telephone*). Mr. Day, please.
Reno calling—Mr. Day? My God, he must
live by the phone. Just hold the— (PEGGY
leaps to the phone.)

PEGGY. Hello, John. (*Clears her throat of a
sob.*) No, I'm not sick. That is, I am sick!
That is, I'm sick to my stomach. Oh, John!
I'm going to have a baby— Oh, darling, are
you?— Oh, darling, do you?— Oh, darling,
so am I! So do I! Course, I forgive you.—
Yes, precious. Yes, lamb. On the very next
train! John? (*A kiss into the phone. It is
returned.*) Oh, Johnny, when I get back,
things are going to be so different—! John do

you mind if I reverse the charges? (*Hangs up.*) I can't stay for supper. I've got to pack.

MARY. When you get back—don't see too much of the girls.

PEGGY. Oh, I won't, Mary. It's all their fault we're here.

MARY. Not—entirely.

PEGGY. Good-bye! Oh, I'm so happy, I could cry. (*Exits, right.*)

MIRIAM. Getting wise, aren't you?

MARY. Know all the answers.

MIRIAM. Then, why're you here?

MARY. I had plenty of advice, Miriam. (*The telephone rings.* MIRIAM *goes to it.*)

MIRIAM. Hello. No, we completed that call, operator. (*Hangs up.*)

MARY. Cigarette?

MIRIAM (*suddenly*). Listen.

MARY. There's nothing you can say I haven't heard.

MIRIAM. Sure? I come from a world where a woman's got to come out on top—or it's just too damned bad. Maybe I got a new slant.

MARY (*wearily*). All right, Miriam. Talk to me about my—lawful husband. Talk to me about security— What does it all come to? Compromise.

MIRIAM. What the hell? A woman's compromised the day she's born.

MARY. You can't compromise with utter defeat. He doesn't want me.

MIRIAM. How do you know?

MARY. How do I know—why else am I here?

MIRIAM (*a pause. Then, mock-tragically*). Because you've got no guts, Mary Haines. It happened to me—I lost my man, too.

MARY (*smiling*). You?

MIRIAM. Oh, it only happened once. Got wise to myself after that. Look, how did I lose

him? We didn't have enough dough to married. I wouldn't sleep with him until did. I had ideals—God knows where I 'em. I held out on him—(*Sighs.*) Can beat it? I liked him a lot better than ever liked anybody since. I never held again— What'd my Romeo do? Got him another girl. I made a terrible stink. W shouldn't I? I should. But what I ou not to have done was say—good-bye. I like you.

MARY. I don't understand.

MIRIAM. Then get a load of this. I shoul licked that girl where she licked me—in hay.

MARY. Miriam!

MIRIAM. That's where you win in the round. And if I know men, that's still (ter's Last Stand. (MARY *walks away f her.*) Shocked you? You're too moc You're ashamed. O.K., sister. But my of love is that love isn't ashamed in noth

MARY (*turning to her*). A good argum Miriam. So modern. So simple. Sex cause, sex the cure. It's too simple, Mir Your love battles are for—lovers—or pr sionals. (*Gently.*) Not for a man and wo who've been married twelve quiet years! I don't mean I wouldn't love Stephen's a around me again. But I wouldn't recap if I could, our—young passion. That the wonderful young thing we had. ' was part of our youth, like the—babies. not the thing that made him my husb that made me his wife—Stephen needed He *needed* me for twelve years. Ste doesn't need me any more.

MIRIAM. I get it. (*Phone rings.*) That's I'm marrying this guy Fowler. He need like hell. If I don't marry him he'll (himself to death in a month, the poor ◌

MARY (*at the telephone*). Yes? No, o tor, we completed—you say, New Yo calling Mrs. Haines? I'll take that call— MIRIAM.) Stephen!

MIRIAM. Listen, make him that speech just made me!

MARY (*radiant*). I knew he'd call. I when the last moment came, he'd reali needed me.

IAM. For God's sake, tell him that *you*
l him!

Y. Hello—hello? Stephen? Mary. Yes.
very cheerful. It's so good to hear your
e, Stephen. I—why, yes, it's scheduled
tomorrow at 12—but, Stephen, I can—
ightened) but, Stephen! No—of course
haven't seen the papers. How could I,
here? (*There is a long pause.*) Yes, I'd
er *you* told me. Of course I understand
position you're both in. No, I'm not bit-
not bitter at all—I—I hope you'll both
ery happy. No, I have no plans, no plans
l—Stephen, do you mind if I hang up?
d-bye, Stephen—Good-bye—

MIRIAM. He's marrying her?

MARY. Oh, God, why did I let this happen? We were married. We were one person. We had a good life. Oh, God, I've been a *fool!*

MIRIAM. Sure you have. Haven't we all, sister?

MARY. But she doesn't love him. I *do*. That's the way it is. (*She goes to the window, and looks out. There is a pause. Then, violently*) But it's not ended if your heart doesn't say so. It's not ended!

CURTAIN

ACT THREE

SCENE I

arly evening, two years later. CRYSTAL'*s bathroom. Left, a black marbleized tub with ed shower-curtains. In a niche, back of the tub, a gilded French telephone. Right, a -skirted dressing table, covered with glittering toilet bottles and cosmetic jars. Towel-s piled with embroidered bath-towels. Center, a door to* CRYSTAL'*s bedroom. As the ain rises,* CRYSTAL *is lolling in the bath, reading a magazine, smoking as* HELENE, ic French maid, enters.*

NE. Madame has been soaking an hour.

TAL (*rudely*). So what?

NE. But, monsieur—

TAL. Monsieur is going out with me and friends, whether he likes it or not. Has kid gone home yet?

NE. Mademoiselle Mary has just finished supper with her daddy. Madame, mon- is so anxious that you say good night er.

TAL. Listen, that kid doesn't want to ne beddy-bye any more than I do. He's for two years to cram us down each 's throats. Let her go home to her mom- (*Passes* HELENE *a brush.*) Here—scrub me day I'm going to slap that kid down. too— (*As* HELENE *scrubs too hard.*) You're taking my skin off—Oh, I'm so I I could—(*Hurls the soap across the* .) Helene, never marry a man who's ted a "good woman." He's as cheerful man who's murdered his poor old er. (*Telephone rings.*) Get out! And,

Helene, when Mrs. Fowler comes, keep her downstairs, if you have to *sit* on her. (*Exit* HELENE. CRYSTAL *picks up the telephone. Her voice melts.*) Hello, darling, I'm in the tub. I'm shrivelled to a peanut waiting for this call. No, I'm not afraid of a shock. You ought to know— Oh, Buck, I'm going to miss you like nobody's business. I can't tell you what it did to me, locking the door on our little apartment— I'll say we had fun! Coma ti-yi-yippy, what? Oh, no, say anything you like. This is the one place where I have some privacy— (CRYSTAL'*s back is to the door. She does not hear a brief rap.*) Listen, baby, must you really go to the coast? Oh, the hell with Mr. Goldwyn. (*Enter* LITTLE MARY. *She stands hesitantly against the door.*) Listen, you don't have to tell me what you sacrificed to have a movie career. I've seen that cartoon you married. If Flora was ever a Countess, I'm the Duchess of Windsor. Well, Buck, maybe she's not such a half-wit, but— (*Sees* LITTLE MARY.) Oh—call me back in two minutes. I've had a small interruption. (*Hangs up.*) Who told you to come in here?

LITTLE MARY (*politely*). Daddy. Good night. (*Turns to go.*)

CRYSTAL (*sweetly*). Oh, don't go, darling. Hand me that brush.

LITTLE MARY (*gently*). Please?

CRYSTAL. Please. (LITTLE MARY *gives her the brush.*)

LITTLE MARY. Good night. (*Goes to the door.*)

CRYSTAL. My, you're in a hurry to tell Daddy about it.

LITTLE MARY. About what?

CRYSTAL. My talk on the telephone.

LITTLE MARY. I don't understand grown-ups on the telephone. They all sound silly. Good night.

CRYSTAL. Good night, who? (*A pause.*) You've been told to call me Aunty Crystal. (*A pause.*) Why don't you do it?

LITTLE MARY (*still edging to the door*). Yes.

CRYSTAL. Yes, what?

LITTLE MARY (*lamely*). Yes, good night.

CRYSTAL (*angry*). You sit down!

LITTLE MARY. Oh, it's awfully hot in here. I've got my coat on.

CRYSTAL. You heard me! (LITTLE MARY *sits on the stool before the dressing table, squirms.*) We're going to have this out. I've done my damn—my level best to be friends with you, but you refuse to co-operate.

LITTLE MARY. What?

CRYSTAL. Co-operate.

LITTLE MARY (*nodding mechanically*). Co-operate.

CRYSTAL (*exasperated*). Answer my question. You don't like me. Why?

LITTLE MARY (*rising*). Well, good night, Crystal—

CRYSTAL. I said, why?

LITTLE MARY (*very patiently*). Listen, Crystal, my mother told me I wasn't to be rude to you.

CRYSTAL. For the last time, young lady, yo give me one good reason why you dor like me.

LITTLE MARY. I never said I didn't like yo Crystal.

CRYSTAL. But you don't like me, do you?

LITTLE MARY. No, but I never *said* so. I' been very polite, Crystal, considering you something awful!

CRYSTAL. Wait till your father hears this!

LITTLE MARY (*suddenly defiant*). Listen Daddy doesn't think you're so wonder any more!

CRYSTAL. Did he tell you that?

LITTLE MARY. No. Daddy always preten you're all right, but he's just ashamed have Mother know what a mean, silly w he's got. And I don't tell Mother what think, because you've made her cry enou Crystal. So I'm not going to co-operate ev

CRYSTAL. Get out!

LITTLE MARY (*goes to the door, then tur rather superior*). And *another* thing, I thi this bathroom is perfectly ridiculous! Go night, Crystal! (*Exits. The telephone rin* CRYSTAL *grabs it, irritable.*)

CRYSTAL. Yes, darling— That Haines b God, she gets under my skin!— No, didn't hear anything. What good woul do her, anyhow? You're off in the morni and Lord knows we've been discree What? You are? (*Giggling.*) Dining w the first Mrs. Haines?— Well, darling, off the gin. It makes you talk too mucl Well, just be careful, darling. (*Enter* SYL *without knocking. She wears an elabo evening gown, and carries a cocktail. T two years have had no appreciable effect* SYLVIA. *She is her old Act One self aga.*

SYLVIA. Yoohoo! May I come in?

CRYSTAL (*in the telephone*). No, this is the Aquarium. It's Grand Central Stat (*Hangs up.*)

SYLVIA. Who was that?

CRYSTAL. A wrong number.

SYLVIA. You were talking to a man

STAL. Pass me that sponge.—Please.

VIA (*waiting on* CRYSTAL). Oh, Crystal, know you can trust me.

STAL. And that eye cup.

VIA. There must be someone. After all, known Stephen for years. He's really your type. I often wonder how you two together. I was telling my psycho-analyst ut it. You know, I've got to tell him rything.

STAL. That must be an awful effort.

VIA. I don't mind discussing myself. But ing about my friends does make me feel oyal. He says Stephen has a Guilt Com-

STAL. What?

VIA (*cheerfully*). He says men of Ste-'s generation were brought up to be-e that infidelity is a sin. That's why he wed Mary to divorce him, and that's why married you, Crystal. He had to marry just to convince himself he was not a al monster.

STAL. Yes? Well, if Stephen is a sexual ster, psycho-analysis is through.

VIA. And he says you've got a Cinder-Complex. He says most American wo-have. They're all brought up to believe marriage to a rich man should be their in life. He says we neither please the nor function as child-bearing animals—

TAL (*bored and angry*). Will you func-yourself into the bedroom?

IA (*hurt*). I don't think that's the way lk to me, after all I've done for you. en you married Stephen you didn't v a soul. It wasn't easy to put *you* over. ybody was on Mary's side.

TAL. They still are. They never miss a ce to remind me what a noble, useful an Mary has become since she left hen.

A (*comforting*.) My dear, she's miser-' Why, she never sees a soul.

TAL. She's having a dinner party tonight.

A. Edith told me. She's going. And .

CRYSTAL. Flora?

SYLVIA. The Countess de Lage. Mrs. Buck Winston? My God, I have to laugh when I think of Flora actually turning that cowboy into a movie star. Of course he's not my type, but he's positively the Chambermaid's Delight—

CRYSTAL (*fiercely*). Will you shut up?

SYLVIA. But, Crystal—

CRYSTAL. I said shut up— (*Calling.*) Helene!

SYLVIA. Well, I think you're very ungrateful!

CRYSTAL. Well, take it up with your psycho-analyst. (HELENE *enters.*) Helene, draw the curtains. I want to take a shower. (SYLVIA *goes to the door as* HELENE *draws the curtains.*) That's right, Sylvia—wait in the bedroom.

SYLVIA (*sees the scales, decides to weigh herself*). Oh, dear, I've lost another pound. I must remember to tell my analyst. You know, everything means something. (*The shower goes on.* HELENE *exits.* SYLVIA *gets off the scales. During the following monologue, she goes to* CRYSTAL's *dressing-table, where she examines all the bottles and jars.*) But even my analyst says no woman should try to do as much as I do. He says I attach too much value to my feminine friendships. He says I have a Damon and Pythias Complex. I guess I have given too much of myself to other women. He says women are natural enemies— (*Picks up bottle.*) Why, Crystal, I thought you didn't touch up your hair— (*Sniffing perfume.*) My dear, I wouldn't use this. You smell it on every tart in New York. That reminds me—(*Going to the shower-curtains*)—if you do have an affair, Crystal, for heaven's sake, be discreet. Remember what Howard did to me, the skunk. (*Peeking in.*) My, you're putting on weight. (*Going back to dressing-table, she sits down, and begins to pry in all the drawers.*) But men are so mercenary. They think they own you body and soul, just because they pay the bills— I tried this cream. It brought out pimples— Of course, Crystal, if you were smart, you'd have a baby. It's the only real hold a woman has—(HELENE *enters.*)

HELENE. Monsieur says will madame be long?

SYLVIA. Can't you see she's rushing?—
(HELENE *exits. The shower goes off.*) Men
are so selfish! When you're only making
yourself beautiful for them. (*Opens another
drawer.*) I wish I could find a man who
would understand my need for a companion—(*Finds a key, examines it.*) Why, Crystal, what are *you* doing with a key to the
Gothic Apartments? (CRYSTAL's *head pops
from behind the curtain.*)

CRYSTAL. What?— Oh— (*Nervously.*) Oh,
that! (*Playing for time.*) Throw me a towel,
Sylvia!

SYLVIA (*bringing her towel*). That's where
Howard had me followed. The doorman
there is a professional blackmailer! (CRYSTAL
*has wrapped herself in a big towel, now
steps from behind the shower-curtains and
sits on the rim of the tub to dry her legs.*)
I asked my psycho-analyst about him, and
he said blackmailers are really perverts who
can't think of a good perversion. So they
blackmail people instead.

CRYSTAL (*going to the dressing-table.*) Really? Well, he can't blackmail me now. (*As

she passes SYLVIA, she lightly snatches
key from her.*) The Gothic Apartments
where Stephen and I had to go before
divorce. I keep it for sentimental reaso
(*Smiling, she drops the key back in
drawer, locks it.*)

SYLVIA. Poor Stephen! My dear, I thought
night how tired he looked, and old. Crys
I've told you everything. Tell me: how l
do you think you can be faithful to Stephe

CRYSTAL (*making up her face*). Well,
plays funny tricks. The urge might hit
tomorrow.

SYLVIA. I doubt it, pet. You're a typ
blonde.

CRYSTAL. So what?

SYLVIA (*loftily*). Most *blondes* are frigi

CRYSTAL. Really? Well, maybe that's ju
dirty piece of *brunette* propaganda!

CURTAIN

SCENE II

Eleven o'clock the same night. MARY's *bedroom. A charming, simple room. Left, a*
to the dressing-room. Right, a door to the hall. As the curtain rises, JANE *is arran*
a number of evening wraps on the bed. MIRIAM, MARY *and* NANCY *are entering.*

MIRIAM. Thanks, baby, a lot! I never was
at a wetter dinner.

MARY. It was a success. I left Reno two years
ago today. This was a memorial dinner for
you old Renoites, and your new husbands.

MIRIAM. I get it. Listen, there's no soap eating out your heart, sister!

NANCY. Mary, if I had a heroine in one of
my books who behaved the way you do, my
two readers would never believe it. No one
man is worth it.

MIRIAM. Say, the whole Racquet Club's not
worth it— Speaking of my dear husband
Howard—the skunk—can I have a whiskey
and soda?

NANCY. Make it two. (JANE *exits, right.*)

MIRIAM. I lay off when Howard's arou
I'm weaning him from the bottle by
stages. He's in the secondary stage no

NANCY. What stage is that?

MIRIAM. He puts ice in.

MARY. How's matrimony, Miriam? Ma
a go of it?

MIRIAM. I'm doing a reconstruction job
makes Boulder Dam look like an egg
(*Enter* PEGGY, *right.*)

PEGGY. Oh, Mary, can't we get off to
party? I have to get home early. Little
always wakes up. Little John said the o
thing the other day. (*A dramatic pa*
He said da-da—!

cy. When does he enter Columbia? (*En-*
jane *with tray and highballs.*)

ɪʏ. Jane, tell Mrs. Winston the ladies are
ɪy to go.

ᴇ. Mrs. Winston, ma'am, is drinking
ɪ the gentlemen.

ʏ. Well, tell her to come up. (*Exit*
ᴇ.)

ᴀᴍ. What's the hurry? Two more snoot-
, and Flora will float up on her own
th. (*Enter* ᴇᴅɪᴛʜ, *right.*)

ʜ (*petulantly*). Mary, I wish you had
levator in this house. It's so difficult to
ᴋ upstairs in my condition.

ʏ. Edith, are you Catholic or just care-

ʜ. Mary, isn't this your old furniture?

ʏ. Yes.

ʜ. I think you should get rid of it.
re's nothing that keeps a woman so in
dumps as sleeping in a bed with old
ᴄiations. Mary, you're carrying this nun-
business too far. How do you expect
ɴd anyone else, if you don't make an
t?

ʏ. I don't want anyone, Edith. (*Mock*
ᴀl.) I hate men! Men are awful—

ʜ. Oh, they're not all like Stephen, dear.

ʏ. I saw plenty of men when I came
from Reno. They're all alike. They
ɪ leave you at your own front door with-
ᴀ wrestling-match.

ɪ. You know I asked Phelps about that
I said, "Why does a man always act
ᴀ Don Juan in a taxi?" And he said it
ᴀ hang-over from their bachelor days
ᴀ a man's sex life was conditioned by the
of the meter.

ᴍ. It beats me how in a taxi, the nicest
ᴜrns into Harpo Marx.

. Mary, want to hear something about
ᴀ? (ᴍᴀʀʏ, ᴍɪʀɪᴀᴍ, ɴᴀɴᴄʏ *and* ᴘᴇɢɢʏ:
ᴀ, *No!*") Well, Sylvia's going to a
ᴏ-analyst. She says you destroyed all
ɪth in friendship.

ᴍᴀʀʏ. As if any woman needed to go to a
psycho-analyst to find out she can't trust women.

ᴇᴅɪᴛʜ. Mary, you've grown awfully hard
since you deserted your old friends.

ᴍᴀʀʏ. Isn't "wise" the word? I'm beginning
to understand women.

ɴᴀɴᴄʏ. Too bad! It's the beginning of woman's inhumanity to woman.

ᴇᴅɪᴛʜ (*moving to door, left*). Oh, they're
going to talk philosophy, Peggy. Come on
in here while I powder my nose.

ᴘᴇɢɢʏ. Edith, did I tell you how little John
said da-da?

ᴇᴅɪᴛʜ. Listen, I wouldn't care if *this* one
stood up and sang the Star-Spangled Banner!
(*They exit, as enter* ᴍʀs. ᴍᴏʀᴇʜᴇᴀᴅ, *in street
clothes, right.*)

ᴍʀs. ᴍᴏʀᴇʜᴇᴀᴅ. Oh, hello, girls! Hello, dear.
Party over?

ᴍᴀʀʏ. Enjoy the movies, Mother?

ᴍʀs. ᴍᴏʀᴇʜᴇᴀᴅ. I wish I could make up my
mind whether or not I like Shirley Temple.
(*Enter the* ᴄᴏᴜɴᴛᴇss ᴅᴇ ʟᴀɢᴇ, *right. She is a
tangle of tulle and jewels. She has a slight
"edge" on.*)

ᴄᴏᴜɴᴛᴇss. Such a lovely dinner! It's so wonderful to see all our lives temporarily settled!

ᴍᴀʀʏ. My mother, Mrs. Morehead, Mrs.
Winston. Mrs. Buck Winston.

ᴍʀs. ᴍᴏʀᴇʜᴇᴀᴅ (*trying to place the name*).
Buck Winston?

ᴍᴀʀʏ. The movie star.

ᴍʀs. ᴍᴏʀᴇʜᴇᴀᴅ. Ah, yes! (*Pleasantly.*) My
granddaughter adores your son on the screen.

ᴄᴏᴜɴᴛᴇss (*good-naturedly*). I daresay the
public does see Buck as just a boy. And it
is a trifle absurd *me* being married to a
movie star. But, Mrs. Morehead, you
wouldn't believe how many of my Newport
friends who ridiculed Buck when I married
him positively claw for invitations to Hollywood. Mais là, East is East and West is
West, but I always say Le Cinema is the
Great Leveller!

MRS. MOREHEAD. You don't say! (*Edges to the hall-door.*)

COUNTESS. Mrs. Morehead, do whip into something, and come along with Mary to my party. The Casino Roof. Everyone's clamored to come. I have no idea who's going to be there.

MRS. MOREHEAD. Well, you're sure to know somebody. (*To* MARY.) Later, dear? (MARY *nods,* MRS. MOREHEAD *escapes, right.*)

COUNTESS (*gathering her wrap*). Mary, you're not coming?

MARY. I'm very tired, Flora.

COUNTESS. Oh, you're cross because Buck's had a wee droppie.

MIRIAM. Don't be modest, Flora. Your ducky is stinko.

COUNTESS. I do wish he wouldn't drink straight gin. You know, he's not allowed to. Mr. Goldwyn put that in the new contract.

MIRIAM. I wish I'd had my marriage license drawn up by Mr. Goldwyn.

COUNTESS. Mary, do come. This is *really* our farewell party. I'm never coming back to New York.

MARY. What's wrong with New York, Flora?

COUNTESS. Well, when Buck isn't working we're not going to live anywhere. (*Whispering.*) Mary, can I trust you?

MARY. Of course, Flora!

COUNTESS (*to the others*). You will keep this just between the four of us?

MIRIAM. Shoot, Flora, it's a nationwide hookup!

COUNTESS (*settling herself beside* MARY *on the foot of the bed*). Well, you know how Buck was? (*Wistfully*) So—so impassioné?

MIRIAM. The boy had something.

COUNTESS (*tartly*). Well, he hasn't got it any more, Miriam! First, I thought it was just gin, interfering with his libido— (*Tear-*

fully) But now I think Buck is deceiv me—

NANCY. How incredible!

COUNTESS. Well, I have no proof. Except comes home every afternoon smelling strange perfume.

MARY. Where does he say he's been?

COUNTESS. Visiting his horse. But Trixie shipped to Hollywood last week. You member, I was photographed with her in baggage-car? Now he says he's been g to the Grand Central Gymnasium. B telephoned today. Some great oaf answe I said: "Is Buck Winston there?" He s "Who? No." So I said: "My dear good he comes every day." So he said: "My take, lady, he's inside now boxing with dolph Valentino."

MARY. Poor Flora!

COUNTESS (*practical*). That's why I thin safer just to keep floating around.

MARY. I understand—l'amour.

COUNTESS. L'amour, yes, but jamais, (*sh her lucid moments*) jamais *lopsided* an

MARY (*laughing*). Lopsided amour is t than no amour at all. Flora, let him m fool of you. Let him do anything he w as long as he stays. He's taking the tr to deceive you. (*Half to herself.*) And took the trouble, he really must have ca

NANCY. The Voice of Experience.

MIRIAM (*to* COUNTESS). Come on, chin

NANCY. That's right. Both of them! (PEGGY *and* EDITH.)

COUNTESS (*rising*). Oh, cheries, you n it! I was just saying—now will you this just among the six of us?—I su Buck of being unfaithful. Of cours my own fault. I should have had watched. The way I did all the oth wish I'd found out where he's had apartment!

PEGGY. An apartment—?

COUNTESS. Where would you expect h go? Central Park? Why, it's winter.

GY. Oh, I've always heard people went
hotels.

UNTESS. But, cherie, *Buck* couldn't go to a
tel. You know what would happen. At
: most inopportune moment someone
uld say: "Mr. Winston, may I have your
:ograph?" It happened to us on our wed-
g night. I would have sent for the man-
·r, but it was the manager asking for the
:ograph. Ah, well, off to Hollywood in
morning! That's safe! (*Moving to door.*)
ar Mr. Hays will protect me from Diet-
h and Harlow. (*Exits, right.*)

TH (*getting her wrap*). Darling, you real-
won't come to Flora's party?

RY. No, Edith!

TH. Then I can tell you. Of course, I
ow how you feel about your Ex—and his
w Deal—though I think you'd be glad
s so happy.

RY. I am.

TH. Sylvia telephoned tonight. She and
ystal and Stephen are going on to the
of with a theatre party. Well, darling, I
i't feel much like going myself. I loathe
s dress. My husband says I look as though
ere going to sing in it. (*Exits, right.*)

NCY. Think I'll go, too, Mary! It's a good
ince to study Park Avenue's flora and
ina. And I'm writing a new book. It's
led "Gone with the Ice-man," or "Sex
s No Place in the Home." (*Exits with
GY.*)

IAM (*to* MARY). Listen, Queen, change
ir mind! Let's go on to the party!

RY. No, Miriam.

IAM. Well, I'm going. Wish you could
the cooing-fest Howard and I put on
Sylvia— Shall I spit in Crystal's eye for
1? (MARY *shakes her head.*) You're pass-
up a swell chance, sister! Where I spit
grass grows ever! ·(*Exits.* JANE *enters,
ht.* MARY *begins to unfasten her dress,
es off her jewels, lays them on the dres-
.*)

RY. Jane, turn down my bed.

IE. Yes, ma'am. (MARY *goes into the bou-
r, left.*)

MARY (*off-stage*). Did Mary have a nice
time with her father?

JANE (*turning down the bed*). Well, ma'am,
you know how she is when she comes home.

MARY (*off-stage*). I'm afraid she's never going to get used to it.

JANE. She takes after you, ma'am, if you'll
pardon me. Always brooding. Sometimes,
ma'am, I think it would be better if she
didn't see her father. Or maybe, ma'am—
though it's none of my business—if you
could find some nice man—(*Enter* MRS.
MOREHEAD, *right, in a wrapper and slippers.*)

MRS. MOREHEAD. Going to bed, darling?

MARY (*off-stage*). Yes, Mother.

MRS. MOREHEAD. Shall we chat for a moment?
Jane, I'll have a cigarette.

JANE (*surprised*). Mrs. Morehead!

MRS. MOREHEAD. Those dreadful women
made me nervous. Why Mrs. Haines tole-
rates them even once a year is beyond me!

MARY (*entering, in a nightgown*). An object
lesson. Smoking, Mother?

MRS. MOREHEAD. Oh, you, too?

MARY. Me, too?

MRS. MOREHEAD. I just felt that spooky pinch.
You'd think after ten years your father's
ghost might have grown more tolerant.

JANE. Good night, ma'am. (*Switches off
side-lights.*)

MARY *and* MRS. MOREHEAD. Good night, Jane.
(*Exit* JANE. MARY *gets into bed, opens a
book, flips through it.*)
MRS. MOREHEAD (*sitting on the bed*). Good
book?

MARY. Don't know. Nancy just gave it to me.
It's about—love. Poetry. All about love.
(*Reads*) "When love beckons to you, follow him, though his ways are hard and
steep. And when his wings enfold you, yield
to him— Though his voice may shatter your
dreams as the North Wind lays waste the
garden."

MRS. MOREHEAD. Well, all I can say is, that's very tactless of Nancy. (*Suddenly*) Oh, Mary, I wish you could find—

MARY (*slams book shut*). Some nice man. We've been all over that before, Mother. I had the only one I ever wanted, I lost him—

MRS. MOREHEAD. It wasn't entirely your fault.

MARY. If I hadn't listened to everyone, everything but my own heart!

MRS. MOREHEAD. He loved her.

MARY. He still does. Though you know, Mother, I'm just beginning to doubt it.

MRS. MOREHEAD. Why?

MARY. Because so many people, like Edith, make a point of telling me how much he loves her. Oh, Mother, I'm terribly tired.

MRS. MOREHEAD. Well, do cheer up, darling. Living alone has its compensations. You can go where you please, wear what you please and eat what you please. I had to wait twenty years to order the kind of meal I liked! Your father called it bird-food— And, heaven knows, it's marvelous to be able to sprawl out in bed, like a swastika. Good night, darling.

MARY. Good night, Mother.

MRS. MOREHEAD. Don't read by that light. You'll hurt your eyes. (*Exits.* MARY *props herself against the pillows, begins to read.*)

MARY. "But if in your fear you would seek only love's peace and love's pleasure, then it is better for you to pass out of love's threshing-floor, into the seasonless world; where you shall laugh, but not all of your laughter, and weep, but not all of your tears." (*Enter* LITTLE MARY, *in a nightgown, barefooted, and very sleepy.*)

LITTLE MARY. Mother?

MARY. Darling, what's the matter?

LITTLE MARY (*goes to the bed*). I had a bad dream!

MARY. Darling, what was it?

LITTLE MARY. I forget. Let me crawl in with you, Mother.

MARY (*helping her in*). I'm so restless.

LITTLE MARY. I don't mind if you kick m[e]. You know, that's the only good thing abo[ut] divorce; you get to sleep with your moth[er]. (*She kisses her. A pause.*) I taste lip-stic[k].

MARY. I haven't washed yet. Good nig[ht], darling.

LITTLE MARY. You know, you're a very sy[m]pathetic mother.

MARY. Am I?

LITTLE MARY. Oh, yes. So would you j[ust] tickle my back?

MARY. All right. But go to sleep— (*A paus[e]*)

LITTLE MARY. She's so silly!

MARY. Who?

LITTLE MARY. Crystal.

MARY. Ssh—

LITTLE MARY. I told Daddy so tonight.

MARY. Oh, you mustn't hurt Daddy's fe[el]ings.

LITTLE MARY. Mother?

MARY. Ssh!

LITTLE MARY. I think Daddy doesn't love [her] as much as you any more.

MARY. What makes you think so, Mary?

LITTLE MARY. He told me so after I s[aw] Crystal.

MARY. What?

LITTLE MARY. But he said I mustn't tell y[ou] because, naturally, why do you care how [she] feels. (*A pause*) Oh, don't stop tickli[ng], Mother. (*A pause*) Mother?

MARY. Yes.

LITTLE MARY. What's anyone want with [a] telephone in the bathroom?

MARY. I don't know. Sssh!

LITTLE MARY. Crystal has one. She was a[w]ful mad when I walked in on her while [she] was talking.

MARY. Sleep, Mary!

LITTLE MARY. Mother, who's the Duchess of Windsor?

MARY. What a question!

LITTLE MARY. Well, Crystal said on the telephone if somebody else was a Countess, she was the Duchess of Windsor!

MARY. Really!

LITTLE MARY. Good night, Mother.

MARY. Good night, baby. (*A pause.*)

LITTLE MARY. I wonder if it was the same man you had for dinner.

MARY. Maybe, ssh!

LITTLE MARY. I thought so.

MARY (*curiously*). If who was the same man?

LITTLE MARY. Crystal was talking to, so lovey-dovey.

MARY (*protestingly*). Oh, Mary!

LITTLE MARY. Well, the front part was the same, Mother.

MARY (*a pause*). The front part of what?

LITTLE MARY. His name, Mother!

MARY (*taking her by the shoulders*). What are you talking about?

LITTLE MARY. That man Crystal was talking in the bathtub.

MARY (*half shaking her*). Mary, what do you mean?

LITTLE MARY. I mean his front name was *Buck*, Mother! (MARY *gets quickly out of bed, rings bell on table.*) Oh, Mother, what are you doing?

MARY. Go to sleep, darling. (*Begins to pull on her stockings.*)

LITTLE MARY. Grown-ups are so sudden. Are you dressing?

MARY. Yes, Mary.

LITTLE MARY. You forgot you were invited to a party?

MARY. Almost, Mary.

LITTLE MARY. What are you going to do when you get there, Mother?

MARY. I don't know yet. But I've got to do something.

LITTLE MARY. Well, have a good time! (*Rolls over. Then suddenly sits up.*) Mother!

MARY. Yes?

LITTLE MARY. I remember now I had something to tell you!

MARY (*eagerly*). Yes?

LITTLE MARY (*dolefully*). I was awfully rude to Crystal.

MARY. I'll forgive you this time. (*Enter* JANE.)

JANE. You ring, ma'am?

MARY. Yes. My evening dress, Jane, and a taxi—and don't stand there gaping! Hurry! Hurry!

CURTAIN

SCENE III

Later, the same night. The Powder Room at ₊he Casino Roof. The decoration is r
tawdry and modernistic. Right, a swinging door from the lobby. Left, another to
washrooms. The rest of the wall-space, left and right, is taken up by counter-like dr
ing-tables and mirrors. The rear wall is a great window overlooking the glitter of m
night Manhattan. An over-stuffed sofa and an armchair upholstered in moderni
fabric. Near the door, right, a screen hides the coat-rack. By this, a chair for SADIE
little old woman in a black maid's uniform and apron. As the curtain rises, SADIE
reading a tabloid, which she puts down when two flashily dressed GIRLS *enter fr*
the lobby. They check their wraps.

FIRST GIRL. It's jammed.

SECOND GIRL. Oh, my boy-friend'll get a table.
(*Enter two* SOCIETY WOMEN. *They move di-*
rectly across the stage to the washroom.)

FIRST WOMAN. My dear, won't he let you?

SECOND WOMAN. No, he won't.

FIRST WOMAN. How incredibly foul!

SECOND WOMAN. I'm heartbroken. But I have
to be philosophical; after all, missing one
winter in Palm Beach really won't kill me.
(*Enter* "CIGARETTES," *a pretty girl in a white*
satin blouse and short black skirt. She car-
ries a tray of cigarettes.)

FIRST GIRL (*moving left*). Thought you and
the boy-friend had a row?

SECOND GIRL. We did.

FIRST GIRL. What about?

SECOND GIRL. His wife.

FIRST GIRL. His wife? What right has she
got to butt in?

SECOND GIRL. He's got some cockeyed idea
that after twenty years he can't kick her
out. (*They exit, left.*)

CIGARETTES. Jeepers, why don't they get sick
of this joint night after night! Same music,
same act, same faces.

SADIE. They like familiarity. It gives them
confidence.

CIGARETTES. I'll say they like familiarity.
Most of them shoving around that floor
would be more comfortable with each other
in bed.

SADIE. In bed? If they was to get that over,
what would they use for conversation? (*En-*

ter a DOWAGER *and a* DEBUTANTE, *right. T*
move directly across stage.)

DOWAGER. —dancing like that! What
those boys think of you?

DEBUTANTE (*wearily*). Oh, Mother.

DOWAGER. Guzzling champagne like th
After all I spent on your education!

DEBUTANTE. Oh, Mother.

DOWAGER. It's one thing to come out.
quite another to go under the table! (*T*
exit, left.)

SADIE. —Getting married, dearie?

CIGARETTES (*sinking, very tired, on the a*
of a chair). As soon as Mike gets a j
It ain't fair! Why, we could get married
have a family on that coat— Sadie, wh'd
say if I was to tell you I'm a Commyan

SADIE. I'd say ya was bats. I was a Tov
sendite. Where'd it get me? (*Enter*
COUNTESS, *piloted by* NANCY *and* MIRI
She is tight and tearful. MIRIAM *and* NA
get her, with some difficulty, to the so

COUNTESS (*tacking*). How could Buck
such a thing to me! Oh, the Dr. Jekyll!
Mr. Hyde! Which was which?

MIRIAM. Pipe down or you'll put an aw
dent in his career, Flora.

COUNTESS. What of my career? I've had
husbands. Buck's the first one who
told me what he really thought of me-
public.

NANCY. It takes all kinds of husbands
round out a career like yours, Flora.

COUNTESS. He told me he'd been decei
me for months. Right in the middle of

gan-Grinder. (*Kicks off shoes.*) Oh, I
so—superfluous!

RIAM (*to* SADIE). A bromo-seltzer.

JNTESS. Bromo-seltzer? Qu'-est-que c'est
e ca?

NCY. It will settle your—superfluity. Flora,
he tell you the lady's name?

JNTESS (*indignant*). Certainly not, Nancy.
's not that drunk.

RIAM (*as* SADIE *exits, right*). And another
nk for Mr. Winston!

JNTESS. No, Miriam. He wouldn't tell me
name, because she's a married woman.
ck is very proletarian, but he's not a
inder. He just said *she* was a natural
nde.

NCY. That ought to narrow down the field
isiderably.

JNTESS. He said she was pretty as a paint-
wagon.

RIAM. Oh, you're not such a bad calliope.
ip out of it, Flora. You know, you're
ng to forgive him.

JNTESS (*firmly*). I'd forgive unfaithful-
s, but not base ingratitude. I rescued
1 from those prairies. I married him.
iat thanks do I get? (*Wailing.*) He says
ll be a cockeyed coyote if he'll herd an old
f like me back to the coast!

NCY. Let this be your lesson. Don't let
r next husband become financially inde-
dent of you.

JNTESS. Now, don't lecture me, Nancy.
ry time I marry I learn something. This
taught me once and for all—you can't
ect *noblesse oblige* from a cowboy—
ing up) Ohhh, my eyes! They're full of
scara.

NCY (*helping her off the couch. To* MIR-
). We've got to get her home. Get Buck,
meet us in the lobby.

IAM (*exits, right*). We're headin' for the
round-up!

JNTESS. If there's a telephone in here I'm
ng to call up Mr. Goldwyn. (*Exits, left,
h* NANCY, *as* SADIE, *with a bromo-seltzer,
rs, right, followed by* CIGARETTES.)

ARETTES. What's it all about?

SADIE (*picks up* COUNTESS' *shoes, as she
crosses, left*). Some man.

CIGARETTES. Bet he isn't worth it.

SADIE. You can always collect on that one.
(*Exits, left, as re-enter, left, the* DOWAGER
and the DEBUTANTE.)

DOWAGER. —Laughing and joking with those
boys like that!

DEBUTANTE. Yes, Mother.

DOWAGER. What can they think of you?

DEBUTANTE. Yes, Mother.

DOWAGER. And don't think I didn't overhear
that Princeton boy call me an old drizzle-
puss, either! (*Exits, right.*)

SADIE (*enters, left; to* CIGARETTES). She wants
gin in her bromo-seltzer. (*Enter* MARY *and*
MIRIAM, *right.*)

MIRIAM (*protesting*). Crystal's not in here.
I don't think she's in the joint.

MARY. She's coming. I know it.

MIRIAM. So what are you going to do when
you find her? (SADIE *takes* MARY'S *wrap.*)

MARY. I don't know. But I've got to find her
tonight. Buck's going to Hollywood in the
morning.

MIRIAM. Say, why don't you settle this matter
with Stephen?

MARY. I have no proof, I tell you! But if
Buck is as drunk as you say, he'll give away
something.

MIRIAM. Listen, he's been trying all night
to give Flora away to the doorman. Got a
twenty-dollar bill?

MARY. Yes.

MIRIAM. That'll lock him in the men's room
till we need him. (*Exits, right, with* MARY,
as enter, left, the two SOCIETY WOMEN. *They
cross the stage.*)

FIRST WOMAN. Not three pounds?

SECOND WOMAN. Three pounds!

FIRST WOMAN. How divine! Aren't you ecstatic?

SECOND WOMAN. Yes, but it's the moral satisfaction. Just bananas and milk for one whole

week! That called for enormous character! (*They exit, right.*)

CIGARETTES (*to* SADIE). Enormous character! Well, she'll need it, all right. Comes the Revolution, she'll diet plenty! (*Enter* PEGGY *and* EDITH, *right. They powder, at the mirror, right.*)

PEGGY. I wish I hadn't come.

EDITH. Well, your husband didn't want you to.

PEGGY (*goes for her wrap*). Flora was disgusting!

EDITH. But it was funny. Even the kettle drummer was laughing.

PEGGY. You never miss anything. (SADIE *gives* EDITH *and* PEGGY *their wraps.*)

EDITH. My dear, who could stand the life we lead without a sense of humor? But Flora is a fool. Always remember, Peggy, it's matrimonial suicide to be jealous when you have a really good reason.

PEGGY. Edith, don't you ever get tired of giving advice?

EDITH. Listen, Peggy, I'm the only happy woman you know. Why? I don't ask Phelps or any man to understand me. How could he? I'm a woman. (*Pulls down her corset.*) And I don't try to understand them. They're just animals. Who am I to quarrel with the way God made them? I've got security. So I put my faith in the law. And I say: "What the hell?" And let nature take its course —it's going to, anyway. (*They exit, right, as enter the two* GIRLS, *left.*)

SECOND GIRL (*powdering at the mirror, left*). —So there we were on Sattiday night and it's Atlantic City. And he says: "I gotta go home tomorrow, baby!" And I says: (*Pulls up her stockings.*) "Why dja got to?" And he says: "My wife always expects me home on Easter Sunday." So I says: "What's she expect ya to do? Lay an egg?"

FIRST GIRL. They got no sentiment. (*Enter, right, a* GIRL, *in distress. The shoulder strap of her very low décolletage has broken.*)

GIRL IN DISTRESS (*to* SADIE). Have you got a safety pin? I was never so embarrassed! (SADIE *gets pin.*)

SECOND GIRL (*crossing, right*). So I told hi "I had a great career until you made give up the stage, you lunkhead. For wha A couple of cheesy diamond bracelets? lousy car, which every time it breaks do you got to have the parts shipped over fr Italy. (*The* GIRLS *exit.*)

GIRL IN DISTRESS. So he says, "Don't lo now, you've just dropped something!" (*E ter* CRYSTAL *and* SYLVIA, *right. They m to check their wraps with* SADIE.)

SADIE. Just a minute, please.

SYLVIA (*they go to mirror, left*). Stephen in a mood.

CRYSTAL. He can take it and like it.

GIRL IN DISTRESS (*to* SADIE). Does it sh now?

SADIE. Not what it did before, miss.

GIRL IN DISTRESS. Thank you. (*She ex right.* SADIE *takes* CRYSTAL's *and* SYLVI wraps.)

CRYSTAL. Is my mouth on straight?

SYLVIA. Crystal, you didn't come here to somebody, did you?

CRYSTAL. Oh, Sylvia, can't you lay off t for a minute? (*Enter* MARY *and* MIRI left.)

MARY (*moving forward resolutely*). M Haines, this is a great pleasure!

CRYSTAL (*turning*). I beg your pardon?

MARY. Such a lovely party! I was afraid weren't coming. (*Introducing* CRYSTAL MIRIAM, MIRIAM *and* SYLVIA) Mrs. Fow Mrs. Haines, Mrs. Fowler, Mrs. Fowler.

MIRIAM (*graciously*). Chawmed.

SYLVIA (*bridling*). This is humiliating.

MARY. Modern life is complicated. Wl you came in I was just telling Miriam—

CRYSTAL. Oh, come along, Sylvia. The l is tight.

SYLVIA. Mary, when did you begin drinki

MARY (*to* CRYSTAL). Early in the eveni with Mr. Winston. You *know* Mr. Winst don't you?

CRYSTAL (*at the door*). I'm afraid I don'

LVIA. Of course you do, Crystal. I intro-
ced you to him. Don't you remember?

RYSTAL. Oh, yes, a cocktail party.

ARY. Well, he's in the lobby now, waiting
r someone, Mrs. Haines, and drunker than
u can possibly imagine. You'd find him
ry difficult to handle, in front of Stephen.
RYSTAL *suddenly changes her mind about
ing into the lobby, moves toward the
ashroom.*)

LVIA. Crystal, where are you going?

YSTAL. I won't stand here and listen to
ivel!

ARY. I wouldn't go in there, either, Mrs.
aines. His wife's in there now, having
sterics. She's found out that Buck has
en deceiving her.

YSTAL. Really! What has that to do with
e?

ARY. A good deal, I'm afraid. You seem to
the woman.

LVIA (*delighted*). Why, Crystal!— *Are
u?*

YSTAL. If he used my name, it's a lie! He's
st the cheap sort— I'll tell my husband.

ARY. You'll have to. Tomorrow it will be
mmon gossip. I don't think Stephen will
e it.

LVIA. Oh, Crystal, he's going to loathe it!
t my psycho-analyst is going to adore it.

YSTAL (*going to her*). What are you try-
g to do? Pin something on me, in front
witnesses?

LVIA. Whatever she's driving at, Crystal—
ointing to MIRIAM)—that little tramp put
up to it!

YSTAL (*to* SYLVIA). Keep out of this!

RIAM. Yeah, check it, Sylvia, we're minor
gue this evening.

YSTAL. All right, Mrs. Haines, you've been
ening to the ravings of a conceited fool.
hat did he tell you?

RY (*playing for time, or inspiration*).
ally, Mrs. Haines, this is very embarras-
g.

CRYSTAL (*brazening it out*). Yes, Mrs.
Haines, isn't it? Exactly what do you think
you know about me?

MARY. Everything! (*A pause.* CRYSTAL
laughs.)

CRYSTAL. Then why are you standing here
talking to me? You ought to be outside
spilling it to Stephen. You're bluffing. Come
along, Sylvia!

MARY (*also moving to door.* CRYSTAL *stops*).
That's very good advice. I will tell Stephen.

CRYSTAL. Oh, he wouldn't believe you.

SYLVIA. Oh, you can't tell, Crystal! He's terribly fond of Mary.

CRYSTAL. Now get this straight, Mrs. Haines.
I like what I got, and I'm going to keep it.
You handed me your husband on a silver
platter. (*Enter* NANCY, *left.*) But I'm not
returning the compliment. I can't be stam-
peded by gossip. What you believe and what
Stephen believes will cut no ice in a divorce
court. You need proof and you haven't got
it. When Mr. Winston comes to his senses,
he'll apologize. And Stephen will have no
choice, but to accept—my explanations. Now
that's that! Good night!

MARY (*desperately*). I hope Mrs. Winston
will accept your explanations.

CRYSTAL. What have I got to explain to her?

MARY (*with a conviction she does not feel*).
What about the apartment?

CRYSTAL. What apartment?

MARY. You know as well as I do.

CRYSTAL. Oh, stop trying to put two and
two together—

MARY. Oh, Mrs. Winston did that. She had
you watched—she's seen you both.

CRYSTAL (*defiantly*). Where?

MARY. Going in, and coming out!

CRYSTAL. Going in and coming out *where?*
(*A pause.*) You're lying!

SYLVIA (*warningly*). I wouldn't be so sure,
Crystal!

MIRIAM. Sounds like the McCoy to me, Crystal.

CRYSTAL. Shut up!

SYLVIA. Oh, Crystal, why didn't you confide in me? (CRYSTAL *turns to the door again, triumphant*.)

MARY (*dismayed*). Sylvia, didn't she?

SYLVIA. Certainly *not!* (CRYSTAL *smiles, very pleased with herself*.) She's the cat that walks alone. (*Goes to* CRYSTAL.) Why, Crystal, I could have told you some place *much safer* than the Gothic Apartments!

CRYSTAL (*exploding*). Why, you big, loud-mouthed idiot!

SYLVIA. How dare you!

CRYSTAL. I'd like to slap your stupid face.

SYLVIA (*backing up*). Oh, Mary, how dare she?

MIRIAM. Oh, I've got a job to do on Flora. (*She pats* SYLVIA *affectionately*.) Kiss you when I get back, Sylvia. (*Exits, left*.)

NANCY. And I'll explain the facts of life to Stephen. (NANCY *exits, right*.)

CRYSTAL (*to* MARY, *fiercely*). You're trying to break up my marriage!

SYLVIA. The way you did hers, you floosie!

CRYSTAL (*nasty*). Well, maybe you're welcome to my—left-overs.

MARY (*calmly*). I'll take them, thank you.

SYLVIA. Why, Mary, haven't you any *pride?*

MARY. That's right. No, no pride; that's a luxury a woman in love can't afford. (*Enter* COUNTESS *and* MIRIAM, *left*. MIRIAM *goes to* SADIE, *gets the* COUNTESS' *and her own wraps*.)

COUNTESS (*rushing for* CRYSTAL). Oh, mon Dieu, mon Dieu!

MARY (*stopping her*). Flora, it's really t[ ] bad—

COUNTESS (*to* CRYSTAL). You—you paint[ ] wagon!

CRYSTAL. So you're determined to have[ ] scandal, Mrs. Haines.

COUNTESS. I'm the one who's going to h[ ] the scandal. Why, Mary, she's no m[ ] a blonde naturelle than I am. What's [ ] creature's name? Miriam forgot to tell [ ]

MARY. Mrs. Stephen Haines, currently.

COUNTESS. Is that the thing Stephen left y[ ] for? Well, cherie, all I can say is, you're [ ] idiot! I hope I never live to see the [ ] when an obvious piece like that conqu[ ] *me* on the champs d'amour! (*She exits, ri[ ] followed by* MIRIAM.)

CRYSTAL (*to* MARY). That damn fool di[ ] know. (SADIE *gives* MARY *her wrap*.)

MARY. I'm afraid she didn't. (*Enter* NAN[ ] *right*.)

NANCY. There's a gentleman called [ ] Haines. He says he's been waiting a l[ ] time for his wife— (CRYSTAL *moves to* [ ] *her wrap*.)

MARY (*stepping between her and* SADIE). [ ] him, *I* am coming. (*Exit* NANCY *quick[ ]*)

SYLVIA. Mary, what a dirty female trick[ ]

CRYSTAL. Yes! From the great, noble l[ ] woman! You're just a cat, like all the [ ] of us!

MARY. Well, I've had two years to shar[ ] my claws. (*Waves her hand gaily to* SYLV[ ] Jungle-red, Sylvia! Good night, lad[ ] (*Exits*.)

CURTAIN

Yes, My Darling Daughter

BY MARK REED

To

ANN AND FRANK

CAST OF CHARACTERS

(In order of appearance)

As produced at the Playhouse, New York City, on February 9, 1937, by Alfred Liagre, Jr.

ELLEN MURRAY	Peggy Conklin
LEWIS MURRAY	Charles Bryant
CONSTANCE NEVINS	Violet Heming
MARTHA	Margaret Curtis
ANN WHITMAN MURRAY	Lucile Watson
TITUS JAYWOOD	Nicholas Joy
DOUGLAS HALL	Boyd Crawford

The play was staged by Mr. de Liagre. The settings were by Raymond Sovey. ~~~e poem in Act II was written for the play by Abby Shute Merchant.

SCENES

T ONE: Living-room of the Murray summer home, New Canaan, Conn. A Friday afternoon in late June.

T Two: Ann's "Office." The same afternoon.

T THREE: The living-room again. The following Monday morning.

ACT ONE

SCENE: *There is no gilt-letter sign or bronze plaque at the entrance to the Murrays' summer home. It is not known as "Rosebank," "Triple Oaks," or even "Nine-acres." Your car, turning from the main highway, passes under a quarter-mile arch of beeches and maples, then draws up to what was once a plain rectangular stone manor house. Wings, thrown out on either end, take care of the modern necessities of housing and feeding week-end guests. At the front of the house the century-old trees give way to a broad lawn, and beyond, across several misty ridges, Long Island Sound is visible. A guest, on the particular day this play starts, would see, on the edge of the lawn, the somewhat disturbing sight of three Italian labourers constructing a cement dam at the end of a lily pond . . . the object apparently being, when the water backs up, to form a pool for swimming.*

Entering the house, this same guest would pass along a wide central hall, papered with old-fashioned "landscape" paper, and step through an archway into the living-room. It is dignified, hospitable. The woodwork throughout is painted a soft green; and the formal soapstone fireplace, set in the panelled wall (actor's right), suggests at once that this room is in the old part of the house.

The fireplace is filled with June flowers, and backed against it, not too close for free passage behind, is a library table and a long comfortable couch. Facing the couch is a large stuffed chair. Both wear summer covers of a soft-toned cretonne. Balancing this furniture group, left center, is a drum table flanked on either side with arm chairs. Right and left of the arch, stand two very large mahogany bookcases. Upstage from the fireplace, a door leads to the dining-room and rear of house. Left, two French windows open out upon the terrace; the draperies, like those of the arch, are a delicate yellow and intensify the afternoon sunlight which floods the terrace and the hall.

The furnishings and ornaments are the accretion of taste and travel. Books and magazines are scattered about, not by servants, but by people who have enjoyed reading them. Above all else, you feel t room has been lived in; the furniture h been hauled about for charades, the fir place has known a thousand fires, wh men and women have gathered aroun sipped good liquor, and talked out the thoughts vigorously, if not always intel gently. In brief, a room which has ass ciated long enough with human beings acquire a mellow and gracious human of its own.

At Rise: ELLEN *is discovered sitting on t couch, hunting up references in a ve scholarly-looking book. An alert, slend well-built girl of twenty-two, her chart are rather obscured by her dress and p ture. She wears blue denim overalls, r sandals, tortoise-shell glasses. Her bobb hair is at loose ends. On a tea table befo the sofa are several books and a pad a pencil. After the curtain rises, she goes the bookcase, gets two additional boo and comes back to the sofa.* LEWIS MURR *enters from the hall.*

LEWIS *is genial, well-tanned, tall, abo forty-eight. His outstanding characteris is a hearty, playful bluntness which or narily is amusing; but occasionally, wh it takes the form of questions, can le to embarrassing moments. He wears informal yachting costume and hat p paratory to departure*

LEWIS. Oh, hello, Ellen.

ELLEN. (*Without looking up.*) He Dad. Had your lunch?

LEWIS. I had lunch in town. Your mo er's not in her office.

ELLEN. No?

LEWIS. Where the devil is she?

ELLEN. Where she can't be disturbed. (LEWIS *crosses to upper French windo takes a look around the terrace, then turns.*)

LEWIS. What you reading?

ELLEN. I'm brushing up on my Cons tution. (*She lifts her glasses to her fo head and looks up.*) You know, D those fifteen judges have me worried. you think he can get away with it?

WIS. I suppose so. He generally does. With considerable feeling.) I wish he'd nd more time on his stamp collection. Ie opens door, right, and calls.) Ann! , Annie! I'm back! (Then, coming wn to ELLEN:) Where the hell is she?

LEN. Mother's simply got to get that ry finished before people begin to ar- e.

WIS. Who'll come on a Friday?

LEN. A Mr. Jaywood for one. Peter's eady gone to meet him.

WIS. Jaywood? Never heard of him.

LEN. He's an important literary agent.

WIS. (Getting the significance of this.) h! By the way, your Aunt Connie is k East. She phoned this morning she'd out.

LEN. I suppose she wants to tell us ut her latest divorce.

WIS. Your mother ought to be told. If nnie's coming out to tell us about her orce, somebody ought to be here to en to her.

LEN. I'll be here, Dad. Now will you ase go sail your boat?

WIS. Thought you were going to Hart- d.

LEN. I am, but not until five o'clock.

WIS. In that case, I'd better give you a s. (He does so.) Good-bye, pet. Have a d time, and behave yourself.

LEN. (Affectionately.) Thanks, Dad. e same to you.

WIS. (Starts to go, stops.) Aw, be a d sport. Come across. . . .

NNIE. (In hallway, outside.) Hello! Is body home?

WIS. Damn! There's Connie already. a low hoarse whisper.) Quick, so I sneak out. Where's your mother?

LEN. Never you mind. Go say Hello your sister.

WIS. (Not moving.) Hi, Connie! (CON-

NIE NEVINS *enters. She is stylish, chic, still young-looking at thirty-five. Basically a gay, affectionate, fun-loving sort of woman, she has not let a rather embittering marital career get her down.*)

CONNIE. Hello, Lewis! (*She goes to him.*)

LEWIS. Hello, Connie!

CONNIE. I didn't expect to find you here.

LEWIS. Been waiting an hour, especially to see you. (*He kisses her perfunctorily, then begins to fire questions without much regard for her answers.*) How are you anyway?

CONNIE. Pretty well, considering. . . .

LEWIS. Have a nice judge?

CONNIE. A dear.

LEWIS. Hotel good?

CONNIE. The food was terrible. I had to keep reminding myself I didn't go to Reno to eat.

LEWIS. Who you going to marry next?

CONNIE. (*With slightly embarrassed laugh.*) That's the problem. . . .

ELLEN. (*Flat on couch.*) Oh, Dad, shut up! You're nothing but a question mark.

CONNIE. (*Aware of* ELLEN *for the first time.*) Ellen darling! (*She expects to kiss* ELLEN, *but the latter keeps on reading and only raises a hand for her to shake.*) You look well. (*Inspects her more closely.*) Or don't you look well?

ELLEN. (*Tersely.*) I don't know how I look; I feel fine.

CONNIE. (*To* LEWIS.) I called up Ann after I called you, but Martha said I couldn't talk to her.

LEWIS. Oh, absolutely out of the question!

CONNIE. (*Startled.*) Ann's not sick?

LEWIS. (*Lugubriously.*) I'm afraid Ann's lost to me forever.

CONNIE. Why, Lewis! What's happened?

ELLEN. Nothing! Mother's hid herself to write a love story, that's all.

CONNIE. I'm glad she's gone back to love. I never can understand her articles about Women in Business, and Women in Marriage, and Women out of Marriage . . . except I've a vague idea they're all aimed at me. What made her go back to fiction after all these years?

ELLEN. (*Pointing to* LEWIS.) That! He felt Mother was getting too independent, so he's disciplining her.

LEWIS. Ellen! Play fair!

ELLEN. Why not tell the truth? You are.

LEWIS. Connie. it's this way. Last week my own sweet, dutiful, loving Annie ordered our duck pond made into a swimming pool. After I expressly told her we couldn't afford it. So this week she's writing a love story to pay the bill.

CONNIE. Can't you afford a swimming pool?

LEWIS. This is a matter of principle. I don't have to be firm with my Annie very often; but when I am firm, by God! I'm granite.

CONNIE. One minute you men go broke to give us a pearl necklace, the next you tell us our extravagance has ruined you . . . a woman doesn't know where she gets off.

LEWIS. My Annie knows where she gets off . . . don't forget that!

CONNIE. I'll admit you two seem to get along.

LEWIS. We're celebrating our twenty-third anniversary next week. Drop around.

CONNIE. Think of it! Remember Father said you and a woman like Ann wouldn't last it out a month. . . .

LEWIS. My father was an old-fashioned man.

ELLEN. Lord, Father, what's so modern about you?

LEWIS. The brilliant way I handle the modern woman. (MARTHA *enters. She is a demure and noiseless Scotch maid in a green dress.*)

MARTHA. Pardon, sir.

LEWIS. What's on your mind, Martha

MARTHA. I've brought in Mrs. Nevi bags.

CONNIE. Where do you suppose Ann w want to put me?

LEWIS. Oh, why not take your regu room!

MARTHA. That's for Mr. Jaywood, sir.

LEWIS. How about the room next to ou

MARTHA. Folks are expected for that, t

LEWIS. Hang around, Connie, we'll you somewhere. (CONNIE *looks at watch.*)

CONNIE. I must have a place to cha now. I've an appointment for four . . . my very best dress.

LEWIS. Ellen, what room *can* she have

ELLEN. I don't know what Mother's pl are.

CONNIE. Maybe I better go back to Waldorf.

LEWIS. You'll do no such thing. A si of mine, just back from Reno, you rate best room in the house. (*To* MARTH Tell Mrs. Murray she must come h at once.

MARTHA. I don't know where she is, Nobody's seen her this whole day.

LEWIS. (*Angrily, to* ELLEN.) This da nonsense must stop! Produce your motl (ELLEN *consults her wrist watch and cides her mother has worked long enoug*

ELLEN. (*To* MARTHA.) She's out betw the vegetable garden and the pump ho under a beach umbrella.

LEWIS. (*To* MARTHA.) Don't you co back here without her!

MARTHA. (*As she exits to terrace.*) right, sir.

CONNIE. (*Apologetically.*) I'm sorry to set . . .

LEWIS. (*Interrupting, heartily.*) No, yo not either. Sit down. Rest your Fre

eels! Want a highball? (ELLEN *rises with*
armful of books.)

CONNIE. No thanks. (*Then to* ELLEN.)
Darling, what are all those books for?

ELLEN. (*Taking books back to book-*
ase.) I just carry them around for exer-
ise.

CONNIE. (*Sitting on sofa.*) I'm crazy to
ear about your graduation.

ELLEN. (*Prosaically, as she puts books*
way.) Oh, the weather was fine, except
ne day it rained possibly an hour. I was
anded a diploma. That's about all there
as to it.

CONNIE. I hoped to get back East in time
o be there.

ELLEN. Sorry you didn't. (*She returns*
nd sits on couch.)

CONNIE. What man did you take? (*To*
EWIS.) That sweet Jackie Whipple, I'll
et.

ELLEN. I didn't take a man.

CONNIE. You didn't take a man?

ELLEN. Nope.

CONNIE. Why, when I graduated from
'iss Spence's I asked seven and eleven
me. Seven, come eleven! Remember,
ewis?

EWIS. (*With a touch of weariness.*) Yes,
remember.

ELEN. Men in droves don't interest me.

CONNIE. But, darling, I can't understand.
girl at Commencement simply has to
ve a man to walk with under the Cam-
s elms in the moonlight. . . .

ELEN. I didn't feel the necessity.

CONNIE. Lewis, I'm worried. It's not nor-
al.

ELEN. (*Turning angrily.*) Connie, you
orry about *your* love life, and I'll worry
out *mine.*

EWIS. (*Sharply, though amused.*) Mind
ur manners, daughter. (*He moves to*
, *to watch for* ANN.)

ELLEN. Sorry.

CONNIE. *You* forgive *me.* I didn't mean
to hurt you.

ELLEN. You didn't. I daresay I *am* peculiar. Personally, I think a woman's a fool
to try and build her happiness around a
man.

CONNIE. (*A trace too sweetly.*) Really,
Ellen, do tell me. I'm in a position this
minute where I yearn to know. What else
can the average woman build her happiness around?

ELLEN. Plenty of things! (ANN *enters*
*from the terrace. The name "*ANN WHIT-
MAN MURRAY*" has for years carried con-*
siderable prestige in the newspaper and
feminist world; but in appearance ANN
looks merely a very comfortable, human,
motherly sort of person . . . with a grow-
ing tendency to be stout. At the moment
she wears a cotton blouse and garden
skirt, neither any too clean, a large sun
hat and old straw sandals. Her face is
streaked with dirt, and strands of loose
hair tend to get in her eyes. Yet despite
this external untidiness, she strikes one
instantly as a personality and a profoundly
charming woman.)

LEWIS. (*Heartily, in a rich Irish brogue.*)
Well, well, Mrs. Lewis Murray, and is it
gardening you have been? (ANN *crosses,*
ignoring her husband as though he did
not exist.)

ANN. Connie! This is grand!

CONNIE. (*Sincere affection in her voice.*)
Ann, my dear!

ANN. Don't kiss me. I'm filthy. I've been
writing a love story with one hand and
weeding parsnips with the other. Did you
have a terrible time?

CONNIE. Not so bad!

LEWIS. She looks a lot better than she
did after her last divorce.

ANN. The main point is: did you get it?

CONNIE. I'm free as air.

ANN. (*Sinking into stuffed chair a n d*
lighting a cigarette.) I'd like to be free
as air myself.

LEWIS. Not if I know it. You haven't a chance!

ELLEN. Mother, do go change, please. You're a sight.

CONNIE. I don't mind.

LEWIS. Yes, Annie, as soon as you wash your face I'd like to kiss you good-bye and go to Larchmont.

ANN. (*Indicating* LEWIS.) Who is that odd-looking man over in the sailor suit who keeps interrupting?

LEWIS. (*Grinning broadly.*) Let me introduce myself. It's me, Annie. Your husband.

ANN. What are you hanging around here for?

LEWIS. For my wife to kiss me good-bye. I'm a very eccentric man. I love my wife. . .

ANN. (*Interrupting.*) Oh, we can't talk till I get rid of him. (*She goes to* LEWIS *and kisses him lightly.*) Good-bye, Commodore.

LEWIS. Good-bye, Annie.

ANN. Hope you get a good ducking!

LEWIS. You peeved at me?

ANN. I am . . . extremely peeved.

LEWIS. Kiss me again. I may get drowned.

ELLEN. Father, will you stop making a sentimental idiot of yourself? You come along with me. (*She takes him by the arm and leads him into the hall.*)

LEWIS. (*Calling back.*) See you at dinner, Connie.

CONNIE. If I can get back in time. (LEWIS *and* ELLEN *disappear,* ANN *settles back comfortably in her chair.*)

ANN. Light yourself a cigarette, Connie, and tell me everything.

CONNIE. (*Lighting cigarette.*) Ann, it's been a tremendous experience. Tremendous! I've come back full of ideas. You know during my first divorce how I got

all weepy and hurt; then the next time when Ted went off with that mouse-coloured blonde, of course I got bitter and drank a lot, and was all kinds of a damn fool. Well, this time I took myself in hand and did some thinking.

ANN. Grand!

CONNIE. I studied those women out there, Ann, ninety percent of them, one look and you'd see why they couldn't hold a man six months unless they had money. There was even more drinking this time than last.

ANN. Really?

CONNIE. I said to myself: Connie Nevin, you don't belong in this gang.

ANN. You don't, you know, Connie.

CONNIE. That's why it's been such an experience. I've found myself. At last I know what I want and why I haven't been happy. From now on I'm going to simplify my life.

ANN. I see.

CONNIE. I'm going to live in the country and have a garden and enjoy all the simple pleasures the way you do. Look, Ann, you and Lewis haven't had a row?

ANN. Not a serious one.

CONNIE. He's a beast to make you write a love story.

ANN. It was my own mistake.

CONNIE. He has money enough for five swimming pools. I wouldn't stand for it.

ANN. Well, he said he couldn't afford it . . . we've had extra expenses with both Roger and Ellen . . . then I saw Joe Bambarra weeping around without any work and nine children, and got soft hearted.

CONNIE. All the same, I'd be furious with Lewis.

ANN. I'd been furious with him it he had let himself be coaxed into paying a bill . . . when I was wrong. I wouldn't want a husband I could twist around my little finger.

CONNIE. If he's around your little finger, you know where he is. (*She consults her wrist watch.*) Ann, is it all right if I fly . . . shortly?

ANN. Of course.

CONNIE. I'm having tea at the club with Glen.

ANN. (*Trying to be enthusiastic.*) Are you? Glen Williams?

CONNIE. You've probably guessed I would anyway . . . but I want you to be the first to know. Glen and I are going to be married next week.

ANN. Next week? I thought you were going to simplify your life?

CONNIE. I am.

ANN. But you said you'd found yourself?

CONNIE. I have.

ANN. Suppose you lose yourself again?

CONNIE. It isn't as though I didn't know Glen awfully well . . . I mean *awfully well*.

ANN. I know you mean *awfully well*. So why the rush? Wait a bit before you marry again. Take a trip. Enjoy a vacation from the masculine sex.

CONNIE. I've just had a six months' vacation. If I dangle Glen any longer, I might lose him.

ANN. If he mislays as easily as that, maybe it would be just as well.

CONNIE. We're so in love.

ANN. Wait. See if you are.

CONNIE. I don't need to. I told you. I've analyzed myself. I've dug into my character with knives. I'm a very affectionate person at heart. Don't you think so?

ANN. Yes, I do. It's made me overlook a lot.

CONNIE. I know. You've stood by the old *divorcée*. Most sisters-in-law wouldn't.

ANN. You see, I like you.

CONNIE. Ann, can I be married here?

ANN. Why not?

CONNIE. (*She crosses to the fireplace.*) I were married in a happy home . . . right here in front of your fireplace . . . it might bring me luck. I can't endure the thought of any more church weddings.

ANN. (*Drily.*) It's certainly worth a try.

CONNIE. Maybe next Wednesday or Thursday. Glen and I will make definite arrangements this afternoon.

ANN. Just let me know a day in advance. (*The phone rings.*)

ELLEN. (*Offstage, rear.*) I'll take it, Mother.

ANN. I'm trying to persuade Ellen to be my secretary for a while. (ELLEN *enters and picks up receiver on small table, left of arch.*)

ELLEN. (*Into phone.*) Hello. Yes, this is Ann Whitman Murray's residence. I'm very sorry. Mrs. Murray is not in right now. I'm her secretary . . . suppose you give me the message. I see. Yes. The fifteenth. (*Makes a note.*) Yes. Yes. I'll ring back and give you an answer as soon as I have talked with Mrs. Murray. (*She hangs up the receiver and comes down to* ANN.) It's a Mr. Henry Folsom. He wants to know will you talk ten minutes at a rally on July fifteenth.

ANN. What's the rally around?

ELLEN. It's the League against War and Fascism.

ANN. All right . . . if I'm free.

ELLEN. Your calendar's in the office. I'll go look. (*She goes out.*)

ANN. (*Calling after her.*) Find out who the other speakers are . . . and if I better wear armour plate.

ELLEN. All right, Mother.

CONNIE. Is Ellen going blind?

ANN. Not to my knowledge.

CONNIE. Why the hideous glasses?

ANN. They're just study glasses. She doesn't wear them all the time.

474 ...he looks so pale and intellectual. ...knows a woman nowadays needs co...rains she can muster up; but that's ...son she shouldn't continue to look ...o. The poor child said she didn't have ...ngle man at her Commencement.

ANN. She could have.

CONNIE. (*Incredulously.*) And didn't!

ANN. She did invite one boy, I believe, but at the last minute he didn't come.

CONNIE. Why not?

ANN. Don't ask me. She is keeping her own counsel this spring . . . at times to the point of being sullen.

CONNIE. You'd be sullen if you weren't popular with men.

ANN. (*Amused.*) Would I?

CONNIE. Ann, I have too much respect for your judgment to think of interfering, but do you mind a suggestion?

ANN. I'd welcome one.

CONNIE. If she were my daughter I'd rush her tomorrow to some good beauty consultant, then to a really intelligent dressmaker.

ANN. (*Vaguely.*) I think she has several Schiaparelli's.

CONNIE. You'd never guess it to look at her. After all, our family does have some position. Why shouldn't Ellen have the benefit of it? Seriously, Ann, why don't you have her come out?

ANN. She has just come out of college. Can she go back in and come out again?

CONNIE. Why not? It's too terrible for her to become a private secretary. If you're going to be nursemaid to a man, you might as well be married to him. (ANN *smiles.*) Smile if you want. I'm telling you God's solemn truth. You take off Ellen's glasses, show her a few attractive men, and in six months she'd bloom like a tea rose.

ANN. Connie, you're grand. After all you've been through, you still advocate the sly, primitive female hunt for man.

CONNIE. I don't care whether Ellen hunts.

All I say is that it's a shame to let a girl with so many possibilities develop into a freak, maybe a crank.

ANN. Like her mother.

CONNIE. (*Conscience-stricken.*) Ann, dear I didn't mean that. You're not.

ANN. My good woman, if I had a dime for every time I'd been called a crank, could balance the national budget.

CONNIE. Anyway, you're not *now*. Since you married Lewis you've been growing more feminine steadily.

ANN. (*Delighted.*) You encourage me Maybe by the time I'm seventy-five, I'll be sex-y. (ELLEN *enters hurriedly.*)

CONNIE. Er, do think over what I've said

ANN. (*Studying* ELLEN *thoughtfully.*) already am.

ELLEN. (*Who has waited for them to sto talking.*) Mother, you simply must dres Peter's back. I think with your Mr. Ja wood. He looks horribly English and ultr (*Both* ANN *and* CONNIE *rise.*)

CONNIE. Where you going to bunk me me?

ANN. Ellen's away till Monday. You ca have her room.

CONNIE. (*To* ELLEN.) Do you mind?

ELLEN. Of course not. Move right I'm all packed.

ANN. Tell Mr. Jaywood I'll be down in jiffy.

ELLEN. Mother, give me fifteen minu alone with him.

ANN. Why should I?

ELLEN. Because I've always wanted meet an International Literary Agent.

ANN. Let's go this way. (CONNIE *and* A *start, right.*)

ELLEN. (*Running after them.*) He (*She hands* ANN *her garden hat.*) A Mother, for Heaven's sake wash beh your ears!

ANN. (*Meekly.*) I generally do, dear.

NIE *and* ANN *exit.* ELLEN *leisurely re-
es her glasses and puts them in case;
s down her skirt; then crosses to mir-
left, and arranges her hair. The reis not style, but she does possess a
in breathless charm.* MARTHA *enters.*)

THA. Miss Ellen, Mr. Jaywood.

N. Show him in. And Martha: bring
whiskey and soda at once. (MARTHA
s *and goes out.* ELLEN *waits eagerly.
appears followed by* MARTHA. *He is a
tly alert Englishman in his early for-
He wears a conservative business
MARTHA *sees him safely through the
way, then disappears from sight.*)

N. I suppose we'll have to introduce
elves. I'm Ellen Murray.

(*As they shake hands.*) I'm Titus
ood. How do you do?

N. (*Briskly, quite unabashed.*) Swell
came early. I've been hoping desper-
you would.

I'm flattered.

N. Do sit down. There are cigarettes
our elbow.

(*Taking cigarette*) Thanks.

N. (*Offering him light.*) Mother says
are an old friend of hers.

Not so old. About five weeks. I
your mother in May at a literary tea.

N. (*Somewhat taken back.*) In May!
t the impression . . . Oh well, it
n't matter. (*She stops, then says
ly.*) If you'll forgive me, I'm going
lunge right ahead.

By all means. Let's not stop now...
RTHA *enters with tray.*)

N. Place it here, Martha. (MARTHA
tray beside ELLEN *and goes out.*) I
ed us whiskey and soda, or would
prefer something else?

Whiskey and soda suits me per-
.

N. Two fingers or three? (*She pours
key.*)

(*Smiling at her intense eagerness.*)

I think I shall need three. (ELLEN *starts
to put ice in drink.*) No ice, thanks.

ELLEN. (*Pouring soda.*) Mother said you
were English. (*Hands him glass.*)

JAY. Thanks.

ELLEN. Comfortable?

JAY. I'm enjoying all the sensations of the
prodigal son.

ELLEN. Then I'm coming straight to the
point.

JAY. Point? Is there a point?

ELLEN. Mr. Jaywood, I've just graduated
from college. The customary thing would
be for me to play up to you all this week-
end, put myself across as hard as I could
. . . then just before you leave, ask you
to help me get a job.

JAY. I wish, Miss Murray, you'd stick
to your American customs. I'd much prefer to be "played up to" till Monday.

ELLEN. But I'm not going to be home
this week-end.

JAY. Oh, that's too bad.

ELLEN. I've got to visit a classmate in
Hartford. Her father runs a paper there.
I'd a lot rather stay here and talk with
you. I've a million questions to ask you
about Maugham, and Priestly and all the
other authors you handle. Unfortunately
I made this date before I knew Mother
had asked you out.

JAY. Naturally you can't look for work
in two places the same week-end.

ELLEN. No, not very well. Will you excuse me if I talk about myself?

JAY. I think it would be charming.

ELLEN. Of course, I was editor of the
"Lit" and all that sort of junk, and of
course, I've learned all I can from Mother.
You see, I want to be one of the best
all-round newspaper women that ever
drew breath, like Anne O'Hare McCor-
mick or Dorothy Thompson.

JAY. Splendid.

ELLEN. You needn't if you don't want to,
but I thought perhaps you'd give me let-

ters to two or three editors. I wouldn't mind going on a magazine . . . anything to get a start. You don't have to say anything very good about me . . . just enough so I can get one foot inside an editor's door.

JAY. That will make it easier.

ELLEN. I wish you'd stop looking so amused. After all, I have already sold stuff.

JAY. (Surprised.) You have? What?

ELLEN. Oh, a few poems . . . at the large sum of two dollars each. I wish there was money in poetry.

JAY. A lot of poets wish that.

ELLEN. Then, of course, I've sold quite a few articles on education and politics.

JAY. Politics? How's your thousand-page novel?

ELLEN. Fine. How's yours? (JAY smiles.) Really, it's no credit to me. Mother and I get into awful arguments. She sells what she says to liberal papers, and I sell what I say to conservatives.

JAY. Haven't you your viewpoints reversed?

ELLEN. When it comes to being liberal, Mother's got me licked six ways. She's just as radical as when she wrote for the *Masses* in Greenwich Village and headed Suffrage Parades. You know, she used to be a famous feminist when she was young. Incidentally, Mr. Jaywood, Mother's been in jail nineteen times.

JAY. That's a very nice record.

ELLEN. I suppose the reason I'm conservative is on account of Father. He's half Dutch. Have you ever met him?

JAY. No, I never have.

ELLEN. I think you'll like him. Can you imagine? Mother an Iowa hog and corn farmer and Father Dutch Social Register! What do you suppose that makes me?

JAY. Let's hope it makes you a good all-round newspaper woman.

ELLEN. You mean you'll really help me get a job? (JAY nods.) Look, Mr. Jaywood,

I want to get this job on my own. won't mention who my mother is, you?

JAY. A g r e e d. There's one quest though, before I commit myself to a se of introductory letters. . . .

ELLEN. Ask me anything.

JAY. Are you engaged?

ELLEN. (With unexpected vehemence should hope not!

JAY. I've introduced girls to jobs be Almost invariably within a year or tw get an irate phone call: "Dammit, J they say, "just as I got that woman tr ed, she's up and leaving me to hav child!"

ELLEN. Oh, I don't think I'll hav child.

JAY. Well, you watch your step! (MAI enters.)

MARTHA. Miss Ellen, there's a Mr. D las Hall outside that says . . .

ELLEN. (Interrupting angrily.) W that man doing here?

MARTHA. (Prosaically.) He's waiting the steps.

ELLEN. Tell him I can't see him. I to leave the house immediately. (MA exits. ELLEN turns to JAY. She has los poise. Her one desire is to flee.) I si must go. You've been awfully helpf wish I could stay and get really acquainted.

JAY. My ambition is to be asked again.

ELLEN. If Mother doesn't ask you, come out and see me. (Extends hand, vously.) Good-bye. It's been grand. .

JAY. Hasn't it? Your indomitable y refreshes me.

ELLEN. (Stopping abruptly.) I bet wrote poetry once.

JAY. Did I? Why?

ELLEN. I don't know. There was s thing about that line. And you see

ressed by the word "youth." (DOUGLAS
L enters. "DOUG" *is an attractive, force-*
young man of around twenty-five. His
hes are of good material and cut, but
-worn. MARTHA *hovers in the back-*
und.)

G. (*With touch of defiance.*) Hi,
n! (*She does not answer.*) Forgive my
ging in.

N. (*Recovering.*) Mr. Jaywood, much
regret the necessity, may I introduce
Hall?

How do you do.

G. How are you, sir. (*A pause.*
her ELLEN *nor* DOUGLAS *can find any-*
g to say. JAY *senses he is between two*
gerents who yearn to open fire.)

(*Blandly.*) Perhaps this would be
xcellent moment for me to unpack.

N. Do you mind?

Not at all.

N. Martha, you know Mr. Jaywood's
n?

THA. Your mother said he was to
the Sound view.

N. (*To* JAY.) Mother will be down
soon.

(*Bowing gravely.*) Mr. Hall, it's
a rare pleasure.

. Thank you. (JAY *exits after* MAR-
)

N. (*With cool sarcasm.*) So you *are*
to leave Boston?

. Listen, Ellen, we've no time to be

N. I'm not sore. I merely commented
he fact that though you couldn't pos-
leave Boston last week, you are able
ave this week.

. Yes? Well, let me comment on the
that when I tell a girl I can't get to
ace, I don't care to be insulted with
e for twenty-five dollars.

N. Insulted?

. I said "insulted"!

ELLEN. But I thought we were friends.

DOUG. So did I.

ELLEN. Well, then . . . didn't you understand?

DOUG. Why didn't you do a little understanding yourself? You knew I was strapped.

ELLEN. Obviously, else why wire you
money?

DOUG. Yes, and you know why I wired
it back.

ELLEN. Frankly, I don't.

DOUG. I'm no paid escort.

ELLEN. That's pretty cheap.

DOUG. The letter you wrote me was pretty
cheap too. (*Fumbles in his pocket.*) Maybe you'd like to refresh your memory.

ELLEN. I kept a carbon copy.

DOUG. You say you understand people's
psychology.

ELLEN. I try to.

DOUG. Good God, then! Didn't you realize I couldn't come because I wasn't in
the mood? I'd have been a gloom in all
that Commencement gaiety. It wasn't the
actual carfare. Lord, I'd have pawned my
watch and hitch-hiked.

ELLEN. Exactly! You didn't want to come.

DOUG. Sure I wanted to come.

ELLEN. Then why didn't you?

DOUG. I told you.

ELLEN. You were too proud.

DOUG. Damn right I was too proud. Think
I'd humiliate you?

ELLEN. I'd rather be humiliated than . . .
than disappointed.

DOUG. I felt you'd have enough other
men.

ELLEN. Oh, I had plenty.

DOUG. Then what are you sore about?

ELLEN. I'm not sore. Is that what you
came to find out?

DOUG. No, I came to say good-bye.

ELLEN. Good-bye. Awfully glad you dropped in. (*She sits on couch and turns her back.*)

DOUG. Listen, Ellen, for God's sake, be a human being, will you? I've come to say good-bye, because I'm going to Belgium.

ELLEN. (*Blankly.*) Belgium?

DOUG. Yes. You remember Belgium, don't you?

ELLEN. What are you talking about? How can you leave your job?

DOUG. Oh, it wasn't so hard to leave... especially after I got your twenty-five-dollar wire. I've chucked architecture.

ELLEN. Doug! That's terrible!

DOUG. The hell with it! What do I want with that profession? After six years' study and work, it won't pay me enough even to go and see the girl I love graduate! (*At the words "I love," ELLEN gives him a surprised look, then turns away.*) Well, it's out! My idea was to tell you later... a little more romantically. Ellen, you've looked right to me from the day I met you. I love you. I'm heart-sick over you. That's why that damn telegram burned me up. (*He studies her face anxiously.*)

ELLEN. That's what I couldn't understand. Why should my telegram burn you up? I mean if we *both* cared for each other.

DOUG. Say, you mean you actually do? Oh, darling! (*She nods. He takes her into his arms. They kiss, shyly, then more eagerly.*)

ELLEN. Oh, Doug, this past month has been pure hell.

DOUG. I'll say it has.

ELLEN. Anyway, everything is all right now.

DOUG. Well, it's better. (*She breaks away from him.*)

ELLEN. That's so. You're leaving. You don't have to go for some time, do you?

DOUG. I sail Monday at midnight.

ELLEN. Monday! Can't you put it off

DOUG. Impossible. I've got to start w July first. It's a ten-day boat. I can make it.

ELLEN. But we've everything to talk c We haven't made any plans yet.

DOUG. We can do a lot of planning tween now and Monday night.

ELLEN. But I'm catching a train in than an hour.

DOUG. Where you going?

ELLEN. Edith Colby's. I agreed to stay Monday. Say, I might get you invited,

DOUG. Swell!

ELLEN. No, that wouldn't be so g There's going to be masses of people al We couldn't be by ourselves. I guess better call it off. . . .

DOUG. Well, if you don't mind. . . .

ELLEN. You can stay here. No, th be a crowd here. I've given up my r to Connie, already. The house will se How long will you have to be gone

DOUG. I've signed up for two years.

ELLEN. Two years? Do you feel it's to stay away from . . . from Americ long?

DOUG. I couldn't get the job if I d

ELLEN. Do you realize that just we've discovered we care, we're about separated. It might be forever.

DOUG. Oh, no, it won't.

ELLEN. Well, I'm not going to Har that's settled!

DOUG. Good girl! (*She crosses tho fully.*)

ELLEN. I have it. I *will* go to Har

DOUG. Say, make up your mind.

ELLEN. I mean suppose I *start* for ford, then you join me, and I won't

DOUG. Won't they expect you?

ELLEN. I'll wire them I can't come. would give us three whole days tog

G. (*Uneasily.*) Together? Er, where?

EN. I don't know. Somewhere! Some
cottage maybe . . . with a lake and
anoe. We could cook our own meals,
smoke and talk, and plan our whole
together.

G. I don't know about that. (*He
ses to left, worried and uncomfortable.*)

N. What's the matter? Have I shock-
ou?

G. No, it's not that.

N. In marriage everything depends
getting off to a right start.

. This might not be such a swell

N. I mean we've been separated so
h and had so many misunderstand-
. Before you go, I think it's terribly
ortant we settle every point we could
bly fight about after you're gone.

. Something to that.

N. I know a little lake outside Lanes-
. We used to drive over from college.
e are several darling cottages on it. I
w we could hire one. The season
n't start till the Fourth. There wouldn't
hree people around the entire lake.

. Three people is plenty sometimes.
n't want you to lose your reputation.

N. I won't . . . if we plan things
ully.

. I still don't quite like the idea.

N. Maybe you think I've done some-
like this before.

. Of course not.

N. (*Solemnly.*) Doug, this is an emer-
y measure.

. God, I wish we could marry.

N. Well, if we can't, we can't! And
think we're entitled to something . . .
thing beautiful and set apart. Some-
we can cling to after you're gone!
t you?

. Yes, but . . .

ELLEN. Doug, be frank. What do you
really feel? Does . . . does my willingness
to go like this make me seem cheap?

DOUG. What do you think I am? (*He
rises and takes her by the shoulders affectionately.*) Makes you seem precious. What
I don't like is . . . it's a bit underhanded.

ELLEN. Whose earthly business is it, except yours and mine?

DOUG. You've got a mother, you know.

ELLEN. I don't think she'd mind particularly. . . .

DOUG. (*Surprised.*) Why not?

ELLEN. I mean, under the circumstances.
Mother's tremendously advanced. Not, of
course, that I'd want her to know. . . .

DOUG. I wish we had more time to think
it over.

ELLEN. So do I, but we haven't. Well,
what shall we do?

DOUG. I think you're right, Ellen. We'll
go.

ELLEN. Oh, I'm glad.

DOUG. So am I. (*Their voices lower, and
take an a brisk secretive quality.*)

ELLEN. How'd you get here?

DOUG. I borrowed my cousin's car. I'm
making my headquarters with him till I
sail.

ELLEN. When does he expect you back?

DOUG. When he sees me. I've got a couple
of visits to make. How far is a place called
Silver Mine from here?

ELLEN. About six miles.

DOUG. (*Looking at watch.*) Your train
goes at five? (ELLEN *nods.*) I can just make
it. There's a Yale man lives at Silver Mine
said he'd buy my drafting instruments.

ELLEN. Oh, Doug, you must let me pay.

DOUG. No, I'm financing this little expedition.

ELLEN. Let's both finance it. . . .

DOUG. No.

ELLEN. Fifty-fifty, I insist. . . .

DOUG. No.

ELLEN. I just received a twenty-dollar check for writing an article.

DOUG. Well, all right. I'll be right back. (*He kisses her.*) Darling, it seems impossible you and I should have scrapped so.

ELLEN. (*Very seriously.*) Maybe our love was clarifying itself.

DOUG. Maybe. Good-bye. (*He starts up to door.*)

ELLEN. (*Stopping him.*) Doug, I do think we can work this out, don't you?

DOUG. Of course we can, darling. A college education must be good for something. (*He hurries out.* ELLEN *follows and calls after him.*)

ELLEN. Drive carefully! We haven't time to get arrested! (*He disappears.* ELLEN *comes back, center and stands for a moment, getting her feet on solid ground again. Then she utters a contented sigh, and starts around the drum table towards the hall.* ANN *enters from right. She has changed into afternoon dress and done her hair. The result is a well-groomed, much more sophisticated-looking woman.*)

ANN. What have you done with Mr. Jaywood?

ELLEN. (*Starting, as though caught with the family jewels.*) Oh, hello, Mother! He . . . he went to his room. (*She regains her poise.*) We had a grand talk. I asked him for some letters of introduction. . . .

ANN (*In disapproving tone.*) The moment he stepped inside the house?

ELLEN. I know. I apologized. I told him I'd have waited till Monday if I hadn't been going away.

ANN. Ellen, we don't use our guests.

ELLEN. (*In joking tone.*) Mother, suppose Mr. Jaywood thought you were entertaining him this week-end in order to sell your story. Aren't you worried stiff?

ANN. (*With calm assurance.*) No, dear, I am not.

ELLEN. Anyway, I invited him out a[s] to see me. . . . (JAY *enters. He has chan[ged] to grey flannel trousers and sport coat.*)

ANN. Oh, how do you do, Mr. Jaywo[od?] I'm so glad you could come this aftern[oon.] Please forgive me for not being down.

JAY. That's quite all right. Your daug[hter] has been entertaining me.

ANN. Ellen tells me she asked you [for] some letters.

JAY. I'll be glad to help her.

ANN. I'm sorry. She shouldn't have [done] it.

JAY. I liked her frankness.

ANN. Well, I don't. I'm out of pati[ence] with this current mania for frankness. [It's] just a cold-blooded excuse to say what [you] please, do what you please, and get [what] you please, without regard for the [com-] mon decencies.

ELLEN. (*Eagerly.*) Mother, there's an [ar-] ticle in that. Here I am, just out of col[lege.] It's terribly hard to get a job. A[n] important person like Mr. Jaywood c[omes] along . . . should I, or should I not, [tell] him frankly how good I am and ask [his] help? And if I don't tell him how [good] I am, and ask his help, would I, or w[ould] I not, be a spineless idiot who ough[t to] end her days in the gutter?

ANN. Suppose you change your cl[othes] and start for Hartford.

ELLEN. Okay. (*In archway she turns. [Her] manner is most innocent and casual.*) [By] the way, Mother, I've altered my [plans] slightly. Doug Hall showed up just [now] out of the blue.

ANN. Really? I wish I'd got a loo[k at] him.

ELLEN. He said he'd come back and [take] me to the train.

ANN. Did you tell Peter he won't be [need-] ed?

ELLEN. Not yet. I will. See you bot[h be-] fore I go. . . . (*She exits.*)

JAY. I like her, Ann.

, I do myself ... most of the time. ...sionally, when that brain of hers gets ...active, I wish I'd given birth to a nice ...y-headed little moron ... with a lisp!

I doubt if you could. (*Lightly.*) Of ...se I haven't seen your husband yet. ...*laughs.*)

(*Impulsively.*) Jay, it's grand you ...l get out this afternoon. Will you have ...ink?

I've still part of what Ellen gave

Did that daughter of mine ply you ...whiskey?

She was jolly hospitable.

What do they teach them at college ...days ... to be night-club hostesses? ...one else is coming till tomorrow. It'll ...us time for a real talk.

(*With mock solemnity.*) Frankly, ...I'm afraid this week-end will be ...thing of an ordeal for me.

(*Surprised.*) Ordeal? Indeed?

It's not easy to visit an old sweet-. A chap looks about, and realizes ...happy home, this gracious wife and ...y daughter might ... with better luck ...have been his. It makes for melan- ...in a single man at times.

I imagine it might.

(*Brightly.*) On the other hand, it ...work the other way. A man realizes ...he has escaped. Why only last Mon- ...morning, I left a home over in Jersey ...laughing like a hyena.

Don't you start any hyena laughs ...d here!

No danger!

You said you never married, didn't

Yes. I've had a few flutters, but you ...the big palpitation.

I must have been. I meet you ac- ...ally at a tea, and find you've been ...nerica three years ... without looking ...p.

JAY. I made inquiries the day I landed. Unfortunately, not in the right social sphere. I asked around Washington Square. One person told me positively you were dead.

ANN. What did I die of?

JAY. It was no joke, I can tell you. I walked slowly under the Arch and started up Fifth Avenue. The next I knew I was on Riverside Drive. There, in the twilight, I buried my youth ... and my love ... right next to Grant's Tomb! Later on, of course, I heard you'd married a wealthy banker. It seemed better to let it go at that.

ANN. (*With faint sarcasm.*) Oh, much better.

JAY. (*After a pause.*) Er, you never got to England?

ANN. Several times.

JAY. Without looking me up?

ANN. I tried to. I decided probably you didn't get through the war.

JAY. Yes, I got through.

ANN. When we were in London, several years ago, Lewis dragged me to the Tomb of the Unknown Soldier. Know what I thought as I stood there?

JAY. I can't imagine.

ANN. I thought: "My heavens! for all I know, this may be Jay!" I burst into tears. Lewis was thoroughly irritated. He made me walk ten paces behind ... so I wouldn't disgrace him. (*A pause.*)

JAY. (*Drily.*) We both seem to have shed some unnecessary tears!

ANN. Oh, I loathe sentiment.

JAY. (*Briskly.*) We must stop. It's aging me rapidly.

ANN. Yes, it's aging me, too. I want to show you the farm. Let's stroll, shall we?

JAY. (*Rising.*) Delighted.

ANN. Jay, I can't get used to you ... not in a corduroy suit.

JAY. I say, do you remember that corduroy suit? It popped into my head upstairs just now. I wore it from 1908 to 1913 inclusively. The pants moaned when I walked.

ANN. And whistled when you ran!

JAY. Jove, that was a pair of pants.

ANN. Oh, sentiment again . . . !

JAY. Where is this farm?

ANN. Oh, it's just occurred to me. (*She goes to archway and looks up-stairs.*) I really must wait and say good-bye to Ellen. Do you mind?

JAY. Of course not. (*Sees photograph on table between windows.*) Is this your son?

ANN. Yes, that's Roger. I'm sorry you won't see him. He left on Monday for Canada to be a counsellor in a boys' camp.

JAY. Nice manly chap.

ANN. Yes, he's like his father.

JAY. Tell me, Ann, your husband . . . this Lewis, who dragged you away from my tomb . . . does he know about me?

ANN. Jay! As if that sort of thing mattered among adult people today.

JAY. Lewis is quite adult?

ANN. Of course he is. I know you'll like him. He's out playing with his boat right now. He'll be back before long.

JAY. I shall look forward to meeting the man who domesticated Ann Whitman.

ANN. (*With unexpected sharpness.*) I don't like that word "domesticated." Do I look domesticated?

JAY. Yes, you've mellowed, Ann. You're . . . softer.

ANN. You're the second person today to tell me I'm soft. I know what's done it. It's that accursed love story.

JAY. How's it coming?

ANN. I've been out in the garden since eight this morning trimming it with moonlight.

JAY. Gray dawn is better, Ann. (dawn is frightfully popular in fiction season.

ANN. I'll run my moonlight into da But what has me tearing my hair is . . . the 1939 model.

JAY. That shouldn't be so difficult, two children.

ANN. They're no help at all. Ellen I argue ourselves hoarse over everyth else, but when it comes to love, she se indifferent. Children nowadays don't s to want to discuss it.

JAY. Maybe all the love problems settled.

ANN. I hope so. (CONNIE *enters hurrie She has changed into a very smart d* JAY *rises.*)

CONNIE. Ann, darling, I'm off.

ANN. What in the world is keeping F upstairs?

CONNIE. She seems to be finding problem what to pack.

ANN. Oh, you two haven't met. Nevins, may I introduce Mr. Jaywoo

JAY. Mrs. Nevins, how do you do.

CONNIE. How do you do.

ANN. Mr. Jaywood has come out brighten up our week-end.

CONNIE. How thrilling!

MARTHA. (*Entering from right.*) Ex me, Mrs. Murray.

ANN. Yes, Martha?

MARTHA. Peter wants to know is Ellen nearly ready.

ANN. Tell Peter he won't be nee Martha. A friend is driving Miss Elle Stamford. (MARTHA *exits.*)

CONNIE. (*Unaccountably interest* Really, Ann? Who?

ANN. A boy from Boston.

CONNIE. (*Thoughtfully.*) I see (*She towards door, right, with mounting*

n.) Ann, do you mind walking out to
car with me?

(*Settling herself comfortably.*) I
certainly do. Why should I?

IE. It's about Ellen.

Shall I . . . ? (*He starts for the ter-*
)

Nonsense, Mr. Jaywood. Connie's
ys being mysterious.

IE. Ann, please!

It can't be as important as all that!

IE. There's no time to argue. Ann,
e simply got to do something. I'm
Ellen isn't going to Hartford at all.
going off somewhere with this boy
right now!

Connie Nevins, do you know what
e saying?

(*Starting to go.*) If you'll excuse
. .

No, you've heard part. I prefer that
hear the rest. (JAY *comes back.*)

IE. When I came back into Ellen's
just now, she had started to re-pack
ags completely.

What of it? I always pack the things
n't want first.

IE. She'd taken out her party dresses
her white evening coat, and was put-
in riding breeches and heavy shoes.
said she thought she'd probably do
hiking than dancing.

Why get suspicious over that?

IE. I didn't, until I put this boy and
riding breeches together . . . well, er,
know what I mean.

I still see nothing to justify . . .

IE. Ann, I may not know much, but

I do know a week-end date when I see
one. Her expression had completely
changed. Her eyes were all shining and
starry. She had that look, you know . . .

ANN. I know. Anticipatory.

CONNIE. Exactly. I felt you ought to know
about it at once. (*She turns to* JAY.) No
doubt you think I'm a meddling old aunty.

JAY. Quite the contrary.

CONNIE. (*To* ANN.) I've got to fly. I don't
know when I'll be back. I imagine Glen
will want to go on somewhere for dinner.
(*Turning back in archway.*) Good-bye,
Mr. Jaywood. Don't wait up for me, Ann.
(*She exits.*)

ANN. (*Calling after her.*) You know
where the key is?

CONNIE. (*Outside.*) Yes, I know. Good-
bye.

ANN. (*Turning to* JAY, *after a pause.*)
You must have seen this boy. Did he look
like a week-ender?

JAY. He looked like a very decent chap.

ANN. This thing does have a kind of
plausibility to it. An affair's the one subject on earth on which Connie is a final
authority. (*Getting worked up, she rises.*)
Maybe Ellen thinks she's being modern.
Maybe she's just a love-sick child. Jay, what
shall I do?

JAY. I'm hardly qualified to say. . . .

ANN. You've been around, haven't you?

JAY. My dear Ann, not to the point of
being a mother.

ANN. I'm going upstairs to ask a few
questions. Make yourself comfortable. (*She
turns in archway.*) And pray for me. (*She
goes out.* JAY *shrugs his shoulders ex-
pressively.*)

CURTAIN

ACT TWO

e: *A comfortable and much-used up-*
room commonly known in the MUR-
family as "Mother's Office." There are
y shelves of books and bound maga-

zines. *Upstage, right center, is a large
old-fashioned desk on which are two
phones and a typewriter. Left, is a fireplace with a couch in front of it. Rear,*

two dormer windows open out with a view into the lower branches of a large maple tree. Sunlight filters through the green leaves. Right, is the only entrance. About the room are pictures, photographs, artistic knick-knacks, such as might be collected in a lifetime. The door and windows are open, with a breeze blowing through. The abstract effect is of a cool, mellow, summer-time interior in an old house set among large trees.

ANN. (*Speaking offstage, right.*) Ellen, come and say good-bye before you go.

ELLEN. (*Faintly, in distance.*) Of course, Mother.

ANN. I'll be in the office. (ANN *enters. She has just come up-stairs from receiving* CONNIE'S *news. For a moment she stands by her desk, trying to decide what to do; then she lights a cigarette and waits, looking towards the door expectantly. The suspense becomes too much; she moves about the room, finally ending up at the window. The fear assails her that* ELLEN *may leave without coming in. She crosses to the door and listens.*)

ANN. (*At length.*) Ellen! You aren't going to forget that I want to see you.

ELLEN. (*In distance.*) I'll be right there, Mother. (ANN *returns to desk, snubs out her cigarette nervously and waits.* ELLEN *enters. She wears a light summer travelling suit and appears extremely piquant and self-possessed.* ANN *watches her cross anxiously without speaking.*) Good-bye, old dear. (*She kisses* ANN, *who does not respond. If* ELLEN *notes this she does not show it. Her voice is gay.*) Think you'll be able to protect yourself from interruptions without me?

ANN. I think so.

ELLEN. That idiotic story's about done, isn't it?

ANN. Almost.

ELLEN. Crazy to read it. Well, see you Monday. . . .

ANN. Ellen, I'd like to talk to you a moment.

ELLEN. I haven't much time.

ANN. Your Mr. Hall hasn't returned has he?

ELLEN. He'll be here in a minute.

ANN. (*In tone of authority.*) Well, the door, and wait for him here, ple

ELLEN. Why, if you wish. . . . (*She the door and returns, doing plent thinking on the way.* ANN *watches with a troubled expression. Catchin* LEN's *glance she tries to smile reassu ly, then she nerves herself, and take plunge.*)

ANN. Ellen, I . . . I dislike to be ob to talk seriously . . . especially when y about to leave . . . but . . .

ELLEN. (*Nervously, hoping to bea to it.*) If it's about hitting up Mr. Jay for those letters, I'm sorry. I supp was cold-blooded and not at all polite but I don't think he minded. You him say my frankness made a hit.

ANN. I want you to be frank with too.

ELLEN. I always am.

ANN. And I hope you always will b *pause. She moves articles on desk nervously.*) You know, dear, up t present moment, you and I have a got along very well without my ever ing to fall back on the fact . . . th that I'm your mother. . . .

ELLEN. Dear, you act hurt about thing!

ANN. No.

ELLEN. I admit I'm trying every know to get a job, but you must see I get much experience sticking aroun house here as your secretary . . .

ANN. I see it perfectly.

ELLEN. I'd really love to work wit . . . if it were practical.

ANN. That's not what I asked you i Ellen, hasn't there been an unexp change in your plans this past half

ELLEN. (*Looking away from* ANN.) no! What plans?

To visit Edith in Hartford.

N. No, why should there be?

You were all packed. Then you up-stairs, throw out your party gowns put in riding breeches and what seems e a costume for an extremely rough -end.

N. (Crossing to behind couch.) Good t, Mother! Can you see around cor- and through walls?

No, but I'm blessed with a sister- w who can.

N. Connie?

Yes.

N. (Angrily.) Why doesn't Connie her own business?

(Gently.) I appreciate it is a great to ask you to confide in anyone, but u are facing a problem . . . can't we it over?

N. I think one's private life is one's te life, and I felt you thought so, too.

I do, only . . .

N. Only Connie got to work on you with her nasty mind!

That's not fair. . . .

N. You know perfectly well that time Connie looks at a man her goes down to ten!

(Taken back by the truth of this rk.) If you feel that way about Con- er . . . life, I am rather surprised you . . .

N. (Indignantly, crossing to right.) e's no comparison.

I'm glad.

N. The way she flits from one male other is positively biological!

She is trying desperately hard to . . . love.

N. Of course, if that's your idea of

It's not. I am trying to find out

yours. (A pause.) You are planning not to go to Hartford, aren't you? (A pause. ELLEN studies the carpet, then in one pent-up outburst.)

ELLEN. Mother, Doug and I've had a terrible time. We've both been at cross purposes and only making each other miserable, then suddenly we got a complete understanding and realized how much we mean to each other . . . and bang! Just like that, Doug announced that Monday he had to go away and I wouldn't see him for two years!

ANN. Where has he got to go?

ELLEN. Belgium.

ANN. Why Belgium?

ELLEN. He has a job there.

ANN. Two years is not so long.

ELLEN. Sometimes it's forever.

ANN. Of course, there is the quaint old custom of marriage.

ELLEN. How could we marry? Mother, there's just no use discussing it. My mind is made up. We talked it over. This is absolutely the only chance we may ever have to be together . . . and nothing's going to stop us. I'm sorry if you're going to let yourself get upset, but you have Connie to blame for that, and really deep down in your heart, Mother, I think you do understand, don't you?

ANN. Suppose you meet someone who recognizes you?

ELLEN. We'll look out. We're going to a little lake in Lanesville. There won't be a soul there.

ANN. Ellen, it's not as simple for you as you make it sound, unless . . .

ELLEN. Unless what?

ANN. Unless this is not the first time. . . .

ELLEN. Put your mind to rest. It is.

ANN. (Rising.) That makes my duty all the more clear to me. I'm sorry, I know how miserably unhappy it will make you at first.

ELLEN. (*Interrupting.*) Mother, I simply won't be stopped by you or anybody else!

ANN. What do you think your father would say?

ELLEN. Does he have to know?

ANN. We have shared your virtues and your sins equally so far.

ELLEN. I know I must sound awfully underhanded and tricky but, you know, I did intend to tell you eventually.

ANN. (*Gently sarcastic.*) Oh, did you?

ELLEN. Sometime when we were alone and feeling confidential over a cocktail, or late some night by the fire . . .

ANN. That would have been considerate. You could tell me too, if I didn't like it, I could lump it!

ELLEN. After all it's none of your business.

ANN. You just get that idea out ⁄of your head, Ellen. You are my business. You and Roger. True, I've puttered around a little the past twenty years at writing and lecturing; but my real thought and my real concern have been over you and Roger. You're all I have to show for my life. That's why, when half my business gets it into its head to go into bankruptcy, I feel I do have something to say about it.

ELLEN. It's so funny to hear *you* get sentimental.

ANN. I'm sorry if what I've said strikes you as humorous.

ELLEN. I used the wrong word. I mean odd . . . because usually you're so rational.

ANN. No matter how you meant it . . . even if I do appear just an old-fashioned mother . . . you can't go off with this boy, and that's the end of it!

ELLEN. You mean you're going to take a moral stand?

ANN. If you wish to call it that.

ELLEN. I'm sorry. There's one thing I thought you could never be, and that's a hypocrite.

ANN. Darling, please! Let's not start ing names!

ELLEN. (*Going up to book-shelves, of desk.*) I said I didn't think you be one . . . if you stopped and thoug over. (*She selects a small thin book.*)

ANN. I'm afraid I don't know quite you mean.

ELLEN. Listen, Mother! (*She comes to ANN, finds a page, and begins to r* It was blustering March but a son Spring
Piped high through the Village. Our gering
Hearts revolted from sidewalk meeti
From park-bench trysts; from c greetings.
All we asked of the gods above.
Was a place we could be alone with love.
   Yet there's always a moment the relent.
Some optimistic editor sent
Me thirty dollars . . . enough for re
Oh, that was the moment our fort were blessed,
For Twenty-one Barrows Street got d sessed!
   While I bearded the landlord, you ried to borrow,
Tony the Iceman's two-wheeled bar
And we trundled my Japanese prints your chair,
Clothes, books and brass candlesticks the Square. . . .
   Oh yes, I smile now that I write
Only . . . I'll never forget the delight
How you'd come rushing in of nigh
Burning with zeal for Woman's Rig
To find me, probably, just as hot
Over Capital's errors and Labour's
We took our life strong, in Barrows S
And did we love it? And wasn't it s
For the Spring Song piped high, our busy tongues flew,
That you were with me and I was you!
   Ah, we had it all, then, all of I delight;
   Good talk, good food, good fire b
   And peace . . . and a kind bed at

(*A pause.* ELLEN *looks to see the the poem has had upon* ANN.) It's alive and beautiful, isn't it?

(*Evasively.*) In a way.

N. I think it's one of John Bliss's poems. (ANN *doesn't answer.* ELLEN *on couch.*) The Village meant some- in those days, didn't it? Oh, Mother, imagine what it must have been! all together for a table d'hôte at the ou . . . John Reed, and Max, and e Dreiser and "Jig" Cook or perhaps were all broke so you were at Polly's or maybe they were all there except . . . and someone rushes in and says: at do you know? John Bliss just called from Paterson! The police knocked Whitman down and they've thrown n jail!" Then everybody got as excited ything, and they all rushed around g to borrow money to bail you out!

(*Sharply.*) Where'd you hear all

N. I didn't hear it. I imagined it.

You didn't imagine those names.

N. Oh, I had to read up, of course.

What do you mean: you had to up, *of course?*

N. For my thesis in Senior English.

I don't quite get the connection,

N. You see, I didn't want to write one of the conventional cut-and-dried ry topics, so I talked it over with -sticks . . . of course he knows you're nother. . . .

Chop-sticks?

N. Professor Lingley. He always car- his own chop-sticks in a little case he goes to a Chinese restaurant. He by all means write about what I was interested in.

Did he, indeed?

N. So I wrote on "The Contribution reenwich Village to the Cause of lom in American Art and Morals." lousy title, don't you think?

Extremely lousy.

N. (*Excitedly.*) I've been dying to

talk it over, but you've been so busy since I came home. You know I got thrill after thrill. Almost everything we've got now, that we take as a matter of course . . . bobbed hair, tea-rooms, better art, poetry, votes for women, freedom of speech and sex . . . is due to you pioneer women.

ANN. Maybe not all to our credit!

ELLEN. That's what I meant . . . it's so ridiculous for you to start going back on yourself now.

ANN. At my age we know more about the world's limitations than at twenty.

ELLEN. I was referring specifically to Doug and me.

ANN. Oh!

ELLEN. Because after all, I suppose you and John Bliss . . . (ANN *turns sharply.*) I mean you did face the same problem . . . only, of course, in a prudish Victorian society . . . now, didn't you?

ANN. (*Swallowing, uncomfortably.*) Well.

ELLEN. Mother, you idiot, don't look so fussed. Suppose you and he did live to- gether . . . what of it? (ANN *rises and moves to right.*) I think you were abso- lutely justified. (ANN *pulls herself together.*)

ANN. I'm afraid your sources of informa- tion were rather unreliable.

ELLEN. (*Coolly.*) I don't think so. I checked up pretty thoroughly.

ANN. (*Weak tone.*) Checked up!

ELLEN. John Bliss wrote "Twenty-one Barrows Street" in 1911 at the time he was living there; and from other sources I found at least a dozen references to John and Ann. There was no other important Ann in the village but you, and his name was never linked with that of any other girl.

ANN. (*Angrily.*) Look here, Ellen, do you think it was quite cricket to prowl around in your mother's past with a college pro- fessor?

ELLEN. What kind of an egg do you think I am?

ANN. I'm beginning to wonder.

ELLEN. I didn't put your affair in the thesis.

ANN. I daresay I should render you thanks.

ELLEN. Mother, you're taking this oddly.

ANN. I . . . I feel odd.

ELLEN. All you've got to do is be consistent.

ANN. Er, I see.

ELLEN. After all, we're just a couple of females discussing woman's problems.

ANN. (*With great patience.*) Ellen, this whole talk of ours must stop. Whether I am consistent or not has nothing to do with what you are planning to do. It's totally different. You don't know what you are talking about.

ELLEN. (*Rising, indignantly.*) Of course I know what I'm talking about. Mother, what's come over you? You sound like some ordinary conventional matron who doesn't know the facts of life! Why, you and Aunt Connie have done all the pioneer work that makes what I want to do not worth a passing comment!

ANN. Now I know you're a little fool if you think your Aunt Connie is a pioneer.

ELLEN. Is that so? Connie came out of school in 1919. The aviators were coming back from France. Speakeasies had begun to open up. I'll bet Connie was flaming youth!

ANN. Connie's private life is her private life.

ELLEN. Exactly, and mine is mine! (*Going to* ANN *eagerly.*) That's the whole point, Mother! That's the principle you fought and struggled for! That's what Connie and all the rest put in practice! And now when a perfectly decent emergency arises, when I want to take advantage of the very thing you worked for, you say "naughty-naughty"! (*A horn sounds outside.*) Mother, there he is!

ANN. (*Desperately.*) How can I make you see the difference? Maybe I did lead a pretty free life. But I had left home . . . my

mother was dead . . . and I was a lot ⟨older⟩ than you.

ELLEN. You were exactly . . . (*She ⟨cal⟩culates rapidly.*) twenty-four when ⟨you⟩ lived with John Bliss. What's two ye⟨ars?⟩

ANN. I was ten years more mature⟨.⟩

ELLEN. Oh, I don't know.

ANN. (*Ignoring this.*) What's more, ⟨now⟩ you're still dependent on your fathe⟨r for⟩ support. At that time I was a reporte⟨r on⟩ the old *World*. As soon as you get a ⟨job,⟩ why then I suppose you can do what⟨ever you⟩ want, even if your father and I don'⟨t ap⟩prove. . . .

ELLEN. Mother, of all the illogical p⟨ea⟩cock! If I was two years older, and ⟨you⟩ were dead, and I had a job . . . ! ⟨A⟩ horn sounds again.) Yes, yes, I'm com⟨ing.⟩

ANN. (*Moving between* ELLEN *and ⟨the⟩ door.*) Ellen, you're not to stir one ⟨step⟩ out of this room.

ELLEN. It . . . it's going to be aw⟨ful if⟩ we quarrel, isn't it?

ANN. It is!

ELLEN. When I'm so in love and ⟨have⟩ been so unhappy, how you can ⟨be so⟩ utterly, inhumanly lacking in sympath⟨y—⟩

ANN. I do sympathize.

ELLEN. You don't! You're like all th⟨e oth⟩er blue-noses. Everything is just duck⟨y for⟩ you to do, but all wrong for every⟨one⟩ else!

ANN. Ellen, please!

ELLEN. If there's one thing I loath⟨e it's⟩ a hypocrite . . . and now you . . . I th⟨ought⟩ you stood for something! Plenty of m⟨others⟩ would be stupid, I know, but I . . . ⟨She⟩ *breaks down, sits in desk chair and b⟨egins⟩ to cry.*) I counted on you.

ANN. (*Also near tears.*) Please, ⟨dear,⟩ please . . . don't cry! We . . . we'll ⟨work⟩ this out together some way.

ELLEN. Sorry . . . I said . . . what I ⟨did.⟩

ANN. Forget it. (*Horn again.* ELLEN ⟨dries⟩ *her eyes and blows her nose.*)

.. How are my eyes?

Fine! How are mine?

.. (*Coldly, ignoring this invitation
..aternize.*) I'll call up Monday. Mean-
.. you and Dad talk it over and decide
..her you ever want me in the house
.. (ANN *puts her hand on* ELLEN'*s
..der and forces her back into the
..*)

Ellen you're running the risk of a
..le disillusionment. I wonder if I can
..in. You know, we women have con-
..ble moral sense when we *don't* love
..n. Mighty little when we *do*. With a
.. it's the opposite. If he *doesn't* care
.. girl, he's without scruples. If he *does*
..he is likely to develop a moral code
.. the angels can live up to. Suppose
.. gets moral and turns against you?

.. He won't!

How do you know he isn't just
.. g advantage of . . . of your generosity?

.. (*Rising, impatiently.*) Oh, that's
..shioned! He's not taking advantage
.. any more than I'm taking advantage
..n.

Do you realize I've never so much
..n this boy?

.. He's a man, not a boy. And I
.. saw your lover!

Dear, at least introduce him to me.
.. not much to ask.

.. It would only be awkward.

Are you ashamed of him . . . or of

.. You're just trying to work on me.
..now perfectly well I've always been
.. of you . . . until today.

Until today.

.. Now you're hurt! Mother, there's
.. keeping this up.

Do me one last favour, dear. Bring
..p for five minutes.

.. But he thinks you *don't know.*

I won't know.

ELLEN. He might suspect. He thinks you
think he's taking me to the train at Stamford.

ANN. I shall do nothing to shatter that
illusion. I promise.

ELLEN. Word of honour?

ANN. My word of honour.

ELLEN. Well, very well. (*Turning at
door.*) But this will make absolutely no
difference in my intentions. (ELLEN *exits.*)

ANN. Oh, oh . . . ! (*She crosses to the
desk quickly and speaks into the house
phone.*) Martha? Martha, will you please
serve tea at once. In the office! And Martha, before you do that, find Mr. Jaywood
and ask him to come up. He was in the
living-room. And Martha, tea will be for
four. That's right! Hurry! (ANN *takes
books and cigarettes from the tea table
and puts them on mantel. She picks up
book of poems from the couch and starts
to cross, right. Midway she stops, and
glances at the poem* ELLEN *read, then shuts
the book sharply and replaces it on the
shelf. A knock at the door finds her by
the couch again.*) Come in quickly and
close the door. (JAY *enters.*) Jay, I'm at
my wits' end.

JAY. (*After closing door.*) There was
some truth in the week-end clue?

ANN. Plenty! Boston has a job in Belgium.
They've apparently had a series of quarrels
with a reconciliation this afternoon, and he
has to sail Monday to be gone two years!

JAY. The poor devils.

ANN. Jay, what am I going to do?

JAY. You can't let her go, of course.

ANN. How can I stop her?

JAY. You and your husband will have to
stand firm.

ANN. Lewis is in the middle of Long
Island Sound . . . he can't stand firm
there . . . and they're about to start.

JAY. You're top hole with her, Ann. I
can't believe she'll go against your express
wishes.

ANN. I tried my express wishes. They failed utterly. Jay, in this room, not five minutes ago, I stood before my daughter a fallen woman. She knows . . . how shall I put it? . . . that I, too, have had unhallowed moments.

JAY. That's not possible!

ANN. She has done research on my past . . . with the help of a college professor.

JAY. Good Lord, Ann!

ANN. To make my ignominy complete, she even read me "Twenty-one Barrows Street" . . . and read it beautifully.

JAY. Does she link you with me?

ANN. Heavens, no! (*She sits on the couch behind tea table.*) Look, Jay, I fought for time. She's bringing the boy up to see me. I want you to stand by.

JAY. Of course, though, frankly, I don't see . . .

ANN. I'm serving tea. That'll take time.

JAY. And nerves of steel!

ANN. It's to be a perfectly respectable tea. I promised. Nobody knows anything about anyone. I thought maybe some way we could show him up, or show free love up, or show something up! (*Someone knocks, right.*) Don't stand there, looking helpless! Open the door! (JAY *opens the door.* ELLEN *enters, followed by* DOUG.)

ELLEN. (*Much relieved to see a third party.*) Oh, hello, Mr. Jaywood. This is grand.

JAY. Er, I dropped up, er . . . to read your mother's story.

ELLEN. Mother, I want you to meet Mr. Douglas Hall.

ANN. How do you do, Mr. Hall. I asked Ellen to invite you in for a moment. It seemed extremely inhospitable to let you wait outside . . . like a taxi, or something.

DOUG. I'm afraid I did honk like a taxi. I thought perhaps Ellen didn't hear me.

ANN. She had some last-minute packing to do. (ELLEN *flashes* ANN *an angry look.* MARTHA *enters with tray on which are tea things.*) Do sit down, children. Mr. Jay-

wood, being very English, insisted I him some tea. Perhaps you'll join us, Hall. Will you sit over here? (ANN on couch, left.)

ELLEN. Really, Mother, we haven't

ANN. (*Placidly.*) When does your leave, dear?

ELLEN. (*Sulkily.*) Five-fifteen.

ANN. You've oceans of time. (DOUG ELLEN *exchange looks. He crosses to before fireplace and sits.* JAY *sits rig couch.*) Come along. Sit by me. (E *sits right of* ANN.) Lemon, Mr. Hall?

DOUG. Thanks . . . and two lumps! *prepares tea throughout the next spe until all are served.*)

ANN. Ellen?

ELLEN. No, thanks, Mother.

ANN. Mr. Jaywood?

JAY. Just plain, thanks.

ANN. (*Politely, to* DOUG.) Is your near here?

DOUG. I haven't any home. I'm m my cousin's home my headquarters week-end.

ANN. Oh, are you? How pleasant!

DOUG. Yes, very pleasant . . . it's central. I have a lot of errands i vicinity.

ANN. Errands?

DOUG. (*Nervously.*) Before I sail fo gium.

ANN. Belgium?

DOUG. I'm sort of liquidating my tion. I've already sold my Encyclo Britannica and my drafting instru And I still have two pairs of skiis, Beta Kappa key, and about a tho architectural plates that I hope to c on before Monday night.

ANN. Doesn't an architect need pla

DOUG. I'm through with that trade years ago I got fifteen dollars a wee spring I'm working for nothing; ne boss admitted he'd expect me to pay a salary. (JAY *chuckles*.)

. What work do you expect to take in Belgium?

G. (*Embarrassed at having to mention it*.) I . . . I'm going over to represent azor blade concern.

. Oh! That's splendid!

. The Belgians could do with a few e razor blades.

G. That's my idea, sir. I'm trying to the job a social significance.

. It seems a pity to give up architec-

G. (*He looks at* ELLEN.) Not if a man ats a home and a wife.

. Marriage interests you, Mr. Hall?

G. (*Cautiously*.) In a general sort of . You can't expect a woman to wait and forever.

. Yes, the girls today are extremely atient.

EN. Some of them were impatient in r day, too, Mother.

. Imprudent was the word then, dear.

EN. (*Who can face no more*.) Doug, ought to get started. (DOUG *rises to go*. stops him.)

. Mr. Hall, I've been running over criminal record.

G. (*Gasping*.) Oh, really?

. There was a Judge Hall once in vidence. . . .

G. That was my father. At one time, was Police Court Judge. Later he ame Supreme Court Justice.

. I knew it! It all comes back. Mr. l, once your father gave me thirty days.

G. I'm awfully sorry.

. Nonsense! I deserved it. I was as onventional as Bernard Shaw and I at to jail at the drop of a hat! Hasn't n told you?

DOUG. (*Much embarrassed*.) Why, er . . . no.

ELLEN. (*Hastily*.) Mother, we haven't time . . . I'll miss my train.

ANN. Mr. Hall, this has been so nice. Do feel free to drop in any time.

DOUG. I'm afraid I'll be pretty far away for that. Anyway, thanks. (*To* JAY.) Good-bye. (JAY *shakes hands with him*.)

JAY. Good-bye.

ELLEN. Good-bye, Mother.

DOUG. (*To* ELLEN.) Did you have any bags?

ELLEN. They're in my room. I'll show you.

ANN. Oh, Mr. Hall! Why can't you stay with us over Sunday? Ellen would love to have you.

ELLEN. Mother, I'm going to Hartford.

ANN. Oh, so you are.

DOUG. Good-bye, Mrs. Murray. Good-bye, sir. (*He bows awkwardly then exits after* ELLEN.)

ANN. Wasn't I a nice muddle-headed old fool of a mother!

JAY. Ann, why that speech about getting arrested in Providence?

ANN. Did you notice how troubled the boy was at taking my daughter out from under my very nose?

JAY. Yes.

ANN. I was trying to put his conscience at ease . . . by sounding a liberal note!

ELLEN. (*Outside*.) I'll be right down, Doug. (*She enters, and stands by the door*.) So long, Mother.

ANN. Come in, dear. (ELLEN *comes forward reluctantly*.) Ellen, I liked him. I liked his courage. I forgot to ask: is he a Communist?

ELLEN. No, he isn't!

ANN. (*With a smile at her vehemence*.) Well, even so. I still like him. He's attempting to pull through on his own initiative. Ellen, I'm a fool; but then I always was. I'm going to stick to my principles. Go off with this boy. (*A pause; then huskily.*) My dear, I give you my blessing.

ELLEN. Mother, do you realize Mr. Jaywood is here?

ANN. Oh, dear, so he is . . . well, anyway he was also present when Connie came down and told me.

ELLEN. Couldn't she use a little tact! It's a nice state of affairs when private and sacred things have to be blurted out before everybody. Mother, you're not fair . . . serving tea in that Park Avenue manner, and then . . . (*She looks at* JAY *and stops.*)

JAY. I assure you, Ellen, your romance will lie, er . . . tenderly and close within my breast. (*She stares at him. Silently her lips and forefinger accentuate the words "tenderly and close within my breast."*) What's the matter?

ELLEN. That line scans. Several of the things you said downstairs . . . ! You're a poet. You're John Bliss.

ANN. Nonsense!

ELLEN. I might have known it. I felt you two had known each other a long time!

JAY. My name is Titus Jaywood. Want to see my baptismal certificate?

ELLEN. Who'd write poetry under a name like Jaywood! (*To* ANN, *with simple frankness.*) I certainly am glad to get this point cleared up. You know, I worked my head off trying to find out what had become of him. I bet I wrote a dozen letters.

JAY. What did they reply?

ELLEN. They said you were missing.

JAY. I am . . . poetically.

ELLEN. Why'd you change your name back.

JAY. You were on the correct scent. No New York editor would bother to read poems of American mines and steel mills written by an Englishman named Titus Jaywood; whereas, he would jump at the opportunity to buy an English novel from Jaywood, Ltd.

ELLEN. Naturally. Mother, you don't tend to stop me now do you?

ANN. I told you I didn't. Besides, this b may never come back. Anything may ha pen in Europe in the next two years.

ELLEN. That's what I meant.

ANN. Well, then go quickly before I gain my commonsense. Go. Climb hi Walk hand in hand under the stars. Ma love. This may be your one great hour earth. Go. I'll stand by you.

ELLEN. Oh, Mother, I won't go . . . you say I shouldn't!

ANN. Get out of here . . . quick!

ELLEN. (*To* JAY.) It's been grand me ing you . . . especially since I know w you really are.

JAY. I've enjoyed meeting you.

ELLEN. (*to* ANN, *kissing her.*) Good-b (*Then, impulsively.*) Oh, Mother, I ne realized how much I loved you! (A *clasps her fiercely in her arms.*)

ANN. Ellen, dear . . . it's all right. all right. Don't let a thing worry you. stand by you.

ELLEN. Don't *you* worry.

ANN. I won't. Good-bye. (ELLEN *goes. pause.* ANN *looks at* JAY.) Say it, say I'm not a fit mother to bring up a dec girl.

JAY. Now, Ann, I wouldn't go as far that.

ANN. But you think it.

JAY. On the contrary, I think you did wise thing. The boy's good stuff. He w let her down.

ANN. (*Sitting.*) Jay, give me a cigare I'm going to bawl.

JAY. Pull yourself together. (*He lig cigarette for her. She takes handkerc. from his breast pocket, dabs her ey* You know perfectly well that a high-min romance, conceived more in the spirit poetry than of legality, is just about noblest work of man . . . and woman this had to come, I think you are to

gratulated that when it did come, your
ghter acted with so much dignity and
feeling.

. Oh, shut up your Mayfair cynicism!
w it's all over, I realize I haven't acted
have just because I'm a liberal thinker.
re likely it's because I'm a selfish cow-

. Now, really, Ann . . . !

. When we first talked she got angry.
called me a hypocrite and a look came
her eyes. I couldn't endure the thought
losing her respect . . . of deliberately
ving myself off the pedestal on which
had placed me!

. (*With a protesting gesture.*) Now,
1 . . .

. (*From behind her handkerchief.*)
's like her father. When she turns, she
s hard! Oh, it's all such a mess. I'm
1 a mess! You're such a mess!

. (*Sharply, in a gay tone.*) I resent
. I'm a well-ordered human being,
king clearly, a good judge of correct
stic values . . . both in fiction and in
! And so are you!

. Oh, stop trying to cheer me up . . . !
NNIE's *voice is heard outside.*)

NIE. Ann, are you there?

. Heavens! What's *she* back for?

NIE. (*Still outside.*) May I come in?

. I suppose so. . . . (CONNIE *enters,*
h excited.)

NIE. Do you realize what has hap-
ed?

. Aren't they serving tea at the club
more?

NIE. Glen left word he was tied up in
rt. He's going to phone me here.

. Oh!

NIE. (*Returning to the subject.*) I
ant happened to Ellen. Driving back
assed a most rattly-looking car and in
was Ellen and that young man. I
ldn't believe my eyes. I supposed, of
rse, you had brought her to her senses
this time.

JAY. (*When* ANN *doesn't answer.*) But
we have.

CONNIE. Really?

JAY. Mr. Hall was merely driving Ellen
to her train at Stamford. They lost their
nerve. It was a complete victory for law
and order.

CONNIE. They were headed north, not towards Stamford.

JAY. Naturally. They missed the train at
Stamford . . . so they . . . (*He sees her
smiling, and ends lamely.*) Oh, I can't lie!

CONNIE. You can lie all right, but not
well. (*To* ANN.) You poor dear! I'd never
believed Ellen . . . deliberately against
your will . . .

ANN. (*Smiling wanly.*) Not just now . . .
please!

CONNIE. I was so amazed to see them driving past me . . . wouldn't you like me to
bathe your head?

ANN. No, thanks!

CONNIE. Maybe some spirits of ammon-
ia . . . ?

ANN. No, really, I'm all right. . . .

JAY. (*To* ANN's *rescue.*) Connie! (CONNIE
turns.) Do you mind if I call you Connie?

CONNIE. I've had so many last names it's
the only one I'm sure to answer to.

JAY. How about a cup of tea?

CONNIE. I'd love one. (*She sits on couch,
to right of* JAY.)

JAY. How many lumps?

CONNIE. Merely lemon. (*Watches* JAY
pour.) You handle a tea pot with exquisite
skill. Are you a bachelor?

JAY. I suppose I am.

CONNIE. Don't you *know*?

JAY. I am . . . definitely.

CONNIE. Well, I won't hold it against
you. I always enjoy tea poured by contented
bachelors.

JAY. (*Indicating* ANN's *untouched cup.*) Freshen you up?

ANN. No, thanks. Connie, I don't think we will tell Lewis anything about what has happened this afternoon.

CONNIE. It would be a terrible blow. He adores Ellen.

ANN. I'd like it to be a private secret between us three. . . .

CONNIE. Suppose Lewis should start hurling questions that awful way he does.... I'd never be able to keep it from him.

ANN. I know you wouldn't. But he won't have any reason to hurl questions if nothing is said.

CONNIE. Heaven knows I don't want to say anything more.

ANN. Then it's agreed?

CONNIE. Of course. As a matter of fact, I called myself names all the way into Greenwich. I never peached on a person before in my life. But Ann, she's such a kid, and we'd been talking about her, I did feel you ought to know . . . then you could do as you please.

ANN. You were dead right. You told me, and I have done as I please!

CONNIE. (*Startled.*) Done as you please! Ann Murray, do you mean to sit there and tell me you deliberately . . . ?

JAY. Cake, Connie!

CONNIE. (*Accepting both the cake and the hint.*) You're right; you're both right. I'm getting straight-laced. (*She sees cake is rich and puts it back on plate.*) No, thanks. I swear another trip to Reno and I'll be positively conventional. . . . (*The phone rings.*)

ANN. Excuse me.

CONNIE. (*Rising excitedly.*) It's probably for me, Ann.

ANN. (*Into phone.*) Hello. Yes. Yes, she's here. I'll call her.

CONNIE. (*Eagerly.*) Is it Glen?

ANN. It talks like a lawyer.

CONNIE. (*Into phone.*) Hello. Hello, d[·] Oh, that's quite all right. Of course! I ca[·] wait to see you. (*Pause.*) Your voice d[·] sound tired. (*Pause; during next speec[·]* CONNIE's *tone changes from enthusiasm [·] a dull, stunned quality.*) Glen, yo[·] joking. I see. I've heard that alibi bef[·] Oh, much better not to see each other [·] all. A real inspiration on your part, [·] so much easier for you. (*Long pau[·]* Well, you might have been man eno[·] to meet me as you promised and tell [·] to my face! Oh, you're right! The t[·] phone does lessen the shock. Yes. Go[·] bye. (*Mechanically she hangs up the ph[·] A pause. Her lips quiver, as she fights [·] self-control, then she laughs.*) Well, v[·] Connie, take that on the chin!

ANN. (*Going to her.*) You poor d[·] That's a rotten dirty trick to play!

CONNIE. God, Ann! And I thought [·] was the real thing at last!

ANN. Perhaps it's better to find it out [·] than later.

CONNIE. It saves flying to Reno. (*A pa[·] she wipes her eyes.*) Ann, it just can'[·] done. You can't give your love to [·] many men. They hold you cheap. (LE[·] *appears in doorway. Her voice begin[·] get shrill and hysterical.*) That's wh[·] know I was so absolutely right in tel[·] you about Ellen. You ought to have s[·] ped her. You ought to have prevented [·] making the damn fool stinking mess [·] her life that I have made of mine! (*[·] breaks down completely.*)

LEWIS. Well, well, what kind of a [·] party is this?

CONNIE. (*Rushing past him.*) Excuse [·] (*She exits.* ANN *goes to* LEWIS.)

ANN. (*Trying to appear casual.*) Yo[·] home early, dear.

LEWIS. (*Also trying to appear casu[·] Just had to get back to my Annie! [·] kisses her.*)

ANN. That means the wind died do[·]

LEWIS. Enough so I could use it for [·] excuse.

. Mr. Jaywood, this is my husband.
looks like an admiral but under the
guise he's just a banker.

. (*As they shake hands.*) How do
 do.

JIS. How do you do. You the chap
's going to sell Ann's love story?

. Well, I hope so.

JIS. How long you and Ann known
 other?

. Let's see. We met sometime in May.

JIS. Huh! She's in a bad money jam.
 you can sell it?

. A good yarn by a well-known name
ly fails to find a market.

JIS. My Annie should write a wicked
 story.

. (*Turns and looks at* ANN.) Er, quite.
N *hands* LEWIS *a cup of tea.*)

. Will you have some tea, dear?

JIS. Thanks. (*Her hand trembles as
takes the cup.*) Ann, you're upset. And
nnie in tears! What's happened since I
 my happy home two hours ago?

N. Not much.

JIS. Well, let's hear it!

. I've had my tea, Ann. If you'll ex-
e me, I'll dress for dinner.

N. Don't bother to dress. Stay and
t. . . . (*She signals him to stay.*)

JIS. (*Turning, heartily to* JAY.) Hell
old man, we're informal here. Don't
her to dress. (*He smiles engagingly.*)
t give me five minutes alone with my
e, that's all. (*At the door,* JAY *turns
 shakes his finger warningly to* ANN
ind LEWIS' back and says silently.*)

. I wouldn't tell him . . . at least no
re than you have to. (LEWIS *turns in
e to notice.* JAY *changes his gesture
 a farewell wave and exits.*)

JIS. Annie, old girl, what is all this?
 pause; she does not answer.*) Come on
v. (*He leans over couch and kisses her.*)
l Papa all about it.

ANN. Connie's lawyer friend just broke
off with her over the phone. It was pretty
cruel.

LEWIS. Hasn't he seen her since she came
back?

ANN. No.

LEWIS. My Lord! Won't we ever get Connie permanently married?

ANN. We don't seem to.

LEWIS. (*Sitting, right of couch.*) Well,
Glen Williams was no fatal loss. He plays
a filthy game of golf.

ANN. I think she counted on improving
his golf after they were married.

LEWIS. Oh, did she? (*He looks at* ANN
sharply.) How is Ellen mixed up in all this?

ANN. Ellen?

LEWIS. Connie was telling you it was
absolutely necessary Ellen should be told
so she wouldn't make a mess of her life.
Or something like that. I don't see any
connection, do you?

ANN. Maybe, remotely. Sort of the horrible example idea, I suppose.

LEWIS. Apparently she'd already told Ellen . . . as I recall.

ANN. Had she? I didn't catch all Connie
said, she was so hysterical.

LEWIS. But Ellen's already gone, hasn't
she?

ANN. Yes.

LEWIS. Then if Connie just got this message over the phone, how could she tell
Ellen?

ANN. Oh, Lord, Lewis, I don't know.
Does it matter so much right now?

LEWIS. Annie, you don't have secrets from
me very often . . . but when you do, they
stick out all over you.

ANN. I'll tell you sometime.

LEWIS. (*In a level, determined tone.*) I
think I'd prefer to know now. (*A pause;
she does not answer.*) Something serious
has happened, I can tell. If you don't feel

like discussing it right now, suppose I talk with Connie . . . (*He rises and starts to go.*)

ANN. (*In alarm.*) No, don't do that!

LEWIS. Why not?

ANN. Connie doesn't know the real situation. If you must wring the truth out of anyone, you'd better wring it out of me. Sit down! (*She beckons and he sits beside her on the couch.*) There! Lewis, during our entire married life, I think what has endeared you to me more than anything else, has been your broadmindedness and sympathy with my . . . my liberal ideas.

LEWIS. Oh, get on, Ann. I know I'm broadminded.

ANN. I just thought I'd remind you.

LEWIS. Ann, come to the point.

ANN. I'm trying to.

LEWIS. Well, what is it?

ANN. Oh, God, I can't tell you!

LEWIS. (*Getting worried.*) It can't be so serious. Ann; you tell me, or I'll bat you one.

ANN. Lewis, that Boston boy who failed Ellen at Commencement turned up this afternoon. They've gone off together for the week-end.

LEWIS. Well, what of it? Whose house? Someone we know, isn't it?

ANN. They're not going to anybody's house. They're just going off together alone. (*Pause. He looks blank.*) You know the meaning of the phrase, don't you, Lewis?

LEWIS. You mean they're going off *together . . . alone?*

ANN. That's what I mean.

LEWIS. Ellen's not that kind. A vulgar cheap week-end!

ANN. This is on a very high plane. Really, it is, dear. They didn't find out they loved each other till this afternoon . . . and the young man's leaving for two years.

LEWIS. How did *you* learn so much ab it?

ANN. The young man called for a ment. His name is Hall.

LEWIS. Oh, you're imagining this! probably took her to the train.

ANN. Ellen told me they were going.

LEWIS. Why didn't you stop her?

ANN. I did try.

LEWIS. You mean she defied you?

ANN. Why, no . . . not exactly. Natur I tried to talk it over calmly with her.

LEWIS. Ann, we've got to find them . before it's too late. (*He starts for the do*

ANN. (*Going to him hastily.*) Lewis, can't go rushing after her. You'd only ridiculous . . .

LEWIS. (*Stopping.*) Well, we must something.

ANN. Dear, I know how you love spring into action, but this is one occas where if nothing is done, nothing happen.

LEWIS. Do you mean Ellen delibera told you, and then walked out of house?

ANN. Lewis, will you please stop fee you've got to do something about it think our duty is to be sympathetic understanding, and let them work their own destiny . . . !

LEWIS. Don't tell me you were sym thetic!

ANN. Not at first, perhaps!

LEWIS. Ann, are you crazy? Did you a girl of twenty-two talk you into a th like this? You should have stopped her you had to tie her. Don't you love her

ANN. Of course I love her.

LEWIS. That's a pretty way to show it.

ANN. (*Quietly.*) Ellen has exactly as m right to love as you have yourself. All can do, as parents, is prepare her to e cise that right intelligently and decer In fact, our work is over.

wis. Did she *say* that?

n. (*Turning away.*) No, I did.

wis. Well, how did she win you over? (ann *doesn't answer.*) What did she say? ou didn't talk about the weather, did a? (ann, *back to him. busies herself ind couch with her hair.*) You're too ious to drop this matter. I think I *will* to Connie. (*Again he starts for the or.*)

n. Lewis, wait a minute! Maybe you're ht. We've faced everything together so , We might as well continue.

wis. My God! What else is there to ?

n. (*Taking his arm.*) When you mar- l me . . . *before* you married me . . . had no illusions you were the first n in my life, did you? You took me what I was.

wis. Of course I did.

n. Well, then . . .

wis. But you were different . . . you re *you*.

n. Exactly.

wis. What do you mean, "exactly"?

n. I mean I was in rather an incon- ent position when it came to stopping en.

wis. If there's one thing a parent doesn't e to be . . . it's consistent!

n. It's wiser with a girl of Ellen's ntality.

wis. She wouldn't know. . . . (*Struck h a sudden idea.*) You mean she does w?

n. More about me than I do myself.

wis. I see. How'd she ever hear?

n. She's been writing a thesis on "The ntribution of Greenwich Village to the se of Freedom in American Art and rals" . . . and naturally, she discovered I, among others, had contributed my

lewis. This is a hell of a time to be funny.

ann. I didn't mean to be.

lewis. But you admit it's right.

ann. Right or wrong, I don't know. Justi- fiable anyway!

lewis. (*Exploding.*) By God, my father spoke the truth! He warned me. He was a wiser bird than I was.

ann. You know your father was a con- servative old fool. You've told me so a hundred times.

lewis. Huh! I can hear him now. (*Quotes in severe hard tone.*) "So, Lewis, you don't mind if the mother of your children is a woman of loose morals!" (*He strides to behind couch, and back.*)

ann. (*Angrily, following him.*) My mor- als aren't loose. I've never looked at another man since I married you. You've got to be fair. You're not going to take any high and mighty attitude with me and get away with it.

lewis. I can't understand. I should think when Ellen found she had a mother like you . . .

ann. (*Interrupting, coolly.*) I took care I had a rather beautiful love affair. . . .

lewis. (*Savagely.*) I don't want to hear about it.

ann. I don't intend to tell you. It's pretty late in the day, Lewis, for you to be jealous over a twenty-five-year-old romance!

lewis. I suppose you helped your daughter pick out a pleasant place to go.

ann. I wasn't consulted in the matter.

lewis. She told you where she was going though, didn't she? (ann *does not an- swer.*) I see she did.

ann. Lewis, they won't be discovered. I don't think there's a chance.

lewis. Where is this place? (*A pause.*) I said: where is this place?

ann. I don't know . . . exactly. I won't tell you anyway.

LEWIS. Naturally, I suppose not! (*Balked, he crosses to the desk. He stands for a moment, thinking, then he returns to* ANN.) I'll ask you once more. Will you tell me where Ellen was going?

ANN. No, I won't. At least, not till you've cooled off.

LEWIS. Very well. (*He turns to go.*)

ANN. Where are you going? Dinner's at seven.

LEWIS. I certainly don't intend to sit opposite *you* at dinner tonight. (*She runs to him, and seizes his coat by both lapels furiously, as though to shake him.*)

ANN. Darling, you big fool, will you come to your senses! I didn't want to tell you. You insisted. Now the least you can do is stand by me, so we can help Ellen over this tough spot . . . ! (*He frees him from her grasp.*)

LEWIS. I'm going to talk with Connie after that I can be reached at my Club

ANN. Oh, don't be such a stuffed sh Run off to your Club to sulk! I'm asha of you!

LEWIS. With your perverted moral se I daresay you are. (*He goes out, slamm the door. For a moment* ANN *stands moti less, then she mutters a disgusted "O She sees the untidy tea tray. Mechanic. she picks it up and starts for the door.*

ANN. (*Angry and unhappy, through suggestion of tears.*) Oh, goddamn anyway!

CURTAIN

ACT THREE

Scene: The living-room again. It is ten o'clock the following Monday morning. A bright sunlight floods the terrace outside. The curtains blow about briskly in quite a stiff breeze.

At Rise: JAY *enters from the terrace followed by* MARTHA *with a breakfast tray.* JAY *wears a blue coat with gray trousers, and a vivid crimson scarf around his throat. He stands by the table, left, wets his finger and sticks it up above his head to test the breeze.*

JAY. This seems a quiet spot. I'll finish here. (MARTHA *puts tray on table.* JAY, *about to sit, notices a music-box on table between windows. He winds it and sets it going. The strains of a sprightly waltz begin to tinkle off.*)

MARTHA. Is there anything else?

JAY. Have you a copy of *The Times* knocking about?

MARTHA. Yes, there's one knocking about over here. (*She goes to table before the fireplace and brings back a newspaper.*)

JAY. Thanks, that's fine! (JAY *watches* MARTHA *exit, then he opens his paper, and begins to read while he sips his coffee, a picture of unruffled contentment.* CONNIE

enters from the hall, in smart white tume with trousers and bolero jacket fect. She looks cheerfully seductive.)

CONNIE. Good morning, Jay. Don't up.

JAY. Hello. Excellent morning!

CONNIE. Why breakfast in here?

JAY. I started on the lawn, but the w raised a surf on my coffee. (*A pause. begins to whistle an accompaniment to music. She studies him thoughtfully. steals a sly glance at his newspaper.*)

CONNIE. You're a maddening man.

JAY. I beg your pardon. Will you h some coffee!

CONNIE. I mean being so disagree cheerful, when everybody else in the h is practically in mourning.

JAY. Perhaps my orchestra is a bit I'll turn it off. (*He turns off the m box, and for the first time gets a squ look at* CONNIE.) As a matter of fact, look moderately cheerful yourself.

CONNIE. I've made it a rule not to h more than one good cry over any man.

Y. (*Not caring to pursue this subject.*)
t's see: you said you didn't want any
ffee?

NNIE. No, I didn't. (*She picks up the
ffee pot.*) May I pour you some more?

Y. No, thanks.

NNIE. Do you mind if I use your cup?

Y. Not at all. (*She pours herself some
ffee.*)

NNIE. There, aren't we cozy?

Y. (*Changing subject.*) Have you seen
n this morning?

NNIE. I went in before I rame down.
e is terribly upset at Lewis' attitude. Do
u suppose Ellen will bring that young
n home with her?

Y. Er, it's not customary, is it?

NNIE. It may be. This younger genera-
n is too much for me. In my days we
d at least a shred of decency. (*She re-
ves outside jacket, revealing a well-
ned back, then puts jacket on couch,
ht.*) At least we *knew* we were kicking
er the traces. But Ellen apparently thinks
at she is doing is all in the day's work.
AY *smiles.*) Frankly, don't you find it
her shocking?

Y. Other people's affairs of the heart
ver shock me. Sometimes they bore me;
metimes they nauseate me; but they never
ock me.

NNIE. Don't my three husbands shock
u?

Y. Not in the slightest.

NNIE. (*Coquettishly.*) Oh, just a tiny

Y. (*Firmly.*) Not one iota. (*A pause.
sips glass of water.* CONNIE *studies
, getting up courage to ask a personal
estion. She seats herself opposite him.*)

NNIE. Jay, how have you solved your
e life?

Y. (*Choking slightly.*) Well, n o w,
lly . . .

NNIE. I'm envious. Here the rest of us

are, embroiled in sex up to our necks . . .
while you loll about and enjoy life. How
do you get that way? You really *never*
married?

JAY. No, never.

CONNIE. Don't you get desperately lonesome? Don't you feel you just must have
somebody who thinks you're wonderful . . .
even if you know you're not?

JAY. I manage to struggle along without
admiration.

CONNIE. You live alone?

JAY. Yes. I've a very small penthouse in
the East Fifties.

CONNIE. Without even a mother or a
canary.

JAY. Not even a guppy.

CONNIE. How appalling!

JAY. Oh, I forgot to mention it; I do have
a Filipino chap who comes in and cooks
for me.

CONNIE. (*Seductively.*) No love in your
life at all?

JAY. Oh, plenty of love! I manage to read
from twenty to thirty love stories a day.
That's about all the love I can endure. By
night I'm ready for a prize fight . . . or
maybe to sit on the terrace and watch the
sunset and the East River shipping!

CONNIE. Reading love stories doesn't af-
fect me that way.

JAY. You should read bad ones!

CONNIE. But you're missing so much, Jay.
A family and children . . . romance . . .
passion!

JAY. I know. One pays a price for everything . . . even contentment!

CONNIE. There! I knew you must have
a philosophy. I've tried "a short life and
a gay one" and "love is all." Now I believe I'll try yours. Contentment! A bachelor woman living in a penthouse with
her books and her sunsets and her friends.

JAY. I recommend it highly.

CONNIE. The only problem is friends. They're not so easy.

JAY. True!

CONNIE. Jay, I'd like you for a friend.

JAY. Er, that's awfully nice of you . . . !

CONNIE. I need a wise well-poised friend terribly . . . someone to watch the East River shipping with . . . someone who isn't interested in love, at least actively. Jay, do me a favour . . . ask me up to your terrace some evening.

JAY. Why, er . . . of course.

CONNIE. You're not conventional?

JAY. God forbid!

CONNIE. Maybe you're clandestine!

JAY. No, I'm not that either.

CONNIE. Then do please, like a good fellow . . . give me a ring . . . some evening when you're not going to a prize fight.

JAY. Why, that'll be fine!

CONNIE. My number is Rhinelander 4-3333.

JAY. That's an interesting number.

CONNIE. Doesn't it interest you enough to take it down?

JAY. I can remember it.

CONNIE. It's very easy to remember. Four times three. It's the only four of a kind in the book that adds up to an even dozen. You can't forget it.

JAY. (*Gloomily.*) I'm sure I can't. . . .

CONNIE. More coffee, darling? (*He looks up, startled. She is embarrassed.*) Oh! Sorry. It slipped out . . . from long habit. (ANN *enters. She appears gay and casual, but underneath she is heavy-hearted and worried.*)

ANN. Good morning.

JAY. Hello, Ann.

ANN. Have you both had breakfast?

JAY. Just finished.

ANN. I'll take away the tray.

CONNIE. Let me do it, Ann. (*She pic up tray and starts, right.*)

ANN. Was everything satisfactory, sir?

JAY. Fine, thanks.

CONNIE. (*Excitedly.*) Ann, I've an ide I believe I've reached that stage in woman's life where she starts a tea-roo (*She kicks door open, like a waitress, ar exits with a flourish.*)

ANN. How is she taking *her* tragedy?

JAY. (*Drily.*) I'm afraid she has fully covered.

ANN. I know. She always does, poor de Yet, Jay, she would make the right man splendid wife, and when it comes to ru ning a house . . .

JAY. May I interrupt?

ANN. (*Smiling.*) If you must. . . .

JAY. I don't want to marry her, if y don't mind.

ANN. No?

JAY. No.

ANN. Oh.

JAY. Look here, did you "sic" her on this morning?

ANN. No.

JAY. Oh.

ANN. Yet you'll have to admit . . .

JAY. I do. I also admit she has given her phone number. It adds up to an ev dozen.

ANN. (*With a chuckle.*) The minx! (*S sits right of table.*)

JAY. Now tell me your troubles.

ANN. My troubles aren't speaking to unless a third person is present.

JAY. I say, that's carrying it a bit far

ANN. Have you seen the man this mo ing?

JAY. A moment. He's gone to Greenw for a minister.

N. The devil he has!

Y. Also to see about a marriage license.

N. The dear, befuddled lamb! And I ppose in case Ellen refuses to be made good woman, he'll bring along a snow-rm, too, to cast her out into!

Y. I don't think he means it that way. e feels . . .

N. He feels moral, that's what he feels . superior, capable of leading the entire nale sex back to the Gay Nineties. The ea of his trying to marry Ellen off like me wanton! (*She begins to walk back d forth.*) I feel the old malignant spirit rging within! I'm going to strike a blow feminine emancipation on the top of wis' head that will . . .

Y. (*Sharply.*) Ann!

N. (*Subsiding meekly.*) You're right. hacking Lewis won't help Ellen. Tell ., has your Paris man telephoned you t?

Y. He was out. He's to call me here soon as he gets back.

N. I'm awfully sorry you had to be ixed up in all this. Go back to town. the call comes, I'll relay it on to you. . . .

Y. Frothingham's in this country for ly a couple of days. We can't risk miss-g him.

N. Ellen might blurt out something out you and me.

Y. She'll be loyal.

N. You can't tell . . . if she gets ex-ed. Lewis would be sure to make a fool himself. Why should you stay and be miliated?

Y. I'll wait for the phone call . . . if all the same?

N. Oh, *I'd* prefer to have you here. I'm tting in a mood in which I'd like to nfront Lewis with all my lovers.

Y. You never had any besides me, Ann. n't get boastful.

N. Then, I'm in a mood in which I sh I'd had more!

JAY. You're in a mood in which you're going to spill the fat in the fire if you don't take care. (LEWIS *enters. He wears a plain business suit, and appears very busy and self-righteous.*)

LEWIS. Hello, Jaywood. (JAY *waves an acknowledgment.*)

ANN. (*Sweetly.*) Good morning, Lewis.

LEWIS. (*Looking squarely at her.*) Huh!

ANN. Huh . . . yourself!

JAY. (*Diplomatically, to* LEWIS.) Er, what luck?

LEWIS. Not bad. I talked with the Mayor. He called up the License Bureau and ar-ranged to have the five-day ruling over-looked.

ANN. (*Pleasantly.*) So you are going to insult your daughter as soon as she enters your house?

LEWIS. What do you mean, insult my daughter?

JAY. I say . . . ! I suspect I'm in the way again.

LEWIS. Nonsense. (*He signals him to stay.*)

ANN. (*At the same time.*) A clergyman and a marriage license waiting on the doorstep sounds like an insult to me.

LEWIS. I'm merely helping her out.

ANN. I'd wait till she asks for your help.

LEWIS. If she loves him, she must want to marry him.

ANN. The young man's salary won't be thirty a week.

LEWIS. I'll put him in the bank.

ANN. He has signed a contract.

LEWIS. My lawyer can get him out of that.

ANN. Lewis, let him have his adventure with the razor blades. It's much bigger.

LEWIS. He's had adventure enough. This morning he assumes his responsibilities. . . .

ANN. Provided he appears. . . .

LEWIS. George! Well, I can get him on the phone . . . or at the boat.

ANN. Lewis, you look like a man I never met before.

LEWIS. You've looked pretty much of a stranger yourself these past few days. (*He glares at* ANN. *A pause.*)

JAY. (*Uncomfortably.*) Er, I'll stroll out and see how the roses are getting along. . . .

LEWIS. Don't go, old man. Glad to have you around. Mighty helpful!

JAY. Even so, I think I'll take a breathing spell. (*He exits to terrace.*)

ANN. You see. You embarrass everybody. You're emotionally *gauche!*

LEWIS. Huh!

ANN. Lewis, dear, don't you realize Ellen has undergone a rather . . . how shall I put it for your correct ears . . . a rather revolutionary physical experience since Friday?

LEWIS. (*Squirming.*) I don't know anything about that.

ANN. No, I don't suppose you do. That's why I'm telling you. I think it's only fair we give Ellen a little time to . . . to brood and dream, before she takes her next step.

LEWIS. Meanwhile this young man leaves the country.

ANN. Well, what of it? Ellen can sail later . . . if she still wants to.

LEWIS. If she *still* wants to! Exactly! It's phrases like that I can't understand, Ann. You've got the goddamnedest attitude.

ANN. I'm only trying . . .

LEWIS. Know what you remind me of? The way I was last fall when Roger made the football team . . . just like his old man. By Jingo, you're proud of Ellen.

ANN. I am. She's beginning to be a person in her own right.

LEWIS. You're swaggering all over the place because she has made the free-love team.

ANN. (*Bursts out laughing.*) Just like h old woman! Look out, Lewis, you'll smi

LEWIS. (*Refusing to smile.*) What yo never did get through your head is th this is basically a conventional world. A ways has been, always will be. Buck tl conventions and you pay for it sooner later.

ANN. Did *I* pay for it? I was rewarded.

LEWIS. How?

ANN. I got *you.*

LEWIS. There's no use arguing with yo At any rate, you know where I stand.

ANN. You don't stand anywhere. You' lying down, back in the Dark Ages.

LEWIS. (*Starting on a new tack.*) Dar it, Ann, take our own case. This old lo of yours bobbing up has nearly got us the rocks, and you know it!

ANN. (*Startled, in a small voice.*) Whi old lover?

LEWIS. I don't know. Any of 'em! All 'em!

ANN. I don't think my old lovers ne bother you.

LEWIS. They make me want to wring yo neck!

ANN. Well that's a risk a woman has run if she marries a man with a narr mind.

LEWIS. Thanks!

ANN. You're quite welcome. (CONNIE ters hurriedly from the hall.)

CONNIE. (*Crossing to* ANN *in suppres excitement.*) Hello, Lewis..

LEWIS. Hello, Connie.

CONNIE. (*Whispers audibly to* ANN.) El is back. She came in a taxi.

ANN. (*Coolly, in normal tone.*) Is alone?

CONNIE. Yes. Er, if you'll excuse me, go up and pack. (*She starts for the d right.*)

LEWIS. Connie, I want you here.

CONNIE. Frankly, Lewis, I'd prefer not to meet her. I hate scenes. . . .

LEWIS. I want the family here. There may be a great deal to do, and we'll have only a short time in which to do it.

CONNIE. Do what?

LEWIS. Lewis feels he'd enjoy marrying Ellen over my dead body.

CONNIE. (*To* LEWIS.) You'll break up your whole family.

LEWIS. I assure you, if a wedding takes place it will be in an atmosphere of family love and effection.

CONNIE. (*Yearning to flee.*) Really, Ann . .

ANN. Stay, dear. There's safety in numbers. (ELLEN *enters.*)

ELLEN. Hello, everybody! (ELLEN *starts at the sight of* LEWIS, *then tries to appear casual. She drops her suitcase by the bookcase, right.*) Hello, Mother.

ANN. Hello darling. (*She puts her arms around* ELLEN *and holds her close.*)

ELLEN. Dad, why aren't you at the office?

LEWIS. I had a few things at home to tend to.

ELLEN. Did you have a good week-end, Mother?

ANN. Very pleasant. Did you?

ELLEN. Deadly!

CONNIE. (*Drily.*) That's too bad!

ELLEN. The Colbys may run a newspaper, but Lord! They are antiques. Prayers before Sunday dinner! Dad, can you imagine?

LEWIS. No, dear, but I see you can. (ELLEN *hesitates for a split second, then plunges on.*)

ELLEN. Anyway the *Hartford Register* is definitely out.

ANN. (*Affecting keen interest.*) Really, dear? Why?

ELLEN. It's all births and deaths and local politics. It doesn't give half a page to world affairs. I want to get on a more sophisticated sheet.

LEWIS. (*Scornfully at word "sophisticated."*) Huh!

ELLEN. Gee, I'm hungry. (*To* ANN.) Wonder if I can have some bacon and eggs.

ANN. Of course.

ELLEN. I had to grab breakfast at seven to make my train. (ELLEN *starts for door, right.*)

LEWIS. (*Sharply.*) Ellen!

ELLEN. Yes?

LEWIS. You come back here.

ELLEN. Why, Dad, what's the matter?

LEWIS. You didn't go to Hartford. (*A pause.* ELLEN *comes back and looks from* ANN *to* LEWIS.)

ELLEN. Does Dad know?

ANN. He does, I regret to say.

ELLEN. But, Mother, you said you'd stand by.

ANN. And I intend to. But you see, dear, after you left things became so involved. . . .

ELLEN. Connie, you ought to be taken out and shot!

LEWIS. That's enough of that attitude.

CONNIE. Ellen, I'm frightfully sorry. I felt . . .

ELLEN. Couldn't you think back a bit? In your day you did a little pioneering yourself.

CONNIE. (*Trying to laugh it off.*) I've never even seen a covered wagon in my life.

ELLEN. You're a fine one to talk! If you weren't rich, and Dad's sister, and too old, you'd have been put in a home for delinquent girls years ago!

CONNIE. (*Explosively.*) Well . . . !

ANN. Ellen Murray . . . !

ELLEN. She had it coming to her.

LEWIS. Ellen, I told you . . . !

ELLEN. Okay, I see my mistake. I just shouldn't have come back to this house. I had too much confidence in my family, that's all! (*She starts to go.*)

LEWIS. (*Stops her and puts his arm around her waist.*) Now, Ellen, hold on. No, you didn't. Your old Dad wants to help. He's taking all the circumstances into consideration. In fact, he is mighty sympathetic.

ELLEN. (*Looking at him doubtfully.*) Are you sure you are?

LEWIS. Positive. Now tell me . . . deep down in your heart . . . are you quite happy about this situation?

ELLEN. Yes, I am.

LEWIS. You two are both deeply in love, aren't you?

ELLEN. Of course we are. (*Indignantly.*) What do you think?

LEWIS. I think maybe I can help you.

ELLEN. I don't know what you can do . . . unless you start rebuilding the economic system, and a lot of people are ahead of you on that already.

LEWIS. Have you considered marrying this Mr. Douglas . . . ?

ANN. (*Helpfully.*) Mr. Hall, Lewis.

LEWIS. Mr. Hall . . . before he sails?

ELLEN. Of course, I haven't! We don't even dare consider it until after he gets back.

LEWIS. By the way, where is your, er . . . friend?

ELLEN. You mean Doug? He stopped in Stamford for a shave. He still doesn't know that any of you know, and he's terribly sunk over leaving. Will you all be generous enough to act as though our miserable little romance hadn't been flaunted before the general public?

LEWIS. Huh!

ELLEN. Mother, do make Father behave himself, won't you?

ANN. I hope we can all behave.

ELLEN. I've got to dress. I'm going town to help Doug shop. You know, th man hasn't but two pairs of socks to h name. . . . (*The phone rings.* LEWIS a swers it.*)

LEWIS. (*Into phone.*) Hello. . . . Y One minute. I'll put him on the wire. . (LEWIS *crosses to terrace.* ELLEN *goes b hind table to pick up gloves and purse, th starts for hall.*)

ANN. Ellen!

ELLEN. Yes?

ANN. I think this may concern you, de

ELLEN. (*Coming back to* ANN.) Me?

LEWIS. (*Calling.*) Oh, Jaywood! Ne York calling! (JAY *enters.*)

LEWIS. They're holding the line for yc

JAY. (*Spotting* ELLEN.) Cheerio!

ELLEN. Hello!

JAY. (*Into phone.*) Hello. Hello, Fro old bean! What I called about particula was this. Have you a place in your Pa office for an A-1 American girl?

LEWIS. Good idea. (*He comes to table a listens eagerly.*)

JAY. (*Into phone.*) No favour to me; I doing you the favour. No, but she has be published. Has a decided flair for nev paper work. Speaks French. Two summe in Europe. She is Ann Whitman Murra daughter. . . .

ELLEN. You promised not to tell.

JAY. (*Into phone.*) But understand th She won't take the job unless she gets on her own. Perfectly satisfactory, I sho say. Fine! I'll bring her in for lunch. .

ELLEN. I'm lunching with Doug.

JAY. (*Into phone.*) Oh, Froth! She ca wait till lunch. We'll be in your office twelve. Righto! (*He hangs up the receiv and turns to* ELLEN.) The Paris edit of the *Herald Tribune.* Office dog. Ab twenty dollars a week. Would you be int ested?

ELLEN. I might. What do you think, Mother?

ANN. Decide as you think best, dear. It's your own problem.

LEWIS. (*Briskly, beaming with satisfaction.*) This fits right into my plan . . . (*He catches her expression, then quickly.*) subject, of course, to your approval. We'll motor to Greenwich about four and have a quiet family wedding. Dr. Whitaker is available, he tells me, at that hour. Then a nice quiet little supper which your loving mother will arrange . . . and you're off on the *Queen Mary* at midnight! Now isn't that neat?

ELLEN. (*With sarcasm.*) Very neat. Doug sailing *steerage* on the *Laconia*.

LEWIS. Oh! Well I'll give you a bridal suite for a wedding present.

ELLEN. So that's the angle? The wayward daughter has returned, and you're going make an honest woman of her.

LEWIS. (*Patient, with effort.*) Now, now . . no such idea entered my head . . . nor your mother's.

ANN. It certainly didn't.

LEWIS. We merely realized how miserable you'd be separated from Mr. Douglas. . . .

ELLEN. (*Interrupting.*) Mr. Hall, Dad!

LEWIS. . . . Mr. Hall for two years; then your mother intimated to Mr. Jaywood . . .

ELLEN. (*Again interrupting.*) Dad, it doesn't listen right.

LEWIS. Well, you wanted a newspaper job . . . so there you are: exactly what you wanted.

ELLEN. I tell you what I think I'll do, Father. I'll take the *job*. (ANN *smiles broadly to* CONNIE.)

LEWIS. (*Squirming uncomfortably.*) Er, I'm not sure that would be wise unless you were married.

ELLEN. Dad, don't you see? I can't hang myself around Doug's neck. Suppose I should get sick or get fired. He'd worry himself to death over a wife he couldn't support!

CONNIE. After all, your father would be glad . . .

ELLEN. (*Interrupting.*) To dole out money to us! Not on your life! When we marry we'll be independent.

CONNIE. You might consider your mother.

ELLEN. You see what I'm fighting for, don't you, Mother?

ANN. Indeed I do, dear. Make your own decisions.

ELLEN. I intend to.

ANN. Of course you must realize that in Paris you'll be working alone at a difficult job in a foreign background. What's more, you may at any moment be plunged into a revolution or a war!

ELLEN. (*Eagerly.*) That's just what I want . . . a chance to study, to see why the world is so cock-eyed.

LEWIS. Why not stay home and study your mother?

ANN. Or your father!

ELLEN. (*Turning to* JAY.) Where'll I meet you for that twelve o'clock appointment? (*She crosses to him by drum table.*)

LEWIS. They won't give you the job, unmarried.

ELLEN. (*To* JAY.) Your man didn't ask if I was "Mrs." did he?

JAY. (*Evasively.*) Single girls, you know! Paris! They are a bit of a risk!

ELLEN. So you advocate marriage, too?

JAY. Well, er . . . it does sound so.

ELLEN. You of all people!

JAY. I know. I know.

LEWIS. (*Suspiciously.*) See here, Ellen, why attack Mr. Jaywood? (ELLEN *realizes she has said too much. She steals a quick look at* ANN.)

ELLEN. No reason. I guess I'm attempting to think things out too honestly for my own good or anybody else's. Please forgive me.

ANN. Eller., I thought you said you had to go up and dress.

ELLEN. It's all right, Mother. Don't worry, I'm just going. (*She exits.*)

LEWIS. (*To* ANN.) You actually encouraged her to take that job. Are you crazy?

ANN. I think it's an excellent opportunity . . . whether she marries, or whether she doesn't.

LEWIS. My God! First you help her to a week-end affair, now you help her to continue it all over Europe!

CONNIE. Lewis, you only irritate Ann . . . and make things worse.

ANN. (*Placidly, rising.*) I wouldn't allow such a superficial thinker to irritate me. (*To* LEWIS.) I know what I'm about. I've seen this boy and you haven't. (*She goes upstairs.*)

LEWIS. (*Wearily to* JAY.) I could do with a drink. How about you? (*He goes to his private hiding-place in book-case, right, and produces bottle of whiskey and two glasses.*)

JAY. I feel I should be getting into town.

CONNIE. (*Eagerly.*) Jay, I'm driving in town myself. Why don't you go with me? I'd love company.

JAY. Kind of you, but . . .

CONNIE. I drive beautifully. I'll go tell Peter to drive my car around. I'll be ready in ten minutes. (*She exits right.*)

JAY. I think I will take a drink. (*Indicating* LEWIS *has poured enough.*) Whoa! (LEWIS *pours himself a glass.*)

LEWIS. Nice of you, old man, to wangle Ellen that Paris job.

JAY. Glad to be of service. (*They drink.*)

LEWIS. Er, now she's got it, do us one more favour, will you?

JAY. Of course . . . what?

LEWIS. See she doesn't get it.

JAY. (*Looking in direction* ANN *departed.*) Well, I don't know . . .

LEWIS. Your friend is particular whom h hires, isn't he?

JAY. You mean call him up and say I'v discovered your daughter is, er . . . a b of a frip? (*He sits on lower end of couch*

LEWIS. (*With a groan.*) God, no, that wo do. (*He takes a drink.*) Jaywood, I'm a co fused and unhappy man. (*Sits on couch* Tell me: is morality dead and I don't kno it?

JAY. On the contrary, if I were a fathe I suspect I'd have feelings much like you (*Warming to the subject.*) You know, i always been a pet theory of mine that me are much more moral than women.

LEWIS. (*Bluntly.*) Are you moral?

JAY. (*Cheerfully.*) Oh, rather!

LEWIS. Huh! (*He glances at* JAY *shrew ly.*) I noticed both Ellen and Ann a peared surprised when you came out support of this marriage. "You of people!" Ellen said.

JAY. (*Affecting surprise.*) Did Ellen s that? I didn't notice.

LEWIS. You know damn well you notice You got red as a turkey cock.

JAY. (*Embarrassed.*) Er, well, the tru is, I have been rather a gay dog in n time.

LEWIS. (*Suspiciously.*) Indeed?

JAY. (*Hastily.*) In London, you know.

LEWIS. How would Ellen hear about tha

JAY. About what?

LEWIS. About your being a gay dog London?

JAY. Er, I fear my reputation may ha been somewhat international.

LEWIS. Huh! (*He rises and crosses to ce ter.* MARTHA *enters from the hall.*)

MARTHA. Excuse me, sir.

LEWIS. What do you want?

MARTHA. There's a Mr. Hall to see M Ellen, sir.

s. (*With mounting anger.*) Show
in here, Martha.

THA. Yes, sir. (*She exits.*)

Easy does it, old boy!

s. I intend to be diplomatic. (DOUG
·s. *At sight of* LEWIS, *he stops dead in
racks. He would like to run. Then he*
JAY *and crosses to him, much relieved.*)

. Oh, hello, Mr. Haywood. Nice to
you again.

(*As they shake hands.*) Nice to see
Mr. Hall, may I introduce Mr. Murray
Ellen's father.

. (*He hesitates, then gives* LEWIS *a
y athletic hand-shake.*) It's a privilege
eet you, sir.

s. Huh! Thanks.

. I dropped in to see if Ellen had re-
d from Hartford yet.

s. Yes, she's back. (*An awkward
·.*)

. Has she been back long?

s. About fifteen minutes, I should
shouldn't you, Jaywood?

(*Coming out of his revery.*) Er,
? Oh, about fifteen or twenty. (*Looks
atch.*) Nearer twenty. (LEWIS *consults
vatch.*)

s. Yes, nearer twenty. (DOUG *consults
·atch. It is a large-sized popular brand.
s and* JAY *bend forward to compare
·me with theirs.* DOUG *hastily pockets
vatch. An awkward pause.*)

Will you have a drink?

No, thanks. (*To* LEWIS.)I'm won-
g if Ellen has had time to tell you
. . or maybe she phoned.

. No, she didn't phone.

(*He looks at* JAY, *then decides to
the plunge.*) You see, Mr. Murray,
allen pretty deeply in love with Ellen,
before I left Friday, we decided to
ie engaged . . . of course with your
it. . . .

LEWIS. Frankly, Mr. Hall, in your particular case don't you feel the word engagement is a slight, er . . . error in terminology?

DOUG. You mean on account of my going
away for so long?

LEWIS. I had in mind the fact you'd been
away.

DOUG. Been away?

LEWIS. I said "been away."

JAY. (*With warning gesture.*) Easy.

LEWIS. Mr. Hall, unfortunately I wasn't
at home when you dropped in for tea.

DOUG. (*Politely.*) I was disappointed to
find you away.

LEWIS. (*Explosively.*) How in the name
of heaven can a well-born, clean-cut, apparently decent young chap like you stand
there and look me in the eye . . . (*Noticing* JAY'S *worried expression.*) No, suppose we drop that phase of the matter....

DOUG. I'd prefer you continue.

LEWIS. I . . . you . . . (*The subject is
too difficult for him. He gives up.*) Nothing important, my boy. Some other time
. . . when we're better acquainted.

DOUG. (*Coolly.*) I'm driving in town directly with Ellen, sir, and I sail at midnight.
If you have anything to say, I wish you'd
say it now.

LEWIS. Er, Mr. Hall, my daughter's happiness means a great deal to me. I don't
want to jeopardize it. Probably I am, as
my wife frequently reminds me, narrow-
minded. Anyway, my personal opinion is
that you behaved like a . . .

JAY. (*Warningly.*) Easy does it.

LEWIS. (*In a milder tone.*) . . . damn cad.

JAY. (*To* DOUG.) In brief, he knows you
spent the week-end with his daughter.

DOUG. I thought that was what he was
driving at.

LEWIS. Correct! That's it.

DOUG. Did Ellen just tell you?

LEWIS. No, I've known it for some time.

DOUG. Some time? That's impossible.

LEWIS. I knew it last Friday.

DOUG. Then why didn't you stop us?

LEWIS. I didn't get the news until after you had gone.

DOUG. (*Thoroughly mystified.*) But Ellen assured me . . . why we all had tea together . . . nobody knew then.

JAY. A few of us were in on it.

DOUG. Did Mrs. Murray know?

JAY. Oh, definitely.

DOUG. Before we started?

JAY. Yes.

DOUG. Do you mean to say that Mrs. Murray sat there all the time, served tea and talked nonsense . . . ?

JAY. That's right.

DOUG. Did *you* know?

JAY. Oh, yes!

DOUG. What kind of a family is this?

JAY. They're extremely nice people, Mr. Hall.

DOUG. (*To* LEWIS.) Say, why didn't some of you raise a row? Then naturally, I wouldn't have thought of going.

LEWIS. Not much courage, eh?

DOUG. Oh, I've plenty of courage. I admit if a person didn't know the facts, my conduct might seem kind of rotten; but frankly, I think you have only yourselves to blame. You know I'm beginning to get pretty good and sore about this!

LEWIS. By God! You needn't get sore . . . ! (CONNIE *enters right. She notices the general air of suppression and tension.*)

CONNIE. Oh, excuse me. I'm just after my cigarette case. I'm going right up to pack. (*She takes case from table, and starts for archway, only to find herself face to face with* DOUG.)

JAY. Mrs. Nevins, may I introduce Hall?

CONNIE. Mr. Hall?! Oh, how do you I've often heard the family speak of yo

DOUG. You're Aunt Connie?

CONNIE. I am Connie.

DOUG. (*Bluntly to* CONNIE.) I suppose know, too.

CONNIE. Know what?

DOUG. About our trip to Lanesville.

CONNIE. Er, just vaguely. . . .

DOUG. And you didn't tell your own what you know, and advise her ne go!

CONNIE. Why, no!

DOUG. I can only repeat: what a fa

LEWIS. (*Angrily.*) If you don't like family, you're at liberty to leave. Tl the door.

DOUG. Oh no, I don't go yet. What w that make *me*?

CONNIE. That's hard to say. At the ment you seem an extremely impo young man. . . . (ANN *enters fron hall.*)

ANN. Oh, good morning, Mr. Hall.

DOUG. (*Tersely, a stag at bay.*) morning.

ANN. (*Chattily.*) We saw you driv Ellen will be right along. Won't yo down?

DOUG. No!

ANN. (*Offended by his tone.*) I beg pardon.

DOUG. Mrs. Murray, I'm afraid we' yond the point where we can be po each other. I'll tell you frankly: pretty mad.

ANN. Lewis is exasperating, but . .

DOUG. (*Interrupting.*) I'm not so n him. It's you. . . .

Me?

s. (*Gloatingly.*) You, Mrs. Murray.

(*To* DOUG.) My dear boy, I've tried
sympathetic. . . .

. (*Interrupting.*) What kind of a
an are you to serve a man tea when
he time you know he is running off
your daughter? Where were your
erly instincts?

Under control, Mr. Hall!

Don't you think it's pretty tough
llen and me to be let in for any such
ition as this?

(*All sympathy.*) Of course I do, bless
heart. Lewis! Ellen begged you not
l him we knew.

. I didn't. He dragged it out of me.

Yes, and another point you've over-
d. My reputation!

Your reputation? Oh, I see. (ANN
nd of sofa, right.)

s. News of your reputation won't
any farther.

Everybody I've met so far seems to
it. . . . (ELLEN *enters, furious. She
hanged hurriedly.*)

. So you have told him . . . the
nt my back was turned! Oh, darling,
e just trying to spoil everything. I'm
Let's get out of here. . . . .

Oh, no!

. (*Stopped short by his tone.*) What
u mean, "Oh, no!"?

We talk this out right here and

. Not before everybody. (JAY *and
E murmur apologies.*)

E. Come, Jay. . . . (*They start to*

Don't one of you leave this room.
t them all here.

E. Oh!'

LEWIS. See here . . .

ELLEN. Why, Doug, what's come over
you?

DOUG. I want them to hear me propose to
you.

ELLEN. But, Doug, you ought to know
you don't have to propose to me.

DOUG. Darling, they think I've misled
you.

ELLEN. What do we care what they think?

DOUG. Don't you understand, it's the wrong
way to look at it. I care too much for
you to . . . to . . . to . . .

ELLEN. We don't need to go into that
now. Listen, Doug, we've had a grand
piece of luck. Through Mr. Jaywood, I
may be able to get a job on the *Paris
Herald.* Isn't that a break? A newspaper
job one week out of college! Aren't you
excited?

DOUG. Say, it might work out at that. (*He
turns to* LEWIS.) We could get married and
Ellen could come over later.

LEWIS. We thought she might even sail
with you.

DOUG. I see no objection.

ELLEN. I see plenty. It's out of the question. Anyway, we can talk it over on the
boat.

DOUG. Ellen, I'm sorry. I can't let you
take the same boat with me. . . .

ELLEN. Why not? You didn't buy it, did
you?

DOUG. Ellen, you and I are going to be
married here, right now, today, where your
family can watch . . . or you're not going
to see me for two years. . . . .

ELLEN. Darling, you're just having a moral
spasm. It'll pass. (*He makes gesture of
protest.*)

DOUG. Ellen, I'll have to insist. Either you
marry me today, or it's good-bye for *more*
than two years.

ELLEN. I won't be forced . . . by you, or any of the rest of you. I know: you've all been working on him.

CONNIE. I'd say he's been working on us.

ELLEN. (*Turning back.*) Doug, I can't marry you like this.

DOUG. Ellen!

ELLEN. In fact, I *won't* marry you like this.

DOUG. (*Weakly, overwhelmed.*) That sounds final.

ELLEN. It is.

DOUG. Then good-bye.

ELLEN. Good-bye.

DOUG. (*Turning to* LEWIS.) Sorry. At least you'll admit I've tried. . . .

LEWIS. Hall, you've acted mighty fine. No father could ask more. (DOUG *backs toward archway. He takes one final look at* ELLEN *to see if there is chance of her relenting.*)

DOUG. (*Awkwardly.*) Pleased to have you all. (*He hurries out.*)

CONNIE. Good-bye, Mr. Hall.

JAY. Good-bye, old boy. (*A pause one knows what to say.* ELLEN, *mise unhappy, turns to* ANN *in appeal.*)

ELLEN. Mother, what do you think?

ANN. (*In pleasantly vigorous tone think, when a man makes such a fuss being seduced . . . a nice girl oug marry him. (It is the tiny filip need decide* ELLEN.)

ELLEN. Maybe you're right. (*Cal. Doug! Doug, wait a minute! (She and runs out.*) (ANN *turns to* LEWI gives a nod of profound satisfaction, that says: "There you are, I handle in my own way. What are you k about?" She extends her arms. He itates, then extends his. They embr hearty congratulation as the Curtain I*

END OF PLAY

Three Men On A Horse

BY JOHN CECIL HOLM AND GEORGE ABBOTT

*"To Equipoise,
that good old horse."*

"THREE MEN ON A HORSE" was first produced by Alex Yokel at The Playhouse
New York City on January 30, 1935. The play was staged by Mr. Abbott, the
ngs were designed by Boris Aronson, and the cast was as follows:

AUDREY TROWBRIDGE	Joyce Arling
THE TAILOR	J. Ascher Smith
ERWIN TROWBRIDGE	William Lynn
CLARENCE DOBBINS	Fleming Ward
DELIVERY BOY	Nick Wiger
HARRY	James Lane
CHARLIE	Millard Mitchell
FRANKIE	Teddy Hart
PATSY	Sam Levene
MABEL	Shirley Booth
MOSES	Richard Huey
GLORIA	Edith Van Cleve
AL	Garson Kanin
HOTEL MAID	Margaret Mullen
MR. CARVER	Frank Camp

SCENES

ACT I

e 1. The living room of the Trowbridge House, Ozone Heights, New Jersey.
e 2. A bar room in the basement of the Lavillere Hotel, New York City.

ACT II

e 1. Ozone Heights.
e 2. A room in the Lavillere Hotel.

ACT III

e 1. Ozone Heights.
e 2. The Hotel Room.

ACT ONE

SCENE I

Scene: The living room of the Trowbridge house, Ozone Heights, New Jersey.

A typical standardized house. There is a stairway leading up, a door to the kitchen and a front door.

ORCHESTRA *plays "Just a Love Nest."*
At rise: AUDREY TROWBRIDGE *enters from the kitchen. She carries a plate of toast which she places on a bridge table. We also see coffee, orange-juice, etc.* AUDREY *is wearing a red print house-dress. She is about twenty-five. As she crosses to the foot of the stairs she examines the sole of one bedroom slipper.*

AUDREY. *(Calling.)* Erwin.

ERWIN. *(Off.)* Yes.

AUDREY. The paint you put on the kitchen floor isn't dry yet.

ERWIN. Well, I didn't expect it would be. It says on the can it takes forty-eight hours.

AUDREY. Oh. Anyway I set up the bridge table in the living room. Breakfast is all ready.

ERWIN. All right. *(Buzzer rings.* AUDREY *opens door, admits the* TAILOR.*)*

AUDREY. Oh, yes. Just a minute. *(Calls.)* Erwin.

ERWIN. *(Off.)* Yes.

AUDREY. The man is here for your suit. Will you bring it down?

ERWIN. All right. Just a second.

AUDREY. *(Over her shoulder.)* Just a second!

ERWIN. *(Pause.)* Here it comes. *(Suit lands at* AUDREY'S *feet.* AUDREY *cleans out pockets of pocket-handkerchief, pipe, matches and a little note-book.)*

AUDREY. The last time I sent this suit I forgot to take out a white handkerchief with a blue border and it never came back.

TAILOR. I'll tell him about it.

AUDREY. *(As the* TAILOR *is leaving.)* It was a good handkerchief. *(She looks through*

note-book—is shocked and distressed—
up stairs—goes to phone cautiously. ▮
up phone.)* Give me forty-two W—
four. *(Sits.)* Hello, Clarence . . . *(Wea▮*
I wonder if you could come over ▮
minute. I just found something that's ▮
me. . . . You will. . . . Oh, thanks. *(H▮*
up. Wipes tear away, blows nose, ▮
calls.)* Erwin, breakfast is ready.

ERWIN. *(Upstairs.)* All right, dear.
DREY *blows nose and looks straight a▮*
ERWIN *comes quickly down the stair▮*
into room. He is dressed, except fo▮
necktie. He is the model little comm▮
I thought of another verse while I ▮
shaving. Darned good, too— *(Sits at t▮*
What's the matter, dear, something ▮
your eye?

AUDREY. I'll be all right.

ERWIN. Gee, that's too bad. It's thi▮
spell we're having. Dust everywhere.

AUDREY. Better drink your coffee ▮
it's too cold.

ERWIN. *(Sits.)* Oh, yes. *(Starts ▮
Pause.)*

AUDREY. You forgot your necktie.

ERWIN. *(Looks.)* Necktie? So I have▮
I couldn't decide which tie to wear.

AUDREY. You need new ones, I gues▮

ERWIN. No, no. I have plenty. Ge▮
late— *(Looking at wrist watch.)*

AUDREY. *(Crossing to the table.)* Yo▮
me you'd stay home from the offic▮
day this week.

ERWIN. I know I did, sweetheart—▮
not today. How in the name of ▮
can I turn out sixty-seven Mother'▮
greetings?

AUDREY. *(Suddenly; hopefully.)* You▮
write them in the country. We co▮
for a drive. *(Sits.)*

ERWIN. No. No. I know I couldn'▮
never been able to write in the cou▮
the birds and the butterflies, distract▮
(Suddenly.) —wait— *(Writing.)*

and the butterflies send you a greeting.
ring and today in mem'ry we're meet-
Mother's Day Number Eleven. Yes,
all right—well, that's another one.
all that "To Mother on Mother's
— (*Starts gulping breakfast. She goes
ndow.*) What's the matter?

Y. I'm expecting Clarence, that's all.

. I wish you'd have him visit when
ot here; he gets me upset—he laughs
—calls me the Poet of Dobbins Drive.

Y. He doesn't understand. He's a
ss man.

. Business man? Every time I look
e window, I see forty-six empty houses
e's built and can't sell. My greeting
verses are read from Asbury Park to
, Washington.

Y. Well, I'm not going to be happy
one Heights—after today.

. (*Looks.*) Why, has something
ned?

Y. Yes—something has. Erwin—

. I wish you wouldn't say Erwin in
one of voice, Audrey. I know my
is Erwin, but it makes me feel what-
as happened has something to do
me.

. It has.

Why, Audrey—

Y. I discovered it before you came

About me? (AUDREY *nods.*) Why
, what is it?

. I'm going to wait until brother
ere.

Do you have to have him here to
e what it is?

. Yes . . . Erwin, you don't love
y more. (*Sits—cries.*)

(*Crosses right.*) Why, Audrey, of
I love you. Maybe I don't walk up
y, "Audrey, I love you," every time
you . . . (*Sits.*) but you know how
Gosh, I don't know how other hus-
act. But I always do the best I can

and we seem to get along all right. If I've
done anything that's wrong I'd rather have
you tell me than tell your brother. (*Turns
front.*) I wish you wouldn't start the day
off like this. It's hard to write my verses
if I'm in the wrong mood, you know that.
Come on, dear, tell Erwin what it is so he
can explain and get to the office. . . .

AUDREY. Well, this morning the man came
for your blue suit—and I gave it to him.

ERWIN. Well . . . why are we so excited
about it? You were the one who said it
needed cleaning. (CLARENCE *enters room.
Looks at tie-less collar on* ERWIN. CLARENCE
*is about thirty-five. A small town business
man. A check book, pen and pencil in his
breast pocket and when the jacket is open
we see several lodge emblems.*)

CLARENCE. Well, good morning, what's
happened? Oh, just getting up?

AUDREY. Good morning—Clarence.

CLARENCE. Hello, sis—you look all upset.
Has he been doing anything to you?

ERWIN. I haven't done a thing that I know
of. I was just having breakfast. It's something about my suit. My blue suit. Audrey
sent it out to be cleaned.

CLARENCE. You being funny?

ERWIN. Maybe you think it's funny. I
don't. I should be at the office and my wife
tells me I don't love her any more.

CLARENCE. What has that got to do with
a blue suit?

AUDREY. I sent it out to be cleaned, and—
(*Takes notebook from pocket and crosses
to* CLARENCE.) I found this note-book in
the coat pocket.

ERWIN. Oh, that book. Is that what upset
you . . .

AUDREY. (*Holds up hand; goes to* CLAR-
ENCE. *Flips pages through.*) Look at those
names . . . Shirley, May, Lena Wee, Bam-
bola, Nell McClatchy, Squeeze . . . not one
or two, Clarence, but pages of them . . .
look at those telephone numbers . . . Jamaica
six-three-two-one. . . .

ERWIN. (*As* AUDREY *returns to davenport.*)
But darling!

CLARENCE. My gosh, say. What are you keeping . . . a harem?

ERWIN. Wait, dear. (*Meekly.*) I can explain. It's only a hobby.

AUDREY. Only a hobby. Oh— (*Sits—cries.*)

ERWIN. They're horses.

CLARENCE. Horses, huh—

AUDREY. Horses!

ERWIN. Horse racing.

CLARENCE. Oh, is that it?

ERWIN. Yes!

CLARENCE. (*Stalking toward* ERWIN.) I always knew you had some secret vice. I was telling Audrey just the other day . . .

ERWIN. I don't play them.

CLARENCE. Then what do you do?

ERWIN. I dope them out.

CLARENCE. For who? For what?

ERWIN. For fun. I do it on the bus on the way to the office to pass the time. Like some people do cross-words. . . .

CLARENCE. Oh, you do?

ERWIN. Yes—one day I came across a racing paper on the bus and I found out that the fellow who doped them out wasn't so good. So the next day I did it myself for fun . . . and I've been keeping track of them in that book.

AUDREY. (*Stands.*) But Erwin, you haven't explained all these numbers.

ERWIN Certainly I have, sweetheart. (*Takes book.*) Listen, here, I wrote on one page Jamaica—six—that's the sixth race. And then two-three-one. The two, three, and one was in the order I thought the entries would finish. On this other page is the way they did finish. (*Turning page.*)

CLARENCE. (*Looking at book.*) You mean you guessed them right?

ERWIN. (*Like a little boy.*) Sure.

AUDREY. But that doesn't explain this number. (*Looking at book.*) This eight ninety-six point fifty—

ERWIN. It isn't a number. That's w[hat] made the week of January twentiet[h] two dollars a bet. Eight hundred ninety-six dollars and fifty cents.

AUDREY. You made that and never [told] me?

ERWIN. Only on paper, sweetheart. I'd never bet on a horse. You know couldn't afford that. (*To* CLARENCE.) —in the back of the book is what I w[ould] have made on a four horse parlay, pl[aying] two dollars a day fourteen thousand d[ollars] and fifty cents since January first. It's [what] you call mental betting.

CLARENCE. (*Looking in book; bus[iness] like.*) So you win on paper. (*Takes b[ook]*)

ERWIN. (*Going back to his break[fast.]*) But I wouldn't bet on a horse with[out] money.

CLARENCE. But on paper with two [dollar] bets you've made a few thousand d[ollars.] Suppose you did put two dollars [on a] horse? And the horse paid three to on[e] you would have six dollars beside[s the] original two dollars you bet.

ERWIN. Yes. But suppose the horse [didn't] win, I'd be out two dollars. Two [dollars] is a lot of money to us, Clarence.

CLARENCE. (*Slowly as he crosses t[o his] place.*) But according to your little [book] here, you couldn't have picked many [horses] that lost or you wouldn't have run up [these] figures.

ERWIN. Oh! yes. I have. Now last [Satur]day, going to town, I went throug[h the] entries in the morning paper and [picked] out horses one-two-three in all the [races] and the one I picked in the fourth [race] fell down and finished out of the [money] and one lost his rider and three [were] scratched.

CLARENCE. How about the other hor[ses?]

ERWIN. (*Eating.*) Oh, they finish[ed all] right.

CLARENCE. One-two-three?

ERWIN. One-two-three.

CLARENCE. (*Turning away.*) How [long] have you been doing this, Erwin?

‑IN. Only since the first of the year.

‑RENCE. Well, that's long enough.

‑IN. That isn't very long—

‑RENCE. I mean that's long enough to ‑ it away.

‑IN. Sock what away?

‑RENCE. (*Going to the table.*) Come on ‑, Erwin. I've been around. I can see ‑ugh you.

‑IN. I don't know what you mean, ‑ence.

‑ENCE. How many savings accounts ‑ you, Erwin?

‑IN. You mean banks?

‑ENCE. Yes, banks.

‑IN. Only one. The Bowery Savings ‑k.

‑ENCE. How much you got in there?

‑IN. It's down to twenty-two dollars ‑

‑ENCE. Say, Erwin, you're as plain as ‑o me. You've been playing the horses ‑ January—you've won a pile of money ‑u don't want anyone to know about ‑o what do you do? You cry poor. So ‑ think you're broke.

‑N. I am broke.

‑ENCE. I'll bet you've got about six dif‑ ‑t bank accounts under "non de plums."

‑EY. Why Erwin—

‑N. But I haven't, honest, I wish I

‑ENCE. (*Sits.*) Now listen—you might ‑omorrow, Erwin, and nobody knows ‑t those bank accounts but you. Think ‑udrey.

‑N. But honest, Clarence, I haven't ‑money. I don't know how you can ‑ up things like this. Gee—if I had a ‑ like yours, I'd write detective stories. ‑y do this for fun—it's just a hobby— ‑like—like golf—or—or tropical fish.

‑NCE. Is that the truth?

ERWIN. That's the truth, Clarence!

CLARENCE. Great grief, man. Why don't you bet?

ERWIN. That would spoil it all.

CLARENCE. (*Baffled.*) Do you mean to tell me you can pick horses, that win every day, and be satisfied with paper profits?

ERWIN. Yes.

CLARENCE. Why?

ERWIN. Because I did bet once.

AUDREY. Why, when was that, Erwin?

ERWIN. Well, that was a long time ago . . . I guess it doesn't hurt to tell about it now. We'd only been married a little while. You wanted something and I wanted to get it for you . . . you said it was too expensive. . . .

CLARENCE. What happened to the horse?

ERWIN. Oh, he lost.

AUDREY. Oh.

ERWIN. He was a good horse, though. One of the fellows at the office showed me a telegram right from the jockey who was going to ride in the race, saying, "It's a sure thing and to play right on the nose. . . ." So I did. I took ten dollars out of my envelope. . . . That was the time I told you my pocket was picked—remember? I was only making thirty then—

CLARENCE. So you thought the race was fixed, huh?

ERWIN. I didn't know anything about that. But he sure was a good horse . . . maybe something went wrong. Just as the race was about to start . . . this horse broke the barrier and ran all the way around the track before they could catch him . . . so they brought him back to the post . . . when the race started he was so tired he just stayed there.

CLARENCE. How do you pick these horses, Erwin?

ERWIN. When I get on the bus, I just look through the entries and pick out the ones I like. I guess you'd call it playing hunches.

CLARENCE. Just for the fun of it. I guess a lot of people do that. I'll bet you even know what's going to win today.

ERWIN. Sure. I figured it out last night on the bus coming home—but I only figured the first race—Brass Monkey—is going to win it.

CLARENCE. Brass Monkey—

ERWIN. Sure, he's a good horse.

AUDREY. I'm awfully sorry, Erwin, I suspected you of anything wrong.

ERWIN. (*Going to her.*) That's all right, darling. I'd never do anything behind your back, you know that.

CLARENCE. But great grief, Erwin, you don't seem to have any initiative. No other man would have let a chance like that slip through his fingers—why don't you bet?

ERWIN. (*Turning.*) I don't think it would be moral for me to bet—we haven't enough money—

CLARENCE. That's ridiculous—why don't you make some? I told you I'd give you a percentage if you sold one of my houses—

AUDREY. That's sweet of you, Clarence.

ERWIN. I don't think I could sell one. Maybe Audrey could. I don't like them. (*Turns and goes toward door.*)

CLARENCE. What do you mean you don't like them?

ERWIN. I don't like them, that's all, and I couldn't sell anything I don't like.

AUDREY. (*Rising.*) What's wrong with them?

ERWIN. (*Trapped.*) There isn't anything wrong with them exactly, but well—there is too much water in the cellar.

CLARENCE. (*Going to* ERWIN.) Now I don't want any minor criticisms from you after that porch you tacked on the house—I built a beautiful row of houses all alike, and you tacked that thing on. You put this house out of step, you know that?

ERWIN. Now listen, Clarence— (*Changing his mind as* CLARENCE *turns.*) Never mind, I'm late. (*Starts.*)

AUDREY. Wait a minute, Erwin.

ERWIN. What's the matter, darling? have to go to work.

AUDREY. Don't you think you better a ogize to Clarence before you go?

ERWIN. Apologize? For what?

AUDREY. For being so rude.

ERWIN. Rude?

AUDREY. Yes. About the houses. Erw

ERWIN. Well, I apologize—but I don't water in the cellar—I don't think it a anything to a house. (*Buzzer rings.* ER opens door.*)

BOY. Number one Dobbins Drive?—

ERWIN. That's right.

BOY. Package for Mrs. Trowbridge. (*H. ing* ERWIN *package.*)

ERWIN. There she is there. . . . (*S. out.*)

BOY. C. O. D. Forty-eight dollars.

ERWIN. What?

AUDREY. I bought some dresses, darlin

ERWIN. C. O. D. Forty-eight dollars? I are we going to pay it—what made do that?

CLARENCE. I told her she needed decent clothes. That's why, and since found out a few things today, I guess I right.

ERWIN. We can't afford it— (*To* Take them back, son. (*Giving him* age.*)

BOY. I can't take them back. They've altered.

AUDREY. That's right, Erwin. It was a They'd cost sixty-five next week. I s you seventeen dollars. Darling, you I didn't have anything to wear.

ERWIN. Nothing to wear! All I seem is pay for dresses and hats . . . and m insurance. (*Crosses to cabinet, take. "Household Budget Book." Looks thr book.*)

ENCE. Don't yell at my sister like that.

N. Nothing to wear. (*Reads.*) Listen
nineteen twenty-nine—six dresses—four
—Nineteen thirty—seven dresses—five
—Nineteen thirty-one, thirty-two and
y-three—eight, nine, and ten dresses
five, four, and eight hats respectively,
ether, that's forty dresses and thirty-
hats. I should be in the hat business
ad of trying to get some place.

EY. Darling, it does sound like a lot,
ow, but that's since Nineteen twenty-
—some of those hats I couldn't wear
use my hair was growing back and
didn't fit.

N. Here's my hat—five dollars it cost
in Nineteen thirty-one and it's good
gh for me, Fall, Winter, Spring and
mer— (*Puts on hat.*) and look at it.

ENCE. Women's things are different—
women buy—

N. Well, look at it.

EY. I'm looking. I have a right to
a dress or two. I've saved a little
y from the budget and anyway how
know you haven't been betting on the
s.

NCE. Yes, there's a lot of things about
'd like to know—

N. My Gosh, don't I bring home my
every week? You know I never bet
horse or anything.

AUDREY. (*Going to* CLARENCE.) Oh, Clarence, let's not argue any more—

CLARENCE. (*Enfolding* AUDREY.) Don't worry, Audrey. I'll pay for the dresses.

ERWIN. Oh, no you won't. I don't want you to pay for anything. (*Goes to cabinet, takes tobacco tin. He takes out bills.*) Here, this is for your dresses. This ten was going to be for a split bamboo weakfishing outfit. These three tens were going to be for a motor trip for the two of us and this ten was supposed to become a panama and a pair of sport shoes—but pay for the dresses. Don't forget to get a receipt. (*Picks up box and puts it back in cabinet.*)

AUDREY. Where are you going?

ERWIN. To the office—I'm late.

AUDREY. You've forgotten your necktie.

ERWIN. What's the difference. Who cares how I look? To Hell with the tie.

AUDREY. Erwin.

ERWIN. And to Hell with this house.

CLARENCE. What?

AUDREY. Erwin! You'll hurt Clarence's feelings.

ERWIN. And I won't apologize. (*Rushing past delivery boy and out door.*)

AUDREY. (*Calls.*) Erwin.

BLACKOUT AND CURTAIN.

SCENE II

: A bar-room in the Lavillere Hotel.
bar is upstage, two thirds the distance.
hone booth to the right. Elevator door
nally across from booth. Door to
room off right out of view. Stairs
nter leading to the street. This is really
asement of the Lavillere Hotel.

: About three in the afternoon.

ise: HARRY the bartender is behind the
CHARLIE and FRANKIE seated at table
right. They have racing sheets spread
n table. FRANKIE is about half the size
ARLIE. His feet just touch the floor.
ears a derby and is smoking a large
CHARLIE is smoking a cigarette. His
hat is pushed back off his forehead.

HARRY. What'll you have, the same?

CHARLIE. Just make it one beer this time. (*Counts change.*) We'll split it, Frankie. (*To* HARRY.) We don't want to break a bill if we can help it—maybe we can figure out a horse to play on in this third race.

HARRY. That's all right by me.

FRANKIE. Geez, you'd think Patsy would call up or somethin'.

CHARLIE. It don't take all day to hock a belt buckle.

FRANKIE. Maybe it wasn't gold after all.

CHARLIE. He paid enough for it.

HARRY. (*As he brings beer to table.*) It just goes to show you how the luck will go. Lobster one day—beans the next. You three fellows were sittin' pretty—how much was it you ran up to last month?

CHARLIE. About four hundred bucks. Aw —we'll have it again.

FRANKIE. Sure.

HARRY. Geez, I could almost open my own place with that. I was tellin' the manager the other day—now the trouble with this place is—it looks too much like a speakeasy—if a thing is legal it should look legal —that's what I say—and another thing— when anybody takes a room at this hotel they don't come in here much—if they want to have a party—they take the bottle to the room. (*The phone rings.* HARRY *goes into booth.*)

CHARLIE. (*Counting money.*) Two, three, four, five, six. Well, I know how I'm goin' to play my six bucks.

FRANKIE. Yeah?

CHARLIE. Yeah, I'm playin' the surest thing I know . . . three bucks on Rose Cross to show.

FRANKIE. But Charlie, Rose Cross won't pay back anything much even if she wins . . . if you lay three bucks to place, you'd only get about ninety cents—so if she shows, you're lucky to get two bits.

CHARLIE. Listen, we got to reserve our capital. Two bits is breakfast money anyways. How d'ya think we're going to eat? We can't get credit for a bet any more— let alone feed money. You know that!

FRANKIE. But, you're puttin' up half your roll. Suppose Rose Cross don't come in?

CHARLIE. There's only five horses in the race. She ought to show at least— This is a Hell of a spot to be in. I wish Patsy would come back. Sometimes he gets some good ideas. Even Mabel ain't in her room. Did she go out with Patsy?

FRANKIE. No, she's doin' the same thing— she took out all her dresses and a parasol that's got a gold top. It's a good thing Patsy's got Mabel—he got forty-five bucks on that bracelet of hers yesterday.

CHARLIE. What do you mean "it's a g[ood] thing Patsy's got Mabel"? He bought that stuff for her, didn't he?

FRANKIE. What I mean is—she's a g[ood] investment. (HARRY *goes to bar.* ER[WIN] *enters slowly down the stairs.*) She's a kid, Mabel.

CHARLIE. Yeah, she's all right—well, Hell with all that. I got to bet.

HARRY. That was Gus on the phone. [He] wanted to find out if anybody wante[d to] bet the third race.

CHARLIE. Who copped that second?

HARRY. Fairweather.

CHARLIE. Brass Monkey took the first [—] paid eight to one. (*Looks at paper.*)

HARRY. (*Looks at slip of paper.*)

CHARLIE. Musta been a sleeper.

HARRY. What'll it be?

ERWIN. (*Looking around.*) I don't [think] I'll meet anybody here—

HARRY. What'll you have?

ERWIN. Scotch.

FRANKIE. I don't think I want to bet t[o]

CHARLIE. Now listen, we didn't play y[ester]day nor the day before—we got t[o bet] today. We might as well break the ic[e.]

ERWIN. (*To* HARRY.) Hey, I should [go to] the office.

HARRY. Takin' a couple hours for 1[unch] huh?

ERWIN. No. I mean I should have be[en at] the office this morning.

HARRY. Oh.

CHARLIE. We could play it like this[—] we put two dollars on Rose Cross to [win] then we put—now let's see . . .

HARRY. I guess you can always do [what] you like when you're in business for [your]self.

ERWIN. Gosh, sometimes I wish I w[as in] business for myself.

HARRY. I thought you was.

IN. No, that's the trouble. I should
been at the office a long time ago.
me have another drink.

RY. It's none of my business, brother,
don't you think you should go to the
while you're able to navigate?

IN. (*Waves idea aside.*) I don't think
ever go to the office again. (*Rests chin
elbow at bar as his attention is drawn
able.*)

Y. Oh. (*As if to say "It's as bad as
"*)

LIE. Maybe we should pass up the
. Does anything look good in the
th?

RY. (*To* ERWIN.) They been sittin'
for an hour tryin' to decide on a horse
ay.

IN. Do you know them?

Y. Sure. They live in this hotel.

IN. Do you think they'd mind if I
them a horse?

Y. What's that again?

N. I said, do you think they would
if I gave them a tip on the third race?

Y. Do you play the horses, too?

N. Me? No.

Y. Oh. Well, you see they're down to
e bucks and I think it might be better
ey made a choice themselves—because
ey lost they wouldn't feel so good.

N. You mean they wouldn't like me?

Y. That's it.

KIE. (ERWIN *turns. Throws down
g paper.*) Aw, Hell, do what you like,
lie. I don't see anything good. I think
wait for Patsy. He might have some-

LIE. All right. I'm playin Rose Cross.

N. (*Looks in book. Weaves to table.*)
se me, gentlemen, I see you're inter-
in horses. You should play Semester
e third race.

LIE. Yeah.

FRANKIE. Wheredja get that?

ERWIN. Oh, I have it right here.

FRANKIE. Semester ain't rated much with the boys.

HARRY. Hey! You better come back here and finish your drink.

CHARLIE. One of them long shot guys.

FRANKIE. Looks like a nut.

CHARLIE. Say, Harry, you better see if he can pay for his drinks. He might want to pay you with a tip.

ERWIN. You fellows have the wrong opinion of me. I was just trying to do you a favor. (*Pulls bill out of wallet.*) Look, twenty dollars. I can pay for more drinks than I ever drank in my whole life. (*To* HARRY.) Don't get me wrong. I don't drink much. But, did you ever feel blue?

HARRY. Sure. Lots of times.

ERWIN. That's just the way I feel today. I got off the bus—and I just didn't care any more—I should be at the office—but my wife and brother-in-law—you married?

HARRY. No.

ERWIN. Then you haven't got a brother-in-law. I got off the bus and I started for the office—and then I just didn't care any more.

CHARLIE. I'll put a dollar to win and one to show. Rose Cross.

FRANKIE. It's your six bucks, not mine. (CHARLIE *starts for booth.*)

ERWIN. You should really play Semester.

CHARLIE. If it's all the same to you, Pal, I'll play Rose Cross. (*Goes into booth.*)

ERWIN. (*Back to* HARRY.) That's the trouble. Nobody pays much attention to me. I think I'll have another drink. (HARRY *pours drink.*) Say, Harry . . . your name is Harry, isn't it?

HARRY. Yes.

ERWIN. (*Patting* HARRY *on shoulder.*) You are a very understanding sort of fellow— How would *you* like to play Semester in the third race just to see what would happen?

HARRY. (*Laughs.*) I know what would happen.

ERWIN. Don't you bet on horses?

HARRY. Say, I wouldn't bet on a horse if I was ridin' him myself.

CHARLIE. Just got it down in time. (*Returns to table.*)

ERWIN. Harry, you're a gentleman. I'd like to see you make some money.

HARRY. So would I.

ERWIN. (*Takes out book.*) Now let's see what I have for the fourth race.

PATSY. (*Enters from street. He is very dapper in a blue suit, grey suede shoes and light hat. He has an air of authority.*) Hello, Harry.

HARRY. Hello, Patsy. The boys was worried about you.

PATSY. (*Sits.*) I been all over town. Interestin' how many guys never heard of you before when they know you lost your roll. Well, Frankie, what did you do?

FRANKIE. Nothin'.

CHARLIE. Frankie was waitin' to see if you knew somethin' good. I just played two bucks on Rose Cross.

PATSY. Two bucks?

CHARLIE. We only got twelve between us. Did you get much on your buckle?

PATSY. Couple bucks. Mabel come in yet?

CHARLIE. No—an' I called her room for you.

PATSY. Thanks. She's trying to raise something too.

ERWIN. (*Weaving to table.*) I was telling them they should play Semester in the third race.

PATSY. (*To boys.*) Who's he?

CHARLIE. Just some drunk.

ERWIN. (*Standing in the middle of the room. More to himself.*) Semester in the third. Hasty Belle in the fourth. (*Suddenly he feels sick.*)

HARRY. Hey—right back in there, brot

ERWIN. Oh. (*Heads for lavatory. E Phone rings.* HARRY *shuts door after h*

HARRY. Geez, the country's full of a teurs. That guy shouldn't drink much.

CHARLIE. That's Gus. (*Goes into boo*

PATSY. He don't look like a drinker to

FRANKIE. He looks like a goof.

HARRY. No. He's a nice guy.

CHARLIE. (*Comes out of booth.*) Well be hit on the nose.

PATSY. What's the matter?

CHARLIE. Guess who won that ra Semester.

PATSY. Well, what about it?

CHARLIE. Didn't you hear him? He's trying to give us Semester for the las minutes.

FRANKIE. Say, how did that guy kno

HARRY. He kept looking in a little bo

PATSY. What book?

HARRY. H re it is. This book.

PATSY. (*Crosses to bar.*) Let's see. (*T book.* CHARLIE *and* FRANKIE *follow.*) —he's got them all figured out.

CHARLIE. What do you mean figured

PATSY. Here's yesterday's winners, an day before—pages of races— My God. got Brass Monkey for today—he come so did Fairweather and Semester.

FRANKIE. Aw, he maybe wrote them after the races was run.

HARRY. Wrote them down nuts. I l him tell you to bet Semester before yo the result.

CHARLIE. Yeah, that's right.

FRANKIE. (*Leans on bar.*) Maybe l handicapper.

PATSY. Now you know he don't lool a handicapper.

HARRY. He said somethin' about wo in an office.

LIE. What's he got for the fourth?

Y. Hasty Belle. He's got the fourth,
, sixth, seventh and eighth figured out.

KIE. Hasty Belle, huh, maybe we
t to lay two bucks on him.

. Two bucks, nothin'. We'll play the
s. (FRANKIE *takes book*.)

LIE. Wait a minute! Maybe it's a new
of a racket.

. To Hell with that. How much you

LIE. I still got four bucks. I ain't been
place.

KIE. I got six left.

. And I got eight. (*Pulls out money*.)
put up your ten between you, that's
een bucks altogether. You take it
d to Gus, Frankie, while this guy's
ere.

KIE. But we don't know anything
t him.

. Maybe he runs a service or some-
You go on around and I'll go in and
to him.

Y. I'll bet he's sick as a pup.

. What the Hell do I care.

KIE. But suppose the horse loses.

. If he does Mabel will be in with
dough in time for the next race. It
n't be the first time we ever lost,
it? Now you go on around and I'll
this guy busy in here. (*Going toward
.*")

KIE. (*Up steps*.) All right. What's
ame of the horse again?

. Hasty Belle.

IE. (*On landing*.) I'll lay the eight-
ucks, but I ain't responsible if this
don't come in. (*He goes*.)

. He kept tryin' to give *me* a horse.

. I'll see if he's still conscious.
.)

HARRY. (CHARLIE *sits at table*.) It will be
interestin' to know what the Hell this is
all about. He kept askin' me if I was married—now what would that have to do with
horses? Hey, I don't want to forget to
collect for those drinks.

MABEL. (*Enters from street. She is an ex-
Follies girl. A little faded and quite dumb*.)
Hello, boys.

CHARLIE. H'ya Mabel.

MABEL. Patsy told me to meet him here.
We had some business to talk over.

CHARLIE. That's all right, Mabel, we know
where you been.

MABEL. (*Sitting at the table*.) Kinda embarrassing, isn't it, to always be hockin'
things. Well, it's all over now. I haven't
anything left to hock except the dress I got
on. It wouldn't be worth much. . . . I
couldn't hock it anyway because I haven't
anything else left to wear . . . you know in
case I had to go out some place.

CHARLIE. Oh, I think you can keep that,
Mabel.

MABEL. Hasn't Patsy come in yet?

CHARLIE. Sure, he's come in. He's in there.
(*Gestures with thumb*.)

MABEL. Oh! I'll wait for him then.

CHARLIE. He's pretty busy.

MABEL. Sure, I guess he is.

CHARLIE. I mean he's got somebody with
him.

MABEL. Somebody with him—in the—in
there?

CHARLIE. Yeah—some guy.

MABEL. What kind of a guy, Charlie?

CHARLIE. Oh, he's all right. He's a friend
of Patsy's.

MABEL. Do I know him?

CHARLIE. I don't think so. You see—he
knew Patsy in the old days—you know—
and he heard how the luck was—and . . .
and—he just dropped in to tip Patsy off
on some fixed races so Patsy could get
straightened out. Isn't that right, Harry?

HARRY. That sounds all right, Charlie.

MABEL. You mean he fixes them?

CHARLIE. Yeah, that's it . . . he fixes them.

MABEL. But why are they in the Johnnie?

CHARLIE. Well, he got sick from the heat and some bum liquor. . . . I mean he ain't used to drinkin'. Patsy used to be his best friend— He's holding his head. (MOSES *stops elevator and steps out.* MOSES *is the colored elevator boy. He is quite a big boy. About twenty-eight.*)

FRANKIE. (*Enters.*) I put in that bet. Hello, Mabel.

MABEL. Hello—

FRANKIE. Where are they?

MABEL. They're in the Johnnie.

MOSES. One pint rye, bottle ginger ale. (*Looks at table.*) Good afternoon.

FRANKIE. (*Sitting at table.*) Hello, Moses—

MOSES. How is the horses?

CHARLIE. O. K. How are the numbers?

MOSES. (*As he goes to bar.*) Fine and dandy. I is playin' a combination I seen on a two dollar bill today. I just see it.

HARRY. (*Gives him order.*) Somebody havin' a party?

MOSES. The couple in three twelve just wakin' up— (*Going back with tray.*) Mr. Charlie, I was on the third floor and the maid asked me if it was all right to make up your room and I said yeah— (*Goes into elevator.*)

CHARLIE. Thanks, Moses.

PATSY. (*Enters.*) He's pretty sick. Did you lay the bets, Frankie?

FRANKIE. On the nose.

PATSY. That's right. Well, Mabel, how did you make out.

MABEL. (*Rising and crossing to* PATSY.) I went down to this place on Eighth Avenue like you told me and I unwrapped the dresses . . .

PATSY. Yeah?

MABEL. . . . which were very good as recall . . . and he said they wasn't so and I told him they was and then he they was out of style and I showed him price tags with the date on which was last week and he said, "How much do want?" and I said, "How much do think they're worth?" and he said isn't the question, he said he might be to sell them for forty dollars but that was only worth eight dollars to him a said that wasn't the right attitude to and he said, "The Hell with the atti will you take the eight bucks?"

PATSY. Did you take it?

MABEL. Yes.

PATSY. Good.

MABEL. (*Gives him money.*) Then I a somebody on the street where I coul a parasol with a gold head and they s would have to go to the assay office I said I wouldn't do that. (*Crosses; p elevator bell.*)

CHARLIE. Ertznay . . . you can sell any place.

FRANKIE. Gold? Certainly you can that any place. That's the basic n ain't it?

PATSY. Frankie, take this eight bucks put it on More Anon in the fifth.

CHARLIE. More Anon?

FRANKIE. (*As he crosses to* PATSY.) B don't know the results of the fourth or anything. How do we know—

PATSY. I know a lot now. I been t to him.

FRANKIE. All right then, if you're (*Starts to go.*) The fourth is on pretty

PATSY. We'll call up. (FRANKIE *goes u stairs. Elevator door opens.*)

MOSES. Goin' up?

MABEL. Yeah, my feet are tired. I'm up to change my shoes, Patsy. Gee, I think it's swell about this friend of fixin' the races for us so we can get again.

SY. Yeah . . . yeah. . . . Sweetheart,
't that somethin'. We'll see you later
n.

BEL. All right. (*Goes. Elevator rises.*)

SY. What didja tell her, Charlie, so
know?

ARLIE. I told her he was a friend of
Irs who was fixin' some races for you
ause he heard how you was broke . . .
two is old buddies . . . he used to be
r best friend.

SY. (ERWIN *enters.* PATSY *goes to him.*)
w do you feel now, Erwin? (*Turns to*
s.) His name is Erwin.

RRY. I knew it would be somethin' like
t.

VIN. (PATSY *leads him to chair.*) I think
el a little bit better now.

SY. (CHARLIE *rises.*) Sit down in this
e chair.

ARLIE. I hope he don't have to leave
n.

SY. He's not leavin'. He's stayin' here
he gets straightened out.

VIN. I forgot to pay for the drinks.

RRY. (*Coming around to him.*) Aw,
's all right.

VIN. How much is it?

RY. One dollar, even.

VIN. Can you break a twenty?

RY. Sure. (*Takes bill to register.*)

NKIE. (*Enters. Crosses right to phone*
th; speaks while he dials.) The bets are
I'm calling Gus. It's post time for the
rth. (*Dials phone leaving booth door*
n.)

SY. We had a long talk. His name is
in somebody. He picks those horses for
He says it's a hobby.

RLIE. Hobby, huh?

NKIE. Hello, Gus . . . this is Frankie.
sty Belle is four to one . . . yeah,
. . . ?

HARRY. (*Brings change to* ERWIN.) Gee, I
hope he's not a nut, you know how a guy
can get about horses.

FRANKIE. Yeah, Gus, I'm here . . . they're
at the quarter—

HARRY. Here's your change.

ERWIN. Thanks. (HARRY *goes back to bar.*)

FRANKIE. Yeah, Yeah, Joybird . . . Little
Lie . . . Post Script I got it . . . Hasty
Belle in that order . . .

PATSY. This is the fourth.

CHARLIE. The one Hasty Belle is in.

PATSY. He ain't done much this season.

CHARLIE. Yeah, I know.

ERWIN. (*Opens eyes.*) What's the matter?

PATSY. (*Crosses to both.*) Horse race.

FRANKIE. Joybird up at the half . . . Who
comes up? . . . Little Lie . . . Now Post
Script . . . neck and neck . . . yes . . . still
that way? . . . They're in the stretch . . .
yes, yes . . . He's past (*Turning to others.*)
he's past . . . (*Back to telephone.*) who's
past? . . . Joybird? Hasty Belle . . . passes
Joybird . . . she does. (*Hangs up, turns to*
others.) Hasty Belle wins!!

CHARLIE. Hasty Belle wins.

PATSY. Huh?

ERWIN. What's the matter?

CHARLIE. Hasty Belle wins.

ERWIN. What do you know about that.

CHARLIE. (*Looks at sheet.*) He ran out of
the money last five starts.

PATSY. (*Crossing to bar. Looks at ceiling.*)
Boy! (*Suddenly* FRANKIE, CHARLIE *and*
PATSY *look at* ERWIN.)

ERWIN. (*Embarrassed.*) Well, he won.
(*Searches pocket.*) Where is my little book?

FRANKIE. (*Across table.*) I was holdin' it
for you.

ERWIN. Just make a check beside Hasty
Belle.

HARRY. Here, I'll buy you a drink. (*Puts*
glass on bar.)

ERWIN. I'm not sure I can drink any more.

PATSY. Sure you can. Frankie, collect and put it all on Rip Van Winkle.

FRANKIE. I'll put up the same amount for the three of us. (*Exits.*)

PATSY. (*Pacing back and forth.*) That's the idea—that bracelet don't suit Mabel so hot anyways. I think I'll get her a platinum wrist watch. Don't you want to bet, Erwin?

ERWIN. I never bet.

PATSY. You don't?

ERWIN. No.

ERWIN. I just spent forty-eight dollars.

HARRY. No in here.

ERWIN. No, before I left home. Forty-eight dollars. Now I'm not going fishing. Forty-eight dollars and he's going to buy a platinum rich wast. Women. It's all the same, isn't it, no matter how you look at it?

HARRY. Sure, it's all the same.

ERWIN. (*Rises.*) Well, I think I'll go.

PATSY. Where you goin'?

ERWIN. Oh, I have to be at the office.

CHARLIE. (*Rises to them.*) You can't go to any office like that. (*Turning ERWIN.*)

HARRY. You'll lose your job.

PATSY. Sure. You work, huh? Everybody's goin' to go home pretty soon.

ERWIN. Huh?

PATSY. People who work in offices will be goin' home pretty soon.

ERWIN. Mr. Carver would still be there. He'll be waiting for me.

PATSY. (*Sits. Seats ERWIN. CHARLIE stands.*) Sit down a second, I want to talk to you— How much do you make a week?

ERWIN. Well, I get regular forty dollars and then there's extra. At fifty cents a line sometimes I sell stuff and that brings it up to forty-six or fifty some weeks not counting the postage stamps and the envelo and maybe this week it might come forty-nine.

CHARLIE. (*Sits.*) Don't you want to v and see how these races come out?

ERWIN. Oh, no. I can look at the res on my way home.

PATSY. (*Sits.*) So you make about f bucks a week. That's eight-fifty a day. N why don't you stay here and I'll give j ten per cent on everything I play Charlie and Frankie will too.

CHARLIE. Sure.

ERWIN. That sounds all right as far the money is concerned—

PATSY. What's the matter? We bet horses, that's our business, but you like pick them—so we pay you for it—if bet, say, twenty dollars on a horse and pays back say, eight to one . . . we get hundred and sixty dollars—you get sixt dollars . . . ten per cent . . . that's ab twice as much as you'd make if you worl all day.

CHARLIE. You see—we take a chance suppose the horse loses?

ERWIN. (*Rises.*) Yes . . . but I don't th I want to stay here.

PATSY. Why not . . you can't go to office like that. We'll call up.

CHARLIE. What's the number, Erwin? call him—

ERWIN. B. O. four six seven five two.

PATSY. I'll call your boss and tell him won't be in.

HARRY. I guess he knows that by now.

CHARLIE. We'll tell him anyway.

PATSY. We'll tell him you don't feel g (*Going to phone.*) Charlie. (*Dialing.*) V shall I ask for?

ERWIN. Mr. J. G. Carver.

CHARLIE. (*Into phone.*) Mr. Carver ple Oh, you're Mr. Carver—well, Mr. Car (*To ERWIN.*) What's your last na Erwin?

WIN. Trowbridge.

ARLIE. (*Into phone.*) Erwin Trow-
idge won't be in today . . . (ERWIN *rises*
PATSY *seats him.*) he got sick on his way
the office . . . yeah . . . terrible . . . he's
the drug store now . . . been here for a
ıg time . . . we been workin' over him
. Me! I'm the pharmacist . . . yeah . . .
hat . . . I'll tell him. Goodbye. (*Hangs
—sits left of* ERWIN.) He says that's
K. because there wouldn't be no use
nin' in this late anyways. He says as
ıg as you can get your work done by
norrow that's jake by him. If you don't
l so hot tomorrow you better send them
yways. Does that make sense to you?

WIN. Yes. I should get those verses
itten.

rSY. You a song writer?

WIN. No. Greeting verse. I'm late for
other's Day.

rSY. You're what?

WIN. I have to catch up on Mother's
y.

sY. We understand, Erwin. You got an
irin, Harry? (*Turning to bar.*)

RRY. (*Passes aspirin.*) Sure.

rSY. Now you just sit there and relax.

RRY. On the house. (*As he gives* PATSY
aspirin and glass of water.*)

ARLIE. I'll give it to him. (*Takes them.*)

ıNKIE. (*Runs in.*) Hey, listen, what do
ı think—I played the fifth . . . one-two-
ce . . . like in the book.

sY. Yeah . . . yeah . . . so what?

NKIE. They come in.

sY. One-two-three?

ıNKIE. One-two-three.

ARLIE. Can you top that?

sY. You hear that, Erwin? Go on take
down. What's a headache to you, eh,
vin? You're makin' money. (*Pounding
vIN on back.*)

ıIN. Have I made eight-fifty yet? (*Al-
st choking.*)

PATSY. Eight-fifty! Abc eighty-eight-fifty.
(CHARLIE *returns to bar ith glass and sips
as he crosses.*) How n ch you bet altogether, Frankie?

FRANKIE. (*Looking in book.* PATSY *with
FRANKIE.*) Let's see—I got back on the fifth
at ten each eighty-four and forty-one and
fifteen, that's one hundred and forty dollars
each, plus what we got on Hasty Belle,
that we played on More Anon. Altogether
that brings a total of two hundred and
forty-five dollars each.

CHARLIE. There ain't that much money.
Harry, could you make up a turkey sandwich?

HARRY. (*At bar.*) I haven't sold a turkey
sandwich in a week. How about cheese?

PATSY. We ain't got time to fool around
with food.

FRANKIE. We ought to play all the races
one-two-three.

PATSY. Erwin's only got the fifth figured
that way. Let's see the sheets, Frankie.
(*They start looking at the handicap sheets.*)

ERWIN. (*Who has been sitting with head
in hands.*) Could I have a pencil?

PATSY. (*First looking at boys.*) Sure, sure,
Erwin, here's a pencil.

CHARLIE. Here's some paper—

ERWIN. (*Searching through clothes.*)
Thanks, I have some paper. (ERWIN *goes to
work writing rapidly.*)

PATSY. Got a flash, hey Erwin?

CHARLIE. (*Tapping* PATSY's *arms as the
three retreat upstage.*) We better not talk
much.

FRANKIE. (*Whispering.*) I been looking
through the book and I see Erwin has a
record of parlays but he ain't got none for
today.

CHARLIE. (*Holds up hand.*) Look, he's got
somethin' hot.

PATSY. What you got, Erwin?

ERWIN. (*More to himself.*) I got one.

FRANKIE. Let's have it.

ERWIN. What?

PATSY. (*Slowly returning.*) Let's hear what you got.

ERWIN. Oh. No. You wouldn't be interested in this.

CHARLIE. (*Coming down.*) Sure we would. Let's hear it.

ERWIN. (PATSY *and* CHARLIE *sink down into chairs on each side.*) Well, I think it will do. Here it is.
  "At Christmas Tide your hair was grey
  But memories chased your cares away
  Now lovingly in my simple way
  I send you love on Mother's Day."
Mother's Day Number Sixteen.

PATSY. Yeah . . . yeah . . . that's all right, Erwin. That's elegant — what is that, Erwin?

ERWIN. That's a Mother's Day verse.

PATSY. You mean you just thought that up?

ERWIN. Yes.

PATSY. Since you been sittin' there?

ERWIN. Sure.

PATSY. Geez, can you imagine that, Frankie?

FRANKIE. (*Turns to* HARRY.) Weird, ain't it?

CHARLIE. (*Stands.*) Why don't you ask him about the horses?

PATSY. We thought you was figurin' some parlay. You know, like you have in your book.

ERWIN. No, sir. I have work to do. (*Rises.*) I have fifty more of those to do. How did that one sound? All right?

CHARLIE. (*Pats him.*) That was the nuts. I wish you'd dope out some parlays . . . you know . . . just for fun.

PATSY. (*Knocks* CHARLIE'S *arm down.*) Leave him alone—leave him alone—let him do whatever he wants. (*Seats him down— pushes down.*) You go ahead, Erwin, write some more of them Mother's Day gags. . . . Where's the roll, Frankie? (*Sits.*)

FRANKIE. Here. (*Puts bills on table.*)

CHARLIE. (*Muses.*) You know I like th[ ] (*Sits.*) "At Christmas Tide your hair v[ ] grey."

PATSY. Suppose you run down and w[ ] around and get paid off on the sixth.

FRANKIE. O. K. Patsy. I don't mind at [ ] (*He goes off street door.* MABEL ent[ ] from elevator.*)

PATSY. (MABEL *crosses to* PATSY.) Mab[ ] guess what I got for you. Look. (*Gives [ ] money.*) You can go next door and [ ] your bracelet out of hock.

MABEL. No foolin'. Are you sure if I [ ] it out I won't have to put it back in [ ] morning? I only hocked it yesterday a[ ] I'd feel so funny if I put it back in [ ] morrow.

PATSY. Sugar, you won't ever have to h[ ] that bracelet again. Oh, Mabel, this is [ ] win. Erwin is here to give us a help[ ] hand.

MABEL. Pleased to meet you.

ERWIN. How do you do?

MABEL. (*Sits on* PATSY'S *knees.*) Cha[ ] was telling me about you, how you're go[ ] to fix the races just for us. I think it's [ ] wonderful.

HARRY. Hey, Patsy, how about settin' [ ] up. I'm supposed to work here.

PATSY. Sure, Harry, rye for me, same [ ] Erwin.

CHARLIE. Same here.

MABEL. Rye with plenty of ginger ale[ ] haven't been eatin' regular lately—I d[ ] want to get tight.

PATSY. You're going to eat tonight, Ma[ ]

MABEL. (*Goes to* ERWIN.) Gee, I'm g[ ] you looked us up.

ERWIN. "When I was young and on y[ ] knee—"

MABEL. What?

CHARLIE. Sh-sh.

PATSY. Did you say somethin', Erwin?

WIN. How does that sound?
"When I was young and on your knee
You told a nursery rhyme to me
But now I've grown a man to be
I send my Love in rhyme to Thee."
Writes it down.) Mother's Day Number
*...*venteen.

..BEL. What is that?

..TSY. (*Both rise, cross down right.*) It's
..d of hard to explain. (*Embarrassed to
..ink he is associating with a sentimental
..rse writer.*) That's a sort of a code.
...ise.)

..RRY. There yuh are.

..BEL. Huh!

..TSY. A message.

..BEL. Gee, Patsy, this is swell—it's like
..it's like spies talk in that magazine story
..was readin'— (HARRY *puts drink on bar.*)
..w what was the name of that—

..RRY. Here we are. (*Serves drinks.*)

..TSY. Mabel, how would you like to go
..the Follies tonight?

..BEL. I don't know. Let's go somewheres
..e. There's none of the old crowd in it at
..any more.

..TSY. Bet you could get back if you
..anted to.

..BEL. Do you really think so, Patsy?

..TSY. Sure— (*Pats her hip.*) Take off a
..w pounds—you know—here and there. It
..ould be a cinch. Here you are, Harry.
Gives him bill.) But I got other plans for
..u, Mabel. You don't want to be tied
..wn. How do we know where we'll be—
..ew Orleans, Lexington, Chicago— (HARRY
..gs cash register.*)

..BEL. How do you mean, Patsy? (*Crosses
..*PATSY.*)

..TSY. That depends on what agreement
..e and Erwin can come to. (*Walks to
..reet do'or with* MABEL.) Now you run
..stairs and get your bracelet out and we'll
..lebrate tonight. Just you and me. How
..ould that be? We'll get dressed and have
..nner at Moore's and make a night of it.

MABEL. Get dressed—all right—but this is
the only dress I got.

PATSY. Get another one. (*Pats her behind.
Gives her money.*) Happy days are here
again, huh, Mabel. (MABEL *goes out the
street door.* PATSY *returns to bar.*) She's as
happy as a kid. Buy Erwin another drink,
Harry—on me.

CHARLIE. (*Watching* ERWIN *write.*) How
many of them things do you have to
write?

ERWIN. Fifty more.

CHARLIE. This week?

ERWIN. By tomorrow.

PATSY. Do you think you can do it?

ERWIN. I have to—my job.

PATSY. Job—huh—say, I bet you'll retire
on these ten per cents. (*He crosses—pushes
elevator bell.*)

FRANKIE. (*Runs in.*) I got the sixth.

CHARLIE. The sixth. (*Ad lib.*)

FRANKIE. He come in— (*Tosses bills on
table.*)

PATSY. It ain't true. Look at that, Erwin.
Your brains did that. Don't that make you
excited? (*Sits at the table down left.*)

ERWIN. There's a lot of money there, I
guess. I can see some twenty-dollar bills.

FRANKIE. (HARRY *starts left with drink for
ERWIN and change for* PATSY.) Twenties,
huh? I bet ten each like I said. My Blaze
paid back six-sixty for two so that was
thirty-three dollars each and Rip Van Winkle paid seven-forty for two. That comes
to— (HARRY *sets drink before* ERWIN.)

PATSY. Five times seven-forty.

CHARLIE. (*Excited.*) Thirty-seven . . .

FRANKIE. Altogether it comes to seventy
dollars each.

PATSY. Now you get seven dollars from
me plus what you got before and you get
the same from Frankie and Charlie too.
That's as much as you'd make in a week
writing them Mother's Day Number Fif-
teens. (*Elevator stops.*)

MOSES. Goin' up?

PATSY. You count out the dough, Charlie, I'll be right back. I'm going to celebrate and pay my bill. (*Exits into elevator.*)

CHARLIE. (*Crosses bar.*) That's ten for Frank—ten for Patsy—ten for me. (*Continues this silently as* MABEL *comes in from street.*)

MABEL. (*Enters, sits right.*) I got my bracelet out. (*Holding up arm.*) Hello! Where's Patsy?

CHARLIE. He'll be right back. He went to pay the hotel bill.

MABEL. What bank was all this in?

CHARLIE. Horses.

MABEL. (*Sits and looks at* ERWIN *with genuine admiration. He sips drink.*) You mean you won all this since I left, Erwin?

CHARLIE. This is just from the sixth race.

MABEL. Gee, that must take a lot of nerve —to fix races.

ERWIN. Oh, I don't know.

MABEL. How long did it take you?

ERWIN. About an hour.

MABEL. (*Sits.*) How did you get in this racket, Erwin? On account of Repeal? I'll bet you were making out all right before. I'd never think you were in rackets if I didn't see you here with Patsy and the boys and that roll there. I'll bet you never have to worry about making a living.

FRANKIE. (*Going to bar.*) How about a drink for everybody?

MABEL. Sure.

CHARLIE. O. K.

ERWIN. I don't think I could drink any more.

FRANKIE. I'm buying them. We ought to celebrate.

ERWIN. But I don't feel so good.

MABEL. It wouldn't be any fun if you don't drink too—on account of we'll really be drinking to you—you know what I mean —fixing the races and all that.

ERWIN. All right then. (*Elevator opens*)

FRANKIE. Four drinks.

PATSY. (*Enters from elevator.*) Make five. (*Points to bills.*) How's that look you, Mabel? This mine, Charlie? (*Pickir pile off table.*)

CHARLIE. That's yours.

PATSY. (*Going to* MABEL.) That's fir Mabel, let's see your bracelet. You and n is going to be back in circulation tonigl How's about it?

HARRY. (*Serves drinks.*) Here we are.

MABEL. It feels like old times again, hu Patsy? I was just saying we ought to dri this to Erwin because he's helping us o like this. Come on, Erwin . . . bottoms u (*They all drink.*)

ERWIN. Oh, sure. (*He drinks.*)

PATSY. Sugar, suppose you go along a start to get dolled up, and knock on n door when you're ready.

MABEL. All right, Patsy. Well, goodbye. . (*As she starts to elevator* ERWIN *rises,* tempts to bow, collapses again.*) Oh, Pats I saw a dress in a window I want to sho you later on.

PATSY. Anything you say goes, Mabel . dress, coat, hat . . . I might even name horse after you.

MABEL. Goodbye, Erwin. (*Elevator do closes.*)

PATSY. Say, do you guys realize how luc we are? Twenty-four hours ago we ow ourselves money . . . now look at us . . . got the makings of a million-dollar ba roll. But we got to keep our mouths sh and Erwin has to play along with us. Y hear that, Erwin? (*Drops arm.*) Geez, h passed out.

HARRY. What did you think he was, sponge?

PATSY. Listen, Harry. He's staying he with us tonight. Then he can pick t entries for tomorrow's races, get it?

HARRY. Sure, I get it.

ARLIE. (*Rises and fans* ERWIN *with rac-
sheets.*) Hey, you don't think we'll get
any trouble, do you?

rsy. Trouble? We're doing him a favor.
God, he's been working for fifty cents
ine and here he's already made as much
he would in a week. Ring for the eleva-
, Charlie.

NKIE. But suppose something . . . (ER-
N *topples from chair, they grab him.*) Is
all right? (HARRY *goes to* ERWIN.)

rsy. He's all right. He just passed out.
y Harry?

RRY. Yeah. Yeah. He'll be O. K. He'll
all right.

rsy. (*Catching* HARRY'S *arm.*) Say, you're
t going to say anything about this, are
, Harry?

RRY. Hell, no. I just want you to play
s five bucks for me on the last race. This
the first time I ever came face to face
th a sure thing.

FRANKIE. But suppose somebody finds out
about it?

PATSY. Say, what's the matter with you
guys? You got a yellow streak all of a
sudden? He should be tickled to death.
We're giving him a break. Suppose Leo's
crowd had ever discovered him? He'd
never see his wife again. They'd take him
from track to track like a horse.

CHARLIE. I guess that's right.

PATSY. All we want to do is run up a
bank roll, then to hell with the bookies
. . . I'm going to get myself a stable and
do this thing right.

MOSES. Goin' up.

PATSY. Here, give us a hand, will you,
boys? (*Ad libs.*) Moses, he's a friend of
ours just passed out. He's staying in my
room tonight. (*Ad libs as they put* ERWIN
in the elevator.)

CURTAIN.

ACT TWO

SCENE I

ce: *Ozone Heights.*

me: *The next morning.*

HESTRA *plays "Just a Love Nest" before
tain goes up and as it rises.*

Rise: AUDREY *sits alone, trying not to
. She wipes her eyes, bites her lip, hits
pillow of divan with her fist. The phone
gs. She leaps to her feet and rushes to it.*

DREY. (*In phone.*) Hello. (*Disap-
intedly.*) Oh, yes, good morning, Mrs.
rple. We'd be delighted—at least I think
would—well, I can't ask him just now
e isn't here— Well, he didn't come
me last night—oh, no—nothing wrong
iff.) —only he just didn't come home—
siness of course. . . . He and Mr. Carver
. that's his boss—they have so many
ngs to talk over, I suppose . . . and I'll
him if he comes home today— Oh,
, of course he'll be here—I just slipped.
ank you, Mrs. Marple. (*Hangs up.*)
, Erwin—where are you? (CLARENCE
ers aggressively.)

CLARENCE. Showed up yet? (*She shakes
her head.*) Didn't even phone. (*Shakes her
head.*) Didn't hear from him at all, huh?

AUDREY. (*Between sobs.*) Mrs. Marple
phoned . . .

CLARENCE. Yes?

AUDREY. Invited us to a party, but he may
not even be here. (*Sobs.*)

CLARENCE. Well, if he isn't, I'll go with
you.

AUDREY. Oh, dear. (*Sobs worse.*)

CLARENCE. (*Walks.*) He's the last fellow
in the world I'd expect to do such a thing.

AUDREY. Do what thing?

CLARENCE. But in a way, I always knew
he was that kind.

AUDREY. What are you talking about?

CLARENCE. Did you phone him at the
office?

AUDREY. Erwin doesn't like me to phone his office.

CLARENCE. (*To phone.*) That's just a gag. What's his number? Huh. I can see through that. (*At desk.*) This it?

AUDREY. He won't like it.

CLARENCE. (*Grimly.*) This is just one of the things he isn't going to like. (*In phone.*) Bogardus four six seven five two. I've got quite a few surprising revelations for you.

AUDREY. I don't want any revelations. I just want Erwin.

CLARENCE. (*Sits. In phone.*) I'd like to speak to Mr. Trowbridge—please—Erwin Trowbridge. No? Is that so? . . . Oh, he didn't. I thank you very much—

AUDREY. What did they say?

CLARENCE. (*Rising.*) Mr. Carver isn't there.

AUDREY. Oh, Clarence—I don't care anything about Mr. Carver.

CLARENCE. Neither is Erwin. What's more he didn't come to work at all yesterday.

AUDREY. It's all my fault.

CLARENCE. What do you mean? It's all your fault?

AUDREY. I shouldn't have bought those dresses. I knew he wouldn't like it.

CLARENCE. Oh, what right has a worm like that to ·object anyhow?

AUDREY. (*With tearful dignity.*) Erwin is not a worm—I don't like you to say such things about him.

CLARENCE. I told you not to marry him. Didn't I? Remember what I said to you? I said—"Don't marry him." You were stubborn. All right. I won't say anything about it. It's all past now. You could have married Charley Blanchard, don't forget that—I spotted him as a comer at the first Kiwanis luncheon and where is he now? Seventy-five dollars a week and one per cent of all sales on his hardware accessories in greater New York and northern New Jersey. And where is Erwin?

AUDREY. (*Sobbing.*) I don't know—I wish I did— Oh, Erwin!

CLARENCE. I'll tell you then—he's left y«

AUDREY. He has not.

CLARENCE. I had a feeling there was sor thing funny about him when he went « of here. He wouldn't look me in the e

AUDREY. That wasn't it at all.

CLARENCE. He kept turning away from ı

AUDREY. He doesn't like to look at you he told me so.

CLARENCE. I might have known he'd tr us like that. I help him along—I let h have a house on easy payment plan— everything I can for him—does he come me with a good thing? No—just quie makes his little cleaning and then leaves all flat.

AUDREY. What are you talking about?

CLARENCE. Brass Monkey won yesterda

AUDREY. Who's Brass Monkey?

CLARENCE. The horse— He had a sure ‹ That little book of his was full of sure ti He's been cleaning up. (*Crossing to .* DREY.) All the time he's been playing p« and talking about how he couldn't aff« things, he's been rich—he's had winni enough in the last few weeks to spend rest of his life loafing— He's got depo in a dozen banks—when I saw that li book yesterday it all came across me clea in fact I went down to the bookies in afternoon to put a thousand dollars Brass Monkey and then I was afraid some trickery and I changed my mi God damn it.

AUDREY. Why Clarence, I never heard swear before.

CLARENCE. But the worm had his roll that race—he had every cent—and cleaned up and you'll never see him aga

AUDREY. You don't understand him—y don't understand him at all.

CLARENCE. Why couldn't he have come me as man to man and told me about That would have been the thing to d« No, but he's selfish—keeps it all to him —wouldn't look me in the eye—I kr something was wrong— Eight to one paid—but that worm held out on me,

DREY. He's not a worm. (*Violent.*) You
it up. You treat him awful. (*Telephone*
gs. AUDREY *crosses to it.*) And I don't
me him for getting mad—and he never
ed living in your old house anyhow.
JDREY *answers it.*) Yes?—Oh, oh Mr.
rver—yes, this is Mrs. Trowbridge— No,
haven't. I don't know.

RENCE. Do you want me to talk to
1?

REY. He had the verses with him—a
ig store? . . .

RENCE. What did he say?

REY. Yes, of course I will. (*Hangs up.*)
. Carver is awful mad (*Rises.*) because
verses aren't there yet. He says Erwin
phoned him yesterday from a drug store

and said he didn't feel well— (*Looks up
suddenly.*) He's lying in some hospital—
sick—or in the back of some drug store.
(*Picks up phone.*)

CLARENCE. What are you going to do?

AUDREY. (*In phone.*) Give me the Ozone
Heights Police Department.

CLARENCE. Audrey!

AUDREY. Leave me alone. This is Mrs.
Erwin Trowbridge. Number one Dobbins
Drive. . . . I wish to report a missing
person . . . yes, my husband . . . he didn't
come home last night.

BLACKOUT.

Orchestra plays "All Alone."

SCENE II

ce: The hotel room.

ne: Noon next day. Room in the Lavil-
• Hotel. Door to elevator and hall up
re to left. Door to bathroom up stage
it. Bed up stage right. Window above
d of bed. Night table next to bed. Chif-
be down stage right. Closet down stage
. Telephone on table down stage left.
uirs, etc.

Rise: ERWIN is discovered in bed. He has
union suit. He sits up and groans.
RLIE enters from bathroom with wet
el.

RLIE. (*Crossing to* ERWIN.) How are
?

IN. Where did everybody go?

RLIE. (*Places wet towel on* ERWIN'S
head.) Don't worry—they'll be back.
w's that feel?

IN. Pretty good—but I don't feel so
d.

NKIE. (*Enters from door with tomato
e.* PATSY *follows him a beat later.*) Here,
ik this.

SY. Drink it. (ERWIN *is bewildered.*)
nk all you can.

IN. I don't think I can drink anything.
hs.) Oh, my head. What are all those
ers on the floor?

CHARLIE. (*Picking them up.*) Those jingles
of yours. Don't you remember? You wrote
half the night.

FRANKIE. (*Picking too.*) Three-four-five.

ERWIN. How many did I do?

CHARLIE. I got twenty-two here.

FRANKIE. Six-seven-eight.

PATSY. There's about ten more in the bathroom.

ERWIN. I must have written nearly the
whole sixty-seven.

CHARLIE. You certainly did.

ERWIN. I don't remember anything about
it.

CHARLIE. You kept me awake the whole
night.

PATSY. Feel better now?

ERWIN. (*Nods.*) Say, I must have gotten
drunk. (*Looking around.*) Where am I?

PATSY. You're in the Lavillere Hotel. You
passed out on us last night. We had to
bring you up here.

ERWIN. What time is it?

CHARLIE. It's after twelve o'clock.

ERWIN. What! Thought you said it was daybreak. . . . I must go to the office. (*Starts to get out of bed.* PATSY *pushes him back, giving* CHARLIE *a dirty look.*)

CHARLIE. You can't get up now.

FRANKIE. Easy now, pal.

PATSY. You can't go to the office like that. You look like the devil. You'll lose your job.

ERWIN. But Mr. Carver must have these verses today.

PATSY. He'll have 'em today. One of us will take 'em around. There's nothin' to worry about— (*Winks at boys.*) —I just had him on the phone. He said if you don't feel good—you can stay in bed all day.

ERWIN. I guess I was in a bad way—you see I never drink. Where are my clothes?

CHARLIE. In the bathroom.

ERWIN. (*Looks at bathroom.*) I must go in there a minute. I feel better now that I know the verses are practically done. Do they look all right? (*Sits up.*)

CHARLIE. They're swell. I wish I could say things like that in poetry . . . especially if you're with a gal. It makes it romantic-like—sort of breaks the ice.

ERWIN. Oh, yes.

CHARLIE. You know, you don't want to start right off and say, "How about it, Baby?"

ERWIN. You better get a big envelope and put all the verses in and take them personally to Mr. Carver—he's waiting for them.

PATSY. You take them, Frankie.

FRANKIE. Where is the joint?

ERWIN. The Holly Cheer Greeting Company Incorporated in the Wedgewood Building. You walk down Sixth Avenue—

FRANKIE. I know where it is. I used to know a tomato on the tenth floor.

ERWIN. Our office is Nine Hundred and Nine.

PATSY. (*Going to window.*) O. K. N get dressed and wash up and you'll f like a new man.

ERWIN. Frankie, be sure Mr. Carver g the verses himself.

PATSY. Don't worry about it.

ERWIN. Oh, but it's very important.

PATSY. Listen, you're going to make me money dopin' horses than you ever ma Now go on and get under a cold show so you'll be in shape to pick the hor today. (*Gets out of bed, goes to bathroc door.*)

ERWIN. (*Suddenly. Coming to* PATS Horses? Oh, I don't think I'll have tin I have to call my wife and I must see M Carver later on—

CHARLIE. You can do all that afterwar

PATSY. Go on, get straightened up. Mea time I'll count out that money I owe y

ERWIN. Money?

PATSY. A hundred and twelve dollars— think it is. Yeah, that's right.

ERWIN. You owe me?

PATSY. Certainly. Don't you recall agreement? We said we'd give you per cent of all we won.

ERWIN. I remember something like th (*Sits on foot of bed stage right.*) . . . bu thought you said eight dollars and f cents . . . you mean I made one hund and twelve dollars—on horses!

CHARLIE. That's right.

ERWIN. Well — Gee — I — you mean i picked them again today I might make t much again—?

FRANKIE. Maybe more. (*Sits end bed n* ERWIN.)

ERWIN. But even that much again. T would be two hundred and twenty-f dollars . . . why with that I could Clarence to go to Hell.

CHARLIE. Who's Clarence?

ERWIN. My brother-in-law.

ANKIE. You could tell a lot of people.

WIN. It's just Clarence that I've been nking about.

rsy. Then you mean you'll pick them?

WIN. Yes, (*Rises.*) I—I'd like to very ıch. I'll get dressed. (*Goes into bath-m, starts to close door.*)

rsy. We're set.

ANKIE. Sure. (*Sits.*)

ARLIE. (*Walks to desk.*) I don't know. wouldn't be too certain. I'm worried.

rsy. You're always crabbing. If it's nin' you're afraid of wet feet; if it's nin', the sun gets in your eyes.

ANKIE. What you worried about now? erything is going fine, ain't it?

ARLIE. That's the trouble. Everything going too good. I'm worried. How do we ow? (*Turns.*) For instance, how long it es him to dope 'em out? Maybe he has work on 'em for a couple of weeks ahead time.

rsy. (*Alarmed, goes to bathroom and ens door.*) Say—

WIN. Huh!

rsy. Oh, excuse me—say, how long does take you to dope 'em out? (ERWIN *mum-s.*) Oh. O. K. (*Shuts door and turns to others triumphantly. Sits arm chair.*) out an hour. We got plenty of time.

ANKIE. There's some good races, too.

ARLIE. If he can only pick 'em like yes-day. (MABEL *enters.*)

BEL. (*Crosses, kisses* PATSY, *sits on end bed.*) Hello, I didn't think you'd be up early, Pats.

rsy. Hello, sugar.

BEL. Where's the boy friend?

ANKIE. Gettin' dressed—

rsy. Say, here's another one of them ses. (*Reads it.*) Listen, fellows, do you ow we're associatin' with a genius?

BEL. What's that?

PATSY. Poetry. Erwin's poetry

MABEL. Oh, Gee, I thought he was a guy who fixed horse races.

PATSY. He does. He just does poetry for a hobby.

FRANKIE. Yeah, I better get those around for him. Room Nine-O-Nine he said. We don't want him to lose his job. (*Crosses to desk.*)

PATSY. You know, I feel sorry for that guy. Slavin' everyday. Doin' the same things over and over.

FRANKIE. I can't find a big envelope. (*Looking through desk.*)

CHARLIE. (*At desk.*) They have 'em down-stairs.

PATSY. Listen to this:
"Why was it that I chose to roam
Cross Land and Sea so far from home?
If that be Life— My Mother Dear,
I send this card of Love and Cheer."
Mother's Day Number Thirty-seven. That touches you—you know that—right here.

MABEL. Yeah . . . like when you're seein' a good sad movie . . . geez—

PATSY. You know, this Erwin guy ain't bein' appreciated.

CHARLIE. You mean he's better than he is?

PATSY. I mean he's better than forty bucks . . . do you know any other guys who could sit down and write them gems for forty bucks a week?

FRANKIE. Well, I guess there is some guys . . .

PATSY. You don't know any off hand?

FRANKIE. No.

PATSY. That's just it. We ought to do somethin'. (*Crosses to window.*)

MABEL. Like what?

PATSY. (*Crosses up right.*) Like somethin', anyway. It gets me sore to think a nice guy like him is workin' for a guy like this here fellow he's tellin' about all the time—J. G. Carver. Look up the Holly Cheer Greeting Company. I don't know Mr. Carver, but he's probably a louse. . . .

CHARLIE. What are you goin' to do, anyways? (*Crossing and sitting on bed.*)

PATSY. I'm goin' to get Erwin a raise. I feel for him like my own brother. That's the trouble with people in this world—they get a good thing like him and they take advantage of it.

FRANKIE. Give me Bogardus Four six seven five two. . . . I'll get it for you.

PATSY. Let me have it Let me talk to . . . Mr. Carver . . . just say it's important . . . Hello, Carver . . . this is a very good friend of Mr. Erwin Trowbridge . . . in fact, I'm his manager . . . since yesterday . . . Oh, they're all written . . . they're gems . . . that's what they are . . . well, before I sent them around I thought we'd discuss terms. Those verses are the best verses I have ever read and I've read a lot of verses . . . what I thought was this . . . we might as well talk man to man . . . you're gettin' away with murder . . . forty bucks a week . . . Yeah . . . yeah . . . that's what I call a steal . . . Hello . . . hello . . . he hung up . . . Is that polite? (*Crosses right and turns.*) Is that the way to talk to me that's manager of a poet practically?

CHARLIE. Maybe one of us should go down and punch him in the nose.

FRANKIE. (*Going to* CHARLIE.) No—let's not start any fights . . . not till we make some money.

PATSY. I don't like him. (*Sits arm chair.*) It ain't what he said to me, you understand, but he said for Erwin to go to Hell too.

FRANKIE. (*Sits at desk.*) It looks like Erwin stayed up all night for nothin'.

PATSY. Like Hell he has. The world should see art like that . . . those gems should be put in bar-rooms . . . railroad stations . . . on calendars . . . wait, I got it.

FRANKIE. We ought to have somethin' because if Erwin finds out I haven't taken—

PATSY. Liebowitz!

MABEL. The printer.

PATSY. Jake Liebowitz who did all the classy postal cards for that smoker last month.

FRANKIE. He prints lots of stuff.

PATSY. Suppose it cost us a hundred buc[k] . . . get a couple o' guys to go around s[ ] 'em to factories, clubs, the Y.M.C.A. . . the Y.W.C.A. . . . the Y.M.H.A. and [ ] the railroad stations then . . . railroad s[ ] tions! (*Crossing left.*) Frankie, have y[ ] ever been in a washroom in a railro[ ] station?

FRANKIE. Sure. Haven't you?

PATSY. Lot of times. Well, in those r[ ] road stations . . . not only railroads, [ ] all over . . . you've seen those verses li[ ] . . . "A man's ambition must be small [ ] write his name . . ." (*At phone.*) Kitty . [ ] Patsy . . . tell Moses to come right up h[ ] and bring a big envelope. (*Hangs up.*)

MABEL. . . . and the one about sittin' a[ ] thinkin'.

PATSY. Sure. Well, nobody's thought [ ] commercialize that kind of poetry . [ ] they're gems. That's what that guy can [ ] If he can write serious stuff like he [ ] here, he can write funny stuff too.

FRANKIE. Gee, that's a swell idea. (*Kn[ ] on the door.*)

CHARLIE. Come in. (MOSES *enters.*)

FRANKIE. I'll bet he never thought of t[ ]

MOSES. This all right, Mr. Patsy?

PATSY. Yeah. That's what I want.

FRANKIE. Here, give it to me.

PATSY. Here you are, Moses. Frankie, t[ ] those around to Jake Liebowitz, I'll [ ] him and tell him you're coming.

FRANKIE. O. K. I'll shoot right over.

PATSY. Come around later and I'll g[ ] you a horse. Pennsylvania six seven ei[ ] one one.

MOSES. If it's all the same to you, [ ] Patsy, I'd sooner have a number.

PATSY. Mr. Erwin only has horses.

MOSES. All right then, I guess I'll have [ ] take a horse. (*Exits.*)

TSY. (*In phone.*) Hello . . . Jake? This Patsy. How are you? . . . Well, say ten, you ain't so busy . . . yeah, I know . but listen, I want a special job done . verses . . . no, not singin' verses . . . etry verses . . . you know—"Roses are d" . . . yeah . . . shiney paper, with lace aybe. They'll be there in a couple of inutes. Don't leave before you get them. K. (*Hangs up.*)

ABEL. If you're going to do this, what's win going to get out of it?

TSY. All of it . . . we're only helping m out.

ABEL. Oh, like bein' in business for him- f, huh?

TSY. Sure. All he has to do is write 'em. hen it gets going good . . . he just stays me and picks horses and the verses sell emselves . . . because they're good.

ABEL. That's what I call givin' him a eak.

WIN. (*Enters and sees* MABEL.) Oh, good orning.

ABEL. Hello. I hope you feel better than sterday.

WIN. Well, I guess I do. Maybe I ought go out and get a little breakfast. (*Cross- g to bureau.*)

TSY. (*Going to* ERWIN.) I was just talk- g to Mr. Carver on the phone.

WIN. You were?

TSY. I don't think that he likes you so uch. I could tell by his voice.

WIN. Why, what's happened?

TSY. Somethin' good . . . we're settin' u up in business on your own.

WIN. But what about Mr. Carver?

TSY. To Hell with him. He don't ap- eciate you.

WIN. Doesn't he like my verses?

TSY. I told him I wouldn't even let him e them.

WIN. Why not? What right have you to a thing like that? I'll lose my job. Where e my verses?

PATSY. Wait a minute, Erwin, this is for your good.

ERWIN. (*Rushing past* PATSY.) Where are they? Where are my verses?

PATSY. (*Clutching* ERWIN's *arm.*) Listen, Erwin, we sent them over to Liebowitz.

ERWIN. Who is Liebowitz?

PATSY. He's one of our best friends. He's going to print your verses so they'll be sold all over the country. See.

ERWIN. Please don't. You can't do this to me . . . you fellows might think this is funny, but I'm going to lose my job . . . you don't know what it means to have a job, fifty-two weeks in the year—forty dol- lars a week.

PATSY. Don't you know you rate more than that? Don't you know that big crook is cheating Hell out of you? Here you are starving along on forty a week, while that big piece of salami is living high with high offices in the Wedgewood Building. Sure. And he made it all off you. Now Liebowitz is going to print your verses so that every home . . .

ERWIN. I don't want Liebowitz to print my verses. All I want is to work for Mr. Carver.

PATSY. But he's a louse.

ERWIN. He is not. Don't you say that about Mr. Carver . . . he's the only boss I ever had and I like to work for him. Get me back my verses. (FRANKIE *enters.*)

FRANKIE. Well, everything's O. K.

PATSY. Frankie, you'll have to get the verses back.

FRANKIE. What the Hell is this?

PATSY. You're careless, that's all.

FRANKIE. I can't get 'em back now.

ERWIN. What's happened to my verses?

FRANKIE. Nothing's happened to them. Liebowitz was waitin' for me at the door when I got there and he said, "Congratulate me, Frankie, my daughter is having a baby at the Beth Israel Hospital and my son is being confirmed at the synagogue . . ." so

I congratulated him and he took the verses with him in a taxicab. Say, it's gettin' late, don't you think Erwin ought to start pickin' the horses.

ERWIN. Horses . . I can't even think of horses.

PATSY. (*Going to* FRANKIE.) Erwin can't pick any horses until he gets the verses back.

FRANKIE. Well, what the Hell are we going to do about it?

PATSY. We gotta do something. We gotta get 'em back.

ERWIN. Working hard all my life . . . trying to get some place, trying to build a reputation. (*Sits in chair right.*)

MABEL. (*Rises.*) Don't worry, Erwin. It'll be all right. Boys, you got to find Liebowitz . . . it's a cinch he's in one of two places, his daughter is havin' a baby at the Beth Israel Hospital and his son is being confirmed at the synagogue.

FRANKIE. But suppose he's gone to his home? He said he had to get dressed.

PATSY. I'll take care of that. Mabel is right. We got to find him. We got to keep Erwin happy so his mind can work good and pick the horses. Frankie, you go to the Beth Israel Hospital. And Charlie, you look for him in the synagogue. Come on, boys, get moving . . . and don't forget the name, Frankie, Beth Israel Hospital.

CHARLIE. Why should I have to go to the synagogue? All right. If you say so that makes it right. (*Goes.*)

FRANKIE. Beth Israel . . . Beth Israel . . . (*Goes.*)

PATSY. There now . . . we'll get the verses right back, see, Erwin. . . . Wait till I look up where he lives.

MABEL. You see, Erwin, now there isn't anything to worry about. (*Going to* ERWIN.) Erwin, say look, Patsy . . . he's all pale . . . Erwin . . . I think he's fainted or something.

PATSY. Fainted? Geez.

MABEL. Should I phone down for a doctor?

PATSY. Doctor? No! Give me a hand. P[ut] him on the bed. We don't want any docto[r] around. (*They take him over to the bed[.]* We'll get him a drink—a couple o' drin[k] will fix him up. (*Rushes to telephone.*)

MABEL. Maybe that's all he needs—just [a] pick-me-up.

PATSY. (*In telephone.*) Hello—get me t[he] bar. (ERWIN *opens eyes for a moment.*)

MABEL. Oh, Patsy, look, he just opened h[is] eyes.

PATSY. Say, his health is important now— remember that—we got to take good ca[re] of him.

MABEL. You bet—

PATSY. (*In phone.*) Hello, Harry—Pats[y.] Are you very busy? Well, bring up a bott[le] of rye right away. Yeah. (*Hangs up. Pic[ks] up telephone book.*)

MABEL. (*To* ERWIN.) How do you fe[el] now? (ERWIN *nods.*) Sure—sure, just [a] teensie hangover, that's all.

PATSY. Sure, he'll be all right— Ge[e] there's about a million Liebowitz's—Ab[ra]ham—Benjamin—David—Herman—Isa[ac] —Jacob— (*Picks up receiver.*) Chelsea thr[ee] seven four four.

HARRY. (*Enters.*) You sounded like y[ou] was in a hurry. (*Looks at* ERWIN.) Ge[e] ain't he come to yet?

PATSY. Yeah, but he passed out again.

MABEL. He's about half to, now—but I'[m] makin' him rest.

HARRY. Do you think he can stand anoth[er] drink?

PATSY. Sure, that's just what— Hel[lo] Jake—

HARRY. (*To* MABEL.) Got a corkscrew?

MABEL. Yeah. (*Goes into bathroom.*)

PATSY. Jake, I gotta have those verses ba[ck] —never mind why— Oh—well, how lo[ng] you goin' to be there? —The Hell with t[he] baby. This is a matter of life and death[.] I'll be right over for them— Wait for m[e.] (*Hangs up; grabs hat.*) Work on hi[m]

rry—he's got to pick those horses. Mabel,
n't let Erwin get out of here and don't
  him call anybody up till I get back.
ɪTSY *exits.* HARRY *pours drink.*)

BEL. (*Bringing another glass from bath-
ɔm.*) Pour me one, too, Harry. I feel
ɪd of faint myself. (HARRY *pours one for
BEL.*) I never seen so much excitement.
rinks it down.)

ʀRY. I wish he'd hurry up and come to.
want another horse today.

ʷIN. (*Groans.*) Oh—

ʙEL. Quick, Harry!

ʀRY. (*Forces drink down* ERWIN'S
oat.) Here, drink this.

ʷIN. (*Sitting up.*) Audrey! . . . (*Sees
ɪrry.*) Oh, gosh.

ʀRY. Now, how do you feel?

ʷIN. (*Rises.*) I don't know.

ʀRY. Better get him under the covers.
ɪt his pants off.

ʷIN. (*Alarmed.*) What?

ʙEL. (*Going to* ERWIN.) Sure. (*Starts
unbutton his pants.*)

ʷIN. Hey, don't—no, no, no. Please.

ʙEL. What's the matter?

ʷIN. It tickles.

ʀRY. Better let me do it. (*Pulls his pants
—puts ERWIN *in bed. Phone rings.*)

ʷIN. I'm all right.

ʀRY. Sure you are.

ʙEL. (*Answering phone.*) Hello . . .
ɑh . . . he's here—well he just got here—
'ʾs helpin' me—he's—all right—I'll tell
m. (*Hangs up.*) You got some customers
 the bar, Harry—you better go down.

ʀRY. (*Tucking* ERWIN *in.*) Who was
ɑt?

ʙEL. Mac.

ʀRY. Ah—nuts to him. (*To* ERWIN.)
 hat do you think of Mad Hatter in the
 st race today, Erwin?

ERWIN. I don't know.

HARRY. Well, take your time. But don't
forget me, will you?—and if there's any
little thing I can do for you, you let me
know.

MABEL. You better hop down there or
Mac'll be yappin' some more. (MABEL *goes
to dresser, gets drink, crosses to bed.*)

HARRY. That damn bar—it's a nuisance.
(*Exits.*)

MABEL. Gee, it's awful nice of you to stay
here and help Patsy like you been doin'.

ERWIN. I was desperate or I wouldn't have
done such a thing.

MABEL. But if you know how much we
liked to have you here—I don't mean just
the boys, I mean more particularly just
myself personally.

ERWIN. Give me back my pants.

MABEL. What's the matter?

ERWIN. I ought to call up my wife.

MABEL. Not just now, Erwin—I don't
want you to get out of bed. You might
faint again.

ERWIN. I ought to call her. I've punished
her enough. She'll be worried.

MABEL. But listen now, pet, just wait till
Patsy gets back, will you? 'Cause I promised
him I wouldn't let you call anybody.

ERWIN. Yes, but I haven't been home all
night.

MABEL. She must be used to that.

ERWIN. Oh, no, she isn't.

MABEL. You're a good deal different than
most men then. God knows Patsy's liable to
disappear for a week at a time. But he's
awfully good to me though— You ought
to see all the swell things he gave me when
I quit the Follies for him! . . . Two weeks
later they tried a four horse parlay at Sara-
toga and we lost everything—I didn't have
a nightgown left, to my name.

ERWIN. Oh! That must have been terrible.

MABEL. Well, it's just the breaks. Now, it
looks as though things is brightening up
again since you come into my life.

ERWIN.   Where's my pencil—quick— (*He writes.*)

MABEL.   What is it? You got the first race? (ERWIN *shakes his head.*) Let's see. (*She takes the paper and reads.*)
   "My soul was sad as darkest night.
   But now the world seems fair and bright
   Because you came so true and fine.
   Oh, stay and be my Valentine."

ERWIN.   Valentine's Day Number One. It doesn't do any hurt to get ahead of schedule.

MABEL.   Yeah. If you're ahead then you're a fast worker, is that it?

ERWIN.   What?

MABEL.   Never mind. (*Reads.*) "Stay and be my Valentine." Gee, that's wonderful! . . . I'm crazy about poetry.

ERWIN.   I don't get much time to write real poetry. I've been so busy with my Mother's Day verses.

MABEL.   Oh . . . gee, I haven't heard from Mom in a long time—of course I haven't written to her lately—maybe I ought to send her one of them . . . a verse . . . it might make her feel good . . . you see, I ain't sure she's my mother. (*Business of taking drink.*)

ERWIN.   Oh, but she'd feel good anyway.

MABEL.   I guess so. I haven't seen her since I came to New York to go on the stage.

ERWIN.   Did you really used to be on the stage?

MABEL.   Yeah, I used to be in the Follies. I'd like to get back in show business but Patsy doesn't think I look as good as I used to. (*Stands up and pats her hips.*) Don't you think I could get back if I worked hard?

ERWIN.   Sure, I'll bet you could. Of course I've never seen a Follies girl close to before —only from the balcony. You look all right to me.

MABEL.   Do I really, Erwin?

ERWIN.   Why yes—yes—you're beautiful.

MABEL.   Gee, I like you . . . just think— maybe I have read one of your poems in a magazine—like a movie magazine—and

here I am standing talking to you . . guess that's what you call romantic. G I'm pretty jealous of your wife, you kn it?

ERWIN.   You are? Why?

MABEL.   Havin' you all to herself—I'm j thinkin' how wonderful it would be travel around the country with you— tenin' to your poetry and helpin' you ma a lot of money bettin' on the horses.

ERWIN.   Oh, but I wouldn't bet—t would spoil everything.

MABEL.   Well, I mean—just enough for fur coat and stuff like that.

ERWIN.   But I don't think I could tell wh ones are going to win if I ever started b ting on them.

MABEL.   Well anyhow, you could make lot of money if you wanted to just wi words for songs like they have in sho . . . lyrics.

ERWIN.   You think so?

MABEL.   Sure. Say, lots of times I sa words in the chorus that wasn't half good as that.

ERWIN.   Did you sing in the Follies?

MABEL.   Yeah— did a specialty once. Wa me to show you? (*He nods.*) Say, I'd anything for you. (*Goes to radio.*) 'Cau I'm crazy about poetry, that's why. (*Tur radio on. Tries a few steps.*) I may not so good till I get limbered up. (*Radio beg to talk.*) I'll see if I can get my dress off I guess among friends it's all right, hu (*Starts to take off dress.*)

ANNOUNCER.   Two tablets daily and assu yourself a perfect health and a happy c age— The Press Radio News Report w be brought to you at five P. M. At t time we present Ivan Aronson and jazzy cossacks in a program of dance mu —"Take it away Ivan!" (*Music.*)

ERWIN.   What is? (MABEL *crosses righ* Maybe I ought to telephone my wife.

MABEL.   Don't you want to see my danc

ERWIN.   Yes, I do.

EL. (*Gets music.*) Here we go. Now, ⸱re the audience. I come out, you see, ⸱ a big spot on me. (*Dances.*) The other ⸱are jealous 'cause I got a specialty— ⸱ *kicks, exposing all.*) Of course this ⸱st a rough idea—

⸱N. Say, that's good!

EL. This is my finish. (*Whirls across ⸱. Turns off radio. Leans against bu-⸱*)

⸱N. What's the matter?

EL. (*Breathless.*) Out of practice . . . ⸱n't done this for so long . . . got dizzy.

⸱N. (*Jumps out of bed and helps ⸱L to bed where she sits.*) I'll give you ⸱ink. (*Pours drink.* PATSY *enters while ⸱N is giving* MABEL *a drink. He stands ⸱or and looks. He has the verses in his ⸱.*)

⸱Y. What the Hell's this?

⸱N. Have you got my verses?

⸱. Yeah.

⸱N. She was doin' a dance—and all of ⸱dden—she got dizzy.

⸱. Oh yeah.

⸱N. Yes.

⸱. . (*Walks slowly toward* MABEL.) ⸱get your dress on and go back to your ⸱.

⸱L. What's the matter, Patsy?

⸱. I said get your dress on and go ⸱ to your room.

⸱L. He wanted to phone his wife ⸱— (*She rises and takes dress from ⸱*

⸱. All right, never mind the lip— ⸱ack to your room. (*As* MABEL *backs ⸱ door.*) You're just good and lucky ⸱'t take a poke at you. Go on.

⸱L. But, Patsy—

⸱. Get out. Get out before I kick ⸱ teeth in—you crooked little punk.

⸱L. Geez, you never talked to me like ⸱ before. (*She goes out almost in tears ⸱ng dress.*)

ERWIN. I hope you don't think—(PATSY *tears verses.*) Hey, stop that—

PATSY. Get those on and take yourself **out** of here.

ERWIN. Hey, my verses!

PATSY. (*Throws pants at him.*) Get your pants on and get out of here before I lose my temper . . . you double-crossin' little . . .

ERWIN. My verses! (*He goes to bathroom; locks door.*) (PATSY, *in a rage, tears verses some more.* CHARLIE *and* FRANKIE *enter together.*)

CHARLIE. Hey, what the Hell did you do to Mabel? She's cryin' in the hall.

FRANKIE. Geez, I never seen a girl cry so much.

PATSY. I didn't do a thing to her, but I should have. (*Points toward bathroom, keeps one verse to tear.*) Can you imagine?

FRANKIE. What?

PATSY. And me thinkin' he was a sap.

CHARLIE. Well what's happened?

PATSY. What the Hell do you think?

FRANKIE. (*Crossing to center.*) She said she was just tryin' to be nice to him till you got back.

PATSY. Yeah. Nice is right. Took three weeks and a diamond bracelet to get her that nice to me.

CHARLIE. Well, you told her to hold him didn't you?

FRANKIE. Yeah—maybe she didn't like it no better than you did. Maybe she just seen her duty, that's all.

PATSY. Aw—it's my fault, I suppose, for leavin' them alone together.

CHARLIE. No, but you can trust Mabel— geez, I never could get nowhere with her—

PATSY. What?

CHARLIE. I mean—if I'd tried. No, you just mistook the looks of things.

FRANKIE. Where's Erwin?

PATSY. In there.

CHARLIE. What didja do to him?

PATSY. I told him to get dressed and get the Hell out of here.

FRANKIE. (*Crossing up to door.*) He ain't gone yet, is he?

PATSY. No. But he will as soon as he gets dressed.

CHARLIE. How about the horses for today?

PATSY. We'll select our own.

CHARLIE. (*Closes in.*) And lose our shirts! Now listen, wise guy, he's just as much ours as he is yours.

FRANKIE. (*Coming down to* PATSY.) That's what I say. You can't throw him out—just because you think your girl happened to go for him. And you ain't even sure—you couldn't prove it in a court of law.

PATSY. How would you feel if your girl happened to do that?

FRANKIE. To do what?—how do you know she did anything?—and suppose she did— what I mean is—well, Gee—you know, a guy like Erwin. That wouldn't be much of anything. (PATSY *slams chair and crosses left.*)

CHARLIE. Sure— Gee, you don't mean to tell me you're worried about a guy like him.

PATSY. Worried? What's that got to do with it? God! there's such a thing like decency, ain't there? It don't look right to me to come back and find some guy in his underpants passin' my girl drinks—it don't look right.

CHARLIE. She was just stallin' for time. (PATSY *paces back and forth.*)

FRANKIE. (*Following him.*) Sure, she was just trying to keep him from phoning his wife. Geez, she was willin' to come through for you and you don't even appreciate it. Ain't that the kind of a girl you want— ain't that loyalty, huh?

CHARLIE. What more do you want? She's always played ball with you.

PATSY. Yeah—but—

CHARLIE. What more do you want? S only tryin' to keep this guy on the so's you can make enough money to a house and settle down with her.

PATSY. Yeah?

CHARLIE. That's what she said.

FRANKIE. And besides, Harry helped his pants off, you know that, don't you

PATSY. No.

CHARLIE. Sure. That don't sound very sual to me.

FRANKIE. You sap. You ought to be bu right in the nose for makin' her cry way.

PATSY. Was she really crying?

CHARLIE. Was she cryin'— Geez!

PATSY. (*Goes right to phone.*) Hel give me Mabel's room. (FRANKIE *drink.* CHARLIE *sees verses on floor, them up.*)

CHARLIE. What the Hell happened to verses?

PATSY. Oh, I got sore. . . . Hello, M . . . Now listen, honey, stop crying. Well, I didn't mean it—but I couldn't it—you know how I feel about you I just didn't like the looks of things. Well, it did look bad to me when I in. . . . Now listen, I want you to dry eyes and forget all about it . . . Yeah I'll tell you what I want to do. . . . Put on that pretty dress I bought you terday and go out and look at apartn . . . All right, look at a house, wha Hell do I care . . . Papa wouldn't you that way, it's just 'cause Papa you.

CHARLIE. Papa gives me a pain in hang up, will you, you said enough

PATSY. (*Hangs up.*) Gee, she *was* c

FRANKIE. Listen, boys, quit foolin' a about women and all that sort of tr let's get down to something import now, how about those horses?

CHARLIE. Yeah, it's after one o'clock

. Aw, it only takes him about an

LIE. Well, we ought to get him start-
Bathroom door opens. ERWIN *enters,*
s to bureau. Puts on coat.)

KIE. Hey, where you goin'?

N. I'm goin' to the office.

KIE. (*Rushing to* ERWIN. *Shocked.*)
ou wouldn't do a thing like that!

N. (*Heading for* PATSY.) Where's my
?

IE. (*Stops him.*) No, but wait a
e—let's talk it over, that's all.

N. (*Passing him.*) I haven't time.

. Now, listen, Erwin, I'm sorry I
to you the way I did. It did look
e bad—but I'm goin' to square every-
I just been talking to Mabel.

. (*To* PATSY.) You ought to be
ed of yourself. She's too good for

. It's all right pal, it's all right—
just forgot myself.

. Where'd you put my verses?

IE. After all, Erwin, you got nothing
t Frankie and me, have you?

. No, no, I haven't, but—

IE. Geez, we nursed you back to
and everything like you was a baby
—

You wouldn't walk out on us after
ay we took care of you. (*Takes him*
els.) Listen, Erwin, didn't you ever
our temper?

. Yes, I did.

Well, that's me—and I'm sorry. If
alk out on us now the boys will hold
inst me for the rest of my life.
say I insulted you and that's why
ft us.

I have to get to the office. I'm late
nd Mr. Carver is going to be up-
aybe he won't even give me my job
ter the way you talked to him—

PATSY. (*Tough.*) He'll give it to you, if
I have to go down and—

CHARLIE. Nix, nix. (FRANKIE *goes up*
right.)

PATSY. We'll buy the joint and let you
run it.

ERWIN. I don't want to run it—I just want
to work for Mr. Carver. Anyhow, I have
to go and explain to him.

CHARLIE. Couldn't you just dope out the
horses before you go?

ERWIN. No.

FRANKIE. I'm disappointed in you, Erwin,
I thought we could trust you. I certainly
did.

ERWIN. (*Worried.*) Well, I'd like to help
you. . . .

PATSY. (*Acting the martyr while the others*
gesture encouragements.) It's all right,
Erwin—I must give you your ten per cent
before you go. (*Counts out money.*)

ERWIN. What, Well—I—

PATSY. If you feel like letting us down I
wouldn't want to be the one to interfere.
Here you are. A hundred and twelve bucks!
Sorry it ain't more, but I thought we was
going to have longer to work on it. Might
have got up into some real coin if you
would have stayed with us today.

CHARLIE. Yes, I guess your share today
would have been a thousand dollars or so.

FRANKIE. Yeah—it's too bad. (*Knock.*)

PATSY. (*Tough.*) Who is it?

MABEL. (*Sticks her head in.*) Did you say
come in?

PATSY. (*Sweet loud kiss.*) Oh, come in,
honey. (*She enters in new dress.*) You're
just in time to say good-bye to Erwin.

MABEL. (*Alarmed.*) Goodbye?

PATSY. He thinks I didn't treat you right,
so he's walking out on us.

MABEL. (*Rushing to* ERWIN.) Aw.

ERWIN. I'd like to stay, honest, I would,
I feel terrible about it, but—

MABEL. Oh, Erwin, I can't bear to have you go.

FRANKIE. If you'd just dope out a couple of horses before you go.

PATSY. I tell you what, Erwin; here's the solution to the whole proposition: you can't take these verses back to the office like this, they're all torn—you just sit down and wait a few minutes while we copy 'em for you.

ERWIN. Well—

CHARLIE. (*Picks up verses and sits.*) Sure, we'll do it—then we can all part the best of friends.

FRANKIE. Sure—move over—give me a couple of those.

PATSY. And while you're waiting for us to do it you can just pass the time figuring a couple of horses.

ERWIN. I can help copy verses.

PATSY. No, no, we tore 'em up, we'll copy 'em. You figure horses— Give me some of those, will you— You figure horses. Give him a pencil, Mabel.

MABEL. Sure. Here's a pencil—Erwin. And there's the *Telegraph*.

ERWIN. Well, all right—I'll try.

MABEL. I knew you would—now—sit right here.

PATSY. That's the boy.

CHARLIE. I always said he was a regular fellow.

PATSY. You bet, you can count on Erwin.

MABEL. Oh yeah, he'll come through all right.

CHARLIE. Good Old Erwin!

FRANKIE. All right boys, don't talk so much. Let him concentrate. (ERWIN *thinks, crosses legs.*)

MABEL. Is there anything I can do?

CHARLIE. Yeah, go into your dance.

PATSY. Shut up.

CHARLIE. Well, don't be bustin' up thoughts.

PATSY. Well, who's talkin'—you are.

MABEL. Yeah, he's doin' all the—

FRANKIE. Shut up, all of you.

CHARLIE. Come on now, let's not argu much, get busy on these verses. (ER tears off slip of paper.)

FRANKIE. Sure. (ERWIN looks at pa shaking head.) No good, huh, Erwin? ERWIN crams paper under pillow.)

PATSY. Leave him alone. Leave him a

FRANKIE. No, but he wrote one down put it under the pillow.

ERWIN. It isn't anything. It's no goo

CHARLIE. (Reading slip, gets prop ERWIN.) Equipoise.

PATSY. Equipoise. Runs in the fourth,

FRANKIE. Equipoise. That's the one I going to pick.

ERWIN. But it doesn't count, I tell y

CHARLIE. Why don't it?

ERWIN. I don't know.

CHARLIE. It's no good?

ERWIN. No!

CHARLIE. (They all rise.) He ain't to come through—I can feel it.

PATSY. (Going to ERWIN.) He is so. wouldn't let me down, would you, E

ERWIN. It's no use.

PATSY. What do you mean, it's no Now, Erwin, you ain't going to ge couraged?

ERWIN. I can't figure them out just here. I've always done them on a bu

CHARLIE. Well, just imagine you're bus.

PATSY. Geez, no wonder he couldn't of 'em sittin' there on that louzy bed— over here by the window, Erwin. T more like a bus. (Rushing ERWIN o

low. ERWIN *demurs.*) Slip that chair
r him, Frankie. Give him that pencil
paper. Just try—just concentrate. Now,
pretend you're on the bus, see. Just
ntrate. (*He concentrates. They watch*
CHARLIE *is in rear of* ERWIN.)

LIE. (*Gently, to give atmosphere but
o break the spell.*) Fares, please—have
fares ready— (PATSY *wants to swing
m.* ERWIN *jumps up.*)

N. (*Steps down.*) It's no use. I can't
t. (CHARLIE *follows to the right of
N.*)

. But you don't try, Erwin.

N. I've tried before. I'm not kidding.
only come to me on a bus.

LIE. Would a taxi do? A nice taxi
a radio?

N. No.

. Hell, a taxi is better than a bus any
And we can get one quicker.

N. (*Shakes his head.*) Only on a bus.

. All right. Frankie, go down and
e the rear seat of the Coney Island
Tell them to throw out all them
es. Get the best lookin' bus you can.

N. Now, wait a minute. . . . I hope
not going to think I'm awfully par-
r—but you see, I couldn't do them on
oney Island bus.

. For God's sake—why not?

N. Because I've always done them
e bus that goes to Ozone Heights.

LIE. Where do you get one of them?

(*Crossing to* CHARLIE.) No— No—

IE. We could just change the sign.

(*Yelling.*) No— No— No—

.. If you fellows would let him do
own way—

Yeah, that's what we're going to
ow shut up!

. Why—(ERWIN *looks up at them,
ed by the sharp tone.*)

PATSY. Well, ain't that right—they're getting you flustered, ain't they, kid?

ERWIN. I am getting kind of mixed up.
You see, usually, just for fun, I figure them
out going home.

PATSY. All right—that's easy—now you'd
like to go home, wouldn't you?

ERWIN. Yes, I would.

PATSY. All right, that's what you're going
to do.

CHARLIE. (*Going down right. Sotto voce.*)
Goodbye, we'll never see him again.

PATSY. You're going out and get on your
regular bus just like you always do. Mabel
and Frankie, they'll go with you. We'll be
copying verses—but in the meantime—
you'll be taking a nice ride and then you
can drop in and see the wife . . . tell her
everything is fine.

ERWIN. Yes, I'd like to do that.

PATSY. But just before you tell her, see,
phone us what horses to bet on. We'll be
right here copying your verses and waiting
for the dope.

ERWIN. (*Crossing left.*) All right. Let's
get started. Come on, Frankie—

CHARLIE. And Erwin, no looking out of
windows—just horses.

PATSY. Unless you hurry we ain't going
to make the first race as it is.

ERWIN. Where's my necktie?

CHARLIE. You never had none.

FRANKIE. Take mine.

PATSY. Keep it on. I got plenty. (*Takes
ties from bureau drawer—throws on bed.*)
Help yourself.

ERWIN. Oh, thanks.(*As he selects a brilliant red tie.*)

PATSY. Frankie, take the *Telegraph*.

FRANKIE. Where the Hell is it?

MABEL. Here it is on the bed. Erwin was
sittin' on it.

PATSY. Have you got a pencil, Erwin?

CHARLIE. Have you got your little black book?

PATSY. Yeah!

FRANKIE. I've got it right here.

PATSY. Stick it in his pocket.

ERWIN. I'll bet my wife will be surprised when she sees this necktie.

PATSY. Get going. Get going.

ERWIN. Where's my hat?

CHARLIE. Here you are—

FRANKIE. (*Dashes to dresser; gets h* I'll get it for you. Ring for the elev Mabel. (CURTAIN *starts down.*)

MABEL. (*They rush him out.*) All r but hurry.

ERWIN. Seems as if I'd been away for

PATSY. Get on the right bus, Erwin.

CHARLIE. Treat him nice. Buy him a s

CURTAIN

ACT THREE

SCENE I

Place: Ozone Heights.
ORCHESTRA *plays "Just A Love Nest."*
At Rise: GLORIA *and* AL *cross downstage left off left. The room is littered with newspapers.* CLARENCE *is peeking out the door. He jumps to the window to watch someone outside.* AUDREY *comes downstairs in a new dress.*

CLARENCE. They took a picture of the house. (AUDREY *dry-eyed and repressed, walks across room and sits.*) Wouldn't it be wonderful if they'd put that in the paper? (*Points to paper on floor.*) That *Newark Star* gave us a very bad write-up. . . . Nothing about Dobbins Drive . . . just said a versifier of Ozone Heights is missing. (*Notices* AUDREY.) You didn't need to get all dressed up—she said she'd take your picture just as you were.

AUDREY. I got dressed up for Mr. Carver, not for her. I'm sure that Erwin would want me to look as well as I can.

CLARENCE. Well, from time to time I've said things against J. G. Carver, but I take 'em all back. His heart is in the right place or he wouldn't be coming out here. Gee, I wonder if I could interest him in a house.

AUDREY. He isn't coming out here about houses he's coming out about Erwin.

CLARENCE. Well, if I've got to support you the rest of your life, the least I can get out of this is maybe a sale or two. (*Snaps*

fingers and sits.) Or a tip on a h Doggone, if Erwin was going to walk that way you would have thought he c at least have left a *hot tip.* He's prob out at some bookie's right now put his money on the winners—gosh, wouldn't I give to know which ones!

AUDREY. You don't have to support the rest of your life, so don't say that a And if you must keep on making rem that Erwin has run away, then I'll to ask you not to come in my house more.

CLARENCE. Why, sis! (*Front door a and* GLORIA GRAY, *reporter on the "Ne Gazette" enters, followed by* AL, *the p grapher.*)

GLORIA. Now, Mrs. Trowbridge, if y just stand over here. (AUDREY *crosse davenport.*) Have you got a handkerc

AUDREY. (*Turning.*) Handkerchief?

GLORIA. Yes, you ought to be crying know—

AUDREY. I'm not going to cry any m

CLARENCE. She cried terrible this mor But she's a brave little woman.

GLORIA. "Brave little woman." Ther very trenchant phrase—remind me t that, will you, Al?

CLARENCE. Want me in the picture? (GLORIA *favors him with a cold smile then turns away.*)

Still—(*Snaps picture.*)

IA. That's fine. Now just one more.
ll take another one brave. That's just
ood. We've had half a dozen weeping
s this week anyhow—(*To* CLARENCE.)
're the brother of the missing man, are
?

RENCE. No, I'm the brother of the
of the missing man, and I'm the owner
his row of houses here.

IA. They're very attractive.

RENCE. They're all alike.

IA. I noticed that.

Still—

IA. (*Giving* CLARENCE *a look.*) All
t, Al, shoot him just for luck.

ENCE. Let's see where'll we a—(*Picks
hair planning to sit for the picture.*)

Still—

ENCE. (*Holding chair in the air.*) Oh,
sn't ready—

IA. That's all right—you looked wor-
—just the right expression.

ENCE. I am worried—he was a fine
w—

EY. (*Crossing to telephone table.*)
, here's the picture of Erwin—I hate
art with it— It's the only one I've
—

IA. Oh, we'll send it back in good
ition— (*Writes on the face.*) Here
are, Al— (*Tosses it to* AL.)

EY. But of course, if it'll help to find
in . . .

IA. Sure it will. Somebody might
nize him—and—you'll get a lot of
le who think they do. I'll promise
that—

ENCE. If you'd print a description I
ld think it might help. When he left
he was wearing a grey suit, brown
black shoes. . . .

EY. And no necktie.

IA. No necktie—(AUDREY *shakes*
.) Why was that?

AUDREY. He was in a hurry. He was late.

GLORIA. Often do that, does he?

AUDREY. (*Shakes head.*) No—it's the first
time.

GLORIA. And—this the first time he ever
stayed away from home overnight? (AUD-
REY *nods.*) And the first time he ever
went to work without a necktie?

AL. Doesn't look like a date—

GLORIA. Who asked you? (*Changes tone.*)
Any suspicious letters or phone calls from
women?

AUDREY. Erwin wasn't like that. He was
different!

GLORIA. Different—

AL. Hey, Toots. (AL *shows* GLORIA ERWIN'S
*picture as though to prove he wasn't like
that.*)

GLORIA. Oh— (*Buzzer rings.*)

AUDREY. (*Helplessly to* CLARENCE.) If that's
the neighbors—

CLARENCE. Let me— (*Opens door.* CAR-
VER, *an irascible old gentleman, stands
there, wearing seedy Prince Albert and
grey striped trousers.*) Yes.

CARVER. (*Handing* CLARENCE *his hat and
coming center.*) How do you do? My name
is Carver— *Where's Erwin?*

AUDREY. (*Clutching his hand and shaking
it.*) Oh, Mr. Carver, it's so nice of you to
come out here. This is my brother, Mr.
Dobbins, and this is Miss Gloria Gray of
the *Newark Gazette,* and that's—I don't
believe I know your—name—

GLORIA. Just Al, pay no attention to him.

AUDREY. Mr. Carver is my husband's boss.

CARVER. (*Recovering from the handshakes
of* GLORIA *and* CLARENCE.) Where's Erwin?

GLORIA. (*Making notes.*) Oh sure—J. G.
Carver— Right?

CARVER. What's the difference? Where is
Erwin?—that's the point.

CLARENCE. Well, I'll tell you my theory,
J. G.

CARVER. Who?

CLARENCE. J. G.? Isn't that correct?

CARVER. My name is Carver—call me Carver, Mr. Carver, or Hey You—but don't call me J.G.

GLORIA. (Offering hand.) My pal.

CARVER. (Waving it away.) No. No.—No nonsense— Where's Erwin?

AUDREY. The detective was here this morning and he said he thought they could trace him. He said lots of men disappear every day—especially married men about Erwin's age.

CARVER. Foolish talk. Foolish talk.

AUDREY. He said they generally turned up in hospitals saying they lost their memory—

CARVER. A lot of pish-posh— Now here's a man that's a reliable citizen, see—worth more than you or you or any of you— in his way. He's gone!! Where? Nobody knows. It's a silly country. Man phones me, says he's Erwin's manager— Why don't they trace him. 'Cause they're a lot of fools. Make a lot of mystery out of nothing—I know where he is.

GLORIA. Where?

CARVER. (Shakes finger.) Writing verses for a rival concern.

AUDREY. Oh, but Mister—

CARVER. Don't talk. Don't argue. I've figured it out. Thought I didn't appreciate him just 'cause I didn't pat him on the back every minute—along comes some sneak—gives him a lot of sugar and steals him away—no justice anywhere—never was —never will be.

GLORIA. But he'd hardly keep it a secret from his wife.

CARVER. 'Fraid of his wife?

AUDREY. Oh, no.

CARVER. Don't argue. Afraid of you. 'Fraid of that man over there—don't know who he is.

CLARENCE. Why, Mr. Carver, I'm—

CARVER. And I don't care. 'Fraid of ev body—just a poet. Just lives in him (Taps forehead.) Afraid of me, even. fact is, that none of you can deny, gone—(Shakes finger.) and Mother's deadline is tomorrow. But I happen know my rights. I've fought competi before and I can do it again. (Phone rin Answer that. And if it's for me, I'm (AUDREY starts for phone, but CLARE takes it. CLARENCE goes to phone an seen but not heard talking.)

CARVER. (Coming down stage.) Er wasn't so good at first. He had the feel the warmth and the inspiration to b top-notch greeting card man, but he di have the technique. I taught him a knew—I worked and struggled to b him up, up the ladder and then some steals him from me. (Goes to the foo divan.)

CLARENCE. (In phone.) Well, you ca you want to.

AUDREY. What is it?

CLARENCE. (In phone.) Well, we know took the bus for New York, but go a if you want to. (Hangs up.)

AUDREY. What was that?

CLARENCE. The Boy Scouts at Eaglev

CARVER. What do they want?

CLARENCE. They want to drag the Ea ville Pond for Erwin.

AUDREY. What?

CLARENCE. I told them he wouldn't there—but they said they'd never dra a pond before and they wanted to c anyway.

GLORIA. The Eagleville Pond—wher that?

CLARENCE. It's right down the street.

GLORIA. Come on, Al. We might use —(Starts for door.)

CLARENCE. It's right next to my pro —(GLORIA, CLARENCE and AL go out.)

AUDREY. (Crosses right.) I'm sure I wouldn't want to work for anybod

Mr. Carver—he was always saying
he liked being in your office and how
erful you were.

ER. I didn't come here to listen to a
f sentimental nonsense.

EY. No, sir.

ER. What I want to know is—did he
 any verses around?

EY. He took them with him—

ER. I mean any old ones? Things he
going to throw away maybe?

EY. He wouldn't let me touch his
—he was very particular about that.

ER. Stuff—stuff—stuff — nonsense—
 cares? Did he leave any papers
d?

EY. He had a little room way up in
ttic where it would be quiet and his
 is all covered with papers—

ER. All right—all right—show me.

EY. But I don't know—

ER. Anything he did while working
e is my property. (AUDREY *starts up
follows.*)—Go ahead with you (AUD-
tarts up the stairs) Easter—I wouldn't
-got a man can write good Easter
—but Mother's Day is Erwin's spec-
-nobody in the office has got his
—(*They go out of sight and we hear
continue to grumble as the voices
farther away.*) Printers have to have
roof way in advance—if I'm late then
charge me overtime . . . overtime,
e time, all kinds of time . . . bunch
oks—can't plan anything—raise prices
 'em more every year, get less work
 year—the whole country is going to
ogs as fast as it can go. (*Upstairs a
slams, shutting off the then distant
*) (ERWIN *enters, followed by* MABEL
RANKIE.)

. This the place?

. Dearie. (ERWIN *opens front door.*)

. Oh, it's cute.

. Dearie.

IE. Ain't she to home?

ERWIN. (*Sad.*) I guess not.

MABEL. (*Crossing right.*) Most likely went
to a movie.

ERWIN. Guess so. Thought maybe she'd
be worried about me, but—

FRANKIE. No—no—she wouldn't be worried.

ERWIN. Of course, maybe she's upstairs
and can't hear me—(*Starts up.*)

FRANKIE. (*Grabbing* ERWIN.) No, wait—
listen—before you do anything else, you
got to phone Patsy.

ERWIN. Well.

FRANKIE. You promised, didn't he, Mabel?

MABEL. (*Crossing to door.*) Sure you did.

FRANKIE. What's the matter, Erwin? You
got them selections, ain't you?

ERWIN. (*Coming back.*) Yes, I told you
I had—Dearie.

FRANKIE. Well, you're acting kind of
funny.

ERWIN. No, I'm not: honest I'm not.

FRANKIE. Where's your phone? (ERWIN
points to it.)

MABEL. (*At door.*) Hey, look—there's a
lot of people up there.

FRANKIE. (*Pulls her in.*) Never mind
what anybody's doing—keep working on
him, will you?

MABEL. (*Shaking him off.*) Well, Erwin's
going to phone.

ERWIN. Sure, I'm going to—I just wonder where my wife is, that's all.

FRANKIE. Well, geez, this phoning is much
more important, you know that, Erwin—
you can look for your wife later. Shall I
call the number for you?

ERWIN. No. I'll do it. (*Going to phone.*)
You don't see a note around for me, do
you? (MABEL *and* FRANKIE *look about.*)
You'd think she'd have left a note. (*In
phone.*) Hello—I want— (*Rises.*)

FRANKIE. What's the matter?

MABEL. (*In phone.*) Pennsylvania six five eight nine two—

ERWIN. (*Running to* FRANKIE.) Suppose Audrey's mad! Suppose she's gone back to live with her mother.

FRANKIE. She hasn't. She don't even like her mother—she likes you better—what the Hell—

MABEL. Hello—Kitty, give me Patsy's room—

FRANKIE. (*Exasperated.*) Look—everything is around here, ain't it? If she'd gone away she'd pack up, wouldn't she? Sure.

MABEL. (*In phone.*) This is me. He's here. Get a paper and pencil.

ERWIN. Well. I guess that's right.

FRANKIE. She's just gone out to get a little fresh air— that's all. You want her to be healthy don't you?

MABEL. (*Passes phone.*) Here you are. Patsy's waiting.

ERWIN. (*Taking phone from* MABEL.) Hello—yes, this is Erwin— What? Oh—oh, yes. Just a minute. I've got them—(*Gets out book to read list.* FRANKIE *pulls a paper out of his pocket to compare lists.*) For the first race Sunador—second Frolic—third Motto—fourth Mr. Khayyam—Well, that's all . . . yes, I know, but I didn't figure the rest of them yet . . . I thought I'd get the others on the way back.

FRANKIE. (*To* MABEL—*holding his list.*) I missed every one.

MABEL. What do you mean?

FRANKIE. I thought I'd see if there was anything in this bus business for me, too, maybe—so you know when I went to the rear seat and sat by myself?—I was trying to dope 'em, and I wrote 'em down all right but, I didn't hit a single one—(*Crumples paper, throws it on floor and walks to window.*) well, that shows it ain't just the bus anyhow.

ERWIN. Certainly I will—but I have my verses to think of too, you know—and—(*AUDREY enters from stairs.*)

FRANKIE. (*Seeing* AUDREY.) Oh—how you?

AUDREY. Erwin.

ERWIN. (*Grins.*) Hello, dear—I was l ing for you. I yoo-hooed a couple of t but— (*In phone.*) Well, goodbye, I v to talk to my wife. Dearie— (*Hangs rises and crosses to her.*) These are friends.

AUDREY. Oh, Erwin— (*Rushes to arms.* ERWIN *looks at the others ple* FRANKIE *gestures I-told-you-so.*) I've wo so—I couldn't imagine— (*Draws b* Where have you been?

ERWIN. Up at the hotel with them—AUDREY *looks at* MABEL.) him. Oh D —I've got so much to tell you—

FRANKIE. Listen Erwin—them last races. (*Coming between* ERWIN *and* REY.)

ERWIN. Oh yes, of course—I can't you everything now, because we ha hurry right back again.

MABEL. Well, don't you think we l get started—

AUDREY. Is anything wrong?

ERWIN. No, no, everything's fine. I'm going to give you a lot of mo over a hundred dollars.

AUDREY. I don't need any money, E

ERWIN. I'm going to give it to you how. (*Searches through clothes.*)

AUDREY. Where'd you get it?

ERWIN. (*They start to drag* ERWIN The horses.

AUDREY. Horses?

ERWIN. Yes. In my little book, you l It's been quite a source of revenue ju advising. (CLARENCE *appears in center*

CLARENCE. Well, well, well—

ERWIN. But don't tell him.

CLARENCE. (*Coming down.*) Don't t what?

ʟ. (*Going to* AUDREY.) I think your
is swell, Mrs. Trowbridge. I'd just
o own it myself. (*Going up center.*)

ᴋɪᴇ. (*Grabs him.*) Say, I don't want
h you, Erwin, but—

ɴ. Yes, we must get started.

ɴᴄᴇ. You going away already?
e you been?

ʏ. Erwin, you'll be back?

ɴ. Oh sure.

ᴋɪᴇ. He'll be back on the bus—
day—back and forth—you know . . .
bing him by arm.)

ɴ. Audrey.

ɪᴇ. Remember your promise, Erwin.

ɴ. Yes, yes, I know. I know. Oh,
minute. (*Breaks away. Rushes back*
s AUDREY.) See you tomorrow— (MA-
FRANKIE *and* ERWIN *hurry out.*)

ɴᴄᴇ. Where's he gone?

ʏ. (*Rushes to window, calling.*)
a.

ɴᴄᴇ. (*Follows.*) Where'd he get the
ʏ? What'd he say? What's he doing?
did he mean—don't tell me?

ʏ. Oh, dear—

ɴᴄᴇ. Where's he gone? Where's he
? Who are those people with him?

ʏ. (*Starts.*) He didn't even tell me
he was . . .

ɴᴄᴇ. (*Stops her.*) And why did he
on't tell me"?—what is it he doesn't
me to know? He's got a horse, that's
d he won't tell me.

ʀ. (*Enters from above.*) I found a
odds and ends that Erwin had ap-
ly discarded as not good enough—
think I can use them—I'll have to.

ʏ. Oh, Mr. Carver—I forgot to tell

ʀ. What do you mean?

ʏ. Erwin was here—he just left.

ʀ. Where? Where's he gone? (*Rush-*
)

AUDREY. (*Starts after.*) They went up that
way, I think. (*Outside.* CARVER *and* AUDREY
exeunt. CLARENCE *goes to door, then turns
and sees paper left on floor by* FRANKIE.
*He picks it up, unfolds and reads, his eyes
bulge with excitement.* CARVER *re-enters,
followed by* AUDREY.)

CLARENCE. Huh.

CARVER. (*Coming down.*) It's your fault—
it's all your fault. You should have called
me. No wonder Erwin isn't farther ahead
in the world. He's got an incompetent
wife—that's what's the matter. You don't
know where he is. Let him get away without finding out where he is.

CLARENCE. I know where he is.

CARVER. What? What'd you say?

CLARENCE. He's at the Lavillere Hotel.

CARVER. Where's that? Whoever heard of
such a place? What are you talking about?
How do you know?

CLARENCE. They dropped this paper.

CARVER. They? Who's they?

CLARENCE. There was a man and woman
with him.

CARVER. Oh, so that's it—unscrupulous
competitors—trying to ruin my Mother's
Day output—I'll show 'em—I can fight for
my rights—I'll show 'em— (*He jams on
his hat and goes.*)

CLARENCE. He thinks they want Erwin's
verses, but I know better. Look— (*Shows
paper.*)

AUDREY. What's that?

CLARENCE. Horses. That's what he didn't
want you to tell me, isn't it?

AUDREY. Yes, but—

CLARENCE. I found this on the floor— It's
their list of the winning horses— Thought
he'd hold out on me, did he—well, I'll
show him— (*Stands.*)

AUDREY. What are you going to do?

CLARENCE. (*Gets phone.*) I'm going to bet
my shirt.

BLACKOUT

ORCHESTRA *plays "Horses."*

SCENE II

Place: The hotel room.

Time: The same afternoon.

At Rise: HARRY, MOSES, PATSY, CHARLIE *and a* CHAMBERMAID *are copying verses. The maid is a Swede.*

CHARLIE. (*Rising from bed and looking over* PATSY's *shoulder.*) I ain't so sure Mr. Carver is going to like your handwriting.

PATSY. (*At desk.*) What's the matter with it?

CHARLIE. Plenty.

PATSY. To Hell with Carver.

CHARLIE. (*Pointing to* CHAMBERMAID.) Why don't you do it like her?

PATSY. Aw—she writes like a pansy.

CHARLIE. That's the way you're supposed to write. (*Sarcastic.*) The idea is so that somebody else can read it, see?

PATSY. The idea is get 'em done by the time Erwin gets back, that's all.

CHARLIE. (*Walking toward bed.*) Yeah, but we want him to like the job, don't we? We got to keep him contented? My God—look at what Moses is doing—what language you writing that in? African?

PATSY. Who appointed you foreman anyhow? (*Goes to phone.*) Get busy instead of criticizing so much. The thing is to be able to say they are copied.

CHARLIE. (*Sits.*) Get to work yourself, you tore 'em up. I'm tired—

PATSY. What're you so tired about?

CHARLIE. Do you think it's easy to find a synagogue?

PATSY. (*Suddenly.*) Geez, we forgot all about the second race— (*In phone.*) Let me talk to Gus. (*Sharply, in phone.*) Well, listen, Kitty, keep this wire open all the time, will you? This is important. To Hell with Mr. Shapiro—which is more important—cloaks and suits or horses?—well, I'm tellin' you—

MOSES. (*Looking up from bed whe⟩ has been seated.*) Lord a' mercy. (⟨ starts out.*)

PATSY. Where you going?

MOSES. Somebody is pushin' that bell through the elevator, Mr. Patsy, but ⟩ back. (*Gives* CHARLIE *paper.*) I got thi⟩ all straight exceptin' one word down ⟩ in the corner. (*Exits.*)

HARRY. I got an extra word here. ⟩ does he need?

CHARLIE. Something to rhyme wit⟩ me see— (*Reading.*) "We trudged⟩ way on Sundays"—something to ⟨ with Sundays.

HARRY. (*Looking at his piece of p⟩ No. The word I have here is "blue-b⟩

CHARLIE. The only word I can thi⟩ is "undies" but I don't suppose ⟩ would want to use that.

PATSY. (*In phone.*) Gus, how is it— (*Turning to others.*) "Frolic" in th⟩ ond race. (*They all cheer.*)

HARRY. Atta baby. (*Jumps up, s⟩ papers.*)

CHARLIE. Hey, look· out for them ⟩

HARRY. I'm one hundred and four ⟨ to the good. Yeah—

PATSY. Pipe down, will you. (*In p⟩ That all goes on Motto in the third.⟩ it's a parlay. What the Hell do you ⟩ —we're pikers? . . . What are you ⟩ in' about? . . . Well, don't forge⟩ ain't the only bookie . . . What's th⟩ ter? You yellow?

CHARLIE. Come on, Harry, help m⟩ them up. (*Starts to pick up papers⟩

HARRY. I got to listen.

CHARLIE. Suppose Erwin comes bac⟩ finds they ain't ready. He's liable ⟩ up on us before we get the last ra⟨ of him.

HARRY. Geez, that's right. We got t⟩ about the future. (*Stooping to p⟩ verses.*)

. (*Back to phone.*) Sure we got a
n—but he ain't here now. We sent
out to get some air. . . . How much?
others.*) He wants to buy a piece of
n.

BERMAID. (*Alarmed.*) What?

RLIE and HARRY *are amused by the*
BERMAID'S *expression.*)

. (*Into phone.*) Never mind how we
im—we own him, that's all. What's
offer for ten per cent? . . . Well, he
missed yet, has he? Wait till you pay
n this four horse parlay and you'll
so. . . . We wouldn't even consider
fer like that. (*Hangs up.*) A lousy
grand for ten per cent of Erwin.

LIE. Maybe we ought to take it.

. What for?

LIE. Well, supposing something went
g?

. What're you talking about?

LIE. Supposing this guy Erwin's
ng out on us.

. Why you . . .

LIE. No, but listen, what does he
us over the phone . . . Mr. Khayyam
and what does he give us under the
v . . . Equipoise.

. What of it? Maybe that's the way
arms himself up. (*Phone.*)

. There's your poetry. Geez, a hun-
and four dollars. I think I'll buy
a necktie.

LIE. He's got a necktie.

. (*In phone.*) Yeah? (*Turns to*
.) It's Mac, he wants you to come
down.

. Huh. Tell him I took the day off.
im I've resigned.

He's quit. He's too rich to work.

. (*Strolling back and forth.*) I can't
hered with that small time stuff . . .
want is to be able to follow Erwin
' for the rest of my life.

PATSY. (*In phone.*) . . . and don't keep
callin' us up, we want this wire open.
(*Hangs up.*)

HARRY. I guess that surprised him, huh?
I don't think I was meant to be a barkeep
anyway.

PATSY. Now to Hell with all that. Let's
get this stuff copied.

HARRY. Sure. All right. I'm just as anxious as you are. After all I got some rights
to Erwin ain't I? Who discovered him in
the first place?

MOSES. (*Enters.*) Yes sir, but I don't know
if they . . .

CARVER. (*Enters.*) Never mind about that
boy . . . Who's in charge here?

PATSY. Who are you?

CARVER. My name's J. G. Carver in case
you're interested . . . and I'm here to tell
you I know my rights.

CHARLIE. I guess you got the wrong room,
brother.

CARVER. Don't try to shilly-shally with me.
I've had the call traced. I know all about
what's been going on here from A to Z.
You kept him here all right . . .

HARRY. We what?

CARVER. (*Crossing to* HARRY.) You've been
stealing his verses, the very verses he'd
been working on under my instructions. I
know what you're doing . . . all of you
. . . Yes, and you too. (*To* MAID.)

MAID. I tink I better go now.

PATSY. Stay where you are, keep copying.
(MAID *sits.*)

CARVER. You can all hear what I have to
say . . . and if I don't get action any other
way, the United States court will hear
about it, let that be understood . . .

PATSY. What the Hell is it you want?

CARVER. I want Erwin Trowbridge.

HARRY. (*Jumps up.*) What?

CHARLIE. (*Pulls him back.*) Take it easy.

CARVER. I want him back in his office by tomorrow morning, or I'll have supoenas enough flying around here to make your eyes water. (*Phone rings.*) If that's for me, I'm out— There's no individualism in an organization like this . . . it's a bad thing for him.

PATSY. It's the third race, boys. Bounce him out of here.

CARVER. I ain't afraid of you fellows or any other greeting card company in the United States.

PATSY. Pipe down, will you.

CARVER. (*Struggles.*) I'll fight all of you.

PATSY. Did you hear us, pipe down . . . get him out of here, will you, boys? The bum's rush. Want me to miss this race? (CHARLIE *and* HARRY *grab him by the seat of his pants, knocking his hat off.* MOSES *picks up hat.*)

CHARLIE. Come on, Bo . . . scram.

HARRY. Leave him to me, I can handle him.

CARVER. Take your hands off me.

MOSES. Here's your hat.

PATSY. (*At phone.*) Coming down the stretch, eh? Who's in the lead?

CARVER. I'll have you blackguards in jail. Every one of you.

HARRY. I've thrown out tougher guys than you.

CHARLIE. Don't hold back . . . I'll give you the boot.

MOSES. Better take your hat. (CHARLIE *and* HARRY *rush* CARVER *out door.*)

MAID. I've found the last line.

PATSY. (*Rises. In phone.*) Motto huh?

HARRY. (*Re-entering.*) He won't be back.

PATSY. Motto wins.

HARRY. Motto?

PATSY. We won . . . we won. Hold on a minute, Gus.

HARRY. (*As* CHARLIE *returns.*) Motto Charlie.

CHARLIE. He won, huh?

CARVER. (*Throws open door.*) I've in business since eighteen ninety-((CHARLIE *slams door shut.*)

CHARLIE. Out and stay out.

MAID. That's the last one. Is there thing else?

PATSY. (*Extracting five dollar bill.*) Here's a fin for you. Go down and on Mr. Khayyam in the fourth race.

MAID. Please Mr.—if it's all the sam you—I got a place that's much (*Sticks it down shirt front.*)

CARVER. (*At door.*) Don't forget wha code says about unfair competition.

PATSY. Harry, take that guy downstair throw him in the street. Give him a will you, Moses? (HARRY *exits.*)

MOSES. Mr. Patsy, I wish you wo mix me up in this thing on accou the race problem.

PATSY. Maybe you're right. (MOSES MAID *exit.*)

PATSY. (*Back to phone.*) Listen, G all rides on Mr. Khayyam—the wo what? . . . All right—then half o what do I care—I'll bet the rest with . . . No, I'm not crazy. (*With hand phone; to* CHARLIE.) Go down and half the dough with Eddie.

CHARLIE. Maybe we oughtn't to be half, Patsy, what d'ya say? Equipois pretty good horse, Patsy, what abo Well, I'm only thinkin'—

PATSY. Has Erwin missed yet?

CHARLIE. No-o-o, but—

PATSY. Then do what I tell you ar lect on the straight bets—get going

CHARLIE. Just the same— (*Goes to* But I'm worried. (*Exits.*)

PATSY. (*Back to phone.*) . . . Yea kind of money don't interest us. E a gold mine . . . we ain't selling

hicken feed . . . all right, all right—
:now my number. (*Hangs up.* MABEL
entered before the end of PATSY'S
h.)

L. (*Coming down to* PATSY.) I seen
.tsy—I seen it.

, Seen what?

L. Our little dream house.

, Oh. Where's Erwin?

.. He's downstairs with Frankie. Oh,
—it's gorgeous—you ought to been
—there was the nicest curtains and
pictures and a real garden and a
to sit on—and a second floor—only
n't go up and Erwin says he wants
. it.

(*Going to the right away from*
O. K. Buy it. Just don't bother me,
all.

.. Patsy, don't you think we ought
married if we're going to live in
se?

We'll get married. You can get
:d any day— (*Going to phone.*) but
a four horse parlay on the fire and
lon't come up often.

. They come up too often—they
up and hit you right in the face.

What do you mean by that?

. I mean I want you to buy this
before everything goes back into

IE. (*Enters followed by* ERWIN.)
s the matter with the elevator? We
· walk up.

, Are my verses copied?

I think you'll find everything in
>ndition, Erwin.

IE. (PATSY *crosses to* FRANKIE.) Who
he first race?

(ERWIN *goes to the bed.*) We won
st three. Charlie's out collectin' the
t bets now. We got a parlay—ridin'
, Khayyam. (*Going back to desk.*)

FRANKIE. (*Sits on end bed.*) Did you hear
that, Erwin—we copped the first three.

ERWIN. (*He is looking at verses.*) What?

FRANKIE. The first three come in.

ERWIN. Oh.

MABEL. I was tellin' Patsy about the house,
Erwin, he says we'll buy it.

ERWIN. (*Looking at verses.*) Gee, I can
hardly read these. (*Telephone.*)

PATSY. (MABEL *goes right of* ERWIN. *Answering it.*) Hello— Oh, hello, Gus, now
you're talkin' turkey . . . we can close the
deal on those terms . . . sure . . . well,
Erwin is worth that much . . . he's just
like money in the bank. . . . All right—
we'll incorporate—but listen, I'm president.
(*Hangs up.*) That was Gus. They've come
around. I made them guys appreciate Erwin's true value.

FRANKIE. I'll bet we'll make a half million with him.

ERWIN. Oh, this is terrible.

PATSY. What's the trouble?

MABEL. What's the matter, Erwin?

ERWIN. Look at this!

MABEL. The handwriting?

ERWIN. No. The words. Those aren't my
words at all. (CHARLIE *enters.*)

PATSY. Well.

CHARLIE. I collected the straight bets and
the parlay stands. Geez, they certainly are
afraid of us—Gus had to lay off with three
bookies.

ERWIN. Oh, Mr. Carver would die if he
saw this—I'd lose my job.

MABEL. Looks like one of yours, Charlie.

CHARLIE. What's the trouble? (*Coming
down left.*)

ERWIN. I couldn't write anything like
this—

CHARLIE. Write what? Let's see.

ERWIN. It doesn't even scan.

PATSY. (*At desk.*) Well, come on boys, let's not have any fuss—let's just fix it, that's all.

CHARLIE. I did fix it.

ERWIN. I don't want anything fixed—I just wanted them copied.

CHARLIE. But we lost the last line.

PATSY. (*Comes center.*) What is it? (*Takes verses. Reads.*)
"I wonder if the old church stands
Where we trudged our way on Sundays;
I recall how we sat with folded hands"

ERWIN. That part's all right—see—but the rest of it.

PATSY. (*Takes paper and reads.*) "So now I don't ever get drunk no more on Tuesdays or Mondays." (*Looks at Erwin.*) That's no good, huh?

ERWIN. It's awful.

CHARLIE. It's the right idea, ain't it? He's thinkin' of his mother, see—

ERWIN. It's no good—

FRANKIE. (*Going to* CHARLIE.) Yeah, you got a crust monkeying with Erwin's verses.

CHARLIE. I was only tryin' to help out—

PATSY. (*Crossing to the right.*) Well, come on, Erwin—just put in your words. What's the stew about?

ERWIN. I can't think what it was myself now. You got me so upset.

FRANKIE. There, you see—you got him all upset, you mug.

MABEL. What you cheap-skates ought to do is hire some first-class poet to do Erwin's verses for him—then he wouldn't have to worry so much.

PATSY. (*Crossing back to desk.*) When this four-horse parlay comes in we'll hire Longfellow.

MABEL. You couldn't hire Longfellow—'cause he's dead—I think he is.

CHARLIE. Here. It all comes to thirty-three hundred dollars. That's on the straight bets. I'm keeping mine. Here's twenty-two hundred.

PATSY. (*Taking money.*) O.K. Now E gets three hundred and thirty.

ERWIN. I do? All that?

PATSY. (*Going to* ERWIN.) That nothin'. Wait till Mr. Khayyam c through to make that four-horse pa Here you are, Erwin—three hundred thirty dollars.

ERWIN. It doesn't seem right. (*Stu bills into pocket.*)

MABEL. The way you got to figure it is, Erwin, that we wouldn't have money if it wasn't for you.

PATSY. Well, we might have—

MABEL. Yeah, we might—but we ably wouldn't. You helped, that's sure

PATSY. Erwin is always going to ge cut, don't worry. And when this fo race comes through—

CHARLIE. *If* this fourth race co through—

ERWIN. (*Turns and looks at him. E and* PATSY *look at* CHARLIE, *then at other.*) Yes. I see what you mean. T pretty good. (*Laughs.*)

PATSY. (*Alarmed.*) Wait a minute.

ERWIN. (*Looking at verses.*) It's f how one line could get lost that way.

PATSY. Never mind about that poetr just a minute, will you, Erwin?

ERWIN. (*Absently, pieces of paper i hand.*) What?

PATSY. Let's just concentrate on this fourth race, I mean—

ERWIN. Of course.

PATSY. We can't lose. Can we, Erw

ERWIN. No—I don't think so.

PATSY. Mr. Khayyam is your sele isn't he?

ERWIN. Oh, yes—that's the horse. paper.) There!—the line—there's the

PATSY. Stop changing the subject.

LIE. (*Crossing to* ERWIN.) Do you
k we should shift to Equipoise?

N. No.

LIE. Then why did you write his
e on a piece of paper?

N. I didn't—

LIE. Oh, you didn't—what about this?
shes *paper*.)

N. (*Takes paper*.) Oh, that?

LIE. Yeah, that. Why did you hide it
r the pillow?

N. Oh, that was when I was sitting
he bed trying to dope them and I
n't sure I could do it—so I wrote
poise two or three times just to see
it would look—but I didn't think it
ed so good.

Y. Oh, you wasn't sure.

N. No— Don't you see— I'm sur-
d at you fellows—you were all right
rday, when I was sick and you took
of me and all that—but now you're
ng greedy.

Y. I notice you took your ten per cent.

N. Oh, yes indeed.

Y. You wouldn't by any chance be
in' of crossin' us, would you, Erwin?

N. No—of course not— Oh no—

Y. All right, boys, everything goes on
Khayyam.

LIE. How much you betting, Erwin?

N. Oh, I wouldn't bet.

Y. What do you mean? Which way
dn't you bet?

N. No. I wouldn't bet on anything.
would spoil it.

EL. Sure. Erwin explained that to

Y. Shut up. (*To* ERWIN.) I thought
be you ought to bet on this nag, Er-
—you doped him.

N. But don't you see, if I did—

PATSY. No, I don't see a thing except that
if he's good enough for us to put our shirts
on—he's good enough for you too. Just
give your bet to Frankie and he'll take it
over with him. (FRANKIE *rises*.)

ERWIN. Well it'll spoil all my fun—
(CHARLIE *crosses to window*.) but of course
—if you buy the house—then I won't be
riding on the bus anymore anyway— Well,
I think I'll bet two dollars.

CHARLIE. Two dollars!

PATSY. What are you doing—kidding?

ERWIN. No, I'm serious— I think he'll
win. I want to bet two dollars.

PATSY. Well, this is a Hell of a joke. We
got eleven thousand dollars on Mr.
Khayyam and you want to bet a deuce.
You can't think much of the horse.

ERWIN. I certainly do—I picked him.

PATSY. Well, then play something worth
while.

ERWIN. Oh, I see what you mean. Here
Frankie—put ten dollars on his nose.
(*Counts it*.)

PATSY. Frankie didn't hear you.

CHARLIE. No, he's deaf.

FRANKIE. They think you ought to put
up some real dough, Erwin.

MABEL. I don't think you ought to make
him bet, boys.

PATSY. Well, we're going to, whether you
think so or not. I wouldn't go so far
as to say that Charlie's right about you,
but a good-sized bet from you would make
me think his heart is in the right place.

ERWIN. All right—here—put a hundred
dollars on Mr. Khayyam to show.

PATSY. To show, huh—he's good enough
for us to have all we got on his nose and
you want to play a lousy century note
to show. (*Knocks* ERWIN's *arm down*.)

FRANKIE. You better hurry up if you want
to get this down.

PATSY. Shut up. You're goin' to play what
you got—on the nose.

ERWIN. You mean all my ten per cents?

PATSY. All your ten per cents. Hand it over.

ERWIN. (*Hands roll to* PATSY.) Well—all right—here you are.

PATSY. (*Gives him money.*) Put that on Mr. Khayyam for Erwin—right on the nose.

ERWIN. Hey, wait—my money from the Bowery Savings Bank is in that.

PATSY. The Hell with it. If he's good enough for us he's good enough for you— every nickel. Go on, Frankie.

FRANKIE. O.K. I got to hurry. (*Goes out.*) (*When* FRANKIE *opens door to go out we see* CLARENCE *standing in hall. He looks in and sees* ERWIN.)

CLARENCE. (*Entering. To* ERWIN. *Comes in.*) There he is. Hiding from me, you sneak. You low down cheat. You couldn't come out and fight like a man. You had to trick me—you crook.

PATSY. Hey, wait a minute.

CLARENCE. He pretends he knows all about horse races. He's got a list. He's got a little black book.

PATSY. Yeah—we know all about that.

CLARENCE. He cleaned me out. He tricked me. He left a list on the floor—knew I'd find it—

ERWIN. That's not the facts at all.

CLARENCE. You double-crossing, Mother's Day crook—I went to the bank—drew all my money out— I'm cleaned—lost every cent.

PATSY. Who is this guy?

ERWIN. He's my brother-in-law.

CLARENCE. Yesterday he had them right— all winners—just to lead me on— (HARRY *enters.*) just to make me bet.

PATSY. You're just in time, Harry. Push this guy downstairs, will you?

HARRY. Be glad to oblige, Mr. Patsy. (*To* CLARENCE.) Come on— (*Takes his arm.*)

CLARENCE. Now just a minute, I do[n't] know who you gentlemen are but I[']d like to introduce myself.

HARRY. Tough guy, huh— (*Grabs him [by the] pants and rushes him out.*)

CLARENCE. What's the idea? (*As th[ey] exit.*)

PATSY. So you'd double-cross your ow[n] brother-in-law?

ERWIN. No, I didn't—honestly. He j[ust] made a mistake, that was all I would[n't] cheat anybody—(*Pause—they look at him[.]*) You fellows believe me, don't you?

PATSY. (*Drily.*) Sure.

CHARLIE. (*Disregarding* ERWIN.) I t[old] you we shouldn't put everything on M[r.] Khayyam—(*Pause.*) Well, what are [we] going to do?

PATSY. It's too late to do anything. (*Loo[ks] at watch.*) It's past time. I'll go down [to] Gus's so I can collect as soon as—I mean [when] Mr. Khayyam comes in. You stay here.

CHARLIE. Don't worry—I'll take care [of] him. (*Crosses and sits near desk.*) (PATSY *exits.*)

ERWIN. Gee, you fellows are getting pre[tty] serious. I haven't missed yet, have I?

CHARLIE. (*More to himself.*) Eleven tho[u]sand dollars.

ERWIN. Well, I suppose Mr. Carver [is] waiting for me—I better get my verses [to]gether and—Get over there—

CHARLIE. You stay here.

ERWIN. But I can't, I—

CHARLIE. Until after the race.

ERWIN. But Charlie.

CHARLIE. (*Makes a gesture of finality a[nd] sits by the door.*) After the race.

ERWIN. (*Poetic.*) After the race (*si[ghs]*) after the race—
That ought to lead to something. (*Ta[kes] pencil and paper.*) Oh, I can't even thi[nk] any more.

EL. (*Turns on radio.*) Maybe I can
the race on here. (MABEL *turns on*
ng stations.)

IN. It's WMCA at the top of the dial
think. (*She gets the station.*)

OUNCER. . . . and took the first turn in
order. War Glory, Good Advice,
lies' Man and Mr. Khayyam.

RLIE. (*At the same time.*) That's it—
l it.

EL. (*To* CHARLIE.) Is this our race?

RLIE. Yeah—they're on their way.

OUNCER. At the quarter . . . War Glory,
d Advice, Mr. Khayyam there in that
er now. Lady's Man going up . . . yes,
Farino. Good Advice is holding that
l, jockey Meade using his head. There
are at the half, Good Advice, War
ry, Mr. Khayyam. Mr. Khayyam driv-
now—rushing in there. Ah, there's a
ble, a spill. Chase Me stumbled, throw-
the jockey, Slate. Slate's all right.
t's the three quarter pole. Mr. Khay-
now leading with Lady's Man coming
and War Glory right behind. There
come fast into the stretch. Looks like
ttle shoving there . . . no, all right. At
stretch coming down there with a
, Equipoise passes Mr. Khayyam, Sun
her right behind. Yes, yes, that's the
sh. Equipoise wins. Equipoise, the
itney horse with Workman up. Mr.
ayyam second and Sun Archer closed
to get third and in the money. Those
backed Equipoise had something to
thankful for today.
BEL *turns off radio.*)

IN. Well, that's too bad.

RLIE. Yes, it's just too bad.

EL. (*Slowly crosses to window.*) Ah,
, I'm just sick—you know it—I'm just.
to the stomach.

IN. Well, the handicappers were right
ey all thought Equipoise would win.
ll, that's what makes it interesting.
ANKIE *enters. Crosses to radio.*)

RLIE. Where's Patsy?

FRANKIE. He's coming.

CHARLIE. You guys wouldn't listen to me.
Didn't I tell you all along—I had a hunch
something like this would happen.
(PATSY *enters, comes toward* ERWIN.)

ERWIN. (*Rises.*) I suppose you want your
necktie back now.

PATSY. I want more than that.

ERWIN. I feel awfully sorry for you fellows.

PATSY. You better start feeling sorry for
yourself.

CHARLIE. He tried to beat it off to the
office and leave us holding the bag.

FRANKIE. What his brother-in-law said
about him was all true.

CHARLIE. The crook.

MABEL. (*Terrified.*) Boys, what are you
going to do?

PATSY. We'll give him something to remember us by. He knew damn well Equipoise was going to win.

ERWIN. I didn't. That's not so.

PATSY. Well, I'll tell you one thing . . .
he'll never forget that Mr. Khayyam lost.
(*Bing. He hits* ERWIN.)

MABEL. Patsy.

ERWIN. Now wait a minute.

PATSY. Learn you to cross us. (*Grabs him
by the coat and hits again.*)

FRANKIE. Give one for me.

MABEL. Don't—don't.

ERWIN. Don't you think this is a little
drastic?

PATSY. I'll show you what's drastic.

MABEL. Patsy . . . Patsy . . .

PATSY. You keep out of it. (*Shoving her
aside.*)

MABEL. Don't hit him again.

PATSY. I ain't started yet. Get a loud station, Frankie.
(FRANKIE *turns on radio.*)

CHARLIE. (*Grabs* MABEL *and holds her.*) Here. Don't try to interfere. That ain't going to do any good.

MABEL. No . . . No . . .

PATSY. Listen, I ain't even begun. (*Radio is heard.*)

CHARLIE. Wait a minute.

ANNOUNCER. Something going on down at the judges stand and no bets are being paid until the official announcement. Looks like a disqualification to me.

PATSY. What?

CHARLIE. Listen.

ANNOUNCER. . . . I was all wrong, folks,— I was all wrong. Equipoise did not win after all—the judges have been in a huddle down there at the stand—what excitement —wait a minute folks,—what is it, Perry? —here's the latest announcement—I just got it—Equipoise disqualified—Mr. Khayyam declared the official winner—Sun Archer second and Lady's Man third. Mr. Khayyam paid twelve to one
(FRANKIE *snaps it off. He turns to the others with a naive grin.*

PATSY. We won. (*They look at* ERWIN. PATSY *goes to him apologetically.*) Gee, I'm awfully sorry, Erwin—

ERWIN. You—(ERWIN *hits him a belt in the jaw.* PATSY *staggers back more from surprise than force.*)

PATSY. Hey, what's the idea?

MABEL. You had it coming to you.

CHARLIE. (*Pushing him about.*) Yeah, I don't blame Erwin. What's the idea of hitting him that way?

ERWIN. Yes, what's the idea? You make me good and mad. (*Takes a swing at* PATSY. PATSY, *mad, would defend himself.*)

CHARLIE. (*Pushing him away.*) Don't hit him, Patsy—he'll quit us.

(CLARENCE *opens center door and comes in, ad libbing. He sees* ERWIN *swinging on* PATSY, *who is apparently afraid of him. He is astounded.* ERWIN *turns and sees* CLARENCE—*full of new-born confidence he*

rushes at him. CLARENCE *runs out in and slams door.* ERWIN *turns and gets breath, leaning against door. Hercules cleaned the Aegean Stables.*)

PATSY. (*At desk.*) Come on, Erwin, d be sore. Announcers don't make mist like that often—and geez, we had shirts up.

AUDREY. (*Opens door, sees* ERWIN.) Th you very much—Erwin! I want to tal you—It's very important. What did do to Clarence?

ERWIN. Oh, that big—

AUDREY. Please forgive him—he's lost his money—he's so upset—
(CLARENCE *and* CARVER *appear center.*)

ERWIN. Oh, Mr. Carver—

AUDREY. And, Erwin, will you do n favor—?

ERWIN. Sure!

AUDREY. Will you speak to Mr. Carve

ERWIN. Why—

CARVER. (*Coming left of* ERWIN.) Erw

ERWIN. Yes, Mr. Carver—I'm sorry I-

CARVER. Have these men a contract you?

ERWIN. Oh no—no—they just—

CARVER. Who gave you your start?

ERWIN. You did, Mr. Carver.

CARVER. Who taught you the busin
(HARRY *enters, goes between* CARVER PATSY.)

HARRY. What do I do for the fifth?

CARVER. Don't interrupt!

HARRY. What do you mean, don't i rupt? (*Slaps* CARVER.) Who do you t you are?

ERWIN. Don't talk to Mr. Carver that

HARRY. (*Meek.*) Oh, all right, Erwi you say so. But what do I do in the f

PATSY. Shut up.

es. (*Enters with sheaf of money.*) Boy, I ride home on a cloud of glory.

in. Get back on your elevator.

es. Oh . . . yes sir, Mr. Erwin.

rey. (*In admiration.*) Erwin.

in. I'm sorry we've been interrupted, Carver.

er. I'm going to have the room with north light repainted and redecorated you can have that to work in, and I'm g to get you a new desk and put your e on the door and I'll give you sixty rs a week.

in. Sixty?

er. Seventy-five. (*Phone rings.*) I'm onference . . . telephones, telephones all day long . . . haven't I had enough ble . . . I'm sorry, Erwin, I'm sorry. *one rings again.*)

y. O.K. for me to answer that call, in?

in. Sure, go ahead. (PATSY *does so.*)

ey. Erwin, please do me a favor . . . ack to Mr. Carver. I know you'll be ier that way.

PATSY. They want to buy twenty per cent of you, Erwin. They've doubled their offer.

ERWIN. Yes. That's all right, except I won't be able to dope them anymore.

PATSY. Why not, why won't you?

ERWIN. Cause you made me bet.

PATSY. What's the difference?

ERWIN. Well, you can't dope them for money. You just have to do it for fun. I told you that. I wouldn't have any idea who was going to win now. (*Puts hand to his head.*)

AUDREY. What's the matter, Erwin? Do you want Clarence to leave the room?

ERWIN. Mr. Carver, have you got a pencil?

CARVER. (*Hurrying to get it.*) Yes, Erwin, yes, my boy, what is it?

ERWIN. Take this down:
    The race is o'er
    We've won my lad
    Love and kisses
    to dear ol' Dad.
(*Raises one finger indicating Father's Day Number One.*)

CURTAIN AND MUSIC

The Children's Hour

BY LILLIAN HELLMAN

FOR

D. HAMMETT

WITH THANKS

THE CHILDREN'S HOUR was produced and directed by Herman Shumlin
Maxine Elliott's Theatre, New York, on November 20, 1934. The settings
re designed by Aline Bernstein.

CAST

(In the order of their speech)

PEGGY ROGERS	Eugenia Rawls
MRS. LILY MORTAR	Aline McDermott
EVELYN MUNN	Elizabeth Seckel
HELEN BURTON	Lynne Fisher
LOIS FISHER	Jacqueline Rusling
CATHERINE	Barbara Leeds
ROSALIE WELLS	Barbara Beals
MARY TILFORD	Florence McGee
KAREN WRIGHT	Katherine Emery
MARTHA DOBIE	Anne Revere
DOCTOR JOSEPH CARDIN	Robert Keith
AGATHA	Edmonia Nolley
MRS. AMELIA TILFORD	Katherine Emmet
A GROCERY BOY	Jack Tyler

ACT I

Living-room of the Wright-Dobie School.
Late afternoon in April.

ACT II

Scene I. Living-room at Mrs. Tilford's. A few hours later.
Scene II. The same. Later that evening.

ACT III

The same as Act I. November.

THE CHILDREN'S HOUR

ACT ONE

SCENE: *A room in the Wright-Dobie School for girls, a converted farm-house eigh*
miles from the town of Lancet. It is a comfortable, unpretentious room used as an a
noon study-room and at all other times as the living-room.

A large door Left Center faces the audience. There is a single door Right. Against
back walls are bookcases. A large desk is at Right; a table, two sofas, and eight or
chairs.

It is early in an afternoon in April.

AT RISE: MRS. LILY MORTAR *is sitting in a large chair Right Center, with her*
back and her eyes closed. She is a plump, florid woman of forty-five with obvio
touched-up hair. Her clothes are too fancy for a class-room.

Seven girls, from twelve to fourteen years old, are informally grouped on chairs
sofa. Six of them are sewing with no great amount of industry on pieces of white mate
One of the others, EVELYN MUNN, *is using her scissors to trim the hair of* ROSALIE,
sits, nervously, in front of her. She has ROSALIE's *head bent back at an awkward a*
and is enjoying herself.

The eighth girl, PEGGY ROGERS, *is sitting in a higher chair than the others. Sh*
reading aloud from a book. She is bored and she reads in a singsong, tired voice.

PEGGY (*reading*). "It is twice blest; it bless-eth him that gives and him that takes: 'tis mightiest in the mightiest; it becomes the throned monarch better than his crown; his sceptre shows the force of temporal power, the attribute to awe and majesty, where-in . . ." (MRS. MORTAR *suddenly opens her eyes and stares at the hair-cutting. The children make efforts to warn* EVELYN. PEGGY *raises her voice until she is shouting.*) "doth sit the dread and fear of kings; but mercy is above . . ."

MRS. MORTAR. Evelyn! What are you doing?

EVELYN (*inanely. She lisps*). Uh—nothing, Mrs. Mortar.

MRS. MORTAR. You are certainly doing some-thing. You are ruining the scissors, for one thing.

PEGGY (*loudly*). "But mercy is above. It . . ."

MRS. MORTAR. Just a moment, Peggy. It is very unfortunate that you girls cannot sit quietly with your sewing and drink in the immortal words of the immortal bard. (*She sighs.*) Evelyn, go back to your sewing.

EVELYN. I can't get the hem thtraight. Hon-eth, I've been trying for three weekth, but I jutht can't do it.

MRS. MORTAR. Helen, please help Evelyn with the hem.

HELEN (*rises, holding up the garment*
LYN *has been working on. It is soiled*
shapeless, and so much has been cut off
it is now hardly large enough for a chil
five. Giggling.) She can't ever wear
Mrs. Mortar.

MRS. MORTAR (*vaguely*). Well, try to
something with it. Make some hand
chiefs or something. Be clever abou
Women must learn these tricks. (*To*
GY.) Continue. "Mightiest in the mi
est."

PEGGY. "'Tis mightiest in the mightie
becomes the throned monarch better
his crown; his sceptre—his sceptre sh
the force of temporal power, the attri
to awe and majesty, wherein—"

LOIS (*from the back of the room ch*
softly and monotonously through the
vious speech). Ferebam, ferebas, fer
ferebamus, ferebatis, fere, fere—

CATHERINE (*two seats away, the*
propped in front of her). Fere*bant.*

LOIS. Ferebamus, ferebatis, fere*bant.*

MRS. MORTAR. Who's doing that?

PEGGY (*the noise ceases. She hurries*
"Wherein doth sit the dread and fea
kings; but mercy is above this sceptred s

enthroned in the hearts of kings, it is
ttribute to God himself—"

, MORTAR (*sadly, reproachfully*). Peggy,
t you imagine yourself as Portia? Can't
read the lines with some feeling, some
? (*Dreamily.*) Pity. Ah! As Sir Henry
to me many's the time, pity makes the
ess. Now, why can't *you* feel pity?

GY. I guess I feel pity.

. Ferebamus, ferebatis, fere—fere—
—

HERINE. Fere*bant,* stupid.

. MORTAR. How many people in this
m are talking? Peggy, read the line
in. I'll give you the cue.

GY. What's a cue?

. MORTAR. A cue is a line or word given
actor or actress to remind them of their
t speech.

EN (*softly*). To remind *him* or *her*.

ALIE (*a fattish girl with glasses*). Weren't
ever in the movies, Mrs. Mortar?

. MORTAR. I had many offers, my dear.
the cinema is a shallow art. It has no—
— (*vaguely.*) no fourth dimension. Now,
gy, if you would only try to submerge
rself in this problem. You are pleading
the life of a man. (*She rises and there are
t sighs from the girls, who stare at her
h blank, bored faces. She recites ham-
y, with gestures.*) "But mercy is above
sceptred sway; it is enthroned in the
rts of kings, it is an attribute to God him-
; and earthly power doth then show likest
d's when mercy seasons justice."

s (*almost singing it*). Utor, fruor, fungor,
ior, and vescor take the dative.

HERINE. Take the *ablative.*

s. Oh, dear. Utor, fruor, fung—

s. MORTAR (*to LOIS, with sarcasm*). You
e something to tell the class?

s (*apologetically*). We've got a Latin
m this afternoon.

s. MORTAR. And you intend to occupy
sewing and elocution hour learning what
uld have been learnt yesterday?

CATHERINE (*wearily*). It takes her more than yesterday to learn it.

MRS. MORTAR. Well, I cannot allow you to interrupt us like this.

CATHERINE. But we're finished sewing.

LOIS (*admiringly*). I bet you were good at Latin, Mrs. Mortar.

MRS. MORTAR (*conciliated*). Long ago, my dear, long ago. Now, take your book over by the window and don't disturb our enjoyment of Shakespeare. (CATHERINE *and* LOIS *rise, go to window, stand mumbling and gesturing.*) Let us go back again. "It is an attribute of—" (*At this point the door opens far enough to let* MARY TILFORD, *clutching a slightly faded bunch of wild flowers, squeeze cautiously in. She is fourteen, neither pretty nor ugly. She is an undistinguished-looking girl, except for the sullenly dissatisfied expression on her face.*) "And earthly power doth then show likest God's when mercy seasons justice. We do pray for mercy, and that same prayer doth teach—"

PEGGY (*happily*). You've skipped three lines.

MRS. MORTAR. In my entire career I've never missed a line.

PEGGY. But you did skip three lines. (*Goes to* MRS. MORTAR *with book.*) See?

MRS. MORTAR (*seeing* MARY *sidling along wall toward other end of the room, turns to her to avoid* PEGGY *and the book*). Mary!

HELEN (*in whisper to* MARY). You're going to catch it now.

MRS. MORTAR. Mary!

MARY. Yes, Mrs. Mortar?

MRS. MORTAR. This is a pretty time to be coming to your sewing class, I must say. Even if you have no interest in your work you might at least remember that you owe me a little courtesy. Courtesy is breeding. Breeding is an excellent thing. (*Turns to class.*) Always remember that.

ROSALIE. Please, Mrs. Mortar, can I write that down?

MRS. MORTAR. Certainly. Suppose you all write it down.

PEGGY. But we wrote it down last week. (MARY *giggles*.)

MRS. MORTAR. Mary, I am still awaiting your explanation. Where have you been?

MARY. I took a walk.

MRS. MORTAR. So you took a walk. And may I ask, young lady, are we in the habit of taking walks when we should be at our classes?

MARY. I am sorry, Mrs. Mortar. I went to get you these flowers. I thought you would like them and I didn't know it would take so long to pick them.

MRS. MORTAR (*flattered*). Well, well.

MARY (*almost in tears*). You were telling us last week how much you liked flowers, and I thought that I would bring you some and—

MRS. MORTAR. That was very sweet of you, Mary; I always like thoughtfulness. But you must not allow anything to interfere with your classes. Now run along, dear, and get a vase and some water to put my flowers in. (MARY *turns, sticks out her tongue at* HELEN, *says* "A-a-a," *and exits Left*.) You may put that book away, Peggy. I am sure your family need never worry about your going on the stage.

PEGGY. I don't want to go on the stage. I want to be a lighthouse-keeper's wife.

MRS. MORTAR. Well, I certainly hope you won't read to him. (*The laughter of the class pleases her.* PEGGY *sits down among the other girls, who are making a great show of doing nothing.* MRS. MORTAR *returns to her chair, puts her head back, closes her eyes*.)

CATHERINE. How much longer, O Cataline, are you going to abuse our patience? (*To* LOIS.) Now translate it, and for goodness' sakes try to get it right this time.

MRS. MORTAR (*for no reason*). "One master passion in the breast, like Aaron's serpent, swallows all the rest." (*She and* LOIS *are murmuring during* KAREN WRIGHT'S *entrance.* KAREN *is an attractive woman of twenty-eight, casually pleasant in manner, without sacrifice of warmth or dignity. She smiles at the girls, goes to the desk. With her entrance there is an immediate change*

in the manner of the girls: they are fond [of] her and they respect her. She gives MOR[TAR,] whose quotation has reached her, an [an]noyed look.)

LOIS. "Quo usque tandem a*butere*. . . ."

KAREN (*automatically*). "Abutere." (*Op[ens] drawer in desk*). What's happened to y[our] hair, Rosalie?

ROSALIE. It got cut, Miss Wright.

KAREN (*smiling*). I can see that. A [new] style? Looks as though it has holes i[n it.]

EVELYN (*giggling*). I didn't mean to d[o it] that bad, Mith Wright, but Rothalie'th [got] funny hair. I thaw a picture in the pa[per] and I wath trying to do it that way.

ROSALIE (*feels her hair, looks pathetically [at]* KAREN). Oh, what shall I do, Miss Wrig[ht?] (*Gesturing*.) It's long here, and it's sh[ort] here and—

KAREN. Never mind. Come up to my ro[om] later and I'll see if I can fix it for you.

MRS. MORTAR. And hereafter we'll have [no] more haircutting.

KAREN. Helen, have you found your brace[let?]

HELEN. No, I haven't, and I've loo[ked] everywhere.

KAREN. Have another look. It must be [in] your room somewhere. (MARY *comes [in] Right, with her flowers in a vase. W[hen] she sees* KAREN, *she loses some of her as[sur]ance.* KAREN *looks at the flowers in [sur]prise*.)

MARY. Good afternoon, Miss Wright. (*[Sits] down, looks at* KAREN, *who is staring h[ard] at the flowers*.)

KAREN. Hello, Mary.

MRS. MORTAR (*fluttering around*). Pe[ggy] has been reading Portia for us. (PE[GGY] *sighs*.)

KAREN (*smiling*). Peggy doesn't like Por[tia.]

MRS. MORTAR. I don't think she quite ap[pre]ciates it, but—

KAREN (*patting* PEGGY *on the head*). W[ell,] I didn't either. I don't think I do [now.] Where'd you get those flowers, Mary?

MORTAR. She picked them for me.
rriedly.) It made her a little late to
, but she heard me say I loved flowers,
she went to get them for me. (*With*
gh.) The first wild flowers of the sea-

EN. But not the very first, are they,
y?

Y. I don't know.

EN. Where did you get them?

Y. Near Conway's cornfield, I think.

EN. It wasn't necessary to go so far.
re was a bunch exactly like this in the
age can this morning.

MORTAR (*after a second*). Oh, I can't
eve it! What a nasty thing to do! (*To*
Y.) And I suppose you have just as
an excuse for being an hour late to
kfast this morning, and last week— (*To*
EN.) I haven't wanted to tell you these
gs before, but—

EN (*hurriedly, as a bell rings off stage*).
re's the bell.

(*walking toward door*). Ad, ab, ante,
de, inter, con, post, præ— (*Looks up at*
EN.) I *can't* seem to remember the rest.

EN. Præ, pro, sub, super. Don't worry,
. You'll come out all right. (LOIS *smiles*,
. MARY *attempts to make a quick exit.*)
t a minute, Mary. (*Reluctantly* MARY
s back as the girls file out. KAREN *moves*
small chairs, clearing the room as she
s.) Mary, I've had the feeling—and I
't think I'm wrong—that the girls here
e happy; that they liked Miss Dobie
me, that they liked the school. Do you
k that's true?

Y. Miss Wright, I have to get my Latin
.

EN. I thought it was true until you
e here a year ago. I don't think you're
happy here, and I'd like to find out
. (*Looks at* MARY, *waits for an answer*,
none, shakes her head.*) Why, for exam-
do you find it necessary to lie to us so
n?

Y (*without looking up*). I'm not lying.
ent out walking and I saw the flowers

and they looked pretty and I didn't know
it was so late.

KAREN (*impatiently*). Stop it, Mary! I'm
not interested in hearing that foolish story
again. I *know* you got the flowers out of
the garbage can. What I do want to
know is why you feel you have to lie
out of it.

MARY (*beginning to whimper*). I *did* pick
the flowers near Conway's. You never believe me. You believe everybody but me.
It's always like that. Everything I say you
fuss at me about. Everything I do is wrong.

KAREN. You know that isn't true. (*Goes to*
MARY, *puts her arm around her, waits until
the sobbing has stopped.*) Look, Mary, look
at me. (*Raises* MARY'S *face with her hand.*)
Let's try to understand each other. If you
feel that you *have* to take a walk, or that
you just *can't* come to class, or that you'd
like to go into the village by yourself, come
and tell me—I'll try and understand.
(*Smiles.*) I don't say that I'll always agree
that you should do exactly what you want to
do, but I've had feelings like that, too—
everybody has—and I won't be unreasonable
about yours. But this way, this kind of lying
you do, makes everything wrong.

MARY (*looking steadily at* KAREN). I got
the flowers near Conway's cornfield.

KAREN (*looks at* MARY, *sighs, moves back
toward desk and stands there for a moment*). Well, there doesn't seem to be any
other way with you; you'll have to be punished. Take your recreation periods alone
for the next two weeks. No horseback-riding
and no hockey. Don't leave the school
grounds for any reason whatsoever. Is that
clear?

MARY (*carefully*). Saturday, too?

KAREN. Yes.

MARY. But you said I could go to the boat-
races.

KAREN. I'm sorry, but you can't go.

MARY. I'll tell my grandmother. I'll tell her
how everybody treats me here and the way
I get punished for every little thing I do.
I'll tell her, I'll—

MRS. MORTAR. Why, I'd slap her hands!

KAREN (*turning back from door, ignoring* MRS. MORTAR's *speech. To* MARY) Go upstairs, Mary.

MARY. I don't feel well.

KAREN (*wearily*). Go upstairs now.

MARY. I've got a pain. I've had it all morning. It hurts right here (*pointing vaguely in the direction of her heart.*) Really it does.

KAREN. Ask Miss Dobie to give you some hot water and bicarbonate of soda.

MARY. It's a bad pain. I've never had it before.

KAREN. I don't think it can be very serious.

MARY. My heart! It's my heart! It's stopping or something. I can't breathe. (*She takes a long breath and falls awkwardly to the floor.*)

KAREN (*sighs, shakes her head, kneels beside* MARY. *To* MRS. MORTAR). Ask Martha to phone Joe.

MRS. MORTAR (*going out*). Do you think—? Heart trouble is very serious in a child. (KAREN *picks* MARY *up from the floor and carries her off Right. After a moment* MARTHA DOBIE *enters Center. She is about the same age as* KAREN. *She is a nervous, high-strung woman.*)

KAREN (*enters Right*). Did you get Joe?

MARTHA (*nodding*). What happened to her? She was perfectly well a few hours ago.

KAREN. She probably still is. I told her she couldn't go to the boat-races and she had a heart attack.

MARTHA. Where is she?

KAREN. In there. Mortar's with her.

MARTHA. Anything really wrong with her?

KAREN. I doubt it. (*Sits down at desk and begins to mark papers.*) She's a problem, that kid. Her latest trick was kidding your aunt out of a sewing lesson with those faded flowers we threw out. Then she threatened to go to her grandmother with some tale about being mistreated.

MARTHA. And, please God, Grandma would believe her and take her away.

KAREN. Which would give the school a swell black eye. But we ought to do something.

MARTHA. How about having a talk ˙ Mrs. Tilford?

KAREN (*smiling*). You want to do it? (ˢ THA *shakes her head.*) I hate to do it. ˢ been so nice to us. (*Shrugging her sʰ ders.*) Anyway, it wouldn't do any g She's too crazy about Mary to see her fˢ very clearly—and the kid knows it.

MARTHA. How about asking Joe to say sˢ thing to her? She'd listen to him.

KAREN. That would be admitting that can't do the job ourselves.

MARTHA. Well, we can't, and we migʰ well admit it. We've tried everything we think of. She's had more attention than other three kids put together. And we haven't the faintest idea what goes oˢ side her head.

KAREN. She's a strange girl.

MARTHA. That's putting it mildly.

KAREN (*laughs*). It's funny. We always about the child as if she were a gr woman.

MARTHA. It's not so funny. There's s thing the matter with the kid. That's true ever since the first day she came. causes trouble here; she's bad for the girls; I don't know what it is—it's a fe I've got that it's wrong somewhere—

KAREN. All right, all right, we'll talk it with Joe. Now what about our other peˢ sance?

MARTHA (*laughs*). My aunt the act What's she been up to now?

KAREN. Nothing unusual. Last night at ner she was telling the girls about she lost her trunks in Butte, Montana, how she gave her best performance of lind during a hurricane. Today in the k en you could hear her on what Sir H said to her.

MARTHA. Wait until she does Hedda G standing on a chair. Sir Henry taugʰ to do it that way. He said it was a te great acting.

KAREN. You must have had a gay childl

MARTHA (*bitterly*). Oh, I did. I did, in God, how I used to hate all that—

EN. Couldn't we get rid of her soon, tha? I hate to make it hard on you, she really ought not to be here.

THA (after a moment). I know.

EN. We can scrape up enough money end her away. Let's do it.

THA (goes to her, affectionately pats her). You've been very patient about it. sorry and I'll talk to her today. It'll ably be a week or two before she can be y to leave. Is that all right?

EN. Of course. (Looks at her watch.) you get Joe himself on the phone?

THA. He was already on his way. Isn't lways on his way over here?

EN (laughs). Well, I'm going to marry some day, you know.

THA (looking at her). You haven't ed of marriage for a long time.

EN. I've talked of it with Joe.

THA. Then you are thinking about it— ?

EN. Perhaps when the term is over. By time we ought to be out of debt, and school should be paying for itself.

THA (nervously playing with a book on table). Then we won't be taking our tion together?

EN. Of course we will. The three of us.

THA. I had been looking forward to e place by the lake—just you and me— way we used to at college.

EN (cheerfully). Well, now there will be e of us. That'll be fun, too.

THA (after a pause). Why haven't you me this before?

EN. I'm not telling you anything we en't talked about often.

THA. But you're talking about it as soon .

EN. I'm glad to be able to. I've been in with Joe a long time. (MARTHA crosses indow and stands looking out, her back KAREN. KAREN finishes marking papers ' rises.) It's a big day for the school. alie's finally put an "l" in could.

MARTHA (in a dull, bitter tone, not turning from window). You really are going to leave, aren't you?

KAREN. I'm not going to leave, and you know it. Why do you say things like that? We agreed a long time ago that my marriage wasn't going to make any difference to the school.

MARTHA. But it will. You know it will. It can't help it.

KAREN. That's nonsense. Joe doesn't want me to give up here.

MARTHA (turning from window). I don't understand you. It's been so damned hard building this thing up, slaving and going without things to make ends meet—think of having a winter coat without holes in the lining again!—and now when we're getting on our feet, you're all ready to let it go to hell.

KAREN. This is a silly argument, Martha. Let's quit it. You haven't listened to a word I've said. I'm not getting married tomorrow, and when I do, it's not going to interfere with my work here. You're making something out of nothing.

MARTHA. It's going to be hard going on alone afterwards.

KAREN. For God's sake, do you expect me to give up my marriage?

MARTHA. I don't mean that, but it's so— (Door Center opens and DOCTOR JOSEPH CARDIN comes in. He is a large, pleasant-looking, carelessly dressed man of about thirty-five.)

CARDIN. Hello, darling. Hi, Martha. What's the best news?

MARTHA. Hello, Joe.

KAREN. We tried to get you on the phone. Come in and look at your little cousin.

CARDIN. Sure. What's the matter with her now? I stopped at Vernie's on the way over to look at that little black bull he bought. He's a baby! There's going to be plenty of good breeding done in these hills.

KAREN. You'd better come and see her. She says she has a pain in her heart. (Goes out Right.)

CARDIN (*stopping to light a cigarette*). Our little Mary pops up in every day's dispatches.

MARTHA (*impatiently*). Go and see her. Heart attacks are nothing to play with.

CARDIN (*looks at her*). Never played with one in my life. (*Exits Right.*)

(MARTHA *walks around room and finally goes to stare out window.*)
(MRS. MORTAR *enters Right.*)

MRS. MORTAR. *I* was asked to leave the room. (MARTHA *pays no attention.*) It seems that I'm not wanted in the room during the examination.

MARTHA (*over her shoulder*). What difference does it make?

MRS. MORTAR. What difference does it make? Why, it was a deliberate snub.

MARTHA. There's very little pleasure in watching a man use a stethoscope.

MRS. MORTAR. Isn't it natural that the child should have me with her? Isn't it natural that an older woman should be present? (*No answer.*) Very well, if you are so thick-skinned that you don't resent these things—

MARTHA. What are you talking about? Why, in the name of heaven, should *you* be with her?

MRS. MORTAR. It—it's customary for an older woman to be present during an examination.

MARTHA (*laughs*). Tell that to Joe. Maybe he'll give you a job as duenna for his office.

MRS. MORTAR (*reminiscently*). It was I who saved Delia Lampert's life the time she had that heart attack in Buffalo. We almost lost her that time. Poor Delia! We went over to London together. She married Robert Laffonne. Not seven months later he left her and ran away with Eve Cloun, who was playing the Infant Phenomenon in Birmingham—

MARTHA. Console yourself. If you've seen one heart attack, you've seen them all.

MRS. MORTAR. So you don't resent your aunt being snubbed and humiliated?

MARTHA. Oh, Aunt Lily!

MRS. MORTAR. Karen is consistently rude [to] me, and you know it.

MARTHA. I know that she is very polite [to] you, and—what's more important—[very] patient.

MRS. MORTAR. Patient with me? I, who h[ave] worked my fingers to the bone!

MARTHA. Don't tell yourself that too of[ten,] Aunt Lily; you'll come to believe it.

MRS. MORTAR. I *know* it's true. Where co[uld] you have gotten a woman of my reputa[tion] to give these children voice lessons, elo[cu]tion lessons? Patient with me! Here [I] donated my services—

MARTHA. I was under the impression [you] were being paid.

MRS. MORTAR. That small thing? I used [to] earn twice that for one performance.

MARTHA. The gilded days. It was very [ex]travagant of them to pay you so m[uch.] (*Suddenly tired of the whole thing.*) Yo[u're] not very happy here, are you, Aunt Lily[?]

MRS. MORTAR. Satisfied enough, I guess, [for] a poor relation.

MARTHA (*makes a motion of distaste*). [So] you don't like the school or the farm o[r—]

MRS. MORTAR. I told you at the beginn[ing] you shouldn't have bought a place like t[his.] Burying yourself on a farm! You'll regre[t it.]

MARTHA. We like it here. (*After a [mo]ment.*) Aunt Lily, you've talked about L[on]don for a long time. Would you like [to] go over?

MRS. MORTAR (*with a sigh*). It's been tw[en]ty years, and I shall never live to se[e it] again.

MARTHA. Well, you can go any time you l[ike.] We can spare the money now, and it [will] do you a lot of good. You pick out the [boat] you want and I'll get the passage. (*She [has] been talking rapidly, anxious to end [the] whole thing.*) Now that's all fixed. Y[ou'll] have a grand time seeing all your old frie[nds,] and if you live sensibly I ought to be a[ble] to let you have enough to get along [on.] (*She begins to gather books, notebooks, [and] pencils.*)

s. MORTAR (*slowly*). So you want me to
ve?

RTHA. That's not the way to put it. You've
nted to go ever since I can remember.

s. MORTAR. You're trying to get rid of me.

RTHA. That's it. We don't want you
und when we dig up the buried trea-
e.

s. MORTAR. So? You're turning me out?
my age! Nice, grateful girl you are.

RTHA. Oh, my God, how can anybody
l with you? You're going where you
nt to go, and we'll be better off alone.
at suits everybody. You complain about
farm, you complain about the school,
u complain about Karen, and now you
ve what you want and you're still looking
something to complain about.

s. MORTAR (*with dignity*). Please do not
se your voice.

RTHA. You ought to be glad I don't do
rse.

s. MORTAR. I absolutely refuse to be
pped off three thousand miles away.
not going to England. I shall go back
the stage. I'll write to my agents tomor-
w, and as soon as they have something
d for me—

RTHA. The truth is I'd like you to leave
n. The three of us can't live together,
l it doesn't make any difference whose
lt it is.

s. MORTAR. You wish me to go tonight?

RTHA. Don't act, Aunt Lily. Go as soon
you've found a place you like. I'll put
money in the bank for you tomorrow.

s. MORTAR. You think I'd take your
ney? I'd rather scrub floors first.

RTHA. I imagine you'll change your mind.

s. MORTAR. I should have known by this
e that the wise thing is to stay out of
r way when *he's* in the house.

RTHA. What are you talking about now?

s. MORTAR. Never mind. I should have
own better. You always take your spite
t on me.

MARTHA. Spite? (*Impatiently.*) Oh, don't
let's have any more of this today. I'm tired.
I've been working since six o'clock this
morning.

MRS. MORTAR. Any day that he's in the house
is a bad day.

MARTHA. When *who* is in the house?

MRS. MORTAR. Don't think you're fooling
me, young lady. I wasn't born yesterday.

MARTHA. Aunt Lily, the amount of disconnected unpleasantness that goes on in your
head could keep a psychologist busy for
years. Now go take your nap.

MRS. MORTAR. I know what I know. Every
time that man comes into this house, you
have a fit. It seems like you just can't stand
the idea of them being together. God knows
what you'll do when they get married.
You're jealous of him, that's what it is.

MARTHA (*her voice is tense and the previous
attitude of good-natured irritation is gone*).
I'm very fond of Joe, and you know it.

MRS. MORTAR. You're fonder of Karen, and
I know that. And it's unnatural, just as unnatural as it can be. You don't like their
being together. You were always like that
even as a child. If you had a little girl
friend, you always got mad when she liked
anybody else. Well, you'd better get a beau
of your own now—a woman of your age.

MARTHA. The sooner you get out of here,
the better. Your vulgarities are making me
sick and I won't stand for them any longer.
I want you to leave— (*At this point there
is a sound outside the large doors Center.
MARTHA breaks off, angry and ashamed.
After a moment she crosses to the door and
opens it.* EVELYN *and* PEGGY *are to be seen
on the staircase. For a second she stands still
as they stop and look at her. Then, afraid
that her anger with her aunt will color anything she might say to the children, she
crosses the room again and stands with her
back to them.*)

MARTHA. What were you doing outside the
door?

EVELYN (*hurriedly*). We were going upthtairth, Mith Dobie.

PEGGY. We came down to see how Mary
was.

MARTHA. And you stopped long enough to see how we were. Did you deliberately listen?

PEGGY. We didn't mean to. We heard voices and we couldn't help—

MRS. MORTAR (*fake social tone*). Eavesdropping is something nice young ladies just don't do.

MARTHA (*turning to face the children*). Go upstairs now. We'll talk about this later. (*Slowly shuts door as they begin to climb the stairs.*)

MRS. MORTAR. You mean to say you're not going to do anything about that? (*No answer. She laughs nastily.*) That's the trouble with these new-fangled notions of discipline and—

MARTHA (*thoughtfully*). You know, it's really bad having you around children.

MRS. MORTAR. What exactly does that mean?

MARTHA. It means that I don't like them hearing the things you say. Oh, I'll "do something about it," but the truth is that this is their home, and things shouldn't be said in it that they can't hear. When you're at your best, you're not for tender ears.

MRS. MORTAR. So now it's my fault, is it? Just as I said, whenever he's in the house you think you can take it out on me. You've got to have some way to let out steam and— (*Door opens Right and* CARDIN *comes in.*)

MARTHA. How is Mary? (MRS. MORTAR, *head in air, gives* MARTHA *a malicious half-smile and makes what she thinks is majestic exit Center.*)

MRS. MORTAR. Good day, Joseph.

CARDIN. What's the matter with the Duchess? (*Nods at door Center.*)

MARTHA. Just keeping her hand in, in case Sir Henry's watching her from above. What about Mary?

CARDIN. Nothing. Absolutely nothing.

MARTHA (*sighs*). I thought so.

CARDIN. I could have managed a better faint than that when I was six years old.

MARTHA. Nothing the matter with her at then?

CARDIN (*laughs*). No, ma'am, not a th Just a little something she thought up

MARTHA. But it's such a silly thing to She knew we'd have you in. (*Sighs.*) Ma she's not so bright. Any idiots in your f ily, Joe? Any inbreeding?

CARDIN. Don't blame her on me. It's ano side of the family. (*Laughs.*) You can l at Aunt Amelia and tell: old New Engl stock; never married out of Boston; thinks honor and dinner's at eight th Yes, ma'am, we're a proud old breed.

MARTHA. The Jukes were an old family, Look, Joe, have you any idea what is matter with Mary? I mean, has she alw been like this?

CARDIN. She's always been a honey. A Amelia's spoiling hasn't helped any, eit

MARTHA. We're reaching the end of our i with her. This kind of thing—

CARDIN (*looking at her*). Aren't you tal this too seriously?

MARTHA (*after a second*). I guess I am. you stay around kids long enough and won't know what to take seriously, eit But I do think somebody ought to tall Mrs. Tilford about her.

CARDIN. You wouldn't be meaning me n would you, Miss Dobie?

MARTHA. Well, Karen and I were talk about it this afternoon and—

CARDIN. Listen, friend, I'm marrying Ka but I'm not writing Mary Tilford in contract. (MARTHA *moves slightly.* CAI *takes her by the shoulders and turns around to face him again. His face is gr his voice gentle.*) Forget Mary for a i ute. You and I have got something to f about. Every time anything's said a marrying—about Karen marrying me— —(*She winces.*) There it is. I'm fond of I always thought you liked me. What is know how fond you are of Karen, but marriage oughtn't to make a great dea difference—

MARTHA (*pushing his hands from her sh ders*). God damn you. I wish— (*She her face in her hands.* CARDIN *watches*

*ilence, mechanically lighting a cigarette.
en she takes her hands from her face, she
ls them out to him. Contritely.)* Joe,
se, I'm sorry. I'm a fool, a nasty, bitter—

OIN *(takes her hands in one of his, pat-
them with his other hand).* Aw, shut
*(He puts an arm around her, and she
·s her head against his lapel. They are
·ding like that when* KAREN *comes in
ht.)*

THA *(to* KAREN, *as she wipes her eyes).*
·r friend's got a nice shoulder to weep on.

EN. He's an admirable man in every
. Well, the angel child is now putting
clothes back on.

THA. The angel child's influence is
·ad even while she's unconscious. Her
·n-mates were busy listening at the door
·le Aunt Lily and I were yelling at each
·r.

EN. We'll have to move those girls away
· one another. *(A bell rings from the
of the house.)*

THA. That's my class. I'll send Peggy
Evelyn down. You talk to them.

EN. All right. *(As* MARTHA *exits Center,
EN goes toward door Right. As she
·es* CARDIN *she kisses him.)* Mary! *(MARY
·s door, comes in, stands buttoning the
of her dress.)*

·IN *(to* MARY*).* How's it feel to be back
· the grave?

·y. My heart hurts.

·IN *(to* KAREN*).* Science has failed. Try
·irbrush.

·y. It's *my* heart, and it hurts.

·N. Sit down.

·y. I want to see my grandmother. I
·t to— *(*EVELYN *and* PEGGY *timidly enter
·er.)*

·N. Sit down, girls, I want to talk to you.

·y. We're awfully sorry, really. We just
·'t think and—

·N. I'm sorry too, Peggy. *(Thought-
·.)* You and Evelyn never used to do
·s like this. We'll have to separate you

EVELYN. Ah, Mith Wright, we've been together almotht a year.

KAREN. It was evidently too long. Now don't
let's talk about it. Peggy, you will move
into Lois's room, and Lois will move in
with Evelyn. Mary will go in with Rosalie.

MARY. Rosalie hates me.

KAREN. That's a very stupid thing to say.
I can't imagine Rosalie hating anyone.

MARY *(starting to cry).* And it's all because
I had a pain. If anybody else was sick they'd
be put to bed and petted. You're always
mean to me. I get blamed and punished
for everything. *(To* CARDIN.*)* I do, Cousin
Joe. All the time for everything. *(*MARY
by now is crying violently and as KAREN
half moves toward her, CARDIN, *who has been
frowning, picks* MARY *up and puts her down
on the couch.)*

CARDIN. You've been unpleasant enough to
Miss Wright. Lie here until you've stopped
working yourself into a fit. *(Picks up his
hat and bag, smiles at* KAREN.*)* I've got to
go now. She's not going to hurt herself
crying. The next time she faints, I'd wait
until she got tired lying on the floor. *(Passing* MARY, *he pats her head. She jerks away
from him.)*

KAREN. Wait a minute. I'll walk to the car
with you. *(To girls.)* Go up now and move
your things. Tell Lois to get her stuff ready.
(She and CARDIN *exit Center. A second after
the door is closed,* MARY *springs up and
throws a cushion at the door.)*

EVELYN. Don't do that. She'll hear you.

MARY. Who cares if she does? *(Kicks table.)*
And she can hear that, too. *(Small orna-
ment falls off table and breaks on floor,
EVELYN and PEGGY gasp, and MARY's bravado
disappears for a moment.)*

EVELYN *(frightened).* Now what are you
going to do?

PEGGY *(stooping down in a vain effort to
pick up the pieces).* You'll get the devil now.
Dr. Cardin gave it to Miss Wright. I guess
it was kind of a lover's gift. People get
awfully angry about a lover's gift.

MARY. Oh, leave it alone. She'll never know
we did it.

PEGGY. *We* didn't do it. You did it yourself.

MARY. And what will you do if I say *we* did do it? (*Laughs.*) Never mind, I'll think of something else. The wind could've knocked it over.

EVELYN. Did you really have a pain? one.

MARY. Oh, stop worrying about it. I'll get out of it.

EVELYN. Yeh. She'th going to believe that

MARY. I fainted, didn't I?

PEGGY. I wish I could faint sometimes. I've never even worn glasses, like Rosalie.

MARY. A lot it'll get you to faint.

EVELYN. What did Miss Wright do to you when the clath left?

MARY. Told me I couldn't go to the boat-races.

EVELYN. Whew!

PEGGY. But we'll remember everything that happens and we'll give you all the souvenirs and things.

MARY. I won't let you go if I can't go. But I'll find some way to go. What were *you* doing?

PEGGY. I guess we shouldn't have done it, really. We came down to see what was happening to you, but the doors were closed and we could hear Miss Dobie and Mortar having an awful row. Then Miss Dobie opens the door and there we were.

MARY. And a lot of crawling and crying you both did too, I bet.

EVELYN. We were thort of thorry about lithening. I gueth it wathn't—

MARY. Ah, you're always sorry about everything. What were they saying?

PEGGY. What was who saying?

MARY. Dobie and Mortar, silly.

PEGGY (*evasively*). Just talking, I guess.

EVELYN. Fighting, you mean.

MARY. About what?

EVELYN. Well, they were talking about M tar going away to England and—

PEGGY. You know, it really wasn't very to've listened, and I think it's worse to

MARY. You do, do you? You just don't me and see what happens. (PEGGY *sig*

EVELYN. Mortar got awful thore at that thaid they juth wanted to get rid of and then they thtarted talking about Cardin.

MARY. What about him?

PEGGY. We'd better get started moving; Wright will be back first thing we kno

MARY (*fiercely*). Shut up! Go on, Ev

EVELYN. They're going to be married.

MARY. Everybody knows that.

PEGGY. But everybody doesn't know Miss Dobie doesn't want them to get ried. How do you like that? (*The opens and* ROSALIE WELLS *sticks her in.*)

ROSALIE. I have a class soon. If you're g to move your things—

MARY. Close that door, you idiot. (Ros *closes door, stands near it.*) What do want?

ROSALIE. I'm trying to tell you. If ye going to move your things—not that I you in with me—you'd better start now. Miss Wright's coming in a mi

MARY. Who cares if she is?

ROSALIE (*starts for door*). I'm just te you for your own good.

PEGGY (*getting up*). We're coming.

MARY. No. Let Rosalie move our thing

ROSALIE. You crazy?

PEGGY (*nervously*). It's all right. E and I'll get your things. Come on, Ev

MARY. Trying to get out of telling me, Well, you won't get out of it that wa down and stop being such a sissy. Ro you go on up and move my things and say a word about our being down her

ROSALIE. And who was your French yesterday, Mary Tilford?

ᴿʏ (*laughing*). You'll do for today. Now
ᴏn, Rosalie, and fix our things.

ᴀʟɪᴇ. You crazy?

ʀʏ. And the next time we go into town,
let you wear my gold locket and buckle.
'll like that, won't you, Rosalie?

ᴀʟɪᴇ (*draws back, moves her hands ner-
sly*). I don't know what you're talking
ut.

ʀʏ. Oh, I'm not talking about anything
ᴘarticular. You just run along now and
ind me the next time to get my buckle
locket for you.

ᴀʟɪᴇ (*stares at her a moment*). All right,
do it this time, but just 'cause I got
ᴅ disposition. But don't think you're
ᴦg to boss me around, Mary Tilford.

ʀʏ (*smiling*). No, indeed. (ʀᴏsᴀʟɪᴇ *starts
door.*) And get the things done neatly,
ᴀlie. Don't muss my white linen bloom-
- (*The door slams as* ᴍᴀʀʏ *laughs.*)

ʏɴ. Now what do you think of that?
ᴀt made her tho agreeable?

ʀʏ. Oh, a little secret we got. Go on, now,
t else did they say?

ᴦʏ. Well, Mortar said that Dobie was
ᴏus of them, and that she was like that
ᴎ she was a little girl, and that she'd
ᴦr get herself a beau of her own because
as unnatural, and that she never wanted
ᴘody to like Miss Wright, and that was
ᴀtural. Boy! Did Miss Dobie get sore
ᴀt!

ʏɴ. Then we didn't hear any more.
ᴣy dropped a book.

ʏ. What'd she mean Dobie was jealous?

ᴦʏ. What's unnatural?

ʏɴ. Un for not. Not natural.

ᴦʏ. It's funny, because everybody gets
ʀied.

ʀʏ. A lot of people don't—they're too
.

ᴦʏ (*jumps up, claps her hand to her
ᴛh*). Oh, my God! Rosalie'll find that
of *Mademoiselle de Maupin*. She'll
like the dickens.

ʀ. Ah, she won't say a word.

EVELYN. Who getth the book when we
move?

MARY. You can have it. That's what I was
doing this morning—finishing it. There's
one part in it—

PEGGY. What part? (ᴍᴀʀʏ *laughs.*)

EVELYN. Well, what wath it?

MARY. Wait until you read it.

EVELYN. Don't forget to give it to me.

PEGGY. It's a shame about being moved. I've
got to go in with Helen, and she blows her
nose all night. Lois told me.

MARY. It was a dirty trick making us move.
She just wants to see how much fun she
can take away from me. She hates me.

PEGGY. No, she doesn't, Mary. She treats
you just like the rest of us—almost better.

MARY. That's right, stick up for your crush.
Take her side against mine.

PEGGY. I didn't mean it that way.

EVELYN (*looks at her watch*). We'd better
get upthtairth.

MARY. I'm not going.

PEGGY. Rosalie isn't so bad.

EVELYN. What you going to do about the
vathe?

MARY. I don't care about Rosalie and I don't
care about the vase. I'm not going to be here.

EVELYN *and* PEGGY (*together*). Not going
to be here! What do you mean?

MARY (*calmly*). I'm going home.

PEGGY. Oh, Mary—

EVELYN. You can't do that.

MARY. Can't I? You just watch. (*Begins to
walk around the room.*) I'm not staying
here. I'm going home and tell Grandma I'm
not staying any more. (*Smiles to herself.*)
I'll tell her I'm not happy. They're scared
of Grandma—she helped 'em when they
first started, you know—and when she tells
'em something, believe me, they'll sit up
and listen. They can't get away with treating me like this, and they don't have to
think they can.

PEGGY (*appalled*). You just going to walk out like that?

EVELYN. What are you going to tell your grandmother?

MARY. Oh, who cares? I'll think of something to tell her. I can always do it better on the spur of the moment.

PEGGY. She'll send you right back.

MARY. You let me worry about that. Grandma's very fond of me, on account my father was her favorite son. I can manage *her* all right.

PEGGY. I don't think you ought to go, really, Mary. It's just going to make an awful lot of trouble.

EVELYN. What'th going to happen about the vathe?

MARY. Say I did it—it doesn't make a bit of difference any more to me. Now listen, you two got to help. They won't miss me before dinner if you make Rosalie shut the door and keep it shut. Now, I'll go through the field to French's, and then I can get the bus to Homestead.

EVELYN. How you going to get to the thtreet-car?

MARY. Taxi, idiot.

PEGGY. How are you going to get out of here in the first place?

MARY. I'm going to walk out. You know where the front door is, or are you too dumb even for that? Well, I'm going right out that front door.

EVELYN. Gee, I wouldn't have the nerve.

MARY. Of course you wouldn't. You'd let 'em do anything to you they want. Well, they can't do it to me. Who's got any money?

EVELYN. Not me. Not a thent.

MARY. I've got to have at least a dollar for the taxi and a dime for the bus.

EVELYN. And where you going to find it

PEGGY. See? Why don't you just wait u your allowance comes Monday, and t you can go any place you want. Maybe that time—

MARY. I'm going today. *Now.*

EVELYN. You can't *walk* to Lanthet.

MARY (*goes to* PEGGY). You've got mo You've got two dollars and twenty cents.

PEGGY. I—I—

MARY. Go get it for me.

PEGGY. No! No! I won't get it for you.

EVELYN. You can't have *that* money, Ma

MARY. Get it for me.

PEGGY (*cringes, her voice is scared*). I w I won't. Mamma doesn't send me muc lowance—not half as much as the re you get—I saved this so long—you too from me last time—

EVELYN. Ah, she wantth that bithycle bad.

PEGGY. I haven't gone to the movi haven't had any candy, I haven't had thing the rest of you get all the tim took me so long to save that and I—

MARY. Go upstairs and get me the mon

PEGGY (*hysterically, backing away from* I won't. I won't. I won't. (MARY ma sudden move for her, grabs her left and jerks it back, hard and expertly. P screams softly. EVELYN tries to take M arm away. Without releasing her hol PEGGY, MARY slaps EVELYN's face. EVELY gins to cry.*)

MARY. Just say when you've had enou

PEGGY (*softly, stiflingly*). All—all right get it. (MARY smiles, nods her head a Curtain falls.*)

ACT TWO

SCENE I

CENE: Living-room at MRS. TILFORD'S. *It is a formal room, without being cold or gant. The furniture is old, but excellent. The exit to the hall is Left; glass doors Right l to a dining-room that cannot be seen.*

T RISE: Stage is empty. Voices are heard in the hall.

THA (*off-stage*). What are *you* doing ? Well, come on in—don't stand there ing at me. Have they given you a holi- or did you just decide you'd get a bet- dinner here? (AGATHA *enters Left, fol- ed by* MARY. AGATHA *is a sharp-faced d, no longer young, with a querulous e.*) Can't you even say hello?

Y. Hello, Agatha. You didn't give me ance. Where's Grandma?

HA. Why aren't you in school? Look our face and clothes. Where have you ?

Y. I got a little dirty coming home. I ed part of the way through the woods.

HA. Why didn't you put on your middy se and your old brown coat?

Y. Oh, stop asking me questions. ere's Grandma?

HA. Where ought any clean person be his time of day? She's taking a bath.

Y. Is anybody coming for dinner?

HA. She didn't say anything about you ing.

Y. How could she, stupid? She didn't w.

HA. Then what are you doing here?

Y. Leave me alone. I don't feel well.

HA. Why don't you feel well? Who ever d of a person going for a walk in the ds when they didn't feel well?

Y. Oh, leave me alone. I came home be- e I was sick.

HA. You look all right.

Y. But I don't feel all right. (*Whining.*) 't even come home without everybody ing at me.

HA. Don't think you're fooling me, g lady. You might pull the wool over

some people's eyes, but—I bet you've been up to something again. (*Stares suspiciously at* MARY, *who says nothing.*) Well, you wait right here till I tell your grandmother. And if you feel so sick, you certainly won't want any dinner. A good dose of rhubarb and soda will fix you up. (*Exits Left.*)

(MARY *makes a face in the direction* AGATHA *has gone and stops sniffling. She looks ner- vously around the room, then goes to a low mirror and tries several experiments with her face in an attempt to make it look sick and haggard.*)

(MRS. TILFORD, *followed by* AGATHA, *enters Left.* MRS. TILFORD *is a large, dignified wo- man in her sixties, with a pleasant, strong face.*)

AGATHA (*to* MRS. TILFORD, *as she follows her into the room*). Why didn't you put some cold water on your chest? Do you want to catch your death of cold at your age? Did you have to hurry so?

MRS. TILFORD. Mary, what are you doing home? (MARY *rushes to her and buries her head in* MRS. TILFORD'S *dress, crying.* MRS. TILFORD *lets her cry for a moment while she pats her head, then puts an arm around the child and leads her to a sofa.*)

MRS. TILFORD. Never mind, dear; now stop crying and tell me what is the matter.

MARY (*gradually stops crying, fondling* MRS. TILFORD'S *hand, playing on the older wo- man's affection for her*). It's so good to see you, Grandma. You didn't come to visit me all last week.

MRS. TILFORD. I couldn't, dear. But I was coming tomorrow.

MARY. I missed you so. (*Smiling up at* MRS. TILFORD.) I was awful homesick.

MRS. TILFORD. I'm glad that's all it was. I was frightened when Agatha said you were not well.

AGATHA. Did I say that? I said she needed a good dose of rhubarb and soda. Most likely she only came home for Wednesday night fudge cake.

MRS. TILFORD. We all get homesick. But how did you get here? Did Miss Karen drive you over?

MARY. I—I walked most of the way, and then a lady gave me a ride and—(*Looks timidly at* MRS. TILFORD.)

AGATHA. Did she have to walk through the woods in her very best coat?

MRS. TILFORD. Mary! Do you mean you left without permission?

MARY (*nervously*). I ran away, Grandma. They didn't know—

MRS. TILFORD. That was a very bad thing to do, and they'll be worried. Agatha, phone Miss Wright and tell her Mary is here. John will drive her back before dinner.

MARY (*as* AGATHA *starts toward telephone*). No, Grandma, don't do that. Please don't do that. Please let me stay.

MRS. TILFORD. But, darling, you can't leave school any time you please.

MARY. Oh, please, Grandma, don't send me back right away. You don't know how they'll punish me.

MRS. TILFORD. I don't think they'll be that angry. Come, you're acting like a foolish little girl.

MARY (*hysterically, as she sees* AGATHA *about to pick up the telephone*). Grandma! Please! I can't go back! I can't! They'll kill me! They will, Grandma! They'll kill me! (MRS. TILFORD *and* AGATHA *stare at* MARY *in amazement. She puts her head in* MRS. TILFORD's *lap and sobs.*)

MRS. TILFORD (*motioning with a hand for* AGATHA *to leave the room*). Never mind phoning now, Agatha.

AGATHA. If you're going to let her— (MRS. TILFORD *repeats the gesture.* AGATHA *exits Right, with offended dignity.*)

MRS. TILFORD. Stop crying, Mary.

MARY (*raising her head from* MRS. TILFORD's *lap*). It's so nice here, Grandma.

MRS. TILFORD. I'm glad you like being h[ere] with me, but at your age you can hard[ly] (*More seriously.*) What made you say [such] a terrible thing about Miss Wright and [Miss] Dobie? You know they wouldn't hurt [you].

MARY. Oh, but they would. They— (*Breaks off, looks around as if hunting f[or a] clue to her next word; then dramatically[.] I* fainted today!

MRS. TILFORD (*alarmed*). Fainted?

MARY. Yes, I did. My heart—I had a p[ain] in my heart. I couldn't help having a p[ain] in my heart, and when I fainted righ[t in] class, they called Cousin Joe and he [said] I didn't. He said it was maybe only [that] I ate my breakfast too fast and Miss Wr[ight] blamed me for it.

MRS. TILFORD (*relieved*). I'm sure if Jos[eph] said it wasn't serious, it wasn't.

MARY. But I did have a pain in my hea[rt,] honest.

MRS. TILFORD. Have you still got it?

MARY. I guess I haven't got it much [any] more, but I feel a little weak, and I [was] so scared of Miss Wright being so m[ean] to me just because I was sick.

MRS. TILFORD. Scared of Karen? Nons[ense.] It's perfectly possible that you had a p[ain,] but if you had really been sick your Co[usin] Joseph would certainly have known it. [It's] not nice to frighten people by pretendi[ng to] be sick when you aren't.

MARY. I didn't *want* to be sick, but I'm [al]ways getting punished for everything.

MRS. TILFORD (*gently*). You mustn't ima[gine] things like that, child, or you'll grow u[p to] be a very unhappy woman. I'm not g[oing] to scold you any more for coming h[ome] this time, though I suppose I should. [Run] along upstairs and wash your face [and] change your dress, and after dinner [John] will drive you back. Run along.

MARY (*happily*). I can stay for dinner?

MRS. TILFORD. Yes.

MARY. Maybe I could stay till the fir[st of] the week. Saturday's your birthday a[nd I] could be here with you.

MRS. TILFORD. We don't celebrate my b[irth]day, dear. You'll have to go back to s[chool] after dinner.

y. But— (*She hesitates, then goes up to* TILFORD *and puts her arms around the* r *woman's neck. Softly.*) How much do love me?

TILFORD (*smiling*). As much as all the ds in all the books in all the world.

y. Remember when I was little and you to tell me that right before I went to ? And it was a rule nobody could say her single word after you finished? You to say: "Wor-rr-ld," and then I had to my eyes tight.

TILFORD. And sometimes you were ghty and didn't shut them.

y. I miss you an awful lot, Grandma.

TILFORD. And I miss you, but I'm afraid Latin is too rusty—you'll learn it better chool.

y. But couldn't I stay out the rest of this ? After the summer maybe I won't d it so much. I'll study hard, honest, —

TILFORD. You're an earnest little coaxer, it's out of the question. Back you go ght. (*Gives* MARY *a playful slap.*) Let's have any more talk about it now, and have no more running away from l ever.

y (*slowly*). Then I really have to go there tonight?

TILFORD. Of course.

y. You don't love me. You don't care her they kill me or not.

TILFORD. Mary.

y. You don't! You don't! You don't care happens to me.

TILFORD (*sternly*). But I *do* care that e talking this way.

y (*meekly*). I'm sorry I said that, Grand- I didn't mean to hurt your feelings. s *her arms around* MRS. TILFORD's *neck.*) ive me?

TILFORD. What made you talk like that?

y (*in a whisper*). I'm scared, Grandma, scared. They'll do dreadful things to

MRS. TILFORD. Dreadful? Nonsense. They'll punish you for running away. You deserve to be punished.

MARY. It's not that. It's not anything I do. It never is. They—they just punish me any-how, just like they got something against me. I'm afraid of them, Grandma.

MRS. TILFORD. That's ridiculous. What have they ever done to you that is so terrible?

MARY. A lot of things—all the time. Miss Wright says I can't go to the boat-races and— (*Realizing the inadequacy of this reply, she breaks off, hesitates, hunting for a more telling reply, and finally stammers.*) It's—it's after what happened today.

MRS. TILFORD. You mean something else be-sides your naughtiness in pretending to faint and then running away?

MARY. I *did* faint. I didn't pretend. They just said that to make me feel bad. Anyway, it wasn't anything that I did.

MRS. TILFORD. What was it, then?

MARY. I can't tell you.

MRS. TILFORD. Why?

MARY (*sulkily*). Because you're just going to take their part.

MRS. TILFORD (*a little annoyed*). Very well. Now run upstairs and get ready for dinner.

MARY. It was—it was all about Miss Dobie and Mrs. Mortar. They were talking awful things, and Peggy and Evelyn heard them and Miss Dobie found out, and then they made us move our rooms.

MRS. TILFORD. What has that to do with you? I don't understand a word you're saying.

MARY. They made us move our rooms. They said we couldn't be together any more. They're afraid to have us near them, that's what it is, and they're taking it out on me. They're scared of you.

MRS. TILFORD. For a little girl you're imagin-ing a lot of big things. Why should they be scared of me? Am I such an unpleasant old lady?

MARY. They're afraid you'll find out.

MRS. TILFORD. Find out what?

MARY (*vaguely*). Things.

MRS. TILFORD. Run along, Mary. I hope you'll get more coherent as you get older.

MARY (*slowly starting for door*). All right. But there're a lot of things. They have secrets or something, and they're afraid I'll find out and tell you.

MRS. TILFORD. There's not necessarily anything wrong with people having secrets.

MARY (*coming back in the room again*). But they've got funny ones. Peggy and Evelyn heard Mrs. Mortar telling Miss Dobie that she was jealous of Miss Wright marrying Cousin Joe.

MRS. TILFORD. You shouldn't repeat things like that.

MARY. But that's what she said, Grandma. She said it was unnatural for a girl to feel that way.

MRS. TILFORD. What?

MARY. I'm just telling you what she said. She said there was something funny about it, and that Miss Dobie had always been like that, even when she was a little girl, and that it was unnatural—

MRS. TILFORD. Stop using that silly word, Mary.

MARY (*vaguely realizing that she is on the right track, hurries on*). But that was the word *she* kept using, Grandma, and then they got mad and told Mrs. Mortar she'd have to get out.

MRS. TILFORD. That was probably not the reason at all.

MARY (*nodding vigorously*). I bet it was, because honestly, Miss Dobie does get cranky and mean every time Cousin Joe comes, and today I heard her say to him: "God damn you," and then she said she was just a jealous fool and—

MRS. TILFORD. You have picked up some very fine words, haven't you, Mary?

MARY. That's just what she said, Grandma, and one time Miss Dobie was crying in Miss Wright's room, and Miss Wright was trying to stop her, and she said that all right, maybe she wouldn't get married right away if—

MRS. TILFORD. How do you know all this?

MARY. We couldn't help hearing beca[use] they—I mean Miss Dobie—was talking [aw]ful loud, and their room is right [next] to ours.

MRS. TILFORD. Whose room?

MARY. Miss Wright's room, I mean, and [you] can just ask Peggy and Evelyn whether [they] didn't hear. Almost always Miss D[obie] comes in after we go to bed and stays a [long] time. I guess that's why they want to [get] rid of us—of me—because we hear th[em.] That's why they're making us move [our] room, and they punish me all the time f[or—]

MRS. TILFORD. For eavesdropping, I sh[ould] think. (*She has said this mechanically. [With] nothing definite in her mind, she is ma[king] an effort to conceal the fact that* MARY'[s de]*scription of the life at school has sho[cked] her.*) Well, now I think we've had en[ough] gossip, don't you? Dinner's almost re[ady] and I can't eat with a girl who has su[ch a] dirty face.

MARY (*softly*). I've heard other things, [too.]

MRS. TILFORD (*abstractedly*). What? [What] did you say?

MARY. I've heard other things. Plent[y of] other things, Grandma.

MRS. TILFORD. What things?

MARY. Bad things.

MRS. TILFORD. Well, what were they?

MARY. I can't tell you.

MRS. TILFORD. Mary, you're annoying [me] very much. If you have anything to [say,] then say it and stop acting silly.

MARY. I mean I can't say it out loud.

MRS. TILFORD. There couldn't possib[ly be] anything so terrible that you couldn'[t say] it out loud. Now either tell the truth [or be] still.

MARY. Well, a lot of things I don't u[nder]stand. But it's awful, and sometimes [they] fight and then they make up, and [Miss] Dobie cries and Miss Wright gets mad [and] then they make up again, and ther[e are] funny noises and we get scared.

MRS. TILFORD. Noises? I suppose you [all] have a happy time imagining a murd[er.]

Y. And we've seen things, too. Funny
gs. (*Sees the impatience of her grand-
her.*) I'd tell you, but I got to whisper

, TILFORD. Why must you whisper it?

Y. I don't know. I just got to. (*Climbs
he sofa next to* MRS. TILFORD *and begins
spering. At first the whisper is slow and
tant, but it gradually works itself up to
excited talking. In the middle of it* MRS.
ORD *stops her.*)

TILFORD (*trembling*). Do you know
t you're saying? (*Without answering,
goes back to the whispering until the
woman takes her by the shoulders and
her around to stare in her face.*) Mary!
you telling me the truth?

. Honest, honest. You just ask Peggy
Evelyn and— (*After a moment* MRS.
ORD *gets up and begins to pace about
oom. She is no longer listening to* MARY,
keeps up a running fire of conversa-
) They know, too. And maybe there're
kids who know, but we've always been
tened and so we didn't ask, and one
t I was going to go and find out, but I
scared and we went to bed early so we
dn't hear, but sometimes I couldn't
it, but we never talked about it much,
se we thought they'd find out and—
Grandma, don't make me go back to that
awful place.

TILFORD (*abstractedly*). What? (*Starts
ove about again.*)

. Don't make me go back to that
. I just couldn't stand it any more.
y, Grandma, I'm so unhappy there,
f only I could stay out the rest of the
why, then—

MRS. TILFORD (*makes irritated gesture*). Be
still a minute. (*After a moment.*) No, you
won't have to go back.

MARY (*surprised*). Honest?

MRS. TILFORD. Honest.

MARY (*hugging* MRS. TILFORD). You're the
nicest, loveliest grandma in all the world.
You—you're not mad at me?

MRS. TILFORD. I'm not mad at you. Now go
upstairs and get ready for dinner. (MARY
kisses her and runs happily out Left. MRS.
TILFORD *stands staring after her for a long
moment; then, very slowly, she puts on her
eyeglasses and crosses to the phone. She dials
a number.*) Is Miss Wright—is Miss Wright
in? (*Waits a second, hurriedly puts down
the receiver.*) Never mind, never mind.
(*Dials another number.*) Dr. Cardin, please.
Mrs. Tilford. (*She remains absolutely motionless while she waits. When she does
speak, her voice is low and tense.*) Joseph?
Joseph? Can you come to see me right
away? Yes, I'm perfectly well. No, but it's
important, Joseph, very important. I must
see you right away. I—I can't tell you over
the phone. Can't you come sooner? It's not
about Mary's fainting—I said it's not about
Mary, Joseph; in one way it's about Mary—
(*Suddenly quiet.*) But will the hospital take
so long? Very well, Joseph, make it as soon
as you can. (*Hangs up the receiver, sits for
a moment undecided. Then, taking a breath,
she dials another number.*) Mrs. Munn,
please. This is Mrs. Tilford. Miriam? This
is Amelia Tilford. I have something to tell
you—something very shocking, I'm afraid—
something about the school and Evelyn and
Mary—

CURTAIN

SCENE II

ENE: *The same as Scene I. The curtain has been lowered to mark the passing of
hours.*

RISE: MARY *is lying on the floor playing with a puzzle.* AGATHA *appears lugging
ets and pillows across the room. Almost at the door, she stops and gives* MARY
noyed look.

A. And see to it that she doesn't get
ood quilt all dirty, and let her wear
green pyjamas.

Who?

AGATHA. Who? Don't you ever keep your
ears open? Rosalie Wells is coming over to
spend the night with you.

MARY. You mean she's going to sleep *here*?

AGATHA. You heard me.

MARY. What for?

AGATHA. Do I know all the crazy things that are happening around here? Your grandmother phoned Mrs. Wells all the way to New York, three dollars and eighty-five cents and families starving, and Mrs. Wells wanted to know if Rosalie could stay here until tomorrow.

MARY (*relieved*). Oh. Couldn't Evelyn Munn come instead?

AGATHA. Sure. We'll have the whole town over to entertain you.

MARY. I won't let Rosalie Wells wear my new pyjamas.

AGATHA (*exits as the front door-bell rings*). Don't tell me what you won't do. You'll act like a lady for once in your life. (*Off-stage.*) Come on in, Rosalie. Just go on in there and make yourself at home. Have you had your dinner?

ROSALIE (*off-stage*). Good evening. Yes'm.

AGATHA (*off-stage*). Hang up your pretty coat. Have you had your bath?

ROSALIE (*off-stage*). Yes, ma'am. This morning.

AGATHA (*off-stage*). Well, you better have another one. (*She is climbing the stairs as* ROSALIE *comes into the room.* MARY, *lying in front of the couch, is hidden from her. Gingerly* ROSALIE *sits down on a chair.*)

MARY (*softly*). Whoooooo. (ROSALIE *jumps.*) Whooooooo. (ROSALIE, *frightened, starts hurriedly for the door.* MARY *sits up, laughs.*) You're a goose.

ROSALIE (*belligerently*). Oh, so it's you. Well, who likes to hear funny noises at night? You could have been a werewolf.

MARY. A werewolf wouldn't want you.

ROSALIE. You know everything, don't you? (MARY *laughs.* ROSALIE *comes over, stands staring at puzzle.*) Isn't it funny about school?

MARY. What's funny about it?

ROSALIE. Don't act like you can come home every night.

MARY. Maybe I can from now on. (R[olls] over on her back luxuriously.) Maybe [I'm] never going back.

ROSALIE. Am I going back? I don't wan[t to] stay home.

MARY. What'll you give to know?

ROSALIE. Nothing. I'll ask Mamma.

MARY. Will you give me a free T. L. [if I] tell you?

ROSALIE (*thinks for a moment*). All ri[ght.] Lois Fisher told Helen that you were [very] smart.

MARY. That's an old one. I don't take i[t.]

ROSALIE. You got to take it.

MARY. Nope.

ROSALIE (*laughs*). You don't know, any[way.]

MARY. I know what I heard, and I k[now] Grandma phoned your mother in New Y[ork] to come and get you right away. Yo[u're] just going to spend the night here. I [wish] Evelyn could come instead of you.

ROSALIE. But what's happened? Peggy [and] Helen and Evelyn and Lois went hom[e last] night, too. Do you think somebody's [got] scarlet fever or something?

MARY. No.

ROSALIE. Do *you* know what it is? H[ow did] you find out? (*No answer.*) You're al[ways] pretending you know everything. Y[ou're] just faking. (*Flounces away.*) Never m[ind,] don't bother telling me. I think curios[ity is] very unladylike, anyhow. I have no [con-]cern with your silly secrets.

MARY. Suppose I told you that I just [might] have said that you were in on it?

ROSALIE. In on what?

MARY. The secret. Suppose I told you t[hat I] *may have* said that you told me abou[t it?]

ROSALIE. Why, Mary Tilford! You can['t do] a thing like that. I didn't tell you [about] anything. (MARY *laughs.*) Did you tell [your] grandmother such a thing?

MARY. Maybe.

ROSALIE. Did you?

MARY. Maybe.

LIE. Well, I'm going right up to your
dmother and tell her I didn't tell you
hing—whatever it is. You're just try-
to get me into trouble and I'm not go-
to let you. (*Starts for door.*)

Y. Wait a minute, I'll come with you.

LIE. What for?

Y. I want to tell her about Helen Bur-
bracelet.

LIE (*sits down suddenly*). What about

Y. Just that you stole it.

LIE. Shut up. I didn't do any such thing.

Y. Yes, you did.

LIE (*tearfully*). You made it up. You're
ys making things up.

Y. You can't call me a fibber, Rosalie
s. That's a kind of a dare and I won't
a dare. I guess I'll go tell Grandma,
vay. Then she can call the police and
ll come for you and you'll spend the
of your life in one of those solitary
ns and you'll get older and older, and
you're very old and can't see any-
, they'll let you out maybe with a big
on your back saying you're a thief,
your mother and father will be dead
you won't have any place to go and
beg on the streets—

LIE. I didn't steal anything. I borrowed
racelet and I was going to put it back
on as I'd worn it to the movies. I
meant to keep it.

. Nobody'll believe that, least of all the
. You're just a common, ordinary
Stop that bawling. You'll have the
house down here in a minute.

LIE. You won't tell? Say you won't tell.

. Am I a fibber?

IE. No.

. Then say: "I apologize on my hands
nees."

IE. I apologize on my hands and knees.
play with the puzzle.

. Wait a minute. Say: "From now on,
alie Wells, am the vassal of Mary Til-

ford and will do and say whatever she tells
me under the solemn oath of a knight."

ROSALIE. I won't say that. That's the worst
oath there is. (MARY *starts for the door.*)

Mary! Please don't—

MARY. Will you swear it?

ROSALIE (*sniffling*). But then you could tell
me to do anything.

MARY. And you'd have to do it. Say it quick
or I'll—

ROSALIE (*hurriedly*). From now on, I, Rosalie Wells, am the vassal of Mary Tilford
and will do and say whatever she tells me
under the solemn oath of a knight. (*She
gasps, and sits up straight as* MRS. TILFORD
enters.)

MARY. Don't forget that.

MRS. TILFORD. Good evening, Rosalie, you're
looking very well.

ROSALIE. Good evening, Mrs. Tilford.

MARY. She's getting fatter every day.

MRS. TILFORD (*abstractedly*). Then it's very
becoming. (*Door-bell rings.*) That must be
Joseph. Mary, take Rosalie into the library.
There's some fruit and milk on the table.
Be sure you're both fast asleep by half past
ten. (*Leans down, kisses them both.* ROSALIE
starts to exit Right, sees MARY, *stops and
hesitates.*)

MARY. Go on, Rosalie. (*Waits until* ROSALIE
reluctantly exits.) Grandma.

MRS. TILFORD. Yes?

MARY. Grandma, Cousin Joe'll say I've got
to go back. He'll say I really wasn't— (CAR-
DIN *enters and she runs from the room.*)

CARDIN. Hello, Amelia. (*Looks curiously at
the fleeing* MARY.) Mary home, eh?

MRS. TILFORD (*watching* MARY *as she leaves*).
Hello, Joseph. Sit down. (*He sits down,
looks at her curiously, waits for her to
speak.*) Whisky?

CARDIN. Please. How are you feeling? Headaches again?

MRS. TILFORD (*puts drink on table*). No.

CARDIN. Those are good powders. Bicarbonate of soda and water. Never hurt anybody
yet.

MRS. TILFORD. Yes. How have you been, Joseph?

CARDIN. My good health is monotonous.

MRS. TILFORD (*vaguely, sparring for time*). I haven't seen you the last few weeks. Agatha misses you for Sunday dinners.

CARDIN. I've been busy. We're getting the results from the mating-season right about now.

MRS. TILFORD. Did I take you away from a patient?

CARDIN. No. I was at the hospital.

MRS. TILFORD. How's it getting on?

CARDIN. Just the same. No money, badly equipped, a lousy laboratory, everybody growling at everybody else— Amelia, you didn't bring me here to talk about the hospital. We're talking like people waiting for the muffins to be passed around. What's the matter with you?

MRS. TILFORD. I—I have something to tell you.

CARDIN. Well, out with it.

MRS. TILFORD. It's a very hard thing to say, Joseph.

CARDIN. Hard for you to say to *me*? (*No answer.*) Don't be worried about Mary. I guessed that she ran home to tell you about her faint. It was caused by nothing but bad temper and was very clumsily managed, at that. Amelia, she's a terribly spoilt—

MRS. TILFORD. I heard about the faint. That's not what is worrying me.

CARDIN (*gently*). Are you in some trouble?

MRS. TILFORD. We all are in trouble. Bad trouble.

CARDIN. We? Me, you mean? Nothing's the matter with me.

MRS. TILFORD. When did you last see Karen?

CARDIN. Today. This afternoon.

MRS. TILFORD. Oh. Not since seven o'clock?

CARDIN. What's happened since seven o'clock?

MRS. TILFORD. Joseph, you've been engaged to Karen for a long time. Are your plans any more definite than they were a [...] ago?

CARDIN. You can get ready to buy the [...] ding present. We'll have the wedding h[...] if you don't mind. The smell of clean [...] girls and boiled linen would worry me[...]

MRS. TILFORD. Why has Karen decide[...] suddenly to make it definite?

CARDIN. She has not suddenly decided [...] thing. The school is pretty well on its [...] and now that Mrs. Mortar is leaving—

MRS. TILFORD. I've heard about their put[...] Mrs. Mortar out.

CARDIN. Putting her out? Well, maybe. [...] a nice sum for a trip and a promise th[...] good niece will support you the rest of [...] life is an enviable way of being put o[...]

MRS. TILFORD (*slowly*). Don't you fin[...] odd, Joseph, that they want so much t[...] rid of that silly, harmless woman?

CARDIN. I don't know what you're tal[...] about, but it isn't odd at all. Lily M[...] is not a harmless woman, although [...] knows she's silly enough. She's a nasty, [...] some, spoilt old bitch. If you're formi[...] Mortar Welfare Society, you're wasting [...] time. (*Gets up, puts down his glass.*) [...] not like you to waste your time. Now, w[...] it that's really on your mind?

MRS. TILFORD. You must not marry K[...]

CARDIN (*shocked, he grins*). You're a [...] impertinent old lady. Why must I—[...] *tates her*) not marry Karen?

MRS. TILFORD. Because there's somet[...] wrong with Karen—something hor[...] (*The door-bell is heard to ring loud [...] long.*)

CARDIN. I don't think I can allow you t[...] things like that, Amelia.

MRS. TILFORD. I have good reason for s[...] it. (*Breaks off as she hears voices off-st[...] Who is that?

KAREN (*off-stage*). Mrs. Tilford, Agat[...] she in?

AGATHA (*off-stage*). Yes'm. Come on [...]

MRS. TILFORD. I won't have her here.

CARDIN (*angrily*). What are you ta[...] about?

TILFORD. I won't have her here.

IN (*picks up his hat*). Then you don't t me here either. (*Turns to face* KAREN, , *with* MARTHA, *has rushed in.*) Darling, t?—

N (*stops when she sees him, puts her d over her eyes*). Is it a joke, Joe?

THA (*with great force to* MRS. TILFORD). ve come to find out what you are doing.

IN (*kissing* KAREN). What is it?

N. It's crazy! It's crazy! What did she for?

IN. What are you talking about? What ou mean?

TILFORD. You shouldn't have come here.

IN. What is all this? What's happened?

N. I tried to reach you. Hasn't she told

IN. Nobody's told me anything. I n't heard anything but wild talk. What , Karen? (*She starts to speak, then bly shakes her head.*) What's happened, ha?

THA (*violently*). An insane asylum has let loose. How do we know what's ened?

IN. What was it?

N. We didn't know what it was. No- would talk to us, nobody would tell ything.

HA. I'll tell you, I'll tell you. You see u can make any sense out of it. At er-time Mrs. Munn's chauffeur said Evelyn must be sent home right away. alf past seven Mrs. Burton arrived to us that she wanted Helen's things d and that she'd wait outside because idn't want to enter a place like ours. minutes later the Wells's butler came osalie.

N. What was it?

HA. It was madhouse. People rushing d out, the children being pushed into

N (*quiet now, takes his hand*). Mrs. rs finally told us.

N. What? What?

KAREN. That—that Martha and I have been —have been lovers. Mrs. Tilford told them.

CARDIN (*for a moment stands staring at her incredulously. Then he walks across the room, stares out of the window, and finally turns to* MRS. TILFORD). Did you tell them that?

MRS. TILFORD. Yes.

CARDIN. Are you sick?

MRS. TILFORD. You know I'm not sick.

CARDIN (*snapping the words out*). Then what did you do it for?

MRS. TILFORD (*slowly*). Because it's true.

KAREN (*incredulously*). You think it's true, then?

MARTHA. You fool! You damned, vicious—

KAREN. Do you realize what you're saying?

MRS. TILFORD. I realize it very well. And—

MARTHA. You realize nothing, nothing, nothing.

MRS. TILFORD. And that's why I don't think you should have come here. (*Quietly, with a look at* MARTHA.) I shall not call you names, and I will not allow you to call me names. It comes to this: I can't trust myself to talk about it with you now or ever.

KAREN. What's she talking about, Joe? What's she mean? What is she trying to do to us? What is everybody doing to us?

MARTHA (*softly, as though to herself*). Pushed around. We're being pushed around by crazy people. (*Shakes herself slightly.*) That's an awful thing. And we're standing here— (CARDIN *puts his arm around* KAREN, *walks with her to the window. They stand there together.*) We're standing here taking it. (*Suddenly with violence.*) Didn't you know we'd come here? Were we supposed to lie down and grin while you kicked us around with these lies?

MRS. TILFORD. This can't do any of us any good, Miss Dobie.

MARTHA (*scornfully imitating her*). "This can't do any of us any good." Listen, listen. Try to understand this: you're not playing with paper dolls. We're human beings, see? It's our lives you're fooling with. *Our* lives.

That's serious business for us. Can you understand that?

MRS. TILFORD (*for the first time she speaks angrily*). I can understand that, and I understand a lot more. *You've* been playing with a lot of children's lives, and that's why I stopped you. (*More calmly.*) I know how serious this is for you, how serious it is for all of us.

CARDIN (*bitterly*). I don't think you do know.

MRS. TILFORD. I wanted to avoid this meeting because it can't do any good. You came here to find out if I had made the charge. You've found out. Let's end it there. *I don't want you in this house.* I'm sorry this had to be done to you, Joseph.

CARDIN. I don't like your sympathy.

MRS. TILFORD. Very well. There's nothing I mean to do, nothing I want to do. There's nothing anybody can do.

CARDIN (*carefully*). You have already done a terrible thing.

MRS. TILFORD. I have done what I had to do. What they are may possibly be their own business. It becomes a great deal more than that when children are involved.

KAREN (*wildly*). It's not true. Not a word of it is true; can't you understand that?

MRS. TILFORD. There won't be any punishment for either of you. But there mustn't be any punishment for me, either—and that's what this meeting is. This—this thing is your own. Go away with it. I don't understand it and I don't want any part of it.

MARTHA (*slowly*). So you thought we would go away?

MRS. TILFORD. I think that's best for you.

MARTHA. There must be something we can do to you, and, whatever it is, we'll find it.

MRS. TILFORD. That will be very unwise.

KAREN. You are right to be afraid.

MRS. TILFORD. I am not afraid, Karen.

CARDIN. But you *are* old—and you *are* irresponsible.

MRS. TILFORD (*hurt*). You know that's not true.

KAREN (*goes to her*). I don't want to h anything to do with your mess, do you h me? It makes me feel dirty and sick to forced to say this, but here it is: there i a single word of truth in anything yo said. We're standing here defending selves—and against what? Against a lie great, awful lie.

MRS. TILFORD. I'm sorry that I can't bel that.

KAREN. Damn you!

CARDIN. But you can believe this: the worked eight long years to save eno money to buy that farm, to start that sch They did without everything that yo people ought to have. You wouldn't k about that. That school meant thing them: self-respect, and bread and butter, honest work. Do you know what it is to so hard for anything? Well, now it's g (*Suddenly hits the side of the table his hand.*) What the hell did you do it

MRS. TILFORD (*softly*). It had to be done

CARDIN. Righteousness is a great thing.

MRS. TILFORD (*gently*). I know how must feel.

CARDIN. You don't know anything a how I feel. And you don't know how feel, either.

MRS. TILFORD. I've loved you as much loved my own boys. I wouldn't have sp them; I couldn't spare you.

CARDIN (*fiercely*). I believe you.

MARTHA. What is there to do to you? V can we do to you? There must be s thing—something that makes you feel way we do tonight. You don't want part of this, you said. But you'll get a More than you bargained for. (*Sudde* Listen: are you willing to stand by e thing you've said tonight?

MRS. TILFORD. Yes.

MARTHA. All right. That's fine. But don' the idea we'll let you whisper this lie: made it and you'll come out with it. S it to your town of Lancet. We'll *make* shriek it—and we'll make you do it court room. (*Quietly.*) Tomorrow, Mrs ford, you will have a libel suit on hands.

TILFORD. That will be very unwise.

N. Very unwise—for you.

TILFORD. It is you I am thinking of. frightened for you. It was wrong of to brazen it out here tonight; it would iminally foolish of you to brazen it out iblic. That can bring you nothing but I am an old woman, Miss Dobie, and I seen too many people, out of pride, act at pride. In the end they punish them-
s.

HA. And you feel that you are too old punished? That we should spare you?

TILFORD. You know that is not what ant.

N (*turns from the window*). So you a child's word for it?

HA (*looks at him, shakes her head*). w it, too.

N. That is really where you got it? I believe—it couldn't be. Why, she's a

HA. She's not a child any longer.

N. Oh, my God, it all fits so well now. girl has hated us for a long time. ever knew why, we never could find There didn't seem to be any reason—

HA. There wasn't any reason. She hates body and everything.

N. Your Mary's a strange girl, a bad There's something very awful the mat-ith her.

TILFORD. I was waiting for you to say Miss Wright.

T. I'm telling you the truth. We should told it to you long ago. (*Stops, sighs.*) use.

HA. Where is she? Bring her out here t us hear what she has to say.

TILFORD. You cannot see her.

N. Where is she?

TILFORD. I won't have that, Joseph.

N. I'm going to talk to her.

TILFORD. *I won't have her go through that again.* (*To* KAREN *and* MARTHA.) ame here demanding explanations. It who should have asked them from

you. You attack me, you attack Mary. I've told you I didn't mean you any harm. I still don't. You claim that it isn't true; it may be natural that you should say that, but I *know* that it is true. No matter what you say, you know very well that I wouldn't have acted until I was absolutely sure. All I wanted was to get those children away. That has been done. There won't be any talk about it or about you—I'll see to that. You have been in my house long enough. Get out.

KAREN (*gets up*). The wicked very young, and the wicked very old. Let's go home.

CARDIN. Sit down. (*To* MRS. TILFORD.) When two people come here with their lives spread on the table for you to cut to pieces, then the only honest thing to do is to give them a chance to come out whole. Are you honest?

MRS. TILFORD. I've always thought so.

CARDIN. Then where is Mary? (*After a moment she moves her head to door Right. Quickly* CARDIN *goes to the door and opens it.*) Mary! Come here. (*After a moment* MARY *appears, stands nervously near door. Her manner is shy and afraid.*)

MRS. TILFORD (*gently*). Sit down, dear, and don't be afraid.

MARTHA (*her lips barely moving*). *Make* her tell the truth.

CARDIN (*walking about in front of* MARY). Look: everybody lies all the time. Sometimes they have to, sometimes they don't. I've lied myself for a lot of different reasons, but there was never a time when, if I'd been given a second chance, I wouldn't have taken back the lie and told the truth. You're lucky if you ever get that chance. I'm telling you this because I'm about to ask you a question. Before you answer the question, I want to tell you that if you've l—, if you made a mistake, you must take this chance and say so. You won't be punished for it. Do you get all that?

MARY (*timidly*). Yes, Cousin Joe.

CARDIN (*grimly*). All right, let's get started. Were you telling your grandmother the truth this afternoon? The exact truth about Miss Wright and Miss Dobie?

MARY (*without hesitation*). Oh, yes. (KAREN *sighs deeply*, MARTHA, *her fists closed tight, turns her back to the child.* CARDIN *smiles as he looks at* MARY.)

CARDIN. All right, Mary, that was your chance; you passed it up. (*Pulls up a chair, sits down in front of her.*) Now let's find out things.

MRS. TILFORD. She's told you. Aren't you through?

CARDIN. Not by a long shot. You've started something, and I'm going to finish it for you. Will you answer some more questions, Mary?

MARY. Yes, Cousin Joe.

MARTHA. Stop that sick, sweet tone. (MRS. TILFORD *half rises;* CARDIN *motions her back.*)

CARDIN. Why don't you like Miss Dobie and Miss Wright?

MARY. Oh, I do like them. They just don't like me. They never have liked me.

CARDIN. How do you know?

MARY. They're always picking on me. They're always punishing me for everything that happens. No matter what happens, it's always me.

CARDIN. Why do you think they do that?

MARY. Because—because they're—because they— (*Stops, turns.*) Grandma, I—

CARDIN. All right, we'll skip that one. Did you get punished today?

MARY. Yes, and it was just because Peggy and Evelyn heard them and so they took it out on me.

KAREN. That's a lie.

CARDIN. Sssh. Heard what, Mary?

MARY. Mrs. Mortar told Miss Dobie that there was something funny about her. She said that she had a funny feeling about Miss Wright, and Mrs. Mortar said that was unnatural. That was why we got punished, just because—

KAREN. That was not the reason they got punished.

MRS. TILFORD (*to* MARTHA). Miss Dobie?

MARTHA. My aunt is a stupid woman. What she said was unpleasant; it was said to annoy me. It meant nothing more than that.

MARY. And, Cousin Joe, she said that e[very] time you came to the school Miss Dobie [was] jealous, and that she didn't want you to [get] married.

MARTHA (*to* CARDIN). She said that, too. [For] God's sake, can't you see what's happeni[ng?] This—this child is taking little things, [little] family things, and making them have me[an]ings that— (*Stops, suddenly regards* M[ARY] *with a combination of disgust and inter*[est.]) Where did you learn so much in so [little] time?

CARDIN. What do you think Mrs. M[ortar] meant by all that, Mary?

MRS. TILFORD. Stop it, Joseph!

MARY. I don't know, but it was always [sort] of funny and she always said things like [that] and all the girls would talk about it w[hen] Miss Dobie went and visited Miss Wr[ight] late at night—

KAREN (*angrily*). And we go to the m[ovies] at night and sometimes we read at n[ight] and sometimes we drink tea at night. T[hese] are guilty things, too, Mrs. Tilford.

MARY. And there are always funny so[unds] and we'd stay awake and listen becaus[e we] couldn't help hearing and I'd get fr[ight]ened because the sounds were like—

MARTHA. Be still!

KAREN (*with violence*). No, no. You [don't] want her still now. What else did you h[ear?]

MARY. Grandma, I—

MRS. TILFORD (*bitterly to* CARDIN). You[r'e] trying to make her name it, aren't yo[u?]

CARDIN (*ignoring her, speaks to* MARY[).] [Go] on.

MARY. I don't know; there were just so[unds.]

CARDIN. But what did you think they w[ere?] Why did they frighten you?

MARY (*weakly*). I don't know.

CARDIN (*smiles at* MRS. TILFORD). She d[oesn't] know.

MARY (*hastily*). I saw things, too. One [night] there was so much noise I thought [some]body was sick or something and I l[ooked] through the keyhole and they were k[issing] and saying things and then I got scare[d be]cause it was different sort of and I—

RTHA (*her face distorted, turns to* MRS. FORD). That child—that child is sick.

REN. Ask her again how she could see us.

DIN. How could you see Miss Dobie and ss Wright?

RY. I—I—

S. TILFORD. Tell him what you whispered ne.

RY. It was at night and I was leaning vn by the keyhole.

REN. *There's no keyhole on my door.*

S. TILFORD. What?

EN. There—is—no—keyhole—on—my— r.

RY (*quickly*). It wasn't her room, Grand-, it was the other room, I guess. It was s Dobie's room. I saw them through keyhole in Miss Dobie's room.

DIN. How did you know anybody was Miss Dobie's room?

RY. I told you, I told you. Because we rd them. Everybody heard them—

THA. I share a room with my aunt. It n the first floor at the other end of the se. It is impossible to hear anything from e. (*To* CARDIN.) Tell her to come and for herself.

TILFORD (*her voice shaken*). What is Mary? Why did you say you saw ugh a keyhole? *Can* you hear from your n?—

Y (*starts to cry*). Everybody is yelling e. I don't know what I'm saying with ybody mixing me all up. I did see it! d see it!

TILFORD. *What* did you see? *Where* you see it? I want the truth, now. The , whatever it is.

IN (*gets up, moves his chair back*). We go home. We are finished here. (*Looks nd.*) It's not a pleasant place to be.

TILFORD (*angrily*). Stop that crying, y. Stand up. (MARY *gets up, head down, crying hysterically.* MRS. TILFORD *goes stands directly in front of her.*)

TILFORD. *I want the truth.*

Y. All—all right.

MRS. TILFORD. What is the truth?

MARY. It was Rosalie who saw them. I just said it was me so I wouldn't have to tattle on Rosalie.

CARDIN (*wearily*). Oh, my God!

MARY. It *was* Rosalie, Grandma, she told us all about it. She said she had read about it in a book and she knew—

CARDIN (*picks up his hat*). We'll go now. Good night, Amelia, and good-by.

MARY (*desperately*). You ask Rosalie. You just ask Rosalie. She'll tell you. We used to talk about it all the time. That's the truth, that's the honest truth. She said it was when the door was open once and she told us all about it. I was just trying to save Rosalie, and everybody jumps on me.

MRS. TILFORD (*to* CARDIN). Please wait a minute. (*Goes to library door.*) Rosalie!

CARDIN. You're giving yourself an awful beating, Amelia, and you deserve whatever you get.

MRS. TILFORD (*stands waiting for* ROSALIE, *passes her hand over her face*). I don't know. I don't know, any more. Maybe it's what I do deserve. (*As* ROSALIE, *frightened, appears at the door, making bows to everybody, she takes the child gently by the hand, brings her down Center, talking nervously.*) I'm sorry to keep you up so late, Rosalie. You must be tired. (*Speaks rapidly.*) Mary says there's been a lot of talk in the school lately about Miss Wright and Miss Dobie. Is that true?

ROSALIE. I—I don't know what you mean.

MRS. TILFORD. That things have been said among you girls.

ROSALIE (*wide-eyed, frightened*). What things? I never—I—I—

KAREN (*gently*). Don't be frightened.

MRS. TILFORD. What was the talk about, Rosalie?

ROSALIE (*utterly bewildered*). I don't know what she means, Miss Wright.

KAREN. Rosalie, Mary has told her grandmother that certain things at school have been—er—puzzling you girls. You, particularly.

ROSALIE. History puzzles me. I guess I'm not very good at history, and Helen helps me sometimes, if that—

KAREN. No, that's not what she meant. She says that you told her that you saw certain —certain acts between Miss Dobie and myself. She says that once, when the door was open, you saw us kissing each other in a way that—(*Unable to bear the child's look, she turns her back.*) women don't kiss one another.

ROSALIE. Oh, Miss Wright, I didn't, didn't, I didn't. I *never* said such a thing.

MRS. TILFORD (*grimly*). That's true, my dear?

ROSALIE. I never saw any such thing. Mary always makes things up about me and everybody else. (*Starts to weep in excitement.*) I never said any such thing ever. Why, I never even could have thought of—

MARY (*staring at her, speaks very slowly*). Yes, you did, Rosalie. You're just trying to get out of it. I remember just when you

said it. I remember it, because it was th day Helen Burton's bracelet was—

ROSALIE (*stands fascinated and fearful, loo ing at* MARY). I never did. I—I—you just—

MARY. It was the day Helen's bracelet w stolen, and nobody knew who did it, an Helen said that if her mother found ou she'd have the thief put in jail.

KAREN (*puzzled, as are the others, by t sudden change in* ROSALIE'S *manner*). Ther nothing to cry about. You must help us telling the truth. Why, what's the matte Rosalie?

MARY. Grandma, there's something I've g to tell you that—

ROSALIE (*with a shrill cry*). Yes. Yes. I d see it. I told Mary. What Mary said w right. I said it, I said it— (*Throws hers on the couch, weeping hysterically;* MART stands leaning against the door; KAREN, CA DIN, *and* MRS. TILFORD *are staring at* ROSAL MARY *slowly sits down as the Curtain fall.*

ACT THREE

SCENE: *the same as Act One. Living-room of the school.*

AT RISE: *The room has changed. It is not actually dirty, but it is dull and dark a uncared for. The windows are tightly shut, the curtains tightly drawn.* KAREN *is sitti in a large chair, Right Center, feet flat on floor.* MARTHA *is lying on the couch, her fa buried against the pillows, her back to* KAREN. *It is a minute or two after the rise of t curtain before either speaks.*

MARTHA. It's cold in here.

KAREN. Yes.

MARTHA. What time is it?

KAREN. I don't know. What's the difference?

MARTHA. None. I was hoping it was time for my bath.

KAREN. Take it early today.

MARTHA (*laughs*). Oh, I couldn't do that. I look forward all day to that bath. It's my last touch with the full life. It makes me feel important to know that there's one thing ahead of me, one thing I've *got* to do. You ought to get yourself something like that. I tell you, at five o'clock every day you comb your hair. How's that? It's better for

you, take my word. You wake up in t morning and you say to yourself, the da not entirely empty, life is rich and full: five o'clock I'll comb my hair. (*They back into silence. A moment later the pho rings. Neither of them pays the slight attention to it, until the ringing becomes insistent. Then* KAREN *rises, takes the ceiver off, goes back, and sits down.*)

KAREN. It's raining.

MARTHA. Hungry?

KAREN. No. You?

MARTHA. No, but I'd like to be hungry aga Remember how much we used to eat college?

KAREN. That was ten years ago.

MARTHA. Well, maybe we'll be hungry in other ten years. It's cheaper this way.

KAREN. What's the old thing about time be-more nourishing than bread?

MARTHA. Yeah? Maybe.

KAREN. Joe's late today. What time is it?

MARTHA (*turns to lie on her side*). We've en sitting here for eight days asking each her the time. Haven't you heard? There 't any time any more.

KAREN. It's been days since we've been out this house.

MARTHA. Well, we'll have to get off these airs sooner or later. In a couple of months ey'll need dusting.

KAREN. What'll we do when we get off?

MARTHA. God knows.

KAREN (*almost in a whisper*). It's awful.

MARTHA. Let's not talk about it. (*After a* ment.) What about eggs for dinner?

KAREN. All right.

MARTHA. I'll make some potatoes with on-is, the way you used to like them.

KAREN. It's a week ago Thursday. It never med real until the last day. It seems real ough now, all right.

MARTHA. Now and forever after.

KAREN (*suddenly*). Let's go out.

MARTHA (*turns over, stares at her*). Where

KAREN. We'll take a walk.

MARTHA. Where'll we walk?

KAREN. Why shouldn't we take a walk? We n't see anybody, and suppose we do, what it? We'll jus—

MARTHA (*slowly gets up*). Come on. We'll through the park.

KAREN. They might see us. (*They stand king at each other.*) Let's not go. (MAR-
goes back, lies down again.) We'll go orrow.

MARTHA (*laughs*). Stop kidding yourself.

KAREN. But Joe says we've got to go out. He s that all the people who don't think it's true will begin to wonder if we keep hiding this way.

MARTHA. If it makes you feel better to think there *are* such people, go ahead.

KAREN. He says we ought to go into town and go shopping and act as though—

MARTHA. Shopping? That's a sound idea. There aren't three stores in Lancet that would sell us anything. Hasn't he heard about the ladies' clubs and their meetings and their circulars and their visits and their—

KAREN (*softly*). Don't tell him.

MARTHA (*gently*). I won't. (*There are foot-steps in the hall, and the sound of something being dragged.*) There's our friend. (*A GRO-CERY BOY appears lugging a box. He brings it into the room, stands staring at them, giggles a little. Walks toward KAREN, stops, eamines her. She sits tense, looking away from him. Without taking his eyes from KAREN, he speaks.*)

GROCERY BOY. I knocked on the kitchen door, but nobody answered.

MARTHA. You said that yesterday. All right. Thanks. Good-by.

KAREN (*unable any longer to stand the stare*). Make him stop it.

GROCERY BOY. Here are the things. (*Giggles, moves toward MARTHA, stands looking at her. Suddenly MARTHA thrusts her hand in the air.*)

MARTHA. I've got eight fingers, see? I'm a freak.

GROCERY BOY (*giggling*). There's a car com-in' here. (*Gets no answer, starts backing out of door, still looking. Familiarly.*) Good-by. (*Exits.*)

MARTHA (*bitterly*). You still think we should go into town.

KAREN. I don't know. I don't know about anything any more. (*After a moment.*) Martha, Martha, Martha—

MARTHA (*gently*). What is it, Karen?

KAREN. What are we going to do? It's all so cold and unreal and awful. It's like that dark hour of the night when, half awake, you struggle through the black mess you've been dreaming. Then, suddenly, you wake up and you see your own bed or your own nightgown and you know you're back again in a solid world. But now it's all the nightmare; there is no solid world. Oh, Martha, *why* did it happen? *What* happened? What are we doing here like this?

MARTHA. Waiting.

KAREN. For what?

MARTHA. I don't know.

KAREN. We've got to get out of this place. I can't stand it any more.

MARTHA. You'll be getting married soon. Everything will be all right then.

KAREN (*vaguely*). Yes.

MARTHA (*looks up at the tone*). What is it?

KAREN. Nothing.

MARTHA. There mustn't be anything wrong between you and Joe. Never.

KAREN. (*without conviction*). Nothing's wrong. (*As footsteps are heard in the hall, her face lights up.*) There's Joe now. (MRS. MORTAR, *small suitcase in hand, stands in the doorway, her face pushed coyly forward.*)

MRS. MORTAR. And here I am. Hello, hello.

MARTHA (*she has turned over on her back and is staring at her aunt. She speaks to* KAREN). The Duchess, isn't it? Returned at long last. (*Too jovially.*) Come on in. We're delighted to see you. Are you tired from your journey? Is there something I can get you?

MRS. MORTAR (*surprised*). I'm very glad to see you both, and (*looks around*) I'm very glad to see the old place again. How is everything?

MARTHA. Everything's fine. We're splendid, thank you. You're just in time for tea.

MRS. MORTAR. You know, I should like some tea, if it isn't too much trouble.

MARTHA. No trouble at all. Some small sandwiches and a little brandy?

MRS. MORTAR (*puzzled finally*). Why, Martha.

MARTHA. Where the hell have you been?

MRS. MORTAR. Around, around. I had a most interesting time. Things—

MARTHA. Why didn't you answer my te grams?

MRS. MORTAR. Things have changed in theater—drastically changed, I might s

MARTHA. *Why didn't you answer my te grams?*

MRS. MORTAR. Oh, Martha, there's your te per again.

MARTHA. Answer me and don't bother ab my temper.

MRS. MORTAR (*nervously*). I was movi around a great deal. (*Conversationall* You know, I think it will throw a very vealing light on the state of the new thea when I tell you that the Lyceum in Roch ter now has a toilet back-stage.

MARTHA. To hell with the toilet in Rochest Where were you?

MRS. MORTAR. Moving around, I tell you.

KAREN. What difference does it all ma now?

MRS. MORTAR. Karen is quite right. Let gones be bygones. As I was saying, ther an effete something in the theater now, a that accounts for—

MARTHA (*to* KAREN). Isn't she wonderf (*To* MRS. MORTAR.) Why did you refuse come back here and testify for us?

MRS. MORTAR. Why, Martha, I didn't ref to come back at all. That's the wrong w to look at it. I was on a tour; that's a mo obligation, you know. Now don't let's t about unpleasant things any more. I'll up and unpack a few things; tomorro plenty of time to get my trunk.

KAREN (*laughs*). Things have changed he you know.

MARTHA. She doesn't know. She expected walk right up to a comfortable fire and down and she very carefully waited u the whole thing was over. (*Leans forwa speaking to* MRS. MORTAR.) Listen: Ka Wright and Martha Dobie brought a li suit against a woman called Tilford beca her grandchild had accused them of h ing what the judge called "sinful sex knowledge of one another." (MRS. MORT *holds up her hand in protest, and* MART *laughs.*) Don't like that, do you? Well great part of the defense's case was ba remarks made by Lily Mortar, actress in ⌐ toilets of Rochester, against her niece, ⌐rtha. And a greater part of the defense's ⌐e rested on the telling fact that Mrs. Mor⌐ would not appear in court to deny or ex⌐in those remarks. Mrs. Mortar had a ⌐ral obligation to the theater. As you prob⌐ly read in the papers, we lost the case.

⌐s. MORTAR. I didn't think of it that way, ⌐rtha. It couldn't have done any good for ⌐ of us to get mixed up in that unpleasant ⌐toriety— (*Sees* MARTHA's *face. Hastily*) ⌐t now that you've explained it, why, I ⌐ see it your way, and I'm sorry I didn't ⌐ne back. But now that I am here, I'm ⌐ing to stand shoulder to shoulder with ⌐. I know what you've gone through, but ⌐ body and heart *do* recover, you know. ⌐ be here working right along with you ⌐ we'll—

⌐RTHA. There's an eight o'clock train. Get ⌐ it.

⌐s. MORTAR. Martha.

⌐RTHA. You've come back to pick the bones ⌐. Well, there aren't even bones anymore. ⌐ere's nothing here for you.

⌐s. MORTAR (*sniffling a little*). How can ⌐ talk to me like that?

⌐RTHA. Because I hate you. I've always hat⌐ you.

⌐s. MORTAR (*gently*). God will punish you ⌐ that.

⌐RTHA. He's been doing all right.

⌐s. MORTAR. When you wish to apologize, ⌐ill be temporarily in my room. (*Starts* ⌐ *exit, almost bumps into* CARDIN, *steps* ⌐*k with dignity.*) How do you do?

⌐DIN (*laughs*). Look who's here. A little ⌐, aren't you?

⌐s. MORTAR. So it's you. Now, I call *that* ⌐al. A lot of men wouldn't still be here. ⌐ey would have felt—

⌐RTHA. Get out of here.

⌐EN (*opening door*). I'll call you when ⌐ time for your train. (MRS. MORTAR *looks* ⌐*er, exits.*)

⌐DIN. Now, what do you think brought ⌐ back?

⌐EN. God knows.

MARTHA. I know. She was broke.

CARDIN (*pats* MARTHA *on the shoulder*). Don't let her worry you this time, Martha. We'll give her some money and get rid of her. (*Pulls* KAREN *to him.*) Been out today, darling?

KAREN. We started to go out.

CARDIN (*shakes his head*). Feel all right? (KAREN *leans over to kiss him. Almost imperceptibly he pulls back.*)

KAREN. Why did you do that?

MARTHA. Karen.

CARDIN. Do what?

KAREN. Draw back that way.

CARDIN (*laughs, kisses her*). If we sit around here much longer, we'll all be bats. I sold my place today to Foster.

KAREN. You did what?

CARDIN. We're getting married this week. Then we're going away—all three of us.

KAREN. You can't leave here. I won't have you do this for me. What about the hospital and—

CARDIN. Shut up, darling, it's all fixed. We're going to Vienna and we're going quick. Fischer wrote that I can have my old place back.

KAREN. No! No! I'm not going to let you.

CARDIN. It's already done. Fischer can't pay me much, but it'll be enough for the three of us. Plenty if we live cheap.

MARTHA. I couldn't go with you, Joe.

CARDIN. Nonsense, Martha, we're all going. We're going to have fun again.

KAREN (*slowly*). You don't want to go back to Vienna.

CARDIN. No.

KAREN. Then why?

CARDIN. Look: I don't want to go to Vienna; I'd rather have stayed here. But then you don't want to go to Vienna; you'd rather have stayed here. Well, to hell with that. We *can't* stay here, and Vienna offers enough to eat and sleep and drink beer on. Now don't object any more, please, darling. All right?

KAREN. All right.

MARTHA. I can't go. It's better for all of us if I don't.

CARDIN (*puts his arm around her*). Not now. You stay with us now. Later on, if you want it that way. All right?

MARTHA (*smiles*). All right.

CARDIN. Swell, I'll buy you good coffee cakes and take you both to Ischl for a honeymoon.

MARTHA (*picking up grocery box, she starts for door*). A big coffee cake with a lot of raisins. It would be nice to like something again. (*Exits.*)

CARDIN (*with a slightly forced heartiness*). I'll be going back with a pretty girl who belongs to me. I'll show you off all over the place—to Dr. Engelhardt, and the nurse at the desk, and to the fat gal in the cake shop, and to Fischer. (*Laughs.*) The last time I saw him was at the railroad station. He took me back of the baggage car. (*With an imitation of an accent.*) "Joseph," he said, "you'll be a good doctor; I would trust you to cut up my Minna. But you're not a great doctor, and you never will be. Go back where you were born and take care of your sick. Leave the fancy work to the others." I came home.

KAREN. You'll be coming home again some day.

CARDIN. No. Let's not talk about it. (*After a moment.*) You'll need some clothes?

KAREN. A few. Oh, your Dr. Fischer was so right. This is where you belong.

CARDIN. I need an overcoat and a suit. You'll need a lot of things—heavy things. It's cold there now, much colder than you'd expect—

KAREN. I've done this to you. I've taken you away from everything you want.

CARDIN. But it's lovely in the mountains, and that's where we'll go for a month.

KAREN. They—*they've* done it. They've taken away every chance we had. Everything we wanted, everything we were going to be.

CARDIN. And we've got to stop talking like that. (*Takes her by the shoulders.*) We've got a chance. But it's just one chance, and if we miss it we're done for. It means that we've got to start putting the whole business

behind us now. *Now,* Karen. What you've done, you've done—and that's that.

KAREN. What *I've* done?

CARDIN (*impatiently*). What's been done you.

KAREN. What did you mean? (*When the is no answer.*) What did you mean wh you said .What you've done....?

CARDIN (*shouting*). Nothing. Nothin (*Then very quietly.*) Karen, there are a of people in this world who've had b trouble in their lives. We're three of tho people. We could sit around the rest of o lives and exist on that trouble, until in t end we had nothing else and we'd wa nothing else. That's something I'm not co ing to and I'm not going to let you come

KAREN. I know. I'm sorry. (*After a m ment.*) Joe, can we have a baby right awa

CARDIN (*vaguely*). Yes, I guess so. Althou we won't have much money now.

KAREN. You used to want one right awa You always said that was the way y wanted it. There's some reason for yo changing.

CARDIN. My God, we *can't* go on like th Everything I say to you is made to me something else. We don't talk like peo any more. Oh, let's get out of here as f as we can.

KAREN (*as though she is finishing the s tense for him*). And every word will ha a new meaning. You think we'll be able run away from that? Woman, child, lo lawyer—no words that we can use in saf any more. (*Laughs bitterly.*) Sick, hi tragic people. That's what we'll be.

CARDIN (*gently*). No, we won't, darli Love is casual—that's the way it should We must find that out all over again. must learn again to live and love like otl people.

KAREN. It won't work.

CARDIN. What?

KAREN. The two of us together.

CARDIN (*sharply*). Stop talking like that

KAREN. It's true. (*Suddenly.*) I want you say it now.

RDIN. I don't know what you're talking
out.

REN. Yes, you do. We've both known for a
ng time. I knew surely the day we lost
e case. I was watching your face in court.
was ashamed—and sad at being ashamed.
y it now, Joe. Ask it now.

RDIN. I have nothing to ask. Nothing—
Quickly.) All right. Is it—was it ever—

REN (*puts her hand over his mouth*). No.
artha and I have never touched each other.
ulls his head down on her shoulder.)
at's all right, darling. I'm glad you asked.
n not mad a bit, really.

RDIN. I'm sorry, Karen, I'm sorry. I didn't
ean to hurt you, I—

REN. I'll say it for you. You wanted to wait
til it was all over, you really never want-
to ask at all. You didn't know for sure;
u thought there might be just a little
th in it all. (*With great feeling.*) You've
en good to me and loyal. You're a fine
an. (*Afraid of tears, she pats him, walks
ay.*) Now go and sit down, Joe. I have
lot of things to say. They're all mixed up
d I must get them clear.

RDIN. Don't let's talk any more. Let's for-
t and go ahead.

REN (*puzzled*). Go ahead?

RDIN. Yes, Karen.

REN. You believe me, then?

RDIN. Of course I believe you. I only had
hear you say it.

REN. No, no, no. That isn't the way
ings work. Maybe you believe me. I'd
ver know whether you did or not. You'd
ver know whether you did, either. We
uldn't do it that way. Can't you see what
uld happen? We'd be hounded by it all
r lives. I'd be frightened, always, and in
e end my own fright would make me—
uld make me hate you. (*Sees slight move-
ent he makes.*) Yes, it would; I know it
uld. I'd hate you for what I thought I'd
ne to you. And I'd hate myself, too. It
uld grow and grow until we'd be ruined
it. (*Sees him about to speak.*) Ah, Joe,
u've seen all that yourself. You knew it
st.

CARDIN (*softly*). I didn't mean it that way;
I don't now.

KAREN (*smiles*). You're still trying to spare
me, still trying to tell yourself that we
might be all right again. But we won't be
all right. Not ever, ever, ever. I don't know
all the reasons why. Look, I'm standing
here. I haven't changed. (*Holds out her
hands.*) My hands look just the same, my
face is the same, even my dress is old. We're
in a room we've been in so many times before; you're sitting where you always sit;
it's nearly time for dinner. I'm like everybody else. I can have all the things that
everybody has. I can have you and a baby,
and I can go to market, and we can go to
the movies, and people will talk to me and
—(*Suddenly notices the pain in his face.*)
Oh, I'm sorry. I mustn't talk like that.
That couldn't be true any more.

CARDIN. It could be, Karen. We'll make it
be like that.

KAREN. No. That's only what we'd like to
have had. It's what we can't have now. Go
home, darling.

CARDIN (*with force*). Don't talk like that.
No matter what it is, we can't leave each
other. I can't leave you—

KAREN. Joe, Joe. Let's do it now and quick;
it will be too hard later on.

CARDIN. No, no, no. We love each other.
(*His voice breaks.*) I'd give anything not to
have asked that question, Karen.

KAREN. It had to be asked sooner or later—
and answered. You're a good man—the best
I'll ever know—and you've been better to
me than— But it's no good now, for either
of us; you can see that.

CARDIN. It can be. You say I helped you.
Help me now; help me to be strong and
good enough to— (*Goes towards her with
his arms out.*) Karen!

KAREN (*drawing back*). No, Joe! (*Then,
as he stops*) Will you do something for me?

CARDIN. Anything but leave you.

KAREN. Will you—will you go away for two
days—a day—and think this all over by
yourself—away from me and love and pity?
Will you? And then decide.

CARDIN (*after a long pause*). Yes, if you want, but it won't make any difference. We will—

KAREN. Don't say anything. Please go now. (*She sits down, smiles, closes her eyes. For a moment he stands looking at her, then slowly puts on his hat.*) And all my heart goes with you.

CARDIN (*at door, leaving*). I'll be coming back. (*Exits, slowly, reluctantly, closing door.*)

KAREN (*a moment after he has gone*). No, you won't. Never, darling. (*Stays as she is until* MARTHA *enters Right.*)

MARTHA (*goes to lamp, lights it*). It gets dark so early now. (*Sits down, stretches, laughs.*) Cooking always makes me feel better. Well, I guess we'll have to give the Duchess some dinner. When the hawks descend, you've got to feed 'em. Where's Joe? (*No answer.*) Where's Joe?

KAREN. Gone.

MARTHA. A patient? Will he be back in time for dinner?

KAREN. No.

MARTHA (*watching her*). We'll save dinner for him, then. Karen! What's the matter?

KAREN (*in a dull tone*). He won't be back any more.

MARTHA (*speaking slowly and carefully*). You mean he won't be back any more tonight.

KAREN. He won't be back at all.

MARTHA (*quickly, walks to* KAREN). What happened? (KAREN *shakes her head.*) What happened, Karen?

KAREN. He thought that we had been lovers.

MARTHA (*tensely*). I don't believe you. (*Wearily* KAREN *turns her head away.*)

KAREN. All right.

MARTHA (*automatically*). I don't believe it. He's never said a word all these months, all during the trial—(*Suddenly grabs* KAREN *by the shoulders, shakes her.*) Didn't you tell him? For God's sake, didn't you tell him it wasn't true?

KAREN. Yes.

MARTHA. He didn't believe you?

KAREN. I guess he believed me.

MARTHA (*angrily*). Then what have y[ ] done?

KAREN. What had to be done.

MARTHA. It's all wrong. It's silly. He'll [ ] back in a little while and you'll clear it [ ] up—(*Realizes why that can't be, covers h[ ] mouth with her hand.*) Oh, God, I want[ ] that for you so much.

KAREN. Don't. I feel sick to my stomach.

MARTHA (*goes to couch opposite* KAREN, *p[ ] her head in her arms*). What's happened [ ] us? What's really happened to us?

KAREN. I don't know. I want to be slee[ ] I want to go to sleep.

MARTHA. Go back to Joe. He's strong; he[ ] understand. It's too much for you this wa[ ]

KAREN (*irritably*). Stop talking about [ ] Let's pack and get out of here. Let's ta[ ] the train in the morning.

MARTHA. The train to where?

KAREN. I don't know. Some place; any pla[ ]

MARTHA. A job? Money?

KAREN. In a big place we could get som[ ] thing to do.

MARTHA. They'd know about us. We've be[ ] famous.

KAREN. A small town, then.

MARTHA. They'd know more about us.

KAREN (*as a child would say it*). Isn't the[ ] anywhere to go?

MARTHA. No. There'll never be any place [ ] us to go. We're bad people. We'll sit. W[ ] be sitting the rest of our lives wonderi[ ] what's happened to us. You think this sce[ ] is strange? Well, get used to it; we'll [ ] here for a long time. (*Suddenly pinc[ ]* KAREN *on the arm.*) Let's pinch each oth[ ] sometimes. We can tell whether we're s[ ] living.

KAREN (*shivers, listlessly gets up, starts m[ ] ing a fire in the fireplace*). But this isn'[ ] new sin they tell us we've done. Other p[ ] ple aren't destroyed by it.

RTHA. They are the people who believe it, who want it, who've chosen it. We n't like that. We don't love each other. *uddenly stops, crosses to fireplace, stands king abstractedly at* KAREN. *Speaks cas-ly.*) I don't love you. We've been very se to each other, of course. I've loved ⌐ like a friend, the way thousands of wo-n feel about other women.

REN (*only half listening*). The fire's nice.

RTHA. Certainly that doesn't mean any-ng. There's nothing wrong about that. ⌐ perfectly natural that I should be fond you, that I should—

REN (*listlessly*). Why are you saying all s to me?

RTHA. Because I love you.

REN (*vaguely*). Yes, of course.

RTHA. I love you that way—maybe the y they said I loved you. I don't know. 'aits, gets no answer, kneels down next KAREN.) Listen to me!

EN. What?

RTHA. *I have loved you the way they said.*

REN. You're crazy.

RTHA. There's always been something ong. Always—as long as I can remember. ⌐ I never knew it until all this happened.

EN (*for the first time looks up, horri-*). Stop it!

RTHA. You're afraid of hearing it; I'm re afraid than you.

EN (*puts her hands over her ears*). I ⌐'t listen to you.

RTHA. Take your hands down. (*Leans* *, pulls* KAREN's *hands away.*) You've got now it. I can't keep it any longer. I've to tell you how guilty I am.

EN (*deliberately*). You are guilty of hing.

RTHA. I've been telling myself that since night we heard the child say it; I've been ying I could convince myself of it. I t, I can't any longer. It's there. I don't w how, I don't know why. But I did you. I do love you. I resented your mar-e; maybe because I wanted you; maybe

I wanted you all along; maybe I couldn't call it by a name; maybe it's been there ever since I first knew you,—

KAREN (*tensely*). It's a lie. You're telling yourself a lie. We never thought of each other that way.

MARTHA (*bitterly*). No, of course *you* didn't. But who says I didn't? I never felt that way about anybody but you. I've never loved a man— (*Stops. Softly.*) I never knew why before. Maybe it's that.

KAREN (*carefully*). You are tired and sick.

MARTHA (*as though she were talking to her-self*). It's funny; it's all mixed up. There's something in you, and you don't know it and you don't do anything about it. Sudden-ly a child gets bored and lies—and there you are, seeing it for the first time. (*Closes her eyes.*) I don't know. It all seems to come back to *me*. In some way I've ruined your life. I've ruined my own. I didn't even *know*. (*Smiles.*) There's a big difference be-tween us now, Karen. You feel sad and clean; I feel sad and dirty. (*Puts out her hand, touches* KAREN's *head.*) I can't stay with you any more, darling.

KAREN (*in a shaken, uncertain tone*). All this isn't true. We'll pretend you never said it; you'll have forgotten it tomorrow.

MARTHA. Tomorrow? That's a funny word. In all those years to come, Karen, we would have had to invent a new language, as chil-dren do, without words like tomorrow.

KAREN (*crying*). Go and lie down, Martha. You'll feel better.

MARTHA (*looks around the room, slowly, carefully. She is very quiet. Exits Right, stands at door for a second looking at* KAREN, *then slowly shuts the door behind her*). Yes. I think I will feel better. (KAREN *sits alone without moving. There is no sound in the house until, a few minutes after* MARTHA's *exit, a shot is heard. The sound of the shot should not be too loud or too strong; the act has not been sensational. For a few seconds after the noise has died out,* KAREN *does not move. Then, suddenly, she springs from the chair, crosses the room, pulls open door Right. Almost at the same moment footsteps are heard on the staircase.*)

MRS. MORTAR. What was that? Where is it? (*Enters door Center, frightened, aimlessly moving about.*) Karen! Martha! Where are you? I heard a shot. What was— (*Stops as she sees* KAREN *reappear Right. Walks toward her, still talking. Stops when she sees* KAREN's *face.*) What—what is it? (KAREN *moves her hands, shakes her head slightly, passes* MRS. MORTAR, *and goes toward window.* MRS. MORTAR *stares at her for a moment, rushes past her through door Right. Left alone,* KAREN *leans against the window.* MRS. MORTAR *re-enters crying. After a minute.*) What shall we do? What shall we do?

KAREN (*in a toneless voice*). Nothing.

MRS. MORTAR. We've got to get a doctor— right away. (*Goes to phone, nervously, fumblingly starts to dial.*)

KAREN (*without turning*). There isn't any use.

MRS. MORTAR. We've got to do something. Oh, it's awful. Poor Martha. I don't know what we can do— (*Puts phone down, collapses in chair, sobs quietly.*) You think she's dead—

KAREN. Yes.

MRS. MORTAR. Poor, poor Martha. I can't realize it's true. Oh, how could she—she was so—I don't know what—(*Looks up, still crying, surprised.*) I'm—I'm frightened.

KAREN. Don't cry.

MRS. MORTAR. I can't help it. How can I help it? (*Gradually the sobs cease, and she sits rocking herself.*) I'll never forgive myself for the last words I said to her. But I was good to her, Karen, and you know God will excuse me for that once. I always tried to do everything I could. (*Suddenly.*) Suicide's a sin. (*No answer. Timidly.*) Shouldn't we call somebody to—

KAREN. In a little while.

MRS. MORTAR. She shouldn't have done it, she shouldn't have done it. It was because of all this awful business. She would have got a job and started all over again—she was just worried and sick and—

KAREN. That isn't the reason she did it.

MRS. MORTAR. What—why—?

KAREN (*wearily*). What difference does it make now?

MRS. MORTAR (*reproachfully*). You're not crying.

KAREN. No.

MRS. MORTAR. What will happen to me? haven't anything. Oh, she wouldn't ha wanted me, no matter what she said, to su fer and starve. I know she wouldn't ha wanted that.

KAREN. She was very good to you; she w good to us all.

MRS. MORTAR. Oh, I know she was, Kare and I was good to her too. I did everythi I could. I—I haven't any place to go.

KAREN (*without malice*). When the haw descend, they must be fed. You'll be tak care of.

MRS. MORTAR (*after a few seconds of silence I'm afraid. It seems so queer—in the ne room. (*Shivers.*)

KAREN. Don't be afraid.

MRS. MORTAR. It's different for you. You young.

KAREN. Not any more. (*The sound of t door-bell ringing.* MRS. MORTAR *jumps.* K REN *doesn't move. It rings again.*)

MRS. MORTAR (*nervously*). Who is it? (*T bell rings again.*) Shall I answer it? (*KAR shrugs.*) I think we'd better. (*Exits do the hall through Center doors. Returns a minute followed by* MRS. TILFORD's ma AGATHA, *who stands in the door.*) It's a v man. (*No answer.*) It's a woman to see y Karen. (*Getting no answer, she turns AGATHA.*) You can't come in now; we had a—we've had trouble here.

AGATHA. Miss Karen, I've *got* to speak to y

KAREN (*turns slowly, mechanically*). A; tha.

AGATHA (*goes to* KAREN). Please, Miss Kar We've tried so hard to get you. I be phoning all the time. Please, please let come in. Just for a minute, Miss Kar Please—

MRS. MORTAR. Who wants to come in he

AGATHA. Mrs. Tilford. (*Looks at* KARE Don't you feel well? (*KAREN shakes head.*) You ain't mad at *me*?

MRS. MORTAR. That woman can't come here. She caused all—

KAREN. I'm not mad at you, Agatha.

ATHA. Can I—can I get you something?

REN. No.

ATHA. You poor child. You look like you
: a pain somewhere. (*Hesitates, takes*
REN's *hands.*) I only came 'cause she's
bad off. She's got to see you, Miss Ka-
ı, she's just got to. She's been sittin' out-
e in the car, hoping you'd come out. She
ı't get Dr. Joe. He—he won't talk to her
y more. I wouldn't a come—I always been
your side—but she's sick. If only you
ıld see her, you'd let her come for just
ninute.

REN. I couldn't do that, Agatha.

ATHA. I don't blame you. But I had to
l you. She's old. It's going to kill her.

REN (*bitterly*). Kill her? Where is Mrs.
.ford?

ATHA. Outside.

REN. All right.

ATHA (*presses* KAREN's *arm*). You always
n a good girl. (*Hurriedly exits.*)

S. MORTAR. You going to allow that wo-
n to come in here? With Martha lying
re? How can you be so feelingless? (*She*
rts to cry.) I won't stay and see it. I
n't have anything to do with it. I'll never
  that woman— (*Rushes sobbing from the*
m.)

    second after, MRS. TILFORD *appears in*
 doorway *Center. She is a sick woman;*
 old woman. Her face, her walk, her
ce have changed. She is feeble.*)

S. TILFORD. Karen, let me come in. (*With-*
  turning, KAREN *bows her head.* MRS. TIL-
RD *enters, stands staring at the floor.*)

REN. Why have you come here?

S. TILFORD. I had to come. (*Stretches out*
  hand to KAREN, *who does not turn. She*
ps her hand.*) I know now; I know it
sn't true.

REN. What?

S. TILFORD (*carefully*). I know it wasn't
e, Karen.

REN (*stares at her, shudders*). You know
 vasn't true? I don't care what you know.
 doesn't matter any more. If that's what
ı had to say, you've said it. Go away.

MRS. TILFORD (*puts her hand to her throat*).
I've *got* to tell you.

KAREN. I don't want to hear you.

MRS. TILFORD. Last Tuesday Mrs. Wells
found a bracelet in Rosalie's room. The
bracelet had been hidden for several months.
We found out that Rosalie had taken the
bracelet from another girl, and that Mary—
(*Closes her eyes.*) that Mary knew that and
used it to force Rosalie into saying that she
had seen you and Miss Dobie together. I—
I've talked to Mary. I've found out. (KAREN
suddenly begins to laugh, high and sharp.)
Don't do that, Karen. I have only a little
more to say. I've talked to Judge Potter.
He will make all arrangements. There will
be a public apology and an explanation.
The damage suit will be paid to you in full
and—and any more that you will be kind
enough to take from me. I—I must see that
you won't suffer any more.

KAREN. We're not going to suffer any more.
It's all too late. Martha is dead. (MRS. TIL-
FORD *gasps, shakes her head as though to*
shake off the truth, feebly falls into a chair,
and covers her face. KAREN *watches her for*
a minute.) So you've come here to relieve
your conscience? Well, I won't be your con-
fessor. It's choking you, is it? (*Violently.*)
And you want to stop the choking, don't
you? You've done a wrong and you have to
right that wrong or you can't rest your head
again. You want to be "just," don't you,
and you wanted us to help you be just?
You've come to the wrong place for help.
You want to be a "good" woman again,
don't you? (*Bitterly.*) Oh, I know. You
told us that night you had to do what you
did. Now you "have" to do this. A public
apology and money paid, and you can sleep
again and eat again. That done and there'll
be peace for you. You're old, and the old are
callous. Ten, fifteen years left for you. But
what of me? It's a whole life for me. A
whole God-damned life. (*Suddenly quiet,*
points to door Right.) And what of her?

MRS. TILFORD (*she is crying*). You are still
living.

KAREN. And I don't know why.

MRS. TILFORD (*with a tremendous effort to*
control herself). I didn't come here to relieve myself. I swear to God I didn't. I
came to try—to try anything. I knew there

wasn't any relief for me, Karen, and that there never would be again. (*Tensely.*) But what I am or why I came doesn't matter. The only thing that matters is you and— You, now.

KAREN. There's nothing for me any more.

MRS. TILFORD. Oh, let's try to make something for you. You're young and I—I can help you.

KAREN (*smiles*). You can help me?

MRS. TILFORD (*with great feeling*). Take whatever I can give you. Take it for yourself and use it for yourself. It won't bring me peace, if that's what's worrying you. (*Smiles.*) Those ten or fifteen years you talk about! I hope it won't be that long. But however long it is, it will be in darkness. And I won't blame you if that gives you pleasure.

KAREN. It doesn't now. I'm too tired to want even that. (*Almost tenderly.*) You will have a hard time ahead, won't you?

MRS. TILFORD. Yes.

KAREN. Mary?

MR. TILFORD. I don't know.

KAREN. You can send her away.

MRS. TILFORD. No. I could never do that. Whatever she does, it must be to me and no one else. She's—she's—

KAREN. Yes. Your very own, to live with the rest of your life. They will be years of darkness; you're right. (*For a moment she watches* MRS. TILFORD's *face.*) It's over for me now, but it will never end for you. She's harmed us both, but she's harmed you more, I guess. (*Sits down beside* MRS. TILFORD.) I'm sorry.

MRS. TILFORD (*clings to her*). Then you'll try for yourself.

KAREN. All right.

MRS. TILFORD. You and Joe.

KAREN. No. We're not together anymore.

MRS. TILFORD (*looks up at her*). Did I do that, too?

KAREN. I don't think anyone did anything, any more.

MRS. TILFORD (*makes a half-movement rise*). I'll go to him right away.

KAREN. No, it's better now the way it is.

MRS. TILFORD. But he must know what know, Karen. You must go back to him.

KAREN (*smiles*). No, not any more.

MRS. TILFORD. You must, you must—(*Se her face, hesitates.*) Perhaps later, Kare

KAREN. Perhaps.

MRS. TILFORD (*after a moment in wh they both sit silent*). Come away from h now, Karen. (KAREN *shakes her head.*) Y can't stay with—(*Moves her hand towa door Right.*)

KAREN. When she is buried, then I will

MRS. TILFORD. You'll be all right?

KAREN. I'll be all right, I suppose. Good-now. (*They both rise.* MRS. TILFORD *spea pleadingly.*)

MRS. TILFORD. You'll let me help yo You'll let me try?

KAREN. Yes, if it will make you feel bett

MRS. TILFORD (*timidly*). And you—you take the money?

KAREN (*tired*). If you want it that way

MRS. TILFORD (*with great feeling*). Oh y oh yes, Karen. (*Unconsciously* KAREN *beg to walk toward the window.*)

KAREN (*suddenly*). Is it nice out?

MRS. TILFORD. It's been cold. (KAREN *op the window slightly, sits on the ledge.* M TILFORD *with surprise*) It seems a li warmer, now.

KAREN. It feels very good. (*They smile each other.*)

MRS. TILFORD. You'll write me some tin

KAREN. If I ever have anything to say. Go by, now.

MRS. TILFORD. You will have. I know Good-by, my dear. (KAREN *smiles, sha her head as* MRS. TILFORD *exits. She d not turn, but a minute later she raises hand.*)

KAREN. Good-by.

CURTAIN

Tobacco Road

BY JACK KIRKLAND

From the novel by Erskine Caldwell

ORIGINAL CAST OF CHARACTERS

As they appeared in the first performance, December 4, 1933, at the Forty-ghth Street Theatre, New York City.

DUDE LESTER .... Sam Byrd
ADA LESTER .... Margaret Wycherly
JEETER LESTER .... Henry Hull
ELLIE MAY .... Ruth Hunter
GRANDMA LESTER .... Patricia Quinn
LOV BENSEY .... Dean Jagger
HENRY PEABODY .... Ashley Cooper
SISTER BESSIE RICE ....Maude Odell
PEARL .... Reneice Rehan
CAPTAIN TIM .... Lamar King
GEORGE PAYNE .... Edwin Walter

Produced and directed by Anthony Brown

Settings by Robert Redington Sharpe

ACT I
Late Afternoon

ACT II
Next Morning

ACT III
Dawn, the Following Day.

The entire action of the play takes place at the farm of Jeeter Lester, situated n a tobacco road in the back country of Georgia.

TOBACCO ROAD

ACT ONE

TIME: *The Present.*

PLACE: *The back country, Georgia—thirty miles or so from Augusta. It is a famished desolate land, once given over to the profitable raising of tobacco, then turned into small cotton plantations, which have been so intensively and stupidly cultivated as to exhaust the soil. Poverty, want, squalor, degeneracy, pitiful helplessness and grotesque, tragic lust have stamped a lost, outpaced people with the mark of inevitable end. Unequipped to face a changing economic program, bound up in traditions, ties, and prejudices, they unknowingly face extinction. It is a passing scene, contemporary and fast fading, hurling the lie at nature's mercy and challenging a god who reputedly looks after his own. Grim humor pervades all, stalking side by side with tragedy on the last short mile which leads to complete, eventual elimination. The pride and hope of a once aggressive group, pioneers in a great new world, thus meet ironic conclusion. The world moves on, unmindful of their ghosts.*

SCENE: *The squalid shack of* JEETER LESTER, *where live his wife, his mother, and two children, last of a multiple brood and last of many generations of deep Georgia crackers. Left stage, angled to curtain line, is the front of the cracked and bleeding house. A small porch, one step up from the yard, projects beyond the building front. Rear, running parallel with the curtain line and disappearing—Left, behind the house, and, Right behind a clump of bushes—is the immediate section of the Tobacco Road. Center stage, from road rear to foots, is a sandy yard. Right center stage is a leafless chinaberry tree under which is a broken, weatherworn bench. Downstage from this, to within two feet of the curtain line, is a well structure, behind which, masking Right stage to curtain, is a broken corn crib. A sprawling, broken log fence separates the yard from the road beyond which fields of sedge brush stretch away in the distance.*

AT RISE: JEETER, *dressed in dirty, torn overalls and dark shirt, an old, battered hat on his head, and heavy, worn boots on his feet, is sitting on the edge of the porch, trying vainly to patch a rotted inner tube. He is really concentrating on his work, but that does not hinder an almost constant run of chatter, most of it a complaining monotone. Standing in the yard and hurling a ball, which he retrieves on the rebound, against the side of the house, upstage beyond the porch, is* DUDE, *last son of* JEETER *to remain at home.* DUDE *is just sixteen, dirty, skinny, and not too bright. He is dressed like his father in dirty overalls and a shirt. Underfeeding has had its effect on both* JEETER *and* DUDE. *They are scrawny and emaciated.* DUDE *continues thumping the ball against the house and catching it on the rebound in spite of the fact that the old boards aren't capable of much resistance. The ball hits the house several times before* JEETER *complains.*

JEETER. Stop chunkin' that ball against that there old house, Dude. You've clear about got all the weatherboards knocked off already. (DUDE, *ignoring him, throws the ball three more times.*) Don't you never do what I tell you? Quit chunkin' that ball at them there weatherboards. The durned old house is going to pitch over and fall on the ground one of these days if you don't stop doing that.

DUDE (*casually*). Aw, go to hell, you dried-up old clod. Nobody asked you nothin'. (*Throws ball again.*)

JEETER (*an edge of supplication in his voice*). Now, Dude, is that a way to treat your old Pa? You ought to sort of help me out instead of always doing somethin' contrary. You ought to be helping me fix up this old inner tube instead of chunkin' that ball at that old house all the time.

DUDE. That there old inner tube ain't going to stay fixed noway. You might just as well quit tryin'.

JEETER. Maybe you're right. Maybe I ought to try filling the tires with cotton hulls and drivin' on them that way. A man told me that was the way to do it.

DUDE (*between throwing the ball*). That old automobile ain't no good. It ain't got

600

rn on it no more and there ain't no sense
ivin' an automobile unless you got a horn.

ETER. It had one of the prettiest horns in
e country when it was new.

DE. Well, it ain't got no horn now, and
don't hardly run neither.

ETER. It used to be one of the prettiest run-
n' and prettiest soundin' automobiles you
er saw. I used to put you children in it
d let you blow the horn all you liked.

DE. That was so long ago it ain't doing
e no good now.

ETER. That old automobile is just about the
st of my goods. It looks like a man can't
ve any goods no more.

DE (*suddenly—fierce*). Some day I'm
ping to have me a new automobile. I'm
ping to have me a new automobile and a
w horn on it and I'm going to ride
rough the country just a raisin' of hell.
GRANDMA LESTER, *an old, bent hag in rag-*
d, black clothes comes around the far
rner of the house just as DUDE *throws his*
ll with particular viciousness, almost strik-
g her. In fright, she drops to her knees and
egins crawling downstage toward the
rch. DUDE *catches the ball on the rebound*
d prepares to hurl it again.) Look out
the way, old woman, or I'll knock your
ad off. (DUDE *hurls the ball against the*
use just above the old woman as she
awls, whimpering, along the ground in
e direction of the porch steps. He takes
vage delight in her fears. She moves pain-
lly and slowly and he has time for two
rows before she reaches the comparative
fety of the steps, under which she crawls.)

ETER. Now, Dude, is that a way to act
ward your old grandma? You got her
ared half to death.

DE. Aw, shut up. You wish she was dead
st as much as anybody, even if she is your
vn ma.

ETER. Now, Dude . . . I never wished no
rm to nobody.

DE. You're a dirty old liar. You don't
en give her nothing to eat.

ETER. I don't give her nothing because
ere ain't nothing.

DUDE. Even when there is you don't give it
to her. You needn't go telling me you don't
want her dead.

JEETER. Now, Dude, is that a way to talk?
It don't seem to me like that's a way a son
should talk to his father.

DUDE. Then keep your mouth out of it when
nobody's asked you nothing. (DUDE *throws*
the ball against the house, beginning his
game again. JEETER *resumes work on the*
inner tube, sitting on the patch. GRANDMA
comes slowly from under the edge of the
porch, rises and starts cautiously to move
around DUDE *in the direction of the Tobacco*
Road. She is carrying an old gunny sack.)

DUDE (*seeing the old woman and stopping*).
Where you going now? There ain't no use
you picking up firewood today. There ain't
going to be anything to eat. (*The* OLD WO-
MAN *shuffles on toward Right rear hole in*
the log fence. DUDE *looks after her, the spirit*
of hurt in his heart and mind.) You better
run, old woman, I'm going to chunk this
ball at you. (*He holds ball to throw. She*
sees his gesture, moves more quickly,
stumbles, falls, get up.) Look out now, I'm
going to hit you in the head—I'm going to
hit you in the head. (GRANDMA *stumbles*
again in her hurry, but this time doesn't rise,
continuing her exit on hands and knees.
DUDE *is on the point of throwing the ball at*
her, when his eye catches the torn cover
and checks him. He looks at the ball more
closely.) Goddamn, just look at that ball.
Just look at what that old house done to that
ball.

JEETER (*wiggling on tube to make the patch*
stick). Let me see it here. (DUDE *hands him*
the ball. He looks at it and shakes his head.)
Yes, sir, it's plumb wore out.

DUDE (*taking back the ball, holding it up,*
and looking at it). It ain't even round no
more. That old house just about ruined it
for good. (*Sits on ground, inspecting ball.*)

JEETER. Looks like about everything around
here is wore out. Seems like the Lord just
ain't with us no more at all.

DUDE. I'm going down to Fuller tomorrow
and steal me a new ball. That's what I'm
going to do.

JEETER. Stealing is powerful sinful, Dude. I
wouldn't want you doing that. I guess steal-

ing is about the most sinful thing a man can do.

DUDE. Go on, you old liar. You're always stealing something if you can find it.

JEETER. Now, Dude! Maybe I have been a powerful sinner in my time, but ain't nobody never been sorrier than me when he's done something against the Lord.

DUDE. You're always praying and shouting after you been stealing something, but that ain't never stopped you from doing it. I'd like to hear you tell me of one time when it stopped you. Just tell me. (*Pauses while* JEETER *fiddles with inner tube.*) You just won't tell me—that's what.

JEETER (*avoiding the issue, pulls at the patch, which comes off in his hand*). Just look at that old inner tube. . . . (*Inspects it for an instant, tosses it aside.*) Well, I guess there ain't no use trying to fix that no more. Looks to me like I got to figure some other way of getting a load of wood down to Augusta. (*Yawns, stretches.*) I got to do some thinking about that. (*Lies back on porch, tilting his hat over his eyes.* DUDE *continues to pound ball on rock.*) I know what I'm going to do. I'm going down to Fuller one of these days and borrow me a mule. I expect I could take a load of wood to Augusta almost every day that way.

DUDE (*laughs*). Ho! Ho! Ain't nobody going to loan you a mule. You can't even get seed-cotton and guano to plant a crop with.

JEETER. Never you mind now. That way I could do about everything I wanted. When I wasn't hauling wood I could cultivate the fields. That's what a man ought to be doing anyway. When February comes like this and the ground gets right for plowing a man ought to be planting in the ground and growing things. That's what the Lord intended a man should do. But he can't do much without a mule to plow with. (*Nods his head, sits up.*) Yes, sir, that's what I'm going to do. I'm going down to Fuller or maybe even McCoy one of these days and borrow me a mule. (*Lies down on his back again, tilting hat over his eyes.*) I got to do some thinking about that. (DUDE *makes no comment, concentrating on pounding the ball back into shape. Hits it twice on the ground.*)

DUDE. Goddamn that old house. This b never will get round no more. (*Enter A through doorway on to the porch and ta ing in* JEETER'*s recumbent form with quick, irritated glance.* ADA *is a thin, gau pellagra-ridden woman. Her shapeless dr is dirty and ragged. She was never a beau and pellagra and forty years of living w* JEETER *have not helped to improve her a pearance. Her hair is a stringy, colorl gray-brown. She shambles rather th walks, and leans against anything stro enough to bear her weight. An inevita snuff stick protrudes from her lips. S speaks when* DUDE *stops pounding the b to inspect it again.*)

ADA. What are you doing laying down th on the porch, Jeeter Lester? Ain't you goi to haul no wood to Augusta?

JEETER (*pushing back hat and sitting Even in that short time he has fallen asle He regards his wife vaguely*). What's th

ADA. When you going to haul some wood Augusta?

JEETER (*sinking back*). I'm aiming to ta a load over there tomorrow or the next d

DUDE. The hell he is, Ma. He's just tryi to lie out of it.

JEETER. Now, Dude.

ADA. You're just lazy, that's what's wro with you. If you wasn't lazy you could h a load every day, and I'd have me so snuff when I wanted it most.

JEETER. I ain't no durn wood-chopper. I a farmer. The wood-choppers hauling wo to Augusta ain't got no farming to take their time like I has. Why, I expect I going to grow near about fifty bales of c ton this year.

ADA. That's the way you talk every y about this time, but you don't never started.

JEETER. This year I'm going to get at Dude and me'll burn the broom sedge the fields one of these days and it wo take long then to put in a crop.

ADA. I been listening to you talk like that long I don't believe nothing you say n It's a big old whopping lie.

ER. Now leave me be, Ada. I'm going
art in the morning. Soon as I get all
ields burned off I'll go borrow me some
s. I wouldn't be surprised if me and
e growed more than fifty bales of cotton
year, if I can get me some seed-cotton
guano.

. Who's going to give you seed-cotton
guano this year any more than they did
year or the year before, or the year be-
that?

ER. God is aiming to provide for me.
getting ready right now to receive His
ty.

You just lay there and see! Even the
ren has got more sense than you has.
't they go off and work in the mills as
as they was big enough? If I wasn't
d I'd go up there right now and make
ome money, myself, just like you ought
doing.

ER (intensely—sitting bolt upright). It's
ed, you saying that, Ada. City ways
God-given. It wasn't intended for a
with the smell of the land in him to
n a mill in Augusta.

It's a whole lot better to live in the mills
it is to stay out here on the Tobacco
and starve to death.

, Cuss the hell out of him, Ma.

ER (sadly. Again lying down). The
sends me every misery He can think
st to try my soul. He must be aiming to
mething powerful big for me because
ure tests me hard. I reckon He figures
an put up with my own people I can
to fight back at the devil.

Humph! If He don't hurry up and do
thing about it, it will be too late. My
stomach gives me a powerful pain all
ong when I ain't got the snuff to calm

ER (without moving). Yes, I reckon you
en folks is about near as hungry as I
sure feel right sorry for you women
(Pulls hat over his eyes and dozes off
. Enter ELLIE MAY right on Tobacco
. ELLIE MAY is eighteen, and not un-
tive as to figure. Her eyes are good;
air is brown. The outstanding feature,
ver, is a slit lip, red and fiery, the open-
unning from about the center of the lip

to the left side of her nose. When she speaks,
which is seldom, she has the garbled pro-
nunciation and nasal emphasis of those
afflicted with a harelip. She is barefoot and
hatless, and her light cotton dress is old,
rumpled, and streaked with dirt. She comes
forward shyly, like a frightened doe, her
eyes watching the three other people. She
only comes in as far as the chinaberry tree,
half edging behind it.)

ADA. You talk like an old fool. . . . Where
you been there, Ellie May?

ELLIE MAY. No place, Ma.

ADA (eagerly). You didn't maybe go to see
Pearl, did you?

ELLIE MAY. No, Ma.

ADA (more to herself than to anyone). I
declare I don't know what's got into that
girl. I ain't seen hide nor hair of her since
she and Lov got married.

DUDE (with deliberate cruelty). Why should
Pearl want to see you?

ADA. She loves her old Ma, that's why.

DUDE. Well, she ain't been back, has she?

ADA. Pearl is different. There ain't one of the
whole seventeen she's like.

DUDE (pointedly—leering). She sure ain't
like the rest of us, all right. . . . What was
you doing, Ma, horsing around some man
besides that old fool over there?

ADA. You ain't no right talking like that to
your old Ma, Dude Lester. The Lord will
strike you dead one of these days.

DUDE. I ain't afraid of the Lord. He ain't
never done nothing for me one way or the
other. . . .

ADA. If you was a good son, you wouldn't
be saying things like that. You'd be helping
to get rations and snuff for your old Ma. I
declare to goodness I don't know when I've
had enough to eat. It's getting so if I had a
stylish dress to be buried in I'd like to lie
down right now and die.

DUDE (with vicious humor). You ain't never
going to get a new dress to die in. You're
going to die and be buried in just what you
got on. They're going to bury you in that
same old dress.

ADA. Now, Dude, don't start fooling with your old Ma like that. (JEETER *is aroused and straightens up sleepily.* ELLIE MAY *moves a step nearer the porch, but is still close to the chinaberry tree.* DUDE *gets to his feet, leering with joy at the effect of his cruel tormenting.* ADA *steps down from the porch, but one hand still holds the upright.*)

DUDE. I ain't fooling. I guess I know . . . Yeh, and they're going to bury Pa just like he is, too. They're going to lay you in the corn crib and then they're going to bury you both just like you is.

JEETER (*plaintively*). What are you saying, Dude? You're always saying that when you know how I feel about it. They ain't going to lay me in no corn crib. Lov swore to me he'd dig a hole and put me right in it.

DUDE. What do I care what Lov promised? I know what they're going to do.

ADA. Make him say they ain't, Jeeter.

JEETER. Dude, you can't let them do that. My Pa was laid in the corn crib before they buried him and the rats ate off half his face. You can't let them do that to me.

DUDE. What you so worried about? You'll be dead, anyhow.

JEETER. My old Pa was dead and I know he minded.

DUDE. There ain't no rats in that old corn crib no more. There ain't been no corn in there for five years. They've all gone away.

JEETER. They'll come back, when they know I'm layin' there. They got it in good and heavy for me because there ain't been no corn in that old crib all this time. They'll just be waitin' to come back when I'm dead and eat off me when I can't do nothing to keep 'em away.

DUDE. What do I care about that?

ADA. You're the only boy left to see your old Ma is buried in a stylish dress. You got to swear to me, Dude.

DUDE (*getting up*). I ain't going to swear to nothing.

JEETER (*coming forward a few steps*). Now, Dude, boy—

DUDE. Aw, go to hell. What do I care [a]bout you? (*Turns—starts to chant*). You're [going] to die and get laid in the corn crib—y[ou're] going to die and get laid in the corn [crib.]

JEETER (*threateningly*). You shut up, [you] Lester. You shut up your mouth.

DUDE (*continuing chant, walking to[ward] gate*). You're going to die and get laid i[n the] corn crib—you're going to die, etc. (J[EETER] *rushes at* DUDE.)

JEETER (*striking weakly at* DUDE'S b[ack]. Shut up. You hear me—shut up!

DUDE (*turning—blocking blows ea[sily]*. What you trying to do, you old fool[? Get] away from me. (*Pushes* JEETER, *who* [stum]*bles back, failing.*) You keep away fro[m me] when I tell you. (*Turns—breaks agai[n into]* *chant.*) You're going to die and get la[id in] the corn crib . . . etc. (*Exits.*)

ADA (*plaintively*). Dude, you come [back] here. You can't go off like that w[ithout] making a promise to your old Ma. (*Ada is* answered only by DUDE'S grim chant, [va]nishing in the distance. JEETER gets up[, goes] back to the porch and sits, abstractedly [pick]ing up the inner tube and working[. He sits] ADA at bench.)

JEETER (*after a pause*). I reckon Du[de's] about the worst child of the whol[e lot.] Seems like a boy would have the [proper] respect for his old Pa.

ADA. I know Lizzie Belle'd help me [get a] stylish dress if I could find out whe[re she] is at. She used to love her old Ma a[nd] Clara might help some, too. She used [to tell] me how pretty I looked when I comb[ed my] hair mornings and put on a clean [dress.] I don't know if the others would w[ant to] help none or not. It's been such a long [time] since I saw the rest of them I've just [about] forgot what they was like. Seems like [I can't] recall their names even.

JEETER. Lizzie Belle might be makin[g a lot] of money over in the mills. Maybe if [I was] to find her and ask her about it, she [might] come sometime and bring us a little n[ow.] I know Bailey would. Bailey was just [about] the best of all the boys.

ADA. Reckon any of the children is

ER. Some, I reckon. . . . But Tom ain't
. I know that for sure. I ain't got
nd to doing it yet, but one of these
I'm going over to Burke County and
im. Everybody in Fuller tells me he's
ing cross ties out of the camp by the
on load day and night. From what
le say about him he's a powerful rich
now. He sure ought to give me some
ey.

When you see Tom tell him that his
Ma would like to see him. You tell him
I said he was near about the best of the
e seventeen. Clara and Lizzie Belle was
t the best, I reckon, but Tom and
y led the boys when it came to being
children. You tell Tom I said he was
best and maybe he'll send me some
ey for a stylish dress.

ER. Pearl is the prettiest. Ain't none of
ther gals got pretty yellow hair like she
Nor them pale blue eyes, neither.

Pearl is my real favorite. But I wish
come to see me sometime. What do
hink makes her stay away since she got
ied, Jeeter?

ER. There never was no telling what
was going to do. You was much like
ourself in that respect when you was
e or thirteen.

Do you think she's happy married to

R. Happy? I don't know anything
that. When a gal is mated to a man
all there is to it.

Maybe she should've gone off to
sta like the others done, even if she
cared. That's where a pretty girl ought
. She ought to be where there's pretty
s and shoes to wear and windows to
t.

R. I don't agree to that. People that's
on the land should stay on the land.
Lord intended such. I made her go to
with Lov because that was the best
for her to do.

Humph! Well, it might be she's satis-
Maybe she don't care about seeing her
Ma right now. When girls is satisfied
ometimes don't like to talk about their

husbands any more than they do when they
ain't satisfied.

JEETER. Pearl don't talk none anyway.
Reckon she talk to Lov, Ada?

ADA. When girls sleep in the bed with their
husbands they usually talk to them, I've discovered.

JEETER. By God and by Jesus you was certainly in no hurry to talk to me even then.

ADA. I'll go down to see her one of these days
if she don't come to see me. You go see
Lov, too. It's time you done that.

JEETER. Don't bother me about that now.
I got to figure out some way to plant me a
crop this year. (*Leans against upright.*) I
got to do some thinking about that right
away. (JEETER *pulls hat over his eyes and
promptly goes to sleep.* ADA *shakes her head.*
ELLIE MAY *starts out gate, but* ADA *sees her.*)

ADA. Ellie May! Hey you, Ellie May! You
come inside and fix up the beds. They ain't
been made all day and somebody's got to
do something around here. (ELLIE MAY *turns
and reluctantly starts toward house, when*
DUDE *enters excitedly from Right and comes
to right of porch.*)

DUDE. Hey, Lov's coming! Lov's coming
down the road. (ELLIE MAY *crosses to right
end of fence; looks down road.*)

JEETER (*drowsily*). What?

ADA (*kicks* JEETER). Wake up, you old
fool—Lov's coming. Maybe he wants to talk
about Pearl.

JEETER. What do I care about that now? By
God, woman, can't you see I'm thinking?

DUDE. He's toting a croker sack that's got
something in it.

JEETER (*suddenly wide awake*). A croker
sack! (*Rises.*) What does it look like in
that croker sack, Dude?

DUDE. He's just coming over the ridge now
and I couldn't make out. But nobody carries
a sack that ain't got nothing good in it.
(JEETER *runs to the fence and looks over
it down the road.* ELLIE MAY *also goes to
the fence, but as far right stage from the
others as possible. Enter* GRANDMA LESTER
with a sackful of twigs which she drags

along the ground. She does not even glance at the others, who are gazing in the opposite direction down the road, but crosses to the porch, releases the sack, and sits, pressing her hands to her side in pain and swaying back and forth.)

JEETER (*peering over fence*). By God and by Jesus, that's Lov all right. Do you think them's turnips he's toting, Dude? Do you think them's turnips in that croker sack?

DUDE. It's something all right.

JEETER (*delighted*). By God and by Jesus, ·I just been waiting to have me some turnips.

ADA. If them's turnips do you reckon he'll let me have some?

JEETER. I'll mention it when I talk to him, but I don't know how he'll take it. He must have paid a good stiff price if they's winter turnips.

DUDE. Lov ain't giving away nothing he paid a good stiff price for.

JEETER. I ain't concerning myself about that. Lov and me think a heap of each other.

DUDE. If he don't give you none, is you going to try and steal some?

JEETER (*admonishingly*). Now, Dude! Stealing is about the most sinful thing a man can do. The Lord don't have no truck with stealing. (ELLIE MAY *giggles foolishly.* JEETER *turns to her.*) Get away from that fence, Ellie May. Lov ain't likely to come in here at all if he sees that face of yours. (ELLIE MAY *giggles foolishly again and moves behind chinaberry tree, from where she peaks.* GRANDMA LESTER *shuffles downstage and flattens herself against the corner of the porch nearest the curtain line.* JEETER *and* DUDE *stretch far over the fence to watch* LOV's *approach.*)

ADA. Is he near about here, Jeeter?

JEETER. Near about. He's just about here now.

ADA. Is them turnips?

JEETER. By God, if they ain't, I sure is doing a hell of a lot of stretching for nothing. (JEETER *gives his full attention to the approaching man for a second, then turns and motions to the others.*)

JEETER. Get away from that fence—a you. Come on, sit down. Act unconcer (JEETER *goes to side of house;* ADA *to* well; DUDE *sits on fence. Enter* LOV BEN LOV *is a man about thirty, dressed in grimed overalls and wearing a dirty, fl hat. When he removes the hat to wipe sweat from his face a shock of unruly is seen rising above a sunburned face.* not unattractive in his dull, slow way, his body shows the result of hard work a reasonable amount of food. He is n big man, but he is stronger and better ished than either* DUDE *or* JEETER. *He ca a partly filled gunny sack over his shou Caution and suspicion mark his every n in dealing with the* LESTERS, *and this evidence now as he comes into the sc*

JEETER (*hiding his eagerness by trying casual*). Hi there, Lov.

LOV. Hi. (*He moves on beyond them to Center stage.*)

JEETER. Ain't seen you in a long time.

LOV. No. (*He stops near the gate, and bag.*)

JEETER. You must be plumb wore out t that croker sack. Come in off the To Road and rest yourself.

LOV. I ain't tired.

JEETER. You must of come a far piece you come from down Fuller way.

LOV. Umm.

JEETER. Come inside and get yours drink.

LOV. I ain't thirsty.

JEETER (*with calculated amiability*). was just talking about you, Lov. We seen you since a way long the first winter. How is you and Pearl getti down there at the coal chute?

ADA (*a trace of anxiety*). Pearl—is s right?

LOV. Humph! (*He glances suspiciou all of them.*) I want to talk to you,

JEETER. Sure. Come inside the yard a down. No use toting that croker sack

e talking. (LOV *repeats his glance of
cion, but comes hesitatingly inside and
s the sack against fence near gate. He
's in front of it, guarding it.* JEETER
to make his voice casual, but every eye
e stage is on that sack, giving the lie
eir pretended indifference.*) What you
n that croker sack, Lov? (*Innocently,
v doesn't answer.*) I heard it said that
people has got turnips this year. (LOV's
narrow with suspicion and he backs
more protectively against the sack.*)

(*shrewdly*). It's Pearl I want to talk
u about.

She ain't sick, is she?

suddenly angry). By God, she's some-
! (*He lets himself to ground, sitting
e turnips and gripping neck of sack.*)

.R (*archly*). Why don't you go over on
orch? That ain't no place to sit.

I'll sit right where I is.

.R (*agreeably*). What you got to say
, Lov? You must have a heap to say,
that sack all this way to do it.

I sure has. You got to talk to Pearl.
s what I got to say.

R. What's that gal up to? I never could
stand her. What's she done now?

It's just like she done ever since she
down to live with me at the chute, only
etting pretty durn tired of it by this
All the niggers make fun of me be-
of the way she treats me.

R. Pearl is just like her Ma. Her Ma
to do the queerest things in her time.

sharply). Is you treating her right?

That ain't got a goddamn thing to do
t. She's married to me, ain't she?

R. You got leave of the county. I re-
er that all right.

Then why the hell don't she act like
ght to? Every time I want to have her
d, she runs off in the broom sedge.
on't talk to me, neither, and she won't
nothing I want to eat.

R. Great day in the morning, now
do you think makes her do that?

LOV. I don't know and I don't care. But I
call it a hell of a business.

JEETER. About the cooking you is just about
right. But when it comes to not talking I
don't see no harm in that. Ada, there, didn't
used to talk neither, but, by God and by
Jesus, now you can't make her shut up.

LOV (*stubbornly*). I want Pearl to talk to me.
I want her to ask me if my back is sore
when I come home from the chute, or if
it's going to rain, or when I is going to get
a hair cut. There's a hell of a lot of things
she could ask me about, but she don't talk
at all.

JEETER. Maybe you don't try the right way
to make her.

LOV. I tried kicking her and I tried pouring
water on her and chunking rocks and sticks
at her, but it don't do no good. She cries
a lot when she's hurt, but, by God, I don't
call that talking.

ADA. Don't you dare hurt her, Lov Bensey.

LOV. You keep out of this. I guess I know
my rights. (*He pauses, looking belligerently
from* ADA *to* JEETER.) And they is something
else she don't do neither.

JEETER. For one little gal they sure is a heap
of things she don't do. What else don't she
do, Lov?

LOV. She don't sleep in the bed with me,
that's what. (*Viciously to* ADA.) And what
you got to say about that?

JEETER (*much more interested*). Now that's
something. By God and by Jesus, that's
something.

LOV (*turning back to* JEETER). She ain't
never slept in the bed. It's a durn pallet on
the floor she sleeps on every night. Now
what I say is, what the hell is the sense in
me marrying a wife if I don't get none of
the benefits?

ADA. If you don't like what she's doing, you
send her right home and get yourself
another girl. Her old Ma will look after her.

LOV. No. I ain't going to do that neither. I
want Pearl. She's about the prettiest piece
in the whole country and I want her.

JEETER. You give her time and she'll get in the bed.

LOV. By God. I already give her enough time. Right now I feel like I got to have me a woman. (*He looks at* ELLIE MAY. ELLIE MAY *catches his glance and giggles. She begins the wriggling movement, which at the right time brings her near* LOV.)

JEETER. I know how you feel, Lov. When the time to plow and put seed in the ground comes along a man feels just like that. Even at this day and age I could do a little of that myself.

LOV. Well, then, you go down and talk to her. You tell her to stop sleeping on that durn pallet and get in the bed—and tell her to talk to me, too, by God.

JEETER. I might do that if I felt you was ready and willing to do something for me in return.

LOV (*suspiciously*). What do you mean by that, Jeeter?

JEETER (*unable longer to restrain himself*). By God and by Jesus, Lov, what you got in that croker sack? I been looking at it ever since you been here and I sure got to know.

LOV. I don't see what that's got to do with it?

JEETER. What is they, I tell you!

LOV (*after a short pause for emphasis and a hard, proud glance around*). Turnips, by God. (*His announcement causes a noticeable reaction on everyone. Their bodies stiffen and lean forward—a look of greed appears in their faces. But wisely they refrain from taking any actual steps forward. Instinctively they wait for* JEETER *to see it through. Only* ELLIE MAY *forgets her hunger in the sharpening force of passion brought on by proximity to* LOV, *and continues her sex-conscious wriggling.*)

JEETER (*keyed up, but holding himself in*).

Turnips! Where'd you get turnips, Lov?

LOV. Wouldn't you like to know?

JEETER. Turnips is about the thing I want most of all right now. I could just about eat me a whole croker sackful between now and sundown.

LOV. Well, don't look to me to give you because I ain't.

JEETER. That's a mean thing to say, Lo[v] a whopping mean thing to say to Pearl' Pa.

LOV. To hell with that. I had to pay cents for this many in a sack and I ha walk clear to the other side of Fuller to them.

JEETER. I was thinking maybe you an could fix up some sort of trade. I coul down to your house and tell Pearl she' to sleep in the bed, and you could giv some of them—

LOV. No, by God. You're Pearl's Daddy you ought to make her behave for not

JEETER. By God and by Jesus, Lov, oughtn't to talk to me like that. I jus to have me some turnips. I ain't had a turnip since a year ago this spring. A turnips I raised this year has got damn-blasted green-gutted worms in

LOV. I don't see what that's got to do Pearl one way or another. I gave you dollars when she came to live with m that's enough.

JEETER. Maybe it was then, but it ain't We is about starved around here. Wha made turnip-worms for I can't make appears to me like He just naturally ha it in good and heavy for a poor m worked all the fall last year digging patch of ground to grow turnips in when they're getting about big enou pull up and eat, along come them blasted green-gutted worms and bore to the middle of them. (LOV *is entire different to* JEETER'S *plea. Cruelly he a turnip from the sack and takes a bi Chewing the bite to the agony of the ing* LESTERS, *he points the stub of the at the wriggling* ELLIE MAY, *sitting ground near the bench and looking a with avid eyes. She giggles.*)

LOV. Now if Pearl was anything lik May there, she wouldn't act like she You go down and tell her to act lik May.

JEETER. Is you in mind then to m trade with them turnips?

(*eating*). I ain't trading turnips with
dy.

ER. That's a hell of a thing to say, Lov.
wanting turnips God himself knows
bad.

Go over to Fuller and buy yourself
, then. I went over there to get mine.

ER. Now, Lov, you know I ain't got a
y to my name. You got a good job
there at the chute and it pays you a
of money.

I don't make but a dollar a day. House
takes up near about all that and eating
est of it.

ER. Makes no difference. You don't
to sit there and let me starve, do you?

I can't help it if you do. The Lord
at us with equal favor, they say. He
me mine and if you don't get yours
etter go talk to Him about it.

You give him hell, Lov. If he wasn't
rn lazy he'd do something instead of
ng about it all the time. He's the laziest
f-a-bitch I ever seen.

ER. My children all blame me because
sees fit to make me poverty-ridden,
They and their Ma is all the time cuss-
ne because we ain't got nothing to eat.
n't my fault that Captain John shut
on giving us rations and snuff, and
went away and died.

indifferently). It ain't my fault neither.

ER. I worked all my life for Captain
Lov. I worked harder than any four
s niggers in the field; then the first
I knowed he came down here one
ing and says he can't be letting me
o more rations and snuff at the store.
that he sells all the mules and goes
Augusta to live. He said there wasn't
e trying to run a farm no more—fifty
or one plow. He told me I could stay
e land as long as I liked, but that ain't
me no good. Ain't no work I can find
for hire and I can't raise a crop of my
because I ain't got no mule and I ain't
o credit. (LOV's *attention turns from*
R *to* ELLIE MAY, *whose wriggling move-
is bringing her inch by inch closer to

him.) That's what I'm wanting to do powerful strong right now—raise me a crop.
When the winter goes and when it gets
time to burn off the broom sedge in the
fields, I sort of want to cry. I reckon it is
the smell of the sedge smoke this time of
year near about drives me crazy. Then
pretty soon all the other farmers start plowing. That's what's the worst. When the
smell of that new earth turning over behind
the plows strikes me, I get all weak and
shaky. It's in my nature—burning broom
sedge and plowing in the ground this time
of year. I did it for near about fifty years,
and my Pa and his Pa before him was the
same kind of men. Us Lesters sure like to
stir up the earth and make plants grow in
it. The land has got a powerful hold on
me, Lov. (LOV *is giving his full attention to*
ELLIE MAY *now, a half-eaten turnip arrested
on its way to his mouth.* ELLIE MAY *leans
back until she rests on the ground and continues her wriggling and squealing.* LOV
begins to edge toward her. DUDE *watches
them closely.*)

DUDE. Hey, Pa.

JEETER. Shut up, Dude. It didn't always
used to be like it is now, neither, Lov. I can
remember a short time back when all the
merchants in Fuller was tickled to give me
credit. Then all of a sudden Captain John
went away and pretty soon the sheriff comes
and takes away near about every durn piece
of goods I possessed. He took every durn
thing I had, excepting that old automobile
and the cow. He said the cow wasn't no
good because she wouldn't take no freshen-
ing, and the automobile wasn't no good
neither. I reckon he was right, too, because
the automobile won't run no more and the
cow died.

DUDE (*throwing a broken piece of weather-
boarding at* JEETER). Hey, you.

JEETER (*angrily*). What you want, Dude?
What's the matter with you—chunking
weather-boarding at me like that?

DUDE. Ellie May's horsing. That's horsing
from way back yonder, hey, Pa?

JEETER (*giving the action conscious attention for the first time*). By God and by
Jesus, Lov, has you been paying attention to
what I was saying? You ain't answered me
about them turnips yet.

DUDE. Lov ain't thinking about no turnips. He's wanting to hang up with Ellie May. Look at her straining for him. She's liable to bust a gut if she don't look out. (*It's* JEETER'S *turn now to be indifferent to conversation. He watches while* LOV *creeps several yards from the turnip sack up to* ELLIE MAY *and awkwardly begins to fondle her. Their backs meet and rub together in a primitive love gesture. Slowly and silently,*

JEETER *puts aside the inner tube which he has been holding and vaguely trying to fix, and gets to his feet. Inch by inch he begins edging toward the sack.* LOV *has worked his way around in back of* ELLIE MAY *and his hands are around her, stroking her arms and legs.*)

JEETER (*moves closer and closer to the sack, unseen by* LOV. *Only* ADA *and* GRANDMA LESTER *notice him.* DUDE *is too occupied watching* LOV *and* ELLIE MAY). By God, Lov ain't never got that close before. He said he wouldn't never get close enough to Ellie May to touch her with a stick. But he ain't paying no mind to that now. I bet he don't even know she's got a slit-lip on her. If he does know it, he don't give a good goddamn. (*And now* JEETER *makes his play. In one swift lunge he crosses the intervening distance and grabs up the sack.* LOV *sees him, turns swiftly, and reaches for him, but misses. He starts to rise as* JEETER *backs a step away, but* ELLIE MAY *grabs his legs, tripping him up. Before he can shake her off,* ADA *hurries from the well, picking up a stick on the way.* GRANDMA LESTER *totters from her place, also brandishing a stick. The two* OLD WOMEN *move down on* LOV *to help* ELLIE MAY.)

LOV. Drop them turnips, Jeeter! Drop them turnips. (ELLIE MAY, *quicker than* LOV, *practically leaps on top of him, holding him down. They roll and struggle.*)
(*To* ELLIE MAY).
Get off me, you. Get off me. (LOV *struggles to rise.* ADA *and* GRANDMA *slap and jab at him with their sticks.*)

JEETER (*at the gate*). You tell Pearl I said be good to you, Lov. I'll be down to see about that first thing in the morning. (*He exits, running.*)

LOV. Goddamn you! (LOV, *by dint of great effort, throws off the women, literally hurl-*

ing ELLIE MAY *to the ground and dash[   ] the gate. He stops there, looking down[   ] road, trying to spy* JEETER.)

DUDE. Ain't no use trying to catch Pa. [   ] run off in the brush and there ain't no[   ] can catch Pa when he runs off in the b[   ] (LOV *realizes the truth of* DUDE'S *stater[   ] and, winded and panting, leans agains[   ] fence, making no effort to run.* ELLIE [   ] lies on the ground, also breathing hard[   ] her eyes still are on* LOV.)

ADA. Go on back to Ellie May, Lov. Don[   ] scared of her. You might even get to lik[   ] and let Pearl come back here to me. [   ] *doesn't answer, pulling a huge co[   ] handkerchief from his pocket and w[   ] his streaming face.* DUDE *moves to the f[   ] center.*)

DUDE. How many scoops-full does that [   ] 17 freight engine empty at the chute [   ] morning, Lov? Looks to me like [   ] freight engines takes on twice as much [   ] as the passenger ones does. (LOV *pay[   ] attention.* ADA *goes back to the porch.* GR[   ] MA LESTER *picks up her sack of twigs, groaning, goes into the house.*) Why [   ] the firemen blow the whistles more [   ] they do, Lov? If I was a fireman I'd pu[   ] whistle cord near about all the time. ([   ] *makes noise like locomotive whistle.[   ] turns from the fence, goes back int[   ] yard, recovers his hat, glances at* ELLIE [   ] who lies sprawled on the ground. The[   ] turns and starts off.* DUDE *follows* LOV *t[   ] gate.* LOV *finishes adjusting his overall[   ] crosses to the gate,* DUDE *following.*) [   ] is you going to buy yourself an autom[   ] Lov? You make a heap of money [   ] chute. You ought to get one that has [   ] great big horn on it. (*Repeats locom[   ] sound. Ecstatically.*) Whistles and [   ] sure make a pretty sound. (*Ignoring [   ]* LOV *exits through the gate and dow[   ] road.*) I reckon Lov don't feel much [   ] talking today.

ADA. Dude, you run right out in the [   ] and find your Pa before he eats up all [   ] turnips. (DUDE *starts.*) See you bring [   ] of them back to your old Ma, too. DUDE. ADA *watches him through the [   ] then calls.*) Ellie May . . . Ellie May

ELLIE MAY (*looking up—blinking*). Ma.

You get inside the house and fix up
beds like I told you a long time ago.
[E] MAY *stretches and yawns, showing*
[di]sposition to move.) I declare to good-
there ain't nobody around here got
[m]otion enough to do anything. Now you
[in]side the house and do like I tell you.
[Y]ou hear me? Come on.

[ADA] MAY (*slowly getting to her feet*). All
[right]—I'm coming. (*Enter* HENRY PEABODY,
[a ma]n who, except for his voice and slight
[differ]ence in his dress, might well be JEETER.
[He is] in very excited. He doesn't come into
[the y]ard, but hangs over the fence. ELLIE
[MAY promptly sits again.*)

[HENR]Y. Hey you, Ada. Is Jeeter home?

[ADA (*s]haking her head negatively*). He went
[off i]nto the brush a little while back. I'm
[expec]ting him pretty soon, but I ain't cer-
[tain.]

[HENR]Y. You tell him I was here.

[ADA.]What's got you so excited, Henry Pea-
[body]? I ain't seen you hurry like that since
[you w]as a boy.

[HENR]Y. I ain't got time to tell you about
[no]w, but you tell Jeeter I been here and
[I'll st]op again on my way home. (*Enter*
[ ]BESSIE RICE, *a rather portly woman of*
[ ]forty, She is dressed in a faded apron
[and w]ears a sunbonnet over her large, round
[face.]BESSIE *is one of the brood of itinerant*
[wome]n preachers peculiar to certain sections
[of the]deep South. She owes allegiance to no
[churc]h, and her creed and method of divine
[preachi]ng are entirely her own. She is loud
[and su]re of voice, and is generally accepted
[at he]r own value by the God-fearing in-
[stinc]ts among whom she moves. She enters
[the wa]y of the gate, coming inside the yard,
[and ta]kes off her sunbonnet, fanning her-
[self as] she gives her greeting.*)

[BESSIE.] Good evening, Brother Henry—good
[evenin]g, Sister Ada. The Lord's blessing
[be wit]h you.

[HENRY]. Good evening, Sister Bessie. . . .
[But]I got to be rushing off. (*Starts off.*)

[BESSIE.] What's hurrying you, Brother Hen-
[ry? Y]ou been sinning against the Lord?

[HENRY]. No, praise God, but I got to hurry.
[(*Exits.*)

BESSIE (*calling after him*). I'm coming
down to your house for preaching and praying one of these days, Brother Henry.
(*There is no answer and she turns to* ADA.)
Now what do you suppose that Henry Peabody's been up to? I bet he's been a powerful wicked man here of late to hurry off
like that. Looks like the devil's got into
him sure.

ADA. Come inside, Bessie. I reckon Jeeter
will be right glad to see you.

BESSIE. I'll be right pleased to, Sister. I
reckon I walked near about three miles
getting here. (*Walks to the porch, stands for
a second.*)

ADA. Set down.

BESSIE. Has you got a chair, Sister? My poor
back's so weary it feels like it's mighty near
breaking in half.

ADA. H'mm. (*She exits into house.* BESSIE,
looking around and fanning herself, sees
ELLIE MAY. ELLIE MAY *giggles.*)

BESSIE. How is you, child? God be with
you. (*She goes onto the porch singing the
hymn "Shall We Gather at the River." Mid-
way in the song* ADA *returns from the house
dragging an old rocking chair which she
thumps down.* BESSIE *abruptly stops singing. To* ADA.) Bless you, Sister. (*She sits,
rocking back and forth, fanning herself.* ADA
*stands on the ground, leaning against the
porch upright, chewing on her snuff stick.*)
Where is Jeeter at this time of day, Sister
Ada? Has that man been up to something
sinful again?

ADA. He's out in the broom sedge, eating up
turnips he stole from Lov a while back.

BESSIE. Lord, O Lord, he's been stealing
again. Jeeter's a powerful sinful man. Ain't
no sin like stealing. . . . Was they good
eating winter turnips, Sister?

ADA. I reckon.

BESSIE. Lord forgive us our sins, and particularly forgive Jeeter. . . . Is he coming
back with any of them turnips, Ada?

ADA. I told Dude to fetch him before he
eats them all up. Maybe he will and maybe
he won't.

BESSIE. Dude will do right by the Lord. Dude's a mighty fine boy, Sister.

ADA. Humph.

BESSIE. We got to be careful against delivering him to the Hardshell Baptists, though. They're sinful people. They don't know the working of the Lord like I does.

ADA. What do you call your religion, Sister Bessie? You ain't never said what name you called it.

BESSIE. It ain't got a name. I generally just call it "Holy." It's just me and God. God talks to me in prayer and I answer Him back. I get most things done that way.

ADA. I want you to say a prayer for Pearl before you go away, Bessie. I reckon Lov's mad about Jeeter stealing his turnips and he might beat Pearl more than he ought to.

BESSIE. I'll be right happy to say a prayer for Pearl. But she ought to pray for herself, too. That sometimes helps a lot with the Lord.

ADA. Pearl don't talk to nobody except me— not even the Lord. I reckon what praying's done for her has got to be done by somebody else.

BESSIE. I'll mention that to the Lord and see if he'll let loose her tongue. There's sin someplace in her or she'd talk like everybody else. The Lord didn't intend for a woman not to talk.

ADA. Ellie May don't talk much, either. But that's because of her lip. It sounds funny when she talks.

BESSIE. There's been a powerful lot of sinning among you Lesters, or Ellie May wouldn't have that lip. One way or another I reckon you Lesters is about the most sinful people in the country. (*They are interrupted by the offstage sound of* JEETER *and* DUDE *quarreling.*)

DUDE (*offstage*). You ain't the only one that likes turnips. I ain't had no more to eat this week than you has.

JEETER (*offstage*). You had five already.
DUDE. Give me some more. Do you hear me?

JEETER. You don't need no more.

DUDE. I'll wham you. (*At this point J[*] comes running to the gate. He ha[*] pockets filled with turnips.* DUDE *is rig[*] his heels and catches him in the gate, th[*] one arm around him from behind and [*] him as he extracts turnips from his p[*] with his right hand.*)

JEETER (*trying to free himself*). Stop[*] Dude, you stop that!

DUDE (*laughing at him*). Ho! Ho! You[*] hurt nobody. You're as weak as an o[*] (*Pushes* JEETER, *who falls on the g[*] near the corner of the house.* DUDE *c[*] to right of gate eating a turnip.*)

JEETER (*lying on ground*). Now tha[*] you're going to git. (*Picks himself u[*]

BESSIE (*oracularly*). You been sinning [*] Jeeter Lester.

JEETER (*seeing* BESSIE *for the first [*] Sister Bessie! The good Lord be p[*] (*He rushes to the porch.*) I knowec[*] would send His angel to take away m[*] You come just at the right time.

BESSIE. The Lord always knows the [*] time. I was at home sweeping ou[*] kitchen when He come to me and [*] "Sister Bessie, Jeeter Lester is doing [*] thing evil. You go to his house anc[*] for him right now before it's too l[*] looked right back at the Lord and [*] "Lord, Jeeter Lester is a powerful [*] man, but I'll pray for him until the[*] goes clear back to hell." That's what [*] Him and here I is.

JEETER (*dancing ecstatically in front [*] SIE'S *chair on the porch*). I knowed th[*] Lord wouldn't let me slip and fall [*] devil's hands. I knowed it! I knowed[*]

BESSIE. Ain't you going to give me a [*] Jeeter? I ain't had much to eat lately. [*] is hard for the good and bad alike.

JEETER. Sure, Bessie. (JEETER *selects [*] of the largest, gives them to* BESSIE. [*] to ADA.) Here you is, Ada. (*Gives he[*] As others get theirs,* GRANDMA *enters,[*] to* JEETER, *and starts pulling at his c[*] BESSIE.) I wish I had something to g[*] to take home, Sister. When I had p[*]

:o give Brother Rice a whole armful of
:ns and potatoes at a time. Now I ain't
:thing but a handful of turnips, but I
ashamed of them. The Lord growed
and His doings is good enough for

(*with full mouth*). Praise be the

R *and* ADA. Amen, Sister! Amen.

(*finishing her turnip with a sigh*).
the call of the Lord. Let's have a little
. (BESSIE *gets up and crosses to the
of the yard,* JEETER *following, as does
d* GRANDMA LESTER, *who groans as she
.* ELLIE MAY *and* DUDE *sit on the porch,
the turnips and watching.*) Some
make an objection to kneeling down
aving prayer out of doors. They say,
Bessie, can't we go in the house and
ust as good?" And do you know what
I say, "Brothers and Sisters, I ain't
ed to pray out here in the open. I
folks passing along the road to know
'm on God's side. It's the old devil
always whispering about going in the
out of sight." That's what I tell them.
the way I stick up for the Lord.

. Praise the Lord.

Let's get ready to pray. (*They all
*) Sister Ada, is you still suffering from
y?

ll the time. (JEETER *and* ADA *bow
eads and close their eyes, but* GRAND-
STER *stares straight ahead, her eyes
her head raised a bit.* BESSIE *nods to
en prays.*)

Dear God, here I is again to offer a
rayer for sinful people. Jeeter Lester
s family want me to pray for them
The last time helped a whole lot, but
let the devil get hold of him today
: went and done a powerful sinful
He stole all of Lov's turnips. They're
out all et up now, so it's too late to
iem back. That's why we want to
r Jeeter. You ought to make him stop
; like he does. I never seen a more
; man in all my days. Jeeter wants to
ut it seems like the devil gets hold
as soon as we get through praying
i. You ain't going to let the old
devil tell You what to do, is You? The Lord
ought to tell the devil what he should do.
. . . And Sister Ada has got the pleurisy
again. You ought to do something for her
this time sure enough. The last time didn't
help none too much. If You'll make her
well of it she'll quit the devil for all time.
Won't you, Sister Ada?

ADA. Yes, Lord.

BESSIE. And old Mother Lester has got a
misery in her sides. She's in pain all the
time with it. She's kneeling down right
now, but she can't do it many more times.
. . . You ought to bless Ellie May, too.
Ellie May has got that slit in her lip that
makes her an awful sight to look at. (ELLIE
MAY *buries her face in her hands.* DUDE *looks
at her and grins.*)

JEETER. Don't forget to pray for Pearl, Sister
Bessie. Pearl needs praying for something
awful.

BESSIE. I was just going to do that. Sister
Ada told me to pray Lov wouldn't beat her
too hard because of them turnips you stole.

JEETER. It ain't that. It's what Pearl's done
herself.

BESSIE. What has Pearl done sinful, Brother
Jeeter?

JEETER. That was what Lov spoke to me
about today. He says Pearl won't talk to
him and she won't let him touch her. When
night comes she gets down and sleeps on
a durn pallet on the floor, and Lov has got
to sleep in the bed by himself. That's a
pretty bad thing for a wife to do, and God
ought to make her quit it.

BESSIE. Brother Jeeter, little girls like Pearl
don't know how to live married lives like
we grown-up women do. So maybe if I was
to talk to her myself instead of getting God
to do it, she would change her ways. I expect I know more about what to tell her
than He does, because I been a married woman up to the past summer when my former husband died. I expect I know all about
it. God wouldn't know what to tell her.

JEETER. Well, you can talk to her, but maybe if you asked God about it He might help
some, too. Maybe He's run across gals like
that before, though I don't believe there's

another durn gal in the whole country who's as contrary-minded about sleeping in the bed as Pearl is. (DUDE *stands up and takes his ball from his pocket.*)

BESSIE. Maybe it wouldn't hurt none if I was to mention it.

JEETER. That's right. You speak to the Lord about it, too. Both of you together ought to get something done. (DUDE *hurls the ball against the house and catches it.* JEETER *speaks angrily*). Quit chunking that there ball against that old house, Dude. Don't you see Sister Bessie's praying. I declare I wish you had more sense.

DUDE. Aw, go to hell.

BESSIE. Now, Dude. . . . (*Waits until he stops.*) Now, Lord, I've got something special to pray about. I don't ask favors unless they is things I want pretty bad, so this time I'm asking for a favor for Pearl. I want You to make her stop sleeping on a pallet on the floor while Brother Lov has to sleep by himself in the bed. I was a good wife to my former husband. I never slept on no pallet on the floor. Sister Ada here don't do nothing like that. And when I marry another man, I ain't going to do that neither. I'm going to get in bed just as big as my new husband does. So You tell Pearl to quit doing that.

JEETER. What was that you was saying, Sister Bessie? Didn't I hear you say you was going to marry yourself a new husband?

BESSIE. Well, I ain't made up my mind yet. I been looking around some, though.

JEETER. Now if it wasn't for Ada there . . .

BESSIE (*giggling*). You hush up, Brother Jeeter. How'd you know I'd take you anyway? You're pretty old, ain't you?

JEETER. Maybe I is and maybe I ain't, but if I is I ain't too old for that.

ADA (*stiffly*). I reckon you'd better finish up the prayer. You ain't done like I asked you about Pearl yet.

BESSIE. So I ain't. . . . Please, Lord, Sister Ada wants me to ask You not to let Lov beat up Pearl too much. And I guess that's

about all. . . . Save us from the devil a

JEETER. Hey, wait a minute. You clea got to say a little prayer for Dude. Yo Dude out all around.

DUDE. No, sir, not me, you don't. I want no praying. (BESSIE *jumps up and to* DUDE. *Clutching him by the arr starts dragging him back to the pr circle.*)

BESSIE. Come on, Dude. Come and with me.

DUDE (*angrily*). I don't want to do t don't want no praying for me. (BESSI one arm around his waist, holding him close, and with her free hand strok shoulder.)

BESSIE (*tenderly*). I got to pray for Dude. The Lord didn't leave you o more than He did Ellie May. (*She but keeps his legs encircled in her* Come on now. All of us has got to prayer some time or another. (DUDE the pressure of her arms on his legs stimulating and exciting, and he begin gling and squirming.)

JEETER. Quit that jumping up and Dude. What ails you? (DUDE *puts h around her neck and begins rubbin as she is rubbing him.*)

BESSIE. You kneel down beside me a me pray for you. You'll do that, won Dude?

DUDE (*snickering*). Hell, I don't damn if I do. (*He kneels, continu keep his arms about her, and she kee arms around him.*)

BESSIE. I knowed you would want pray for you, Dude. It will help y shed of your sins like Jeeter did. (*Clo eyes, lifts her head.*) Dear God, I'm You to save Brother Dude from th and make a place for him in heaven. all. Amen.

JEETER. Praise the Lord, but that durn short prayer for a sinner like (*He gets to his feet.* BESSIE *and* DU tinue to hold each other.)

BESSIE (*smiling fondly at* DUDE.) Dud need no more praying for. He's jus and he's not sinful like us grown-up

<table>
<tr><td>

ₐR. Well, maybe you're right. But I sort
·ollect the Bible says a son shouldn't
·his Ma and Pa like he does other
·e.

· (*stroking* DUDE's *hair*). Dude won't
·at again. He's a fine boy, Dude is.
·ould make a handsome preacher, too.
·mighty like my former husband in his
·er days. (*She and* DUDE *stop kneeling,*
·t *on the ground and continue to hold*
·other.*)

ₐR. Dude's about sixteen years old now.
·makes him two years younger than
·May. He'll be getting a wife pretty
·I reckon. All my other male children
·ed early in life, just like the gals done.
·wasn't for Ellie May's lip she'd been
·ed as quick as any. Men here around
·all want to marry gals about eleven
·elve years old, like Pearl was. Ada,
·was just turning twelve when I mar-
·er.

· The Lord intended all of us should
·ted. He made us that way. My former
·nd was just like the Lord in that
·t. They both believed in the same
·when it came to mating.

ₐ. I reckon the Lord did intend for us
·get mated, but He didn't take into
·t a woman with a slit in her mouth
·llie May's got.

· The Lord's ways is wise, Jeeter.

ₐ. Well, maybe, but I don't believe He
·he right thing by her when He opened
·· lip. That's the only contrary thing I
·aid about the Lord, but it's the truth.
·use is a slit like that for? You can't
·hrough it, and you can't whistle
·h it, now can you? It was just mean-
·· His part when He done that—just
·meanness.

· You shouldn't talk about the Lord
·at. He knows what He done it for.
·d the best reason in the world for
·it.

· What reason?

· Maybe I ought not to say it, Jeeter.

· You sure ought to tell me if you tell
·y. I'm her Pa.

</td><td>

BESSIE. He done that to save her pure body
from you, Brother Jeeter.

JEETER. From me?

BESSIE (*nodding*). He knowed she would
be safe in this house when He made her
like that. He knowed that you was once
a powerful sinner, and that you might be
again.

JEETER. That's the truth. I used to be a
powerful sinful man in my time. I reckon
at one time I was the most powerful sinful
man in the whole country. Now you take
them Peabody children over across the field.
I reckon near about all of them is half
mine, one way or another.

BESSIE. You wait till I finish accusing you,
Jeeter, before you start lying out of it.

JEETER. Praise God, I ain't lying out of it.
I just told you how powerful sinful I once
was.

BESSIE. Don't think the Lord didn't know
about it.

JEETER (*chuckles; crossing to well*). Henry
Peabody didn't know nothing about it,
though.

ADA. Humph.

JEETER (*turns Left; really noticing* BESSIE's
and DUDE's *goings on*). Say, Sister Bessie,
what in hell is you and Dude doing? You
and him has been squatting there, hugging
and rubbing of the other, for near about
half an hour. (BESSIE *manages as much of
a blush as she is capable of.*)

BESSIE (*removing* DUDE's *arm from around
her waist, trying to rise*). The Lord was
speaking to me. (DUDE *replaces his arm
about her waist.*) He was telling me I ought
to marry a new husband.

JEETER. He didn't tell you to marry Dude,
did he?

BESSIE. Dude would make a fine preacher.
He would be just about as good as my
former husband was, maybe better. He is
just suitable for preaching and living with
me. Ain't you, Dude?

DUDE (*quickly*). You want me to go home
with you now? (*Takes a step toward her.*)

</td></tr>
</table>

BESSIE. Not now, Dude. I'll have to ask the Lord if you'll do. (*Crosses Left of* DUDE.) He's sometimes particular about his male preachers, especially if they is going to marry women preachers. I got to pray over it first—(*with a knowing glance at* DUDE) and Dude, you pray over it, too.

DUDE (*giggles in embarrassment*). Aw, like hell I will. (*Crosses to Left of gate.*)

JEETER (*crossing to* DUDE). What's the matter with you, Dude? Didn't you hear Sister Bessie tell you to pray over that? You is the luckiest man alive. What's the matter with you, anyway? Great day in the morning, if you ain't the goddamdest boy I ever heard tell of. (JEETER *starts down Left;* DUDE *crosses to Right of gate. Enter* HENRY PEABODY. *He comes running to the gate.*)

PEABODY (*coming to gate*). Hey, you, Jeeter —Jeeter.

JEETER (*crosses to* PEABODY). What's the matter, Henry?

PEABODY. Didn't Ada tell you nothing?

JEETER. She didn't tell me nothing.

PEABODY. Didn't she tell you I was here before?

JEETER (*impatiently*). No. What is it you've got to say?

PEABODY. It's big news, Jeeter.

JEETER. Well, start telling it. It ain't going to do me no good keeping it to yourself.

PEABODY (*impressively*). Captain John's coming back.

JEETER (*shocked*). Captain John! Captain John's dead.

PEABODY. Well, not Captain John, but his boy is.

JEETER. He is! (*Turning on* ADA.) Do you heart that, Ada? Captain John's coming back!

ADA. He didn't say Captain John. H[e] Captain John's boy.

JEETER. That don't make no difference tain Tim is Captain John's boy, ain (*To* PEABODY.) He figures on giving to the farmers again, don't he?

PEABODY. I reckon so. That's what ever thinks. He's down in Fuller now, bu be around about here tomorrow.

JEETER. God be praised. I knowed the was aiming to provide (*To* ADA.) what has you got to say now, w Didn't I tell you I was going to plan crop this year? (*To* DUDE, *as* ADA *shru doesn't answer.*) Hey, you, Dude. G in the fields and start burning off that sedge. You go to the far side and I'll the near. We're going to burn off fields this year. We're going to grow biggest crop you ever seen.

PEABODY. Well, I got to be going, J reckon I'll burn off my own fields no self. (JEETER *nods and he exits.*)

JEETER. Good-by, Henry. . . . Now in that house, Ada, and fix us someth eat. We're going to be hungry wh come back.

ADA. There ain't nothing to fix.

JEETER. You're the contrariest womar seen. By God and by Jesus, if you ain do like I tell you and quit saying al damn fool things. . . . Come on, Dud tain John's boy has got to see we is a when he comes around tomorrow. H now . . . come on. (JEETER *climbs ove Left, in his hurry, exiting down the T Road.* DUDE *gives a hungry glance at then hurries to the gate and exits.* BESS *to fence and calls after* DUDE.)

BESSIE. Hey, you, Dude. Don't you You pray like I told you and I'll here in the morning and let you (*Turns to* ADA *with a benevolent Something tells me the Lord is going Dude a whole lot.

CURTAIN

ACT TWO

NE: *Same as Act One.*

E: *The following day.*

RISE: *It is still early morning and the amber glow of dawning day haunts the scene.*
, as time passes, the light comes on fuller and brighter until full day has arrived.
e curtain rises, no one is seen, the rotting house enjoying the dawn in solitude.
moment, however, BESSIE *enters swiftly through the gate, crosses to the porch, and*
ers loudly on the door with her fists.

, Dude. . . . Hey, you, Dude. . . .
(She waits impatiently a few seconds,
ng first to the upstage corner of the
then to the window downstage of the
Then she flings open the door and
nside.) Where is you, Dude? (JEETER,
ng and scratching, sticks his head out
window and rubs his mouth with the
f his hand before speaking. He is still
but is wearing, already, his tattered
lthough the rest of his body is, ap-
ly, as naked as a blue jay.)

. What you want with Dude this time
, Bessie?

, Never you mind. I want Dude. . . .
you, Dude. *(She exits through the*
calling.) Dude. . . . You, Dude.
R draws back from the window, look-
side, as BESSIE'S *voice continues, off.)*
is you, Dude? . . . (For an instant
ge is empty. Then DUDE *enters Left*
Tobacco Road and crosses yard to the
here he draws up water and drinks.
ys no attention to BESSIE'S *occasionally*
d cry for him. Enter JEETER *through*
use door. He is getting into his over-
nd is carrying his shirt, also socks and
in his hands. He sees DUDE.)

. Hey, you, Dude, where you been?
's been looking all over for you. (DUDE
t answer, continuing to drink water.
drops shoes and socks and slips into
s.) She just about tore up every bed in
use. Why don't you tell her where
?

Aw, to hell with her. *(Drinks.)*

. *(dressing).* By God and by Jesus,
seen a woman so anxious to see any-
I reckon she wants to get married to
ter all. *(Glances up as* DUDE *doesn't*
.) Is you thinking about getting your-
rried to her if that's what she wants?

DUDE. Aw, what do I want to do that for?

JEETER. You sure looked like you was set
on doing that yesterday—all that hugging
and rubbing of the other. What do you
think about that now, Dude?

DUDE. Aw, hell, it don't always look the
same to a man in the morning.

BESSIE *(off).* Dude! . . . Hey, you, Dude.

JEETER. Listen to her yelling. She must of
gone clear through to the backyard by this
time. Why don't you answer her, Dude?
Where was you when she went looking in
the bed for you? Where was you anyway?

DUDE. Out in the fields.

JEETER *(excitedly).* What about them fields?
Is they finished burning?

DUDE *(nodding).* Most. Them to the north is
still burning some.

JEETER. I is sure glad to hear that. We want
to be ready to start the plowing and planting when Captain John's boy comes around
today.

BESSIE *(off).* Dude. . . . Where is you, Dude?
(BESSIE *enters around upstage corner of*
house, sees DUDE.) There you is! *(Crosses*
swiftly to him. He glances at her, but keeps
his back to her as she comes up.) Didn't you
hear me call you? *(Affectionately—putting*
her arms around his waist from the rear.)
Don't you know I been looking for you,
Dude boy? *(Her arms tighten in a sudden*
and sharp squeeze that causes the water to
slosh from the bucket he is holding.)

DUDE. Hey, now look what you made me go
and do.

BESSIE. Now that ain't nothing, Dude. Ain't
you glad to see me? *(She presses him*
closer.) Don't that make you feel good?

DUDE (*grinning*). H'mm. (*He puts down the bucket, turns and embraces her. Their posture is awkward and amusing. On the steps, JEETER continues to pick his feet and slowly put on shoes and socks, the while he watches the amorous couple.*)

JEETER. You must be figuring on getting married after all, Bessie. (BESSIE *starts to smooth down* DUDE'S *wet hair.* ADA *appears in doorway,* ELLIE MAY *at window.*)

BESSIE (*confidentially—nodding affirmatively*). The Lord told me to do it. I asked Him about it last night and He said, "Sister Bessie, Dude Lester is the man I want you to wed. Get up early in the morning and go to the Lester place and marry Dude the first thing." That's what He said, so I got out of bed and ran up here as fast as I could, because the Lord don't like to be kept waiting. (BESSIE *affectionately regards* DUDE *who grins self-consciously.*)

JEETER. You hear what the Lord told Sister Bessie. What do you think of doing now, Dude?

DUDE. Shucks! I don't know.

JEETER. What's ailing you? Ain't you man enough?

DUDE. Maybe I is, and maybe I ain't.

BESSIE. There ain't nothing to be scared of, Dude. You'll like being married to me because I know how to treat men fine. (DUDE *hesitates.* ADA *moves forward from doorway and rests against the porch upright.* GRANDMA LESTER *appears around the upstage corner of the house but keeps crouched and hidden so as not to attract attention.*)

JEETER. Well, is you going to do it, Dude?

DUDE (*self-consciously*). Aw, hell, what do I want to go marry her for? (DUDE *pulls ball out of his pocket and throws it against house.* BESSIE *glances swiftly at* DUDE'S *averted face, then plays her trump card. She turns to* JEETER.)

BESSIE (*wisely to* JEETER). Do you know what I is going to do, Jeeter?

JEETER. What?

BESSIE. I is going to buy me a new automobile. (*The effect of this on all of them is electric.* JEETER *comes quickly to his feet,* and DUDE *stops throwing ball with s[ ] awed interest.*)

JEETER. A new automobile? A sure e[ ] brand-new automobile?

BESSIE (*nodding*). A brand-new one. ([ ] *shakes her head emphatically.* DUDE [ ] *at her wide-eyed and unbelieving.*)

JEETER. Is you got money?

BESSIE (*proudly*). Eight hundred dolla[ ]

JEETER. Eight hundred dollars! Wher[ ] you get all that money, Bessie?

BESSIE (*nodding*). My former husban[ ] that in insurance and when he died I [ ] and put it in the bank.

JEETER. That sure is a heap of mon[ ] didn't think there was that much real n[ ] in the whole country.

ADA. You ain't going to spend all that [ ] new automobile, is you?

BESSIE (*nodding*). Dude and me wan[ ] best there is. Don't we, Dude? (DUD[ ] *only look at her wide-eyed.*)

ADA. It don't seem right to me. It see[ ] me like if you wanted to do right you'[ ] some of that money to Dude's old M[ ] Pa. We could sure use it for snuff and [ ]

BESSIE. No, Sister Ada, the Lord [ ] intend for it to be used like that. [ ] tended I should use it to carry on the p[ ] ing and the praying. That's what I'm [ ] ing the new automobile for, so Dud[ ] me can drive around when we take a [ ] to go somewheres in the Lord's wor[ ]

JEETER. Sister Bessie's right, Ada. [ ] ain't nothing like working for the L[ ] don't make no difference to us abou[ ] money noway. Captain John's boy, C[ ] Tim, is back now and I'll get all the [ ] I need.

ADA. Humph. You is sure mighty [ ] handed with something you ain't g[ ]

JEETER. Never you mind about her, I [ ] When you going to buy that new [ ] mobile?

BESSIE. I'm going over to Fuller and [ ] right now. (*Glances at* DUDE *eagerly.*) is, if Dude and me gets married.

ER. What do you say to that now,
? Will you be wanting to marry Sister
e and ride around the country preach-
nd praying in a new automobile?

Will it have a horn on it?

. I reckon it will. Don't all new auto-
es have horns?

Can I drive it?

. That's what I'm buying it for.

Can I drive it all the time?

. Sure, Dude. I don't know how to
an automobile.

Then why the hell not?

(*joyfully hugging him and trying to
him*). Oh, Dude! (DUDE *escapes from
mbrace and begins to put on his shoes.*)

When is you and Dude going to do all
iding around and preaching and pray-
Is you going to get married before or

. Before. We'll walk over to Fuller
now and buy the new automobile and
get married.

ER. Is you going to get leave of the
ty, or is you just going to live along
ut it?

E. I'm going to get the license for mar-
.

ER. That costs about two dollars. Is you
wo dollars? Dude ain't—Dude ain't got
ng.

E. I ain't asking Dude for one penny
oney. I'll attend to that part myself. I've
ight hundred dollars in the bank and
v more besides. Dude and me won't
nothing to worry about. Will we,
?

(*impatiently*). Naw. Come on. We
got no time to lose. (DUDE *starts to walk
, while* BESSIE *is delayed arranging her
walking more slowly to the gate.*)

You'll have to make Dude wash his
very once in a while, Bessie, because if
don't he'll dirty up the quilts. Some-
he don't wash himself all winter long,
he quilts get that dirty you don't know
to go about the cleaning of them.

BESSIE (*pleasantly to* DUDE, *who is waiting
at the gate*). Is you like that, Dude?

DUDE (*impatiently*). If we is going to buy
that new automobile, let's buy it.

ADA. Dude is just careless like Pa. I had the
hardest time learning him to wear his socks
in the bed, because it was the only way I
could keep the quilts clean. Dude is just
going on the way his Pa done, so maybe
you'd better make him wear his socks, too.

BESSIE. That's all right. Me and Dude'll
know how to get along fine. (*Exit* DUDE.
Exit BESSIE.)

ADA (*calling after* BESSIE *and* DUDE). If you
get down around where Pearl lives, I wish
you'd tell her that her Ma sure would like
to see her again. (JEETER, ADA, *and* ELLIE
MAY *move to fence to look after* DUDE *and*
BESSIE. *Even* GRANDMA LESTER *looks from
behind the trunk of the chinaberry tree.*)

JEETER (*shakes his head emphatically*). That
Dude is the luckiest man alive. (*Directly to
others*). Now, ain't he? . . . He's going to
get a brand-new car to ride around in and
he's going to get married all at the same
time. There's not many men get all that in
the same day, I tell you. There ain't nobody
else that I know of between here and the
river who has got a brand-new automobile.
And there ain't many men who has a wife
as fine-looking as Sister Bessie is, neither.
Bessie makes a fine woman for a man—
any man, I don't care where you find him.
She might be just a little bit more than
Dude can take care of, though. Now if it
was me, there wouldn't be no question of it.
I'd please Sister Bessie coming and going
right from the start, and keep it up clear
to the end.

ADA (*in disgust*). Huh!

JEETER (*speaks now to* ELLIE MAY). Now
you, Ellie May, it's time you was finding
yourself a man. All my other children has
got married. It's your time next. It was your
time a long while ago, but I make allow-
ances for you on account of your face. I
know it's harder for you to mate up than it
is for anybody else, but you ought to get
out and find yourself a man to marry right
away. It ain't going to get you nowhere
fooling around with Lov like you was
doing, because he's married already. He
might have married you if it wasn't for the

way you looked, but don't show your face too much and it won't stop the boys from getting after you. (*He pauses, and to his amazement* ELLIE MAY *bursts into heart-broken sobs, hiding her face in her hands.*) What's the matter? What's the matter with you, Ellie May? (*Still sobbing,* ELLIE MAY *runs to the gate and exits down the road.* JEETER *turns helplessly to* ADA.) Now I never seen the likes of that before. I wonder what I said to make her carry on like that? (JEETER *sits on porch.*) I declare to goodness I don't know what gets into women folks sometimes. There ain't never no way to figure them out. (*Starts to lie down, but* ADA *is in the way.*) By God and by Jesus, woman, can't you move over when a man wants to lay down?

ADA. Ain't you going to take no wood to Augusta today?

JEETER. Are you going to start that talk again? Ain't I told you Captain Tim is coming and I'm going to plant me a crop? I've got to save my strength for that.

ADA. Humph! There ain't a bite in the house, and nobody never saved their strength by not eating.

JEETER. Never mind that now. Captain Tim will fix that. Anyhow, I couldn't make that old automobile go even if I wanted to.

ADA. Do you reckon Dude and Bessie will let you take a load in their new car?

JEETER. I ain't aiming to carry no more wood to Augusta. But I sure is going to take a ride in that new car. I reckon I'll be riding clear over into Burke County one of these days to see Tom.

ADA. If you see him you might mention that his old Ma sure would like a stylish dress to die in. I know he won't stand back with his money for a little thing like that.

JEETER. I'll mention it, but I don't know how he'll take it. I expect he's got a raft of children to provide for.

ADA. Reckon he has got some children?

JEETER. Maybe some.

ADA. I sure would like to see them. I know I must have a whole heap of grandchildren somewhere. I'm bound to have, with all them boys and girls off from home.

JEETER. Clara has got a raft of childre bet. She was always talking about ha them. And they say over in Fuller Lizzie Belle has got a lot of them, to don't know how other folks know n about such things than I do. Looks li ought to be the one who knows most a my own children. (*Enter* LOV, *who st just inside gate, panting heavily and l ing at* ADA *and* JEETER. JEETER *glances and sees* LOV, *whose heaving chest haunted eyes make him believe* LOV *come for revenge for stealing the turni* Lov, *by God!* (*He springs to his feet darts for the downstage corner of the u*

LOV (*through quick breathing*). Never n running, Jeeter. I ain't going to hurt

JEETER (*at corner of house, still read run*). Ain't you peeved about me stea them turnips yesterday?

LOV (*wearily*). I don't care about tha more.

JEETER. What's the matter with you, I You look like you run all the way I What's wrong with you, anyway? *doesn't answer and sits.*) Is you sick? *nods negatively.*)

ADA (*higher note—stepping forward*). Pearl! That's what it is—it's Pearl! *looks at her and nods. She comes for hysterically.*)

JEETER. What's the matter with her, I

LOV. She run off.

ADA. No! She didn't! She wouldn't done that without seeing her Ma first.

LOV (*coming forward—shaking head*). just run off.

JEETER. How do you know, Lov? M she's just hiding in the woods some

LOV (*shakes his head*). Jones Peabody her walking along the road to Augusta morning.

ADA. Augusta!

LOV. He said he stopped and asked where she was going, but she wouldn't to him. She just kept on going.

ADA (*fiercely to* LOV). You done somet to her. Don't tell me you didn't.

No, I didn't, Ada. I woke up early this
ing and looked at her down on that
on the floor and I just couldn't stand
longer. I got down and hugged her
y arms. I wasn't going to hurt her. I
wanted to hold her for a minute. But
ot loose from me and I ain't seen her
. (ADA *rocks, heartbroken, on the*
.)

ER. Well, I figured that she was going
n off to Augusta one of these days, only
was always afraid before.

Jones Peabody said she acted like she
about scared to death this morning.
perately.) I got to get her back, Jeeter.
t got to get her back.

ER. Ain't much use you figuring on
All them girls went off all of a sudden.
ie Belle up and went to Augusta just
that. (*He snaps his fingers.*)

Ain't there something I can do, Jeeter?

ER. About the best thing you can do,
is let her be.

If I was to go up to Augusta and find
do you reckon she'd let me bring her
home to stay? . . . Reckon she would,
r?

ER. I wouldn't recommend that. You'll
your time down there at the chute while
was looking for her, and if you was
ing her back she'd run off again twice
ick.

She might get hurt up there.

ER. Lizzie Belle and Clara took care of
selves all right, didn't they?

Pearl ain't like them.

ER. In many ways she ain't, but in many
s, too. She wasn't never satified living
n here on the Tobacco Road. She's just
Lizzie Belle and Clara and the other
in that respect. I can't call all their
es right now, but it was every durn one
em, anyhow. They all wanted stylish
es.

Pearl never said nothing to me about
ting stylish clothes. She never said any-
g to me at all.

ER. It's just like I said. They're like
Ma. Ada there ain't satisfied neither,

but she can't do nothing about it. I broke her
of wanting to run off, but them gals was
more than I could take care of. There was
too durn many of them for one man to
break. They just up and went.

LOV (*thinking aloud*). I sort of hate to lose
her, for some reason or another. All them
long yellow curls hanging down her back
always made me hate the time when she
would grow up and be old.

JEETER. That sure ain't no lie. Pearl had the
prettiest yellow hair of any gal I ever saw.
I wish Ada had been that pretty. Even when
Ada was a young gal she was that durn
ugly it was a sin. I reckon I ain't never seen
an uglier woman in the whole country.

LOV. I been the lonesomest man in the whole
country for the longest time, Jeeter. Ain't
there something you can do to get her back
again?

JEETER. I might try something, but it
wouldn't do no good. One way or another
I've said about everything I can to that girl,
but she won't even answer me. She won't
talk to nobody but her Ma. It wouldn't do
no good for me to do anything, even if you
could find her.

LOV. Ada, will you? . . . (*Sees hopelessness
of help from* ADA. *Abjectly*). Well, I've got
to get back to the chute. That morning
freight will be coming along pretty soon
now and it always empties all the scoops.
They raise hell if they ain't filled up again.
(*Turns; crosses to gate; leans against post.*)

JEETER. I sure am glad you wasn't riled
about the turnips, Lov. I meant to go down
first thing this morning and talk to you
about that, but Dude and Bessie went off
to get married and I forgot all about it.
Did you hear about that, Lov? Dude and
Bessie went off to Fuller to get married and
buy them a new automobile all at the same
time. Now ain't that something! (LOV *nods.*)

LOV. If you happen to see or hear anything
about Pearl, you let me know. (LOV *exits
down road Left.*)

JEETER (*turning back to* ADA, *who still sits
on the porch, staring blankly into space*).
Lov sure is a funny one. He just can't think
about anything but Pearl. It looks to me
like he wouldn't want a gal that won't stay
in the bed with him. I don't understand

him at all. I don't understand Pearl, for that matter, neither. I'd of bet almost anything she would have come up here and told us good-by before running off. But it's like I always said. Coming or going, you can't never tell about women. (*Looks at* ADA, *hoping she'll talk to him. Crosses closer to her, but her eyes stare straight ahead. Finally he hits her gently with the back of his hand.*) That's all right, Ada. (*He crosses to fence, Left, climbs it, glances back at her.*) If Captain John's boy comes along, you tell him I'll be back soon. I'm going to look at them fields. (JEETER *exits.* ADA *sits staring ahead, her eyes holding a depth of suffering. Suddenly there is an offstage cry from* JEETER *and she turns to look toward the gate.*)

JEETER (*off—calling*). Ada—Ada! (*Lower, but still off.*) Come on, child—come on. (*He appears at the edge of the gate, pulling someone after him.* ADA, *eyes wide with wonder, stands up.*) Come on—there ain't nothing to be afraid of. Your old Pa ain't going to hurt you. (*He pulls* PEARL *through the gate.*) Look, Ada—look what I found hiding in the broom sedge.

ADA (*lifts her hands, palms turned up, toward her daughter*). Pearl!

PEARL. Ma!! (*Pulling away from* JEETER, PEARL *rushes across stage and flings herself, sobbing, into her mother's arms.* JEETER, *eager and alive with excitement and admiration, comes up to the two women.* PEARL *is a beautiful child. She looks at least sixteen, in spite of the fact that she is much less than that, and is almost as tall as* ADA. *She is barefoot, and wears only a shabby, dark gray calico dress. Her hair hangs down over her shoulders like a cloud of spun gold.* ADA *soothes her.*)

ADA. There, now—there, now, don't cry. You got your old Ma again.

JEETER (*prancing around* PEARL). Now ain't that somethin'! I was just turning to go across the fields when I saw that yellow head of hers moving in the broom sedge and there she was. If she hadn't stumbled I never would of caught her. Ain't she pretty! She's about the prettiest piece in the whole country. . . .

ADA. Go away, Jeeter.

JEETER (*who hasn't the slightest inte*[*] *of going away*). Ain't she growed son[] the past year, though? She's most a g[] woman by now. (*Moves* PEARL's *dres*[] *better to see her figure.*) By God an[] Jesus if she ain't.

ADA (*sharply—slapping* JEETER's []— *away*). Stop that, Jeeter.

JEETER. What for? She is, ain't she? []— how white and gold she looks with [] yellow hair hanging down her back. [] What are you standing there crying [] Pearl? Why didn't you go on to Aug[] like you started to anyway? Was [] scared? Was that it, Pearl?

ADA. She wanted to see her old Ma first. [] PEARL.) That was it, wasn't it, child? ([] *nods, her head still on her mother's shou*[] *and* ADA *speaks to* JEETER.) There, yo[] that, Jeeter. Now you go on away like [] you. She ain't going to talk none [] you're here.

JEETER. I got to speak to her about [] first. Now that she ain't run away [] have to begin treating him right.

ADA. Hush up, Jeeter. Maybe she ain't [] to go back and live with Lov at all. [] because she didn't go all the way to Aug[] don't mean she's going to stay with [] again.

JEETER. What's that? Now you w[] minute. That ain't right. When a g[] mated up with a man she's got to live [] him.

ADA. Mind your own business, Jeeter.[]

JEETER. I is minding my own business[] minding my business and Lov's bus[] too. A gal's got no right to act like P[] been acting. No, sir. I say Pearl has g[] go back and live in the house with Lo[] let him have his rights with her.

ADA (*angrily*). Now you listen to me, [] Lester. You keep out of this. If I sa[] Pearl can do just like she wants. You [] got the right to tell her what she's got []

JEETER. What! Who you talking to, [] way? I'm her Pa, ain't I?

ADA. No, you ain't.

JEETER. What?

That's what.

ER. By God and by Jesus! Do you know you're saying, woman?

I sure do. You ain't her Pa. You never and never will be.

ER (*lightly amazed*). Well, by damn— what do you think of that?

Whatever made you think you was, vay? Do you think a lazy old fool like could be the Daddy of a gal like Pearl?

ER (*without rancor*). Well, I thought that now and then. She didn't look to ike none of the Lesters I ever heard of.

There ain't no Lester in her. Her real vouldn't have no truck with any of

ER. It wasn't that Henry Peabody down oad, was it?

(*with disgust*). No.

ER. I didn't think it was. He couldn't a pretty piece like Pearl for a child more than I could. Who was it, Ada?

Nobody you ever knew. He came from n Carolina and was on his way to s.

ER. H'mm. I don't remember nobody that. I must of been in Fuller, or even ve in Augusta at the time.

You was down seeing Captain John a mule to plow with.

ER. By God and by Jesus, I remember I remember that old mule just like I mber that old cow I used to have. Re- ber that old mule, Ada?

I reckon.

ER. It was the last one I ever got off ain John. Pretty soon after that he d up to Augusta and I ain't heard a from him since, until now when his s coming back. (*To* PEARL.) Did you about that, Pearl? Captain John's boy ning back this morning and I'm going ant me a crop this year sure.

Pearl ain't interested in that now.

R (*indignantly*). Well, she ought to verybody ought to be when they's been and raised on the land like I was. Cap-

tain John was and Captain John's boy that comes after him is interested just as much, you'll find out. You can't keep nobody like Captain John or me away from the land forever.

ADA. Shut up, Jeeter. Can't you see Pearl is all wore out? If Jones Peabody saw her on the road to Augusta she must of walked about ten miles this morning to get here. (*To* PEARL.) Is you hungry, Pearl? (PEARL *shakes her head affirmatively.*)

JEETER (*watching the girl with disapproval*). Now what's the sense to all that shaking of your head? (*Mimics her.*) What's the meaning of all that? It's plain to see you ain't no child of mine all right. Coming and going us Lesters has always talked about as much as anybody in the whole country. Can't you speak up?

ADA. Quit your nagging, Jeeter. You know what she means all right. She's hungry. You get busy and find her something to eat.

JEETER. Ain't you got no sense at all, Ada? How can I get her something to eat when there ain't even nothing for myself.

ADA. You got something yesterday from Lov when *you* was hungry.

JEETER. Is you aiming to make me steal again, woman? (ADA *shrugs.*) Well, if you is I ain't. The Lord's a wise old somebody. He's watching around the corner every minute for just such as that. You can't fool Him about stealing. . . . Besides there ain't nothing between here and Fuller to steal noway.

ADA. I heard tell Morgan Prior bought hisself a sack of corn meal down to McCoy the other day.

JEETER. Corn meal! I ain't et corn meal since—(*Checks himself.*) No, sir! Maybe he did and maybe he didn't, but I ain't going near Morgan Prior's house no matter what the circumstance. I promised the Lord—

ADA (*shrewdly*). They say he's got some bacon and fat back, too.

JEETER. Woman, you is a sinner in the eyes of God! . . . (*Whistles.*) Morgan Prior must be a powerful rich man to have all that to eat. Maybe if I went down there and asked him he might let me borrow some for a little while.

ADA. Humph! I don't build no hopes on that. Morgan Prior ain't going to let you borrow nothing.

JEETER. I don't see why he oughtn't. The Lord says the rich should share their bounty with the poor. You come along with me, Ada, and we'll see if Morgan Prior is ready to do like the Lord says.

ADA. Me? What do you want me for?

JEETER. Don't you know nothing, woman? If I want to borrow me something from Morgan Prior somebody's got to talk to him at the front door, while I go around to the back, don't they? (*A full, belligerent pause.*) Now hurry up. Morgan Prior might be out early plowing the fields and it would be an almighty temptation and a sin if we borrowed something when he wasn't at home.

ADA. You go get my old hairbrush first. Pearl ain't brushed her hair this morning.

JEETER (*eagerly*). Is she going to do that?

ADA (*with an abrupt nod*). While I'm gone off. (JEETER *exits quickly into house.*)

PEARL (*gripping* ADA). Oh, Ma, don't go off from me.

ADA (*comforting her*). There now. You don't need to worry no more. Your old Ma's looking out for you from now on. You don't have to go back and live with Lov no matter what Jeeter says.

PEARL. I don't never want to go back!

ADA. You don't have to. But one of these days you got to go down to Augusta to live. I've made up my mind to that.

PEARL. I'm scared, Ma. (JEETER *enters with hairbrush.*)

JEETER (*eagerly*). Here you is, Ada. Great day, we ought to see something now! Lov says there ain't a prettier piece in the whole country than Pearl when she's brushing her hair and I'm inclined to agree with him.

ADA (*snatching brush*). Go along, Jeeter. Don't think you're going to stay around here all day watching Pearl.

JEETER. Lord, Ada, don't get so peeved. I ain't doing nothing.

ADA. No, and you never would if I di make you. Hurry up now. You go al I'll catch up with you down the road.

JEETER. Well—(*Reluctantly crossing gate.*) Pearl, if Captain John's boy co here, you tell him I won't be gone long. tell him I got a little business down the and to wait right here for me. (*Exits.*)

ADA. Now you listen to me, honey. T ain't no sense you being scared about g off to Augusta. All my other gals went t or someplace else to live and they don' gret it.

PEARL (*fervently*). I want to stay here you.

ADA. Never you mind that. I ain't goin be here long. One of these days I'm g to die.

PEARL. No—no, you ain't!

ADA. That's all right, honey. It don't m —only sometimes I do wish I had r stylish dress to be buried in.

PEARL. I'll get you a stylish dress, Ma. H I will.

ADA. Don't you care about me. You g look out for yourself. You got to have : to put on and shoes and dresses to wear the gals in Augusta.

PEARL. I don't want none.

ADA. Sure you do. You don't want to here like your old Ma, raising a ra children and no snuff to calm you v there ain't nothing to eat. None of my children was as pretty as you, or as si neither, when you want to talk, and if can do it you can do it. (JEETER *appear Tobacco Road.*)

JEETER. Hey, you, Ada. Is you comin ain't you?

ADA. I heard you, I'm coming. (*Gets Speaks to* PEARL.) Now, honey, you think about that while I'm gone. And fret none. I won't be off long. (*Enter GR MA LESTER from around house, as* ADA *cr to gate.*) Hey, you, old woman. You g in the broom sedge and pick up some s for the fire. We might be wanting to around here pretty soon now. (*To* PE/ Fix up your hair now, honey. (ADA *exits GRANDMA LESTER hurries to the porch*

; her old croker sack *from beneath it.*
L watches her. Straightening up, the old
·an looks long at PEARL. *Hobbling for-*
d she tries to touch the girl's hair, but
L backs away from her. GRANDMA LESTER
;, her eyes reflecting her deep hurt and
·ppointment. For a moment more she
·s at the girl, then turns and shuffles off.
L stands looking after her, and when
OLD WOMAN *has quite gone, she goes to*
well and dips her brush in the bucket.
has taken a stroke or two with the brush
·n she suddenly stops and listens. The
·ence hears nothing, but she does. Mov-
·quickly in back of the well, she drops to
knees, listening and waiting. Presently
RY PEABODY *enters down the road, run-*
·. He glances inside the yard, sees noth-
·and then comes through the gate to the
·h. Pushing open the door he calls in-
·)

·ODY. Jeeter—hey, you, Jeeter—Ada. . . .
to hell with them. (*No answer and he*
·es down from the porch and goes to up-
·e corner of the house; he glances around.
·ng nothing, then, he moves quickly to
·gate and exits. Slowly and cautiously
·L now comes around from behind the
·, runs to the road to see if PEABODY *has*
·, then comes back to the porch and sits,
·back to the gate, brushing her hair. She
·preoccupied she does not hear LOV *enter*
·tly on the Tobacco Road. He sees her.
·pauses. He moves silently through the
·across the yard on the balls of his feet
·stands in back of her, watching. Sud-
·y he reaches down and takes her hand
·ly as it makes a stroke with the brush.
·leaps to her feet, panic-stricken, to run
·but his hold is too strong and he pulls
·back.)

(*pleading*). Don't run off, Pearl. I ain't
g to hurt you. (*She won't answer or*
·at him.) If you only wouldn't run
·y, I'd leave hold of you now and just
·h you brush your hair again. I'd rather
you do that than anything I can think
There ain't nobody got pretty hair like
I used to sit on the porch and watch
·ugh the window when you was comb-
·and brushing it and I just couldn't keep
·eyes off it. Will you promise you won't
·off again if I leave you go? (*Pause as*
·aits for her to answer.) Won't you talk
·e? Won't you say nothing to me at all?
·don't know how I been missing you

since you run off. I didn't mean nothing by
what I done this morning. It's just that you
won't stay in the bed with me or talk to me.
Sometimes I just shake all over, for wanting
to squeeze you so hard. I keep on thinking
how pretty your eyes is early in the morning. They's pretty any time of the day, but
early in the morning they's the prettiest
things a man could ever want to look at.
Won't you come back again sometime? You
won't even have to stay in the bed with
me. Will you come back if I do that, Pearl?
(*He waits, but still there is no answer.*)
Remember that last pretty I got for you?
I can remember like it was yesterday. They
was green beads on a long string and when
'you put them around your neck I swear to
God if it didn't make you about the prettiest girl I ever heard tell about. (*Pitiful
enthusiasm.*) I tell you what . . . one of these
days we'll ride up to Augusta and buy you
a hat—and a stylish dress, too. Would you
like to do that? Maybe Dude and Bessie
will take us in the new automobile they're
buying today. Did you know about that,
Pearl? Dude and Bessie is getting married
and is buying a new automobile. (*Not a
flicker of interest shows in* PEARL'S *impressive expression.* LOV *has a dream.*) A
new automobile! That's what we'll get one
of these days, and we'll ride all over the
whole country faster than that old No. 7
passenger ever thought of going—(*In the
excitement stimulated by imagination,* LOV
has released his hold on PEARL'S *wrist and
she has sprung clear of him. His pleading,
broken cry falls on unhearing ears. Swiftly—
much more swiftly than his clumsiness will
permit him to follow—she steps away from
the porch, whirls, and dashes to the gate.*)
Pearl! (*Just as* PEARL *reaches the gate,* ADA
*appears and the girl throws herself into her
mother's arms.*)

PEARL. Ma! Ma! (ADA *says nothing, but over*
PEARL'S *shoulder her eyes fasten malevolently
on the innocent* LOV. *Appearances are against
him, he knows it, and he is so emotionally
upset his sense of guilt gains upper hand.
For a full pause they regard each other.*)

LOV (*pitifully apologetic*). I didn't do nothing, Ada. We was just talking. I didn't hurt
her none. (ADA *pushes* PEARL *behind her,
picks up stick, and advances grimly and
silently on him. He takes an involuntary
step back.*) I just wanted her to come back
and live in the house with me. (ADA *comes*

up to him, her fury blazing in her eyes. The stick falls across LOV's *hunched shoulders. He stands his ground, but lowers his head and raises his arms to protect himself.* PEARL *is thrilled.*) Don't do that, Ada—don't do that. (*Her answer is to strike him again. Enter* JEETER, *carrying a couple of small packages. His eyes light up as he sees the action.*)

JEETER. Great day in the morning, will you look at that! What you beating Lov for, Ada? What's he done to make you beat him like that?

LOV. I ain't done nothing, Jeeter—(*He is stopped by a whack.*)

JEETER. By God and by Jesus, maybe you ain't, but you sure is getting a beating for it just the same. I don't remember when I ever seen such a good, round beating as you is getting right this minute. (LOV *gives ground slowly, so that* ADA *misses now and again.*)

LOV. I tell you I ain't done nothing!

JEETER. That don't stand to reason to me. In my experience I found that people usually get what's coming to them in this world or the next and it looks to me like right now you is getting yours in this.

LOV. I swear to God I ain't, Jeeter.

JEETER. Do you hear that, Ada? Lov says he ain't done nothing. What have you got to say about that?

ADA. Shut up.

JEETER. By God, woman, don't talk like that. Put down that stick, do you hear me? You has already done one whopping big sin today. You ought to be mighty sorry to do another. (LOV *manages to grab* ADA's *stick and stop the attack.* JEETER *nods approval.*) I'm glad to see you do that, Lov. That was no way for Ada to treat you. But what did you do to her anyway to make her keep hitting you with that old stick all the time?

LOV. I only wanted Pearl to come back and live with me.

ADA (*holding* PEARL). Pearl ain't never going back and live with you. There ain't no use you trying to make her, either. She's going to Augusta just like she set out to do this morning and nothing you do can stop her.

LOV. I'm her husband, ain't I? I can [ ] her and by God I will!

ADA (*belligerently*). You just try it.

JEETER. There ain't no sense you tryin[ ] carry your point, Lov. Ada made up [ ] mind Pearl's going to Augusta and [ ] ain't nothing I know can change it.

LOV. You can't be letting Pearl do tha[ ] ain't right.

JEETER. Right or wrong ain't got nothir[ ] do with it where Ada is concerned. J[ ] little while ago she made me borrow s[ ] thing when Morgan Prior wasn't at [ ] house. That's about the biggest sin a wo[ ] can make a man do, but she don't care r[ ] There ain't no use talking to her about [ ] or wrong.

LOV. Augusta ain't no place for a gi[ ] pretty as she is.

JEETER. I sure would like to stand in [ ] way, but I ain't got no more right [ ] that—(*Snaps his finger characteristica[ ] *Ada's the one you got to talk to, about [ ]

LOV. Ada's her Ma, but you're her Pa, [ ] you?

JEETER. By God and by Jesus, no! Ada [ ] was horsing around big as you please [ ] some man while I was down borrowin[ ] a mule one time. That don't make me [ ] Pa no more than you is.

LOV. You took care of her until she [ ] married to me. That's the same thing.

JEETER. No, it ain't. The Lord don't [ ] no recognition of that. The Lord is a [ ] old somebody. He said His flesh is His [ ] That don't make no provision for [ ] horsing around while I'm down borro[ ] me a mule. (*Enter* ELLIE MAY, *who [ ] bashfully behind tree when she sees [ ]*

ADA. You might just as well go away, [ ] I ain't lettin' Pearl go back with yo[ ] matter how much you talk, less'n she w[ ] to. . . . And I don't reckon she want[ ]

LOV. Pearl—won't you come back? (P[ ] *shrinks farther back.* LOV *glances plead[ ] at* ADA.) Ada—(LOV *glances helplessly [ ] *ADA *to* PEARL, *then lowers his head [ ] reaches down to pick up his hat, which[ ] fallen off. He dusts it off on his knee [ ] is starting away when* JEETER *stops h[ ]*

ᴇᴛᴇʀ. Hold on there, Lov. No sense you
ng off without a gal just because Pearl
n't want to go with you. Why don't you
ᴇ Ellie May there? (ᴇʟʟɪᴇ ᴍᴀʏ, *behind
chinaberry tree, giggles and puts her
n over her mouth to hide the torn lip.
ᴠ glances from* ᴊᴇᴇᴛᴇʀ *to* ᴇʟʟɪᴇ ᴍᴀʏ, *then
k to* ᴊᴇᴇᴛᴇʀ *again. Without a word he
ls his hat tighter and again starts off.
ᴇᴛᴇʀ takes a step forward as he sees* ʟᴏᴠ's
ifference.* ʟᴏᴠ *takes another step and
ᴇᴛᴇʀ follows.*) Ellie May's got to get a
n somewhere. When me and Ada's dead
d gone there won't be nobody to watch
r her. The niggers would haul off and
ᴇ here by the dozen. The niggers would
her in no time if she was here by her-
f. (ᴇʟʟɪᴇ ᴍᴀʏ *sets up her giggling and
iggling again and* ʟᴏᴠ *once more regards
objectively and solemnly.*)

ᴠ (*looking away from* ᴇʟʟɪᴇ ᴍᴀʏ. *He
aks stubbornly*). I want Pearl.

ᴇᴛᴇʀ (*exasperated*). By God and by
us, you know you ain't going to get Pearl,
what's the sense going on talking about
t? Now Ellie May there's got a lot of—

ᴠ. Ellie May's got that ugly looking face.
ʟɪᴇ ᴍᴀʏ, *standing in* ʟᴏᴠ's *path, giggles
d squirms.* ʟᴏᴠ *looks at her hard as* ᴊᴇᴇᴛᴇʀ
tinues.*)

ᴇᴛᴇʀ. You and her was hugging and rub-
g of each other to beat all hell just yester-
. Wouldn't you like to do that some
re?

ᴠ (*still looking hard at* ᴇʟʟɪᴇ ᴍᴀʏ). No,
God! I want Pearl or nothing. (*He moves
t her and exits.* ᴊᴇᴇᴛᴇʀ *shakes his head
he watches* ʟᴏᴠ *disappear down the
d.*)

ᴇʀ (*chiefly to* ᴀᴅᴀ). Now that's some-
ng I can't understand at all. It looks to
when a man loses one gal he'd be thank-
to get another—hey, stop that! What you
ng there, Ellie May? (*His sentence has
n broken by* ᴇʟʟɪᴇ ᴍᴀʏ's *attack on* ᴘᴇᴀʀʟ.
pushes* ᴘᴇᴀʀʟ *to the ground, picks up
stick* ᴀᴅᴀ *dropped after beating* ʟᴏᴠ, *and
bors her pretty sister furiously.* ᴊᴇᴇᴛᴇʀ
s forward to stop her, but he is slower
n the infuriated* ᴀᴅᴀ, *who grabs the stick
y from* ᴇʟʟɪᴇ ᴍᴀʏ *and starts beating her
urn.* ᴇʟʟɪᴇ ᴍᴀʏ *fights back for a moment.
ɴᴅᴍᴀ ʟᴇsᴛᴇʀ enters furtively and goes*

*behind the chinaberry tree where she ob-
serves scene.*)

ᴀᴅᴀ (*swinging stick sharply*). I'll show
you—I'll show you. (ᴇʟʟɪᴇ ᴍᴀʏ *gives up the
unequal fight and flees through the gate and
Left down road.* ᴘᴇᴀʀʟ *gets up and seeks
protection behind her mother.*) Don't you
worry none, Pearl. She won't do that no
more. (*She starts dusting off* ᴘᴇᴀʀʟ's *dress.*)

ᴊᴇᴇᴛᴇʀ (*shaking his head*). Great day in
the morning! I never seen such beating one
of the other as I seen here today. What do
you suppose Ellie May done that for, Ada?
(ᴀᴅᴀ *shoots him a baleful glance, but the
disdainful reply she is forming is checked
by the sudden muffled blast of a motor car
horn. All of them look up. The horn, louder,
sounds again.* ᴊᴇᴇᴛᴇʀ's *face lights up.*)
That's Dude! That's Dude and Bessie in
that new automobile. (ᴊᴇᴇᴛᴇʀ *goes through
gate, works to center stage, and looks down
the road.* ᴀᴅᴀ *crosses to fence and looks.
Even* ᴘᴇᴀʀʟ *is moved by sudden interest and
goes to the fence. Only* ɢʀᴀɴᴅᴍᴀ ʟᴇsᴛᴇʀ
comes further in, taking her place downstage of the well, where she huddles, listening and waiting.*) Here they come! Just look
at them! It's a brand-new automobile, all
right—just look at that shiny black paint!
Great day in the morning! Just look at them
coming yonder! (*The horn sounds again—
closer.* ᴊᴇᴇᴛᴇʀ *speaks with pride.*) Listen to
Dude blow that horn. Don't he blow it
pretty, though? (ᴇʟʟɪᴇ ᴍᴀʏ *enters Left and
flashes down the Tobacco Road on a dead
run, exiting Right to meet the car.*)

ᴀᴅᴀ. Ain't that the prettiest sight to see,
Pearl? Look at that dust flying up behind.
It makes it look like a big black chariot,
running away from a cyclone. (*The horn
sounds again, to the same rhythm of an
engineer blowing a locomotive whistle.*)

ᴊᴇᴇᴛᴇʀ. That's Dude driving it and blowing
the horn, too. (*Mounting excitement.*) Hi,
there, Dude! Hi, Bessie. (*Swinging down
from the fence, he runs through gate and
exits down road toward car. The horn continues to sound.* ᴀᴅᴀ, ᴘᴇᴀʀʟ, *and* ɢʀᴀɴᴅᴍᴀ
ʟᴇsᴛᴇʀ *wait, watching. We hear* ᴊᴇᴇᴛᴇʀ *returning before we see him.*) By God, Bessie,
I been seeing you come a far piece off in that
new automobile. (ʙᴇssɪᴇ *and* ᴊᴇᴇᴛᴇʀ *enter.*)
In all my days I never seen a finer looking
machine. Is it real brand new?

BESSIE (*vigorously and proudly*). I paid the whole eight hundred dollars for it. (*The horn sounds.*)

JEETER (*listens to* DUDE, *then speaks*). By God and by Jesus, it sure does make me feel happy again to know there's such a handsome automobile around. Don't you reckon you could take me for a little trip, Bessie? I sure would like to go off in it for a piece.

BESSIE (*looking pretentiously at marriage license she carries*). I reckon when Dude and me gets back you can go riding.

JEETER. Where is you and Dude going to, Bessie?

BESSIE (*proudly*). We're going to ride around like married folks.

ADA. Did you and Dude get married in Fuller?

BESSIE. Not all the way. I got leave of the county, however. It cost two dollars to do that little bit. (*Waves license at them.*) There's the paper to show it.

ADA. Ain't you going to get a preacher?

BESSIE. I is not! Ain't I a preacher of the gospel? I'm going to do it myself. Ain't no Hardshell Baptist going to fool with us.

JEETER. I knowed you would do it the right way. You sure is a fine woman preacher, Sister Bessie. (DUDE· *blows horn again.* JEETER *smiles complacently.*) That there old Dude sure does like fooling around with that there old horn.

BESSIE (*a bit peeved*). He's been doing that about every minute all the way up from Fuller. Looks to me like he'd want to stop now that we is about to do the rest of the marrying.

ADA. Did you and Dude have any trouble getting leave from the county?

BESSIE. None to speak of. At first the man said Dude was too young and that I'd have to get the consent of his Ma and Pa. I told him the Lord said for me to marry Dude, but he told me that didn't make no difference. So I started praying right then and there, and pretty soon the man said if I would just stop he'd do anything I wanted.

JEETER. You sure is a powerful pray-er, all right, Sister Bessie. You is about the best

pray-er and Dude is about the best aut[o]mobile driver in the country. Coming a[nd] going that makes you just about equ[al] (*Enter* DUDE *lugging, with quite some noi[se,] a torn off, dented fender.* JEETER *whirls [to] look at him.*) Great day, Dude, what y[ou] got there? Ain't that a fender off your ne[w] car?

DUDE (*dropping fender without concern*[).] Uh-huh.

JEETER. Now how did that happen? D[id] you run into something?

DUDE. We was coming back from Fuller a[nd] I was looking out at a big turpentine sti[ll] and then the first thing I knowed we w[as] smashed smack bang into the back of [a] two-horse wagon.

JEETER. Didn't hurt the running of the au[to]mobile, though, did it?

DUDE. Naw. It runs like it was brand n[ew] yet. The horn wasn't hurt none at all. [It] blows just as pretty as it did at the start.

JEETER (*nodding in agreement*). Don't p[ay] no attention to it, Bessie. Just leave it be a[nd] you'll never know that machine was a[ny] different than when you got it.

BESSIE. That's right. I ain't letting it wo[rry] me none, because it wasn't Dude's fa[ult.] He was looking at the big turpentine s[till] alongside the road, when the wagon got [in] our way. The nigger driving it ought [to] have had enough sense to move over.

JEETER. Was you blowing the horn th[en,] Dude?

DUDE. Not right then I wasn't. I was b[usy] looking at that big still. I never saw one t[hat] big nowhere. It was most as big as a co[rn] liquor still, only it wasn't so shiny-looki[ng.]

BESSIE (*bending down and wiping dust fr[om] fender with her skirt*). It's a shame to [see] the new car smashed up so soon, howe[ver.] It was brand new not more than an h[our] ago.

DUDE. It was that damn nigger. If he had[n't] been asleep on the wagon it wouldn't h[ave] happened at all. He was plumb asleep ti[ll I] woke him up and threw him out in [the] ditch.

JEETER. He didn't get hurt much, did [he?]

DUDE. I don't know about that. The wagon turned over on him and smashed him some. His eyes was wide open all the time, but I couldn't make him say nothing. He looked like he was dead.

JEETER. Niggers will get killed. Looks like here just ain't no way to stop it. (DUDE *takes out ball and hurls it against house.*)

ADA. When is you and Dude going to go on with the marrying?

BESSIE (*turning from fender and resuming her aggressive manner*). Right this minute. (*Smooths her skirt. Unrolls license again.*) Come on, Dude.

DUDE (*turning impatiently with ball in hand*). What you want to do now?

BESSIE. Marry us.

DUDE. Didn't you get that all done at the courthouse in Fuller?

BESSIE (*still extending his end of license*). That wasn't all. We got to get married in the sight of the Lord.

DUDE. Humph! (*Throws ball again.*)

JEETER. By God and by Jesus, Dude, stop dunking that ball against that old house and do what Bessie tells you.

DUDE. I want to take a ride.

BESSIE. We got plenty of time to ride around after we is married.

DUDE. Will we go then?

BESSIE. Yes, Dude.

DUDE. Is you sure?

BESSIE. Sure, Dude.

DUDE. What the hell, then. Then what do I do?

BESSIE (*extending license*). You hold your end of the license while I pray. (DUDE *gingerly takes one end of license, and* BESSIE *the other.* BESSIE *lowers her head and closes her eyes for several seconds of silent prayer, while* DUDE *looks down on her with a slight, rather perplexed frown. Presently* BESSIE *lifts her head, but her eyes are still closed as she intones.*) I marry us man and wife. So be it.

That's all, God. Amen. (*She opens her eyes and smiles gently up at* DUDE.)

DUDE (*pulling away*). Come on.

BESSIE. I got to pray now. You kneel down on the ground while I make a little prayer. (BESSIE *and others all kneel and* DUDE *reluctantly follows, still watching her with his expression of bored annoyance.*) (*Praying*). Dear God, Dude and me is married now. We is wife and husband. Dude, he is an innocent young boy, unused to the sinful ways of the country, and I am a woman preacher of the gospel. You ought to make Dude a preacher, too, and let us use our new automobile in taking trips to pray for sinners. You ought to learn him how to be a fine preacher so we can make all the goats into sheep. That's all this time. We're in a hurry now. Save us from the devil and make a place for us in heaven. Amen. (*She opens her eyes and smiles brightly at* DUDE.)

JEETER (*jumping up*). Bless the Lord, that was one of the prettiest marriages I ever seen. Dude sure got hisself good and wed, didn't he, Ada?

ADA. Humph!

JEETER (*goes to* BESSIE *and kisses her*). Praise God, Sister Bessie, that Dude is a lucky man. I'd sure like to be in his place right now.

BESSIE (*laughing coyly*). Be still, you old sinner.

JEETER (*to* DUDE). Yes, sir, Dude, boy. You sure is lucky to get a fine woman like Bessie.

DUDE (*shaking him off*). Aw, shut up, you old fool. (BESSIE *raps on the porch and* JEETER *turns to look at her.*)

JEETER. What you knocking on the porch for, Bessie? (*She raps again and* JEETER's *face clears.*) Great day! Now, why didn't I think of that? . . . You, Dude—can't you see how bad Sister Bessie wants to go into the house?

DUDE. What for?

JEETER. Never you mind what for. (*He starts pushing* DUDE.)

BESSIE (*taking* DUDE's *arm*). Just for now. Come on, Dude.

DUDE. You said we was going for a ride.

BESSIE. We can go after a little while.

JEETER (*pushing him harder*). What's the matter with you, Dude? Go on in with Sister Bessie. (*Slowly and grudgingly* DUDE *allows himself to be shoved and pulled on to the porch. At the door he pauses.*)

DUDE. This is a hell of a time to be going indoors. (BESSIE *and* DUDE *exit into the house, the door closing.* JEETER *stands almost center stage, his eyes shining with excitement.* ELLIE MAY *crosses quickly to the window and draws herself up on her toes, her fingers on the sill, as she tries to look into the house.* JEETER *crosses to window and pulls* ELLIE MAY *away.*)

JEETER. You got no business trying to see inside. Sister Bessie and Dude is married. (*Shoving* ELLIE MAY *aside, he promptly pulls himself up on the sill to see.* ELLIE MAY *suddenly turns and crosses swiftly toward porch, where* ADA *leans against an upright.* PEARL *stands on the ground at the edge of the porch near her mother.*)

ELLIE MAY (*passing* PEARL). Come on around to the back. (PEARL *hesitates for an instant, then joins her, and the two girls exit around upstage corner of house.* JEETER *hasn't much success seeing into the window, and he suddenly stops trying and scampers around the upstage corner of the house. He returns almost immediately with a chopping block on which he climbs to see into the room. A smile of approval beams on his weathered face.*)

JEETER. Sister Bessie sure is a fine-looking woman, ain't she, Dude?

BESSIE (*appearing at window*). Get away from there, Jeeter Lester.

JEETER. What's the matter, Bessie? I ain't done nothing.

BESSIE. Never you mind. You get away from there.

JEETER. Now don't get peeved, Bessie. This time of year puts a queer feeling into a man. I feel that way every late February and early March. No matter how many children a man's got, he always wants to get more.

BESSIE. That don't matter. I don't want to have nothing to do with you. You is an old sinner.

JEETER (*complacently*). Yes, I reckon I is. I reckon I is one of the biggest sinners in the whole country. (*Suddenly changes and roars.*) But, by God and by Jesus, woman— what's a man going to do! (DUDE *comes up to window and starts pushing at* JEETER *a. enter* CAPTAIN TIM *and* GEORGE PAYNE.)

DUDE. Get away from there, you old fool, o— I'll wham you one.

TIM (*amused*). Well, Jeeter, what's all th— excitement?

JEETER (*turning on block*). Captain John' boy!—Captain Tim! (JEETER *steps from th box and runs swiftly to meet* TIM *at th gate, almost frantic with excitement.* AD *stands on the porch, eying the strangers in passively and sucking on her snuff brush The old* GRANDMOTHER *peers out from b hind the protecting well.* TIM *extends h hand as* JEETER *comes running up.*)

TIM. How are you, Jeeter, how are you?

JEETER (*eagerly*). Captain Tim, I sure glad to see you!

TIM. Jeeter, this is Mr. Payne, from August

PAYNE. How do you do, Mr. Lester?

JEETER. Morning, sir.

TIM (*seeing* ADA *on porch*). That's Ada, is— it? Good morning, Ada.

ADA (*coldly*). Morning.

TIM (*indicating* DUDE). I don't recognize t' boy, Jeeter. Which one is he?

JEETER. That's Dude.

TIM. Oh, yes. I remember Dude now. (DUDE.) Hello there, Dude. Do you reme ber me?

DUDE (*impudently*). Naw! (*Giggles s consciously.*)

JEETER. That there next to Dude is Sis Bessie. They just married themselves bef you came.

PAYNE. Married *themselves*?

JEETER. Sister Bessie is a woman preacl and she done it.

PAYNE (*dubiously*). I see.

(*to* DUDE). Well, congratulations, Dude. ...ngratulations, Sister Bessie. (*To* JEETER.) ...Dude the only one of your children left, ...ter?

...TER. Ellie May and Pearl is around some-...ce.

...I (*looking about*). Well, the place hasn't ...nged much. What keeps it from falling ...wn, Jeeter?

...TER. Praise God, Captain Tim, I don't ...ow. I expect it will one of these days. . . . ...w you come on the porch and sit down. ... Dude, you bring some chairs out here.

...NE. Don't bother. I'm afraid we won't ...able to stay very long.

...TER. Ain't no bother at all. Could you do ...h a drink of water, Captain Tim?

...I. Thanks, Jeeter. (PAYNE *crosses up Left,* ...ncing about the property and inspecting ...house.*)

...TER (*crossing to well for water*). Dude, ...a go do what I told you. (*While* JEETER ...etting the water,* PAYNE *glances around ...iously. His eyes meet* TIM's *and he shakes ...head to suggest his reaction to the sur-...ndings.* DUDE *pulls a chair on to the ...ch.*) Here you is. (*Crossing to* TIM *with ...per of water.*)

...I. Much obliged. (*Drinks.*)

...TER. I sure is glad to see you back, Cap-...n. I knowed you couldn't stay away from ...land any more than your Daddy could. ...ybe city ways is all right for a short time, ...t when they start cleaning off the fields ...d burning the broom sedge, a man ain't ...ppy unless he can be seeing it and be ...ng it, too.

...I. You must be getting pretty old, Jeeter. ...think you'd be tired of it by this time.

...TER. No, sir. I is ready to do just as big ...day's work as the next one. Ada there is ...vays saying I is lazy, but there ain't no ...th in that when it comes to planting a ...p.

...I (*going to well and putting cup down*). ...w have crops been lately?

...TER. Praise God there ain't been none in ...en years. We just ain't been able to get ...dit down here on the Tobacco Road.

Ain't nobody got no mony. By God and by Jesus, I is glad ʹou came back to provide that again.

TIM (*turning—surprised*). What?

JEETER. Yes, sir, Captain Tim. I was just tell-ing Ada a short time back that the Lord was aiming to take care of me out of His bounty. I wasn't thinking about you at the time, but soon as I heard you was here again Dude and me set to burning off the fields. Them north fields is burning some right this minute.

TIM (*after a glance at* PAYNE). Well, I don't know how that idea got around. I'm sure sorry, but I'm—well, Jeeter, I'm afraid I can't help you. I'm in pretty much the same fix you are.

JEETER (*unbelieving*). What's that, Captain Tim?

TIM (*turning to* PAYNE). You'd better tell him, Payne.

PAYNE. Well, you see, Mr. Lester, I'm from the bank in Augusta. We're down here to collect money, not lend it.

JEETER. You mean I can't have no credit to grow me a crop this year?

PAYNE. I'm afraid not.

JEETER. But I just got to have credit. Me and my folks is starving out here on the Tobacco Road.

PAYNE. Well, then you ought to be glad we came. We're ready to help you to get away from here to where you have a chance of making a living.

JEETER. I don't want to get away from here. If you mean go off and work in the mills, I say, by God and by Jesus, no!—I ain't going to do it.

PAYNE. But if you're really starving—

JEETER. That ain't got nothing to do with it. Captain John said I could live here as long as I wanted. He said he couldn't give me credit at the stores in Fuller no more, but he told me I could stay here and live until I died. You know that, Captain Tim.

TIM. Yes, Jeeter, I remember, and that was all right as long as the land was ours. But it's not any more. I had to borrow money on every farm we owned around here and now I can't pay it back. Like your grand-daddy used to own the land and Captain John took it over, the bank's doing it with me.

JEETER (*heatedly*). I don't understand that. This was my daddy's place and his daddy's before him, and I don't know how many Lesters before that. There wasn't no nothing here in the whole country before they came. They made that road out there hauling tobacco kegs fifteen miles down the ridge to the river. Now I don't own it and you don't own it and it belongs to a durn bank that ain't never had nothing to do with it even.

TIM. That's the way things just seem to happen, Jeeter.

JEETER. Praise God, it ain't the way things just happen. It's the rich folks in Augusta that's doing it. They don't work none, but they get all the money us farmers make. One time I borrowed me three hundred dollars from a loan company there to grow a crop and when I gave them interest and payments and every other durn thing they could think of I didn't make but seven dollars the whole year working every day. By God, that ain't right, I tell you. God won't stand for such cheating much longer. He ain't so liking of the rich people as they think He is. God, He likes the poor.

PAYNE. Now, Mr. Lester. We don't want to be hard on you old farmers, but we're going to try putting this whole section under scientific cultivation and there wouldn't be any use for you.

JEETER. Why not? If you is going to grow things on the land, why can't I stay right here and do it, too? I'd work for you just like I did for Captain John and no nigger ever worked harder than that.

PAYNE. I'm afraid that's impossible.

DUDE. What did I tell you, you old fool? No-body ain't going to give you nothing.

JEETER. You shut up, Dude Lester. You shut up and get away from here. Captain Tim ain't going to let them send me away. Is you, Captain Tim?

PAYNE. Be reasonable, Mr. Lester. You've proved you can't get along here. Why don't you move your family up to Augusta or

across the river in South Carolina where t mills are?

JEETER. No! By God and by Jesus, no! Tha one thing I ain't never going to do. The durn cotton mills is for the women folks work in. I say it's a hell of a job for a m to spend his time winding strings on spoo

PAYNE. It shouldn't be any harder than t ing to grow a crop here. Even if you get one, you can't make enough out of to live on.

JEETER. I don't care. God made the land, l you don't see Him building no durn cott mills.

PAYNE. That hasn't anything to do with You old farmers are all the same. You do realize that times have changed.

JEETER. That's no concern of mine. I is rea to look after my own like the Bible says, that don't include no goddam mill! (*Tu ing to* TIM.) Please, Captain Tim, don't them make me do that. I'm like to die pr soon now, anyway, but up there I'd go fore my time. You ain't going to let them that to me, is you?

TIM. Lord, Jeeter, what can I do? That's to Mr. Payne now. (*Turning to* PAYN How about it, Payne? Couldn't you something for this man?

PAYNE. I'm sorry, Mr. Harmon, but if made an exception for one we'd have to all of them. Of course, if he could pay ren

JEETER. Rent! No use asking that. I coul pay no rent. Praise God, I hasn't even money to buy food with.

TIM. What about your children? Coul one of them help you?

JEETER. I don't know where none of th is except Tom—(*A sudden idea.*) By C and by Jesus—Tom!

TIM. I remember Tom. What's Tom doi

JEETER. They say down in Fuller he' powerful rich man now. They tell me hauls all the ties for the railroad. (*Turn* PAYNE.) How much money would you wanting for rent, mister?

PAYNE. Well—this place ought to be we a hundred dollars a year.

TER. That's a heap of money, but Tom
[ou]ght to be ready to help out his old Pa
[at] a time like this. When would you be
[wa]nting that hundred dollars?

[O]NE. We ought to be starting back early
[tom]orrow.

[JEE]TER. I got time for that. Tom's only
[kin] in Burke County. (*Turns and calls.*)
[He]y, you, Dude. You and Bessie get in that
[new] automobile and ride over and see Tom.
[Yo]u tell him his old Pa has got to have a
[hun]dred dollars. Don't lose no time about
[doi]ng it neither.

[DUD]E (*jumping off porch—eager for a ride*).
[Com]e on, Bessie. We is going for a ride.
[Be]ssie *hesitates, glancing back into the
[hou]se.*)

[JEE]TER. You hurry up there, Bessie. Ain't
[no] time to be thinking about going in the
[hou]se now. (*With a last disappointed
[gla]nce, BESSIE comes down off the porch.
[DUD]E moves ahead of her to the gate.*)

TIM. Don't you think you ought to go and
speak to Tom yourself, Jeeter?

JEETER. He might not like that so much.
He might have changed some since he was
a boy. He'll talk to Dude and Bessie, though.
(BESSIE *and* DUDE *disappear down the road,
and* JEETER *runs to the gate to call after
them.*) Hey, you, Dude. You tell Tom his
old Pa needs that money powerful bad. You
tell him we ain't got anything to eat here,
either, and his Ma needs snuff to calm her
stomach with. (*Turns back to* TIM.) Tom
was just about the best of all the boys. I
reckon Bailey was the best, but Tom was
good, too. He always said he was going
to make a heap of money. (*The horn sounds
off in* DUDE'S *inimitable manner.* JEETER
speaks proudly.) That's Dude doing that.
Don't he blow the horn pretty, though? Just
listen to it. (*The horn sounds again, somewhat fainter, and* JEETER *again smiles with
pride at* TIM.) That's Dude. (*He is listening again as the* CURTAIN *falls.*)

ACT THREE

SCENE: *The same.*

[T]IME: *Dawn the following morning.*

[A]T RISE: JEETER, *shoeless, is discovered asleep on the porch, his back against one of the
[upr]ights, head slumped forward on his chest. Again the early sun spreads its soft golden
[glo]w, soon to become a fierce white glare as the morning advances.* JEETER *awakens ab-
[rup]tly, as one does who all night has tried to fight off sleep, and crosses swiftly to the
[gat]e, where he gazes off Right stage down the empty, silent road. Disappointed, he comes
[bac]k into the yard to the well, where he performs his casual morning ablutions, using,
[as a]lways, his shirt for a towel. Fingers through his hair serve as a comb for his scraggly
[hai]r; his hat goes back on his head. He is ready for the day. Again he crosses to the road,
[whe]re his anxious gaze once more sweeps the horizon Right for a glimpse of* DUDE *and
[BES]SIE.* ADA *appears on the porch, pressing her sides to ease the early morning pains of a
[bod]y that sleep can no longer refresh.*

[...]. Is they coming yet?

[JEE]TER. No. (*Comes inside to porch where
[he s]its and starts putting on shoes.*) By God
[and] by Jesus, I don't understand that. They
[bee]n gone long enough to go to Burke
[Cou]nty and back three times over.

[ADA]. It's that Bessie. She ain't going to hurry
[hom]e just because you want her to.

[JEE]TER. They must of seen Tom all right if
[the]y been gone this long. Maybe he made
[the]m stay all night. Do you think he done
[that], Ada?

ADA. Maybe he did and maybe he didn't.
But if he asked them, you can bet that
Bessie stayed all right. She ain't going to
come home as long as there is any other
place to go.

JEETER. What is you so peeved at Bessie for?
She's a fine woman preacher.

ADA. She's a old hussy, that's what she is.

JEETER. Now what makes you say that? Sister Bessie is—

ADA. Don't tell me what she is. I know.
Walking around here so uppity because she

bought herself that new automobile. Why didn't she buy us some rations and snuff instead of spending all that money. That's what a good woman preacher would have done.

JEETER. She wants that new automobile to carry on the preaching and the praying. Women preachers ain't like the rest of us. They is got the Lord's work to do.

ADA. Humph. Looks to me like the Lord's work would be done better if she bought Dude's Ma a stylish dress. The Lord would understand that.

JEETER (suddenly and impatiently). Say, when is we going to eat this morning, anyway? Ain't there none of that meal left we borrowed from Morgan Prior yesterday?

ADA (crossly). There's some meal all right, but there ain't no kindling wood. Ellie May's ready to cook it as soon as she gets some.

JEETER. You tell Ma Lester to go get it then.

ADA. Ma Lester ain't here.

JEETER. Where is she?

ADA. I don't know. She didn't sleep in the bed last night.

JEETER. H'mm. Maybe she went out in the broom sedge yesterday and couldn't get back. Maybe she even died out there.

ADA. Maybe. She ain't never stayed away before.

JEETER. I'll go out and look around one of these days. . . . Well, you tell Ellie May to go out and get some wood. I sure got to have my chicory before long. . . .

ADA (calling inside house). Ellie May—Ellie May!

ELLIE MAY (off—in house). What you want, Ma?

ADA. You go out in the fields and get some sticks for the fire.

ELLIE MAY (off). Oh, make that old woman go.

ADA. She ain't here.

ELLIE MAY (complaining). Well, where she?

ADA. She's likely dead. You go on do l I tell you. (ELLIE MAY enters yawning scratching her head.)

ELLIE MAY. Why don't you make Pearl She don't never do nothing.

ADA. Never you mind now. I got other thi for Pearl to do.

ELLIE MAY. Aw, gee!

JEETER. You hurry up. I is near about dy for my chicory.

ELLIE MAY (complaining). Can't I even me a drink of water?

JEETER. All right, you get you some wa then get along. But keep away from th north fields. They might be burning so yet. That's probably what happened to y old Grandma. The fire come up on her a she couldn't get away from it. (He is fil with sudden energy, gets up, crosses to road, and looks down it, shakes his he ELLIE MAY drinks leisurely from the wa dipper.) By God and by Jesus, they ought be back with that money before this. F thing you know Captain Tim and that m will be along here looking for it.

ADA (calling into house—ignoring JEETE Pearl—Pearl, git up, honey. Come out h and freshen up. We'll be having somethi to eat pretty soon now. Bring that old bri with you, too. I want to pretty up your h (ELLIE MAY hears ADA and takes the dip slowly down from her mouth. She look ADA, her face livid with unspoken rage. S denly she flings the dipper at ADA, the wa spilling. JEETER, coming through the g regards ELLIE MAY with anger.)

JEETER. Great day in the morning, wh the meaning of all that! (ELLIE MAY, di garding JEETER, looks at her mother u blazing eyes, her breath coming hard. returns the look with level coldness. EL MAY's throat contracts with half-stifled s and she turns and rushes to the gate. starts down the Tobacco Road Left w something she sees offstage stops her. For instant she is rigid, then, with the first p nounced sob, she turns, and exits Right, r ning down the road. JEETER follows EL MAY with a puzzled glance, then turns ADA.)

ETER. Now if that ain't the durndest gal.
hat do you suppose made her turn around
e that for? (*He answers his own curi-
ty by crossing to the road and looking off
ft. He turns back with some surprise.*)
Lov coming down the road.

. Don't you let him come in here.

ETER. What the hell, woman. He ain't
ing to do no harm. He looks too durned
ed.

. He ain't going to have Pearl.

TER. Who said he was? I just said he was
ning down the road.

(*calling inside*). Pearl, Lov's coming.
y where you is and get ready to run case
starts trying to get at you. (ADA *shuts the
r and stands with her back to it.*)

TER. Great day, he's toting something
in. Now whatever could be in that any-
y? I bet you one thing, by God—it ain't
nips! (*Twitching with eagerness he
es inside the yard and takes his familiar
ce, hanging over the fence, his back to
audience, straining to see down the
d.*) Whatever he's got, I sure could use
e, even if I can't see it. I certainly is
py Lov and me is friends about this time.

. Humph! The only way you'll ever get
thing from him is stealing it.

TER. No, sir! The Lord forgave me for
t before and I ain't going to risk his
th again.

. Humph.

TER (*again stretching over fence to peer
n the road*). Now, Ada, don't be too
d on Lov and I might be able to prevail
him to give us a little something.

. Then he better keep away from Pearl.

ETER *waves her quiet and turns back to
fence, but he restrains his eagerness, as
did in the first act, so that* LOV *will not
frightened off.* LOV *enters disconsolately,
ying a small flour sack, the bottom of
ch bulges somewhat from an object the
of a brick.*)

TER (*casually*). Hi, there, Lov. (LOV
s.)

(*after a pause*). I want to talk to you,
er.

JEETER. Sure, Lov. Come inside and rest
yourself. (LOV *slowly comes through the
gate.*) What you got in that sack, Lov?
What you got there anyway?

LOV (*after a significant pause and a glance
from* JEETER *to* ADA *and back to* JEETER.
Knowing the bombshell effect of his words).
Salt pork.

JEETER (*electrified*). Salt pork! Lord a'-
mighty! I ain't had salt pork since the Lord
himself knows how long. Is you going to
give me some of that, Lov? I sure could do
with a small piece about this time.

LOV. Take it. (*He holds sack to the astounded* JEETER.)

JEETER (*unbelieving*). Take it? You mean
take it all?

LOV. I bought it for that.

JEETER (*taking sack*). Great day in the
morning, I never heard of such bounty!
(*Turns.*) Did you hear that, Ada? Lov has
give me all this salt pork.

ADA (*coldly*). What does he want for it?

JEETER. He don't want nothing for it. Lov
just give it to me, that's all.

ADA. Ask him.

JEETER (*doubtfully*). Well now . . . What
have you got to say about that, Lov? *Is
you after something from me in return for
this salt pork?*

LOV. I want to talk to you about Pearl.

ADA. That's just what I thought. Well, you
ain't going to have her back. No use you
trying to talk Jeeter into it, neither. He ain't
got nothing to say about it. You give him
back that salt pork, Jeeter.

JEETER. Now, Ada, there ain't no sense in
being hasty about this matter. What you say
is right, but there can't be no harm in talking about it.

ADA. You just want to hold on to that salt
pork.

JEETER. Now, Ada—

LOV (*with sudden desperation*). I got to have
Pearl back, Jeeter, no matter what you said
yesterday. I just got to have her back.

JEETER. Now, Lov, we talked all about that before. I told you—

LOV. I don't care what you told me. Maybe you ain't Pearl's real Pa, but you got the right of her.

JEETER. I wish I could agree with you on that matter, Lov, but it ain't right in the eyes of God.

LOV. I'll pay you, Jeeter. I'll give you a dollar every week out of the money I make at the chute.

JEETER (whistles). That's a heap of money, Lov, and coming and going I might have considered it a short time back. But I ain't going to need money bad enough now to make me fly against the wrath of the Lord. Dude and Bessie is over with Tom right this minute and he'll be sending me all the money I want for my needs.

LOV. I'll give you two dollars.

JEETER. Two dollars a week! Now, Lov Bensey, you quit tempting me.

LOV (with sudden fury). By God, I want my wife. (ADA plants her back more firmly against the door and the movement tells LOV where PEARL is. He takes a few steps to the edge of the porch. ADA's arms raise to cover the door.)

ADA. You come any closer, and I'll call to her to run off. (LOV, checked by the threat, stops, his sudden anger cooling.)

LOV (defeated). No, don't do that. (JEETER takes this opportunity to hide the sack behind the well. LOV slowly turns to JEETER.) Jeeter, I don't see how I can make it more than two dollars every week. But that's a heap of money.

JEETER. Praise God, I know it, Lov.

ADA. Get out of here, Lov Bensey—get out. (LOV slowly turns and crosses to the gate; JEETER keeps himself in front of the well to lessen any chance of LOV seeing and remembering the salt pork. LOV exits Left. JEETER waits until LOV has gone, then runs to the fence and looks after him.)

JEETER. He's gone all right. He's gone and forgot that salt pork, too. (Running back to the well, he picks up the sack and takes out

the pork.) Now ain't that something! Th[...] must be near about two pounds. Lov su[...] is a generous provider. (Crosses to ADA[...] There you is, Ada. You fix up some of t[...] with the corn meal when Ellie May com[...] back with the kindling. (ADA takes the sac[...] She has moved away from the door on LO[...] exit and is in her usual position, leani[...] against an upright.) Now what do y[...] think's happened to Ellie May, anywa[...] What's happened to Dude and Bessie [...] that matter? By God and by Jesus, th[...] ought to be back with that money befo[...] this.

ADA. What is you going to do with t[...] money, Jeeter?

JEETER (pausing with foot half raised to [...] on other shoe. He is outraged). What i[...] going to do? Is you crazy, woman! I got[...] give it to that man with Captain Tim.

ADA. Humph! That don't make no sense[...] me.

JEETER. Great day in the morning, you[...] crazy! That money's going to keep me [...] land, ain't it? That money's going to let[...] stay here and raise a crop. By God and [...] Jesus, what do you mean there ain't no se[...] in that?

ADA. You give the money to that man a[...] what has you got left? Nothing! You a[...] got no seed cotton to plant in the fields, y[...] ain't got nothing to eat and you ain't[...] better off than you was before.

JEETER. I ain't aiming to be better off. [...] aiming to keep my land.

ADA. You're an old fool, Jeeter Lester. W[...] that money we could get us a place to [...] up in Augusta. Maybe we could even buy[...] an automobile like Bessie's. (Wisely.) [...] wouldn't have to worry none about be[...] laid in the corn crib when you die neit[...] Ain't no telling what's going to happen[...] you stay here.

JEETER. Shut up! You just say that to s[...] me into doing what you want. Well, I a[...] going to be laid in no corn crib, and I a[...] going to work in no cotton mill neither[...]

ADA. Maybe you wouldn't have to w[...] none up there. (Glances toward door.) M[...] be Ellie May and Pearl could do that. P[...]

ld like that a lot. She wouldn't be scared
oing if her old Ma went.

ER. You ain't thinking about my wants
n you talk like that. It's Pearl you is
king about. Well, you can take her if
's what you want, and leave me here
e. I was born here on the land, and by
l and by Jesus that's where I'll die.

(*fiercely*). I hope you do. I hope you
and they lay you in the corn crib and
rats eat off your face just like they done
r Pa.

ER (*rising—threatening and furious,
ng his shoe to strike her*). Goddam you,
nan! (*The horn, sounded in* DUDE's *in-
able style, checks* JEETER's *descending
. Radiance replaces black fury in his
as he hears it again.*) Here they is.
t's them, all right. That's Dude blowing
old horn. (PEARL *and* ELLIE MAY *enter
o porch. Hobbling because of the one
*, JEETER *crosses to the gate, where he
s and starts to pull on his shoe, while
horn continues its bleat.* JEETER's *shoe
on with difficulty. Once or twice he
s off with it half on, but is so impeded
he stops and works on it again. The
stops.* JEETER, *giving up the job of
ing on the shoe while standing, plumps
he ground, puts it on, and gets through
gate, starting down the road Right,
n* BESSIE *enters.*) Here you is, Bessie. I
waiting all night and day for you and
e to come back. Where you been any-
?

E (*proudly*). In Augusta.

ER. Augusta! Didn't you go see Tom?

E. We saw Tom first. Then we rode up
ugusta and had us a honeymoon.

ER. Honeymoon? What the hell is
?

E. A honeymoon is when two people is
ried and they get in the bed together.

ER. Where did you do that?

E (*proudly*). At a hotel.

ER. Great day in the morning! Didn't
take a heap of money?

E. It took two bits.

JEETER. Hear that, Ada? Dude and Bessie
stayed at a hotel in Augusta.

ADA (*dourly*). Did they bring us anything
back?

BESSIE. I didn't have no money left to do
that. That two bits was the last piece of
money I had.

ADA. Humph! Looks to me like you might
have brought some snuff back to Dude's old
Ma instead of wasting money like that.
(*Enter* DUDE *carrying broken headlight.*)

JEETER. Now, Ada, you let Bessie alone.
(*Sees* DUDE.) Here you is, Dude. Bessie just
told us about staying all night in Augusta—
(*Sees headlight.*) Great day, just look at that
old headlight. What done that?

DUDE. A goddam old pine tree. That's what.

JEETER (*inspecting light*). H'mm. Was you
looking where you was going?

DUDE. I just looked back once and there it
was—smack in front of me.

JEETER. Well, it don't look like it's going
to be much good no more.

DUDE. If I had me an ax, I'd have chopped
that tree down right then and there.

JEETER. I wouldn't concern myself much
about it. One headlight is plenty to drive
with.

DUDE. Oh, to hell with it. (*He drops light
on ground, crosses to gate.*) It's just the way
that pine tree got in front of me, that's all.

JEETER. Looks like they will do that sometimes. Hey, Dude. Where is the money
Tom sent me?

DUDE. Tom didn't send you no money. Why
the hell did you think he would anyway?
(*Exits.*)

JEETER. Hey, Dude—(*Turning back to* BES-
SIE.) Dude's lying, ain't he, Bessie?

BESSIE (*nodding*). Tom ain't at all like he
used to be, Jeeter.

JEETER (*desperately*). Now, Bessie—don't
fool with me. Give me the money.

BESSIE. There ain't no money, Jeeter. Tom
just didn't send any—that's all.

JEETER. You is crazy, woman. He did send it. Tom wouldn't do that to me.

BESSIE. Yes, he did, Jeeter. He's a wicked man, Tom is.

JEETER. No, sir, I don't believe it. You is got the money and I want it. Give it to me, hear me—give it to me.

BESSIE. I ain't got it, Jeeter.

JEETER. You is a liar. That's what you is— an old liar. Tom did send it. (*Enter* DUDE *rolling an auto wheel.* JEETER *rushes over to him inside the gate and grabs him.*) Dude, give me that money—hear me, give me that money.

DUDE (*shaking him off*). Didn't I tell you once! There ain't no money. Now get away from me and shut up. (*Bends over wheel, his back half to* BESSIE.)

JEETER. No. Tom wouldn't do that. He was my special boy. You just didn't go see him.

DUDE. We saw him all right. We saw him and he said to tell you to go to hell. (BESSIE *grabs him by the neck and shakes him so that the wheel falls to the ground.* DUDE *is furious.*) Damn you, turn loose of me. (*Shakes free.*) What the hell you doing?

BESSIE. You shouldn't have told Jeeter that. That's a wicked thing to say.

DUDE. I didn't say it— Tom said it. And you keep off me. I didn't do nothing to you.

BESSIE. Praise the Lord, you won't be fit to preach a sermon next Sunday if you cuss like that. Good folks don't want to have God send them sermons by cussing preachers.

DUDE. All right, I won't cuss no more. But don't you go jumping on my neck no more neither. (*He picks up wheel and rolls it against fence near the other broken pieces of the automobile, and sits.* JEETER *sits on fence, staring blankly ahead.* PEARL *and* ELLIE MAY *exit into the house.*)

ADA. What does Tom look like now? Has he changed much?

BESSIE. He looks a lot like Jeeter. There ain't much resemblance in him and you.

ADA. Humph! There was a time when I'd have declared it was the other way around.

BESSIE. Maybe one time, but now he lo[oks] more like Jeeter than Jeeter does hisself.

ADA. What did he say when you told h[im] you and Dude was married?

BESSIE. He didn't say nothing much. Loo[ks] to me like he didn't care one way or [the] other.

DUDE (*over his shoulder from where he [sits] back to audience, appraising the dama[ged] parts*). Tom said she used to be a two[-bit] slut when he knowed her. (*With a bo[und]* BESSIE *is on his neck again, choking h[im.] He jerks away from her quickly and pus[hes] his hand at her face, getting up, threat[en-] ing.*) Goddam you! You keep off me.

BESSIE (*tenderly as she backs off*). N[o,] Dude, you promised me you wasn't goin[g to] cuss no more.

DUDE. Then, by God, quit choking me. [I'm] getting damned sick and tired of you do[ing] that.

BESSIE. You shouldn't talk like that a[bout] the woman you is mated to.

DUDE. Well, that's what Tom said. He [said] it right to you and you didn't do noth[ing.] Why didn't you do something to him i[f he] was telling a lie?

BESSIE. Tom is a wicked man. The L[ord] punishes wicked men like that.

DUDE. Well, then, you let the Lord pu[nish] me and keep your hands off my neck. (D[UDE] *pulls wheel down and begins trying [to] straighten spokes by pulling on them [with] his hands and pounding them with a h[and-] sized rock.*)

ADA. Did Tom say he had any children[?]

BESSIE. He didn't mention it if he had. [He] didn't seem to want to talk very much, [not] even when I told him you and Jeeter di[dn't] have meal nor meat in the house.

DUDE (*looking up from his work*). He [just] said he didn't give a damn and went [on] driving his team of ox.

ADA (*briskly—pleased*). Well, I reckon [I'd] better be getting ready to go off, Jeeter.

JEETER. What?—(*Snapped back from [his] stunned silence.*) No, I ain't going, I [tell] you.

(*exasperated*). Tom didn't send you no
|ney. How you going to stay here?

|TER. By God, I'm going to stay, that's all.
|A, *realizing the uselessness of arguing
|h him, turns and exits into the house.
|SIE *turns to* DUDE *and watches him
|·k*.)

|SIE. Do you reckon you'll ever get that
|eel straight again, Dude?

|E (*crossly*). I'm trying, ain't I?

|TER (*abstractedly, pointing to wheel*).
|.at done that?

|·E. Remember that old pine tree that
|ted the headlight?

|TER Um.

|E. Well, I was backing away from that
| some durn fool left a pile of cross ties
|.t where I'd run smack into them.

|TER (*easily*). Well, now what do you
|·k?

|E. It busted the back of the car in, too.

|SIE. It looks like everything's trying to
| my new automobile. Ain't nothing
| it was when I paid eight hundred dol-
|for it in Fuller just yesterday.

|TER. It ain't hurt the running of it none,
|·gh, has it? It runs good yet.

|·IE. I reckon so, but it makes a powerful
|·f noise when it's running up hill—and
|·n hill, too.

|·E. That's because we was running it
|·hout oil. The man at the gasoline station
| something was burned out inside.

|TER. That's a pity.

|·E. It runs pretty good, though, even if it
|· make all that racket.

|TER. Some automobiles is like that.
|·nps down from fence, suddenly his old
|·again*.) By God and by Jesus, now why
|·'t I think of that before. Quit pounding
|·hat old wheel, Dude. You come with

|·E (*still sitting*). What you want to do
|·? I done enough running around for
|·morning.

JEETER. You get up from there and do like
I say. You and me is going to start hauling
wood to Augusta right this minute.

DUDE. You're just an old fool. That old
machine of yours can't carry no wood to
Augusta.

JEETER. No, but that there new one can.
You come on.

DUDE. What do I want to haul wood to
Augusta for?

JEETER. So I can get me some money for the
bank—that's what for.

DUDE. You ain't going to get no hundred
dollars for no load of wood, or nothing else
like it.

JEETER. I can get a couple of dollars maybe,
and every day doing that I can get me more
than a hundred.

BESSIE. You stop right where you is, Jeeter.
You ain't going to use my new automobile
for no such purpose.

JEETER. Now, Bessie, ain't I always shared
what I had with you and your former husband? You ain't going to see me lose my
land, is you?

BESSIE. That ain't no concern of mine.
Hauling wood in my new machine would
punch holes in the seat and the top just like
it done to your old one.

JEETER. I won't let it hurt it none.

BESSIE. It's already broke up enough. I ain't
going to let you do it.

JEETER. Now, Bessie—

BESSIE. You can't have it and that's all.

JEETER (*with heat*). That's a hell of a way
to act toward me. You ain't got the mercy
of the Lord in you. I say you is a hell of a
woman preacher.

BESSIE (*angrily*). You shut up cussing at me,
Jeeter Lester.

JEETER. I won't. You is an old bitch, that's
what you is. You is an old bitch.

BESSIE (*with equal fury*). You is an old
bitch, too. You is an old son-of-a-bitch. All
you Lesters is sons-of-bitches. (DUDE *looks
up amused*.)

JEETER (*coming up to her threateningly*). Get off my land. If I can't borrow me that automobile, you get off my land.

BESSIE. It ain't your land. It's the bank's land and *you* got to get off it.

JEETER. It's the old Lester place, and I ain't going to get off it while I'm alive. But durned if I can't run you off—(*Enter* PEARL *from house with small, blackened pot.*) Now git!—You hear me, gi—(JEETER *sees* PEARL, *who has hesitated on the porch at sight of the quarrel, and suddenly stops his tirade, the hand raised to strike* BESSIE *halted in midair.* PEARL *comes down from the porch and crosses to the well,* JEETER's *eyes following her and his hand slowly lowering to his side. The fury in his eyes dies to a strange, puzzled, contemplative expression.* DUDE, *who has been amused by the quarrel, a smile wreathing his face, follows his father's glance curiously, but without enlightenment.* BESSIE *glances from* JEETER *to* PEARL *and back to* JEETER *again, a frown wrinkling her forehead.*)

BESSIE. What's the matter with you, you old fool? Has you lost your mind?

JEETER (*suddenly turning away from regarding* PEARL *at the well, smiling at* BESSIE, *and moving away a few steps*). Ain't no sense you and me fighting, Bessie. You and me always thought a heap of each other. You can stay here just as long as you has a mind to.

BESSIE. H'mm. (*Suspicious and uncompromising.*) You ain't going to have the use of my new automobile to haul wood to Augusta.

JEETER. I gave up thinking about that a long time back. Don't concern yourself about that no more. However, I might be wanting you and Dude to take a little trip for me pretty soon now. Will you do that?

BESSIE (*suspiciously*). Maybe. What you want us to do?

JEETER. Never you mind. It won't be far.

BESSIE. Well, if it ain't far.

JEETER. It won't hardly take no time. (*Crosses to* DUDE.) How is you getting on there, Dude?

DUDE (*back trying to straighten spoke*). Maybe it will be all right. It don't m[atter] matter if all the spokes ain't straight.

JEETER. Umm. (*Out of the corner of his* [eye] JEETER *watches* PEARL, *who, having fi*[lled] *the kettle, crosses back from well to ho*[use] *and exits.* JEETER *leaves his place at the fe*[nce] *and nonchalantly ambles to the porch* [and] *leans, taking out his knife and whittling* *a piece of broken weather-boarding.* [Al-] *though he tries to appear at ease, his te*[nse-] *ness is apparent, and occasional swift glar*[ces] *at the door reveal his real interest.*)

DUDE (*hitting at spokes with a stone har*[der] *than before*). This is a hell of a job.

JEETER. Don't worry too much about t[hat.] The wheels of my old machine wa[sn't] straight much after the first few days an[d it] didn't hurt the running of it hardly any[.]

BESSIE. I don't like my new car busted [up] like that though. (*Indicating headlig*[ht.]) Look there, Dude. There ain't hardl[y a] piece of glass left in that headlight.

DUDE. Don't I know it. Goddam it, can't [you] let me be? Can't you see I'm trying to [fix] this old wheel?

BESSIE. Now, Dude, is that a way to t[alk?] Good folks don't want to go and he[ar a] Sunday sermon by a cussing preache[r. I] thought you wasn't going to swear no m[ore.]

DUDE. Then don't be always poking aro[und.] Go sit down someplace. (*Enter* PEARL [with] *pan.* JEETER *watches her sharply as [she] crosses to well.*)

JEETER (*pretending interest*). When's [Dude] going to start being a preacher, Bessie? (*Fol-* *lows* PEARL *slowly to well.*)

BESSIE. He's going to preach a little s[weet] sermon next Sunday. I is already tel[ling] him what to say when he preaches.

JEETER. Dude might make a fine [young] preacher at that under your direction[, al-] though I never thought he had right g[ood] sense. I used to think he was goin[g to] stay on the land like I always done, b[ut I] reckon he'll be better off riding around [the] country preaching and praying with [you.] (*Edges forward a bit as* PEARL *fills [her] bucket and starts back to door. Wi[th a] spring* JEETER *is at* PEARL's *side and g[rabs]*

firmly by the wrist. The bucket falls—
girl's cry rings out, as she makes a
~erate effort to pull away and run.*)

~L. Ma! (BESSIE *and* DUDE *whirl around
~ook.*)

~ER. Hey, Dude—you and Bessie ride
~n to the chute and get Lov. Tell him
~t Pearl for him. (*The door flies open
~an infuriated* ADA *takes in the scene.
~rushes down on* JEETER *and begins
~ng at him furiously.*)

You let her be—you let her be!

~ER (*pushing off* ADA *with his free hand*).
~ry up there, Dude. You tell Lov if he's
~ready to pay that two dollars a week
~nake Pearl go back and live with him.

~E. Jeeter, that ain't the right thing to

~ER (*fighting off* ADA). Maybe it wasn't
~t before, but it sure is now. You get the
~out of here!

~: (*grabbing* BESSIE). Come on. (DUDE
~pulls BESSIE *through gate.*)

~(*clawing at* JEETER *and yelling at* DUDE).
~'t you go, Dude—don't you go.

~ER. Go on, Dude. You do like I tell
~(DUDE *and* BESSIE *exit Right.* ADA *strikes
~EETER, but when she sees* DUDE *and
~E exit, she suddenly stops her attack
~runs after them.*)

Don't go, Dude. Wait! Wait! (ADA
~. PEARL *continues to scratch and fight
~ist* JEETER, *her gasping sobs the only
~d she utters.* JEETER *holds her, but looks
~n direction the others have gone. For
~nstant there is silence, broken only by
~'s sobs. Then the sound of an engine
~ing up and the blare of a horn come
~the road below, and hard on this rings
~he high shriek of a woman in agony.
~n the scream cuts the silence, and even
~'s sobs are hushed, as she and* JEETER
~. Suddenly she again struggles to free
~lf in a frenzy of effort to be with her
~er, but* JEETER'S *hold does not relax.
~ing is spoken, no voice is heard, for a
~pause. Then, on hands and knees,
~ing along the Tobacco Road and whim-
~g like a hurt puppy, comes* ADA. PEARL'S
~gles cease and she stands, horrified, still*

in JEETER's *grasp, as* ADA *continues forward.
At the gate her strength deserts her, and she
sinks to her side, now dragging herself along
by her arms alone, until she is in the yard.*)

PEARL. Ma! . . . Let me go, goddam you—
let me go. (*But* JEETER *holds fast,* DUDE *and*
BESSIE *come running up to fence outside,
followed by* ELLIE MAY. DUDE *leans over the
fence, looking at his mother. There is no
grief in his voice, only calm explanation.*
JEETER *holds* PEARL, *who stands transfixed.*)

DUDE. We was backing on to the road and
she got in the way. I guess the wheels ran
over her. (ADA *makes a last movement forward and a stifled groan comes from her
crushed, wracked body as she props herself
on her arm. A sob escapes* PEARL *and she
tries to pull away from* JEETER.)

ADA. Let her go, Jeeter. Let her come to me.

JEETER. Praise God, I'd like to do that for
you, Ada, but she'll run away.

ADA. Just let her come close to me, that's
all. (JEETER *yields several steps, so that*
PEARL, *kneeling, can reach out her hand to
touch* ADA. ELLIE MAY *enters and stands outside the fence.*)

PEARL (*kneeling—touching her mother—
sobbing*). Ma! Ma! Don't die. You can't,
Ma—you can't!

ADA. That's all right, Pearl. I was going
pretty soon now anyway. (*Glances around
as best she can.*) I wish I had that stylish
dress to be buried in, though. Reckon you
can get me one, Jeeter?

JEETER. I sure would like to promise you
that, Ada, but it ain't likely.

PEARL. I'll get you one, Ma. I'll get you one.

ADA (*matter-of-factly, without either self-
pity or bitterness*). Never mind, honey. I
never really thought I'd get it. It would have
sort of pleased me, though. (*Pauses, looks
at* PEARL, *then* JEETER.) Let her go, Jeeter?
I never asked for nothing before, but now
I'm going to die.

JEETER. I sure would like to, Ada, but I'm
going to die pretty soon myself now. I feel
it inside me. But I got to die on the land.
Don't you understand? If I don't hold on to
her for Lov I won't be able to do that.

ADA. Please, Jeeter, don't make her go back.

JEETER. Praise God, Ada, I got to.

ADA. All my life I been working for you. I picked cotton in the fields and turned over the furrows. I took care of your house and raised your children, and now when I'm going to die you won't even do what I want you to.

JEETER. My concern is with the living. The dead has to look out for themselves.

ADA. You're a sinful man, Jeeter Lester. You're a sinful man, and you're going to hell. (*Holds out arm to* PEARL.) Come here, child. Just put your arm around me so I can sit up. (JEETER *allows* PEARL *to come close enough to* ADA, *so that her free arm goes around her mother, and* JEETER'S *hand works close to* ADA'S *mouth. Suddenly* ADA *leans forward the few necessary inches and her teeth sink into* JEETER'S *hand. With a smothered exclamation* JEETER *jerks back his hand, releasing* PEARL. *With flashing quickness the girl is on her feet. A dash carries her through the gate before* JEETER *recovers from the shock of his pain. Pausing,* PEARL *looks back at her mother, propped on her arm in the yard.*)

PEARL. Good-by, Ma. (JEETER *springs forward toward her, but with a last wave of her hand,* PEARL *flashes down the road and is gone.* JEETER *reaches the fence, makes to run after her, then stops, realizing the hopelessness of overtaking the girl.* ADA, *holding herself up with her last strength, sees his defeat. A low laugh escapes her and she rolls forward on her face and is dead.* JEETER *slowly turns and comes back inside. He stops to look down at* ADA *for a moment and then crosses to the porch where he sits. His hand doesn't hurt much now, but he continues to hold it.* LOV *enters.*)

DUDE. Hi there, Lov. Jeeter was looking for you, but I guess it's too late now. Pearl's done gone.

LOV (*after a pause, indicating* ADA). What's the matter with her?

DUDE. Me and Bessie run over her in the new automobile a while back.

LOV. Is she hurt bad?

DUDE. Looks like she's dead. (LOV *comes [_]side, kneels down, looks at* ADA. *Then g[_] up to* JEETER.)

LOV. Ada's dead, Jeeter. (JEETER *nods,[_] dazed. Crossing to* ADA, *he stands over[_] for a long pause. At last he speaks.*)

JEETER. Lov, you and Dude go out in[_] fields and find the best place to bury [_] Make a deep hole—Ada would like that. [_] Bessie, you do some praying, too. It wo[_] please Ada a whole lot.

BESSIE. Praise the Lord, I'll be glad [_] Brother Jeeter. (LOV, DUDE, *and* BESSIE *[_] ELLIE MAY *moves forward tentatively [_] JEETER *notices her.*)

JEETER. Ellie May, you better go dow[_] Lov's house and fix it up for him. He'[_] coming home to supper tonight and [_] cook him what he wants. Be nice to him[_] maybe he'll let you stay. He'll be wan[_] a woman pretty bad now. (ELLIE M[_] frantic with delight, drops her sticks [_] crosses on a run down the road. Just be[_] she exits, she stops and looks back.*)

ELLIE MAY. Good-by, Pa. (JEETER *n[_] ELLIE MAY *exits, running.* JEETER *l[_] down at* ADA.)

JEETER. You shouldn't have done that, [_] One way and another it didn't do anyt[_] much good except maybe Pearl. (*For a [_] second* JEETER *looks down at* ADA, *the[_] crosses to the porch and sits. He bends d[_] slowly, takes a pinch of the earth betw[_] his fingers and rubs it into dust. He[_] back, leaning against the upright, and [_] his hat forward over his eyes. It is the s[_] posture he has assumed so many time[_] fore when he has suddenly and unexpec[_] fallen asleep. For a moment he continue[_] stractedly to rub the dirt between his fin[_] Then all movement ceases. Seconds of [_] ber silence pass. A rotten shingle falls [_] the sagging porch, and the* CURTAIN [_] slowly.*)

THE END

Of Mice And Men

BY JOHN STEINBECK

CAST OF CHARACTERS

This play was first presented by Sam H. Harris at the Music Box Theatre the evening of November 23, 1937, with the following cast:

GEORGE	Wallace Ford
LENNIE	Broderick Crawford
CANDY	John F. Hamilton
THE BOSS	Thomas Findlay
CURLEY	Sam Byrd
CURLEY'S WIFE	Claire Luce
SLIM	Will Geer
CARLSON	Charles Slattery
WHIT	Walter Baldwin
CROOKS	Leigh Whipper

Staged by George S. Kaufman
Settings by Donald Oenslager

SYNOPSIS OF SCENES

ACT I

Scene I. A Sandy bank of the Salinas River. Thursday night.
Scene II. The interior of a bunkhouse. Late Friday morning.

ACT II

Scene I. The same as Act I, Scene II. About seven-thirty Friday evening.
Scene II. The room of the stable buck, a lean-to. Ten o'clock Saturday evening.

ACT III

Scene I. One end of a great barn. Mid-afternoon, Sunday.
Scene II. Same as Act I, Scene I.

Time: The present.
Place: An agricultural valley in Southern California.

OF MICE AND MEN

ACT ONE

SCENE I

Thursday night.
A sandy bank of the Salinas River sheltered with willows—one giant sycamore rig
upstage.
The stage is covered with dry leaves. The feeling of the stage is sheltered and qu
Stage is lit by a setting sun.
Curtain rises on an empty stage. A sparrow is singing. There is a distant sound
ranch dogs barking aimlessly and one clear quail call. The quail call turns to a warni
call and there is a beat of the flock's wings. Two figures are seen entering the stage in sin
file, with GEORGE, *the short man, coming in ahead of* LENNIE. *Both men are carry*
blanket rolls. They approach the water. The small man throws down his blanket roll,
large man follows and then falls down and drinks from the river, snorting as he drin

GEORGE (*irritably*). Lennie, for God's sake, don't drink so much. (*Leans over and shakes* LENNIE.) Lennie, you hear me! You gonna be sick like you was last night.

LENNIE (*dips his whole head under, hat and all. As he sits upon the bank, his hat drips down the back*). That's good. You drink some, George. You drink some too.

GEORGE (*kneeling and dipping his finger in the water*). I ain't sure it's good water. Looks kinda scummy to me.

LENNIE (*imitates, dipping his finger also*). Look at them wrinkles in the water, George. Look what I done.

GEORGE (*drinking from his cupped palm*). Tastes all right. Don't seem to be runnin' much, though. Lennie, you oughtn' to drink water when it ain't running. (*Hopelessly.*) You'd drink water out of a gutter if you was thirsty. (*He throws a scoop of water into his face and rubs it around with his hand, pushes himself back and embraces his knees.* LENNIE, *after watching him, imitates him in every detail.*)

GEORGE (*beginning tiredly and growing angry as he speaks*). God damn it, we could just as well of rode clear to the ranch. That bus driver didn't know what he was talkin' about. "Just a little stretch down the highway," he says. "Just a little stretch"—damn near four miles. I bet he didn't want to stop at the ranch gate. . . . I bet he's too damn lazy to pull up. Wonder he ain't too lazy to stop at Soledad at all! (*Mumbling.*) Just a little stretch down the road.

LENNIE (*timidly*). George?

GEORGE. Yeh . . . what you want?

LENNIE. Where we goin', George?

GEORGE (*jerks down his hat furiously*). you forgot that already, did you? So I to tell you again! Jeez, you're a cr bastard!

LENNIE (*softly*). I forgot. I tried not forget, honest to God, I did!

GEORGE. Okay, okay, I'll tell you again. (*With sarcasm.*) I ain't got nothin' to Might just as well spen' all my time tel you things. You forgit 'em and I tell again.

LENNIE (*continuing on from his last spee* I tried and tried, but it didn't do no goo remember about the rabbits, George!

GEORGE. The hell with the rabbits! You c remember nothing but them rabbits. remember settin' in that gutter on How Street and watchin' that blackboard?

LENNIE (*delightedly*). Oh, sure! I remen that . . . but . . . wha'd we do th I remember some girls come by, and says—

GEORGE. The hell with what I says! You member about us goin' in Murray Ready's and they give us work cards bus tickets?

LENNIE (*confidently*). Oh, sure, George I remember that now. (*Puts his hand his side coat-pocket; his confidence vani Very gently.*) . . . George?

GEORGE. Huh?

NNIE (*staring at the ground in despair*). n't got mine. I musta lost it.

ORGE. You never had none. I got both of here. Think I'd let you carry your own rk card?

NNIE (*with tremendous relief*). I thought ut it in my side pocket. (*Puts his hand his pocket again.*)

RGE (*looking sharply at him; and as he ks,* LENNIE *brings his hand out of his ket.*) Wha'd you take out of that pocket?

NNIE (*cleverly*). Ain't a thing in my ket.

RGE. I know there ain't. You got it in your d now. What you got in your hand?

NIE. I ain't got nothing, George! Honest!

RGE. Come on, give it here!

NIE (*holds his closed hand away from RGE*). It's on'y a mouse!

RGE. A mouse? A live mouse?

NIE. No . . . just a dead mouse. (*Worly.*) I didn't kill it. Honest. I found it. und it dead.

RGE. Give it here!

NIE. Leave me have it, George.

RGE (*sternly*). Give it here! (LENNIE ctantly gives him the mouse.*) What do want of a dead mouse, anyway?

NIE (*in a propositional tone*). I was ng it with my thumb while we walked g.

GE. Well, you ain't pettin' no mice while walk with me. Now let's see if you can mber where we're going. (GEORGE ws it across the water into the brush.*)

NIE (*looks startled and then in embarnent hides his face against his knees*). got again.

GE. Jesus Christ! (*Resignedly.*) Well, , we are gonna work on a ranch like one we come from up north.

NIE. Up north?

GE. In Weed!

NIE. Oh, sure I remember—in Weed.

GEORGE (*still **with exaggerated patience***). That ranch we're goin' to is right down there about a quarter mile. We're gonna go in and see the boss.

LENNIE (*repeats as a lesson*). And see the boss!

GEORGE. Now, look! I'll give him the work tickets, but you ain't gonna say a word. You're just gonna stand there and not say nothing.

LENNIE. Not say nothing!

GEORGE. If he finds out what a crazy bastard you are, we won't get no job. But if he sees you work before he hears you talk, we're set. You got that?

LENNIE. Sure, George . . . sure, I got·that.

GEORGE. Okay. Now when we go in to see the boss, what you gonna do?

LENNIE (*concentrating*). I . . . I . . . I ain't gonna say nothing . . . jus' gonna stand there.

GEORGE (*greatly relieved*). Good boy, that's swell! Now say that over two or three times so you sure won't forget it.

LENNIE (*drones softly under his breath*). I ain't gonna say nothing . . . I ain't gonna say nothing. . . . (*Trails off into a whisper.*)

GEORGE. And you ain't gonna do no bad things like you done in Weed neither.

LENNIE (*puzzled*). Like I done in Weed?

GEORGE. So you forgot that·too, did you?

LENNIE (*triumphantly*). They run us out of Weed!

GEORGE (*disgusted*). Run us out, hell! We run! They was lookin' for us, but they didn't catch us.

LENNIE (*happily*). I didn't forget that, you bet.

GEORGE (*lies back on the sand, crosses his hands under his head. And again* LENNIE *imitates him*). God, you're a lot of trouble! I·could get along so easy and nice, if I didn't have you on my tail. I could live so easy!

LENNIE (*hopefully*). We gonna work on a ranch, George.

GEORGE. All right, you got that. But we're gonna sleep here tonight, because . . . I want to. I want to sleep out. (*The light is going fast, dropping into evening. A little wind whirls into the clearing and blows leaves. A dog howls in the distance.*)

LENNIE. Why ain't we goin' on to the ranch to get some supper? They got supper at the ranch.

GEORGE. No reason at all. I just like it here. Tomorrow we'll be goin' to work. I seen thrashing machines on the way down; that means we'll be buckin' grain bags. Bustin' a gut liftin' up them bags. Tonight I'm gonna lay right here an' look up! Tonight there ain't a grain bag or a boss in the world. Tonight, the drinks is on the . . . house. Nice house we got here, Lennie.

LENNIE (*gets up on his knees and looks down at* GEORGE, *plaintively*). Ain't we gonna have no supper?

GEORGE. Sure we are. You gather up some dead willow sticks. I got three cans of beans in my bindle. I'll open 'em up while you get a fire ready. We'll eat 'em cold.

LENNIE (*companionably*). I like beans with ketchup.

GEORGE. Well, we ain't got no ketchup. You go get the wood, and don't you fool around none. Be dark before long. (LENNIE *lumbers to his feet and disappears into the brush.* GEORGE *gets out the bean cans, opens two of them, suddenly turns his head and listens. A little sound of splashing comes from the direction that* LENNIE *has taken.* GEORGE *looks after him; shakes his head.* LENNIE *comes back carrying a few small willow sticks in his hand.*) All right, give me that mouse.

LENNIE (*with elaborate pantomime of innocence*). What, George? I ain't got no mouse.

GEORGE (*holding out his hand*). Come on! Give it to me! You ain't puttin' nothing over. (LENNIE *hesitates, backs away, turns and looks as if he were going to run. Coldly*). You gonna give me that mouse or do I have to take a sock at you?

LENNIE. Give you what, George?

GEORGE. You know goddamn well, what! I want that mouse!

LENNIE (*almost in tears*). I don't know w I can't keep it. It ain't nobody's mouse didn' steal it! I found it layin' right besi the road. (GEORGE *snaps his fingers sharp and* LENNIE *lays the mouse in his hand.* wasn't doin' nothing bad with it. Just stre ing it. That ain't bad.

GEORGE (*stands up and throws the mouse far as he can into the brush, then he ste to the pool, and washes his hands*). Y crazy fool! Thought you could get aw with it, didn't you? Don't you think I co see your feet was wet where you went the water to get it? (LENNIE *whimpers l a puppy.*) Blubbering like a baby. Je Christ, a big guy like you! (LENNIE *tries control himself, but his lips quiver and face works with an effort.* GEORGE *puts hand on* LENNIE's *shoulder for a momer* Aw, Lennie, I ain't takin' it away just meanness. That mouse ain't fresh. Besi you broke it pettin' it. You get a mouse th fresh and I'll let you keep it a little wh

LENNIE. I don't know where there is no ot mouse. I remember a lady used to give to me. Ever' one she got she used to giv to me, but that lady ain't here no m

GEORGE. Lady, huh! . . . Give me th sticks there. . . . Don't even remember v that lady was. That was your own A Clara. She stopped givin' 'em to you. always killed 'em.

LENNIE (*sadly and apologetically*). They so little. I'd pet 'em and pretty soon t bit my fingers and then I pinched t head a little bit and then they was c . . . because they was so little. I wish v get the rabbits pretty soon, George. T ain't so little.

GEORGE. The hell with the rabbits! Come let's eat. (*The light has continued to go of the scene so that when* GEORGE *lights fire, it is the major light on the stage.* GE *hands one of the open cans of bean* LENNIE.) There's enough beans for men.

LENNIE (*sitting on the other side of the speaks patiently*). I like 'em with ketc

GEORGE (*explodes*). Well, we ain't got Whatever we ain't got, that's what want. God Almighty, if I was alone, I c live so easy. I could go get a job of v and no trouble. No mess . . . and v

e end of the month c— , I could take
y fifty bucks and go into town and get
hatever I want. Why, I could stay in a
t-house all night. I could eat any place I
int. Order any damn thing.

NNIE (*plaintively, but softly*). I didn't
int no ketchup.

ORGE (*continuing violently*). I could do
at every damn month. Get a gallon of
hiskey or set in a pool room and play
rds or shoot pool. (LENNIE *gets up to his
ees and looks over the fire, with fright-
ed face.*) And what have I got? (*Dis-
stedly.*) I got *you.* You can't keep a job
d you lose me every job I get!

NNIE (*in terror*). I don't mean nothing,
orge.

ORGE. Just keep me shovin' all over the
untry all the time. And that ain't the
rst—you get in trouble. You do bad
ngs and I got to get you out. It ain't
d people that raises hell. It's dumb ones.
e shouts.) You crazy son-of-a-bitch, you
ep me in hot water all the time. (LENNIE
trying to stop GEORGE's flow of words
th his hands. Sarcastically.) You just
nta feel that girl's dress. Just wanta pet
ike it was a mouse. Well, how the hell'd
know you just wanta feel her dress?
w'd she know you'd just hold onto it
e it was a mouse?

NIE (*in panic*). I didn't mean to, George!

RGE. Sure you didn't mean to. You didn't
an for her to yell bloody hell, either. You
n't mean for us to hide in the irrigation
ch all day with guys out lookin' for us
h guns. Alla time it's something you
n't mean. God damn it, I wish I could
you in a cage with a million mice and
them pet *you.* (GEORGE's *anger leaves him
denly. For the first time he seems to see
expression of terror on* LENNIE's *face.
looks down ashamedly at the fire, and
neuvers some beans onto the blade of his
ket-knife and puts them into his mouth.*)

NIE (*after a pause*). George! (GEORGE
posely does not answer him.) George?

RGE. What do you want?

NIE. I was only foolin', George. I don't
t no ketchup. I wouldn't eat no ketchup
was right here beside me.

GEORGE (*with a sullenness of shame*). If they
was some here you could have it. And if
I had a thousand bucks I'd buy ya a bunch
of flowers.

LENNIE. I wouldn't eat no ketchup, George.
I'd leave it all for you. You could cover
your beans so deep with it, and I wouldn't
touch none of it.

GEORGE (*refusing to give in from his sullenness, refusing to look at* LENNIE.) When I
think of the swell time I could have without
you, I go nuts. I never git no peace!

LENNIE. You want I should go away and
leave you alone?

GEORGE. Where the hell could you go?

LENNIE. Well, I could . . . I could go off
in the hills there. Some place I could find a
cave.

GEORGE. Yeah, how'd ya eat? You ain't got
sense enough to find nothing to eat.

LENNIE. I'd find things. I don't need no nice
food with ketchup. I'd lay out in the sun
and nobody would hurt me. And if I found
a mouse—why, I could keep it. Wouldn't
nobody take it away from me.

GEORGE (*at last he looks up*). I been mean,
ain't I?

LENNIE (*presses his triumph*). If you don't
want me, I can go right in them hills, and
find a cave. I can go away any time.

GEORGE. No. Look! I was just foolin' ya.
'Course I want you to stay with me. Trouble
with mice is you always kill 'em. (*He
pauses.*) Tell you what I'll do, Lennie. First
chance I get I'll find you a pup. Maybe you
wouldn't kill it. That would be better than
mice. You could pet it harder.

LENNIE (*still avoiding being drawn in*). If
you don't want me, you only gotta say so.
I'll go right up on them hills and live by
myself. And I won't get no mice stole from
me.

GEORGE. I want you to stay with me. Jesus
Christ, somebody'd shoot you for a coyote
if you was by yourself. Stay with me. Your
Aunt Clara wouldn't like your runnin' off
by yourself, even if she is dead.

LENNIE. George?

GEORGE. Huh?

LENNIE (*craftily*). Tell me—like you done before.

GEORGE. Tell you what?

LENNIE. About the rabbits.

GEORGE (*near to anger again*). You ain't gonna put nothing over on me!

LENNIE (*pleading*). Come on, George . . . tell me! Please! Like you done before.

GEORGE. You get a kick out of that, don't you? All right, I'll tell you. And then we'll lay out our beds and eat our dinner.

LENNIE. Go on, George. (*Unrolls his bed and lies on his side, supporting his head on one hand.* GEORGE *lays out his bed and sits cross-legged on it.* GEORGE *repeats the next speech rhythmically, as though he had said it many times before.*)

GEORGE. Guys like us that work on ranches is the loneliest guys in the world. They ain't got no family. They don't belong no place. They come to a ranch and work up a stake and then they go in to town and blow their stake. And then the first thing you know they're poundin' their tail on some other ranch. They ain't got nothin' to look ahead to.

LENNIE (*delightedly*). That's it, that's it! Now tell how it is with us.

GEORGE (*still almost chanting*). With us it ain't like that. We got a future. We got somebody to talk to that gives a damn about us. We don't have to sit in no barroom blowin' in our jack, just because we got no place else to go. If them other guys gets in jail, they can rot for all anybody gives a damn.

LENNIE (*who cannot restrain himself any longer. Bursts into speech*). But not us! And why? Because . . . because I got you to look after me . . . and you got me to look after you . . . and that's why! (*He laughs.*) Go on, George!

GEORGE. You got it by heart. You can do it yourself.

LENNIE. No, no. I forget some of the stuff. Tell about how it's gonna be.

GEORGE. Some other time.

LENNIE. No, tell how it's gonna be!

GEORGE. Okay. Some day we're gonna the jack together and we're gonna have little house, and a couple of acres and cow and some pigs and . . .

LENNIE (*shouting*). And live off the of the land! And have rabbits. Go George! Tell about what we're gonna ha in the garden. And about the rabbits in cages. Tell about the rain in the winter . and about the stove and how thick cream is on the milk, you can hardly cut Tell about that, George!

GEORGE. Why don't you do it yoursel you know all of it!

LENNIE. It ain't the same if I tell it. Go now. How I get to tend the rabbits.

GEORGE (*resignedly*). Well, we'll have big vegetable patch and a rabbit hutch chickens. And when it rains in the wi we'll just say to hell with goin' to we We'll build up a fire in the stove, and around it and listen to the rain comin' d on the roof—Nuts! (*Begins to eat with knife.*) I ain't got time for no more. (falls to eating. LENNIE *imitates him, spill a few beans from his mouth with et bite.* GEORGE, *gesturing with his kni* What you gonna say tomorrow when boss asks you questions?

LENNIE (*stops chewing in the middle bite, swallows painfully. His face cont with thought*). I . . . I ain't gonna a word.

GEORGE. Good boy. That's fine. Say, ma you're gittin' better. I bet I can let tend the rabbits . . . specially if you member as good as that!

LENNIE (*choking with pride*). I can member, by God!

GEORGE (*as though remembering someth points his knife at* LENNIE's *chest*). Ler I want you to look around here. Think can remember this place? The ranc 'bout a quarter mile up that way. Just fo the river and you can get here.

LENNIE (*looking around carefully*). Su can remember here. Didn't I remember not gonna say a word?

GEORGE. 'Course you did. Well, look, Lennie, you just happen to get in trouble, I want you to come right here and hide in the brush.

LENNIE (*slowly*). Hide in the brush.

GEORGE. Hide in the brush until I come for you. Think you can remember that?

LENNIE. Sure I can, George. Hide in the brush till you come for me!

GEORGE. But you ain't gonna get in no trouble. Because if you do I won't let you tend the rabbits.

LENNIE. I won't get in no trouble. I ain't gonna say a word.

GEORGE. You got it. Anyways, I hope so. (GEORGE *stretches out on his blankets. The light dies slowly out of the fire until only the faces of the two men can be seen.* GEORGE *is still eating from his can of beans.*) It's gonna be nice sleeping here. Lookin' up ... at the leaves ... Don't build no more fire. We'll let her die. Jesus, you feel free when you ain't got a job—if you ain't hungry. (*They sit silently for a few moments. A night owl is heard far off. From* across the river there comes the sound of a coyote howl and on the heels of the howl all the dogs in the country start to bark.)

LENNIE (*from almost complete darkness*). George?

GEORGE. What do you want?

LENNIE. Let's have different color rabbits, George.

GEORGE. Sure. Red rabbits and blue rabbits and green rabbits. Millions of 'em!

LENNIE. Furry ones, George. Like I seen at the fair in Sacramento.

GEORGE. Sure. Furry ones.

LENNIE. 'Cause I can jus' as well go away, George, and live in a cave.

GEORGE (*amiably*). Aw, shut up.

LENNIE (*after a long pause*). George?

GEORGE. What is it?

LENNIE. I'm shutting up, George. (*A coyote howls again.*)

CURTAIN

SCENE II

Late Friday morning.

The interior of a bunkhouse.

Walls, white-washed board and bat. Floors unpainted.

There is a heavy square table with upended boxes around it used for chairs. Over each bunk there is a box nailed to the wall which serves as two shelves on which are the private possessions of the working men.

On top of each bunk there is a large noisy alarm clock ticking madly.

The sun is streaking through the windows. Note: Articles in the boxes on wall are soap, talcum powder, razors, pulp magazines, medicine bottles, combs, and from nails on the sides of the boxes a few neckties.

There is a hanging light from the ceiling over the table, with a round dim reflector on it.

The curtain rises on an empty stage. Only the ticking of the many alarm clocks is heard.

CANDY, GEORGE and LENNIE are first seen passing the open window of the bunkhouse.

CANDY. This is the bunkhouse here. Door's on this side. (*The latch on the door and* CANDY *enters, a stoop-shouldered man. He is dressed in blue jeans and a denim coat. He carries a big push broom in his left hand. His right hand is gone at the wrist. He grasps things with his right arm between arm and side. He walks into the room followed by* GEORGE *and* LENNIE. *Conversationally.*) The boss was expecting you last night. He was sore as hell when you wasn't here to go out this morning. (*Points with his handless arm.*) You can have them two beds there.

GEORGE. I'll take the top one ... I don't want you falling down on me. (*Steps over to the bunk and throws his blankets down. He looks into the nearly empty box shelf over it, then picks up a small yellow can.*) Say, what the hell's this?

CANDY. I don't know,

GEORGE. Says "positively kills lice, roaches and other scourges." What the hell kinda beds you givin' us, anyway? We don't want no pants rabbits.

CANDY (*shifts his broom, holding it between his elbow and his side, takes the can in his left hand and studies the label carefully*). Tell you what . . . last guy that had this bed was a blacksmith. Helluva nice fellow. Clean a guy as you'd want to meet. Used to wash his hands even *after* he et.

GEORGE (*with gathering anger*). Then how come he got pillow-pigeons? (LENNIE *puts his blankets on his bunk and sits down, watching* GEORGE *with his mouth slightly open.*)

CANDY. Tell you what. This here blacksmith, name of Whitey, was the kinda guy that would put that stuff around even if there wasn't no bugs. Tell you what he used to do. He'd peel *his* boiled potatoes and take out every little spot before he et it, and if there was a red splotch on an egg, he'd scrape it off. Finally quit about the food. That's the kind of guy Whitey was. Clean. Used to dress up Sundays even when he wasn't goin' no place. Put on a necktie even, and then set in the bunkhouse.

GEORGE (*skeptically*). I ain't so sure. What da' ya say he quit for?

CANDY (*puts the can in his pocket, rubs his bristly white whiskers with his knuckles*). Why . . . he just quit the way a guy will. Says it was the food. Didn't give no other reason. Just says "give me my time" one night, the way any guy would. (GEORGE *lifts his bed tick and looks underneath, leans over and inspects the sacking carefully.* LENNIE *does the same with his bed.*)

GEORGE (*half satisfied*). Well, if there's any grey-backs in this bed, you're gonna hear from me! (*He unrolls his blankets and puts his razor and bar of soap and comb and bottle of pills, his liniment and leather wristband in the box.*)

CANDY. I guess the boss'll be out here in a minute to write your name in. He sure was burned when you wasn't here this morning. Come right in when we was eatin' breakfast and says, "Where the hell's them new men?" He give the stable buck hell, too. Stable buck's a nigger.

GEORGE. Nigger, huh!

CANDY. Yeah. (*Continues.*) Nice fellow t Got a crooked back where a horse kick him. Boss gives him hell when he's m But the stable buck don't give a damn abc that.

GEORGE. What kinda guy is the boss?

CANDY. Well, he's a pretty nice fella fo boss. Gets mad sometimes. But he's pr nice. Tell you what. Know what he d Christmas? Brung a gallon of whiskey ri in here and says, "Drink hearty, boys, Chr mas comes but once a year!"

GEORGE. The hell he did! A whole gallc

CANDY. Yes, sir. Jesus, we had fun! T let the nigger come in that night. Well, a little skinner name Smitty took after nigger. Done pretty good too. The g wouldn't let him use his feet so the nig got him. If he could a used his feet Sm says he would have killed the nigger. guys says on account the nigger go crooked back Smitty can't use his f (*He smiles in reverie at the memory.*)

GEORGE. Boss the owner?

CANDY. Naw! Superintendent. Big land c pany. . . . Yes, sir, that night . . . he co right in here with a whole gallon . . . h right over there and says, "Drink hea boys," . . . he says. . . . (*The door op Enter the* BOSS. *He is a stocky man, dre in blue jean trousers, flannel shirt, a b unbuttoned vest and a black coat. He u a soiled brown Stetson hat, a pair of h heeled boots and spurs. Ordinarily he his thumbs in his belt.* CANDY, *shuffling wards the door, rubbing his whiskers his knuckles as he goes.*) Them guys come. (CANDY *exits and shuts the door hind him.*)

BOSS. I wrote Murray and Ready I wa twc men this morning. You got your slips?

GEORGE (*digs in his pockets, produces slips, and hands them to the* BOSS). they are.

BOSS (*reading the slips*). Well, I see it w Murray and Ready's fault. It says right on the slip, you was to be here for this morning.

RGE. Bus driver give us a bum steer. We
to walk ten miles. That bus driver says
was here when we wasn't. We couldn't
mb no rides. (GEORGE *scowls meaningly*
ENNIE *and* LENNIE *nods to show that he
erstands.*)

. Well, I had to send out the grain
ns short two buckers. It won't do any
d to go out now until after dinner.
'd get lost. (*Pulls out his time book,
ns it to where a pencil is stuck between
eaves. Licks his pencil carefully.*) What's
r name?

RGE. George Milton.

. George Milton. (*Writing.*) And what's
s?

RGE. His name's Lennie Small.

. Lennie Small. (*Writing.*) Le's see, this
e twentieth. Noon the twentieth . . .
kes positive mark. Closes the book and
it in his pocket.*) Where you boys
workin'?

GE. Up around Weed.

(*to* LENNIE). You too?

GE. Yeah. Him too.

(*to* LENNIE). Say, you're a big fellow,
you?

GE. Yeah, he can work like hell, too.

He ain't much of a talker, though, is

GE. No, he ain't. But he's a hell of a
worker. Strong as a bull.

NIE (*smiling*). I'm strong as a bull.
RGE *scowls at him and* LENNIE *drops
ead in shame at having forgotten.*)

(*sharply*). You are, huh? What can
do?

GE. He can do anything.

(*addressing* LENNIE). What can you
(LENNIE, *looking at* GEORGE, *gives a
nervous chuckle.*)

GE (*quickly*). Anything you tell him.
a good skinner. He can wrestle grain

bags, drive a cultivator. He can do anything.
Just give him a try.

BOSS (*turning to* GEORGE). Then why don't
you let *him* answer? (LENNIE *laughs.*)
What's he laughing about?

GEORGE. He laughs when he gets excited.

BOSS. Yeah?

GEORGE (*loudly*). But he's a goddamn good
worker. I ain't saying he's bright, because
he ain't. But he can put up a four hundred
pound bale.

BOSS (*hooking his thumbs in his belt*). Say,
what you sellin'?

GEORGE. Huh?

BOSS. I said what stake you got in this guy?
You takin' his pay away from him?

GEORGE. No. Of course I ain't!
BOSS. Hell, I never seen one guy take so
much trouble for another guy. I just like
to know what your percentage is.

GEORGE. He's my . . . cousin. I told his ole
lady I'd take care of him. He got kicked
in the head by a horse when he was a kid.
He's all right. . . . Just ain't bright. But
he can do anything you tell him.

BOSS (*turning half away*). Well, God knows
he don't need no brains to buck barley
bags. (*He turns back.*) But don't you try
to put nothing over, Milton. I got my eye
on you. Why'd you quit in Weed?

GEORGE (*promptly*). Job was done.

BOSS. What kind of job?

GEORGE. Why . . . we was diggin' a cesspool.

BOSS (*after a pause*). All right. But don't
try to put nothing over 'cause you can't get
away with nothing. I seen wise guys before. Go out with the grain teams after
dinner. They're out pickin' up barley with
the thrashin' machines. Go out with Slim's
team.

GEORGE. Slim?

BOSS. Yeah. Big, tall skinner. You'll see him
at dinner. (*Up to this time the* BOSS *has been
full of business. He has been calm and*

suspicious. In the following lines he relaxes, but gradually, as though he wanted to talk but felt always the burden of his position. He turns toward the door, but hesitates and allows a little warmth into his manner.) Been on the road long?

GEORGE (*obviously on guard*). We was three days in 'Frisco lookin' at the boards.

BOSS (*with heavy jocularity*). Didn't go to no night clubs, I 'spose?

GEORGE (*stiffly*). We was lookin' for a job.

BOSS (*attempting to be friendly*). That's a great town if you got a little jack, Frisco.

GEORGE (*refusing to be drawn in*). We didn't have no jack for nothing like that.

BOSS (*realizes there is no contact to establish; grows rigid with his position again*). Go out with the grain teams after dinner. When my hands work hard they get pie and when they loaf they bounce down the road on their can. You ask anybody about me. (*He turns and walks out of bunkhouse.*)

GEORGE (*turns to* LENNIE). So you wasn't gonna say a word! You was gonna leave your big flapper shut. I was gonna do the talkin'. . . . You goddamn near lost us the job!

LENNIE (*stares hopelessly at his hands*). I forgot.

GEORGE. You forgot. You always forget. Now, he's got his eye on us. Now, we gotta be careful and not make no slips. You keep your big flapper shut after this.

LENNIE. He talked like a kinda nice guy towards the last.

GEORGE (*angrily*). He's the boss, ain't he? Well, he's the boss first an' a nice guy afterwards. Don't you have nothin' to do with no boss, except do your work and draw your pay. You can't never tell whether you're talkin' to the nice guy or the boss. Just keep your goddamn mouth shut. Then you're all right.

LENNIE. George?

GEORGE. What you want now?

LENNIE. I wasn't kicked in the head w[ith] no horse, was I, George?

GEORGE. Be a damn good thing if you w[as]. Save everybody a hell of a lot of trou[ble].

LENNIE (*flattered*). You says I was y[our] cousin.

GEORGE. Well, that was a goddamn lie. A[nd] I'm glad it was. Why, if I was a rela[tion] of yours—(*He stops and listens, then s[teps] to the front door, and looks out.*) Say, w[hat] the hell you doin', listenin'?

CANDY (*comes slowly into the room. B[y a] rope, he leads an ancient drag-footed, b[lind] sheep dog. Guides it from running int[o a] table leg, with the rope. Sits down o[n a] box, and presses the hind quarters of the dog down*). Naw . . . I wasn't listenin'. I was just standin' in the shade a min[ute] scratchin' my dog. I jest now finis[hed] swamping out the washhouse.

GEORGE. You was pokin' your big nose [in] our business! I don't like nosey guys.

CANDY (*looks uneasily from* GEORGE [to] LENNIE *and then back*). I jest come there[.] I didn't hear nothing you guys was sayi[n'] ain't interested in nothing you was sa[y.] A guy on a ranch don't never listen. [An'] he don't ast no questions.

GEORGE (*slightly mollified*). Damn r[ight] he don't! Not if the guy wants to [keep] workin' long. (*His manner changes*). Th[at's] a helluva ole dog.

CANDY. Yeah. I had him ever since he w[as a] pup. God, he was a good sheep dog, w[hen] he was young. (*Rubs his cheek with [his] knuckles.*) How'd you like the boss?

GEORGE. Pretty good! Seemed all right.

CANDY. He's a nice fella. You got ta [take] him right, of course. He's runnin' this ra[nch.] He don't take no nonsense.

GEORGE. What time do we eat? Ele[ven] thirty? (CURLEY *enters. He is dresse[d in] working clothes. He wears brown h[igh] heeled boots and has a glove on his [left] hand.*)

CURLEY. Seen my ole man?

NDY. He was here just a minute ago, rley. Went over to the cookhouse, I nk.

RLEY. I'll try to catch him. (*Looking over the new men, measuring them. Unsciously bends his elbow and closes his nd and goes into a slight crouch. He lks gingerly close to* LENNIE.) You the w guys my ole man was waitin' for?

ORGE. Yeah. We just come in.

RLEY. How's it come you wasn't here s morning?

ORGE. Got off the bus too soon.

RLEY (*again addressing* LENNIE). My ole n got to get the grain out. Ever bucked ley?

ORGE (*quickly*). Hell, yes. Done a lot of

RLEY. I mean him. (*To* LENNIE.) Ever cked barley?

ORGE. Sure he has.

RLEY (*irritatedly*). Let the big guy talk!

ORGE. 'Spose he don't want ta talk?

RLEY (*pugnaciously*). By Christ, he's gotta k when he's spoke to. What the hell you vin' into this for?

ORGE (*stands up and speaks coldly*). Him l me travel together.

RLEY. Oh, so it's that way?

ORGE (*tense and motionless*). What way?

LEY (*letting the subject drop*). And you n't let the big guy talk? Is that it?

ORGE. He can talk if he wants to tell you thing. (*He nods slightly to* LENNIE.)

NNIE (*in a frightened voice*). We just e in.

LEY. Well, next time you answer when 're spoke to, then.

RGE. He didn't do nothing to you.

LEY (*measuring him*). You drawin' cards hand?

GEORGE (*quietly*). I might.

CURLEY (*stares at him for a moment, his threat moving to the future*). I'll see you get a chance to ante, anyway. (*He walks out of the room.*)

GEORGE (*after he has made his exit*). Say, what the hell's he got on his shoulder? Lennie didn't say nothing to him.

CANDY (*looks cautiously at the door*). That's the boss's son. Curley's pretty handy. He done quite a bit in the ring. The guys say he's pretty handy.

GEORGE. Well, let 'im be handy. He don't have to take after Lennie. Lennie didn't do nothing to him.

CANDY (*considering*). Well . . . tell you what, Curley's like a lot a little guys. He hates big guys. He's alla time pickin' scraps with big guys. Kinda like he's mad at 'em because *he* ain't a big guy. You seen little guys like that, ain't you—always scrappy?

GEORGE. Sure, I seen plenty tough little guys. But this here Curley better not make no mistakes about Lennie. Lennie ain't handy, see, but this Curley punk's gonna get hurt if he messes around with Lennie.

CANDY (*skeptically*). Well, Curley's pretty handy. You know, it never did seem right to me. 'Spose Curley jumps a big guy and licks him. Everybody says what a game guy Curley is. Well, 'spose he jumps 'im and gits licked, everybody says the big guy oughta pick somebody his own size. Seems like Curley ain't givin' nobody a chance.

GEORGE (*watching the door*). Well, he better watch out for Lennie. Lennie ain't no fighter. But Lennie's strong and quick and Lennie don't know no rules. (*Walks to the square table, and sits down on one of the boxes. Picks up scattered cards and pulls them together and shuffles them.*)

CANDY. Don't tell Curley I said none of this. He'd slough me! He jus' don't give a damn. Won't ever get canned because his ole man's the boss!

GEORGE (*cuts the cards. Turns over and looks at each one as he throws it down*). This guy Curley sounds like a son-of-a-bitch to me! I don't like mean little guys!

CANDY. Seems to me like he's worse lately. He got married a couple of weeks ago. Wife lives over in the boss's house. Seems like Curley's worse'n ever since he got married. Like he's settin' on a ant-hill an' a big red ant come up an' nipped 'im on the turnip. Just feels so goddanm miserable he'll strike at anything that moves. I'm kinda sorry for 'im.

GEORGE. Maybe he's showin' off for his wife.

CANDY. You seen that glove on his left hand?

GEORGE. Sure I seen it!

CANDY. Well, that glove's full of vaseline.

GEORGE. Vaseline? What the hell for?

CANDY. Curley says he's keepin' that hand soft for his wife.

GEORGE. That's a dirty kind of a thing to tell around.

CANDY. I ain't quite so sure. I seen such funny things a guy will do to try to be nice. I ain't sure. But you jus' wait till you see Curley's wife!

GEORGE (begins to lay out a solitaire hand, speaks casually). Is she purty?

CANDY. Yeah. Purty, but—

GEORGE (studying his cards). But what?

CANDY. Well, she got the eye.

GEORGE (still playing at his solitaire hand). Yeah? Married two weeks an' got the eye? Maybe that's why Curley's pants is fulla ants.

CANDY. Yes, sir, I seen her give Slim the eye. Slim's a jerkline skinner. Hell of a nice fella. Well, I seen her give Slim the eye. Curley never seen it. And I seen her give a skinner named Carlson the eye.

GEORGE (pretending a very mild interest). Looks like we was gonna have fun!

CANDY (stands up). Know what I think? (Waits for an answer. GEORGE doesn't answer.) Well, I think Curley's married himself a tart.

GEORGE (casually). He ain't the first. Bl[ack] queen on a red king. Yes, sir . . . the[re's] plenty done that!

CANDY (moves towards the door, leading [the] dog out with him). I got to be settin' out [the] wash basins for the guys. The teams'll [be] in before long. You guys gonna buck barl[ey?]

GEORGE. Yeah.

CANDY. You won't tell Curley nothing I sa[id?]

GEORGE. Hell, no!

CANDY (just before he goes out the door, [he] turns back). Well, you look her over, mis[ter.] You see if she ain't a tart! (He exi[ts.])

GEORGE (continuing to play out his solita[ire.] He turns to LENNIE). Look, Lennie, [. . .] here ain't no set-up. You gonna have trou[ble] with that Curley guy. I seen that kind [be-] fore. You know what he's doin'. He's ki[nda] feelin' you out. He figures he's got [you] scared. And he's gonna take a sock at y[ou] first chance he gets.

LENNIE (frightened). I don't want [no] trouble. Don't let him sock me, George!

GEORGE. I hate them kind of bastards. I s[een] plenty of 'em. Like the ole guy says: "Cu[rley] don't take no chances. He always figure[s to] win." (Thinks for a moment.) If [he] tangles with you, Lennie, we're goin' [in] the can. Don't make no mistake about t[hat.] He's the boss's kid. Look, you try to k[eep] away from him, will you? Don't never sp[eak] to him. If he comes in here you move c[lear] to the other side of the room. Will you [re-] member that, Lennie?

LENNIE (mourning). I don't want no trou[ble.] I never done nothing to him!

GEORGE. Well, that won't do you no go[od] if Curley wants to set himself up fo[r a] fighter. Just don't have nothing to do w[ith] him. Will you remember?

LENNIE. Sure, George . . . I ain't gonna [say] a word. (Sounds of the teams comin[g in] from the fields, jingling of harness, cr[eak] of heavy laden axles, men talking to [and] cussing the horses. Crack of a whip and f[rom] a distance a voice calling.)

SLIM'S VOICE. Stable buck! Hey! Stable b[uck!]

GEORGE. Here come the guys. Just don't say nothing.

LENNIE (*timidly*). You ain't mad, George?

GEORGE. I ain't mad at you. I'm mad at this here Curley bastard! I wanted we should get a little stake together. Maybe a hundred dollars. You keep away from Curley.

LENNIE. Sure I will. I won't say a word.

GEORGE (*hesitating*). Don't let 'im pull you in—but—if the son-of-a-bitch socks you—let him have it!

LENNIE. Let him have what, George?

GEORGE. Never mind. . . . Look, if you get in any kind of trouble, you remember what I told you to do.

LENNIE. If I get in any trouble, you ain't gonna let me tend the rabbits?

GEORGE. That's not what I mean. You remember where we slept last night. Down by the river?

LENNIE. Oh, sure I remember. I go there and hide in the brush until you come for me.

GEORGE. That's it. Hide till I come for you. Don't let nobody see you. Hide in the brush by the river. Now say that over.

LENNIE. Hide in the brush by the river. Down in the brush by the river.

GEORGE. If you get in trouble.

LENNIE. If I get in trouble.

A brake screeckes outside and a call: "stable buck, oh, stable buck!" "Where the hell's that goddamn nigger?" Suddenly CURLEY'S WIFE is standing in the door. Full, heavily rouged lips. Wide-spaced, made-up eyes, her fingernails are bright red, her hair hangs in little rolled clusters like sausages. She wears a cotton house dress and red mules, on the insteps of which are little bouquets of red ostrich feathers. GEORGE and LENNIE look up at her.)

CURLEY'S WIFE. I'm lookin' for Curley!

GEORGE (*looks away from her*). He was in here a minute ago but he went along.

CURLEY'S WIFE (*puts her hands behind her back and leans against the door frame so that her body is thrown forward*). You're the new fellas that just come, ain't you?

GEORGE (*sullenly*). Yeah.

CURLEY'S WIFE (*bridles a little and inspects her fingernails*). Sometimes Curley's in here.

GEORGE (*brusquely*). Well, he ain't now!

CURLEY'S WIFE (*playfully*). Well, if he ain't, I guess I'd better look some place else. (LENNIE *watches her, fascinated.*)

GEORGE. If I see Curley I'll pass the word you was lookin' for him.

CURLEY'S WIFE. Nobody can't blame a person for lookin'.

GEORGE. That depends what she's lookin' for.

CURLEY'S WIFE (*a little wearily, dropping her coquetry*). I'm jus' lookin' for somebody to talk to. Don't you never jus' want to talk to somebody?

SLIM (*offstage*). Okay! Put that lead pair in the north stalls.

CURLEY'S WIFE (*to* SLIM, *offstage*). Hi, Slim!

SLIM (*voice offstage*). Hello.

CURLEY'S WIFE. I—I'm trying to find Curley.

SLIM'S VOICE (*offstage*). Well, you ain't tryin' very hard. I seen him goin' in your house.

CURLEY'S WIFE. I—I'm tryin' to find Curley. *and* LENNIE). I gotta be goin'! (*She exits hurriedly.*)

GEORGE (*looking around at* LENNIE). Jesus, what a tramp! So, that's what Curley picks for a wife. God Almighty, did you smell that stink she's got on? I can still smell her. Don't have to see *her* to know she's around.

LENNIE. She's purty!

GEORGE. Yeah. And she's sure hidin' it. Curley got his work ahead of him.

LENNIE (*still staring at the doorway where she was*). Gosh, she's purty!

GEORGE (*turning furiously at him*). Listen to me, you crazy bastard. Don't you even look at that bitch. I don't care what she says or what she does. I seen 'em poison before, but I ain't never seen no piece of jail bait worse than her. Don't you even smell near her!

LENNIE. I never smelled, George!

GEORGE. No, you never. But when she was standin' there showin' her legs, you wasn't lookin' the other way neither!

LENNIE. I never meant no bad things, George. Honest I never.

GEORGE. Well, you keep away from her. You let Curley take the rap. He let himself in for it. (*Disgustedly.*) Glove full of vaseline. I bet he's eatin' raw eggs and writin' to patent-medicine houses.

LENNIE (*cries out*). I don't like this place. This ain't no good place. I don't like this place!

GEORGE. Listen—I don't like it here no better than you do. But we gotta keep it till we get a stake. We're flat. We gotta get a stake. (*Goes back to the table, thoughtfully.*) If we can get just a few dollars in the poke we'll shove off and go up to the American River and pan gold. Guy can make a couple dollars a day there.

LENNIE (*eagerly*). Let's go, George. Let's get out of here. It's mean here.

GEORGE (*shortly*). I tell you we gotta stay a little while. We gotta get a stake. (*The sounds of running water and rattle of basins are heard.*) Shut up now, the guys'll be comin' in! (*Pensively.*) Maybe we ought to wash up. . . . But hell, we ain't done nothin' to get dirty.

SLIM (*enters. He is a tall, dark man in blue jeans and a short denim jacket. He carries a crushed Stetson hat under his arm and combs his long dark damp hair straight back. He stands and moves with a kind of majesty. He finishes combing his hair. Smoothes out his crushed hat, creases it in the middle and puts it on. In a gentle voice*). It's brighter'n a bitch outside. Can't hardly see nothing in here. You the new guys?

GEORGE. Just come.

SLIM. Goin' to buck barley?

GEORGE. That's what the boss says.

SLIM. Hope you get on my team.

GEORGE. Boss said we'd go with a jerk-line skinner named Slim.

SLIM. That's me.

GEORGE. You a jerk-line skinner?

SLIM (*in self-disparagement*). I can snap 'em around a little.

GEORGE (*terribly impressed*). That kinda makes you Jesus Christ on this ranch, don' it?

SLIM (*obviously pleased*). Oh, nuts!

GEORGE (*chuckles*). Like the man says, "Th boss tells you what to do. But if you wan to know how to do it, you got to ask th mule skinner." The man says any guy tha can drive twelve Arizona jack rabbits wit a jerk line can fall in a toilet and come u with a mince pie under each arm.

SLIM (*laughing*). Well, I hope you get o my team. I got a pair a punks that don know a barley bag from a blue ball. Yo guys ever bucked any barley?

GEORGE. Hell, yes. I ain't nothin' to screa about, but that big guy there can put more grain alone than most pairs can.

SLIM (*looks approvingly at* GEORGE). Y guy's travel around together?

GEORGE. Sure. We kinda look after ea other. (*Points at* LENNIE *with his thum* He ain't bright. Hell of a good work though. Hell of a nice fella too. I've know him for a long time.

SLIM. Ain't many guys travel around gether. I don't know why. Maybe eve body in the whole damn world is scared each other.

GEORGE. It's a lot nicer to go 'round wit guy you know. You get used to it an' t it ain't no fun alone any more. (*E* CARLSON. *Big-stomached, powerful man.* head still drips water from scrubbing dousing.*)

CARLSON. Hello, Slim! (*He looks at* GEO *and* LENNIE.)

м. These guys just come.

кLSON. Glad to meet ya! My name's Carl-
ь.

ʀGE. I'm George Milton. This here's Len-
Small.

ĸLSON. Glad to meet you. He ain't very
all. (*Chuckles at his own joke.*) He ain't
all at all. Meant to ask you, Slim, how's
ɪr bitch? I seen she wasn't under your
gon this morning.

м. She slang her pups last night. Nine of
a. I drowned four of 'em right off. She
ıldn't feed that many.

кLSON. Got five left, huh?

м. Yeah. Five. I kep' the biggest.

кLSON. What kinda dogs you think they
ına be?

м. I don't know. Some kind of shepherd,
uess. That's the most kind I seen around
e when she's in heat.

кLSON (*laughs*). I had an airdale an' a guy
vn the road got one of them little white
ozy dogs, well, she was in heat and the
locks her up. But my airedale, named
m he was, he et a woodshed clear down
the roots to get to her. Guy come over
day, he's sore as hell, he says, "I
uldn't mind if my bitch had pups, but
rist Almighty, this morning she slang a
er of Shetland ponies. . . ." (*Takes off
hat and scratches his head.*) Got five
os, huh! Gonna keep all of 'em?

м. I don' know, gotta keep 'em awhile,
hey can drink Lulu's milk.

ьsoN (*thoughtfully*). Well, looka here,
n, I been thinkin'. That dog of Candy's
o goddamn old he can't hardly walk.
ıks like hell. Every time Candy brings
t in the bunkhouse. I can smell him
or three days. Why don't you get Candy
hoot his ol' dog, and give him one of
n pups to raise up? I can smell that dog
ıle off. Got no teeth. Can't eat. Candy
s him milk. He can't chew nothing else.
l leadin' him around on a string so he

don't bump into things . . . (*The triangle
outside begins to ring wildly. Continues for
a few moments, then stops suddenly.*)
There she goes! (*Outside there is a burst
of voices as a group of men go by.*)

SLIM (*to* LENNIE *and* GEORGE). You guys
better come on while they's still somethin'
to eat. Won't be nothing left in a couple
of minutes. (*Exit* SLIM *and* CARLSON, LENNIE
watches GEORGE *excitedly.*)

LENNIE. George!

GEORGE (*rumpling his cards into a pile*).
Yeah, I heard 'im, Lennie . . . I'll ask 'im!

LENNIE (*excitedly*). A brown and white
one.

GEORGE. Come on, let's get dinner. I don't
know whether he's got a brown and white
one.

LENNIE. You ask him right away, George, so
he won't kill no more of 'em!

GEORGE. Sure! Come on now—le's go. (*They
start for the door.*)

CURLEY (*bounces in, angrily*). You seen a
girl around here?

GEORGE (*coldly*). 'Bout half an hour ago,
mebbe.

CURLEY. Well, what the hell was she doin'?

GEORGE (*insultingly*). She *said* she was lookin' for you.

CURLEY (*measures both men with his eyes
for a moment*). Which way did she go?

GEORGE. I don't know. I didn't watch her
go. (CURLEY *scowls at him a moment and
then turns and hurries out the door.*) You
know, Lennie, I'm scared I'm gonna tangle
with that bastard myself. I hate his guts!
Jesus Christ, come on! They won't be a
damn thing left to eat.

LENNIE. Will you ask him about a brown
and white one? (*They exeunt.*)

CURTAIN

ACT TWO

SCENE I

About seven-thirty Friday evening.
Same bunkhouse interior as in last scene.
The evening light is seen coming in through the window, but it is quite dark in t
interior of the bunkhouse.
From outside comes the sound of a horseshoe game. Thuds on the dirt and occasion
clangs as a shoe hits the peg. Now and then voices are raised in approval or derisio
"That's a good one." . . . "Goddamn right it's a good one." . . . "Here goes for a ring
I need a ringer." . . . "Goddamn near got it, too."
SLIM and GEORGE come into the darkening bunkhouse together. SLIM reaches up a.
turns on the tin-shaded electric light. Sits down on a box at the table. GEORGE takes
place opposite.

SLIM. It wasn't nothing. I would of had to drown most of them pups anyway. No need to thank me about that.

GEORGE. Wasn't much to you, mebbe, but it was a hell of a lot to him. Jesus Christ, I don't know how we're gonna get him to sleep in here. He'll want to stay right out in the barn. We gonna have trouble keepin' him from gettin' right in the box with them pups.

SLIM. Say, you sure was right about him. Maybe he ain't bright—but I never seen such a worker. He damn near killed his partner buckin' barley. He'd take his end of that sack (*a gesture*) pretty near kill his partner. God Almighty, I never seen such a strong guy.

GEORGE (*proudly*). You just tell Lennie what to do and he'll do it if it don't take no figuring. (*Outside the sound of the horseshoe game goes on: "Son of a bitch if I can win a goddamn game." . . . "Me neither. You'd think them shoes was anvils."*)

SLIM. Funny how you and him string along together.

GEORGE. What's so funny about it?

SLIM. Oh, I don't know. Hardly none of the guys ever travels around together. I hardly never seen two guys travel together. You know how the hands are. They come in and get their bunk and work a month and then they quit and go on alone. Never seem to give a damn about nobody. Jest seems kinda funny. A cuckoo like him and a smart guy like you traveling together.

GEORGE. I ain't so bright neither or I would be buckin' barley for my fifty and found. I was bright, if I was even a little bit sma I'd have my own place and I'd be bring in my own crops 'stead of doin' all the wo and not gettin' what comes up out of ground. (*He falls silent for a moment.*)

SLIM. A guy'd like to do that. Sometimes like to cuss a string of mules that was own mules.

GEORGE. It ain't so funny, him and me go round together. Him and me was both bo in Auburn. I knowed his aunt. She took h when he was a baby and raised him When his aunt died Lennie jus' come alo with me, out workin'. Got kinda used each other after a little while.

SLIM. Uh huh.

GEORGE. First I used to have a hell of a of fun with him. Used to play jokes on because he was too dumb to take care himself. But, hell, he was too dumb e to know when he had a joke played on h (*Sarcastically.*) Hell, yes, I had fun! M me seem goddamn smart alongside of h

SLIM. I seen it that way.

GEORGE. Why, he'd do any damn thin tole him. If I tole him to walk over a c over he'd go. You know that wasn't so da much fun after a while. He never got m about it, neither. I've beat hell out of l and he could bust every bone in my b jest with his hands. But he never lifte finger against me.

SLIM (*braiding a bull whip*). Even if socked him, wouldn't he?

GE. No, by God! I tell you what made
stop playing jokes. One day a bunch of
s was standin' aroun' up on the Sacra-
to river. I was feelin' pretty smart. I
as to Lennie and I says, "Jump in."

. What happened?

GE. He jumps. Couldn't swim a stroke.
damn near drowned. And he was so nice
ne for pullin' him out. Clean forgot I
him to jump in. Well, I ain't done
in' like that no more. Makes me kinda
tellin' about it.

. He's a nice fella. A guy don't need
ense to be a nice fella. Seems to be some-
s it's jest the other way round. Take a
smart guy, he ain't hardly ever a nice

GE (stacking the scattered cards and
ing his solitaire game ready again). I
got no people. I seen guys that go round
the ranches alone. That ain't no good.
y don't have no fun. After a while they
mean.

(quietly). Yeah, I seen 'em get mean.
en 'em get so they don't want to talk to
ody. Some ways they got to. You take
unch of guys all livin' in one room an'
od they got to mind their own business.
t the only private thing a guy's got is
re he come from and where he's goin'.

GE. 'Course Lennie's a goddamn nuis-
most of the time. But you get used to
' round with a guy and you can't get rid
im. I mean you get used to him an' you
get rid of bein' used to him. I'm sure
pin' at the mouth. I ain't told nobody
his before.

. Do you want to git rid of him?

GE. Well, he gets in trouble all the time.
use he's so goddamn dumb. Like what
ened in Weed. (He stops, alarmed at
t he has said.) You wouldn't tell no-
?

(calmly). What did he do in Weed?

GE. You wouldn't tell?—No, 'course you
ldn't.

. What did he do?

GE. Well, he seen this girl in a red
s. Dumb bastard like he is he wants to
h everything he likes. Jest wants to feel

of it. So he reaches out to feel this red
dress. Girl lets out a squawk and that gets
Lennie all mixed up. He holds on 'cause
that's the only thing he can think to do.

SLIM. The hell!

GEORGE. Well, this girl squawks her head
off. I'm right close and I hear all the yellin',
so I comes a-running. By that time Lennie's
scared to death. You know, I had to sock
him over the head with a fence picket to
make him let go.

SLIM. So what happens then?

GEORGE (carefully building his solitaire
hand). Well, she runs in and tells the law
she's been raped. The guys in Weed start
out to lynch Lennie. So there we sit in an
irrigation ditch, under water all the rest
of that day. Got only our heads stickin' out
of water, up under the grass that grows
out of the side of the ditch. That night we
run outa there.

SLIM. Didn't hurt the girl none, huh?

GEORGE. Hell, no, he jes' scared her.

SLIM. He's a funny guy.

GEORGE. Funny! Why, one time, you know
what that big baby done! He was walking
along a road—(Enter LENNIE through the
door. He wears his coat over his shoulder
like a cape and walks hunched over.) Hi,
Lennie. How do you like your pup?

LENNIE (breathlessly). He's brown and white
jus' like I wanted. (Goes directly to his bunk
and lies down. Face to the wall and knees
drawn up.)

GEORGE (puts down his cards deliberately).
Lennie!

LENNIE (over his shoulder). Huh? What
you want, George?

GEORGE (sternly). I tole ya, ya couldn't bring
that pup in here.

LENNIE. What pup, George? I ain't got no
pup. (GEORGE goes quickly over to him,
grabs him by the shoulder and rolls him
over. He picks up a tiny puppy from where
LENNIE has been concealing it against his
stomach.)

LENNIE (quickly). Give him to me, George.

GEORGE. You get right up and take this pup
to the nest. He's got to sleep with his

mother. Ya want ta kill him? Jes' born last night and ya take him out of the nest. Ya take him back or I'll tell Slim not to let you have him.

LENNIE (*pleadingly*). Give him to me, George. I'll take him back. I didn't mean no bad thing, George. Honest I didn't. I jus' want to pet him a little.

GEORGE (*giving the pup to him*). All right, you get him back there quick. And don't you take him out no more. (LENNIE *scuttles out of the room.*)

SLIM. Jesus, he's just like a kid, ain't he?

GEORGE. Sure he's like a kid. There ain't no more harm in him than a kid neither, except he's so strong. I bet he won't come in here to sleep tonight. He'll sleep right alongside that box in the barn. Well, let him. He ain't doin' no harm out there. (*The light has faded out outside and it appears quite dark outside. Enter* CANDY *leading his old dog by a string.*)

CANDY. Hello, Slim. Hello, George. Didn't neither of you play horseshoes?

SLIM. I don't like to play every night.

CANDY (*goes to his bunk and sits down, presses the old blind dog to the floor beside him*). Either you guys got a slug of whiskey? I got a gut ache.

SLIM. I ain't. I'd drink it myself if I had. And I ain't got no gut ache either.

CANDY. Goddamn cabbage give it to me. I knowed it was goin' to before I ever et it. (*Enter* CARLSON *and* WHIT.)

CARLSON. Jesus, how that nigger can pitch shoes!

SLIM. He's plenty good.

WHIT. Damn right he is.

CARLSON. Yeah. He don't give nobody else a chance to win. (*Stops and sniffs the air. Looks around until he sees* CANDY's *dog.*) God Almighty, that dog stinks. Get him outa here, Candy. I don't know nothing that stinks as bad as ole dogs. You got to get him outa here.

CANDY (*lying down on his bunk, reaches over and pats the ancient dog, speaks softly*).

I been round him so much I never not how he stinks.

CARLSON. Well, I can't stand him in he That stink hangs round even after h gone. (*Walks over and stands looking do at the dog.*) Got no teeth. All stiff w rheumatism. He ain't no good to y Candy. Why don't you shoot him?

CANDY (*uncomfortably*). Well, hell, I ł him so long! Had him since he was a p I herded sheep with him. (*Proudly.*) Y wouldn't think it to look at him now. was the best damn sheep dog I ever se

GEORGE. I knowed a guy in Weed that ł an airedale that could herd sheep. Lear it from the other dogs.

CARLSON (*sticking to his point*). Loo Candy. This ole dog jus' suffers itself all time. If you was to take him out and sh him—right in the back of the head . (*Leans over and points.*) . . . right th why he never'd know what hit him.

CANDY (*unhappily*). No, I couldn't do t I had him too long.

CARLSON (*insisting*). He don't have no no more. He stinks like hell. Tell you w I'll do. I'll shoot him for you. Then it w be you that done it.

CANDY (*sits up on the bunk, rubbing whiskers nervously, speaks plaintively* had him from a pup.

WHIT. Let 'im alone, Carl. I ain't a g dog that matters. It's the way the guy f about the dog. Hell, I had a mutt one wouldn't a traded for a field trial poir

CARLSON (*being persuasive*). Well, Ca ain't being nice to him, keeping him a Lookit, Slim's bitch got a litter right n I bet you Slim would give ya one of th pups to raise up, wouldn't ya, Slim?

SLIM (*studying the dog*). Yeah. You have a pup if you want to.

CANDY (*helplessly*) Mebbe it would h (*After a moment's pause, positively.*) A don't mind taking care of him.

CARLSON. Aw, he'd be better off dead. way I'd shoot him he wouldn't feel noth I'd put the gun right there. (*Points* his toe.) Right back of the head.

WHIT. Aw, let 'im alone, Carl.

CARLSON. Why, hell, he wouldn't even quiver.

WHIT. Let 'im alone. (*He produces a magazine.*) Say, did you see this? Did you see this in the book here?

CARLSON. See what?

WHIT. Right there. Read that.

CARLSON. I don't want to read nothing. . . . It'll be all over in a minute, Candy. Come

WHIT. Did you see it, Slim? Go on, read it. Read it out loud.

SLIM. What is it?

WHIT. Read it.

SLIM (*reads slowly*). "Dear Editor: I read your mag for six years and I think it is the best on the market. I like stories by Peter Rand. I think he is a whing-ding. Give us more like the Dark Rider. I don't write many letters. Just thought I would tell you I think your mag is the best dime's worth I ever spen'." (*Looks up questioningly.*) What you want me to read that for?

WHIT. Go on, read the name at the bottom.

SLIM (*reading*). "Yours for Success, William Tenner." (*Looks up at* WHIT.) What ya want me to read that for?

CARLSON. Come on, Candy—what you say?

WHIT (*taking the magazine and closing it impressively. Talks to cover* CARLSON). You can't remember Bill Tenner? Worked here about three months ago?

SLIM (*thinking*). Little guy? Drove a cultivator?

WHIT. That's him. That's the guy.

CARLSON (*has refused to be drawn into this conversation*). Look, Candy. If you want me to, I'll put the old devil outa his misery right now and get it over with. There ain't nothing left for him. Can't eat, can't see, can't hardly walk. Tomorrow you can pick of Slim's pups.

SLIM. Sure . . . I got a lot of 'em.

CANDY (*hopefully*). You ain't got no gun.

CARLSON. The hell, I ain't. Got a Luger. It won't hurt him none at all.

CANDY. Mebbe tomorrow. Let's wait till tomorrow.

CARLSON. I don't see no reason for it. (*Goes to his bunk, pulls a bag from underneath, takes a Luger pistol out.*) Let's get it over with. We can't sleep with him stinking around in here. (*He snaps a shell into the chamber, sets the safety and puts the pistol into his hip pocket.*)

SLIM (*as* CANDY *looks toward him for help*). Better let him go, Candy.

CANDY (*looks at each person for some hope.* WHIT *makes a gesture of protest and then resigns himself. The others look away, to avoid responsibility. At last, very softly and hopelessly*). All right. Take him.
(*He doesn't look down at the dog at all. Lies back on his bunk and crosses his arms behind his head and stares at the ceiling.* CARLSON *picks up the string, helps the dog to its feet.*)

CARLSON. Come, boy. Come on, boy. (*To* CANDY, *apologetically.*) He won't even feel it. (CANDY *does not move nor answer him.*) Come on, boy. That's the stuff. Come on. (*He leads the dog toward the door.*)

SLIM. Carlson?

CARLSON. Yeah.

SLIM (*curtly*). Take a shovel.

CARLSON. Oh, sure, I get you.
(*Exit* CARLSON *with the dog.* GEORGE *follows to the door, shuts it carefully and sets the latch.* CANDY *lies rigidly on his bunk. The next scene is one of silence and quick staccato speeches.*)

SLIM (*loudly*). One of my lead mules got a bad hoof. Got to get some tar on it. (*There is a silence.*)

GEORGE (*loudly*). Anybody like to play a little euchre?

WHIT. I'll lay out a few with you. (*They take places opposite each other at the table but* GEORGE *does not shuffle the cards. He ripples the edge of the deck. Everybody looks over at him. He stops. Silence again.*)

SLIM (*compassionately*). Candy, you can have any of them pups you want. (*There is no answer from* CANDY. *There is a little gnawing noise on the stage.*)

GEORGE. Sounds like there was a rat under there. We ought to set a trap there. (*Deep silence again.*)

WHIT (*exasperated*). What the hell is takin' him so long? Lay out some cards, why don't you? We ain't gonna get no euchre played this way.
(GEORGE *studies the backs of the cards. And after a long silence there is a shot in the distance. All the men start a bit, look quickly at* CANDY. *For a moment he continues to stare at the ceiling and then rolls slowly over and faces the wall.* GEORGE *shuffles the cards noisily and deals them.*)

GEORGE. Well, let's get to it.

WHIT (*still to cover the moment*). Yeah ... I guess you guys really come here to work, huh?

GEORGE. How do you mean?

WHIT (*chuckles*). Well, you come on a Friday. You got two days to work till Sunday.

GEORGE. I don't see how you figure.

WHIT. You do if you been round these big ranches much. A guy that wants to look over a ranch comes in Saturday afternoon. He gets Saturday night supper, three meals on Sunday and he can quit Monday morning after breakfast without turning a hand. But you come to work on Friday noon. You got ta put in a day and a half no matter how ya figure it.

GEORGE (*quietly*). We're goin' stick around awhile. Me and Lennie's gonna roll up a stake. (*Door opens and the Negro stable buck puts in his head. A lean-faced Negro with pained eyes.*)

CROOKS. Mr. Slim.

SLIM (*who has been watching* CANDY *the whole time*). Huh? Oh, hello, Crooks, what's the matter?

CROOKS. You tole me to warm up tar for that mule's foot. I got it warm now.

SLIM. Oh, sure, Crooks. I'll come right out and put it on.

CROOKS. I can do it for you if you want, Mr. Slim.

SLIM (*standing up*). Naw, I'll take care of my own team.

CROOKS. Mr. Slim.

SLIM. Yeah.

CROOKS. That big new guy is messing rou your pups in the barn.

SLIM. Well, he ain't doin' no harm. I g him one of them pups.

CROOKS. Just thought I'd tell ya. He's tak 'em out of the nest and handling 'em. T won't do 'em no good.

SLIM. Oh, he won't hurt 'em.

GEORGE (*looks up from his cards*). If t crazy bastard is foolin' round too m jus' kick him out. (SLIM *follows the sta buck out.*)

WHIT (*examining his cards*). Seen the kid yet?

GEORGE. What kid?

WHIT. Why, Curley's new wife.

GEORGE (*cautiously*). Yeah, I seen her.

WHIT. Well, ain't she a lulu?

GEORGE. I ain't seen that much of her.

WHIT. Well, you stick around and keep y eyes open. You'll see plenty of her. I ne seen nobody like her. She's just workin everybody all the time. Seems like s even workin' on the stable buck. I d know what the hell she wants.

GEORGE (*casually*). Been any trouble s she got here? (*Obviously neither ma interested in the card game.* WHIT *lays do his hand and* GEORGE *gathers the card and lays out a solitaire hand.*)

WHIT. I see what you mean. No, they been no trouble yet. She's only been he couple of weeks. Curley's got yellow jac in his drawers, but that's all so far. E time the guys is around she shows up. S lookin' for Curley. Or she thought she somethin' layin' around and she's loo for that. Seems like she can't keep away f guys. And Curley's runnin' round like lookin' for a dirt road. But they ain' no trouble.

GEORGE. Ranch with a bunch of guys ain't no place for a girl. Specially like

IT. If she's give you any ideas you ought come in town with us guys tomorrow ht.

RGE. Why, what's doin'?

IT. Just the usual thing. We go in to old y's place. Hell of a nice place. Old Susy . laugh. Always cracking jokes. Like she s when we come up on the front porch Saturday night: Susy opens the door and yells over her shoulder: "Get your coats girls, here comes the sheriff." She never s dirty neither. Got five girls there.

RGE. What does it set you back?

IT. Two and a half. You can get a shot of skey for fifteen cents. Susy got nice chairs set in too. If a guy don't want to flop, y, he can just set in them chairs and e a couple or three shots and just pass time of day. Susy don't give a damn. ain't rushin' guys through, or kicking m out if they don't want to flop.

RGE. Might go in and look the joint r.

IT. Sure. Come along. It's a hell of a lot un—her crackin' jokes all the time. Like says one time, she says: "I've knew ple that if they got a rag rug on the r and a kewpie doll lamp on the phono-ph they think they're runnin' a parlor se." That's Gladys's house she's talkin' ut. And Susy says: "I know what you s want," she says: "My girls is clean," she . "And there ain't no water in my skey," she says. "If any you guys want ook at a kewpie doll lamp and take your nce of gettin' burned, why, you know re to go." She says: "They's guys round e walkin' bowlegged because they liked ook at a kewpie doll lamp."

RGE. Gladys runs the other house, huh?

IT. Yeah. (*Enter* CARLSON. CANDY *looks at* .)

LSON. God, it's a dark night. (*Goes to his k; starts cleaning his pistol.*)

IT. We don't never go to Gladys's. dys gits three bucks, and two bits a shot she don't crack no jokes. But Susy's place lean and she got nice chairs. A guy can in there like he lived there. Don't let Manila Goo-Goos in, neither.

GEORGE. Aw, I don't know. Me and Lennie's rollin' up a stake. I might go in and set and have a shot, but I ain't puttin' out no two and a half.

WHIT. Well, a guy got to have some fun sometimes. (*Enter* LENNIE. LENNIE *creeps to his bunk and sits down.*)

GEORGE. Didn't bring him back in, did you, Lennie?

LENNIE. No, George, honest I didn't. See?

WHIT. Say, how about this euchre game?

GEORGE. Okay. I didn't think you wanted to play. (*Enter* CURLEY *excitedly.*)

CURLEY. Any you guys seen my wife?

WHIT. She ain't been here.

CURLEY (*looks threateningly about the room*). Where the hell's Slim?

GEORGE. Went out in the barn. He was goin' put some tar on a split hoof.

CURLEY. How long ago did he go?

GEORGE. Oh, five, ten minutes. (CURLEY *jumps out the door.*)

WHIT (*standing up*). I guess maybe I'd like to see this. Curley must be spoilin' or he wouldn't start for Slim. Curley's handy, god-damn handy. But just the same he better leave Slim alone.

GEORGE. Thinks Slim's with his wife, don't he?

WHIT. Looks like it. 'Course Slim ain't. Least I don't think Slim is. But I like to see the fuss if it comes off. Come on, le's go.

GEORGE. I don't want to git mixed up in nothing. Me and Lennie got to make a stake.

CARLSON (*finishes cleaning gun, puts it in his bag and stands up*). I'll look her over. Ain't seen a good fight in a hell of a while. (WHIT *and* CARLSON *exeunt.*)

GEORGE. You see Slim out in the barn?

LENNIE. Sure. He tole me I better not pet that pup no more, like I said.

GEORGE. Did you see that girl out there?

LENNIE. You mean Curley's girl?

GEORGE. Yeah. Did she come in the barn?

LENNIE (*cautiously*). No—anyways I never seen her.

GEORGE. You never seen Slim talkin' to her?

LENNIE. Uh-uh. She ain't been in the barn.

GEORGE. Okay. I guess them guys ain't gonna see no fight. If they's any fightin', Lennie, ya get out of the way and stay out.

LENNIE. I don't want no fight. (GEORGE *lays out his solitaire hand.* LENNIE *picks up a face card and studies it. Turns it over and studies it again.*) Both ends the same. George, why is it both ends the same?

GEORGE. I don't know. That jus' the way they make 'em. What was Slim doin' in the barn when you seen him?

LENNIE. Slim?

GEORGE. Sure, you seen him in the barn. He tole you not to pet the pups so much.

LENNIE. Oh. Yeah. He had a can of tar and a paint brush. I don't know what for.

GEORGE. You sure that girl didn't come in like she come in here today?

LENNIE. No, she never come.

GEORGE (*sighs*). You give me a good whorehouse every time. A guy can go in and get drunk and get it over all at once and no messes. And he knows how much it's goin' set him back. These tarts is jus' buckshot to a guy. (LENNIE *listens with admiration, moving his lips, and* GEORGE *continues.*) You remember Andy Cushman, Lennie? Went to grammar school same time as us?

LENNIE. The one that his ole lady used to make hot cakes for the kids?

GEORGE. Yeah. That's the one. You can remember if they's somepin to eat in it. (*Scores up some cards in his solitaire playing.*) Well, Andy's in San Quentin right now on account of a tart.

LENNIE. George?

GEORGE. Huh?

LENNIE. How long is it goin' be till we git that little place to live on the fat of the land?

GEORGE. I don't know. We gotta get a b stake together. I know a little place we c get cheap, but they ain't givin' it awa (CANDY *turns over and watches* GEORGE.)

LENNIE. Tell about that place, George.

GEORGE. I jus' tole you Jus' last night.

LENNIE. Go on, tell again.

GEORGE. Well, it's ten acres. Got a windmi Got a little shack on it and a chicken ru Got a kitchen orchard. Cherries, appl peaches, 'cots and nuts. Got a few berri There's a place for alfalfa and plenty wat to flood it. There's a pig pen. . . .

LENNIE (*breaking in*). And rabbits, Georg

GEORGE. I could easy build a few hutch And you could feed alfalfa to them rabbi

LENNIE. Damn right I could. (*Excitedly* You goddamn right I could.

GEORGE (*his voice growing warmer*). A we could have a few pigs. I'd build a smok house. And when we kill a pig we cou smoke the hams. When the salmon run the river we can catch a hundred of 'e Every Sunday we'd kill a chicken or rabb Mebbe we'll have a cow or a goat. And t cream is so goddamn thick you got to c it off the pan with a knife.

LENNIE (*watching him with wide ey softly*). We can live off the fat of the la

GEORGE. Sure. All kinds of vegetables in t garden and if we want a little whiskey can sell some eggs or somethin'. And wouldn't sleep in no bunkhouse. Nobo could can us in the middle of a job.

LENNIE (*begging*). Tell about the hou George.

GEORGE. Sure. We'd have a little house. A a room to ourselves. And it ain't enou land so we'd have to work too hard. Me six, seven hours a day only. We would have to buck no barley eleven hours a d And when we put in a crop, why we'd there to take that crop up. We'd know w come of our planting.

LENNIE (*eagerly*). And rabbits. And take care of them. Tell how I'd do th George.

ORGE. Sure. You'd go out in the alfalfa
ch and you'd have a sack. You'd fill up
sack and bring it in and put it in the
bit cages.

NIE. They'd nibble and they'd nibble, the
y they do. I seen 'em.

ORGE. Every six weeks or so them does
uld throw a litter. So we'd have plenty
bits to eat or sell. (*Pauses for inspiration.*)
d we'd keep a few pigeons to go flying
nd and round the windmill, like they
e when I was a kid. (*Seems entranced.*)
d it'd be our own. And nobody could can
If we don't like a guy we can say: "Get
hell out," and by God he's got to do it.
d if a friend come along, why, we'd have
extra bunk. Know what we'd say? We'd
, "Why don't you spen' the night?" And
God he would. We'd have a setter dog
l a couple of striped cats. (*Looks sharply
LENNIE.*) But you gotta watch out them
s don't get the little rabbits.

NIE (*breathing hard*). You jus' let 'em
. I'll break their goddamn necks. I'll
ash them cats flat with a stick. I'd smash
l flat with a stick. That's what I'd do.
hey sit silently for a moment.*)

DY (*at the sound of his voice, both* LEN-
and GEORGE *jump as though caught in
e secret*). You know where's a place like
t?

ORGE (*solemnly*). S'pose I do, what's that
you?

DY. You don't need to tell me where it's
Might be any place.

ORGE (*relieved*). Sure. That's right, you
ldn't find it in a hundred years.

DY (*excitedly*). How much they want
a place like that?

ORGE (*grudgingly*). Well, I could get it
six hundred bucks. The ole people that
ns it is flat bust. And the ole lady needs
dicine. Say, what's it to you? You got
thing to do with us!

DY (*softly*). I ain't much good with only
e hand. I lost my hand right here on the
ch. That's why they didn't can me. They
e me a job swampin'. And they give me
o hundred and fifty dollars 'cause I lost
hand. An' I got fifty more saved up
ht in the bank right now. That's three

hundred. And I got forty more comin' the
end of the month. Tell you what . . . (*He
leans forward eagerly.*) S'pose I went in
with you guys? That's three hundred and
forty bucks I'd put in. I ain't much good,
but I could cook and tend the chickens and
hoe the garden some. How'd that be?

GEORGE (*his eyes half closed, uncertainly*).
I got to think about that. We was always
goin' to do it by ourselves. Me an' Lennie.
I never thought of nobody else.

CANDY. I'd make a will. Leave my share to
you guys in case I kicked off. I ain't got no
relations nor nothing. You fellas got any
money? Maybe we could go there right now.

GEORGE (*disgustedly*). We got ten bucks
between us. (*He thinks.*) Say, look. If me
and Lennie work a month and don't spend
nothing at all, we'll have a hundred bucks.
That would be four forty. I bet we could
swing her for that. Then you and Lennie
could go get her started and I'd get a job
and make up the rest. You could sell eggs
and stuff like that. (*They look at each other
in amazement. Reverently.*) Jesus Christ, I
bet we could swing her. (*His voice is full of
wonder.*) I bet we could swing 'er.

CANDY (*scratches the stump of his wrist
nervously*). I got hurt four years ago. They'll
can me pretty soon. Jest as soon as I can't
swamp out no bunkhouses they'll put me
on the county. Maybe if I give you guys my
money, you'll let me hoe in the garden, even
when I ain't no good at it. And I'll wash
dishes and little chicken stuff like that. But
hell, I'll be on our own place. I'll be let to
work on our own place. (*Miserably.*) You
seen what they done to my dog. They says
he wasn't no good to himself nor nobody
else. But when I'm that way nobody'll shoot
me. I wish somebody would. They won't do
nothing like that. I won't have no place to
go and I can't get no more jobs.

GEORGE (*stands up*). We'll do 'er! God damn,
we'll fix up that little ole place and we'll
go live there. (*Wonderingly.*) S'pose they
was a carnival, or a circus come to town or
a ball game or any damn thing. (CANDY *nods
in appreciation.*) We'd just go to her. We
wouldn't ask nobody if we could. Just say
we'll go to her, by God, and we would. Just
milk the cow and sling some grain to the
chickens and go to her.

LENNIE. And put some grass to the rabbits. I wouldn't forget to feed them. When we gonna to do it, George?

GEORGE (*decisively*). In one month. Right squack in one month. Know what I'm gonna do? I'm goin' write to them ole people that owns the place that we'll take 'er. And Candy'll send a hundred dollars to bind her.

CANDY (*happily*). I sure will. They got a good stove there?

GEORGE. Sure, got a nice stove. Burns coal or wood.

LENNIE. I'm gonna take my pup. I bet by Christ he likes it there. (*The window, center backstage, swings outward.* CURLEY'S WIFE *looks in. They do not see her.*)

GEORGE (*quickly*). Now don't tell nobody about her. Jus' us three and nobody else. They'll liable to can us so we can't make no stake. We'll just go on like we was a bunch of punks. Like we was gonna buck barley the rest of our lives. And then all of a sudden, one day, bang! We get our pay and scram out of here.

CANDY. I can give you three hundred right now.

LENNIE. And not tell nobody. We won't tell nobody, George.

GEORGE. You're goddamn right we won't. (*There is a silence and then* GEORGE *speaks irritably.*) You know, seems to me I can almost smell that carnation stuff that goddamn tart dumps on herself.

CURLEY'S WIFE (*in the first part of the speech by* GEORGE *she starts to step out of sight but at the last words her face darkens with anger. At her first words everybody in the room looks around at her and remains rigid during the tirade*). Who you callin' a tart! I come from a nice home. I was brung up by nice people. Nobody never got to me before I was married. I was straight. I tell you I was good. (*A little plaintively.*) I was. (*Angrily again.*) You know Curley. You know he wouldn't stay with me if he wasn't sure. I tell you Curley is sure. You got no right to call me a tart.

GEORGE (*sullenly*). If you ain't a tart, what you always hangin' round guys for? You got a house an' you got a man. We don't want no trouble from you.

CURLEY'S WIFE (*pleadingly*). Sure I go[t] man. He ain't never home. I got nobody talk to. I got nobody to be with. Think I [c] just sit home and do nothin' but cook Curley? I want to see somebody. Just see '[e]m] an' talk to 'em. There ain't no women can't walk to town. And Curley don't t[a]me to no dances now. I tell you I jus' w[ant] to talk to somebody.

GEORGE (*boldly*). If you're just friendly w[hat] you givin' out the eye for an' floppin' y[er] can around?

CURLEY'S WIFE (*sadly*). I just wanta be ni[ce]. (*The sound of approaching voices:* "Y[ou] don't have to get mad about it, do you?" "I ain't mad, but I just don't want no m[ore] questions, that's all. I just don't want [no] more questions.*"

GEORGE. Get goin'. We don't want no troub[le]. (CURLEY'S WIFE *looks from the window a[nd] closes it silently and disappears. Enter* SL[IM] *followed by* CURLEY, CARLSON *and* W[HIT.] SLIM'S *hands are black with tar.* CUR[LEY] *hangs close to his elbow.*)

CURLEY (*explaining*). Well, I didn't m[ean] nothing, Slim. I jus' ast you.

SLIM. Well, you been askin' too often. [I'm] gettin' goddamn sick of it. If you can't l[ook] after your own wife, what you expect m[e to] do about it? You lay off of me.

CURLEY. I'm jus' tryin' to tell you I di[dn't] mean nothing. I just thought you might [a] saw her.

CARLSON. Why don't you tell her to stay [the] hell home where she belongs? You let [her] hang around the bunkhouses and pr[etty] soon you're goin' to have somethin' on y[our] hands.

CURLEY (*whirls on* CARLSON). You keep [out] of this 'less you want ta step outside.

CARLSON (*laughing*). Why you godda[mn] punk. You tried to throw a scare into S[lim] and you couldn't make it stick. Slim thro[wed] a scare into you. You're yellow as a fr[og] belly. I don't care if you're the best b[oxer] in the country, you come for me and I'll k[ick] your goddamn head off.

WHIT (*joining in the attack*). Glove ful[l of] vaseline!

CURLEY (*glares at him, then suddenly s[niffs] the air, like a hound*). By God, she's bee[n]

e. I can smell— By God, she's been in
e. (*To* GEORGE.) You was here. The other
ys was outside. Now, God damn you—
 talk.

RGE (*looks worried. He seems to make
his mind to face an inevitable situation.
wly takes off his coat, and folds it
ost daintily. Speaks in an unemotional
notone*). Somebody got to beat the hell
a you. I guess I'm elected. (LENNIE *has
n watching, fascinated. He gives his high,
vous chuckle.*)

RLEY (*whirls on him*). What the hell you
ghin' at?

NIE (*blankly*). Huh?

RLEY (*exploding with rage*). Come on,
 big bastard. Get up on your feet. No big
-of-a-bitch is gonna laugh at me. I'll show
 who's yellow.

NNIE *looks helplessly at* GEORGE. *Gets up
 tries to retreat upstage.* CURLEY *follows
hing at him. The others mass themselves
front of the two contestants:* "That ain't
 way, Curley—he ain't done nothing to
." . . . "Lay off him, will you, Curley.
 ain't no fighter." . . . "Sock him back,
 guy! Don't be afraid of him!" . . . "Give
 a chance, Curley. Give him a chance."

NIE (*crying with terror*). George, make
 leave me alone, George.

RGE. Get him, Lennie. Get him! (*There is
arp cry. The gathering of men opens and
RLEY is flopping about, his hand lost in
NIE's hand.*) Let go of him, Lennie. Let
 ("He's got his hand!" . . . "Look at that,
 you?" . . . "Jesus, what a guy!" LENNIE
ches in terror the flopping man he holds.
NIE's face is covered with blood.* GEORGE
s LENNIE *in the face again and again.
LEY is weak and shrunken.*) Let go his
d, Lennie. Slim, come help me, while
 guy's got any hand left. (*Suddenly
NIE lets go. He cowers away from
RGE.*)

NIE. You told me to, George. I heard
 tell me to. (CURLEY *has dropped to the
r.* SLIM *and* CARLSON *bend over him and
 at his hand.* SLIM *looks over at* LENNIE
 horror.*)

M. We got to get him to a doctor. It
s to me like every bone in his hand is
ed.

LENNIE (*crying*). I didn't wanta. I didn't
wanta hurt 'im.

SLIM. Carlson, you get the candy wagon out.
He'll have to go into Soledad, and get his
hand fixed up. (*Turns to the whimpering
LENNIE.*) It ain't your fault. This punk had
it comin' to him. But Jesus—he ain't hardly
got no hand left.

GEORGE (*moving near*). Slim, will we git
canned now? Will Curley's ole man can us
now?

SLIM. I don't know. (*Kneels down beside
CURLEY.*) You got your sense enough to
listen? (CURLEY *nods.*) Well, then you listen.
I think you got your hand caught in a
machine. If you don't tell nobody what happened, we won't. But you jest tell and try
to get this guy canned and we'll tell everybody. And then will you get the laugh!
(*Helps* CURLEY *to his feet.*) Come on now.
Carlson's goin' to take you in to a doctor.
(*Starts for the door, turns back to* LENNIE.)
Le's see your hands. (LENNIE *sticks out both
hands.*) Christ Almighty!

GEORGE. Lennie was just scairt. He didn't
know what to do. I tole you nobody ought
never to fight him. No, I guess it was Candy
I tole.

CANDY (*solemnly*). That's just what you
done. Right this morning when Curley
first lit into him. You says he better not fool
with Lennie if he knows what's good for
him. (*They all leave the stage except* GEORGE
and LENNIE *and* CANDY.)

GEORGE (*to* LENNIE, *very gently*). It ain't your
fault. You don't need to be scairt no more.
You done jus' what I tole you to. Maybe you
better go in the washroom and clean up
your face. You look like hell.

LENNIE. I didn't want no trouble.

GEORGE. Come on—I'll go with you.

LENNIE. George?

GEORGE. What you want?

LENNIE. Can I still tend the rabbits, George?
(*They exeunt together, side by side, through
the door of the bunkhouse.*)

CURTAIN

SCENE II

Ten o'clock Saturday evening.

The room of the stable buck, a lean-to off the barn. There is a plank door upsta center; a small square window center right. On one side of the door a leather worki bench with tools racked behind it, and on the others racks with broken and partly mena harnesses, collars, hames, traces, etc. At the left upstage Crooks' bunk. Over it two shel On one a great number of medicines in cans and bottles. And on the other a num of tattered books and a big alarm clock. In the corner right upstage a single-barreled sh gun and on the floor beside it a pair of rubber boots. A large pair of gold spectacles ha on a nail over Crooks' bunk.

The entrance leads into the barn proper. From that direction and during the wh scene come the sounds of horses eating, stamping, jingling their halter chains and n and then whinnying.

Two empty nail kegs are in the room to be used as seats. Single unshaded small-cand power carbon light hanging from its own cord.

As the curtain rises, we see CROOKS sitting on his bunk rubbing his back with linime He reaches up under his shirt to do this. His face is lined with pain. As he rubs flexes his muscles and shivers a little.

LENNIE appears in the open doorway, nearly filling the opening. Then CROOKS, sens his presence, raises his eyes, stiffens and scowls.

LENNIE smiles in an attempt to make friends.

CROOKS (*sharply*). You got no right to come in my room. This here's my room. Nobody got any right in here but me.

LENNIE (*fawning*). I ain't doin' nothing. Just come in the barn to look at my pup, and I seen your light.

CROOKS. Well, I got a right to have a light. You go on and get out of my room. I ain't wanted in the bunkhouse and you ain't wanted in my room.

LENNIE (*ingenuously*). Why ain't you wanted?

CROOKS (*furiously*). 'Cause I'm black. They play cards in there. But I can't play because I'm black. They say I stink. Well, I tell you all of you stink to me.

LENNIE (*helplessly*). Everybody went into town. Slim and George and everybody. George says I got to stay here and not get into no trouble. I seen your light.

CROOKS. Well, what do you want?

LENNIE. Nothing . . . I seen your light. I thought I could jus' come in and set.

CROOKS (*stares at LENNIE for a moment, takes down his spectacles and adjusts them over his ears; says in a complaining tone*). I don't know what you're doin' in the barn anyway. You ain't no skinner. There's no

call for a bucker to come into the barn at You've got nothing to do with the horses mules.

LENNIE (*patiently*). The pup. I come to my pup.

CROOKS. Well, God damn it, go and see y pup then. Don't go no place where you a wanted.

LENNIE (*advances a step into the ro remembers and backs to the door aga* I looked at him a little. Slim says I ain' pet him very much.

CROOKS (*the anger gradually going out of voice*). Well, you been taking him out of nest all the time. I wonder the ole lady d move him some place else.

LENNIE (*moving into the room*). Oh, don't care. She lets me.

CROOKS (*scowls and then gives up*). Com in and set awhile. Long as you won't out and leave me alone, you might as set down. (*A little more friendly.*) All boys gone into town, huh?

LENNIE. All but old Candy. He jus' set the bunkhouse sharpening his pencils. sharpening and figurin'.

CROOKS (*adjusting his glasses*). Figu What's Candy figurin' about?

NIE. 'Bout the land. 'Bout the little
e.

oKS. You're nuts. You're crazy as a
ge. What land you talkin' about?

NIE. The land we're goin' to get. And
ttle house and pigeons.

oKS. Just nuts. I don't blame the guy
're traveling with for keeping you out
sight.

NIE (*quietly*). It ain't no lie. We're
na do it. Gonna get a little place and
on the fat of the land.

oKS (*settling himself comfortably on
bunk*). Set down. Set down on that nail

NIE (*hunches over on the little barrel*).
think it's a lie. But it ain't no lie. Ever'
d's the truth. You can ask George.

oKS (*puts his dark chin on his palm*).
travel round with George, don't you?

NIE (*proudly*). Sure, me and him goes
place together.

oKS (*after a pause, quietly*). Sometimes
alks and you don't know what the hell
talkin' about. Ain't that so? (*Leans for-
.*) Ain't that so?

NIE. Yeah. Sometimes.

oKS. Just talks on. And you don't know
t the hell it's all about.

NIE. How long you think it'll be before
pups will be old enough to pet?

oKS (*laughs again*). A guy can talk to
and be sure you won't go blabbin'. A
le of weeks and them pups will be all
. (*Musing.*) George knows what he's
t. Just talks and you don't understand
ng. (*Mood gradually changes to ex-
ent.*) Well, this is just a nigger talkin'
a busted-back nigger. It don't mean
ng, see. You couldn't remember it
ay. I seen it over and over—a guy
ng to another guy and it don't make
fference if he don't hear or understand.
thing is they're talkin'. (*He pounds
nee with his hand.*) George can tell
crewy things and it don't matter. It's
he talkin'. It's just bein' with another
that's all. (*His voice becomes soft and
ious.*) S'pose George don't come back

no more? S'pose he took a powder and
just ain't comin' back. What you do then?

LENNIE (*trying to follow* CROOKS). What?
What?

CROOKS. I said s'pose George went into town
tonight and you never heard of him no more
(*Presses forward.*) Just s'pose that.

LENNIE (*sharply*). He won't do it. George
wouldn't do nothing like that. I been with
George a long time. He'll come back tonight. . . . (*Doubt creeps into his voice.*)
Don't you think he will?

CROOKS (*delighted with his torture*). Nobody
can tell what a guy will do. Let's say he
wants to come back and can't. S'pose he
gets killed or hurt so he can't come back.

LENNIE (*in terrible apprehension*). I don't
know. Say, what you doin' anyway? It ain't
true. George ain't got hurt.

CROOKS (*cruelly*). Want me to tell you
what'll happen? They'll take you to the
booby hatch. They'll tie you up with a
collar like a dog. Then you'll be jus' like me.
Livin' in a kennel.

LENNIE (*furious, walks over towards*
CROOKS). Who hurt George?

CROOKS (*recoiling from him with fright*).
I was just supposin'. George ain't hurt. He's
all right. He'll be back all right.

LENNIE (*standing over him*). What you
supposin' for? Ain't nobody goin' to s'pose
any hurt to George.

CROOKS (*trying to calm him*). Now set
down. George ain't hurt. Go on now, set
down.

LENNIE (*growling*). Ain't nobody gonna
talk no hurt to George.

CROOKS (*very gently*). Maybe you can see
now. You got George. You know he's comin' back. S'pose you didn't have nobody.
S'pose you couldn't go in the bunkhouse
and play rummy, 'cause you was black.
How would you like that? S'pose you had
to set out here and read books. Sure, you
could play horseshoes until it got dark, but
then you got to read books. Books ain't no
good. A guy needs somebody . . . to be near
him. (*His tone whines.*) A guy goes nuts
if he ain't got nobody. Don't make no dif-

ference who it is as long as he's with you. I tell you a guy gets too lonely, he gets sick.

LENNIE (*reassuring himself*). George gonna come back. Maybe George come back already. Maybe I better go see.

CROOKS (*more gently*). I didn't mean to scare you. He'll come back. I was talkin' about myself.

LENNIE (*miserably*). George won't go away and leave me. I know George won't do that.

CROOKS (*continuing dreamily*). I remember when I was a little kid on my ole man's chicken ranch. Had two brothers. They was always near me, always there. Used to sleep right in the same room. Right in the same bed, all three. Had a strawberry patch. Had an alfalfa patch. Used to turn the chickens out in the alfalfa on a sunny morning. Me and my brothers would set on the fence and watch 'em—white chickens they was.

LENNIE (*interested*). George says we're gonna have alfalfa.

CROOKS. You're nuts.

LENNIE. We are too gonna get it. You ask George.

CROOKS (*scornfully*). You're nuts. I seen hundreds of men come by on the road and on the ranches, bindles on their back and that same damn thing in their head. Hundreds of 'em. They come and they quit and they go on. And every damn one of 'em is got a little piece of land in his head. And never a goddamn one of 'em gets it. Jus' like heaven. Everybody wants a little piece of land. Nobody never gets to heaven. And nobody gets no land.

LENNIE. We are too.

CROOKS. It's jest in your head. Guys all the time talkin' about it, but it's jest in your head. (*The horses move restlessly. One of them whinnies.*) I guess somebody's out there. Maybe Slim. (*Pulls himself painfully upright and moves toward the door. Calls.*) That you, Slim?

CANDY (*from outside*). Slim went in town. Say, you seen Lennie?

CROOKS. You mean the big guy?

CANDY. Yes. Seen him around any place?

CROOKS (*goes back to his bunk and s down, says shortly*). He's in here.

CANDY (*stands in the doorway, scratchi his wrist. Makes no attempt to enter*). Loc Lennie, I been figuring something o About the place.

CROOKS (*irritably*). You can come in if y want.

CANDY (*embarrassed*). I don't know. 'Cou if you want me to.

CROOKS. Oh, come on in. Everybody's com in. You might just as well. Gettin' to b goddamn race track. (*He tries to conceal pleasure.*)

CANDY (*still embarrassed*). You've got a n cozy little place in here. Must be nice have a room to yourself this way.

CROOKS. Sure. And a manure pile under window. All to myself. It's swell.

LENNIE (*breaking in*). You said about place.

CANDY. You know, I been here a long ti An' Crooks been here a long time. Thi the first time I ever been in his room.

CROOKS (*darkly*). Guys don't come i colored man's room. Nobody been here Slim.

LENNIE (*insistently*). The place. You about the place.

CANDY. Yeah. I got it all figured out. can' make some real money on them rak if we go about it right.

LENNIE. But I get to tend 'em. George I get to tend 'em. He promised.

CROOKS (*brutally*). You guys is just kid yourselves. You'll talk about it a hell lot, but you won't get no land. You'll swamper here until they take you out box. Hell, I seen too many guys.

CANDY (*angrily*). We're gonna do it. Ge says we are. We got the money right i

CROOKS. Yeah. And where is George n In town in a whorehouse. That's w your money's goin'. I tell you I seen it pen too many times.

CANDY. George ain't got the money in t The money's in the bank. Me and Le

l George. We gonna have a room to our-
ves. We gonna have a dog and chickens.
gonna have green corn and maybe a
.

OKS (*impressed*). You say you got the
ney?

DY. We got most of it. Just a little bit
re to get. Have it all in one month.
orge's got the land all picked out too.

OKS (*exploring his spine with his hands*).
never seen a guy really do it. I seen guys
rly crazy with loneliness for land, but
ry time a whorehouse or a blackjack
ne took it away from 'em. (*Hesitates and
speaks timidly.*) If you guys would
nt a hand to work for nothin'—just his
p, why I'd come and lend a hand. I ain't
crippled I can't work like a son-of-a-
h if I wanted to.

RGE (*strolls through the door, hands in
kets, leans against the wall, speaks in a
-satiric, rather gentle voice*). You
ldn't go to bed like I told you, could
, Lennie? Hell, no—you got to get out
society an' flap your mouth. Holdin' a
vention out here.

NIE (*defending himself*). You was gone.
ere wasn't nobody in the bunkhouse. I
t done no bad things, George.

RGE (*still casually*). Only time I get any
ce is when you're asleep. If you ever get
kin' in your sleep I'll chop off your head
a chicken. (*Chops with his hand.*)

OKS (*coming to* LENNIE's *defense*). We
jus' settin' here talkin'. Ain't no harm
hat.

RGE. Yeah. I heard you. (*A weariness has
ed on him.*) Got to be here ever' minute,
 less. Got to watch ya. (*To* CROOKS.) It
t nothing against you, Crooks. We just
n't gonna tell nobody.

DY (*tries to change subject*). Didn't you
e no fun in town?

RGE. Oh! I set in a chair and Susy was
kin' jokes an' the guys was startin' to
e a little puny hell. Christ Almighty—I
r been this way before. I'm jus' gonna
out a dime and a nickel for a shot an'
ink what a hell of a lot of bulk carrot
you can get for fifteen cents.

CANDY. Not in them damn little envelopes—
but bulk seed—you sure can.

GEORGE. So purty soon I come back. I can't
think of nothing else. Them guys slingin'
money around got me jumpy.

CANDY. Guy got to have *some* fun. I was to a
parlor house in Bakersfield once. God Almighty, what a place. Went upstairs on a
red carpet. They was big pitchers on the
wall. We set in big sof' chairs. They was
cigarettes on the table—an' they was *free*.
Purty soon a Jap come in with drinks on a
tray an' them *drinks* was free. Take all you
want. (*In a reverie.*) Purty soon the girls
come in an' they was jus' as polite an' nice
an' quiet an' purty. Didn't seem like
hookers. Made ya kinda scared to ask 'em.
. . . That was a long time ago.

GEORGE. Yeah? An' what'd them sof' chairs
set you back?

CANDY. Fifteen bucks.

GEORGE (*scornfully*). So ya got a cigarette
an' a whiskey an' a look at a purty dress an'
it cost ya twelve and a half bucks extra.
You shot a week's pay to walk on that red
carpet.

CANDY (*still entranced with his memory*).
A week's pay? Sure. But I worked weeks all
my life. I can't remember none of them
weeks. But . . . that was nearly twenty
years ago. And I can remember that. Girl
I went with was named Arline. Had on a
pink silk dress.

GEORGE (*turns suddenly and looks out the
door into the dark barn, speaks savagely*).
I s'pose ya lookin' for Curley? (CURLEY's
WIFE *appears in the door.*) Well, Curley
ain't here.

CURLEY'S WIFE (*determined now*). I know
Curley ain't here. I wanted to ast Crooks
somepin'. I didn't know you guys was here.

CANDY. Didn't George tell you before—we
don't want nothing to do with you. You
know damn well Curley ain't here.

CURLEY'S WIFE. I know where Curley went.
Got his arm in a sling an' he went anyhow.
I tell ya I come out to ast Crooks somepin'.

CROOKS (*apprehensively*). Maybe you better
go along to your own house. You hadn't
ought to come near a colored man's room.

I don't want no trouble. You don't want to ask me nothing.

CANDY (*rubbing his wrist stump*). You got a husband. You got no call to come foolin' around with other guys, causin' trouble.

CURLEY'S WIFE (*suddenly angry*). I try to be nice an' polite to you lousy bindle bums—but you're too good. I tell ya I could of went with shows. An'—an' a guy wanted to put me in pitchers right in Hollywood. (*Looks about to see how she is impressing them. Their eyes are hard.*) I come out here to ast somebody somepin' an'—

CANDY (*stands up suddenly and knocks his nail keg over backwards, speaks angrily*). I had enough. You ain't wanted here. We tole you, you ain't. Callin' us bindle stiffs. You got floozy idears what us guys amounts to. You ain't got sense enough to see us guys ain't bindle stiffs. S'pose you could get us canned—s'pose you *could*. You think we'd hit the highway an' look for another two-bit job. You don't know we got our own ranch to go to an' our own house an' fruit trees. An' we got friends. That's what we got. Maybe they was a time when we didn't have nothing, but that ain't so no more.

CURLEY'S WIFE. You damn ol' goat. If you had two bits, you'd be in Soledad gettin' a drink an' suckin' the bottom of the glass.

GEORGE. Maybe she could ask Crooks what she come to ask an' then get the hell home. I don't think she come to ask nothing.

CURLEY'S WIFE. What happened to Curley's hand? (CROOKS *laughs.* GEORGE *tries to shut him up.*) So it wasn't no machine. Curley didn't act like he was tellin' the truth. Come on, Crooks—what happened?

CROOKS. I wasn't there. I didn't see it.

CURLEY'S WIFE (*eagerly*). What happened? I won't let on to Curley. He says he caught his han' in a gear. (CROOKS *is silent.*) Who done it?

GEORGE. Didn't nobody do it.

CURLEY'S WIFE (*turns slowly to* GEORGE). So *you* done it. Well, he had it comin'.

GEORGE. I didn't have no fuss with Curley.

CURLEY'S WIFE (*steps near him, smiling*). Maybe now you ain't scared of him no more.

Maybe you'll talk to me sometimes n Ever'body was scared of him.

GEORGE (*speaks rather kindly*). Look didn't sock Curley. If he had trouble, it a none of our affair. Ask Curley about Now listen. I'm gonna try to tell ya. tole you to get the hell out and it don't no good. So I'm gonna tell you another w Us guys got somepin' we're gonna do. If y stick around you'll gum up the works ain't your fault. If a guy steps on a rou pebble an' falls an' breaks his neck, it a the pebble's fault, but the guy wouldn' did it if the pebble wasn't there.

CURLEY'S WIFE (*puzzled*). What you tall about pebbles? If you didn't sock Cur who did? (*She looks at the others, t steps quickly over to* LENNIE.) Where'd get them bruises on your face?

GEORGE. I tell you he got his hand caugh a machine.

LENNIE (*looks anxiously at* GEORGE, spe miserably). He caught his han' in a mach

GEORGE. So now get out of here.

CURLEY'S WIFE (*goes close to* LENNIE, spe softly and there is a note of affection in voice*). So . . . it was you. Well . . . ma you're dumb like they say . . . an' maybe you're the only guy on the ranch with g (*She puts her hand on* LENNIE's shoul He looks up in her face and a smile gr on his face. She strokes his shoulder.*) Yo a nice fella.

GEORGE (*suddenly leaps at her ferociou grabs her shoulder and whirls her arou Listen . . . you! I tried to give you a br Don't you walk into nothing! We a gonna let you mess up what we're gonna You let this guy alone an' get the hell of here.

CURLEY'S WIFE (*defiant but slightly frigh ed*). You ain't tellin' me what to do. (BOSS appears in the door, stands legs spr thumbs hooked over his belt.*) I got a r to talk to anybody I want to.

GEORGE. Why, you—(GEORGE, *furiously,* close—his hand is raised to strike her. cowers a little.* GEORGE stiffens, seeing frozen in position. The others see* BOSS Girl retreats slowly.* GEORGE's hand d slowly to his side—he takes two slow b ward steps. Hold the scene for a mom

CURTAIN

ACT THREE

SCENE I

[M]id-afternoon Sunday.

[O]ne end of a great barn. Backstage the hay slopes up sharply against the wall. High in [the] upstage wall is a large hay window. On each side are seen the hay racks, behind [whi]ch are the stalls with the horses in them. Throughout this scene the horses can be [hear]d in their stalls, rattling their halter chains and chewing at the hay.

[T]he entrance is downstage right.

[T]he boards of the barn are not close together. Streaks of afternoon sun come between [the] boards, made visible by dust in the air. From outside comes the clang of horseshoes [on] the playing peg, shouts of men encouraging or jeering.

[In] the barn there is a feeling of quiet and humming and lazy warmth. Curtain rises [on] LENNIE sitting in the hay, looking down at a little dead puppy in front of him. He [puts] out his big hand and strokes it clear from one end to the other.

[LEN]NIE (*softly*). Why do you got to get [kill]ed? You ain't so little as mice. I didn' [boun]ce you hard. (*Bends the pup's head up [and] looks in its face.*) Now maybe George [ain't] gonna let me tend no rabbits if he [find]s out you got killed. (*He scoops a little [holl]ow and lays the puppy in it out of sight [and] covers it over with hay. He stares at the [mou]nd he has made.*) This ain't no bad [thin]g like I got to hide in the brush. I'll tell [Geo]rge I found it dead. (*He unburies the [pup] and inspects it. Twists its ears and works [his f]ingers in its fur. Sorrowfully.*) But he'll [kno]w. George always knows. He'll say: [“Yo]u done it. Don't try to put nothin' over [on m]e.” And he'll say: “Now just for that [you] don't get to tend no—you-know-whats.” [(His] anger rises. Addresses the pup.*) God [dam]n you. Why do you got to get killed? [You] ain't so little as mice. (*Picks up the pup [and] hurls it from him and turns his back on [it. H]e sits bent over his knees moaning to [him]self.*) Now he won't let me. . . . Now he [won']t let me. (*Outside there is a clang of [hors]eshoes on the iron stake and a little [chor]us of cries. LENNIE gets up and brings [the] pup back and lays it in the hay and sits [dow]n. He mourns.*) You wasn't big enough. [The]y tole me and tole me you wasn't. I [didn']t know you'd get killed so easy. Maybe [Geo]rge won't care. This here goddamn little [son-]of-a-bitch wasn't nothin' to George.

[CAND]Y (*voice from behind the stalls*). Len- [nie,]where you at? (*LENNIE frantically buries [the] pup under the hay. CANDY enters ex- [cited]ly.*) Thought I'd find ya here. Say . . . [I be]en talkin' to Slim. It's okay. We ain't

gonna get the can. Slim been talkin' to the boss. Slim tol' the boss you guys is good buckers. The boss got to move that grain. 'Member what hell the boss give us las' night? He tol' Slim he got his eye on you an' George. But you ain't gonna get the can. Oh! an' say. The boss give Curley's wife hell, too. Tole her never to go near the men no more. Give her worse hell than you an' George. (*For the first time notices* LENNIE's *dejection.*) Ain't you glad?

LENNIE. Sure.

CANDY. You ain't sick?

LENNIE. Uh-uh!

CANDY. I got to go tell George. See you later. (*Exits.* LENNIE, *alone, uncovers the pup. Lies down in the hay and sinks deep in it. Puts the pup on his arm and strokes it.* CURLEY'S WIFE *enters secretly. A little mound of hay conceals* LENNIE *from her. In her hand she carries a small suitcase, very cheap. She crosses the barn and buries the case in the hay. Stands up and looks to see whether it can be seen.* LENNIE *watching her quietly tries to cover the pup with hay. She sees the movement.*)

CURLEY'S WIFE. What—what you doin' here?

LENNIE (*sullenly*). Jus' settin' here.

CURLEY'S WIFE. You seen what I done.

LENNIE. Yeah! you brang a valise.

CURLEY'S WIFE (*comes near to him*). You won't tell—will you?

LENNIE (*still sullen*). I ain't gonna have nothing to do with you. George tole me. I ain't to talk to you or nothing. (*Covers the pup a little more.*)

CURLEY'S WIFE. George give you all your orders?

LENNIE. Not talk nor nothing.

CURLEY'S WIFE. You won't tell about that suitcase? I ain't gonna stay here no more. Tonight I'm gonna get out. Come here an' get my stuff an' get out. I ain't gonna be run over no more. I'm gonna go in pitchers. (*Sees* LENNIE'S *hand stroking the pup under the hay.*) What you got there?

LENNIE. Nuthing. I ain't gonna talk to you. George says I ain't.

CURLEY'S WIFE. Listen. The guys got a horse-shoe tenement out there. It's on'y four o'clock. Them guys ain't gonna leave that tenement. They got money bet. You don't need to be scared to talk to me.

LENNIE (*weakening a little*). I ain't supposed to.

CURLEY'S WIFE (*watching his buried hand*). What you got under there?

LENNIE (*his woe comes back to him*). Jus' my pup. Jus' my little ol' pup. (*Sweeps the hay aside.*)

CURLEY'S WIFE. Why! He's dead.

LENNIE (*explaining sadly*). He was so little. I was jus' playin' with him—an' he made like he's gonna bite me—an' I made like I'm gonna smack him—an'—I done it. An' then he was dead.

CURLEY'S WIFE (*consoling*). Don't you worry none. He was just a mutt. The whole country is full of mutts.

LENNIE. It ain't that so much. George gonna be mad. Maybe he won't let me—what he said I could tend.

CURLEY'S WIFE (*sits down in the hay beside him, speaks soothingly*). Don't you worry. Them guys got money bet on that horseshoe tenement. They ain't gonna leave it. And tomorra I'll be gone. I ain't gonna let them run over me. (*In the following scene it is apparent that neither is listening to the other*

and yet as it goes on, as a happy tone [in]creases, it can be seen that they are grow[ing] closer together.*)

LENNIE. We gonna have a little place [an'] raspberry bushes.

CURLEY'S WIFE. I ain't meant to live like t[his.] I come from Salinas. Well, a show co[me] through an' I talked to a guy that was i[n it.] He says I could go with the show. My [ol'] lady wouldn't let me, 'cause I was on'y [fif]teen. I wouldn't be no place like this [if I] had went with that show, you bet.

LENNIE. Gonna take a sack an' fill it [up] with alfalfa an'—

CURLEY'S WIFE (*hurrying on*). 'Nother t[ime] I met a guy an' he was in pitchers. W[ent] out to the Riverside Dance Palace with h[im.] He said he was gonna put me in pitch[ers.] Says I was a natural. Soon's he got bac[k to] Hollywood he was gonna write me abou[t it.] (*Looks impressively at* LENNIE.) I never [got] that letter. I think my ol' lady stole it. W[ell,] I wasn't gonna stay no place where they s[tole] your letters. So I married Curley. Met [him] out to the Riverside Dance Palace too.

LENNIE. I hope George ain't gonna be m[ad] about this pup.

CURLEY'S WIFE. I ain't tol' this to nob[ody] before. Maybe I oughtn' to. I don't like C[ur]ley. He ain't a nice fella. I might a sta[yed] with him but last night him an' his ol' m[an] both lit into me. I don't have to stay h[ere.] (*Moves closer and speaks confidentia[lly.*]) Don't tell nobody till I get clear away. [I'll] go in the night an' thumb a ride to H[olly]wood.

LENNIE. We gonna get out a here purty s[oon.] This ain't no nice place.

CURLEY'S WIFE (*ecstatically*). Gonna g[o in] the movies an' have nice clothes—all t[hem] nice clothes like they wear. An' I'll se[t in] them big hotels and they'll take pitcher[s of] me. When they have them openings I'[ll] an' talk in the radio . . . an' it won't [cost] me nothing 'cause I'm in the pitcher. (*[Puts] her hand on* LENNIE'S *arm for a mome[nt.*]) All them nice clothes like they wear . . . [be]cause this guy says I'm a natural.

LENNIE. We gonna go way . . . far a[way] from here.

CURLEY'S WIFE. 'Course, when I run away from Curley, my ol' lady won't never speak to me no more. She'll think I ain't decent. That's what she'll say. (*Defiantly.*) Well, we really ain't decent, no matter how much my ol' lady tries to hide it. My ol' man was a drunk. They put him away. There! Now I told.

LENNIE. George an' me was to the Sacramento Fair. One time I fell in the river an' George pulled me out an' saved me, an' then we went to the Fair. They got all kinds of stuff there. We seen long-hair rabbits.

CURLEY'S WIFE. My ol' man was a signpainter when he worked. He used to get drunk an' paint crazy pitchers an' waste paint. One night when I was a little kid, him an' my ol' lady had an awful fight. They was always fightin'. In the middle of the night he come into my room, and he says, "I can't stand this no more. Let's you an' me go away." I guess he was drunk. (*Her voice takes on a curious wondering tenderness.*) I remember in the night—walkin' down the road, and the trees was dark. I was pretty sleepy. He picked me up, an' he carried me on his back. He says, "We gonna live together. We gonna live together because you're my own little girl, an' no stranger. No arguin' and fightin'," he says, "because you're my little daughter." (*Her voice becomes soft.*) He says, "Why you'll bake little cakes for me, and I'll paint pretty pitchers all over the wall." (*Sadly.*) The morning they caught us . . . an' they put him away. (*Pause.*) I wish we'd a' went.

LENNIE. Maybe if I took this here pup an' throwed him away George wouldn't never know.

CURLEY'S WIFE. They locked him up for a week, and in a little while he died.

LENNIE. Then maybe I could tend the rabbits without no trouble.

CURLEY'S WIFE. Don't you think of nothing but rabbits? (*Sound of horseshoe on metal.*) Somebody made a ringer.

LENNIE (*patiently*). We gonna have a house an' a garden, an' a place for alfalfa. And I take a sack and get it all full of alfalfa, and then I take it to the rabbits.

CURLEY'S WIFE. What makes you so nuts about rabbits?

LENNIE (*moves close to her*). I like to pet nice things. Once at a fair I seen them long-hair rabbits. And they was nice, you bet. (*Despairingly.*) I'd even pet mice, but not when I could get nothin' better.

CURLEY'S WIFE (*giggles*). I think you're nuts.

LENNIE (*earnestly*). No, I ain't. George says I ain't. I like to pet nice things with my fingers. Soft things.

CURLEY'S WIFE. Well, who don't? Everybody likes that. I like to feel silk and velvet. You like to feel velvet?

LENNIE (*chuckling with pleasure*). You bet, by God. And I had some too. A lady give me some. And that lady was—my Aunt Clara. She give it right to me. . . . (*Measuring with his hands.*) 'Bout this big a piece. I wish I had that velvet right now. (*He frowns.*) I lost it. I ain't seen it for a long time.

CURLEY'S WIFE (*laughing*). You're nuts. But you're a kinda nice fella. Jus' like a big baby. A person can see kinda what you mean. When I'm doin' my hair sometimes I jus' set there and stroke it, because it's so soft. (*Runs her fingers over the top of her head.*) Some people got kinda coarse hair. You take Curley, his hair's just like wire. But mine is soft and fine. Here, feel. Right here. (*Takes* LENNIE'S *hand and puts it on her head.*) Feel there and see how soft it is. (LENNIE'S *fingers fall to stroking her hair.*) Don't you muss it up.

LENNIE. Oh, that's nice. (*Strokes harder.*) Oh, that's nice.

CURLEY'S WIFE. Look out now, you'll muss it. (*Angrily.*) You stop it now, you'll mess it all up. (*She jerks her head sideways and* LENNIE'S *fingers close on her hair and hang on. In a panic.*) Let go. (*She screams.*) You let go. (*She screams again. His other hand closes over her mouth and nose.*)

LENNIE (*begging*). Oh, please don't do that. George'll be mad. (*She struggles violently to be free. A soft screaming comes from under* LENNIE'S *hand. Crying with fright.*) Oh, please don't do none of that. George gonna say I done a bad thing. (*He raises his hand* from her mouth and a hoarse cry escapes. Angrily.) Now don't. I don't want you to yell. You gonna get me in trouble just like George says you will. Now don't you do that. (She struggles more.) Don't you go yellin'. (He shakes her violently. Her neck snaps sideways and she lies still. Looks down at her and cautiously removes his hand from over her mouth.) I don't wanta hurt you. But George will be mad if you yell. (When she doesn't answer he bends closely over her. He lifts her arm and lets it drop. For a moment he seems bewildered.) I done a bad thing. I done another bad thing. (He paws up the hay until it partly covers her. The sound of the horseshoe game comes from the outside. And for the first time LENNIE seems conscious of it. He crouches down and listens.) Oh, I done a real bad thing. I shouldn't a did that. George will be mad. And . . . he said . . . and hide in the brush till he comes. That's what he said. (He picks up the puppy from beside the girl.) I'll throw him away. It's bad enough like it is.

(He puts the pup under his coat, creeps to the barn wall and peers out between the cracks and then he creeps around to the end of the manger and disappears. The stage is vacant except for CURLEY'S WIFE. She lies in the hay half covered up and she looks very young and peaceful. Her rouged cheeks and red lips make her seem alive and sleeping lightly. For a moment the stage is absolutely silent. Then the horses stamp on the other side of the feeding rack. The halter chains clink and from outside men's voices come loud and clear.)

CANDY (offstage). Lennie! Oh, Lennie, you in there? (He enters.) I been figurin' some more, Lennie. Tell you what we can do. (Sees CURLEY'S WIFE and stops. Rubs his white whiskers.) I didn't know you was here. You was tol' not to be here. (He steps near her.) You oughn't to sleep out here. (He is right beside her and looks down.) Oh, Jesus Christ! (Goes to the door and calls softly.) George, George! Come here . . . George!

GEORGE (enters). What do you want?

CANDY (points at CURLEY'S WIFE). Look.

GEORGE. What's the matter with her? (Steps up beside her.) Oh, Jesus Christ! (Kneels beside her and feels her heart and her wrist.

Finally stands up slowly and stiffly. From this time on through the rest of the scen GEORGE is wooden.)

CANDY. What done it?

GEORGE (coldly). Ain't you got any ideas (CANDY looks away.) I should of knew. guess way back in my head I did.

CANDY. What we gonna do now, George What we gonna do now?

GEORGE (answering slowly and dully). Gue . . . we gotta . . . tell . . . the guys. Guess w got to catch him and lock him up. We can let him get away. Why, the poor bastar would starve. (He tries to reassure himself Maybe they'll lock him up and be nice him.

CANDY (excitedly). You know better'n tha George. You know Curley's gonna want get him lynched. You know how Curley

GEORGE. Yeah. . . . Yeah . . . that's right know Curley. And the other guys too. (looks back at CURLEY'S WIFE.)

CANDY (pleadingly). You and me can that little place, can't we, George? You a me can go there and live nice, can't w Can't we? (CANDY drops his head and lo down at the hay to indicate that he know

GEORGE (shakes his head slowly). It somethin' me and him had. (Softly.) think I knowed it from the very first. I th I knowed we'd never do her. He used like to hear about it so much. I got fo to thinkin' maybe we would. (CANDY st to speak but doesn't.)

GEORGE (as though repeating a lesson). work my month and then I'll take my bucks. I'll stay all night in some lousy house or I'll set in a pool room until ev body goes home. An' then—I'll come an' work another month. And then I'll fifty bucks more.

CANDY. He's such a nice fellow. I didn't t he'd a done nothing like this.

GEORGE (gets a grip on himself and stra ens his shoulders). Now listen. We gott the guys. I guess they've gotta bring in. They ain't no way out. Maybe they hurt him. I ain't gonna let 'em hurt Le

rply.) Now you listen. The guys might
I was in on it. I'm gonna go in the
house. Then in a minute you come out
yell like you just seen her. Will you do
So the guys won't think I was in on it?

Y. Sure, George. Sure, I'll do that.

GE. Okay. Give me a couple of minutes
And then you yell your head off. I'm
now. (GEORGE *exits.*)

Y (*watches him go, looks helplessly
at* CURLEY'S WIFE; *his next words are in
w and in anger*). You goddamn tramp.
done it, didn't you? Everybody knowed
mess things up. You just wasn't no
. (*His voice shakes.*) I could of hoed
e garden and washed dishes for them
. . . . (*Pauses for a moment and then
into a sing-song repeating the old
s.*) If there was a circus or a baseball
e . . . we would o' went to her . . . just
to hell with work and went to her.
they'd been a pig and chickens . . . and
e winter a little fat stove. An' us jus'
' there . . . settin' there. . . . (*His eyes
with tears and he goes weakly to the
nce of the barn. Tries for a moment to
a shout out of his throat before he
eds.*) Hey, you guys! Come here! Come

side the noise of the horseshoe game
. The sound of discussion and then the
s come closer: "What's the matter?"
"Who's that?" . . . "It's Candy." . . .
ething must have happened." Enter
and* CARLSON, *Young* WHIT *and* CURLEY,
KS in the back, keeping out of attention
. And last of all* GEORGE. GEORGE *has
n his blue denim coat and buttoned it.
black hat is pulled down low over his
"What's the matter?" . . . "What's
ened?")*

esture from* CANDY. *The men stare at
EY'S* WIFE. SLIM *goes over to her, feels
wrist and touches her cheek with his
rs. His hand goes under her slightly
ed neck.* CURLEY *comes near. For a
ent he seems shocked. Looks around
essly and suddenly he comes to life.*)

EY. I know who' done it. That big son-
itch done it. I know he done it. Why,
body else was out there playing horse-
. (*Working himself into a fury.*) I'm
a get him. I'm gonna get my shotgun.
, I'll kill the big son-of-a-bitch myself.

I'll shoot him in the guts. Come on, you
guys. (*He runs out of the barn.*)

CARLSON. I'll go get my Luger. (*He runs out
too.*)

SLIM (*quietly to* GEORGE). I guess Lennie
done it all right. Her neck's busted. Lennie
could o' did that. (GEORGE *nods slowly. Half-
questioning.*) Maybe like that time in Weed
you was tellin' me about. (GEORGE *nods.
Gently.*) Well, I guess we got to get him.
Where you think he might o' went?

GEORGE (*struggling to get words out*). I don't
know.

SLIM. I guess we gotta get him.

GEORGE (*stepping close and speaking passionately*). Couldn't we maybe bring him in
and lock him up? He's nuts, Slim, he never
done this to be mean.

SLIM. If we could only keep Curley in. But
Curley wants to shoot him. (*He thinks.*)
And s'pose they lock him up, George, and
strap him down and put him in a cage, that
ain't no good.

GEORGE. I know. I know.

SLIM. I think there's only one way to get
him out of it.

GEORGE. I know.

CARLSON (*enters running*). The bastard stole
my Luger. It ain't in my bag.

CURLEY (*enters carrying a shotgun in his
good hand. Officiously*). All right, you
guys. The nigger's got a shotgun. You take
it, Carlson.

WHIT. Only cover around here is down by
the river. He might have went there.

CURLEY. Don't give him no chance. Shoot
for his guts, that'll double him over.

WHIT. I ain't got a gun.

CURLEY. Go in and tell my old man. Get a
gun from him. Let's go now. (*Turns
suspiciously on* GEORGE.) You're comin'
with us, fella!

GEORGE. Yeah. I'll come. But listen, Curley,
the poor bastard's nuts. Don't shoot him,
he didn't know what he was doin'.

CURLEY. Don't shoot him! He's got Carlson's Luger, ain't he?

GEORGE (*weakly*). Maybe Carlson lost his gun.

CARLSON. I seen it this morning. It's been took.

SLIM (*looking down at* CURLEY'S WIFE). Curley, maybe you better stay here with your wife. (*The light is fading into evening.* CURLEY *hesitates. Seems almost to weaken, then he hardens again.*)

CURLEY. Naw, I'm gonna shoot the guts of that big bastard, I'm gonna get him self. Come on, you guys.

SLIM (*to* CANDY). You stay here then, Ca The rest of us better get goin'. (*They out,* SLIM *and* GEORGE *last. Exeunt all* CANDY. *He squats in the hay, watching face of* CURLEY'S WIFE.)

CANDY. Poor bastard.

CURTAIN

ACT THREE

SCENE II

Evening.
The river bank again.
Light from the setting sun shines on the low brown hills. Among the trees by the r the shade is deep with evening feeling.
Sounds: distant barking of dogs and the quiet call of quail.
The curtain rises on an empty stage.
There is a sudden whistle of evening wind that stirs the trees and scuds the leave. the ground.
The stage is still again. LENNIE *enters as silently as a bear. He is bent over and u On stage he looks behind him. Then he takes from under his coat the dead pup, la on the ground and, going to the river, lies on his stomach and drinks.*
He returns to the dead pup, sits down beside it.

LENNIE. George gonna give me hell . . . I bet. I . . . won't tell him. I'll bury him. (*Begins to scoop a hole in the sand in front of him. Softly.*) But I didn't forget, you bet. I come right here. Hide in the brush an' wait for George. (*Works carefully at his little grave, shaping the hole. At last he picks up the pup and lays it in the hole. Mourning.*) He gonna give me hell. He gonna wish he was alone. (*Adjusts the puppy in the hole, turning it around to make it fit better. Defiantly.*) Well . . . I can go right up in the hills an' find a cave. 'Course I wouldn't never have no ketchup. (*Begins packing sand down carefully about the pup, patting it as he does in beat with his words.*) I'll—go—away—go—away. (*Every word a pat. Fills the grave carefully, smooths the sand over it.*) There now. (*Gathers leaves and scatters them over the place. Gets up on his knees and cocks his head to inspect the job.*) Now. I won't never tell George. (*Sinks back to a sitting position.*) He'll know. He always knows.

(*Far off sound of voices approaching. ' come closer during the scene. Sudd there is the clicking warning of a quail and then the drum of the flock's w* GEORGE *enters silently, but hurriedly.*)

GEORGE (*in a hoarse whisper*). Get in tules—quick.

LENNIE. I ain't done nothing, George. *voices are very close.*)

GEORGE (*frantically*). Get in the tules—d you. (*Voices are nearly there.* GEORGE pushes LENNIE down among the tules. tops rustle showing his crawling progr*

WHIT (*offstage*). There's George. (*En Better not get so far ahead. You ain' a gun. (*Enter* SLIM, CARLSON, BOSS, CU and three other ranch hands. They are a with shotguns and rifles.*)

CARLSON. He musta come this way. ' prints in the sand was aimed this wa

(*has been regarding* GEORGE). Now
. We ain't gonna find him stickin' in a
ch this way. We got to spread out.

.EY. Brush is pretty thick here. He might
ying in the brush. (*Steps toward the*
. GEORGE *moves quickly after him.*)

(*Seeing the move speaks quickly*).
—(*pointing*)—up there's the county
an' open fields an' over there's the high-
. Le's spread out an' cover the brush.

. Slim's right. We got to spread.

. We better drag up to the roads an'
drag back.

.EY. 'Member what I said—shoot for
;uts.

. Okay, move out. Me an' George'll go
o the county road. You guys gets the
way an' drag back.

. If we get separated, we'll meet here.
ember this place.

.EY. All I care is getting the bastard.
e men move offstage right, talking. SLIM
GEORGE *move slowly upstage listening to*
voices that grow fainter and fainter.)

(*softly to* GEORGE). Where is he?
RGE *looks him in the eyes for a long*
ent. Finally trusts him and points with
humb toward the tules.)

. You want—I should—go away?
RGE *nods slowly, looking at the ground.*
starts away, comes back, tries to say
thing, instead puts his hand on GEORGE's
der for a second, and then hurries off
ge.)

GE (*moves woodenly toward the bank*
the tule clump and sits down). Lennie!
tules shiver again and LENNIE *emerges*
ing.)

IE. Where's them guys goin'? (*Long*
e.)

GE. Huntin'.

IE. Whyn't we go with 'em? I like
n'. (*Waits for an answer.* GEORGE *stares*
s the river.) Is it 'cause I done a bad
?

GE. It don't make no difference.

LENNIE. Is that why we can't go huntin' with
them guys?

GEORGE (*woodenly*). It don't make no difference. . . . Sit down, Lennie. Right there.
(*The light is going now. In the distance*
there are shouts of men. GEORGE *turns his*
head and listens to the shouts.)

LENNIE. George!

GEORGE. Yeah?

LENNIE. Ain't you gonna give me hell?

GEORGE. Give ya hell?

LENNIE. Sure. . . . Like you always done
before. Like—"If I didn't have you I'd take
my fifty bucks . . ."

GEORGE (*softly as if in wonder*). Jesus Christ,
Lennie, you can't remember nothing that
happens. But you remember every word
I say!

LENNIE. Well, ain't you gonna say it?

GEORGE (*reciting*). "If I was alone I—could
live—so easy. (*His voice is monotonous.*)
I could get a job and not have no mess. . . ."

LENNIE. Go on, go on! "And when the end
of the month come . . ."

GEORGE. "And when the end of the month
come, I could take my fifty bucks and go
to—a cat-house. . . ."

LENNIE (*eagerly*). Go on, George, ain't you
gonna give me no more hell?

GEORGE. No!

LENNIE. I can go away. I'll go right off in
the hills and find a cave if you don't want
me.

GEORGE (*speaks as though his lips were stiff*).
No, I want you to stay here with me.

LENNIE (*craftily*). Then tell me like you
done before.

GEORGE. Tell you what?

LENNIE. 'Bout the other guys and about us!

GEORGE (*recites again*). "Guys like us got no
families. They got a little stake and then
they blow it in. They ain't got nobody in the
world that gives a hoot in hell about 'em!"

LENNIE (*happily*). "But not *us*." Tell about us now.

GEORGE. "But not us."

LENNIE. "Because . . ."

GEORGE. "Because I got you and . . ."

LENNIE (*triumphantly*). "And I got you. We got each other," that's what, that gives a hoot in hell about us. (*A breeze blows up the leaves and then they settle back again. There are the shouts of men again. This time closer.*)

GEORGE (*takes off his hat; shakily*). Take off your hat, Lennie. The air feels fine!

LENNIE (*removes his hat and lays it on the ground in front of him*). Tell how it's gonna be. (*Again the sound of men.* GEORGE *listens to them.*)

GEORGE. Look acrost the river, Lennie, and I'll tell you like you can almost see it. (LENNIE *turns his head and looks across the river.*) "We gonna get a little place . . . (*Reaches in his side pocket and brings out* CARLSON's *Luger. Hand and gun lie on the ground behind* LENNIE's *back. He stares at the back of* LENNIE's *head at the place where spine and skull are joined. Sounds of men's voices talking offstage.*)

LENNIE. Go on! (GEORGE *raises the gun, but his hand shakes and he drops his hand on to the ground.*) Go on! How's it gonna be? "We gonna get a little place. . . ."

GEORGE (*thickly*). "We'll have a cow. And we'll have maybe a pig and chickens—and

down the flat we'll have a . . . little of alfalfa. . . ."

LENNIE (*shouting*). "For the rabbits!"

GEORGE. "For the rabbits!"

LENNIE. "And I get to tend the rab[b]

GEORGE. "And you get to tend the rab[b]

LENNIE (*giggling with happiness*). "An[d] on the fat o' the land!"

GEORGE. Yes. (LENNIE *turns his head. Q[uick]ly.*) Look over there, Lennie. Like yo[u] really see it.

LENNIE. Where?

GEORGE. Right acrost that river there. [Can] you almost see it?

LENNIE (*moving*). Where, George?

GEORGE. It's over there. You keep lo[okin',] Lennie. Just keep lookin'.

LENNIE. I'm lookin', George. I'm lo[okin'.]

GEORGE. That's right. It's gonna be nice [.] Ain't gonna be no trouble, no fights[. No] body ever gonna hurt nobody, or steal [from] 'em. It's gonna be—nice.

LENNIE. I can see it, George. I can s[ee it.] Right over there! I can see it! (GEORGE [fires.] LENNIE *crumples; falls behind the b[rush.] The voices of the men in the distance[.]*)

CURTAIN

Dead End

BY SIDNEY KINGSLEY

*"The contrast of affluence and wretchedness is like dead
and living bodies chained together."*

THOMAS PAINE.

CHARACTERS

GIMPTY	MR. JONES
T.B.	KAY
TOMMY	JACK HILTON
DIPPY	LADY WITH DOG
ANGEL	THREE SMALL BOYS
SPIT	SECOND CHAUFFEUR
DOORMAN	SECOND AVENUE BOYS
OLD LADY	MRS. MARTIN
OLD GENTLEMAN	PATROLMAN MULLIGAN
FIRST CHAUFFEUR	FRANCEY
"BABY-FACE" MARTIN	G-MEN
HUNK	POLICEMEN
PHILIP GRISWALD	PLAINCLOTHESMAN
GOVERNESS	INTERNE
MILTY	MEDICAL EXAMINER
DRINA	SAILOR
MR. GRISWALD	A CROWD

ACT ONE

DEAD END of a New York street, ending in a wharf over the East River. To the left is a high terrace and a white iron gate leading to the back of the exclusive East River Terrace Apartments. Hugging the terrace and filing up the street are a series of squalid tenement houses.

Beyond the wharf is the East River, covered by a swirling scum an inch thick. A brown river, mucky with floating refuse and offal. A hundred sewers vomit their guts into it. Up-town of the wharf as we float down Hell Gate, the River voices its defiant protest in fierce whirlpools and stumbling rapids, groaning. Further down, we pass under the arch of the Queensboro Bridge, spired, delicate, weblike in superstructure, powerful and brutal in the stone and steel which it plants like uncouth giant feet on the earth. In its hop, skip, and jump over the River it has planted one such foot on the Island called Welfare, once the home of hospital, insane asylum, and prison, now being dismantled, an eyesore to the fastidious who have recently become its neighbors. And here on the shore, along the Fifties is a strange sight. Set plumb down in the midst of slums, antique warehouses, discarded breweries, slaughter houses, electrical works, gas tanks, loading cranes, coal-chutes, the very wealthy have begun to establish their city residence in huge, new, palatial apartments. The East River Terrace is one of these. Looking up this street from the vantage of the River, we see only a small portion of the back terrace and a gate; but they are enough to suggest the towering magnificence of the whole structure. The wall is of rich, heavy masonry, guarded at the top by a row of pikes. Beyond the pikes, shutting off the view of the squalid street below, is a thick edging of lush green shrubbery. And beyond that, a glimpse of the tops of gaily colored sun umbrellas. Occasionally the clink of glasses and laughter filter through the shrubs. The exposed sidewalk of the tenement is whitewashed and ornamented with an elaborate, ivy-covered trellis to hide its ugliness. The gate posts are crowned with brass ship lanterns, one red, one green. Through the gate is a catwalk which leads to a floating d where the inhabitants of this apartr moor their boats and yachts.

Contrasting sharply with all this rich is the miseased street below, filthy, str with torn newspapers and garbage the tenements. The tenement houses close, dark and crumbling. They cr each other. Where there are curtain the windows, they are streaked and fo where there are none, we see throug hideous, water stained, peeling wall-p and old broken-down furniture. The escapes are cluttered with gutted mattr and quilts, old clothes, bread-boxes, bottles, a canary cage, an occasional p plant struggling for life.

To the right is a huge, red sand ho standing on stilts of heavy timber se stories tall. Up the street, blocking view, is a caterpillar steam shovel. Be it, way over to the west, are the sky-s ing parallelepipeds of Radio City. An way between two tenements, tied tog by drooping lines of wash, gives us a tant glimpse of the mighty Empire Building rearing its useless mooring t a quarter of a mile into the clouds.

At the juncture of tenement house terrace is a police call-box; at the jun of the street and wharf is a police sta ion bearing the warning, "Dead En The boards of the wharf are weather en and deeply grained; the piles are sta green with algae to where the water and brown above. A ladder nailed t beams dips down into the river. The light tossed from the waves dances a the piles to the musical lap of the u Other river sounds counter-point orchestration: the bells and the wh the clink and the chug of passing bo

A gang of boys are swimming in the s age at the foot of the wharf, splas about and enjoying it immensely. of them wear torn bathing trunks, are nude. Their speech is a rhyt shocking jargon that would put a t driver to blush.

re are a few onlookers. A fat, greasy
…AN leans out of a tenement window.
… is peeling an orange and throwing
… peels into the street. A sensitive-faced
…ng MAN, in a patched, frayed shirt,
…n at the neck, is sitting on one of the
…s. In his lap is a drawing board. Occa-
…ally he will work feverishly, using pen-
…and triangular ruler, then he will let
…pencil droop, and stare out over the
…r with deep-set eyes, dream-laden,
…dy.

…ubercular-looking BOY about sixteen is
…near the hopper, pitching pennies to
…sidewalk. There is a splash of water,
…ud derisive laugh, and up the ladder
…bs a BOY, lean, lithe, long-limbed,
…-nosed, his cheeks puffed with water.
…ching the top of the ladder, he leans
…and squirts out the water. A yelp
…w. He laughs again and cries:
…tcha dat time!"

… BOYS come running down the street
…rd the wharf. One, a tiny Italian with
…eat shock of blue-black hair, is dangling
…oe box almost as big as himself; the
…r, a gawky Polack, head shaven, cret-
…s, adenoidal, is slapping his thigh with
…led newspaper as he runs. They shout:
…ya, Tommy?"

…MY. H'lo Angel! H'lo Dippy! (ANGEL
…ings his box, and starts tearing off his
…es. A squat boy with a brutish face,
…bubbling from his nostrils, climbs up
… TOMMY. As he reaches the top and
…the others, he shouts in a mocking
…-song, "Dopey Dippy, dopey Dippy,
…y Dippy!")

…Y. Shat ap, will ya, Spit!

…(*Spitting through his teeth at* DIPPY,
…is stripping his jersey over his head.)
…t inna belly-button! (*Laughs and*
…bs onto the wharf to sprawl next to
…MY. DIPPY *mumbles and wipes out his*
…l with his finger.)

…MY. Lay off 'im, why doncha?

…I'll knock 'im innis eye!

…MY. Wassamattuh? Yuh a wise guy
boy scout? C'mon in, Dippy!

ANGEL. Howza wawda, Tommy?

TOMMY. Boy! Duh nuts!

SPIT. Geeze, great!

ANGEL. Cold?

TOMMY. Nah. Swell. Jus' right. (*Wiping
off some of the river filth that has clung
to him.*) Boy, deah's a lot a junk inna
wawda tuhday!

DIPPY. (*Pointing to some dirt on* SPIT's
back.) Wat's at? (*He touches* SPIT, *smells
his finger and makes a wry face.*) Pee—
ew, whadda stink! (SPIT *plucks off a huge
gob of filth and throws it at* DIPPY. DIPPY
whines.) What yuh wanna do dat fuh?

SPIT. Aw, I'll mobilize yuh!

TOMMY. Leave 'im alone! (*To* DIPPY.)
Whyn't yuh keep yuh trap shut, huh?

DIPPY. He trew dat crap on me! I wuz…

TOMMY. O.K. O.K. O.K. (*Pointing at
some imaginary object near the sand hopper.*) Hey, felluhs, look! (*All look off.*
TOMMY *sticks his forefinger next to* SPIT's
averted nose.) Hey, Spit! (SPIT *turns his
head and bumps his nose on* TOMMY's
finger. The boys laugh.) Nex' time leave
'im alone, see? (*The cadaverous-looking
lad picks up his pennies, and comes down
to the others, boasting, "Boy I git a
crack all a time!"*)

TOMMY. (*Rising.*) Yeah? Aw right, T.B.,
I'll pitch yuh.

T.B. O.K. C'mon.

TOMMY. Lemme a couple.

T.B. Yuh ain' got 'ny?

TOMMY. Come on! I'll pay yuh back.
(TOMMY *and* T.B. *go up to the hopper and
pitch pennies to the sidewalk.*)

SPIT, (*Turning to* DIPPY, *makes a swipe
at him.* DIPPY *backs away.*) Two fuh flinchin' . . . two fuh flinchin'!

DIPPY. I di' not.

SPIT. Yuh did so.

DIPPY. I di' not.

ANGEL. Whyn't cha choose? Choose 'im! Choose fer it!

SPIT. (*Scrambling to his feet.*) O.K. Odds!

ANGEL. Go on!

DIPPY. Evens! (SPIT *and* DIPPY *match fingers.*) Once fuh me. See? Cheatin' shows!

SPIT. Come on! Once fuh me. Twice fuh me. An' tree fuh me. Cheatin' shows? Yeah. Boy, ahl knock yuh fer a loop!

ANGEL. Go on, Dippy, yuh lost. Yuh git yer lumps.

DIPPY. (*Whining.*) Hey, Tommy. . . .

SPIT. (*Grabbing* DIPPY's *rolled newspaper.*) Come on! (*He bangs* DIPPY *twice on the head.*)

DIPPY. Ow! . . . Ow! . . . Ow! Ah, yuh louse. Yuh didn't have tuh hit me so hahd. Wid all his might he hit me. Wid all his might, duh son uva bitch!

TOMMY. (*Still absorbed in pitching pennies with* T.B.) Whyn't yuh pick on a kid who kin fight back?

SPIT. Aw-ww!

TOMMY. Ah! (*The* DOORMAN, *a giant in powder-blue uniform with gilt buttons and braid, opens the gate of the apartment house, crosses to the end of the sidewalk and blows a whistle, then signals to someone up the street to come down. He turns to speak to an aristocratic* OLD GENTLEMAN *and* OLD LADY *who appear in the gateway of the East River Terraces.*)

DOORMAN. I'm so sorry, ma'am, but it'll only be for a day or two.

OLD LADY. That's quite all right.

OLD GENTLEMAN. (*Arthritic, grumpy, walking slowly and with effort.*) It isn't at all. There's no reason why we should have to walk half a block to the car. (*A* COLORED MAN *in chauffeur's uniform comes down the sidewalk.*)

DOORMAN. I'm so sorry, sir.

OLD LADY. That's quite all right. (*She pauses a moment, surveying the boys.*) Look at this!

OLD GENTLEMAN. Humph! I've seen from the balcony.

ANGEL. Hey, look, guys! Dey usin' a b daw.

TOMMY. I wonduh why.

DIPPY. (*Familiarly, to the young man u is sketching.*) Duh yuh know, Gimp Hey, Gimpty?

GIMPTY. What?

DIPPY. Duh yuh know why?

GIMPTY. Why what?

DIPPY. Why dey usin' a back daw.

GIMPTY. Are they?

DIPPY. Yeah.

GIMPTY. No . . . no, I don't. (*The* ORED CHAUFFEUR *salutes the* OLD MAN *offers him an arm to lean on.*)

CHAUFFEUR. Good afternoon sir, I'm s I couldn't drive the car around the . . .

OLD LADY. That's all right, Jordan. L at these youngsters! Aren't they sweet

OLD GENTLEMAN. Sweet? Yes . . . fro distance! (*They walk up the street, of sight. A passing tug blasts the air its fog horn.* TOMMY, *having won at pe pitching, puts the pennies in the pocke his trousers, which are hanging on hopper.* T.B. *disconsolate, goes to* ANG

T.B. Dat cleans me. I dunno. I kin al git a crack when I'm playin' by my (*He watches* ANGEL, *who is fussing a scrap of newspaper and some stra brown substance.*) Whatcha got deah

ANGEL. It's a dried up hawse-ball.

T.B. Whatcha doin'?

ANGEL. I'm gonna make some cigare Some guy tole me—yuh kin make c ettes outa dem.

T.B. Yeah?

ANGEL. Yeah. I'm gonna try it.

T.B. I never hoid a dat.

ANGEL. It's good. Some guy tole me,

MY.   Aw, yuh crazy.

EL.   Naw . . . it's good.

Deah wuz a guy at rifawm school
e used tuh smoke marywanna. Yuh
w what dat is? Dope. It's like dope.
dope. It gives yuh dreams.

EL.   Didja try it?

Nah. I can't smoke on accoun' a my
. It gits me. I cough like anyt'ing.

EL.   (*Rises and crosses to* GIMPTY.)
, Gimpty, got a match?

(*Murmurs.*) My pratt and your face.
's a good match! (*Laughs to himself.*)

PTY.   What for?

Y.   He's makin' cigarettes outta hawse-
.

PTY.   Out of what?

EL.   Hawse-balls.

PTY.   Throw it away, you crazy fool.
 want to get sick?

EL.   I kin smoke. Whadda yuh tink I
?

PTY.   Listen. I read about a guy once
 smoked that stuff. You know what
pened to him.

EL.   What?

PTY.   Great, big things grew right out
his head.

EL.   (*Turning away from* GIMPTY, *with
ust.*) Aw—w—w, go wan.

PTY.   Listen . . . if I give you a good
, will you throw that away?

EL.   (*Turning back eagerly.*) Sure!

PTY.   (*Appropriates* ANGEL's *horrible
rette and throws it into the water; then
s a sack of tobacco from his pocket,
ptly rolls a cigarette and holds it out
ANGEL.*) Here! Stick out your tongue.
GEL *licks the paper.* GIMPTY *completes
ing the cigarette and gives it to him.*)
re you are! Now don't try that again.
'll get sick as a dog. Remember . . .
tellin' you.

ANGEL.   (*Proudly exhibiting his cigarette.*)
Boy! Hey, felluhs, look! Gimpty gimme
a butt. (*To* T.B.) Gimme a light, T.B. (T.B.
*fishes some matches from his pocket and
lights* ANGEL's *cigarette.*)

DIPPY.   (*Dashing over to* GIMPTY.) Me
too, Gimpty! Gimme! Yew know me! Yew
know me! (DIPPY, TOMMY *and* SPIT *descend
on* GIMPTY, *swarming over him like a
horde of locusts. They hold out their hands
and beg plaintively.* "*Give us one! Yew
know us, Gimpty.*")

GIMPTY.   No! No! No more! Beat it! That's
all! (*They only plead the louder.*) I said
that's all. Don't you understand English?
You want a boot in the behind? (TWO
MEN *come down the street. One, tall,
young, rather good-looking in a vicious
way: the other, older, shorter, squat, a
sledge-hammer build. The first has thin
nervous lips, narrow agate eyes, bloodshot.
A peculiarly glossy face, as if the skin had
been stretched taut over the cheekbones
which are several sizes too large for the
lean jaw underneath. Here is a man given
to sudden volcanic violences that come
and are gone in a breath. His movements
are sharp, jerky; his reflexes exaggerated,
those of a high-strung man whose nerves
are beginning to snap under some constant
strain. He covers it, though, with a cocky
swagger. He walks leaning forward, hips
thrown back, almost as if out of joint.
He wears a gray, turned-down fedora, an
expensive suit, sharpy style, the coat a bit
too tight at the waist, pleated trousers, and
gray suede shoes. His squat companion is
dressed almost identically, but was not
designed to wear such clothes. His trousers
hang on his hips, revealing a bulge of
shirt-waist between vest and trouser-top,
his barrel of a chest is too thick for his
jacket, his arms too long for the sleeves.
His huge fingers you notice at once! Thick
stubs sticking out of the shapeless bags
of his hands like the teats of a cow. The
two men come down almost to the edge
of the wharf. The tall one lights a cigarette, looks about, smiles, shakes his head,
and talks* sotto voce *to his companion.*)

TOMMY.   (*To* GIMPTY.) Aw, ta hell wid
yuh! Cheap skate! (*The boys walk away,

disgusted. GIMPTY *rolls another cigarette, lights it, and returns to his drawing-board.*)

SPIT. Yeah, ta hell wid 'im!

DIPPY. Yeah, ta hell wid 'im!

SPIT. (*Crosses to his clothes, which are hanging from a nail on the hopper.*) I dun need hisn. I gotta stack a butts I picked up I'm savin'.

TOMMY. Give us one.

DIPPY. Yeah! Give us one!

SPIT. Nah. I'm savin' 'em.

TOMMY. Don' be a miser. (SPIT *takes out a tobacco tin, opens it, exposing a rare collection of cigarette ends gleaned from the streets. Grudgingly he hands* TOMMY *and* DIPPY *a butt each, then selects a choice one for himself.*) Gimme a light, T.B. (*They all light up and puff away with huge satisfaction.*)

ANGEL. (*Suddenly aware of the two strangers.*) Shine, mistah? (*The tall fellow shakes his head and turns away.*) A good shine. Come on! (*To the other.*) Yew? (*The squat man glares at him and growls,* "Yuh cockeyed? Can't yuh see we got one?")

ANGEL. (*Turns away, muttering.*) Aw ... call at a shine? (*The* DOORMAN *comes to the gate and holds it open. A* GOVERNESS, *accompanied by a well-dressed, delicate-featured, little boy, comes out of the Terrace Apartments. The* GOVERNESS *talks with a marked French accent. She nods to the* DOORMAN.)

GOVERNESS. Good afternoon.

DOORMAN. Good afternoon, ma'am.

GOVERNESS. But ... where is our chauffeur?

DOORMAN. I think he's on the corner with the cab-drivers. Shall I get him?

GOVERNESS. Never mind. (*To the little boy.*) Wait here. *Attends moi ici, mon cheri.* (*The* DOORMAN *goes in, closing the gate behind him. The little boy, surveying the curious scene, answers, a bit distracted,*

"All right, I'll ..." *When he opens mouth, he shows a shiny, gold orthodo brace.*)

GOVERNESS. *Mais, Philippe! En françai.*

PHILIP. (*Obediently.*) *Oui, mademois j'attendrais.*

GOVERNESS. *Très bien. J'y reviendrai suite ... dans deux minutes.*

PHILIP. *Oui, oui, mademoiselle.* (*She ries up the sidewalk and out of sight.*)

TOMMY. Wee-wee! He's godda go wee-v (*All the boys shout with laughter.*)

DIPPY. Do a swan-dive, Tommy. At's I like.

TOMMY. O.K. Hole my butt. (*He ha his cigarette to* DIPPY.) Hey, kid! I yew! Hey, wee-wee! (PHILIP *looks at hi* Yuh wanna see sumpm? A swan-d Watch! (TOMMY *dashes off, under hopper. We hear his* "Whe-e-e" *an splash. The boys cluck approval.*)

PHILIP. What's so wonderful about tl

ANGEL. Aw, yuh fat tub a buttuh, more'n yew kin do.

PHILIP. That shows how much you kn

T.B. I bet a dollar he can't even swin

PHILIP. I can too.

T.B. Ah, balonee!

PHILIP. Balonee yourself! We've a poo there and I swim every day ... with struction.

SPIT. Aw, bushwah! (TOMMY *appears the ladder.* DIPPY *hands him his cigare.*

DIPPY. He sez dey godda pool in ere

TOMMY. How wuzat swan-dive?

DIPPY. He sez it wuz lousy.

TOMMY. (*Climbing over the parapet crossing to* PHILIP, *belligerently.*) Oh, ye What wuza mattuh wid it? Kin yew betta?

PHILIP. A trillion times.

TOMMY. Awright. Lessee yuh.

IP. Where?

MY. Heah!

IP. Here?

MY. Yeah, heah. Yew hoid me. Yew deef. (*Turns to the others.*) His eahs hlap, dat's it! (*They roar with laugh-*

IP. I wouldn't swim here.

He's yelluh, dat's what! Dat's what! s godda yelluh streak up 'is back a wide.

IP. It's dirty here.

Y. (*Shocked.*) Doity!

(*Very indignant.*) Doity! He sez y. He sez it's doity! I'll sock 'im!

EL. Lil fairy!

. Wassamattuh? Yuh sca'd yuh git a loit on yuh?

IP. Besides, I haven't got my suit.

MY. Well, go in bareass.

Yeah, wassamattuh wid bareass?

IP. And besides, I'm not allowed to.

Y. (*Sing-song.*) Sissy, sissy, sucks his nma's titty!

IP. Sticks and stones may break my es, but names will never hurt me. (*The s crowd him back against the gate.*)

MY. Ah, ahl spit in yuh eye an' vn yuh. Hey, what's at junk yuh got /uh mout . . . like a hawse?

IP. It's a brace, to make my teeth ight.

MY. Wha-a-at? I could do dat wit wallop! (*The gang roar with laughter.*)

IP. You try and you'll be arrested.

. Yeah?

MY. (*Contemptuously.*) Look who's na arrest us!

IP. My uncle's a judge.

MY. Balonee!

PHILIP. Did you ever hear of Judge Gris- wald?

ANGEL. So what? So I know a guy whose brudduh's a detective. He'll git us out.

T.B. Yeah? Did yuh evuh hear a Judge Poikins! Well, he's a frien' a mine, see? He sent me to rifawm school once.

DOORMAN. (*Appears, bellowing.*) What's the matter? Get away from here, you! (*They scatter, razzing him. He turns to* PHILIP.) Were they bothering you?

PHILIP. No, I don't pay any attention to them. (*The* DOORMAN *opens the gate and both he and* PHILIP *go in. The boys laugh and mock them.* DIPPY, *preoccupied with the phenomena of his body, suddenly dis- covers a lone hair on his chest.*)

DIPPY. Boy! Gee! Hey, I godda hair! (*He caresses it, proudly.* T.B. *comes over, in- spects the hair, admires it, then suddenly plucks it out, and runs away laughing and holding up the trophy.* DIPPY *yips, first with pain, then with rage.* TOMMY *finds an old discarded broom in the litter under the hopper. He balances it skillfully on the palm of his hand.*)

SPIT. Gese, I'm hungry!

TOMMY. Me too!

ANGEL. Boy, I'm so hungry I could eat a live dog.

DIPPY. (*Looks up from his wounded chest.*) Boy, I could eat a hot dog.

ANGEL. Wid sour-kraut!

DIPPY. Yeah.

ANGEL. (*Licking his lips and patting his belly.*) Yum.

SPIT. Hey, should we go tuh Schultzie's 'n' see if we kin snitch sumpin?

TOMMY. (*Balancing the broom.*) Nah, Schultzie's wise tuh us.

ANGEL. We could try some udduh staws.

TOMMY. (*Still balancing the broom.*) Nah, dey're all wise tuh us. Duh minute we walk in 'ey ask us wadda we want. If we had some dough, while one uv us wuz buyin' sumpm de udduh guys could swipe some stuff, see? I got faw cents, but 'at ain' enough. (*He drops the broom, and becomes the man of action.*) Anybody got any dough heah? Hey, yew, Angel, yuh got some?

ANGEL. No, I ain'.

TOMMY. Come on! Don' hole out!

ANGEL. Honest! I didn' git no customah dis mawnin'.

TOMMY. Weah's' 'is pants? Look in 'is pants! (T.B. *and* SPIT *rush to the hopper, grab* ANGEL's *pants, and start rifling the pockets.* ANGEL *follows them, yelling.*)

ANGEL. Hey! Git outa deah! Git outa deah!

T.B. Nuttn but a couple a stamps 'n' a boy-scout knife.

SPIT. (*Taking the knife himself.*) Oh baby, kin I have dis?

ANGEL. (*Follows* SPIT.) No, I need it.

SPIT. No, yuh don't.

ANGEL. Aw, Spit, gimme my knife!

SPIT. (*Mocking his accent.*) Watsa ma'? Piza Taliana? (*He spits at him.*) Right inee ear! Ha!

ANGEL. (*Backs a step and wipes out his ear with a finger.*) Ah, yuh louse! Ast me fuh sumpm sometime 'n' see watcha git.

TOMMY. Giv'im 'is knife!

SPIT. Da hell I will!

ANGEL. Aw, Spit, gimme my knife! Tommy, make 'im, will yuh?

TOMMY. Gimme dat knife!

SPIT. What fuh?

TOMMY. (*Makes a fist and waves it in front of* SPIT's *nose.*) Fuh dis...right in yuh bugle! (*He grabs the knife and examines it.*) Gese, dat's a knife! Five blades! Boy, I'd like one like 'at. (*Enter from the lower tenement door, a young* BOY *of about twelve, a bit timid, neatly dressed, obvious semitic features.*)

ANGEL. Aw, Tommy, I need it. I g⌐ use it. Honest!

TOMMY. (*Gives him his knife.*) H⌐ Stop squawkin'! Don' say I nevuh ⌐ yuh nuttin'!

ANGEL. Tanks, Tommy. Dat's white.⌐

TOMMY. (*Good-naturedly.*) Ah, shat⌐ (*To* DIPPY, *who sits reflectively picking⌐ nose.*) Hey, Dippy! Pick me a big j⌐ one! (DIPPY *grins, rolls the resinous m⌐ into a little ball, and flicks it at* TO⌐ TOMMY *laughs, and trots up the stree⌐ join the others who are seated on a ⌐ ment stoop. The* TALL MAN *turns from⌐ conversation with his companion, and ⌐ to* DIPPY, "*Hey, you!*")

DIPPY. What?

THE TALL ONE. Wanna run a errand⌐ me?

THE SQUAT ONE. (*Offers.*) I'll go, c⌐ What is it?

DIPPY. Sure. Wheah?

THE TALL ONE. (*Points to a tener⌐ house up the block.*) 418...fourth ⌐ ...Mrs. Martin. Tell her a friend a⌐ wants a see her here.

DIPPY. O.K. 418? O.K. (*He trots off⌐*

GIMPTY. (*Who has looked up at the so⌐ of* THE TALL ONE's *voice.*) Don't I k⌐ you from somewhere? (*The stran⌐ lips compress—"no".*) I could've sⱯ⌐ I...

SQUAT MAN. (*Comes over and mutter⌐ a thick voice full of threat.*) He said⌐ didn' he? (*The other restrains him w⌐ touch on the arm.*)

GIMPTY. Sorry. (*He looks down at⌐ drawing. The two walk away, and s⌐ leaning against the wall, talking in ⌐ tones. The boys on the stoop sudd⌐ notice the little Jewish boy who is pee⌐ over the wharf.*)

T.B. Hey, look! Deah's 'at new kid⌐ moved aroun' a block.

SPIT. 'At's 'at Jew kid! (*They rise ⌐ come down toward him.*)

MMY. Hey, kid!

GEL. Hey, kid!

JEWISH BOY. (*Looks up.*) Wadda
want?

T. Come heah, Ikey! Come on! Don'
so slow. (*He comes over, eager to join
m, yet scared.*)

MMY. Yew da noo kid onna block,
tcha?

JEWISH BOY. Yeah.

MMY. Watsya name?

JEWISH BOY. Milton. Milton Schwartz.

MMY. Yuh wanna belong tuh are gang?

TY. (*Eagerly.*) Yeah. Shuah.

MMY. Got 'ny dough? Yuh godda be
etiated.

TY. I god tree sants.

MMY. Gimme it!

T. (*Prodding him in the ribs.*) Give
uh 'im!

(*Prodding him harder and pulling
around.*) Go on!

MMY. (*Pulling him back.*) Come on!
n' hole out! (MILTY *fishes out three
ts and hands them to* TOMMY.) 'At's all
got?

TY. Yeah.

T. Sure?

TY. Hones'.

MMY. Soich 'im! (*They start to go
ough his pockets.*)

TY. (*Turns his pockets inside out.*)
n'! Yuh don' haf tuh. Look!

T. Ah, you punk!

MMY. Listen, yew! If yuh wanna belong
dis gang, yuh godda git a quatuh.

TY. A quatuh? Wheah ahm gonna
a quatah fum?

T. Fum yuh ole lady.

TY. She woodn gimme no quatuh.

SPIT. Yuh know wheah she keeps huh
money, doncha?

MILTY. Dat's a sin tuh steal.

SPIT. (*Mocking his accent.*) Whassamat-
tuh, Ikey?

MILTY. Don' make fun on me. I can' help
it.

SPIT. (*Contemptuously.*) Yuh scared tuh
snitch a quatuh? Geese, she won' fin out.

MILTY. Yes, she would.

SPIT. (*Still mocking him.*) Oh, she counts
huh money all a time, huh, Jakey Ikey?

MILTY. Stop dat! Gimme back my tree
sants. I don' wanna hang out wid youse.

TOMMY. (*To* SPIT.) Yuh godda watch-
pocket, aincha?

SPIT. Yeah.

TOMMY. Guard dis dough! (*He hands the
money to* SPIT, *who puts it in his pocket.
They walk away, completely ignoring*
MILTY.)

MILTY. (*Follows them, murmuring tremu-
lously.*) Gimme back my tree sants!

SPIT. (*Whispers to the others.*) Let's cockalize him!

ANGEL. Wadda yuh say, Tommy?

TOMMY. O.K.

T.B. Come on! (ANGEL *crosses nonchalantly behind* MILTY, *then crouches on his
hands and knees unnoticed. The others
turn and slowly approach him. Suddenly*
TOMMY *pushes* MILTY, *who stumbles backward and trips over* ANGEL, *feet flying up.
They all pounce on the prostrate boy, pin
his arms and legs to the ground, unbutton
his pants, pull up his shirt.*)

TOMMY. Gimme some a dat doit!

SPIT. (*Scoops up a handful of dirt.*) Heah!
(*They rub it into* MILTY's *groin. He kicks
and screams, hysterically laughing at the
sensation. When he's through rubbing in
the filth,* TOMMY *coughs up a huge wad
of saliva and spits on* MILTY's *organ. Each
of them spit, once round the circle. The*
TALL ONE *and the* SQUAT ONE *laugh. A tat-*

too of heels running down the street! A whirlwind hits the group, and the boys are dispersed right and left. The whirlwind is a girl not much bigger than TOMMY, *with a face resembling his—pushed up nose and freckles. She slaps and pulls and pushes the boys, who scatter away, laughing and shouting. She stands there, eyes blazing.*

TOMMY. Aw scram, will yuh, Drina, Scram!

DRINA. Shut up! (*She helps* MILTY *to his feet, brushes him off, and wipes his face, comforting him. On second glance she is not the child she seemed. Her simple dress, her hair combed back of the ears and held in place with a cheap celluloid clasp, her lithe, boyish figure combine to create the illusion of a very young girl. When she comforts* MILTY, *however, it is apparent in the mature quality of her solicitude that she is much older—in her earlier twenties. The* TALL ONE *grins at her. She throws him a contemptuous side glance and rebukes him sharply.*)

DRINA. You ought to be ashamed of yourself, standing there and letting them pile up on this kid.

TOMMY. Aw, Drina, will yuh butt outa dis?

DRINA. (*To the snivelling boy.*) Are you hurt? (*To the* TALL ONE.) Why didn't you stop 'em?

THE TALL ONE. What fer? It'll do 'im good.

DRINA. (*Furiously.*) Oh, yeah? I suppose it'll do you good if I crack your face, huh?

THE TALL ONE. Oh, lady, yuh scare me!

DRINA. Fresh guy, huh?

THE SQUAT ONE. (*Walks over to her, his face screwed up in disgust.*) Shut yuh big mouth or I'll . . .

THE TALL ONE. (*Sharply.*) Hunk! Cut it! (HUNK *obeys instantly. They walk away to the bulwark.*)

TOMMY. Aw, Drina, why dontcha butt outa my business?

DRINA. Wait till I get you home, I'll s[.] you butt out of . . . (TOMMY *scratches* [.] *head. She places her hands on her hips* [.] *frowns.*) What are you scratchin' y[.] head for? Are you buggy again? ([.] *authoritative, maternal concern gives* [.] *the air of a little girl playing house.*)

TOMMY. Aw, git out a heah or I'll [.] yuh one!

DRINA. That's fine talk, Tommy . . . [.] you one! (*He scratches again.*) There go again! Scratchin'! (*She crosses to hi[.]* Come on home! I'm gonna wash y[.] head.

TOMMY. Aw, lemme alone. All a time bodderin' me. . . . (*Runs away from* DR[.] *and climbs up the hopper like a mon[.] out of her reach.*)

DRINA. (*To* GIMPTY.) Pete, why didn't [.] stop 'em?

GIMPTY. I'm sorry, Drina. I didn't n[.] what was happenin'. I was thinkin' ab[.] somethin'.

DRINA. Yeah? (*She turns to* TOMMY, *da[.] ling high on his perch.*) Tommy, did [.] go to school today?

TOMMY. Sure.

DRINA. If you're lying, Tommy, I'll [.] you.

TOMMY. (*Wiggling his toes at her.*) [.] nuts!

DRINA. (*To* MILTY, *who is still sobbir[.]* What's the matter? Did they hurt you[.]

MILTY. Dey took my money.

DRINA. They did? How much?

MILTY. Tree sants.

DRINA. Tommy!

TOMMY. What?

DRINA. Did you take this boy's three ce[.]

TOMMY. Nope.

DRINA. You did so!

TOMMY. I di' not!

DRINA. You did so!

MMY. Well, I ain't got it.

NA. Who has? Who's got it? (*To* GEL.) You?

GEL. Not me. (DRINA *looks accusingly* T.B.)

. (*Walks away, indignantly.*) Don' k at me!

MMY. Go on, Spit, giv 'im back 'is tree ts.

NA. (*Turns on* SPIT.) Oh, so you're the e! Come on!

T. (*Thumbs his nose.*) Like hell I will.

NA. Come on!

T. Frig you!

NA. (*Flaring.*) I'll crack you . . . you like that!

T. Ah, I'll sock yuh inna' tit. (*She acks him. He clenches his fist and draws back ready to swing.*)

MMY. (*Jumps from the hopper and hes at* SPIT, *fists clenched, arms raised in hting position.*) Cut dat out yuh louse!

T. Well . . . she smacked me foist. smacked me foist. No dame kin smack foist an' get away wid it.

MY. Give 'er dat dough.

T. What fuh?

MY. Give her da dough. Dat's what .

T. Yeah?

MY. Yeah.

T. Ah, yuh mudduh's chooch!

MY. Ah, yuh fadduh's doop!

NA. Keep quiet, Tommy! (*To* SPIT.) me on! *Come on!*

MY. Hurry up! Give 'er dat dough! use. SPIT *grudgingly gives her the mon-* TOMMY *drops his hands and returns to hopper, whistling.* DRINA *hands the ney back to* MILTY.)

NA. Here.

MILTY. Tanks!

DRINA. That's all right. You look like a nice boy. Stay away from them. They're no good. They're bums.

SPIT. (*Sullen, but seeking an ally.*) Come on, Angel. Y'ain' bin in yet. Wanna go in?

ANGEL. O.K.

SPIT. Last one in's a stinkin' rotten egg! (*They rush off and jump into the water with great splashes.* T.B. *remains near the hopper, watching. Off right voices are heard. A tall, lean, soft-spoken gentleman, middle-aged, wearing shell-rimmed glasses and carrying a pipe appears at the gate. He is followed by a plumpish man of about the same age.* PHILIP *opens the gate for them, smiling.*)

PHILIP. Hello, daddy!

PHILIP'S FATHER. Hello, son. Shoulders back! (PHILIP *straightens.*) Attaboy. Where's Jeanne?

PHILIP. She went to find Charles.

PHILIP'S FATHER. Oh? And where's he?

PHILIP. I don't know.

PHILIP'S FATHER. (*Goes up the street, looks into the tenement hallway. He shakes his head in disapproval and turns to his companion.*) Say, Jones! Look at this at our back door! (JONES *nods.*)

DRINA. (*To* GIMPTY.) You let them take his money without even interfering. Shame on you!

GIMPTY. I told you I didn't notice what was happening. My mind was on somethin' else.

DRINA. Ah, you're always sticking up for them. (*To* TOMMY.) Tommy! I'm gonna get some kerosene and clean your head right away.

TOMMY. Aw—w—w.

DRINA. Don't aw—w—w me! (*She walks up the street.* TOMMY *jumps down from the hopper and dives into the water.*)

PHILIP'S FATHER. Hm! Whose property is this?

JONES. I think J. and J. I'm not sure, Griswald.

GRISWALD. Why don't they keep it in repair?

JONES. What for? It's valuable stuff as it is. No upkeep.

GRISWALD. (*Gasps at the stench that comes out of the building.*) Phew! What do they do? Use this hallway as a latrine?

JONES. Probably.

GRISWALD. Hm! Terrible!

JONES. Well, these people have to live some place.

GRISWALD. (*Groping in his coat pockets.*) Hm. Forgot my tobacco pouch. Will you run up and get it for me, son?

PHILIP. Sure, daddy! Where is it?

GRISWALD. Now, let me see. I think it's . . . I'd better go myself. (*Turns to* JONES.)

JONES. I'll go up with you.

GRISWALD. We'll be down in a minute. Ask Charles to wait for us.

PHILIP. Certainly, daddy.

GRISWALD. Thanks, son. (*They go off into the apartment house.* DIPPY *comes running down the sidewalk.*)

DIPPY. I fuhgot. Wot wuzat name? Moitle?

THE TALL ONE. Martin! (HUNK *cautions him with a tug.* GIMPTY'S *head jerks up. He stares at the* TALL ONE.)

HUNK. Maybe I better go.

THE TALL ONE. O.K. 418, fourth floor. (*To* DIPPY.) Nevuh mind, kid. (*To* HUNK.) And while yuh at it, look in at tailor's I tole yuh.

HUNK. (*Nods.*) Check! (*Exit* HUNK *up the sidewalk.*)

DIPPY. I'll go. I'll go git her.

THE TALL ONE. Beat it!

DIPPY. Don' I git nuttin'? I went part a da way.

THE TALL ONE. Nuttin' fer nuttin'. Be it!

DIPPY. Ah, dat's a lousy trick tuh play a kid.

THE TALL ONE. (*Raises his foot to ki DIPPY.*) Come on! . . . (DIPPY *runs to t ladder, grumbling, climbs over, yells.*)

DIPPY. Hey! Yew! (*The* TALL ONE *tur to look.*) Go tuh hell! (*And he quick jumps into the water. The* TALL ONE *laug comes down to the edge of the wharf, a watches* DIPPY *splash away.*)

GIMPTY. (*Snaps his fingers. Sudden collection.*) Martin! Baby-face Martin!

THE TALL ONE. (*Wheels to face* GIMPT one hand reaching under his coat for shoulder holster.*) I ain't Martin, you b tard!

GIMPTY. Don't you recognize me?

MARTIN. O.K. Yew asked fer it an' y git it!

GIMPTY. I'm Gimpty. . . . Remember?

MARTIN. Gimpty?

GIMPTY. Sure, Baby-face. I . . .

MARTIN. Sh! Shat ap! My name's Jo son. Git it? Johnson.

GIMPTY. We were kids here. Don't y remember? I was one of the gang.

MARTIN. (*Squints at him carefully fo long time.*) Yeah.

GIMPTY. You don't have to worry ab me.

MARTIN. I ain't worryin' about you. worryin' about me. (*His hand emer slowly from under his coat.*) You wuz funny kid who used to mind my clot when I went swimmin'.

GIMPTY. Yeah.

MARTIN. Yeah. 'At's right. Kin yuh keep yer lips buttoned up?

GIMPTY. I guess so.

MARTIN. Yuh guess so! Yuh better f out. And God damn quick!

IPTY. You know me, Marty, I . . . (*A
n comes out of the East River Terrace.*)

RTIN. Sh! (MARTIN *waits till the man
out of hearing, then relaxes.*) O.K. Ony,
a tellin' yuh, if it wuz anybody else, so
p me God, I'd . . . (*Gestures with
mb and forefinger, as if reaching for
gun.*)

IPTY. Thanks. . . . What did you do
your face?

RTIN. Operation. Plastic, dey call it.

IPTY. Oh! And you dyed your hair,
.

RTIN. Yeah. I guess yuh read about me.

IPTY. Sure. You're the headliner these
ys.

RTIN. God damn right; (*Pauses. Looks
und reminiscently and nods toward the
st River Terrace Apartments.*) Hey, dat's
nethin' new, ain't it?

IPTY. No. It's been up a couple of years.

RTIN. Yeah? What is it?

IPTY. One of the swellest apartment
ases in town.

RTIN. Yuh don' tell me! Well, what
yuh know!

IPTY. Yeah. You have to have blue
od, a million bucks, and a yacht to live
there, or else you have to . . . (*Breaks
, moodily.*)

RTIN. What?

IPTY. Oh, nothin'.

RTIN. Come on! I don' like 'at. If
're gonna say it, say it.

IPTY. It's nothin'. You see over there?
ey got a floatin' dock.

RTIN. Yeah. . . . What's it doin' there?
ht by de ole wharf. We used to pee
r deah . . . remember?

IPTY. Yeah.

RTIN. Uh-huh. (*Regards* GIMPTY *quiz-
ally.*) What's your racket?

IPTY. I'm an architect.

MARTIN. What's dat?

GIMPTY. I design houses.

MARTIN. Yuh don' say! What do yuh
know! Little Gimpty, an' look at 'im! An
architect! Well, I always knew yuh'd come
trew. Yuh had somethin' here, kid! (*Taps
his head.*) Yep. Well, I'm glad tuh see
yuh doin' O.K., Gimpty. Not like dese
udder slobs. Yuh must be in a big dough,
huh?

GIMPTY. (*Laughs.*) Nine out of ten archi-
tects are out of work.

MARTIN. Yeah?

GIMPTY. Yeah.

MARTIN. So what da hell's a good?

GIMPTY. That's the question. Don't ask
me. I don't know. . . . Strictly speakin'
I'm not even an architect. You see, before
you're an architect, you got to build a
house, an' before anybody'll let you build
'em a house, you got to be an architect.

MARTIN. Sounds screwy.

GIMPTY. Yeah, I guess it is. Besides, nobody's building any more, anyway.

MARTIN. An' fer dat yuh had to go tuh
high school?

GIMPTY. College, too.

MARTIN. College? Yuh went to college?

GIMPTY. Six years.

MARTIN. Six years? Why, yuh son uv a
bitch, yuh're marvelous!

GIMPTY. Well, I won a scholarship, and
Mom worked like hell . . . and here I am.
I was doin' a little work for the govern-
ment, but . . .

MARTIN. Oh, yeah?

GIMPTY. No . . . don't get excited. . . .
On a slum clearance project. But that folded up. I'm on home relief now.

MARTIN. Oh! (*A man comes down the
street and enters the tenement. He bangs
the door.* MARTIN *starts and looks back
jerkily.*)

GIMPTY. Say, is it so smart for you to come here? With that big reward.

MARTIN. I ain' here. I'm out West. Read da papers.

GIMPTY. Have you seen your mother yet?

MARTIN. No. Dat's one reason why I come back. I ain't see dee old lady 'n seven years. I kind a got a yen. Yuh know?

GIMPTY. Sure. . . . I saw her here day before yesterday.

MARTIN. Yeah? I taught she might be aroun'. How's she look?

GIMPTY. All right.

MARTIN. Gese. Seven years! Since a day I come out a reform school. Say, yew came down 'ere wid her tuh meet, me, didn' cha?

GIMPTY. Yeah.

MARTIN. Sure. 'At's right.

GIMPTY. Well, you've gone a long way since then.

MARTIN. Yeah.

GIMPTY. You know, Marty, I never could quite believe it was you.

MARTIN. Why not?

GIMPTY. To kill eight men?

MARTIN. Say, what ta hell a yuh tryin' tuh do? Tell me off, yuh bastard. Why, I'll . . .

GIMPTY. No, Marty. . . .

MARTIN. Say, maybe yuh changed, huh? Maybe yuh become a rat. Maybe yuh'd like tuh git dat faw grand at's up fuh me. . . .

GIMPTY. You know better.

MARTIN. I'm not so sure. Fawty-two hundred bucks is pretty big dough fer a joik like yew.

GIMPTY. You can trust me.

MARTIN. Den don' gimme any a dat crap! What ta hell did yuh tink I wuz gonna do, hang aroun' 'is dump waitin' fer Santa Claus tuh take care a me, fer Chris' sake? Looka yew! What a yew got? Six years

yuh went tuh college an what da hell yuh got? A lousy handout a thoity buc' a month! Not fer me! I yain't like ye punks . . . starvin' an' freezin' . . . f… what? Peanuts? Coffee an'? Yeah, I g… mine, but I took it. Look! (*Pulls at h… shirt.*) Silk. Twenty bucks. Look a d… (*Pulls at his jacket.*) Custom tailored— hundred an' fifty bucks. Da fat a da la… I live off of. An' I got a flock a dam… at'd make yew guys water at da mou… At'd make yew slobs run off in a da… corner when yuh see dere pichure an pl… pocket-pool.

GIMPTY. Ain't you ever scared?

MARTIN. Me? What of? What ta hell, y… can't live faever. Ah, I don' know. Su… Sometimes I git da jitters. An' sometin… I git a terrific yen tuh stay put, an' . … Ah, ta hell wid it! Say, do yew rememb… dat kid Francey?

GIMPTY. Francey?

MARTIN. She wuz my goil when we w… kids.

GIMPTY. Oh, yeah. She was a fine girl… remember.

MARTIN. Yew bet. Ey don' make no m… like her. I know. I had 'em all. Yuh a… seen her around, have yuh?

GIMPTY. No.

MARTIN. Hoid anythin' about her?

GIMPTY. No.

MARTIN. Gee, I got a terrific yen tuh… dat kid again. At's why I come back h… I wonder what she's doin'. Maybe she… married. Nah, she couldn'! Maybe she di… Nah, not Francey! She had too much o… ball, too much stuff . . . guts. Yeah,… wuz like me. Nuttin' kin kill Baby-f… Martin an nuttin' kin kill her. Not Franc… Gese, I wonder what's become a her?

GIMPTY. She's the girl whose uncle o… a tailor shop around the corner, isn't s… (MILTY *strolls over to the parapet* … *stands looking into the water.*)

MARTIN. Yeah. Yuh remember her no…

GIMPTY. Sure I remember her, all right.

RTIN. I tole Hunk, he's one a my boys,
look in 'ere an' see if he could git her
dress. Gese, I gotta see dat kid again!
IT *climbs out of the water, goes to* MILTY
d *in one sweep of his arm, tears* MILTY's
open.)

T. Tree bagger!

LTY. Stop dat!

T. (*Threatening him.*) What?

MMY. (*Follows* SPIT *over the parapet.*)
v, cut it out, Spit. We gave im enough
one time.

T. I'll knock 'im intuh da middle a
xt week!

MMY. (*Tearing open* SPIT's *fly.*) Home
n! (*The rest of the* KIDS *climb out of the
ter.* MILTY *joins them in laughing at
T's discomfiture.)

T. (*Turning on* MILTY.) What a yuh
ghin' at?

PY. Yeah, what?

T. Sock 'im, Dippy.

PY. Aw, I could lick im wid one han'
d behin' my back. (*Taps* MILTY's *should-
with his clenched fist in rhythm to.*)
ee, six, nine, da fight is mine, I kin lick
w any ole time. Tree, six, nine, da . . .

LTY. Git outa heah. Lemme alone. (*He
ings at* DIPPY, *who retreats frightened.*)

T. (*Grabbing* MILTY *roughly by his
rt.*) Oh . . . a tough guy, huh?

MMY. I said leave 'im alone. We give
enough fuh one time.

T. (*Releases* MILTY *and goes to* TOMMY
eateningly.*) Wheah da hell a yuh come
, all a time tellin' me what tuh do?

MMY. I'll put yew out like a light.

T. (*Spitting at* TOMMY.) Right inna
se!

MMY. (*Ducks, and the wad of saliva
s over his head.*) Miss! Now yuh git
lumps!

T. Try it! Wanna make somethin' out
it? Come on! Come on! (*He starts

dancing in front of TOMMY, *waves his fists
and mutters dire threats.* TOMMY *suddenly
gives him one terrific blow and* SPIT *collapses, his nose bleeding.*)

GIMPTY. Hey!

TOMMY. Hay fuh hosses! It wuz comin'
tuh him. (*To* MILTY, *patting his back.*)
O.K. kid! Yew kin stick aroun'. (HUNK
enters down the sidewalk.)

T.B. Hey, Tommy, len' me a couple a my
pennies. I wanna practice pitchin'.

TOMMY. O.K. (*They pitch pennies from
the hopper to the sidewalk.*)

MARTIN. (*To* GIMPTY.) Da kids aroun'
here don' change! (*Turns, meets* HUNK's
suspicious stare at GIMPTY; *to* HUNK.) He
ain' nuttin' tuh worry about.

HUNK. It's your funeral as well as mine.

MARTIN. Did yuh git huh address?

HUNK. Yuh mudder's out. Deah wuz no
answer.

MARTIN. Francey. What about huh?

HUNK. Dee old joker said ee didn't know,
but ee gimme da address of her aunt in
Brooklyn. She might know.

MARTIN. Well, hop a cab an' git it.

HUNK. (*Making a wry face.*) Brooklyn?

MARTIN. Yeah.

HUNK. Oh, hell!

MARTIN. Come on! Stop crappin' aroun'.

HUNK. Awright. (*Exit up the sidewalk.*)

SPIT. (*To* PHILIP, *who has appeared on
the terrace to watch the fight.*) Whadda
yuh lookin' at, huh? Yuh nosey lil . . .

PHILIP. Nosey nothing. It's a free country,
isn't it?

TOMMY. Hey, wee-wee, what ah yuh, a
boy 'r a goil?

T.B. He's a goil, cantcha see?

PHILIP. I'm a man! (T.B. *razzes him
loudly.* PHILIP *razzes loudly back.*)

T.B. Wassamattuh? Yew a wise guy?

PHILIP. Yes, I am.

T.B. Oh, yeah?

PHILIP. I can name all the Presidents of the United States. Can you?

T.B. What? Tommy kin . . .

PHILIP. Ah-h-h!

TOMMY. I used to be able tuh.

T.B. Ah, I bet yuh. I bet yuh a dollar ee kin. I bet yuh . . .

PHILIP. All right.

T.B. Aw right what?

PHILIP. I'll bet you a dollar.

T.B. What?

PHILIP. (*Takes a dollar bill from his pocket and proudly waves it aloft.*) Put up your dollar!

DIPPY. Gese, a buck!

T.B. (*Slaps his cheek in amazement.*) A whole real live dollar . . . my gawd! (ANGEL *and* SPIT, *impressed, exclaim and whistle.*)

PHILIP. Aw, you haven't even got a dollar.

T.B. Yeah, well . . . show 'im, Tommy, anyway. Show 'im! Jus' show 'im up, will yuh?

PHILIP. Washington, Adams, Jefferson. Go on! Name the next three!

TOMMY. Madison . . . Harrison . . . no . . ,

PHILIP. Wrong!

TOMMY. Well, I used tuh know em. I fergit.

PHILIP. Aw-w.

TOMMY. Well, who cares, anyway? Yuh li'l sissy! Let's cockalize 'im! Whadda yuh say? Come on! (*Chorus of approval. They start climbing up the wall, but the* DOORMAN *appears just in time.*)

DOORMAN. Get out of here! (*He gives them a dirty look, then exits, closing the gate.*)

TOMMY. Wait till I git yew . . . I'll fix your wagon! Come heah, guys. We gotta

git dat kid away from deah. We gotta him. . . . (*The gang all huddle ab* TOMMY, *whispering. Three smaller bo straggle down the street and sit on curb. They try to insinuate their way i the conclave.*)

TOMMY. (*To the three smaller* BOYS.) H whata yew want? (*The three smaller b don't answer, but are ready for a figh* Angel, tell yuh kid brudder tuh git hell outa heah!

ANGEL. Beat it!

TOMMY. Go home and tell yuh mud she wants yuh!

ANGEL. (*Rises, rushes the kids. The sm est stops to fight him, but* ANGEL ro them and they flee up the sidewalk.*) I crazy brudduh a mine! (DRINA *enters do the street, carrying a can of kerosene.*)

MARTIN. Well, keep yer nose clean, Gin ty, an' yer lips buttoned up tight, see?

GIMPTY. Forget it! (MARTIN *exits up sidewalk, eyeing* DRINA *as she passes hir*

DRINA. Come on, Tommy.

TOMMY. Not now, I'm busy.

DRINA. Tommy, don't be like that, you? You can't go around with a head of live stock.

TOMMY. I ain't got no bugs.

DRINA. (*Grabbing him, as he pulls awa* Let me see . . . come here! (*She exami his head.*) Whew! You ain't! You got army witha brass band. Come on hom

TOMMY. Wassamattuh wid tuhnight?

DRINA. Tonight I got a strike meetin' don't know what time I'll be home.

TOMMY. Aw, yew an' yuh lousy meeti

DRINA. It ain't no fun for me, Tom Come on an' let's get you cleaned up.

TOMMY. Aw, Drina!

DRINA. I don't like it any more than do.

TOMMY. Gese, look it! (*He points up street, and* DRINA *relaxes her hold on h*

TOMMY *rushes off under the hopper and dives into the water with a "Whee-ee." The other* KIDS *laugh and then straggle up the street to sit in a huddle on the doorstep of a tenement house.*)

DRINA. Tommy!

GIMPTY. (*Laughs.* DRINA *looks at him. He smiles understandingly.*) You've got a tough job on your hands, Drina.

DRINA. (*Peering over the wharf, following* TOMMY *with her eyes.*) He's really a good kid.

GIMPTY. (*Also watches* TOMMY, *whom we can hear thrashing the water with a clockwork, six-beat crawl.*) Sure.

DRINA. Just a little wild.

GIMPTY. Hey . . . Tommy's got a good crawl-kick!

DRINA. (*Calling.*) Tommy! Come on! (TOMMY *shouts under the water, making a noise like a seal.* DRINA *laughs against her will.*) What are you gonna do with a kid like that?

GIMPTY. (*Laughs.*) I don't know.

DRINA. (*Seating herself on the parapet, next to* GIMPTY.) It's not that he's dumb, either. I went to see his teacher yesterday. She said he's one of the smartest pupils she's got. But he won't work. Two weeks he played hookey.

GIMPTY. I don't blame him.

DRINA. I can't seem to do anything with him. It was different when Mom was alive. She could handle him . . . and between us we made enough money to live in a better neighborhood than this. If we win this strike, I'm gonna move, get him outa here the first thing.

GIMPTY.. Yeah. That's the idea.

DRINA. (*Noticing his drawings.*) What've you got there? More drawings?

GIMPTY. Couple a new ideas in communal housing. Here! see? (*He passes the drawing pad to her.*)

DRINA. (*Studies them and nods admiringly.*) Yeah. Thty're beautiful houses, Pete.

But what's the good? Is anybody going to build them?

GIMPTY. No.

DRINA. (*Handing back the drawings.*) So what?

GIMPTY. All my life I've wanted to build houses like these. Well . . . I'm gonna build 'em, see? Even if it's only on paper.

DRINA. A lot of good they'll do on paper. Your mother told me you've even given up looking for a job lately.

GIMPTY. (*Suddenly bitter and weary.*) Sure. What's the use? How long have you been on strike now?

DRINA. A month.

GIMPTY. Pickeetin' an' fightin' an' broken heads. For what?

DRINA. For what? For two dollars and fifty cents a week extra. Eleven dollars a month, Pete. All toward rent. So's Tommy an' I can live in a decent neighborhood.

GIMPTY. Yeah. You're right there. I've seen this neighborhood make some pretty rough guys. You've heard about Baby-face Martin? He used to live around here.

DRINA. Yeah. I read about it.

GIMPTY. I used to know him.

DRINA. You did? What was he like? (TOMMY *climbs up out of the water, breathless. He lies on the parapet, listening.*)

GIMPTY. As a kid, all right . . . more than all right. Yeah, Drina, the place you live in is awfully important. It can give you a chance to grow, or it can twist you—(*he twists an imaginary object with grim venom*)—like that. When I was in school, they used to teach us that evolution made men out of animals. They forgot to tell us it can also make animals out of men.

TOMMY. Hey, Gimpty.

GIMPTY. Yeah?

TOMMY. What's evilushin? (*He clambers along the parapet and lies on his stomach in front of* DRINA.)

GIMPTY. (*Looks at* TOMMY *a moment, smiles, and comes out of his dark mood.*) What's evolution, Tommy? Well, I'll tell you. A thousand million years ago we were all worms in the mud, and that evolution made us men.

DRINA. And women!

GIMPTY. And women.

TOMMY. An' boys and goils?

GIMPTY. And boys and girls.

TOMMY. Ah, I wuzn't even born a tousan' million years ago.

GIMPTY. No, but your great, great, great, great grandfather and mother were; and before them their great, great, great, great grandfather and mother were worms.

TOMMY. Blah-h-h!

DRINA. (*Impressed.*) It's like God!

GIMPTY. It is God! Once it made dinosaurs—animals as big as that house.

TOMMY. As big as at?

DRINA. Sure.

TOMMY. Wow!

GIMPTY. Then it didn't like its work and it killed them. Every one of them! Wiped 'em out!

TOMMY. Boy! I'd like tuh see one a dem babies.

GIMPTY. I'll show you a picture some time.

TOMMY. Will yuh?

GIMPTY. Sure.

TOMMY. At'll be swell, Gimpty. (SPIT *appears on the ladder and stops to listen, hanging from the top rung.*)

GIMPTY. Once evolution gave snakes feet to walk on.

TOMMY. Snakes? No kiddin'!

SPIT. (*Sings in mockery.*) Te-da-da-da-da-bushwah, te-da-da bushwah!

TOMMY. Shat ap! Right innee eye! (*He spits.* SPIT *jumps back into the water.*)

DRINA. Tommy, cut that out! See? You'[re] like an animal.

TOMMY. Well . . . he does it tuh all udduh kids. . . . Anyhow, what happen[s] tuh duh snakes' feet?

GIMPTY. Evolution took 'em away. T[he] same as ostriches could once fly. I bet y[ou] didn't know that.

TOMMY. No.

GIMPTY. Well, it's true. And then it to[ok] away their power to fly. The same as [it] gave oysters heads.

TOMMY. Oysters had heads?

GIMPTY. Once, yeah.

TOMMY. Aw-w!

DRINA. Sh, listen!

GIMPTY. Then it took them away. "N[ow] men," says Evolution, "now men"—(*no[w] to* DRINA, *acknowledging her contrib[u]tion*)—"and women . . . I made you wa[lk] straight, I gave you feeling, I gave y[ou] reason, I gave you dignity, I gave you [a] sense of beauty, I planted a God in yo[ur] heart. Now let's see what you're going [tuh] do with them. An' if you can't do an[y]thing with them, then I'll take 'em away. Yeah, I'll take away your reason [as] sure as I took away the head of the oyst[er] and your sense of beauty as I took aw[ay] the flight of the ostrich, and men will cra[wl] on their bellies on the ground like snak[es] . . . or die off altogether like the dinosa[urs]." (*A very attractive, smartly-groomed* YOU[NG] LADY *in a white linen suit comes out of [the] gate. She brings a clean coolness into t[he] sweltering street. She has a distincti[ve] lovely face; high forehead, patrician no[se] relieved by a warm, wide, generous mou[th] and eyes that shut and crinkle at the c[or]ners when she smiles—which she is doi[ng] now.*)

TOMMY. Gee!

GIMPTY. That scare you?

TOMMY. Wow!

ANGEL. (*Who has been sitting on [the] tenement steps up the streeet watching T[ommy] and* DIPPY *climb the tractor, notices [the]*

nan come out of the gate.) Hey, Gimp-
heah's yuh goil friend!

PTY. Oh, hello, Kay!

. Hello, Pete. (*Her manner is simple,
ct, poised and easy. She is a realist;
chichi, no pretense. And she is ob-
sly very fond of* GIMPTY.)

Y. (*To* T.B.) Hey, Gimpty's goil fren
e outa deah.

(*Rising.*) No kid! No kid!

EL. Gee whiz! (*The* THREE BOYS
ter down to KAY.)

Y. Do yew live in deah?

PTY. (*Embarrassed.*) Hey!

(*Laughs.*) Yes.

EL. Have dey really got a swimmin'
in at joint?

Yes. A big one.

Y. Ah yew a billionairess?

No.

. Millionairess?

No.

TY. Hey-y-y!

L. Den what a yuh doin' comin' out
ah?

A. Angelo! (*To* KAY.) Don't mind

(*Smiling.*) Oh, he's all right.

. I got it. She's a soivant goil.

Nah, she's too swell-dressed all a
(KAY *laughs.*)

TY. (*Squirming with embarrass-
.*) Look! Will you kids beat it! Scram!
outa here! Go on!

A. Come on, Tommy! I'm gonna
your head.

TY. (*Crawling over to the ladder.*)
Hey, Gimpty . . . 'at evilushin guy . . .

RY. What about him?

RY. Did he make everything?

GIMPTY. Yeah.

TOMMY. Bugs too?

GIMPTY. Yeah.

TOMMY. (*To* DRINA.) Deah yuh ah! God
makes bugs an' yew wanna kill 'em.
(*Gently chiding her as if she were a
naughty child.*) Is 'at nice? (*He dives off
the ladder into the water.*) Whee-e-e!

KAY. He's very logical.

DRINA. Yeah. That part's all right, but
he's very lousy too, an' that part ain't. (*She
calls.*) Tommy! Come on! (*More splashing
of the water from* TOMMY.)

DIPPY. Whee! Look! He's a flyin' fish! Do
dat again, Tommy! Wait, I'm comin',
Tommy! (*He mounts the parapet.*) Look a
me! I'm divin' . . . a backjack! (*He stands
poised for a backjack, then looks back and
downward, fearfully. It's awfully high.*)
Wait a minute! Wait . . . wait! (*He climbs
two rungs down the ladder. Looks down.
Nods. This is better.*) I'm divin' a backjack! Watch out, Tommy! (*He jumps
sprawling out of sight. A tremendous
splash.* KAY *looks over the parapet laughing.* DIPPY *calls up.*) How wuz at?

KAY. Beautiful!

T.B. Stinks! (*He walks off toward the
hopper arm in arm with* ANGEL. TWO
GIRLS *come out of the Terrace, and walk up
the street, chattering.* T.B. *and* ANGEL *follow them, mimicking their mincing walk,
and making indecent remarks. One of the
GIRLS stops and turns to slap* ANGEL. *The
BOYS laugh and run off behind the hopper.
The* TWO GIRLS *go up the street, one indignant, the other giggling.* KAY *has picked
up* GIMPTY's *drawings and is admiring
them.* DRINA *stares enviously at* KAY, *at her
modish coiffure, at her smart suit, at her
shoes.* KAY *becomes conscious of the scru-
tiny and turns.* DRINA, *embarrassed, drops
her eyes, then calls to* TOMMY.)

DRINA. Tommy! Coming?

TOMMY. (*From the water.*) No-o-o!

DRINA. Well, I'm going home. I can't wait
here all day. (*She goes.*)

GIMPTY. They're using the back entrance
to-day. . . .

KAY. (*Handing him the drawing pad.*) Yes. There's some trouble in front. They've ripped up the whole street. (*She looks out across the River, and breathes deep.*) It's a grand day, isn't it?

GIMPTY. Yeah.

KAY. Oh! . . . I was talking to some of Jack's friends last night. I thought they could find something for you. (*Produces a business card from her pocket.*) Here's a man who said you might come up and speak to him. Here's his card.

GIMPTY. (*Takes the card from her, and reads it.*) Del Block. Oh, yeah . . . he's a good man. Thanks! Gee! Thanks!

KAY. I don't know if it'll help much.

GIMPTY. This is swell of you! (*He looks at her a moment, lost in admiration. Then, shyly, with a good deal of hesitation and groping for the right words.*) I was telling Mom about you last night. I been kind of going around the house like a chicken with its head chopped off . . . and Mom asked me why. So I told her.

KAY. What?

GIMPTY. Oh, just a little about you. How we'd got to talking here, and meeting every day, and what great friends we've become. How you've been trying to help me. And . . . that I worship you!

KAY. You didn't!

GIMPTY. Well, I do. Do you mind?

KAY. (*Deeply toched.*) Mind? You fool! What'd she say?

GIMPTY. She said you sounded like a very, real, good person.

KAY. Good? Did you tell her all about me? About Jack?

GIMPTY. Yeah.

KAY. Your mother must be a sweet woman. I'd like to meet her some time.

GIMPTY. (*Enthusiastically.*) She'd be tickled. Will you?

KAY. Right now, if you like.

GIMPTY. Well, she's out for the afternoon.

KAY. Oh!

GIMPTY. Maybe I can get her down h day after tomorrow, huh?

KAY. (*Pauses, then, a bit depressed.*) may not be here then. I may leave ton row.

GIMPTY. Tomorrow?

KAY. Night. Jack's going 'on a fish trip. He wants me with him.

GIMPTY. Isn't that sudden?

KAY. He's been planning it for some ti

GIMPTY. How long will you be gone?

KAY. About three months.

GIMPTY. That's a long time.

KAY. Yes. (*Down the street strides a v dressed, rather handsome man in his e forties, hard lines around the eyes. At moment he is hot and uncomfortable. eyes the tenements curiously as he p them. The* DOORMAN *appears as he s to enter the gate. He asks the* DOORMA *a cultured, quiet voice, "What happe in front?"*)

DOORMAN. I'll tell you, Mr. Hilton. see, the gas mains . . .

KAY. (*Rises.*) Hello, Jack!

HILTON. (*Turns around, sees* KAY. prised.*) Hello! What're you doing h (*He crosses to her.*)

KAY. Oh, I just came out.

HILTON. (*Takes off his panama, wipe sweat band and mops his brow wi handkerchief.*) Phew! It's been a hell day, arranging things at the office. I've made the plans for the trip. E thing's set. The boat's in shape. I've t to Captain Swanson. (DIPPY *climbs up the parapet, talking to himself.*)

DIPPY. Hooray fuh me! I did a back (*To* GIMPTY.) Wuz 'at good, Gimpty?

GIMPTY. All right!

DIPPY. (*To* KAY.) Hey, Gimpty's friend, wuz at good?

. Beautiful. (DIPPY, *patting his chest* ~~l~~ *gloating "Attaboy, Dippy!" goes back* ~~o~~ *the water.* HILTON *is puzzled and an-* ~~ed~~. *He looks at* KAY.)

~~T~~ON. What's all this about?

~~.~~ Nothing.

~~T~~ON. (*His voice begins to rasp.*) Come ~~Let's~~ go in.

~~.~~ It's nice out. I'd like to take a walk

~~T~~ON. You'll do that later. Come on!

~~.~~ I have a little headache. I want to ~~out~~ a few minutes more.

~~T~~ON. Take an aspirin and you'll be all ~~t~~. Come on!

~~.~~ Please!

~~T~~ON. We've a million things to do.

~~.~~ You go ahead. I'll be right in.

~~T~~ON. (*Casts a glance at* GIMPTY.) ~~t's~~ the big attraction out here?

~~.~~ Nothing.

~~T~~ON. Then stop acting like a prima-~~na~~ and come on in.

~~.~~ Plase don't make a fuss.

~~T~~ON. (*Suddenly loses his temper and* ~~s~~.) It's not me . . . it's you! Damn it, ~~been~~ tearing around all day like a mad-~~,~~ and I come home and find you be-~~ng~~ like a cheap . . .

~~.~~ Jack!

~~T~~ON. (*Bites his lip, controls himself,* ~~mutters~~ curtly.) All right. Stay there! ~~goes~~ in. KAY *follows him to the gate,* ~~es~~ there, uncertain. Then indulges in ~~omentary~~ flash of temper herself.)

Oh . . . let him! (*She returns slow-*

~~T~~Y. Is that the guy?

~~.~~ Yes. (*Then, not to be unfair.*) Don't ~~e~~ him by this. He's really not so bad. ~~going~~ to be sorry in a few minutes. ~~so~~ darn jealous. His wife gave him ~~etty~~ raw deal. You can't blame him

GIMPTY. (*Suddenly inflamed.*) All right! If it were anybody else, all right! But you? He can't treat *you* like that!

KAY. (*Sits there a while in silence, think-ing. Finally, she speaks, slowly, almost in explanation to herself.*) I've been living with Jack a little over a year now. He isn't usually like this. You see, he really loves me.

GIMPTY. He has a funny way of showing it.

KAY. He wants me to marry him.

GIMPTY. Are you going to?

KAY. I don't know.

GIMPTY. Do you love him?

KAY. I like him.

GIMPTY. Is that enough?

KAY. I've known what it means to scrimp and worry and never be sure from one minute to the next. I've had enough of that . . . for one lifetime.

GIMPTY. (*Intensely.*) But Kay, not to look forward to love . . . God, that's not living at all!

KAY. (*Not quite convincing.*) I can do without it.

GIMPTY. That's not true. It isn't, is it?

KAY. (*Smiles wryly.*) Of course not.

(*A very stout* LADY *with much bosom, comes out of the gate, fondling a tiny, black dog.*)

TOMMY. (*Clambering over the parapet, sees the dog and chuckles.*) Look a dat cockaroach, will yuh? Hey, lady, wheah didja git dat cockaroach?

FAT LADY. Well, of all the little! . . . (TOMMY *starts to bark. The dog yaps back, and struggles to escape. The others* BOYS *climb up and bark in various keys. The three* SMALLER BOYS *appear and join in the medley. The stout* LADY *is distraught. She shouts at them, but to no avail.*) Get away from here, you little beasts!

SPIT. In yuh hat, fat slob! (*And he con-tinues barking.*)

FAT LADY. Wha-a-at? Doorman! (*To the frantic dog.*) Quiet, Buddy darling! Quiet! Doorman! (*The* DOORMAN *comes out on the run and chases the boys away. They run en masse to the hopper.* TOMMY *climbs up on it. The* SMALLER BOYS *retire to the steps of an upper tenement doorway.* MR. GRISWALD, PHILIP, *and* MR. JONES *come out of the East River Terrace Apartments.*)

GRISWALD. What's the matter?

DOORMAN. Those kids! They're terrible, sir.

PHILIP. They wanted to hit me, too, daddy!

GRISWALD. Oh, yes? Why? What did you do to them? (*Smiles at* JONES.)

PHILIP. Nothing.

GRISWALD. Sure?

PHILIP. Honest, daddy, I didn't say anything to them.

DOORMAN. It's all their fault, sir.

FAT LADY. They're really horrible brats. And their language! . . .

TOMMY. (*Hanging from the hopper.*) Ah, shat ap, yuh fat bag a hump!

GRISWALD. You touch him again and I'll break your necks.

TOMMY. Balls to yew, faw eyes!

GRISWALD. (*To* PHILIP, *as he takes his arm and walks him up the street.*) The next time you hit them back.

PHILIP. But they all pile up on you, daddy.

GRISWALD. Oh, is that so? Well, I think I'm going to buy you a set of gloves and teach you how to box. (*They continue up the sidewalk, followed by* JONES.)

PHILIP. Will you, daddy? (THE GOVERNESS *and a young* CHAUFFEUR *in maroon livery meet them.*)

GOVERNESS. Bonjour, monsieur!

CHAUFFEUR. (*Saluting.*) I'm sorry to keep you waiting, sir, but . . .

GRISWALD. (*Waves them ahead.*) Th all right. Never mind. (*To* PHILIP.) next time someone attacks you, you'll able to defend yourself.

MR. JONES. That's the idea!

TOMMY. (*Shouts up the street after the* Yeah! Wid ee army an' navy behin' (*Gang laughs and shouts.* TOMMY ju down from the hopper. The FAT L waddles across to KAY.)

TOMMY. Come 'ere, guys, I got a sch how we kin git dat kid an' cockalize (*They gather in a huddle.*)

ANGEL. How?

TOMMY. (*Subsiding to a whisper.*) I we git 'im inna hallway, an' . . .

FAT LADY. The little Indians! T oughtn't to be allowed in the street decent people. (*Exit the* DOORMAN, clo the gate.)

GIMPTY. No? What would you do them?

FAT LADY. Send them all away.

GIMPTY. Where?

FAT LADY. I'm sure I don't know.

GIMPTY. Huh! (*Great outburst of la ter from the huddle.*)

T.B. Dat'll woik! You'll see! Dat'll git

TOMMY. Wait! Shat ap! I got maw . (*The conclave becomes a whispered again.*)

FAT LADY. The little savages! They'r wicked. It's born in them: They in it.

GIMPTY. (*Suddenly bursts out, a bitter sonal note in his passion.*) Inherita Yeah. You inherit a castle thirty st over the river, or a stinkin' hole in ground! Wooden heads are inherited, not wooden legs . . . nor legs twiste rickets! (*The* FAT LADY *is completely t aback by this unexpected antipathy. looks at* KAY, *gasps, and walks away, high, patting her animal.* KAY smile GIMPTY *sadly, sympathetically.*)

TY. I'm sorry.

(*Touches his hand.*) Oh, Pete! (*An- outburst. The three smaller* BOYS *have down and joined the fringe of the dle.*)

MY. Dey're back again! Angel, will tell yuhr kid brudduh tuh git tuh outa heah? (ANGEL *swings at the st of the* BOYS, *who kicks him in the , spits at him, and runs away, thumb- his nose.* ANGEL *chases the* BOYS *part e way up the street, then returns rub- his shin and shaking his head.*)

L. 'At crazy kid brudduh a mine, gonna kill 'im when I git 'im home! e huddle reorganizes.*)

TY. Gosh, I wish we could be alone minute!

Pete, I've thought of that so many s. I've wanted to invite you inside, . . .

TY. You couldn't, of course.

Cock-eyed, isn't it? Couldn't we go ur place?

TY. Gee, I! . . . No, you wouldn't it.

Why not?

TY. It's an awful dump. It would ss you.

Oh!

TY. I'd love to have you, Kay, but ashamed to let you see it. Honestly.

(*Rises and offers him her hand.*) Pete, that's silly. I wasn't born in a

pent house. Come on! (*With the aid of a cane he rises. They walk up the street. For the first time we notice that one of his legs is withered and twisted—by rick- ets.* MILTY *rises and crosses to within a few steps of the huddle.*)

MILTY. (*Timidly.*) Hey.

TOMMY. What?

MILTY. Look, I . . . (*He approaches* TOM- MY *slowly.*) If yuh want, I t'ink I kin snitch 'at quatuh fuh yuh. (*The chug of an approaching tug-boat is faintly heard.*)

TOMMY. (*Thinks it over.*) O.K., Milt! O.K. Den yuhr inna gang, see? (*Turns to the others.*) Anybody gits snotty wid Milt, gits snotty wid me, see? (*To* MILTY.) Now git dat quatah. Come on, git duh lead outa yuh pants! (*The chug-chug grows louder.*)

MILTY. (*Jubilant.*) O.K., Tommy! (*Runs off into the tenement house. The chug- chug grows louder.*)

TOMMY. See? He's a good kid. He loins fast. Remember da time I moved aroun' heah? I wuz wearin' white socks an' I wouldn't coise, so yuh all taught I wuz a sissy. (*The chug-chug grows louder.*)

DIPPY. 'Cept me, Tommy.

TOMMY. Yeah, 'cept yew. Everybody else I hadda beat da pants off a first. (*Down to business again.*) Now here's how we git wee-wee. Yew, T.B.. . . . (*His voice is drowned out by the chug-chug-chug- chug—*)

CURTAIN

ACT TWO

E: *The same, the following day, lit brilliant afternoon sun. The boys are ng poker with an ancient deck of , greasy and puffed, inches thick. h sticks are their chips. Their faces rave and intense. They handle their familiarly, carressing them like old lers.*

N *lounges against the terrace wall and es them with grim nostalgia.*

ANGEL. (*Throwing two match sticks into the pot.*) I'll open fuh two. Hey, Spit, it's rainin'. Come on, decorate da mahogany!

T.B. (*Adds his two.*) O.K. I'm in.

SPIT. (*Follows suit.*) Heah's my two. Dippy.

DIPPY. (*Tosses in his match sticks, de- liberately, one at a time.*) I'm in.

ANGEL. (*Slapping down two cards.*) Gimme . . . two.

SPIT. (*Deals.*) Aw, he's got tree uva kin'.

T.B. (*Throws away one.*) Gimme one. Make it good. (SPIT *deals him one.*)'

ANGEL. Ah, yuh ain' got nuttin'.

SPIT. He's got a monkey. I ain' takin' any. How many fuh yew, Dippy?

DIPPY. (*Studies his hand with grave deliberation.*) I'll take five.

SPIT. Yuh can' take five.

DIPPY. (*The mental effort contorts his face.*) Faw.

SPIT. Yuh kin ony take tree.

DIPPY. (*After considerable hesitation.*) Gimme one!

ANGEL. (*Inclining his head toward* T.B.) Say, T.B., feel 'at bump I got. Feel it!

T.B. (*Explores* ANGEL's *head with a finger.*) Wow! Feel 'at bump Angel's got!

DIPPY. (*Leans over and feels the bump.*) Boy! 'At's like 'n egg!

SPIT. Wheah juh git it?

ANGEL. Me ole man give it tuh me.

DIPPY. Fuh what?

ANGEL. Fuh nuttin. Just like 'at, fuh nuttin. Last night me ole man cumzin drunk.

SPIT. (*Impatiently.*) Cum on, cum on . . . whadda yuh do?

ANGEL. (*Raps his knuckles on the sidewalk.*) I blow.

T.B. (*Raps.*) I blow.

SPIT. (*Raps.*) I blow, too. Dippy?

DIPPY. (*Raps.*) I blow.

T.B. Whatcha got?

ANGEL.. (*Reveals a pair of Jacks.*) A pair of Johnnies. You?

T.B. (*Exhibits two pair, twos and threes.*) Two pair. Deuces and trays. (*He reaches for the pot.*)

ANGEL. Aw hell!

SPIT. Wait a minute! (*Lays down t*⟨*h*⟩ tens.) Read 'em an' weep! Judge Shm⟨ . . . thoity days!

DIPPY. I guess I ain' got nuttin. (⟨ *gleefully rakes in the match sticks. E*⟨ TOMMY, *kicking a tin can before him.* ⟨ BOYS *greet him.*)

TOMMY. Hi yuh, guys. Howza wawda⟨

SPIT. Cold.

TOMMY. Whatcha playin' fuh?

SPIT. Owins. Wanna play?

TOMMY. (*Starts undressing.*) Deal me ⟨ next han'. Who's winnin'?

T.B. I yam.

TOMMY. How much?

T.B. Twenty-eight matches.

TOMMY. Twenty-eight cents . . . boy, ⟨ putty good! Hey, didja heah about it⟨

SPIT. What?

ANGEL. About what? ⎫
DIPPY. What, Tommy? ⎭ } *Together*

TOMMY. Dincha heah? Boy, deah w⟨ big fight at da Chink laundry las' ni⟨

ANGEL. No kiddin'!

TOMMY. Yeah.

DIPPY. How did it staht, Tommy?

TOMMY. Oh . . . a couple handkuh⟨ got snotty. (*They all roar with laugh*⟨ Did wee-wee show up yet?

DIPPY. No, Tommy.

ANGEL. Don' worry. I bin on a loo⟨ furrim.

DIPPY. Yeah, we bin on a lookout fu⟨

ANGEL. So, like I wuz tellin' yuh, ⟨ night me old man comes in stinkin' d⟨ So he stahts beatin' hell outa me ole ⟨ Boy, he socks 'er all ovah da place! ⟨ *laughs.*)

TOMMY. What da hell a yuh laughin⟨ Dat ain' so funny.

EL. No, dat ain' so funny. Cause den picks up a chair and wants a wallop wid it.

Y. Whatcha do den?

EL. So I grabs a kitchen knife . . . dat . . . an' I sez, "Touch me, yuh louse, I give yuh dis."

Yeah?

EL. Yeah, yeah, I did. So he laughs, so aughs, so he falls on a flaw, an' he goes sleep . . . so he snores—(*Imitates a ing snore*)—like at. Boy, wuz ee k! Boy, he wuz stinkin'! (*Enter* MILTY n *the sidewalk.*)

Y. Hello, Tommy!

MY. Hi yuh, Milty! How's evyting?

Y. Swell.

MY. Attaboy. (MILTY *goes to* MARTIN.)

TIN. Well?

Y. She wuz deah. I tole huh. She not tuh come up. She said tuh meet down heah.

TIN. O.K. Heah, kid, buy yerself a Royce. (*He gives* MILTY *a half-dollar.*)

Y. Gee!

Whatcha git?

Y. Oh, momma! Haffa buck!

(*Shouting quickly.*) Akey! Akey! es!

. (*Also shouting quickly, topping nd holding up crossed fingers.*) Fens! key! No akey!

(*Throws down his cards and rises teningly.*) I said akey. Come on, s.

Y. Yuh didn't have yuh finguhs d.

Don' han' me dat balonee! Gimme its.

. Yuh didn't cross yuh finguhs.

(*Thrusting his face into* MILTY'S.) he two bits 'r I kick yuh ina slats.

MILTY. Yeah?

SPIT. Yeah.

MILTY. Ah, yuh mudduh's chooch!

SPIT. Ah, yuh fadduh's doop!

MILTY. Hey, Tommy, do I gotta givim?

TOMMY. Naw. He didn' have 'is finguhs crossed.

SPIT. I'll choose yuh fer it.

MILTY. Whadduh yuh tink I yam, a dope?

SPIT. Ah, yuh damn jip ahdist!

MILTY. Look who's talkin'!

SPIT. Ah, yew stink on ice!

TOMMY. Stan' up tuh him, Milty! Stan' up tuh him.

MILTY. (*Suddenly thrusts his jaw forward.*) Watsamatteh? Yew wanna fight?

SPIT. Yeah.

MILTY. Join ee ahmy! . . . Ha! (*The boys roar at* SPIT.)

SPIT. (*Raising a fist and twisting his face fiercely.*) Ah!

MILTY. (*Raising his fist and returning the grimace.*) Ah!

SPIT. (*Fiercer in grimace and growl.*) Mah!

MILTY. (*Tops him.*) Wah! (*They stand there a moment, glaring at each other in silence, fists raised, faces almost touching, then* SPIT *turns in disgust and sits down again to his cards.*)

TOMMY. (*Grins at* MILTY's *triumph.*) Kimmeah, Milty! Yuh wanna play?

MILTY. I dunna how.

TOMMY. Kimmeah, watch me. I'll loin yuh. (*Two strange, tough-looking* BOYS *come down the street. They pause, watch a moment, confer, then wander over to the group.*)

FIRST BOY. Hey, which one a youse guys is a captain a dis gang?

TOMMY. (*Doesn't even deign to look up.*) Who wantsa know?

SECOND BOY. Weàh fum da up da blocks.

TOMMY. Second Avenya gang?

FIRST BOY. Yeah.

TOMMY. (*Assorting his cards.*) Yeah? Well, go take a flyin' jump at ta moon!

SECOND BOY. Whoza leaduh?

TOMMY. Me. What about it? I pass. (*Throws down his cards, rises, turns to the enemy.*) Wanna make sumpm out uv it?

SECOND BOY. (*A bit frightened.*) Yew tell 'im.

FIRST BOY. Yuh wanna fight are gang?

TOMMY. Sure. (*Turns to his gang.*) O.K. felluhs? Yuh wanna fight da Second Aven-yoo gang? (*They approve raucously.* TOM-MY *turns back to the emissaries.*) Sure!

FIRST BOY. O.K. On are block?

TOMMY. Yeah. O.K.

SECOND BOY. Satiday?

TOMMY. (*Asks the gang.*) O.K., Satiday, felluhs? (*They shout approval.*) Faw o'clock? (*A little bickering about time, but they agree.*) O.K. We'll be up deah Satiday faw o'clock an' boy, we'll kick the stuffin's outa youse!

SECOND BOY. Yeah?

TOMMY. Yeah! No bottles 'r rocks, jus' sticks 'n' bare knucks. Flat sticks. No bats.

SECOND BOY. Sure.

TOMMY. O.K.?

SECOND BOY. O.K.!

TOMMY. O.K. Now git da hell out a heah befaw I bust yuh one! Scram! (*The two* BOYS *run off. From a safe distance they yell.*)

FIRST BOY. Nuts tuh yew! Son uva bitch! son uva bitch!

SECOND BOY. Satiday! We be waitin' faw yuh. We kick da pants offa yuh! (TOMMY *picks up a rock, hurls it after them.* DIPPY *rises, does the same.* MARTIN *laughs.*)

ANGEL. (*First noticing* MARTIN.) Sh mistuh?

MARTIN. O.K., kid. (ANGEL *moves his down to* MARTIN *and begins to shine shoes.*)

SPIT. (*Sneers at* DIPPY.) Look at 'im tr will yuh? Like a goil. Yuh godda g ahm? Cantcha trow a rock even?

DIPPY. Yeah. Kin yew trow bettuh?

SPIT. (*Picks up a rock, rises, looks f target. He spots a flower pot on a escape.*) Watch! See at flowuh pot? throws the rock and breaks the pot.*)

TOMMY. Pot shot! Pot shot!

MARTIN. Say, at wuz good pitchin'. kids like tuh git some dope on gang f in'?

ANGEL. Sure! Hey, felluhs, come h (*They crowd about* MARTIN.)

MARTIN. Foist ting is tuh git down oiliuh' an yuh. . . . (GIMPTY *enters d the sidewalk, whistling cheerfully.*) H Gimpty!

GIMPTY. Hello.

MARTIN. (*Continues the lesson.* GI *stops and listens.*) Oiliuh an yuh said, Dey won't be ready fuh yuh. En I yuh kids what yuh wanna do. Git of old electric bulbs, see? Yuh trow an den yuh trow a couple a milk b . . . an' some a dee udder kids git an' den yuh charge 'em.

TOMMY. Yeah, but we made up no bottles, ony bare knucks an' sticks.

MARTIN. Yuh made up! Lissen, kid when yuh fight, dee idee is tuh wi don' cut no ice how. An' in gang fig remember, take out da tough guys T'ree aw faw a yuh gang up on 'im. one a yuh kin git behin' 'im an' slug A stockin' fulla sand an' rocks is goo dat. An' if ey're lickin' yuh, pull a Give 'em a little stab in ee arm. Ey' like hell an' run.

TOMMY. Yeah, but we made up no k Gese, 'at ain' fair. . . .

PTY. What's a matter with you? What
you trying to teach these kids?

RTIN. Yew shut yer trap. (*To* TOMMY.)
sen. If yuh wanna win, yuh gotta make
yer own rules, see?

IMY. But we made up dat . . .

RTIN. Yuh made up . . .

IMY. We kin lick 'em wid bare knucks
fair and square.

TIN. Lissen, kid . . . Ere ain' no fair
ere ain' no square. It's winnah take all.
it's easier tuh lick a guy by sluggin'
fum behin' 'en it is by sockin' it out
'im toe tuh toe. Cause if yuhr lickin'
en he pulls a knife on yuh, see? En
ah are yuh?

IMY. Den I pull a knife back on him.

TIN. Yeah, but what's a good unless
got one an' know how tuh use it?

MY. I know how tuh.

PTY. Don't pay any attention to him,
s!

TIN. Yew lookin' fer a sock in a puss?

PTY. If you kids listen to that stuff,
ll get yourselves in Dutch.

MY. Aw, shat ap. (*The boys razz*
PTY.)

TIN. Git out a heah, yuh monkey!
PTY, *angry but impotent, walks away.*
TIN *turns to the boys again.*) See what
ean?

MY. Yeah, well, if I had a knife . . .

Y. Angel's godda knife.

EL. Aw, I need it. (MARTIN *hands*
L *a dime for the shine.*)

MY. Yuh kin jus' loan it tuh me. I'll
it back tuh yuh.

L. No, yuh won't. Honest, I need it.
Give it tuh him! Go on, or I'll crack
one!

L. No!

MY. Nevuh mind . . . tuh hell wid

T.B. (*To* ANGEL.) Ah, yuh stink on ice!

ANGEL. Aw, shat ap!

T.B. Shat ap yuhself!

MILTY. Look, Angel, I tell yuh what. Ahl
give yuh a quarteh fuh it. Whadda yuh
say?

ANGEL. Sure!

MILTY. (*To* MARTIN.) Change, Misteh?

MARTIN. Yeah. . . . (*He gives* MILTY *two
quarters in exchange for the half, then
rises. A newspaper in the gutter catches
his attention. He frowns, picks it up, reads
it, wandering off to the tenement stoop,
where he sits on a step, absorbed in the
newspaper item.* ANGEL *runs to the hopper,
finds his trousers, fumbles in the pocket,
produces the knife and returns with it. He
completes the transaction with* MILTY, *who
hands the knife to* TOMMY.)

MILTY. Heah, Tommy.

TOMMY. (*Rises.*) Wha' faw?

MILTY. Fuh a present.

TOMMY. Yuh mean yuh givin' it tuh me?

MILTY. Yeah. Yuh kin keep it.

TOMMY. Gee, t'anks, Milty! Gese, 'at's
swell . . . t'anks!

MILTY. Aw, dat's nuttin.

TOMMY. Aw, dat's a whole lot. T'anks!
Gee! (CHARLES, *the chauffeur, enters from
the gate of the East River Terrace, followed by* PHILIP.)

T.B. Hey, Tommy . . . ! (*He points to*
PHILIP. *The gang gathers under the hopper, in huddled consultation.*)

PHILIP. I think I'll wait here, Charles.

CHARLES. Wouldn't you rather come with
me to the garage?

PHILIP. No.

CHARLES. But your mother said . . .

PHILIP. I'll wait here for them.

CHARLES. Yes, sir. (*Exit* CHARLES *up the
street.* PHILIP *examines his wrist-watch os-*

tentatiously. KAY *appears on the terrace, finds a space in the shrubbery, leans over the balustrade, and signals to* GIMPTY.)

KAY. Pete!

GIMPTY. (*Rising and crossing toward her, beaming.*) Hello, Kay! How are you feeling?

KAY. All right. And you?

GIMPTY. Like a million dollars!

KAY. I'll be down in a second. (*She disappears behind the shrubs. The conclave finished, all the boys saunter off in different directions, pretending disregard of* PHILIP. TOMMY, *whistling a funeral dirge, signals* T.B. *with a wink and a nod of the head.* T.B. *approaches* PHILIP *casually.*)

T.B. Hello, what time is it?

PHILIP. Half past four.

T.B. T'anks. Gee, dat's a nice watch yuh got deah. What kine is it?

PHILIP. A Gruen.

T.B. Boy, 'at's as nice as 'n Ingersoll. (*Coughs, then proudly tapping his chest, boasts.*)—T.B. I got T.B.

TOMMY. (*On the tenement stoop.*) Hey, felluhs, come on inna hall heah. I got sumpm great tuh show yuhs. Come on, T.B. (*They all whip up loud, faked enthusiasm.*)

T.B. O.K. (*To* PHILIP.) Yuh wanna come see?

TOMMY. Nah, he can't come. Dis is ony fuh da gang. (*The others agree volubly that* PHILIP *can't join them in the mystery.*)

T.B. Aw, why not? He's a good kid.

TOMMY. (*Supported by a chorus of "Nahs".*) Nah, he can't see dis. Dis is ony fuh da gang.

PHILIP. What is it?

T.B. Gee, I can't tell yuh . . . but it's . . . gese, it's sumpm great!

TOMMY. (*To* T.B.) Come on! Git da lead out a yuh pants!

T.B. Too bad dey won' letcha see it. B yuh nevuh saw anyting like dat.

PHILIP. Well, I don't care. I can't anyw I'm waiting for my father and moth We're going to the country.

T.B. It'll ony take a minute. . . . F felluhs, let 'im come 'n' see it, will y He's O.K.

TOMMY. (*Consenting with a great s of reluctance.*) Well . . . awright. Let come. (TOMMY *enters the tenement, foll ed by the others.*)

T.B. Come on.

PHILIP. I don't know. I expect my . . .

T.B. Awright, it's yuhr loss! (T.B. s up the sidewalk.)

PHILIP. Wait! Wait! I'm coming! (R to catch up with T.B. As they reach steps and enter, T.B. pushes him in doorway, spits on his hands and foll him in. KAY enters.)

GIMPTY. (*Beams. He is very hap* Hello!

KAY. Hello, darling. (*There is a s strain in her voice and attitude, w manifests itself in over-kindness and much gentleness, as if she were tryin mitigate some hurt she is about to him. They sit on the coping.*)

GIMPTY. Well . . . I got up early morning and went down to a stac offices looking for a job.

KAY. That's swell. Did you find one?

GIMPTY. Not yet. But I will. Wait see.

KAY. Of course you will.

GIMPTY. Thanks to you. (SPIT *runs the hallway, stops a second on the walk, looking about, then grabs a barrel stave, whacks his hand wit whistles, and runs back into the tene hallway.*)

KAY. Did you see Del Block?

GIMPTY. Yep.

KAY. Didn't he have anything for yo

PTY. Oh, we had a nice talk. He's a
y interesting guy. He showed me some
his work. He's done some pretty good
ff. (*Grins.*) He asked me if I knew
ere he could find a job. (*They both have
laugh at this.*) He thinks you're pretty
ell, too.

. Pete . . . you've got to get some-
ng.

PTY. I will.

. I didn't know how important it was
il yesterday.

PTY. Hey, there!

. I used to think we were poor at home
ause I had to wear a made-over dress
a prom. Yesterday I saw the real thing.
hadn't seen it, I couldn't have believed
I dreamt of it all night . . . the filth,
smells, the dankness! I touched a wall
it was wet. . . . (*She touches her
er-tips, recalling the unpleasant tactile
sation. She shivers.*)

PTY. That house was rotten before I
born. The plumbing is so old and
ken . . . it's been dripping through the
lding for ages.

. What tears my heart out is the
ught that you have to live there. It's
fair! It's not right!

PTY. I's not right that anybody should
like that, but a couple a million of
do.

. Million?

PTY. Yeah, right here in New York
New York with its famous skyline . . .
Empire State, the biggest God-damned
ding in the world The biggest tomb-
e in the world! They wanted to build
nonument to the times. Well, there it
bigger than the pyramids and just as
y tenants. (*He forces her to smile with
. Then he sighs, and adds, hopelessly.*)
onder when they'll let us build houses
men to live in? (*Suddenly annoyed
himself.*) Ah, I should never have let
see that place!

. I'm glad you did. I know so much
e about you now. And I can't tell you

how much more I respect you for coming
out of that fine, and sweet . . . and sound.

GIMPTY. (*His eyes drop to his withered
limb.*) Let's not get started on that.
(PHILIP *can be heard sobbing in the tenement hallway. He flings open the door and
rushes out, down the street into the apartment, crying convulsively, his clothes all
awry. The gang follows him from the
hallway, yelling and laughing.*)

TOMMY. (*Holding* PHILIP's *watch.*) Come
on, let's git dressed an' beat it!

SPIT. Let's grab a quick swim foist.

TOMMY. Nah!

SPIT. Come on!

MILTY. Betteh not. . . .

SPIT. (*Rushes off under the hopper and
dives into the water.*) Las' one in's a
stinkin' rotten egg!

TOMMY. (*Throws the watch to* T.B.)
Guard 'at watch and lay chickee! (*All the
boys except* T.B. *dive into the water.*)

GIMPTY. When I see what it's doing to
those kids I get so mad I want to tear down
these lice nests with my fingers!

KAY. You can't stay here. You've got to
get out. Oh, I wish I could help you!

GIMPTY. But you have. Don't you see?

KAY. No. I'm not that important.

GIMPTY. Yes, you are!

KAY. I mustn't be. Nobody must. For your
own good, you've got to get out of here.

GIMPTY. I will, damn it! And if I do . . .
maybe I'm crazy . . . but will you marry
me?

KAY. Listen!

GIMPTY. Don't get me wrong. I'm not
askin' you to come and live there with
me. But you see, if. . . .

KAY. Listen! First I want you to know
that I love you . . . as much as I'll allow
myself to love anybody. Maybe I shouldn't
have gone with you yesterday. Maybe it

was a mistake. I didn't realize quite how much I loved you. I think I ought to leave tonight.

GIMPTY. Why?

KAY. Yes, I'd better. (*The chug of a small boat is heard.*)

GIMPTY. Why?

KAY. I'd better get away while we can still do something about this.

GIMPTY. How will that help?

KAY. If I stay, I don't know what will happen, except that . . . we'll go on and in the end make ourselves thoroughly miserable. We'd be so wise to call it quits now.

GIMPTY. Gee, I don't see it.

KAY. I do, and I think I'm right. (*Pause. She looks out over the river.*) There's the boat.

GIMPTY. (*Pauses. Turns to look.*) Is that it?

KAY. Yes.

GIMPTY. (*Irrelevantly, to conceal his emotion. In a dull monotone.*) It's a knockout. I'm crazy about good boats. They're beautiful, because they're designed to work. That's the way houses should be built . . . like boats.

KAY. Pete, will you be here . . . tonight . . . before I leave? (MARTIN *looks up from his newspaper to eye* KAY.)

GIMPTY. Don't go, Kay. I'll do anything. Isn't there some way . . . something?

KAY. (*Hopelessly.*) What? (*Rises.*) I guess I'll go in now, and get my things ready . . . I'll see you later? (*She presses his shoulder and exits.* MARTIN *rises, throws down his newspaper and approaches* GIMPTY.)

MARTIN. (*Sucks his lips, making a nasty, suggestive sound.*) Say . . . dat's a pretty fancy lookin' broad. High class, huh? How is she? Good lay? (GIMPTY *glares at him.* MARTIN *laughs.*) Well, fer Chris' sake, what's a matter? Can't yuh talk?

GIMPTY. Cut it out, Martin. Just cut out!

MARTIN. Lissen, kid, why don' yuh wise tuh yerself? Dose dames are p[u] overs, fish fuh duh monkeys!

GIMPTY. (*Half rising, furious.*) I said it out!

MARTIN. (*Roughly pushes him back.*) down, yew! (*A chuckle of contemp[t]* Look what wantsa fight wid me! L[ook] Gimpty wansa fight wid me! Wassa[matter] tuh, Gimpty? Wanna git knocked [off?] (HUNK *slouches down the street, follo[wed] in a painfully weary shuffle by a ga[unt,] raw-boned, unkempt woman, sloppy [and] disheveled. Her one garment an anc[ient] house dress retrieved from some garb[age] heap, black with grease stains. Her [legs] are stockingless, knotted and bulging [with] blue, twisted, cord-like veins. Her feet s[how] through the cracks in her house slipp[ers.] In contrast to the picture of general d[ecay] is a face that looks as if it were car[ved] out of granite; as if infinite suffering [had] been met with dogged, unyielding stren[gth.]*)

HUNK. Hey! (*She comes to a dead [stop] as she sees* MARTIN. *There is no other [sign] of recognition, no friendliness on her [face.] She stares at him out of dull, hostile ey[es.]*)

MARTIN. (*Face lights, he grins. He s[teps] rapidly toward her.*) Hello, Mom! [How] are yuh? (*Pause.*) It's me. (*No reco[gni-] tion.*) I had my face fixed. (*There [is a] moment of silence. She finally speaks i[n an] almost inaudible monotone.*)

MRS. MARTIN. Yuh no good tramp!

MARTIN. Mom!

MRS. MARTIN. What're yuh doin' he[re?]

MARTIN. Aintcha glad tuh see me? (*[She] suddenly smacks him a sharp crack a[cross] the cheek.*)

MRS. MARTIN. That's how glad I am.

MARTIN. (*Rubs his cheek, stunned by [the] unexpected reception. He stammers.*) [That's] a great hello.

MRS. MARTIN. Yuh dog! Yuh stinkin' low dog yuh!

RTIN. Mom! What kin' a talk is 'at?
e, Mom ...

. MARTIN. Don't call me Mom! Yuh
t no son a mine. What do yuh want
n me now?

TIN. Nuttin'. I just ...

. MARTIN. (*Her voice rises, shrill, hys-
al*) Then git out a here! Before I crack
goddam face again. Git out a here!

TIN. (*Flaring.*) Why, yuh ole tramp,
lled a guy fer lookin' at me da way
are!

. MARTIN. (*Stares at him and nods
ly. Then quietly.*) Yeah ... You're a
r all right ... You're a murderer ...
're a butcher, sure! Why don't yuh
e me ferget yuh? Ain' I got troubles
ugh with the cops and newspapers
erin' me? An' Johnny and Martha ...

TIN. What's a mattuh wid 'em?

MARTIN. None a yer business! Just
e us alone! Yuh never brought nothin'
trouble. Don't come back like a bad
y! ... Just stay away and leave us
e ... an' die ...but leave us alone!
turns her back on him, and starts to

TIN. Hey, wait!

MARTIN. (*Pauses.*) What?

TIN. Need any dough?

MARTIN. Keep yer blood money.

TIN. Yuh gonna rat on me ... gonna
a cops?

MARTIN. No. They'll get yuh soon
gh.

TIN. Not me! Not Martin! Huh, not
-face Martin!

MARTIN. (*Mutters.*) Baby-face! Baby-
I remember ... (*She begins to sob,
hing her stomach.*) In here ... in
Kickin'! That's where yuh come
. God! I ought to be cut open here
ivin' yuh life ... murderer!!! (*She
es away, up the street, weeping quietly.
N stands there looking after her for
g time. His hand goes to his cheek.*

HUNK *comes down to him, clucking sympathetically. A boat whistle is heard.*)

HUNK. How da yuh like 'at! Yuh come
all away across a country jus' tuh see yer
ole lady, an' what da yuh git? Crack inna
face! I dunno, my mudder ain' like dat.
My mudder's always glad tuh see me. ...

MARTIN. (*Low, without turning.*) Shut
up! Gese, I must a been soft inna head, so
help me!

HUNK. Yuh should a slugged 'er one.

MARTIN. Shut up! I must a bin crazy inna
head. I musta bin nuts.

HUNK. Nah! It's jus' she ain' gota heart.
Dat ain' ...

MARTIN. (*Turns on* HUNK, *viciously, barking.*) Screw, willyuh? Screw! *Exit* HUNK
up the sidewalk. Martin. (*Turns, looking
after his mother. Turns slowly onto the
sidewalk, then notices* GIMPTY.) Kin yuh
pitchure dat?

GIMPTY. What did you expect ... flags
and a brass band?

MARTIN. (*Suddenly wheels and slaps*
GIMPTY.) Why—yew—punk!

GIMPTY. What's the idea?

MARTIN. Dat's ee idea ... fer shootin'
off yer mout'. I don' like guys 'at talk outa
toin. Not tuh me!

GIMPTY. Who the hell do you think you
are?

MARTIN. (*Claws his fingers and pushes*
GIMPTY's *face against the wall.*) Why, yuh
lousy cripple, I'll ...

GIMPTY. (*Jerks his head free of* MARTIN's
clutch.) Gee, when I was a kid I used to
think you were something, but you're rotten ... see? You ought to be wiped out!

MARTIN. (*His face twitching, the veins on
his forehead standing out, kicks* GIMPTY's
crippled foot and shouts.) Shut up!

GIMPTY. (*Gasps in pain, glaring at* MAR-
TIN. *After a long pause, quietly, deliberately.*) All right. O.K., Martin! Just wait!

MARTIN. What? (*Reaches for his shoulder holster.*) What's 'at?

GIMPTY. Go on! Shoot me! That'll bring 'em right to you! Go on!

MARTIN. (*Hesitates. He is interrupted by the excited voices of* GRISWALD *and* PHILIP. *Cautiously he restrains himself and whispers.*) I'll talk to yuh later. I'll be waitin' right up thuh street, see? Watch yuh step. (GRISWALD *appears behind the gate with* PHILIP, *who is sobbing. The* GOVERNESS *tries to quiet* PHILIP *while she dabs his face with her handkerchief.* MARTIN *goes up the street.*)

GRISWALD. It's all right, son! Now stop crying! What happened? Stop crying! Tell me just what happened?

GOVERNESS. *Attends, mon pauvre petit . . . 'ere, let me wipe your face . . . attends, attends!*

PHILIP. They hit me with a stick!

GRISWALD. A stick!

PHILIP. (*Spread-eagling his arms.*) That big!

GRISWALD. (*Furious.*) I'll have them locked up . . . I swear I'll send them to jail. Would you know them if you saw them?

PHLIP. Yes, daddy.

GRISWALD. (*To the* GOVERNESS.) You should have been with him. After yesterday . . .

GOVERNESS. I told him to stay in the garden. Madame said it was all right and she asked me to help Clara with the curtains in his room. (SPIT *starts up the ladder, followed by the other boys.* DIPPY *is frozen. He is blue and shaking with cold. His teeth are chattering.*)

DIPPY. Look, I'm shiverin'. My teet' 'r' knockin'.

TOMMY. Yeah. Yuh lips 'r' blue! Yuh bettuh git dressed quick, aw yuh'll ketch cold. (*Looks down at* MILTY *who is climbing the ladder, behind him.*) How do yuh like it, Milty?

MILTY. (*Grins from ear to ear.*) Swell! (*As the boys appear over the parapet,* T.B. *rises from under the hopper, points to* GRISWALD, *and calls the danger-cry.*)

T.B. Chikee! Putzo! Hey, felluhs! Chi[kee!] Tommy! (PHILIP *sees the boys and po[ints] them out to* GRISWALD.)

PHILIP. There they are! They're the o[nes!] (*Points out* TOMMY.) He's the leader!

GRISWALD. That one?

PHILIP. Yes. (SPIT, DIPPY, MILTY and [AN-] GEL *dash to the hopper, all yelling "C[hik-] ee!" They gather up their clothes and [run] madly up the street, followed by* T.B. T[OM-] MY, *stooping to pick up his clothes, tr[ips,] falls and is grabbed by* GRISWALD, *[who] shakes him violently.*)

GRISWALD. What right did you have [to] beat this boy? What makes you think [you] can get away with that?

TOMMY. (*Struggling to escape.*) Le[mme] go! Lemme go, will yuh? I didn' do [no-] tin' . . . lemme go!

PHILIP. (*Jumping up and down with [ex-] citement.*) He's the one! He's got [my] watch, daddy!

TOMMY. (*Tries to break away and ge[ts to] PHILIP.*) I have not, yuh fat li'l bastid!

GOVERNESS. (*Frightened, screams.*) [Phil-] ippe, come 'ere!

GRISWALD. (*Jerks* T[O]MMY *back.*) Oh, [no!] Not this time! I'll break your neck!

PHILIP. He's the one!

GRISWALD. Give me that watch!

TOMMY. I yain't got it!

PHILIP. He has! He's got it!

GRISWALD. (*Turns to the* GOVERNESS, [per-] emptorily.) Jeanne! Call an officer! (*[To]* TOMMY *again.*) Give me that watch!

TOMMY. (*Frightened by the police thr[eat.]* I yain't got it. Honest, I yain't! (*Sudden[ly] shouts up the street for help.*) Hey, fell[uhs!] (*The* GOVERNESS *stands there, paralyze[d.]*)

GRISWALD. Jeanne, *will* you call an of[ficer!] Come on! Hurry!

GOVERNESS. *Oui, oui, monsieur!* (*She [goes] up the sidewalk in a stiff-legged trot.*)

TOMMY. (*Stops struggling for a mom[ent.]* Aw, Mister, don't toin me ovuh tu[h]

s, will yuh? I won' touch 'im again.
 do it to allee udduh kids, an 'ey do it
 us. Dat ain' .nuttin'.

swald. No? I ought to break your
k.

ıMY. Oh, yeah? (*He suddenly pulls
y, almost escaping.* griswald *puts more
ssure on the arm.* tommy *calls to the
g.*) Hey, felluhs! (griswald *twists his
 double.* tommy *begins to cry with
, striking at* griswald.) Yuh joik! Ow,
, breakin' my ahm! Hey, Gimpty!

 pty. Have a heart! You're hurting that
 You don't have to . . .

wald. Hurt him! I'll kill him! (milty
 down the street, holding out the
ch.)

ıy. Heah yuh ah! Heah's duh watch!
ve 'im go misteh! He didn' do nuttin'!
ve 'im go! (*He starts pounding* gris-
.d. tommy *frees his hand.* griswald
ks his arm around tommy *in a strangle-
, and with the free arm pushes* milty
y.)

wald. (*To* milty.) Get out of here,
 . . .

ıMY. Hey, yer chokin' me! Yer chok-
ne! (*Both hands free, he gropes in the
sers he has clung to. Suddenly he
luces an open jackknife and waves it.*)
k out! I gotta knife. I'll stab yuh!
swald *only holds him tighter, trying
 apture the knife. A flash of steel!* gris-
 groans and clutches his wrist, re-
ng tommy. tommy *and* milty *fly up
street.* griswald *stands there stunned,
ng at his bleeding wrist.*)

iP. Daddy! Daddy! Daddy! (*He be-
to sob at the sight of blood. The
MAN comes out of the gateway and
imediately excited.*)

MAN. What's the matter?

vALD. (*Jerking his head toward the
ng boys.*) Catch those boys! (*The
MAN lumbers up the street in pursuit.
vALD takes a handkerchief from his
t pocket and presses it to his wrist.
d seeps through.* griswald, *self-con-
d now, tries to quiet the sobbing*

philip.) It's all right, son, it's all right!
No, no, no! Now stop crying. Let me
have your handkerchief!

gimpty. Are you hurt?

griswald. What do you think?

gimpty. Can I help?

griswald. It's a little late for that now.

philip. (*Fishes out a crumpled handkerchief and hands it to his father.*) Here.

griswald. Haven't you a clean one?

philip. No.

gimpty. You can have mine.

griswald. Never mind. (*To* philip, *who
puts his own handkerchief back.*) You
should always carry two clean handker-
chiefs. Put your hand in my pocket. You'll
find one there. No, the other pocket.
(philip *finds the handkerchief. The* governess *comes down the sidewalk with a
policeman.*)

policeman. What's the matter?

griswald. Plenty.

governess. (*Sees the blood and shrieks.*)
Oh! He's bleeding! (*To* philip.) *Qu'est ce
qui passe, mon petit?*

philip. That boy stuck him with a knife!

governess. (*To* griswald.) *Mon Dieu!*
Are you hurt, monsieur? (griswald *ignores her and tightens the bandage.*)

policeman. Is it deep?

griswald. Deep enough.

policeman. Better let me make a tourni-
quet.

griswald. Never mind.

policeman. Who did it?

griswald. One of these hoodlums around
here. I want that boy arrested.

policeman. Sure. Do you know who he
was?

griswald. No.

governess. Can I help you, monsieur?

GRISWALD. Yes. Go up and call Dr. Merriam at once. I'm afraid of infection. (*The* DOORMAN *returns, empty-handed, puffing, and mopping his brow.* GRISWALD *frowns.*) Where is he?

DOORMAN. (*Panting.*) Phew . . . I couldn't catch them.

GRISWALD. (*Angry.*) You let them go?

DOORMAN. I tried, sir. They were like little flies . . . in and out . . . Just when I thought I had one of them . . . he ran down the cellar . . . I went after him, but he got away. . . .

GRISWALD. Officer, I want you to find that boy and arrest him. Understand?

POLICEMAN. (*Takes out a notebook and pencil.*) Well, that ain't gonna be so easy, you know.

GRISWALD. Never mind. That's your job! It's pretty serious that a thing like this can happen on your beat in broad daylight.

POLICEMAN. Well, I can't be everywhere at once.

GRISWALD. Before he stabbed me, he and some others beat up my boy and stole his watch. You should have been around some of that time.

POLICEMAN. (*Annoyed at his officiousness. Brusquely.*) Well . . . what's your name?

GRISWALD. My name's Griswald . . . I live here. (*Nods toward the East River Terrace.*)

POLICEMAN. What did the boy look like?

GRISWALD. He was about so high . . . black hair . . . oh, I don't know. I didn't notice. Did you, son?

PHILIP. One of them coughs.

POLICEMAN. Didn't you notice anything else?

PHILIP. No.

GRISWALD. Jeanne?

GOVERNESS. Let me see . . .

POLICEMAN. How was he dressed?

GOVERNESS. They'd been in swimm— here. They were practically naked . . . filthy. And their language was 'orrible

GRISWALD. (*Irritated.*) He knows that, knows that! What were they like, thou; Didn't you see?

GOVERNESS. It all happened so quickly didn't have a chance to, monsieur.

PHILIP. He hit me with a stick.

POLICEMAN. Hm!

GRISWALD. (*Suddenly a bit faint.*) T men can tell you better. They saw it. Jea— will you please call Dr. Merriam r away? I'm feeling a little sick.

GOVERNESS. Oui, monsieur! Come, I ippe! (*She goes in, accompanied by* PHI

GRISWALD. I don't want to make trouble, officer, but I want that boy ca and arrested. Understand?

POLICEMAN. I'll do the best I can. (GRISWALD. *The* POLICEMAN *mutters.*) I v der who the hell that guy thinks he is

DOORMAN. (*Impressively, rolling the s on his tongue.*) Mr. Griswald. (CHA the chauffeur, saunters down the sidew

POLICEMAN. What of it?

DOORMAN. Don't you know? He's J Griswald's brother.

POLICEMAN. (*His attitude changes.*)

DOORMAN. (*To the* CHAUFFEUR, *who reached the gate.*) Oh, I don't think Griswald'll be using the car now. He just hurt.

CHARLES. Wha-a-at? What happened?

DOORMAN. He was stabbed. It's a story. I'll tell you later.

CHARLES. (*Concerned.*) Well, will you him and see if he wants me?

DOORMAN. (*Starting off.*) Yeah.

POLICEMAN. Hey, wait!

DOORMAN. I'll be right out, officer. Griswald may need him.

POLICEMAN. Oh, all right. (DOORMAN CHARLES *go in through the gate.*)

ARLES. What happened?

ORMAN. These kids around here have
en raising an awful rumpus all day, and
st now one of them . . . (*Their voices
off.*)

LICEMAN. (*To* GIMPTY.) Did you see the
ds who did this?

IPTY. I didn't notice them.

LICEMAN. You come around here often?

IPTY. Yes.

LICEMAN. Didn't you recognize any of
1?

IPTY. No.

LICEMAN. Can you describe 'em?

IPTY. Not very clearly.

LICEMAN. (*Annoyed.*) Well, what were
y like?

IPTY. About so high . . . dirty an'
:ed. . . .

ICEMAN. (*Impatiently.*) And they sock-
that young jalopee in the eye. Yeah. I
that much myself. But that might be
/ kid in this neighborhood. Anything
?

IPTY. No.

ICEMAN. (*Slaps his book shut.*) Why
hell didn't I learn a trade? (*He starts
vard the gate.* DRINA *comes down the
et and approaches* GIMPTY. *She looks
d and bedraggled. She has an ugly
ise' on her forehead.*)

IPTY. (*To* DRINA.) Hey, what's the mat-
with your head?

NA. (*Looking at the* POLICEMAN *and
ing her voice.*) We were picketing the
e, an' some lousy cop hit me.

ICEMAN. (*Wheels around, insulted.*)
at's that?

NA. (*Deliberately.*) One a you lousy
s hit me.

ICEMAN. You better watch your lan-
ge or you'll get another clout!

IA. Go on and try it!

GIMPTY. (*Urging discretion.*) Sh!

POLICEMAN. Listen! I'm in no mood to be
tampered with. I'm in no mood! . . . Not
by a lousy Red.

DRINA. (*Quietly.*) I ain't no Red.

POLICEMAN. (*Thick-skulled.*) Well, you
talk like one.

DRINA. Aw nuts!

POLICEMAN. You were strikin', weren't
you?

DRINA. Sure. Because I want a few bucks
more a week so's I can live decent. God
knows I earn it!

POLICEMAN. (*Who has had enough.*) Aw,
go on home! (*He turns and goes in the
gate, addressing someone.*) Hey, Bill, I
wanna see you. . . . (*Pause.*)

DRINA. (*To* GIMPTY.) We were only picketing. We got a right to picket. They
charged us. They hit us right and left.
Three of the girls were hurt bad.

GIMPTY. I'll give you some advice about
your brother.

DRINA. I was just lookin' for him. Did
you see him?

GIMPTY. Tell him to keep away from
here . . . or he's in for a lot of trouble.

DRINA. (*Sits down, exhausted, and sighs.*)
What's he done now?

GIMPTY. Plenty.

DRINA. What?

GIMPTY. Just tell him to keep away.

DRINA. Gosh, I don't know what to do
with that boy! (*A passing boat hoots
twice.* DRINA *ponders her problem a moment.*) There's a feller I know . . . is always askin' me to marry him. . . . Maybe
I ought to do that, hm? . . . For Tommy
. . . he's rich. . . . What should I do?

GIMPTY (*Disinterested, too absorbed in his
own problem.*) That's up to you.

DRINA. Most of the girls at the store are
always talkin' about marryin' a rich guy.
I used to laugh at 'em. (*She laughs now
at herself.*)

GIMPTY. Maybe they're right.

DRINA. (*Looks at him.*) That doesn't sound like you.

GIMPTY. No? How do you know what goes on inside of me?

DRINA. (*Shakes her head and smiles sadly.*) I know.

GIMPTY. (*Curtly.*) Smart girl!

DRINA. (*Very tender and soft. She knows he's suffering.*) What's the matter?

GIMPTY. Nothing.

DRINA. I understand.

GIMPTY. You can't.

DRINA. Why can't I? (*Suddenly exasperated.*) Sometimes, for a boy as bright as you, with your education, you talk like a fool. Don't you think I got a heart too? Don't you think there are nights when I cry myself to sleep? Don't you think I know what it means to be lonely and scared and to want somebody? God, ain't I human? Am I so homely that I ain't got a right to . . .

GIMPTY. No, Drina! I think you're a swell girl. You are.

DRINA. (*Turns away, annoyed at his patronage.*) Oh, don't give me any of that taffy! You don't even know I'm alive!

GIMPTY. Why do you say that?

DRINA. What's the difference? It don't matter. . . . Only I hate to see you butting your head against a stone wall. You're only going to hurt yourself.

GIMPTY. What're you talking about?

DRINA. You know. . . . Oh, I think that lady's beautiful . . . and I think she's nice. . . .

GIMPTY. (*Angry.*) Look! Will you be a good girl and mind your own business?

DRINA. She's not for you!

GIMPTY. Why not? (*The POLICEMAN comes out of the East River Terrace, notebook and pencil in hand. He goes to GIMPTY.*)

POLICEMAN. Well, I got something work on, anyway. . . . Do you know kid named Tommy something arou here? (*DRINA starts, but checks herself.*

GIMPTY. No.

POLICEMAN. They heard the others him Tommy. (*Jerks his head toward gate.*) You know what he's liable to With his pull? Have me broke, may The first thing I know, I'll be pound a lousier post than this! Harlem, may Get a knife in my back. . . . (*Looks from his notebook, to DRINA.*) Hey, yo

DRINA. What?

POLICEMAN. You live around here?

DRINA. (*Very docile, frightened.*) Yes.

POLICEMAN. Know a kid named Tom something?

DRINA. No . . . no, I don't.

POLICEMAN. (*Studying his notes.*) I'll c him. I'll skin him alive!

DRINA. (*Finally ventures.*) What'd he

POLICEMAN. Pulled a knife on some muck-a-muck in there.

DRINA. No!

POLICEMAN. Yeah. Ah, it don't pay to nice to these kids. It just don't pay.

DRINA. Was the man hurt?

POLICEMAN. Yeah. It looks like a pr deep cut. Lord, he's fit to be tied! I n seen a guy so boined up! (*DRINA turns goes up the street, restraining her imp to run. The POLICEMAN jabbers on, c plainingly.*) This is a tough enough cinct . . . but Harlem?—There's a l precinct! A pal of mine got killed t last year. Left a wife and a couple of k

GIMPTY. Is that so?

POLICEMAN. Yeah.

GIMPTY. Too bad! (*As the idea begin take form.*) Well . . . maybe you can c Baby-face Martin or one of those fell and grab off that forty-two-hundred-d reward.

POLICEMAN. Yeah.

IPTY. Then you could retire.

ICEMAN. Yeah, you could do a lot on t.

IPTY. Yeah, I guess you could. . . . . . . tell me something . . .

ICEMAN. What?

IPTY. Supposin' . . . supposin' a fellow ew where that . . . er . . . Baby-face rtin is located. How would he go about orting him . . . and making sure of not ting gypped out of the reward?

ICEMAN. Just phone police headquarters . or the Department of Justice direct. ey'd be down here in two minutes. (*He ks at* GIMPTY *and asks ironically.*) Why? u don't know where he is, do you?

IPTY. (*Smiles wanly back at him.*) lorado, the newspapers say. . . . No, I s just wonderin'.

ICEMAN. Well, whoever turns that guy is taking an awful chance. He's a killer.

IPTY. Well . . . you can't live forever. *passing tug shrieks its warning signal. d shrieks again.* MARTIN *walks, cat- ted, down the street.*)

ICEMAN. That's right. (GIMPTY *turns, s* MARTIN, *and rises.*)

IPTY. (*To the* POLICEMAN.) Excuse me.

ICEMAN. Sure. (GIMPTY *crosses to the er side of the street, and walks away, tending not to notice* MARTIN.)

RTIN. Hello, Gimpty! (GIMPTY *accel- tes his pace and hobbles off.* MARTIN ks his teeth for a second, thinking. Then adopts an amiable smile and approaches POLICEMAN.) Kinda quiet today, ain' officer?

ICEMAN. Not with these kids around.

RTIN. (*Jerks his head in* GIMPTY'S *di- tion.*) Dat's a nice feller. Friend of mine. UNK *has entered from up the street t after* GIMPTY'S *exit. He is lighting a ar, when he sees* MARTIN *in friendly versation with the arch. enemy. He nds there, transfixed, match to cigar.*)

ICEMAN. I had quite a talk with him.

MARTIN. (*Fishing.*) What about?

POLICEMAN. Oh . . . about these kids here.

MARTIN. Zat all?

POLICEMAN. Say, that's plenty! (*He puts his notebook in his pocket.*) You don't happen to know a kid around here named Tommy something, do you?

MARTIN. (*Shakes his head.*) Uh-uh!

POLICEMAN. Well, I'll catch him all right! (*He strides up the sidewalk.* MARTIN *watches him, then laughs. The match burns* HUNK'S *fingers. He drops it.*)

HUNK. Jesus!

MARTIN. (*Laughing.*) A pal a mine.

HUNK. Dat's crazy.

MARTIN. Dey don' know me . . . wid dis mug.

HUNK. (*Sighs. This is too much for him. Then he remembers his errand.*) Say, dat dame is heah.

MARTIN. Who?

HUNK. Er . . Francey, or whatevah yuh call huh.

MARTIN. She is?

HUNK. Yeah. I got 'er waitin' on a cor- ner. (*Puzzled.*) I dunno what yuh wanna bodder wid a cheap hustlah like dat fuh.

MARTIN. (*Sharply.*) Wha da yuh mean? Francey ain' no hustlah!

HUNK. (*Skeptical.*) No?

MARTIN. No.

HUNK. (*Smiles weakly.*) O.K. My mis- take. We all make mistakes, boss. Dat's what dey got rubbuhs on ee end a pencils faw. (*Laughs feebly.*)

MARTIN. Pretty cute, ain' cha? Maybe yuhr a mistake. Maybe yuhr liable tuh git rubbed out yuhself.

HUNK. (*Frightened.*) I'll git huh now. (*He starts off. A young girl comes down the street, an obvious whore of the lowest class, wearing her timeless profession de- fiantly. A pert, pretty little face still show-*

ing traces of quality and something once sweet and fine. Skin an unhealthy pallor, lips a smear of rouge. Her mop of dyed red hair is lustreless, strawy, dead from too much alternate bleach and henna. She carries herself loosely. Droop-shouldered. Voluptuous S-shaped posture. There are no clothes under her cheap, faded green silk dress, cut so tight that it reveals the nipples of her full breasts, her navel, the "V" of her crotch, the muscles of her buttocks. She has obviously dressed hastily, carelessly; one stocking streaked with runs dribbles down at the ankle. She accosts HUNK, *impatiently.*)

FRANCEY. Hey, what ta hell's ee idear, keepin' me standin' on a corner all day? I'm busy. I gotta git back tuh da house. Yuh want Ida tuh break my face? (MARTIN *looks at her.*)

MARTIN. Francey! Jesus, what's come over yuh?

FRANCEY. (*Turning sharply to* MARTIN.) How do yew know my name? Who are yew? (*Impatiently.*) Well, who th' hell . . . (*Then she recognizes him, and gasps.*) Fuh th' love a God! Marty!

MARTIN. (*Never taking his eyes off the girl.*) Yeah. Hunk . . . scram! (HUNK *goes up the street, stops at the tenement stoop and lounges there, within ear shot.*)

FRANCEY. (*Eagerly.*) How are yuh, Marty?

MARTIN. Read duh papers!

FRANCEY. Yuh did somethin' to yuh face.

MARTIN. Yeah. Plastic, dey call it.

FRANCEY. They said yuh wuz out aroun' Coloraduh—th' noospapuhs! Gee, I'm glad to see yuh! (MARTIN *slips his arm around her waist and draws her tight to his body. As his lips grope for hers,* FRANCEY *turns her face away.* MARTIN *tries to pull her face around. She cries furiously:* No . . . don' kiss me on a lips!)

MARTIN. (*Releasing her, puzzled.*) What? What's a matter? (*He can't believe this. He frowns.*) I ain't good enough for yuh?

FRANCEY. (*Quickly.*) No. It ain't dat. It ain't yew. It's me. I got a sore on my mouth. Fuh yuhr own good, I don't w yuh to kiss me, dat's why.

MARTIN. I ain't nevuh fuhgot da way y kiss.

FRANCEY. (*Wistfully.*) I ain't niethuh. (laughs.) Go on! You wit all yer fa dames. Where do I come off?

MARTIN. Dey don't mean nuttin'.

FRANCEY. Dat chorus goil . . . what's name?

MARTIN. Nuttin'. She ain't got nuttin' no guts, no fire. . . . But yew been boin in my blood . . . evuh since . . .

FRANCEY. An' yew been in mine . . . yuh wanna know.

MARTIN. Remembuh dat foist night . on a roof?

FRANCEY. Yeah, I remembuh . . . da was full a stars, an' I was full a drea ideas. Dat was me foist time. I was fo teen, goin' on fifteen.

MARTIN. Yeah. It wuz mine too. It w terrific. Hit me right wheah I live . . . my back wuz meltin'. An I wuz so sc when yuh started laffin' an' cryin', cr like. . . . (*They both laugh, enjoying memory, a little embarrassed by it.*)

FRANCEY. Yeah.

MARTIN. Gee, I nevuh wuz so sca'd 'at time.

FRANCEY. Me too.

MARTIN. (*Draws her to him again, m gently.*) Come eah! Close to me!

FRANCEY. (*Acquiescing.*) Ony don' me on a lips!

MARTIN. Closuh! (*They stand there moment, bodies close, passionate.* MAR buries his face in her hair.*)

FRANCEY. (*Eyes closed, whispers.*) Ma

MARTIN. Dose times unduh da stairs. .

FRANCEY. A couple a crazy kids we w We wuz gonna git married. I bough ring at da five an' dime staw.

MARTIN. Yeah, Ony we didn' have mo enough fuh de license. Gee, it seems

tiddy. We wuz talkin' about it right
ah.

NCEY. Yestiddy! It seems like a million
ths!

RTIN. (*As voices are heard coming
m the East River Terrace.*) Wait! (*They
arate. He draws his hat over his eyes
d turns away as a young couple come
t of the gate and walk up the street.*)

L. So many people standing around.
hat's all the excitement? What's happen-
?

N. The elevator man said someone was
bbed.

L. Really? Who was it, do you know?

N. Mr. Griswald, I think he said.
elfth floor.

L. Oh! Yes? Did he say who did it?

N. He said one of the kids around
e somewhere. . . . (*When they are well
t of sight,* FRANCEY *clutches* MARTIN'S
n.*)

NCEY. Marty, listen! Yuh got ta take
e a yuhself. Yuh gotta go way an' hide.
lon' want 'em to git yuh! I don' wan'
n to git yuh!

RTIN. Whatsa diffrince wheah I go?
got thuh finger on me everywheah. Ah,
g 'em.

NCEY. Dey won't reco'nize yuh. Dey
n't. Even I didn't.

RTIN. Yeah, but yuh can' change ese,
ancey. Look! (*He holds up his fingers.
e tips are yellow and scarred.*) Tree
es I boined 'em wid acid an' t'ings. No
od. Dere are some t'ings yuh can't
nge. But I'll tell yuh what. . . I'll scram
t a heah.. I'll scram . . . if yew come
t me.

NCEY. Ah, what do yuh want me fer?
broken-down hoor.

RTIN. Shut up!

NCEY. I wouldn' be good fuh yuh.

RTIN. I know what I want.

NCEY. (*Laughs crazily.*) Yeah. Dis is

a swell pipe-dream I'm havin'! I'm Minnie
de Moocher kickin' a gong aroun'!

MARTIN. Listen! I got de dough now, kid.
We kin do it now.

FRANCEY. But I'm sick, Marty! Don't yuh
see? I'm sick!

MARTIN. What's a matter wid yuh?

FRANCEY. (*Almost inaudibly.*) What do
yuh think? (MARTIN *looks at her for a long
time. He sees her. The nostalgic dream is
finished. His lips begin to curl in disgust.*)

MARTIN. Why didncha git a job?

FRANCEY. Dey don' grow on trees!

MARTIN. Why didncha starve foist?

FRANCEY. Why didnchou? (MARTIN *makes
no effort to conceal his growing disgust.
Turns away.*)

FRANCEY. (*Suddenly shouts, fiercely, at
the top of her lungs.*) Well, what ta hell
did yuh expect?

MARTIN. I don' know. (*A passing tug
shrieks hoarsely. The echo floats back.*)

FRANCEY. (*Quietly, clutching at a hope.*)
Maybe . . . if yuh got da dough . . . yuh
git a doctuh an' he fixes me up . . .

MARTIN. Nah. Once at stuff gits in yuh
. . . nah! (*Again the tug shrieks and is
answered by its echo. He reaches into his
inner breast pocket, extracts a fat roll of
bills, peels off several and hands them to
her.*) Heah. Buy yerself somethin'.

FRANCEY. (*Her eyes suddenly glued to the
money.*) Baby! Dat's some roll yuh got.
Yuh cud choke a hoss wid dat.

MARTIN. (*Thrusting it at her.*) Heah!

FRANCEY. (*Takes the money.*) Is it hot?

MARTIN. Yeah. Bettah be careful where
yuh spend it.

FRANCEY. Sure.

MARTIN. An' keep yuh lips buttoned up!

FRANCEY. I wouldn' tell on yuh, Marty.
Not if dey tied me ta wild hosses, I
wouldn't.

MARTIN. Bettuh not.

FRANCEY. (*Folds her money, still fascinated by the huge roll of bills in his hand. Her voice takes on a peculiar whining, wheedling quality.*) Honey!

MARTIN. Yeah?

FRANCEY. Cud yuh spare another twenty bucks? I godda . . .

MARTIN. No!

FRANCEY. Aw, come on, dearie!

MARTIN. No!

FRANCEY. Don' be a tightwad!

MARTIN. (*Reaching the limit of his disgust.*) What ta hell do yuh tink I am? Some guy yuh got up in yuh room? I'll . . . (*He raises his hand, ready to slap her. Again the shriek of a tug, and the echo.*)

FRANCEY. (*Quickly, frightened.*) Nah, fergit it, Marty! I wuz just . . .

MARTIN. Awright! Awright! Now beat it!

FRANCEY. O.K., Marty. (*She starts to go, pauses, turns back.*) Fer old times' sakes, will yuh do me a favor? Please?

MARTIN. (*Shoves the money back into his pocket.*) No!

FRANCEY. Not dat.

MARTIN. What?

FRANCEY. Will yuh kiss me? Heah? Ona cheek? Jus' fuh old times' sakes? Come on. (*He hesitates. She comes close, presses her cheek against his lips. He pecks her cheek, and turns away, scowling. She laughs, a low bitter laugh, at his obvious disrelish.*) Thanks! (*She goes up the street slowly, her purse swinging carelessly, her body swaying invitation, the tired march of her profession. The shriek of the tug is drawn out and distant now. The echo lingers.* MARTIN *spits and wipes the kiss off his lips with a groan of distaste.*)

HUNK. (*Comes down the sidewalk, slowly.*) Well?

MARTIN. Huh?

HUNK. See?

MARTIN. Yeah. Yeah!

HUNK. Twice in one day. Deah yuh I toldja we shouldn' a come back. But wouldn' lissen a me. Yuh nevuh lissen me.

MARTIN. Yeah.

HUNK. (*Trying to console him.*) I kn how yuh feel, Marty. Les go back St. Louis, huh? Now dat dame yuh deah—Deedy Cook—Now dat wuz broad. Regaler. Bet she's waitin fuh . . . wid welcome ona doormat.

MARTIN. Awright! Don talk about dam Hunk, will yuh? Fuhget 'em. All cats l alike inna dahk. Fuhget 'em. (*A little comes out of the gate bouncing a rub ball.* MARTIN *looks at her, thinks a mome turns to watch her go up the street. sucks his teeth a moment, thinking.*)

HUNK. Listen, Marty . . . Let's git o heah. Too many people know yuh he Whaddaya say?

MARTIN. Sh! I'm thinkin'. (*Pause.*)

HUNK. Well, guess I'll go shoot a gam pillpool. (*Starts to go up the street.*)

MARTIN. (*Motions him back, turns stare at the Terrace Apartments.*) Wa minute . . . (HUNK *returns.*) Yuh kn Hunk. (*He shakes a thumb at the Ap ment.*) Der's a pile a tin in ere.

HUNK. Yeah.

MARTIN. Didja see what dese kids did h today?

HUNK. No.

MARTIN. Ey got one a dese rich little squ in a hallway, slapped him around an' bed his watch.

HUNK. So what? (*A man appears on terrace, watches them for a second, then slips away. Two men come down street talking casually, one of them into the tenement, the other, waiting him, wanders over back of the hopper is hidden from view.*)

MARTIN. (*Glances at them, lowers voice.*) Maybe we kin pull a snatch kidnap one a dese babies.

HUNK. We're too hot. Foolin' round kids ain' our racket.

RTIN. Scared?

NK. No . . . ony . . . I . . . .

RTIN. Stop yuh yammerin'! Git a hold
Whitey. See wot he knows about duh
gs in heah! (HUNK *hesitates.*) Come on,
nk, git goin'!

NK. O.K. Yuh duh boss! (*He goes re-
antly. The tap of* GIMPTY'S *cane on the
walk is heard approaching, its rhythmic
k ominous.* GIMPTY *appears, tight-lipped,
e, grim.* MARTIN *smiles out of one cor-
of his lips, and throws him a concilia-
greeting.*)

RTIN. Hello, Gimpty! (GIMPTY *turns
ay without answering.* MARTIN, *amused,
ghs. He is suddenly in a good mood.
e man who spied on him from the
ace appears in the gateway and catches
IPTY'S eye.* GIMPTY *points his cane at
RTIN. The good mood passes.* MARTIN'S
brows pull together in one puzzled
e.*)

RTIN. What's eatin' yuh, wise guy?
he man behind the gate draws a revol-
comes quickly up behind* MARTIN *and
s the gun in his back.*)

MAN. Get em up, Martin! The Depart-
nt of Justice wants you!

RTIN. What ta hell . . . ! (*Tries to
n, but the revolver prods him back.*)

IAN. Come on, get 'em up!

RTIN. (*Hands up.*) I ain't Martin. My
ne's Johnson. Wanna see my license?
e slides his hand into his breast pocket.*)

IAN. If you're smart, you'll behave your-
!

RTIN. (*Wheels around, draws his gun,
fires in one motion.*) No, yuh don't
. (*The* G MAN *drops his gun, crumples
o the sidewalk holding his belly and
king.* MARTIN *turns to face* GIMPTY, *who
backed away to the hopper.* MARTIN,
face black and contorted, aims at* GIMP-
) So yuh ratted, yuh. . . . (*From be-
d the hopper and the tenement door-
y guns explode. Two other* G MEN
ear and descend on* MARTIN, *firing as
y come.* MARTIN *groans, wheels, and*

*falls, his face in the gutter, his fingers
clawing the sidewalk. One of the* G MEN
*goes to aid his wounded comrade. The
other* G MAN *stands over* MARTIN's *body,
pumping bullet after bullet into him, literally nailing him to the ground. The* G
MAN *kicks him to make sure he's dead.
No twitch!* MARTIN *lies there flat. The*
G MAN *takes out a handkerchief, picks up*
MARTIN's *gun gingerly, wraps it in the
handkerchief, puts it in his pocket.*)

SECOND G MAN. Where'd he get you, Bob?
Come on, sit up here! (*Helps him to sit
against the coping.* FIRST G MAN *presses his
hand in agony to his wound. From the
street there is a rising babble of voices.
Tenement windows are thrown up, heads
thrust out; the curious crowd to the edge
of the terrace, come to the gate, run down
the street, collect in small groups, discussing the macabre scene in excited, hushed
murmur. A* LADY *comes out of the gate,
sees the dead man, screams hysterically,
and is helped off by the* DOORMAN. *The*
POLICEMAN *comes tearing down the street,
revolver drawn. He forces his way through
the crowd.*)

POLICEMAN. Out a my way! Look out!
(*To the* THIRD G MAN.) What's this?

THIRD G MAN. (*Taking out a badge in a
leather case from inside his coat pocket
and holding it up.*) It's all right, officer.
Department of Justice! (*Replaces the
badge.*)

POLICEMAN. What happened? Who's this
guy?

THIRD G MAN. Baby-face Martin.

POLICEMAN. Is that him?

THIRD G MAN. Yep.

POLICEMAN. Gese, I was talkin' to him a
couple a minutes ago.

SECOND G MAN. Get an ambulance, quick!
Will you?

POLICEMAN. (*Crosses to the police box,
opens it.*) Box 10 . . . Mulligan. Send
ambulance! Make all notifications! Baby-
face Martin was just shot by Federal men.
He winged one of 'em . . . I don't know . . .
yeah . . . here. Gese, I was talking to him

myself a few minutes ago ... Hell, Sarge, I couldn't recognize him. His face is all made over. (*He hangs up. The shrill siren of a radio car mounts to a crescendo, mingles with the screech of brakes, and is suddenly silent. Two more policemen dash on, forcing their path through the crowd. They are followed by* SPIT, *wearing a single roller skate. He edges his way to the front of the crowd.*)

SECOND POLICEMAN. Hi, Mulligan. What have yuh got here?

MULLIGAN. Baby-face Martin!

THIRD POLICEMAN. Did you git him?

MULLIGAN. No such luck. The Federal men got him. He winged one of them. (*Gestures toward the wounded* G MAN.)

SECOND POLICEMAN. Did you notify the house?

MULLIGAN. Yeah. I gave em everything ... Lend us a hand, will yuh. Git rid of this crowd. (MULLIGAN *stands by* MARTIN's *body, writing in a notebook. The other* POLICEMEN *push back the crowd.* SPIT *slips through, and looks at the dead man with scared curiosity.*)

SECOND POLICEMAN. (*Pushing the crowd.*) Break it up! This is no circus. Come on, break it up!

GIRL IN THE CROWD. Don't push me!

SECOND POLICEMAN. Well, go on home! Go on, break it up!

SECOND G MAN. (*To the wounded agent.*) How you feelin', Bob?

FIRST G MAN. Lousy.

SECOND G MAN. You'll be O.K.

FIRST G MAN. I don't know ... I don't know! I should've plugged him right away ... in the back. You don't give a snake like that a break. ... Anyway, we got him! That's something!

SECOND G MAN. Sure you did, Bob. You'll get cited for this.

FIRST G MAN. That's just dandy! That's just dandy! Give the medal to my old lady for the kids to play with ..., an' remember

they once had an old man who was a . hero!

THIRD G MAN. Aw, cut it, Bob. You'll O.K. Don't talk like that!

DOORMAN. (*Pushing through the crow* Officer! Officer!

MULLIGAN. Get outa here! You with rest of them. Come on, get back!

DOORMAN. Officer, this is important! Th one of the boys ... there, that one! H one of the gang!

MULLIGAN. What boy? What the hell you talkin' about?

DOORMAN. The one who stabbed Griswald.

MULLIGAN. What? Oh, where?

DOORMAN. (*Pointing.*) That one the He's one of the gang.

MULLIGAN. Are you sure?

DOORMAN. Yes ... yes ... I'll swear it!

MULLIGAN. Come here! Hey you! (*R over to* SPIT, *grabs his arm. The murr of the crowd rises.*)

SPIT. Lemme go! I didn' do nuttin. L me go!

SECOND POLICEMAN. What is this kid to do with it?

MULLIGAN. That's somethin' else. (* clang of an approaching ambulance co to a sudden halt. Enter, pushing their down the street, an* INTERNE *carryin doctor's bag, followed by an* AMBULA MAN *carrying a folded stretcher, which closes a pillow and a rolled blanket. murmur of the crowd hushes.*)

INTERNE. Hello, Mulligan.

MULLIGAN. Hello, doc. (*To* SECOND POL MAN.) Hold this kid a minute. (SEC POLICEMAN *grabs* SPIT's *arm and drags back to the crowd on the sidewalk.*)

INTERNE. What's up? (*He comes d to the body.*)

MULLIGAN. Just got Baby-face Mar (*The murmur rises again as the new spread.*)

ᴛᴇʀɴᴇ. You did? (*He glances at the*
dy.) He won't need me!

ᴄᴏɴᴅ ɢ ᴍᴀɴ. Hey, doc, look at this
n! (*The* ɪɴᴛᴇʀɴᴇ *kneels to the wounded*
n, examines his wound, sponges it,
ces a pad over it.) It's not bad, is it,
:?

ᴇʀɴᴇ. (*Cheerfully.*) Not very bad, but
'd better rush him off to the hospital.
re, somebody help get him on the
ᴇtcher. (*The* ᴀᴍʙᴜʟᴀɴᴄᴇ ᴍᴀɴ *opens the*
ᴇtcher, places the pillow at the head.
ᴏɴᴅ ɢ ᴍᴀɴ *and* ᴍᴜʟʟɪɢᴀɴ *lift the*
unded ɢ ᴍᴀɴ *carefully and lay him on*
stretcher with words of encouragement.
ᴇ ᴀᴍʙᴜʟᴀɴᴄᴇ ᴍᴀɴ *unrolls the blanket*
ᴇr him. ꜱᴇᴄᴏɴᴅ ɢ ᴍᴀɴ *and the* ᴀᴍʙᴜ-
ᴄᴇ ᴅʀɪᴠᴇʀ *carry the wounded man up*
sidewalk calling "Gangway." The
ʀᴅ ɢ ᴍᴀɴ *accompanies them, holding*
wounded man's hand and talking to
n. The crowd open a path, and stare,
ir murmur silenced for a moment.)

ʟʟɪɢᴀɴ. (*Pointing to Baby-face.*) Want
look at this guy, doc?

ᴇʀɴᴇ. (*Kneels by the body, rips open*
coat and vest, cursorily inspects the
unds, rolls back the eyelid, applies a
hoscope to the heart.) Phew! They cer-
ᴉly did a job on him! Nothing left to
k at but chopped meat. God, they
ɪn't leave enough of him for a good
ᴠ.! (*Rises, takes pad and pencil from*
pocket, glances at ᴍᴜʟʟɪɢᴀɴ's *shield,*
ᴇs.) Mulligan . . . 10417 . . . 19th pre-
ᴄt. Have you got his pedigree?

ʟʟɪɢᴀɴ. (*Reading from his own note-*
k.) Joe Martin. 28. White . . . U.S.
ᴛ., 9 in. 170 lbs. Unmarried. Occupation
. (*Shrugs his shoulders.*)

ᴇʀɴᴇ. All right. Dr. Flint. Mark him
ᴅ.A.!

ʟʟɪɢᴀɴ. (*Writing.*) Dead . . . on . . .
ᴠal. . . . (*Enter, pushing their way*
ᴜgh the crowd, the ᴍᴇᴅɪᴄᴀʟ ᴇxᴀᴍɪɴᴇʀ,
ᴏwed by the ᴘᴏʟɪᴄᴇ ᴘʜᴏᴛᴏɢʀᴀᴘʜᴇʀ. *The*
ᴘᴛᴏɢʀᴀᴘʜᴇʀ opens his camera, adjusts
ᴅ photographs the body from several
ᴅes.)

ᴇʀɴᴇ. (*As the* ᴇxᴀᴍɪɴᴇʀ *approaches.*)
ᴏ, doc!

ᴇxᴀᴍɪɴᴇʀ. Hello, Doctor. So they finally
got him, did they?

ɪɴᴛᴇʀɴᴇ. Yes, they sure did.

ᴇxᴀᴍɪɴᴇʀ. It's about time. What have you
got on him?

ɪɴᴛᴇʀɴᴇ. Twelve gunshot wounds. Five
belly, four chest, three head. (*Picks up his*
bag and goes. The ᴇxᴀᴍɪɴᴇʀ *inspects the*
body.)

ᴍᴜʟʟɪɢᴀɴ. (*To the* ᴅᴏᴏʀᴍᴀɴ.) Hey, find
something to cover this up with. (*The*
ᴅᴏᴏʀᴍᴀɴ *nods and disappears through the*
gateway. ᴍᴜʟʟɪɢᴀɴ *turns to the* ᴛʜɪʀᴅ
ᴘᴏʟɪᴄᴇᴍᴀɴ, *who is still holding back the*
crowd.) Hey, Tom! Stand by while I go
through this bum! (*He kneels, and goes*
through ᴍᴀʀᴛɪɴ's *pockets, handing his*
findings to the ᴛʜɪʀᴅ ᴘᴏʟɪᴄᴇᴍᴀɴ *who jots*
them down in his notebook. ᴍᴜʟʟɪɢᴀɴ
takes a ring off ᴍᴀʀᴛɪɴ's *finger.*) Diamond
ring. Look at that rock! (*He hands it to*
the ᴛʜɪʀᴅ ᴘᴏʟɪᴄᴇᴍᴀɴ *who pockets it, and*
makes a note. ᴍᴜʟʟɪɢᴀɴ *extracts* ᴍᴀʀᴛɪɴ's
wad of bills.) And this roll of bills! What
a pile! You count it!

ᴇxᴀᴍɪɴᴇʀ. Through with him, boys?

ᴍᴜʟʟɪɢᴀɴ. (*Rising.*) Yeah.

ᴘʜᴏᴛᴏɢʀᴀᴘʜᴇʀ. One second! (*Takes a last*
photograph.)

ᴇxᴀᴍɪɴᴇʀ. Well, as soon as the wagon
comes, send him down to the morgue. I'll
look him over in the morning. Mulligan,
you report to me there first thing in the
morning, too.

ᴍᴜʟʟɪɢᴀɴ. Yes, sir. (*The* ᴇxᴀᴍɪɴᴇʀ *goes.*
The ᴘʜᴏᴛᴏɢʀᴀᴘʜᴇʀ *folds his camera and*
follows.)

ᴡᴏᴍᴀɴ ɪɴ ᴛʜᴇ ᴄʀᴏᴡᴅ. (*To the* ꜱᴇᴄᴏɴᴅ
ᴘᴏʟɪᴄᴇᴍᴀɴ, *who is holding* ꜱᴘɪᴛ.) Officer!
What did this boy have to do with it?
Why are you holding him?

ꜱᴇᴄᴏɴᴅ ᴘᴏʟɪᴄᴇᴍᴀɴ. Never mind. Stand
back!

ꜱᴘɪᴛ. Lemme go! I didn't do nuttin'!
Whadda yuh want?

ᴍᴜʟʟɪɢᴀɴ. (*Goes to* ꜱᴘɪᴛ.) You're one of
the gang who beat up a boy here today and
stabbed his father, ain't you?

SPIT. No, I yain't. I did'n 'ave nuttn tuh do wid it. It wuz a kid named Tommy McGrath. (*The murmur of the crowd fades as they all listen.*)

MULLIGAN. Tommy McGrath! Where does he live?

SPIT. On Foist Avenoo between Fifty-toid and Fifty-fawt.

MULLIGAN. Sure?

SPIT. Yeah.

MULLIGAN. (*To the* SECOND POLICEMAN.) Take this kid around there, will yuh? Get ahold a Tommy McGrath. He's wanted for stabbin some guy. I got to wait for the morgue wagon.

SECOND POLICEMAN. O.K. (*Drags* SPIT *through the crowd.*) Come on! You show

us where he lives and we'll let you go. (*they go off, the murmur of the crow rises again. The* THIRD G MAN *crosses* GIMPTY, *who is leaning against the hopp white and shaking. The* DOORMAN *com out with an old discarded coat, the g braid ravelled and rusty, the cloth di and oil-stained.* MULLIGAN *takes it fr him.*)

THIRD G MAN. (*To* GIMPTY.) Good wo Mac: Come over to the office and pick your check. (*He makes his way up street.* MULLIGAN *throws the coat o* MARTIN's *body. The murmur of the cro rises high. A boat horn in the river bello hoarsely and dies away.*)

CURTAIN

ACT THREE

SCENE: *The same. That night. A very dark night. From the dock the sounds of a gay party, music, babble, laughter.* GIMPTY, *a bent silhouette, sits on the coping leaning against the terrace wall. There's a lamp shining up the street. The lights from the tenement windows are faint and yellow and glum. The lanterns on the gateposts, one red, one green, are lit and look very decorative. There's a blaze of fire crackling out of an old iron ash-can in the center of the street. The* BOYS *hover over it, roasting potatotes skewered on long sticks. Their impish faces gleam red one minute and are wiped by shadows the next as they lean over the flames.*

ANGEL. (*Gesturing wildly.*) All uv a sudden da shots come . . . bing . . . bing . . . bam . . . biff . . .

T.B. (*Superior.*) I hoid da shots foist. I wuz jus walkin' up . . .

ANGEL. (*Angrily.*) Yuh di'not.

T.B. I did so.

ANGEL. Yuh tought it wuz a rivitin' machine, yuh said.

T.B. I di'not.

ANGEL. (*Tops him.*) Yuh did so.

T.B. (*Tops him.*) I di'not.

ANGEL. (*Tops him.*) Yuh did so.

T.B. (*Tops him.*) Ah, yuh muddr chooch!

ANGEL. (*Tops him.*) Yeah, yuh faddr doop!

T.B. (*Crescendo.*) Fongoola! (DIPPY r down the street waving two potatoes.)

DIPPY. Hey, guys, I swiped two n mickeys. Look!

ANGEL. Boy, 'at's good!

SPIT. O.K. Put 'em in.

DIPPY. Wheah's Tommy?

SPIT. Put 'em in!

DIPPY. Dis big one's mine, remembuh

SPIT. Put 'em in, I said!

DIPPY. Don' fugit, dis big one's mine

SPIT. Shat ap!

DIPPY. Yeah . . . yew . . . yew shat a

SPIT. Wha-a-at?

DIPPY (*Cowed, moves away from sp* Wheah's Tommy?

ANGEL. I dunno. He didn' show up ye

. (*Reflectively, referring to* MARTIN.)
papuhs said dey found twenty gran' in
pockets.

GEL. Twenty G's. Boy 'at's a lot a
ugh!

T. Boy, he must a bin a putty smaht
y.

. Baby-face? Sure! He wuz a tops.
blic enemy numbuh one. Boy, he had
ts. He wasn' a scared a nobody. Boy, he
uld knock 'em all off like dat . . . like
yt'ing! Boy, like nuttn! (DIPPY *takes a*
k from the can and holds it against his
ulder, pointed at ANGEL, *maneuvering it*
if it were a machine gun.)

PY. (*Makes a rapid, staccato bleating*
und.) Ah-ah-ah-ah-ah! Look, I godda
chine gun! Ah-ah-ah-ah!

GEL. (*Pointing his kazoo at* DIPPY.)
ng Bang!

PY. (*Sore.*) Nah, yuh can't do dat.
h'r dead. I shot yuh foist.

GEL. (*Ignores that salient point, raises*
kazoo again, takes dead aim at DIPPY.)
ng!

PY. (*Lets loose with his improvised*
chine gun.*) Ah-ah-ah-ah! Deah. Now I
tcha! Now yuh dead!

GEL. Bang!

PY. (*Disgusted.*) Aw-w-w! (*He throws*
stick into the fire and turns away.*)

. Gese . . . what I could do wid twenty
!

GEL. What?

T. Snot!

. Yeah, I bet I could buy a boat like
, huh? (*He points off toward the dock.*)

GEL. Look! Dey got lights an' flags an'
sic!

T. Dey got some hot party on, hey
ys?

PY. Look! Look! Dey're dancin'!
avorts about with an imaginary partner,
king ribald gestures and singing.*) Yuh're
top, yuh're da coliseum. Hey! I'm

dancin'! Look, felluhs! Look on me! I'm
dancin'! Look on me! (*He whirls around*
and looks at them for approval.)

T.B. (*Sour-faced.*) Sit down! Yew stink!
(DIPPY *stops grinning and dancing simultaneously. He sits down, squelched.*)

ANGEL. Twenty grand! . . .

SPIT. Yeah . . . so what't it got 'im?

ANGEL. Yeah. Yuh see duh pitchuh uv 'is
broad inna papuhs? Deedy Cook aw
sump'm . . .

T.B. Boy, some nice nooky, huh?

SPIT. Boy, she's got some contrac's now! I
heah she's gonna do a bubble dance in a
boilesque, I t'ink.

ANGEL. Yeah. My fadduh took one look
at huh pitchuh. So 'ee said 'ee'd let 'em
shoot 'im too, fuh half an hour wid a
fancy floozy like dat. So my mudduh gits
mad. So she sez dey wouldn' haf tuh shoot
cha. Haf an hour wid at cockamamee
yuh'd be dead! (*They all laugh.*) So she
spills some boilin' watuh on 'im. So 'ee
yells like a bastid an' runs outa da house
mad. (MILTY *comes down the sidewalk,*
breathless with excitement.)

MILTY. Hey, felluhs, yuh know what?

ANGEL. What?

SPIT. Snot!

MILTY. Balls tuh yew!

SPIT. Ah, I'll mobilize yuh!

MILTY. Yuh know what, guys? Duh cops
ah wise tuh Tommy.

ANGEL. Gese!

T.B. No kid! No kid!

SPIT. Aw, bushwah!

MILTY. No bushwah! Deah' lookin' fuh
'im. He tole me hisself. (*To* SPIT.) Fot
smelleh! Dey went up tuh his house. Some
guy snitched.

T.B. No kid!

SPIT. Did dey git 'im?

MILTY. Nah. Tommy's too wise fuh dem.
Dey come in tru de daw. He goes out tru

de fire-escape, down a yahd, oveh de fence, trus de celleh, up de stayuhs, out dee udduh street.

SPIT. Wheah's he now?

MILTY. He's hidin' out.

SPIT. Wheah?

MILTY. Wheah duh yuh tink, wheah? Wheah dey don' ketch 'im, dat's wheah.

SPIT. Ah, dey'll ketch 'im.

MILTY. Dey don' ketch Tommy so quick.

SPIT. (Nervously, looking into the fire.) How're de mickeys comin'?

T.B. Gese, I bet a dollah dey sen' 'im tuh rifawm school.

SPIT. Sure. Dat's what dey do.

DIPPY. Yeah, dat's what. Ain' it, T.B.?

T.B. Yeah. Dey sent me tuh rifawm school fuh jus' swipin' a bunch a bananas. An' 'ey wuz all rotten too, most a dem.

MILTY. I pity duh guy who snitched. Tommy's layin' fuh him, awright.

DIPPY. Does 'ee know who?

SPIT. (Trying to change the subject.) Hey, guys, duh mickeys ah awmost done!

ANGEL. (Fishing out his potato and poking it with his kazoo.) Nah, not yet. Look, dis one's hard inside.

DIPPY. (Reaches to feel ANGEL's mickey.) Yeah. Like a rock . . . Ouch! Dat's hot! (Licks his fingers.)

ANGEL. (Dipping the mickey back into the embers.) Gese, poor Tommy! If dey ketch 'im, he don' git no maw mickeys like dis fer a long time.

DIPPY. Dey git mickeys in rifawm school, don' dey?

T.B. Slop dey git, slop . . . unless dey git some dough tuh smeah da jailies wid.

SPIT. Aw, shat ap! All a time yuh shoot yuh mout' off about rifawm school . . . like yew wuz 'ee on'y one who evuh went.

DIPPY. Yeah. Yew wuz on'y deah six mont's.

ANGEL. Tom'll git two yeahs.

DIPPY. T'ree, maybe, I bet.

MILTY. Gese, dat's lousy.

SPIT. Ah, shat ap, will yuh?

T.B. Yeah, nevuh mind. Yuh loin a barr a good tings in rifawm school. (The DOORMAN comes out of the gate, exasperated)

DOORMAN. Now I'm not going to tell yc again!

SPIT. Ah, go frig! ⎫
T.B. Deah're awmost done. ⎬ Simultaneously
ANGEL. Jus' a li'l while. ⎭

DOORMAN. No! Get away from here . . all of you . . . right now!

GIMPTY. (Approaches the DOORMAN ar addresses him in a voice tight and hoars hardly recognizable.) Did you give her n note?

DOORMAN. Yes. She said she'd be out a moment.

GIMPTY. Thanks. (He retires to sit aga in the shadows.)

DOORMAN. If you kids don't beat it, I' going to call a' cop! (Turns to the gate

SPIT. Aw, hold yuh hawses!

DOORMAN. (Wheels about, threateningly Wha-a-at?

SPIT. (Scared.) Nuttn. (A LADY in eve ing gown and a MAN in tuxedo come dou the street, talking quietly. The WOMA laughs. As they reach the gate, the DOC MAN touches his hat.)

DOORMAN. Good evening.

MAN AND WOMAN. Good evening. (T DOORMAN follows them through the ga way.)

SPIT. (When the DOORMAN is well out earshot.) Ah, yuh louse, I'll mobilize yu (The boys all roar.)

ANGEL. Hey, de fire's dyin' down.

T.B. Yeah, we need maw wood.

IT. Let's scout aroun' an' soich out some
aw wood. I'll stay heah an' guard de
ickeys.

B. Me too.

IT. Yew, too, balls!

B. What's a mattuh wid me?

IT. What's a mattuh wit yew? Yew
nk on ice, 'at's what's a mattuh wit' yew!

B. Yeah, well, yew ain' no lily a da
lley.

IT. Go on now, or yuh git dis mickey
. red hot . . . up yuh bunny!

B. Yeah? (*He begins to cough.*)

IT. Yeah! Wanna make sumpm otov it?

B. If it wasn't fuh my T.B. . . .

IT. Ah, dat's a gag. Anytime yuh put it
aight up tuh. 'im, he goes . . . (*Imitates
e cough.*) My T.B. . . . . Balls!

B. Oh, yeah? . . . Look, smart guy!
He has been holding his hand to his lips.
e coughs again, spits, opens his hand,
lds it out and displays a bloody clot in
e palm. Proudly.) Blood! (*The boys
sp.*)

GEL. Wow!

B. Smart guy!

IT. Ah, I could do dat. Yuh suck yuh
ut'!

PPY. (*Sucks his mouth audibly, spits*
o his hand.) I can't . . . I can't. How do
h do it? (*DRINA comes down the street,*
s the boys and hurries to them.)

LTY. Hello, Drina.

NA. Did you see Tommy? (*There is
ired, desperate quality in her tone.*)

LTY. No.

NA. (*To* DIPPY.) Did you?

PY. Nope.

NA. Did anybody see him? He hasn't
en home at all.

LTY. No. Nobody saw 'im, Drina.

DRINA. (*Tired, very tired.*) Thanks.
Thanks, Milty. (*She notices* GIMPTY *and
approaches him.*)

ANGEL. (*In a whisper.*) Whyn't yuh tell
huh?

MILTY. (*Also whispering.*) No. Tommy
said no.

SPIT. (*Aloud.*) Ah, balonee!

MILTY. (*Whispers.*) Sh! Shat ap!

SPIT. (*Deliberately loud.*) Who fuh! I'll
give yuh yuh lumps in a minute.

DRINA. (*To* GIMPTY.) Pete, did you see
Tommy?

GIMPTY. What?

DRINA. My brother? Have you seen him
at all?

GIMPTY. Oh! No.

DRINA. Gee, he hasn't showed up yet. The
cops are looking for him. I'm scared to
death.

GIMPTY. I'm sorry.

SPIT. Hey, Drina! Milty knows, but he
won't tell!

DRINA. (*Turns quickly.*) Does he?

MILTY. No.

SPIT. He does.

MILTY. (*Quietly to* SPIT.) Ah, yuh louse!
(*Aloud to* DRINA.) I do not!

SPIT. (*To* MILTY.) I'll mobilize yuh! (*To*
DRINA.) He does so. (DRINA *takes* MILTY *by
both shoulders and shakes him.*)

DRINA. Milty, please tell me if you know
. . . please! I'm half crazy.

MILTY. Tommy said not tuh tell.

DRINA. (*Pleading.*) But I wouldn't hurt
him. You know that. It's for his good. I've
got to talk to him. I've got to find out
what we're gonna do. (*Pause.*) Milty,
you've gotta tell me . . . please!

MILTY. (*Reluctantly.*) Aw right! Come
on. . . .

DRINA. (*As they go up the street.*) How is
he? Is he all right? Is he hurt or anything?

MILTY. Nah!

DRINA. Why didn't he come home?

MILTY. Don' worry, Drina. Dey won' catch 'im. (*They're out of sight and the voices fade off.*)

SPIT. Hey, Angel. You stay heah wid me. Youse guys git some wood. Go on!

DIPPY. O.K. Watch my mickey.

T.B. Mine too. (DIPPY *and* T.B. *exit up the sidewalk.*)

DIPPY. Me, I'm goin' ovuh on Toid Avenoo.

T.B. I'm goin' ovuh tuh Schultzie's.

DIPPY. Naw, whyn't cha go ovuh on Second Avenoo? (*Their voices fade away.*)

SPIT. Hey, Angel, yew stay heah an' guard dose mickeys.

ANGEL. Wheah yuh goin?

SPIT. I'm gonna trail Milty an' fin' out wheah Tommy is.

ANGEL. What faw?

SPIT. None a yuh beeswax! (*He lopes up the street.* ANGEL *watches him for a while, puzzled, then fishes his kazoo from a pocket, relaxes by the fireside, and hums into the instrument. A shadow detaches itself from the hopper and creeps stealthily toward* ANGEL. *It whispers "Psst! Hey! Angel!"* ANGEL *wheels around, startled.*)

ANGEL. Tommy! Gese!

TOMMY. (*His face glowing red as he leans over the fire toward* ANGEL.) Sh! Shat ap! (*In a hoarse whisper.*) Wheah ah da guys? (*They both talk in whispers.*)

ANGEL. Dey went tuh look fuh wood.

TOMMY. What?

ANGEL. Fuh wood. Maw wood. Milty jus' took yuh sistuh . . .

TOMMY. Is Spit wit de guys?

ANGEL. Yeah.

TOMMY. O.K.

ANGEL. Milty jus' took yuh sistuh tuh y[e] hideout.

TOMMY. He did? De louse!

ANGEL. Whatcha gonna do, Tommy?

TOMMY. Run away . . . so de bulls do[n'] git me.

ANGEL. (*Impressed.*) Gese!

TOMMY. (*Quietly.*) But foist I'm gonn[a] ketch de guy who snitched. Do yuh kno[w] who it wuz?

ANGEL. Me? No.

TOMMY. (*Flaring.*) Don' lie tuh me . . [.] I'll kill yuh!

ANGEL Yew know me, Tommy.

TOMMY. O.K. I tink I'm wise tuh wh[o] done it.

ANGEL. Who?

TOMMY. Spit.

ANGEL. Yuh tink so?

TOMMY. Yeah.

ANGEL. Gese!

TOMMY. Now I'm gonna hide, see? Rig[ht] back a deah. (*Points up behind the ho[p]per.*) If yuh let on I'm heah . . . (*Omin[i]ously.*) I'll put yuh teet' down yuh tro[at.]

ANGEL. Aw, Tommy, yuh know me . [. .] yuh know me!

TOMMY. O.K. Den do like I tell yu[h.] When Spit comes back, yew tell 'im li[ke] dis . . . Duh guy I stabbed wuz down he[ah] lookin' fuh Spit tuh givvim five bucks f[uh] snitchin' on who done it. Yuh got [it] straight?

ANGEL. Duh guy what he got stabbed . [. .] wuz down heah lookin' fuh Spit . . . [tuh] givvim five bucks fuh snitchin' on w[ho] done it.

TOMMY. Right.

ANGEL. O.K.

TOMMY. An' rememba . . . yew let on [I'm] heah, I'll . . .

GEL. Aw, Tommy, yew know me.

MMY. Aw right. Jus' do like I tole yuh.

GEL. Whadda yuh gonna do tuh Spit if done it? (TOMMY *takes a knife from* *pocket, and nips open the blade. The* *elight runs along the blade. It looks* *ght and sharp and hard.* TOMMY *grimly* *ws it diagonally across his cheek.* ANGEL *unts.*) Mark a de squealuh?

MMY. (*Snaps the blade home and pock-* *the knife.*) Right.

GEL. Gese!

MMY. Now, go on playin' yuh kazoo *e nuttn happened . . . like I wuzn't* ah. (*Footsteps and voices from the gate.* MMY *ducks and melts into the shadows* *the hopper.* ANGEL *plays his kazoo a bit* *entatiously. The* DOORMAN *opens the* *e.* KAY *appears in a shimmering evening* *wn, lovely and scented.*)

MPTY. (*His voice dull and tired.*) Hello, ay!

Y. Hello, Pete! (GIMPTY *looks past* KAY *the* DOORMAN.) Yes?

ORMAN. Ma'am?

Y. Anything you want?

ORMAN. Oh no . . . no, ma'am. Excuse *. (Exit.)*

MPTY. I sent you a note this afternoon. d you get it?

Y. Yes, I was out. I didn't get back till *e.* I'm so sorry, Pete. Forgive me.

MPTY. Forget it! (*Two couples in even-* *clothes come down the street. They* *all hectic, gay, and a trifle drunk. They* *et* KAY *merrily. She laughs and jests* *th them, tells them she'll join them* *ortly, and in the gate they go. Not,* *wever, without one or two backward* *nces at* GIMPTY. *Their chatter, off, ends* *a burst of laughter that fades away.* KAY *ns to* GIMPTY.)

Y. What a brawl that's turning into!

MPTY. Yeah. It seems like quite a party.

Y. Yes, it is.

GIMPTY. (*After a pause, in a voice so low,* *it can scarcely be heard.*) Kay . . . did you hear what happened here this afternoon?

KAY. What do you? . . .

GIMPTY. The shooting.

KAY. (*Making talk. Evading.*) Oh, yes. And we just missed it. It must have been exciting. I'm . . .

GIMPTY. I didn't miss it.

KAY. No? . . . Oh, tell me . . . was it very? . . .

GIMPTY. (*Begins to give way to the terror* *and remorse pent up in him.*) It was pretty horrible.

KAY. Oh . . . of course.

GIMPTY: Horrible!

KAY. (*Realizing by his tone that some-* *thing dreadful lies in all this, she becomes* *very tender and soothing.*) Pete, give me your hand. Come here. (*She leads him to* *the edge of the wharf.*) Sit down. . . . Now, what happened?

GIMPTY. I'd rather not talk about it for a minute.

KAY. If it upsets you, let's not talk about it at all.

GIMPTY. Yes, I've got to . . . but not for a minute. . . .

KAY. All right. (*Underneath them, the* *River splashes against the bulwark. Off,* *on the yacht, the band is playing a soft,* *sentimental melody. The chatter and the* *laughter from the party float faintly over* *the water. They sit there for a long time* *just staring across the river, at its lights,* *at the factories and signs on the opposite* *shore, at the bridge with its glittering* *loops, at the string of ghostly barges silent-* *ly moving across the river. For a long time.* *Then she speaks, quietly*)

KAY. I love the river at night. . . . It's beautiful . . . and a bit frightening.

GIMPTY. (*Stares down at the black water* *swirling under him. He begins to talk,* *faster and faster, trying to push back into his unconscious the terror that haunts him, to forget that afternoon if only for a few seconds.*) It reminds me of something . . . . What is it? . . . Oh, yeah . . . when I was a kid. In the spring the sudden sun showers used to flood the gutters. The other kids used to race boats down the street. Little boats: straws, matches, lollipop-sticks. I couldn't run after them, so I guarded the sewer and caught the boats to keep them from tumbling in. Near the sewer . . . sometimes, I remember . . . a whirlpool would form. . . . Dirt and oil from the street would break into rainbow colors . . . iridescent. . . . (*For a moment he does escape.*) Beautiful, I think . . . a marvel of color out of dirty water. I can't take my eyes off it. And suddenly a boat in danger. (*The terror in him rises again.*) I try to stop it. . . . Too late! It shoots into the black hole of the sewer. I used to dream about falling into it myself. The river reminds me of that. . . . Death must be like this . . . like the river at night. (*There is no comfort in her big enough for his needs. They sit in brooding silence, which is finally interrupted by the* DOOR-MAN's *voice, off.*)

DOORMAN. Miss Mitchell came out here only a moment ago. Yes, there she is now. (*The* DOORMAN *and a* SAILOR *come out of the gate.*)

SAILOR. Miss Mitchell?

KAY. Yes?

SAILOR. Mr. Hilton says we're ready to cast off. We're waiting for you, ma'am.

KAY. Tell him I'll be there in a minute.

SAILOR. Yes'm. (*Exit* SAILOR.)

DOORMAN. (*Turns to* ANGEL, *who is still hovering over the fire.*) Why don't you kids beat it?

ANGEL. Aw-w!

DOORMAN. All right! I'll fix you! (*He strides off up the street.*)

GIMPTY. (*Desperately.*) Kay, there's still time. You don't have to go.

KAY. (*Finality in her quiet voice.*) I'm afraid I do.

GIMPTY. Listen . . . I knew where Marti was. And I told the police.

KAY. You? How did you recognize him

GIMPTY. I used to know him when I w a kid.

KAY. Oh!

GIMPTY. I know it was a stinkin' thin to do.

KAY. No. It had to be done.

GIMPTY. There was a reward.

KAY. Yes, I know. I read about it. That a break for you, Pete. You can help yo mother now. And you can live decently.

GIMPTY. How about you?

KAY. This isn't the miracle we were loo ing for.

GIMPTY. (*After a long pause.*) No. I gue you're right.

KAY. How long would it last us? Perha a year, then what? I've been through that. I couldn't go through it again.

GIMPTY. I guess it's asking too much.

KAY. (*Softly, trying to make him see t picture realistically, reasonably.*) It's n all selfishness, Pete. I'm thinking of y too. I could do this. I could go and li with you and be happy—(*And she mea it*)—and then when poverty comes . . and we begin to torture each other, wh would happen? I'd leave you and go ba to Jack. He needs me too, you see. I pretty certain of him. But what wou become of you then? That sounds pret bitchy, I suppose.

GIMPTY. No . . . no, it's quite right. didn't see things as clearly as you did. just that I've been . . . such a dope.

KAY. No! It's just that we can't ha everything . . . ever. (*She rises.*)

GIMPTY. Of course.

KAY. Good-bye, darling.

GIMPTY. (*Rises.*) Good-bye, Kay. Have pleasant trip.

(One sob escaping her.) Oh, Pete,
ve me if I've hurt you. Please forgive

PTY. Don't be foolish. You haven't
me. It's funny, but you know, I never
estly expected anything. I didn't. It
really just a . . . whimsy I played on
elf.

Pete.

TY. Yes?

Will you stay here and wave good-
to me when the boat goes?

TY. Naturally. I expected to.

Thanks. *(She kisses him.)* Take
of yourself! *(She goes quickly.* GIMPTY
ws her to the gate, standing there,
*ing through the bars, catching a last
pse of her.* SPIT *trots down the street.)*

He wuzn't deah.

L. No?

Nah. Milty's a lot of bushwah. I
yuh. *(He looks at the fire. Spits into
*NGEL *glances backward at the shadows
r the hopper.)

L. Hey, Spit!

What?

L. Dey wuz a guy heah . . . *(*T.B.
ars, dragging an egg crate.)

Look what I got! Whew! Boy, dat'll
*p like wildfire!

Babee! Dat's good!

L. Yeah! Dat's swell! *(They smash
*he crate by jumping on it. Then they
off the slats and break them across the
, The noise of the crashing and splint-
* exhilarates them. They laugh and
er.* DIPPY *enters, puffing and grunt-
dragging an old discarded automo-
seat by a rope.)*

. *(Proud of his contribution.)* Hey,
*'ink dis'll boin? I t'ink it'll boin, don'
? Boy, like a house afire I bet.

L. Nah, dat'll stink up da place.

DIPPY. *(Disappointed.)* Aw gese, I dragged it a mile. I dragged it fuh five blocks.
It wuz way ovuh by Toid Avenoo. *(The
*BOYS *throw some of the wood into the
fire. It flares up with a great crackling.
Tongues of flame shoot up out of the can.
The band on the boat plays, "Anchors
Aweigh!" There is much laughter and
shouting of "Bon Voyage!" "Have a
pleasant trip," etc. from the party who
have disembarked. The bells and the
whistles of the boat blow, the engines
throb, and the propellers churn the water.
*GIMPTY *stands strained and tense, looking
off, through the gate.)*

T.B. Hey, look! Look! Duh boat! She's
goin' like sixty. Babee! *(They rush over
to the gate.)*

ANGEL. Boy, dat's some boat! Dat's a
crackerjack.

DIPPY. Yeah. *(He imitates the sound of
the bells, the foghorn, the engine.)* Clang,
clang! Oooh! Ch, ch, ch! Poo! Poo! I'm a
boat! Look, felluhs! I'm a boat. Ch! Ch!
Ch! *(He shuffles around, hands fore and
aft.)*

ANGEL. *(Points at the departing boat.)*
Lookit duh dame wavin' at us.

DIPPY. *(Waves vigorously.)* Yoo, hoo!
Yoo hoo!

T.B. She ain't wavin' at us, yuh dope.

SPIT. At Gimpty.

T.B. How'd yuh like tuh be on 'at boat?

DIPPY. Boy! I bet yew cud cross 'ee ocean
in 'at boat. Yuh cud cross 'ee ocean in 'at
boat, couldn't yuh, Gimpty?

GIMPTY. What?

DIPPY. Yuh cud cross 'ee ocean in 'at boat,
couldn't yuh? *(*ANGEL *returns to the fire
and pokes around in it.)*

GIMPTY. Oh, yeah, I guess you could.

T.B. A cawse yuh could, yuh dope, anybody knows 'at.

SPIT. *(Sees* ANGEL *fishing out a mickey.)*
Hey, watcha doin'?

ANGEL. (*Testing his mickey.*) My mickey's done. Dey're done now, felluhs! (*The sounds of the yacht die off in the distance.*)

SPIT. Look out! Look out! Wait a minute! (*They all rush to haul out their mickeys. SPIT pushes them aside, and spears the biggest potato with a stick.*)

DIPPY. Hey, Spit, dat big one's mine. Remembuh . . . I swiped it!

SPIT. Shat ap, yuh dope! (*He punches DIPPY, who begins to snivel.*)

DIPPY. If Tommy wuz heah, yuh wouldn't do dat.

SPIT. Nuts tuh yew! Who's got da salt?

ANGEL. (*Takes a small packet of newspaper from his shoeshine box.*) Heah, I got it! (*The salt is passed around. They eat their mickeys with much smacking of the lips.*)

DIPPY. (*Who has gotten the smallest mickey.*) Ahl git even witcha!

SPIT. Nuts!

DIPPY. Yew wait till yuh ast me tuh do sumpm fuh yew some day. Jus' wait. See watcha git!

SPIT. (*Spits at DIPPY.*) Right innee eye!

DIPPY. (*Wiping his eye.*) Ah, yuh louse!

ANGEL. (*Remembering the conspiracy. Slowly and deliberately, between munches.*) Hey, Spit.

SPIT. What?

ANGEL. Dey wuz a guy heah . . . yuh know da guy what Tommy stabbed? . . . Well, he wuz heah.

SPIT. What fuh?

ANGEL. He wuz lookin' fuh yew.

SPIT. Fuh me?

ANGEL. Yeah.

SPIT. What faw?

ANGEL. He said he wuz gonna give yuh five bucks fuh snitchin' on who done it.

SPIT. Wheah izee? Wheah'd ee go?

DIPPY. Did yew snitch on Tommy?

SPIT. Sure. Sure I did. (*A chorus of approval follows this confession. SPIT and doubles up his fists. To DIPPY.) Wh it to yuh?

DIPPY. Nuttn'! (*SPIT looks at ANGEL.*)

ANGEL. Nuttn'!

T.B. Yew snitched on Tommy! Gese!

SPIT. Aw, shat ap, 'r I'll give yuh y lumps! (*He turns, looking for the b factor.*) Wheah'd he go? Which way want dat five bucks. (*TOMMY runs f behind the hopper, leaps onto SPIT's b bearinᵹ him to the ground.*)

TOMMY. (*Sits astride SPIT, his knees ning SPIT's arms down.*) Yuh'll git it, stool pigeon! In a pig's kapooch yuh w

DIPPY. Tommy!

ANGEL. Gese! ⎱ *Simultaneously*

T.B. Wow! ⎰

TOMMY. Ahl give yuh sumpm yuh w fuhgit so easy. Say yuh prayuhs, yuh lᵒ

SPIT. Lemme go! Lemme go!

TOMMY. Oh, no, yuh don't!

SPIT. Aw, Tommy, I didn' mean tuh. had me! De cops had me! What cou do?

TOMMY. Yuh know watcha gonna git it? (*He takes out his knife. SPIT sq with terror. TOMMY jams his hand SPIT's mouth.*) Shat ap!

DIPPY. What's ee gonna do?

ANGEL. Gash his cheek fum heah heah!

T.B. No kid!

ANGEL. Yeah!

DIPPY. Gee whiz! Wow!

SPIT. (*Crying and pleading.*) To don't, will yuh? I'll give yuh dose wheels I swiped. I'll give yuh me sta I'll give yuh me immies. I'll give yu five bucks. Ony lemme go, will yuh?

MY. Dis time yuh don' git away wid easy, see?

, Hey, felluhs! Hey, Gimpty! He's got nife!

PTY. (*Notices for the first time what's ening.*) Stop that, you crazy kid!

MY. No!

PTY. (*Starts toward* TOMMY.) Let him Tommy!

MY. Come near me, Gimpty, an' I'll it tuh yew. Stay back, or I'll give it 'im right now! (*He places the knife t at* SPIT's *throat.* GIMPTY *stops short.*)

TY. Getting easy, isn't it?

MY. Yeah, it's a cinch.

PTY. Let him up, Tommy!

MY. No!

TY. Tommy, give me that knife!

MY. No!

TY. Sell it to me! I'll buy it from you!

MY. No!

TY. What's a matter? You a yellow-, Tommy?

MY. Who's a yeller-belly?

TY. Only a yellow-belly uses a knife, my. You'll be sorry for this!

MY. Well, he squealed on me! (MILTY DRINA *come down the street.*)

Y. I dunno. He wuz heah befaw . . . st! (*Seeing the fight, he rushes to* MY *and* SPIT.) Wassamattuh, Tommy?

A. (*Rushing to* TOMMY *and* SPIT.) my! Tommy! Where've you been?

Drina! Drina, he's godda knife! He ts a stab me!

MY. (*Slaps* SPIT.) Shat ap!

A. Tommy! . . . Give me that knife! What's the matter with you? Aren't in enough hot water now? Don't you rstand what you're doing? (*Screams.*) me that knife!

GIMPTY. Go on, Tommy! (*Pause.*)

TOMMY. (*Reluctantly hands the knife to* DRINA.) Heah! (*He rises, releasing* SPIT. *As* SPIT *scrambles to his feet,* TOMMY *kicks him in the rump, yelling.*) Beat it, yuh son uv a . . . (SPIT *runs up the sidewalk.*)

DRINA. (*Sharply.*) Sh, Tommy!

SPIT. (*From a safe distance, turns.*) Tuh hell witcha, yuh bastid! (*Then he redoubles his speed, disappearing around the corner.*)

TOMMY. I'll kill yuh! (*He starts after* SPIT, *but* DRINA *grabs his arm, and pulls him back.*)

DRINA. Tommy, behave yourself!

TOMMY. But 'ee squealed on me, Drina!

DRINA. That's no excuse for this. Now it's knives! (*She snaps the blade shut.*) What'll it be next? What's happening to you, Tommy?

TOMMY. I wuz ony gonna scare 'im.

DRINA. (*Grasps him by the shoulders and shakes him to emphasize what she's saying.*) Listen to me! The cops came up to the house ten minutes ago. They were lookin' for you. You stabbed some man! Why! *Why!* (TOMMY *turns away.*) Don't you see what you're doing? They'll send you to jail, Tommy?

TOMMY. (*All the fight gone.*) No, dey won't. Dey gotta ketch me foist.

DRINA. What do you mean?

TOMMY. I'm gonna run away.

DRINA. Run away? Where to?

TOMMY. I dunno.

DRINA. Where?

TOMMY. Dere a plenty a places I kin hitch tuh. Lots a guys do.

DRINA. And what are you gonna eat? Where you gonna sleep?

TOMMY. I'll git along.

DRINA. How?

SIDNEY KINGSLEY

TOMMY. I dunno. Some way. I'll snitch stuff. I dunno. (*Belabored and uncertain.*) Aw, lemme alone!

DRINA. I can see what's gonna happen to you. (*Fiercely.*) You'll become a bum!

TOMMY. Aw right! I'll become a bum, den!

DRINA. (*Hurls the knife onto the sidewalk, and screams.*) That's fine! That's what mamma worked her life away for! That's what I've worked since I was a kid for! So you could become a bum! That's great!

TOMMY. (*Shouting back.*) Aw right! It's great! Well, gese, whadda yuh want me tuh do? Let da cops git me an' sen' me up the rivuh, Drina? I don' wanna be locked up till I'm twenty-one. Izzat what yuh want me tuh do?

DRINA. (*Suddenly very soft and tender, maternally.*) No, darling, no. I won't let that happen. I won't let them touch you, Tommy. Don't worry.

TOMMY. Well, what else kin we do?

DRINA. I'll run away with you, Tommy. We'll go away, together, some place.

TOMMY. No, Drina, yuh couldn't do dat. Yer a goil. (*Pause.*) Yuh know what? Maybe, if I give myself up, an' tell em I didn' mean tuh to do it, an if I swear on a Bible I'll nevuh do it again, maybe dey'll let me go.

DRINA. No, Tommy, I'm not gonna let you give yourself up. No!

TOMMY. Yeah, Drina. (*Enter* DOORMAN *with a* POLICEMAN.)

DOORMAN. (*Pointing to the boys.*) There!

POLICEMAN. (*Roars.*) Get ta hell out a here! Go wan home!

T.B. Chickee da cop! (*The* BOYS *scatter.* DIPPY *and* T.B. *duck into the tenement doorway.* ANGEL *and* MILTY *scramble under the hopper. To the* DOORMAN.) Get some water! Put this out. (MULLIGAN, *the policeman, turns to the cringing figures under the hopper.*) Yuh wanna set fire to these houses? Lemme ketch you doin' this

again and I'll beat the b'jesus out a y (*He slaps the blazing can with his n stick to punctuate the warning. Sp fly up.*)

TOMMY. (*Slowly.*) Yuh know, Drina tink 'at's what I ought tuh do.

DRINA. (*Holding him tight, terrified. a hoarse whisper.*) No. I won't let you that.

TOMMY. Yeah. (*He detaches her arm, goes to* MULLIGAN.) Hey, mister!

MULLIGAN. What do you want? Come beat it!

TOMMY. Wait a minute! I'm Tor McGrath.

MULLIGAN. What of it? (*The other creep back.*)

TOMMY. I'm da kid dat stabbed dat today.

MULLIGAN. What!!! (*He grabs* TOM arm. *The* DOORMAN *comes running ove verify this.*)

TOMMY. (*His voice shrill and trem.* Yeah. He wuz chokin' me an breakin' ahm . . . so I did it.

MULLIGAN. So, you're the kid. I bin in' fuh you.

DOORMAN. (*Who has been staring at* MY, *suddenly elated.*) That's him all r That's him! Wait, I'll call Mr. Gris He'll tell you! (*He rushes off through gateway.*)

MULLIGAN. All right. I'll keep him Don't you worry.

DRINA. (*Goes to* MULLIGAN, *plead* Tommy! No, no, they can't take hin him go, officer! Please!

MULLIGAN. I can't do that, miss.

DRINA. He didn't know what he wa ing. He's only a baby.

MULLIGAN. You tell it to the judge. it to the judge.

DRINA. (*Trying to wrench* TOMMY No! Let him go! Let him go!

LIGAN. (*Pushes her away roughly.*) away. Don't try that! (*To* GIMPTY.) better take her away or she'll get hurt.

TY. Drina, come here.

A. No.

LIGAN. In a minute I'll take her to station-house, too.

AY. Aw, Drina, cut it out, will yuh? ain' gonna help.

TY. He's right, you know.

(*Sidles over to* TOMMY, *whispering.*) Tommy if yuh go tuh rifawmatory, up a guy named . . .

LIGAN. (*Shoving* T.B. *away.*) Git outa (T.B. *flies across the street.*)

A. Yes, of course he's right. I'm so I just don't know what I'm . . .

MAN (*Enters with* MR. GRISWALD.) Mr. Griswald, I'm sure it's the boy. WALD *pushes him aside, and walks ly to* MULLIGAN.)

ALD. So you've caught him.

IGAN. Yes, sir.

A. He gave himself up!

WALD. Let me look at him. (*He looks hingly at* TOMMY's *face and nods.*) this is the boy, all right.

IGAN. Good.

A. He gave himself up.

ALD. (*Turns to her.*) What's that?

. (*Trying desperately to be calm.*) is sister!

ALD. Oh. Well . . . a fine brother e got.

IGAN. (*To* ANGEL *and* MILTY, *who crept to the foreground.*) Come on, ut a here! Beat it! (*They scramble again under the hopper.*)

. Listen, mister! Give him another e. . . . (*She clutches his arm. He s and draws his breath in pain.*) , will you?

GRISWALD. Careful of that arm!

DRINA. Oh! I'm sorry. . . . Give him another chance! Let him go!

GRISWALD. Another chance to what? To kill somebody?

TOMMY. I won' evuh do it again. Yew wuz chokin' me an' I wuz seein' black aready, an' I . . .

DRINA. Have a heart, mister! He's only a kid. He didn't know what he was doing.

GRISWALD. No?

DRINA. No.

GRISWALD. Then you should have taught him better.

DRINA. (*Her impulse is to fight back, but she restrains herself.*) Listen! He's a good boy. And he's got brains. Ask his teacher . . . Miss Judell, P.S. 59. He used to get A,A,A . . . all the time. He's smart.

GRISWALD. Then I can't see any excuse at all for him.

DRINA. (*Flaring.*) All right! He made a mistake! He's sorry! What's so terrible about that?

GIMPTY. Sh! Drina!

GRISWALD. I have a gash half an inch deep in my wrist. The doctor is afraid of infection. What do you say to that?

DRINA. (*With such effort at self-control that she trembles.*) I'm sorry! I'm awfully sorry!

GRISWALD. Sorry! That won't help, will it?

DRINA. Will it help to send him to reform school?

GRISWALD. I don't know. It'll at least keep him from doing it to someone else.

DRINA. But you heard him. He swore he wouldn't ever do it again.

GRISWALD. I'm afraid I can't believe that. He'll be better off where they'll send him. They'll take him out of the gutters and teach him a trade.

DRINA. (*Explodes again.*) What do you know about it?

GRISWALD. I'm sorry. I've no more time. I can't stand here arguing with you. (*To* MULLIGAN.) All right, officer! I'll be down to make the complaint. (*Starts to exit.*)

GIMPTY. (*Stepping in front of* GRISWALD *and blocking his path.*) Wait a minute, mister!

GRISWALD. Yes?

GIMPTY. May I talk to you a moment?

GRISWALD. There's no use, really.

GIMPTY. Just a moment, please?

GRISWALD. Well, what is it?

GIMPTY. You know what happened here today? A man was shot . . . killed.

GRISWALD. You mean that gangster?

GIMPTY. Yes.

GRISWALD. What about it?

GIMPTY. I killed him.

GRISWALD. You what?

MULLIGAN. He's crazy. (*To* GIMPTY.) What are you trying to do?

GIMPTY. It was I who told them where to find him.

GRISWALD. Well, that may be so. Then you were doing your duty. It's simple enough. And I'm doing mine.

DRINA. (*Hysterically.*) No! It ain't the same! Martin was a butcher, he was like a mad dog. He deserved to die. But Tommy's a baby . . .

GIMPTY. Please! That's not the point!

DRINA. It is!

MULLIGAN. (*To* ANGEL *and* MILTY, *who are back again.*) How many times have I gotta tell you! . . . (*They retreat.*)

GIMPTY. Yes, maybe it is. Anyway, I turned him over for my own selfish reasons. And yet the thing I did, Griswald, was nothing compared to what you're doing. . . . Yeah . . . Martin was a killer, he was bad, he deserved to die, true! But I knew him when we were kids. He had a lot of fine stuff. He was strong. He had

courage. He was a born leader. He [e] had a sense of fair play. But living in [the] streets kept making him bad. . . . Then [he] was sent to reform school. Well, they formed him all right! They taught him [the] ropes. He came out tough and hard [and] mean, with all the tricks of the trade.

GRISWALD. But I don't see what yo[u're] driving at.

GIMPTY. I'm telling you! That's [where] you're sending this kid to.

GRISWALD. I'm afraid there's no alte[rna-] tive.

DRINA. Are you so perfect? Didn't [you] ever do anything you were sorry for la[ter]? (*Screams.*) God! Didn't anybody ever [for-] give you for anything?

GRISWALD. (*Looks at her in silence f*[*or a*] *moment.. Then, gently, and sympathe*[*tical-*] *ly.*) Of course. I'm sorry. I'm very s[orry.] Believe me, I'm not being vindictive. [I'm] not punishing him for hurting me. A[s far] as this goes—(*Touches his band*[*aged*] *wrist.*)—I would forgive him gladly. [But] you must remember that I'm a father [and] that today he, unprovoked, beat my [boy] with a stick and stole his watch. T[here] are other boys like mine. They've g[ot to] be protected, too. I feel awfully sorr[y for] you, but your brother belongs in a [re-] formatory. (*To* MULLIGAN.) All r[ight,] officer! (*He shakes his head and disap*[*pears*] *in the gateway.*)

DRINA. (*With a cry of despair.*) W[ait!]

MULLIGAN. All right! Let's go! (*To* [TOM-] MY.) Come along.

T.B. (*Edges over to* TOMMY.) Hey, [Tom-] my, wait! Look up a guy named Sm[...]

MULLIGAN. Get away from here. [I'll] bounce one off your head!

TOMMY. (*Looking back to* DRINA.) [Don't] worry, Drina. I ain' scared.

DRINA. (*Trying to smile for* TOMMY.) [Of] course not, darling. I'm coming with [you.] (*Starts up.*)

LIGAN. Yeah, I think you better. Come (*He calls over his shoulder to the* DOOR-.) Put out that fire!

RMAN. Oh, yes . . . yes, officer! (*Hur-off, through the gate.* MULLIGAN *and* MY *go up the street.* DRINA *starts to* w. T.B. *catches her arm.*)

Drina! Drina! Wait!

A. No, I can't, I gotta . . .

It's important. It's about Tommy!

A. (*Turns.*) What?

(*Very knowing and very helpful. been through this before.*) Look, aa, dere's a guy at rifawm school named key . . . like dat, Smokey, dey call Smokey. Yew tell Tommy tuh be nice him and give im t'ings like cigarettes lat. Cause dis guy Smokey, he knows t of swell rackets fuh Tommy when its out . . . cause Tommy's a wise kid . .

A. (*Scared, helpless, begins to sob.*) Mom, why did you leave us? I don't w what to do, Mom. I don't know re to turn. I wish I was dead and ed with you.

(*Puzzled by this unexpected reac-to his good advice.*) What's a mattuh? t'd I say? I didn' say nuttin'. What'd y?

TY. Sh! Shut up! (*He goes to* DRINA, is sobbing her heart out, and puts otective arm around her.*) You poor You poor kid. Stop crying. Stop ag now.

A. I'm all right. I'll be all right in a te.

TY. Now you stop crying and listen e. Tomorrow morning you meet me t here at half past nine. We're going ntown. We're going to get the best er in this city, and we'll get Tommy

A. But that'll cost so much!

TY. Don't worry about that. We'll im out.

DRINA. Do you really think so?

GIMPTY. I know so.

DRINA. Oh, God bless you . . . you're so . . . (*She breaks into sobs again.*)

GIMPTY. Now, now. You go along now and stick by Tommy.

DRINA. (*Controlling herself.*) You've been so awfully good to us, I . . . I hate to ask for anything else, but . . .

GIMPTY. Sure, what is it?

DRINA. I wish you'd come along with us now. I know if you're there . . . they wouldn't dare touch . . . (*Her voice catches.*) Tommy!

GIMPTY. Me? I'm nobody. I can't . . .

DRINA. I wish you would. Please?

GIMPTY. (*Softly.*) All right. (*They go up the street, his arm still around her, his cane clicking on the sidewalk even after they've disappeared from sight. Awed by the scene, the kids gather about the fire again.*)

ANGEL. Gese, wadda yuh tink'll happen tuh Tommy?

MILTY. Dey'll git 'im off. Dey'll git 'im off. Yuh'll see.

T.B. Even if dey don't, yuh loin a barrel a good tings at rifawm school. Smokey once loined me how tuh open a lock wid a hair pin. Boy! It's easy! It's a cinch! I loined one-two-three, but now I fuhgit . . . (*The* DOORMAN *appears uncoiling a garden hose. He pushes* ANGEL *aside, points the nozzle into the can, and releases the stream. The fire hisses, spits, and dies. A thick pillar of smoke ascends skyward out of the can.*)

ANGEL. (*Looks upward, entranced.*) Holy smokes!

DIPPY. Whee!

ANGEL. Look a dat!

T.B. Boy! Right up tuh duh sky!

ANGEL. Right up tuh duh stahs!

DIPPY. How high ah dey? How high ah duh stahs?

DOORMAN. (*Turning back at the gate.*) And you rats better not start any more trouble, if you know what's good for you! (*He goes in. The boys wait till he is out of ear-shot, then they hurl a chorus of abuse.*)

MILTY. Gay cock of'm yam! ⎫
ANGEL. Fongoola! ⎬ *Simultaneously*
DIPPY. Nuts ta yew! ⎪
T.B. In yuhr hat! ⎭

(ANGEL *plays a mocking tune on his kazoo.* T.B. *sings the lyrics.* To da da da da bushwah. Te da da bushwah.)

ANGEL. Ahl goul him!

DIPPY. (*Laughs.*) Yeah. (*After this outburst, there is a long pause. They watch the smoke curling upward.*)

MILTY. (*Softly.*) Gee! Looka dat smoke!

T.B. Dat reminds me—all a time at fawm school Smokey usta sing a song a[l] Angel—"If I had de wings of a An[g] (*They laugh.*)

MILTY. Angel ain't got no wings.

DIPPY. Real ones got wings. I saw it pitcha once. (ANGEL *starts playing "* had the wings of an angel" on his kaz[*]

T.B. Dat's right. Dat's it! (*In a qua[*] voice he accompanies* ANGEL.) If I ha[d] wings of a angel. Ovuh dese prison [w] I wud fly . . . (*The others join in, s[*] ing the song.*) Straight tuh dee yahn[*] my muddah. Ta da da, da da . . . [*] *passing tramp steamer hoots mournf*[*] *The smoke continues to roll out of* [*] *can, as their cacophony draws out* [*] *funereal end.*) Da . . . da . . . da [*] dum.

CURTAIN

Bury The Dead

BY IRWIN SHAW

"...*what is this world that*
you cling to it?"

———

To My Mother

———

CAST OF CHARACTERS

PRIVATE DRISCOLL
PRIVATE MORGAN
PRIVATE LEVY
PRIVATE WEBSTER
PRIVATE SCHELLING
PRIVATE DEAN
JOAN BURKE
BESS SCHELLING
MARTHA WEBSTER

JULIA BLAKE
KATHERINE DRISCOLL
ELIZABETH DEAN
Generals One, Two and Three.
A Captain, a Sergeant, and four infantrymen,
    employed as a burial detail.
A Priest, a Rabbi, a Doctor.
A Reporter and an Editor.
Two Whores.

COPYRIGHT, 1936, BY IRWIN SHAW

TIME

The second year of the war that is to begin tomorrow night.

SCENE

The stage is in two planes—in the foreground, the bare stage, in the rear, not too far back, going the entire length of the stage, a platform about seven feet above the level of the stage proper. No properties are used to adorn the stage save for some sandbags, whole and split, lying along the edge of the raised platform and some loose dirt also on the platform. The entire platform is painted dull black. It is lighted by a strong spotlight thrown along it at hip-height from the right wing. It is the only light on the stage. The platform is to represent a torn-over battlefield, now quiet, some miles behind the present lines, where a burial detail, standing in a shallow trench dug in the platform, so that the audience sees them only from the hip up, are digging a common grave to accommodate six bodies, piled on the right of the platform, wrapped in canvas. A sergeant stands on the right, on the edge of the grave, smoking. . . . The soldier nearest him, in the shallow trench, stops his digging . . . .

FIRST SOLDIER. Say, Sergeant, they stink . . . . (*Waving his shovel at the corpses*) Let's bury them in a hurry. . . .

SERGEANT. What the hell do you think you'd smell like, after you'd been lyin' out for two days—a goddamn lily of the valley? They'll be buried soon enough. Keep digging.

SECOND SOLDIER. (*Scratching himself.*) Dig and scratch! Dig and scratch! What a war! When you're not diggin' trenches you're diggin' graves. . . .

THIRD SOLDIER. Who's got a cigarette? I'll take opium if nobody's got a cigarette.

SECOND SOLDIER. When you're not diggin' graves you're scratchin' at fleas. By God, there're more fleas in this army than . . .

FIRST SOLDIER. That's what the war's made for—the fleas. Somebody's got to feed 'em. . . .

FOURTH SOLDIER. I used to take a sho[wer] every day. Can you imagine?

SERGEANT. All right, Mr. Lifebuoy, [we'll] put your picture in the *Saturday Eve[ning] Post*—in color!

SECOND SOLDIER. When you're not scra[tchin'] in' at fleas, you're bein' killed. Tha[t's a] helluva life for a grown man.

THIRD SOLDIER. Who's got a cigarette? [I'll] trade my rifle—if I can find it—fo[r a] cigarette. For Christ's sake, don't [they] make cigarettes no more? (*Leaning, m[elan]choly, on his shovel*) This country's [gone] to the dogs for real now. . . .

SERGEANT. Lift dirt, soldier. Come [on.] This ain't no vacation.

THIRD SOLDIER. (*Disregarding him.*) [I] heard of guys packin' weeds and [corn] flop into cigarettes in this man's a[rmy.] They say it has a tang. (*Reflectively*) [Got] to try it some day. . . .

SERGEANT. Hurry up! (*Blowing on [his] hands*) I'm freezin' here. I don't wa[nt to] hang around all night. I can't feel my [toes] no more. . . .

FOURTH SOLDIER. I aint felt my fee[t for] two weeks. I ain't had my shoes off in [two] weeks. (*Leaning on his shovel*) I wo[nder] if the toes're still connected. I wear [a size 9] shoe. Aristocratic foot, the salesman al[ways] said. Funny—going around not knowin' whether you still got toe[s or] not. . . . It's not hygienic really. . .

SERGEANT. All right, friend, we'll [make] sure the next war you're in is run hyg[ienic.]

FOURTH SOLDIER. In the Spanish-Ame[rican] War more men died of fever than . . .

FIRST SOLDIER. (*Beating viciously at [some-] thing in the grave*) Get him! Get [him!] Kill the bastard!

FOURTH SOLDIER. (*Savagely*) He's co[min'] this way! We've got him cornered!

SOLDIER. Bash his brains out!

ND SOLDIER. You got him with that
(*All the soldiers in the grave beat
, yelling demoniacally, triumphantly.*)

GEANT. (*Remonstrating*) Come on
, you're wasting time. . . .

SOLDIER. (*Swinging savagely*) There.
fixed him. The god-damn . . .

RTH SOLDIER. (*Sadly*) You'd think the
d at least wait until the stiffs were
rground.

SOLDIER. Did you ever see such a fat
n your whole life? I bet he ate like
rse—this one.

EANT. All right, all right. You're not
in' the war against rats. Get back to
business.

SOLDIER. I get a lot more pleasure
' rats than killin' them. (*Gesture to-
the front lines.*)

EANT. Rats got to live, too. They don't
v no better.

SOLDIER. (*Suddenly scooping up rat
his shovel and presenting it to* SER-
T) Here you are, Sergeant. A little
n of our regard from Company A.

EANT. Stop the smart stuff! I don't
it.

SOLDIER. (*Still with rat upheld on
el*) Ah, Sergeant, I'm disappointed.
rat's a fine pedigreed animal—fed
on the choicest young men the United
s turned out in the last twenty years.

EANT. Come on, wise guy. (FIRST
ER *goes right on.*)

SOLDIER. Notice the heavy, powerful
lders to this rat, notice the well-cov-
flanks, notice the round belly—bank
s, mechanics, society-leaders, farmers
od feeding— (*Suddenly he throws the
way*) Ah—I'm gettin' awful tired of
I didn't enlist in this bloody war to
o bloody grave-digger!

ANT. Tell that to the President. Keep
n'.

SECOND SOLDIER. Say, this is deep enough.
What're we supposed to do—dig right
down to hell and deliver them over first-
hand?

SERGEANT. A man's entitled to six feet a'
dirt over his face. We gotta show respect
to the dead. Keep diggin'. . . .

FOURTH SOLDIER. I hope they don't put
me too far under when my turn comes. I
want to be able to come up and get a
smell of air every once in so often.

SERGEANT. Stow the gab, you guys! Keep
diggin'. . . .

FIRST SOLDIER. They stink! Bury them!

SERGEANT. All right, Fanny. From now on
we'll perfume 'em before we ask you to
put them away. Will that please you?

FIRST SOLDIER. I don't like the way they
smell, that's all. I don't have to like the
way they smell, do I? That ain't in the
regulations, is it? A man's got a right
to use his nose, ain't he, even though he's
in this god-damn army. . . .

SERGEANT. Talk respectful when you talk
about the army, you!

FIRST SOLDIER. Oh, the lovely army . . .
(*He heaves up clod of dirt.*)

SECOND SOLDIER. Oh, the dear army . . .
(*He heaves up clod of dirt.*)

THIRD SOLDIER. Oh, the sweet army . . .
(*He heaves up clod of dirt.*)

FIRST SOLDIER. Oh, the scummy, stinking,
god-damn army . . . (*He heaves up three
shovelfuls in rapid succession.*)

SERGEANT. That's a fine way to talk in
the presence of death. . . .

FIRST SOLDIER. We'd talk in blank verse
for you, Sergeant, only we ran out of it
our third day in the front line. What do
you expect, Sergeant, we're just common
soldiers . . .

SECOND SOLDIER. Come on. Let's put 'em
away. I'm getting blisters big enough to
use for balloons here. What's the difference? They'll just be turned up anyway,
the next time the artillery wakes up. . . .

SERGEANT. All right! All right! If you're in such a hurry—put 'em in. . . . (*The soldiers nearest the right-hand edge of the grave jump out and start carrying the bodies over, one at each corner of the canvas. The other soldiers, still in the trench, take the bodies from them and carry them over to the other side of the trench, where they lay them down, out of sight of the audience.*)

SERGEANT. Put 'em in neat, there. . . .

FIRST SOLDIER. File 'em away alphabetically, boys. We may want to refer to them, later. The General might want to look up some past cases.

FOURTH SOLDIER. This one's just a kid. I knew him a little. Nice kid. He used to write dirty poems. Funny as hell. He don't even look dead. . . .

FIRST SOLDIER. Bury him! He stinks!

SERGEANT. If you think *you* smell so sweet, yourself, Baby, you oughta wake up. You ain't exactly a perfume-ad, soldier. (*Laughter.*)

THIRD SOLDIER. Chalk one up for the Sergeant.

FIRST SOLDIER. You ain't a combination of roses and wistaria, either, Sergeant, but I can stand you, especially when you don't talk. At least you're alive. There's something about the smell of dead ones that gives me the willies. . . . Come on, let's pile the dirt in on them. . . . (*The* SOLDIERS *scramble out of the grave.*)

SERGEANT. Hold it.

THIRD SOLDIER. What's the matter now? Do we have to do a dance around them?

SERGEANT. We have to wait for chaplains . . . . They gotta say some prayers over them.

FIRST SOLDIER. Oh, for Christ's sake ain't I ever going to get any sleep tonight?

SERGEANT. Don't begrudge a man his prayers, soldier. You'd want 'em, wouldn't you?

FIRST SOLDIER. God, no. I want to sleep peaceful when I go. . . . Well, where are

they? Why dont they come? Do we to stand here all night waiting for guys to come and talk to God about fellers?

THIRD SOLDIER. Who's got a cigar (*Plaintively.*)

SERGEANT. Attention! Here they are Roman-Catholic priest and a rabbi in.)

PRIEST. Is everything ready?

SERGEANT. Yes, Father . . .

FIRST SOLDIER. Make it snappy! I'm ful tired.

PRIEST. God must be served slowly son. . . .

FIRST SOLDIER. He's gettin' plenty of vice these days—and not so slow, e He can stand a little rushin'. . . .

SERGEANT. Shut up, soldier.

RABBI. Do you want to hold your vices first, Father?

SERGEANT. There ain't no Jewish bo there. (*Gesture to grave*) Reverend, I think we'll need you.

RABBI. I understand one of them is n Levy.

SERGEANT. Yes. But he's no Jew.

RABBI. With that name we won't tak chances. Father, will you be first?

PRIEST. Perhaps we had better wait. is an Episcopal bishop in this sector expressed the desire to conduct a service here. He's doing that in all s he is visiting. I think we had better for him. Episcopal bishops are rathe sitive about order. . . .

RABBI. He's not coming. He's havin supper.

FIRST SOLDIER. What does God do the bishop has his supper?

SERGEANT. If you don't keep quiet bring you up on charges.

FIRST SOLDIER. I want to get it over Bury them! They stink!

sт. Young man, that is not the way
ılk about one of God's creatures. . . .

' soldier. If that's (*Gesture to grave*)
of God's creatures, all I can say is,
slippin' . . .

sт. Ah, my son, you seem so bitter. . . .

' soldier. For God's sake, stop talk-
ınd get this over with. I want to throw
over them! I can't stand the smell of
! Sergeant, get 'em to do it fast. They
got no right to keep us up all night.
got work to do tomorrow. . . . Let
say their prayers together! God'll be
to understand. . . .

sт. Yes. There is really no need to
ng it. We must think of the living
ell as the dead. As he says, Reverend,
will be able to understand. . . . (*He
's at the head of the grave, chants the
prayer for the dead. The* RABBI *goes
nd to the other end and recites the
ew prayer. In the middle of it, a
a is heard, low, but clear. The chants
on. Another groan is heard.*)

soldier. (*While the Hebrew and
go on*) I heard a groan. (*The* RABBI
PRIEST *continue*) I heard a groan!

ANT. Shut up, soldier! (*The Latin
Hebrew go on.*)

soldier. (*Gets down on one knee
ide of grave and listens. Another
*) Stop it! I heard a groan . . .

ANT. What about it? Can you have
without groans? Keep quiet! (*The
rs go on undisturbed. Another groan.
FIRST* soldier *jumps into the grave.*)

soldier. It's from here! Hold it!
aming) Hold it! Stop those god-
ied parrots! (*Throws a clod of dirt
d of trench*) Hold it! Somebody down
groaned. . . . (*A head appears slowly
the trench rim at the left end, a
stands up, slowly facing the rear. All
nen sigh—the service goes on.*)

ANT. Oh, my God . . .

soldier. He's alive. . . .

ANT. Why the hell don't they get
things straight? Pull him out!

FIRST SOLDIER. Stop them! (*As the services go on*) Get them out of here! Live
men don't need them. . . .

SERGEANT. Please, Father, this has nothing
to do with you. . . . There's been some
mistake. . . .

PRIEST. I see. All right, Sergeant. (*He and
RABBI join, hand in hand, and leave. Nobody notices them. All the men are hyp-
notically watching the man in the trench,
arisen from the dead. The* CORPSE *passes
his hand over his eyes. The men sigh—
horrible, dry sighs. . . . Another groan is
heard from the left side of trench.*)

FIRST SOLDIER. (*In trench*) There! (*Pointing*) It came from there! I heard it! (*A
head, then shoulders appear over the rim
of trench at left side. The* SECOND CORPSE
*stands up, passes his hands over eyes in
same gesture which drew sighs from the
men before. There is absolute silence as
the men watch the arisen corpses. Then,
silently, a corpse rises in the middle of the
trench, next to the* FIRST SOLDIER. *The
FIRST SOLDIER screams, scrambles out of
the trench in rear, and stands, bent over,
watching the trench, middle-rear. There
is no sound save the very light rumble of
the guns. One by one the* CORPSES *arise and
stand silently in their places, facing the
rear, their backs to the audience. The
SOLDIERS don't move, scarcely breathe, as,
one by one, the* CORPSES *appear. They stand
there, a frozen tableau. Suddenly, the
SERGEANT talks.*)

SERGEANT. What do you want?

FIRST CORPSE. Don't bury us.

THIRD SOLDIER. Let's get the hell out of
here!

SERGEANT. (*Drawing pistol*) Stay where
you are! I'll shoot the first man that moves.

FIRST CORPSE. Don't bury us. We don't
want to be buried.

SERGEANT. Christ! (*To men*) Carry on!
(*The men stand still*) Christ! (*The SER-
GEANT rushes off, calling*) Captain! Captain! Where the hell is the Captain? (*His
voice fades, terror-stricken. The* SOLDIERS
*watch the corpses, then slowly, all to-
gether, start to back off.*)

SIXTH CORPSE. Don't go away.

SECOND CORPSE. Stay with us.

THIRD CORPSE. We want to hear the sound of men talking.

SIXTH CORPSE. Don't be afraid of us.

FIRST CORPSE. We're not really different from you. We're dead.

SECOND CORPSE. That's all. . . ?

FOURTH. All—all . . .

FIRST SOLDIER. That's all . . . ?

THIRD CORPSE. Are you afraid of six dead men? You, who've lived with the dead, the so-many dead, and eaten your bread by their side when there was no time to bury them and you were hungry?

SECOND CORPSE. Are we different from you? An ounce or so of lead in our hearts, and none in yours. A small difference between us.

THIRD CORPSE. Tomorrow or the next day, the lead will be yours, too. Talk as our equals.

FOURTH SOLDIER. It's the kid—the one who wrote the dirty poems.

FIRST CORPSE. Say something to us. Forget the grave, as we would forget it. . . .

THIRD SOLDIER. Do you—do you want a cigarette? (SERGEANT re-enters with CAPTAIN.)

SERGEANT. I'm not drunk! I'm not crazy, either! They just—got up, all together— and looked at us. . . . Look—look for yourself, Captain! (The CAPTAIN stands off to one side, looking. The men stand at attention.)

SERGEANT. See?

CAPTAIN. I see. (He laughs sadly) I was expecting it to happen—some day. So many men each day. It's too bad it had to happen in my company. Gentlemen! At ease! (The men stand at ease. The CAPTAIN leaves. The guns roar suddenly. Fadeout.)

The spotlight is turned on to the lower stage, right, below the platform on which the action, until now, has taken place.

Discovered in its glare are three GENE[RALS] around a table. The CAPTAIN is stan[ding] before them, talking.

CAPTAIN. I'm only telling the Gen[erals] what I saw.

FIRST GENERAL. You're not making [it] up, Captain?

CAPTAIN. No, General.

SECOND GENERAL. Have you any p[roof,] Captain?

CAPTAIN. The four men in the buria[l de-]tail and the Sergeant, Sir.

THIRD GENERAL. In time of war, Cap[tain,] men see strange things.

CAPTAIN. Yes, General.

SECOND GENERAL. You've been drin[king,] Captain.

CAPTAIN. Yes, General.

SECOND GENERAL. When a man has [been] drinking, he is not responsible for [what] he sees.

CAPTAIN. Yes, General. I am not re[spon-]sible for what I saw. I am glad of th[at. I] would not like to carry that burden, [too,] with all the others. . . .

FIRST GENERAL. Come, come, Captain, [con-]fess now. You were drinking and [you] walked out into the cold air over a [battle] just lately won and what with the l[iquor] and the air and the flush of victory . [. .]

CAPTAIN. I told the General what I [saw.]

SECOND GENERAL. Yes, we heard. W[e for-]give you for it. We don't think an[y the] worse of you for taking a nip. It's [only] natural. We understand. So take an[other] drink with us now and forget [your] ghosts. . . .

CAPTAIN. They weren't ghosts. They [were] men—killed two days, standing in [their] graves and looking at me.

FIRST GENERAL. Captain, you're beco[ming] trying. . . .

CAPTAIN. I'm sorry, Sir. It was a [terrible] sight. I saw them and what are the [Gen-]erals going to do about it?

ND GENERAL. Forget it! A man is tak-
or dead and put in a grave. He wakes
his coma and stands up. It happens
y day—you've got to expect such things
war. Take him out and send him to
ospital!

AIN. Hospitals aren't for dead men.
at are the Generals going to do about
?

D GENERAL. Don't stand there croak-
"What are the Generals going to do
t them?" Have 'em examined by a
r. If they're alive send them to a
ital. If they're dead, bury them! It's
simple.

AIN. But . . .

D GENERAL. No buts, Sir!

AIN. Yes, Sir.

D GENERAL. Take a doctor down with
Sir, and a stenographer. Have the
r dictate official reports. Have them
essed. And let's hear no more of it.

AIN. Yes, Sir. Very good, Sir. (*Wheels*
out.)

ND GENERAL. Oh, and Captain . . .

AIN. (*Stopping*) Yes, Sir.

ND GENERAL. Stay away from the
.

AIN. Yes, Sir. Is that all, Sir?

D GENERAL. That's all.

AIN. Yes, Sir. (*The light fades from*
ENERALS. *It follows the* CAPTAIN *as*
alks across the stage. The CAPTAIN
takes out a bottle. Takes two long
. Blackout.*)

guns rumble, growing louder. They
been almost mute during GENERALS'
. The light is thrown on the burial
again, where the DOCTOR is seen ex-
ng the CORPSES in their graves. The
R is armed with a stethoscope and is
ed by a soldier stenographer, two of
OLDIERS, impressed as witnesses, and
APTAIN. The DOCTOR is talking, as he
from the first man.*

DOCTOR. Number one. Evisceration of the lower intestine. Dead forty-eight hours.

STENOGRAPHER. (*Repeating*) Number one. Evisceration of the lower intestine. Dead forty-eight hours. (*To witnesses*) Sign here. (*They sign.*)

DOCTOR. (*On the next man*) Number two. Bullet penetrated the left ventricle. Dead forty-eight hours.

STENOGRAPHER. Number two. Bullet penetrated the left ventricle. Dead forty-eight hours. (*To witnesses*) Sign here. (*They sign.*)

DOCTOR. (*On the next* CORPSE) Number three. Bullets penetrated both lungs. Severe hemorrhages. Dead forty-eight hours.

STENOGRAPHER. (*Chanting*) Number three. Bullets penetrated both lungs. Severe hemorrhages. Dead forty-eight hours. Sign here. (*The witnesses sign.*)

DOCTOR. (*On next* CORPSE) Number four. Fracture of the skull and avulsion of the cerebellum. Dead forty-eight hours.

STENOGRAPHER. Number four. Fracture of the skull and avulsion of the cerebellum. Dead forty-eight hours. Sign here. (*The witnesses sign.*)

DOCTOR. (*Moving on to next* CORPSE) Number five. Destruction of the genito-urinary system by shell-splinters. Death from hemorrhages. Dead forty-eight hours. Ummn. (*Looks curiously at* CORPSE's *face*) Hum . . . (*Moves on.*)

STENOGRAPHER. Number five. Destruction of the genito-urinary system by shell-splinters. Death from hemorrhages. Dead forty-eight hours. Sign here. (*The witnesses sign.*)

DOCTOR. (*On the next* CORPSE) Number six. Destruction of right side of head from supra-orbital ridges through jaw-bone. Hum. You'd be a pretty sight for your mother, you would. Dead forty-eight hours . . .

STENOGRAPHER. Number six. Destruction of right side of head from supra-orbital ridges through jaw-bone. You'd be a pretty sight for your mother you would. Dead forty-eight hours. Sign here.

DOCTOR. What are you doing there?

STENOGRAPHER. That's what you said, Sir. . . .

DOCTOR. I know. Leave out—"You'd be a pretty sight for your mother you would . . ." The Generals wouldn't be interested in that.

STENOGRAPHER. Yes, Sir. Sign here. (*The witnesses sign.*)

DOCTOR. Six, is that all?

CAPTAIN. Yes, Doctor. They're all dead? (*The* FOURTH CORPSE *offers the* THIRD SOLDIER *a cigarette. The* THIRD SOLDIER *hesitates a second before taking it, then accepts it with a half-grin.*)

THIRD SOLDIER. Thanks, Buddy. I—I'm awful sorry—I—Thanks . . . (*He saves cigarette.*)

DOCTOR. (*Eyes on* FOURTH CORPSE *and* THIRD SOLDIER) All dead.

CAPTAIN. A drink, Doctor?

DOCTOR. Yes, thank you. (*He takes the proffered bottle. Drinks long from it. Holds it, puts stethoscope in pocket with other hand. Stands looking at the* CORPSES, *lined up, facing the rear, nods, then takes another long drink. Silently hands bottle to* CAPTAIN, *who looks around him from one* CORPSE *to another, then takes a long drink. Blackout.*)

Spotlight on the GENERALS, *facing the* CAPTAIN *and the* DOCTOR. *The* FIRST GENERAL *has the* DOCTOR's *reports in his hands.*

FIRST GENERAL. Doctor!

DOCTOR. Yes, Sir.

FIRST GENERAL. In your reports here you say that each of these six men is dead.

DOCTOR. Yes, Sir.

FIRST GENERAL. Then I don't see what all the fuss is about, Captain. They're dead— bury them. . . .

CAPTAIN. I am afraid, Sir, that that can't be done. . . . They are standing in their graves. They refuse to be buried.

THIRD GENERAL. Do we have to go that again? We have the doctor's re[port] They're dead. Aren't they, Doctor?

DOCTOR. Yes, Sir.

THIRD GENERAL. Then they aren't stan[ding] in their graves, refusing to be buried, they?

DOCTOR. Yes, Sir.

SECOND GENERAL. Doctor, would you k[now] a dead man if you saw one?

DOCTOR. The symptoms are easily re[cog]nized.

FIRST GENERAL. You've been drin[king] too. . . .

DOCTOR. Yes, Sir.

FIRST GENERAL. The whole damned a[rmy] is drunk! I want a regulation annou[nced] tomorrow morning in all regiments. [No] more liquor is to be allowed within tw[o] miles of the front line upon pain of d[eath]. Got it?

SECOND GENERAL. Yes, General. But how'll we get the men to fight?

FIRST GENERAL. Damn the fighting! [We] can't have stories like this springing [up.] It's bad for the morale! Did you [hear] me, Doctor, it's bad for the morale [and] you ought to be ashamed of yourself[.]

DOCTOR. Yes, Sir.

THIRD GENERAL. This has gone far en[ough.] If it goes any farther, the men wi[ll get] wind of it. We have witnessed certif[icates] from a registered surgeon that these [men] are dead. Bury them! Waste no more [time] on it. Do you hear me, Captain?

CAPTAIN. Yes, Sir. I'm afraid, Sir, t[hat I] must refuse to bury these men.

THIRD GENERAL. That's insubordin[ation,] Sir. . . .

CAPTAIN. I'm sorry, Sir. It is not w[ithin] the line of my military duties to bury [men] against their will. If the General will [only] think for a moment he will see tha[t it] is impossible. . . .

T GENERAL. The Captain's right. It
ht get back to Congress. God only
ws what *they'd* make of it!

RD GENERAL. What are we going to
hen?

T GENERAL. Captain, what do you sug-
?

AIN. Stop the war.

RUS OF GENERALS. Captain!

T GENERAL. (*With great dignity*) Cap-
, we beg of you to remember the
vity of the situation. It admits of no
ty. Is that the best suggestion you can
:e, Captain?

AIN. Yes. But I have another— If
Generals would come down to the
ve themselves and attempt to influence
e—ah—corpses—to lie down, perhaps
would prove effective. We're seven
s behind the line now and we could
en the roads to protect your arrival....

T GENERAL. (*Coughing*) Umm—uh—
ally, of course, that would be—uh . . .
'll see. In the meantime it must be
t quiet! Remember that! Not a word!
ody must know! God only knows
it would happen if people began to
ect we couldn't even get our dead to
down and be buried! This is the god-
indest war! They never said anything
ut this sort of thing at West Point.
iember, not a word, nobody must know,
:t as the grave, *mum! ssssh!* (*All the*
ERALS *repeat the ssssh after him.*)

light fades—but the hiss of the GEN-
Ls *hushing each other is still heard as
light falls on another part of the
e proper, where two soldiers are on
t in the front lines, behind a barricade
sandbags. The sound of guns is very
ng. There are flashes of gun-fire.*

INS. (*A soldier past forty, fat, with a
-belly and graying hair showing under
helmet*) Did you hear about those guys
won't let themselves be buried, Char-

RLEY. I heard. You never know what's
na happen next in this lousy war.

BEVINS. What do you think about it,
Charley?

CHARLEY. What're they gettin' out of it,
that's what I'd like to know. They're just
makin things harder. I heard all about
'em. They stink! Bury 'em. That's what
I say.

BEVINS. I don't know, Charley. I kinda
can see what they're aimin' at. Christ, I
wouldn't like to be put six foot under
now, I wouldn't. What the hell for?

CHARLEY. What's the difference?

BEVINS. There's a difference, all right. It's
kinda good, bein' alive. It's kinda nice,
bein' on top of the earth and seein' things
and hearin' things and smellin' things....

CHARLEY. Yeah, smellin' stiffs that ain't
had time to be buried. That sure is sweet.

BEVINS. Yeah, but it's better than havin'
the dirt packed onto your face. I guess
those guys felt sorta gypped when they
started throwin' the dirt in on 'em and
just couldn't stand it, dead or no dead.

CHARLEY. They're dead, ain't they? Nobody's puttin' them under while they're
alive.

BEVINS. It amounts to the same thing,
Charley. They should be alive now. What
are they—a parcel of kids? Kids shouldn't
be dead, Charley. That's what they musta
figured when the dirt started fallin' in on
'em. What the hell are they doin' dead?
Did they get anything out of it? Did anybody ask them? Did they want to be
standin' there when the lead poured in?
They're just kids, or guys with wives and
young kids of their own. They wanted to
be home readin' a book or teachin' their
kid c-a-t spells cat or takin' a woman out
into the country in a open car with the
wind blowin'. . . . That's the way it musta
come to them, when the dirt smacked on
their faces, dead or no dead. . . .

CHARLEY. Bury them. That's what I say
. . . . (*There is the chatter of a machine
gun off in the night.* BEVINS *is hit. He
staggers.*)

BEVINS. (*Clutching his throat*) Charley—Charley . . . (*His fingers bring down the top sandbag as he falls. The machine gun chatters again and* CHARLEY *is hit. He staggers.*)

CHARLEY. Oh, my God . . . (*The machine gun chatters again. He falls over* BEVINS. *There is quiet for a moment. Then the eternal artillery again. Blackout.*)
A baby spotlight, white, picks out the FIRST GENERAL, *standing over the prone forms of the two soldiers. He has his fingers to his lips.*

FIRST GENERAL. (*In a hoarse whisper*) Sssh! Keep it quiet! Nobody must know! Not a word! Sssh! (*Blackout.*)

A spotlight picks out another part of the stage—a newspaper office. EDITOR *at his desk,* REPORTER *before him, hat on head.*

REPORTER. That's the story! It's as straight as a rifle-barrel, so help me God.

EDITOR. (*Looking down at manuscript in hand*) This is a freak, all right. I never came across anything like it in all the years I've been putting out a newspaper.

REPORTER. There never was anything like it before. It's somethin' new. Somethin's happening. Somebody's waking up. . . .

EDITOR. It didn't happen.

REPORTER. So help me God, I got it straight. Those guys just stood up in the grave and said, "The hell with it, you can't bury us!" God's honest truth.

EDITOR. (*Picks up telephone*) Get me Macready at the War Department. . . . It's an awfully funny story. . . .

REPORTER. What about it? It's the story of the year— the story of the century—the biggest story of all time—men gettin' up with bullets in their hearts and refusin' to be buried. . . .

EDITOR. Who do they think they are—Jesus Christ?

REPORTER. What's the difference? That's the story! You can't miss it! You goin' to put it in? Lissen—are you goin' to put it in?

EDITOR. Hold it! (*Into telephone*) M ready!

REPORTER. What's he got to do with

EDITOR. I'll find out. What are you so about? . . . Hello? Macready? Hansen fr the New York . . . Yeah. . . . Listen, M ready, I got this story about the six g who refuse to be . . . Yeah. . . .

REPORTER. What does he say?

EDITOR. Okay, Macready. Yeah, if th the way the Government feels about it. Yeah. . . .

REPORTER. Well?

EDITOR. (*Putting down telephone*) No

REPORTER. Holy god-damn, you got People got a right to know.

EDITOR. In time of war, people have right to now nothing. If we put it in, be censored anyway.

REPORTER. Ah, this is a lousy business.

EDITOR. Write another human inte story about the boys at the front. Tha keep you busy. You know . . . that about how the boys in the front-line s "I Can't Give You Anything but Lo before they go over the top. . . .

REPORTER. But I wrote that last week.

EDITOR. It made a great hit. Write it ag

REPORTER. But these guys in the gr Boss. Lloyds are giving three to one t won't go down. That's a story!

EDITOR. Save it. You can write a book memoirs twenty years from now. M that "I Can't Give You Anything but Lc story a thousand words, and make it s py. The casualty lists run into two p today' and we got to balance them something. . . . (*Blackout*)

Rumble of guns. The spotlight illumin the grave on the platform, where CORPSES *are still standing, hip-deep, fa the rear. The burial squad is there, and* CAPTAIN, *and the* GENERALS.

CAPTAIN. There they are. What are Generals going to do about them?

FIRST GENERAL. (*Pettishly*) I see them. Stop saying "What are the Generals going o do about them?"

SECOND GENERAL. Who do they think they are?

THIRD GENERAL. It's against all regulations.

FIRST GENERAL. Quiet, please, quiet. Let's not have any scenes. . . . This must be handled with authority—but tactfully. I'll talk to them! (*He goes over to brink of grave*) Men! Listen to me! This is a strange situation in which we find ourselves. I have no doubt but that it is giving you as much embarrassment as it is us. . . .

SECOND GENERAL. (*Confidentially to* THIRD GENERAL) The wrong note. He's good on rtillery, but when it comes to using his head, he's lost. . . . He's been that way ever since I knew him.

FIRST GENERAL. We're all anxious to get this thing over with just as quickly and quietly as possible. I know that you men re with me on this. There's no reason why we can't get together and settle this jig time. I grant, my friends, that it's unfortunate that you're dead. I'm sure that you'll all listen to reason. Listen, too, to the voice of duty, the voice that sent you here to die bravely for your country. Gentlemen, our country demands of you that you lie own and allow yourselves to be buried. Must our flag fly at half-mast and droop the wind while you so far forget your uty to the lovely land that bore and nursed you? I love America, gentlemen, its lls and valleys. If you loved America as do, you would not . . . (*He breaks down, overcome*) I find it difficult to go on. (*He uses*) I have studied this matter and me to the conclusion that the best thing r all concerned would be for you men lie down peaceably in your graves and ow yourselves to be buried. (*He waits. The* CORPSES *do not move.*)

THIRD GENERAL. It didn't work. He's not m enough. You've got to be firm from e beginning or you're lost.

FIRST GENERAL. Men, perhaps you don't understand. (*To* CORPSES) I advise you to ow yourselves to be buried. (*They stand, motionless*) You're dead, men, don't you realize that? You can't be dead and stand there like that. Here . . . here . . . I'll prove it to you! (*He gets out* DOCTOR's *reports*) Look! A doctor's reports. Witnessed! Witnessed by Privates McGurk and Butler. (*He reads the names*) This ought to show you! (*He waves the reports. He stands on the brink of the grave, middle-rear, glaring at the* CORPSES. *He shouts at them*) You're dead, officially, all of you! I won't mince words! You heard! We're a civilized race, we bury our dead. Lie down! (*The* CORPSES *stand*) Private Driscoll! Private Schelling! Private Morgan! Private Levy! Private Webster! Private Dean! Lie down! As Commander-in-Chief of the Army as appointed by the President of the United States in accordance with the Constitution of the United States, and as your superior officer, I command you to lie down and allow yourselves to be buried. (*They stand, silent and motionless*) Tell me— What is it going to get you, staying above the earth? (*Not a sound from the* CORPSES) I asked you a question, men. Answer me! What is it going to get you? If I were dead I wouldn't hesitate to be buried.

Answer me . . . what do you want? What is it going to get you . . . (*As they remain silent*) Tell me! Answer me! Why don't you talk? Explain it to me, make me understand . . .

SECOND GENERAL. (*In whisper to* THIRD GENERAL, *as* FIRST GENERAL *glares hopelessly at the* CORPSES.) He's licked. It was a mistake—moving him off the artillery.

THIRD GENERAL. They ought to let me handle them. I'd show 'em. You've got to use force.

FIRST GENERAL. (*Bursting out—after walking along entire row of* CORPSES *and back*) Lie down! (*The* CORPSES *stand, immobile. The* GENERAL *rushes out, moaning*) Oh, God, oh, my God . . . (*Blackout.*)

Spotlight, red, picks out two WHORES, *dressed in the uniform of their trade, on a street corner.*

FIRST WHORE. I'd lay 'em, all right. They oughta call me in. I'd lay em. There wouldn't be any doubt in anybody's mind after I got through with 'em. Why don't they call me in instead of those Generals? What do Generals know about such things? (*Both* WHORES *go off into fits of wild laughter*) Call the War Department, Mabel, tell 'em we'll come to their rescue at the prevailing rates. (*Laughs wildly again*) We're willing to do our part, like the papers say—share the burden! Oh, my Gawd, I ain't laughed so much . . . (*Laugh again. A* MAN *crosses their path. Still laughing, but professional*) Say, Johnny, Johnny, what'cha doin' tonight? How'd ya like . . . ? (*The* MAN *passes on. The women laugh*) Share the burden—Oh, my Gawd . . . (*They laugh and laugh and laugh, clinging to each other. . . . Blackout. But the laughter goes on.*)

The spotlight illuminates the grave— SOLDIERS *of burial detail are sitting around a covered fire.* SECOND SOLDIER *is singing "Swing Low, Sweet Chariot."*

THIRD SOLDIER. This is a funny war. It's rollin' downhill. Everybody's waitin'. Personally, I think it's those guys there that . . . (*He gestures to grave.*)

SERGEANT. Nobody asked you. You're not supposed to talk about it.

FIRST SOLDIER. Regulation 2035a . . .

SERGEANT. Well, I just told ya. (SECOND SOLDIER *starts to sing again.* SERGEANT *breaks in on him*) Say, lissen, think about those guys there. How do you think they feel with you howlin' like this? They got more important things to think about.

SECOND SOLDIER. I won't distract 'em. I got an easy-flowin' voice.

SERGEANT. They don't like it. I can tell.

FIRST SOLDIER. Well, I like to hear him sing. And I'll bet they do, too. I'm gonna ask 'em . . . (*He jumps up.*)

SERGEANT. Now, lissen! (FIRST SOLDIER *slowly approaches the grave. He is embarrassed, a little frightened.*)

FIRST SOLDIER. Say, men, I . . . (CAPTAIN *comes on.* FIRST SOLDIER *stands at attention.*)

CAPTAIN. Sergeant . . .

SERGEANT. Yes, Sir!

CAPTAIN. You know that none of the men is to talk to *them*. . . .

SERGEANT. Yes, Sir. Only, Sir . . .

CAPTAIN. All right. (*To* FIRST SOLDIER) Get back there, please.

FIRST SOLDIER. Yes, Sir! (*He salutes and goes back.*)

SERGEANT. (*Under his breath to* FIRST SOLDIER) I warned ya.

FIRST SOLDIER. Shut up! I wanna lissen to what's goin' on there! (CAPTAIN *has meanwhile seated himself on the edge of the grave and has brought out a pair of eye-glasses with which he plays as he talks.*)

CAPTAIN. Gentlemen, I have been asked by the Generals to talk to you. My work is not this . . . (*He indicates his uniform*) I am a philosopher, a scientist, my uniform is a pair of eye-glasses, my usual weapon test-tubes and books. At a time like this perhaps we need philosophy, need science. First I must say that your General has ordered you to lie down.

FIRST CORPSE. We used to have a General.

THIRD CORPSE. No more.

FOURTH CORPSE. They sold us.

CAPTAIN. What do you mean—sold you?

FIFTH CORPSE. Sold us for twenty-four yards of bloody mud.

SIXTH CORPSE. A life for four yards of bloody mud.

CAPTAIN. We had to take that hill. General's orders. You're soldiers. You understand.

FIRST CORPSE. We understand now. The real estate operations of Generals are always carried on at boom prices.

SIXTH CORPSE. A life for four yards of bloody mud. Gold is cheaper, and rubies, jewels, pearls and rubies. . . .

THIRD CORPSE. I fell in the first yard. . .

SECOND CORPSE. I caught on the wire and hung there while the machine gun stitched me through the middle to it. . . .

FOURTH CORPSE. I was there at the end and thought I had life in my hands for another day, but a shell came and my life dripped into the mud.

SIXTH CORPSE. Ask the General how he'd like to be dead at twenty. (*Calling, as though to the* GENERALS) Twenty, General, twenty . . .

CAPTAIN. Other men are dead.

FIRST CORPSE. Too many.

CAPTAIN. Men must die for their country's sake—if not you, then others. This has always been. Men died for Pharaoh and Cæsar and Rome two thousand years ago and more, and went into the earth with their wounds. Why not you . . . ?

FIRST CORPSE. Men, even the men who die for Pharaoh and Cæsar and Rome, must, in the end, before all hope is gone, discover that a man can die happy and be contentedly buried only when he dies for himself or for a cause that is his own and not Pharaoh's or Cæsar's or Rome's. . . .

CAPTAIN. Still—what is this world, that you cling to it? A speck of dust, a flaw in the skies, a thumb-print on the margin of a page printed in an incomprehensible language. . . .

SECOND CORPSE. It is our home.

THIRD CORPSE. We have been dispossessed by force, but we are reclaiming our home. It is time that mankind claimed its home, this earth—its home. . . .

CAPTAIN. We have no home. We are strangers in the universe and cling, desperate and grimy, to the crust of our world, and if there is a God and this His earth, we must be a terrible sight in His eyes.

FOURTH CORPSE. We are not disturbed by the notion of our appearance in the eyes of God. . . .

CAPTAIN. The earth is an unpleasant place and when you are rid of it you are well out of it. Man cheats man here and the only sure things are death and despair. What use, then, to remain on it once you have the permission to leave?

FIFTH CORPSE. It is the one thing we know.

SIXTH CORPSE. We did not ask permission to leave. Nobody asked us whether we wanted it or not. The Generals pushed us out and closed the door on us. Who are the Generals that they are to close the door on us?

CAPTAIN. The earth, I assure you, is a mean place, insignificantly miserable. . . .

FIRST CORPSE. We must find out for ourselves. That is our right.

CAPTAIN. Man has no rights. . . .

FIRST CORPSE. Man can make rights for himself. It requires only determination and the good-will of ordinary men. We have made ourselves the right to walk this earth, seeing it and judging it for ourselves.

CAPTAIN. There is peace in the grave. . . .

THIRD CORPSE. Peace and the worms and the roots of grass. There is a deeper peace than that which comes with feeding the roots of the grass.

CAPTAIN. (*Looks slowly at them, in turn*) Yes, gentlemen . . . (*Turns away and walks off.* FIRST SOLDIER *moves slowly up to the grave.*)

FIRST SOLDIER. (*To the* CORPSES) I . . . I'm glad you . . . you didn't . . . I'm glad. Say, is there anything we can do for you?

SERGEANT. Lissen, soldier!

FIRST SOLDIER. (*Passionately, harshly*) Shut up, Sergeant! (*Then very softly and warmly to* FIRST CORPSE) Is there anything we can do for you, Friend?

FIRST CORPSE. Yeah. You can sing . . . (*There is a pause in which the* FIRST SOLDIER *turns around and looks at the* SECOND SOLDIER, *then back to the* FIRST CORPSE.

Then the silence is broken by the SECOND SOLDIER's *voice, raised in song. It goes on for a few moments, then fades as the light dims.*)

Colored spotlights pick out three BUSINESS MEN *on different parts of the stage.*

FIRST BUSINESS MAN. Ssh! Keep it quiet!

THIRD BUSINESS MAN. Sink 'em with lead. . . .

SECOND BUSINESS MAN. Bury them! Bury them six feet under!

FIRST BUSINESS MAN. What are we going to do?

SECOND BUSINESS MAN. We must keep up the morale.

THIRD BUSINESS MAN. Lead! Lead! A lot of lead!

SECOND BUSINESS MAN. What do we pay our Generals for?

CHORUS OF BUSINESS MEN. Ssssh! (*Blackout*)
Spotlight on the congregation of a church, kneeling, with a PRIEST *praying over them.*

PRIEST. O Jesus, our God and our Christ, Who has redeemed us with Thy blood on the Cross at Calvary, give us Thy blessing on this holy day, and cause it that our soldiers allow themselves to be buried in peace, and bring victory to our arms, enlisted in Thy Cause and the cause of all righteousness on the field of battle . . . Amen . . . (*Blackout*.)

FIRST GENERAL. (*In purple baby spotlight*) Please, God, keep it quiet . . .

(*Spotlight on newspaper office.*)

REPORTER. Well? What are you going to do?

EDITOR. Do I have to do anything?

REPORTER. God damn right you do. . . . They're still standing up. They're going to stand up from now till Doomsday. They're not going to be able to bury soldiers any more. It's in the stars. . . . You got to say something about it. . . .

EDITOR. All right. Put this in. "It is alleged that certain members of an infantry regiment refuse to allow themselves to be buried. . . . "

REPORTER. Well?

EDITOR. That's all.

REPORTER. (*Incredulous*) That's all?

EDITOR. Yes, Christ, isn't that *enough?* (*Blackout*.)

Spotlight on a radio-loudspeaker. A VOICE *mellow and beautiful, comes out of it.*

THE VOICE. It has been reported that certain American soldiers, killed on the field of battle, have refused to allow themselves to be buried. Whether this is true or not the Coast-to-Coast Broadcasting System feel that this must give the American public an idea of the indomitable spirit of the American doughboy in this war. We cannot rest until this war is won—not even our brave dead boys . . . (*Blackout*.)

Guns. Spotlight on FIRST GENERAL *and* CAPTAIN.

FIRST GENERAL. Have you got any suggestions . . . ?

CAPTAIN. I think so. Get their women. . .

FIRST GENERAL. What good'll their women do?

CAPTAIN. Women are always conservative. It's a conservative notion—this one of lying down and allowing yourself to be buried when you're dead. The women will fight the General's battle for them—in the best possible way—through their emotions. . . . It's the General's best bet. . . .

FIRST GENERAL. Women— Of course! You've got it there, Captain! Get out the women! Get them in a hurry! We'll have these boys underground in a jiffy. Women! By God, I never thought of it. . . . Send out the call. . . . Women! (*Fadeout*.)

A baby spotlight on the loudspeaker. The VOICE *again, just as mellow, just as persuasive.*

VOICE. We have been asked by the War Department to broadcast an appeal to the women of Privates Driscoll, Schelling, Morgan, Webster, Levy, and Dean, reported dead. The War Department requests that the women of these men present themselves at the War Department Office immediately. It is within their power to do a great service to their country. . . (*Blackout*.)

The spotlight illuminates the FIRST GENERAL, *where he stands, addressing women.*

ST GENERAL. Go to your men . . . talk them . . . make them see the error of ir ways, ladies. You women represent at is dearest in our civilization—the red foundations of the home. We are ting this war to protect the foundations the homes of America! Those founda- s will crumble utterly if these men of rs come back from the dead. I shudder think of the consequences of such an , Our entire system will be mortally ck. Our banks will close, our buildings apse . . . our army will desert the field l leave our fair land open to be overrun the enemy. Ladies, you are all Gold r mothers and wives and sweethearts. u want to win this war. I know it. I w the high fire of patriotism that burns women's breasts. That is why I have led upon you. Ladies, let me make this r to you. If you do not get your men lie down and allow themselves to be ied, I fear that our cause is lost. The den of the war is upon your shoulders w. Wars are not fought with guns and wder alone, ladies. Here is your chance do your part, a glorious part. . . . You fighting for your homes, your children, r sisters' lives, your country's honor. u are fighting for religion, for love, for decent human life. Wars can be fought l won only when the dead are buried l forgotten. How can we forget the dead o refuse to be buried? And we *must* get them! There is no room in this rld for dead men. They will lead only the bitterest unhappiness—for you, for m, for everybody. Go ladies, do your ty. Your country waits upon you. . . . *ackout.)*

tlight immediately illuminates the ce where PRIVATE SCHELLING, CORPSE o, *is talking to his wife.* MRS. SCHELLING *spare, taciturn woman, a farmer's wife, o might be twenty or forty or anything between.*

s SCHELLING. Did it hurt much, John?

ELLING. How's the kid, Bess?

s. He's fine. He talks now. He weighs nty-eight pounds. He'll be a big boy. l it hurt much, John?

SCHELLING. How is the farm? Is it going all right, Bess?

BESS. It's going. The rye was heavy this year. Did it hurt much, John?

SCHELLING. Who did the reapin' for you, Bess?

BESS. Schmidt took care of it—and his boys. Schmidt's too old for the war and his boys are too young. Took 'em nearly two weeks. The wheat's not bad this year. Schmidt's oldest boy expects to be called in a month or two. He practises behind the barn with that old shotgun Schmidt uses for duck.

SCHELLING. The Schmidts were always fools. When the kid grows up, Bess, you make sure you pump some sense into his head. What color's his hair?

BESS. Blond. Like you. . . . What are you going to do, John?

SCHELLING. I would like to see the kid— and the farm—and . . .

BESS. They say you're dead, John. . . .

SCHELLING. I'm dead, all right.

BESS. Then how is it . . . ?

SCHELLING. I don't know. Maybe there's too many of us under the ground now. Maybe the earth can't stand it no more. You got to change crops sometime. What are you doing here, Bess?

BESS. They asked me to get you to let yourself be buried.

SCHELLING. What do you think?

BESS. You're dead, John. . . .

SCHELLING. Well . . . ?

BESS. What's the good . . . ?

SCHELLING. I don't know. Only there's something in me, dead or no dead, that won't let me be buried.

BESS. You were a queer man, John. I never did understand what you were about. But what's the good . . . ?

SCHELLING. Bess, I never talked so that I could get you to understand what I wanted while I—while I—before . . . Maybe now . . . There're a couple of things, Bess, that I ain't had enough of. Easy things, the things you see when you look outa your window at night, after supper, or when you wake up in the mornin'. Things you smell when you step outside the door when summer's on and the sun starts to turn the grass brown. Things you hear when you're busy with the horses or pitchin' the hay and you don't really notice them and yet they come back to you. Things like the fuzz of green over a field in spring where you planted wheat and it's started to come out overnight. Things like lookin' at rows of corn scrapin' in the breeze, tall and green, with the silk flying off the ears in the wind. Things like seeing the sweat come out all over your horse's fat flank and seein' it shine like silk in front of you, smelling horsey and strong. Things like seein' the loam turn back all fat and deep brown on both sides as the plough turns it over so that it gets to be awful hard walkin' behind it. Things like taking a cold drink of water outa the well after you've boiled in the sun all afternoon, and feelin' the water go down and down into you coolin' you off all through from the inside out. . . . Things like seein' a blond kid, all busy and serious, playin' with a dog on the shady side of a house. . . . There ain't nothin' like that down here, Bess. . . .

BESS. Everything has its place, John. Dead men have theirs.

SCHELLING. My place is on the earth, Bess. My business is with the top of the earth, not the under-side. It was a trap that yanked me down. I'm not smart, Bess, and I'm easy trapped—but I can tell now . . . I got some stories to tell the farmers before I'm through—I'm going to tell 'em. . . .

BESS. We could bury you home, John, near the creek—it's cool there and quiet and there's always a breeze in the trees. . . .

SCHELLING. Later, Bess, when I've had my fill of lookin' and smellin' and talkin' . . . . A man should be able to walk into his grave, not be dragged into it. . . .

BESS. How'll I feel—and the kid—w you walkin' around—like—like that . .

SCHELLING. I won't bother you. . . . I wo come near you. . . .

BESS. Even so. Just knowin' . . .

SCHELLING. I can't help it. This is so thin' bigger'n you—bigger'n me. It's so thin' I ain't had nothin' to do with st in'. . . . It's somethin' that just grew outa the earth—like—like a weed—a flow Cut it down now and it'll jump up i dozen new places. You can't stop it. 1 earth's ready for it. . . .

BESS. You were a good husband, Jo For the kid—and me—won't you?

SCHELLING. (Quietly) Go home, B Go home! (Blackout.)
The spotlight picks out CORPSE NUM FIVE, PRIVATE LEVY, where he stands the grave, with his back to the audie His woman, a pert, attractive young la is sitting next to him, above him, fac him, talking to him.

JOAN. You loved me best, didn't you, H ry—of all of them—all those women— loved me the best, didn't you?

LEVY. (FIFTH CORPSE) What's the dif ence, now?

JOAN. I want to know it.

LEVY. Its not important.

JOAN. It's important to me. I knew ab the others, about Doris and that shi eyed Janet. . . . Henry you're not a man, are you, Henry?

LEVY. No, I'm all shot away inside.

JOAN. Must wars always be fought in mud like this? I never expected it to l like this. It . . . it looks like a dump he

LEVY. You've gotten your shoes mud They're pretty shoes, Joan.

JOAN. Do you think so, Henry? The lizard. I like them too. It's so hard to a good pair of shoes nowadays.

LEVY. Do you still dance, Joan?

AN. Oh, I'm really much better than I
ed to be. There are so many dances
ck home nowadays. Dances for orphan
lief and convalescent hospitals and Vic-
ry Loans. I'm busy seven nights a week.
sold more Victory Loans than any other
rl in the League. I got a helmet . . .
e of *their* helmets . . . one with a bullet-
le in it, for selling eleven thousand dol-
rs' worth.

vy. Out here we get them for nothing,
the million—bullet-holes and all.

AN. That sounds bitter. You shouldn't
und bitter.

vy. I'm sorry.

AN. I heard Colonel Elwell the other
y. You know Colonel Elwell, old
nthony Elwell who owns the mill. He
ade a speech at the monthly Red Cross
nquet and he said that that was the
ce thing about this war, it wasn't being
ught bitterly by our boys. He said it
as just patriotism that kept us going.
e's a wonderful speaker, Colonel Elwell;
cried and cried. . . .

vy. I remember him.

AN. Henry, do you think we're going
win the war?

vy. What's the difference?

AN. Henry! What a way to talk! I
n't know what's come over you. Really,
don't. Why, the papers say that if *they*
in the war, they'll burn our churches
d tear down our museums and . . . and
pe our women. (LEVY *laughs*) Why are
u laughing, Henry?

vy. I'm dead, Joan.

AN. Yes. Then why—why don't you let
em bury you?

vy. There are a lot of reasons. There
ere a lot of things I loved on this
rth. . . .

AN. A dead man can't touch a woman.

vy. The women, yes—but more than
uching them. I got a great joy just from
tening to women, hearing them laugh,
atching their skirts blow in the wind,

noticing the way their breasts bounced up
and down inside their dresses when they
walked. It had nothing to do with touching them. I liked to hear the sound of their
high heels on pavements at night and the
tenderness in their voices when they walked past me arm in arm with a young man.
You were so lovely, Joan, with your pale
hair and long hands.

JOAN. You always liked my hair. (*A
pause*) No woman will walk arm in arm
with you, Henry Levy, while you cheat the
grave.

LEVY. No. But there will be the eyes of
women to look at and the bright color
of their hair and the soft way they swing
their hips when they walk before young
men. These are the things that mean life
and the earth to me, the joy and the pain.
These are the things the earth still owes
me, now when I am only thirty. Joy and
pain—to each man in his own way, a full
seventy years, to be ended by an unhurried fate, not by a colored pin on a General's map. What do I care for the colored
pins on a General's map?

JOAN. They are not only pins. They mean
more. . . .

LEVY. More? To whom? To the Generals
—not to me. To me they are colored pins.
It is not a fair bargain—this exchange of
my life for a small part of a colored pin. . . .

JOAN. Henry, how can you talk like that?
You know why this war is being fought.

LEVY. No. Do you?

JOAN. Of course, everybody knows. We
must win! We must be prepared to sacrifice our last drop of blood. Anyway,
what can you do?

LEVY. Do you remember last summer,
Joan? My last leave. We went to Maine.
I would like to remember that—the sun
and the beach and your soft hands—for
a long time.

JOAN. What are you going to do?

LEVY. Walk the world looking at the fine,
long-legged girls, seeing in them something
deep and true and passionately vital, lis-

tening to the sound of their light voices with ears the Generals would have stopped with the grave's solid mud. . . .

JOAN. Henry! Henry! Once you said you loved me. For the love of me, Henry, go into the grave. . . .

LEVY. Poor Joan. (*Stretches out his hand tenderly as if to touch her.*)

JOAN. (*Recoiling*) Don't touch me. (*Pause*) For love of me.

LEVY. Go home, Joan! *Go home!* (*Black-out.*)
The spotlight picks out the THIRD CORPSE,

PRIVATE MORGAN, *and* JULIA BLAKE, *he with his back to the audience, standing in the grave, she above and to the right.* JULIA *sobs.*

MORGAN. Stop crying, Julia. What's the sense in crying?

JULIA. No sense. Only I can't stop crying.

MORGAN. You shouldn't have come.

JULIA. They asked me to come. They said you wouldn't let them bury you—dead and all. . . .

MORGAN. Yes.

JULIA. (*Crying*) Why don't they kill me too? I'd let them bury me. I'd be glad to be buried—to get away from all this . . I—I haven't stopped crying for two weeks now. I used to think I was tough. I never cried. Even when I was a kid. It's a wonder where all the tears can come from. Though I guess there's always room for more tears. I thought I was all cried out when I heard about the way they killed Fred. My kid brother. I used to comb his hair in the morning when he went to school . . . I—I . . . Then they killed you. They did, didn't they?

MORGAN. Yes.

JULIA. It's hard to know like this. I—I know, though. It—it makes it harder, this way, with you like this. I could forget easier if you . . . But I wasn't going to say that. I was going to listen to you. Oh, my darling, it's been so rotten. I get drunk. I

hate it and I get drunk. I sing out lou and everybody laughs. I was going throug your things the other day—I'm crazy . . I go through all your things three tim a week, touching your clothes and readin your books. . . . You have the nicest cloth . . . . There was that quatrain you wro to me that time you were in Boston a . . . First I laughed, then I cried, then . It's a lovely poem—you would have bee a fine writer: I think you would ha been the greatest writer that ever . . . I. Did they shoot your hands away, darling

MORGAN. No.

JULIA. That's good. I couldn't bear it anything happened to your hands. Was bad, darling?

MORGAN. Bad enough.

JULIA. But they didn't shoot your han away. That's something. You learn how be grateful for the craziest things now days. People have to be grateful for som thing and it's so hard, with the war a all. . . . Oh, darling, I never could thi of you dead. Somehow you didn't see to be made to be dead. I would feel be ter if you were buried in a fine green fie and there were funny little flowers jum ing up around the stone that said, "Walt Morgan, Born 1913, Died 1937." I cou stop getting drunk at night and singi out loud so that people laugh at me. T worst thing is looking at all the books y piled up home that you didn't read. Th wait there, waiting for your hands to cor and open them and . . . Oh, let them bu you, let them bury you . . . There's not ing left, only crazy people and cloth that'll never be used hanging in the clos . . . Why not?

MORGAN. There are too many books haven't read, too many places I have seen, too many memories I haven't ke long enough. . . . I won't be cheated them. . . .

JULIA. And me? Darling, me . . . I ha getting drunk. Your name would look well on a nice simple chunk of marble a green field. "Walter Morgan, Beloved Julia Blake . . . " With poppies and dais and those little purple flowers all arou

e bottom, and . . . (*She is bent over,*
most wailing. There is the flash of a
n in her hand, and she totters, falls)
ow they can put my name on the cas-
lty lists, too. . . . What do they call those
rple flowers, darling . . . ? (*Blackout.*)

he spotlight follows KATHERINE DRISCOLL
she makes her way from CORPSE *to*
RPSE *in the grave, looking at their faces.*
e looks first at CORPSE SIX, *shudders,*
vers her eyes and moves on. She stops
CORPSE FIVE.

THERINE. I'm Katherine Driscoll. I—
n looking for my brother. He's dead.
re you my brother?

TH CORPSE. No. (KATHERINE *goes on to*
RPSE FOUR, *stops, looks, moves on to*
RPSE THREE.)

THERINE. I'm looking for my brother.
y name is Katherine Driscoll. His
me—

IRD CORPSE. No. (KATHERINE *goes on,*
nds irresolutely before CORPSE TWO.)

THERINE. Are you . . . ? (*Realizing it*
't *her brother. Goes on to* CORPSE ONE)
n looking for my brother. My name is
therine Driscoll. His name—

ISCOLL. I'm Tom Driscoll.

THERINE. Hel—Hello. I don't know
u. After fifteen years— And . . .

ISCOLL. What do you want, Katherine?

THERINE. You don't know me either,
you?

ISCOLL. No.

THERINE. It's funny—my coming here
talk to a dead man—to try to get him
do something because once long ago
was my brother. They talked me into
I don't know how to begin. . . .

ISCOLL. You'll be wasting your words,
therine. . . .

THERINE. They should have asked some-
e nearer to you—someone who loved
u—only they couldn't find anybody. I
s the nearest, they said. . . .

DRISCOLL. That's so. You were the nearest. . . .

KATHERINE. And I fifteen years away. Poor
Tom . . . It couldn't have been a sweet
life you led these fifteen years.

DRISCOLL. It wasn't.

KATHERINE. You were poor, too?

DRISCOLL. Sometimes I begged for meals.
I wasn't lucky. . . .

KATHERINE. And yet you want to go back.
Is there no more sense in the dead, Tom,
than in the living?

DRISCOLL. Maybe not. Maybe there's no
sense in either living or dying, but we
can't believe that. I travelled to a lot of
places and I saw a lot of things, always
from the black side of them, always workin' hard to keep from starvin' and turnin'
my collar up to keep the wind out, and
they were mean and rotten and sad, but
always I saw that they could be better and
some day they were going to be better,
and that the guys like me who knew that
they were rotten and knew that they could
be better had to get out and fight to make
it that way.

KATHERINE. You're dead. Your fight's over.

DRISCOLL. The fight's never over. I got
things to say to people now—to the people
who nurse big machines and the people
who swing shovels and the people whose
babies die with big bellies and rotten bones.
I got things to say to the people who leave
their lives behind them and pick up guns
to fight in somebody else's war. Important things. Big things. Big enough to lift
me out of the grave right back onto the
earth into the middle of men just because
I got the voice to say them. If God could
lift Jesus . . .

KATHERINE. Tom! Have you lost religion,
too?

DRISCOLL. I got another religion. I got a
religion that wants to take heaven out of
the clouds and plant it right here on the
earth where most of us can get a slice of
it. It isn't as pretty a heaven—there aren't
any streets of gold and there aren't any
angels, and we'd have to worry about sew-

erage and railroad schedules in it, and
we don't guarantee everybody'd love it,
but it'd be right here, stuck in the mud of
this earth, and there wouldn't be any entrance requirement, like dying to get into
it. . . . Dead or alive, I see that, and it
won't let me rest. I was the first one to
get up in this black grave of ours, because
that idea wouldn't let me rest. I pulled
the others with me—that's my job, pulling
he others . . . They only know what they
want—I know how they can get it. . . .

KATHERINE. There's still the edge of ar-
rogance on you.

DRISCOLL. I got heaven in my two hands
to give to men. There's reason for arro-
gance. . . .

KATHERINE. I came to ask you to lie down
and let them bury you. It seems foolish
now. But . . .

DRISCOLL. It's foolish, Katherine. I didn't
get up from the dead to go back to the
dead. I'm going to the living now. . . .

KATHERINE. Fifteen years. It's a good thing
your mother isn't alive. How can you say
good-bye to a dead brother Tom?

DRISCOLL. Wish him an easy grave, Katherine. . . .

KATHERINE. A green and pleasant grave
to you, Tom, when finally . . . finally . . .
green and pleasant. (*Blackout.*)

The spotlight illuminates PRIVATE DEAN,
the SIXTH CORPSE, *where he stands with his
back to the audience, listening to his
mother, a thin, shabby, red-eyed woman of
about forty-five, sitting above and to the
right, in the full glare of the spotlight.*
DEAN *is in shadow.*

MRS. DEAN. Let me see your face, son . . .

DEAN. You don't want to see it, mom . . .

MRS. DEAN. My baby's face. Once, before
you . . .

DEAN. You don't want to see it, mom. I
know. Didn't they tell you what happened
to me?

MRS. DEAN. I asked the doctor. He said
a piece of shell hit the side of your head—
but even so. . . .

DEAN. Don't ask to see it, mom.

MRS. DEAN. How are you, son? (DEA[N]
laughs a little—bitterly) Oh, I forgot.
asked you that question so many tim[e]
while you were growing up, Jimmy. L[et]
me see your face, Jimmy—just once. . .

DEAN. How did Alice take it when sh[e]
heard . . . ?

MRS. DEAN. She put a gold star in he[r]
window. She tells everybody you were g[o]
ing to be married. Is that so?

DEAN. Maybe. I liked Alice.

MRS. DEAN. She came over on your birt[h]
day. That was before this—this happene[d]
She brought flowers. Big chrysanthemum[s]
Yellow. A lot of them. We had to p[ut]
them in two vases. I baked a cake. I dor[t]
know why. It's hard to get eggs and fi[ne]
flour nowadays. My baby, twenty yea[rs]
old . . . Let me see your face, Jimm[y]
boy. . . .

DEAN. Go home, mom. . . . It's not doir[g]
you any good staying here. . . .

MRS. DEAN. I want you to let them bu[ry]
you, Baby. It's done now and over.
would be better for you that way. . . .

DEAN. There's no better to it, mom—a[nd]
no worse. It happened that way, that's a[ll]

MRS. DEAN. Let me see your face, Jimm[y]
You had such a fine face. Like a go[od]
baby's. It hurt me when you started [to]
shave. Somehow, I almost forget what y[ou]
looked like, Baby. I remember what y[ou]
looked like when you were five, wh[en]
you were ten—you were chubby and fa[t]
and your cheeks felt like little silk cushio[ns]
when I put my hand on them. But I do[n't]
remember how you looked when you we[nt]
away with that uniform on you and th[e]
helmet over your face. . . . Baby, let [me]
see your face, once. . . .

DEAN. Don't ask me . . . You don't wa[nt]
to see. You'll feel worse—forever . . .
you see . . .

MRS. DEAN. I'm not afraid. I can look [at]
my baby's face. Do you think mothers [can]
be frightened by their children's . . .

DEAN. No, mom . . .

RS. DEAN. Baby, listen to me, I'm your
other. . . . Let them bury you. There's
mething peaceful and done about a grave.
fter a while you forget the death and you
member only the life before it. But this
ay—you never forget. . . . it's a wound
alking around forever, without peace.
or your sake and mine and your father's
, . Baby . . .

AN. I was only twenty, mom. I hadn't
ne anything. I hadn't seen anything. I
ver even had a girl. I spent twenty years
actising to be a man and then they
lled me. Being a kid's no good, mom.
ou try to get over it as soon as you can.
ou don't really live while you're a kid.
ou mark time, waiting. I waited, mom—
t then I got cheated. They made a speech
d played a trumpet and dressed me in
uniform and then they killed me.

RS. DEAN. Oh, Baby, Baby, there's no
ace this way. Please, let them . . .

EAN. No, mom . . .

RS. DEAN. Then once, now, so that I can
member—let me see your face, my baby's
ce . . .

EAN. Mom, the shell hit close to me.
ou don't want to look at a man when a
ell hits close to him.

RS..... DEAN. Let me see your face, Jim-
y . . .

EAN. All right, mom . . . Look! (*He
rns his face to her. The audience can't
e his face, but immediately a spotlight,
hite and sharp, shoots down from di-
ctly above and hits* DEAN's *head.* MRS.
EAN *leans forward, staring. Another spot-
ght shoots down immediately after from
e extreme right, then one from the left,
en two more, from above. They hit with
e impact of blows and* MRS. DEAN *shud-
ers a little as they come, as though she
ere watching her son being beaten. There
absolute silence for a moment. Then
RS. DEAN starts to moan, low, painfully.
he lights remain fixed and* MRS. DEAN's
oans rise to a wail, then to a scream.
he leans back, covering her eyes with her
nds, screaming. Blackout. The scream
rsists, fading, like a siren fading in the
istance, until it is finally stilled.*)

The spotlight on CORPSE THREE, PRIVATE
WEBSTER, *and his wife, a dumpy, sad little
woman.*

MARTHA WEBSTER. Say something.

WEBSTER. What do you want me to say?

MARTHA. Something—anything. Only talk.
You give me the shivers standing there
like that—looking like that. . . .

WEBSTER. Even now—after this—there's
nothing that we can talk to each other
about.

MARTHA. Don't talk like that. You talked
like that enough when you were alive—
It's not my fault that you're dead. . . .

WEBSTER. No.

MARTHA. It was bad enough when you
were alive—and you didn't talk to me and
you looked at me as though I was always
in your way.

WEBSTER. Martha, Martha, what's the difference now?

MARTHA. I just wanted to let you know.
Now I suppose you're going to come back
and sit around and ruin my life altogether?

WEBSTER. No. I'm not going to come back.

MARTHA. Then what . . . ?

WEBSTER. I couldn't explain it to you,
Martha. . . .

MARTHA. No! Oh, no—you couldn't explain it to your wife. But you could explain
it to that dirty bunch of loafers down at
that damned garage of yours and you could
explain it to those bums in the saloon on
F Street. . . .

WEBSTER. I guess I could. (*Musing*)
Things seemed to be clearer when I was
talking to the boys while I worked over
a job. And I managed to talk so people
could get to understand what I meant
down at the saloon on F Street. It was
nice, standing there of a Saturday night,
with a beer in front of you and a man
or two that understood your own language next to you, talking—oh, about Babe
Ruth or the new oiling system Ford was
putting out or the chances of us gettin'
into the war. . . .

MARTHA. It's different if you were rich and had a fine beautiful life you wanted to go back to. Then I could understand. But you were poor . . . you always had dirt under your finger nails, you never ate enough, you hated me, your wife, you couldn't stand being in the same room with me. . . . Don't shake your head, I know. Out of your whole life, all you could remember that's good is a beer on Saturday night that you drank in company with a couple of bums. . . .

WEBSTER. That's enough. I didn't think about it then . . . but I guess I was happy those times.

MARTHA. You were happy those times . . . but you weren't happy in your own home! I know, even if you don't say it! Well, I wasn't happy either! Living in three damned rooms that the sun didn't hit five times a year! Watching the roaches make picnics on the walls! Happy!

WEBSTER. I did my best.

MARTHA. Eighteen-fifty a week! Your best! Eighteen-fifty, condensed milk, a two-dollar pair of shoes once a year, five hundred dollars' insurance, chopped meat, God, how I hate chopped meat! Eighteen-fifty, being afraid of everything—of the landlord, the gas company, scared stiff every month that I was goin' to have a baby! Why shouldn't I have a baby? Who says I shouldn't have a baby? Eighteen-fifty, no baby!

WEBSTER. I woulda liked a kid.

MARTHA. Would you? You never said anything.

WEBSTER. It's good to have a kid. A kid's somebody to talk to.

MARTHA. At first . . . In the beginning . . . I thought we'd have a kid some day.

WEBSTER. Yeah, me too. I used to go out on Sundays and watch men wheel their kids through the park.

MARTHA. There were so many things you didn't tell me. Why did you keep quiet?

WEBSTER. I was ashamed to talk to you. I couldn't give you anything.

MARTHA. I'm sorry.

WEBSTER. In the beginning it looked fine. I used to smile to myself when walked beside you in the street and oth men looked at you.

MARTHA. That was a long time ago.

WEBSTER. A kid would've helped.

MARTHA. No, it wouldn't. Don't fc yourself, Webster. The Clarks downsta have four and it doesn't help them. O man Clark comes home drunk every Sa urday night and beats 'em with his sha ing strap and throws plates at the o lady. Kids don't help the poor. Nothi helps the poor! I'm too smart to have sic dirty kids on eighteen-fifty. . . .

WEBSTER. That's it. . . .

MARTHA. A house should have a bal But it should be a clean house with a f icebox. Why shouldn't I have a bab Other people have babies. Even now, wi the war, other people have babies. Th don't have to feel their skin curl eve time they tear a page off the calend They go off to beautiful hospitals in love ambulances and have babies between c ored sheets! What's there about them th God likes that He makes it so easy *them* to have babies?

WEBSTER. They're not married to mecha ics.

MARTHA. No! It's not eighteen-fifty them. And now . . . now it's worse. Yo twenty dollars a month. You hire yours out to be killed and I get twenty dolla a month. I wait on line all day to get loaf of bread. I've forgotten what but tastes like. I wait on line with the ra soaking through my shoes for a pou of rotten meat once a week. At night go home. Nobody to talk to, just sittii watching the bugs, with one little lig because the Government's got to sa electricity. You had to go off and leave to that! What's the war to me that I ha to sit at night with nobody to talk t What's the war to you that you had to off and . . . ?

WEBSTER. That's why I'm standing now, Martha.

ARTHA. What took you so long, then?
hy now? Why not a month ago, a year
o, ten years ago? Why didn't you stand
) then? Why wait until you're dead?
ou live on eighteen-fifty a week, with
e roaches, not saying a word, and then
hen they kill you, you stand up! You
ol!

EBSTER. I didn't see it before.

ARTHA. Just like you! Wait until it's
) late! There's plenty for live men to
and up for! All right, stand up! It's about
ne you talked back. It's about time all
ou poor miserable eighteen-fifty bastards
ood up for themselves and their wives
d the children they can't have! Tell 'em
to stand up! Tell 'em! *Tell 'em* (*She
rieks. Blackout.*)

spotlight picks out the FIRST GENERAL.
e has his hands to his lips.

RST GENERAL. It didn't work. But keep
quiet. For God's sake, keep it quiet....
Blackout.)

*spotlight picks out the newspaper office,
e* REPORTER *and the* EDITOR.

PORTER. (*In harsh triumph*) It didn't
ork! Now, you've got to put it in! I knew
wouldn't work! Smear it over the head-
es! It didn't work!

ITOR. Put it in the headlines.... They
on't be buried! (*Blackout — Voices
ll....*)

DICE. (NEWSBOY *spotted*) It didn't work!
xtra! It didn't work!

DICE. (*In dark. Hoarse whisper*) It
dn't work! They're still standing....
omebody do something....

DICE. (*Spotted, a clubwoman type*)
omebody do something....

DICE. (NEWSBOY *spotted*) Extra! They're
ill standing....

DICE. (CLUBWOMAN) Don't let them back
ito the country....

EPORTER. (*Spotted. Triumphantly.*) They're
anding. From now on they'll always
and! You can't bury soldiers any more
... (*Spotted, a group, owners of the next
ur voices.*)

VOICE. They stink. Bury them!

VOICE. What are we going to do about
them?

VOICE. What'll happen to our war? We
can't let anything happen to our war....

VOICE. (*A* PRIEST, *facing the three men*)
Pray! Pray! God must help us! Down on
your knees, all of you and pray with your
hearts and your guts and the marrow of
your bones....

VOICE. (REPORTER *spotted, facing them
all*) It will take more than prayers. What
are prayers to a dead man? They're standing! Mankind is standing up and climbing
out of its grave.... (*Blackout.*)

VOICE. (*In dark*) Have you heard...?
It didn't work...,

VOICE. (*In dark*) Extra! Extra! It didn't
work! They're still standing! (*Spotted*, MRS.
DEAN, MRS. SCHELLING, JULIA BLAKE.)

MRS. DEAN. My baby....

MRS. SCHELLING. My husband....

JULIA BLAKE. My lover.... (*Blackout.*)

VOICE. (*In dark*) Bury them! They stink!
(*The next set of characters walks through
a stationary spotlight.*)

VOICE. (*A* FARMER) Plant a new crop!
The old crop has worn out the earth.
Plant something besides lives in the old
and weary earth....

VOICE. (*A* NEWSBOY, *running*) Extra! It
didn't work!

VOICE. (*A* BANKER. *Frantic*) Somebody do
something! Dupont's passed a dividend!

VOICE. (*A* PRIEST) The Day of Judgment
is at hand....

VOICE. (*The* FIRST WHORE) Where is
Christ? (*Blackout.*)

VOICE. (*In dark*) File 'em away in alpha-
betical order.... (*Spotlight on a man in
academic robes, reading aloud from behind a table, after he adjusts his glasses.*)

VOICE. We don't believe it. It is against
the dictates of science. (*Blackout—Spot on
SECOND GENERAL.*)

SECOND GENERAL. Keep it quiet! (MRS. SCHELLING *walks in front of him. The others follow.*)

BESS SCHELLING. My husband. . . .

JULIA BLAKE. My lover. . . .

MRS. DEAN. My baby. . . . (*Blackout.*)

VOICE. (*A* CHILD) What have they done with my father? (*Spot on* BANKER *at telephone.*)

BANKER. (*Into phone*) Somebody do something. Call up the War Department! Call up Congress! Call up the Roman Catholic Church! Somebody do something!

VOICE. We've got to put them down!

REPORTER. (*Spotted*) Never! Never! Never! You can't put them down. Put one down and ten will spring up like weeds in an old garden. . . . (*Spots at various parts of the stage.*)
VOICE. (*The* THIRD GENERAL) Use lead on them, lead! Lead put 'em down once, lead'll do it again! Lead!

VOICE. Put down the sword and hang the armor on the wall to rust with the years. The killed have arisen.

VOICE. Bury them! Bury the dead!

VOICE. The old demons have come back to possess the earth. We are lost. . . .

VOICE. The dead have arisen, now let the living rise, singing. . . .

VOICE. Do something, for the love of God, do something. . . .

VOICE. Extra! They're still standing.

VOICE. Do something!

VOICE. (*In dark*) We will do something. . . .

VOICE. Who are you?

VOICE. (PRIEST *in spot*) We are the Church and the voice of God. The State has tried its ways, now let the Church use the ways of God. These corpses are possessed by the devil, who plagues the lives of men. The Church will exorcise the devil from these men, according to its ancient rite, and they will lie down in their graves like children to a pleasant slee rising no more to trouble the world living men. The Church which is t Voice of God upon this earth, amen. . . (*Blackout.*)

CHORUS OF VOICES. Alleluia, alleluia, sir . . . . (*The scream of the bereft moth fades in, reaches its height, then dies a as the holy procession of priests mov solemnly on with bell, book and candl A* PRIEST *sprinkles the* CORPSES *with ho water, makes the sign of the cross ov them and begins in the solemn Latin the service. At the end he goes into En lish—his voice rising in ritualistic passion* PRIEST. I exorcise thee, unclean spirit, the name of Jesus Christ; tremble, O Sata thou enemy of the faith, thou foe of ma kind, who hast brought death into th world, who hast deprived men of lif and hast rebelled against ` justice, th seducer of mankind, thou root of evil, th source of avarice, discord, and env (*Silence. Then the* CORPSES *begin to laug lightly, horribly. There is a sign from t living men present, and the priestly pr cession goes off, its bell tinkling. T laughter goes on. Blackout. The* VOIC *again. . . .*)

VOICE. No. . . .

VOICE. NO!

VOICE. It didn't work. . . .

VOICE. We are deserted by God for o evil ways. It is the new flood, witho rain. . . .

NEWSBOY. They're licked.

VOICE. This isn't 1918! This is today!

VOICE. See what happens tomorrow!

VOICE. Anything can happen now! An thing!

VOICE. They're coming. We must st them!

VOICE. We must find ways, find means

VOICE. (*The* REPORTER, *exulting*) They coming! There will be no ways, no mean

SEMI-CHORUS. (*Mocking*) What are y going to do?

RUS. *What are you going to do?*
ey laugh sardonically.)

RD GENERAL. Let me have a machine
! Sergeant! A machine gun! (*A bolt
ight comes down to a machine gun set
he left of the grave, mid-way between
edge of the grave and the wings. The
ERALS are clustered around it.*)

RD GENERAL. I'll show them! This is
t they've needed!

T GENERAL. All right, all right. Get it
with! Hurry! But keep it quiet!

RD GENERAL. I want a crew to man this
. (*Pointing to* FIRST SOLDIER) You!
e over here! And you! You know
t to do. I'll give the command to
. . .

T SOLDIER. Not to me, you won't. . . .
is over me. I won't touch that gun.
e of us will! We didn't hire out to
o butcher of dead men. Do your own
pping. . . .

D GENERAL. You'll be court-martialed!
'll be dead by tomorrow morning. . . .

T SOLDIER. Be careful, General! I may
a notion to come up like these guys.
's the smartest thing I've seen in this
y. I like it. . . . (*To* DRISCOLL) What
say, Buddy?

OLL. It's about time. . . . (*The* THIRD
RAL draws his gun, but the other GEN-
hold his arm.*)

T GENERAL. Stop it! It's bad enough as
! Let him alone! do it yourself! Go
d, do it!

D GENERAL. (*Whispers*) Oh, my God
. (*He looks down at gun, then slowly
down on one knee behind it. The
GENERALS slide out behind him. The
SES come together in the middle of the
e, all facing the gun. THIRD GENERAL
les with the gun. VOICES call.*)

RTER. Never, never, never!

A. Walter Morgan, Beloved of Julia
e, Born 1913, Died 1937.

DEAN. Let me see your face, Baby?

THA WEBSTER. All you remember is a
of beer with a couple of bums on
day night.

KATHERINE DRISCOLL. A green and pleasant
grave . . .

BESS SCHELLING. Did it hurt much, John?
His hair is blond and he weighs twenty-
eight pounds.

JOAN. You loved me best, didn't you,
Henry? . . . best . . .

VOICE. Four yards of bloody mud . . .

VOICE. I understand how they feel, Charlie.
I wouldn't like to be underground . . .
now . . .

REPORTER. Never, never!

VOICE. Never!

MARTHA WEBSTER. Tell 'em all to stand
up! Tell 'em! *Tell 'em!* (*The* CORPSES *begin to walk toward the left end of the
grave, not marching, but walking together,
silently. The* THIRD GENERAL *stiffens, then
starts to laugh hysterically. As the* CORPSES
*reach the edge of the grave and take their
first step out, he starts firing, laughing
wildly, the gun shaking his shoulders
violently. Calmly, in the face of the chattering gun, the* CORPSES *gather on the brink
of the grave, then walk soberly, in a little
bunch, toward the* THIRD GENERAL. *For a
moment they obscure him as they pass
him. In that moment the gun stops. There
is absolute silence. The* CORPSES *pass on,
going off the stage, like men who have
leisurely business that must be attended to
in the not too pressing future. As they pass
the gun, they reveal the* THIRD GENERAL,
*slumped forward, still, over the still gun.
There is no movement on the stage for a
fraction of a second. Then, slowly, the*
FOUR SOLDIERS *of the burial detail break
ranks. Slowly they walk, exactly as the*
CORPSES *have walked, off toward the left,
past the* THIRD GENERAL. *The last* SOLDIER,
as he passes the THIRD GENERAL, *deliberately, but without malice, flicks a cigarette butt at him, then follows the other*
SOLDIERS *off the stage. The* THIRD GENERAL
*is the last thing we see, huddled over his
quiet gun, pointed at the empty grave, as
the light dims—in the silence.*)

Curtain

The Fall of The City

A Verse Play for Radio

BY ARCHIBALD MacLEISH

For

A. B. L. and R. A. L.

The first performance over the air occurred Sunday Evening, April 11, 19
from 7 to 7:30 Eastern Standard Time, over the Columbia Broadcasting Syst
Network.

Production under the direction of Irving Reis, director of the Colum
Workshop.

CAST OF CHARACTERS

VOICE OF STUDIO DIRECTOR	House Jameson
VOICE OF ANNOUNCER	Orson Welles
VOICE OF DEAD WOMAN	Adelaide Klein
VOICE OF FIRST MESSENGER	Carleton Young
VOICE OF ORATOR	Burgess Meredith
VOICE OF SECOND MESSENGER	Dwight Weist
VOICE OF PRIEST	Edgar Stehli
VOICE OF GENERAL	William Pringle
VOICES OF ANTIPHONAL CHORUS.	Guy Repp Brandon Peters Karl Swenson Dan Davies Kenneth Delmar

CITIZENS, DANCERS, PRIESTS, SOLDIERS, ETC.

Music composed and directed by Bernard Herman.

Crowd supervision by William N. Robson.

Editorial supervision by Brewster Morgan.

Stage management by Earl McGill.

THE FALL OF THE CITY

CE OF THE STUDIO DIRECTOR *(orotund and
fessional).*

ies and gentlemen:
  broadcast comes to you from the city
eners over the curving air have heard
m furthest-off frontiers of foreign
ours—
untain Time: Ocean Time: of the is-
nds:
waters after the islands—some of them
aking
ere noon here is the night there: some
ere noon is the first few stars they see or
ie last one.

three days the world has watched this
ty—
for the common occasions of brutal
ime
the usual violence of one sort or another
oronations of kings or popular festivals:
for stranger and disturbing reasons—
resurrection from death and the tomb
a dead woman.

n day for three days there has come
the door of her tomb at noon a woman
iried!

terror that stands at the shoulder of our
ne
ches the cheek with this: the flesh
inces.
re have been other omens in other cities
never of this sort and never so credible.

time like ours seemings and portents
gnify.
s is a generation when dogs howl and
e
crawls on the skull with its beast's
reboding.
men now alive with us have feared.
have smelled the wind in the street that
anges weather.
have seen the familiar room grow un-
miliar:
order of numbers alter: the expectation
t the expectant eye. The appearance de-
ilts with us.

in this city the wall of the time cracks.

ake you now to the great square of this
y. . . .

e shuffle and hum of a vast patient

*crowd gradually rises: swells: fills the back-
ground.)*

VOICE OF THE ANNOUNCER *(matter-of-fact).*

We are here on the central plaza.
We are well off to the eastward edge.
There is a kind of terrace over the crowd
  here.
It is precisely four minutes to twelve.
The crowd is enormous: there might be ten
  thousand:
There might be more: the whole square is
  faces.
Opposite over the roofs are the mountains.
It is quite clear: there are birds circling.
We think they are kites by the look: they
  are very high. . . .

The tomb is off to the right somewhere—
We can't see for the great crowd.
Close to us here are the cabinet ministers:
They stand on a raised platform with awn-
  ings.
The farmers' wives are squatting on the
  stones:
Their children have fallen asleep on their
  shoulders.
The heat is harsh: the light dazzles like
  metal.
It dazes the air as the clang of a gong
  does. . . .

News travels in this nation:
There are people here from away off—
Horse-raisers out of the country with brooks
  in it:
Herders of cattle from up where the snow
  stays—
The kind that cook for themselves mostly:
They look at the girls with their eyes hard
And a hard grin and their teeth show-
  ing. . . .

It is one minute to twelve now:
There is still no sign: they are still waiting:
No one doubts that she will come:
No one doubts that she will speak too:
Three times she has not spoken.

*(The murmur of the crowd changes—
not louder but more intense: higher.)*

THE VOICE OF THE ANNOUNCER *(low but with
increasing excitement).*

Now it is twelve: now they are rising:
Now the whole plaza is rising:

Fathers are lifting their small children:
The plumed fans on the platform are motionless. . . .

There is no sound but the shuffle of shoe
  leather . . .

Now even the shoes are still. . . .

We can hear the hawks: it is quiet as that
  now. . . .

It is strange to see such throngs so silent. . . .

Nothing yet: nothing has happened. . . .

Wait! There's a stir here to the right of us:
They're turning their heads: the crowd
  turns:
The cabinet ministers lean from their bal-
  cony:
There's no sound: only the turning. . . .

(*A woman's voice comes over the silence of
the crowd: it is a weak voice but penetrat-
ing: it speaks slowly and as though with
difficulty.*)

THE VOICE OF THE DEAD WOMAN

First the waters rose with no wind. . . .

THE VOICE OF THE ANNOUNCER (*whispering*).

Listen: that is she! She's speaking!

THE VOICE OF THE DEAD WOMAN

Then the stones of the temple kindled
Without flame or tinder of maize-leaves. . . .

THE VOICE OF THE ANNOUNCER (*whispering*).

They see her beyond us: the crowd sees
  her. . . .

THE VOICE OF THE DEAD WOMAN

Then there were cries in the night haze:
Words in a once-heard tongue: the air
Rustling above us as at dawn with herons.

Now it is I who must bring fear:
I who am four days dead: the tears
Still unshed for me—all of them: I
For whom a child still calls at nightfall.

Death is young in me to fear!
My dress is kept still in the press in my bed-
  chamber:

No one has broken the dish of the dead
  woman.
Nevertheless I must speak painfully:
I am to stand here in the sun and speak

(*There is a pause. Then her voice comes
again loud, mechanical, speaking as by
rote.*)

The city of masterless men
Will take a master.
There will be shouting then:
Blood after!

(*The crowd stirs. Her voice goes on weak
and slow as before.*)

Do not ask what it means: I do not know
Only sorrow and no hope for it.

THE VOICE OF THE ANNOUNCER

She has gone. . . . No, they are still looking

THE VOICE OF THE DEAD WOMAN

It is hard to return from the time past
  have come
In the dream we must learn to dream where
  the crumbling of
Time like the ash from a burnt string h
Stopped for me. For you the thread st
  burns:
You take the feathery ash upon your finger
You bring yourselves from the time past
  it pleases you.

It is hard to return to the old nearness .

Harder to go again. . . .

THE VOICE OF THE ANNOUNCER

    She is gone.
We know because the crowd is closing.
All we can see is the crowd closing.
We hear the releasing of held breath—
The weight shifting: the lifting of s
  leather.
The stillness is broken as surface of w
  is broken—
The sound circling from in outward.

(*The murmur of the crowd rises.*)

Small wonder they feel fear.
Before the murders of the famous kin
Before imperial cities burned and fell—

: dead were said to show themselves and
›eak.
en dead men came disaster came. Pres-
 atiments
 t let the living on their beds sleep on
 ke dead men out of death and gave them
 ›ices.
 ancient men in every nation knew this.

›ICE OVER THE CROWD

 terless men . . .

›ICE OVER THE CROWD

 en shall it be . . .

ICE OVER THE CROWD

 terless men
 take a master . . .

ICE OVER THE CROWD

 t has she said to us . . .

ICE OVER THE CROWD

 en shall it be . . .

ICE OVER THE CROWD

 terless men
 take a master.
 d after . . .

ICE OVER THE CROWD

 t has she said to us . . .

ES TOGETHER

 d after!

*: voices run together into the excited
 of the crowd. The Announcer's voice
 .d over it.)*

VOICE OF THE ANNOUNCER

 are milling around us like cattle that
 ell death.
 whole square is whirling and turning
 d shouting.
 of the ministers raises his arms on the
 .tform.

No one is listening: now they are sounding
  drums:
Trying to quiet them likely: No! No!
Something is happening: there in the far
  corner:
A runner: a messenger: staggering: people
  are helping him:
People are calling: he comes through the
  crowd: they are quieter.
Only those on the far edge are still shouting:
Listen! He's here by the ministers now!
  He is speaking. . . .

THE VOICE OF THE MESSENGER

There has come the conqueror!
I am to tell you.
I have raced over sea land:
I have run over cane land:
I have climbed over cone land.
It was laid on my shoulders
By shall and by shan't
That standing by day
And staying by night
Were not for my lot
Till I came to the sight of you.
Now I have come.

Be warned of this conqueror!
This one is dangerous!
Word has out-oared him.
East over sea-cross has
All taken—
Every country.
No men are free there.
Ears overhear them.
Their words are their murderers.
Judged before judgment
Tried after trial
They die as do animals:—
Offer their throats
As the goat to her slaughterer.
Terror has taught them this!

Now he is here!

He was violent in his vessel:
He was steering in her stern:
He was watching in her waist:
He was peering in her prow:
And he dragged her up
Nine lengths
Till her keel lodged
On this nation.

Now he is here
Waylaying and night-lying.
If they hide before dark

He comes before sunup.
Where hunger is eaten
There he sits down:
Where fear sleeps
There he arises.

I tell you beware of him!
All doors are dangers.
The warders of wealth
Will admit him by stealth.
The lovers of men
Will invite him as friend.
The drinkers of blood
Will drum him in suddenly.
Hope will unlatch to him:
Hopelessness open.

I say and say truly
To all men in honesty
Such is this conqueror!
Shame is his people.
Lickers of spittle
Their lives are unspeakable:
Their dying indecent.

Be well warned!
He comes to you slightly
Slanting and sprinting
Hinting and shadowing:
Sly is his hiding:—
A hard lot:
A late rider:

Watch! I have said to you!

THE VOICE OF THE ANNOUNCER

They are leading him out: his legs give:
Now he is gone in the crowd: they are
    silent:
No one has spoken since his speaking:

They stand still circling the ministers.
No one has spoken or called out:—
There is no stir at all nor movement:
Even the farthest have stood patiently:
They wait trusting the old men:
They wait faithfully trusting the answer.
Now the huddle on the platform opens:
A minister turns to them raising his two
    arms. . . .

THE VOICE OF THE ORATOR

Freemen of this nation!
The persuasion of your wills against your
    wisdom is not dreamed of.
We offer themes for your consideration.

What is the surest defender of liberty?
Is it not liberty?
A free people resists by freedom:
Not locks! Not blockhouses!

The future is a mirror where the past
Marches to meet itself. Go armed tow
    arms!
Peaceful toward peace! Free and with mu
    toward freedom!
Face tomorrow with knives and tomorro
    knife-blade.
Murder you foe and your foe will be m
    der!—
Even your friends suspected of false-spe
    ing.
Hands on the door at night and the fl
    boards squeaking.

Those who win by the spear are the sp
    toters.
And what do they win? Spears! What
    is there?
If their hands let go they have nothing
    hold by.
They are no more free than a paralytic p
    ped against a tree is.

With the armored man the arm is up
    by the weapon:
The man is worn by the knife.

Once depend on iron for your freedom
    your
Freedom's iron!
Once overcome your resisters with force
    your
Force will resist you!—
You will never be free of force.
Never of arms unarmed
Will the father return home:
The lover to her loved:
The mature man to his fruit orchard
Walking at peace in that beauty—
The years of his trees to assure him.
Force is a greater enemy than this
    queror—
A treacherous weapon.

Nevertheless my friends there *is* a wea
Weakness conquers!

Against chainlessness who breaks?
Against wall-lessness who vaults?
Against forcelessness who forces?

Against the feather of the thistle
Is blunted sharpest metal.
No edge cuts seed-fluff.

s conqueror unresisted
conquer no longer: a posturer
ing his blows upon burdocks—
ting his guard against shadows.
kers will sound among road-menders:
ers be stifled by laundresses:
se guffaws among chambermaids.
dened with rage he will roar.
will sweat in his uniform foolishly.
will disappear: no one hear of him!

re *is* a weapon my friends.
n conquers!

VOICE OF THE ANNOUNCER (*the Orator's
unintelligible under it*).

sh you could all see this as we do—
whole plaza full of these people—
r colorful garments—the harsh sun-
ht—
water-sellers swinging enormous
urds—
orator there on the stone platform—
temple behind him: the high
ramid—
hawks overhead in the sky teetering
to the windward: swift to the down-
nd—
houses blind with the blank sun on
m. . . .

VOICE OF THE ORATOR

e is a weapon.
on and truth are that weapon.

this conqueror come!
him no hindrance!
r his flag and his drum!
ds . . . win!

VOICE OF THE ANNOUNCER

e's the shout now: he's done:
climbing down: a great speech:
're all smiling and pressing around
n:
women are squatting in full sunlight:
're opening packages: bread we'd say
the look—
bread: bread wrapped between corn
ves:
're squatting to eat: they're quite con-
ted and happy:
en are calling their men from the
nny stones:

There are flutes sounding away off:
We can't see for the shifting and moving—
Yes: there are flutes in the cool shadow:
Children are dancing in intricate figures.

(*A drum and flute are heard under the
voice.*)

Even a few old men are dancing.
You'd say they'd never feared to see them
dancing.
A great speech! really great!
Men forget these truths in passion:
They oppose the oppressors with blind
blows:
They make of their towns tombs: of their
roofs burials:
They build memorial ruins to liberty:
But liberty is not built from ruins:
Only in peace is the work excellent. . . .

That's odd! The music has stopped. There's
something—
It's a man there on the far side: he's point-
ing:
He seems to be pointing back through the
farthest street:
The people are twisting and rising: bread
in their fists. . . .
We can't see what it is. . . . Wait! . . . it's
a messenger.
It must be a messenger. Yes. It's a message
—another.
Here he is at the turn of the street trotting:
His neck's back at the nape: he looks tired:
He winds through the crowd with his
mouth open: laboring:
People are offering water: he pushes away
from them:
Now he has come to the stone steps: to the
ministers:
Stand by: we're edging in. . . .

(*There are sounds of people close by:
coughs: murmurs. The Announcer's voice
is lowered.*)

Listen: he's leaning on the stone: he's speaking.

THE VOICE OF THE MESSENGER

There has come . . . the Conqueror. . . .

I am to tell you . . .

I have run over corn land:
I have climbed over cone land:
I have crossed over mountains. . . .

It was laid on my shoulders
By shall and by shan't
That standing by day
And staying by night
Were not for my lot
Till I came to the sight of you. . . .

Now I have come.

I bear word:
Beware of this conqueror!

The fame of his story
Like flame in the winter-grass
Widens before him.
Beached on our shore
With the dawn over shoulder
The lawns were still cold
When he came to the sheep meadows:—
Sun could not keep with him
So was he forward.
Fame is his sword.

No man opposing him
Still grows his glory.
He needs neither foeman nor
Thickset of blows to
Gather his victories—
Nor a foe's match
To earn him his battles.

He brings his own enemy!

He baggages with him
His closet antagonist—
His private opposer.
He's setting him up
At every road corner—
A figure of horror
With blood for his color:
Fist for his hand:
Reek where he stands:
Hate for his heat:
Sneers for his mouth:
Clouts for his clothes:
Oaths if he speak:—
And he's knocking him down
In every town square
Till hair's on his blade
And blood's all about
Like dust in a drouth
And the people are shouting
Flowers him flinging
Music him singing
And bringing him gold
And holding his heels
And feeling his thighs
Till their eyes start

And their hearts swell
And they're telling his praises
Like lays of the heroes
And chiefs of antiquity.

Such are his victories!
So does he come:
So he approaches. . . .

(*A whisper rustles through the cro*

No man to conquer
Yet as a conqueror
Marches he forward. . . .

(*The whisper is louder.*)

Stands in your mountains. . . .

(*A murmur of voices.*)

Soon to descend on you!

(*A swelling roar.*)

THE VOICE OF THE ANNOUNCER

That touched them! That frightened th
Some of them point to the east hills:
Some of them mock at the ministers: '
dom!'
'Freedom for what? To die in a rat tr
They're frantic with anger and plain
They're sold out they say. You can
them.
'Down with the government! Down
the orators!
'Down with liberal learned minds!
'Down with the mouths and the l
tongues in them!
'Down with the lazy lot! They've sol
'We're sold out! Talking has done
us!' . . .
They're boiling around us like mullet
smell shark.
We can't move for the mob: they're
with terror. . . .

A LOUD VOICE (*distant*).

God-lovers!
Think of your gods!

Earth-masters!
Taste your disasters!

Men!
Remember!

THE VOICE OF THE ANNOUNCER

There's a voice over the crowd somew
They hear it: they're quieting down.

t's the priests!

 see them now: it's the priests on the
yramid!

ere might be ten of them: black with
heir hair tangled.

 smoke of their fire is flat in the quick
vind:

ey stand in the thick of the smoke by
he stone of the victims:

eir knives catch in the steep sun: they
re shouting:
en!—

ES OF THE PRIESTS

n to your gods rememberers!

NGLE VOICE

the world be saved by surrendering the
orld: Not otherwise shall it be saved.

ES OF THE PRIESTS

n to your gods rememberers!

NGLE VOICE

evil be overcome by the coming over of
il: Your hearts shall be elsewhere.

ES OF THE PRIESTS

n to your gods rememberers!

ES OF THE PRIESTS (*antiphonally*).

n to your gods!
    The conqueror cannot take you!
n to your gods!
    The narrow dark will keep you!

n to your gods!
    In god's house is no breaking!

n to your gods!
    In god's silences sleep is!

up your will with the gods!
    Stones cannot still you!

up your will with the gods!
    Blade cannot blind you!

up your will with the gods!
    Danger departs from you!

VOICE OF THE ANNOUNCER

a wonderful thing to see this crowd
ponding.

Even the simplest citizens feel the emotion.
There's hardly a sound now in the square.
    It's wonderful:
Really impressive: the priests there on the
    pyramid:
The smoke blowing: the bright sun: the
    faces—

A SINGLE VOICE

In the day of confusion of reason when all
    is delusion:
In the day of the tyrants of tongues when
    the truth is for hire:
In the day of deceit when ends meet:
Turn to your gods!

In the day of division of nations when hope
    is derision:
In the day of the supping of hate when the
    soul is corrupted:
In the day of despair when the heart's bare:
Turn to your gods!

(*A slow drum beat.*)

THE VOICE OF THE ANNOUNCER

A kind of dance is beginning: a serpent of
    people:
A current of people coiling and curling
    through people:
A circling of people through people like
    water through water. . . .

CHANTING VOICES (*to the drums*).

Out of the stir of the sun
Out of the shout of the thunder
Out of the hush of the star . . .
Withdraw the heart.

THE VOICE OF THE ANNOUNCER (*the chant
and drums under*).

A very young girl is leading them:
They have torn the shawl from her bare
    breast:
They are giving her flowers: her mouth
    laughs:
Her eyes are not laughing. . . .

CHANTING VOICES

Leave now the lovely air
To the sword and the sword-wearer—
Leave to the marksman the mark—
Withdraw the heart.

THE VOICE OF THE ANNOUNCER (*the chant and drums louder*).

She's coming . . . the drums pound . . . the crowd
Shrieks . . . she's reaching the temple . . . she's climbing it. . .
Others are following: five: ten . . .
Hundreds are following . . . crowding the stairway. . . .
She's almost there . . . her flowers have fallen . . .
She looks back . . . the priests are surrounding her. . . .

(*The drums suddenly stop: there is an instant's silence: then an angry shout from the crowd.*)

THE VOICE OF THE ANNOUNCER

Wait! Wait! Something has happened!
One of the ministers: one of the oldest:
The general: the one in the feathered coat:—
He's driving them down with the staff of a banner:
He's climbed after them driving them down:
There's shouting and yelling enough but they're going:
He's telling them off too: you can hear him—

A DEEP VOICE (*chatter of the crowd under it*).

Men! Old men! Listen!
Twist your necks on your nape bones!
The knife will wait in the fist for you.
There is a time for everything—
Time to be thinking of heaven:
Time of your own skins!

Cock your eyes to the windward!

Do you see smoke on those mountains?
The smoke is the smoke of towns.
And who makes it? The conqueror!
And where will he march now? Onward!
The heel of the future descends on you!

THE VOICE OF THE ANNOUNCER

He has them now: even the priests have seen it:
They're all looking away here to the east.
There's smoke too: filling the valleys: like thunderheads! . . .

THE VOICE OF THE GENERAL

You are foolish old men.

You ought to be flogged for your fooli ness.
Your grandfathers died to be free
And you—you juggle with freedom!
Do you think you're free by a law
Like the falling of apples in autumn?

You thought you were safe in your liberti
You thought you could always quibble!
You can't! You take my word for it.
Freedom's the rarest bird!
You risk your neck to snare it—
It's gone while your eyeballs stare!

Those who'd lodge with a tyrant
Thinking to feed at his fire
And leave him again when they're fed
Plain fools or were bred to it—
Brood of the servile races
Born with the hang-dog face. . . .

THE VOICE OF THE ANNOUNCER

They're all pointing and pushing togeth
The women are shouldering baskets: bre children. . . .
They smell smoke in the air: they sr terror. . . .

THE VOICE OF THE GENERAL (*louder over increasing sound*).

There's nothing in this world worse—
Empty belly or purse or the
Pitiful hunger of children—
Than doing the Strong Man's will!

The free will fight for their freedom.
They're free men first. They feed
Meager or fat but as free men.
Everything else comes after—
Food: roof: craft—
Even the sky and the light of it!

(*The voices of the crowd rise to a tumu sounds—drums: shouts: cries.*)

THE VOICE OF THE ANNOUNCER

The sun is yellow with smoke . . . town's burning. . . .
The war's at the broken bridge. . . .

THE VOICE OF THE GENERAL (*shouting*)
You! Are you free? Will you fight?

ere are still inches for fighting!

ere is still a niche in the streets!

ı can stand on the stairs and meet him!

 can hold in the dark of a hall!

 can die!

   —or your children will crawl for it!

 VOICE OF THE ANNOUNCER (*over the ult*).

y won't listen. They're shouting and reaming and circling.
 square is full of deserters with more ming.
ry street from the bridge is full of de-rters.
y're rolling in with the smoke blowing hind them.
 plaza's choked with the smoke and e struggling of stragglers.
y're climbing the platform: driving the inisters: shouting—
  speaks and another:

VOICES OF CITIZENS

city is doomed!
   There's no holding it!

the conqueror have it! It's his!

age is his! It's his century!

institutions are obsolete.
marches a mile while we sit in a eeting.

ions and talk!
berative walks beneath the ivy and the eepers!

age demands a made-up mind.
conqueror's mind is decided on every-ing.

doubt comes after the deed or never.

knows what he wants for his want's at he knows.
gone before they say he's going.
come before you've barred your house.

one man: we are but thousands!

can defend us from one man?

Bury your arms! Break your standards!

Give him the town while the town stands!

THE VOICE OF THE ANNOUNCER

They're throwing their arms away: their
  bows are in bonfires.
The plaza is littered with torn plumes:
  spear-handles. . . .

THE VOICES OF CITIZENS

Masterless men! . . .

Masterless men
Must take a master! . . .

Order must master us! . . .

Freedom's for fools:
Force is the certainty!

Freedom has eaten our strength and corrupted our virtues!

Men must be ruled!

Fools must be mastered!

Rigor and fast
Will restore us our dignity!

Chains will be liberty!

THE VOICE OF THE ANNOUNCER

The last defenders are coming: they whirl
  from the streets like
Wild leaves on a wind: the square scatters
  them.
Now they are fewer—ten together or five:
They come with their heads turned: their
  eyes back.

Now there are none. The street's empty—
  in shadow.
The crowd is retreating—watching the
  empty street:
The shouts die.

    The voices are silent.

      They're watching. . . .

They stand in the slant of the sunlight
  silent and watching.
The silence after the drums echoes the drum
  beat.

Now there's a sound. They see him. They
  must see him!
They're shading their eyes from the sun:
  there's a rustle of whispering:
We can't see for the glare of it. . . . Yes!
  Yes! . . .
He's there in the end of the street in the
  shadow. We see him!
He looks huge—a head taller than anyone:
Broad as a brass door: a hard hero:
Heavy of heel on the brick: clanking with
  metal:
The helm closed on his head: the eyeholes
  hollow.

He's coming! . . .
          He's clear of the shadow! . . .
                  The sun takes him.

They cover their faces with fingers. They
  cower before him.
They fall: they sprawl on the stone. He's
  alone where he's walking.
He marches with rattle of metal. He
  tramples his shadow.
He mounts by the pyramid—stamps on the
  stairway—turns—
His arm rises—his visor is opening. . . .

(*There is an instant's breathless silence:
then the voice of the Announcer low—
almost a whisper.*)

                  There's no one! . . .
There's no one at all! . . .
                  No one! . . .
                  The helmet is hollow!
The metal is empty! The armor is empty! I
  tell you
There's no one at all there: there's only the
  metal:
The barrel of metal: the bundle of armor.
  It's empty!

The push of a stiff pole at the nipple wo
  topple it.

They don't see! They lie on the pavi
  They lie in the
Burnt spears: the ashes of arrows. They
  there . . .
They don't see or they won't see. They
  silent. . . .

The people invent their oppressors: t
  wish to believe in them.
They wish to be free of their freedom:
  leased from their liberty:—
The long labor of liberty ended!
                  They lie there!

(*There is a whisper of sound. The
nouncer's voice is louder.*)

Look! It's his arm! It is rising! His a
  rising!
They're watching his arm as it rises. T
  stir. They cry.
They cry out. They are shouting. The
  shouting with happiness.
Listen! They're shouting like troops
  victory. Listen—
'The city of masterless men has foun
  master!'
You'd say it was they were the conque
  they that had conquered.

A ROAR OF VOICES

The city of masterless men has fou
  master!
The city has fallen!
The city has fallen!

THE VOICE OF THE ANNOUNCER (*flat*).

The city has fallen. . . .

Golden Boy

BY CLIFFORD ODETS

For Luise

GOLDEN BOY was first presented by the Group Theatre at the Belasco
Theatre on the evening of November 4th, 1937, with the following members
of the Group Theatre Acting Company:

(In order of speech)

TOM MOODY	Roman Bohnen	EDDIE FUSELI	Elia Kazan
LORNA MOON	Frances Farmer	PEPPER WHITE	Harry Bratsburg
JOE BONAPARTE	Luther Adler	MICKEY	Michael Gordon
TOKIO	Art Smith	CALL BOY	Bert Conway
MR. CARP	Lee J. Cobb	SAM	Martin Ritt
SIGGIE	Jules Garfield	LEWIS	Charles Crisp
MR. BONAPARTE	Morris Carnovsky	DRAKE	Howard Da Silva
ANNA	Phoebe Brand	DRISCOLL	Charles Niemeyer
FRANK BONAPARTE	John O'Malley	BARKER	Karl Malden
ROXY GOTTLIEB	Robert Lewis		

Direction by HAROLD CLURMAN
Settings by MORDECAI GORELIK

SCENES

ACT ONE

SCENE 1. The office of Tom Moody.
SCENE 2. The Bonaparte home. That night.
SCENE 3. The office. Two months later.
SCENE 4. A park bench. A few nights later.
SCENE 5. The Bonaparte home. Midnight, six weeks later.

ACT TWO

SCENE 1. A gymnasium. Five months later.
SCENE 2. The park bench. A few nights later.
SCENE 3. The office. The following day.
SCENE 4. A dressing room in the Arena. Six weeks later.

ACT THREE

SCENE 1. The office. Six months later.
SCENE 2. The dressing room. The following night.
SCENE 3. The Bonaparte home. Several hours later.

GOLDEN BOY

ACT ONE

SCENE I

The small Broadway office of Tom Moody, *the fight manager.*
The office is scantily furnished, contains desk, chairs, telephone and couch. With Moo[dy]
at present is his girl, Lorna Moon. *There is a certain quiet glitter about this girl, and*
she is sometimes hard, it is more from necessity than choice. Her eyes often hold a s[ad]
sad glance. Likewise Moody's *explosiveness covers a soft, boyish quality, and at the sa[me]*
time he possesses a certain vulnerable quality which women find very attractive.
The time is eighteen months ago.
As the lights fade in, we catch these two at the height of one of their frequent fights[.]

MOODY. Pack up your clothes and go! Go! Who the hell's stopping you?

LORNA. You mean it?

MOODY. You brought up the point yourself.

LORNA. No, I didn't!

MOODY. Didn't you say you had a good mind to leave me?

LORNA. No, I said—

MOODY. You said you were going to pack!

LORNA. I said I feel a tramp and I don't like it. I want to get married, I want—

MOODY. Go home, Lorna, go home! I ain't got time to discuss it. Gimme some air. It's enough I got my wife on my neck.

LORNA. What does she say?

MOODY. Who?

LORNA. Your wife—your sweet Goddam Monica!

MOODY. She wants five thousand dollars to give me the divorce. (LORNA *laughs.*) I don't see that it's funny.

LORNA. Look, Tom, this means as much to me as it does to you. If she's out of the way, we can get married. Otherwise I'm a tramp from Newark. I don't like the feeling.

MOODY. Lorna, for pete's sake, use your noodle! When I get rid of Monica, we'll marry. Now, do I have to bang you on the nose to make you understand?

LORNA. Go to hell! . . . But come back to-night. (MOODY's *answer is to look at her, then smile, then walk to her. They kiss.*)

MOODY. If I had the money, I'd buy [you] something—I don't know what—a big [os]trich feather! If Kaplan wins tonight, [I'll] take you dancing at the Park.

LORNA. He won't win.

MOODY. How do you know? *I* don't kn[ow] —how do *you* know?

LORNA. Are you crazy? Do you think y[our] Mr. Kaplan can go ten rounds with [the] Baltimore Chocolate Drop?

MOODY. How do I know?

LORNA. It's the Twentieth Century, To[m,] no more miracles. (MOODY's *face turns wor*]*ried.* LORNA *smiles.*) You know what I [like] about you—you take everything so ser[ious.]

MOODY. Who will if I don't? I've been [on] the gold standard for eight years. This [used] to be a gorgeous town. New York was [lousy] with money. Kaplan gets four hun[dred] bucks tonight. In the old days, that [was] nothing. Those were the days when I [had] Marty Welch, the heavyweight contend[er,] Cy Webster who got himself killed [in a] big, red Stutz. In '27 and 8 you cou[ldn't] go to sleep—the town was crawling [with] attractions. . . .

LORNA. My mother died in '28.

MOODY. I haven't had a break in y[ears.] "Carry me back to old Virginny"—t[hat's] how I feel. There isn't much of a fu[ture.] (*Suddenly despondent,* MOODY *goes ba[ck to]* *his desk.*)

LORNA. I was fooling.

LORNA. Do you think I'd leave you?

MOODY. What about?

DY. Why not? I'm an old man. What
I give you?

NA. A bang on the nose for a start. But
t can I give you?

DY. A boy who can fight. Find me a
l black boy and I'll show you a mint.

NA. Are good boys so hard to find?

DY. Honest to God, you make me sick
ny stomach! What do you think I took
p to Philadelphia? What do you think
ent to Chicago? Wasn't i up in Boston
a week? You think good boys are laying
nd like pop-corn? I'd even take a ban-
weight, if I found one.

NA. How about a nice lady fighter with
ard— (*Preparing to leave.*) Well, I'll
you tonight, Moody.

DY (*thoughtfully*). I'd give me right
for a good black boy.

NA. Let me have your right eye for a
ute. (*She kisses his eye.* MOODY *begins
embrace her—she eludes his grasp.*)
t's to keep you hot. But if the truth
known—"yours till hell freezes over."

DY. I need you, I need you, Lorna—I
l you all the time. I'd like to give you
ything you want. Push your mouth
. . . . (LORNA *holds her face to his; he
s her. Suddenly a youth is standing at
office door.* LORNA *sees him and breaks
.*)

(*breathing quickly*). Mr. Moody . . .

DY (*spinning around*). Don't you knock
n you come in an office?

Sometimes I knock, sometimes I don't.

DY. Say your piece and get the hell out!

I just ran over from the gym . . .

DY. What gym?

Where Kaplan trains. He just broke his
l. . . . (MOODY *stiffens to attention.*)
a fact.

DY (*grasping the phone*). Is Tokio over
? My trainer?

He's looking after Kaplan. (MOODY *be-
to dial the phone but abruptly changes
nind and replaces the phone.*)

MOODY. You can put me in the bug-house
right now. Moody is the name, folks—step
right up and wipe your shoes! Ah, that
Kaplan! That phonus bolonus! (*He sits at
his desk in despair.*) Now I have to call up
Roxy Gottlieb and cancel the match. His
club's in the red as it is.

BOY. I don't think it's necessary to cancel,
Tom.

MOODY (*aware of the* BOY *for the first time*).
Oh, you don't? Who the hell are you? And
who the hell are you to call me Tom? Are
we acquainted?

BOY. I wrote you a couple of letters. I can
do that stretch.

MOODY. What stretch?

BOY. Why don't you let me take Kaplan's
place tonight?

MOODY (*sarcastically*). Go slow and tell me
again . . . what?

BOY (*coolly*). I can take Kaplan's place. . . .

MOODY. You mean you want to fight the
Baltimore Chocolate Drop? *You?* (*The* BOY
remains silent. MOODY *comes out from behind his desk and stands face to face with
the* BOY. *With sudden discovery.*) You're
cock-eyed too.

BOY (*quietly*). Can't you fix it up with Roxy
Gottlieb?

MOODY (*suddenly*). Looka, kid, go home,
kid, before I blame Kaplan's glass mitts on
you. Then you won't like it, and I won't
like it, and Miss Moon here, she won't like
it.

BOY (*turning to* LORNA). How do you do,
Miss Moon. (LORNA *smiles at the* BOY's *quiet
confidence.*) I need a good manager, Mr.
Moody. You used to be tops around town—
everyone says so. I think you can develop
me. I can fight. You don't know it, but I can
fight. Kaplan's been through for years. He
may be the best fighter in your stable, but
he's a stumble-bum for the younger boys
growing up. Why don't you give me this
chance, Tom?

MOODY. I don't want you calling me Tom!
(*He glares at the* BOY *and then returns to
the desk and telephone.*)

BOY. I'm waiting for your answer. (MOODY's *answer is an exasperated glance as he begins to dial the phone. The* BOY *half approaches the desk.*) There are forty-three thousand minutes in a month—can't you give me five?

MOODY. I'll give you this phone in the head in a minute! Who are you? What the hell do you want? Where do you fight?

BOY (*with cool persistence*). We ought to get together, Tom.

MOODY. I don't want you calling me Tom. You're brash, you're fresh, you're callow—and you're cock-eyed! In fact, you're an insult to my whole nature! Now get out! (MOODY *turns back to the phone and begins dialing again. The* BOY *stands there, poised on his toes, not sure of his next move. He turns and looks at* LORNA. *She nods her head and gives him a faint smile of encouragement. On phone.*) This is Tom Moody . . . is Tokio there? . . . (*He hangs up the phone and holds the instrument thoughtfully.*) Tokio's on his way over.

BOY. The Baltimore Chocolate Drop is not as good as you think he is. (MOODY *suddenly whirls around and holds the telephone high over his head in a threatening gesture. The* BOY *steps back lightly and continues.*) I've studied his style for months; I've perfected the exact punch to quench his thirst. Did you ever watch closely? (*Acting it out.*) He likes to pull your lead—he hesitates for a second—he pulls your lead—he slips his face away and then he's in. Suppose you catch that second when he hesitates—he's open for the punch!

MOODY (*sarcastically*). And what do you do with his left hook?

BOY (*simply*). Avoid it.

MOODY (*lowering the phone*). Looka, you idiot, did you ever hear of Phil Mateo?

BOY. I heard of him.

MOODY. The Chocolate Drop marked him lousy in twelve minutes and ten seconds. Was Kid Peters within your ken? And did you ever hear of Eddie Newton? The Chocolate gave him the blues in two rounds. And Frisco Samuels and Mike Mason. . . .

BOY. Did you ever hear of me?

MOODY (*sarcastically*). No, who are you? I would honestly like to know—who are you?

BOY (*quietly*). My name is Bonapa[rte] (MOODY *howls with laughter, and even* L[OR]NA, *sympathetic to the* BOY, *laughs. The* [BOY] *continues.*) I don't think it's funny. . . .

MOODY. Didn't that name used to get y[ou] a little giggle in school? Tell the tru[th,] Bonaparte. Didn't it?

BOY. Call me Joe.

MOODY (*laughing*). And your eyes . [. .] Didn't they used to get a little giggle t[oo?]

JOE. You don't seem as intelligent a[s I] thought you were.

LORNA (*to the laughing* MOODY, *seeing* BOY's *pain*). Stop it, Tom.

MOODY (*laughing*). You can't blame [me,] Bonaparte. . . . I haven't laughed for ye[ars.]

JOE. I don't like it. . . . I don't want [you] to do it. (*Suddenly* JOE *grabs* MOODY *by* [the] *coat lapels.* MOODY, *surprised, shakes* [him] *off. At the same time a small, quiet* [man] *enters the office. He is* TOKIO, MOO[DY's] *trainer.*)

JOE. I'm sorry I did that, Tom. We ou[ght] to be together, Tom—not apart.

MOODY. Tokio, did you send this kid h[ere?]

TOKIO. No.

MOODY. Take him out before I brain h[im!] (*He storms back to his desk.*)

TOKIO (*after looking at the* BOY). You [know] about Kaplan?

MOODY. This idiot told me. It's the en[d of] everything! I'm off my top with the w[hole] thing! Kaplan was our meal-ticket, I'm [up] to the throat in scandal, blackmail, perj[ury] and all points west!

TOKIO (*turning to* JOE). You oughta [be] ashamed to show your face in this offi[ce.]

JOE. If Kaplan's mother fed him milk [he] wouldn't have those brittle bones.

MOODY. ? ? ? ?

TOKIO (*to* MOODY). This is the boy who [did] it to Kaplan.

MOODY. ? ? ?

TOKIO. I went down for an apple a[nd] come back and Kaplan's sparring with [this] kid—picked him up in the gym. The

ing I know, Kaplan's down on the floor
th a busted mitt.

E (*modestly*). I took it on the elbow.

OODY. ! ! (*Silence finally.*)

RNA. Where do you come from, Bona-
rte?

E. Here.

RNA. How old are you?

E. Twenty-one—tomorrow.

OODY (*after a look at* LORNA). Fight much?

E. Enough.

OODY. Where?

E (*fabricating*). Albany, Syracuse . . .

RNA. Does Roxy Gottlieb know you?

E. I never fought at his club.

OODY (*harshly*). Does he know you?

E. No. (TOKIO *and* MOODY *look at each*
er. The phone rings.)

OODY (*on the phone*). Hello. . . . "What's
s you hear?" . . . You hear the truth,
xy. . . . He bust his mitt again. . . . I
'1't help it if you got *fifty* judgments on
ur club. . . . The same to you. . . . Your

mother, too! (*Keeping his eyes on* BONA-
PARTE.) If you tie up your big flabby mouth
for a minute, I'll give you some news. I'm
in a position to do you a big favor. I got a
replacement—*better* than Kaplan . . . Bonaparte. . . . No, Bon-a-parte. (*Holds hand*
over mouthpiece and asks BOY.) Is that
crap?

JOE. No, that's my name.

MOODY (*back at phone*). That's right, like
in Napoleon. . . . (*Looks the* BOY *over ap-*
praisingly.) One hundred and thirty . . .

JOE. Three.

MOODY. Hundred and thirty-three. Your customers'll eat him up. I'll bring him right
over . . . you can take my word—the kid's
a cock-eyed wonder . . . *your* mother too!
(*He hangs up and turns around.* JOE *is the*
focus of all eyes.) It's revenge on somebody
—maybe God.

JOE (*quietly*). I think you'll be surprised.

MOODY (*sadly*). Do your worst, kid. I've
been surprised by experts.

JOE. Don't worry, Tom.

MOODY. Call me Tom again and I'll break
your neck!

QUICK FADEOUT

SCENE II

Later that night.

The combination dining and front room of the Bonaparte home. A round dining-room
ble, littered with newspapers, is lighted from directly above like a billiard table. Plaster
sts of Mozart and Beethoven are on the sideboard. A cage of love birds at the other
e of the room. Sitting at the table are two men: MR. BONAPARTE, *the father of* JOE,
d a Jewish friend, a MR. CARP, *who owns the local candy and stationery store.*

As the lights fade in, MR. BONAPARTE *turns his newspaper.* MR. CARP *is slowly pouring*
er from a bottle. He begins to sip it as SIGGIE, MR. BONAPARTE's *son-in-law, enters from*
kitchen. He is barefooted, dressed in an undershirt, trousers and hung-down suspen-
rs. He brings his own beer and glass, which he begins to fill with an expert's eye. In
silence, MR. CARP *takes a long, cool sip of beer combined with a murmur of relish.*

RP (*finally*). I don't take it easy. That's
trouble—if I could only learn to take it
y. . . .

GIE. What do you call it now, what you're
ng?

RP. Say, it's after business hours.

GIE. That's a business? A man who runs
candy store is an outcast of the world.

Don't even sell *nickel* candies—*penny* candies!

CARP. And your taxicab business makes you
higher in the social scale?

SIGGIE. So I'm an outcast too. Don't change
the subject. Like my father-in-law here—he's
always changing the subject when I get a
little practical on him. (*Putting his beer*

on the table and scratching himself under the arms like a monkey.) You—I'm talking about you, Mr. Bonaparte.

MR. BONAPARTE *(suddenly shooting out two words).* Ha ha! *(He then resumes his reading.)*

SIGGIE. Every time I talk money, he gives me that horse laugh. Suppose you bought me a cab—I could pay it off by the week.

MR. BONAPARTE *(who talks with an Italian accent).* I don't go in taxicab business.

SIGGIE. I am married to your daughter and when you do this little thing, you do it for her and me together. A cab in two shifts is a big source of profit. Joe takes the night shift. I'm a married man so you don't expect me to take the night shift. *(ANNA, SIGGIE's wife, in a night-gown, pokes her head in at the door.)*

ANNA. Come to bed, Siggie. You'll wake up the whole neighborhood. *(ANNA disappears.)*

SIGGIE. See? I'm a married man! You don't expect me to take the night shift.

MR. BONAPARTE *(having heard this talk for months).* No, Siggie . . . no.

SIGGIE. No, what?

MR. BONAPARTE. No taxicab.

SIGGIE. Don't you wanna help your own family, Foolish? After all, Joe's your own son—he's a man, no kid no more—

MR. BONAPARTE. Tomorrow's twenty-one.

SIGGIE. If he don't work he'll turn into a real bum. Look how late he's staying out at night.

MR. BONAPARTE. I don't expects for Joe to drive taxi.

SIGGIE. He's got to do something. He can drive like a fire engine. Why not?

MR. BONAPARTE. He gonna do something.

SIGGIE. What? Play his violinsky in the backyards?

ANNA *(looking in at the door again).* Come to bed, Siggie! Poppa, don't talk to him so he'll come to bed! *(ANNA disappears again.)*

SIGGIE *(annoyed).* Women! Always buzzing around. *(MR. BONAPARTE's only answer is to turn over the newspaper on the table before him.)*

CARP *(reflectively).* Women . . . the less we have to do with women the better. A Schopenhauer says, "Much ado about nothing . . . the comedy of reproduction." *(He wags his head bitterly.)* Women . . . !

SIGGIE. I'm hungry, but I ain't got the heart to go in the kitchen again. It reminds me of how my wife slaves for this family of crazy wops! A fine future for an intelligent woman!

MR. BONAPARTE. She'sa your wife, but also my daughter. She'sa not so intelligent as you say. Also, *you* are not so intelligent!

SIGGIE. You can't insult me, I'm too ignorant! *(ANNA now comes fully into the room. She is buxom, energetic, good-natured and adenoidal.)*

ANNA. Poppa, why don't you let Siggie come to bed? Looka him, walking around barefooted!

MR. BONAPARTE. I don't stop him. . . .

SIGGIE. Sure he stops me—he stops me every night. I'm worried. I don't sleep. It's my Jewish disposition. He don't wanna help me out, your old man. He wants me to drive company cab and submit to the brutalities of the foremen all my life. I could be in a healthy little enterprise for myself, but your old man don't wanna help me out.

ANNA. Why don't you buy Siggie a cab, poppa? You got the cash.

SIGGIE. Buy it for Siggie and Joe.

ANNA. For Siggie and Joe—it don't have to be a new one.

SIGGIE *(after giving his wife a stabbing glance).* Sure, even an old one—the way they recondition them now-a-days—

MR. BONAPARTE. Children, gone to bed.

SIGGIE. Don't tell a lie—how much you got in the bank?

MR. BONAPARTE *(with a smile).* Millions.

SIGGIE. Four thousand?

MR. BONAPARTE. No.

GGIE. Three? (MR. BONAPARTE *shakes his
ead.*) Three? . . .

NA. What's your business how much he's
t?

GGIE. Shut up, Duchess! Am I asking for
y health? If I wanna take you out of the
tchen, is that the gratitude I get? You
d your father, you get my goat! I'm sore!

NA. Come to bed, Siggie.

GGIE. "Come to bed, come to bed!" What
e hell's so special in bed. (ANNA's *answer
a warm prolonged giggle.*) It's a con-
iracy around here to put me to bed. I'm
rning one thing: if matters go from
orse to worse, don't ever expect me to
pport this family, I'm warning!

R. BONAPARTE (*smiling kindly*). We have-a
ceive the warning. We are in a conspiracy
ainst you—go to bed. (*He turns back to
s newspaper.* SIGGIE *sees he has lost again
d now turns on his wife.*)

GGIE. Who asked you to stick in your two
nts about second-hand cabs? As long as
n not gonna get it, I'll tell you what I
nt—a first-class job, fresh from the fac-
y. (*He suddenly swats her on the head
th a rolled-up newspaper. She hits him
ck. He returns her blow.*)

NA. Don't be so free with your hands!
e hits her again. She hits him back.*) You
some nerve, Siggie!

GIE (*hitting her again*). The next time
break your neck—I'm super-disgusted
th you!

. BONAPARTE (*standing up*). Stop this . . .

GIE (*turning to him*). And with you, I'm
er-finished! (*Turning back to his wife.*)
out here with this Unholy Alliance—
sleep alone tonight. (*He starts for the
r.* MR. BONAPARTE *puts his arm around
NA who begins to sob.*)

. BONAPARTE. Hit your wife in private,
in public!

P. A man hits his wife and it is the first
to fascism!

GIE (*to* CARP). What are you talking
ut, my little prince! I love my wife. You
't stop talking how you hate yours.
ow to MR. BONAPARTE.) And as for you,

don't make believe you care!—Do I have to
fall on my knees to you otherwise? We wanna raise a family—it's a normal instinct.
Take your arm off her.

ANNA (*suddenly moving over to* SIGGIE).
That's right, poppa. He can hit me any
time he likes.

SIGGIE (*his arm around her*). And we don't
want you interfering in our affairs unless
you do it the right way!

ANNA. That's right, poppa—you mind your
g.d. business! (MR. BONAPARTE *repressing a
smile, slowly sits.*)

SIGGIE. In the bed, Duchess.

ANNA (*with a giggle*). Good night.

MR. BONAPARTE *and* MR. CARP. Good night.
(*She exits. After a belligerent look at the
pair at the table,* SIGGIE *follows her.*)

MR. BONAPARTE (*bursting into hushed laughter*). There'sa olda remark—never interfere
in the laws of nature and you gonna be
happy. Love! Ha ha!

CARP (*gloomily*). Happy? A famous man
remarked in the last century, "Pleasure is
negative."

MR. BONAPARTE. I feela good. Like-a to have
some music! Hey, where'sa my boy, Joe?
(*Looks at his watch; is surprised.*) One
o'clock . . . don't come home yet. Hey, he
make-a me worry!

CARP. You think you got worries? Wait,
you're a young man yet. You got a son,
Joe. He practised on his fiddle for ten years?
He won a gold medal, the best in the city?
They gave him a scholarship in the Erick-
son Institute? Tomorrow he's twenty-one,
yeah?

MR. BONAPARTE (*emphatically*). Yeah!

CARP (*leaning forward and dramatically
making his point*). Suppose a war comes?
Before you know it, he's in the army!

MR. BONAPARTE. Naw, naw! Whata you say!
Naw!

CARP (*wagging his head in imitation*). Look
in the papers! On every side the clouds of
war—

MR. BONAPARTE. My Joe gotta biga talent.
Yesterday I buy-a him present! (*With a*

dramatic flourish he brings a violin case out of the bottom part of the sideboard.)

CARP (*as the case is opened.*) It looks like a coffin for a baby.

MR. BONAPARTE (*looking down at the violin in its case*). His teacher help me to picka him.

CARP (*the connoisseur*). Fine, fine—beautiful, fine! A cultural thing!

MR. BONAPARTE (*touching it fondly*). The mosta golden present for his birthday which I give him tonight.

CARP. How much, if I'm not getting too personal, did such a violin cost you?

MR. BONAPARTE. Twelve hundred dollars.

CARP (*shocked*). What?

MR. BONAPARTE. You're surprised of me? Well, I waita for this moment many years.

CARP (*sitting*). Ask yourself a pertinent remark: could a boy make a living playing this instrument in our competitive civilization today?

MR. BONAPARTE. Why? Don't expect for Joe to be a millionaire. He don't need it, to be millionaire. A good life'sa possible—

CARP. For men like us, yes. But nowadays is it possible for a young man to give himself to the Muses? Could the Muses put bread and butter on the table?

MR. BONAPARTE. No millionaire is necessary. Joe love music. Music is the great cheer-up in the language of all countries. I learn that from Joe. (CARP *sighs as* MR. BONAPARTE *replaces the violin in the buffet.*)

CARP. But in the end, as Schopenhauer says, what's the use to try something? For every wish we get, ten remains unsatisfied. Death is playing with us as a cat and her mouse!

MR. BONAPARTE. You make-a me laugh, Mr. Carp. You say life'sa bad. No, life'sa good. Siggie and Anna fight—good! They love—good! You say life'sa bad . . . well, is pleasure for you to say so. No? The streets, winter a' summer—trees, cats—I love-a them all. The gooda boys and girls, they who sing and whistle—(*Bursts into a moment of gay whistling.*)—very good! The eating and sleeping, drinking wine—very good! I gone around on my wagon and talk to

many people—nice! Howa you like the b[ig] buildings of the city?

CARP. Buildings? And suppose it falls? [A] house fell down last week on Staten Islan[d.]

MR. BONAPARTE. Ha ha, you make me laug[h,] ha ha! (*Now enters* FRANK BONAPARTE, *ol[d]est son of the family, simple, intellige[nt,] observant.*)

MR. BONAPARTE. Hello, Frank.

FRANK. Hello, poppa . . . Mr. Carp . . .

CARP (*nodding*). What's new in the worl[d?]

FRANK (*dropping newspapers to the tab[le] but keeping one for himself*). Read 'em a[nd] weep. March first tomorrow—spring on t[he] way. Flowers soon budding, birds twitt[er]ing—south wind . . . Cannons, bombs a[nd] airplane raids! Where's Joe? Did you gi[ve] him the fiddle yet?

MR. BONAPARTE. No, not in yet. Siggie a[nd] Anna sleep. Hungry?

FRANK (*beginning to undress—putting [his] coat on the back of a chair*). No, I'm tir[ed.] I'll see you in the morning, before I lea[ve.]

CARP. Going away again?

FRANK. South. Tex-tiles. There's hell do[wn] there in textiles. (*He sits on the other s[ide] of the room and looks at a paper.*)

CARP. I don't begin to understand it—t[ex-] tiles! What's it his business if the work[ers] in tex-tiles don't make good wages!

MR. BONAPARTE. Frank, he fighta for eat, [for] good life. Why not!

CARP. Foolish!

MR. BONAPARTE. What ever you got ina y[our] nature to do isa not foolish!

CARP (*flipping over the newspaper*). For [in]stance—look: playing baseball isn't fooli[sh?]

MR. BONAPARTE. No, if you like-a to do.

CARP. Look! Four or five pages—baseba[ll,] tennisball—it gives you an idea what a ci[vil]ization! You ever seen a baseball game[?]

MR. BONAPARTE. No.

CARP (*wagging his head*). Hit a ball, ca[tch] a ball . . . believe me, my friend—nonse[nse!]

FRANK. Poppa, where did you say Joe w[as?]

R. BONAPARTE. Don't know—

RANK. Poppa, you better brace yourself in ur chair!

R. BONAPARTE. What? (FRANK *places the per before* MR. BONAPARTE. *He reads oud.*)

RANK. Looka this, Joe's had a fight. "Flash: hocolate Drop fails to K.O. new cock-ed wonder." Take a look at the picture.

ARP. What?

R. BONAPARTE. What?

RANK. It's my little brother Joie, or I don't now a scab from a picket!

R. BONAPARTE. Had a fight? That is foolish -not possible.

RANK (*pointing with his finger*). There's s name—Bonaparte.

R. BONAPARTE (*puzzled*). Musta be some her boy. (FRANK *suddenly flips over the ewspaper. The others immediately see the ason:* JOE *stands in the entrance, in the adows.*)

OE (*in the shadows*). Gee, you're up te. . . .

R. BONAPARTE. We waita for you. (JOE owly *moves into the light. His face is ruised and over one eye is a piece of ad- sive tape.*)

OE (*seeing their looks*). I had a fight— boy in the park—

R. BONAPARTE. He hit you?

OE. I hit him.

R. BONAPARTE. You hurt?

OE. No. (MR. BONAPARTE *casts a furtive look the direction of the other men.*)

R. BONAPARTE. Whata you fight him for?

OE. Didn't like what he said to me.

R. BONAPARTE. What he said?

OE (*evasively*). It's a long story and I'm red.

R. BONAPARTE (*trying to break a pause of mbarrassment*). I was say to Mr. Carp to- orrow is your birthday. How you like to e so old?

JOE. I forgot about that! I mean I forgot for the last few hours. Where do you think I was? Do you want the truth?

FRANK. Truth is cheap. We bought it for two cents. (*He turns over the paper and shows* JOE *his own face.* JOE *looks at the picture, likes it. General silence.*)

JOE (*finally, belligerently*). Well, what are you going to do about it?

MR. BONAPARTE (*still puzzled*). Abouta what?

JOE (*challengingly*). Tomorrow's my birth-day!

FRANK. What's that got to do with being a gladiator?

JOE (*turning to* FRANK, *with sudden vehe-mence*). Mind your business! You don't know me—I see you once a year; what do you know about me?

FRANK (*smiling*). You're a dumb kid!

MR. BONAPARTE (*starting to his feet*). Hey, waita one-a minute. What'sa for this excite-a-ment?

JOE (*hotly*). I don't want to be criticized! Nobody takes me serious here! I want to do what I want. I proved it tonight I'm good— I went out to earn some money and I earned! I had a professional fight tonight —maybe I'll have some more.

CARP. You honest to God had a fight?

JOE (*glaring at* CARP). Why not?

FRANK (*to* JOE). No one's criticizin'.

MR. BONAPARTE. That's right.

JOE (*half sheepishly*). I don't know why I got so sore. . . .

FRANK. You're expecting opposition all the time—

MR. BONAPARTE. Sit down, Joe—resta you'self.

JOE. Don't want to sit. Every birthday I ever had I sat around. Now'sa time for standing. Poppa, I have to tell you—I don't like myself, past, present and future. Do you know there are men who have wonder-ful things from life? Do you think they're better than me? Do you think I like this feeling of no possessions? Of learning about the world from Carp's encyclopaedia? Frank don't know what it means—he travels around, sees the world! (*Turning to* FRANK.) You don't know what it means to sit around here and watch the months go ticking by! Do you think that's a life for a boy my age? Tomorrow's my birthday! I change my life!

MR. BONAPARTE. Justa like that?

JOE. Just like that!

FRANK. And what do you do with music?

JOE. Who says I'm married to music? I take a vacation—the notes won't run away!

FRANK. You're a mysterious kid. Where did you learn the fighting game?

JOE. These past two years, all over the city —in the gyms—

MR. BONAPARTE. Hey, Joe, you sounda like crazy! You no gotta nature for fight. You're

musician. Whata you say, heh? Whata yo do?

JOE. Let's call it a day.

MR. BONAPARTE. Isa no true whata I say?—

JOE. That's all for tonight. (*His lips tigh ened, he abruptly exits.*)

MR. BONAPARTE (*calling after him*). Ta a gooda sleep, Joe.

FRANK (*smiling*). It looks like the gold bu has visited our house.

CARP (*sadly*). Fortunes! I used to hear it my youth—the streets of America is pave with gold. Say, you forgot to give him t present.

MR. BONAPARTE (*slowly, puzzled*). I don' know . . he say he gonna fight. . . .

SLOW FADEOUT

SCENE III

Two months later; MOODY's *office as seen before.*

MOODY *is pacing back and forth in one of his fuming moods. Those present inclu* LORNA, *stretched out on the couch, blowing cigarette smoke into the air;* TOKIO *sittin quietly on the window sill; and* ROXY GOTTLIEB, *comfortably spread out in the desk cha wearing a big white panama hat which he seldom removes.*

ROXY. They don't like him. They seen him in five fights already. He's a clever boy, that Bonaparte, and speedy—but he's first-class lousy in the shipping department! I bought a piece of him, so I got a right to say it: a mosquito gives out better! Did you read what he wrote in his column, that Drake? He writes he's a regular "brain trust."

LORNA. What's wrong with that?

ROXY. I'll tell you in a capsule: the people who'll pay to watch a "brain trust" you could fit in a telephone booth! Roxy Gott-lieb is telling you!

MOODY. Roxy's right. Joe pulls his punches. Two months already and he don't throw his hands right and he don't throw them enough.

LORNA. Tom, what do you want the boy to do? You surely know by now he's not a slugger. His main asset is his science—he's a student.

ROXY (*loftily*). Excuse me, Miss Moon. the prizefight ring the cash customer do look for stoodents. Einstein lives in a c lege—a wonderful man in *his* line! Als while I think of it, a woman's place is in t hay, not in the office!

MOODY (*indignantly*). Where do you cor off to make a remark like that?

LORNA (*standing up*). At the moment woman's place is in the bar—see you lat (*She looks at the others with a pecul smile and exits.* MOODY *stares at* ROXY w *realizes he has said the wrong thing.*)

MOODY. I'm worried about that boy!

TOKIO. I'd trust him, Tom. Joe knows own needs, as he says. Don't ask him change his style. A style is best when individual, when it comes out of the inr personality and the lay of the muscles a the set of the bones. That boy stands chance to make the best lightweight sir Benny Simon.

ROXY. On *your* nose!

TOKIO. He's got one of the best defenses I ever seen. And speedy as the wind.

MOODY. But he won't fight!

ROXY. A momma doll gives out better!

TOKIO. He's a peculiar duck—I want him thinking he's the best thing in shoe leather.

MOODY. He thinks so now.

TOKIO. I don't like to contradict you, Tom, but he don't. It's seventy-five percent front. If you want the goods delivered you have to treat him delicate, gentle—like a girl.

ROXY. Like a girl? Why didn't you say so before?

MOODY. No, Roxy, not you—you just treat him like a human being.

TOKIO. I think we can begin the build-up now.

MOODY. A road tour?

TOKIO. I'd like to take him around the Middle West, about fifteen bouts.

ROXY (*answering a look from* MOODY). I didn't say no. But will he cooperate?

TOKIO. As soon as I find the password.

MOODY. What's the password to make this kid go in and slug—that's the problem. (*There is a knock at the door.* MOODY *calls.*) Yes? (*The door opens and* MR. BONAPARTE *stands there hesitantly.*)

MR. BONAPARTE (*timidly*). My name is Joe Bonaparte's father. I come-a to see my son's new friends.

MOODY (*expansively*). Come in, sit down, Mr. Bonaparte.

ROXY (*sitting comfortably*). Take a seat.

MR. BONAPARTE. Am I interrupt?

MOODY. Not at all.

ROXY. What's the matter with your boy?

TOKIO (*to* MR. BONAPARTE). This is Mr. Moody and Mr. Gottlieb.

MR. BONAPARTE (*sitting*). Good afternoon.

MOODY. We were just discussing your son.

MR. BONAPARTE. I please to hear. I like find out froma you how's this boxer business for Joe. Whata good in it for him.

MOODY. Your Joe's a very clever fighter.

ROXY. Can you take it? We want to make your boy famous—a millionaire, but he won't let us—won't cooperate. How do you like it?

MR. BONAPARTE. Why? Whatta he do?

ROXY (*going over and facing the old man in a lecturing position*). I'll ask *you*. What does he do? What does he do that's right? *Nothing!* We offer him on a gold platter! Wine, women and song, to make a figure of speech. We offer him *magnitudes!* . . .

MR. BONAPARTE (*waiting*). Yes—?

MOODY. But he won't fight.

MR. BONAPARTE (*puzzled*). He'sa fighta for you, no?

ROXY. You're right—no! Your boy's got unexplored possibilities—*unexplored!* But you can't make a purse out of somebody's ear.

MOODY (*trying to counteract* ROXY's *volubility*). My colleague is trying to say that Joe keeps holding back in the ring.

MR. BONAPARTE. Holda back?

TOKIO. He nurses his self—

MOODY. He keeps holding back—

TOKIO. His defense is brilliant—

MOODY. Gorgeous—!

ROXY. But where's the offense? You take but you can't give. Figure it out—where would you be in a traffic jam? You know how to reverse—but to shift in second or high?—nothing!

MR. BONAPARTE (*quietly to* ROXY). Hey, you talka too much—nobody's contradicta you.

ROXY (*after a momentary setback*). "Everybody'sa contradicta me!" Even you, and I never met you before. (*With a reproachful glance he retires to the desk where he sits and sulks.*)

MR. BONAPARTE (*singling out* TOKIO *as a man to whom he can speak*). Who are you?

TOKIO. Your son's trainer. . . .

MR. BONAPARTE. You interest to helpa my boy?

TOKIO (*respectfully*). Very much. . . .

MR. BONAPARTE. Me too. Maybe not so as plan by these-a gentleman here. I don't say price fight-sa no good for Joe. Joe like-a to be fame, not feel ashame. . . .

TOKIO. Is Joe afraid of his hands?

MR. BONAPARTE. I don't know. You tella me what'sa what . . . I don't know price fight. His hand coulda get hurt?

MOODY. Every fighter hurts his hands. Sometimes they break—

TOKIO. They heal up in no time.

ROXY (*flaring out*). What's so special about hands? I suppose your kid plays piano!

MR. BONAPARTE. Coulda get hurt? Coulda break?

ROXY. So what?

MR. BONAPARTE (*up on his feet*). Hey, you! I don't like-a you! You no interest in my boy! (*Proudly.*) My boy'sa besta violin' in New York!

MOODY (*suddenly sickened*). What . . . ?

MR. BONAPARTE. Yes, play the violin!

MOODY. That's it! . . .

ROXY (*anguished by this stupidity*). If I had hair I'd tear it out! Five hundred fiddlers stand on Broadway and 48th Street, on the corner, every day, rain or shine, hot or cold. And your boy dares—! (*Turning to* MOODY.) How do you like it? (*He waves his hands in despair and retires to the desk, where he sits in fuming disgusted silence.*)

MOODY (*repressing a feeling of triumph*). Your boy's afraid of his hands because he fiddles?

MR. BONAPARTE. Yes, musta be!

TOKIO. Why did you come and tell us this?

MR. BONAPARTE. Because I like-a to help my boy. I like-a for him to try himself out. Maybe thisa better business for him. Maybe not. He mus' try to find out, to see whata he want . . . I don't know. Don't help Joe to tell him I come here. Don't say it. (*He slowly walks to the door.*)

MOODY. That means you won't stand in h[is] way?

MR. BONAPARTE. My boy coulda break b[is] hand? Gentleman, I'ma not so happy as yo[u] . . . no! (*He slowly exits.*)

MOODY (*joyously*). I'm beginning to see th[e] light! Joe's mind ain't made up that th[e] fist is mightier than the fiddle.

ROXY (*bouncing up and down*). I'll make u[p] his mind. For the money that's involve[d] I'd make Niagara Falls turn around and [go] back to Canada.

TOKIO. Don't try to bully him into anythin[g.]

ROXY. In Roxy Gottlieb he met his matc[h.]

MOODY (*explosively*). What the hell's th[e] matter with you, Roxy! Sit down a minut[e] (ROXY *sits*.)

MOODY. As I see it, the job is to handle hi[m] gently, to make him see how much w[e] prize him—to kill his doubts with goodne[ss.]

ROXY. I got it: the password is honey! . [. .]

MOODY. Right! The Middle West tour is o[n.] Tokio goes along to build up a real offe[n-] sive. I take care of the newspapers her[e,] Chris', I thought it was something seriou[s.] I'm getting to feel like 1928 again. Call [it] intuition: I feel like the Resurrection. (*[He] gets up and begins to stroll about.*) On[ce] we're out of the tunnel, with thirty bou[ts] behind us—

ROXY. If you hear a noise, it's my mou[th] watering— (*The telephone rings.* MOO[DY] answers.)

MOODY. Hello? . . . Yeah . . . I think h[e'll] win— (*Hangs up.*) Who do you think th[at] was? (*Imitating.*) "Fuseli is speaking." E[ddie] die Fuseli!

ROXY. Fuseli? What's he want?

MOODY. Will Joe win against Vincenti Tu[es-] day. Tokio, from now on it's your job.

TOKIO. I got faith in the boy.

MOODY (*to* ROXY). I have to ask one thing [:] when Joe comes over from the gym let [me] do the talking.

TOKIO. And don't mention music! (*LOR[NA] enters.*)

LORNA. Shh! Here's Joe. (JOE BONAPARTE *enters the office. Immediately* MOODY *and* ROXY *put on their softest kid gloves. Their methods of salesmanship will shortly become so apparent that both* JOE *and* LORNA *become suspicious.*)

MOODY (*slowly circling around*). Glad to see you, Joe. Joe, you remember in reference to what we were speaking about yesterday? Well . . . we had several friends on the long distance phone. We're booking fifteen out of town bouts for you. Tough ones, too.

ROXY. Tonight I'm calling my Chicago connections.

MOODY. We talked it over with Tokio and he says—well, tell him what you said, Tokio —tell him the truth.

TOKIO. I think you got a wonderful future.

MOODY (*to* TOKIO). Name the names, Tokio.

TOKIO. Well, I said Benny Simon—as good as Simon, I said.

MOODY. Tokio's gonna work with you—help you develop a right—

ROXY. And a left! What'sa right without a left?

MOODY. Tokio thinks that when he brings you back you'll be a contender for Number one.

JOE (*a little defensively*). Really? . . .

MOODY. But *you* have to help *us* help *you.*

ROXY. Could Webster say it better?

MOODY (*softly singing a siren song, his arms around* JOE's *shoulder*). This job needs gorgeous concentration. All your time and thoughts, Joe. No side lines, no side interests—

JOE (*defensively*). I don't go out with girls.

MOODY. You're in the fighting game. It's like being a priest—your work comes first. What would you rather do than fight?

JOE (*defensively*). I don't know what you mean.

MOODY (*carefully picking his words*). Some boys, for instance, like to save their looks. They'd practically throw the fight to keep their nose intact.

JOE (*smiling wryly*). My looks don't interest me. (LORNA *is listening with rapt attention.*)

MOODY (*still singing the siren song*). Then what's holding you back, Joe? You can tell me, Joe. We've set up housekeeping together, Joe, and I want you to tell me if you can't cook a steak—it don't matter. We're married anyway. . . .

JOE (*uneasily*). Who's being put to bed?

MOODY. What do you mean?

JOE. I don't like this seduction scene. (*To* TOKIO) What are they after?

TOKIO. They think you're afraid of your hands.

MOODY. Are you?

JOE. Half . . .

TOKIO. Why?

ROXY (*bouncing up*). Tell the truth!

JOE. What truth?

MOODY (*holding back* ROXY *with a look*). Are you afraid your hands'll bust, Joe? (JOE *remains silent*). What's a busted hand to a *fighter*? You can't go in and do your best if you're scared of your mitts . . . can you? You tell me. . . .

JOE. No. . . .

MOODY. Whyn't you give up outside ideas, Joe?

ROXY (*suddenly, in a loud voice to* TOKIO). You shoulda seen that bunch of musicians on 48th Street before. Fiddlers, drummers, cornetists—not a dime in a car-load. Bums in the park! Oh, excuse me, Tom, I was just telling Tokio— (JOE *is now aware that the others know of the violin. Now he is completely closed to them.* MOODY *sees this. He says to* ROXY:)

MOODY (*wrathfully*). What would you like to say, my fine-feathered friend?

ROXY (*simulating bewilderment*). What's the matter? What happened? (*Receiving no answer, he looks around several times and adds, with a shrug:*) I think I'll run across the street and pick up an eight-cylinder lunch.

MOODY. Sprinkle it with arsenic. Do that for me, for me, sweetheart!!

ROXY (*hurt*). That's a fine remark from a friend. (*He haughtily exits.*)

JOE. What do you want, Mr. Moody?

MOODY. At the moment, nothing. I'm puffed out. See you tomorrow over the gym.

JOE. Maybe I won't be there. I might give up fighting as a bad job. I'm not over-convinced it's what I want. I can do other things. . . .

TOKIO. I'll see you tomorrow at the gym, Joe. (JOE *looks at both the men, says nothing, exits.*) That Mr. Gottlieb is a case. See you later.

MOODY (*not looking up*). Okay. (TOKIO *exits.* LORNA *and* MOODY *are alone. She blows cigarette smoke to the ceiling.* MOODY *puts his feet up on the desk and leans back wearily.*)

MOODY (*snorting through his nostrils*). The password is honey!

LORNA. What was that all about? (*The telephone rings.*)

MOODY (*of the ringing bell*). If that's for me, tear it up. I ain't in, not even for God.

LORNA (*answering*). Hello? . . . (*Putting her hand on the mouthpiece*). It's Mrs. God —your wife. (MOODY *makes a grimace of distaste but picks up the phone and puts on a sweet voice.*)

MOODY. Yes, Monica, darling. . . . Yeah . . . you and your support. . . . You're gonna fifty-buck me to death! . . . Monica, if I

had fifty bucks I'd buy myself a big juic coffin—what?—so throw me in jail. (*H hangs up the phone.*) Bitch! That'll l number three. She means it too.

LORNA. What was that scene with Bon. parte?

MOODY. Sweetheart, the jig is up! Believe or not, Bonaparte's a violinist. Maybe h was on the radio. I don't know what th hell he was. His old man came here an told us. His mitts are on his mind. Yo can't do a thing with a nut like that.

LORNA. Won't he give up the violin?

MOODY. You heard him stalling. This is th end, Lorna. It's our last chance for a decer life, for getting married—we have to mak that kid fight! He's *more* than a mea ticket—he's everything we want and nee from life! (LORNA *goes over and slaps hi on the back.*)

LORNA. Pick up your chin, little man.

MOODY. Don't Brisbane me, Lorna. I' licked. I'm tired. Find me a mouse hole crawl in. . . .

LORNA. Why don't you ask me when yc want something? You got the brains of flea. Do you want Bonaparte to fight?

MOODY. Do I wanna see tomorrow?

LORNA. I'll make him fight.

MOODY. How?

LORNA. How? . . . I'm "a tramp from Nev ark," Tom. . . . I know a dozen ways. .

SLOW FADEOUT

SCENE IV

A few nights later.
JOE *and* LORNA *sit on a bench in the park. It is night. There is carousel music in t distance. Cars ride by in front of the boy and girl in the late spring night. Out of sig a traffic light changes from red to green and back again throughout the scene and ca its colors on the faces of the boy and girl.*

LORNA. Success and fame! Or just a lousy living. You're lucky you won't have to worry about those things. . . .

JOE. Won't I?

LORNA. Unless Tom Moody's a liar.

JOE. You like him, don't you?

LORNA (*after a pause*). I like him.

E. I like how you dress. The girls look
ce in the summer time. Did you ever
and at the Fifth Avenue Library and
atch those girls go by?

RNA. No, I never did. (*Switching the sub-
ct.*) That's the carousel, that music. Did
u ever ride on one of those?

E. That's for kids.

RNA. Weren't you ever a kid, for God's
ke?

E. Not a happy kid.

RNA. Why?

E. Well, I always felt different. Even my
me was special—Bonaparte—and my
es . . .

RNA. I wouldn't have taken that too seri-
is. . . . (*There is a silent pause.* JOE *looks
aight ahead.*)

E. Gee, all those cars . . .

RNA. Lots of horses trot around here. The
h know how to live. You'll be rich. . . .

E. My brother is an organizer for the
I.O.

RNA. What's that?

E. If you worked in a factory you'd know.
d you ever work?

RNA (*with a smile*). No, when I came
t of the cocoon I was a butterfly and
tterflies don't work.

E. All those cars . . . whizz, whizz. (*Now
rning less casual.*) Where's Mr. Moody
night?

RNA. He goes up to see his kid on Tues-
y nights. It's a sick kid, a girl. His wife
ves it at her mother's house.

E. That leaves you free, don't it?

RNA. What are you hinting at?

E. I'm thinking about you and Mr. Moody.

RNA. Why think about it? I don't. Why
ould you?

E. If you belonged to me I wouldn't think
out it.

RNA. Haven't you got a girl?

E. No.

LORNA. Why not?

JOE (*evasively*). Oh . . .

LORNA. Tokio says you're going far in the
fighting game.

JOE. Music means more to me. May I tell
you something?

LORNA. Of course.

JOE. If you laugh I'll never speak to you
again.

LORNA. I'm not the laughing type.

JOE. With music I'm never alone when I'm
alone— Playing music . . . that's like saying, "I am man. I belong here. How do
you do, World—good evening!" When I
play music nothing is closed to me. I'm not
afraid of people and what they say. There's
no war in music. It's not like the streets.
Does this sound funny?

LORNA. No.

JOE. But when you leave your room . . .
down in the street . . . it's war! Music can't
help me there. Understand?

LORNA. Yes.

JOE. People have hurt my feelings for years.
I never forget. You can't get even with
people by playing the fiddle. If music shot
bullets I'd like it better—artists and people
like that are freaks today. The world moves
fast and they sit around like forgotten
dopes.

LORNA. You're loaded with fireworks. Why
don't you fight?

JOE. You have to be what you are—!

LORNA. Fight! See what happens—

JOE. Or end up in the bughouse!

LORNA. God's teeth! Who says you have to
be one thing?

JOE. My nature isn't fighting!

LORNA. Don't Tokio know what he's talking
about? Don't Tom? Joe, listen: be a fighter!
Show the world! If you made your fame
and fortune—and you can—you'd be anything you want. Do it! Bang your way to
the lightweight crown. Get a bank account. Hire a great doctor with a beard—
get your eyes fixed—

JOE. What's the matter with my eyes?

LORNA. Excuse me, I stand corrected. (*After a pause.*) You get mad all the time.

JOE. That's from thinking about myself.

LORNA. How old are you, Joe?

JOE. Twenty-one and a half, and the months are going fast.

LORNA. You're very smart for twenty-one and a half "and the months are going fast."

JOE. Why not? I read every page of the Encyclopædia Britannica. My father's friend, Mr. Carp, has it. A shrimp with glasses had to do something.

LORNA. I'd like to meet your father. Your mother dead?

JOE. Yes.

LORNA. So is mine.

JOE. Where do you come from? The city is full of girls who look as if they never had parents.

LORNA. I'm a girl from over the river. My father is still alive—shucking oysters and bumming drinks somewhere in the wilds of Jersey. I'll tell you a secret: I don't like you.

JOE (*surprised*). Why?

LORNA. You're too sufficient by yourself . . . too inside yourself.

JOE. You like it or you don't.

LORNA. You're on an island—

JOE. Robinson Crusoe . . .
LORNA. That's right—"me, myself, and I." Why not come out and see the world?

JOE. Does it seem that way?

LORNA. Can't you see yourself?

JOE. No. . . .

LORNA. Take a bird's-eye view; you don't know what's right or wrong. You don't know what to pick, but you won't admit it.

JOE. Do you?

LORNA. Leave me out. This is the anatomy of Joe Bonaparte.

JOE. You're dancing on my nose, huh?

LORNA. Shall I stop?

JOE. No.

LORNA. You're a miserable creature. Yo want your arm in *gelt* up to the elbow You'll take fame so people won't laugh scorn your face. You'd give your soul f those things. But every time you turn yo back your little soul kicks you in the teet It don't give in so easy.

JOE. And what does your soul do in perfumed vanity case?

LORNA. Forget about me.

JOE. Don't you want—?

LORNA (*suddenly nasty*). I told you forget

JOE (*quietly*). Moody sent you after me— decoy! You made a mistake, Lorna, for t reasons. I make up my own mind to figl Point two, he doesn't know you don't lo him—

LORNA. You're a fresh kid.

JOE. In fact he doesn't know anything abo you at all.

LORNA (*challengingly*). But you do?

JOE. This is the anatomy of Lorna Mo she's a lost baby. She doesn't know wha right or wrong. She's a miserable creatu who never knew what to pick. But sh never admit it. And I'll tell you why y picked Moody!

LORNA. You don't know what you're talki about.

JOE. Go home, Lorna. If you stay, I'll kn something about you. . . .

LORNA. You don't know anything.

JOE. Now's your chance—go home!

LORNA. Tom loves me.

JOE (*after a long silence, looking ahea* I'm going to buy a car.

LORNA. They make wonderful cars tod Even the lizzies—

JOE. Gary Cooper's got the kind I want saw it in the paper, but it costs too much fourteen thousand. If I found one seco hand—

LORNA. And if you had the cash—

JOE. I'll get it—

LORNA. Sure, if you'd go in and really fight!

JOE (*in a sudden burst*). Tell your Mr. Moody I'll dazzle the eyes out of his head!

LORNA. You mean it?

JOE (*looking out ahead*). Those cars are poison in my blood. When you sit in a car and speed you're looking down at the world. Speed, speed, everything is speed—nobody gets me!

LORNA. You mean in the ring?

JOE. In or out, nobody gets me! Gee, I like to stroke that gas!

LORNA. You sound like Jack the Ripper.

JOE (*standing up suddenly*). I'll walk you back to your house—your hotel, I mean.

(LORNA *stands.* JOE *continues.*) Do you have the same room?

LORNA (*with a sneaking admiration*). You're a fresh kid!

JOE. When you're lying in his arms tonight, tell him, for me, that the next World's Champ is feeding in his stable.

LORNA. Did you really read those Brittannia books?

JOE. From A to Z.

LORNA. And you're only twenty-one?

JOE. And a half.

LORNA. Something's wrong somewhere.

JOE. I know. . . . (*They slowly walk out as*)

FADEOUT

SCENE V

The next week.
It is near midnight in the dining room of the Bonaparte home. An open suitcase rests on the table. SIGGIE *is pouring samples of wine for* LORNA MOON. *He himself drinks appreciatively. To one side sits* MR. BONAPARTE *silently, thoughtfully, watchfully—pretending to read the newspaper.*

SIGGIE. I was fit to be knocked down with a feather when I heard it. I couldn't believe until I seen him fight over at the Keystone last week. You never know what somebody's got in him—like the man with germs—suddenly he's down in bed with a crisis! (JOE *enters with an armful of clothes which he begins to pack in the suitcase.*)

LORNA. Joe's road tour will do him lots of good. (ANNA *enters and takes off an apron. Silence, in which* SIGGIE *and* LORNA *sip their wine.*)

ANNA. How do you like that wine, Miss Moon? My father makes better wine than any Eyetalian in New York. My father knows everything—don't you, poppa? (*With a faint smile,* MR. BONAPARTE *shrugs his shoulders.*)

SIGGIE. We're thinking of sending the old man to a leper colony. . . .

ANNA. Don't my husband say funny things? Tell her what you told the janitor Tuesday, Siggie.

SIGGIE. Never mind, never mind.

ANNA. You know how I met Siggie? He was a United Cigar Store clerk and I walked in for a pack of Camels and the first thing you know he said something funny. It was raw, so I can't say it. He had me laughing from the first. Seven years and I haven't stopped laughing yet. (*She laughs loudly, pleasurably.*) This will be the first time Joe ever went traveling. Was you ever out of New York, Miss Moon?

LORNA. Oh, many times.

ANNA. That's nice. Far?

LORNA. California, Detroit, Chicago. I was an airplane hostess for two months.

ANNA. That's nice—it's a real adventure. I'd like to fly.

SIGGIE. Stay on the ground! Fly! What for? Who do you know up there? Eagles?

ANNA. It must be a wonderful way to see life.

LORNA (*drinking*). I've seen life in all its aspects. (MR. BONAPARTE *stands up with a smile.* LORNA'S *eyes follow him as he exits.*)

LORNA (*to* JOE). I think your father left because he don't like me.

JOE. He likes you.

ANNA. My father likes everybody. He's a very deep man. My father has more friends than any man alive. But best of all he likes his horse, Dolly, who drives the fruit wagon. My father can't sit still on Sunday afternoon—he has to go see what that horse is doing. (*Her eyes catch sight of the suitcase.*) Joe, you don't know how to pack. (*She starts over to assist him.*)

SIGGIE (*querulously*). Rest the feet awhile, Duchess.

ANNA (*explaining her move*). He don't know how to pack. (*Beginning to rearrange the suitcase.* MR. BONAPARTE *returns and hands* JOE *a sweater.*)

MR. BONAPARTE. You forget your good sweater.

JOE. Thanks. (MR. BONAPARTE *sits.* JOE *looks at him sideways.*)

ANNA. When you get out to Chicago, buy yourself some new underwear, Joe. I hear everything's cheaper in Chicago. Is that right, Miss Moon?

LORNA (*after taking another drink*). Chicago? I don't know. I was there only one night—I got news that night my mother died. As a matter of fact, she killed herself.

ANNA. That's very sad.

LORNA. No, my father's an old drunk son-of-a-bitch. Did you ask me about my father?

MR. BONAPARTE (*who has been listening intently*). Yes. . . .

LORNA. Twice a week he kicked my mother's face in. If I let myself go I'd be a drunkard in a year.

ANNA. My father never said one bad word to my mother in her whole lifetime. And she was a big nuisance right up till the day she died. She was more like me, more on the stout side. Take care of your health, Joe, when you're out there. What's better than health?

LORNA (*turning to* MR. BONAPARTE, *with whom she is self-conscious*). The question is, do you like me or do you not?

MR. BONAPARTE (*with a faint smile*). Yes. . .

LORNA. Your family is very cute— Now do you like me?

MR. BONAPARTE. Yes. . . .

LORNA. Why do you look at me that way

MR. BONAPARTE. I don't look special. You gonna travel on those train with my son

LORNA. God's teeth, no! I'm a friend of his manager's, that's all. And a friend of Joe's too.

MR. BONAPARTE. You are in favor for my son to prizefight? (JOE *looks at his father sideways and exits.*)

LORNA. Certainly. Aren't you?

MR. BONAPARTE. Joe has a dream many year to be superior violin'. Was it boyhood thing Was it real? Or is this real now? Those are my question, Miss Moon. Maybe you ar friend to my son. Then I aska you, look out for him. Study him. Help him find what'sa right. Tell me, Miss Moon, when you find out. Help Joe find truthful success Will you do it for me?

LORNA. I'll be glad to keep my eye on him (JOE *enters with slippers, which he put in bag.*)

ANNA (*to* JOE). You could stand some new shirts, too.

SIGGIE. Listen, pop, I'm a natural man an I don't like wise guys. Joe went in the box ing game 'cause he's ashamed to be poor That's his way to enter a little enterprise All other remarks are so much alfalfa! (JOE *locks the bag.*)

ANNA (*taking the wine glass from* SIGGIE hand). Drunk as a horse fly!

JOE. It's getting late and the train won wait.

SIGGIE (*standing up*). My God is success Need I say more? I'm prouda you, Joe Come home a champ. Make enough dough to buy your sister's boy friend a new cal Yes, boys and girls, I'm looking in that ol crystal ball and I see strange and wonderfu events! Yazoo!

ANNA (*giggling*). Drunk as a horse fly!

JOE (*to* SIGGIE). You can't drive us dow to the station in this condition.

SIGGIE. What condition?

ANNA. You're drunk, stupid.

SIGGIE. Shut the face, foolish! Just because I don't hold in my nerves she thinks I'm drunk. If you hold in your nerves you get ulcers. (*To* JOE.) Get your "chapow" and let's go. Or don't you want me to drive you down?

JOE. No.

SIGGIE. I should worry—my cab's in the garage anyway! (*Suddenly he sits.*)

JOE. We'd better start. . . .

LORNA (*to* MR. BONAPARTE). I'd like to have another talk with you some time.

MR. BONAPARTE. Come any time in the evening. You are a very lovely girl. (MR. CARP *stands in the doorway.*) Here is Mr. Carp to say good-bye.

SIGGIE. Come in, my little prince.

CARP (*coming in and shaking hands with* JOE). I wish you good luck in every undertaking.

JOE (*uneasily, because his father is looking at him*). Thanks.

MR. BONAPARTE (*introducing* CARP). Miss Moon, my neighbor, Mr. Carp.

CARP. A pleasure to meet you.

LORNA. Hello. (MR. BONAPARTE *brings the violin case from its hiding place in the buffet.*)

MR. BONAPARTE. Joe, I buy you this some time ago. Don't give cause I don't know whatta you gonna do. Take him with you now. Play for yourself. It gonna remember you your old days of musical life. (JOE *puts down the suitcase and picks up the violin. He plucks the strings, he tightens one of them. In spite of the tension his face turns soft and tender.*)

LORNA (*watching intently*). We better not miss the train—Tokio's waiting.

MR. BONAPARTE (*of violin*). Take him with you, Joe.

JOE. It's beautiful. . . .

MR. BONAPARTE. Practise on the road. (JOE *abruptly turns and with the violin exits.*

The others listen, each standing in his place, as rich violin music comes from the other room. JOE *returns. There is silence as he places the violin on the table in front of his father.*)

JOE (*in a low voice*). Return it, poppa.

ANNA (*hugging* JOE). Have a good trip, Joey.

CARP. Eat in good restaurants. . . . (*There is silence: the* FATHER *and* SON *look at each other. The others in the room sense the drama between the two. Finally:*)

JOE. I have to do this, poppa.

MR. BONAPARTE (*to* JOE). Be careful fora your hands.

JOE. Poppa, give me the word—

MR. BONAPARTE. What word?

JOE. Give me the word to go ahead. You're looking at yesterday—I see tomorrow. Maybe you think I ought to spend my whole life here—you and Carp blowing off steam.

MR. BONAPARTE (*holding himself back*). Oh, Joe, shut your mouth!

JOE. Give me the word to go ahead!

MR. BONAPARTE. Be careful fora your hands!

JOE. I want you to give me the word!

MR. BONAPARTE (*crying out*). *No! No word!* You gonna fight? All right! Okay! But I don't gonna give no word! No!

JOE. That's how you feel?

MR. BONAPARTE. That'sa how I feel! (MR. BONAPARTE's *voice breaks and there is nothing for father and son to do but to clutch each other in a hasty embrace. Finally* MR. BONAPARTE *disentangles himself and turns away.* JOE *abruptly grabs up his suitcase and exits.* LORNA *follows, stopping at the door to look back at* MR. BONAPARTE. *In the ensuing silence* ANNA *looks at her father and shakes her head.* SIGGIE *suddenly lumbers to his feet and sounds off like a chime.*)

SIGGIE. Gong gong gong gong!

ANNA. Gee, poppa . . .

SIGGIE. Come to bed, Anna. . . . Anna-banana . . . (SIGGIE *exits.*)

ANNA. Gee, poppa . . . (*She touches her father sympathetically.*)

MR. BONAPARTE (*without turning*). Gone to bed, Anna. . . . (ANNA *slowly exits.* MR. BONAPARTE *now slowly comes back to the table and looks down at the violin.*)

CARP (*seating himself slowly*). Come, my friend . . . we will have a nice talk on a cultural topic. (*Looking at the violin.*)

You'll work around a number of years b fore you make it up, the price of that fiddl . . . (MR. BONAPARTE *stands looking dow at the violin.*)

CARP (*sadly*). Yes, my friend, what is man As Schopenhauer says, and in the last ana ysis . . .

SLOW FADEOUT

ACT TWO

SCENE I

Six months later. Present in the corner of a gymnasium are ROXY, MOODY, LORNA *an* TOKIO. *They are looking off right, watching* JOE BONAPARTE *work out with a partne From off right come the sounds of typical gym activities: the thud of boxing gloves, t rat-a-tat of the punching bag, and from time to time the general bell which is a sign for rest periods. Tacked on the tin walls are an ad for Everlast boxing equipment, boxir "card" placards, a soiled American flag, some faded exit signs.*

The group watches silently for several seconds after the lights fade in. A BOXER, *wipi his perspiring body with a towel, passes from left to right and looks back at* LORNA legs. As ROXY *watches, his head moves to and fro in the rhythm of* JOE'S *sparring off stag* ROXY *nods his head in admiration.*

ROXY. Tokio. I gotta give the devil his dues: in the past six months you done a noble job!

TOKIO (*calling off*). With the left! A long left, Joe! . . .

LORNA (*looking off*). Joe's a very good-looking boy. I never quite noticed it before. (*The general bell sounds; the boxing din off stage stops.*)

MOODY (*rubbing his hands enthusiastically*). "Let it rain, let it pour! It ain't gonna rain where we're headed for!"

ROXY. I'm tickled to death to see the canary birds left his gloves.

TOKIO. He's the king of all he surveys.

MOODY. Boy, oh, boy, how he surprised them in the Bronx last night! . . . But one thing I can't explain—that knockout he took in Philly five weeks ago.

TOKIO. That night he was off his feed, Tom. Where do you see speed like that? That's style, real style—you can't tag him. And he's giving it with both hands.

MOODY. You don't have to sell me his virtues—I'm sold. Nevertheless, he got tagged in Philly.

TOKIO. Here's what happened there: we r into some man when we're leaving the hot Joe goes pale. I ask him what it is. "Not ing," he says. But I see for myself—a m with long hair and a violin case. When turn the corner, he says, "He's after m he says. As if it's cops and robbers! (*T general bell sounds; the fighting din begi again.*)

ROXY. A kidnapper?

LORNA. Don't be a fool. He was reminded .

ROXY. Speak when spoken to, Miss Moon!

MOODY (*moodily*). And when he got in t ring that night, he kept his hands in I pockets?

TOKIO. Yeah. I didn't mention this before it's not important.

MOODY. But it's still a danger—

TOKIO. No. No.

MOODY. But anyway, we better get him aw from his home. We can't afford no mo possible bad showings at this stage of t game. No more apparitions, like suddenl fiddle flies across the room on wings! (*T group again intently watches* JOE *off stag*

ODY. Ooh! Did you see that? He's pack-
a real Sunday punch in that right. (*Call-
off.*) Hit 'im, Joe, hit 'im! (*As an indis-
t answer comes back.) Ha ha, looka
t, hahaha . . . (*Now turning to* TOKIO.)
at's your idea of a match with Lom-
do?

IO. Can you get it?

ODY. Maybe.

IO. Get it.

ODY. Sure?

IO. It's an easy win, on points at least.
*uring the last few lines a thin dark man
entered. His dark hair is grayed at the
ples, an inarticulate look in his face. He
EDDIE FUSELI, a renowned gambler and
man.*)

IE FUSELI (*approaching the group*). Hel-

Y (*nervously*). Hello, Eddie.

ODY (*turning*). I haven't seen you for a
's age, Fuseli.

IE (*pointing off left*). You got this cer-
boy—Bonaparte. I like his looks. Ameri-
born?

Y. Right from here.

IE (*watching* JOE *off*). Like a cat, never
his position. He appeals to me. (*To*
ODY.) They call you the Brown Fox.
at's your opinion of this boy?

ODY (*coolly, on guard*). Possibilities. . . .

IE (*to* TOKIO). What's your idea?

IO. Tom said it.

IE. Could he get on top?

ODY (*as above*). I can't see that far ahead.
on't read palms.

IE. Could I buy a piece?

ODY. No.

IE (*coolly*). Could I?

ODY. No!

IE (*with a certain tenderness*). I like a
d fighter. I like to see you after, Tom.
* LORNA.) This your girl?

NA (*pertly*). I'm my mother's girl.

EDDIE (*with a small mirthless laugh*). Ha
ha—that's a hot one. (*He coolly drifts out
of the scene on his cat's feet. The general
bell sounds. The din ceases.*)

LORNA. What exhaust pipe did he crawl out
of?

ROXY. I remember this Eddie Fuseli when
he came back from the war with a gun.
He's still got the gun and he still gives me
goose pimples!

MOODY. That Fuseli's a black mark in my
book. Every once in a while he shoots across
my quiet existence like a roman candle!

LORNA. Sell or don't sell. But better be careful, that guy's tough! (*A* FIGHTER, *robed,
hooded with towel, passes across: A* GAMB-
LING TYPE *passes in the opposite direction.
Both look at* LORNA's *legs.*)

MOODY. Give a rat like that a finger and you
lose a hand before you know it!

TOKIO. Did you know Joe bought a car
this morning?

ROXY. What kinda car?

TOKIO. A Deusenberg.

MOODY. One of those fancy speed wagons?

TOKIO (*agreeing*). It cost him five grand,
second-hand.

MOODY (*flaring up*). Am I a step-child
around here? I'm glad you tell me now, if
only outa courtesy!

ROXY (*indignantly*). Whatta you keep a
think like that incognito for?

MOODY. He drives like a maniac! That time
we drove to Long Beach? I almost lost my
scalp! We can't let him drive around like
that! Boy, he's getting a bushel of bad
habits! We gotta be careful. (*The general
bell sounds again; the fighting din stops.*)

MOODY. Here's the truth: our boy can be
the champ in three easy lessons—Lombardo,
Fulton, the Chocolate Drop. But we gotta
be careful!

LORNA. Here he comes. (JOE *enters in bathrobe, taking off his headgear, which* TOKIO
takes from him.)

MOODY (*completely changing his tone*). You
looked very good in there, Joe. You're going

swell and I like it. I'd work more with that long left if I were you.

JOE. Yes, I was speaking to Tokio about that. I feel my form's improving. I like to work. I'm getting somewhere—I feel it better every day.

LORNA. Happy?

JOE (*looking at her intently*). Every day's Saturday!

ROXY (*officiously*). Say, what's this I hear you bought a Deusenberg?

JOE. What's your objection—I might have some fun?

ROXY. I got my wampum on you. I like to know your habits. Ain't I permitted? (JOE *is about to retort hotly when* MOODY *gently takes his arm in an attempt to soothe him.*)

MOODY. Wait a minute, Joe. After all we have your welfare at heart. And after all a Deusenberg can go one fifty per— (EDDIE FUSELI *appears above, unseen by the others. He listens.*)

JOE. Who'd want to drive that fast?

MOODY. And since we're vitally interested in your future—

JOE (*shaking off* MOODY's *arm and saying what is really on his mind*). If you're vitally interested in my future, prove it! Get me some fights—fights with contenders, not with dumb-bunny club fighters. Get me some main bouts in the metropolitan area!—

MOODY (*losing his temper*). For a kid who got kayoed five weeks ago, your mouth is pretty big! (*The general bell sounds; the din begins.*)

JOE. That won't happen again! And how about some mention in the press? Twenty-six bouts—no one knows I'm alive. This isn't a vacation for me—it's a profession! I'm staying more than a week. Match me up against real talent. You can't go too fast for me. Don't worry about autos!

MOODY. We can go too fast! You're not so good!

JOE (*with a boyish grin*). Look at the records! (JOE *abruptly exits.* TOKIO *follows him, first giving the others a glance.*)

MOODY. Boy, oh, boy, that kid's chang

ROXY. He goes past my head like a cold v from the river!

LORNA. But you're gettin' what you wa the contender for the crown!

MOODY. I wish I was sure.

ROXY. Frankenstein! (EDDIE FUSELI *sau down to the others.*)

EDDIE. I thought it over, Tom. I like to a piece of that boy.

MOODY (*angrily*). I thought it over, t not for sale. In fact I had a visitation f Jehovah. He came down on the calm w and He said, "Let there be unity in ownership."

EDDIE (*with a dead face*). I had a visit, He come down in the bar and He ate a zel. And He says, "Eddie Fuseli, I you to buy a piece!"

MOODY (*trying to delay the inevitable*). not see me in my office tomorrow?

EDDIE. It's a cheap office. I get depresse that office.

MOODY (*finally*). I can't make any gu tees about the boy.

EDDIE. How do you mean it, Tom?

MOODY. I don't know what the hell he in the next six months.

ROXY. Eddie, it's like flap-packs—up down—you don't know which side

EDDIE (*with his small mirthless laugh*) ha, that's a good one. You oughta be o radio.

MOODY. No, it's a fact—

ROXY. We had enough headaches alr He's got a father, but how!

EDDIE. Don't want him to fight?

ROXY. His father sits on the kid's hea a bird's nest! (ROXY *puts his hand on E arm.*)

EDDIE. Take your hand off. (ROXY *withdraws.*) Let the boy decide. . . .

MOODY. If you buy in?

EDDIE. Let the boy decide.

DY. Sure! But if he says no— (*Before
DY can finish* JOE *enters.* EDDIE *whirls
und and faces* JOE, *getting his cue from
others. Curiously,* EDDIE *is almost em-
rassed before* JOE. *The bell sounds; the
stops.*)

DY. Joe, this is Eddie Fuseli. He's a
a around town—

E (*facing* JOE, *his back to the others*).
h good connections—

DY. He wantsa buy a piece of you—

E (*whirling around*). I will tell him my-
(*Turning back to* JOE; *with quiet in-
e dignity*). I'm Eyetalian too—Eyetalian
a, but an American citizen. I like to
a piece of you. I don't care for no profit.
uld turn it back to—*you* could take my
e. But I like a good fighter; I like a
d boy who could win the crown. It's the
r-est of my life. It would be a proud
g for me when Bonaparte could win the
vn like I think he can.

DY (*confidently*). It's up to you, Joe, if
uys in.

E (*wooingly*). Some managers can't give
what you need—

DY. Don't say that!

E. *Some* managers can't! I'll see you get
bouts . . . also press notices . . . I know
. You're a boy who needs that. You de-
. . . (*There is a pause;* JOE's *eyes flit
LORNA to the others and back to* EDDIE.)

Not my half.

E. Not your half.

As long as Mr. Fuseli doesn't mix in
rivate life . . . cut it up any way you
Excuse me, I got a date with Miss
senberg. (*The others silently watch* JOE

. A date with who?

Y (*snorting*). Miss Deusenberg!

An automobile. It gives you an idea
a boy—"Miss Deusenberg"!

. How do you like it, Tom? Big bills
le bills?

Y. Don't think you're buying in for an
and an egg.

EDDIE. Take big bills—they're new, they feel
good. See you in that office tomorrow. (*The
bell clangs off stage.* EDDIE *starts off, but
abruptly turns and faces* ROXY *whom he in-
wardly terrifies.*)

EDDIE. It's a trick you don't know, Roxy:
when a bird sits on your head and inter-
feres with the championship, you shoot him
off. All kinds of birds. You be surprised
how fast they fall on the ground. Which is
my intention in this syndicate. (*He smiles
thinly and then moves out of the scene like
a cat.*)

MOODY. I don't like that!

ROXY. I'm not so happy myself at the present
time. How do you like it with our boy for
gratitude? He leaves us here standing in
our brevities!

LORNA. What makes you think you're worthy
of gratitude?

MOODY (*to* LORNA). For pete's sake, pipe
down! Are you with us or against us?

ROXY (*haughtily, to* MOODY). Take my advice, Tom. Marry her and the first year give
her a baby. Then she'll sit in the corner and
get fat and sleepy, and not have such a big
mouth! Uncle Roxy's telling you!

LORNA (*to* ROXY). Couldn't you keep quiet
about the father to that gunman? Go home
and let your wife give *you* a baby!

ROXY. A woman shouldn't interfere—

MOODY. Peace, for chri' sake, peace! Lorna,
we're in a bad spot with Joe. He's getting
hard to manage and this is the time when
everything's gotta be right. I'm seeing Lombardo's manager tomorrow! Now that gunman's on my tail. You have to help me. You
and I wanna do it like the story books,
"happy ever after"? Then help me.

LORNA. How?

MOODY. Go after the boy. Keep him away
from his folks. Get him away from the
buggies—

LORNA. How?

MOODY (*impatiently*). You know how.

ROXY. Now you're talking.

LORNA (*pointing* to ROXY.) You mean the
way I see it on his face?

MOODY. For crying out loud! Where do you come off to make a remark like that?

LORNA. You expect me to sleep with that boy?

MOODY. I could tear your ears off for a remark like that!

ROXY (*discreetly*). I think I'll go grab a corn-beef sandwich. (*He exits.*)

MOODY (*after silence*). Are you mad?

LORNA (*tight-lipped*). No.

MOOD (*seductively*). I'm not a bad guy. Lorna. I don't mean anything bad. . . . All right, I'm crude—sometimes I'm worried and I'm crude. (*The bell clangs; the boxing din stops.*)

MOODY. But what the hell, my heart's in the right place. . . . (*Coming behind her and putting his arms around her as she looks ahead.*) Lorna, don't we both want that s〔 to come up and shine on us? Don't we? I fore you know it the summer'll be he Then it's the winter again, and it's anotl year again . . . and we're not married y See? . . . See what I mean? . . .

LORNA (*quietly*). Yes. . . .

MOODY (*beaming, but with uncertaint〕* That sounds like the girl I used to know

LORNA. I see what you mean. . . .

MOODY (*worried underneath*). You're 〔 still mad?

LORNA (*briefly*). I'm not mad. (*But 〔 abruptly cuts out of the scene, leav〔 MOODY standing there.*)

MOODY (*shaking his head*). Boy, I still d〔 know anything about women! . . .

MEDIUM FADEOUT

SCENE II

A few nights later. LORNA *and* JOE *sit on the same park bench.*

JOE. Some nights I wake up—my heart's beating a mile a minute! Before I open my eyes I know what it is—the feeling that someone's standing at my bed. Then I open my eyes . . . it's gone—ran away!

LORNA. Maybe it's that old fiddle of yours.

JOE. Lorna, maybe it's you. . . .

LORNA. Don't you ever think of it any more —music?

JOE. What're you trying to remind me of? A kid with a Buster Brown collar and a violin case tucked under his arm? Does that sound appetizing to you?

LORNA. Not when you say it that way. You said it different once. . . .

JOE. What's on your mind, Lorna?

LORNA. What's on yours?

JOE (*simply*). You. . . . You're real for me —the way music was real.

LORNA. You've got your car, your career— what do you want with me?

JOE. I develop the ability to knock down anyone my weight. But what point have I made? Don't you think I know that 〔 went off to the wars 'cause someone ca〔 me a name—because I wanted to be 〔 other guys. Now it's happening. . . . I'm 〔 sure I like it.

LORNA. Moody's against that car of yo〔

JOE. I'm against Moody, so we're even.

LORNA. Why don't you like him?

JOE. He's a manager! He treats me li〔 possession! I'm just a little silver min〔 him—he bangs me around with a shove〔

LORNA. He's helped you—

JOE. No, Tokio's helped me. Why 〔 you give him up? It's terrible to have 〔 a Tuesday-night girl. Why don't you be〔 to me every night in the week? Why 〔 you teach me love? . . . Or am I bei〔 fool?

LORNA. You're not a fool, Joe.

JOE. I want you to be my family, my 〔 Why don't you do it, Lorna, why?

LORNA. He loves me.

JOE. I love you!

RNA (*treading delicately*). Well . . . Any-
ay, the early bird got the worm. Anyway,
can't give him anguish. I . . . I know
hat it's like. You shouldn't kick Moody
ound. He's poor compared to you. You're
ve, you've got yourself—I can't feel sorry
you!

E. But you don't love him!

RNA. I'm not much interested in myself.
t the thing I like best about you . . . you
l feel like a flop. It's mysterious, Joe. It
kes me put my hand out. (*She gives him
r hand and he grasps it.*)

E. I feel very close to you, Lorna.

RNA. I know. . . .

E. And you feel close to me. But you're
aid—

RNA. Of what?

E. To take a chance! Lorna, darling, you
n't let me wake you up! I feel it all the
ne—you're half dead, and you don't know

RNA (*half smiling*). Maybe I do. . . .

E. Don't smile—don't be hard-boiled!

RNA (*sincerely*). I'm not.

E. Don't you trust me?

RNA (*evasively*). Why start what we can't
sh?

E (*fiercely*). Oh, Lorna, deep as my voice
l reach—*listen!* Why can't you leave him?
ay?

RNA. Don't pull my dress off—I hear you.

E. Why?

RNA. Because he needs me and you don't—

E. That's not true!

RNA. Because he's a desperate guy who
ways starts out with two strikes against
m. Because he's a kid at forty-two and
're a man at twenty-two.

E. You're sorry for him?

RNA. What's wrong with that?

E. But what do *you* get?

RNA. I told you before I don't care.

E. I don't believe it!

LORNA. I can't help that!

JOE. What did he ever do for you?

LORNA (*with sudden verve*). Would you like
to know? He loved me in a world of enemies, of stags and bulls! . . . and I loved
him for that. He picked me up in Friskin's
hotel on 39th Street. I was nine weeks behind in rent. I hadn't hit the gutter yet, but
I was near. He washed my face and combed
my hair. He stiffened the space between my
shoulder blades. Misery reached out to misery—

JOE. And now you're dead.

LORNA (*lashing out*). I don't know what the
hell you're talking about!

JOE. Yes, you do. . . .

LORNA (*withdrawing*). Ho hum. . . . (*There
is silence. The soft park music plays in the
distance. The traffic lights change. LORNA
is trying to appear impassive. JOE begins to
whistle softly. Finally LORNA picks up his
last note and continues; he stops. He picks
up her note, and after he whistles a few
phrases she picks him up again. This whistling duet continues for almost a minute.
Then the traffic lights change again.*)

LORNA (*beginning in a low voice*). You
make me feel too human, Joe. All I want
is peace and quiet, not love. I'm a tired old
lady, Joe, and I don't mind being what you
call "half dead." In fact it's what I like.
(*Her voice mounting higher.*) The twice I
was in love I took an awful beating and I
don't want it again! (*Now half crying.*) I
want you to stop it! Don't devil me, Joe. I
beg you, don't devil me . . . let me alone.
. . . (*She cries softly. JOE reaches out and
takes her hand; he gives her a handkerchief
which she uses.*)

LORNA (*finally*). That's the third time I cried
in my life. . . .

JOE. Now I know you love me.

LORNA (*bitterly*). Well . . .

JOE. I'll tell Moody.

LORNA. Not yet. Maybe he'd kill you if he
knew.

JOE. Maybe.

LORNA. Then Fuseli'd kill him. . . . I guess I'd be left to kill myself. I'll tell him. . . .

JOE. When?

LORNA. Not tonight.

JOE. Swiftly, do it swiftly—

LORNA. Not tonight.

JOE. Everything's easy if you do it swiftly.

LORNA. He went up there tonight with six hundred bucks to bribe her into divorce.

JOE. Oh . . .

LORNA (sadly). He's a good guy, neat all over—sweet. I'll tell him tomorrow. I'd like a drink.

JOE. Let's drive over the Washington Bridge.

LORNA (standing). No, I'd like a drink.

JOE (standing and facing her). Lorna, when I talk to you . . . something moves in my heart. Gee, it's the beginning of a wonder-ful life! A man and his girl! A warm liv[e] girl who shares your room. . . .

LORNA. Take me home with you.

JOE. Yes.

LORNA. But how do I know you love [me]

JOE. Lorna . . .

LORNA. How do I know it's true? You'll [go] to be the champ. They'll all want you, all [the] girls! But I don't care! I've been underse[a] long time! When they'd put their hands [on] me I used to say, "This isn't it! This i[sn't] what I mean!" It's been a mysterious w[orld] for me! But, Joe, I think you're it! I d[on't] know why, I think you're it! Take me h[ome] with you.

JOE. Lorna!

LORNA. Poor Tom . . .

JOE. Poor Lorna! (The rest is embrace [and] kiss and clutching each other.)

SLOW FADEOUT

SCENE III

The next day: the office. LORNA *and* MOODY *are present. She has a hangover an[d] restless.*

MOODY. Boy, you certainly double-scotched yourself last night. What's the idea, you making a career of drinking in your old age? Headache?

LORNA. No.

MOODY. I won't let you walk alone in the park any more, if you do that.

LORNA (nasty in spite of her best intentions). Well, if you stayed away from your wife for a change . . .

MOODY. It's pretty late to bring that up, isn't it? Tuesday nights—

LORNA. I can't help it—I feel like a tramp. I've felt like a tramp for years.

MOODY. She was pretty friendly last night.

LORNA. Yeah? Did you sleep with her?

MOODY. What the hell's the matter with you, Lorna? (He goes to her. She shrugs away from him.)

LORNA. Keep off the grass! (MOODY *gives [her] a quizzical look, goes back to his desk [and] from there gives her another quizzical loo[k.]*)

MOODY. Why do you drink like that?

LORNA (pointing to her chest). Right her[e] there's a hard lump and I drink to disse[olve] it. Do you mind?

MOODY. I don't mind—as long as you k[eep] your health.

LORNA. Aw, Christ!—you and your he[alth] talks!

MOODY. You're looking for a fight, d[ear] girl!

LORNA. And you'll give it?

MOODY (with a grin). No, I'm feeling [too] good.

LORNA (sitting wearily). Who left you a [for]tune?

MOODY. Better. Monica's seen the light. [The] truth is she's begun to run around wi[th]

ed brewer and now *she* wants the di-
e.

A. Good, now she can begin paying *you.*

DY. She goes to Reno in a few months.

A (*moodily*). I feel like a tramp. . . .

DY. That's what I'm telling you— In
w months we'll be married! (*He laughs
 pleasure.*)

A. You still want to marry me? Don't I
like an old shoe to you?

DY (*coming to her*). Honest, you're so
b!

A (*touched by his boyishness*). You're
veet. . . .

DY. And flash!—I signed Lombardo to-
They meet six weeks from tonight.

A. Goody. . . .

DY (*disappointed by her flippant reac-
but continuing*). I'm still not sure what
show with Lombardo. But my present
y is this: help me get that kid straight.
you speak to him about the driving
night?

A. I didn't see him. . . .

DY. It's very important. A Lombardo
clinches everything. In the fall we ride
o the Chocolate's door and dump him
e gutter! After that . . . I don't like
xaggerate—but the kid's primed! And
and I—Lorna baby, we're set. (*Hap-
*) What do you think of that?

A (*evasively*). You draw beautiful pic-
. (*A knock sounds on the door.*)

Y. Come in. (SIGGIE *enters, dressed in
driver's garb.*)

E. Hello, Miss Moon.

A. Hello. You know Mr. Moody.

E (*to* MOODY). Hello.

Y. What can we do for you?

E. For me you can't do nothing. I'm
I'm here against my better instinct.
*king a roll of money from his pocket
lapping it on the desk.*) He don't want
o part of it! My father-in-law don't
it. Joe sent it up—two hundred bucks

—enough to choke a horse—but he don't
want . it!

MOODY. Why?

LORNA. That's nice he remembers his folks.

SIGGIE. Listen, I got a father-in-law nothing's
nice to him but feeding his horse and giving
a laugh and slicing philosophical salami
across the table! He's sore because Joe don't
come home half the time. As a matter of
fact, ain't he suppose to come to sleep no
more? The old man's worried.

MOODY. That's not my concern.

SIGGIE. I can't see what it's such a worry.
A boy gets in the higher brackets—what's
the worry? He's got enough clothes now
to leave three suits home in the closet.
(*Turning to* LORNA.) It won't hurt if he
sends me a few passes—tell him I said so.

LORNA. How's the wife?

SIGGIE. The Duchess? Still laughing.

LORNA. When you getting that cab?

SIGGIE. Do me a favor, Miss Moon—tell him
I could use this wad for the first instalment.

LORNA. I'll tell him. Tell Mr. Bonaparte I
saw Joe last night. He's fine.

MOODY. I'll see you get some passes.

SIGGIE. Thanks, thanks to both of you. Adios.
(*He exits.*)

LORNA. He and his wife are crazy for each
other. Married . . . they throw each other
around, but they're like love birds. Marriage is something special. . . . I guess you
have to deserve it.

MOODY. I thought you didn't see Joe last
night.

LORNA. I didn't, but why worry his father?

MOODY. The hell with his father.

LORNA. The hell with you!

MOODY (*after a brooding pause*). I'll tell you
something, Lorna. I'm not overjoyed the
way Joe looks at you.

LORNA. How's he look?

MOODY. As if he saw the whole island of
Manhattan in your face, and I don't like it.

LORNA. You thought of that too late.

MOODY. Too late for what?

LORNA. To bawl me out.

MOODY. Who's bawling you out?

LORNA. You were about to. Or warn me. I don't need warnings. (*Coasting away from the argument.*) If you saw Joe's father you'd like him.

MOODY. I saw him.

LORNA. If you knew him you'd like him.

MOODY. Who wantsa like him? What do I need him for? I don't like him and I don't like his son! It's a business—Joe does his work, I do mine. Like this telephone—I pay the bill and I use it!

LORNA. He's human. . . .

MOODY. What're we fighting about?

LORNA. We're fighting about love. I'm trying to tell you how cynical I am. Tell the truth, love doesn't last—

MOODY (*suddenly quietly serious*). Everything I said about *Joe*—the opposite goes for you. Love lasts . . . if you want it to. . . . I want it to last. I need it to last. What the hell's all this struggle to make a living for if not for a woman and a home? I don't kid myself. I know what I need. I need you, Lorna.

LORNA. It has to end. . . .

MOODY. What has to end?

LORNA. Everything.

MOODY. What're you talking about?

LORNA. I oughta burn. I'm leaving you. . . .

MOODY (*with a sick smile*). That's what you think.

LORNA (*not looking at him*). I mean it.

MOODY (*as above*). I mean it too.

LORNA (*after looking at him for a moment*). You can't take a joke?

MOODY (*not knowing where he stands*). It all depends. . . . I don't like a joke that pushes the blood down in my feet.

LORNA (*coming to him and putting her arms around his neck*). That's true, you're pale.

MOODY. Who's the man?

LORNA (*heartsick, and unable to tell [him] the truth*). There's no man, Tom . . . e[ven] if there was, I couldn't leave you. ([*She*] looks at him, unable to say more.)

MOODY (*after a pause*). How about s[ome] lunch? I'll buy it. . . .

LORNA (*wearily*). Where would I put [it,] Tom?

MOODY (*impulsively*). In your hat! ([*And*] suddenly he embraces her roughly and k[isses] her fully and she allows it. JOE walks [into] the office, EDDIE FUSELI behind him. T[hey] break apart.)

JOE. The first time I walked in here [it] was going on. It's one long duet aro[und] here.

MOODY. Hello.

EDDIE (*sardonically*). Hello, Partner. [. . .] (LORNA *is silent and avoids* JOE's loo[k.])

JOE. How about that fight with Lombar[do?]

MOODY. Six weeks from tonight.

JOE. He's gonna be surprised.

MOODY (*coolly*). No one doubts it.

JOE (*sharply*). I didn't say it was doub[ted.]

MOODY. Boy, everyone's off his feed to[day!] It started with the elevator boy—next [it's] Lorna—now it's you! What are *you* [sore] about?

LORNA (*trying to turn the conversation [from]* JOE). Siggie was here looking for you. [Your] father's worried—

JOE. Not as much as my "manager" wo[rries] me.

MOODY. I don't need you to tell me ho[w to] run my business. I'll book the matches [. . .]

JOE. That doesn't worry me.

MOODY. But you and your speeding wo[rry] me! First it's music, then it's motors. Ch[ances] next it'll be girls and booze!

JOE. It's girls already.

LORNA. Joe—

JOE (*bitterly*). Certainly! By the dozen[s!]

IE. Haha—that's a hot one. Don't ask which is worst—women or spiders.

NA. Siggie left this money—your father n't take it. Siggie says buy him a cab— E *takes the money*.)

IE. Your relative? I'll get him a cab.) MOODY.) How about a flock of bouts Bonaparte over the summer?

DY (*bitterly*). All he wants—practice ts—to make him a better "artiste."

IE. That is what we like. (JOE *is looking* ORNA.)

DY. "We?" Where do *I* come in?

IE. You push the buttons, the *right* but-. I wanna see Bonaparte with the crown.

DY (*sarcastically*). Your concern touches deep in my heart!

IE. What's the matter, Tom? You get- tired?

DY (*coolly*). I get tired, don't you?

IE. Don't get tired, Tom . . . not in a ial time.

DY. Get him to give up that Deusenberg.

E (*after looking at* JOE). That's his . . .

DY. His fun might cost your crown.

(*suddenly, to* LORNA). Why did you kiss ?

DY (*to* JOE). It's about time you shut mouth and minded your own goddam ness. Also, that you took some orders.

(*suddenly savage*). Who are you, God?

DY. Yes! I'm your maker, you cock-eyed er rat! Outa sawdust and spit I made I own you—without me you're a blank! r insolence is gorgeous, but this is the I'm a son of a gun! What're you so rior about?

E. Don't talk so quick, Tom. You don't w . . .

DY. I wouldn't take the crap of this last ight months from the President him- Cut me up in little pieces, baby—but me!

EDDIE (*quietly*). You could get cut up in little pieces.

MOODY (*retiring in disgust*). Sisst!

EDDIE. You hear me?

MOODY (*from his desk*). You wanna manage this boy? Help yourself—do it! I'll sell my piece for half of what it's worth. You wanna buy?

EDDIE. You are a funny man.

MOODY. Gimme twenty thousand and lemme out. Ten, I'll take ten. I got my girl. I don't need crowns or jewels. I take my girl and we go sit by the river and it's everything.

JOE. What girl?

MOODY. I'm not on speaking terms with you! (*To* EDDIE.) Well?

EDDIE. It would be funny if your arms got broke.

JOE. Wait a minute! Lorna loves me and I love her.

MOODY (*after looking from* JOE *to* LORNA *and back*). Crazy as a bat! (*He laughs.*)

JOE (*frigidly*). Is it so impossible?

MOODY. About as possible as hell freezes over. (*He and* JOE *simultaneously turn to* LORNA.)

JOE. Tell him. . . .

LORNA (*looking* JOE *in the face*). I love Tom. Tell him what? (JOE *looks at her intently. Silence.* JOE *then turns and quietly exits from the office.* MOODY *shakes his head with a grin.*)

MOODY. Eddie, I take everything back. I was a fool to get sore—that boy's a real nutsy-Fagan! (*He offers his hand.* EDDIE *looks at it and then viciously slaps it down.*)

EDDIE (*repressing a trembling voice*). I don't like no one to laugh at that boy. You call a boy like that a rat? An educated boy? What is your idea to call him cock-eyed? When you do it in front of me, I say, "Tom don't like himself" . . . for Bonaparte is a good friend to me . . . you're a clever manager for him. That's the only reason I take your slop. Do your business, Tom. (*To* LORNA.) And that goes for you, too! No tricks, Miss Moon! (*He slowly exits.* MOODY *stands there thoughtfully.* LORNA *moves to the couch.*)

MOODY. I'm a son of a gun!

LORNA. I feel like I'm shot from a cannon.

MOODY. Why?

LORNA. I'm sorry for him.

MOODY. Why? Because he's a queer?

LORNA. I'm not talking of Fuseli. (*Sudd*—— LORNA's *eyes flood with tears.* MOODY *t her hand, half sensing the truth.*)

MOODY. What's wrong, Lorna? You ca me. . . .

LORNA. I feel like the wrath of God.

MOODY. You like that boy, don't you?

LORNA. I love him, Tom.

SLOW FADEOUT

SCENE IV

Six weeks later.
    A dressing room before the Lombardo fight. There are a couple of rubbing tables i room. There are some lockers and a few hooks on which hang pieces of clothing. A to the left leads to the showers; a door to the right leads to the arena.
    As the lights fade in, MR. BONAPARTE *and* SIGGIE *are sitting to one side, on a wooden bench.* TOKIO *is fussing around in a locker. A fighter,* PEPPER WHITE, *h already bandaged, is being rubbed down by his trainer-manager,* MICKEY. *Throughou scene is heard the distant Roar of* THE CROWD *and the clanging of the bell.*

MR. BONAPARTE (*after a silence of intense listening*). What is that noise?

SIGGIE. That's the roar of the crowd.

MR. BONAPARTE. A thousand people?

SIGGIE. Six thousand.

PEPPER WHITE (*turning his head as he lies on his belly*). Nine thousand.

SIGGIE. That's right, nine. You're sitting under nine thousand people. Suppose they fell down on your head? Did you ever think of that? (*The outside door opens;* EDDIE FUSELI *enters. The distant bell clangs.* EDDIE *looks around suspiciously, then asks* TOKIO:)

EDDIE. Where's Bonaparte?

TOKIO. Still with the newspapermen.

EDDIE (*unpleasantly surprised*). He's what?

TOKIO. Tom took him upstairs—some sports writers.

EDDIE. A half hour before a fight? What is Moody trying to do?

TOKIO. Tom's the boss.

EDDIE. Looka, Tokio—in the future you are gonna take your orders from me! (*Pointing to* SIGGIE *and* MR. BONAPARTE.) Who is this?

TOKIO. Joe's relatives.

EDDIE (*going over to them*). Is thi father?

MR. BONAPARTE (*somberly*). Yes, this father.

SIGGIE. And this is his brother-in-law sent passes up the house. We just got I thought it was in Coney Island—it's I looked at the tickets. Believe it or the old man never seen a fight in his Is it human?

EDDIE (*coldly*). Shut your mouth a mi This is The Arena—Bonaparte is fight good man tonight—

SIGGIE. Ahh, that Lombardo's a bag of

EDDIE. When Bonaparte goes in there him to have one thing on his mind—ing! I hope you understand me. An' like to find you here when I return! I you understand that. . . . (*After a full g at them* EDDIE *gracefully exits.*)

SIGGIE. That's a positive personality!

TOKIO. That's Eddie Fuseli.

SIGGIE. Momma-mia! No wonder I sr gun powder! (*Turning to* MR. BONAP/ Pop, that's a paradox in human beh shoots you for a nickel—then for fifty [buc]ks he sends you flowers!

[TOK]IO (*referring to the distant bell*). That's next bout.

[SIGG]IE (*to* MR. BONAPARTE). Come on, we [do]n't wanna miss the whole show.

[MR.] BONAPARTE. I waita for Joe.

[SIGG]IE. You heard what Fuseli said—

[MR.] BONAPARTE (*with somber stubbornness*). [I wa]nna wait!

[SIGG]IE. Listen, pop, you—

[MR.] BONAPARTE (*with sudden force*). I say [I wa]nna wait!!

[SIGG]IE (*handing* MR. BONAPARTE *a ticket*). [Tic]ket. (*Shrugging.*) Good-bye, you're let-[ting] flies in! (SIGGIE *exits jauntily.* MR. BONA-[PAR]TE *silently watches* TOKIO *work over the* [figh]ter's *materials. A* SECOND *comes in, puts* [a pa]il *under the table where* TOKIO *hovers,* [then] *exits.* PEPPER WHITE, *his head turned,* [wat]ches MR. BONAPARTE *as he hums a song.*)

[PEP]PER. Oh, Sweet Dardanella, I love your [h]arem eyes,
Sweet Dardanella, I'm a lucky fellow [to] get such a prize. . . .

[(to] MR. BONAPARTE.) So you're Bonaparte's [th]e boy, Buddy? Why didn't you say so [befo]re? Come over and shake my hand. [(MR.] BONAPARTE *does so.*)

[PEP]PER. Tell Bonaparte I like to fight him.

[MR.] BONAPARTE. Why?

[PEP]PER. I like to beat him up.

[MR.] BONAPARTE (*naïvely, not amused*). Why? [You] don't like him?

[PEP]PER. Don't kid me, Buddy! (A CALL BOY [appear]s in at the door.)

[CALL] BOY. Pepper White! Ready, Pepper [Whi]te! (CALL BOY *exits.* PEPPER WHITE *slips* [off t]he table and begins to change his shoes.)

[PEPP]ER (*to* MR. BONAARTE). When I get back [I'll e]xplain you all the ins and outs. (A SEC-[OND] *enters, takes a pail from* MICKEY *and* [exits.] LORNA *enters.*)

[PEPP]ER (*indignantly*). Who told girls to [come] in here?!

LORNA. Modest? Close your eyes. Is Moo-dy . . . ? (*Suddenly seeing* MR. BONAPARTE.) Hello, Mr. Bonaparte!

MR. BONAPARTE (*glad to see a familiar face*). Hello, hello, Missa Moon! Howa you feel?

LORNA. What brings you to this part of the world?

MR. BONAPARTE (*somberly*). I come-a to see Joe. . . .

LORNA. Why, what's wrong?

MR. BONAPARTE (*with a slow shrug*). He don't come-a to see me. . . .

LORNA. Does he know you're here?

MR. BONAPARTE. No. (LORNA *looks at him sympathetically.*)

LORNA (*finally*). It's a three-ring circus, isn't it?

MR. BONAPARTE. How you mean?

LORNA. Oh, I mean you . . . and him . . . and other people . . .

MR. BONAPARTE. I gonna see how he fight.

LORNA. I owe you a report. I wish I had good news for you, but I haven't.

MR. BONAPARTE. Yes, I know . . . he gotta wild wolf inside—eat him up!

LORNA. You could build a city with his ambition to be somebody.

MR. BONAPARTE (*sadly, shaking his head*). No . . . burn down! (*Now the outside door is thrust open—the distant bell clangs.* JOE *enters, behind him* MOODY *and* ROXY. JOE *stops in his tracks when he sees* LORNA *and his father together—the last two persons in the world he wants to see now. His hands are already bandaged, a bathrobe is thrown around his shoulders.*)

JOE. Hello, poppa. . . .

MR. BONAPARTE. Hello, Joe. . . .

JOE (*turning to* TOKIO). Throw out the girls —this isn't a hotel bedroom!

MOODY. That's no way to talk!

JOE (*coldly*). I talk as I please!

MOODY (*angrily*). The future Mrs. Moody—

JOE. I don't want her here!

LORNA. He's right, Tom. Why fight about it? (*She exits.*)

JOE (*to* MOODY). Also, I don't want to see writers again before a fight; it makes me nervous!

ROXY (*softly, for a wonder*). They're very important, Joe—

JOE. *I'm* important! My mind must be clear before I fight. I have to think before I go in. Don't you know that yet?

ROXY (*suddenly*). Yeah, we know—you're a stoodent—you gotta look in your notes.

JOE. What's funny about that? I do, *I do!!*

ROXY (*retreating*). So I said you do! (PEPPER WHITE *comes forward, about to exit; to* MOODY.)

PEPPER. How 'bout a bout with Napoleon?

MOODY. On your way, louse!

PEPPER (*with a grin*). Pickin' setups? (JOE *suddenly turns and starts for* PEPPER. TOKIO *quickly steps in between the two boys.*)

TOKIO. Save it for the ring! (*The two fighters glare at each other.* JOE *slowly turns and starts back for the table.*)

PEPPER. You think he'll be the champ? Where'd you ever read about a cock-eye champ? (JOE *spins around, speeds across the room—*PEPPER *is on the floor!* MICKEY *now starts for* JOE. TOKIO *starts for* MICKEY. PEPPER *gets up off the floor and finds himself occupied with* MOODY. *For a moment the fight is general.* EDDIE FUSELI *enters. All see him. The fighting magically stops on the second.*)

EDDIE. What'sa matter? Cowboys and Indians? (*To* PEPPER.) Out! (MICKEY *and* PEPPER *sullenly exit.*)

EDDIE (*to* MOODY). I'm lookin' for you! You're a manager and a half! You and your fat friend! (*Meaning* ROXY.) You think this boy is a toy?

JOE. Eddie's the only one here who understands me.

MOODY. Who the hell wantsa understand you! I got one wish—for Lombardo to give you the business! The quicker he taps you off tonight, the better! You gotta be took

down a dozen pegs! I'm versus you! C[o]pletely versus!

EDDIE (*quietly, to* MOODY). Moody, y[our] brains is in your feet! This is how [to] handle a coming champ, to give him [the] jitters before a bout? Go out and take s[ome] air! . . . (*Seeing* EDDIE'S *quiet deadli[ness]* MOODY *swallows his wrath and exits;* R[OXY] *follows with pursed lips.*)

EDDIE. Lay down, Joe—take it easy. ([He] *sits on a table.*)

EDDIE. Who hurt you, Joe? Someone [hurt] your feelings?

JOE. Everything's all right.

EDDIE. Tokio, I put fifty bucks on B[ona]parte's nose for you. It's my apprecia[tion] to you. . . .

TOKIO. Thanks.

EDDIE (*of* MR. BONAPARTE). Whatta [you] want me to do with him?

JOE. Leave him here.

EDDIE. Tell me if you want something.

JOE. Nothing.

EDDIE. Forget that Miss Moon. Stop loo[kin'] down her dress. Go out there and [get] Lombardo! Send him out to Woodla[wn!] Tear his skull off! . . . as I know Bona[parte] can do it! (EDDIE *gives* MR. BONAPAR[TE] *sharp look and exits. There is silence in[ten]sified by the distant clang of the bell [and] the muted roar of* THE CROWD. TOKIO [looks] *over at* MR. BONAPARTE *who has been sil[ently] seated on the bench all this time.*)

JOE (*not quite knowing what to say*). [How] is Anna, poppa?

MR. BONAPARTE. Fine.

JOE. Siggie watching the fights?

MR. BONAPARTE. Yes. . . .

JOE. You look fine. . . .

MR. BONAPARTE. Yes, feela good. . . .

JOE. Why did you send that money b[ack?] (*There is no answer.*) Why did you [come] here? . . . You sit there like my [con]science. . . .

MR. BONAPARTE. Why you say so?

, Poppa, I have to fight, no matter what
say or think! This is my profession! I'm
for fame and fortune, not to be different
rtistic! I don't intend to be ashamed of
life!

BONAPARTE (*standing up*). Yeah, I un-
tanda you. . . .

Go out and watch the fights.

BONAPARTE (*somberly*). Yeah . . . you
t. Now I know . . . is'a too late for
ic. The men musta be free an' happy for
ic . . . not like-a you. Now I see whatta
are . . . I give-a you every word to
t . . . I sorry for you. . . . (*Silence. The
int roar of* THE CROWD *climbs up and
down; the bell clangs again.*)

10 (*gently*). I'll have to ask you to
e, Mr. Bonaparte. . . .

BONAPARTE (*holding back his tears*).
. . . I hope-a you win every fight. (MR.
APARTE *slowly exits. As he opens and
es the door the roar of* THE CROWD *swells
or an instant.*)

10. Lay down, Joe. There's five minutes
to tune you up.

(*in a low voice*). That's right, tune me
. . . (JOE *stretches out on his stomach
TOKIO's *busy hands start up the back
is legs.*)

10 (*working with steady briskness*). I
r worried less about a boy . . . in my
You're a real sweetheart. . . . (*Suddenly
begins to cry in his arms.* TOKIO *looks
n, momentarily hesitates in his work—
slowly goes ahead with his massaging
ds. The* BOY *continues to shake with si-
sobs. Again the bell clangs in the dis-
e.*)

10 (*in a soft caressing voice*). You're
ing good, honey. Maybe I never told
that before. I seen it happen before.
ntinuing the massaging.*) It seems to
pen sudden—a fighter gets good. He
easy and graceful. He learns how to
himself—no energy wasted . . . he slips
slides—he travels with the punch. . . .
sure, I like the way you're shaping up.
KIO *continues massaging.* JOE *is silent.
sobbing stops. After a moment* TOKIO
inues.*) What was you saying about
bardo's trick? I understood you to say

he's a bull's-eye for a straight shot from the
inside. I think you're right, Joe, but that
kind of boy is liable to meet you straight-on
in a clinch and give you the back of his
head under the chin. Watch out for that.

JOE. He needs a straight punch. . . . (JOE
*suddenly sits up on the table, his legs dang-
ling.*)

JOE. Now I'm alone. They're all against me
—Moody, the girl . . . you're my family now,
Tokio—you and Eddie! I'll show them all
—nobody stands in my way! My father's
had his hand on me for years. No more. No
more for her either—she had her chance!
When a bullet sings through the air it has
no past—only a future—like me! Nobody,
nothing stands in my way! (*In a sudden
spurt of feeling* JOE *starts sparring around
lightly in a shadow boxing routine.* TOKIO
smiles with satisfaction. Now the roar of THE
CROWD *reaches a frenzied shriek and hangs
there. The bell clangs rapidly several times.
The roar of* THE CROWD *settles down again.*)

TOKIO. That sounds like the kill. (JOE *draws
his bathrobe around him and prances on his
toes.*)

JOE. I'm a new boy tonight! I could take two
Lombardos! (*Vigorously shaking out his
bandaged hands above his head.*) Hallelujah! We're on the Millionaire Express tonight! Nobody gets me! (*The door is thrust
open and a* CALL BOY *shouts.*)

CALL BOY. Bonaparte, ready. Bonaparte,
ready. (PEPPER WHITE *and* MICKEY *enter as
the* CALL BOY *speeds away.* PEPPER *is flushed
with victory.*)

PEPPER (*to* JOE). Tell me when you want it;
you can have it the way I just give it to
Pulaski! (JOE *looks* PEPPER *in the face,
flexes his hands several times and suddenly
breaks out in laughter, to* PEPPER's *astonishment.* JOE *and* TOKIO *exit.* PEPPER *throws off
his robe and displays his body.*)

PEPPER. Look me over—not a mark. How
do you like that for class! I'm in a hurry
to grab a cab to Flushing.

MICKEY (*impassively*). Keep away from her.

PEPPER. I don't even hear you.

MICKEY. Keep away from her!

PEPPER. I go for her like a bee and the
flower.

MICKEY (*in a droning prophetic voice*). The flower is married. Her husband is an excitable Armenian from the Orient. There will be hell to pay! Keep away from her! (*Now in the distance is heard the indistinct high voice of the announcer.*)

PEPPER. You oughta get me a fight with that cock-eye Napoleon—insteada sticking your nose where it don't belong! I could slaughter him in next to nothing.

MICKEY (*impassively*). If you could make his weight and slaughter him, you'd be the next world's champ. But you can't make his weight, you can't slaughter him, and you can't be the champ. Why the hell don't you take a shower? (*The bell clangs—in the arena,* JOE's *fight is on.*)

PEPPER (*plaintively, beginning to dress at his locker*). If my girl don't like me without a shower, I'll tell her a thing or two.

MICKEY. If her husband don't tell you first. (*The roar of* THE CROWD *swells up as the door opens and* MR. BONAPARTE *enters. He is unusually agitated. He looks at* PEPPER *and* MICKEY *and sits on a bench. The roar of* THE CROWD *mounts higher than before, then drops.*)

PEPPER (*to* MR. BONAPARTE). What's the matter with you?

MR. BONAPARTE (*shaking his head*). Don't like to see . . .

PEPPER (*delighted*). Why? Your boy gettin' smeared?

MR. BONAPARTE. They fighta for money, no?

MICKEY. No, they're fighting for a noble cause—

MR. BONAPARTE. If they wasa fight for cause or for woman, woulda not be so bad.

PEPPER (*still dressing behind the locker door*). I fight for money and I like it. I don't fight for under a thousand bucks. Do I, Mickey?

MICKEY. Nope.

PEPPER (*boasting naïvely*). I didn't fight for under a thousand for five years. Did I, Mickey?

MICKEY (*impassively*). Nope.

PEPPER. I get a thousand bucks tonight, don't I?

MICKEY. Nope.

PEPPER (*up like a shot*). How much? I much tonight?

MICKEY. Twelve hundred bucks.

PEPPER. What? Mickey, I oughta bust in the nose. How many times do I hav say I don't fight for under one thou bucks! (*To* MR. BONAPARTE.) Now you what I'm up against with this manager

MICKEY (*impassively*). Okay, you'll g thousand.

PEPPER. I better, Buddy! That's all I sa better! (*To* MR. BONAPARTE.) I tell hi want to fight your kid and he don't l finger. (*The roar of* THE CROWD *cresce and drops down again.*)

MICKEY. You don't rate no fight with B parte. (*To* MR. BONAPARTE, *of* PEPPER.) an old man, a fossil!

MR. BONAPARTE. Who?

MICKY. Him—he's twenty-nine.

MR. BONAPARTE. Old?

MICKEY. In this business, twenty-nine i cient.

PEPPER. My girl don't think so.

MICKEY. Keep away from her. (*The of* THE CROWD *mounts up to a det shriek.*)

PEPPER. Wow, is your boy getting schloc

MR. BONAPARTE. My boy isa' win.

PEPPER. Yeah, and that's why you away?

MR. BONAPARTE. Whatta the difference w a win? Is terrible to see!

PEPPER (*grinning*). If I wasn't in a h I'd wait around to help pick up your Joie's head off the floor. (*He draws sport shirt.*)

MICKEY (*to* PEPPER). What are you wea a polo shirt on a winter night for?

PEPPER. For crying out loud, I just bo it! . . . So long, Mr. Bonaparte.

MR. BONAPARTE. I aska you please—w happen to a boy's hands when he fig longa time?

ER (*holding up his fists*). Take a look [m]ine—I got a good pair. See those [kn]kles? Flat!

BONAPARTE. Broke?

ER. Not broke, flat!—pushed down!

BONAPARTE. Hurt?

ER. You get used to it.

BONAPARTE. Can you use them?

ER. Go down the hall and look at Pu-

[B]ONAPARTE. Can you open thees-a hands?

ER. What for?

BONAPARTE (*gently touching the fists*). [St]rong, so hard . . .

ER. You said it, Buddy. So long, Buddy. [To] MICKEY.) Take my stuff.

[MICK]EY. Sam'll take it after. Keep away [from] her! (PEPPER *looks at* MICKEY *with a* [ma]*nic grin and exits followed by* MICKEY.)

[B]ONAPARTE (*to himself*). So strong . . . [u]seless . . . (*The roar of* THE CROWD [mou]*nts up and calls for a kill.* MR. BONA-[parte] *trembles. For a moment he sits quiet-* [on] *the bench. Then he goes to the door* [of th]*e shower room and looks around at* [b]*oxing paraphernalia. In the distance* [a] *bell begins to clang repeatedly.* MR. [BONA]*PARTE stares in the direction of the* [noise]*. He goes to the exit door.* THE CROWD [ch]*eering and howling.* MR. BONAPARTE [wai]*tes a moment at the door and then* [slow]*ly walks back to the bench, where he* [sits.] *Head cocked, he listens for a moment.* [The r]*oar of* THE CROWD *is heated, demand-* [ing a]*nd hateful. Suddenly* MR. BONAPARTE [rise]*s to his feet. He is in a murderous* [rage]*. He shakes his clenched fist in the* [direct]*ion of the noise—he roars aloud. The* [roar] *of* THE CROWD *dies down. The door* [opens], PEPPER'*s second,* SAM, *enters, softly* [whist]*ling to himself. Deftly he begins to* [put] *together* PEPPER'*s paraphernalia.*)

BONAPARTE. What'sa happen in the [ring?]

Knockout.

[B]ONAPARTE. Who?

SAM. Lombardo's stiff. (MR. BONAPARTE *slowly sits. Softly whistling,* SAM *exits with the paraphernalia. The outside door is flung open. In come* JOE, TOKIO, MOODY *and* ROXY, *who is elated beyond sanity.* JOE'*s eyes glitter; his face is hard and flushed. He has won by a knockout.*)

ROXY (*almost dancing*). My boy! My darling boy! My dear darling boy! (*Silently* JOE *sits on the edge of the table, ignoring his father after a glance. His robe drops from his shoulders.* ROXY *turns to* MOODY.)

ROXY. How do you like it, Tom? He knocks him out in two rounds!

MOODY (*stiffly, to* JOE). It's good business to call the sports writers in—

ROXY. That's right, give a statement! (MOODY *gives* JOE *a rapid glance and hurriedly exits.*)

ROXY. I'm collecting a bet on you. All my faith and patience is rewarded. (*As he opens the door he almost knocks over* EDDIE FUSELI.) Haha! How do you like it, Eddie? Haha! (*He exits.* EDDIE FUSELI *closes the door and stands with his back to it.* TOKIO *moves up to* JOE *and begins to remove a glove.*)

TOKIO (*gently*). You're a real sweetheart. . . . (TOKIO *removes the sweaty glove and begins to fumble with the lace of the other one.* JOE *carefully moves this glove out of* TOKIO'*s reach, resting it on his opposite arm.*)

JOE (*almost proudly*). Better cut it off. . . . (MR. BONAPARTE *is watching tensely.* EDDIE *watches from the door.*)

TOKIO. . . . Broke? . . .

JOE (*holding the hand out proudly*). Yes, it's broke. . . . (TOKIO *slowly reaches for a knife. He begins carefully to cut the glove.*)

JOE. Hallelujah! It's the beginning of the world! (MR. BONAPARTE, *lips compressed, slowly turns his head away.* EDDIE *watches with inner excitement and pleasure;* JOE *has become a fighter.* TOKIO *continues with his work.* JOE *begins to laugh loudly, victoriously, exultantly—with a deep thrill of satisfaction.*)

SLOW FADEOUT

ACT THREE

SCENE I

MOODY's *office, six months later. Present are* MOODY, *acting the persuasive salesman w two sports writers,* DRAKE *and* LEWIS; ROXY GOTTLIEB *being helpful in his usual mann* TOKIO, *to one side, characteristically quiet . . . and* JOE BONAPARTE. BONAPARTE *sits on desk and diffidently swings his legs as he eats a sandwich. His success has added a cer bellicocity to his attitude; it has changed his clothing to silk shirts and custom-made su*

MOODY. He's got his own style. He won't rush—

ROXY. Nobody claims our boy's Niagara Falls.

DRAKE (*a newspaperman for twenty years*). Except himself!

MOODY. You newspaper boys are right.

DRAKE. We newspaper boys are always right!

MOODY. He won't take chances tomorrow night if he can help it. He'll study his man, pick out flaws—then shoot at them.

JOE (*casually*). It won't matter a helluva lot if I win late in the bout or near the opening. The main thing with Bonaparte is to win.

DRAKE (*dryly*). Well, what does Bonaparte expect to do tomorrow night?

JOE (*as dryly*). Win.

MOODY. Why shouldn't we have a win from the Chocolate Drop? Look at our record!—

LEWIS (*good-natured and slow*). We just wanna get an impression—

MOODY. Seventeen knockouts? Fulton, Lombardo, Guffey Talbot—?

JOE. Phil Weiner . . .

MOODY. Weiner?

ROXY. That's no powderpuff hitter!

LEWIS. In this fight tomorrow night, can you name the round?

JOE. Which round would you like?

DRAKE. You're either a genius or an idiot!

MOODY. Joe don't mean—

DRAKE (*sharply*). Let him talk for hims

JOE (*getting off the desk*). Listen, Dra I'm not the boy I used to be—the hon moon's over. I don't blush and stamm these days. Bonaparte goes in and slugs v the best. In the bargain his brain is be than the best. That's the truth; why deny

DRAKE. The last time you met Chocolate never even touched him!

JOE. It's almost two years since I "ne even touched him." Now I know how

MOODY. What Joe means to say—

DRAKE. He's the genuine and only mo cock-eyed wonder!

JOE. What good is modesty? I'm a figh The whole essence of prizefighting is modesty! "I'm better than you are—prove it by breaking your face in!" W do you expect? A conscience and a n smile? I don't believe that bull the me inherit the earth!

DRAKE. Oh, so it's the earth you want!

JOE. I know what I want—that's my ness! But I don't want your guff!

DRAKE. I have two sons of my own—I boys. But I'm a son-of-a-bitch if I can s ach your conceit!

MOODY (*trying to save the situation*). serve a helluva rum Collins across street—

DRAKE. Bonaparte, I'll watch for Wat with more than interest!

MOODY. Why don't we run across f drink? How 'bout some drinks?

DRAKE. Tom, you can buy me twenty d and I still won't change my mind a him. (*He exits.*)

VIS (*smiling*). You're all right, Bonate.

. Thanks....

VIS (*clinching a cigarette at the desk*). w's that big blonde of yours, Tom?

ODY. Fine.

VIS. How does she feel about the wedding ls? Sunday is it? (*This is news to* JOE, *l* MOODY *knows it is.*)

ODY (*nervously*). Happy, the way I am. ah, Sunday.

Y. How about the drinks? We'll drink everybody's health!

VIS (*to* JOE). Good luck tomorrow.

. Thanks, . . . (*They exit,* MOODY *throw- a resentful look at* JOE. JOE *and* TOKIO *left. In the silence* JOE *goes back to the nains of his lunch.*)

IO. That Drake is a case.

(*pushing the food away*). They don't ke cheesecake the way they used to when vas a boy. Or maybe I don't like it any re. When are they getting married?

IO. Moody? Sunday.

. Those writers hate me.

IO. You give them too much lip.

(*looking down at his clenched fists*). rather give than take it. That's one rea- I became a fighter. When did Moody his divorce?

IO. Few weeks ago. . . . (*Cannily.*) Why 't you forget Lorna?

(*as if not understanding*). What?

IO. I'll say it again . . . why not forget ? (*No answer comes.*) Joe, you're loaded h love. Find something to give it to. ur heart ain't in fighting . . . your *hate* is. t a man with hate and nothing else . . . s half a man . . . and half a man . . . no man. Find something to love, or some-. Am I stepping on your toes?

(*coldly*). I won't be unhappy if you nd your business.

TOKIO. Okay. . . . (TOKIO *goes to the door, stops there.*) Watch your dinner tonight. No girls either.

JOE. Excuse me for saying that—

TOKIO (*with a faint smile*). Okay. (TOKIO *opens the door and* LORNA MOON *enters.* TOKIO *smiles at her and exits. She carries a pack of newspapers under her arm.* JOE *and she do not know what to say to each other—they wish they had not met here.* LORNA *crosses and puts the newspapers on the desk. She begins to bang through the desk drawers, looking for the scissors.*)

JOE. I hear you're making the leap tomorrow....

LORNA. Sunday. . . .

JOE. Sunday. (*Intense silence.*)

LORNA (*to say anything*). I'm looking for the scissors....

JOE. Who're you cutting up today?

LORNA (*bringing out the shears*). Items on Bonaparte, for the press book. (*She turns and begins to unfold and clip a sheet of newspaper.* JOE *is at a loss for words.*)

JOE (*finally*). Congratulations....

LORNA (*without turning*). Thanks. . . . (*In a sudden irresistible surge* JOE *tears the papers out of* LORNA'*s hands and hurls them behind the desk. The two stand facing each other.*)

JOE. When I speak to you, look at me!

LORNA. What would you like to say? (*They stand face to face, straining. Finally*:)

JOE. Marry anyone you like!

LORNA. Thanks for permission!

JOE. Queen Lorna, the tramp of Newark!

LORNA. You haven't spoken to me for months. Why break your silence?

JOE. You're a historical character for me—dead and buried!

LORNA. Then everything's simple; go about your business.

JOE. Moody's right for you—perfect—the mating of zero and zero!

LORNA. I'm not sorry to marry Tom—

JOE (*scornfully*). That's from the etiquette book—page twelve: "When you marry a man say you like it!"

LORNA. I know I could do worse when I look at you. When did you look in the mirror last? Getting to be a killer! You're getting to be like Fuseli! You're not the boy I cared about, not you. You murdered that boy with the generous face—God knows where you hid the body! I don't know you.

JOE. I suppose I never kissed your mouth—

LORNA. What do you want from me? Revenge? Sorry—we're all out of revenge today!

JOE. I wouldn't look at you twice if they hung you naked from a Christmas tree! (*At this moment* EDDIE FUSELI *enters with a pair of packages. He looks intently at* LORNA, *then crosses and puts the packages on the desk. He and* JOE *are dressed almost identically.* LORNA *exits without a word.* EDDIE *is aware of what has happened but begins to talk casually about the packages.*)

EDDIE. This one's your new headgear. This is shirts from Jacobs Brothers. He says the neck bands are gonna shrink, so I had him make sixteens—they'll fit you after one washing. (*Holding up a shirt.*) You like that color?

JOE. Thanks.

EDDIE. Your brother-in-law drove me over. Picked him up on 49th. Don't you ever see them no more?

JOE (*sharply*). What for?

EDDIE. What'sa matter?

JOE. Why? You see a crowd around here, Eddie?

EDDIE. No.

JOE. That's right, you don't! But I do! I see a crowd of Eddies all around me, suffocating me, burying me in good times and silk shirts!

EDDIE (*dialing the telephone*). You wanna go to the Scandals tonight? I got tickets. (*Into the telephone.*) Charley? Fuseli is speaking. . . . I'm giving four to five on Bonaparte tomorrow. . . . Four G's worth.

. . . Yes. (*Hanging up the phone.*) gonna be a good fight tomorrow

JOE (*belligerently*). How do you know?

EDDIE. I know Bonaparte. I got eighte thousand spread out on him tomorrow nig

JOE. Suppose Bonaparte loses?

EDDIE. I look at the proposition from sides—I know he'll win.

JOE. What the hell do you think I am? machine? Maybe I'm lonely, maybe—

EDDIE. You wanna walk in a parade? Eve body's lonely. Get the money and you're so lonely.

JOE. I want some personal life.

EDDIE. I give Bonaparte a good personal l I got loyalty to his cause. . . .

JOE. You use me like a gun! Your loyal to keep me oiled and polished!

EDDIE. A year ago Bonaparte was a roo with a two-pants suit. Now he wears best, eats the best, sleeps the best. He wa down the street respected—the golden b They howl their heads off when Bonapa steps in the ring . . . and I done it for hi

JOE. There are other things. . . .

EDDIE. There's no other things! Don't thi so much—it could make you very si You're in this up to your neck. You o me a lot—I don't like you to forget. Y better be on your toes when you step that ring tomorrow night. (EDDIE *turns a begins to dial the telephone.*)

JOE. Your loyalty makes me shiver. (*starts for the door.*)

EDDIE. Take the shirts.

JOE. What do I want them for? I can o wear one at a time. . . . (EDDIE *speaks i the phone.*)

EDDIE. Meyer? . . . Fuseli is speaking. . I'm giving four to five on Bonaparte to row. . . . Two? . . . Yeah. . . . (*Ab to exit,* JOE *stands at the door and watc* EDDIE *as he calmly begins to dial the ph again.*)

MEDIUM FADEOUT

SCENE II

The next night.
The lights fade in on an empty stage. We are in the same dressing room as seen in Act
two. Far in the distance is heard the same roar of THE CROWD. *The distant bell clangs*
menacingly. The room is shadows and patches of light. The silence here has its own ugly
sad quality.
LORNA MOON *enters. She looks around nervously; she lights a cigarette; this reminds her*
rouge her lips; she puffs the cigarette. The distant bell clangs again. EDDIE FUSELI *enters,*
pale and tense. He sees LORNA *and stops short in his tracks. There is an intense silence as*
they look at each other.

LORNA. How's the fight?

EDDIE. I like to talk to you.

LORNA. Is Joe still on his feet?

EDDIE. Take a month in the country, Miss
Moon.

LORNA. Why?

EDDIE (*repressing a murderous mood*). Give
the boy . . . or move away.

LORNA. I get married tomorrow. . . .

EDDIE. You heard my request—give him or
—

LORNA. Don't Moody count?

EDDIE. If not for Bonaparte they'd find you
in a barrel long ago—in the river or a
bush!

LORNA. I'm not afraid of you. . . . (*The dis-*
tant bell clangs.)

EDDIE (*after turning his head and listening*).
That's the beginning of the eighth. Bonaparte's unsettled—fighting like a drunken
sailor. He can't win no more, unless he
knocks the Chocolate out. . . .

LORNA (*at a complete loss*). Don't look at
me . . . what'd you . . . I . . .

EDDIE. Get outa town! (THE ROAR OF THE
CROWD *mounts to a demand for a kill.*)

EDDIE (*listening intently*). He's like a bum
tonight . . . and a bum done it! You! (*The*
roar grows fuller.) I can't watch him get
slaughtered. . . .

LORNA. I couldn't watch it myself. . . . (*The*
bell clangs loudly several times. THE ROAR
OF THE CROWD *hangs high in the air.*) What's
happening now?

EDDIE. Someone's getting murdered. . . .

LORNA. It's me. . . .

EDDIE (*quietly, intensely*). That's right . . .
if he lost . . . the trees are ready for your
coffin. (THE ROAR *of* THE CROWD *tones*
down.) You can go now. I don't wanna
make a scandal around his name. . . . I'll
find you when I want you. Don't be here
when they carry him in.

LORNA (*at a complete loss*). Where do you
want me to go?

EDDIE (*suddenly releasing his wrath*). Get
outa my sight! You turned down the sweetest boy who ever walked in shoes! You
turned him down, the golden boy, that king
among the juven-niles! He gave you his
hand—you spit in his face! You led him on
like Gertie's whoore! You sold him down
the river! And now you got the nerve to
stand here, to wait and see him bleeding
from the mouth!—

LORNA. Fuseli, for God's sake—

EDDIE. Get outa my sight!

LORNA. Fuseli, please—

EDDIE. Outa my sight, you nickel whoore!
(*Completely enraged and out of control,*
EDDIE *half brings his gun out from under*
his left armpit. JOE *appears in the doorway.*
Behind him are ROXY, MOODY *and a* SEC-
OND.)

JOE. Eddie! (EDDIE *whirls around. The*
others enter the room. In the ensuing silence,
MOODY, *sensing what has happened, crosses*
to LORNA.)

LORNA (*quietly*). What happened?

ROXY. What happened? (*He darts forward*
and picks up JOE'S *arm in the sign of vic-*

tory. The arm drops back limply.) The monarch of the masses!

EDDIE (*to the* SECOND). Keep everybody out. Only the newspaper boys. (*The* SECOND *exits and closes the door.* JOE *sits on a table. Physically he is a very tired boy. There is a high puff under one eye; the other is completely closed. His body is stained with angry splotches.*)

TOKIO (*gently*). I have to hand it to you, Joe. . . .

ROXY (*explaining to the frigid* EDDIE, *elaborately*). The beginning of the eighth: first the bell! Next the Chocolate Drop comes out like a waltz clog, confident. Oh, he was so confident! Haha! The next thing I know the Chocolate's on the floor, the referee lifts our arm, we got on our bathrobe and we're here in the dressing room! How do you like it?

EDDIE (*narrowly*). I like it.

TOKIO (*taking off* JOE's *gloves*). I'll have you feelin' better in a minute. (*After which he cuts the tapes.*)

JOE. I feel all right.

EDDIE (*to* TOKIO). Gimme his gloves.

MOODY (*wary of* JOE). That's a bad lump under your eye.

JOE. Not as bad as the Chocolate Drop got when he hit the floor!

ROXY. Darling, how you gave it to him! Not to my enemies!

JOE. 'Twas a straight right—with no trimmings or apologies! Aside from fouling me in the second and fifth—

MOODY. I called them on it—

ROXY. I seen the bastard—

JOE. That second time I nearly went through the floor. I gave him the fury of a lifetime in that final punch! (EDDIE *has taken the soggy boxing gloves for his own property.* TOKIO *is daubing the bruise under* JOE's *eye.*) And did you hear them cheer! (*Bitterly, as if reading a news report.*) Flash! As thousands cheer, that veritable whirlwind Bonaparte—that veritable cock-

eye wonder, Bonaparte—he comes from hind in the eighth stanza to slaughter Chocolate Drop and clinch a bout with champ! Well, how do you like me, bo Am I good or am I good?

ROXY. Believe *me*!

TOKIO (*attempting to settle* JOE). You w the right for a crack at the title. You wo fair and clean. Now lay down. . . .

JOE (*in a vehement outburst*). I'd l to go outside my weight and beat up whole damn world!

MOODY (*coldly*). Well, the world's your ter now!

TOKIO (*insistently*). Take it easy. Lem fix that eye, Joe— (*Now a bustling li Irishman,* DRISCOLL, *hustles into the roor*

DRISCOLL. Who's got the happy boy's glov

EDDIE. Here . . . why? (DRISCOLL *rapi takes the gloves, "breaks" and exami them.*)

TOKIO. What's the matter, "Drisc"?

JOE. What's wrong?

DRISCOLL (*handing the gloves back to DIE*). Chocolate's a sick boy. Your ha are clean. (DRISCOLL *hustles for the door. is up and to him.*)

JOE. What happened?

DRISCOLL (*bustling*). It looks like the Pr of Baltimore is out for good. Change y clothes.

JOE. How do you mean?

DRISCOLL. Just like I said—out! (DRISC *pats* JOE's *shoulder, hustles out, closing door in* JOE's *face.* JOE *slowly sits on nearest bench. Immediately* TOKIO *come him, as tender as a mother.*)

TOKIO. You didn't foul him—you're a cl fighter. You're so honest in the ring stupid. If something's happened, it's accident. (*The others stand around stunn not knowing what to do or say.*)

MOODY (*very worried*). That's right, the nothing to worry about.

ROXY (*ditto*). That's right. . . .

. Gee. . . . (JOE *stands up, slowly crosses
room and sits on the table, head in his
ads, his back to the others. No one knows
at to say.*)

DIE (*to* MOODY). Go out there and size up
situation. (MOODY, *glad of the opportu-
y to leave the room, turns to the door
ich is suddenly violently thrust open.*

RKER, *the* CHOCOLATE DROP'S *manager,
shes* MOODY *into the room with him, leav-
the door open. From outside a small
up of curious people look in.* BARKER,
eft of his senses, grabs* MOODY *by the coat
el.*)

RKER. Do you know it? Do you know it?

OODY. Now wait a minute, Barker— (BAR-
R *runs over to* JOE *and screams:*)

RKER. You murdered my boy! He's dead!
u killed him!

KIO (*getting between* JOE *and* BARKER).
t a minute!

RKER (*literally wringing his hands*). He's
ad! Chocolate's dead!

KIO. We're very sorry about it. Now pull
urself together. (EDDIE *crosses the room
d slams the door shut as* BARKER *points
accusing finger at* JOE *and screams:*)

RKER. This dirty little wop killed my boy!

DIE (*coming to* BARKER). Go back in your
m.

RKER. Yes he did!! (EDDIE'S *answer is to
ove* BARKER *roughly toward the door,
eping.*) Yes, he did!!

DIE. Get out before I slug your teeth apart!

E (*jumping to his feet*). Eddie, for God
es, don't hit him! Let him alone! (EDDIE
mediately desists.* BARKER *stands there, a
eping idiot.*)

OODY. Accidents can happen.

RKER. I know . . . know . . .

OODY. Chocolate fouled us twice.

RKER. I know, I know. . . . (BARKER *stam-
rs, gulps and tries to say something more.
ddenly he dashes out of the room. There
a long silent pause during which* JOE *sits
wn again.*)

EDDIE. We'll have to wait for an investigation.

TOKIO (*to* JOE). Don't blame yourself for
nothing. . . .

JOE. That poor guy . . . with those sleepy
little eyes. . . .

ROXY (*solemnly*). It's in the hands of God,
a thing like that. (LEWIS, *the sports writer,
tries to enter the room.*)

EDDIE (*herding him out*). Stay outside. (*To*
MOODY.) See what's happening? (MOODY *immediately leaves.*) Everybody out—leave
Bonaparte to calm hisself. I'll watch the
door.

TOKIO. Don't worry, Joe. (*He exits, followed
by* ROXY. EDDIE *turns and looks at* LORNA.)

EDDIE. You too, Miss Moon—this ain't no
cocktail lounge.

LORNA. I'll stay here. (EDDIE *looks at her
sharply, shifts his glance from her to* JOE
and back again; he exits.) Joe. . . .

JOE. Gee, that poor boy. . . .

LORNA (*holding herself off*). But it wasn't
your fault.

JOE. That's right—it wasn't my fault!

LORNA. You didn't mean it!

JOE. That's right—I didn't mean it! I
wouldn't want to do that, would I? Everybody knows I wouldn't want to kill a man.
Lorna, you know it!

LORNA. Of course!

JOE. But I *did* it! That's the thing—I *did* it!
What will my father say when he hears I
murdered a man? Lorna, I see what I did.
I murdered myself, too! I've been running
around in circles. Now I'm smashed! That's
the truth. Yes, I was a real sparrow, and I
wanted to be a fake eagle! But now I'm
hung up by my finger tips—I'm no good—
my feet are off the earth!

LORNA (*in a sudden burst, going to* JOE).
Joe, I love you! We love each other. Need
each other!

JOE. Lorna darling, I see what's happened!

LORNA. You wanted to conquer the world—

JOE. Yes—

LORNA. But it's not the kings and dictators who do it—it's that kid in the park—

JOE. Yes, that boy who might have said, "I have myself; I am what I want to be!"

LORNA. And now, tonight, here, this minute —finding yourself again—that's what makes you a champ. Don't you see that?

JOE. Yes, Lorna—yes!

LORNA. It isn't too late to tell the world good evening again!

JOE. With what? These fists?

LORNA. Give up the fighting business!

JOE. Tonight!

LORNA. Yes, and go back to your music—

JOE. But my hands are ruined. I'll never play again! What's left, Lorna? Half a man, nothing, useless. . . .

LORNA. No, *we're* left! Two together! We have each other! Somewhere there must be happy boys and girls who can teach us way of life! We'll find some city wh poverty's no shame—where music is crime!—where there's no war in the stre —where a man is glad to be himself, to l and make his woman herself!

JOE. No more fighting, but where do we g

LORNA. Tonight? Joe, we ride in your c We speed through the night, across the pa over the Triboro Bridge—

JOE (*taking* LORNA's *arms in his trembl hands*). Ride! That's it, we ride—clear head. We'll drive through the night. Wl you mow down the night with headligl nobody gets you! You're on top of world then—nobody laughs! That's i speed! We're off the earth—unconnect We don't have to think!! That's what spee for, an easy way to live! Lorna darling, w burn up the night! (*He turns and as begins to throw his street clothes out of locker.*)

MEDIUM FADEOUT

SCENE III

Late the same night.

In the Bonaparte home sit EDDIE FUSELI, MOODY, ROXY *and* SIGGIE, *drinking homem wine, already half drunk.* MR. BONAPARTE *stands on the other side of the room, look out of the window.* FRANK *sits near him, a bandage around his head.*

MOODY *is at the telephone as the lights fade in.*

MOODY (*impatiently*). . . . 'lo? Hello! . . .

SIGGIE. I'll tell you why we need another drink. . . .

ROXY. No, I'll tell you. . . .

MOODY (*turning*). Quiet! For Pete's sake! I can't hear myself think! (*Turning to the phone.*) Hello? . . . This is Moody. Any calls for me? Messages? . . . No sign of Miss Moon? . . . Thanks. Call me if she comes in—the number I gave you before. (*Hanging up and returning to his wine glass; to* MR. BONAPARTE.) I thought you said Joe was coming up here!

MR. BONAPARTE. I say maybe. . . .

MOODY (*sitting*). I'll wait another fifteen minutes. (*He drinks.*)

SIGGIE. Here's why we need another dri it's a night of success! Joe's in those lo brackets from now on! We're gonna m to a better neighborhood, have a bun kids! (*To* MR. BONAPARTE.) Hey, pop wish we had a mortgage so we could pa off! To the next champ of the world! (GIE *lifts his glass; the others join him.*)

ROXY. Bonaparte.

EDDIE. Don't you drink, Mr. Bonaparte?

SIGGIE. You, too, Frank—it's all in the fa ily. (MR. BONAPARTE *shrugs and comes do accepting a glass.*)

ROXY. It's in the nature of a celebration!

MR. BONAPARTE. My son'sa kill a man night—what'sa celebrate? What'sa go be, heh?

GIE. Ahh, don't worry—they can't do him
:hing for that! An accident!

DIE (*coldly, to* MR. BONAPARTE). Listen,
old news. It's been out on the front page
o-three hours.

. BONAPARTE. Poor color' boy . .

ODY. Nobody's fault. Everybody's sorry—
give the mother a few bucks. But we
: the next champ! Bottoms up. (*All drink,*
ANK *included.*)

XY (*to* MR. BONAPARTE). You see how a
y can make a success nowadays?

. BONAPARTE. Yeah . . . I see.

DIE (*resenting* MR. BONAPARTE's *attitude*).
» we bother you? If I didn't think Joe was
:e I don't come up. I don't like nobody
gimme a boycott!

. BONAPARTE (*going back to the window*).
:lpa you'self to more wine.

GIE (*to* EDDIE). Leave him alone—he don't
l social tonight.

ODY. Don't worry, Mr. Bonaparte. Looka
:—take a lesson from me—I'm not wor-
d. I'm getting married tomorrow—*this
ernoon!*—I don't know where my girl is,
t I'm not worried! What for? We're all
clover up to our necks!

GIE. Shh . . . don't wake up my wife.
OODY *suddenly sits heavily; jealousy be-
is to gnaw at him despite his optimism.*
XY *takes another drink.* EDDIE *asks* FRANK,
·opos *of his bandaged head:*)

DIE. What's that "Spirit of '76" outfit for?

GIE (*grinning to* EDDIE). Didn't you hear
1at he said before? They gave it to him
a strike—

DIE (*to* FRANK). You got a good build—
1 could be a fighter.

ANK. I fight. . . .

DIE. Yeah? For what?

ANK. A lotta things I believe in. . . .
DDIE *looks at* FRANK *and appreciates his
ality.*)

DIE. Whatta you get for it?

XY (*laughing*). Can't you see? A busted
ıd!

FRANK. I'm not fooled by a lotta things Joe's
fooled by. I don't get autos and custom
made suits. But I get what Joe don't.

EDDIE. What don't he get? (MR. BONAPARTE
comes in and listens intently.)

FRANK (*modestly*). The pleasure of acting
as you think! The satisfaction of staying
where you belong, being what you are . . .
at harmony with millions of others!

ROXY (*pricking up his ears*). Harmony?
That's music! the family's starting up music
again!

FRANK (*smiling*). That's right, that's music— (*Now* MOODY *emphatically stamps his
glass down on the table and stands.*)

MOODY. What's the use waiting around!
They won't be back. (*Bitterly.*) Lorna's got
a helluva lotta nerve, riding around in Long
Island with him! Without even asking me!

SIGGIE. Long Island's famous for the best
eating ducks.

EDDIE (*to* MOODY). You got the champ—
you can't have everything.

MOODY. What's that supposed to mean?

EDDIE (*coldly*). That girl belongs to Bonaparte. They're together now, in some road-
house . . . and they ain't eating duck!

MOODY (*finally, unsteadily*). You don't know
what you're talking about!

EDDIE. Moody, what do you figger your interest is worth in Bonaparte?

MOODY. Why?

EDDIE (*without turning*). Roxy . . . are you
listening?

ROXY. Yeah. . . .

EDDIE. 'Cause after tonight I'd like to handle
Bonaparte myself.

MOODY. . . . Your gall is gorgeous! But I
got a contract. . . .

ROXY. Eddie, have a heart—I'm holding a
little twenty percent. . . . (*Out of sheer
rage* MOODY *drinks more wine;* ROXY *follows
his example.*)

FRANK (*to* EDDIE). How much does Joe own
of himself?

EDDIE. Thirty percent. After tonight I own the rest.

MOODY. Oh, no! No, sir-ee!!

EDDIE. You're drunk tonight! Tomorrow!

MR. BONAPARTE (*coming forward*). Maybe Joe don't gonna fight no more, after tonight....

EDDIE. Listen, you creep! Why don't you change your tune for a minute!

ROXY (*to* MR. BONAPARTE). What're YOU worried about?

MR. BONAPARTE. My boy usta coulda be great for all men. Whatta he got now, heh? Pardon me fora nota to feel so confident in Joe'sa future! Pardon me fora to be anxious....

EDDIE (*standing up*). I don't like this talk!

SIGGIE. Sit down, pop—you're rocking the boat! Shh! Shh! (*He slips out of the room.*)

ROXY. Does anyone here know what he's talking about?

FRANK. He's trying to say he's worried for Joe.

ROXY. But why? Why? Don't he realize his kid's worth a fortune from tonight on? (*After giving* EDDIE *a quick glance.*) Ain't he got brains enough to see two feet ahead? Tell him in Italian—he don't understand our language—this is a festive occasion! To Bonaparte, the Monarch of the Masses! (*The telephone rings.*)

MOODY (*triumphantly, to* EDDIE). That's my hotel! You see, you were all wrong! That's Lorna! (*Speaking into the telephone.*) Hello? . . . No. . . . (*Turning to* MR. BONAPARTE.) It's for you. (MOODY *extends the telephone in* MR. BONAPARTE's *direction, but the latter stands in his place, unable to move. After a few seconds,* FRANK *sees this and briskly moves to the telephone, taking it from* MOODY. *In the meantime* MOODY *has begun to address* EDDIE *with drunken eloquence. Wavering on his feet.*) There's a constitution in this country, Eddie Fuseli. Every man here enjoys life, liberty and the pursuit of happiness!

FRANK (*speaking into the telephone*). Yes? . . . No, this is his son. . . . (MR. BONAPARTE

watches FRANK *mutely as he listens at t telephone.*)

MOODY. There's laws in this country, Fuse —*contracts!* We live in a civilized world-

FRANK (*loudly, to the others*). Keep qui (*Resumes listening.*) Yes . . . yes. . . .

ROXY (*to* EDDIE). And there's a God in he ven—don't forget it!

FRANK (*on the telephone*). Say it again. . (*He listens.*) Yes. . . .

MOODY (*to* EDDIE). You're a killer! A m tries to do his best—but you're a kill (FRANK *lowers the telephone and com down to the others.*)

FRANK. You're all killers! (MR. BONAPAR *advances a step toward* FRANK.)

MR. BONAPARTE. Frank . . . is it . . . ?

FRANK. I don't know how to tell you, p pa....

MR. BONAPARTE (*hopefully*). Yes? . . .

FRANK. We'll have to go there—

EDDIE. Go where?

FRANK. Both of them . . . they were kil in a crash—

EDDIE. Who?! What?!

FRANK. They're waiting for identification Long Island, Babylon.

EDDIE (*moving to* FRANK). What are y handing me?! (EDDIE, *suddenly knowing truth, stops in his tracks. The telephone erator signals for the telephone to be placed. The mechanical clicks call* FRANK attention; he slowly replaces the instrumen

MOODY. I don't believe that! Do you h me? I don't believe it—

FRANK. What waste! . . .

MOODY. It's a goddam lie!!

MR. BONAPARTE. What have-a you pect? . . .

MOODY (*suddenly weeping*). Lorna! . . .

MR. BONAPARTE (*standing, his head hig Joe. . . . Come, we bring-a him home . where he belong....

SLOW FADEOUT

Stage Door

BY EDNA FERBER AND GEORGE S. KAUFMAN

STAGE DOOR was produced by Sam H. Harris at the Music Box Theatre, New York, on Thursday night, October 22nd, with the following cast:

OLGA BRANDT	Sylvia Lupas	KENDALL ADAMS	Margot Stevenson
BERNICE NIEMEYER	Janet Fox	FRANK	William Andrews
SUSAN PAIGE	Lili Zehner	TERRY RANDALL	Margaret Sullavan
MATTIE	Dorothea Andrews	SAM HASTINGS	Robert Thomsen
MARY HARPER (Big Mary)	Beatrice Blinn	JIMMY DEVEREAUX	Alex Courtney
MARY McCUNE (Little Mary)	Mary Wickes	FRED POWELL	Walter Davis
MADELEINE VAUCLAIN	Grena Sloan	LOU MILHAUSER	Edmund Dorsay
JUDITH CANFIELD	Lee Patrick	DAVID KINGSLEY	Onslow Stevens
ANN BRADDOCK	Louise Chaffee	KEITH BURGESS	Richard Kendrick
MRS. ORCUTT	Leona Roberts	MRS. SHAW	Helen Ray
KAYE HAMILTON	Frances Fuller	DR. RANDALL	Priestly Morrison
PAT DEVINE	Virginia Rousseau	ELLEN FENWICK	Judith Russell
LINDA SHAW	Jane Buchanan	TONY GILLETTE	Draja Dryden
JEAN MAITLAND	Phyllis Brooks	LARRY WESTCOTT	Tom Ewell
BOBBY MELROSE	Juliet Forbes	BILLY	William Atlee
LOUISE MITCHELL	Catherine Laughlin	ADOLPH GRETZL	Ralph Locke

THE SCENES

ACT I

SCENE 1 Main Room of the Footlights Club. Somewhere in the West Fifties, New York.
SCENE 2 One of the bedrooms. A month later.

ACT II

SCENE 1 Again the main room. A year later.
SCENE 2 The same. Two months later.

ACT III

SCENE 1 The same. The following year. A Sunday morning.
SCENE 2 The same. About two weeks later. Midnight.

STAGE MANAGER—*E. John Kennedy*

STAGE DOOR

ACT ONE

SCENE I

The Footlights Club. A club for girls of the stage.

It occupies an entire brownstone house in the West Fifties, New York. One of thos[e] old houses whose former splendor has departed as the neighborhood has changed.

The room we see is the common living room. It is comfortably furnished with unrelate[d] but good pieces, enlivened by a bit of chintz. The effect is that of charm and livabilit[y] what with the piano, a desk, a fireplace with a good old marble mantel. Prominently hun[g] is a copy of a portrait of Sarah Bernhardt, at her most dramatic. There is a glimpse [of] hallway with a flight of stairs. Near the stairway is a hall table that holds mail, message[s] papers; an occasional hat is thrown there.

It is an October evening, just before the dinner hour. The girls are coming hom[e] from matinees, from job-hunting, they are up and down the stairs, and presently the[y] will be out again on dinner dates, playing the evening performances, seeing a movie.

Two girls are in the room at the moment, one at the piano, the other at a writing des[k.] The girl at the piano, OLGA BRANDT, is dark, intense, sultry-looking.

BERNICE NIEMEYER, at the desk, is a young girl definitely not of the ingenue typ[e.] This is at once her cross and (in her opinion) her greatest asset as an actress.

For a moment nothing is heard but the music. The girl at the piano is playing, beau[ti]fully and with exquisite technique, Chopin's Opus 9, No. 2.

A girl comes in from the street door, stops for a quick look through the mail, tosses "Hi!" into the room, and goes on up the stairs. SUSAN PAIGE.

The piano again.

BERNICE (*to* OLGA). What's that you're playing?

OLGA (*her Russian origin evident in her accent*). Chopin.

BERNICE. How did you learn to play like that?

OLGA. Practice. Practice.

BERNICE. How long did it take you?

OLGA (*out of patience*). Oh! (*A little discordant crash of the keys.*)

BERNICE. Well, I was just asking. (*The telephone rings as* MATTIE, *the maid, is descending the stairs, a little pile of towels over her arm.*)

(MATTIE *is colored, about thirty, matter-of-fact, accustomed to the vagaries of a houseful of girls, and tolerant of them.*)

MATTIE. Hello! . . . Yes, this the Footlights Club. . . . (*To the girls in the room.*) Miss Devine come in yet? (*A negative shake of the head from* OLGA, *and a muttered "uh-uh" from* BERNICE.) No, she ain't. (*She hangs up.*)

BERNICE. Was it a man? (*Meanwhile voic[es] are heard as the street door opens.* "Oh, n[o] let's have dinner here and go to a movie[.]" "Well, all right.")

BERNICE (*pursuing her eternal queries*[)]. Who's that?

OLGA (*a shade of impatience*). Big and Littl[e] Mary. (BIG *and* LITTLE MARY—MARY HARP[ER] *and* MARY MCCUNE—*come into view in t[he] doorway. There is a wide gap in statu[re] between the two. One comes about to t[he] other's elbow.*)

BIG MARY. What time is it? Dinner rea[dy] yet?

BERNICE. Where've you been? Seeing ma[n]agers?

LITTLE MARY (*drooping*). Yeh. We're dea[d.]

BIG MARY. We've been in every manager's [of]fice on Broadway.

BERNICE. Is anybody casting?

BIG MARY. How do *we* know? We on[ly] got in to see *one* of them.

ᴇʀɴɪᴄᴇ. Which one? Who'd you see?

ʟɪᴛᴛʟᴇ ᴍᴀʀʏ. Rosenblatt.

ᴇʀɴɪᴄᴇ. What's he doing?

ʙɪɢ ᴍᴀʀʏ. Take it easy. It's all cast. (*Her tone implies that this is the stereotyped managerial reply.*)

ʟɪᴛᴛʟᴇ ᴍᴀʀʏ. All except a kid part—ten years old.

ᴇʀɴɪᴄᴇ (*eagerly*). I could look ten years old! (*She becomes a dimpled darling.*)

ʟɪᴛᴛʟᴇ ᴍᴀʀʏ. No. Big Mary had the same idea, and she's littler than you are.

ʙɪɢ ᴍᴀʀʏ. You're almost as tall as Little Mary. (*The* ᴍᴀʀʏs *go up the stairs.*)

ᴇʀɴɪᴄᴇ. Listen, why is the little one called Big Mary and the big one Little Mary?

ᴏʟɢᴀ. Nobody knows. Will you for heaven's sake stop asking questions?

ᴇʀɴɪᴄᴇ. Oh, all right. . . . Where've you been? (*The last remark is addressed to a newcomer who stands in the doorway. She is* ᴍᴀᴅᴇʟᴇɪɴᴇ ᴠᴀᴜᴄʟᴀɪɴ, *a languid beauty, who runs through a sheaf of letters to discover if there is any mail for her.*) (*The telephone rings.* ʙᴇʀɴɪᴄᴇ *picks it up.*)

ᴇʀɴɪᴄᴇ. Footlights Club! . . . (*To* ᴏʟɢᴀ) Terry Randall come in? (*As she shakes her head*) Not yet. (*Hangs up.*)

ᴍᴀᴅᴇʟᴇɪɴᴇ. I saw her sitting in Berger's office. I guess she gives up hard.

ᴇʀɴɪᴄᴇ (*alert at once*). Is Berger doing any casting? (*Another girl comes in the street door and dashes upstairs at break-neck speed.* ʙᴏʙʙʏ ᴍᴇʟʀᴏsᴇ.)

ᴍᴀᴅᴇʟᴇɪɴᴇ. Listen, if you'd make the rounds once in a while, instead of sitting on your bustle and writing letters—

ᴇʀɴɪᴄᴇ (*up the stairs*). I make the rounds, but all you see is the office boys.

ᴍᴀᴅᴇʟᴇɪɴᴇ. Well, who do you think sees the letters?

ᴇʀɴɪᴄᴇ. Well, if they won't see you and won't read the letters, where do you go from there?

ᴍᴀᴅᴇʟᴇɪɴᴇ (*calling after her*). If you find out I wish you'd tell me.

ᴍᴀᴛᴛɪᴇ (*in the dining-room doorway*). Either you girls eating home?

ᴍᴀᴅᴇʟᴇɪɴᴇ. I'm not.

ᴍᴀᴛᴛɪᴇ. Anyhow, it's ready. (*Goes.*)

ᴏʟɢᴀ (*continues playing*). Yes, yes.

ᴍᴀᴅᴇʟᴇɪɴᴇ. Look, you don't want to go out tonight, do you? I've got an extra man.

ᴏʟɢᴀ (*a shake of the head*). I am rehearsing.

ᴍᴀᴅᴇʟᴇɪɴᴇ. Tonight?

ᴏʟɢᴀ (*with bitterness*). Tonight! I must play the piano for a lot of chorus girls to sing and dance. (*She plays and even sings in a wordless imitation of their infantile tones; a few scornful bars of the music to which the chorus girls are expected to sing and dance. Then she rises, furiously.*) That's what I am doing tonight—and every night! And for that I studied fifteen years with Kolijinsky! (*She storms into the dining room.*)

ᴍᴀᴅᴇʟᴇɪɴᴇ (*mildly astonished at this outburst*). Well, look, all I did was ask you if you wanted to go out tonight. (*A new figure appears in the doorway. It is* ᴊᴜᴅɪᴛʜ ᴄᴀɴ-ꜰɪᴇʟᴅ, *hard, wise, debunked. She has picked up a letter from the hall table.*)

ᴊᴜᴅɪᴛʜ (*with dreadful sweetness*). Oh, goody, goody, goody! I got a letter from home!

ᴍᴀᴅᴇʟᴇɪɴᴇ. Hello, Judith!

ᴊᴜᴅɪᴛʜ (*averting her gaze from the letter as she opens it, she brings herself to look at it with a courageous jerk of the head.*) (*A little laugh of false gayety as the letter meets every expectation.*) Mmmmm! Pa got laid off. (*Turns a page.*) My sister's husband has left her. (*Her eye skims a line or two.*) And one of my brothers slugged a railroad detective. . . . I guess that's all. Yes. Lots of love and can you spare fifty dollars.

ᴍᴀᴅᴇʟᴇɪɴᴇ. Nothing like a letter from home to pick you up. . . . Look, Judy, what are you doing tonight?

ᴊᴜᴅɪᴛʜ (*who has dropped onto a couch, whisked off her pump, and is pulling out the toe of her stocking*). I don't know. Why?

ᴍᴀᴅᴇʟᴇɪɴᴇ. I've got an extra man.

JUDITH (*brightening*). You mean dinner?

MADELEINE. Yes. Fellow from back home in Seattle. He's in the lumber business. He's here for a convention.

JUDITH. Sounds terrible.

MADELEINE. No, he isn't bad. And he's got this friend with him, so he wanted to know if I could get another girl.

JUDITH. Is the friend also in the lumber business?

MADELEINE. I don't know. What's the difference!

JUDITH. He'll be breezy. "Hello, Beautiful!"

MADELEINE. If we don't like it we can go home early.

JUDITH. Well— (*Weighing it.*) —do we dress?

MADELEINE. Sure!

JUDITH. Okay. I kind of feel like stepping out tonight.

MADELEINE (*going toward the stairs*). Swell. We'd better start. It's getting late.

JUDITH (*tugging at her stocking*). I'll be ready. (MADELEINE *disappears.*)
(JUDITH *wriggles her cramped toes, sighs.*)
(*Still another girl,* ANN BRADDOCK, *has come down the stairs and goes toward the dining room. She is wearing a hat and carrying her coat, which she tosses onto the piano as she passes.*)

ANN. Going in to dinner?

JUDITH. Got a date.

ANN. Well, that's all right for you—you're not working. But I can't go out to dinner, and run around, and still give my best to the theater. After all, you never see Kit Cornell dashing around. (*Righteously, she goes into the dining room.*)

JUDITH (*mutters at first*). Kit Cornell! (*Then raises her voice as the portrait on the wall gives her an idea*). What about Bernhardt! I suppose *she* was a home girl! (*From above stairs and descending the stairway the voice of the House Matron is heard.*)

MRS. ORCUTT. Yes, I'm sure you're going to be most comfortable here. Both of your

roommates are lovely girls. Now if you'll just— (*Sees* JUDITH.) Oh— (MRS. ORCUTT *is a woman of about forty-six. In her manner and dress you detect the flavor of a theatrical past. Her dress is likely to have too many ruffles, her coiffure too many curls. She is piloting a fragile and rather wispy girl whose eyes are too big for her face. We presently learn that her name is* KAYE HAMILTON.) Uh—this is Judith Canfield, one of our girls— I'm so sorry, I'm afraid I didn't—

KAYE. Kaye Hamilton.

MRS. ORCUTT. Oh, yes. Miss Hamilton is planning to be with us if everything—uh—she'll room with Jean and Terry, now that Louise is leaving.

JUDITH. That'll be swell. Excuse me. (*Shoe in hand, she limps toward the stairs.*)

MRS. ORCUTT (*a little gracious nod*). Now, that's our dining room. (*A gesture toward it.*) Dinner is served from six to seven, because of course the girls have to get to the theater early if they're working. Now, let me see. You're in the same room with Terry and Jean, so that's only twelve-fifty a week, including the meals. I suppose that will be all right.

KAYE. Yes, thank you.

MRS. ORCUTT. Now, about the reference. (*She looks at a piece of paper she has been holding.*) I'll have that all looked up in the morning.

KAYE. Morning! Can't I come in tonight?

MRS. ORCUTT. I'm afraid not. You see—

KAYE. But I've got to come in tonight. I've got to. (*A girl comes in at the street door, passes through the hallway and goes rapidly up the stairs, humming as she goes.* PAT DEVINE. *Halfway up the stairs we hear her call* "Yoo-hoo!")

MRS. ORCUTT (*after the interruption*). Well—uh—it's a little irregular. However . . Did you say your bags were near by?

KAYE. Yes. That is, I can get them

MRS. ORCUTT (*reluctantly*). Well, then, I suppose it's all right. . . . Now, we have certain little rules. As you know, this is a club for stage girls. I assume you are on the stage.

AYE. Yes. Yes. I'm not working now, but hope ...

MRS. ORCUTT. I understand. . . . Now about callers—men callers, I mean—

AYE. There won't be any men.

MRS. ORCUTT. Oh, it's quite all right. We like you to bring your friends here. But not after eleven-thirty at night, and—of course—only in this room.

AYE. I understand.

MRS. ORCUTT. I try very hard to make the girls feel that this is a real home. I was one of them myself not many years back, before I married Mr. Orcutt. Helen Romayne? Possibly you remember?

AYE. I'm afraid I—

MRS. ORCUTT. That's quite all right. I think that covers everything. If you wish to go and get your bags—Mattie! (*Peering toward the dining room.*) Will you come here a minute?

MATTIE. Yes, ma'am!

MRS. ORCUTT (*she gently pilots* KAYE *toward the doorway*). Now, each girl is given a door key, and there's a little charge of twenty-five cents in case they're lost. Well, good-by, and I'll expect you in a very short time. (*As* MATTIE *has appeared in the dining-room doorway* BERNICE *comes downstairs; crosses the living room.*)

BERNICE. What have we got for dinner, Mattie?

MATTIE. We got a good dinner.

BERNICE (*as she disappears*). Smells like last night. Is it? (*The sound of the front door closing.* MRS. ORCUTT, *very businesslike, returns.*)

MRS. ORCUTT. Now, Mattie, there's a new girl coming in as soon as Louise Mitchell leaves. You'll only have a few minutes to get that room straightened up.

MATTIE. Yes, ma'am.

MRS. ORCUTT. Let's see, Terry Randall isn't in yet, is she?

MATTIE. No, ma'am.

MRS. ORCUTT. Well, if I don't see her be sure to tell her there's a new girl moving in with

her and Jean. Don't forget fresh paper in the bureau drawers, and— (*Down the stairs like an angry whirlwind comes* LINDA SHAW. *She is clutching a dressing gown about her. Her hair is beautifully done, she is wearing evening slippers; obviously she is dressed for the evening except for her frock.*)

LINDA. Mattie, isn't my dress pressed yet?

MATTIE. Oh! Was you wanting it right away?

LINDA. Right away! When did you *think* I wanted it?

MATTIE. Well, I'll do it right this minute.

LINDA. Oh, don't bother! I'll do it myself! (*Storms out.*)

MATTIE (*following after her*). You never give it to me till pretty near half-past five. (*The telephone rings.* MRS. ORCUTT *answers.*)

MRS. ORCUTT. Footlights Club! . . . Yes, she is. . . . The Globe Picture Company? . . . Mr. Kingsley himself? . . . Just a minute. (*Impressed.*) I'll get her right away. . . . (*Calls toward the stairs.*) Jean! Oh, Jean! (*A voice from above.*)

JEAN. Yes!

MRS. ORCUTT (*in hushed tones*). Mr. Kingsley of the Globe Picture Company wants to talk to you.

JEAN. All right.

MRS. ORCUTT (*back to telephone*). She'll be right down. (*She lays down the receiver with a tenderness that is almost reverence, and takes a few steps away, looking toward the stairway. As* JEAN *appears,* MRS. ORCUTT *affects an elaborate nonchalance and disappears into dining room.*)

(JEAN MAITLAND *is a beautiful girl in her early twenties. She is, perhaps, a shade too vivacious. A better actress off than on. Her hair is blonde, and that toss of her head that shakes back her curls is not quite convincing. An opportunist; good-natured enough when things go her way; she has definite charm and appeal for men.*)
(JEAN *throws her all into her voice as she greets the man at the telephone.*)

JEAN. Hello! Mr. Kingsley! How perfectly— (*Obviously she is met by a secretary's voice. Dashed by this, her tone drops to below normal.*) Yes, this is Miss Maitland. Will you put him on, please? (*Again she gathe· all her forces and even tops her first performance.*) Hello! Mr. Kingsley! How wonderful! . . . Well, *I* think it's pretty wonderful. With all the thousands of people at that party I didn't think you'd remember *me.* . . . Yes, I know you said that, but in your business you must meet a million beautiful girls a day. . . . Well, anyhow, half a million. . . . (*Coyly.*) Dinner! You don't mean tonight! Oh! . . . Yes, I did have, but it's nothing I can't break . . . Oh, but I want to. I'd love to. . . . What time? . . . Yes, I'll be ready. I suppose we're dressing? . . . Yes, I'd love to. All right. Good-by. (*As she hangs up the receiver, figures pop out of the vantage points from which they have been listening.* BERNICE *and* ANN *come out of the dining room with* MRS. ORCUTT; *cloppity-clop down the stairs come* BIG *and* LITTLE MARY *and* BOBBY MELROSE. BOBBY *is a soft Southern belle, fluffy, feminine. At the moment she is in a rather grotesque state of metal hair curlers, cold cream and bathrobe.*)

BIG MARY (*a squeal of excitement*). Jean!

BERNICE. I'm dying!

LITTLE MARY. Tell us about it!

BOBBY. What time is he coming?

MRS. ORCUTT. Well, Jeanie, does this mean we're going to lose you to pictures?

BOBBY. Aren't you palpitating?

BERNICE. How soon is he coming? Can I see him?

JEAN. Now listen, you girls, no fair hanging around!

LITTLE MARY. Aw!

JEAN. You've got to promise me—no parading.

BIG MARY. Big-hearted Bertha!

BERNICE. I'll bet you'll let Terry meet him.

JEAN. Well, Terry's different.

ANN. All this fuss about a man! I wouldn't lift my little finger to meet him. (*She stalks into the dining room.*)

LITTLE MARY. She's oversexed!

MRS. ORCUTT (*still among her souvenirs*). David Kingsley! You know, he was Al

Woods' office boy when I played *The Wo ·n in Room 13.*

BERNICE (*not much interested*). Really? (*T JEAN*) What are you going to wear?

JEAN. I wonder if Pat'll let me have he rose taffeta.

BERNICE. Sure she would.

JEAN. And I'll wear Kendall's evening coa

MRS. ORCUTT (*insistent*). When he becam a producer he wanted me for his first pla But by that time I had married Mr. Orcutt— (*From abovestairs comes the sound of hal a-dozen voices haphazardly singing: "Her Comes the Bride!" The group in the room once knows what this means, and their a tention is turned toward the stairs.*)

BIG MARY. Oh, here's Louise!

BERNICE. Louise is going!

BOBBY. Oh, my goodness, I promised to hel her pack.

LITTLE MARY. Let's get some rice and thro it!

BIG MARY. Oh, for heaven's sake, that's sill (FRANK, *the houseman, comes down th stairs laden with bags. He is* MATTIE's hu band—thirty-five or so. Close on FRANK heels comes* LOUISE MITCHELL *in travelin clothes, and wearing a corsage of gardenia She is accompanied by three girls. One susan, a student at an acting school. Th others are* PAT DEVINE, *a night-club dance and* KENDALL ADAMS, *of the Bosto Adamses.*)
(MATTIE, *broadly grinning and anticipator comes to the dining-room doorway.*)
(LOUISE *is ushered into the room on a wa of melody.*)

MRS. ORCUTT. Well, my dear, and so th moment has come. But when you see ho saddened we are, you will realize that par ting is sweet sorrow, after all. (JUDIT comes down the stairs, followed by MAD LEINE. Both in dishabille.*)

JUDITH. Well, Mitchell, you're finally gettin the hell out of here, huh?

MRS. ORCUTT. Judith! That seems to me har ly the spirit.

JUDITH. Sorry.

LOUISE. Judy doesn't mean anything.

FRANK (*in the doorway*). Shall I get you taxi, Miss Louise?

LOUISE. Oh, yes, thank you, Frank. (*The moment of departure has come. She looks about her for a second.*) Well, I guess there's no use in my trying to— Why, where's Terry? I thought she was down here.

KENDALL. Isn't she here?

SUSAN. No.

JEAN. She hasn't come in yet.

LOUISE. Oh, dear, I can't go without seeing Terry.

BERNICE. What's she up to, anyhow? I haven't seen her for days.

JEAN. I don't know. She's gone before I'm awake in the morning.

LOUISE. Well, anyhow, I guess I'd better get out of here before I bust out crying. You've all been just too darling for words, every single one of you— (LINDA, *having retrieved her dress, flashes through the hall and makes for the stairs.*) Who's that? Oh, good-by, Linda. I'm going. (LINDA, *no part of this, tosses a "good-by" over her shoulder as she goes up the stairs.*) And no matter how happy I am, I'll never forget you, and thanks a million times for the perfume, Pat, and you, Susan, for the compact, and all of you that clubbed together and gave me the exquisite nightgown.

BERNICE (*accepting the credit*). Oh, that's all right.

LOUISE. So—I hope I'll make a better wife than I did an actress. I guess I wasn't very good at that—

BIG MARY (*stoutly*). You were so!

LITTLE MARY. You were swell!

LOUISE. I guess I wasn't *very* swell or I wouldn't be getting mar— (*Catches herself.*) —that is, any girl would be glad to give up the stage to marry a wonderful boy like Bob—anyway, I certainly am. Goodness, when I think that for two whole years he's waited back there in Appleton, I guess I'm pretty lucky.

BIG MARY (*obliging, but not meaning it*). Yes. (*The faces about her, while attentive, do not reflect full belief in Louise's good fortune.*)

LOUISE. Well, if any of you ever come out that way with a show, why, it's only a hundred miles from Milwaukee. Don't forget I'll be Mrs. Robert Hendershot by that time, and Wisconsin's perfectly beautiful in the autumn—the whole Fox River Valley—it's beautiful— (*It's no use. She cannot convince even herself, much less the rather embarrassed young people about her. The situation is miraculously saved by the slam of the street door and the electric entrance of a new and buoyant figure.*)
(TERRY RANDALL *has the vivid personality, the mobile face of the born actress. She is not at all conventionally beautiful, but the light in her face gives to her rather irregular features the effect of beauty. High cheekbones, wide mouth, broad brow.*)

TERRY (*breathless*). LOUISE! Dar-ling! I was so afraid you'd be gone. I ran all the way from Forty-sixth Street. Nothing else in the world could have kept me—look— what do you think! I've got a JOB! (*This announcement is greeted with a chorus of excited exclamations. "You haven't! . . Who with? . . . Tell us about it! . . . Terry, how wonderful! . . . Tell us all about it!"*) I will in a minute. . . . Louise, what a darling crazy hat! I just love it on you.

LOUISE. Oh, Terry, have you really got a job! What in?

JEAN. Who is it? Berger?

TERRY. Yes.

BERNICE. I thought he was all cast.

TERRY. He was, all except this one part. It's not big, but it's good. It's got one marvelous scene—you know— (*With three attitudes and a series of wordless sounds—one denunciatory, one tender, one triumphant —she amusingly conveys the range of the part.*)
(*From among the group, "It sounds marvelous! . . . Terry, you'll be wonderful!"*)

FRANK (*in the doorway*). Taxi's waiting, Miss Louise.

LOUISE (*a glance at her wrist watch*). Oh, dear, I can't bear to go. How'll I ever know the rest of it? Why did I ever— I've got to go—Terry, baby! (*Throws her arms about* TERRY, *kisses her. There is general*

embracing and good-bys.) Jean! (*She kisses* JEAN, *her other roommate.*) Good-by, good-by! (LOUISE *is hurrying from the room, the others streaming into the hallway to speed her.* "Don't forget us! . . . Send us a piece of wedding cake! . . . We want the deadly details. . . ." (From MRS. ORCUTT) "I hope you'll be very happy, dear child. Good-by . . . Good-by . . . Good-by!")
(MATTIE, *giggling, tosses after* LOUISE *a handful of rice that she has brought from the kitchen.* LOUISE *is gone.*)
(*The girls stream back into the room.*)

KENDALL. When do you go into rehearsal, Terry?

OLGA. Yes, when?

TERRY. Right away!

BERNICE. Gosh, Terry, you certainly got a break. Berger wouldn't even talk to me.

LITTLE MARY. Berger's an awful meany. How'd you get to him, anyway?

TERRY. I just stood there outside his door for a week.

PAT. And it did the trick?

BIG MARY. *I* tried that.

BOBBY. It never helped *me* any.

JUDITH. Me neither. I laid there for a whole afternoon once with "Welcome!" on me.

TERRY. I've had a longer run outside his office than I've had with most shows. This was my second week. I was just going to send out for a toothbrush and a camp chair when suddenly he opened the door. He was going to send out for a toothbrush and a camp chair when suddenly he opened the door. He was going. I said, "Mr. Berger!" That's practically all I've said for two weeks —Mr. Berger. (*She gives an assortment of readings of* "Mr. Berger," *ranging from piteous pleading to imperious command.*)

LITTLE MARY. What did he do?

SUSAN. What happened?

TERRY. He never even stopped. Suddenly I was furious. I grabbed his arm and said, "Listen! You're a producer and I'm an actress. What right have you got to barricade yourself behind closed doors and not see me! And hundreds like me! The greatest actress in the world might be coming up your stairs and you'd never know it."

KENDALL. Terry! What did he say!

TERRY. He said, "Are you the greatest ac tress in the world?" I said, "Maybe." H said, "You don't look like anything to me You're not even pretty and you're just little runt." I said, "Pretty! I suppose Rache was pretty. And what about Nazimova She's no higher than this." (*Indicates level.*) "But on a stage she's any heigh she wants to be."

JUDITH. P.S. She got the job.

TERRY. Yes. (*A deep sigh that conveys he relief at the outcome.*) And when I walke out on Broadway again it seemed the mos glamorous street in the world. Those bea tiful Nedick orange stands, and that lovel traffic at Broadway and Forty-fifth, an those darling bums spitting on the side walk— (*The doorbell rings. Instantaneousl the group is galvanized. The girls realiz the lateness of the hour.*)
(BOBBY *takes a peek out the window.*)

BOBBY. Oh, it's my new young man! Matti tell him I won't be a minute!

MADELEINE. Wait a minute, Mattie! Give u a chance to get upstairs!

JUDITH (*darting after her, gathering he négligée as she goes*). Yes, Mattie. We don want to give him the wrong idea of th house. (*A handful of the girls, squealin for time, dash into the dining room.*)
(JEAN *starts up the stairs with* TERRY.)

JEAN. Terry! What do you think's happene to your little girl friend! I'm having dinne with David Kingsley tonight.

TERRY. Jean, how marvelous! Did he sa anything about a picture test?

JEAN. Not yet, but it must mean he's i terested. Now look, when he gets here want you to come down and meet him, b cause you never can tell. (MATTIE, *havin waited until the coast was clear, now go to the front door. There is the sound of man's voice.* "Is Miss Melrose in?" MATTIE *reply,* "Yes, she is. Come right in.")
(*A* YOUNG MAN *stands in the doorway, trifle ill at ease in these unfamiliar su roundings. He hasn't the look of a Ne Yorker. There is about him the rath graceful angularity and winning simplici of the Westerner.*)

ᴍᴀᴛᴛɪᴇ. You-all can wait in there.

ᴛʜᴇ ʏᴏᴜɴɢ ᴍᴀɴ. Oh, thanks. Just tell her Sam Hastings is calling for her.

ᴍᴀᴛᴛɪᴇ (*as she goes to the dining-room door*). I think she knows about it— She'll be down directly. (ꜱᴀᴍ ʜᴀꜱᴛɪɴɢꜱ *mutters a thank-you as* ᴍᴀᴛᴛɪᴇ *passes into the dining room, closing the doors behind her.*)

Left alone, and not yet at ease, ꜱᴀᴍ ʜᴀꜱᴛ-ɪɴɢꜱ *makes a leisurely survey of the room, rather getting in the way of his own big frame as he turns. He decides, unfortunately, on the least substantial chair in the room and sits gingerly on its edge. At once there is a short sharp crack of protesting wood. He is on his feet like a shot. From above-stairs a snatch of popular song. Swift foot-steps are heard descending the stairs. He gazes expectantly, but it's not his girl. It is* ᴋᴇɴᴅᴀʟʟ, *who is humming a bit of song as she comes. She pauses on the stairs to fix her stocking. She stops abruptly as she sees the stranger. With a glare at the embarrassed* ʜᴀꜱᴛɪɴɢꜱ *she goes into the dining room. Then a peremptory voice shouts from up-stairs; "Judy! You going to stay in the Johnny all night?" He clears his throat and looks away, though there's nothing to look away from.*) (*The doorbell rings.*)

ʙᴇʀɴɪᴄᴇ *comes out of the dining room. Her face brightens as she beholds the young man.*)

ʙᴇʀɴɪᴄᴇ (*summoning all her charm*). Par-don me. You're not Mr. David Kingsley!

ꜱᴀᴍ. No. My name's Hastings. (*With a syl-lable of dismissal,* ʙᴇʀɴɪᴄᴇ *goes on her way, and up the stairs.*)

By this time ᴍᴀᴛᴛɪᴇ *is opening the front door. A voice inquires, "Miss Paige in?" "Yes, come right in."*)

The ʙᴏʏ *who appears is even younger than* ꜱᴀᴍ ʜᴀꜱᴛɪɴɢꜱ. *Perhaps nineteen. Slight, graceful, dark-haired, rather sensitive look-ing.*)

ᴍᴀᴛᴛɪᴇ (*calls from the foot of the stairs*). Miss Susan! (ꜱᴜꜱᴀɴ'ꜱ *voice from upstairs— All right, Mattie!*")

The two ʙᴏʏꜱ *confront each other rather uncertainly. The newcomer in the doorway ventures a mannerly, "How do you do?" "Howdy-do?" There is a little awkward pause.*)

ᴛʜᴇ ɴᴇᴡᴄᴏᴍᴇʀ. My name's Devereaux.

ꜱᴀᴍ. Mine's Hastings.

ᴅᴇᴠᴇʀᴇᴀᴜx. Yes, I recognized you. I saw you in that Keith Burgess play last month.

ꜱᴀᴍ. You sure must have looked quick.

ᴅᴇᴠᴇʀᴇᴀᴜx. I liked that part. You did a lot with it. Too bad the play flopped.

ꜱᴀᴍ. I don't rightly recall you. Have you done anything lately?

ᴅᴇᴠᴇʀᴇᴀᴜx. Last month I played Emperor Jones, and I'm cast now for Hamlet.

ꜱᴀᴍ. Hamlet?

ᴅᴇᴠᴇʀᴇᴀᴜx. I'm at the New York School of Acting. This is my last year.

ꜱᴀᴍ. Oh! And then what?

ᴅᴇᴠᴇʀᴇᴀᴜx. Then I'm going on the stage.

ꜱᴀᴍ. Did you ever try to get a job on the stage?

ᴅᴇᴠᴇʀᴇᴀᴜx. Not yet.

ꜱᴀᴍ. That's more of a career than acting. I've been in New York two years. I'm from Texas. Houston Little Theater. We came up and won a contest, and I stayed. I've had ten weeks' work in two years. Don't ask me how I live. I don't know.

ᴅᴇᴠᴇʀᴇᴀᴜx. You could go back to Texas, couldn't you?

ꜱᴀᴍ. Go back! Oh, no! I'm an actor. (ꜱᴜꜱᴀɴ *runs down the stairs, in street clothes.*)

ꜱᴜꜱᴀɴ. Hello, Jimmy!

ᴅᴇᴠᴇʀᴇᴀᴜx. Hello, Sue. Do you know Mr. Hastings?

ꜱᴜꜱᴀɴ. Howdy-do?

ᴅᴇᴠᴇʀᴇᴀᴜx. Miss Susan Paige. She's up at the school, too. She's going to do Hedda Gabler.

ꜱᴀᴍ. Well, you have to start somewhere.

ꜱᴜꜱᴀɴ (*laughingly*). Yes. (ᴅᴇᴠᴇʀᴇᴀᴜx *says,* "good-by!" *There is a word of farewell from* ʜᴀꜱᴛɪɴɢꜱ *and* ꜱᴜꜱᴀɴ *as the doorbell rings.*)

ᴅᴇᴠᴇʀᴇᴀᴜx (*as he and* ꜱᴜꜱᴀɴ *go into the hall*). Where do you want to eat?

ꜱᴜꜱᴀɴ. How much money have you got?

ᴅᴇᴠᴇʀᴇᴀᴜx. Sixty-five cents.

SUSAN. I've got thirty. That's ninety-five. (*As they open the door they are accosted by a hearty masculine voice, subsequently identified as that of* FRED POWELL. *"This the Footlights Club?"*)

SUSAN. Yes. Won't you just— Mattie! Somebody at the door.

MATTIE (*having appeared in the hallway*). Yes'm, Miss Susan. . . . You gentlemen calling on somebody? (FRED POWELL *and* LOU MILHAUSER *come into view. They are two overhearty Big Business Men out for a holiday. Their derby hats and daytime attire will be a shock to the girls, especially* JUDITH.)

POWELL. Yes, we're calling for Miss Madeleine Vauclain.

MILHAUSER. And her friend.

MATTIE (*at the foot of the stairs*). Miss Madeleine! . . . Couple gentlemen down here say they calling for you and—somebody.

MADELEINE. Coming down!

MATTIE. She's coming down. (*They come into the living room, and finding another man there, offer a tentative greeting; a smile and wave of the hand. Then they look the room over.*)

MILHAUSER. What'd you say this place was? A Home for Girls?

POWELL. Yeah, all actresses. A whole bunch of 'em live here.

MILHAUSER. Kind of a handy place to know about.

POWELL. Yeah.

MILHAUSER (*whisks from his pocket two cellophaned cigars*). Smoke?

POWELL. Thanks. (*As they light up, having tossed the crumpled cellophane jackets to a near-by table,* POWELL *sends a glance of half-inquiry at* SAM. *Hastily, in order to divert any further advances,* SAM *opens his cigarette case and lights a cigarette.*)

MILHAUSER. Certainly is a funny place, New York. Now, you take a layout like this. Wouldn't find it anywhere else in the world.

POWELL. Bet you wouldn't, at that.

MILHAUSER. I—I always thought actress lived in flats or—uh—hotel rooms.

POWELL. Lot of 'em do.

MILHAUSER (*struck by a new thought*) What about men actors—where do th live?

POWELL. I don't know—Lambs' Club, guess.

MILHAUSER. Oh, yeah. (SAM HASTINGS *shi his position a little, throws them a look*). (BOBBY MELROSE, *finally coming down t stairs, saves the situation. She is at her m Southern.*)

BOBBY MELROSE (*from the stairs*). He there, Texas!

SAM (*gathering up his coat and hat*). C hello!

BOBBY. Ah hope Ah didn't keep you waiti

SAM. No! No!

BOBBY. One thing about me, Ah'm alwa prompt. (*The outer door closes. They gone.*)

POWELL. That was a cute little trick.

MILHAUSER. Yeah. . . . Look! What ab this one you've got on the fire for me? S any good?

POWELL. Sure, sure. You leave it to Ma leine.

MILHAUSER. Oh, well, as long as she's go natured. (*There is a rustle of silk on stairway. "Ah!" exclaims* POWELL, *in ant pation and relief.*) (MADELEINE *and* JUDITH *descend the st in full evening regalia, gathered from richest recesses of the club—furs, sil gloves, jewelry.*)

MADELEINE (*furiously, as she catches si of the men's attire*). Well, is this what call dressing?

POWELL. Huh?

MADELEINE. Why didn't you come in ov alls!

POWELL. Now, now, baby. We got snar up in a committee meeting, didn't we, L

MILHAUSER. Sure. Sure.

POWELL. This is Ben Dexter, girls. M Madeleine Vauclain and—uh—

ADELEINE (*sulkily*). This is Miss Canfield.

ILHAUSER (*coming right up to* JUDITH'S *pectations*). Hello, Beautiful! (*Very jo-al.*) How about it? Shall we step out and places?

DITH (*sourly*). Yes, let's.

ILHAUSER. Now don't be like that. We're ing to have a good time.

WELL. Sure we are! The works! (*He is loting* MADELEINE *out to the hallway.*) me on, boys and girls! Where do you int to eat?

ILHAUSER. I got an idea. How about a lit-Italian place?

DITH. Little Italian *nuts!* I want a decent inner. (*A slam of the door. They are ne.*)

ENDALL *comes out of the dining room and sies herself at the mirror.* OLGA *follows, justing her hat and cape as she enters.*)

GA. Kendall, are you going to your show? am rehearsing at the Winter Garden, if u want to walk down.

NDALL. No, it's too early for me. We don't up till eight-fifty.

GA (*with almost too much Slavic bitter-ss*). The Winter Garden! The star pupil Kolijinsky, at the Winter Garden! (*She es.*)

TLE MARY (*who, with the inevitable* BIG RY *at her side, has come into the room t in time to hear this*). Bellyaching, and e's got a job. Look at me. (*She flops into seat.*) Edwin Booth and I retired from stage at practically the same time.

NDALL. I think I'll take a rest before the ht show. Matinee days are frightfully ing. (*She goes up to her room.*)

MARY. Frightfully tiring! Why doesn't go back to Boston, where she belongs! at'd rest her up.

TLE MARY. There ought to be an equity against society girls going on the stage. iss Kendall Adams, daughter of Mr. and s. Roger Winthrop Adams."

MARY. Of Boston and the Lucky Strike . (PAT *and* ANN *come out of the dining m. There is the tinkle of china and silver.*

The doors are shut by MATTIE. *Dinner is over.*)

ANN. What's it like out? It looked rainy when I came in. (*Goes to the hallway for her coat.*)

BIG MARY (*at the window*). No, it's all right. . . . Oh, girls, look! There's the Cadillac again for Linda Shaw.

LITTLE MARY. Is *he* in it?

BIG MARY. No, just the chauffeur, same as always.

PAT. Who's the guy, anyhow? Anybody know?

LITTLE MARY. He doesn't ever come. Just sends the car.

PAT. Well, nice work if you can get it.

ANN (*righteously*). I think it's disgraceful. A nice girl wouldn't want a man to send for her that way. And if you ask me, it gives the club a bad name. (*A warning gesture and a "Pss-s-st!" from* LITTLE MARY *as* LINDA *descends the stairs.*)
(LINDA *is beautifully dressed for the eve-ning. She is wearing the dress whose press-ing had annoyed her; her evening cape is handsomely furred. Enormous orchids.*)

BIG MARY. Oo, Linda! How gorgeous!

LINDA (*pausing reluctantly*). Oh, hello.

LITTLE MARY. Come on in. Let's see you.

BIG MARY. What a marvelous coat, Linda!

PAT. Yes, and a very nifty bit of jack rabbit, if I may say so. (*Her finger outlines a collar in the air.*)

LINDA. Oh, that! Mother sent it to me. It used to be on a coat of hers.

LITTLE MARY. It's lovely.

PAT (*mildly*). Oh—Mother has a nice taste in orchids, too.

LINDA (*baring her fangs*). Yes. Don't you wish you had a mother like mine? (*She sweeps out.*)
(*The two* MARYS *dart to the window.*)

PAT. What would you two do without that window? Why don't you pull up a rocking chair!

ANN. Linda Shaw's comings and goings don't interest me. Girls make such fools of themselves about men! (*She goes.*)

BIG MARY. Say! What do you know about Jean? Having dinner with David Kingsley!

LITTLE MARY. Some girls have all the luck. Where'd she meet him, anyhow?

BIG MARY. Oh, some cocktail party.

PAT. I wish *I* could meet him. He can spot picture material just like that. (*She snaps her fingers.*) He's got an eye like a camera.

LITTLE MARY. Yeh, he picked three picture stars last year. Nobody ever heard of 'em before he sent 'em out there.

PAT. Well, *I'll* never meet him. (*She indulges in an elaborate yawn and stretch.*) Oh, what to do till eleven o'clock. Except sleep.

LITTLE MARY. Anyhow, you've got something to *do* at eleven. . . . Look at us!

BIG MARY. Yeh, you're working.

PAT. I hate it. Hoofing in a night club for a lot of tired business men. The trouble is they're *not* tired and there's no business. (*The doorbell rings.*)

BIG MARY (*at the window*). I think it's David Kingsley! It looks like him.

PAT. Kingsley? Are you sure?

LITTLE MARY (*peering*). Yes, that's him. Look, we'd better get out of the way, hadn't we?

BIG MARY. Yes, I guess so. (PAT, *mindful of her pajamas, also gathers herself together.*)
(BERNICE *descends the stairs with rather elaborate unconcern.*)

BERNICE (*too polite*). Oh, pardon me, I just want to speak to—Frank—about—something— (*She dashes into the dining room.*)
(PAT *stands looking after* BERNICE *for a second. Then as* MATTIE *crosses the hallway to answer the door* PAT *makes her own decision and darts up the stairs.*)
(*A man's voice at the door.*)

KINGSLEY (*in the hall*). Miss Maitland, please.

MATTIE. Yessuh. Come right in.

KINGSLEY. Tell her Mr. Kingsley. (DAV KINGSLEY *enters. Perhaps thirty-six or -seve A man of decided charm and distinctio He is wearing evening clothes. You see h white muffler above the dark topcoat.*)

MATTIE. If you'll just rest yourself—I'll right up. (MATTIE *goes up the stairs with stateliness that indicates her appreciation the caller's importance.*)
(KINGSLEY *glances about the room a b He opens his cigarette case, lights a cig rette.*)
(BERNICE *comes out of the dining roo Her face is turned toward someone in t room she has just left and it is this perso she is addressing, apparently all unawa that anyone (certainly not Kingsley) is the living room. With one quick twist s has altered—or thinks she has altered—t arrangement of her hair so as to make herself a more arresting type.*)

BERNICE. Yes, Mattie, an actress's life is su an interesting one, if you could only see t different types that I do in the course of day, Mattie. For example, an English tress came into an office today. (*Goes su denly very English.*) "My dear Harry, he definitely ripping to see you. Definitely r ping!" And then, Mattie, a little girl fr Brooklyn came in. "Listen, I did write an appurntment! You got a noive!" (*S turns, and to her obvious embarrassm there is* MR. KINGSLEY. *She is a picture pretty confusion.*) Oh, I am so sorry! didn't dream anyone was here.

KINGSLEY (*politely amused*). That's qu all right.

BERNICE (*following up her advantage*). I —Bernice Niemeyer. (KINGSLEY *bows slig ly, murmurs her name.*) Well—I j thought— (*She is dangling at the end her rope.*)
(*Here she is mercifully interrupted by* PA *descent of the stairs. The jacket of* PAT'S *jama suit is missing. Her slim figure is u revealed in the trousers and scant sho sleeved top. Her low-heeled scuffs have be replaced by pert high-heeled mules.*)

PAT. I wonder— (*Makes a slow turn tow* BERNICE—*a turn which by a strange cha serves at the same time to reveal the t points of her figure to the waiting* KINGLE You—you didn't see my book anywh around here, did you?

RNICE (*sourly*). What book? (*She goes
o the stairs.*)

AT *flutters in her quest to a table, goes to
e book-shelf, selects a volume, ruffles its
ges to make sure that the book meets her
ood, then gives a little sigh of delight,
asps the book to her breast and trips up the
airs.*)

KINGSLEY *barely has time to seat himself
ain before another aspirant for his ap-
oval appears.*)

t is MRS. ORCUTT, *who has shed her work-
ay dress for something very grand in the
ay of a silk dinner gown.*)

RS. ORCUTT (*outstretched hands*). David
ingsley! Little David Kingsley!

NGSLEY (*a little bewildered, rises to meet
e emergency*). Why—how do you do!

RS. ORCUTT (*coquettishly*). Surely you re-
ember me.

NGSLEY (*lying bravely*). Of course I do.

RS. ORCUTT. Who am I? (KINGSLEY *has an
stant of panic.*) Now think. Helen who?—

NGSLEY (*catches desperately at this straw*).

S. ORCUTT. —mayne! Helen Romayne!

NGSLEY (*repeating it just the barest flash
hind her*). Helen Romayne. Why, of
urse! Well, what a charming surprise.
agine your remembering me! A scrubby
le kid in the office.

S. ORCUTT. But that little office boy bene one of the most brilliant producers in
theater. Those beautiful plays! I loved
m all.

NGSLEY. So did I. But something hap-
ned to the theater about that time. It was
t of shot from under us.

S. ORCUTT. But you've gone right on.
u've risen to even greater triumphs in
pictures.

NGSLEY (*quietly ironic*). Yes, even greater
umphs. (*A step on the stair.* MRS. ORCUTT
ns.*)

S. ORCUTT. Well—it was lovely seeing you.
ope you'll be coming again.

NGSLEY. I hope so, too. (MRS. ORCUTT
kes her escape as JEAN *appears on the*

stairs, resplendent in her borrowed finery.
PAT's *rose taffeta, and* KENDALL's *evening
wrap.*)

JEAN. So glad to see you, Mr. Kingsley.

KINGSLEY. I'm glad you happened to be free.

JEAN. I guess girls generally manage to be
free when you invite them.

KINGSLEY. You don't think my being in the
motion-picture business may have something
to do with it?

JEAN. Why, Mr. Kingsley, how can you say
such a thing!

KINGSLEY. You think it's all sheer charm,
huh?

JEAN. Of course. . . . Look, would you mind
awfully if I— (*Calls up the stairs.*) Terry!
Come *on!*

TERRY (*from above*). I'm coming.

JEAN. That's Terry Randall, my roommate.
Did you see *Cyclone?* Or *The Eldest Son?*

KINGSLEY. Oh, yes. In *Cyclone*—she was—

JEAN. It was just a tiny part. She came into
the drugstore.

KINGSLEY. Oh, yes. Just a bit, but she was
good. . . . Yes, she was excellent! (TERRY
comes down the stairs.)

(*She is still wearing the plain dark little
dress in which we have previously seen her.
If it were not for the glowing face she would
seem rather drab in comparison to the dazzling* JEAN.)

TERRY (*with great directness*). Well, if you
will come calling at a girls' club, Mr. Kingsley, what can you expect?

KINGSLEY. I didn't expect anything as charming as this.

TERRY. Mm! You *are* in the moving-picture
business, aren't you?

KINGSLEY. I am, Miss Randall. But my soul
belongs to God.

JEAN. Don't you think she'd be good for
pictures, Mr. Kingsley? Look. (*Turning
TERRY's profile to show to the best advantage.*)

TERRY. I think I'd be terrible.

JEAN. Don't talk like that. Of course she's rehearsing now in the new Berger play. That is, she starts tomorrow.

KINGSLEY. Good! I hear it's an interesting play.

TERRY. Do you know the first play I ever saw, Mr. Kingsley?

KINGSLEY. No, what?

TERRY. It was your production of *Amaryllis.*

KINGSLEY. *Amaryllis!* You couldn't have seen that! That was my first production. Ten years ago.

TERRY. I did, though. I was eleven years old, and I saw it at English's Opera House, in Indianapolis. My mother took me. She cried all the way through it, and so did I. We had a lovely time.

KINGSLEY. But *Amaryllis* wasn't a sad play.

TERRY. Oh, we didn't cry because we were sad. Mother cried because it brought back the days when she was an actress, and I cried because I was so happy. You see, we lived seventy-five miles from Indianapolis, and it was the first time I'd ever been in a theater.

JEAN. Now, really, I don't think it's tactful to talk about the theater to a picture man.

TERRY. I'm afraid I'm kind of dumb about pictures. Mother used to say the theater had two offspring—the legitimate stage, and the bastard.

JEAN (*taking* KINGSLEY *by the hand and pulling him from the room*). Come on! And forget I ever introduced her to you. (*He goes, calling, "Good-by, Miss Randall!"*)

TERRY (*calling after him*). Oh, I hope I didn't—

KINGSLEY (*as the door closes on them*). It's all right. I forgive you. (*Left alone,* TERRY *suddenly realizes she has had no dinner. As she goes toward the dining room she calls.*)

TERRY. Mattie! (*She opens the dining-room doors.*) Oh, dear, is dinner over!

MATTIE. Yes. I'm just clearing away.

TERRY. Oh, Mattie darling, could you let me have just anything! Champagne and a little caviar?

MATTIE (*in the dining room*). Well, I'll f[ix] you a plate of something.

TERRY. You're an angel. (KENDALL ADAM[S] *comes down the stairs, dressed for the stree[t]. At sight of* TERRY *she pauses a moment [to] chat.*)

KENDALL. Isn't it splendid, Terry, abo[ut] your getting a job!

TERRY. It seems pretty dazzling to me, aft[er] six months. I only hope it's as big a hit [as] yours.

KENDALL. It's queer about being in a h[it]. You go through everything to get into on[e], and after a few months you're bored with [it]. It's like marriage. (*The doorbell rings[.]* (*Calls.*) It's all right, Mattie, I'll answer [it] . . . Going out, Terry?

TERRY. Not tonight.

KENDALL (*at the street door*). See you lat[er.] (*A voice at the door. "Hello there! Who a[re] you!"* KENDALL'S *voice, a film of ice over [it,] "I beg your pardon!" The man's voice [ex-] plains, "I'm looking for Jean Maitland[."]* KENDALL *calls, "Mattie!" and goes on h[er] way. The call is unheard by* MATTIE.)

(KEITH BURGESS *appears in the archway. [He] is the kind of young man who never we[ars] a hat. Turtle-necked sweater, probably blac[k,] unpressed tweed suit; unshaven.*)

KEITH. Where's Jean Maitland?

TERRY. In a taxi with a big moving-pictu[re] man.

KEITH. She can't be. She had a date w[ith] me.

TERRY. Sorry. It isn't my fault.

KEITH. Who are you?

TERRY. Who wants to know?

KEITH. Are you an actress?

TERRY. Are you dizzy in the morning? [Do] you have spots before the eyes?

KEITH. My name is Keith Burgess.

TERRY. Is it?

KEITH. Don't you know who I am?

TERRY. Yes. You're a playwright, and [you] wrote a play called *Blood and Roses* t[hat] was produced at the Fourteenth St[reet]

eater, and it ran a week and it wasn't
ry good.

ITH. It was the best goddam play that was
er produced in New York! And the one
n writing now is even better.

RRY. Mm! *Two* weeks.

ITH (*vastly superior*). I don't think in
ms of material success. Who cares
ether a play makes money! All that mat-
s is its message!

RRY (*mildly*). But if nobody comes to see
who gets the message?

ITH. I write about the worker! The
sses! The individual doesn't count in
dern society.

RRY. But aren't the masses made up of
dividuals?

ITH. Don't quibble!

RRY. I'm so sorry.

ITH. I ask nothing as an individual. My
rk, my little room—that's all.

RRY. No furniture?

ITH. A table, a bed, a chair. My books.
music. And— (*The doorbell has rung,
d* FRANK *has crossed the hall to answer it.
e voice of* KAYE HAMILTON *is now heard
the door.* KEITH, *accordingly, is forced
suspend for a moment.*)

YE. I'm Miss Hamilton. Kaye Hamilton.

NK. Oh yes. I think Mrs. Orcutt's expect-
you. (MRS. ORCUTT *appears in the hall-
y just in time to greet the new arrival.*)

. ORCUTT. Glad to see you again, Miss
milton. Everything's in readiness for you.
nk, take Miss Hamilton's things right
. Oh! (*As she sees* TERRY *in the living
m.*) Terry, this is Kaye Hamilton, who's
ng to share the room with you and Jean.
rry Randall.

E. I'll try not to be in the way.

RY. Oh, don't start that way! Grab your
re of the closet hooks.

E. Thank you.

. ORCUTT. Now, if you'll just come with
I'll show you where everything is.

TERRY (*as they start up*). Let me know if I
can be of any help.

MRS. ORCUTT (*talking as they ascend*). If you
have a trunk check Frank will take care
of all that for you.

KAYE. No, no, I haven't got a trunk. (*They
are gone.*)
(KEITH, *throughout the above scene, has
been observing* TERRY *with an old-fashioned
eye of appreciation.*)

KEITH. Hey! Turn around! (*She does so,
rather wonderingly.*) You shouldn't wear
your hair like that. It hides your face.

TERRY. Oh, do you notice faces? I thought
you were above all that.

KEITH. I notice everything. Your head's too
big for the rest of you, you've got pretty
legs, but you oughtn't to wear red.

TERRY (*surveying him*). I suppose you're
known as Beau Burgess! What the Well-
Dressed Man Will Wear!

KEITH. Oh, you like snappy dressers, eh?
Monograms and cuff links.

TERRY. No, I don't meet very many monograms.

KEITH (*his gaze roaming around the room*).
What do you live in this place for? Do you
like it?

TERRY. I love it. We live and breathe theater,
and that's what I'm crazy about.

KEITH (*eagerly*). Are you? So am I. What
do you want to *do* in the theater? What
kind of parts do you want to play?

TERRY. I want to play everything I'm not
suited for. Old hags of eighty, and Topsy,
and Lady Macbeth. And what do I get?
Ingenues—and very little of that.

KEITH. Don't take 'em. Wait till you get
what you want.

TERRY. Well, it's a nice idea. But did you
ever hear of this thing called eating?

KEITH. You mustn't think of that. Why, I've
lived on bread and cocoa for days at a time.
If you believe in something you've got to
be willing to starve for it.

TERRY. I'm willing. But you don't know
what it is to be an actress. If you feel some-

thing you can write it. But I can't act un-less they let me. I can't just walk up and down my room, being an actress.

KEITH. It's just as tough for a writer. Sup-pose they won't produce his plays? I write about ironworkers and they want grand dukes. I could write potboilers, but I don't. The theater shouldn't be just a place to earn a living in. It should be thunder and light-ning, and power and truth.

TERRY. And magic and romance!

KEITH. No, no! Romance is for babies! I write about *today!* I want to tear the heart out of the rotten carcass they call life, and hold it up bleeding for all the world to see!

TERRY. How about putting some heart *into* life, instead of tearing it out?

KEITH. There's no place for sentiment in the world today. We've gone past it.

TERRY. I suppose that's why you never hear of *Romeo and Juliet.*

KEITH (*turning away*). That's a woman's argument.

TERRY. Well, I'm a woman.

KEITH (*once more surveying her*). Wh haven't I run into you before? Where' you been all the time?

TERRY. Right here, in and out of every ma ager's office on Broadway.

KEITH. Me too. But I'm going to keep rig on until they listen to me. And you've g to keep right on too!

TERRY. I will! I'm going to! (MATTIE a pears in the dining-room doorway.)

MATTIE. You-all want your dinner now, M Terry? It's ready.

TERRY. Why, I'd forgotten all about it, M tie.

KEITH (*taking control*). Never mind, M tie! . . . How about dinner with me? We go to Smitty's and have a couple of ha burgers.

TERRY (*not at all unwilling*). With onion

KEITH. Sure—onions! . . . Say, what the he your name, anyway? (*They start for door. The two* MARYS *are coming down stairs again, deep in an argument, as usua*)

CURTAIN

SCENE II

One of the bedrooms. A pleasant enough but rather cramped room, with three be three dressers, three small chairs. There is a bathroom door down left, a window cen A door up left leads to hall.

Each dresser reflects something of the personality and daily life of its owner. Stuck in sides of the mirrors are snapshots, photographs, newspaper clippings, telegrams, the programs.

It is night, and through the window we get a glimpse of the city's lights.

At the beginning the room is unoccupied.

KAYE HAMILTON *comes out of the bathroom, closes the door. She is wearing a bathr over her nightgown. Goes to her dresser, which is conspicuously bare of ornaments, sou nirs, or photographs. She opens the dresser top drawer, takes out her handbag, remo her money from a small purse and counts it, a process which doesn't take long. T dollars and sixty cents.*

There is a knock at the door.

KAYE. Yes?

JUDITH (*as she opens the door*). Can I come in? Where's Terry?

KAYE. She isn't back yet. (JUDITH *is wearing sleeping pajamas and she is in the process of doing her face up for the night. A chin strap is tied about her face and ends in a top-knot. A net safeguards her curls.*)

JUDITH. Look, do you think she'd min I borrowed some of her frowners? I fo to get some.

KAYE. I think there's some in her top dra

JUDITH (*as she pulls open the draw* Thanks. . . . You don't go out much nings, do you?

KAYE. No.

JUDITH. Any sign of a job yet?

KAYE. No, not yet.

JUDITH. Something'll turn up. It always does. (*She waits a moment for* KAYE's *answer, but there is none.*) You know, you're a funny kid. You've been here a month, and I don't know any more about you than when you came in. The rest of us are always spilling our whole insides, but you never let out a peep. Nobody comes to see you, no phone calls, never go out nights, you haven't even got a picture on your dresser. Haven't you got any folks? Or a beau or something? (*No sound from* KAYE. JUDITH *turns to glance at her.*) Sorry. My mistake. (*The voices of* BIG *and* LITTLE MARY *are heard in the hall.* BIG MARY: *"Mm, somebody's cooking something."* LITTLE MARY: *"Smells like rarebit."*) *The two* MARYS, *in hats and coats, stick their heads in at the door.*)

LITTLE MARY. Who's cooking? You?

JUDITH. No—Madeleine. Where've you been? Show?

BIG MARY (*dourly*). Yes. We saw the Breadline Players in *Tunnel of Death.*

LITTLE MARY. Come on, let's get some rarebit before it's all gone. (*They disappear down the hallway.*)

JUDITH. Terry's late, isn't she? It's half-past eleven. And she isn't in the last act?

KAYE. She'll be here in a minute. Have you seen the play?

JUDITH. I haven't had time yet. I'm going tomorrow night.

KAYE. I didn't like it very much, but Terry's awfully good. Just a little part, but you always knew she was on. (PAT *appears in the doorway. She is wearing a tailored suit and hat.*)

PAT (*peering around*). Anybody in here? Well, off to the mines.

JUDITH. Hello, Pat. Going to work?

PAT (*wearily*). Yeh, the night shift. (*She does a rather listless floor-show dance step; disappears.*)

KAYE. I wonder what it'd be like, working in a night club. I wish I'd learned to dance.

JUDITH (*intent on her own reflection in the mirror*). Well, with your looks you'll get along all right. (*She wanders over to* KAYE's *dresser.*) Where's your hand mirror? Why, where's the whole set?

KAYE. I haven't got it any more.

JUDITH (*a little too casually*). It was—gold, wasn't it?

KAYE. Uh-huh.

JUDITH. I see. . . . Got any folks you have to support?

KAYE (*quietly*). No, I haven't any folks.

JUDITH. Well, if you want some, I'm the girlie that can fix you up. Five brothers and four sisters, and you couldn't scare up a dollar eighty among the lot. I've got a little sister named Doris. Fifteen, and as innocent as Mata Hari. She's coming to New York next year to duplicate my success.

KAYE (*somewhat wistfully*). I think it would be rather nice, having a little sister with you.

JUDITH. Yeh, only she won't be with me much. Two weeks, and they'll have her in the Home for Delinquent Girls. (TERRY *enters, a drooping figure. A glance at the two occupants of the room. Her back to the door, she slowly closes it behind her and slumps against it.*)

TERRY. Young lady, willing, talented, not very beautiful, finds herself at liberty. Will double in brass, will polish brass, will *eat* brass before very long. Hi, girls!

KAYE. Terry, what's the matter?

TERRY. We closed. Four performances and we closed.

KAYE. Terry, you didn't!

JUDITH. Tonight! But it's only Thursday!

TERRY. Well, it seems you can close on Thursday just as well as Saturday—in fact, it's even better; it gives you two more days to be sunk in.

JUDITH. But it didn't get bad notices. What happened?

TERRY. We just got to the theater tonight, and there it was on the call board. "To the Members of the *Blue Grotto* Company: You are hereby advised that the engagement of the *Blue Grotto* will terminate after to-night's performance. Signed, Milton H. Schwepper, for Berger Productions, Incorporated."

KAYE. Terry, how ghastly!

JUDITH. Just like that, huh?

TERRY. Just like that. We stood there for a minute and read it. Then we sort of got together in the dressing rooms and talked about it in whispers, the way you do at a funeral. And then we all put on our make-up and gave the best damned performance we'd ever given.

JUDITH. Any other job in the world, if you get canned you can have a good cry in the washroom and go home. But show business! You take it on the chin and then paint up your face and out on the stage as gay as anything. "My dear Lady Barbara, what an enchanting place you have here! And what a quaint idea, giving us pigs' knuckles for tea!"

TERRY. Yes, it was awfully jolly. I wouldn't have minded if Berger or somebody had come backstage and said, "Look, we're sorry to do this to you, and better luck next time." But nobody came around—not Berger, or the author, or the director or anybody. They can all run away at a time like that, but the actors have to stay and face it.

JUDITH. You'll get something else, Terry. You got swell notices in this one.

TERRY. Nobody remembers notices except the actors who get them.

KAYE. The movie scouts remember. What about your screen test?

JUDITH. Yes, how about that? Have you heard from it?

TERRY. Oh, I'm not counting on that. They might take Jean. She's got that camera face. But they'll never burn up the coast wires over me.

JUDITH. Jean can't act. You're ten times the actress that she is.

TERRY. Oh, how do you know who's an actress and who isn't! You're an actress if you're acting. Without a job and those lines to say, an actress is just an ordinary person, trying not to look as scared as she feels. What is there about it, anyhow! Why do we all keep trying? (*The door opens and*

BERNICE *enters—rather solemnly. Her mood fits none too well with the definitely pink pajamas that form the basis of her costume, so you gather that it must have to do with a great filmy bit of black something that she has draped around her head and shoulders, and which trails behind her at enormous length. Obviously, she thinks that Modjeska herself could not have achieved a finer characterization.*)

BERNICE. How do I look?

KAYE. Marvelous.

JUDITH. What *are* you?

BERNICE (*in the voice of a woman anywhere between forty and eighty.*) I'm trying out tomorrow. The Theatre Guild is reviving Madame X. (*She goes—the perfect embodiment of Madame X, or anyhow Little Eva.*) (*Meanwhile* MADELEINE *has come down the hall and now stands lounging in the doorway, a plate of food in one hand, a fork in the other.*)

MADELEINE. Anybody want some chop suey? Terry? Kaye?

TERRY. No, thank you.

KAYE. No, thanks.

JUDITH (*tempted by this*). Chop suey? I thought it was rarebit.

MADELEINE. We didn't have any beer, so I'm calling it chop suey. (*She goes.*)

JUDITH. Certainly sounds terrible. (*Turns with a hand on the door.*) Look, I guess you want this closed, huh?

TERRY. Yes, please. (*The door closes. KAYE and* TERRY *are alone. With a sigh* TERRY *again faces reality. Listlessly she begins to undress.* KAYE *is almost ready for bed. As she turns back the bedclothes she pauses to regard* TERRY.)

KAYE. I know how sunk you feel, Terry. It's that horrible letdown after the shock has worn off.

TERRY. The idiotic part of it is that I didn't feel so terrible after that first minute. I thought, well, Keith's coming around after the show, and we'll go to Smitty's and sit there and talk and it won't seem so bad. But he never showed up.

KAYE. Terry, I shouldn't try to advise you where men are concerned. I haven't been

ery smart myself—but this isn't the first
ime he's let you down. Don't get in too
deep with a boy like Keith Burgess. It'll
only make you unhappy.

TERRY. I don't expect him to be like other
people. I wouldn't want him to be. One of
he things that makes him so much fun is
hat he's different. If he forgets an appointment it's because he's working and doesn't
otice. Only—I wish he had come tonight.
*She is pulling her dress over her head as
she talks and her words are partly muffled
until she emerges.*) I needed him so. (*Suddenly her defenses are down.*) Kaye, I'm
frightened. For the first time, I'm frightened. It's three years now. The first year it
didn't matter so much. I was so young. Nobody was ever as young as I was. I thought,
they just don't know. But I'll get a good
part and show them. I didn't mind anything
in those days. Not having any money, or
quite enough food; and a pair of silk stockings always a major investment. I didn't
mind because I felt so sure that that wonderful part was going to come along. But it
wasn't. And suppose it doesn't next year?
Suppose it—never comes?

KAYE. You can always go home. You've
got a home to go to, anyhow.

TERRY. And marry some home-town boy—
like Louise?

KAYE. I didn't mean that, exactly.

TERRY. I can't just go home and plump myself down on Dad. You know what a county doctor makes! When I was little I never
knew how poor we were, because Mother
made everything seem so glamorous—so
much fun. (*All this time* TERRY *has continued her preparations for bed. At one
point in her disrobing she has gone to the
clothes closet, hung up her dress, and slipped
her nightgown over her head. Unseen there,
for a moment, she has gone on talking.*)
Even if I was sick it was a lot of fun, because then I was allowed to look at her
scrapbook. I even used to pretend to be sick,
just to look at it—and that took acting,
with a doctor for a father. I adored that
scrapbook. All those rep-company actors in
wooden attitudes—I remember a wonderful
picture of Mother as Esmeralda. It was the
first part she ever played, and she never
finished the performance.

KAYE. What happened?

TERRY. She fainted, right in the middle of
the last act. They rang down and somebody
said, "Is there a doctor in the house?" And
there was. And he married her.

KAYE. Terry, how romantic!

TERRY. Only first she was sick for weeks and
weeks. Of course the company had to leave
her behind. They thought she'd catch up
with them any week, but she never did.

KAYE. Didn't she ever miss it? I mean afterward.

TERRY. I know now that she missed it every
minute of her life. I think if Dad hadn't
been such a gentle darling, and not so dependent on her, she might have gone off and
taken me with her. I'd have been one of
those children brought up in dressing rooms,
sleeping in trunk trays, getting my vocabu-
lary from stagehands.

KAYE. That would have been thrilling.

TERRY. But she didn't. She lived out the
rest of her life right in that little town, but
she was stage-struck to the end. There never
was any doubt in her mind—I was going to
be an actress. It was almost a spiritual thing,
like being dedicated to the church.

KAYE. I never thought of the theater that
way. I just used it as a convenience, because
I was desperate. And now I'm using it again,
because I'm desperate.

TERRY. Oh, now I've made you blue. I didn't
mean to be gloomy. We're fine! We're elegant! They have to pay me two weeks' salary for this flop. Eighty dollars. We're fixed
for weeks. One of us'll get a job.

KAYE. I can't take any more money from
you. You paid my twelve-fifty last week.

TERRY. Oh, don't be stuffy! I happened to be
the one who was working.

KAYE. I'll never get a job. I'm—I'm no
very good actress.

TERRY. Oh, stop that!

KAYE. And there's nothing else I can do and
nobody I can go back to. Except somebody
I'll never go back to.

TERRY (*facing her*). It's your husband, isn't
it?

KAYE (*looks at* TERRY *a moment, silently*). I ran away from him twice before, but I had to go back. I was hungry, and finally I didn't even have a room. Both times, he just waited. He's waiting now.

TERRY. Kaye, tell me what it is! Why are you afraid of him?

KAYE (*she turns her eyes away from* TERRY *as she speaks*). To most people he's a normal, attractive man. But I know better. Nights of terror. "Now, darling, it wouldn't do any good to kill me. They wouldn't let you play polo tomorrow. Now, we'll open the window and you'll throw the revolver at that lamppost. It'll be such fun to hear the glass smash." And then there were the times when he made love to me. I can't even tell you about that. (*She recalls the scene with a shudder.*)

TERRY. Kaye, darling! But if he's as horrible as that, can't you do something legally?

KAYE (*a desperate shake of her head*). They have millions. I'm nobody. I've gone to his family. They treated me as though *I* were the mad one. They're united like a stone wall.

TERRY. But Kaye, isn't there anybody—what about your own folks? Haven't you got any?

KAYE. I have a father. Chicago. I ran away at sixteen and went on the stage. Then I met Dick—and I fell for him. He was good-looking, and gay, and always doing sort of crazy things—smashing automobiles and shooting at bar-room mirrors. . . . I thought it was funny, then.

TERRY (*reaches out wordlessly to extend a comforting hand*). And I've been moaning about my little troubles.

KAYE. You know, I'd sworn to myself I never was going to bother you with this. Now, what made me do it?

TERRY. I'm glad you did. It'll do you good.

KAYE. Yes, I suppose it will.

TERRY (*taking off her robe*). Well, maybe we might as well get those sheep over the fence. Maybe we'll wake up tomorrow morning and there'll be nineteen managers downstairs, all saying, "You, and only you, can play this part."

KAYE (*as she settles herself for sleep*). I suppose Jean'll be out till all hours.

TERRY. There's a girl who hasn't got any troubles. Life rolls right along for her. . . (*At the window.*) Well, ready to go bye-bye?

KAYE. I suppose I might as well. But I feel so wide awake. (*As* TERRY *opens the window a blast of noise comes up from the street. A cacophony made up of protesting brakes, automobile horns, taxi drivers shouts, a laugh or two.*)
(KAYE *turns out the top light. From her dresser she takes a black eyeshield and adjusts it over her eyes after she is in bed.* TERRY *does the same, then shouts a "Good night!" loudly enough to be heard above the street din.* KAYE's *good night is equally loud. Simultaneously they turn out the bed lights. For a second—but only a second—the room is in darkness. Then the reason for the eyeshades becomes apparent. A huge electric advertising sign on an adjacent roof flashes on, off, on, off, alternately flooding the room with light and plunging it into darkness.*)

TERRY (*shouting*). Funny if we both did get jobs tomorrow!

KAYE. Huh?

TERRY (*louder*). I say, it would be funny we both got jobs tomorrow!

KAYE. Certainly would! (*A moment of silence in the room.*)
(*The door bursts open.* JEAN *comes in bringing with her a quiver of excitement. She is in dinner clothes.*)

JEAN (*she turns on the light*). Terry! Wake up!

TERRY. What's the matter?

JEAN (*slams the window down*). We're the movies!

TERRY. What?

JEAN. Both of us! We're in the movies! They just heard from the Coast!

TERRY. Jean! How do you know? What happened?

JEAN. Mr. Kingsley just got the telegram. They liked the tests, and we're to go to the office tomorrow to sign our contracts. We

ave for the Coast next week! Terry! Can
ou believe it!

AYE. Oh, girls, how exciting!

ERRY (*bewildered*). Yes. Yes. You mean—
ght away?

AN (*hardly' able to contain herself*). Of
ourse we'll only get little parts in the be-
nning. But there's that beautiful check
ery week, whether you work or not. And
e swimming and the sunshine and those
tle ermine jackets up to here. No more
nning around to offices and having them
it in your eye. And a salary raise every
x months if they like us. So at the end of
ree years it begins to get pretty good,
d after five years it's wonderful, and at
e end of seven years it's more money than
ou ever heard of.

RRY. Seven years! What do you mean—
ven years!

AN. Yes, it's a seven-year contract—that
if they take up the options.

RRY. But what about the stage? Suppose
wanted to act?

AN. Well, what do you think this is!
ggling? Motion-picture acting is just as
uch of an art as stage acting, only it's
t up more. You only have to learn about
ine at a time, and they just keep on tak-
g it until you get it right.

RRY (*staring at* JEAN. *A stricken pause.
hen she shakes her head slowly. Her deci-
n is made*). Oh, no.

AN. What?

RRY. I couldn't.

AN. Couldn't what?

RRY. That isn't acting; that's piecework.
ou're not a human being, you're a thing
a vacuum. Noise shut out, human re-
onse shut out. But in the theater, when
u hear that lovely sound out there, then
u know you're right. It's as though they'd
ned on an electric current that hit you
e. And that's how you learn to act.

AN. You can learn to act in pictures. You
ve to do it till it's right.

RRY. Yes, and then they put it in a tin
n—like Campbell's soup. And if you die
next day it doesn't matter a bit. You

don't even have to be alive to act in pictures.·

JEAN. I suppose you call *this* being alive!
Sleeping three in a room in *this* rotten
dump! It builds you up, eh?

TERRY. I'm not going to stay here all my
life! This is only the beginning!

JEAN. Don't kid yourself! You've been here
three years, and then it's three years more,
and then another three, and where are you?
You can't play ingenues forever. Pretty soon
you're a character woman, and then you're
running a boardinghouse, like old Orcutt.
That'll be nice, won't it?

TERRY. I don't know! You make me sound
like a fool, but I know I'm not. All I know
is I want to stay on the stage. I just don't
want to be in pictures. An actress in the
theater—that's what I've wanted to be my
whole life. It isn't just a career, it's a feeling. The theater is something that's gone on
for hundreds and hundreds of years. It's—
I don't know—it's part of civilization.

JEAN (*screaming at her*). All right, you stay
here with your civilization, eating those
stews and tapiocas they shove at us, toeing
the mark in this female seminary, buying
your clothes at Klein's! That's what you
like, eh?

TERRY. *Yes,* I like it!

JEAN. And I suppose you like this insane
racket going on all night! (*She throws open
the window.*)

TERRY (*yelling above the noise*). Yes, I *do.*

JEAN. And that Cadillac car sign going on
and off like a damned lighthouse! (*She
turns off the light. Again we see the flash
of the electric sign, off, on, off, on.*) I suppose you've got to have *that* to be an actress!

TERRY. Yes! Yes! Yes! Yes! Yes!

JEAN (*not stopping for her*). Well, not for
me! I'm going out where there's sunshine
and money and fun and—

TERRY (*shouting above her*). And little ermine swimming pools up to here! (*The
street noise, the flashing light, and their angry shouts are still going on as the curtain
descends.*)

CURTAIN

ACT TWO

SCENE I

The main room of the Footlights Club. It is mid-morning; the sunlight is streaming in.
FRANK, the houseman, is rather listlessly pushing a carpet sweeper, his attention directed toward an open newspaper lying on a chair. He edges nearer and nearer; his movements with the carpet sweeper become slower and slower, until finally they are barely perceptible.
ANN BRADDOCK comes briskly down the stairs with a condescending "Good morning, Frank!" and goes into the dining room, FRANK's response having been an absent-minded mumble.
MATTIE bustles in from the hall, and her face reflects her irritation as she sees her husband's idling at this busy hour of the day. Lips compressed, she marches straight to him, snatches the carpet sweeper from him and goes off with it. FRANK follows meekly after.
Somewhere in the hall, unseen, a clock strikes eleven.
BOBBY MELROSE, gaily singing, skips down the stairs and stops for a look through the mail. She finds a letter that gets her full attention, so that she is absorbed in it as she walks more slowly toward the dining room.

BOBBY. Oh, girls! Here's a letter from Madeleine.

JUDITH (*entering from the dining room*). Where is she this week?

BOBBY. Let's see. This week, Portland and Spokane. Next week, Seattle.

JUDITH. Seattle. That's her home town. (KENDALL ADAMS *dashes down the stairs, struggling into one coat sleeve as she comes. She stops for a quick glance at the mail, shrugging into her coat meanwhile.*) Heh, where're you going?

KENDALL. Rehearsal!

JUDITH. What's the rush?

KENDALL. Late!

JUDITH (*calling after her as she dashes for the door*). You're too conscientious. (*The slam of the door.*) Never gets you anywhere in this business.

TERRY (*coming down the stairs*). Well, what *does* get you anywhere, if I may make so bold?

JUDITH. Clean living, high thinking, and an occasional dinner with the manager.

TERRY (*taking a look through the mail*). What time is it? Shouldn't you be at rehearsal?

JUDITH. No, there's plenty of time. The nuns aren't called until eleven-thirty today.

TERRY (*turning over the envelope in her hand*). Mrs. Robert Hendershot—why, that's Louise! Appleton, Wisconsin. It's a letter from Louise. (*The telephone rings.* TERRY *rips open the envelope and takes a quick look at its pages, which are voluminous.*)

JUDITH (*en route to the telephone*). Maybe it's a Little Stranger. She's been married a year. . . . Hello! . . . She's right here. . . (*Hands the telephone to* TERRY.)

TERRY. Keith? (*Thrusts the letter into* JUDITH'*s hand.*) Here. It's addressed to all of us. (*As* JUDITH *buries herself in the letter* TERRY'*s attention goes to the telephone.* Keith! Isn't this the middle of the night for you! . . . What about? . . . No, I've got to stay free all afternoon on account of Dad . . . I don't know what time he gets here. He's driving with a friend. . . . Yes, all the way from Elvira. Well, you don't have to like it. He will. . . . No, I can't, because he's only here a day and a half, and this afternoon he wants to see Radio City and the Medical Center and the Battery.

JUDITH (*looking up from her letter*). Has he got a bicycle?

TERRY. And don't forget that you've invited us to dinner. . . . No, not at Smitty's. . . Well, Dad and Smitty's just don't go together. And look, darling, don't wear a black shirt and don't be one of the Masons tonight. . . . (SUSAN *runs down the stairs*

nd goes to the dining room with a "Good
morning!" to the girls.) What? . . . Well,
ou can tell me about it at dinner. . . . No,
ve got a radio rehearsal.

UDITH (still with the letter). Say, this is
classic.

ERRY. Well, if it's as vital as all that you
an come up here. . . . That's my brave
oy! (She hangs up.)

UDITH (her first opportunity to read from
he letter). Get this: "I have gained a little
veight, but Bob says I look better not so
crawny. He says maybe I like my own
ooking too much, but then he is always
oking." (To OLGA, who has come out of
he dining room). It's a letter from Louise.

LGA. What does she say?

OBBY (appearing in the dining-room door-
ay). Who said a letter from Louise?

ERRY. Yes, it just came.

UDITH (reading, as ANN and SUSAN come
to the dining-room doorway to hear the
ews.) "Dear Girlies: I guess you all won-
er why I have not written for so long. I
onestly don't know where the year has
one to. First there was the house to fur-
ish. We've got the darlingest six-room
ungalow on Winnebago Street. And then
f course everybody was giving parties for
e, and after that I had to return the obliga-
ons by giving parties for them. We are all
en now. I gave the last one just yesterday
-eighteen girls of the young married set,
ree tables of bridge and one of mah jong,
d two people just talked. The luncheon
as lovely, if I do say so. Everything pink."

LGA. You're making it up.

UDITH. So help me . . . "I am a member
the Ladies' Committee at the Country
lub, which gives wonderful Saturday-
ght dances during the summer." (She
rns to the girls for a moment.) Japanese
nterns. . . . "But do not think that I have
st track of the theater. We take the Mil-
aukee Sentinel daily, and last week we
ove to Milwaukee and saw Walter Hamp-
n in Cyrano."

RRY (reaching for the letter). Let me see!
o now I've told you all my news and
u've got to write me just everything about
e club. What about you, Terry, have you
t a swell part for this season? I thought

I'd die when I saw Jean's picture in Photo-
play, all dressed up like a real movie star
in a little ermine jacket and everything.
Jean a movie star! I've been bragging to all
my friends. Well, if you girls think about
me as much as I do about you, my ears
would be about burned off. We have supper
here around six o'clock, just as you all do
at the club, and when it's over I always
think, well, the girls are all beating it down
to the show shop and making up to go on
and just knocking the audience cold. Only
I don't say it out loud any more because
Bob says, oh, for God's sake, you and your
club! Love to old Orcutt and for goodness'
sakes, write, write, WRITE!"

JUDITH (very low). Wow.

TERRY. Well, I'll never complain again. This
makes my eighteen a week on the radio look
pretty wonderful.

OLGA (as she goes up the stairs). Everything
pink.

BOBBY. We've just been livin' in a bed of
roses.

ANN. I could have told her when she left
it wouldn't work. (BOBBY, ANN and SUSAN
go back to the dining room. TERRY and JU-
DITH remain in the living room.)

JUDITH (getting into her coat). Well, I
might as well get down to the factory.

TERRY. Look, Judith. Think you'll be rehearsing all afternoon?

JUDITH. How do I know! This thing I'm
in is a combination of Ringling Brothers
and the Passion Play. You never know
whether they're going to rehearse us nuns
or the elephants.

TERRY. It's just that I'd love you to meet
my father, if you have time.

JUDITH. Oh, I want to. He sounds like a
cutie.

TERRY. I wonder what's on Keith's mind,
getting up so early.

JUDITH. Nothing, is my guess.

TERRY. Judith! Maybe he sold the play!

JUDITH. Maybe. (Takes the plunge.) Look,
Terry. Where're you heading in with that
guy, anyhow?

TERRY. Why, what do you mean?

JUDITH. *You* know. He's been coming around here for a year, taking all your time, talking about himself, never considering you for a minute. Sold his play! Well, if he has he can thank *you* for it. It's as much your play as his.

TERRY. That isn't true.

JUDITH. Don't tell *me*. It was nothing but a stump speech the way he wrote it. You made him put flesh and blood into it.

TERRY (*quietly*). You're talking about someone you don't understand.

JUDITH. O.K. Forget I ever brought it up. . . . Well—good-by.

TERRY (*rather reserved*). Good-by. (*Takes a couple of typewritten pages out of her handbag.*)

JUDITH. Oh, now you're sore at me. I never can learn to keep my trap shut. But I only said it because I think more of you than anybody else in this whole menagerie. . . . Forgiven?

TERRY. Of course, Judy darling.

JUDITH (*indicating the papers in* TERRY'S *hand*). What's that? Your radio?

TERRY. Mmm.

JUDITH. It makes me boil to think of an actress like you reading radio recipes for a living. (*Peers at the script.*) "Two eggs and fold in the beaten whites." The beaten whites! That's us!

TERRY. Anyhow, it's a living for a few weeks. Aunt Miranda's Cooking Class.

JUDITH. Well, you're a hell of an Aunt Miranda, that's all I can say. . . . (*Goes.*)
(ANN *and* BOBBY *come out of the dining room.* ANN *is carrying a newspaper.*)

ANN (*seeing* TERRY). Did you read about Jean out in Hollywood? They've given her a new contract with a big raise and she's going to play the lead in *Two for Tonight*.

TERRY. Really! (*Looking over* ANN'S *shoulder.*) How marvelous! (*Takes paper from* ANN *and goes into dining room.*)

BOBBY. It's all a matter of cheek bones. You've got to have a face like this. (*She pushes her round little face into hollow curves.*)

ANN (*getting her coat*). What are you doing this morning? Job-hunting?

BOBBY. Uh-huh. Ah thought Ah'd go round to Equity and see what's up on the bulletin board. Maybe there's something new casting.

ANN (*applying her lipstick*). I'm going to try a couple of agents' offices. (*Becomes unintelligible as she paints the cupid's bow.*) Sometimes they know about new things.

BOBBY. What kind of lipstick's that?

ANN. It's a new one. It's called "I'll Never Tell."

BOBBY. Let me see. (*Tries a daub on the back of her hand.*) Mm. It's too orange for me. Ah like Tibiscus—good and red—as if you'd been kicked in the mouth by a mule. (*They gather up their handbags and go.*)
(KAYE *comes down the stairs like a little wraith. Near the foot of the stairs she glances over the railing and it is evident that she is relieved to find the living room empty.*)
(*As she is about to go to the street door* MRS. ORCUTT *swoops down on her with a promptness which indicates that she has been waiting for her.*)

MRS. ORCUTT. Oh, Kaye! Could I speak to you just a minute, please?

KAYE. I'm—just on my way to rehearsal.

MRS. ORCUTT (*as she carefully closes the dining-room door*). I won't detain you but a second. I just want to— (*The door closed.*) You must know how reluctant I always am to speak to you on this subject. I try to be as easy as I can with the girls, but, after all, I have my bills to pay, too.

KAYE. But Mrs. Orcutt, I'm rehearsing. You know that. And I'm sure they like me. And just the minute we open I can start paying off.

MRS. ORCUTT. Yes, I know. But plays are not always successful, and the amount has grown rather large. So, taking everything into consideration, I wonder if you'd mind a little suggestion.

KAYE. No. No.

MRS. ORCUTT. Well, it occurred to me that perhaps it might be wise if you were nd some place a little cheaper. By a lucky hance I think I know the ideal place. Of ourse the girls are a little older, and it's ot strictly a theatrical club—more the commercial professions. However, I think you'll ind it almost as conveniently situated. 'orty-ninth Street, this side of Tenth Avenue. Perhaps, when you have time, you night drop in and look at it. (KAYE *only ods a silent assent.*) Now, now, we mustn't e upset by this. It's just a little talk. (*A ather grim pause which suggests the alternative.*) Now, let's put it out of our minds.. hall we? And let me see a little smile. (*As here is no response from* KAYE, MRS. ORCUTT miles for both.*) There! . . . Well, we both ave our day's work to do. (MRS. ORCUTT oes.)

PAT, *singing blithely, comes down the airs. As she passes* KAYE *she chucks her aily under the chin, says, "H'ya, baby?" by ay of morning greeting, and executes a rief and intricate little dance step, all this ithout pausing on her way to the dining oom.)*

KAYE *stands, a little wooden figure. She rns to go as* TERRY *comes in from the ining room.)*

ERRY. What are you doing—going without ur breakfast?

AYE. I don't want any breakfast. I'm not ngry.

RRY (*on her way to the stairs*). Well, u're just an old fool, rehearsing on an npty stomach. (*As* KAYE *goes the two ARYS come into sight on the stairs, talking they descend. They pass* TERRY *as she es up.*)

G MARY (*in the throes of trying to memore a part.* LITTLE MARY, *who is cueing her, llows with the part in her hand*). "Three eeks now since he first came here. What we know about him—uh—anyhow?" Is ere an "anyhow"?

TLE MARY. Yeh.

MARY. "What do we know about him yhow? Only that he spent twelve years in istralia and that he claims to be your ond cousin—second cousin—second cou—"

TLE MARY. "I tell you—" (*The doorbell gs.*)

BIG MARY. "I tell you there is something mysterious going on in this house." Well, that's all, give me the cue.

LITTLE MARY (*scans the part*). Uh—huh—

BIG MARY. Oh, for heaven's sakes! "We must call the police."

LITTLE MARY. Oh, yeh. "We must call the police."

BIG MARY. Now let's go back and do it right. "I tell you there is something mysterious going on in this house."

LITTLE MARY (*as they go into the dining room*). "We must call the police." (*The outer door is opened and we hear a voice subsequently identified as that of* MRS. SHAW, LINDA'S *mother.*)

MRS. SHAW. Good morning.

MATTIE. How-do.

MRS. SHAW. This is the Footlights Club, isn't it?

MATTIE. Yes, ma'am. Won't you come in?

MRS. SHAW. Oh, thank you. (MRS. SHAW *comes into sight. She is a rather cozy little woman of about fifty-five, plainly dressed, sweet-faced and inclined to be voluble.*) (*She speaks rather confidingly now to* MATTIE.) I'm Mrs. Shaw, Linda's mother. She doesn't know I'm coming. I'm surprising her.

MATTIE. Oh—you Miss Linda's mother! For land's sakes!

MRS. SHAW. She doesn't know I'm here. We live in Buffalo. I just got off the train and came right up. Linda hasn't gone out, I hope?

MATTIE (*as she goes toward the stairs*). No, I haven't seen her around yet.

MRS. SHAW. Well, you just tell her there's somebody here to see her, very important. Only don't tell her it's her mother.

MATTIE. Yes'm. (*She disappears.*) (MRS. SHAW *seats herself and looks about her with bright-eyed interest.*) (SUSAN *comes out of the dining room, and seeing a middle-aged woman in the room nods politely.*)

MRS. SHAW. Good morning.

SUSAN. Good morning.

MRS. SHAW. Are you a little actress?

SUSAN. Yes, sort of.

MRS. SHAW. I'm Linda's mother. I've come to surprise her.

SUSAN. Oh, what fun!

MRS. SHAW. Which one of the girls are you? Perhaps Linda's written me about you.

SUSAN. I'm Susan Paige.

MRS. SHAW. Are you acting a part on Broadway?

SUSAN. I'm in *Petticoat Lane,* but I'm only an understudy.

MRS. SHAW. Understudy?

SUSAN. That means I play the part in case the leading woman gets sick.

MRS. SHAW. Oh! That's nice. And does she get sick often?

SUSAN. Never! (SUSAN *goes up the stairs as* MATTIE *descends.*)
(MATTIE *appears slightly flustered.*)

MATTIE. I'm awful sorry, I must have made a mistake. I guess Miss Linda must have gone out already.

MRS. SHAW. Oh, dear! Does anybody know where she went?

MATTIE (*edging toward the hall*). Well, I'll see—maybe Mrs. Orcutt knows. (*We have not heard the front door open or close, so silently has* LINDA SHAW *entered the house. She is swiftly tiptoeing up the stairs as* MATTIE *turns and sees her.*) There she is! Miss Linda! Miss Linda! (LINDA *has not heeded the first call, but the second one stops her.*) Your ma's here.

MRS. SHAW. Oh, dear, I was going to surprise you.

LINDA (*frozen on the stairs*). Why—Mother!

MRS. SHAW. I guess I have. Well, aren't you going to come down? (*Holds her arms open wide to embrace her daughter.*)
(LINDA *makes a slow and heavy-footed descent, eyeing first her mother, then* MATTIE. *She is wrapped in a camel's-hair ulster, a little too large for her; on her head is a small beret such as might be worn by a man or woman.*)

LINDA. Mother, how—how wonderful. When did—you—

MRS. SHAW. Why, Linda, child, aren't you glad to see me?

LINDA. Of course I am, Mother. (*Kisses her mother quickly.*)

MRS. SHAW (*as she surveys her daughter's strange attire*). Of all the funny getups!

LINDA. Yes, isn't it silly—I— (*She turns to the gaping* MATTIE.) —Mattie, I'm sure you have your work to do. Why don't you run along?

MATTIE (*reluctant to leave*). Yes—Miss Linda. (*She goes.*)

MRS. SHAW. Where did you get that coat? I never saw that coat before.

LINDA. It belongs to—to one of the girls . . . I had to go down to the drugstore.

MRS. SHAW. Why—you've got on evening slippers!

LINDA. I just put on the first thing I could find.

MRS. SHAW. Linda Shaw, if you've run out in your pajamas—

LINDA (*backing away from her mother*). No, I haven't. I— (*She realizes she has made a blunder.*) —Yes, I have. Yes.

MRS. SHAW. Linda, what are you wearing under that coat? (LINDA *stands, holding the coat about her.*) Take off that coat! Take off that— (*She jerks it open so that it slides down the girl's arms and drops to the floor, revealing* LINDA *in a black satin evening dress of extreme cut—the narrowest of shoulder straps, bare shoulders, a deep decolletage, the bodice almost backless.*) Linda!

LINDA. I spent the night with a girl friend.

MRS. SHAW. Oh—Linda!

LINDA. Oh, Mother, don't make a scene!

MRS. SHAW (*with repressed emotion*). Linda, go up and pack your things. You're coming home with me.

LINDA. Oh, no, I'm not.

MRS. SHAW. Linda Shaw!

LINDA. We can't talk here, Mother. And there's no use talking, anyhow. I'm never coming home. I'm twenty-two years old and my life is my own.

MRS. SHAW. Who—who is this man? Are you going to marry him?

LINDA. He *is* married.

MRS. SHAW. I'm going to send for your father. He'll know what to do.

LINDA. Mother, if you make a fuss about this I'll have to leave the club. That girl knows already. And if I leave here I'll go and live with him, and the whole world will know it. Now take your choice. (MRS. ORCUTT *enters, apprehension in her face, steeled for an eventuality. Her quick eye goes from the girl to the mother.*)

MRS. ORCUTT. I'm Mrs. Orcutt, Mrs. Shaw. My maid just told me you were here.

MRS. SHAW. Oh, how do you do, Mrs. Orcutt?

MRS. ORCUTT. I understand you arrived unexpectedly.

MRS. SHAW. Yes, I came down to do a bit of shopping and surprise my little girl, here, and we practically came in together. She spent the night with my niece and her husband—Eighty-sixth Street—they had a rather late party and Linda just decided to— I don't see how these young people stand it. . . . (*A little laugh.*) Doesn't she look silly—this time of day— Linda darling, do run up and change. Why don't you meet me for luncheon at the hotel? Can you do that?

LINDA. Of course, Mother dear.

MRS. SHAW. I'm at the Roosevelt, darling. Shall we say one o'clock?

LINDA (*in quiet triumph*). Yes, Mother darling. (*She goes upstairs.*)

MRS. SHAW. Oh, well, I must run along. I'm only going to be here a day or two and .. Well, good-by.

MRS. ORCUTT (*accompanying her to the door*). Good-by. It's been so nice. I'm always happy to meet the parents of our girls. And I hope that whenever you are in the city you won't fail to drop in on us. Well, good-by. (*As* MRS. ORCUTT *passes back along the hallway* OLGA *descends the stairs. She is wearing a hat, her coat is over her arm. In one hand she has a few sheets of music, in the other a music portfolio. She tosses her coat over to the piano and props a sheet of music on the rack.*)
She sits at the piano, plays a few bars.)

(BERNICE, *in hat and coat, comes down the stairs. She looks in on* OLGA *and listens to the music.*)

BERNICE. Are you going to play that at your concert?

OLGA (*playing*). Yes.

BERNICE. When's it going to be?

OLGA. In the spring.

BERNICE. Whereabouts, Town Hall?

OLGA. Yes, yes.

BERNICE. Are you going to play under your own name?

OLGA. Certainly.

BERNICE. Well, you've got an interesting name—Olga Brandt. It sounds like a musician. But Bernice Niemeyer! I think that's what's holding me back in the theater. Do you know what? I thought maybe I'd take one of those one-word names, the way some actresses do. I thought, instead of Bernice Niemeyer, I'd just call myself—Zara. (BERNICE *goes.*)
(OLGA *continues with her music. The doorbell rings.* MATTIE *answers.*)
(*As the door opens we hear the voice of* DR. RANDALL, TERRY'S *father. His first words are lost under cover of* OLGA'S *music.*)

MATTIE. Just go right in and sit down. I'll tell Miss Terry you're here. (*She goes up the stairs.*)
(DR. RANDALL *is a gentle-looking, gray-haired man touching sixty. There is about him a vague quality—a wistful charm—that is not of the modern professional world.*)
(OLGA, *as he enters, is about to launch herself on the finale of the selection she has been playing. It entails terrific chords, dissonances, and actual physical effort. The length of the keyboard seems scarcely adequate.* DR. RANDALL *stands arrested by this. Three times the music pauses as if finished, each time* DR. RANDALL *steps forward to speak and* OLGA *starts again. He gives a little nod of approval as* OLGA *finishes, rises, and gathers up her music and her coat.* OLGA *acknowledges this with a little inclination of her head, and goes.*)
(*The front door slams on her going. Immediately the dining-room doors open and the two* MARYS *come out, still deep in rehearsal.*)

BIG MARY. "I tell you there is something mysterious going on in this house."

LITTLE MARY. "We must call the police."

BIG MARY (*with no particular expression*). "Last night I heard moans and shrieks, and this morning a dead man was found on the doorstep, his head completely severed."

LITTLE MARY. "What about the blood in the library?" (*They disappear up the stairs.*)

(PAT *emerges from the dining room, intent on mastering a fast and intricate dance routine for which she provides her own music. She catches herself at the sight of a stranger, and scampers up the stairs.*)

(DR. RANDALL *has barely had time to react to these somewhat bewildering encounters when a gay high voice from the stairs calls, "Dad!" and* TERRY *comes running down. She hurls herself into her father's arms.*)

TERRY. Dad! Darling! I couldn't be more surprised.

DR. RANDALL. Glad to see me?

TERRY. Glad! I should say so! It's been almost a year.

DR. RANDALL. Too long, my dear. Too long to be separated. . . . Let me look at you.

TERRY. Bursting with health, Doc.

DR. RANDALL. Mmm. (*Pulls down first one eyelid, then the other.*) Look kind of peaked to me. Eat enough greens?

TERRY. Greens! I'm a regular Miss Popeye. Now let me look at you. Say Ah, say Oh, say you love me. (*He laughs as he kisses her.*) Now come on and tell me everything. How's Aunt Lucy? And is she taking good care of you?

DR. RANDALL. Say, you know Lucy! You'd think I was ten years old.

TERRY. I know. Wear your rubbers, have you got a clean handkerchief. Didn't she fuss about your driving all this way?

DR. RANDALL. Carried on like mad.

TERRY. How did you get here so early? You said afternoon. What happened?

DR. RANDALL. Well, when Stacy invited me to come East with him, I didn't know what kind of driver he was. Turned out he's one of those fellows slows down to eighty going through a town. I dozed off a couple o minutes, once, and missed all of Pennsyl vania.

TERRY. He shouldn't have done it, but i does give me more time with you.

DR. RANDALL. Now maybe you've got thing to do. You weren't expecting me till thre or four.

TERRY. I've got nothing but a silly radi rehearsal. You know—I'm the big butter and-egg girl. I'll be all through by quarter past one. Let's have lunch way up on to of something. Shall we?

DR. RANDALL. That's fine. Gives me time t drop in at the Polyclinic a few minute. Three forty-five West Fiftieth Stree Where's that?

TERRY. It's not five minutes from here. An I'll pick you up at your hotel. Where ar you?

DR. RANDALL. New Yorker. Stacy's idea. Fu of go-getters.

TERRY. After lunch we'll whirl all over tow We'll see everything. Tonight we're goin to the theater, and Keith's taking us to di ner.

DR. RANDALL. Oh, yes. Your young man. want to meet the boy.

TERRY. Now, Dad, remember, he's not lik the boys back in Elvira.

DR. RANDALL. Say, *they're* not like that an more, either.

TERRY. Yes, but Keith's not like anybod you ever met. He's brilliant, and he's wri ten the most marvelous play, and he hat the government and won't wear evenin clothes.

DR. RANDALL. Sounds as if he didn't have nickel.

TERRY. Oh, but he will have! This play w put him over. It's thrilling and beautifu And oh, Dad, I'm going to play the lead.

DR. RANDALL. Why, Tress, that's wonderfu Your mother would have been very prou

TERRY. Of course he hasn't sold the pl yet. But he will. He's bound to.

DR. RANDALL. Say, I'm going to come back and see you in that if it takes my last nickel.

TERRY (*who has been eyeing him a little anxiously*). Dad.

DR. RANDALL. Yes, Tress?

TERRY. You look as though you'd been working too hard. Have you?

DR. RANDALL. I wish I could say I had. But my waiting room looks pretty bleak these days.

TERRY. Isn't anybody sick at all? How about old Mrs. Wainwright?

DR. RANDALL. Yes, folks get sick, all right.

TERRY. Well, then!

DR. RANDALL. Well, it seems just being a medical man isn't enough these days. If you had a cold, we used to just cure the cold. But nowadays, the question is, why did you get the cold? Turns out, it's because, subconsciously, you didn't want to live. And why don't you want to live? Because when you were three years old the cat died, and they buried it in the back yard without telling you, and you were in love with the cat, so, naturally, forty years later you catch cold.

TERRY. But who tells them all this?

DR. RANDALL. Why—uh—young fellow came to town a few months ago; opened up offices.

TERRY. Oh!

DR. RANDALL. Sun lamps, X-ray machines, office fixed up like a power plant. He's the one's looking after Mrs. Wainwright. She's bedridden with sciatica, arthritis and a heart condition, but, fortunately, it's all psychic.

TERRY. Dad, do you mean he's taken your whole practice away from you!

DR. RANDALL. Mm—not as bad as that. The mill folks still come to me.

TERRY. But they haven't any money?

DR. RANDALL. They still have babies.

TERRY. Never you mind. I'm going to buy you the biggest, shiniest, sun-lamp machine ever invented; and fluoroscopes and microscopes and stethoscopes and telescopes. You'll be able to sit in your office and turn a button and look right *through* Mrs. Wainwright, six blocks away.

DR. RANDALL. How about that new doctor? Will it go through him?

TERRY. It'll *dissolve* him. (*The front door slams.* KEITH *strides to the foot of the stairs. The black sweater has given way to a black shirt. Otherwise his costume is about the same. No hat, of course.*)

KEITH (*shouts up the stairs*). Terry!

TERRY. Why—Keith!

KEITH. Oh! I—the door was open. I came right in.

TERRY. Here's Father! He got here this morning.

KEITH (*advancing*). Well! This is indeed a pleasure, sir.

DR. RANDALL. Thank you, young man. I'm glad to know you.

KEITH. Terry has told me so much about you. I've been looking forward to this meeting for a long time, sir.

DR. RANDALL. Oh, that's very good of you.

KEITH (*takes out a crumpled pack of Camels*). May I offer you a cigarette, sir?

DR. RANDALL. Thanks. (*Takes a cigarette.*)

TERRY (*who has been observing all this courtliness with a growing bewilderment*). Keith, Dad doesn't understand that kind of fooling.

KEITH. You never told me, Theresa, that you and your father had such a strong resemblance. The same fine brow, the deepset, thoughtful eyes. Allow me, sir! (*Lights* DR. RANDALL's *cigarette.*)

TERRY. Keith, will you stop it! What is this act, anyhow?

KEITH (*blandly*). It's no act. What are you talking about?

DR. RANDALL (*pats* KEITH *on the shoulder*). I guess you'll do. . . . Well, children, I've got to be off. You said quarter-past one, Terry?

TERRY. Yes, Father. I'll come to your hotel.

DR. RANDALL (*to* KEITH). Understand we're seeing you later. That right?

KEITH (*absent-mindedly*). What? Oh, yes.

TERRY (*as she accompanies her father into the hallway, their arms about each other's shoulders*). I can't tell you how grand it is to have you here, Dad. . . . Now, don't cross against the lights, and promise to take taxis. Don't try to find places by yourself.

DR. RANDALL. All right, all right.

TERRY. I'll be at the hotel at one-fifteen.

DR. RANDALL. I'll be waiting.

TERRY. Good-by, darling.

DR. RANDALL. Good-by. (TERRY *returns to the living room and* KEITH.)

TERRY. Really, Keith, you can be so maddening. What was all that "Yes, sir," and "How are you, sir?"

KEITH. Can't I be polite?

TERRY. One of the least convincing performances I ever saw.

KEITH. That's right. Hit a fellow when he's down.

TERRY. Keith, what's the matter?

KEITH. I come to you in one of the toughest spots I ever was in in my life, and you jump all over me.

TERRY. I'm so sorry. I didn't know. How could I—what's happened? Is it the play?

KEITH (*unhappily*). Yes.

TERRY. They all turned it down?

KEITH (*reluctantly*). N-no.

TERRY. Keith! Tell me!

KEITH (*unwillingly*). I—I could sign a contract this afternoon.

TERRY. You don't mean it! Who with?

KEITH. Gilman.

TERRY (*almost with awe*). Gilman! Why, he's the best there is!

KEITH. That's what makes it so tough.

TERRY. Keith, for heaven's sake, you're not being unreasonable about this! A Gilman production—why, it's—Keith, no matter what he wants you to do, you've got to do it. What's he want you to change? The second act?

KEITH. No. He likes the play all right. He's nuts about it.

TERRY. Well, then, I don't—understand what—

KEITH (*squirming*). I just can't let him have it, that's all.

TERRY (*something clicks in her mind*). Keith! It's me. He doesn't want me.

KEITH. Well—you see—Gilman's got Natalie Blake under contract, and she *is* a big star, and it just happens to be the kind of part she's been looking for—

TERRY (*crushed*). Did you tell him you thought I would be good in it?

KEITH. Of course. I gave him a hell of an argument. But he just won't do it unless Blake is in it.

TERRY. Well then, that's—that. I wouldn't do anything to— I bow out, Keith.

KEITH. Gosh, Terry! You mean you really would do that for me!

TERRY. The play is the important thing, Keith. I love every line of it. You didn't think, after the way we've worked on it for a whole year, that I'd stand in the way, did you?

KEITH. God, you're wonderful, Terry! You're a great kid! I'm crazy about you! (*He embraces her.*)

TERRY (*evading him*). Please, Keith.

KEITH. There isn't one girl in a million would have taken it like this. And I love you for it. Love you, do you hear!

TERRY. Yes, Keith.

KEITH. Well, look— (*He breaks off as* LINDA *comes down the stairs—*LINDA *in a neat little mink cape, and carrying a costly looking dressing case. There is determination written in her face.*)
(*She gives a swift glance down the hall. Then decides to use* TERRY *as her messenger.*)

LINDA. Terry. Terry, will you do something for me?

TERRY (*absorbed in her own thoughts*). What? . . . Oh, hello, Linda.

LINDA. I don't want to see Orcutt. Will you give her a message for me?

TERRY. Yes, of course.

LINDA. Tell her I'm leaving. I'll send for my things this afternoon. And give her this. (*She thrusts some bills into* TERRY's *hand.*) It's for the whole week.

TERRY. Linda, what's the matter? You're moving? Where?

LINDA. You bet I'm moving. Fast. And nobody'll ever know where. (*She goes.*)

KEITH. What was all that about?

TERRY (*collecting herself*). What? . . . I don't know. She's a strange girl.

KEITH. Well, look, I've got to run. Gilman's waiting in the office for me. He's lining up a hell of a cast. I'm going to meet Natalie Blake this evening. I'm having dinner with her and Gilman.

TERRY. Tonight! Keith, you're having dinner with Father and me.

KEITH. Oh, for God's sake, Terry! I get a chance like this with a top manager and a big star, and you expect me to say (*Lapses into an imitation of a nitwit.*) I can't meet you tonight, I got to have dinner with my girl and her papa. That's what you want me to say, I suppose?

TERRY. No—no.

KEITH (*about to leave*). I'll do the best I can. You know that. This whole thing is for you as much as for me. You know that, don't you?

TERRY. Yes.

KEITH. Well, then! Now look, darling— (TERRY's *gaze, chancing to go toward the stairway, sees a quiet little figure stealing up the steps. She halts* KEITH *with a gesture.*)

TERRY. Why, Kaye, what are you doing back? (KAYE *turns on the stair; looks at* TERRY *for a moment without speaking. Then she starts slowly into the room.*)

KAYE. Terry, they let me out.

TERRY. Oh, Kaye!

KAYE. There was another girl rehearsing when I got there. I'm fired.

TERRY. But they can't do that! How long had you been rehearsing?

KAYE. They still could. This was the seventh day.

TERRY. Darling, don't let it upset you. It happens to all of us. (*A realization of her own recent disappointment comes over her.*) To me. It's a part of this crazy business.

KAYE. Terry, I haven't a cent.

TERRY. Who cares! I've still got my radio job. We'll get along.

KAYE (*dully*). Don't try to fool me. I know about the radio job. You've only got two more weeks. I can't take any more money from you. I owe you more than a hundred dollars.

TERRY. What of it! Now look. Have lunch with Dad and me. Come on down to my radio rehearsal.

KAYE. No, I couldn't, Terry. I just—couldn't. Don't you bother about me. I'm all right.

TERRY (*glances at her wrist watch*). Oh, dear, I hate to leave you like this. Don't be low, darling.

KAYE (*as she goes up the stairs*). I'm all right. Thanks, Terry.

TERRY. Oh, I wish I didn't have to— (*She turns to* KEITH.) It meant everything to her.

KEITH. She'll get something else—the season's just begun. . . . Look, darling, you and your dad have a nice dinner some place and leave my ticket at the box office and I'll be along just as soon as I can. Will you do that, sweet?

TERRY (*dully*). Yes.

KEITH. Okay! That's my girl! (*He gives her a hasty kiss.*) You're the swellest kid that ever lived! (*Dashes off; the slam of the door*).

(TERRY *stands for a moment, trying to pull herself together.* KEITH *and his news;* KAYE's *terrible situation; even the strange behavior of* LINDA—*all these are in her mind. Then* MATTIE *comes into the room, intent on tidying up. With ash receptacle and dust cloth, she makes the rounds.*)

TERRY (*mechanically, as she looks down and finds* LINDA's *money in her hand*). Mattie, where's Mrs. Orcutt?

MATTIE. Back in her room. (TERRY *goes.*)

(MATTIE, *continuing her work, hums a snatch of lively song.*)
(*Then suddenly a piercing scream is heard from upstairs.* SUSAN *hurtles down the steps,*

her face distorted with terror. TERRY *rushes back into the room.)*

TERRY. What is it? What is it?

SUSAN. Up in the hall! She drank something! She's—

TERRY. No! No! *(She rushes up the stairs, followed quickly by* MATTIE. MRS. ORCUTT *and* FRANK *rush breathlessly into the room.)*

MRS. ORCUTT. What's the matter? What happened? *(*SUSAN, *unable to speak, gestures toward the upper hallway.* MRS. ORCUTT *and* FRANK *run up.)*

*(*SUSAN, *sobbing, staggers further into the room and drops onto the piano bench, a little huddled figure. Meanwhile we hear frantic voices upstairs: "Kaye, can you hear me?" "Oh, Lord, look at her!" "Kaye, darling, why did you do it?" "Want me to carry her in her room?" "What'd she swallow? What was it?" "Here's the bottle. Don't say nothing on it." "I'll get a doctor!")*

*(*MRS. ORCUTT *comes quickly down the stairs; goes to the phone, dials. Before she can even finish, however,* TERRY *comes slowly into view on the stairs.* MRS. ORCUTT *looks at her; it is almost unnecessary for* TERRY *to speak.)*

TERRY. It's—no use. *(*MRS. ORCUTT *hangs up the receiver mechanically.* TERRY *comes slowly down the remaining steps, her eyes fixed straight ahead of her.)*

MRS. ORCUTT *(in a low voice).* It'll be in all the papers. I never should have let her stay here. I felt it from the start. There was something about her. She was—different from the rest of you.

TERRY. Don't say that! It might have been any one of us. She was just a girl without a job, like— *(She is afraid to finish the sentence.)* It might have been—any one of us. *(*FRANK *and* MATTIE, *huddling together, come into view on the stairs as—*

THE CURTAIN FALLS

SCENE II

Again the living room of the Footlights Club. It is seven o'clock in the evening, about two months later.

Again SAM HASTINGS *is waiting for a tardy* BOBBY. *Obviously it has been a long wait and his patience is frayed. He peers up the stairs, paces the room, crosses to the piano and impatiently fingers a few notes.*

BOBBY *floats down the stairs, as Southern as ever.*

BOBBY. Hello there, honey bun!

SAM. Hello, sugar!

BOBBY *(as she kisses him).* Ah didn't keep you waitin', did Ah?

SAM No. No.

BOBBY *(fussing with his necktie).* Just look at your tie! Ah declare, Ah don't see how Ah can keep on lovin' you, the way you get yourself up.

SAM *(on their way out).* Go on! Everybody knows you're crazy about me.

BOBBY. Ah sure enough am. Ah just can't sleep or eat.

SAM. Honest, honey?

BOBBY. Mhm. Where we going to have dinner? *(They go.)*

(Two MARYS *enter from dining room, crossing to stairs deep in an argument.)*

LITTLE MARY. Well, what do you want to do all evening? I'm sick of movies and you don't want to sit around *here.*

BIG MARY. I'll tell you what. Let's go and see Keith Burgess' play.

LITTLE MARY. Keith Burgess' play! We couldn't get into that. The paper says seats eight weeks in advance and fifty standees last night.

BIG MARY. Then two more won't matter. That's all we want to do—stand up.

LITTLE MARY. Yes, but I don't think we ought to ask.

BIG MARY. Good Lord, you don't want to *pay* do you?

LITTLE MARY. Pay? For theater? You must be out of your mind. (*They go up the stairs.*)
Doorbell. MATTIE *enters from the dining room. Looks back.*)

MATTIE. Did you put a new 'lectric bulb up in Miss Kendall's room?

FRANK (*from dining room*). I will.

MATTIE. Give Miss Terry that telephone message? From Mr. Kingsley.

FRANK. Land sakes, I forgot.

MATTIE. Well, you better tell her—he's important. And you can close up the dining room—everybody's been in that's going to eat. (FRANK *closes the dining-room door.* MATTIE *proceeds to the outer door, and presently we hear her astonished voice.*) Well, I declare! (*The reason for her exclamation becomes apparent as* KEITH BURGESS *comes into the room. He is a figure of splendor in full evening regalia—white tie, top hat, white muffler, beautifully tailored topcoat.*) MATTIE *goes toward the stairs with her astonished gaze so fixed on this dazzling apparition as to make her ascent a somewhat stumbling one.*)

KEITH, *waiting, takes out a platinum-and-gold cigarette case, symbol of his seduction; taps a cigarette smartly, lights it.*)
JUDITH, *the last to finish her dinner, comes out of the dining room eating a large banana. As* KEITH *bursts upon her vision she stops dead, and all progress with the banana is temporarily suspended.*)

KEITH (*removing his hat*). Hello, Judith. JUDITH *advances slowly to him, grasps the hand that holds the hat, moves it up so that the hat is held at about shoulder height, backs up, lifts her skirts a little, and is about to kick when* KEITH, *outraged, breaks his position and walks away from her.*)

JUDITH. Well, if you don't want to play. *Takes the final bite of her banana.*)

KEITH. Pixie, eh? (JUDITH *tosses the banana skin on the floor between them; beckons him enticingly.*)

JUDITH. Come to mama!

MATTIE (*descending the stairs*). Miss Terry'll be right down.

JUDITH (*shakes her head dolefully as she picks up the banana skin*). You were more fun in the other costume.

KEITH. You'd better watch your figure, eating those bananas. Starches and show business don't go together.

JUDITH. They do in my show. I got nothing to compete with but elephants.

KEITH. Are there idiots who really *go* to those childish things—pay money?

JUDITH. Say, you can't have *all* the idiots. You're doing pretty good; give us some of the overflow.

KEITH. I suppose you know we broke the house record last week.

JUDITH. Oh, sure. I stayed up all Saturday night to get the returns.

KEITH (*under his breath*). Wisecracker. (TERRY's *voice is heard as she comes running down the stairs.*)

TERRY. So-o sorry, Mr. Burgess! At the last minute I had a run in my stocking and I had to— (*She stops short as she sees* KEITH's *magnificent effect. She herself is wearing her everyday clothes.*)

JUDITH (*sensing trouble*). Well, I'll—I'll leave you two young people together. (*She gives the effect of tiptoeing out of the room.*)

TERRY (*dazzled*). Keith! How— (*She curtsies to the floor.*) Did you remember to bring the glass slipper?

KEITH. What's the idea, Terry? I told you on the phone we were dressing.

TERRY. I thought you were joking. You said, "We'll dress, of course," and I said, "Of course!" But I didn't dream you were serious.

KEITH. We're going to an opening night! And our seats are third row center!

TERRY. Downstairs?

KEITH. Down— Where do you think?

TERRY. Darling, we've been to openings before, and we always sat in the gallery.

KEITH. Gallery! We're through with the gallery! I've got a table at the Vingt-et-un for dinner, and after the theater we're invited to a party at Gilman's penthouse. You can't go like that!

TERRY. Give me just ten minutes— I'll go up and change. (*She suddenly recollects.*) Oh, dear!

KEITH. What's the matter?

TERRY. I loaned my evening dress to Susan.

KEITH. Oh, for God's— (*Turns away in disgust.*)

TERRY. It's all right. I'll borrow Judy's pink— Oh, no! Olga's wearing it.

KEITH. This is the god-damnedest dump I was ever in! Sordid kind of life! Wearing each other's clothes! I suppose you use each other's toothbrushes, too!

TERRY (*quietly*). Would you rather I didn't go, Keith?

KEITH. I didn't say that I—

TERRY (*still quietly*). Yes—but would you rather?

KEITH. Now you're playing it for tragedy. What's the matter with you, anyhow!

TERRY. There's nothing the matter with me, Keith. I just can't see us as third-row first-nighters. We always went to see the *play*, Keith. That whole crowd—it makes the audience more important than the show.

KEITH. Listen, I don't like those people any better than you do. They don't mean anything to *me*.

TERRY. Then why do you bother with them?

KEITH. They can't hurt me. I watch them as you'd watch a hill of ants. Insects, that's what they are.

TERRY. Keith, you wrote your last play about people you understood and liked. You lived with them, and you knew them, and they gave you something. You'll starve to death in third-row center.

KEITH. I'm going back to them. I'm no fool. They're keeping my room for me just as it was.

TERRY. Keeping it? How do you mean?

KEITH. Oh, I don't want to talk about it now. Come on, let's get out of here.

TERRY. But I've got to know. Do you mean you've moved without even telling me?

KEITH (*decides to face the music*). Well, I was going to break it to you later. I knew

you'd jump on me. But as long as you've gone this far— I'm going to Hollywood.

TERRY. Hollywood!

KEITH. Yes, to write for pictures.

TERRY. No, no, Keith!

KEITH. Now don't start all over again! If you don't watch yourself you'll turn into one of those nagging— (*He stops as KENDALL comes down the stairs. She throws a glance into the room, in passing, and notices KEITH's unusual attire.*)

KENDALL (*impressed and very friendly*). Hel-lo!

KEITH (*with no cordiality*). H'are you?

KENDALL (*senses she has walked into a hornets' nest*). Good-by. (*Beats a hasty retreat via the front door.*)

KEITH. Let's get out of here.

TERRY. Keith, you can't go to Hollywood! I won't let you! You said you'd never go, no matter how broke you were, and now that your play's a big hit you're going.

KEITH. Well, they didn't want me before it was a hit!

TERRY. Keith, listen—

KEITH. I know what you're going to say. All that junk about its shriveling up my soul. Listen! I'm going to use Hollywood. It's not going to use me. I'm going to stay one year at two thousand a week. That's one hundred thousand dollars. I'll write their garbage in the daytime, but at night I'll write my own plays.

TERRY. But will you? That's what I'm afraid of. *Will* you?

KEITH. You bet I will! And in between I'll keep fit with sunshine, and swimming, and tennis, and—

TERRY. Little ermine jackets, up to here.

KEITH. Huh?

TERRY. It doesn't matter.

KEITH. Believe me, they'll never catch m at their Trocaderos or their Brown Derbies

TERRY (*quietly*). When are you going Keith?

KEITH. I don't know. Next week.

TERRY. Well—good-by.

KEITH. What!

TERRY. Good-by, Keith, and good luck. It's been swell. (*She turns; runs swiftly up the stairs.*)

(KEITH *goes to the foot of the stairs and calls.*)

KEITH. Terry! What's the— Terry! . . . Terry! (*Only silence from above. He claps his hat on his head and goes. The door slams loudly after him.*)

(*Immediately on the slam of the door* BERNICE *tiptoes down the stairs with a catlike swiftness and soundlessness. Obviously she has been eavesdropping. A quick, comprehensive look around the room, then she scurries to the window, peers out guardedly, so as not to be seen from the street. Turns back from the window just as the two* MARYS *make swift, silent descents of the stairs. The three at once plunge into an elaborate whispered and pantomimic routine revealing their knowledge of the scene which has just taken place between* TERRY *and* KEITH, *and their unbounded interest in its consequences. "Is he gone?" "Yes." "How's Terry?" "Don't know." "Do you think she can hear us!" "Yes." "Wasn't it terrible!" "I thought I'd die." "Poor Terry!" "I never did like him." "Me neither." "We'd better go back up or she'll be suspicious." "Yes, be very quiet."*)

(*With elaborate caution they start to tiptoe up the stairs again. On the stairway one of them turns to the girl behind her. "Shall we ask her if we can do anything?" "No."*) (*They vanish up the stairs.*)

(*The doorbell rings. From the back of the house we hear* MATTIE'S *complaint to* FRANK: "Land sakes, I been runnin' my laigs off. Cain't you pick yourself up go answer that doorbell once!"*)

(FRANK *appears, getting into his housecoat and casting a resentful glance back at the unseen* MATTIE.)

(*As the door is opened by* FRANK *the voice of* DAVID KINGSLEY *is heard: "Does Miss Terry Randall happen to be in?" "Yessuh, I think so. Will you come right in?"* FRANK *comes into sight. "What's the name, suh?"*)

KINGSLEY. Mr. Kingsley.

FRANK. Oh, yeh. You the gentleman telephoned. I clean forgot to tell Miss Terry.

KINGSLEY. Well, as long as she's here . . .

FRANK. Yessuh. (*Pulls himself together and goes up the stairs.*)

(KINGSLEY *comes into the room. He stands a moment, then takes out his cigarette case and lights a cigarette.*)

(FRANK *comes down again.*)

FRANK. I told her you was here.

KINGSLEY. Oh, thank you.

FRANK. And I told her about the phone call, too. (FRANK *goes about his business as* TERRY *comes down the stairs.*)

TERRY. Why, Mr. Kingsley, how dramatic! You're just in the nick of time.

KINGSLEY. I'm glad of that. What's happened?

TERRY. Oh—sort of an emotional crisis. I dashed upstairs to have a good cry, buried my head in the pillow just the way you're supposed to, and guess what?

KINGSLEY. What?

TERRY. The tears wouldn't come. In fact, I felt sort of relieved and light, as though I'd just got over a fever.

KINGSLEY. How disappointing. Like not being able to sneeze.

TERRY. Perhaps I'll be able to manage it later. Tonight.

KINGSLEY. If a shoulder would be of any —help?

TERRY. You're very kind. I'm afraid I have to fight this out alone. . . . Do take your coat off.

KINGSLEY. Thanks. This is rather a strange hour for me to drop in. I did telephone—

TERRY. Oh, Frank doesn't believe in phone messages.

KINGSLEY. They do in Hollywood. They just called me up. Can you take a plane for California tomorrow?

TERRY. Me! (*He murmurs an assent.*)

KINGSLEY. They didn't say what the part was—sort of character-comedy, I believe. Of course they put the picture in production first and then started looking for a cast— the Alice-in-Wonderland method. At any rate, they want a new face in this particular part; they ran off all the screen tests they had on file, and finally came to that one of yours. So there you are. And—oh, yes—they want to know in twenty minutes. Of course it's only four-thirty on the Coast. (*As he glances at his watch.*)

TERRY. You're joking.

KINGSLEY. No, all important things are decided in twenty minutes out there. The more trivial ones take years. Shall I phone them you'll be there?

TERRY. Why—I don't know.

KINGSLEY. You don't mean to say you're hesitating!

TERRY. But it's fantastic! How can I—

KINGSLEY. Dear child, do you mind if I tell you something? (TERRY *looks up at him.*) I've been watching you for several seasons. You've been in the theater for two —three—what is it?

TERRY. Three.

KINGSLEY. Three years. You've appeared in, perhaps, half-a-dozen plays. I wouldn't call any of them exactly hits—would you? (TERRY *merely shakes her head.*) And one or two of them closed before the week was over.

TERRY. You've been doing a lot of detective work, haven't you?

KINGSLEY. No, I didn't need to. I know all about you.

TERRY. You do! That's a little frightening.

KINGSLEY. It's part of my business—watching the good ones. And you are good. You've got fire and variety and a magnetic quality that's felt the minute you walk on a stage.

TERRY (*as he hesitates*). Oh, don't stop!

KINGSLEY. But off stage you're nothing at all. (TERRY *wishes she had left well enough alone.*) When you walk into an office the average manager doesn't see anything there. You might be the little girl who's come to deliver the costumes. They wouldn't see that spark. If Elizabeth Bergner walked in on them unknown—or Helen Hayes—what would they see! Little anæmic wisps that look as if they could do with a sandwich and a glass of milk. But put them on a stage, and it's as if you had lighted a thou-

sand incandescent bulbs behind their eyes. That's talent—that's acting—that's you!

TERRY. Now I—*am* going to cry.

KINGSLEY. But what if they don't see what's hidden in you? Suppose they never discover you. You might go tramping around for twenty years, and never get your chance. That's the stage.

TERRY. Twenty years!

KINGSLEY. But let's say you go to Hollywood. They'll know what to do with you out there. Light you so as to fill those hollows, only take your— (*He is turning her head this way and that to get the best angle.*)—right profile. That's the good one. Shade the nose a trifle. (*Opens her mouth and peers in as though she were a racehorse.*) Perhaps a celluloid cap over those two teeth. They'd make you very pretty. (TERRY *steals a quick look in the mirror. Her morale is somewhat shaken.*) Then you play in this picture. Fifty million people see you. Fan mail. Next time you get a better part. No tramping up and down Broadway, no worries about money. A seven-year contract, your salary every week whether you work or not. And if you make a really big hit, like Jean, they'll tear up your contract and give you a bigger one.

TERRY (*a sudden idea*). Wouldn't they let me do just one or two pictures, instead of this seven-year thing?

KINGSLEY. I'm afraid not. If you make a big hit they don't want another studio to reap the benefit. That's not unreasonable, is it?

TERRY. No, I suppose not. Oh, dear! Everything you say is absolutely sound and true, but you see, Mr. Kingsley, the trouble with me is—I'm stage-struck. The theater beats me and starves me and forsakes me, but I love it. I suppose I'm just that kind of girl —you know—rather live in a garret with her true love than dwell in a palace with old Moneybags.

KINGSLEY. But it looks as though your true love had kicked you out of the garret.

TERRY. Oh, dear, if there was only somebody. Mr. Kingsley, won't *you* help me? Won't you tell me what to do?

KINGSLEY. Me?

TERRY. Please!

KINGSLEY. But I work for the picture company.

TERRY. But if you didn't.

KINGSLEY (*quietly*). I'd think you ought to tell them to go to hell.

TERRY. What!

KINGSLEY (*indignantly*). Go out there and let them do all those things to you! (*Again he has a finger under her chin, raising her head as he scans her face.*) That lovely little face! And for what? So that a few years from now they can throw you out on the ash heap! The theater may be slow and heartbreaking, but if you build solidly you've got something at the end of seven years, and seventeen years, and twenty-seven! Look at Katharine Cornell, and Lynn Fontanne, and Alfred Lunt. They tramped Broadway in their day. They've worked like horses, and trouped the country, and stuck to it. And now they've got something that nothing in the world can take away from them. And what's John Barrymore got? A yacht!

TERRY. You're wonderful!

KINGSLEY. Are you going to Hollywood?

TERRY. NO!

KINGSLEY. Will you go to dinner?

TERRY. YES!

KINGSLEY. That's really all I came to ask you.

CURTAIN

ACT THREE

SCENE I

A Sunday morning at the Footlights Club. The following October.

The girls are scattered about the room in various informal attitudes and various stages of attire. Pajamas, lounging robes, hair nets, cold cream, wave combs. Four or five Sunday papers, opened and distributed among the girls, are in drifts everywhere; girls are lying on the floor reading bits of this and that; lounging in chairs; coffee cups, bits of toast, a banana or an orange show that Sunday-morning breakfast is a late and movable feast. One of the girls is in riding clothes (KENDALL) and bound for a day in the country. All the girls are present except TERRY.

During the year two new girls have joined the club, and now are sprawled at ease with the others.

OLGA, at the piano, is obliging with the latest popular tune. Now and then a girl rather absent-mindedly sings a fragment of the song, leaving a word half-finished as her attention is momentarily held by something she is reading. A foot is waggled in time to the music. PAT, sprawled full-length on top of the grand piano, is giving a rather brilliant performance of dancing with her legs in the air.

LITTLE MARY, on hands and knees, is making a tour of the recumbent figures in search of a certain theatrical news item. In one hand she holds a half-eaten banana.

LITTLE MARY. Where's the list of next week's openings? (*She finds that* BIG MARY *has the page she wants. She settles down to read over her shoulder.*)

BOBBY. Anybody got a muffin they don't want?

TONY GILLETTE (*one of the new girls*). Here!

BOBBY. Toss! (*The muffin is hurled through the air.*)

MADELEINE (*turning a page of the rotogravure section*). Autumn Millinery Modes. Oh, look at the hats they're going to wear!

SUSAN. Let me see. (*Traverses the distance to* MADELEINE *by two neat revolutions of her entire body, and brings up just behind the outspread papers. Reads:*) "Hats will be worn off the head this winter."

PAT (*a leg suspended in mid-air as her attention is caught by this remark*). Where?

SUSAN. That's what it says. "Hats'll be worn off the head this winter."

BERNICE (*at the desk*). Where're they going to *put* 'em?

LITTLE MARY (*busy with the* American). Did you know that in Ancient Egypt five thousand years ago the women used to dye their hair just like we do?

JUDITH (*furious*). Who's we?

BIG MARY (*to* LITTLE MARY, *who is reading over her shoulder*). Take that banana out of my face, will you!

ELLEN FENWICK (*the other new girl, perusing the department store ads*). "Two-piece Schiaparelli suits—$5.98. You cannot tell the model from the copy."

JUDITH. The hell you can't.

SUSAN (*emerging from the newspaper*). Oh, they're postponing that Lord Byron play because they can't find a leading man.

LITTLE MARY. What are they looking for?

SUSAN. He's got to be young and handsome.

OLGA. There are no handsome men on the stage now any more.

JUDITH. There's a shortage *off* stage, too.

PAT. Looks don't count any more. It's good old sex appeal.

KENDALL. Would you rather go out with a handsome man without sex appeal, or a homely man *with* it?

BERNICE. I'd rather go out with the handsome one.

JUDITH. Sure, and stay *in* with the other one.

ANN (*as* JUDITH's *sally is greeted with a general laugh*). I think you girls are simply disgusting! Men, men, men! It's degrading just to listen to you.

JUDITH. Isn't it though?

BIG MARY. Say, Terry! . . . Where's Terry?

JUDITH. She's still asleep. It's the only chance she gets—Sundays.

BIG MARY. I see that old beau of hers is coming back.

TONY. Who's that?

BIG MARY. Keith Burgess. He used to hang around here all the time.

TONY. Really? What's he like?

JUDITH. He's one of those fellows started out on a soapbox and ended up in a swimming pool.

LITTLE MARY. Terry was crazy about him, all right.

BIG MARY. Yeah.

PAT. And if you ask me, I think she still is.

LITTLE MARY. Really! What makes you think so?

PAT. Somebody just mentioned his name the other day and you ought to've seen her face!

JUDITH. That's not true. She's forgotten he ever lived—that Left-Wing Romeo.

KENDALL. Well, I should think she might, with David Kingsley in the offing. Now, I call *him* attractive!

PAT. Oh, he isn't her type. Anyway, he's just interested in her career.

KENDALL. If it's just her career they eat an awful lot of dinners together.

LITTLE MARY. If it's her art he's got on his mind why doesn't he get her a job? Not much of a career standing behind a sales counter.

BOBBY. Ah think it's perfectly awful the way Terry has to get up at half-past seven every morning. That miserable job of hers.

MADELEINE. It's no worse than what I've got ahead of me.

SUSAN. Well, anyway, you'll be acting.

MADELEINE. Acting! A Number Three Company of *A Horse on You,* playing up and down the West Coast! God! I come to New York to get away from Seattle, and they keep shipping me back there.

BOBBY. You'll be earning some money! Look at Sam and me! We can't make enough to get married. Ah declare Ah'm so bored with livin' in sin.

ANN. Well, really!

LITTLE MARY. Oh, shut up!

JUDITH. Speaking of Seattle, Miss Vauclain, would you be good enough to take that load of lumber off my neck! After all, you put it there.

MADELEINE. It isn't my fault if he fell for you.

PAT. Oh, is Lumber in town again?

JUDITH (*drawing a letter from her pajama pocket*). No; but I've had a warning.

ANN (*impatiently, rising*). Oh, I'm not going to waste my whole Sunday! What time is Jean coming?

MADELEINE. Stick around. What have you got to lose ?

ANN. My time's just as valuable as Jean's is.

MADELEINE. Sure. You're in big demand. Sit down.

ANN. Well, if Jean wants to see me I'm upstairs. I don't find this conversation very uplifting. (*Goes upstairs.*)

OLGA. She should be teaching school, that girl.

TONY. Is Jean Maitland as pretty off the screen as she is on? I've never seen her.

ELLEN. Neither have I.

KENDALL. She's much better looking off. They've made her up like all the rest of them on the screen.

OLGA. I hope she will soon be here. I must be at the Winter Garden at one o'clock.

LITTLE MARY. On Sunday!

OLGA (*bitterly*). On Sunday. (*Goes into a few bars of the newest Winter Garden melody. Something very corny.*)

LITTLE MARY (*anticipating her*). We know! Kolijinsky! (*A voice which we later find is that of* LOUISE MITCHELL HENDERSHOT *calls out from the dining room.*)

LOUISE. What's that you're playing, Olga?

OLGA (*not very clearly heard above the music*). "Hillbilly Sam."

LOUISE (*off*). What?

OLGA. Come in here if you want to talk.

PAT. Yes, stop stuffing yourself and come in here. . . . Hey, Louise!

LOUISE (*as she comes out of the dining room*). I was having some pancakes.

PAT. Listen, you've got to cut out those farmhand breakfasts, now that you're back in New York.

LOUISE (*settles herself in the group*). Imagine getting the *Times* the day it's printed instead of three days later!

JUDITH. You mean you're not lonesome for good old Appleton?

LOUISE. I haven't been so happy in years. (*She turns her attention to the paper.*)

JUDITH. Everything pink.

BIG MARY. Oh, say, Irene Fitzroy has been engaged for the society girl part in *River House*. (*A series of highly interested responses to this announcement.* "No!" "Really!" "That's wonderful!" "She'll be good in it!" "Isn't that exciting!"*)

BERNICE. I could have played that Fitzroy part. I dont know why I couldn't be a society girl. (*Assumes a supercilious expression to prove her fitness for the part.*) (*A chorus of:* "Sure!" . . . "We know" . . . "You're always the type.") A real actress can play anything. I may play the French adventuress in *Love and War*. (*A little chorus of astonishment:* "Really!" "No kidding!")

KENDALL. Do you mean they offered it to you!

BERNICE. Well, not exactly, but I'm writing 'em a letter. (*Another chorus:* "Oh, we see" . . . "Letters!" . . . "You and your letters!") (MATTIE *comes out of the dining room with a large tray. She is intent on gathering up the coffee cups.*)

MATTIE. You-all knows Mrs. Orcutt don't allow you girls to go laying around downstairs in your pajamas.

JUDITH (*dreamily, as she reads*). Don't give it another thought, Mattie. We'll take 'em right off.

MATTIE. Besides, lookit this here room! (*Takes a banana skin off a small bust of Shakespeare, where it has been draped as a hat.*) Banana skins and newspapers and toast! I should think with Miss Jean coming you'd be getting all slicked up. Big moving-picture star. (*She stoops for a hidden coffee cup.*) And fu'thermore, you ain't supposed to eat breakfast in here. What's the dining room foh! (*She goes back to the dining room with her laden tray.*)

MADELEINE (*to* BERNICE). You still writing that letter about yourself?

BERNICE. Look. How many *l*'s are there in allure?

MADELEINE. Why don't you give up, anyhow?

BIG MARY. Yeh, why don't you take up ballet dancing, or something?

BERNICE (*springs suddenly to her feet, her hands clutching the back of the chair behind her*). Don't you say that to me! I'm never going to give up! I'm as good as— (*She realizes that she is making a spectacle of herself.*) Leave me alone.

KENDALL. Oh, they were just kidding. Can't you take a joke? (TERRY *runs down the stairs, stopping halfway to toss a word of greeting to the girls below.*)

TERRY (*a gesture that embraces them all*). Ah! My public!

JUDITH. Well, **Terry, the** Beautiful Shopgirl!

PAT. Thought you were never going to get up.

TERRY. I wouldn't, if it weren't for Jean's coming. . . . Heh, Mattie! (*A "Yes'm," from* MATTIE *in the dining room.*) Draw one in the dark! . . . Oh, isn't Sunday heavenly! (*Stretches luxuriously.*) I woke up at half-past seven; said, "Nope, I don't have to," and went right back to sleep. Not all day long do I have to say, "This blouse is a copy of a little import that we are selling for $3.95. I am sure you would look simply terrible in it."

JUDITH. I'm going to come down there someday and have you wait on me.

TERRY. If you do I'll have you pinched as a shoplifter.

BOBBY. Honest, Terry, Ah don't see how you tolerate that job of yours. Moochin' down there nine o'clock in the mawnin.' Slaving till six, and after.

TERRY. Oh, it isn't so terrible if you keep thinking that next week that part will turn up. I keep on making the rounds.

ELLEN. But when do you have time for it?

TERRY. Lunch hour.

SUSAN. Then when do you eat lunch?

TERRY. Sundays.

PAT. Just goes to show how cuckoo the stage is. You can act rings around all of us. Well— (*Stretching a bit as she makes for the stairs.*) —I guess I'll go up and put the face together. I look like an old popover.

SUSAN. Me too. Don't say anything good while we're gone.

JUDITH. What are you going to do today, Terry, after Jean goes?

TERRY. I don't know. Who's doing what? Kendall, you're going social for the day, h'm?

KENDALL. Yes, I'm going out to Piping Rock.

TERRY. Piping Rock—isn't that where your ancestors landed?

KENDALL. Thereabouts.

JUDITH. Mine landed in Little Rock.

BIG MARY. Oh, say, Terry! The paper says Keith Burgess gets back from the Coast today. Did you know that? (*A little hush. The eyes of the girls are turned toward* TERRY.)

TERRY. Yes, I know. Why do they call California the Coast instead of New York?

LITTLE MARY. I wonder if that sunshine has mellowed him up any.

BOBBY (*holding up a paper*). Girls, here's Jean stepping out of an airplane!

BERNICE (*jumping up*). Oh, let's see it.

BOBBY (*as three or four girls cluster around her. Reads:*) "Blonde Hollywood Screen Star Alights At Newark Airport."

LITTLE MARY. That's a darling costume!

BIG MARY. I don't like her hat.

BERNICE (*reading*). "Lovely Jean Maitland, Popular Screen Actress, Arrives For Rehearsals Of Broadway Stage Play."

JUDITH. That belle certainly is shot with luck.

BOBBY. That's what she is!

JUDITH. First she goes out and knocks 'em cold in pictures, and now she gets starred on Broadway.

BIG MARY. And she isn't even a good actress. (MATTIE *brings* TERRY'S *coffee from the dining room.*)

MATTIE. Here's your coffee, Miss Terry.

TERRY. Thanks, Mattie.

ELLEN. What's she going to do? Quit pictures and stay on the stage?

BIG MARY. No, no. The picture company puts on the play. It's like a personal appearance.

BERNICE (*who has drifted over to the window*). Girls! She's here!

BIG MARY (*darting to the window*). Let's see!

BOBBY. Look at that car, would you!

LOUISE. Isn't it gorgeous!

LITTLE MARY. There she is! She's getting out!

BERNICE. Oohoo! (*Raps on the window.*) Jean! (*With a concerted rush they make for the front door.*)
(*Little Mary:* "She's got on red foxes!" *Bobby:* "She looks marvelous, doesn't she!" *Big Mary:* "I wonder if she's changed!" *Bernice:* "Isn't it exciting!" *Tony:* "Don't forget to introduce me!" *Ellen:* "Yes. Me, too!" *Louise* (*Calling up the stairs*): "Girls! Yoo hoo! She's here!")
(*Meanwhile, on the part of the remaining girls, there is a wild scramble to tidy up the room. Newspapers, cigarette butts, etc.*)

TERRY. Here—pick up the papers! Give them to me! (*With a great bundle of newspapers she dashes into the dining room and out again.*)

MADELEINE. We should have got all dressed up.

JUDITH. Not me. She's seen me worse than this.

OLGA. She will be dressed up enough.

KENDALL. We're acting like a lot of schoolgirls. We'll be asking for her autograph next. (*The squealing in the hallway now mounts to a burst of ecstatic greeting.* "Jean! Jean!" ... "DAR-ling!" ... "WON-derful!" ... "Look grand!" ... "Jean! Welcome home!")

JEAN (*still in the hallway*). Oh, I'm so excited! How darling of you all to be here! (SUSAN *and* PAT *run downstairs.*)
(*From among the group:* "Are you glad to be back? ... You haven't changed a bit." (JEAN *comes into view. Her costume is simple and horribly expensive. Her red fox furs are fabulous, her orchids are pure white.*)

JEAN (*embracing girls*). Hello, girls! Madeleine! Olga, how's the music? Kendall! Hello, Judy! This is worth the whole trip—

TERRY. Jean darling!

JEAN. Terry! (*They embrace.*)

MRS. ORCUTT (*looming up in the dining-room doorway,* FRANK *and* MATTIE *just behind her*). Well, well! My little Jean!

JEAN. Hello, Mrs. Orcutt! Mattie! Frank! (*In turn she throws her arms around all three of them. As she embraces* FRANK *a laugh goes up from the group.*) Well, let me get my breath and have a look at all of you.

BERNICE. It's the same old bunch.

TERRY. No, there are two new ones. Ellen Fenwick and Tony Gillette. Miss Jean Maitland.

TONY. Hello.

PAT (*the trumpet sound*). Ta-da-a-ah!

JEAN. Hello, girls. I hope you don't think I'm crazy—all excited like this.

ELLEN. Oh, no!

TONY. We think you're darling. (BERNICE, *before the mirror, is having a private try-on of* JEAN'S *red fox and orchids. Enchanting effect.*)

JEAN (*in greeting to* ANN, *who has come rather sedately down the stairs*). Ann! I was just going to ask for you.

ANN. My, you look Hollywood!

JEAN (*recalls the two men who have accompanied her, and who are standing in the hallway. One has a huge camera and tri-*

pod). Oh, boys, I'm so sorry. Girls, this is Mr. Larry Westcott, our New York publicity man—and a wonder. And this is Billy—uh—I'm afraid I never heard your last name.

BILLY. Just Billy.

LARRY. Just want to snap a few pictures. Do you mind?

MRS. ORCUTT (*a hand straightening her coiffure*). Not at all.

LARRY. Human-interest stuff.

BERNICE. You mean with us!

JEAN. Of course!

BOBBY. Oh, I've got to go and fix up. (*A chorus of: "So do I!" . . . "I look a fright." . . . "Me, too!" . . . "We'll just be a minute."*)
(*Up the stairs go* BERNICE, BIG *and* LITTLE MARRY, BOBBY, *and* LOUISE.)
(MATTIE *is doing a little sprucing up, preparatory to being photographed, and* FRANK *buttons his house coat.*)

TERRY. Jean darling, aren't you thrilled at doing a play? When do your rehearsals start?

JEAN. On Wednesday.

BILLY (*speaking to* MRS. ORCUTT *and the two servants. He has his electric apparatus in his hand*). I've got a pretty strong light here. All right if I plug in?

FRANK. Yes, sah. I'll show you. (BILLY *and* FRANK *disappear into the hallway toward the rear of the house.*)

LARRY. Pardon me, Miss Maitland. You were going to ask about our taking some shots upstairs. (*Glancing from* JEAN *to* MRS. ORCUTT.)

JEAN. Oh, yes. Do you mind, Mrs. Orcutt? They want to take some stills of me up in my old room.

MRS. ORCUTT. Of course not.

LARRY. You know—Humble Beginnings in The Footlights Club. They love it.

MRS. ORCUTT. I'd be delighted.

TERRY. Wait a minute! I've got my Sunday wash hanging up there. You can't photograph that!

LARRY. Great! Just what we want!

TERRY. All right. But I never thought m underwear would make *Screenland*.

OLGA. So you are a big actress now, e Jean! You are going to be starred in a pla

JEAN. Isn't it silly! I didn't want them t star me in it. I'm scared stiff.

LARRY. She'll be great in it. Look, Miss Mai land, we haven't got a lot of time. M Kingsley is picking you up here at twelv forty-five and then you're meeting M Gretzl.

TERRY. Who?

JEAN. Mr. Gretzl.

JUDITH. What's a Gretzl?

JEAN. He's the Big Boss—Adolph Gretz

LARRY. President of the company.

MRS. ORCUTT. Of course! Adolph Gretzl.

OLGA (*dashing to the piano. Improvises an sings*). Of course Adolph Gretzl, He looks like a pretzl—

JUDITH (*picking it up*). So why should w fretzl—

PAT (*with an accompanying dance step* And fume. Boom-boom. (*She times this la with a couple of bumps.*)
(*The two* MARYS *come dashing down th stairs.*)

LITTLE MARY. We're ready!

LARRY. Okay! Everybody here now?

BIG MARY. Oh, no. There's more yet. (*A foot of stairs.*) Girls! Hurry! (LOUISE's voi from upstairs: "Coming!")

JEAN. Terry darling, when am I going see you? I've got loads to tell you and want to hear all about you. Rehearsals sta Wednesday. How about lunch tomorrow

LARRY. Oh, not tomorrow, Miss Maitlan You're lunching with the press.

JEAN. Oh, dear. Let's see—David Kingsle is taking me to that opening in the evenin . . . How about tea?

LARRY. Not tea! You've got the magazi people. And you've got photographs all da Tuesday.

JEAN (*turns to* TERRY). But I want to see her. How about Wednesday? I'll get away from rehearsal and we'll have lunch. One o'clock?

TERRY. You won't believe it, but my lunch hour's eleven-thirty to twelve-thirty.

JEAN. Eleven-thirty! What do you mean? (*Down come* BOBBY *and* LOUISE, *refurbished.*)

BOBBY. Ah hope we didn't keep you waitin'.

LARRY (*impatiently glancing at his watch*). All right, Miss Maitland.

JEAN. Oh, fine. Now before we start, everybody, I've got a teentsy-weentsy surprise for you.

BIG MARY. Surprise?

JEAN. Billy, will you bring it in?

BOBBY. Bring what in?

LOUISE. What?

JEAN. It's for all of you, dear Mrs. Orcutt, and the whole dear Footlights Club. (BILLY *enters from the hallway, carrying what is evidently a large picture, framed and covered with a rich red drapery which conceals the subject.*)

BOBBY. Oh, look!

KENDALL. How exciting!

PAT. What is it?

TONY. Looks like a picture.

LITTLE MARY. What of, I wonder?

JUDITH. Papa Gretzl.

JEAN. All right, girls?

BOBBY. We're ready! (JEAN *steps forward, and with a sweeping gesture, throws aside the velvet drape. It is a portrait of* JEAN. *All eyelashes, golden hair and scarlet lips.*) (*A series of delighted and semi-delighted exclamations: "It's Jean!" . . . "Lovely!" . . . "How beautiful!" . . . "Darling!"*)

MRS. ORCUTT (*her dismayed glance sweeping the walls*). It's lovely, Jean, lovely! Now, if we can only find a fitting place to hang it.

LARRY. Well, let's see. (*With a look that lights on the Bernhardt portrait and rests there.*)

(JUDITH *makes a gallant gesture of Hail and Farewell toward the Divine Sarah.*)

JUDITH. So long, Sarah!

LARRY. Now, if you'll all just gather round the picture . . . Okay, Billy?

BILLY (*bringing in his camera*). Ready in a second.

LARRY. Now then, Miss Maitland! You stand right there behind the portrait. And—er— (*He gestures toward* MRS. ORCUTT.)

MRS. ORCUTT (*helpfully*). Me?

LARRY. That's right! Right here beside Miss Maitland. And all you girls fill in this space in front. That's it—right in here, all of you. We want a nice little informal group. A nice little— (*He drops back, surveying the group with the eye of an artist. It becomes immediately apparent that it will be a nice group, all right, but that isn't what* LARRY *wants. His concern is* JEAN MAITLAND.) No, no! You'll all have to crouch down. (*He rushes around, pressing them all down on their knees.*) Everybody down! You too, sister! (*This last is addressed to* MRS. ORCUTT, *who gets down with no little difficulty.*) That's fine! And everybody looking at Miss Maitland!

JEAN (*very sweet*). Frank and Mattie have to be in it. Come on, Frank and Mattie! (*They have been looking a little crestfallen and now take their places at the extreme edge, much elated.*)

LARRY. Sure, sure! It wouldn't be a picture without 'em. We want the whole Twilight Club. Now, then, have we got everybody? (*Looks over his shoulder just as* BILLY *turns on his special light.*)

LITTLE MARY. No, no, where's Bernice?

BIG MARY. Bernice isn't here!

BERNICE (*her voice from the top of the stairs*). I'm ready. Here I am! (BERNICE *has seized on this opportunity to register as undiscovered Hollywood star material. She has made herself up to look like a rather smudged copy of Joan Crawford. Her entrance is undulating and regal.*)

PAT. Heh! That's my new dress!

BERNICE. Well, I had to be right, didn't I?

LARRY. Come on, girlie. Right here. (*Immediately* BERNICE *stares out toward the camera.*) No, no! Look at Miss Maitland. Everybody look at Miss Maitland. . . . Ready, Billy?

BILLY. Okay.

LARRY. Hold still now! And everybody look at Miss Maitland! . . . Right! (*Just as the bulb is pressed* BERNICE *makes a lightning full-face turn toward the camera, all smiles, and back again before they can catch her at it.*) Now then! For the pictures upstairs . . . Miss Maitland?

JEAN. Want to come along, girls? (*The girls certainly* do *want to come along, and they do so. Chattering away, the whole procession streams up the stairs—*MRS. ORCUTT, CAMERAMEN, *and all.* FRANK *brings up the rear with the electrical apparatus.* "You-all using this upstairs too, ain't you?" *An answer from* LARRY:"*Yes, bring it right up!*") (TERRY *and* JUDITH, *unable to face a second such scene, remain behind, with only the smiling portrait of* JEAN *as company.*). (*Their eyes meet understandingly. There goes* JEAN.)

TERRY (*blandly*). You're not going to be in the—other pictures?

JUDITH. No, if I'm going to work as an extra I want my five dollars a day.

TERRY. I do hope I left my room looking sordid enough.

JUDITH. Say, what about that play they've got her doing? Do you suppose it's really something?

TERRY. Oh, it is. David Kingsley told me about it. He says it's a really fine and moving play.

JUDITH (*a glance at the portrait*). Then why does he let her do it?

TERRY. He couldn't help it. They got it into their heads out on the Coast. It's Gretzl's idea. What do they care about the theater? They think the stage is something to advertise pictures with.

JUDITH. Listen, Jean can't act. If the play's as good as all that, she'll kill it. It doesn't make sense!

TERRY. Now, Judy, haven't you learned not to— (*Of all people,* KEITH BURGESS *suddenly*

appears in the archway. Though he has been gone a year, he barges right in as though he had left only yesterday. His clothes represent an ingenious blending of the Hollywood style with his own Leftist tendencies. He still wears the sweater, but it is an imported one; the trousers are beautifully tailored, the shirt probably cost eighteen dollars; no necktie, and, of course, no hat.)

KEITH (*his voice heard in the hallway*). Where's Terry Randall? Oh, there you are!

TERRY. Why, hello, Keith!

JUDITH. Well, if it isn't the fatted calf!

KEITH (*surveying the room*). God, a year hasn't made any difference in *this* dump! (*He casts an appraising eye over* TERRY.) What's the matter with you? You're thin and you've got no color.

TERRY. Well, I haven't been having those hamburgers at Smitty's since you left.

KEITH. That reminds me, I haven't had any breakfast. (*He selects a pear from a bowl of fruit on the table.*) Hope this is ripe. . . . Heh! What's her name out there? (*Shouting toward the dining room.*) Bring me a cup of coffee!

JUDITH (*obsequiousness in her tone*). The deviled kidneys are very nice today.

KEITH (*finding the pear too juicy for him*). God! Give me your handkerchief, Terry.

TERRY. You've got one.

KEITH. That's silk. (*Grabs hers.*)

TERRY. Well, Keith, tell us about yourself. Are you back from Hollywood for good?

KEITH. What do you mean? I'm going back there in three days. I've been working on a plan to put the whole studio on a commonwealth basis, with the electricians right on a footing with the executives, and they won't have it.

TERRY. Who won't have it? The executives?

KEITH. The electricians!

TERRY. Well, I must say you look wonderful. All healthy and sunburned, and I never saw such beautiful trousers.

KEITH (*taking a last bite of the pear*). You're looking terrible. (*The core of the pear is*

and, he glances about for some place to
deposit it.)

Lightning-fast, the perfect servant, JUDITH
*is by his side, offering a little ash tray. He
drops the pear core on it without a word.*)

JUDITH. Thank you.

KEITH (*suddenly he notices* JEAN's *portrait*).
What's *this* chromo?

TERRY. It's Cinderella. She's upstairs.

KEITH. Those autograph hounds out there
waiting for her?

JUDITH. No, they want another glimpse of
you.

KEITH. Did it ever occur to you that I didn't
come here to see *you?*

JUDITH. You mean there's no—no hope for
me at all? (*Crushed, she goes into the dining room.*)

TERRY. Well, Keith! Give me an account of
yourself. You've been gone a year—I hardly
know what's happened to you.

KEITH. Why—I wrote you, didn't I?

TERRY. Oh, yes. A postcard from Palm
Springs, showing the cactus by moonlight,
and a telegram of congratulations for my
opening in February, which arrived two
days after we closed.

KEITH. I got mixed up.

TERRY. But tell me—what do you mean
you're only going to be here three days?
Your year's up, isn't it?

KEITH. Yeh, but they wouldn't let me go.
I had to sign for another year.

TERRY. But, Keith, your plays! Aren't you
writing another play?

KEITH. Yes. Sure. I haven't written it yet,
but I will this year.

TERRY. I see. I went to see the picture you
wrote—what was the name of it? *Loads of
Love.*

KEITH. Oh, did you see that? How'd you
like it?

TERRY. Very amusing. Of course, the Masses
got a little crowded out.

KEITH. Masses! It played to eighty million
people. That's masses, isn't it?

TERRY. Yes. Yes, I guess I didn't get the
idea.

KEITH. Now, listen, sweet. You know why
I'm here, don't you?

TERRY. No, I don't. Keith.

KEITH. Well, look! You can't go stumbling
around like this forever. You're not working, are you?

TERRY. Yes.

KEITH. You are? What in?

TERRY. The blouse department of R. H.
Macy & Co.

KEITH. What! You're kidding!

TERRY. I have to live, Keith.

KEITH. Good God! Listen, darling. You
spend years on Broadway and finish up in
Macy's. And look at Jean! Two years in
Hollywood and she's a star.

TERRY. They speed up everything in Hollywood. In two years you're a star, in four
you're forgotten, and in six you're back in
Sweden. (*The doorbell.*)

KEITH. That's the kind of reasoning that's
put you where you are! From now on I'm
going to take charge of you. You're going
to be— (*Breaks off as* MATTIE *crosses the
hall.*) There's always somebody coming into
this place. It's like Grand Central Station.

KINGSLEY (*heard at the door*). Good morning, Mattie.

MATTIE. Morning, Mr. Kingsley.

KINGSLEY (*appearing in the archway*). Hello,
Terry. (*As he sees* KEITH.) Well, hello
there!

KEITH. Hello.

TERRY. David! How nice to see you!

KINGSLEY (*a glance at the portrait*). I see I
missed the ceremony.

TERRY. They're still shooting up on Stage
Six.

KINGSLEY. No, thanks. I'm the official escort,
but there are limits. . . . How are you, Burgess? I heard you were coming back?

KEITH (*none too graciously*). How are you?

KINGSLEY. So you've served your year, h'm? Well, you're an exception. You've had the courage to quit when you said you would.

Another year, and you'd have gone the way they all do. Never written a fine play again. (*A moment of embarrassed silence.*)

TERRY (*rather nervously*). Keith is going back to Hollywood for one more year.

KINGSLEY. Oh. I didn't mean to—

KEITH. It amuses me to hear a fellow like you, who makes his living out of pictures, turn on Hollywood, and attack it. If you feel that way about pictures why do you work in them!

TERRY (*hurriedly*). Well, we can't always do what we want to, Keith. After all, you're working in Hollywood, and I'm selling blouses, and David Kingsley is—

KINGSLEY. No, Terry. He's right. I shouldn't talk that way, and I don't very often. But I'm a little worked up this morning. I reread Jean's play last night. (*A gesture toward* JEAN's *portrait.*) And I realized more than ever what a beautiful play it is. That's what's got me a little low. When picture people come into the theater—when they take a really fine play and put a girl like Jean in it—when they use a play like this for camera fodder, that's more than I can stand. The theatre means too much to me.

KEITH. All right! It's a fine play. And you notice it's Hollywood that's doing it.

TERRY. Oh, Keith, let's not get into an argument.

KEITH. It just shows how little you know about Hollywood. You're five years behind the times. They're *crazy* about fine things. Dickens and Shakespeare—they've got a whole staff digging them up.

TERRY. All right! Let's talk about something else.

KEITH. If you go to a dinner in Hollywood what's the conversation! Books, and politics and art! They never even mention pictures.

KINGSLEY. I suppose they put that on the dinner invitation. Instead of R.S.V.P. it says: Don't mention pictures.

TERRY. Oh, what's got into you two! You're a picture man and you're yelling about the stage, and you're a playright and you're howling about Hollywood!

KINGSLEY. At least I'm honest about it. I work in pictures, but I don't pretend to like it.

KEITH. Who's pretending? I like it and I'm going back there. And what's more, I'm taking Terry with me.

KINGSLEY. What?

TERRY. Keith, don't be absurd!

KEITH. It's time somebody took her in hand and I'm going to do it. I'm going to marry her.

KINGSLEY. Terry, you can't do that!

TERRY (*hopefully*). Why not, David?

KEITH. Look here, you—

KINGSLEY. I've told you why a hundred times. You belong in the theater.

TERRY. Is that the reason! You certainly have told me a hundred times. A thousand! I've sat across a table from you and heard it with the soup and the meat and the coffee. Actress, actress, actress!

KINGSLEY. Of course I've told you. Because you *are* an actress.

TERRY. And I've just realized why. Because you quit the theater yourself, and you've been salving your own conscience by preaching theater to me. That made you feel less guilty, didn't it?

KINGSLEY. Terry, that's not true.

TERRY. Oh, yes, it is. *So* true. Funny I never thought of that before.

KEITH. Look, I've got to get out of here. ... If I may have just a moment. (*He steps between* TERRY *and* KINGSLEY.) When are we going to get married?

TERRY (*in a deadly tone*). When are we going to get married? We are going to get married, Mr. Burgess, when Hollywood to Dunsinane doth come. That's Shakespeare —you know, the fellow they're digging up out there.

KEITH (*stunned*). Huh?

TERRY. It's too late, Keith. When you walked out on me a year ago, you walked out yourself, too. That other Keith was cock-sure and conceited, but he stood for something. What was it—"thunder and lightning and power and truth?" Wasn't that what you said? And "if you believe in something you've got to be willing to starve for it." Well, I believed in it, Keith. (*She turns* her gaze to KINGSLEY, *then her look includes both of them.*) So—I guess that leaves me just a young lady with a career. Or, shall we say—just a young lady? (*She goes slowly up the stairs.*)

CURTAIN

SCENE II

It is midnight, and the main room of the Footlights Club is in semidarkness. There is a pool of light in the hall and on the stairway from the overhead chandelier.

A little later, when the lights go on, we see that Bernhardt has given way to JEAN MAITLAND.

After a moment of stillness there is the sound of the front door opening, and the two MARYS *are heard coming home.*

LITTLE MARY. Well, I didn't like either the play *or* the cast. And I thought Laura Wilcox was terrible.

BIG MARY. She's always terrible. You know how she got the part, don't you?

LITTLE MARY. Sure. Everybody on Broadway knows. The trouble with us is we've been hanging on to our virtue.

BIG MARY. Maybe *you* have. (*They disappear up the stairs.*)

(*Somewhere in the hallway a clock strikes twelve. Then the door is heard to open again.*)

(*We heard the voice of* JUDITH *at the door.*)

JUDITH. Well, good night. And thank you ever so much.

A MAN'S VOICE. Thank *you.* (JUDITH *comes into sight. Not a very spirited figure. Meanwhile we hear the man still talking.*) I certainly had one swell evening, all right. (*With that he comes into sight. And who is it but good old* LOU MILHAUSER, *the lumber man. He is elaborately decked out in evening clothes, in contrast to the simple little street number that* JUDITH *has on.*)

JUDITH (*with a weak smile*). Yes, so did I. What time is it—about two o'clock?

MILHAUSER. No, it's only twelve.

JUDITH. Oh, really? I guess my watch is fast.

MILHAUSER. Look, I'm going to be here all week. What are you doing tomorrow night?

JUDITH. Tomorrow? That's Tuesday—oh, that's my gymnasium night.

MILHAUSER. Well, how about Wednesday?

JUDITH. Wednesday? Oh, I've got friends coming in from Europe. On the—ah—Mauretania.

MILHAUSER. The Mauretania? I thought they took that off.

JUDITH. Did I say Mauretania? Minnetonka.

MILHAUSER. Well, I've got to see you before I go. Of course I'll be back next month.

JUDITH. Next month? Oh, I spend November in the Catskills. My hay fever.

MILHAUSER. Well, I'll call you anyway to-morrow. On a chance. (*He goes.* JUDITH *waits for the closing of the door*).

JUDITH. Swell chance. (*She goes grimly up the stairs, just as* FRANK *comes into the room —a final round of inspection before going to bed.*)

FRANK. Evening, Miss Judith. You in early, ain't you?

JUDITH (*as she disappears*). It may seem early to you. (FRANK *goes on about his business—locks a window, puts out the desk lamp. Then comes a ring of the doorbell.*)

FRANK (*at the door*). Who's there?

KINGSLEY'S VOICE. Hello, Frank.

FRANK (*a change of tone as he opens the door*). Why, Mr. Kingsley!

KINGSLEY (*in the hall*). I hope we didn't wake you up, Frank. May we come in?

FRANK. Yessah, yessah. Pardon my shirt sleeves. I thought one of the young ladies forgot her key. (KINGSLEY *and another man have come into view. The stranger is a short-thickset man who carries himself with great authority in order to make up for his lack of stature. Instinct tells you that this is none other than* ADOLPH GRETZL *himself.*)

KINGSLEY. We wouldn't have bothered you at this hour, but it's terribly important. We want to see Miss Randall.

FRANK. Miss Terry! Why, she goes to sleep early. She got to get up half-past seven.

KINGSLEY (*gently turning* FRANK *around and starting him toward the stairs*). It's all right. Wake her up and ask her to come down.

FRANK. Yessah. You ge'men want to wait in here? (*He turns on the light in the living room, then goes up the stairs.*)

GRETZL (*looking about with disfavor*). I don't like the whole idea. A fine actress don't live in a place like this.

KINGSLEY. But she is a fine actress, Mr. Gretzl.

GRETZL. It don't feel right to me. Something tells me it's no good.

KINGSLEY. Mr. Gretzl, you've had this play in rehearsal for two weeks now. And she can't make the grade. You've got to face it —Jean is a motion-picture actress. And that's all.

GRETZL. She is a beautiful girl. When she comes on the stage they will gasp.

KINGSLEY. You saw that rehearsal tonight. And that's the best she'll ever do.

GRETZL. But she's Jean Maitland! People will come to see Jean Maitland.

KINGSLEY. No, they won't. Theatergoers won't come to see movie stars just because they're movie stars. They've got to act.

FRANK (*coming down the stairs*). Ah woke Miss Terry. She's comin' right down. (*He goes down the hall.*)

KINGLEY. Thank you, Frank. . . . (*Points a stern finger toward the head of the stair.*) Believe me, this girl's an actress.

GRETZL. All right, all right—an actress. Let's see her.

KINGSLEY. She's got presence and authority and distinction! And a beautiful, mobile face. She's exactly right for this play.

GRETZL. If she is such a great beauty and such a wonderful actress, where's she been keeping herself?

KINGSLEY. She's been learning her business.

GRETZL. All right, we'll let her read the part. What else am I here for in the middle of the night? She's got to start tomorrow morning—tonight, even. It's a great big part. Everything depends on it.

KINGSLEY. She can do it. She's young and eager and fresh. Wait till you see her.

GRETZL. That's what I'm— (*He stops as* TERRY RANDALL *comes down the stairs. She is wearing a loose flowing robe over her long white nightgown. Her hair falls over her shoulders; her feet are in low scuffs. She is anything but the dazzling figure described by* KINGLEY.)
(*She comes into the room wordlessly, looking at the two men.*)
(KINGSLEY *advances to her.*)

KINGSLEY. It's sweet of you to come down, Terry. I wasn't sure you would.

TERRY (*looking up at him*). You knew I would, David.

KINGSLEY (*taking her hand and leading her toward* GRETZL.) Terry, this is Mr. Gretzl. This is Terry Randall.

TERRY. How do you do, Mr. Gretzl? (GRETZL *mumbles a greeting. "How do you do?"*

KINGSLEY. Terry, I suppose I needn't tell you why we're here at this hour. Could you start rehearsing tomorrow morning in the play of Mr. Gretzl's, and open in a week—

GRETZL. Wait a minute, Kingsley. Not so fast, there! Let me look at her. (*He slowly describes a half-circle around her, his eye intent on her face. As the inspection finishes she turns her head and meets his gaze. But* GRETZL's *inquiring look is now directed* KINGSLEY.) This is the party you just now described to me!

KINGSLEY (*pulling a typed "part" out of his pocket*). Terry, I know what you can do but Mr. Gretzl doesn't. Will you read a couple of speeches of this—let him hear you?

TERRY (*a little terrified at the thought*). Now?

GRETZL. Of course *now*. That's what I came for.

KINGSLEY. Would you, Terry?

TERRY. I'll try.

KINGSLEY (*giving her the part*). How about this bit here?

TERRY. May I look at it a second, just to—

KINGSLEY. Of course. (*He turns to* GRETZL.) You know, it's rather difficult to jump right into a character.

GRETZL. What's difficult! We do it every day in pictures. . . . Come on, young lady. Well— (*He turns a chair around, seats himself ostentatiously, and beckons* TERRY *to stand directly in front of him and perform.*)

TERRY (*a deep sigh, and takes the plunge. Reads:*) "Look, boys, I haven't got any right to stand up here and tell you what to do. Only maybe I have got a right, see, because, look—" No, that isn't right. "Because, look—" Do you mind if I start all over?

GRETZL (*annoyed*). All right. Start over.

TERRY (*to* KINGSLEY). What's she want them to do?

KINGSLEY. Strike.

TERRY. Oh. Uh— (*She is off again, less certain of herself than ever.*) —"Look boys—" (*A bad start again, but she quickly recovers herself.*) —"Look, boys, I haven't got any right to stand up here and tell you what to do. Only maybe I have got a right, see, because, look, I'm engaged to be married. We were going to be married tomorrow. You all know who it is. He's right here in this hall." (GRETZL *rises abruptly and begins to pace the floor, his hands behind his back.* TERRY *goes on stumblingly:*) —"In this hall. So you fellas vote to go on strike, why, I guess it's no wedding bells for me. Don't kid yourself I don't know what I'm talking about. Because I've been through it before. I've been through it with my old man, and

my brothers, so I ought to know." (GRETZL *has picked up a matchbox from the table, and now strikes a match with a sharp rasping sound and lights a long cigar.*) "It means hungry, and maybe cold, and scared every minute somebody'll come home with a busted head. But which would you'd ruther do? Die quick fighting, or starve to death slow? That's why I'm telling you—strike! Strike! Strike!" (GRETZL *has again seated himself in front of her, and as he throws back his head, the better to survey her, a cloud of cigar smoke is blown upward toward her face.*) —"That's why I'm telling you— strike! Strike! S—" (*She has been choking back a cough, but it now becomes too much for her. She stops and throws the part to the floor. Tears and anger struggle for mastery.*) I can't do it! I can't! I won't go on!

KINGSLEY (*angered*). You're a fool if you do.

GRETZL (*rising and buttoning his coat with a gesture of finality*). You must excuse me. I am a plain-speaking man. I don't want to hurt anybody's feelings, but in my opinion this young lady is not anything at all. Not anything.

TERRY. But, Mr. Gretzl, nobody could give a reading under these conditions. It isn't fair. It isn't possible for an actress—you don't understand.

GRETZL. All right. I don't understand. But I understand my business and I know what I see. So I will say good night, and thank you. Come on, Kingsley.

KINGSLEY. I'm sorry, Terry. No one could look a great actress in bathrobe and slippers. And Mr. Gretzl only knows what he sees.

GRETZL. Are you working for me or against me, Kingsley?

KINGSLEY. I'm working *for* you. What are you going to do about your play tomorrow?

GRETZL. I'm going to throw it into the ash can. All I wanted it for was Jean Maitland. So she could make a picture of it. All right. She'll do something else. I can get plenty of material.

KINGSLEY. It's incredible that anyone should be so stupid.

GRETZL (*rising to his full height*). Mr. Kingsley, you are *out*! You will hear from our lawyers in the morning.

TERRY. Oh, David!

KINGSLEY. It's all right, Terry. Gretzl, if you've lost your interest in the play, how about selling it to me?

GRETZL. I see. You're going back into the theater, eh?

KINGSLEY. I might. Will you sell it to me?

GRETZL. How much?

KINGSLEY. Just what it cost you.

GRETZL. All right. See Becker in the morning. He'll fix it up. Good night.

KINGSLEY. Good night.

GRETZL (*as he goes*). And *I* am the stupid one? Huh!

TERRY. David! David, oh, my dear, you mustn't do this just for me.

KINGSLEY. No, I'm not one of those boys who puts on a play just so that his girl can act in it. . . . By the way, you *are* my girl, aren't you?

TERRY (*brightly*). Oh, yes sir.

KINGSLEY. I just thought I'd ask. (*He takes her in his arms and kisses her.*) You know, I had a couple of nasty weeks, Terry, after you drove me out into the cold.

TERRY. Weeks? It seemed like years. (*Again he embraces her—just as* MRS. ORCUTT *enters, in bathrobe and slippers.*)

MRS. ORCUTT. I'm sorry, Mr. Kingsley, but this is against the rules.

TERRY. Mrs. Orcutt, it's the play!

KINGSLEY. My apologies, Mrs. Orcutt. This may look a little strange. But I came up on business.

MRS. ORCUTT. Frank said there was another gentleman.

TERRY (*gaily*). But he's gone! And, oh, Mrs. Orcutt! I'm going to do the play! (*At the end of this announcement, as she says "play," her hand goes to her mouth, like a little girl's; she is surprised to find herself crying.*)

MRS. ORCUTT. Terry, my child!

KINGSLEY. Darling, you're tired. You must get your sleep. (*There is a farewell kiss, with the full approval of* MRS. ORCUTT.) Good night.

TERRY. Good night.

KINGSLEY. Eleven in the morning, at the Lyceum.

TERRY (*in a low voice*). I'll be there. (KINGSLEY *is gone.*)

MRS. ORCUTT. Terry, dear, I'm so happy for you. Aren't you thrilled?

TERRY (*her eyes glowing*). It was like Victoria. When they came to tell her she was Queen.

MRS. ORCUTT. Dear child! But now you must run along to bed and get your sleep.

TERRY. No, no. I must learn my part. And I must be alone. I want a room by myself tonight. Please, Mrs. Orcutt.

MRS. ORCUTT. I'll see what I can do. (*She goes, first switching off the main light.*) (TERRY *stands alone in the semi-darkened room. A light from a street lamp shines through the window and strikes her face. For a moment she stands perfectly still. Then the realization of her new position comes over her. She seems to take on height and dignity.*)

TERRY. Now that I am Queen, I wish in future to have a bed, and a room, of my own. (*She stands transfixed as the curtain falls.*)

CURTAIN

AUTHORS REPRESENTED

MAXWELL ANDERSON (b. 1888).

White Desert, 1923.
What Price Glory? (with Laurence Stallings), 1924.
First Flight (with Laurence Stallings), 1925.
Outside Looking In, 1925.
The Buccaneer (with Laurence Stallings), 1925.
Saturday's Children, 1927.
Gods of the Lightning (with Harold Hickerson), 1928.
Gypsy, 1929.
Elizabeth, the Queen, 1930.
Night Over Taos, 1932.
Both Your Houses, 1933.
Mary of Scotland, 1933.
Valley Forge, 1934.
Winterset, 1935.
The Wingless Victory, 1936.
High Tor, 1937.
The Masque of Kings, 1937.
The Star Wagon, 1937.
Knickerbocker Holiday, 1938.

PHILIP BARRY (b. 1896).

A Punch for Judy, 1921.
You and I, 1923.
The Youngest, 1924.
In a Garden, 1925.
White Wings, 1926.
John, 1927.
Paris Bound, 1927.
Cock Robin (with Elmer Rice), 1928.
Holiday, 1928.
Hotel Universe, 1930.
Tomorrow and Tomorrow, 1931.
The Animal Kingdom, 1932.
The Joyous Season, 1934.
Bright Star, 1935.
Spring Dance (adapted from play by Eleanor Golden and Eloise Barrangon), 1936.
The Philadelphia Story, 1939.

N. BEHRMAN (b. 1893).

The Second Man, 1927.
Love Is Like That, 1927.
Serena Blandish, 1929.
Meteor, 1929.
Brief Moment, 1931.
Biography, 1932.
Rain from Heaven, 1934.
End of Summer, 1936.
Amphitryon 38 (adapted from comedy by Jean Giraudoux), 1937.

Wine of Choice, 1938.
No Time for Comedy, 1939.

CLARE BOOTHE (b. 1903).

Abide With Me, 1935.
The Women, 1936.
Kiss the Boys Goodbye, 1938.

MARC CONNELLY (b. 1891).

Wisdom Tooth, 1926.
The Wild Man of Borneo (with Herman J. Mankiewicz), 1927.
The Green Pastures, 1930.
The Farmer Takes a Wife (with Frank B. Elser), 1934.

PAUL GREEN (b. 1894).

The No 'Count Boy, 1925; numerous one-act plays produced.
In Abraham's Bosom, 1926.
The Field God, 1927.
The House of Connelly, 1931.
Roll, Sweet Chariot, 1934 (also Tread the Green Grass, produced by "little theatres").
Hymn to the Rising Sun, Unto Such Glory, one-act plays, 1936.
Johnny Johnson, 1936.

LILLIAN HELLMAN (b. 1905).

The Children's Hour, 1934.
Days to Come, 1936.
The Little Foxes, 1939.

JOHN CECIL HOLM (b. 1906).

Three Men on a Horse (with George Abbott), 1935.

GEORGE S. KAUFMAN (b. 1889).

Dulcy (with Connelly), 1921.
To the Ladies (with Connelly), 1922.
Merton of the Movies (with Connelly), 1922.
Helen of Troy N. Y. (book by Kaufman and Connelly), 1923.
The Deep Tangled Wildwood (with Connelly), 1923.
Beggar on Horseback (with Connelly), 1924.
Be Yourself (book by Kaufman and Connelly), 1924.
Minick (with Edna Ferber), 1924.
The Butter and Egg Man, 1925.
The Cocoanuts (book by George S. Kaufman), 1925.
The Good Fellow (with Mankiewicz), 1926.
The Royal Family (with Ferber), 1928.
Animal Crackers (with Morrie Ryskind), 1928.
June Moon (with Ring Lardner), 1929.

The Channel Road (with Alexander Wooll-
cott), 1929.
Strike Up the Band (musical comedy by Mor-
rie Ryskind), 1930.
Once in a Lifetime (with Moss Hart), 1930.
The Band Wagon (with Howard Dietz),
1931.
Of Thee I Sing (with Morris Ryskind), 1931.
Dinner at Eight (with Edna Ferber), 1932.
Let 'Em Eat Cake (with Morris Ryskind),
1933.
The Dark Tower (with Alexander Wooll-
cott), 1933.
Merrily We Roll Along (with Moss Hart),
1934.
First Lady (with Katherine Dayton), 1935.
Stage Door (with Edna Ferber), 1936.
You Can't Take It With You (with Moss
Hart), 1936.
I'd Rather Be Right (with Moss Hart), 1937.
The American Way (with Moss Hart), 1939.

SIDNEY KINGSLEY (b. 1906).

Men in White, 1933.
Dead End, 1935.
Ten Million Ghosts, 1936.

JACK KIRKLAND (b. 1904).

Tobacco Road (dramatization of Erskine
Caldwell's book), 1933.
Tortilla Flat (from the novel by John Stein-
beck), 1937.
I Must Love Someone, 1939.

ARCHIBALD MacLEISH (b. 1892).

Panic, 1935.
The Fall of the City, 1937.
Macbeth, 1937 (radio version).
Air Raid, 1938.

CLIFFORD ODETS (b. 1906).

Awake and Sing, 1935.
Waiting for Lefty, 1935.
Till the Day I Die, 1935.
Paradise Lost, 1935.
Golden Boy, 1937.
Rocket to the Moon, 1938.

MARK REED

She Would and She Did, 1919.
Skyrocket, 1929.
Petticoat Fever, 1935.
Yes, My Darling Daughter, 1937.

IRWIN SHAW (b. 1912).

Bury the Dead, 1936.

Siege, 1937.
The Gentle People, 1939.

ROBERT E. SHERWOOD (b. 1896).

The Road to Rome, 1927.
The Love Nest, 1927.
The Queen's Husband, 1928.
Waterloo Bridge, 1930.
This Is New York, 1930.
Reunion in Vienna, 1931.
The Petrified Forest, 1935.
Idiot's Delight, 1936.
Tovarich (adapted from comedy by Jacques
Deval), 1936.
Abe Lincoln in Illinois, 1938.

JOHN STEINBECK (b. 1902).

Of Mice and Men, 1937.

SPEWACKS (BELLA, b. 1900, and SAMUEL
b. 1900).

The Solitaire Man, 1926.
Poppa, 1928.
The War Song, 1928.
Clear All Wires, 1932.
Spring Song, 1934.
Boy Meets Girl, 1935.
Leave It to Me, 1938.
Miss Swan Expects, 1939.

EDNA FERBER (b. 1887).

Our Mrs. McChesney (with G. V. Hobart
1915.
The Eldest, 1920.
$1200 a Year (with Newman Levy), 192
Minick (with George S. Kaufman), 1924.
The Royal Family (with George S. Kau
man), 1927.
Dinner at Eight (with George S. Kaufman
1933.
Stage Door (with George S. Kaufman), 193

GEORGE ABBOTT (b. 1887).

The Fall Guy (with James Gleason), 1925.
A Holy Terror (with Winchell Smith), 192
Love 'Em and Leave 'Em (with John V.
Weaver), 1926.
Broadway (with Philip Dunning), 1926.
Four Walls (with Dana Burnett), 1927.
Coquette (with Ann Bridgers), 1927.
Ringside (with E. E. Paramore and
Daab), 1928.
Those We Love (adapted with S. K. Laure
1930.
Lilly Turner (adapted with Philip Dunnin
1932.

Heat Lightning (with Leon Abrams), 1933. 1933.

Ladies' Money (adapted with L. Hazard and R. Flournoy), 1934.

Three Men on a Horse (with J. C. Holm), 1935.

On Your Toes (with Rodgers and Hart), 1936.

Sweet River (from *Uncle Tom's Cabin*), 1936.

MOSS HART (b. 1904).

Jonica (with Dorothy Heyward), 1930.

Once in a Lifetime (with George S. Kaufman), 1930.

Face the Music (with Irving Berlin), 1932.

As Thousands Cheer (with Irving Berlin), 1933.

The Great Waltz (adaptation), 1934.

Merrily We Roll Along (with George S. Kaufman), 1934.

Jubilee (with Cole Porter), 1935.

You Can't Take It With You (with George S. Kaufman), 1936.

The Show Is On, 1936.

I'd Rather Be Right (with George S. Kaufman), 1937.

The American Way (with George S. Kaufman), 1939.

A SELECT LIST OF PRODUCED PLAYS [1930-1940]
BY OTHER AUTHORS

EUGENE O'NEILL

Mourning Becomes Electra, 1931.

SIDNEY HOWARD

The Late Christopher Bean (adaptation of French comedy by René Fauchois), 1932.

Dodsworth (adaptation of novel by Sinclair Lewis), 1934.

Yellow Jack, 1934.

ELMER RICE

The Left Bank, 1932.

Counsellor-at-Law, 1931.

JOHN HOWARD LAWSON

Success Story, 1932.

Marching Song, 1937.

RACHEL CROTHERS

Susan and God, 1937.

THORNTON WILDER

Our Town, 1938.

OWEN DAVIS (with **DONALD DAVIS**)

Ethan Frome (adaptation of Edith Wharton's short novel), 1936.

JOE AKINS

The Old Maid (adaptation of story by Edith Wharton), 1935.

SAMSON RAPHAELSON

Accent on Youth, 1936.

JOHN WEXLEY

The Last Mile, 1930.

They Shall Not Die, 1934.

LYNN RIGGS

Green Grow the Lilacs, 1931.

Russet Mantle, 1936.

DU BOSE and DOROTHY HEYWARD

Mamba's Daughters, 1938.

BEN HECHT and CHARLES MacARTHUR

20th Century, 1932.

LAWRENCE LANGNER and ARMINA MARSHALL

The Pursuit of Happiness, 1933.

PAUL OSBORN

The Vinegar Tree, 1930.

On Borrowed Time (adapted from novel by Lawrence Edward Watkin), 1938.

SUSAN GLASPELL

Alison's House, 1930.

VIRGIL GEDDES

Native Ground (published version), Mangled Production, 1932.

From the Life of George Emery Blum (published version), 1934.

LEOPOLD ATLAS

Wednesday's Child, 1934.

ROBERT ARDREY
How to Get Tough About It, 1938.

E. P. CONKLE
200 Were Chosen, 1936.
Prologue to Glory, 1937.

ROBERT TURNEY
Daughters of Atreus, 1936.

GEORGE O'NEIL
American Dream, 1933.

T. S. ELIOT
Murder in the Cathedral, 1935.

EMMET LAVERY
The First Legion, 1934.

WILLIAM SAROYAN
My Heart's in the Highlands, 1939.

STEPHEN VINCENT BENET
The Devil and Daniel Webster, 1939.

HARDIE ALBRIGHT
All the Living (adapted from "*I Knew 3000
Lunatics*," by Dr. Victor Small), 1938.

SINCLAIR LEWIS and JOHN C. MOFFITT
It Can't Happen Here (adapted from the
novel), 1936.

VICTOR WOLFSON
Excursion, 1937.

MARC BLITZSTEIN
The Cradle Will Rock, 1937.
ALBERT MALTZ
Black Pit, 1935.

PAUL PETERS
Stevedore (with George Sklar), 1934.

ALBERT BEIN
Little Ol' Boy, 1933.
Let Freedom Ring (adapted from a novel
Grace Lumpkin), 1935.

ARTHUR ARENT (and staff of Federal The
tre's "Living Newspaper")
Power, 1937.
One-third of a Nation, 1938.

LENORE COFFEE and WILLIAM JOYC
COWEN
Family Portrait, 1937.

ROBERT L. BUCKNER and WALTER HA
Primrose Path (adapted from Victoria Li
coln's novel, "*February Hill*"), 1939.

ARTHUR KOBER
Having Wonderful Time, 1937.

ROSE FRANKEN
Another Language, 1932.

JAMES HAGAN
One Sunday Afternoon, 1933.

LAWRENCE RILEY
Personal Appearance, 1934.

JOHN MURRAY and ALLEN BORETZ
Room Service, 1937.

JULIAN THOMPSON
The Warrior's Husband, 1932.

GILBERT SELDES
Lysistrata (adapted from Aristophanes' co
edy), 1930.

BIBLIOGRAPHY

Selected List of Books on the Contemporary American Theatre, 1930-40

NDERSON, JOHN: *The American Theatre.* New York: The Dial Press, 1938.

An admirable brief introduction to the history of the American theatre with a concluding survey of recent trends.

RCHITECTURE FOR THE NEW THEATRE. Essays by Bel Geddes, Simonson, and others. New York: Theatre Arts, 1935.

LAKE, BEN: *The Awakening of the American Theatre.* New York: Tomorrow Publishers, 1935.

A highly informative pamphlet, dealing with the rise and development of the social or "left" theatre of the 'thirties.

LOCK, ANITA: *The Changing World in Plays and Theatre.* Boston: Little, Brown & Company, 1939.

This study of important social ideas and trends in the modern drama contains detailed studies of a number of contemporary American plays.

RICKER, HERSCHEL L. (Editor) : *Our Theatre Today.* New York: Samuel French, 1936.

A collection of essays on various phases of the theatre.

ROWN, JOHN MASON: *Two on the Aisle: Ten Years of the American in Performance.* New York: W. W. Norton & Co., 1938.

A collection of incisive and excellently written reviews by the brilliant lecturer and critic of The New York Post.

USTIS, MORTON: *Broadway, Inc.: The Theater as Business.* New York: Dodd, Mead & Co., 1934.

layers at Work. New York: Theatre Arts, 1937.

Nine prominent actors and actresses discuss their methods.

LEXNER, ELEANORE: *American Playwrights 1918-1938.* With a Preface by John Gassner. New York: Simon and Schuster, 1939.

An analytical and provocative examination of the important playwrights by a critic who stresses their relation to current social problems and trends.

OZLENKO, WILLIAM (editor) : *The One-Act Play Today.* New York: Harcourt, Brace & Co., 1938.

A symposium by Percival Wilde, Walter Prichard Eaton, Michael Blankfort, Gilbert Seldes, Alfred Kreymborg, Barrett H. Clark, Glenn Hughes, and John Gassner.

AWSON, JOHN HOWARD: *Theory and Technique of Playwriting.* New York: G. P. Putnam's Sons, 1936.

Valuable as a contemporary playwright's analysis of dramatic technique.

ANTLE, BURNS: *The Best Plays* of 1930, 1931, 1932, 1933, 1934, 1935, 1936, 1937, 1938. (A volume for each year.) New York: Dodd, Mead & Company.

Invaluable records of performances of each season, condensations of selected plays, and notes on their authors.

Contemporary American Playwrights. New York: Dodd Mea
. & Co., 1938.
A biographical dictionary of American playwrights; a useful source-book.

McCANDLESS, STANLEY R.: *A Method of Lighting the Stage.* Revised edition. Ne
York: Theatre Arts, 1939.
Modern Stage Design. New York: Theatre Arts, 1935.

MOSES, MONTROSE J. and BROWN, JOHN MASON (editors): *The American Theatr
as Seen by Its Critics.* New York: W. W. Norton & Co., 1934.
A compilation of American criticism, including reviews of the drama betwee
1920 and 1934 by John Anderson, Brooks Atkinson, Robert Benchley, Joh
Mason Brown, Gilbert Gabriel, Percy Hammond, Joseph Wood Krutch, Ric
ard Lockridge, Burns Mantle, George Jean Nathan, Walter Winchell, Sta
Young, and others.

NATHAN, GEORGE JEAN: *The Morning After the First Night.* New York: Alfre
A. Knopf, 1938.
Another collection of scintillating criticism by Mr. Nathan.

QUINN, ARTHUR HOBSON: *A History of the American Drama from the Civil W
to the Present Day.* New York: F. S. Crofts, 1936.
An authoritative history which examines the contemporary drama in some deta

SIMONSON, LEE: *The Stage Is Set.* New York: Harcourt, Brace & Co., 1932.
A notable study of scenic design through the ages, containing illuminatir
comments on current stage-craft and a deeply reasoned analysis of style
contemporary American playwriting.

SKINNER, RICHARD DANA: *Eugene O'Neill: A Poet's Quest.* New York: Longman
Green & Co., 1935.
A comprehensive, if somewhat mystical, study of our major playwright.

TRAUBE, SHEPARD: *So You Want To Go Into the Theatre.* Boston: Little, Brow
& Co., 1936.
A handbook of facts about the contemporary theatre.

WHITMAN, WILLSON: *Bread and Circuses.* New York: Oxford University Pres
1937.
A history of the rise and development of the Federal Theatre.

WINTER, SOPHUS KEITH: *Eugene O'Neill. A Critical Study.* New York: Randor
House, 1934.

Also consult the following periodicals:
Theatre Arts
Theatre Guild Magazine
New Theatre; New Theatre and Film.
Stage
Theatre Workshop
One Act Play Magazine
"Tac"

342147